BASEBALL ALMANAC

Contributing Writers
Dan Schlossberg
Stuart Shea
Mike Tully
Michael Bradley
Pete Palmer
Jeff Kurowski
Bruce Herman

Publications International, Ltd.

Dan Schlossberg is baseball editor for the *Americana Encyclopedia Annual*, columnist for *Legends Magazine*, and contributor to *Petersen's Pro Baseball Yearbook, Street & Smith's Official Baseball Yearbook*, and many other baseball periodicals. The former Associated Press sportswriter has written 15 books, including *The Baseball Catalog* and *The Baseball Book of Why*. He is a co-author of *Players of Cooperstown: Baseball's Hall of Fame*.

Stuart Shea works as a researcher with The Baseball Workshop and is a featured essayist in *The Scouting Report: 1995*. His work has also appeared in *Baseball Legends of All Time, 1001 Fascinating Baseball Facts*, and *1992 Fantasy League Baseball*.

Mike Tully is a former national baseball writer for UPI. He has written six books, including *Leagues and Barons* and *1990-91 Baseball's Hottest Rookies*. His freelance work has appeared in *The National Sports Daily, Sports Illustrated*, and *The New York Times*. He is a co-author of *1994-95 Hockey Almanac*.

Michael Bradley is a freelance writer whose work has appeared in *The Sporting News, The Philadelphia Inquirer*, and a variety of national sports publications.

Pete Palmer edited both *Total Baseball* and *The Hidden Game of Baseball* with John Thorn. Palmer was the statistician for *1994 Golf Almanac, 1994-95 Basketball Almanac*, and *1001 Fascinating Baseball Facts*. He is a member of the Society for American Baseball Research.

Jeff Kurowski is a professional baseball and sports-card price guide coordinator for books and sports-card magazines, including *1995 Baseball Card Price Guide* and *1994-95 Basketball Almanac*. He is the former editor of *Sports Card Price Guide Monthly* and *Sports Collector's Digest Baseball Card Price Guide*. He is also the editor of *The Standard Catalogue of Baseball Cards*.

Bruce Herman is a syndicated columnist for Tribune Media, a consultant to The Topps Company, and a freelance writer based in St. Petersburg, Florida. He has contributed to such publications as *Sports Illustrated, Inside Sports*, and *USA TODAY Baseball Weekly*.

CONTENTS

4

CONTENTS

5

CONTENTS

CONTENTS

CONTENTS

Current Players and Rookie Prospects

In this section you'll find profiles of 800 players—first 600 current players and then 200 rookie prospects. The current players and rookie prospects are in alphabetical order.

  Full major-league statistics are included with the current players. If a player played with two teams in both the American League and the National League in one season, both lines are presented in the "Major League Registers." If the player played with two teams in one league during a season, the statistics were combined to give you accurate information of how each player performed against one league in one season. At the bottom of most of the Major League Registers you'll find a "3 AVE" line. Players who qualified had their last three seasons' statistics averaged for each of the 10 categories. For batters to qualify for this line, they had to accumulate 150 at bats in each season. For starters to qualify, they had to pitch at least 60 innings each season. For relievers to qualify, they had to pitch at least 30 innings each season. If the player did not qualify for all three seasons but for only two years out of the last three, you'll find a "2 AVE" line. These lines give you a straightforward way to help you better predict how these players will do this summer. When calculating the averages, the totals for the 1994 season were increased by approximately 1.41, or 162 divided by 115. This is to provide a more accurate picture of how a player will do over a 162-game schedule.

  The rookie prospects each have a "Professional Register." Included are statistics from each year that the player has been in organized baseball, from the Rookie leagues (**R**), Class-A (**A**), Double-A (**AA**), and Triple-A (**AAA**). If the player has played in the major leagues, each league's performance is also shown (**AL** and **NL**). If during one season a player played with more than one team on one minor league level, or if a player played with more than one AL or NL team, the statistics were combined to give you accurate information of how that player did against one level or against one major league.

  The abbreviations for batters are: **BA** = batting average; **G** = games played; **AB** = at bats; **R** = runs scored; **H** = hits; **2B** = doubles; **3B** = triples; **HR** = home runs; **RBI** = runs batted in; **SB** = stolen bases. The abbreviations for pitchers are: **W** = wins; **L** = losses; **ERA** = earned run average; **G** = games; **CG** = complete games; **S** = saves; **IP** = innings pitched; **H** = hits; **ER** = earned runs; **BB** = bases on balls; **SO** = strikeouts. Note that for innings pitched, a .1 = ⅓ inning pitched, and .2 = ⅔ inning pitched.

  The "Player Summary" box that accompanies each profile is an at-a-glance look at each player. The "Fantasy Value" line suggests a draft price for any of the fantasy baseball games that have mushroomed around the country. The price range is based on $260 budget for a 23-player roster. The "Card Value" line is a general estimate in determining the worth of a Mint 1995 regular-issue (base set) baseball card of that player. This estimate is based mostly on the future value gain of that player's card. Any error, variation, or specialty cards are not taken into account.

JIM ABBOTT

Position: Pitcher
Team: New York Yankees
Born: Sept. 19, 1967 Flint, MI
Height: 6'3" **Weight:** 200 lbs.
Bats: left **Throws:** left
Acquired: Traded from Angels for J.T. Snow, Russ Springer, and Jerry Nielsen, 12/92

Player Summary	
Fantasy Value.	$8 to $10
Card Value	12¢ to 25¢
Will.	keep ball down
Can't	prevent gophers
Expect	strong defense
Don't Expect	high K totals

Suprisingly, Abbott has been a big winner only once in his career. He has command of four pitches: a fastball, a curveball, a forkball, and a changeup. His cut fastball rides in on right-handed hitters, making him almost as effective against righties as he is against lefties. Because he's always around the plate, Abbott yields a high number of home runs, though many come with bases empty. Opposing batters usually average about a hit per inning and three walks per game. He won six of his first eight decisions in 1994 before tailing off. Fearing that Abbott might be tipping his pitches, the Yankees added a special flap to his glove and suggested he throw more changeups. When he's right, he keeps the ball down—resulting in ground outs and double plays. He also is a fine fielder. The former University of Michigan star went right from college to the majors. He pitched a no-hitter for New York in September 1993.

Major League Pitching Register

	W	L	ERA	G	CG	IP	H	ER	BB	SO
89 AL	12	12	3.92	29	4	181.1	190	79	74	115
90 AL	10	14	4.51	33	4	211.2	246	106	72	105
91 AL	18	11	2.89	34	5	243.0	222	78	73	158
92 AL	7	15	2.77	29	7	211.0	208	65	68	130
93 AL	11	14	4.37	32	4	214.0	221	104	73	95
94 AL	9	8	4.55	24	2	160.1	167	81	64	90
Life	67	74	3.78	181	26	1221.1	1254	513	424	693
3 AVE	10	13	3.91	32	5	217.0	221	94	77	117

KURT ABBOTT

Position: Shortstop
Team: Florida Marlins
Born: June 2, 1969 Zanesville, OH
Height: 6' **Weight:** 170 lbs.
Bats: right **Throws:** right
Acquired: Traded from Athletics for Kerwin Moore, 12/93

Player Summary	
Fantasy Value.	$4 to $6
Card Value	12¢ to 20¢
Will	show some power
Can't	wait for walks
Expect	decent defense
Don't Expect	trouble with righties

Given a chance to play every day as a rookie in 1994, Abbott responded by showing major-league ability and displaying surprising power for a shortstop. By June 16, he had 18 extra-base hits—one more than veteran Walt Weiss, his predecessor at shortstop for Florida, had produced during the entire previous season. Abbott even set a Marlins' club record by hitting home runs in four consecutive games. Two of his first-half homers came with the bases loaded. As he gains experience, he should become more selective at the plate (his ratio of strikeouts to walks last year was a ghastly 6-to-1). Abbott also needs to improve his production with runners in scoring position and in late-inning pressure situations. He handled lefty and righty pitching almost equally. Experience should help him improve his defense as he learns where to position himself against opponents. A competent shortstop with good hands, Abbott has a strong arm and can turn the double play. He was voted the Triple-A Pacific Coast League's No. 9 prospect by loop managers in 1993.

Major League Batting Register

	BA	G	AB	R	H	2B	3B	HR	RBI	SB
93 AL	.246	20	61	11	15	1	0	3	9	2
94 NL	.249	101	345	41	86	17	3	9	33	3
Life	.249	121	406	52	101	18	3	12	42	5

MARK ACRE

Position: Pitcher
Team: Oakland Athletics
Born: Sept. 16, 1968   Concord, CA
Height: 6'8"   **Weight:** 235 lbs.
Bats: right   **Throws:** right
Acquired: Signed as a free agent, 8/91

Player Summary	
Fantasy Value.	$6 to $8
Card Value	5¢ to 7¢
Will	throttle righties
Can't	always find plate
Expect	first-class heater
Don't Expect	a closer role

Dennis Eckersley's early struggles last year created an opening in the Oakland bullpen for Acre. The 6'8" former basketball player from New Mexico State immediately won his first four American League decisions. The towering right-hander, signed as an undrafted free agent, advanced to the Athletics after saving 30 games in the minors in 1993. He also averaged about one strikeout per inning that year while pitching in Class-A and Double-A. By the time he reached the majors, scouts rated his fastball the best in the Oakland organization. Acre also throws an outstanding forkball. He dominates right-handed batters and keeps the ball in the park. He averaged only six hits per nine innings last season but sometimes struggled with his control. By early August, Acre had allowed more walks than strikeouts. He also needs to improve his ratio of stranding inherited runners; he stranded about two-thirds last year. Acre could have a future as a bigleague closer, although he will have to improve his performance against left-handed batters to succeed in that role.

Major League Pitching Register

	W	L	ERA	G	S	IP	H	ER	BB	SO
94 AL	5	1	3.41	34	0	34.1	24	13	23	21
Life	5	1	3.41	34	0	34.1	24	13	23	21

RICK AGUILERA

Position: Pitcher
Team: Minnesota Twins
Born: Dec. 31, 1961   San Gabriel, CA
Height: 6'5"   **Weight:** 205 lbs.
Bats: right   **Throws:** right
Acquired: Traded from Mets with Kevin Tapani, Tim Drummond, Jack Savage, and David West for Frank Viola, 7/89

Player Summary	
Fantasy Value.	$25 to $30
Card Value	8¢ to 12¢
Will	convert most chances
Can't	return to starting
Expect	lots of strikeouts
Don't Expect	trouble with control

Because he's a former starter, Aguilera brings a highly varied arsenal of pitches to his job as a closer. Though he's widely considered a fastball-slider pitcher, his best delivery is a split-fingered fastball that dips just as it crosses the plate. Aguilera also throws a curve that makes his rising 90 mph fastball look even faster. In 1993, he retired 27 straight opposing hitters—the equivalent of a perfect game. Aguilera averages more than a strikeout an inning and less than two walks per game. He also helps himself with his fielding, perfected during his days as a collegiate third baseman at Brigham Young. Aguilera had a better than 4.5-1 strikeout-to-walk ratio last season. He keeps the ball in the park and holds runners well. Aguilera rarely blows a save opportunity.

Major League Pitching Register

	W	L	ERA	G	S	IP	H	ER	BB	SO
85 NL	10	7	3.24	21	0	122.1	118	44	37	74
86 NL	10	7	3.88	28	0	141.2	145	61	36	104
87 NL	11	3	3.60	18	0	115.0	124	46	33	77
88 NL	0	4	6.93	11	0	24.2	29	19	10	16
89 NL	6	6	2.34	36	7	69.1	59	18	21	80
89 AL	3	5	3.21	11	0	75.2	71	27	17	57
90 AL	5	3	2.76	56	32	65.1	55	20	19	61
91 AL	4	5	2.35	63	42	69.0	44	18	30	61
92 AL	2	6	2.83	64	41	66.2	60	21	17	52
93 AL	4	3	3.11	65	34	72.1	60	25	14	59
94 AL	1	4	3.63	44	23	44.2	57	18	10	46
Life	56	53	3.29	417	179	866.2	822	317	244	687
3 AVE	2	5	3.18	64	36	67.2	67	24	15	59

MIKE ALDRETE

Position: First base; outfield
Team: Oakland Athletics
Born: Jan. 29, 1961 Carmel, CA
Height: 5'11" **Weight:** 185 lbs.
Bats: left **Throws:** left
Acquired: Signed as a free agent, 3/93

Player Summary	
Fantasy Value	$0
Card Value	5¢ to 7¢
Will	pinch-hit often
Can't	throw very well
Expect	success vs. righties
Don't Expect	much speed

One of the game's most valuable utility players, Aldrete serves as a superb substitute at first base, left field, as a designated hitter, or as a left-handed pinch hitter. For the second straight year, he filled in as the Oakland first baseman when Mark McGwire was injured. Though Aldrete is primarily a singles hitter, he does have occasional pop in his bat. This spray hitter is much more productive against right-handers. He shows fine patience at the plate, striking out moderately more often than he walks, and therefore he thrives on a steady fastball diet. He becomes a much better hitter when he gets ahead in the count. Though he has little speed, Aldrete has the quick reactions that translate to good range in the field, both at first base and in left field. He has a weak arm, however. One of the game's more intelligent players, Aldrete has his bachelor's degree in communications from Stanford.

Major League Batting Register

	BA	G	AB	R	H	2B	3B	HR	RBI	SB
86 NL	.250	84	216	27	54	18	3	2	25	1
87 NL	.325	126	357	50	116	18	2	9	51	6
88 NL	.267	139	389	44	104	15	0	3	50	6
89 NL	.221	76	136	12	30	8	1	1	12	1
90 NL	.242	96	161	22	39	7	1	1	18	1
91 NL	.000	12	15	2	0	0	0	0	1	0
91 AL	.262	85	183	22	48	6	1	1	19	1
93 AL	.267	95	255	40	68	13	1	10	33	1
94 AL	.242	76	178	23	43	5	0	4	18	2
Life	.266	789	1890	242	502	90	9	31	227	19
2 AVE	.254	101	253	36	64	10	1	8	29	2

LUIS ALICEA

Position: Second base
Team: Boston Red Sox
Born: July 29, 1965 Santurce, Puerto Rico
Height: 5'10" **Weight:** 150 lbs.
Bats: both **Throws:** right
Acquired: Traded from Cardinals for Nate Minchey and Jeff McNeely, 12/94

Player Summary	
Fantasy Value	$4 to $6
Card Value	5¢ to 7¢
Will	hit lefties best
Can't	stay injury free
Expect	good clutch bat
Don't Expect	fielding woes

For the last few seasons, Alicea had to fend off challenges for the St. Louis second base job from Geronimo Pena and Jose Oquendo. Alicea displayed the best all-around skills of the trio. He was better defensively than Pena though not as gifted defensively as Oquendo. Alicea has great range and turns the double play well, and he was a better hitter than Oquendo. Though Alicea uses his speed to good advantage on defense, he has yet to master the art of using it as an offensive weapon. He doesn't steal much, and though he has enough speed to beat out infield hits, he does not hit the ball on the ground often enough. He has failed in periodic trials as a leadoff man. He hits well from both sides of the plate and is a threat to hit solid line drives when batting right-handed. A contact hitter with occasional gap power, Alicea walks almost as often as he strikes out. The switch-hitter is at his best in late-inning pressure situations. Alicea is a former All-American from Florida State.

Major League Batting Register

	BA	G	AB	R	H	2B	3B	HR	RBI	SB
88 NL	.212	93	297	20	63	10	4	1	24	1
91 NL	.191	56	68	5	13	3	0	0	0	0
92 NL	.245	85	265	26	65	9	11	2	32	2
93 NL	.279	115	362	50	101	19	3	3	46	11
94 NL	.278	88	205	32	57	12	5	5	29	4
Life	.250	437	1197	133	299	53	23	11	131	18
3 AVE	.269	108	305	40	82	15	7	4	40	6

ROBERTO ALOMAR

Position: Second base
Team: Toronto Blue Jays
Born: Feb. 5, 1968 Ponce, Puerto Rico
Height: 6′ **Weight:** 175 lbs.
Bats: both **Throws:** right
Acquired: Traded from Padres with Joe Carter for Fred McGriff and Tony Fernandez, 12/90

Player Summary	
Fantasy Value	$35 to $40
Card Value	30¢ to 50¢
Will	get on base often
Can't	win home run title
Expect	All-Star selection
Don't Expect	fielding lapses

The 1994 fall of the Blue Jays cannot be blamed on Alomar. The five-time All-Star, making a full recovery from an ankle broken in the Puerto Rican Winter League, remained one of baseball's top performers. A combination of speed and power, he is always among the league leaders in batting average and on-base percentage. His .326 average placed him third in the 1993 AL batting race, trailing only John Olerud and Paul Molitor. Alomar followed with a .480 average in the World Series. Although he has occasional trouble with left-handers, Alomar is a big problem for righties. He makes good contact, walks more often than he strikes out, and is always a threat to steal. In 1993, Alomar led the AL with 15 steals of third. Defensively, he has no equal at his position. His quickness translates into exceptional range. He is a master at turning the double play and knows how to play rival hitters. His rare defensive miscues usually occur on throws.

Major League Batting Register

	BA	G	AB	R	H	2B	3B	HR	RBI	SB
88 NL	.266	143	545	84	145	24	6	9	41	24
89 NL	.295	158	623	82	184	27	1	7	56	42
90 NL	.287	147	586	80	168	27	5	6	60	24
91 AL	.295	161	637	88	188	41	11	9	69	53
92 AL	.310	152	571	105	177	27	8	8	76	49
93 AL	.326	153	589	109	192	35	6	17	93	55
94 AL	.306	107	392	78	120	25	4	8	38	19
Life	.298	1021	3943	626	1174	206	41	64	433	266
3 AVE	.314	152	571	108	179	32	7	12	74	44

SANDY ALOMAR

Position: Catcher
Team: Cleveland Indians
Born: June 18, 1966 Salinas, Puerto Rico
Height: 6′5″ **Weight:** 200 lbs.
Bats: right **Throws:** right
Acquired: Traded from Padres with Chris James and Carlos Baerga for Joe Carter, 12/89

Player Summary	
Fantasy Value	$10 to $13
Card Value	8¢ to 12¢
Will	make good contact
Can't	avoid injury jinx
Expect	solid clutch bat
Don't Expect	fielding woes

Since winning AL Rookie of the Year honors in 1990, Alomar has suffered a never-ending plague of injuries. He's had back, knee, and hand problems; an inflamed rotator cuff; a strained hip flexor; and more. In between, he's made the All-Star Team three times and shown considerable potential both as a hitter and even more as a defensive receiver. Alomar did some of his best hitting with runners in scoring position and in late-inning pressure situations in 1994. He was also a solid .300 hitter against right-handed pitching. Like brother Robby, Sandy is a contact hitter who walks almost as often as he fans. Alomar can also hit the ball out of the park. He nailed about 35 percent of the runners who tried to steal against him last year. Alomar has a strong, accurate arm but needs to unload the ball more quickly. He calls a good game and is especially adept at blocking balls in the dirt.

Major League Batting Register

	BA	G	AB	R	H	2B	3B	HR	RBI	SB
88 NL	.000	1	1	0	0	0	0	0	0	0
89 NL	.211	7	19	1	4	1	0	1	6	0
90 AL	.290	132	445	60	129	26	2	9	66	4
91 AL	.217	51	184	10	40	9	0	0	7	0
92 AL	.251	89	299	22	75	16	0	2	26	3
93 AL	.270	64	215	24	58	7	1	6	32	3
94 AL	.288	80	292	44	84	15	1	14	43	8
Life	.268	424	1455	161	390	74	4	32	180	18
3 AVE	.272	89	308	36	84	15	1	9	40	6

13

MOISES ALOU

Position: Outfield
Team: Montreal Expos
Born: July 3, 1966 Atlanta, GA
Height: 6'3" **Weight:** 180 lbs.
Bats: right **Throws:** right
Acquired: Traded from Pirates with Scott Ruskin and Willie Greene for Zane Smith, 8/90

Player Summary	
Fantasy Value. . . . . $25 to $30
Card Value . . . . 12¢ to 20¢
Will . . . . become MVP contender
Can't . . . . steal many bases
Expect . . . . hitting vs. lefties
Don't Expect . . . . much publicity

Alou is doing for the Expos nowadays what his father, Felipe, did in the 1960s. Moises might just be the best of the Alou bunch, including dad—now Montreal's manager—and uncles Matty and Jesus. Before the 1994 season was half over, Moises had proven himself fully recovered from the dislocated left ankle and broken left fibula he had suffered the previous September. In fact, he had established himself as one of the NL's best left fielders, in a class just behind Barry Bonds. Moving up on the plate slightly increased Alou's coverage and made him one of the league's top hitters. He had two two-homer games three days apart in June. He also had the winning hit for the NL in the 10th inning of the 1994 All-Star Game. A good clutch hitter, Alou killed left-handed pitching in 1994. He has good speed but does not steal much. That speed helps Alou enormously in the outfield, where he gets a great jump and shows a strong throwing arm.

Major League Batting Register

	BA	G	AB	R	H	2B	3B	HR	RBI	SB
90 NL	.200	16	20	4	4	0	1	0	0	0
92 NL	.282	115	341	53	96	28	2	9	56	16
93 NL	.286	136	482	70	138	29	6	18	85	17
94 NL	.339	107	422	81	143	31	5	22	78	7
Life	.301	374	1265	208	381	88	14	49	219	40
3 AVE	.307	134	472	79	145	34	5	19	84	14

WILSON ALVAREZ

Position: Pitcher
Team: Chicago White Sox
Born: March 24, 1970 Maracaibo, Venezuela
Height: 6'1" **Weight:** 175 lbs.
Bats: left **Throws:** left
Acquired: Traded from Rangers with Scott Fletcher and Sammy Sosa for Harold Baines and Fred Manrique, 7/89

Player Summary	
Fantasy Value. . . . . $15 to $18
Card Value . . . . 10¢ to 20¢
Will. . . . . get outs with curve
Can't. . . . . field position well
Expect. . . . . high win totals
Don't Expect . . . . many walks

When Alvarez pitched a 1991 no-hitter in his first start with the White Sox, he was merely providing a preview of things to come. He worked mostly in relief in '92, then suffered such severe control trouble that he received an exile to the minors a year later. By 1994, however, the southpaw finally lived up to his potential. He won his first nine decisions—giving him 15 straight to tie LaMarr Hoyt's 1983-84 club record. Alvarez also became the first Venezuelan pitcher to make a big-league All-Star squad. Free of his previous control problems, Alvarez averaged about six strikeouts and three walks per game. He yielded less hits than innings pitched, held runners close, and maintained about a 2-1 ratio of strikeouts to walks. Alvarez throws four pitches: a fastball that sometimes exceeds 95 mph; a big-breaking curve, which some scouts say is his best pitch; a changeup; and a slider. When he's right, he gets most of his outs by strikeouts and ground balls.

Major League Pitching Register

	W	L	ERA	G	CG	IP	H	ER	BB	SO
89 AL	0	1	0.00	1	0	0.0	3	3	2	0
91 AL	3	2	3.51	10	2	56.1	47	22	29	32
92 AL	5	3	5.20	34	0	100.1	103	58	65	66
93 AL	15	8	2.95	31	1	207.2	168	68	122	155
94 AL	12	8	3.45	24	2	161.2	147	62	62	108
Life	35	22	3.64	100	5	526.0	468	213	280	361
3 AVE	12	7	3.58	33	1	178.2	159	71	91	124

LARRY ANDERSEN

Position: Pitcher
Team: Philadelphia Phillies
Born: May 6, 1953 Portland, OR
Height: 6'3" **Weight:** 205 lbs.
Bats: right **Throws:** right
Acquired: Signed as a free agent, 12/92

Player Summary	
Fantasy Value	$0
Card Value	5¢ to 7¢
Will	strand runners
Can't	retire left-handers
Expect	declining workload
Don't Expect	a healthy '95

The retirement of Charlie Hough left Andersen as the oldest active player in the NL. He continued to baffle right-handed hitters and register high strikeout totals with his nasty slider, however. Andersen also throws a straight fastball and a cut fastball. Injuries interfered with his effectiveness last summer. Because of his high leg kick, Andersen has problems holding runners, which is not a wonderful trait for a relief pitcher—but he compensates by fielding his position well. He's also adept at stranding inherited runners. During his 17-year career, he's helped pitch three teams (the Astros, Red Sox, and Phillies) into postseason play. He's a world-class prankster.

Major League Pitching Register

	W	L	ERA	G	S	IP	H	ER	BB	SO
75 AL	0	0	4.76	3	0	5.2	4	3	2	4
77 AL	0	1	3.14	11	0	14.1	10	5	9	8
79 AL	0	0	7.56	8	0	16.2	25	14	4	7
81 AL	3	3	2.66	41	5	67.2	57	20	18	40
82 AL	0	0	5.99	40	1	79.2	100	53	23	32
83 NL	1	0	2.39	17	0	26.1	19	7	9	14
84 NL	3	7	2.38	64	4	90.2	85	24	25	54
85 NL	3	3	4.32	57	3	73.0	78	35	26	50
86 NL	2	1	3.03	48	1	77.1	83	26	26	42
87 NL	9	5	3.45	67	5	101.2	95	39	41	94
88 NL	2	4	2.94	53	5	82.2	82	27	20	66
89 NL	4	4	1.54	60	3	87.2	63	15	24	85
90 NL	5	2	1.95	50	6	73.2	61	16	24	68
90 AL	0	0	1.23	15	1	22.0	18	3	3	25
91 NL	3	4	2.30	38	13	47.0	39	12	13	40
92 NL	1	1	3.34	34	2	35.0	26	13	8	35
93 NL	3	2	2.92	64	0	61.2	54	20	21	67
94 NL	1	2	4.41	29	0	32.2	33	16	15	27
Life	40	39	3.15	699	49	995.1	932	348	311	758
3 AVE	2	2	3.50	46	1	47.2	42	19	17	47

BRADY ANDERSON

Position: Outfield
Team: Baltimore Orioles
Born: Jan. 18, 1964 Silver Spring, MD
Height: 6'1" **Weight:** 195 lbs.
Bats: left **Throws:** left
Acquired: Traded from Red Sox with Curt Schilling for Mike Boddicker, 7/88

Player Summary	
Fantasy Value	$16 to $19
Card Value	8¢ to 15¢
Will	show power
Can't	handle all lefties
Expect	patience at plate
Don't Expect	glove problems

Anderson's blend of speed and power makes him an excellent leadoff man. He shows good patience at the plate, helping him draw enough walks to produce an on-base percentage 100 points higher than his batting average. He also runs well: On Aug. 8, he stole his 27th consecutive base without getting caught. Anderson can also swing the bat. He had four extra-base hits against Oakland April 26 and two home runs against Toronto exactly two months later. Anderson hits for more power against right-handers but gets more walks against lefties. He thrives on a low fastball diet. Anderson makes more highlight films for his defense than his offense. His leaping catches are already legendary in Baltimore, where he has mastered the art of leaping over the wall to deprive rival hitters of home runs. Anderson's speed serves him well in left, where he shows outstanding range and a good throwing arm. He's also capable of playing center when needed.

Major League Batting Register

	BA	G	AB	R	H	2B	3B	HR	RBI	SB
88 AL	.212	94	325	31	69	13	4	1	21	10
89 AL	.207	94	266	44	55	12	2	4	16	16
90 AL	.231	89	234	24	54	5	2	3	24	15
91 AL	.230	113	256	40	59	12	3	2	27	12
92 AL	.271	159	623	100	169	28	10	21	80	53
93 AL	.262	142	560	87	147	36	8	13	66	24
94 AL	.263	111	453	78	119	25	5	12	48	31
Life	.247	802	2717	404	672	131	34	56	282	161
3 AVE	.266	152	607	99	161	33	8	17	71	40

BRIAN ANDERSON

Position: Pitcher
Team: California Angels
Born: April 26, 1972 Geneva, OH
Height: 6'1" **Weight:** 190 lbs.
Bats: both **Throws:** left
Acquired: First-round pick in 6/93 free-agent draft

Player Summary	
Fantasy Value	$4 to $6
Card Value	25¢ to 50¢
Will	always throw strikes
Can't	thwart rival hitters
Expect	defense to help him
Don't Expect	many Ks

After Anderson won three of his four decisions last spring, teammate Dwight Smith, a former National Leaguer, said the rookie reminded him of a young Greg Maddux. Some scouts see a more obvious parallel with Tom Glavine, who throws from the same side as Anderson. Either comparison is high praise for a kid plucked off the Wright State (Ohio) campus a year before. The third overall pick in the June 1993 amateur draft, Anderson was considered one of the best control pitchers in the lottery. He accepted an Angel offer of $680,000, plus the promise of a quick trip to the majors. After making four starts in the minors, he cracked the California rotation by showing good control and confusing batters with a three-quarters delivery. Although he throws four pitches for strikes, he does not record high strikeout totals. Instead, he induces ground balls and lets his defense do the work. Anderson averaged about four strikeouts and two and one-half walks per game and more than a hit per inning, but he kept the ball in the park. His pickoff move is already one of the league's best.

Major League Pitching Register

	W	L	ERA	G	CG	IP	H	ER	BB	SO
93 AL	0	0	3.97	4	0	11.1	11	5	2	4
94 AL	7	5	5.22	18	0	101.2	120	59	27	47
Life	7	5	5.10	22	0	113.0	131	64	29	51

ERIC ANTHONY

Position: Outfield
Team: Seattle Mariners
Born: Nov. 8, 1967 San Diego, CA
Height: 6'2" **Weight:** 195 lbs.
Bats: left **Throws:** left
Acquired: Traded from Astros for Mike Felder and Mike Hampton, 12/93

Player Summary	
Fantasy Value	$7 to $9
Card Value	6¢ to 10¢
Will	show power in streaks
Can't	hit left-handers hard
Expect	unusual batting style
Don't Expect	great average

Coming to the Kingdome was supposed to work wonders for Anthony's home run stroke. The slugging outfielder seemed delighted to be moving from one of baseball's toughest targets (the fences of the Houston Astrodome) to one of the easiest. But injuries interfered, along with the not-so-easy adjustment to new pitchers and a new league, leaving Anthony with a .237 batting average and only 30 RBI for the shortened 1994 campaign. Anthony's problems are obvious: He fans twice as much as he walks and struggles against southpaw pitching. A streaky hitter, Anthony once produced eight homers in a 35-game stretch for the Astros. His stance is a problem because he uses a leg kick to generate his power. He has some speed but doesn't steal many bases. His speed helps on defense, where he can play any of the three outfield positions. With Jay Buhner entrenched as Seattle's right fielder last summer, Anthony shifted to left and played well.

Major League Batting Register

	BA	G	AB	R	H	2B	3B	HR	RBI	SB
89 NL	.180	25	61	7	11	2	0	4	7	0
90 NL	.192	84	239	26	46	8	0	10	29	5
91 NL	.153	39	118	11	18	6	0	1	7	1
92 NL	.239	137	440	45	105	15	1	19	80	5
93 NL	.249	145	486	70	121	19	4	15	66	3
94 AL	.237	79	262	31	62	14	1	10	30	6
Life	.226	509	1606	190	363	64	6	59	219	20
3 AVE	.242	131	432	53	104	18	2	16	63	5

KEVIN APPIER

Position: Pitcher
Team: Kansas City Royals
Born: Dec. 6, 1967   Lancaster, CA
Height: 6'2"   **Weight:** 190 lbs.
Bats: right   **Throws:** right
Acquired: First-round pick in 6/87 free-agent draft

Player Summary

Fantasy Value	$19 to $22
Card Value	8¢ to 15¢
Will	attempt big comeback
Can't	stymie lefty hitters
Expect	many ground-ball outs
Don't Expect	many gophers

Kansas City's decision to change pitching coaches last summer did not sit well with Appier. When Guy Hansen handled the pitchers, Appier had a 33-16 mark and 2.52 ERA. With Bruce Kison in charge, Appier got off to a poor start. He needed mechanical adjustments to improve his control and combat arm fatigue in April. Things were better by May 25, when Appier fanned 13—one shy of the club record—in five and one-third innings against Texas. His luck didn't last, however. Failing to follow his usual routine of warming with the weather, Appier stumbled into the strike with the highest ERA of his career and a record just one game above .500. Appier is usually able to throw strikes with a fastball, a forkball, a curve, and a slider. When he was pitching at his best, he was handcuffing right-handed hitters, yielding less than eight hits per nine innings, and keeping the ball in the park. The 1993 AL ERA king averages more than eight strikeouts per game.

Major League Pitching Register

	W	L	ERA	G	CG	IP	H	ER	BB	SO
89 AL	1	4	9.14	6	0	21.2	34	22	12	10
90 AL	12	8	2.76	32	3	185.2	179	57	54	127
91 AL	13	10	3.42	34	6	207.2	205	79	61	158
92 AL	15	8	2.46	30	3	208.1	167	57	68	150
93 AL	18	8	2.56	34	5	238.2	183	68	81	186
94 AL	7	6	3.83	23	1	155.0	137	66	63	145
Life	66	44	3.09	159	18	1017.0	905	349	339	776
3 AVE	14	8	2.95	32	3	221.1	181	73	79	180

ALEX ARIAS

Position: Infield
Team: Florida Marlins
Born: Nov. 20, 1967   New York, NY
Height: 6'3"   **Weight:** 185 lbs.
Bats: right   **Throws:** right
Acquired: Traded from Cubs with Gary Scott for Greg Hibbard, 11/92

Player Summary

Fantasy Value	$0
Card Value	8¢ to 12¢
Will	try to make contact
Can't	come through in clutch
Expect	a utility role
Don't Expect	any power

Given limited opportunities as a utility player last year, Arias abandoned his previous habit of selectivity at the plate. Once a player who walked more than he fanned, he reversed that trend—and watched his batting average fall as a result. Used as a three-position infielder by the Marlins, he contributed zero power and did not inject any speed into the lineup. He lost the short-stop job to Kurt Abbott. Arias performed well when pressed into service at short and third base, however. Arias, who can also play second, did his best work at Joe Robbie Stadium, where he actually hit over .300 before the Aug. 12 player strike. Unfortunately, he was ineffective with runners in scoring position and in late-inning pressure situations. At 27, Arias could be at a career crossroads. He apparently needs more activity to stay sharp enough to produce when called upon. Originally a third-round pick of the Cubs in 1987, Arias hit so well in a 32-game trial with Chicago in '92 that the Marlins acquired him just after the expansion draft.

Major League Batting Register

	BA	G	AB	R	H	2B	3B	HR	RBI	SB
92 NL	.293	32	99	14	29	6	0	0	7	0
93 NL	.269	96	249	27	67	5	1	2	20	1
94 NL	.239	59	113	4	27	5	0	0	15	0
Life	.267	187	461	45	123	16	1	2	42	1

JACK ARMSTRONG

Position: Pitcher
Team: Texas Rangers
Born: March 7, 1965 Englewood, NJ
Height: 6'5" **Weight:** 220 lbs.
Bats: right **Throws:** right
Acquired: Signed as a free agent, 1/94

Player Summary	
Fantasy Value	$0
Card Value	5¢ to 7¢
Will	need medical miracle
Can't	prevent gopher balls
Expect	trouble vs. southpaws
Don't Expect	1990's form

Armstrong's return to the AL was placed on hold last year by a torn rotator cuff. The former Cleveland pitcher—who also played for the Reds and Marlins before the Rangers—had been expected to step into the Texas rotation, even though he had losing records in the three previous seasons. Coaches still like Armstrong's potential. He throws a 92-mph fastball as well as a curveball, a slider, and a changeup. He tends to give up too many home runs, however, and has trouble with left-handed hitters. In addition, he had his own personal injury wave even before the rotator cuff problems became public. When he's right, Armstrong gets numerous ground-ball outs and does his best pitching with runners in scoring position. He started the All-Star Game for the NL in 1990, when he won 11 of his first 14 decisions for the Reds. Armstrong has good control, but he sabotages his own efforts with weak fielding and an inability to keep baserunners close.

Major League Pitching Register

	W	L	ERA	G	CG	IP	H	ER	BB	SO
88 NL	4	7	5.79	14	0	65.1	63	42	38	45
89 NL	2	3	4.64	9	0	42.2	40	22	21	23
90 NL	12	9	3.42	29	2	166.0	151	63	59	110
91 NL	7	13	5.48	27	1	139.2	158	85	54	93
92 AL	6	15	4.64	35	1	166.2	176	86	67	114
93 NL	7	17	4.49	36	0	196.1	210	98	78	118
94 AL	0	1	3.60	2	0	10.0	9	4	2	7
Life	40	65	4.58	152	4	786.2	807	400	319	510
2 AVE	8	16	4.56	36	1	181.2	193	92	73	116

RENE AROCHA

Position: Pitcher
Team: St. Louis Cardinals
Born: Feb. 24, 1966 Havana, Cuba
Height: 6' **Weight:** 180 lbs.
Bats: right **Throws:** right
Acquired: Signed as a free agent, 11/91

Player Summary	
Fantasy Value	$12 to $15
Card Value	8¢ to 12¢
Will	retain relief role
Can't	avoid home runs
Expect	fine control
Don't Expect	knuckleballs

A washout as a starting pitcher, Arocha carved his niche in the St. Louis bullpen last season. After moving to the pen on May 10, he posted a 2.36 ERA and 11 saves until he went down with an inflamed elbow. As a reliever, Arocha found he no longer had to pace himself. He threw harder for shorter periods and regained his once-exceptional control. Arocha averaged about two walks and seven strikeouts per nine innings. He does an adequate job of holding runners and fields his position well but doesn't pose a threat as a hitter, though he knows how to bunt. Arocha yields more hits than innings pitched and sometimes has trouble keeping balls in the park. Because of his wide repertoire, however, Arocha keeps hitters guessing. He throws seven pitches, though the Cardinals have put the kibosh on his knuckler for the time being. A forkball and a splitter produce plenty of ground balls when he is on top of his game. Arocha, a defector from the 1991 Cuban national team, was sent to Triple-A immediately in 1992 and compiled a 12-7 record with a 2.70 ERA.

Major League Pitching Register

	W	L	ERA	G	S	IP	H	ER	BB	SO
93 NL	11	8	3.78	32	0	188.0	197	79	31	96
94 NL	4	4	4.01	45	11	83.0	94	37	21	62
Life	15	12	3.85	77	11	271.0	291	116	52	158
2 AVE	8	7	3.87	48	8	152.0	165	66	30	92

ANDY ASHBY

Position: Pitcher
Team: San Diego Padres
Born: July 11, 1967 Kansas City, MO
Height: 6'5" **Weight:** 180 lbs.
Bats: right **Throws:** right
Acquired: Traded from Rockies with Doug
Bochtler and Brad Ausmus for Greg Harris
and Bruce Hurst, 7/93

Player Summary	
Fantasy Value	$10 to $13
Card Value	8¢ to 12¢
Will	show good control
Can't	keep runners close
Expect	wins with support
Don't Expect	return to pen

Before 1994, Ashby was generally regarded as a player with a great arm and a pitcher's body, but someone who couldn't throw strikes. He was once considered the top Phillie pitching product and was a first-round expansion pick by the Rockies. However, both the Phillies and Rockies gave up on him before the Padres, desperate for inexpensive pitchers with experience, gave him a chance to join their rotation. Under no pressure on a last-place team, Ashby prospered. He showed good command of his sinking fastball, cut fastball, curve, and changeup. He also developed enough confidence to throw any of them at any time. After going 48 career starts without a complete game, he threw four in eight starts. In 1994, Ashby allowed less hits than innings pitched and averaged about seven strikeouts and two and one-half walks per game. He dominates right-handed hitters and keeps gopher balls to a minimum. Ashby is an adequate fielder but a light hitter. A poor pickoff move is his biggest problem.

Major League Pitching Register

	W	L	ERA	G	CG	IP	H	ER	BB	SO
91 NL	1	5	6.00	8	0	42.0	41	28	19	26
92 NL	1	3	7.54	10	0	37.0	42	31	21	24
93 NL	3	10	6.80	32	0	123.0	168	93	56	77
94 NL	6	11	3.40	24	4	164.1	145	62	43	121
Life	11	29	5.26	74	4	366.1	396	214	139	248
2 AVE	6	13	4.58	33	3	177.1	186	90	58	124

PAUL ASSENMACHER

Position: Pitcher
Team: Chicago White Sox
Born: Dec. 10, 1960 Detroit, MI
Height: 6'3" **Weight:** 200 lbs.
Bats: left **Throws:** left
Acquired: Purchased from Yankees, 3/94

Player Summary	
Fantasy Value	$1 to $3
Card Value	5¢ to 7¢
Will	strand inherited runners
Can't	let righties hit heater
Expect	sweeping overhand curve
Don't Expect	a closer role

One of baseball's true specialists, Assenmacher has a simple assignment: retire one or two left-handed hitters in key late-inning situations. Because he excels in that role, Assenmacher invariably finishes each season with a higher total of appearances than innings pitched. Though he throws a fastball, a curve, and a changeup, he is known throughout baseball for the effectiveness of his curve. It's a sweeping hook, delivered with an overhand motion and deadly for the left-handed hitters who try to pick it up. Because of the curve, Assenmacher in 1994 averaged nearly eight strikeouts per nine innings. Over that same span, he also yielded seven hits and three and one-half walks. He's stingy with the home run ball and fields his position well but is an easy mark for basestealers. Assenmacher was picked up by the White Sox last year to fill in for Scott Radinsky.

Major League Pitching Register

	W	L	ERA	G	S	IP	H	ER	BB	SO
86 NL	7	3	2.50	61	7	68.1	61	19	26	56
87 NL	1	1	5.10	52	2	54.2	58	31	24	39
88 NL	8	7	3.06	64	5	79.1	72	27	32	71
89 NL	3	4	3.99	63	0	76.2	74	34	28	79
90 NL	7	2	2.80	74	10	103.0	90	32	36	95
91 NL	7	8	3.24	75	15	102.2	85	37	31	117
92 NL	4	4	4.10	70	8	68.0	72	31	26	67
93 NL	2	1	3.49	46	0	38.2	44	15	13	34
93 AL	2	2	3.12	26	0	17.1	10	6	9	11
94 AL	1	2	3.55	44	1	33.0	26	13	13	29
Life	42	34	3.44	575	48	641.2	592	245	238	598
3 AVE	3	3	3.71	68	3	56.1	54	23	22	51

PEDRO ASTACIO

Position: Pitcher
Team: Los Angeles Dodgers
Born: Nov. 28, 1969 Hato Mayor, Dominican Republic
Height: 6'2" **Weight:** 195 lbs.
Bats: right **Throws:** right
Acquired: Signed as a free agent, 11/87

Player Summary

Fantasy Value	$9 to $11
Card Value	6¢ to 10¢
Will	bank on changeup
Can't	finish his starts
Expect	varied repertoire
Don't Expect	less intensity

After leading the Dodgers with 14 wins in 1993, Astacio was expected to produce bigger and better numbers last summer. It didn't happen—partly because the young right-hander didn't enjoy the same success against lefty hitters as he did against right-ies. Astacio certainly has the credentials. In 1994, he averaged six and one-half strike-outs and less than three walks per nine in-nings and yielded less hits than innings pitched. He throws his share of home run balls and has modest success in prevent-ing running backs from stealing. Astacio's arsenal is fine: a sinking fastball, a curveball, and a changeup that acts like a screwball. His running speed helps him as a fielder who's quick to cover first and as a hitter who oc-casionally legs out bunts and infield rollers. Astacio's enthusiasm is obvious: He races off the mound after escaping a jam, pump-ing up the home crowd as well as his team-mates. If his consistency matched that enthusiasm, Astacio would be much more successful. Challenging the hitters more often would help.

BRAD AUSMUS

Position: Catcher
Team: San Diego Padres
Born: April 14, 1969 New Haven, CT
Height: 5'11" **Weight:** 190 lbs.
Bats: right **Throws:** right
Acquired: Traded from Rockies with Doug Bochtler and Andy Ashby for Bruce Hurst and Greg Harris, 7/93

Player Summary

Fantasy Value	$4 to $6
Card Value	8¢ to 12¢
Will	improve his throwing
Can't	avoid striking out
Expect	occasional gap power
Don't Expect	Sandy Alomar

In recent years, the penny-pinching Padres have traded Sandy Alomar and let Benny Santiago move to the Marlins as a free agent. Although he arrived with a reputation for defensive excellence, Ausmus has yet to don that mantle. When he had trouble throwing last year, with only about 30 per-cent of runners caught stealing, the young-ster got a crash course in throwing from coach Bruce Bochy. Ausmus's strong arm, quick release, and all-around catching skills advertised in advance seemed to be ob-scured by occasional lapses in judgement, coupled with an obvious lack of experience. On the offensive end, Ausmus showed some power, as well as exceptional speed for a catcher. Twenty of his first 80 hits went for extra bases, including seven home runs. The Dartmouth product should improve if he reduces his current 2-1 ratio of strike-outs to walks. He hit only eight homers dur-ing a five-year stint in the minors but has shown increasing power and bat speed in recent seasons. He hit .270 at Triple-A in 1993.

Major League Pitching Register

	W	L	ERA	G	CG	IP	H	ER	BB	SO
92 NL	5	5	1.98	11	4	82.0	80	18	20	43
93 NL	14	9	3.57	31	3	186.1	165	74	68	122
94 NL	6	8	4.29	23	3	149.0	142	71	47	108
Life	25	22	3.52	65	10	417.1	387	163	135	273
3 AVE	9	8	3.61	25	4	159.0	148	64	51	106

Major League Batting Register

	BA	G	AB	R	H	2B	3B	HR	RBI	SB
93 NL	.256	49	160	18	41	8	1	5	12	2
94 NL	.251	101	327	45	82	12	1	7	24	5
Life	.253	150	487	63	123	20	2	12	36	7
2 AVE	.252	96	310	41	78	12	1	7	23	5

STEVE AVERY

Position: Pitcher
Team: Atlanta Braves
Born: April 14, 1970 Trenton, MI
Height: 6'4" **Weight:** 180 lbs.
Bats: left **Throws:** left
Acquired: First-round pick in 6/88 free-agent draft

Player Summary	
Fantasy Value	$20 to $25
Card Value	20¢ to 35¢
Will	combine poise, control
Can't	halt rival baserunners
Expect	a comeback season
Don't Expect	losing streaks

Although he'll only be 24 when the 1995 season opens, Avery has already had a fine career. He's had two 18-win seasons, won playoff MVP honors, and pitched in the World Series. Considering those achievements, his 1994 season was disappointing. After his son was born three months prematurely and hospitalized for a long period, Avery altered his between-starts routine so that he could return to his Michigan home. Problems developed with his windup and delivery, as he won only once in 11 starts through July 21 and yielded more home runs and walks than usual. He returned to form just before the strike started. When he's on, Avery is a control pitcher who averages seven strikeouts per game and less hits than innings pitched. A quick worker, he keeps the ball down—inducing ground outs and double plays. Avery is a fine fielder, bunter, and hitter, but has problems holding runners—an unusual flaw for a southpaw. His slow delivery allows runners to get a jump.

Major League Pitching Register

	W	L	ERA	G	CG	IP	H	ER	BB	SO
90 NL	3	11	5.64	21	1	99.0	121	62	45	75
91 NL	18	8	3.38	35	3	210.1	189	79	65	137
92 NL	11	11	3.20	35	2	233.2	216	83	71	129
93 NL	18	6	2.94	35	3	223.1	216	73	43	125
94 NL	8	3	4.04	24	1	151.2	127	68	55	122
Life	58	39	3.58	150	10	918.0	869	365	279	588
3 AVE	13	7	3.38	35	2	223.2	204	84	64	142

BOBBY AYALA

Position: Pitcher
Team: Seattle Mariners
Born: July 8, 1968 Ventura, CA
Height: 6'3" **Weight:** 200 lbs.
Bats: right **Throws:** right
Acquired: Traded from Reds with Dan Wilson for Erik Hanson and Bret Boone, 11/93

Player Summary	
Fantasy Value	$25 to $30
Card Value	8¢ to 15¢
Will	blow righties away
Can't	always locate plate
Expect	many splitters
Don't Expect	fewer saves

Even before inheriting the vacant closer job in Seattle, Ayala was an obvious candidate for the role. With an arsenal of a 95-mph fastball, a slider, and a forkball, he had the variety as well as the velocity to succeed in the late innings. He also led the Double-A Southern League in strikeouts in 1992. Given full-time work by the Mariners, he recorded four wins, 18 saves, and a 2.86 ERA during the 1994 campaign. Last season Ayala fanned three times more men than he walked, kept the ball in the park, and decimated right-handed hitters. He yielded less than seven hits per nine innings while averaging a dozen strikeouts during the same span. His prime problem is occasional wildness. He gave up more than four walks per game last year. His best bet is to keep runners off base. He's neither a good fielder nor practioner of the pickoff move. Ayala is also better suited for starting an inning than entering with runners on, as disposing of inherited runners is not one of his strong suits. He should, however, improve with time.

Major League Pitching Register

	W	L	ERA	G	S	IP	H	ER	BB	SO
92 NL	2	1	4.34	5	0	29.0	33	14	13	23
93 NL	7	10	5.60	43	3	98.0	106	61	45	65
94 AL	4	3	2.86	46	18	56.2	42	18	26	76
Life	13	14	4.56	94	21	183.2	181	93	84	164
2 AVE	6	7	4.37	54	14	88.1	83	43	41	86

CARLOS BAERGA

Position: Second base
Team: Cleveland Indians
Born: Nov. 4, 1968 San Juan, Puerto Rico
Height: 5′11″ **Weight:** 165 lbs.
Bats: both **Throws:** right
Acquired: Traded from Padres with Sandy Alomar and Chris James for Joe Carter, 12/89

Player Summary	
Fantasy Value. . . . . $30 to $35
Card Value . . . . 30¢ to 50¢
Will. . . . . hit right-handers best
Can't . . . . win Gold Glove
Expect . . . . great production
Don't Expect . . . . patience

Before the strike-shortened 1994 season, Baerga had become the first AL second baseman ever to record a .300 batting average, 20 home runs, 100 RBI, and 200 hits in the same season. And he did it two years in a row. Last spring, however, he reported to training camp nearly 15 pounds overweight. The resulting slow start forced Baerga to regroup. He met the challenge with flying colors. By early August, he was on pace to approach those lofty numbers again. Only his on-base percentage stayed down—the result of his refusal to show any patience at the plate. When he got his second walk of the season June 5, it was his first in 134 at bats. Baerga makes good contact and hits to all fields but is much more effective against right-handed pitching. He fattens his batting average with occasional bunts, and he usually succeeds when he tries to steal. He has good range at second, where he shows a strong arm and turns the double play well.

Major League Batting Register

	BA	G	AB	R	H	2B	3B	HR	RBI	SB
90 AL	.260	108	312	46	81	17	2	7	47	0
91 AL	.288	158	593	80	171	28	2	11	69	3
92 AL	.312	161	657	92	205	32	1	20	105	10
93 AL	.321	154	624	105	200	28	6	21	114	15
94 AL	.314	103	442	81	139	32	2	19	80	8
Life	.303	684	2628	404	796	137	13	78	415	36
3 AVE	.316	153	635	104	200	35	3	23	111	12

JEFF BAGWELL

Position: First base
Team: Houston Astros
Born: May 27, 1968 Boston, MA
Height: 6′ **Weight:** 195 lbs.
Bats: right **Throws:** right
Acquired: Traded from Red Sox for Larry Andersen, 8/90

Player Summary	
Fantasy Value. . . . . $35 to $40
Card Value . . . . 30¢ to 50¢
Will . . . . near Triple Crown
Can't . . . . play nine spots
Expect . . . . many All-Star trips
Don't Expect . . . . missed RBI chances

Last summer, Bagwell suddenly became a Triple Crown contender. He had been a fine batter, but he added vast power and superior run production to the mix. He established Houston records for average, homers, RBI, and extra-base hits. He topped the NL in runs and RBI—the first time anyone has done that since Mike Schmidt in 1981. Bagwell was the NL Player of the Month in both June and July. He began hitting the ball hard the minute the season started. He had a career-best 26 RBI in April and improved on that pace. The first big leaguer to reach 100 RBI last year, he hit at a blistering clip against lefties. Once an easy strikeout victim, he learned to become more selective—giving him a high on-base percentage for a power hitter. Bagwell topped the NL in total bases and slugging while ranking second in batting, hits, homers, and on-base average. He is also a superb defensive player. Bagwell's left hand, broken by an Andy Benes pitch Aug. 10, should not hamper his 1995 performance.

Major League Batting Register

	BA	G	AB	R	H	2B	3B	HR	RBI	SB
91 NL	.294	156	554	79	163	26	4	15	82	7
92 NL	.273	162	586	87	160	34	6	18	96	10
93 NL	.320	142	535	76	171	37	4	20	88	13
94 NL	.368	110	400	104	147	32	2	39	116	15
Life	.309	570	2075	346	641	129	16	92	382	45
3 AVE	.319	153	561	103	179	39	4	31	116	15

HAROLD BAINES

Position: Designated hitter
Team: Baltimore Orioles
Born: March 15, 1959 Easton, MD
Height: 6'2" **Weight:** 195 lbs.
Bats: left **Throws:** left
Acquired: Traded from Athletics for Bobby Choinard and Allen Plaster, 1/93

Player Summary	
Fantasy Value.	$8 to $10
Card Value	8¢ to 15¢
Will	produce in the clutch
Can't	handle all southpaws
Expect	long-ball production
Don't Expect	much speed

His knees don't allow him to play the outfield anymore, but Baines can still hit. His 442-foot homer against Toronto last July 30 was the longest ever hit by an Oriole at Camden Yards. Though Baines sometimes struggles against southpaws, he hits well over .300 against right-handers. He has power to the opposite field but is a dead-pull hitter when he hits grounders. That makes him difficult to defense, though some clubs play three infielders on the right side against him. Baines is no threat to bunt or even take an extra base. Stealing is out of the question. His knees have been operated on so often that it is only a matter of time before they will force Baines into retirement.

Major League Batting Register

	BA	G	AB	R	H	2B	3B	HR	RBI	SB
80 AL	.255	141	491	55	125	23	6	13	49	2
81 AL	.286	82	280	42	80	11	7	10	41	6
82 AL	.271	161	608	89	165	29	8	25	105	10
83 AL	.280	156	596	76	167	33	2	20	99	7
84 AL	.304	147	569	72	173	28	10	29	94	1
85 AL	.309	160	640	86	198	29	3	22	113	1
86 AL	.296	145	570	72	169	29	2	21	88	2
87 AL	.293	132	505	59	148	26	4	20	93	0
88 AL	.277	158	599	55	166	39	1	13	81	0
89 AL	.309	146	505	73	156	29	1	16	72	0
90 AL	.284	135	415	52	118	15	1	16	65	0
91 AL	.295	141	488	76	144	25	1	20	90	0
92 AL	.253	140	478	58	121	18	0	16	76	1
93 AL	.313	118	416	64	130	22	0	20	78	0
94 AL	.294	94	326	44	96	12	1	16	54	0
Life	.288	2056	7486	973	2156	368	47	277	1198	30
3 AVE	.285	130	451	61	129	19	0	20	77	0

SCOTT BANKHEAD

Position: Pitcher
Team: New York Yankees
Born: July 31, 1963 Raleigh, NC
Height: 5'10" **Weight:** 185 lbs.
Bats: right **Throws:** right
Acquired: Traded from Red Sox for a player to be named later and cash, 8/94

Player Summary	
Fantasy Value.	$1 to $3
Card Value	5¢ to 7¢
Will	show good control
Can't	think about shoulder
Expect.	few stolen bases
Don't Expect.	back-to-back outings

As a former starter now working mainly in middle relief, Bankhead has the repertoire, composure, and experience to suit the job. A sinker-slider pitcher who uses a curve as his changeup, Bankhead is a fast worker who helps himself with his fielding and pick-off move. Few runners challenge him. The 1984 Olympian yields less hits than innings pitched and averages about three walks and six strikeouts per nine innings. Because of past shoulder problems, Bankhead cannot pitch for long stretches or in consecutive games, nor can he warm up more than once a night. Once on the mound, however, he's a tough competitor who makes his living by pitching inside. He pitched for the Royals, Mariners, and Reds before coming to the Red Sox in 1993. His best year as a starter was in 1989 for Seattle. His shoulder problems recurred the following year.

Major League Pitching Register

	W	L	ERA	G	S	IP	H	ER	BB	SO
86 AL	8	9	4.61	24	0	121.0	121	62	37	94
87 AL	9	8	5.42	27	0	149.1	168	90	37	95
88 AL	7	9	3.07	21	0	135.0	115	46	38	102
89 AL	14	6	3.34	33	0	210.1	187	78	63	140
90 AL	0	2	11.08	4	0	13.0	18	16	7	10
91 AL	3	6	4.90	17	0	60.2	73	33	21	28
92 NL	10	4	2.93	54	1	70.2	57	23	29	53
93 AL	2	1	3.50	40	0	64.1	59	25	29	47
94 AL	3	2	4.54	27	0	37.2	34	19	12	25
Life	56	47	4.09	247	1	862.0	832	392	273	594
3 AVE	5	3	3.58	44	0	62.2	55	25	25	45

WILLIE BANKS

Position: Pitcher
Team: Chicago Cubs
Born: Feb. 27, 1969 Jersey City, NJ
Height: 6'1" **Weight:** 190 lbs.
Bats: right **Throws:** right
Acquired: Traded from Twins for Dave Stevens and Matt Walbeck, 11/93

Player Summary	
Fantasy Value	$2 to $4
Card Value	6¢ to 10¢
Will	learn on the job
Can't	keep consistency
Expect	improving changeup
Don't Expect	stolen bases

For Banks, the 1994 season was an ongoing learning process. For three weeks in May, he sparkled, with a 4-0 record and 1.47 ERA. He blanked the Dodgers on May 24 for his first shutout in 55 career starts. When he's right, Banks mixes his fine fastball and curve with a straight change refined last year by Cub pitching coach Moe Drabowsky. When he hits the right spots, gets the breaking ball over, and keeps hitters off balance by blending his pitches, Banks begins to pay dividends on the ability that once made him Minnesota's No. 1 draft choice. Mechanical problems marred much of his 1994 campaign, however. He was pitching with his left elbow outside the knee, causing him to fall away from the plate in his follow-through. A fly-ball pitcher, Banks in 1994 averaged about a hit per inning and yielded six hits and three and one-half walks per game. He is much more effective against right-handed hitters. Banks is very good at holding runners, but his defense and his batting need some work.

Major League Pitching Register

	W	L	ERA	G	CG	IP	H	ER	BB	SO
91 AL	1	1	5.71	5	0	17.1	21	11	12	16
92 AL	4	4	5.70	16	0	71.0	80	45	37	37
93 AL	11	12	4.04	31	0	171.1	186	77	78	138
94 NL	8	12	5.40	23	1	138.1	139	83	56	91
Life	24	29	4.88	75	1	398.0	426	216	183	282
3 AVE	9	11	4.92	26	0	145.1	154	80	65	101

BRET BARBERIE

Position: Second base
Team: Baltimore Orioles
Born: Aug. 16, 1967 Long Beach, CA
Height: 5'11" **Weight:** 185 lbs.
Bats: both **Throws:** right
Acquired: Traded from Marlins for Jay Powell, 12/94

Player Summary	
Fantasy Value	$8 to $10
Card Value	6¢ to 10¢
Will	surprise with power
Can't	steal bases often
Expect	clutch hitting
Don't Expect	defensive woes

A switch-hitter who's better from the right side, Barberie produces surprising punch for a middle infielder. Though he once hit home runs from both sides of the plate in the same game, he's not a major home run threat, but does collect his share of extra-base hits. Though he fans three times more often than he walks, Barberie has some idea of the strike zone. He also hits well in late-inning pressure spots. Although Barberie has some speed, he hasn't tried to steal much the last couple of years. He is a top-notch fielder at second base. His range extends well to his left, he reacts quickly, and he has an arm that was once considered strong enough to play third base. Playing in one place has helped Barberie, who was once used as a three-position infielder by the Expos and opened the 1992 season as the Montreal third baseman. Injuries have hampered his progress in the past, but he should have a clear road ahead. The Southern Cal graduate was All-Pac-10 and a member of the U.S. Olympic team in 1988.

Major League Batting Register

	BA	G	AB	R	H	2B	3B	HR	RBI	SB
91 NL	.353	57	136	16	48	12	2	2	18	0
92 NL	.232	111	285	26	66	11	0	1	24	9
93 NL	.277	99	375	45	104	16	2	5	33	2
94 NL	.301	107	372	40	112	20	2	5	31	2
Life	.283	374	1168	127	330	59	6	13	106	13
3 AVE	.277	120	395	42	109	18	2	4	34	5

KEVIN BASS

Position: Outfield
Team: Houston Astros
Born: May 12, 1959 Redwood City, CA
Height: 6′ **Weight:** 180 lbs.
Bats: both **Throws:** right
Acquired: Signed as a free agent, 1/93

Player Summary	
Fantasy Value.	$3 to $5
Card Value	6¢ to 10¢
Will	still hit ball hard
Can't	steal much anymore
Expect	good clutch hitting
Don't Expect	a regular spot

Even when the Astros handed their 1994 right-field job to James Mouton, Bass waited in the background, ready to play. When the rookie struggled, the veteran got his chance. Bass responded well—especially against left-handed pitching. He hit well over .300 with runners in scoring position and in late-inning pressure situations last season, and against lefties, his average soared into the .400 range. Always a good clutch hitter, he produced as a pinch hitter as well as a starter. He also contributed on defense, where he showed a good arm, fine range, and sound reactions. He broke into pro ball in 1977, five years before reaching the majors with the Brewers. He's hit home runs from both sides of the plate in the same game four times, a National League record.

Major League Batting Register

	BA	G	AB	R	H	2B	3B	HR	RBI	SB
82 AL	.000	18	9	4	0	0	0	0	0	0
82 NL	.042	12	24	2	1	0	0	0	1	0
83 NL	.236	88	195	25	46	7	3	2	18	2
84 NL	.260	121	331	33	86	17	5	2	29	5
85 NL	.269	150	539	72	145	27	5	16	68	19
86 NL	.311	157	591	83	184	33	5	20	79	22
87 NL	.284	157	592	83	168	31	5	19	85	21
88 NL	.255	157	541	57	138	27	2	14	72	31
89 NL	.300	87	313	42	94	19	4	5	44	11
90 NL	.252	61	214	25	54	9	1	7	32	2
91 NL	.233	124	361	43	84	10	4	10	40	7
92 NL	.269	135	402	40	108	23	5	9	39	14
93 NL	.284	111	229	31	65	18	0	3	37	7
94 NL	.310	82	203	37	63	15	1	6	35	2
Life	.272	1460	4544	577	1236	236	40	113	579	143
3 AVE	.285	121	306	41	87	21	2	7	42	8

KIM BATISTE

Position: Shortstop; third base
Team: Philadelphia Phillies
Born: March 15, 1968 New Orleans, LA
Height: 6′ **Weight:** 193 lbs.
Bats: right **Throws:** right
Acquired: Third-round pick in 6/87 free-agent draft

Player Summary	
Fantasy Value	$0
Card Value	5¢ to 7¢
Will.	swing at anything
Can't.	hold regular job
Expect	some clutch hits
Don't Expect.	polished defense

Although given the chance to win daily duty at both shortstop and third base in recent seasons, Batiste has blown both opportunities. He can't hit breaking balls, can't play consistent defense, and could be the least patient hitter in the major leagues. He went 181 at bats last year before drawing his first walk of the season on July 31. Most pitchers are more patient at the plate. Batiste does his best hitting in late-inning pressure situations but has trouble hitting his weight in several other key categories. He should be much more productive against left-handers, for example; he was in 1993, when he was platooned in the first half of the season. Defensively, his troubles in the 1993 postseason got national exposure. Yet the Phils gave him another look at third when Dave Hollins was sidelined last May. After Batiste made five errors in 11 games, the team shifted Mariano Duncan to the position instead. Despite his strong arm, Batiste won't ever be anything more than a utility infielder.

Major League Batting Register

	BA	G	AB	R	H	2B	3B	HR	RBI	SB
91 NL	.222	10	27	2	6	0	0	0	1	0
92 NL	.206	44	136	9	28	4	0	1	10	0
93 NL	.282	79	156	14	44	7	1	5	29	0
94 NL	.234	64	209	17	49	6	0	1	13	1
Life	.241	197	528	42	127	17	1	7	53	1
2 AVE	.251	85	225	19	57	8	1	3	24	1

JOSE BAUTISTA

Position: Pitcher
Team: Chicago Cubs
Born: July 25, 1964   Bani, Dominican Republic
Height: 6'2"   **Weight:** 205 lbs.
Bats: right   **Throws:** right
Acquired: Signed as a minor-league free agent, 12/92

Player Summary	
Fantasy Value	$3 to $5
Card Value	5¢ to 7¢
Will	usually throw strikes
Can't	quiet left-handed bats
Expect	frequent bullpen calls
Don't Expect	occasional starts

The line drive that broke his wrist Aug. 5 ended Bautista's stated ambition of breaking the Cubs' record for appearances (84 by Ted Abernathy). Bautista was working in his 58th game when the accident occurred. Used strictly in relief after making seven starts the year before, the rubber-armed right-hander showed fine control while allowing slightly more than a hit per inning. He also averaged nearly six strikeouts per game while stranding 70 percent of the runners he inherited. Bautista, whose 2.82 ERA had topped the Cub staff in 1993, had trouble with lefties last year. He also fell victim to the gopher ball—a common problem in Wrigley Field. Bautista usually helps himself with his fielding. His pickoff move is sabotaged by his slow delivery, however. He doesn't add a thing with his bat. Bautista's repertoire—extensive for a middle reliever—includes a fastball, a slider, a curveball, and a forkball that he throws at two different speeds.

Major League Pitching Register

	W	L	ERA	G	S	IP	H	ER	BB	SO
88 AL	6	15	4.30	33	0	171.2	171	82	45	76
89 AL	3	4	5.31	15	0	78.0	84	46	15	30
90 AL	1	0	4.05	22	0	26.2	28	12	7	15
91 AL	0	1	16.88	5	0	5.1	13	10	5	3
93 NL	10	3	2.82	58	2	111.2	105	35	27	63
94 NL	4	5	3.89	58	1	69.1	75	30	17	45
Life	24	28	4.18	191	3	462.2	476	215	116	232
2 AVE	8	5	3.32	70	2	104.2	105	39	25	63

ROD BECK

Position: Pitcher
Team: San Francisco Giants
Born: Aug. 3, 1968   Burbank, CA
Height: 6'1"   **Weight:** 215 lbs.
Bats: right   **Throws:** right
Acquired: Traded from Athletics for Charlie Corbell, 3/88

Player Summary	
Fantasy Value	$40 to $45
Card Value	8¢ to 15¢
Will	seldom blow a save
Can't	prevent gophers
Expect	four good pitches
Don't Expect	uneven control

Rival hitters agree: Rod Beck looks mean. When they see his forkball, they know he has no sympathy for their cause. In three short seasons, Beck has established himself as one of baseball's premier closers. Last July 30, he converted his 25th save in as many chances—a major-league record—and his 67th in 69 career opportunities. Such a performance has landed him on the NL All-Star team in each of the last two seasons. He also throws a sinker, a slider, and a mid-90s fastball, and he succeeds primarily because of uncanny control. He averages one and one-half walks per nine innings and about seven strikeouts over the same span. He also yields about a hit per inning. Since Beck is always around the plate, some of those hits leave the yard. He's adept at holding runners and fielding his position. His lone weakness is that he tires from overwork. Beck averaged 70½ appearances per year in 1992 and 1993. He had fewer save opportunities last summer, yet still finished second in the NL in saves.

Major League Pitching Register

	W	L	ERA	G	S	IP	H	ER	BB	SO
91 NL	1	1	3.78	31	1	52.1	53	22	13	38
92 NL	3	3	1.76	65	17	92.0	62	18	15	87
93 NL	3	1	2.16	76	48	79.1	57	19	13	86
94 NL	2	4	2.77	48	28	48.2	49	15	13	39
Life	9	9	2.45	220	94	272.1	221	74	54	250
3 AVE	3	3	2.18	70	35	80.1	63	19	15	76

STEVE BEDROSIAN

Position: Pitcher
Team: Atlanta Braves
Born: Dec. 6, 1957   Methuen, MA
Height: 6'3"   **Weight:** 210 lbs.
Bats: right   **Throws:** right
Acquired: Signed as a free agent, 3/93

Player Summary	
Fantasy Value	$1 to $3
Card Value	5¢ to 7¢
Will	work in middle innings
Can't	retire all left-handers
Expect	less hits than innings
Don't Expect	a Cy Young

Although he once won a Cy Young Award as a closer (in 1987), Bedrosian was used almost exclusively as a set-up reliever by the 1994 Braves. Age may have been a factor, or perhaps the fact that the veteran right-hander no longer has his once-frightening velocity. Bedrock still depends heavily upon his slider, but also mixes in a fastball and a forkball. His control remains good, and he still yields less hits than innings pitched—a feat he's failed to reach only once in 13 seasons. In 1994, Bedrosian averaged less than eight hits but more than eight strikeouts per nine innings. Right-handed batters are especially vulnerable when Bedrosian is on the mound. He has occasional problems with inherited runners, so he's best at the start of an inning. His pickoff move is the weakest part of his usually sound defense.

Major League Pitching Register

	W	L	ERA	G	S	IP	H	ER	BB	SO
81 NL	1	2	4.44	15	0	24.1	15	12	15	9
82 NL	8	6	2.42	64	11	137.2	102	37	57	123
83 NL	9	10	3.60	70	19	120.0	100	48	51	114
84 NL	9	6	2.37	40	11	83.2	65	22	33	81
85 NL	7	15	3.83	37	0	206.2	198	88	111	134
86 NL	8	6	3.39	68	29	90.1	79	34	34	82
87 NL	5	3	2.83	65	40	89.0	79	28	28	74
88 NL	6	6	3.75	57	28	74.1	75	31	27	61
89 NL	3	7	2.87	68	23	84.2	56	27	39	58
90 NL	9	9	4.20	68	17	79.1	72	37	44	43
91 AL	5	3	4.42	56	6	77.1	70	38	35	44
93 NL	5	2	1.63	49	0	49.2	34	9	14	33
94 NL	0	2	3.33	46	0	46.0	41	17	18	43
Life	75	77	3.31	703	184	1163.0	986	428	506	899
2 AVE	3	2	2.59	57	0	57.1	46	16	20	47

TIM BELCHER

Position: Pitcher
Team: Detroit Tigers
Born: Oct. 19, 1961   Mount Gilead, OH
Height: 6'3"   **Weight:** 210 lbs.
Bats: right   **Throws:** right
Acquired: Signed as a free agent, 2/94

Player Summary	
Fantasy Value	$3 to $5
Card Value	6¢ to 10¢
Will	bank on fastball
Can't	keep ball in park
Expect	ERA to be inflated
Don't Expect	top control

Making a good first impression is a great idea, but it doesn't always turn out that way. Belcher went 0-7 for the Tigers in his first nine starts, failing to win until May 17. Since he's a fly-ball pitcher who doesn't get many strikeouts, Belcher and Tiger Stadium, his new home park, might have been a poor match. He started winning only after reestablishing his fastball, which he sometimes uses on nine out of 10 pitches. Belcher also has a forkball, a slider, and a curve. Throwing them all for strikes posed some problems last year, when he limped into August with more walks than strikeouts. Belcher also yielded more hits than innings pitched and was one of three Tiger starters to throw 20 home run balls before the strike. He helps himself with his glove but has a slow delivery that encourages runners to steal. Though Belcher has won in double figures four times in eight years, his ERA has risen in recent summers.

Major League Pitching Register

	W	L	ERA	G	CG	IP	H	ER	BB	SO
87 NL	4	2	2.38	6	0	34.0	30	9	7	23
88 NL	12	6	2.91	36	4	179.2	143	58	51	152
89 NL	15	12	2.82	39	10	230.0	182	72	80	200
90 NL	9	9	4.00	24	5	153.0	136	68	48	102
91 NL	10	9	2.62	33	2	209.1	189	61	75	156
92 NL	15	14	3.91	35	2	227.2	201	99	80	149
93 NL	9	6	4.47	22	4	137.0	134	68	47	101
93 AL	3	5	4.40	12	1	71.2	64	35	27	34
94 AL	7	15	5.89	25	3	162.0	192	106	78	76
Life	84	78	3.69	232	31	1404.1	1271	576	493	993
3 AVE	12	15	4.76	35	4	221.1	223	117	88	130

STAN BELINDA

Position: Pitcher
Team: Kansas City Royals
Born: Aug. 6, 1966 Huntington, PA
Height: 6'3" **Weight:** 200 lbs.
Bats: right **Throws:** right
Acquired: Traded from Pirates for Dan Miceli and Jon Lieber, 7/93

Player Summary	
Fantasy Value. . . . . $1 to $3
Card Value . . . . 5¢ to 7¢
Will . . . . serve in set-up role
Can't . . . . always throw strikes
Expect. . . . . problems with lefties
Don't Expect. . . . . tight ERA

For three straight seasons, from 1991 to 1993, Belinda was the baron of the bullpen for the Pirates. He was the man inserted most often when the game situation called for a closer. Things changed for Belinda in '93, however, when the economy-minded Pirates peddled the pitcher to the Royals for two prospects. That deal made Belinda a set-up man for incumbent Jeff Montgomery. A sidearmer who augments his fastball with a forkball, Belinda yields less hits than innings pitched. Last year he averaged nearly seven strikeouts per game. But he is often betrayed by poor control and a tired arm. Though he sometimes struggles against left-handed hitters, Belinda fared equally against both righties and lefties last year. That wasn't necessarily good, since his work against right-handers had been far more effective in 1993. Belinda is an adequate fielder but needs work holding runners; his high-kicking delivery gives runners an extra step.

Major League Pitching Register

	W	L	ERA	G	S	IP	H	ER	BB	SO
89 NL	0	1	6.10	8	0	10.1	13	7	2	10
90 NL	3	4	3.55	55	8	58.1	48	23	29	55
91 NL	7	5	3.45	60	16	78.1	50	30	35	71
92 NL	6	4	3.15	59	18	71.1	58	25	29	57
93 NL	3	1	3.61	40	19	42.1	35	17	11	30
93 AL	1	1	4.28	23	0	27.1	30	13	6	25
94 AL	2	2	5.14	37	1	49.0	47	28	24	37
Life	22	18	3.82	282	62	337.0	281	143	136	285
3 AVE	4	3	4.05	58	13	70.1	63	31	27	55

DEREK BELL

Position: Outfield
Team: San Diego Padres
Born: Dec. 11, 1968 Tampa, FL
Height: 6'2" **Weight:** 200 lbs.
Bats: right **Throws:** right
Acquired: Traded from Blue Jays for Darrin Jackson and William Briggs, 3/93

Player Summary	
Fantasy Value. . . . . $20 to $25
Card Value . . . . 8¢ to 15¢
Will. . . . . bid for 30-30 club
Can't. . . . . hack at bad pitches
Expect . . . . better power numbers
Don't Expect . . . . a Gold Glove

If he learns to show more consistent power, Bell could blossom into a 30-30 talent. He still strikes out three times more than he walks, but that's an improvement over his ratio of previous years. Because of his speed, Bell would fatten his average with infield hits if he made contact more often. He's capable of hitting to the opposite field with power but needs to curb a tendency to swing at bad pitches. He's also prone to swinging at the first pitch. Despite those flaws, Bell blossomed into a .300 hitter last year. It was his presence behind No. 2 hitter Tony Gwynn that helped Gwynn hit for the highest average of his distinguished career. Bell is a good baserunner who is rarely thrown out when he tries to steal. That speed also helps him in the outfield, though his play in center was far short of acrobatic. Though he has a strong arm, Bell is better suited for one of the outfield corners. Once vilified in San Diego because he was traded for Darrin Jackson, Bell now delights Padre fans.

Major League Batting Register

	BA	G	AB	R	H	2B	3B	HR	RBI	SB
91 AL	.143	18	28	5	4	0	0	0	1	3
92 AL	.242	61	161	23	39	6	3	2	15	7
93 NL	.262	150	542	73	142	19	1	21	72	26
94 AL	.311	108	434	54	135	20	0	14	54	24
Life	.275	337	1165	155	320	45	4	37	142	60
3 AVE	.282	121	438	57	124	18	1	14	54	22

JAY BELL

Position: Shortstop
Team: Pittsburgh Pirates
Born: Dec. 11, 1965 Eglin Air Force Base, FL
Height: 6'1" **Weight:** 180 lbs.
Bats: right **Throws:** right
Acquired: Traded from Indians for Felix Fermin, 3/89

Player Summary	
Fantasy Value	$10 to $13
Card Value	8¢ to 12¢
Will	move runners over
Can't	stop striking out
Expect	great work vs. lefties
Don't Expect	many stolen bases

A first-time All-Star and Gold Glove winner in 1993, Bell picked up the baton and kept on running last summer. For the second straight season, he devoured left-handed pitching and proved he could win games with bunts as well as hits to the alleys. A solid .300 hitter with runners in scoring position, Bell would almost certainly become a big RBI man if he hit lower than No. 2 in the batting order. At present, however, his role is to bunt runners over, execute the hit-and-run, and set the table. Though he does the job well, he'd be better if he could reduce his 2-1 ratio of strikeouts to walks. Despite that drawback, NL managers polled by *Baseball America* last year rated him the league's top hit-and-run man, No. 2 bunter, and No. 3 defensive shortstop. Though his range is no better than average, Bell compensates with positioning and a fine arm. He homered on his first big-league pitch, with the 1986 Indians.

Major League Batting Register

	BA	G	AB	R	H	2B	3B	HR	RBI	SB
86 AL	.357	5	14	3	5	2	0	1	4	0
87 AL	.216	38	125	14	27	9	1	2	13	2
88 AL	.218	73	211	23	46	5	1	2	21	4
89 NL	.258	78	271	33	70	13	3	2	27	5
90 NL	.254	159	583	93	148	28	7	7	52	10
91 NL	.270	157	608	96	164	32	8	16	67	10
92 NL	.264	159	632	87	167	36	6	9	55	7
93 NL	.310	154	604	102	187	32	9	9	51	16
94 NL	.276	110	424	68	117	35	4	9	45	2
Life	.268	933	3472	519	931	192	39	57	335	56
3 AVE	.283	156	611	95	173	39	7	10	56	9

ALBERT BELLE

Position: Outfield
Team: Cleveland Indians
Born: Aug. 25, 1966 Shreveport, LA
Height: 6'2" **Weight:** 200 lbs.
Bats: right **Throws:** right
Acquired: Second-round pick in 6/87 free-agent draft

Player Summary	
Fantasy Value	$35 to $40
Card Value	30¢ to 50¢
Will	often carry club
Can't	earn Gold Glove
Expect	an MVP Award
Don't Expect	anxiety at bat

After leading the majors with 129 RBI in 1993, Belle became a Triple Crown contender last year. Though he lost a week when he was suspended for using a corked bat, he bounced back strong. When the Aug. 12 walkout began, he ranked second in batting and third in both home runs and RBI. He was also first in total bases, second in slugging and doubles, and third in on-base percentage. A patient hitter who's willing to wait for walks, Belle buries left-handers and excels in the clutch. His two-run homer in the eighth June 30 beat Baltimore 4-2 and was the fifth time he had won a 1994 game with his final swing (four home runs and a single). When he's hot, Belle can carry a club: He had eight hits, seven walks, and a hit-by-pitch during a stretch of 17 at bats last May. A student of hitting, his average stood well over .400 in Jacobs Field before the strike. He's worked hard to improve his play in left field, where he shows good range and an accurate arm.

Major League Batting Register

	BA	G	AB	R	H	2B	3B	HR	RBI	SB
89 AL	.225	62	218	22	49	8	4	7	37	2
90 AL	.174	9	23	1	4	0	0	1	3	0
91 AL	.282	123	461	60	130	31	2	28	95	3
92 AL	.260	153	585	81	152	23	1	34	112	8
93 AL	.290	159	594	93	172	36	3	38	129	23
94 AL	.357	106	412	90	147	35	2	36	101	9
Life	.285	612	2293	347	654	133	12	144	477	45
3 AVE	.302	154	586	100	177	36	2	41	128	15

ANDY BENES

Position: Pitcher
Team: San Diego Padres
Born: Aug. 20, 1967 Evansville, IN
Height: 6'6" **Weight:** 235 lbs.
Bats: right **Throws:** right
Acquired: First-round pick in 6/88 free-agent draft

Player Summary	
Fantasy Value	$15 to $18
Card Value	10¢ to 15¢
Will	bid for K crown
Can't	avoid some gophers
Expect	200 innings pitched
Don't Expect	control woes

The ace of the San Diego staff last summer got little support from his teammates. Although Benes led the National League in strikeouts last summer, he often ended up on the losing end of close decisions. Benes did manage 12 strikeouts and no walks during a 5-2 win at San Francisco June 12 and posted a 7-0 one-hitter against the Mets July 3. Benes averaged about 10 strikeouts, eight hits, and two and one-half walks per nine innings in 1994. He keeps runners close, dominates left-handed hitters, and helps himself with his fielding, bunting, and hitting. He has been known to hit the ball out of the park. Benes yields a few home runs himself, but that's mainly because of his fine control. A fastball-slider pitcher whose heater sinks, Benes has added an excellent changeup to his repertoire. The 1988 Olympian is a workhorse who is always among the league leaders in innings pitched. He had topped 200 innings three straight years before 1994.

Major League Pitching Register

	W	L	ERA	G	CG	IP	H	ER	BB	SO
89 NL	6	3	3.51	10	0	66.2	51	26	31	66
90 NL	10	11	3.60	32	2	192.1	177	77	69	140
91 NL	15	11	3.03	33	4	223.0	194	75	59	167
92 NL	13	14	3.35	34	2	231.1	230	86	61	169
93 NL	15	15	3.78	34	4	230.2	200	97	86	179
94 NL	6	14	3.86	25	2	172.1	155	74	51	189
Life	65	68	3.51	168	14	1116.1	1007	435	357	910
3 AVE	12	16	3.67	34	3	234.1	216	96	73	205

TODD BENZINGER

Position: First base
Team: San Francisco Giants
Born: Feb. 11, 1963 Dayton, KY
Height: 6'1" **Weight:** 190 lbs.
Bats: both **Throws:** right
Acquired: Signed as a free agent, 1/93

Player Summary	
Fantasy Value	$2 to $5
Card Value	5¢ to 7¢
Will	return to bench
Can't	run worth a lick
Expect	occasional power
Don't Expect	patience at plate

The free-agent exit of Will Clark and the spring failure of slugging rookie J.R. Phillips made Benzinger the Giants' first baseman by default. He failed to be a sufficient replacement for Clark. One year after providing punch off the bench in pinch-hitting roles, Benzinger returned to old habits, striking out five times more often than he walked. By the time the starts began, he hadn't hit his weight with runners in scoring position, though he had produced his best work in late-inning pressure situations. Benzinger's brilliance against left-handed pitching in 1993 virtually evaporated last summer. The switch-hitter was suddenly much more impressive against righties. He hit a handful of homers—the Giants expected much more—but brought no speed to the lineup. Benzinger is an adequate defensive first baseman, but he proved previously that he is less than adequate in the outfield.

Major League Batting Register

	BA	G	AB	R	H	2B	3B	HR	RBI	SB
87 AL	.278	73	223	36	62	11	1	8	43	5
88 AL	.254	120	405	47	103	28	1	13	70	2
89 NL	.245	161	628	79	154	28	3	17	76	3
90 NL	.253	118	376	35	95	14	2	5	46	3
91 NL	.187	51	123	7	23	3	2	1	11	2
91 AL	.294	78	293	29	86	15	3	2	40	2
92 NL	.239	121	293	24	70	16	2	4	31	2
93 NL	.288	86	177	25	51	7	2	6	26	0
94 NL	.265	107	328	32	87	13	2	9	31	2
Life	.257	915	2846	314	731	135	18	65	374	21
3 AVE	.261	119	311	31	81	14	2	8	34	2

JASON BERE

Position: Pitcher
Team: Chicago White Sox
Born: May 26, 1971   Cambridge, MA
Height: 6'3"   **Weight:** 185 lbs.
Bats: right   **Throws:** right
Acquired: 36th-round pick in 6/90 free-agent draft

Player Summary	
Fantasy Value	$11 to $14
Card Value	20¢ to 30¢
Will	improve with time
Can't	fine-tune control
Expect	high whiff totals
Don't Expect	a good move

Before he reached the majors in 1993, Bere idolized Roger Clemens, the three-time Cy Young Award winner. Now, the admirer is being compared to his hero. Like Clemens, Bere is a power pitcher who worked hard to reach the majors. He refined his delivery, improved his mechanics, and added 7 mph to his already-quality fastball. The results have been impressive: Bere's 4-2 win over Baltimore June 3 was his 14th in 15 decisions. Ten days later, he fanned 14 while yielding two hits over eight innings to beat Oakland 1-0. In addition to his 94-mph fastball, Bere also throws a curve and a Mike Boddicker-style "foshball" that he uses as a changeup. Bere yielded less than eight hits and more than eight strikeouts per nine innings in 1994. His primary problem is a tendency to yield too many walks, though he has improved from 1991, when he walked 100 batters in 163 innings in Class-A. He also could improve his pickoff move and his defense. A first-time All-Star in 1994, Bere is equally effective against both left- and right-handed hitters.

Major League Pitching Register

	W	L	ERA	G	CG	IP	H	ER	BB	SO
93 AL	12	5	3.47	24	1	142.2	109	55	81	129
94 AL	12	2	3.81	24	0	141.2	119	60	80	127
Life	24	7	3.64	48	1	284.1	228	115	161	256
2 AVE	14	4	3.67	29	1	170.2	138	70	97	154

GERONIMO BERROA

Position: Outfield; first base
Team: Oakland Athletics
Born: March 18, 1965   Santo Domingo, Dominican Republic
Height: 6'   **Weight:** 195 lbs.
Bats: right   **Throws:** right
Acquired: Signed as a free agent, 1/94

Player Summary	
Fantasy Value	$8 to $10
Card Value	8¢ to 12¢
Will	bury left-handers
Can't	help on defense
Expect	power production
Don't Expect	regular spot

Before he was felled by a pulled groin muscle in August, Berroa was one of Oakland's most pleasant surprises of 1994. The career minor leaguer made the most of the chance he was given by his seventh big-league organization. The powerful right-handed hitter, used mostly as a reserve, hit .341 against left-handed pitching and .333 with runners in scoring position until landing on the disabled list. He also had 13 homers and 65 RBI in 340 at bats. Berroa's biggest home run might have been his 10th: a two-run blast that gave the Athletics an 8-7 win over the Yankees on July 5. Though never known for his speed or defense, Berroa even swiped seven bases in nine tries and erred only once while playing 51 games in the field. Berroa's only two previous home runs came for the Braves in 1989. Originally signed by the Blue Jays, he has also played in the majors with the Reds and Marlins. His .300 average in 1994 wasn't totally an illusion; he had three straight .300 seasons in Triple-A from 1991 to '93.

Major League Batting Register

	BA	G	AB	R	H	2B	3B	HR	RBI	SB
89 NL	.265	81	136	7	36	4	0	2	9	0
90 NL	.000	7	4	0	0	0	0	0	0	0
92 NL	.267	13	15	2	4	1	0	0	0	0
93 NL	.118	14	34	3	4	1	0	0	0	0
94 AL	.306	96	340	55	104	18	2	13	65	7
Life	.280	211	529	67	148	24	2	15	74	7

SEAN BERRY

Position: Third base
Team: Montreal Expos
Born: April 22, 1966   Santa Monica, CA
Height: 5'11"   **Weight:** 210 lbs.
Bats: right   **Throws:** right
Acquired: Traded from Royals with Archie Corbin for Chris Haney and Bill Sampen, 8/92

Player Summary	
Fantasy Value	$11 to $14
Card Value	6¢ to 10¢
Will	handle left-handers
Can't	produce in clutch
Expect	occasional homers
Don't Expect	opposite-field hits

Before last season began, the left side of Montreal's infield was viewed with skepticism—even by several members of Expo management. Wil Cordero was considered a clumsy shortstop who might need to shift to third, while Berry was regarded as a competent fielder with a lightweight bat. Fortunately for the Expos, the reviewers were wrong on both counts. Cordero developed into an All-Star, while Berry held his own on both offense and defense. A UCLA product, Berry proved a potent performer against left-handed pitching and a source of more power than predicted. He batted more than 20 points above his career average. Berry could improve his performance by hitting the ball where it is pitched and using the opposite field. He doesn't steal often but is rarely thrown out when he tries. Originally a fourth-round draft pick of the Red Sox, Berry spent parts of two seasons with the Royals before his trade to Montreal.

Major League Batting Register

	BA	G	AB	R	H	2B	3B	HR	RBI	SB
90 AL	.217	8	23	2	5	1	1	0	4	0
91 AL	.133	31	60	5	8	3	0	0	1	0
92 NL	.333	24	57	5	19	1	0	1	4	2
93 NL	.261	122	299	50	78	15	2	14	49	12
94 NL	.278	103	320	43	89	19	2	11	41	14
Life	.262	288	759	105	199	39	5	26	99	28
2 AVE	.271	134	375	55	102	21	2	15	53	16

DAMON BERRYHILL

Position: Catcher
Team: Cincinnati Reds
Born: Dec. 3, 1963   Laguna, CA
Height: 6'   **Weight:** 210 lbs.
Bats: both   **Throws:** right
Acquired: Signed as a free agent, 11/94

Player Summary	
Fantasy Value	$2 to $4
Card Value	5¢ to 7¢
Will	call good game
Can't	win Gold Glove
Expect	best bat vs. lefties
Don't Expect	speed on bases

Although he bats from both sides of the plate, Berryhill blasted left-handed pitchers for an average more than 120 points better than the mark he managed against righties in 1994. In his first American League season, he became Boston's regular receiver. He didn't match the defense of Tony Pena, his predecessor, but Berryhill proved far more potent at the plate. Over the first four months, Berryhill collected 25 extra-base hits, including a half-dozen homers. He hit well over .300 with runners in scoring position and thrived in Fenway Park. He strikes out three times more than he walks, doesn't contribute any speed, and supplies steady but not spectacular defense. He calls a good game—Roger Clemens made Berryhill his personal catcher early on last year—and erases about one-third of those who try to steal against him. He was one of the better receivers in the AL. He was about a .240 career hitter in the NL.

Major League Batting Register

	BA	G	AB	R	H	2B	3B	HR	RBI	SB
87 NL	.179	12	28	2	5	1	0	0	1	0
88 NL	.259	95	309	19	80	19	1	7	38	1
89 NL	.257	91	334	37	86	13	0	5	41	1
90 NL	.189	17	53	6	10	4	0	1	9	0
91 NL	.188	63	160	13	30	7	0	5	14	1
92 NL	.228	101	307	21	70	16	1	10	43	0
93 NL	.245	115	335	24	82	18	2	8	43	0
94 NL	.263	82	255	30	67	17	2	6	34	0
Life	.241	576	1781	152	430	95	6	42	223	3
3 AVE	.246	111	334	29	82	19	2	9	45	0

DANTE BICHETTE

Position: Outfield
Team: Colorado Rockies
Born: Nov. 18, 1963   West Palm Beach, FL
Height: 6'3"   **Weight:** 212 lbs.
Bats: right   **Throws:** right
Acquired: Traded from Brewers for Kevin Reimer, 11/92

Player Summary	
Fantasy Value	$25 to $30
Card Value	12¢ to 20¢
Will	clobber ball at home
Can't	handle all righties
Expect	strong defensive play
Don't Expect	patience at bat

Bichette came to 1994 spring training 22 pounds lighter than he was at the end of the previous season. The immediate result—improved bat speed—allowed him to develop into a candidate for the 30-30 club. On June 27, he had two homers and two steals. On July 17, he solved St. Louis pitching for six RBI. A student of hitting, Bichette has read Ted Williams's *The Science of Hitting* more than 10 times. All of Teddy Ballgame's lessons haven't taken hold, however, because Bichette remains an impatient guess hitter who fans more than three times as often as he walks. His 1994 approach was different because he was very aggressive early on pitches he could handle. The result was selection to the NL All-Star team. Bichette murders left-handed pitching and hits well above .300 in late-inning pressure situations. He is also a standout right fielder with a feared throwing arm. He holds the Rockies' club record of 113 straight games without an error.

CRAIG BIGGIO

Position: Second base
Team: Houston Astros
Born: Dec. 14, 1965   Smithtown, NY
Height: 5'11"   **Weight:** 180 lbs.
Bats: right   **Throws:** right
Acquired: First-round pick in 6/87 free-agent draft

Player Summary	
Fantasy Value	$25 to $30
Card Value	10¢ to 20¢
Will	produce clutch hits
Can't	return to catching
Expect	high on-base average
Don't Expect	poor defensive play

Now that Biggio has become an All-Star second baseman, it's hard to remember that he reached the majors as a catcher who couldn't throw. These days, his defense has earned more than its share of famed Padre announcer Jerry Coleman's gold stars. In fact, Robby Thompson and Biggio are generally considered the heirs to Ryne Sandberg's throne as the best second baseman in the National League. Biggio has good hands, excellent range, fine instincts, and the ability to turn the double play. Biggio's speed helps—on both offense and defense. He beats out numerous infield hits and was nailed only four times in his first 41 steal tries last summer. A good clutch hitter, Biggio batted about .330 with runners in scoring position in 1994. He was also well above .300 against right-handed pitchers and in his home ballpark. Biggio has above-average power for a leadoff man. He also draws enough walks to produce an on-base percentage above .400.

Major League Batting Register

	BA	G	AB	R	H	2B	3B	HR	RBI	SB
88 AL	.261	21	46	1	12	2	0	0	8	0
89 AL	.210	48	138	13	29	7	0	3	15	3
90 AL	.255	109	349	40	89	15	1	15	53	5
91 AL	.238	134	445	53	106	18	3	15	59	14
92 AL	.287	112	387	37	111	27	2	5	41	18
93 NL	.310	141	538	93	167	43	5	21	89	14
94 NL	.304	116	484	74	147	33	2	27	95	21
Life	.277	681	2387	311	661	145	13	86	360	75
3 AVE	.302	139	536	78	162	39	3	21	88	21

Major League Batting Register

	BA	G	AB	R	H	2B	3B	HR	RBI	SB
88 NL	.211	50	123	14	26	6	1	3	5	6
89 NL	.257	134	443	64	114	21	2	13	60	21
90 NL	.276	150	555	53	153	24	2	4	42	25
91 NL	.295	149	546	79	161	23	4	4	46	19
92 NL	.277	162	613	96	170	32	3	6	39	38
93 NL	.287	155	610	98	175	41	5	21	64	15
94 NL	.318	114	437	88	139	44	5	6	56	39
Life	.282	914	3327	492	938	191	22	57	312	163
3 AVE	.294	159	613	106	180	45	5	12	61	36

BUD BLACK

Position: Pitcher
Team: San Francisco Giants
Born: June 30, 1957 San Mateo, CA
Height: 6'2" **Weight:** 188 lbs.
Bats: left **Throws:** left
Acquired: Signed as a free agent, 11/90

Player Summary	
Fantasy Value	$2 to $4
Card Value	5¢ to 7¢
Will	retain rotation berth
Can't	seem to avoid injuries
Expect	command of four pitches
Don't Expect	control woes

Injuries have interfered with Black's career throughout his 14 years in the major leagues. He was disabled four times in his first three years with the Giants and got off to a belated start last year because he was slow to recuperate. His return from September 1993 elbow surgery was compounded by arthroscopic right knee surgery in February 1994. When Black finally returned in June, he won his first three decisions. A healthy Black throws strikes with four pitches: a fastball, a slider, a curve, and a changeup. Though he's not a strikeout pitcher, he succeeds because he yields fewer than three walks per game. Black is prone to throwing gopher balls, however. He also had trouble with left-handed hitters in 1994. Black controls the running game.

Major League Pitching Register

	W	L	ERA	G	CG	IP	H	ER	BB	SO
81 AL	0	0	0.00	2	0	1.0	2	0	3	0
82 AL	4	6	4.58	22	0	88.1	92	45	34	40
83 AL	10	7	3.79	24	3	161.1	159	68	43	58
84 AL	17	12	3.12	35	8	257.0	226	89	64	140
85 AL	10	15	4.33	33	5	205.2	216	99	59	122
86 AL	5	10	3.20	56	0	121.0	100	43	43	68
87 AL	8	6	3.60	29	0	122.1	126	49	35	61
88 AL	4	4	5.00	33	0	81.0	82	45	34	63
89 AL	12	11	3.36	33	6	222.1	213	83	52	88
90 AL	13	11	3.57	32	5	206.2	181	82	61	106
91 NL	12	16	3.99	34	3	214.1	201	95	71	104
92 NL	10	12	3.97	28	2	177.0	178	78	59	82
93 NL	8	2	3.56	16	0	93.2	89	37	33	45
94 NL	4	2	4.47	10	0	54.1	50	27	16	28
Life	117	114	3.77	387	32	2006.0	1915	840	607	1005
2 AVE	9	7	3.82	22	1	135.1	134	58	46	64

WILLIE BLAIR

Position: Pitcher
Team: Colorado Rockies
Born: Dec. 18, 1965 Paintsville, KY
Height: 6'1" **Weight:** 185 lbs.
Bats: right **Throws:** right
Acquired: First-round pick from Astros in 11/92 expansion draft

Player Summary	
Fantasy Value	$0
Card Value	5¢ to 7¢
Will	struggle vs. lefties
Can't	always throw strikes
Expect	work in middle relief
Don't Expect	low ERA

Though scouts have been buzzing about Blair's arm for years, his performance has yet to justify their praise. Wildness has hampered his progress. He allowed opponents to compile a .390 on-base average and four and one-half walks per nine innings in 1994. He also yields too many hits, is prone to allowing homers and gap line drives that result in extra bases, and is dreadful against lefties. A fastball-curveball pitcher who also throws a changeup, Blair has been tried as both a starter and reliever during his two years with the Rockies. While Denver's thin air has been a nightmare for most, Blair has actually had some success working out of the bullpen. He seems to be most effective when facing an opposing lineup only once. In addition, he can throw harder for short stints. Blair fields his position well and has a superb pickoff move for a righty. He's no slouch at the plate either. The Morehead State product began his pro career in the Toronto system in 1986.

Major League Pitching Register

	W	L	ERA	G	S	IP	H	ER	BB	SO
90 AL	3	5	4.06	27	0	68.2	66	31	28	43
91 AL	2	3	6.75	11	0	36.0	58	27	10	13
92 NL	5	7	4.00	29	0	78.2	74	35	25	48
93 NL	6	10	4.75	46	0	146.0	184	77	42	84
94 NL	0	5	5.79	47	3	77.2	98	50	39	68
Life	16	30	4.86	160	3	407.0	480	220	144	256
3 AVE	4	8	4.91	47	1	111.2	132	61	41	76

JEFF BLAUSER

Position: Shortstop
Team: Atlanta Braves
Born: Nov. 8, 1965 Los Gatos, CA
Height: 6'1" **Weight:** 180 lbs.
Bats: right **Throws:** right
Acquired: First-round pick in secondary phase of 6/84 free-agent draft

Player Summary	
Fantasy Value	$10 to $13
Card Value	6¢ to 10¢
Will	seek strong comeback
Can't	duplicate career year
Expect	better on-base average
Don't Expect	great speed

The magic disappeared for Blauser in 1994. Maybe he worried too much about playing out the last year of his contract. Maybe he kept looking over his shoulder at coming prime prospect Chipper Jones. Maybe Blauser tried too hard to duplicate his All-Star year of '93, with its .305 average, 110 runs scored, and .401 on-base percentage. Whatever the reasons, Blauser went bust in almost every department. His average fell nearly 50 points, his on-base percentage fell even more, and his home run power seemed to evaporate. Perhaps Blauser was pressing. Normally a patient hitter who draws lots of walks, he struck out twice for every base on balls. He stopped stealing bases—probably because he reached much less frequently and was afraid of being thrown out. Blauser doesn't run well. His defense is adequate, with positioning, hands, and throwing arm his biggest assets.

Major League Batting Register

	BA	G	AB	R	H	2B	3B	HR	RBI	SB
87 NL	.242	51	165	11	40	6	3	2	15	7
88 NL	.239	18	67	7	16	3	1	2	7	0
89 NL	.270	142	456	63	123	24	2	12	46	5
90 NL	.269	115	386	46	104	24	3	8	39	3
91 NL	.259	129	352	49	91	14	3	11	54	5
92 NL	.262	123	343	61	90	19	3	14	46	5
93 NL	.305	161	597	110	182	29	2	15	73	16
94 NL	.258	96	380	56	98	21	4	6	45	1
Life	.271	835	2746	403	744	140	21	70	325	42
3 AVE	.278	140	492	83	137	26	4	12	61	7

MIKE BLOWERS

Position: Third base
Team: Seattle Mariners
Born: April 24, 1965 Wurzburg, West Germany
Height: 6'2" **Weight:** 210 lbs.
Bats: right **Throws:** right
Acquired: Traded from Yankees for Jim Blueberg and cash, 6/91

Player Summary	
Fantasy Value	$5 to $7
Card Value	5¢ to 7¢
Will	hit left-handers
Can't	avoid errors
Expect	good bat with men on
Don't Expect	patience at plate

With Edgar Martinez healthy again, Blowers didn't see as much third base for the 1994 Mariners as he might have liked. But Seattle found ways to keep his booming bat sharp. He saw action as a first baseman, outfielder, and designated hitter. He also played third when Martinez was resting in the DH spot. When Blowers played, he produced. A better hitter against left-handers, he did his best hitting with runners in scoring position, notching a .347 average in 1994. Blowers would be better if he showed more patience, fanning more than twice for every walk. Though given less playing time last year, his average was almost identical to his 1993 mark. He should get more at bats in '95. In the field, his range, hands, and arm are fine, but he's prone to occasional boots. Originally signed by the Expos, Blowers began his pro career in 1986, three years before he reached the majors with the Yankees.

Major League Batting Register

	BA	G	AB	R	H	2B	3B	HR	RBI	SB
89 AL	.263	13	38	2	10	0	0	0	3	0
90 AL	.188	48	144	16	27	4	0	5	21	1
91 AL	.200	15	35	3	7	0	0	1	1	0
92 AL	.192	31	73	7	14	3	0	1	2	0
93 AL	.280	127	379	55	106	23	3	15	57	1
94 AL	.289	85	270	37	78	13	0	9	49	2
Life	.258	319	939	120	242	43	3	31	133	4
2 AVE	.284	123	380	54	108	21	2	14	63	2

JOE BOEVER

Position: Pitcher
Team: Detroit Tigers
Born: Oct. 4, 1960   St. Louis, MO
Height: 6'1"   **Weight:** 200 lbs.
Bats: right   **Throws:** right
Acquired: Signed as a free agent, 8/93

Player Summary	
Fantasy Value.	$4 to $6
Card Value	5¢ to 7¢
Will	pitch often
Can't	thread needle
Expect	many palmballs
Don't Expect.	closer job

Boever has battled three problems throughout his career: weight, control, and lack of work. When he gets enough work, however, the others seem to diminish in importance. Constant calls keep his palmball sharp, making his fastball and slider seem faster. Boever can make the trick pitch move right or left—depending upon the batter's box occupied by the batter—and is successful when he throws it for strikes. Boever yields less hits than innings but averages only five and one-half strikeouts per game. That means he has to minimize baserunners, keep the ball in the park, and let the defense do its job. He's not always successful at all three. Too erratic to work as a closer, but resilient enough to pitch often, Boever is best utilized as a middle man. He averaged more than 100 relief innings a year for two straight seasons before the strike-shortened '94 campaign.

Major League Pitching Register

	W	L	ERA	G	S	IP	H	ER	BB	SO
85 NL	0	0	4.41	13	0	16.1	17	8	4	20
86 NL	0	1	1.66	11	0	21.2	19	4	11	8
87 NL	1	0	7.36	14	0	18.1	29	15	12	18
88 NL	0	2	1.77	16	1	20.1	12	4	1	7
89 NL	4	11	3.94	66	21	82.1	78	36	34	68
90 NL	3	6	3.36	67	14	88.1	77	33	51	75
91 NL	3	5	3.84	68	0	98.1	90	42	54	89
92 NL	3	6	2.51	81	2	111.1	103	31	45	67
93 AL	6	3	3.61	61	3	102.1	101	41	44	63
94 AL	9	2	3.98	46	3	81.1	80	36	37	49
Life	29	36	3.51	443	44	640.2	606	250	293	464
3 AVE	7	4	3.36	69	3	109.1	106	41	47	66

WADE BOGGS

Position: Third base
Team: New York Yankees
Born: June 15, 1958   Omaha, NE
Height: 6'2"   **Weight:** 197 lbs.
Bats: left   **Throws:** right
Acquired: Signed as a free agent, 12/92

Player Summary	
Fantasy Value.	$8 to $10
Card Value	20¢ to 35¢
Will	vie for batting crown
Can't	count on speed
Expect.	high on-base average
Don't Expect	age to crimp numbers

After two subpar seasons, Boggs bid for his sixth batting title last year. With a .360 average at the All-Star break, Boggs proved he could hit in Yankee Stadium. The longtime Red Sox star no longer needs the inside-out swing he once used to tattoo the Green Monster in Fenway Park's left field. Boggs needs all of his other talents, however. A creature of habit with many superstitions, he usually takes the first pitch. What he does with the others separates him from other hitters. A singles hitter with little speed, he uses the opposite field against lefties but sprays the ball everywhere against righties. He's at his best in clutch situations. He reached double figures in homers for the second time in his 13-year career. Despite limited range, Boggs shows solid glovework at third base and throws well.

Major League Batting Register

	BA	G	AB	R	H	2B	3B	HR	RBI	SB
82 AL	.349	104	338	51	118	14	1	5	44	1
83 AL	.361	153	582	100	210	44	7	5	74	3
84 AL	.325	158	625	109	203	31	4	6	55	3
85 AL	.368	161	653	107	240	42	3	8	78	2
86 AL	.357	149	580	107	207	47	2	8	71	0
87 AL	.363	147	551	108	200	40	6	24	89	1
88 AL	.366	155	584	128	214	45	6	5	58	2
89 AL	.330	156	621	113	205	51	7	3	54	2
90 AL	.302	155	619	89	187	44	5	6	63	0
91 AL	.332	144	546	93	181	42	2	8	51	1
92 AL	.259	143	514	62	133	22	4	7	50	1
93 AL	.302	143	560	83	169	26	1	2	59	0
94 AL	.342	97	366	61	125	19	1	11	55	2
Life	.335	1865	7139	1211	2392	467	49	98	801	18
3 AVE	.301	141	530	77	159	25	2	8	62	1

BARRY BONDS

Position: Outfield
Team: San Francisco Giants
Born: July 24, 1964   Riverside, CA
Height: 6'1"   **Weight:** 185 lbs.
Bats: left   **Throws:** left
Acquired: Signed as a free agent, 12/92

Player Summary	
Fantasy Value	$45 to $50
Card Value	50¢ to $1
Will	mount MVP bid
Can't	avoid Mays comparison
Expect	30-plus homers
Don't Expect	shotgun arm

Bonds began the 1994 campaign with lofty goals: He wanted to win his third straight MVP Award and fourth overall. No previous player had done either. Elbow and shoulder injuries, as well as his team's slow start, made the task more formidable. Anxious to succeed, Bonds became less patient at the plate and his hitting suffered. With Will Clark gone and Robby Thompson hurt, Bonds found he couldn't carry the club alone. But the July signing of Darryl Strawberry helped. Bonds had consecutive two-homer games for the first time on July 15 and 16 and three homers in a game Aug. 2. When the strike started 10 days later, Bonds was just one steal shy of his third 30-30 campaign. NL managers polled by *Baseball America* last year rated him the league's most exciting player and second-best hitter and defensive outfielder. The four-time All-Star has won five consecutive Gold Gloves. There's little he can't do.

Major League Batting Register

	BA	G	AB	R	H	2B	3B	HR	RBI	SB
86 NL	.223	113	413	72	92	26	3	16	48	36
87 NL	.261	150	551	99	144	34	9	25	59	32
88 NL	.283	144	538	97	152	30	5	24	58	17
89 NL	.248	159	580	96	144	34	6	19	58	32
90 NL	.301	151	519	104	156	32	3	33	114	52
91 NL	.292	153	510	95	149	28	5	25	116	43
92 NL	.311	140	473	109	147	36	5	34	103	39
93 NL	.336	159	539	129	181	38	4	46	123	29
94 NL	.312	112	391	89	122	18	1	37	81	29
Life	.285	1281	4514	890	1287	276	41	259	760	309
3 AVE	.320	152	521	121	167	33	3	44	113	36

RICKY BONES

Position: Pitcher
Team: Milwaukee Brewers
Born: April 7, 1969   Salinas, Puerto Rico
Height: 6'   **Weight:** 190 lbs.
Bats: right   **Throws:** right
Acquired: Traded from Padres with Jose Valentin and Matt Mieske for Gary Sheffield, 3/91

Player Summary	
Fantasy Value	$9 to $11
Card Value	8¢ to 12¢
Will	win with guile
Can't	stop hanging curves
Expect	low K frequency
Don't Expect	runners to prevail

When Milwaukee traded Gary Sheffield, fans were perplexed at the package of unknowns it received (Bones, Jose Valentin, and Matt Mieske). They're no longer wondering. All three made major contributions to the 1994 Brewers—none as significant as the one delivered by Bones. Getting high and low strikes with a wide variety of pitches, he threw a 7-0 shutout—his first—at Kansas City April 24. He later made the All-Star team for the first time. Though he's not a power pitcher, Bones won in '94 by yielding less hits than innings, keeping walks to a minimum, and finding as much success against right-handed hitters as lefties. Because his control is so good, he gives up his share of home runs—many with no one on base. Bones throws a fastball that rises, a forkball that sinks, and a curveball that's most effective when it's low. An agile fielder, he made a huge improvement in controlling the running game last year. Given more run support, his record could have been much better.

Major League Pitching Register

	W	L	ERA	G	CG	IP	H	ER	BB	SO
91 NL	4	6	4.83	11	0	54.0	57	29	18	31
92 AL	9	10	4.57	31	0	163.1	169	83	48	65
93 AL	11	11	4.86	32	3	203.2	222	110	63	63
94 AL	10	9	3.43	24	4	170.2	166	65	45	57
Life	34	36	4.37	98	7	591.2	614	287	174	216
3 AVE	11	11	4.22	32	3	202.2	208	95	58	69

BOBBY BONILLA

Position: Third base; outfield
Team: New York Mets
Born: Feb. 23, 1963 New York, NY
Height: 6'3" **Weight:** 230 lbs.
Bats: both **Throws:** right
Acquired: Signed as a free agent, 12/91

Player Summary	
Fantasy Value.	$20 to $25
Card Value	12¢ to 20¢
Will	hit the long ball
Can't	get Gold Glove
Expect	great clutch work
Don't Expect.	fewer strikeouts

Although he'd been an All-Star five times before 1994, Bonilla worked hard to improve last summer. His average went up after sessions with hitting coach Tom McCraw. After coaches Bobby Wine and Mike Cubbage hit Bonilla numerous grounders during the spring, his defense also improved. An outfielder by trade, he accepted full-time duty at third to create outfield space for younger players. The move worked. After making 11 errors in 52 games at third in 1993, he made none in his first 32 games last year. He also knocked in a run in nine straight games in May, breaking the team record shared by Keith Hernandez and Jeff Kent. Bonilla hit well with runners in scoring position and in late-inning pressure spots last year. Though he strikes out often, he also draws enough walks to post a fine on-base average. He hits for a higher average left-handed. Bonilla has a good arm.

Major League Batting Register

	BA	G	AB	R	H	2B	3B	HR	RBI	SB
86 AL	.269	75	234	27	63	10	2	2	26	4
86 NL	.240	63	192	28	46	6	2	1	17	4
87 NL	.300	141	466	58	140	33	3	15	77	3
88 NL	.274	159	584	87	160	32	7	24	100	3
89 NL	.281	163	616	96	173	37	10	24	86	8
90 NL	.280	160	625	112	175	39	7	32	120	4
91 NL	.302	157	577	102	174	44	6	18	100	2
92 NL	.249	128	438	62	109	23	0	19	70	4
93 NL	.265	139	502	81	133	21	3	34	87	3
94 NL	.290	108	403	60	117	24	1	20	67	1
Life	.278	1293	4637	713	1290	269	41	189	750	36
3 AVE	.270	140	503	76	136	26	1	27	84	3

BRET BOONE

Position: Second base
Team: Cincinnati Reds
Born: April 6, 1969 El Cajon, CA
Height: 5'10" **Weight:** 180 lbs.
Bats: right **Throws:** right
Acquired: Traded from Mariners with Erik Hanson for Bobby Ayala and Dan Wilson, 11/93

Player Summary	
Fantasy Value.	$13 to $16
Card Value	10¢ to 15¢
Will.	hit in clutch
Can't	wait for walks
Expect	extra-base hits
Don't Expect	standout defense

Slugging middle infielders are hard to find. That makes one wonder why the Seattle Mariners ditched Boone after half a season. Lou Piniella apparently disliked Boone's tendency to swing for the fences all the time. Nor did Piniella appreciate Boone's defensive play. One man's junk is another man's treasure, however. Enter Cincinnati manager Davey Johnson, who once hit 42 homers in a season while playing second base, and who once tried to make Gregg Jefferies into a second sacker. Johnson suggested Boone play further back on Riverfront's ersatz turf—a move that immediately improved Boone's range—and left him alone at the plate. Finding NL pitching to his liking, Boone responded by blossoming into a .300 hitter, with one-third of his hits going for extra bases. He managed to have a better bat average against right-handers than left-handers—the reverse of what was expected. The first third-generation player in major-league history, Boone made a major contribution to Cincinnati's revival.

Major League Batting Register

	BA	G	AB	R	H	2B	3B	HR	RBI	SB
92 AL	.194	33	129	15	25	4	0	4	15	1
93 AL	.251	76	271	31	68	12	2	12	38	2
94 NL	.320	108	381	59	122	25	2	12	68	3
Life	.275	217	781	105	215	41	4	28	121	6
2 AVE	.297	114	404	57	120	24	2	14	67	3

PAT BORDERS

Position: Catcher
Team: Toronto Blue Jays
Born: May 14, 1963 Columbus, OH
Height: 6'2" **Weight:** 205 lbs.
Bats: right **Throws:** right
Acquired: Sixth-round pick in 6/82 free-agent draft

Player Summary	
Fantasy Value	$2 to $4
Card Value	6¢ to 10¢
Will	succeed in clutch
Can't	be patient at bat
Expect	durability
Don't Expect	top on-base mark

In six seasons as Toronto's No. 1 catcher, Borders has established a reputation for both performance and durability. He led AL receivers in total chances in both 1992 and 1993 and twice topped a dozen homers while working as many as 138 games in a season (twice). As a catcher, Borders calls a good game, blocks potentially wild pitches, protects the plate from incoming runners, and erases about 32 percent of potential basestealers. His errors usually come on rushed throws. Though he's an impatient hitter who whiffs three times more than he walks, Borders often comes through in the clutch. He's also a skilled bunter who knows how to move runners. His power production fell last year after he tried to imitate the batting style of teammate Paul Molitor. As a result, backup Randy Knorr received more playing time. An even bigger worry for Borders was the specter of Triple-A slugger Carlos Delgado, Toronto's "catcher of the future."

Major League Batting Register

	BA	G	AB	R	H	2B	3B	HR	RBI	SB
88 AL	.273	56	154	15	42	6	3	5	21	0
89 AL	.257	94	241	22	62	11	1	3	29	2
90 AL	.286	125	346	36	99	24	2	15	49	0
91 AL	.244	105	291	22	71	17	0	5	36	0
92 AL	.242	138	480	47	116	26	2	13	53	1
93 AL	.254	138	488	38	124	30	0	9	55	2
94 AL	.247	85	295	24	73	13	1	3	26	1
Life	.256	741	2295	204	587	127	9	53	269	6
3 AVE	.248	132	461	40	114	25	1	9	48	1

MIKE BORDICK

Position: Shortstop
Team: Oakland Athletics
Born: July 21, 1965 Marquette, MI
Height: 5'11" **Weight:** 175 lbs.
Bats: right **Throws:** right
Acquired: Signed as a free agent, 7/86

Player Summary	
Fantasy Value	$4 to $6
Card Value	6¢ to 10¢
Will	make good contact
Can't	hit the ball out
Expect	excellent defense
Don't Expect	clutch production

The A's got a bonus when Bordick hit .300 in 1992. He's supposed to make his living as a fielder, not as a hitter. Bordick came down to earth in '93 and continued at the same level of production last summer. He's basically a .250 hitter who has trouble turning on inside pitches. Bordick has little power. He does, however, have a selective approach to hitting, making contact and walking almost as often as he fans. He also has enough speed to reach double figures in steals and rarely gets thrown out. Bordick's speed helps him fatten his average on bunts and infield hits. It also helps in the field, where he's a first-class performer with fine range, a good arm, and the ability to turn two. The one-time three-position utility man has become a fixture at shortstop. Bordick is also a team leader on and off the field. He led the University of Maine to two College World Series in his three years there. He was not drafted after college but was signed after excelling in the summer Cape Cod League.

Major League Batting Register

	BA	G	AB	R	H	2B	3B	HR	RBI	SB
90 AL	.071	25	14	0	1	0	0	0	0	0
91 AL	.238	90	235	21	56	5	1	0	21	3
92 AL	.300	154	504	62	151	19	4	3	48	12
93 AL	.249	159	546	60	136	21	2	3	48	10
94 AL	.253	114	391	38	99	18	4	2	37	7
Life	.262	542	1690	181	443	63	11	8	154	32
3 AVE	.266	158	534	59	142	22	4	3	49	11

CHRIS BOSIO

Position: Pitcher
Team: Seattle Mariners
Born: April 3, 1963 Carmichael, CA
Height: 6'3" **Weight:** 225 lbs.
Bats: right **Throws:** right
Acquired: Signed as a free agent, 12/92

Player Summary	
Fantasy Value	$9 to $11
Card Value	6¢ to 10¢
Will	show fine control
Can't	always keep cool
Expect	200 frames if healthy
Don't Expect	solid performance

After winning a total of 30 games for Milwaukee in 1991 and '92, Bosio made believers out of the Mariners. Signed to a huge contract, he no-hit Boston in his first month with the team. Unfortunately for Seattle, he then spent long stretches on the sidelines with a broken collarbone. Suffice to say that neither of his two seasons with the team have been winning ones. Last year, he went 0-8 on the road before beating Boston July 9. Then he underwent knee surgery. When healthy, Bosio is a control pitcher who doesn't get many Ks. He's much more effective against right-handed hitters, who don't get a good look at his fastballs, sliders, curves, or changeups. Bosio rates pluses for fielding his position and controlling the running game. He rates a minus for controlling his temper. For example, a 1993 outburst sparked a brawl that resulted in round two on the disabled list for the collarbone injury.

Major League Pitching Register

	W	L	ERA	G	CG	IP	H	ER	BB	SO
86 AL	0	4	7.01	10	0	34.2	41	27	13	29
87 AL	11	8	5.24	46	2	170.0	187	99	50	150
88 AL	7	15	3.36	38	9	182.0	190	68	38	84
89 AL	15	10	2.95	33	8	234.2	225	77	48	173
90 AL	4	9	4.00	20	4	132.2	131	59	38	76
91 AL	14	10	3.25	32	5	204.2	187	74	58	117
92 AL	16	6	3.62	33	4	231.1	223	93	44	120
93 AL	9	9	3.45	29	3	164.1	138	63	59	119
94 AL	4	10	4.32	19	4	125.0	137	60	40	67
Life	80	81	3.77	260	39	1479.1	1459	620	388	935
3 AVE	10	10	3.79	30	4	190.1	185	80	53	111

SHAWN BOSKIE

Position: Pitcher
Team: Seattle Mariners
Born: March 28, 1967 Hawthorne, NV
Height: 6'3" **Weight:** 205 lbs.
Bats: right **Throws:** right
Acquired: Traded from Phillies for Fred McNair, 7/94

Player Summary	
Fantasy Value	$1 to $3
Card Value	5¢ to 7¢
Will	get outs on grounders
Can't	stop opposing runners
Expect	luck vs. lefties
Don't Expect	consistent success

After bouncing between the majors and minors for four seasons, Boskie recorded more big-league exposure last summer. During a first-half stint with the Phillies, he recorded his first complete game in more than four seasons. He yielded two hits in seven innings against the Cubs, his first team, on June 1, and worked eight good innings against the same club five days later. Boskie has a live arm, good delivery, and command of four pitches: a curveball, a changeup, a forkball, and a sinking fastball. When he's on, he gets lots of ground-ball outs. He bears down with runners in scoring position and fares well against the left-handers he faces. An infielder turned pitcher, Boskie helps himself with his fielding. He needs work on his pickoff move. Had he steered clear of injuries last summer, he would have made a more important contribution to the Mariners. Boskie has been used as both a starter and reliever in a pro career that began in 1986.

Major League Pitching Register

	W	L	ERA	G	S	IP	H	ER	BB	SO
90 NL	5	6	3.69	15	0	97.2	99	40	31	49
91 NL	4	9	5.23	28	0	129.0	150	75	52	62
92 NL	5	11	5.01	23	0	91.2	96	51	36	39
93 NL	5	3	3.43	39	0	65.2	63	25	21	39
94 NL	4	6	5.01	20	0	88.0	88	49	29	61
94 AL	0	1	6.75	2	0	2.2	4	2	1	0
Life	23	36	4.59	127	0	474.2	500	242	170	250
3 AVE	5	8	4.67	31	0	95.1	96	49	33	55

DARYL BOSTON

Position: Outfield
Team: New York Yankees
Born: Jan. 4, 1963 Cincinnati, OH
Height: 6'3" **Weight:** 195 lbs.
Bats: left **Throws:** left
Acquired: Signed as a free agent, 1/94

Player Summary
Fantasy Value $0
Card Value . . . . 5¢ to 7¢
Will . . . . thrive in platoon
Can't . . . . add speed to game
Expect . . . . occasional homers
Don't Expect . . . . patience at plate

Because of his mediocre outfield defense, plus his inability to hit southpaws, Boston is best used as a left-handed pinch hitter. He usually performs well in that role, since statistics show he does his best work in late-inning pressure situations. After getting off to a slow start with the Yankees last year, Boston rebounded to rip key hits in five games. Though pitchers work him carefully in such spots, he has been known to get himself out. Anxious to produce a big hit, he often flails away at anything—even when it's way out of the strike zone. Used semi-regularly by the Rockies in '93, Boston fanned twice as much as he walked. That ratio slipped to 3-to-1 last year, when he saw less action. Though he's not a basestealer, Boston has enough speed to play anywhere in the outfield. His arm is accurate but not powerful.

Major League Batting Register

	BA	G	AB	R	H	2B	3B	HR	RBI	SB
84 AL	.169	35	83	8	14	3	1	0	3	6
85 AL	.228	95	232	20	53	13	1	3	15	8
86 AL	.266	56	199	29	53	11	3	5	22	9
87 AL	.258	103	337	51	87	21	2	10	29	12
88 AL	.217	105	281	37	61	12	2	15	31	9
89 AL	.252	101	218	34	55	3	4	5	23	7
90 AL	.000	5	1	0	0	0	0	0	0	1
90 NL	.273	115	366	65	100	21	2	12	45	18
91 NL	.275	137	255	40	70	16	4	4	21	15
92 NL	.249	130	289	37	72	14	2	11	35	12
93 NL	.261	124	291	46	76	15	1	14	40	1
94 AL	.182	52	77	11	14	2	0	4	14	0
Life	.249	1058	2629	378	655	131	22	83	278	98
2 AVE	.255	127	290	42	74	15	2	13	38	7

RAFAEL BOURNIGAL

Position: Shortstop
Team: Los Angeles Dodgers
Born: May 12, 1966 Azusa, Dominican Republic
Height: 5'11" **Weight:** 165 lbs.
Bats: right **Throws:** right
Acquired: 19th-round pick in 6/87 free-agent draft

Player Summary
Fantasy Value . . . . $1 to $3
Card Value . . . . 8¢ to 15¢
Will . . . . make good contact
Can't . . . . show strong arm
Expect . . . . dynamic defense
Don't Expect . . . . power explosion

When promoted from Triple-A Albuquerque last summer, Bournigal brought a .332 average and only nine strikeouts in 208 at bats. He had topped the .320 mark for Albuquerque in 1992 and batted .277 the following year. That was good enough for the Dodger front office personnel, who knew all about Bournigal's reputation for defensive excellence and had seen it with their own eyes during spring training exhibition games. Even if he didn't hit in the majors, the brass reasoned, he had to be an improvement over the error-prone Jose Offerman. A contact hitter who walks more often than he fans, Bournigal doesn't collect many extra-base hits. But he delivers the advertised defense. He not only catches anything hit his way but makes up for an average arm with a quick release. His great range allowed him to lead the Pacific Coast League in total chances and double plays in 1993, and he was voted the shortstop with the best tools in the PCL by *Baseball America*.

Major League Batting Register

	BA	G	AB	R	H	2B	3B	HR	RBI	SB
92 NL	.150	10	20	1	3	1	0	0	0	0
93 NL	.500	8	18	0	9	1	0	0	3	0
94 NL	.224	40	116	2	26	3	1	0	11	0
Life	.247	58	154	3	38	5	1	0	14	0

RYAN BOWEN

Position: Pitcher
Team: Florida Marlins
Born: Feb. 10, 1968 Hanford, CA
Height: 6' **Weight:** 185 lbs.
Bats: right **Throws:** right
Acquired: Third-round pick from Astros in 11/92 expansion draft

Player Summary	
Fantasy Value	$0
Card Value	5¢ to 7¢
Will	throw lively fastball
Can't	find the strike zone
Expect	last chance to start
Don't Expect	low ERA

Over the last few years, Bowen has shown flashes of potential but failed to emerge as a reliable starter. Injuries interfered last season, when shoulder problems and a strained side muscle prevented him from holding a spot in Florida's rotation. Bowen's main bugaboo, however, has not been injuries but a lack of control. Though he yields about a hit per inning, he often sabotages his own games by issuing free passes. A fastball-slider pitcher who also throws a good curve, Bowen is more effective against right-handed batters. He holds runners well but can't be considered a good fielder because his delivery leaves him in poor defensive position. No automatic out at the plate, Bowen has been known to poke a few hits, including some for extra bases. His job this year will be to stay healthy, keep ahead of the hitters, and prove he can win on the major-league level. He's getting too old to be considered a prospect. The Astros picked him in the first round of the 1986 free-agent draft.

JEFF BRANSON

Position: Infield
Team: Cincinnati Reds
Born: Jan. 26, 1967 Waynesboro, MS
Height: 6' **Weight:** 180 lbs.
Bats: left **Throws:** right
Acquired: Second-round pick in 6/88 free-agent draft

Player Summary	
Fantasy Value	$1
Card Value	5¢ to 7¢
Will	deliver clutch hits
Can't	cut down Ks
Expect	pinch hits
Don't Expect	everyday job

During the last three seasons, Branson has carved his niche as an all-purpose infielder and valuable left-handed pinch hitter who produces in the clutch. Based upon his previous record, he showed surprising power last year. He still fanned far too frequently, though, averaging about three whiffs for every walk. Branson does his best hitting with runners in scoring position and also handles righties far better than southpaws. He tends to get jammed by inside fastballs and fooled by outside breaking stuff. He'll lunge for pitches outside the strike zone. A 1992 knee injury has eliminated whatever speed Branson had but hasn't effected his fielding. He's best at second and second-best at third but capable of playing anywhere in the infield. He came up through the Cincinnati organization as a shortstop, though his range may be lacking to play there for extended periods. A 1988 U.S. Olympian, he was a Division II All-American out of Livingston (Alabama) University. Branson began in pro baseball a year later.

Major League Pitching Register

	W	L	ERA	G	CG	IP	H	ER	BB	SO
91 NL	6	4	5.15	14	0	71.2	73	41	36	49
92 NL	0	7	10.96	11	0	33.2	48	41	30	22
93 NL	8	12	4.42	27	2	156.2	156	77	87	98
94 NL	1	5	4.94	8	1	47.1	50	26	19	32
Life	15	28	5.38	60	3	309.1	327	185	172	201

Major League Batting Register

	BA	G	AB	R	H	2B	3B	HR	RBI	SB
92 NL	.296	72	115	12	34	7	1	0	15	0
93 NL	.241	125	381	40	92	15	1	3	22	4
94 NL	.284	58	109	18	31	4	1	6	16	0
Life	.260	255	605	70	157	26	3	9	53	4

JEFF BRANTLEY

Position: Pitcher
Team: Cincinnati Reds
Born: Sept. 5, 1963 Florence, AL
Height: 5'11" **Weight:** 180 lbs.
Bats: right **Throws:** right
Acquired: Signed as a free agent, 1/94

Player Summary	
Fantasy Value	$11 to $14
Card Value	5¢ to 7¢
Will	pitch frequently
Can't	omit forkball
Expect	average control
Don't Expect	gopher troubles

Acquired as a set-up man for Rob Dibble, Brantley soon replaced the injured Cincinnati star as the club's top closer. Brantley had saved a total of 34 games for the Giants in 1990 and 1991. He showed last summer that his poor 1993 campaign—when he was moved into the Giants' rotation for a time—was merely an aberration. He does his best work against righty batters, who have trouble with his rising fastball. He gets ground outs with his forkball, while also mixing in a curve and a hard slider. He averaged more than eight strikeouts and less than seven hits allowed over nine innings last year. He keeps the ball in the park and is capable of working often—though he has a history of shoulder problems. He strands most inherited runners, controls the running game with a good pickoff move, and fields his position. His major weakness is an occasional inability to thread the plate. The Reds' signing of Brantley was one of baseball's best bargains.

Major League Pitching Register

	W	L	ERA	G	S	IP	H	ER	BB	SO
88 NL	0	1	5.66	9	1	20.2	22	13	6	11
89 NL	7	1	4.07	59	0	97.1	101	44	37	69
90 NL	5	3	1.56	55	19	86.2	77	15	33	61
91 NL	5	2	2.45	67	15	95.1	78	26	52	81
92 NL	7	7	2.95	56	7	91.2	67	30	45	86
93 NL	5	6	4.28	53	0	113.2	112	54	46	76
94 NL	6	6	2.48	50	15	65.1	46	18	28	63
Life	35	26	3.15	349	57	570.2	503	200	247	447
3 AVE	7	7	3.31	60	9	99.2	81	36	43	84

SID BREAM

Position: First base
Team: Houston Astros
Born: Aug. 3, 1960 Carlisle, PA
Height: 6'4" **Weight:** 220 lbs.
Bats: left **Throws:** left
Acquired: Signed as a free agent, 1/94

Player Summary	
Fantasy Value	$0
Card Value	5¢ to 7¢
Will	pinch-hit often
Can't	employ speed
Expect	clubhouse presence
Don't Expect	former power

Bream gave up years of regular duty to serve as a pinch hitter and understudy to Jeff Bagwell, one of baseball's most durable performers. Bream not only accepted but took to the job with flying colors. Though idled early by foot problems, he blossomed into Houston's best pinch hitter, posting a .406 average (13-for-32) with six walks through the first four months. Over that same span, Bream also topped .400 in the Astrodome, with runners in scoring position, and in late-inning pressure situations. His mark against right-handers was a more mortal .364. A high fastball hitter who likes to pull, Bream has been prone to hot and cold streaks. His power has waned, and his "speed" was only a factor once, when he scored the pennant-winning run for the Braves in the '92 NLCS. Bream remains a superb defensive first baseman.

Major League Batting Register

	BA	G	AB	R	H	2B	3B	HR	RBI	SB
83 NL	.182	15	11	0	2	0	0	0	2	0
84 NL	.184	27	49	2	9	3	0	0	6	1
85 NL	.132	24	53	4	7	0	0	3	6	0
85 NL	.230	50	148	18	34	7	0	6	21	0
86 NL	.268	154	522	73	140	37	5	16	77	13
87 NL	.275	149	516	64	142	25	3	13	65	9
88 NL	.264	148	462	50	122	37	0	10	65	9
89 NL	.222	19	36	3	8	3	0	0	4	0
90 NL	.270	147	389	39	105	23	2	15	67	8
91 NL	.253	91	265	32	67	12	0	11	45	0
92 NL	.261	125	372	30	97	25	1	10	61	6
93 NL	.260	117	277	33	72	14	1	9	35	4
94 NL	.344	46	61	7	21	5	0	0	7	0
Life	.264	1088	3108	351	819	191	12	90	455	50
2 AVE	.260	121	325	32	85	20	1	10	48	5

JOHN BRISCOE

Position: Pitcher
Team: Oakland Athletics
Born: Sept. 22, 1967 La Grange, IL
Height: 6'3" **Weight:** 190 lbs.
Bats: right **Throws:** right
Acquired: Third-round pick in 6/88 free-agent draft

Player Summary	
Fantasy Value	$0
Card Value	8¢ to 12¢
Will	improve
Can't	pinpoint strike zone
Expect	many Ks
Don't Expect	righties to hit

After tasting three cups of coffee with Oakland before 1994, Briscoe was able to enjoy an entire brunch in a big-league bullpen last year. Used exclusively in middle relief, he showed amazing effectiveness against right-handed hitters. Their average against him was only .136. Briscoe also showed an ability to strand inherited runners and keep hits to a minimum (less than six per nine innings) while averaging eight and one-half strikeouts over the same period. Erratic control gave him problems, however—especially when forced to work from behind in the count. Several such pitches caught too much of the plate and disappeared over the outfield wall. He allowed seven home runs last year. Except for 1989, his first full year in pro ball, the Texas Christian University product has resided in the bullpen. At Double-A Huntsville in 1993, he had 16 saves in 30 appearances, with 62 strikeouts and only 16 walks in 38⅔ innings. He also notched six saves, 16 strikeouts, and nine walks at Triple-A Tacoma in nine appearances that year.

Major League Pitching Register

	W	L	ERA	G	S	IP	H	ER	BB	SO
91 AL	0	0	7.07	11	0	14.0	12	11	10	9
92 AL	0	1	6.43	2	0	7.0	12	5	9	4
93 AL	1	0	8.03	17	0	24.2	26	22	26	24
94 AL	4	2	4.01	37	1	49.1	31	22	39	45
Life	5	3	5.68	67	1	95.0	81	60	84	82

RICO BROGNA

Position: First base
Team: New York Mets
Born: April 18, 1970 Turner Falls, MA
Height: 6'2" **Weight:** 200 lbs.
Bats: left **Throws:** left
Acquired: Traded from Tigers for Alan Zinter, 4/94

Player Summary	
Fantasy Value	$4 to $6
Card Value	10¢ to 15¢
Will	produce in clutch
Can't	show patience
Expect	good power
Don't Expect	Griffey Jr.

The real thing or a flash in the pan? Brogna's start last summer made Mets' fans wonder. In a trade of minor-league disappointments, the Mets acquired Brogna for Alan Zinter, a former first-round pick first baseman like Brogna who had a little more power but wasn't as developed as a batter. Brogna languished in Triple-A until the Mets needed a body to replace the injured David Segui. Brogna soon won the job with eye-popping numbers and a display of dazzling defense. He had seven homers, 20 RBI, and a .351 batting average. He produced in late-inning pressure spots and even pounded left-handed pitching. His lone weakness at the plate was impatience, fanning five times more than he walked. Tom McCraw, the New York hitting coach, said Brogna's mannerisms reminded him of Ken Griffey Jr. After all, Brogna was a left-handed batter who showed good power to all fields. He even had a 5-for-5 game on July 25. This is the same guy the Tigers tried to make into a dead-pull hitter. Brogna, Detroit's No. 1 draft pick in 1988, gave up a Clemson football scholarship to play pro baseball.

Major League Batting Register

	BA	G	AB	R	H	2B	3B	HR	RBI	SB
92 AL	.192	9	26	3	5	1	0	1	3	0
94 NL	.351	39	131	16	46	11	2	7	20	1
Life	.325	48	157	19	51	12	2	8	23	1

SCOTT BROSIUS

Position: Third base; infield
Team: Oakland Athletics
Born: Aug. 15, 1966   Hillsboro, OR
Height: 6'1"   **Weight:** 185 lbs.
Bats: right   **Throws:** right
Acquired: 20th-round pick in 6/87 free-agent draft

Player Summary	
Fantasy Value	$6 to $8
Card Value	6¢ to 10¢
Will	generate some pop
Can't	coax walks
Expect	good clutch work
Don't Expect	big on-base mark

In three previous stints with the Athletics, Brosius saw service strictly as a utility man. He played every infield position as well as the outfield. Both his hitting and fielding suffered, leading him to believe he'd never get a chance to crack the lineup. His revival at the plate in the second half of 1993, however, convinced Tony LaRussa to find a spot for Brosius. Installed at third base, an Oakland weak spot, he didn't disappoint. A middle infielder in the minors, he proved adept at charging, fielding, and throwing on the run. He reputation for careless throwing errors evaporated. He showed good hands, good range, and—most importantly—a good bat. On June 29, his ninth-inning homer beat Chuck Finley 1-0. Then on July 16, Brosius smashed a grand slam and a solo homer against Boston for his second five-RBI game. He'd hit better if he were more patient. He fans twice as often as he walks. In late-inning pressure situations, however, he hits well. In 1993 at Triple-A Tacoma, Brosius batted .297 with eight homers and 41 RBI.

Major League Batting Register

	BA	G	AB	R	H	2B	3B	HR	RBI	SB
91 AL	.235	36	68	9	16	5	0	2	4	3
92 AL	.218	38	87	13	19	2	0	4	13	3
93 AL	.249	70	213	26	53	10	1	6	25	6
94 AL	.238	96	324	31	77	14	1	14	49	2
Life	.238	240	692	79	165	31	2	26	91	14
2 AVE	.241	103	335	35	81	15	1	13	47	4

KEVIN BROWN

Position: Pitcher
Team: Texas Rangers
Born: March 14, 1965   McIntyre, GA
Height: 6'4"   **Weight:** 188 lbs.
Bats: right   **Throws:** right
Acquired: First-round pick in 6/86 free-agent draft

Player Summary	
Fantasy Value	$11 to $14
Card Value	6¢ to 10¢
Will	get ground outs
Can't	recapture '92
Expect	first-inning woes
Don't Expect	control problems

Brown's performance declined last summer for the second straight year. A 21-game winner and All-Star starter in 1992, he slipped to 15 wins in '93 before the disaster of '94. Left-handed hitters were eating him alive, and he wasn't fooling righties either. It's tough to win when you're yielding an average of 12 hits per nine innings, as he did last summer. Too many of those hits came in the first inning—a frame Brown would rather forget. He's notoriously bad at the start of games. A sinker-slider pitcher who also throws a straight fastball, a changeup, and an occasional curve, Brown gets lots of ground balls when he's pitching well. He has refined his pickoff move well enough, especially for a right-hander, to control the running game. He also helps himself with his glove. The former Georgia Tech All-American is a durable performer who has topped 200 innings in three of the last four years.

Major League Pitching Register

	W	L	ERA	G	CG	IP	H	ER	BB	SO
86 AL	1	0	3.60	4	0	5.0	6	2	0	4
88 AL	1	1	4.24	4	1	23.1	33	11	8	12
89 AL	12	9	3.35	28	7	191.0	167	71	70	104
90 AL	12	10	3.60	26	6	180.0	175	72	60	88
91 AL	9	12	4.40	33	0	210.2	233	103	90	96
92 AL	21	11	3.32	35	11	265.2	262	98	76	173
93 AL	15	12	3.59	34	12	233.0	228	93	74	142
94 AL	7	9	4.82	26	3	170.0	218	91	50	123
Life	78	64	3.81	187	40	1278.2	1322	541	428	742
3 AVE	15	12	3.89	35	9	246.1	266	106	73	163

JERRY BROWNE

Position: Third base; second base; outfield
Team: Florida Marlins
Born: Feb. 13, 1966 Christiansted, St. Croix, Virgin Islands
Height: 5'10" **Weight:** 170 lbs.
Bats: both **Throws:** right
Acquired: Signed as a free agent, 1/94

Player Summary	
Fantasy Value	$1 to $3
Card Value	5¢ to 7¢
Will	make contact
Can't	slug homers
Expect	high on-base average
Don't Expect	dazzling defense

Because he doesn't hit for power, Browne has long been one of baseball's most underrated players. But his versatility and exceptional patience at the plate make him extremely valuable. He walks twice as often as he fans—yielding a high on-base percentage—and produces with runners in scoring position. When he's ahead in the count, he'll turn fat pitches into doubles by driving them into the gap. Inside heat sometimes gives him trouble, but Browne is a better hitter when he's playing often. That happened last season after Florida decided to shift Gary Sheffield to right and Alex Arias didn't hit enough to hold third. Browne, who also spent some time at second and the outfield, has decent speed but only average range. He has quick reactions and good hands but a below-average throwing arm for a third baseman. He usually hits near the top of the lineup because he has speed and reaches base so often.

Major League Batting Register

	BA	G	AB	R	H	2B	3B	HR	RBI	SB
86 AL	.417	12	24	6	10	2	0	0	3	0
87 AL	.271	132	454	63	123	16	6	1	38	27
88 AL	.229	73	214	26	49	9	2	1	17	7
89 AL	.299	153	598	83	179	31	4	5	45	14
90 AL	.267	140	513	92	137	26	5	6	50	12
91 AL	.228	107	290	28	66	5	2	1	29	2
92 AL	.287	111	324	43	93	12	2	3	40	3
93 AL	.250	76	260	27	65	13	0	2	19	4
94 NL	.295	101	329	42	97	17	4	3	30	3
Life	.272	905	3006	410	819	131	25	22	271	72
3 AVE	.281	110	349	43	98	16	3	3	34	4

TOM BROWNING

Position: Pitcher
Team: Cincinnati Reds
Born: April 28, 1960 Casper, WY
Height: 6'1" **Weight:** 190 lbs.
Bats: left **Throws:** left
Acquired: Ninth-round pick in 6/82 free-agent draft

Player Summary	
Fantasy Value	$0
Card Value	5¢ to 7¢
Will	win if healthy
Can't	escape injury bug
Expect	great location
Don't Expect	stolen bases

Keeping Browning healthy has turned into baseball's version of *Mission: Impossible*. He missed the last three months of 1993 with a broken finger, then he broke his left arm while throwing a pitch in San Diego last May 9. He had previously suffered ruptured knee ligaments, a broken middle finger on his pitching hand, and other disabling mishaps. When healthy, he is a fine starter who works 200 innings per year. A control pitcher, he usually maintains a 3-1 ratio of strikeouts to walks. His repertoire includes a fastball, a curveball, and a changeup. Browning yields more than a hit per inning and is often victimized by the homer. He succeeds because of fine location and an ability to change speeds. He also helps himself with strong defense, a fine pickoff move, and a solid bat. Browning pitched a perfect game against L.A. in 1988.

Major League Pitching Register

	W	L	ERA	G	CG	IP	H	ER	BB	SO
84 NL	1	0	1.54	3	0	23.1	27	4	5	14
85 NL	20	9	3.55	38	6	261.1	242	103	73	155
86 NL	14	13	3.81	39	4	243.1	225	103	70	147
87 NL	10	13	5.02	32	2	183.0	201	102	61	117
88 NL	18	5	3.41	36	5	250.2	205	95	64	124
89 NL	15	12	3.39	37	9	249.2	241	94	64	118
90 NL	15	9	3.80	35	2	227.2	235	96	52	99
91 NL	14	14	4.18	36	1	230.1	241	107	56	115
92 NL	6	5	5.07	16	0	87.0	108	49	28	33
93 NL	7	7	4.74	21	0	114.0	159	60	20	53
94 NL	3	1	4.20	7	2	40.2	34	19	13	22
Life	123	88	3.92	300	31	1911.0	1918	832	506	997
2 AVE	7	6	4.88	19	0	101.0	134	55	24	43

JACOB BRUMFIELD

Position: Outfield
Team: Pittsburgh Pirates
Born: May 27, 1965 Bogalusa, LA
Height: 6′ **Weight:** 180 lbs.
Bats: right **Throws:** right
Acquired: Traded from Reds for Danny Clyburn, 10/94

Player Summary	
Fantasy Value	$1 to $3
Card Value	8¢ to 15¢
Will	make decent contact
Can't	win starting job
Expect	fine speed
Don't Expect	weak effort

One of baseball's most valuable reserves, Brumfield provided a right-handed-hitting alter ego for the left-handed-hitting Deion Sanders last summer for the Reds. Primarily a center fielder, Brumfield brought speed, versatility, and punch to the Cincinnati bench. He's capable of playing all three outfield positions as well as filling in at second base. He's also appeared as a pinch hitter and pinch runner. The Reds didn't lose any defense when Sanders was idled by injury for a spell last year. Brumfield actually has a better throwing arm, plus comparable range—especially on balls hit over his head. He also makes better contact than Sanders. Brumfield hits left-handers well, holds his own in the clutch, and delivers unexpected power. He's a fine hitter when ahead in the count. While he doesn't have Sanders's speed, Brumfield is not slow. He even stole home against Denny Neagle July 10. The Pirates are planning to install Brumfield as a starter. Originally a seventh-round pick by the Cubs in 1983, he missed the 1984 and '85 seasons with injuries.

Major League Batting Register

	BA	G	AB	R	H	2B	3B	HR	RBI	SB
92 NL	.133	24	30	6	4	0	0	0	2	6
93 NL	.268	103	272	40	73	17	3	6	23	20
94 NL	.311	68	122	36	38	10	2	4	11	6
Life	.271	195	424	82	115	27	5	10	36	32

TOM BRUNANSKY

Position: Outfield; designated hitter
Team: Boston Red Sox
Born: Aug. 20, 1960 Covina, CA
Height: 6′4″ **Weight:** 216 lbs.
Bats: right **Throws:** right
Acquired: Traded from Brewers for Dave Valle, 6/94

Player Summary	
Fantasy Value	$1 to $3
Card Value	6¢ to 10¢
Will	deliver some homers
Can't	hit for average
Expect	decent arm
Don't Expect	Ks to stop

Returning to the Red Sox resurrected Brunansky's reputation last summer. He homered in his first swing for Boston and hit another later in the same game. In his first seven BoSox contests, he went 9-for-27. He eventually settled into a more typical regimen of low-average, high-power production. His struggles against southpaws last year were as much a mystery as his failure to crack the Mendoza Line at Fenway Park, usually a hitter's paradise. Part of the problem was an alarming K-to-walk rate of nearly 3-to-1. At his age, Bruno can't hit hard stuff the way he once did. His speed has also faded. He can still throw well enough to play right field.

Major League Batting Register

	BA	G	AB	R	H	2B	3B	HR	RBI	SB
81 AL	.152	11	33	7	5	0	0	3	6	1
82 AL	.272	127	463	77	126	30	1	20	46	1
83 AL	.227	151	542	70	123	24	5	28	82	2
84 AL	.254	155	567	75	144	21	0	32	85	4
85 AL	.242	157	567	71	137	28	4	27	90	5
86 AL	.256	157	593	69	152	28	1	23	75	12
87 AL	.259	155	532	83	138	22	2	32	85	11
88 AL	.184	14	49	5	9	1	0	1	6	1
88 NL	.245	143	523	69	128	22	4	22	79	16
89 NL	.239	158	556	67	133	29	3	20	85	5
90 NL	.158	19	57	5	9	3	0	1	2	0
90 AL	.267	129	461	61	123	24	5	15	71	5
91 AL	.229	142	459	54	105	24	1	16	70	1
92 AL	.266	138	458	47	122	31	3	15	74	2
93 AL	.183	80	224	20	41	7	3	6	29	3
94 AL	.234	64	205	24	48	12	1	10	34	0
Life	.245	1800	6289	804	1543	306	33	271	919	69
3 AVE	.238	103	324	34	77	18	2	12	50	2

STEVE BUECHELE

Position: Third base
Team: Chicago Cubs
Born: Sept. 26, 1961   Lancaster, CA
Height: 6'2"   **Weight:** 190 lbs.
Bats: right   **Throws:** right
Acquired: Traded from Pirates for Danny Jackson, 7/92

Player Summary	
Fantasy Value	$7 to $9
Card Value	6¢ to 10¢
Will	show some power
Can't	avoid striking out
Expect	first-rate defense
Don't Expect	contact hitting

Since coming to the Cubs in 1992, Buechele's offense has not kept pace with his defense. An excellent third baseman who has twice led his league in fielding percentage, he compensates for lack of speed with quick reactions and proper positioning. He has good hands and a strong, accurate arm, though he'll never be mistaken for Matt Williams. As a hitter, Buechele has some power. He hit at least 15 homers in five of his nine big-league seasons before 1994. Though he takes a lot of pitches, he strikes out frequently—averaging nearly three whiffs per walk. His production of extra-base hits fell sharply last summer, even though he played half his games in the friendly confines of Wrigley Field. Pitchers simply refused to feed him low fastballs. Buechele did his best hitting last year with runners in scoring position.

Major League Batting Register

	BA	G	AB	R	H	2B	3B	HR	RBI	SB
85 AL	.219	69	219	22	48	6	3	6	21	3
86 AL	.243	153	461	54	112	19	2	18	54	5
87 AL	.237	136	363	45	86	20	0	13	50	2
88 AL	.250	155	503	68	126	21	4	16	58	2
89 AL	.235	155	486	60	114	22	2	16	59	1
90 AL	.215	91	251	30	54	10	0	7	30	1
91 AL	.267	121	416	58	111	17	2	18	66	0
91 NL	.246	31	114	16	28	5	1	4	19	0
92 NL	.261	145	524	52	137	23	4	9	64	1
93 NL	.272	133	460	53	125	27	2	15	65	1
94 NL	.242	104	339	33	82	11	1	14	52	1
Life	.247	1293	4136	491	1023	181	21	136	538	17
3 AVE	.258	142	487	50	126	22	2	15	67	1

JAY BUHNER

Position: Outfield
Team: Seattle Mariners
Born: Aug. 13, 1964   Louisville, KY
Height: 6'3"   **Weight:** 205 lbs.
Bats: right   **Throws:** right
Acquired: Traded from Yankees with Rick Balabon and Troy Evers for Ken Phelps, 7/88

Player Summary	
Fantasy Value	$15 to $18
Card Value	12¢ to 20¢
Will	hit immense homers
Can't	count on speed
Expect	patience at bat
Don't Expect	weak throws

Once an all-or-nothing slugger, Buhner has become a far superior offensive performer—thanks to hitting tips provided by Lou Piniella, his manager in Seattle last summer. A one-time wild hacker, Buhner now practices so much patience that he walks as often as he strikes out. His on-base percentage has soared along with his batting average. And his power has not been hampered. A low fastball hitter who murders left-handers, Buhner is known for his long-distance blasts. His 1991 Yankee Stadium shot traveled 479 feet. Buhner's presence in the lineup immediately behind Ken Griffey Jr. has been an enormous factor in Junior's 1993 and 1994 production. Though he doesn't run well, Buhner gets good jumps and plays in the right place. In addition, runners have great respect for his powerful right-field throwing arm, which ranks among baseball's best.

Major League Batting Register

	BA	G	AB	R	H	2B	3B	HR	RBI	SB
87 AL	.227	7	22	0	5	2	0	0	1	0
88 AL	.215	85	261	36	56	13	1	13	38	1
89 AL	.275	58	204	27	56	15	1	9	33	1
90 AL	.276	51	163	16	45	12	0	7	33	2
91 AL	.244	137	406	64	99	14	4	27	77	0
92 AL	.243	152	543	69	132	16	3	25	79	0
93 AL	.272	158	563	91	153	28	3	27	98	2
94 AL	.279	101	358	74	100	23	4	21	68	0
Life	.256	749	2520	377	646	123	16	129	427	6
3 AVE	.264	151	537	88	142	25	4	27	91	1

JIM BULLINGER

Position: Pitcher
Team: Chicago Cubs
Born: Aug. 21, 1965   New Orleans, LA
Height: 6'2"   **Weight:** 185 lbs.
Bats: right   **Throws:** right
Acquired: Ninth-round pick in 6/86 free-agent draft

Player Summary

Fantasy Value	$1 to $3
Card Value	5¢ to 7¢
Will	get ground outs
Can't	stop basestealing
Expect	good hitting
Don't Expect	control problems

After posting a 1.73 ERA in his first 15 relief appearances last year, Bullinger found some success as an emergency starter. In his first six starts, his earned run mark was 3.24. In a 6-3 win over the Rockies July 18, Bullinger not only got his first complete game in two years but collected three RBI with a 2-for-4 hitting performance. A converted shortstop who homered in his first Cub at bat, Bullinger is a sinker-slider pitcher whose game plan is to coax ground balls from rival hitters. He averaged three walks and six and one-half strikeouts per nine innings last year while yielding less hits than innings pitched and keeping the ball in the park. He needs to improve his ratio of stranding inherited runners as well as his ability to control the running game. Bullinger credited his 1994 success to advice provided by former Cub pitching coach Dick Pole, who moved on to the Giants in the same capacity. Bullinger should be in a middle-relief role in 1995. In 1993, he notched 20 saves for Triple-A Iowa, after posting 14 for the club in 1992.

Major League Pitching Register

	W	L	ERA	G	S	IP	H	ER	BB	SO
92 NL	2	8	4.66	39	7	85.0	72	44	54	36
93 NL	1	0	4.32	15	1	16.2	18	8	9	10
94 NL	6	2	3.60	33	2	100.0	87	40	34	72
Life	9	10	4.11	87	10	201.2	177	92	97	118
2 AVE	5	5	4.00	43	5	113.0	97	50	51	69

DAVE BURBA

Position: Pitcher
Team: San Francisco Giants
Born: July 7, 1966   Dayton, OH
Height: 6'4"   **Weight:** 240 lbs.
Bats: right   **Throws:** right
Acquired: Traded from Mariners with Bill Swift and Mike Jackson for Kevin Mitchell, 12/91

Player Summary

Fantasy Value	$2 to $4
Card Value	5¢ to 7¢
Will	endure big workload
Can't	always find plate
Expect	many fastballs
Don't Expect	stolen bases

If he ever learns to harness his control, Burba could become one of the league's best set-up men. A fastball-slider pitcher who in 1994 averaged more than 10 strikeouts per nine innings, he also yielded five and one-half walks over the same span. In 1993, he showed more control and had more success. He yields less hits than innings pitched, doesn't throw too many gopher balls, and is capable of working often. The rubber-armed right-hander, who also throws a changeup, was the busiest pitcher on the Giant staff when the strike started last Aug. 12. Burba had already appeared 57 times. One of the pitcher's problems last year was an inability to retire right-handed hitters; he was much more effective against lefties. Although he's only an average fielder, Burba is better than average in controlling the running game, which had been a weak spot for him in 1993. He also rates better than most pitchers with a bat. The Ohio State product was Seattle's second-round pick in the June 1987 draft.

Major League Pitching Register

	W	L	ERA	G	S	IP	H	ER	BB	SO
90 AL	0	0	4.50	6	0	8.0	8	4	2	4
91 AL	2	2	3.68	22	1	36.2	34	15	14	16
92 NL	2	7	4.97	23	0	70.2	80	39	31	47
93 NL	10	3	4.25	54	0	95.1	95	45	37	88
94 NL	3	6	4.38	57	0	74.0	59	36	45	84
Life	17	18	4.39	162	1	284.2	276	139	129	239
3 AVE	5	6	4.49	52	0	90.1	86	45	44	84

JOHN BURKETT

Position: Pitcher
Team: San Francisco Giants
Born: Nov. 28, 1964   New Brighton, PA
Height: 6'3"   **Weight:** 205 lbs.
Bats: right   **Throws:** right
Acquired: Sixth-round pick in 6/83 free-agent draft

Player Summary	
Fantasy Value	$10 to $13
Card Value	6¢ to 10¢
Will	regain winning form
Can't	help with bat
Expect	rebound vs. righties
Don't Expect	control lapses

In the wake of a 22-win season in 1993, Burkett was regarded as the ace of the San Francisco staff. His teammates, though, failed to give him much run support last year. Through the first week of August, he was receiving an average of 3.83 runs per game—not much margin of error for a pitcher who allows more than three and one-half. Burkett's pitching hasn't changed much, relying on control. He averaged two walks, five strikeouts, and just under 10 hits per nine innings while keeping the ball in the park. Burkett fields his position well and does a fair job of holding runners on. His bat is no help at all. Burkett's strength is his command of five different pitches: a forkball, a slider, a curveball, a changeup, and a fastball that sinks. He also gives his team a lot of innings. Burkett's biggest problem last year was his inexplicable difficulty with right-handed hitters. Their average against him was up more than 70 points from the previous season.

Major League Pitching Register

	W	L	ERA	G	CG	IP	H	ER	BB	SO
87 NL	0	0	4.50	3	0	6.0	7	3	3	5
90 NL	14	7	3.79	33	2	204.0	201	86	61	118
91 NL	12	11	4.18	36	3	206.2	223	96	60	131
92 NL	13	9	3.84	32	3	189.2	194	81	45	107
93 NL	22	7	3.65	34	2	231.2	224	94	40	145
94 NL	6	8	3.62	25	0	159.1	176	64	36	85
Life	67	42	3.83	163	10	997.1	1025	424	245	591
3 AVE	14	9	3.70	34	2	215.2	222	88	45	124

ELLIS BURKS

Position: Outfield
Team: Colorado Rockies
Born: Sept. 11, 1964   Vicksburg, MS
Height: 6'2"   **Weight:** 202 lbs.
Bats: right   **Throws:** right
Acquired: Signed as a free agent, 11/93

Player Summary	
Fantasy Value	$16 to $19
Card Value	8¢ to 15¢
Will	provide top defense
Can't	avoid injury
Expect	good power
Don't Expect	emphasis on speed

In his first month with his new team, Burks gave the Rockies the center-field defense they expected. He also gave them a batting explosion that earned NL Player of the Month honors. He homered in his first at bat, against Curt Schilling April 5, and went on to hit .413 with nine homers for the month. In mid-May, however, Burks tore a ligament in his left wrist while checking a swing and sat out more than two months. He's been hurt before, having problems with his knees, shoulders, and back—but has always rebounded. He spends an extra hour stretching and taking treatments before every game and uses a pad for his back on the bench. His biggest improvement in switching leagues was adapting to the NL strike zone and umpires. Burks doesn't steal much anymore, but he still hits with power. A fastball hitter with a short stroke, he fans twice as much as he walks but kills left-handers. Burks earned a Gold Glove in 1990.

Major League Batting Register

	BA	G	AB	R	H	2B	3B	HR	RBI	SB
87 AL	.272	133	558	94	152	30	2	20	59	27
88 AL	.294	144	540	93	159	37	5	18	92	25
89 AL	.303	97	399	73	121	19	6	12	61	21
90 AL	.296	152	588	89	174	33	8	21	89	9
91 AL	.251	130	474	56	119	33	3	14	56	6
92 AL	.255	66	235	35	60	8	3	8	30	5
93 AL	.275	146	499	75	137	24	4	17	74	6
94 NL	.322	42	149	33	48	8	3	13	24	3
Life	.282	910	3442	548	970	192	34	123	485	102
2 AVE	.268	106	367	55	99	16	4	13	52	6

JEROMY BURNITZ

Position: Outfield
Team: Cleveland Indians
Born: April 15, 1969 Westminster, CA
Height: 6′ **Weight:** 190 lbs.
Bats: left **Throws:** right
Acquired: Traded from Mets with Joe Roa for Dave Mlicki, Jerry DiPoto, Paul Byrd, and Jesus Azuaje, 11/94

Player Summary	
Fantasy Value.................	$5 to $7
Card Value	10¢ to 15¢
Will..................	improve with age
Can't........................	hit lefties
Expect	some power
Don't Expect	patience at bat

Great Expectations is not just the title of a Dickens novel but the heading of the scouting report on Burnitz. Once a 30-30 man in the minors, his speed-plus-power potential has excited scouts for years. So far, however, Burnitz has bombed. After beginning 1994 with the Mets, he was exiled in May with a .192 average, seven RBI, and only four extra-base hits in 78 at bats. In addition to missing too many pitches and too many cutoff men, he was considered a low-key guy with a low boiling point. He batted .239 with 14 homers, 49 RBI, and 18 stolen bases at Triple-A Norfolk. Though his performance improved after his return, Burnitz may never be able to boost his average beyond .250. Trying to pull every pitch, he fans far too often—sometimes swinging at pitches far out of the strike zone. He seems overmatched by southpaws and intimidated by clutch situations. On the plus side, the Oklahoma State product has enough speed to stay out of double plays. He runs and throws well enough to become an adequate right fielder. He is young and there is a little time for improvement.

Major League Batting Register

	BA	G	AB	R	H	2B	3B	HR	RBI	SB
93 NL	.243	86	263	49	64	10	6	13	38	3
94 NL	.238	45	143	26	34	4	0	3	15	1
Life	.241	131	406	75	98	14	6	16	53	4

BRETT BUTLER

Position: Outfield
Team: Los Angeles Dodgers
Born: June 15, 1957 Los Angeles, CA
Height: 5′10″ **Weight:** 160 lbs.
Bats: left **Throws:** left
Acquired: Signed as a free agent, 12/90

Player Summary	
Fantasy Value...............	$13 to $16
Card Value	8¢ to 12¢
Will................	bunt for hits
Can't	make great throws
Expect	superb leadoff work
Don't Expect..........	mastery vs. lefties

Age hasn't deterred Butler's reputation as one of baseball's best leadoff men. A fleet contact hitter with extreme patience, his ability to work pitchers for walks translates into a lofty on-base percentage. Anytime he catches the infield playing back, he'll drop a bunt for a base hit. According to NL managers polled by *Baseball America* last year, he's the best bunter in the league. He also invokes the image of Luke Appling, who'd foul off a dozen pitches before slapping a single the opposite way. Butler even had unexpected power last year. He still has the speed for 40 stolen bases, though increasingly he gets caught. Despite his mediocre arm, he is a terrific center fielder whose July 8 catch of a Todd Hundley drive high above the Dodger Stadium wall might have been the grab of his career.

Major League Batting Register

	BA	G	AB	R	H	2B	3B	HR	RBI	SB
81 NL	.254	40	126	17	32	2	3	0	4	9
82 NL	.217	89	240	35	52	2	0	0	7	21
83 NL	.281	151	549	84	154	21	13	5	37	39
84 AL	.269	159	602	108	162	25	9	3	49	52
85 AL	.311	152	591	106	184	28	14	5	50	47
86 AL	.278	161	587	92	163	17	14	4	51	32
87 AL	.295	137	522	91	154	25	8	9	41	33
88 NL	.287	157	568	109	163	27	9	6	43	43
89 NL	.283	154	594	100	168	22	4	4	36	31
90 NL	.309	160	622	108	192	20	9	3	44	51
91 NL	.296	161	615	112	182	13	5	2	38	38
92 NL	.309	157	553	86	171	14	11	3	39	41
93 NL	.298	156	607	80	181	21	10	1	42	39
94 NL	.314	111	417	79	131	13	9	8	33	27
Life	.290	1945	7193	1207	2089	250	118	53	514	503
3 AVE	.307	156	582	92	179	18	11	5	42	39

KEN CAMINITI

Position: Third base
Team: Houston Astros
Born: April 21, 1963 Hanford, CA
Height: 6′ **Weight:** 200 lbs.
Bats: both **Throws:** right
Acquired: Third-round pick in 6/84 free-agent draft

Player Summary	
Fantasy Value	$11 to $14
Card Value	10¢ to 15¢
Will	succeed in clutch
Can't	reduce strikeouts
Expect	brilliant defense
Don't Expect	speed

Caminiti's numbers kept moving up. In his eighth big-league season last summer, he reached a career high in homers even before the player strike started Aug. 12. Hitting behind Jeff Bagwell helped, because pitchers thought the worst was over when Caminiti came to bat. A switch-hitter who's better against right-handers, he produces in the clutch, especially with runners in scoring position. He's also become a more patient hitter, though he still fans too frequently. Caminiti doesn't steal many bases, but he constantly steals hits from rival hitters. He may have been the best fielding third baseman in the 1994 NL, with good hands, above-average range, quick reactions, and a gun for an arm. He's equally adept at charging bunts or racing down the left-field foul line in pursuit of pop flies. The former San Jose State All-American started his career in 1985, four years before he reached the majors to stay.

Major League Batting Register

	BA	G	AB	R	H	2B	3B	HR	RBI	SB
87 NL	.246	63	203	10	50	7	1	3	23	0
88 NL	.181	30	83	5	15	2	0	1	7	0
89 NL	.255	161	585	71	149	31	3	10	72	4
90 NL	.242	153	541	52	131	20	2	4	51	9
91 NL	.253	152	574	65	145	30	3	13	80	4
92 NL	.294	135	506	68	149	31	2	13	62	10
93 NL	.262	143	543	75	142	31	0	13	75	8
94 NL	.283	111	406	63	115	28	2	18	75	4
Life	.260	948	3441	409	896	180	13	75	445	39
3 AVE	.279	145	540	77	151	34	2	17	81	8

TOM CANDIOTTI

Position: Pitcher
Team: Los Angeles Dodgers
Born: Aug. 31, 1957 Walnut Creek, CA
Height: 6′2″ **Weight:** 205 lbs.
Bats: right **Throws:** right
Acquired: Signed as a free agent, 12/91

Player Summary	
Fantasy Value	$7 to $9
Card Value	6¢ to 10¢
Will	work 200 innings
Can't	stall basestealers
Expect	mostly knucklers
Don't Expect	gopher woes

Before the player strike shortened the 1994 season, Candiotti had pitched more than 200 innings eight years in a row. Throwing the knuckleball helps. The veteran uses it often and throws it at three different speeds. To keep batters honest, he mixes in some curves and his version of a "fastball," which seems quick only when compared with the agonizing knuckler. Always around the plate, Candiotti averaged three walks and six strikeouts per game, yielded less hits than innings pitched, and kept the ball in the park in 1994. During a typical game, Candiotti gets better as he goes along. The first inning is often his worst, but he's usually unhittable after the sixth or seventh. Controlling the running game is a tough task for him, though he does have a good pickoff move. He even helps himself at the plate with a few bunts. Candiotti began his pro career in 1979.

Major League Pitching Register

	W	L	ERA	G	CG	IP	H	ER	BB	SO
83 AL	4	4	3.23	10	2	55.2	62	20	16	21
84 AL	2	2	5.29	8	0	32.1	38	19	10	23
86 AL	16	12	3.57	36	17	252.1	234	100	106	167
87 AL	7	18	4.78	32	7	201.2	193	107	93	111
88 AL	14	8	3.28	31	11	216.2	225	79	53	137
89 AL	13	10	3.10	31	4	206.0	188	71	55	124
90 AL	15	11	3.65	31	3	202.0	207	82	55	128
91 AL	13	13	2.65	34	6	238.0	202	70	73	167
92 NL	11	15	3.00	32	6	203.2	177	68	63	152
93 NL	8	10	3.12	33	2	213.2	192	74	71	155
94 NL	7	7	4.12	23	5	153.0	149	70	54	102
Life	110	110	3.46	301	63	1975.0	1867	760	649	1287
3 AVE	10	12	3.42	32	5	211.1	193	80	70	150

JOSE CANSECO

Position: Designated hitter; outfield
Team: Boston Red Sox
Born: July 2, 1964 Havana, Cuba
Height: 6'3" **Weight:** 230 lbs.
Bats: right **Throws:** right
Acquired: Traded from Rangers for Otis Nixon and Luis Ortiz, 12/94

Player Summary	
Fantasy Value	$30 to $35
Card Value	25¢ to 35¢
Will	wreak havoc
Can't	duplicate 40-40 year
Expect	tremendous power
Don't Expect	hits vs. righties

Determined to regain his old status as one of baseball's premier players, Canseco was a study in concentration when the 1994 season started. Healed from elbow surgery, he improved his bat speed and showed much more patience at the plate. He went 10-for-13 with four homers and 10 RBI in a three-game sweep at Boston in June. Later, he had three homers—one of them a 491-footer—and eight RBI in a game against Seattle. It was his seventh multihomer game of the year and 19th of his career. Canseco later became the 16th player to reach 250 homers before his 30th birthday. He still strikes out frequently but also draws a healthy share of walks. He thrived in late-inning pressure spots last year. Canseco steals some bases, though he's not likely to duplicate his 40-40 feat of 1988. Nor is he likely to hurt himself playing the outfield. He was a full-time DH in 1994.

Major League Batting Register

	BA	G	AB	R	H	2B	3B	HR	RBI	SB
85 AL	.302	29	96	16	29	3	0	5	13	1
86 AL	.240	157	600	85	144	29	1	33	117	15
87 AL	.257	159	630	81	162	35	3	31	113	15
88 AL	.307	158	610	120	187	34	0	42	124	40
89 AL	.269	65	227	40	61	9	1	17	57	6
90 AL	.274	131	481	83	132	14	2	37	101	19
91 AL	.266	154	572	115	152	32	1	44	122	26
92 AL	.244	119	439	74	107	15	0	26	87	6
93 AL	.255	60	231	30	59	14	1	10	46	6
94 AL	.282	111	429	88	121	19	2	31	90	15
Life	.267	1143	4315	732	1154	204	11	276	870	149
3 AVE	.264	112	425	76	112	19	1	27	87	11

CRIS CARPENTER

Position: Pitcher
Team: Texas Rangers
Born: April 5, 1965 St. Augustine, FL
Height: 6'1" **Weight:** 185 lbs.
Bats: right **Throws:** right
Acquired: Traded from Marlins for Robb Nen and Kurt Miller, 7/93

Player Summary	
Fantasy Value	$2 to $4
Card Value	5¢ to 7¢
Will	stay in middle relief
Can't	retire lefties
Expect	occasional gophers
Don't Expect	stolen bases

If Carpenter posted better numbers against left-handed hitters, he'd be much more valuable. In 199?, for the second straight season, lefties lit him up for a batting average well above .300. As a result, the University of Georgia product had given up 10½ hits per nine innings by the time the strike began. Too many of those hits left the yard. Though he averages three walks and six strikeouts per nine innings, Carpenter won't recapture his old Cardinal form until he cuts down on the number of hits he allows. The one-time No. 1 draft choice may need to add another pitch to his fastball-slider repertoire. Until then, his success against inherited runners will be negligible. It barely surpassed 50 percent last summer. Carpenter fields his position well, can pitch fairly often, and holds his own with baserunners. But he has yet to pitch as well in the American League as he did in the National League.

Major League Pitching Register

	W	L	ERA	G	S	IP	H	ER	BB	SO
88 NL	2	3	4.72	8	0	47.2	56	25	9	24
89 NL	4	4	3.18	36	0	68.0	70	24	26	35
90 NL	0	0	4.50	4	0	8.0	5	4	2	6
91 NL	10	4	4.23	59	0	66.0	53	31	20	47
92 NL	5	4	2.97	73	1	88.0	69	29	27	46
93 NL	0	1	2.89	29	0	37.1	29	12	13	26
93 AL	4	1	4.22	27	1	32.0	35	15	12	27
94 AL	2	5	5.03	47	5	59.0	69	33	20	39
Life	27	22	3.83	283	7	406.0	386	173	129	250
3 AVE	4	4	3.84	65	3	80.0	77	34	27	51

CHUCK CARR

Position: Outfield
Team: Florida Marlins
Born: Aug. 10, 1968 San Bernardino, CA
Height: 5'10" **Weight:** 165 lbs.
Bats: both **Throws:** right
Acquired: First-round pick from Cardinals in 11/92 expansion draft

Player Summary	
Fantasy Value	$14 to $17
Card Value	10¢ to 15¢
Will	show dazzling speed
Can't	hit with power
Expect	great defense
Don't Expect	patient at bats

Speed isn't everything. Though he can out-run almost everybody, Carr couldn't keep his job as leadoff man. After peaking at .353 on May 20, his average dropped like a stone, settling at .263 as the strike started. His on-base percentage wasn't much better. Carr won't wait for walks, doesn't make good contact, and registers more than three Ks for every base on balls. Though he hits well in late-inning pressure situations, the switch-hitting Carr isn't particularly productive against southpaws. He's also no threat to hit the ball out of the park—with his speed, an inside-the-parker is more likely. Carr had Florida's first five-hit game on May 3 but had few other 1994 highlights. Dropping bunts would fatten his average and allow him to again contend for league leadership in stolen bases (he led with 58 in 1993). Carr's speed gives him great range in center, where he's known for diving catches. He also has a solid arm. An electrifying player, Carr has been a fan favorite in South Florida.

Major League Batting Register

	BA	G	AB	R	H	2B	3B	HR	RBI	SB
90 NL	.000	4	2	0	0	0	0	0	0	1
91 NL	.182	12	11	1	2	0	0	0	1	1
92 NL	.219	22	64	8	14	3	0	0	3	10
93 NL	.267	142	551	75	147	19	2	4	41	58
94 NL	.263	106	433	61	114	19	2	2	30	32
Life	.261	286	1061	145	277	41	4	6	75	102
2 AVE	.265	146	580	80	154	23	2	3	42	52

HECTOR CARRASCO

Position: Pitcher
Team: Cincinnati Reds
Born: Oct. 22, 1969 San Pedro de Macoris, Dominican Republic
Height: 6'2" **Weight:** 175 lbs.
Bats: right **Throws:** right
Acquired: Traded from Marlins with Gary Scott for Chris Hammond, 9/93

Player Summary	
Fantasy Value	$9 to $11
Card Value	15¢ to 25¢
Will	hold hitters at bay
Can't	rely on slider
Expect	moving fastball
Don't Expect	great control

Just before the 1994 season, coaches convinced Carrasco to change the grip on his fastball. Holding it by the seams, the pitcher improved the movement on a pitch already averaging 95 mph. The final piece to the puzzle was added when Jose Rijo helped the rookie with his slider grip during spring training. Combining the sinker and the slider with a confidence that showed no fear of big-league hitters, Carrasco created a stir by jumping from Class-A to the Cincinnati roster. His resemblance to Rijo cannot be ignored. Carrasco in 1994 yielded less than seven hits per nine innings, averaged six and one-half strikeouts over the same span, and kept the ball in the park. He struggled with his control on occasion. He needs to improve against inherited runners and basestealers. On the plus side, Carrasco holds hitters to a microscopic batting average and has the temperament to serve as a closer. One scout who saw him last spring said he had the best arm in the entire league. Carrasco began his pro career in 1988 with the Mets, and he was with Houston and Florida before arriving in Cincy.

Major League Pitching Register

	W	L	ERA	G	S	IP	H	ER	BB	SO
94 NL	5	6	2.24	45	6	56.1	42	14	30	41
Life	5	6	2.24	45	6	56.1	42	14	30	41

MARK CARREON

Position: Outfield; first base
Team: San Francisco Giants
Born: July 9, 1963 Chicago, IL
Height: 6' **Weight:** 195 lbs.
Bats: right **Throws:** left
Acquired: Signed as a free agent, 1/93

Player Summary	
Fantasy Value	$0
Card Value	5¢ to 7¢
Will	show power
Can't	offer solid defense
Expect	clutch hitting
Don't Expect	patience at bat

Carreon doesn't keep his big-league berth because of speed or defense. He survives strictly as a hitter—especially when the game situation calls for a big hit off the bench in the late innings. A prodigious pinch hitter, Carreon has a reputation for coming off the bench and hitting the ball over the fence. He fans three times more than he walks but no one can fault his production with runners in scoring position and in late-inning pressure spots. He usually carves up left-handers, though he did better against righties last year. Carreon can't run a lick, and his defense is far from dazzling—either in right field, where he spent most of his time in the outfield last year, or at first base. You may see him in the American League as a righty designated hitter soon. Carreon still lives off the reputation he established with the Mets, when eight of the 21 homers he hit over five seasons came as a pinch hitter.

Major League Batting Register

	BA	G	AB	R	H	2B	3B	HR	RBI	SB
87 NL	.250	9	12	0	3	0	0	0	1	0
88 NL	.556	7	9	5	5	2	0	1	1	0
89 NL	.308	68	133	20	41	6	0	6	16	2
90 NL	.250	82	188	30	47	12	0	10	26	1
91 NL	.260	106	254	18	66	6	0	4	21	2
92 AL	.232	101	336	34	78	11	1	10	41	3
93 NL	.327	78	150	22	49	9	1	7	33	1
94 NL	.270	51	100	8	27	4	0	3	20	0
Life	.267	502	1182	137	316	50	2	41	159	9
2 AVE	.261	90	243	28	64	10	1	9	37	2

JOE CARTER

Position: Outfield
Team: Toronto Blue Jays
Born: March 7, 1960 Oklahoma City, OK
Height: 6'3" **Weight:** 215 lbs.
Bats: right **Throws:** right
Acquired: Traded from Padres with Roberto Alomar for Fred McGriff and Tony Fernandez, 12/90

Player Summary	
Fantasy Value	$30 to $35
Card Value	25¢ to 35¢
Will	clear fences often
Can't	avoid Ks
Expect	100 RBI
Don't Expect	fine on-base mark

Even the strike didn't keep Carter from reaching 100 RBI for the sixth straight season. He had a record 31 in April and 49 in the first 36 games. By the All-Star break, Carter's RBI count was 80—most by a Blue Jay at the break, topping George Bell's 76 in 1987. Carter remains one of the game's most durable performers. He broke his thumb when hit by a Scott Erickson pitch March 23 but contradicted doctors who predicted he'd be idled eight weeks. Forced to cut down on his big swing, he became more selective at the plate. The result was the RBI explosion. Carter hits well against left-handers. He doesn't have a great on-base percentage, however, because he fans twice as much as he walks. Defensively, he's only adequate in right and not much better in left.

Major League Batting Register

	BA	G	AB	R	H	2B	3B	HR	RBI	SB
83 NL	.176	23	51	6	9	1	1	0	1	1
84 AL	.275	66	244	32	67	6	1	13	41	2
85 AL	.262	143	489	64	128	27	0	15	59	24
86 AL	.302	162	663	108	200	36	9	29	121	29
87 AL	.264	149	588	83	155	27	2	32	106	31
88 AL	.271	157	621	85	168	36	6	27	98	27
89 AL	.243	162	651	84	158	32	4	35	105	13
90 NL	.232	162	634	79	147	27	1	24	115	22
91 AL	.273	162	638	89	174	42	3	33	108	20
92 AL	.264	158	622	97	164	30	7	34	119	12
93 AL	.254	155	603	92	153	33	5	33	121	8
94 AL	.271	111	435	70	118	25	2	27	103	11
Life	.263	1610	6239	889	1641	322	41	302	1097	200
3 AVE	.263	156	613	96	161	33	5	35	128	12

VINNY CASTILLA

Position: Shortstop
Team: Colorado Rockies
Born: July 4, 1967 Oaxaca, Mexico
Height: 6'1" **Weight:** 175 lbs.
Bats: right **Throws:** right
Acquired: Second-round pick from Braves in 11/92 expansion draft

Player Summary	
Fantasy Value	$3 to $5
Card Value	5¢ to 7¢
Will	deliver in clutch
Can't	handle all lefties
Expect	strong arm
Don't Expect	patience at bat

Atlanta manager Bobby Cox still bemoans the loss of Castilla in the expansion draft. Given a chance to play in Colorado, he hit with surprising power during his first two seasons. The 1994 arrival of Walt Weiss turned Castilla into a four-position utility infielder, but he spent the bulk of his time at second and short, in addition to making numerous pinch-hitting appearances. As the strike deadline approached, one-third of Castilla's hits had gone for extra bases. In addition, he was averaging about .360 with runners in scoring position and in late-inning pressure spots. He struggled some against southpaws last summer after hitting them hard in 1993. Part of the problem was impatience at the plate. Castilla takes his rips—even at balls well out of the strike zone. He fans three times more than he walks. Castilla's anxiety sometimes extends to defense, where he's made some careless boots. He has a strong arm, but his lack of speed hampers his range at short. He may be best at third base.

FRANK CASTILLO

Position: Pitcher
Team: Chicago Cubs
Born: April 1, 1969 El Paso, TX
Height: 6'1" **Weight:** 180 lbs.
Bats: right **Throws:** right
Acquired: Sixth-round pick in 6/87 free-agent draft

Player Summary	
Fantasy Value	$0
Card Value	5¢ to 7¢
Will	bid to keep starting
Can't	keep ball in stadium
Expect	inconsistency
Don't Expect	problem with control

Though he spent most of the last four years as a starter for the Cubs, Castillo's performance has been a mystery most of the time. He throws four pitches with reasonably good control but doesn't always locate them well in the strike zone. When they're up, his earned run average rises in direct proportion. A sinker-slider pitcher who also throws a decent curve and a change, Castillo slipped so badly last year that he endured an exile in the minors. He was better when he returned but still ranked at the bottom of the mediocre Cub rotation. Though his ratio of 10 hits per nine innings isn't bad, too many of those hits leave the park. Even when he's ahead in the count, Castillo sometimes has trouble escaping unscathed. His hitting, fielding, and pickoff move are pluses, but that's almost like locking the barn door after the horse is stolen. Castillo has to pitch better before his performance can get much of a boost from other areas. He is running out of chances to impress in the big leagues.

Major League Batting Register

	BA	G	AB	R	H	2B	3B	HR	RBI	SB
91 NL	.200	12	5	1	1	0	0	0	0	0
92 NL	.250	9	16	1	4	1	0	0	1	0
93 NL	.255	105	337	36	86	9	7	9	30	2
94 NL	.331	52	130	16	43	11	1	3	18	2
Life	.275	178	488	54	134	21	8	12	49	4

Major League Pitching Register

	W	L	ERA	G	CG	IP	H	ER	BB	SO
91 NL	6	7	4.35	18	4	111.2	107	54	33	73
92 NL	10	11	3.46	33	0	205.1	179	79	63	135
93 NL	5	8	4.84	29	2	141.1	162	76	39	84
94 NL	2	1	4.30	4	1	23.0	25	11	5	19
Life	23	27	4.11	84	7	481.1	473	220	140	311
2 AVE	8	10	4.02	31	1	173.1	171	78	51	110

TONY CASTILLO

Position: Pitcher
Team: Toronto Blue Jays
Born: March 1, 1963 Lara, Venezuela
Height: 5'10" **Weight:** 188 lbs.
Bats: left **Throws:** left
Acquired: Signed as a free agent, 1/93

Player Summary	
Fantasy Value	$0
Card Value	5¢ to 7¢
Will	triumph vs. lefties
Can't	always find plate
Expect	frequent calls
Don't Expect	closer job

With ace reliever Duane Ward out for the year, the 1994 Blue Jays needed someone to step into the workhorse role. Castillo answered the call. The well-traveled southpaw became the busiest and most effective pitcher in the Toronto pen. Castillo, who does his best work against lefties, in 1994 yielded less hits than innings pitched, kept the ball in the park, and averaged five and one-half strikeouts per game. He is subject to occasional control trouble, however. Castillo was able to hold down his walks-per-nine-innings ratio to about three and one-half last summer, which is good enough. A fastball-slider pitcher who can work often, Castillo helps himself with good defensive play and a competent pickoff move. Originally signed by Toronto in 1983, Castillo spent his first year in pro ball as a starter. He became a reliever in '85. In addition to the Jays, Castillo has pitched in the majors for the Braves and Mets.

Major League Pitching Register

	W	L	ERA	G	S	IP	H	ER	BB	SO
88 AL	1	0	3.00	14	0	15.0	10	5	2	14
89 AL	1	1	6.11	17	1	17.2	23	12	10	10
89 NL	0	1	4.82	12	0	9.1	8	5	4	5
90 NL	5	1	4.23	52	1	76.2	93	36	20	64
91 NL	2	1	3.34	17	0	32.1	40	12	11	18
93 NL	3	2	3.38	51	0	50.2	44	19	22	28
94 AL	5	2	2.51	41	1	68.0	66	19	28	43
Life	17	8	3.60	204	3	269.2	284	108	97	182
2 AVE	5	2	2.81	54	1	73.1	68	23	31	44

ANDUJAR CEDENO

Position: Shortstop
Team: Houston Astros
Born: Aug. 21, 1969 La Romana, Dominican Republic
Height: 6'1" **Weight:** 168 lbs.
Bats: right **Throws:** right
Acquired: Signed as a free agent, 10/86

Player Summary	
Fantasy Value	$8 to $10
Card Value	8¢ to 12¢
Will	develop over time
Can't	learn strike zone
Expect	extra-base power
Don't Expect	Gold Gloves

At times, Cedeno seemed to be treading water last season. Warned not to try to pull every pitch, he sometimes reverted to old habits. After hitting a 443-foot homer April 27, he fell into a 4-for-54 (.074) funk. He fans three times more than he walks, takes a big swing, and whales away at bad pitches. On the plus side, Cedeno has the quick wrists needed to generate good bat speed. He also hits well with runners in scoring position and in late-inning pressure situations. More than one-third of his hits go for extra bases. Not surprisingly, Cedeno handles lefties more easily than righties. He doesn't steal much but does have enough speed to yield good range at short. Cedeno's defense still needs work; he makes too many errors—on booted balls as well as throws—and has the ability to do better. The Astros were disappointed that Cedeno failed to make the same progress last year as the younger, less-experienced Wil Cordero made at shortstop in Montreal.

Major League Batting Register

	BA	G	AB	R	H	2B	3B	HR	RBI	SB
90 NL	.000	7	8	0	0	0	0	0	0	0
91 NL	.243	67	251	27	61	13	2	9	36	4
92 NL	.173	71	220	15	38	13	2	2	13	2
93 NL	.283	149	505	69	143	24	4	11	56	9
94 NL	.263	98	342	38	90	26	0	9	49	1
Life	.250	392	1326	149	332	76	8	31	154	16
3 AVE	.255	119	402	46	103	25	2	9	46	4

WES CHAMBERLAIN

Position: Outfield
Team: Boston Red Sox
Born: April 13, 1966 Chicago, IL
Height: 6'2" **Weight:** 210 lbs.
Bats: right **Throws:** right
Acquired: Traded from Phillies with Mike Sullivan for Billy Hatcher and Paul Quantrill, 5/94

Player Summary	
Fantasy Value	$5 to $7
Card Value	6¢ to 10¢
Will	rake lefties
Can't	rely on speed
Expect	wrong-field power
Don't Expect	patient at bats

Only a few short seasons ago, Chamberlain was regarded as a coming superstar—the centerpiece of a waiver wire blunder that caused the ouster of a Pittsburgh general manager. Times have certainly changed. Chamberlain gained weight after knee surgery, losing whatever running speed he once had. He also gave Philadelphia problems regarding dedication, punctuality, and performance. He was reduced to platoon status before his midseason trade across league lines. Though Chamberlain still hits lefties well, his overall game is crippled by his over-anxious approach to hitting. He fans three times more than he walks and hacks at pitches out of the strike zone. When he does connect, however, Chamberlain has line-drive power—even to the opposite field. He loves a fastball diet. Chamberlain's lack of speed makes him somewhat of a defensive liability. He throws well enough to post double figures in assists, however.

Major League Batting Register

	BA	G	AB	R	H	2B	3B	HR	RBI	SB
90 NL	.283	18	46	9	13	3	0	2	4	4
91 NL	.240	101	383	51	92	16	3	13	50	9
92 NL	.258	76	275	26	71	18	0	9	41	4
93 NL	.282	96	284	34	80	20	2	12	45	2
94 NL	.275	24	69	7	19	5	0	2	6	0
94 AL	.256	51	164	13	42	9	1	4	20	0
Life	.260	366	1221	140	317	71	6	42	166	19
3 AVE	.267	93	296	29	79	19	1	10	41	2

NORM CHARLTON

Position: Pitcher
Team: Philadelphia Phillies
Born: Jan. 6, 1963 Fort Polk, LA
Height: 6'3" **Weight:** 195 lbs.
Bats: both **Throws:** left
Acquired: Signed as a free agent, 2/94

Player Summary	
Fantasy Value	$1
Card Value	6¢ to 10¢
Will	seek major comeback
Can't	keep runners close
Expect	hefty whiff totals
Don't Expect	league saves title

For Charlton, 1994 was a lost season. The Phillies, seeking a closer to replace World Series goat Mitch Williams, signed Charlton in the hope that he'd return from the disabled list by May—10 months after "Tommy John surgery" to repair a torn ligament in his left elbow. During the rehab stint that preceded his scheduled debut, Charlton felt pain in the elbow again. New surgery was performed and the lefty's future was placed on hold. The fact that he's also had past shoulder problems doesn't help. He had been a power pitcher whose arsenal included a fastball, a forkball, and a slider. He saved 44 games over a two-year span in 1992 and 1993. Before his elbow blew out in '93, he had held AL hitters to a .179 batting average and was averaging a league-best 12.46 strikeouts per game. Charlton usually has good control and helps himself with his defense, though he doesn't hold baserunners well. When he's on, he concentrates on blowing batters away.

Major League Pitching Register

	W	L	ERA	G	S	IP	H	ER	BB	SO
88 NL	4	5	3.96	10	0	61.1	60	27	20	39
89 NL	8	3	2.93	69	0	95.1	67	31	40	98
90 NL	12	9	2.74	56	2	154.1	131	47	70	117
91 NL	3	5	2.91	39	1	108.1	92	35	34	77
92 NL	4	2	2.99	64	26	81.1	79	27	26	90
93 AL	1	3	2.34	34	18	34.2	22	9	17	48
Life	32	27	2.96	272	47	535.1	451	176	207	469
2 AVE	3	3	2.79	49	22	58.0	51	18	22	69

DAVE CLARK

Position: Outfield
Team: Pittsburgh Pirates
Born: Sept. 3, 1962 Tupelo, MS
Height: 6'2" **Weight:** 209 lbs.
Bats: left **Throws:** right
Acquired: Signed as a free agent, 1/92

Player Summary	
Fantasy Value	$4 to $6
Card Value	5¢ to 7¢
Will	hit vs. lefties
Can't	cut K totals
Expect	results in clutch
Don't Expect	any speed

A classic example of a late bloomer, Clark came into his own as a hitter in 1994—11 years after he broke into pro ball. It was only his third full year in the majors. Pittsburgh manager Jim Leyland pretty much rescued Clark's career and gave him extensive playing time in right field. Clark did his best hitting in late-inning pressure situations (a .351 average). He also topped .300 against left-handed pitching and at his home park, Three Rivers Stadium. A pull hitter who loves fastballs, Clark has learned the importance of working the count. He still fans twice as much as he walks, but his free-swinging days are behind him. Since Clark has also improved his defense in right field, Leyland had no qualms about making Orlando Merced a first baseman in midseason. Clark throws well enough to play right and no longer makes as many miscues as he once did. He doesn't have great speed but his range is more than adequate.

Major League Batting Register

	BA	G	AB	R	H	2B	3B	HR	RBI	SB
86 AL	.276	18	58	10	16	1	0	3	9	1
87 AL	.207	29	87	11	18	5	0	3	12	1
88 AL	.263	63	156	11	41	4	1	3	18	0
89 AL	.237	102	253	21	60	12	0	8	29	0
90 NL	.275	84	171	22	47	4	2	5	20	7
91 AL	.200	11	10	1	2	0	0	0	1	0
92 NL	.212	23	33	3	7	0	0	2	7	0
93 NL	.271	110	277	43	75	11	2	11	46	1
94 NL	.296	86	223	37	66	11	1	10	46	2
Life	.262	526	1268	159	332	48	6	45	188	12
2 AVE	.284	116	296	48	84	13	2	13	55	2

MARK CLARK

Position: Pitcher
Team: Cleveland Indians
Born: May 12, 1968 Bath, IL
Height: 6'5" **Weight:** 225 lbs.
Bats: right **Throws:** right
Acquired: Traded from Cardinals with Juan Andujar for Mark Whiten, 3/93

Player Summary	
Fantasy Value	$7 to $9
Card Value	8¢ to 12¢
Will	keep fielders alert
Can't	deter some gophers
Expect	decent control
Don't Expect	high K total

Sometimes an injury is a blessing in disguise. Clark proved that point when he went 11-3 in his first 20 starts last summer, after a 1993 stint on the disabled list with a strained back muscle. All Clark did was switch from an abbreviated windup to the over-the-head motion he used in college. Clark also moved a foot to his left on the pitching rubber, making his slider more effective. A fast worker who keeps his fielders alert, Clark also throws a sinking fastball, a forkball, and a changeup. He'll throw any pitch on any count. Though he's not a strikeout pitcher, Clark racked up wins in 1994 by yielding less than three walks per game and just over a hit per inning. He controls the running game well but needs work on his defense. When Clark is right, he has enough stamina to go all the way. He had three complete games in four starts. Clark's superb 1994 season turned sour July 20 when a line drive broke his right wrist. He proved last year that the Indians weren't robbed in the Mark Whiten deal.

Major League Pitching Register

	W	L	ERA	G	CG	IP	H	ER	BB	SO
91 NL	1	1	4.03	7	0	22.1	17	10	11	13
92 NL	3	10	4.45	20	1	113.1	117	56	36	44
93 AL	7	5	4.28	26	1	109.1	119	52	25	57
94 AL	11	3	3.82	20	4	127.1	133	54	40	60
Life	22	19	4.16	73	6	372.1	386	172	112	174
3 AVE	8	6	4.12	25	3	134.1	141	61	39	62

PHIL CLARK

Position: Outfield; first base; catcher
Team: San Diego Padres
Born: May 6, 1968 Crockett, TX
Height: 6' **Weight:** 200 lbs.
Bats: right **Throws:** right
Acquired: Claimed from Tigers on waivers, 4/93

Player Summary	
Fantasy Value	$1
Card Value	6¢ to 10¢
Will	show some power
Can't	add defense
Expect	a utility job
Don't Expect	speed

After impressing the Padres with his power potential in 1993, Clark never got untracked last season. Though he made contact at the plate, his hits—especially those for extra bases—were few and far between. Clark would enhance his value if he showed more patience at the plate, but he refuses to wait for walks. After his .313 performance in '93, management didn't complain. But nothing went right last year. He couldn't hit his weight against right-handers and also slipped badly against southpaws. Too much moving around might have hurt him, since the Padres used him at both infield corners and the outfield in addition to catcher. Clark, an All-Star catcher in two minor leagues, has a strong throwing arm. Chronic knee problems have also slowed his progress. Since Clark adds little speed or defense, his hitting will have to improve for him to remain in the major leagues. If he must play the field, left field is the spot, though he can also pass as an adequate first baseman. Clark's future probably lies as a DH.

Major League Batting Register

	BA	G	AB	R	H	2B	3B	HR	RBI	SB
92 AL	.407	23	54	3	22	4	0	1	5	1
93 NL	.313	102	240	33	75	17	0	9	33	2
94 NL	.215	61	149	14	32	6	0	5	20	1
Life	.291	186	443	50	129	27	0	15	58	4

WILL CLARK

Position: First base
Team: Texas Rangers
Born: March 13, 1964 New Orleans, LA
Height: 6'1" **Weight:** 190 lbs.
Bats: left **Throws:** left
Acquired: Signed as a free agent, 11/93

Player Summary	
Fantasy Value	$25 to $30
Card Value	25¢ to 50¢
Will	slash line drives
Can't	win home run crown
Expect	high on-base mark
Don't Expect	long slumps

Changing leagues posed no problems for Will Clark. He hit .395 in April and supplied his usual strong defense. By mid-May, he was leading the AL with 20 multihit games and was among the league leaders in on-base percentage, batting average, RBI, doubles, runs, and hits. The five-time National League All-Star earned his first AL selection. At strike time, Clark was over .300 in batting, .400 in on-base average, and .500 in slugging. He hits both lefties and righties well. His patient approach helps, as Clark walks more often than he fans. When southpaws pitch him away, he goes with the pitch and hits to the opposite field. When they pitch him inside, he pulls the ball with power. Clark excels with runners in scoring position. An intense competitor, he is proud of the Gold Glove he won in 1991. The former Mississippi State All-American was a member of the 1984 U.S. Olympic team.

Major League Batting Register

	BA	G	AB	R	H	2B	3B	HR	RBI	SB
86 NL	.287	111	408	66	117	27	2	11	41	4
87 NL	.308	150	529	89	163	29	5	35	91	5
88 NL	.282	162	575	102	162	31	6	29	109	9
89 NL	.333	159	588	104	196	38	9	23	111	8
90 NL	.295	154	600	91	177	25	5	19	95	8
91 NL	.301	148	565	84	170	32	7	29	116	4
92 NL	.300	144	513	69	154	40	1	16	73	12
93 NL	.283	132	491	82	139	27	2	14	73	2
94 AL	.329	110	389	73	128	24	2	13	80	5
Life	.302	1270	4658	760	1406	273	39	189	789	57
3 AVE	.305	144	517	85	158	34	2	16	86	7

ROYCE CLAYTON

Position: Shortstop
Team: San Francisco Giants
Born: Jan. 2, 1970 Burbank, CA
Height: 6′ **Weight:** 175 lbs.
Bats: right **Throws:** right
Acquired: First-round pick in 6/88 free-agent draft

Player Summary

Fantasy Value	$14 to $17
Card Value	10¢ to 15¢
Will	bunt for hits
Can't	provide much power
Expect	speed on the bases
Don't Expect	defense to quit

Except for his running game, which remained remarkably potent, Clayton endured a disappointing season in 1994. He strikes out far too frequently and doesn't draw enough walks to maintain a healthy on-base percentage. The righty batter struggles against southpaws, batting only about .175 against them. Clayton could fatten his average by bunting for hits more often but swings away instead. That's not helpful, since he rarely hits anything more than a single even when he connects. His performance in the clutch remains unacceptable; his batting average in late-inning pressure situations over the past two years is well below the Mendoza Line. He has improved his success ratio as a basestealer. Clayton's defense also seems to be improving. His speed gives him tremendous range, and he's learning how to position himself against the hitters. Clayton has good hands and a good arm despite some careless throwing errors. Any comparisons to Barry Larkin are definitely premature.

Major League Batting Register

	BA	G	AB	R	H	2B	3B	HR	RBI	SB
91 NL	.115	9	26	0	3	1	0	0	2	0
92 NL	.224	98	321	31	72	7	4	4	24	8
93 NL	.282	153	549	54	155	21	5	6	70	11
94 NL	.236	108	385	38	91	14	6	3	30	23
Life	.251	368	1281	123	321	43	15	13	126	42
3 AVE	.251	134	471	46	118	16	6	5	45	17

ROGER CLEMENS

Position: Pitcher
Team: Boston Red Sox
Born: Aug. 4, 1962 Dayton, OH
Height: 6′4″ **Weight:** 220 lbs.
Bats: right **Throws:** right
Acquired: First-round pick in 6/83 free-agent draft

Player Summary

Fantasy Value	$20 to $25
Card Value	25¢ to 50¢
Will	win with support
Can't	always find control
Expect	K per inning
Don't Expect	injury-free year

Maybe he's not the pitcher who won three Cy Young Awards in six seasons from 1986 to 1991, but Clemens remains one of baseball's best. He could have sued his Red Sox teammates for nonsupport last summer, when they gave him an average of only 3.88 runs—lowest on the Boston staff—before the August strike started. Clemens in April posted his first shutout in nearly a year and fanned a season-high 12 in a June outing. It was the 57th time he reached double figures in strikeouts. Clemens overcame mechanical flaws created by a 1993 groin injury but then was slowed by a recurrence of the injury. A fastball-slider pitcher who also throws a splitter and a curve, Clemens averages almost a K an inning. He yields six and one-half hits and three and one-half walks per game.

Major League Pitching Register

	W	L	ERA	G	CG	IP	H	ER	BB	SO
84 AL	9	4	4.32	21	5	133.1	146	64	29	126
85 AL	7	5	3.29	15	3	98.1	83	36	37	74
86 AL	24	4	2.48	33	10	254.0	179	70	67	238
87 AL	20	9	2.97	36	18	281.2	248	93	83	256
88 AL	18	12	2.93	35	14	264.0	217	86	62	291
89 AL	17	11	3.13	35	8	253.1	215	88	93	230
90 AL	21	6	1.93	31	7	228.1	193	49	54	209
91 AL	18	10	2.62	35	13	271.1	219	79	65	241
92 AL	18	11	2.41	32	11	246.2	203	66	62	208
93 AL	11	14	4.46	29	2	191.2	175	95	67	160
94 AL	9	7	2.85	24	3	170.2	124	54	71	168
Life	172	93	2.93	326	94	2393.1	2002	780	690	2201
3 AVE	14	12	3.14	32	6	225.2	184	79	76	202

GREG COLBRUNN

Position: First base
Team: Florida Marlins
Born: July 26, 1969 Fontana, CA
Height: 6′ **Weight:** 190 lbs.
Bats: right **Throws:** right
Acquired: Claimed from Expos on waivers, 10/93

Player Summary	
Fantasy Value	$9 to $11
Card Value	5¢ to 7¢
Will	hit in clutch
Can't	wait for walks
Expect	more homers
Don't Expect	southpaw woes

When healthy, Colbrunn has a swing that reminds some observers of Jeff Bagwell. Colbrunn has yet to match Bagwell's numbers or power, but Colbrunn could be on his way. He showed last year that he has finally healed from the elbow problems that cost him huge chunks of the preceding three seasons. Though slowed last year by torn cartilage in his left knee, he produced so well that the Marlins felt no qualms about releasing Orestes Destrade, a 20-homer man in 1993. A great clutch performer, Colbrunn does his best hitting in late-inning pressure situations. He also produces runners in scoring position. Colbrunn kills left-handed pitching and feasts on high fastballs. He'd be even more effective if he showed patience; he fans three times more than he walks. The one-time Montreal "catcher of the future," he has been strictly a first baseman since 1990. Colbrunn is a decent defensive performer at first, though he will never return to backstopper duties because of his reconstructive elbow surgery in 1991.

Major League Batting Register

	BA	G	AB	R	H	2B	3B	HR	RBI	SB
92 NL	.268	52	168	12	45	8	0	2	18	3
93 NL	.255	70	153	15	39	9	0	4	23	4
94 NL	.303	47	155	17	47	10	0	6	31	1
Life	.275	169	476	44	131	27	0	12	72	8
3 AVE	.279	63	180	17	50	10	0	5	28	3

ALEX COLE

Position: Outfield
Team: Minnesota Twins
Born: Aug. 17, 1965 Fayetteville, NC
Height: 6′2″ **Weight:** 175 lbs.
Bats: left **Throws:** left
Acquired: Signed as a free agent, 3/94

Player Summary	
Fantasy Value	$10 to $13
Card Value	5¢ to 7¢
Will	show off great speed
Can't	clear the wall often
Expect	good on-base average
Don't Expect	big stick vs. lefties

A prime example of a platoon player, Cole makes solid contributions against right-handers but is a nonfactor against southpaws. Until last year, Cole was also a washout in the power department. He went 1,317 at bats before connecting for a home run, then hit four in his next 220 trips—giving credence to the 1994 juiced-ball theory. Cole's high average in late-inning pressure situations last year also seemed inflated. Though he can handle breaking stuff, Cole can be overpowered with heat. He's a pesky hitter, however, and is willing to wait for walks and put his speed to work. Cole relies on his speed to overcome occasional mistakes on the basepaths. He improved his success ratio as a basestealer last summer. Cole's speed also helps in center field, where range is his biggest asset. He sometimes misjudges balls, however, and doesn't have a powerful throwing arm. Originally signed by the Cardinals, Cole began his pro career in 1985.

Major League Batting Register

	BA	G	AB	R	H	2B	3B	HR	RBI	SB
90 AL	.300	63	227	43	68	5	4	0	13	40
91 AL	.295	122	387	58	114	17	3	0	21	27
92 AL	.206	41	97	11	20	1	0	0	5	9
92 NL	.278	64	205	33	57	3	7	0	10	7
93 NL	.256	126	348	50	89	9	4	0	24	30
94 AL	.296	105	345	68	102	15	5	4	23	29
Life	.280	521	1609	263	450	50	23	4	96	142
3 AVE	.273	126	379	63	103	11	6	2	24	29

VINCE COLEMAN

Position: Outfield
Team: Kansas City Royals
Born: Sept. 22, 1961 Jacksonville, FL
Height: 6′ **Weight:** 170 lbs.
Bats: both **Throws:** right
Acquired: Traded from Mets with cash for
  Kevin McReynolds, 1/94

Player Summary	
Fantasy Value	$14 to $17
Card Value	6¢ to 10¢
Will	bunt for hits
Can't	show patience
Expect	bid for steals crown
Don't Expect	any power

Given new life by the Royals last year and over the hamstring problems that plagued him during his three-year tenure with the Mets, Coleman stole 40 bases in his first 76 games—surpassing Willie Wilson's 1983 club record for the fastest Royal to reach that number. On Aug. 4, Coleman poked his 12th triple—the most by a Royal since Wilson led the league with 15 in 1987. Coleman posted poor batting and on-base averages last year, though. With a 3-1 ratio of strikeouts to walks, he was bumped from leadoff to No. 2 in the lineup. He'd be infinitely more valuable if he reached by bunts or walks. A walk to Coleman is a double to anyone else. He's rarely erased when he tries to steal. Despite his great range, Coleman is only an average outfielder, and that's being charitable. It was an upset that Coleman revived a career that should have been finished.

Major League Batting Register

	BA	G	AB	R	H	2B	3B	HR	RBI	SB
85 NL	.267	151	636	107	170	20	10	1	40	110
86 NL	.232	154	600	94	139	13	8	0	29	107
87 NL	.289	151	623	121	180	14	10	3	43	109
88 NL	.260	153	616	77	160	20	10	3	38	81
89 NL	.254	145	563	94	143	21	9	2	28	65
90 NL	.292	124	497	73	145	18	9	6	39	77
91 NL	.255	72	278	45	71	7	5	1	17	37
92 NL	.275	71	229	37	63	11	1	2	21	24
93 NL	.279	92	373	64	104	14	8	2	25	38
94 AL	.240	104	438	61	105	14	12	2	33	50
Life	.264	1217	4853	773	1280	152	82	22	313	698
3 AVE	.258	103	406	62	105	15	9	2	31	44

DAVID CONE

Position: Pitcher
Team: Kansas City Royals
Born: Jan. 2, 1963 Kansas City, MO
Height: 6′1″ **Weight:** 190 lbs.
Bats: left **Throws:** right
Acquired: Signed as a free agent, 12/92

Player Summary	
Fantasy Value	$20 to $25
Card Value	12¢ to 25¢
Will	vie for Cy Young
Can't	stop basestealers
Expect	steady control
Don't Expect	hits by righties

After leading the majors in total strikeouts from 1990 to '92, Cone decided to concentrate on control and rely on his defense. As a result, he took home his first Cy Young Award. Baseball's lowest run support (2.94 runs per game) hurt him in 1993, but his teammates compensated last summer. Taking command of his once-fiery temper, the former Met had streaks of eight straight wins and 29 consecutive scoreless innings in 1994. A fastball-forkball pitcher who also uses a curve and a slider, Cone averaged seven hits, seven strikeouts, and less than three walks per nine innings last year. He dominates right-handed hitters and isn't forgiving against lefties either. Though he makes a lot of pickoff throws, his slow delivery handicaps his ability to keep runners close. Cone's defense is only adequate. Originally signed by the Royals, Cone broke into pro ball in 1981.

Major League Pitching Register

	W	L	ERA	G	CG	IP	H	ER	BB	SO
86 AL	0	0	5.56	11	0	22.2	29	14	13	21
87 NL	5	6	3.71	21	1	99.1	87	41	44	68
88 NL	20	3	2.22	35	8	231.1	178	57	80	213
89 NL	14	8	3.52	34	7	219.2	183	86	74	190
90 NL	14	10	3.23	31	6	211.2	177	76	65	233
91 NL	14	14	3.29	34	5	232.2	204	85	73	241
92 NL	13	7	2.88	27	7	196.2	162	63	82	214
92 AL	4	3	2.55	8	0	53.0	39	15	29	47
93 AL	11	14	3.33	34	6	254.0	205	94	114	191
94 AL	16	5	2.94	23	4	171.2	130	56	54	132
Life	111	70	3.12	258	44	1692.2	1394	587	628	1550
3 AVE	17	10	3.03	34	6	248.2	196	84	100	213

JEFF CONINE

Position: Outfield; first base; third base
Team: Florida Marlins
Born: June 27, 1966 Tacoma, WA
Height: 6'1" **Weight:** 220 lbs.
Bats: right **Throws:** right
Acquired: First-round pick from Royals in 11/92 expansion draft

Player Summary	
Fantasy Value.	$19 to $22
Card Value	10¢ to 20¢
Will.	deliver under pressure
Can't	cut down Ks
Expect	more homers
Don't Expect	speed

The comparisons have already started. Florida manager Rene Lachemann says Conine reminds him of Joe Rudi, a good hitter and above-average left fielder who once played for the Athletics. A strong hitter with good bat speed, Conine got help last year from hitting coach Doug Rader, the same man who helped Mark McGwire in Oakland. For Conine, the result was a significant increase in power over his 1993 rookie campaign. The one-time UCLA pitcher produced so well last year that he even made the NL All-Star team. Though he still fans too frequently, Conine hits both righties and lefties hard and comes through in clutch situations. He doesn't have enough speed to become a basestealing threat, but Conine runs well enough to play left field. Once thought of as a stop-gap outfielder, he became a heck of a fly-catcher. Just before the strike, he started taking ground balls at third base, even going to the fall league. Conine tied a big-league record by playing in 162 games as a rookie.

Major League Batting Register

	BA	G	AB	R	H	2B	3B	HR	RBI	SB
90 AL	.250	9	20	3	5	2	0	0	2	0
92 AL	.253	28	91	10	23	5	2	0	9	0
93 NL	.292	162	595	75	174	24	3	12	79	2
94 NL	.319	115	451	60	144	27	6	18	82	1
Life	.299	314	1157	148	346	58	11	30	172	3
2 AVE	.306	162	615	80	188	31	6	19	97	2

STEVE COOKE

Position: Pitcher
Team: Pittsburgh Pirates
Born: Jan. 14, 1970 Kanai, HI
Height: 6'6" **Weight:** 220 lbs.
Bats: right **Throws:** left
Acquired: 35th-round pick in 6/89 free-agent draft

Player Summary	
Fantasy Value.	$1 to $3
Card Value	8¢ to 15¢
Will	display control
Can't	stop gophers
Expect	improvement
Don't Expect	great pickoff move

His style suggests he's a left-handed version of Doug Drabek, but Cooke has yet to emulate the achievements of the former Pirate standout. A curveball specialist who also throws a changeup and a sinking fastball, Cooke suffered through the sophomore jinx last summer. Plagued by the gopher ball (he allowed 21 homers last year), he also yielded 10½ hits per nine innings—a ratio too steep for a pitcher who nets only five strikeouts per game. Though Cooke's control is good (an average of three walks per game), it needs to be better. He won't be a successful starter until he shows dramatic improvement against left-handed hitters. He has to fool hitters to be successful, something he did not do last year. Cooke needs considerable work on his pickoff move—one of baseball's weakest among left-handed starters. His defense is suspect. At least the College of Southern Idaho product knows how to hit and bunt. Cooke needs to recapture his 1993 form, when he led the Pirates in many pitching categories, including starts, innings, and ERA.

Major League Pitching Register

	W	L	ERA	G	CG	IP	H	ER	BB	SO
92 NL	2	0	3.52	11	0	23.0	22	9	4	10
93 NL	10	10	3.89	32	3	210.2	207	91	59	132
94 NL	4	11	5.02	25	2	134.1	157	75	46	74
Life	16	21	4.28	68	5	368.0	386	175	109	216
2 AVE	8	13	4.43	34	3	199.2	214	98	62	118

SCOTT COOPER

Position: Third base
Team: Boston Red Sox
Born: Oct. 13, 1967 St. Louis, MO
Height: 6'3" **Weight:** 205 lbs.
Bats: left **Throws:** right
Acquired: Third-round pick in 6/86 free-agent draft

Player Summary	
Fantasy Value. . . . . $13 to $16
Card Value . . . . 8¢ to 12¢
Will . . . . show more power
Can't . . . . hit southpaws
Expect . . . . patience at plate
Don't Expect . . . . fielding woes

Although shoulder problems hampered his progress last summer, Cooper continued to make major strides. In his third big-league season, he improved both his offense and defense. After batting coach Mike Easler convinced him to stop pulling every pitch, Cooper discovered that most of his power was directed toward center field. He had five RBI while hitting for the cycle against the Royals April 12 and slammed two homers against the Angels April 24. Cooper also posted a pretty good on-base average last season, and he possesses a fine batting eye. Infield coach Frank White improved Cooper's defense by making him stand more upright, then take a step in with the pitch. That compensated for Cooper's lack of speed. He now ranks with the best as a third baseman, with quick reactions, good hands, and a strong throwing arm. Already a two-time All-Star, Cooper should continue his development. He has excellent work habits and a demonstrated willingness to learn.

Major League Batting Register

	BA	G	AB	R	H	2B	3B	HR	RBI	SB
90 AL	.000	2	1	0	0	0	0	0	0	0
91 AL	.457	14	35	6	16	4	2	0	7	0
92 AL	.276	123	337	34	93	21	0	5	33	1
93 AL	.279	156	526	67	147	29	3	9	63	5
94 AL	.282	104	369	49	104	16	4	13	53	0
Life	.284	399	1268	156	360	70	9	27	156	6
3 AVE	.280	142	461	57	129	24	3	11	57	2

JOEY CORA

Position: Second base
Team: Chicago White Sox
Born: May 14, 1965 Caguas, Puerto Rico
Height: 5'8" **Weight:** 155 lbs.
Bats: both **Throws:** right
Acquired: Traded from Padres with Kevin Garner and Warren Newson for Adam Peterson and Steve Rosenberg, 3/91

Player Summary	
Fantasy Value. . . . . $4 to $6
Card Value . . . . 6¢ to 10¢
Will . . . . drive opponents nuts
Can't . . . . generate power
Expect . . . . clever bunts
Don't Expect . . . . a Gold Glove

A contact hitter who walks more often than he fans, Cora supplanted Tim Raines as the White Sox leadoff man last year. Manager Gene Lamont made the move after Cora posted a .365 batting average in June. Lamont reasoned that Cora is adept at working the pitchers and making things happen on the bases, while Raines has more power. On May 10, Cora connected for his third homer in 1,383 at bats. A spray hitter who produces from both sides, Cora is among the top bunters in the game. In 1993, he led the AL with 19 sacrifice bunts and 48 bunts in play. If he hit the ball on the ground more often, he could probably boost his batting average above .300. He's a tough little hitter in clutch situations but can be overpowered by fastballs on occasion. His speed translates into good range at second base. Cora turns the double play well, but he sometimes makes careless throwing errors.

Major League Batting Register

	BA	G	AB	R	H	2B	3B	HR	RBI	SB
87 NL	.237	77	241	23	57	7	2	0	13	15
89 NL	.316	12	19	5	6	1	0	0	1	1
90 NL	.270	51	100	12	27	3	0	0	2	8
91 AL	.241	100	228	37	55	2	3	0	18	11
92 AL	.246	68	122	27	30	7	1	0	9	10
93 AL	.268	153	579	95	155	15	13	2	51	20
94 AL	.276	90	312	55	86	13	4	2	30	8
Life	.260	551	1601	254	416	48	23	4	124	73
2 AVE	.271	140	509	86	138	17	9	2	47	16

WIL CORDERO

Position: Shortstop
Team: Montreal Expos
Born: Oct. 3, 1971   Mayaguez, Puerto Rico
Height: 6'2"   **Weight:** 185 lbs.
Bats: right   **Throws:** right
Acquired: Signed as a free agent, 5/88

Player Summary	
Fantasy Value	$18 to $21
Card Value	12¢ to 20¢
Will	show speed
Can't	hit righties
Expect	20-20-20 year
Don't Expect	a Gold Glove

During 1994 spring training, Cordero made a slight mechanical change with his hitting by holding his hands lower on the bat, moving them up just as he started his swing. That allowed him to see the ball longer by improving his bat speed and enabled him to make better contact. He hit his first career grand slam July 10 against San Diego, played in his first All-Star Game two days later, and broke Hubie Brooks's club record for home runs by a shortstop. Cordero was on pace for a 20-20-20 year (homers, steals, and errors) when the players struck. His improvement was dramatic. For example, over the first four months, he topped .350 against left-handers and in late-inning pressure situations. Cordero's speed allows him to record a high success ratio as a basestealer. Moved to third base at the end of 1993 because of a league-worst 27 errors in 98 games at shortstop, Cordero showed last summer that he can play short in the majors, though his defense still needs work. He has a strong arm, great range, and good hands.

RHEAL CORMIER

Position: Pitcher
Team: St. Louis Cardinals
Born: April 23, 1967   Moncton, New Brunswick, Canada
Height: 5'10"   **Weight:** 185 lbs.
Bats: left   **Throws:** left
Acquired: Sixth-round pick in 6/88 free-agent draft

Player Summary	
Fantasy Value	$2 to $4
Card Value	6¢ to 10¢
Will	remain in rotation
Can't	win without sinker
Expect	great control
Don't Expect	lefties to hit

Staying healthy has been Cormier's primary problem during his three-year career in the majors. He was sidelined for three weeks of 1993 and spent two stints on the 1994 disabled list before Memorial Day. Cormier's ailments included a sore left shoulder and torn back muscle fibers. When healthy, the 1988 Canadian Olympian is a sinkerball specialist with pinpoint control. He yielded about a hit per inning, one and a half bases on balls per nine innings, and six strikeouts per game in 1994. Such numbers suggest a pitcher with a solid record, but Cormier tends to get his pitches up. Eighteen of the 40 hits he surrendered before the strike last year resulted in extra bases. His performance against left-handers should also be better. He even held righties to a lower average than left-handed hitters last year. On the plus side, Cormier keeps runners close and often helps himself with his bat. His fielding could improve. Cormier attended the Community College of Rhode Island.

Major League Batting Register

	BA	G	AB	R	H	2B	3B	HR	RBI	SB
92 NL	.302	45	126	17	38	4	1	2	8	0
93 NL	.248	138	475	56	118	32	2	10	58	12
94 NL	.294	110	415	65	122	30	3	15	63	16
Life	.274	293	1016	138	278	66	6	27	129	28
2 AVE	.274	146	530	74	145	37	3	16	73	17

Major League Pitching Register

	W	L	ERA	G	CG	IP	H	ER	BB	SO
91 NL	4	5	4.12	11	2	67.2	74	31	8	38
92 NL	10	10	3.68	31	3	186.0	194	76	33	117
93 NL	7	6	4.33	38	1	145.1	163	70	27	75
94 NL	3	2	5.45	7	0	39.2	40	24	7	26
Life	24	23	4.12	87	6	438.2	471	201	75	256
2 AVE	9	8	3.97	35	2	166.1	179	73	30	96

DANNY COX

Position: Pitcher
Team: Toronto Blue Jays
Born: Sept. 21, 1959 Northampton, England
Height: 6'4" **Weight:** 225 lbs.
Bats: right **Throws:** right
Acquired: Signed as a free agent, 1/93

Player Summary	
Fantasy Value	$3 to $5
Card Value	5¢ to 7¢
Will	win with sinker
Can't	generate old speed
Expect	first-hitter success
Don't Expect	hits by righties

The injury that idled Cox during the first half of 1994 hurt the Blue Jays almost as much as the year-long absence of Duane Ward. The wily Cox had served the Jays well as Ward's set-up man the year before. Both men were difficult to replace. A sinkerballer with good control, Cox is perfect for middle relief. He strands enemy runners, yields less hits than innings, and keeps the ball in the park. He also maintains a 3-1 ratio of strikeouts to walks. Cox, who mixes a curve and a changeup with the sinker, no longer has the velocity he once showed as a starter. That went out the window with an elbow injury. But he's adept at fooling hitters by changing speeds. A real rally-choker, Cox has good success with first batters. In addition, he makes life difficult for any right-handed hitters he faces. Cox controls baserunners and fields his position well.

Major League Pitching Register

	W	L	ERA	G	S	IP	H	ER	BB	SO
83 NL	3	6	3.25	12	0	83.0	92	30	23	36
84 NL	9	11	4.03	29	0	156.1	171	70	54	70
85 NL	18	9	2.88	35	0	241.0	226	77	64	131
86 NL	12	13	2.90	32	0	220.0	189	71	60	108
87 NL	11	9	3.88	31	0	199.1	224	86	71	101
88 NL	3	8	3.98	13	0	86.0	89	38	25	47
91 NL	4	6	4.57	23	0	102.1	98	52	39	46
92 NL	5	3	4.40	25	3	62.2	66	32	27	48
93 AL	7	6	3.12	44	2	83.2	73	29	29	84
94 AL	1	1	1.45	10	3	18.2	7	3	7	14
Life	73	72	3.51	254	8	1253.0	1235	488	399	685
2 AVE	6	5	3.75	35	3	73.2	70	31	28	66

CHAD CURTIS

Position: Outfield
Team: California Angels
Born: Nov. 6, 1968 Marion, IN
Height: 5'10" **Weight:** 175 lbs.
Bats: right **Throws:** right
Acquired: 45th-round pick in 6/89 free-agent draft

Player Summary	
Fantasy Value	$19 to $22
Card Value	10¢ to 20¢
Will	contribute speed
Can't	always get on base
Expect	solid defense
Don't Expect	return to leadoff

If Curtis coupled his fine speed with more patience at the plate, his value as a leadoff man would soar. Instead, he fans twice as much as he walks and doesn't bunt much for base hits. Curtis stole 91 bases in his first two seasons before his total slipped last summer. The fact that he's thrown out so often suggests that he's still learning and makes mistakes in judgement. The Angels moved him from second to first in the lineup on July 5 but that experiment was short-lived. Just before the strike, Curtis was hitting out of the No. 3 hole. He did reach a career high in home runs. Curtis hits left-handed pitching well and holds his own with runners in scoring position. This former second baseman is also a valuable contributor on defense. Blessed with terrific range, he charges balls and throws with accuracy despite an arm that is only average. He had nine assists before the strike started. In 1992, he led all AL outfielders with 16 assists. Curtis has been described as one of the hardest-working players in baseball.

Major League Batting Register

	BA	G	AB	R	H	2B	3B	HR	RBI	SB
92 AL	.259	139	441	59	114	16	2	10	46	43
93 AL	.285	152	583	94	166	25	3	6	59	48
94 AL	.256	114	453	67	116	23	4	11	50	25
Life	.268	405	1477	220	396	64	9	27	155	116
3 AVE	.267	151	554	82	148	24	4	10	58	42

MILT CUYLER

Position: Outfield
Team: Detroit Tigers
Born: Oct. 7, 1968   Macon, GA
Height: 5'10"   **Weight:** 175 lbs.
Bats: both   **Throws:** right
Acquired: Second-round pick in 6/86 free-agent draft

Player Summary	
Fantasy Value	$1 to $3
Card Value	5¢ to 7¢
Will	provide strong defense
Can't	hit homers
Expect	speed to dominate
Don't Expect	hits vs. righties

If he could steal first base, Cuyler would become an All-Star. He has speed to burn but a weak bat that usually produces U-turns toward the dugout. In his brief career, Cuyler has also shown a penchant for getting hurt. He suffered a severely lacerated and dislocated right ring finger last May 25 while diving back into second base. In 1993, he endured knee problems. The Tigers already had an injured Eric Davis last year. A spray hitter who uses the whole field, Cuyler is so desperate to show off his speed that he hacks at anything near the plate. He was more selective last summer but still fanned far too often for a Punch-and-Judy hitter. His .318 on-base average is not up to par for a leadoff man. He did hit left-handers, however, and had a .300 mark in late-inning pressure situations at the time of the strike. While Cuyler's bat may never make the Hall of Fame, his glove might. He has good reactions, exceptional range, and the ability to outrace balls hit over his head. His arm is only mediocre.

Major League Batting Register

	BA	G	AB	R	H	2B	3B	HR	RBI	SB
90 AL	.255	19	51	8	13	3	1	0	8	1
91 AL	.257	154	475	77	122	15	7	3	33	41
92 AL	.241	89	291	39	70	11	1	3	28	8
93 AL	.213	82	249	46	53	11	7	0	19	13
94 AL	.241	48	116	20	28	3	1	1	11	5
Life	.242	392	1182	190	286	43	17	7	99	68
2 AVE	.228	86	270	43	62	11	4	2	24	11

RON DARLING

Position: Pitcher
Team: Oakland Athletics
Born: Aug. 19, 1960   Honolulu, HI
Height: 6'3"   **Weight:** 195 lbs.
Bats: right   **Throws:** right
Acquired: Traded from Expos for Matt Grott and Russell Cormier, 7/91

Player Summary	
Fantasy Value	$2 to $4
Card Value	6¢ to 10¢
Will	rely on defense
Can't	throw hard
Expect	help with glove
Don't Expect	basestealers

Recovering from a slow start last season, Darling started lasting longer into his games, helping the Athletics return to contention. The veteran right-hander averaged a hit per inning and three walks and six strikeouts per game in 1994, as he became the biggest winner on the Oakland staff. A fastball-forkball pitcher who also throws a curve and a cut fastball, Darling has won in double digits eight times in a 12-year career. A former power pitcher who has lost some velocity, he now depends more upon his defense. That's fine for most pitchers, but Darling gives up more fly balls than grounders. He does help his own cause, however, since he's an agile defender who once won a Gold Glove. He also holds runners very well for a right-hander.

Major League Pitching Register

	W	L	ERA	G	CG	IP	H	ER	BB	SO
83 NL	1	3	2.80	5	1	35.1	31	11	17	23
84 NL	12	9	3.81	33	2	205.2	179	87	104	136
85 NL	16	6	2.90	36	4	248.0	214	80	114	167
86 NL	15	6	2.81	34	4	237.0	203	74	81	184
87 NL	12	8	4.29	32	2	207.2	183	99	96	167
88 NL	17	9	3.25	34	7	240.2	218	87	60	161
89 NL	14	14	3.52	33	4	217.1	214	85	70	153
90 NL	7	9	4.50	33	1	126.0	135	63	44	99
91 NL	5	8	4.37	20	0	119.1	125	58	33	69
91 AL	3	7	4.08	12	0	75.0	64	34	38	60
92 AL	15	10	3.66	33	4	206.1	198	84	72	99
93 AL	5	9	5.16	31	4	178.0	198	102	72	95
94 AL	10	11	4.50	25	4	160.0	162	80	59	108
Life	132	109	3.77	361	36	2256.1	2120	944	860	1521
3 AVE	11	11	4.41	33	4	203.0	208	100	76	115

DANNY DARWIN

Position: Pitcher
Team: Boston Red Sox
Born: Oct. 25, 1955 Bonham, TX
Height: 6'3" **Weight:** 190 lbs.
Bats: right **Throws:** right
Acquired: Signed as a free agent, 12/90

Player Summary	
Fantasy Value	$1
Card Value	5¢ to 7¢
Will	seek comeback
Can't	get lefties out
Expect	gopher woes
Don't Expect	wobbly control

Injuries and advancing age wreaked havoc with Darwin's 1994 statistics. After finishing the previous season with 15 wins in 26 decisions, he was counted on by Boston to be a big-time producer behind Roger Clemens and Frank Viola, but Darwin was disabled by a back injury in June and also endured rib-cage problems. Though he showed his usual fine control, he was devastated by left-handed hitters and plagued by the gopher ball. Over the first four months, he yielded a dozen hits per nine innings. Only solid run support by teammates prevented him from having a losing record. A fastball-slider pitcher who also throws a forkball, Darwin does not get many Ks.

Major League Pitching Register

	W	L	ERA	G	CG	IP	H	ER	BB	SO
78 AL	1	0	4.15	3	0	8.2	11	4	1	8
79 AL	4	4	4.04	20	1	78.0	50	35	30	58
80 AL	13	4	2.63	53	0	109.2	98	32	50	104
81 AL	9	9	3.64	22	6	146.0	115	59	57	98
82 AL	10	8	3.44	56	0	89.0	95	34	37	61
83 AL	8	13	3.49	28	9	183.0	175	71	62	92
84 AL	8	12	3.94	35	5	223.2	249	98	54	123
85 AL	8	18	3.80	39	11	217.2	212	92	65	125
86 AL	6	8	3.52	27	5	130.1	120	51	35	80
86 AL	5	2	2.32	12	1	54.1	50	14	9	40
87 AL	9	10	3.59	33	3	195.2	184	78	69	134
88 AL	8	13	3.84	44	3	192.0	189	82	48	129
89 AL	11	4	2.36	68	0	122.0	92	32	33	104
90 AL	11	4	2.21	48	3	162.2	136	40	31	109
91 AL	3	6	5.16	12	0	68.0	71	39	15	42
92 AL	9	9	3.96	51	2	161.1	159	71	53	124
93 AL	15	11	3.26	34	2	229.1	196	83	49	130
94 AL	7	5	6.30	13	0	75.2	101	53	24	54
Life	145	140	3.56	598	51	2447.0	2303	968	722	1615
3 AVE	11	9	4.14	34	1	165.2	166	76	45	110

DARREN DAULTON

Position: Catcher; first base
Team: Philadelphia Phillies
Born: Jan. 3, 1962 Arkansas City, KS
Height: 6'2" **Weight:** 190 lbs.
Bats: left **Throws:** right
Acquired: 25th-round pick in 6/80 free-agent draft

Player Summary	
Fantasy Value	$18 to $21
Card Value	15¢ to 25¢
Will	produce in clutch
Can't	worry about knees
Expect	100 RBI
Don't Expect	much speed

Catchers who can hit are rare commodities. Over the last three seasons, Daulton has been one of the best. A 100-RBI man in both 1992 and 1993, he was hitting an even .300 last year when he broke his right clavicle during a 2-1 loss to Florida June 28. He was still sidelined at the time the player strike started Aug. 12. A dangerous left-handed hitter, Daulton does his best batting with runners in scoring position. He makes good contact for a power hitter—especially when he doesn't try to pull—and gets enough walks to produce a healthy on-base percentage. A good receiver, Daulton has led the league in total chances and double plays. He calls a good game, blocks the plate well, and snares errant pitches. To preserve his bat, his stamina, and his aching knees (seven operations), Daulton may become a first baseman.

Major League Batting Register

	BA	G	AB	R	H	2B	3B	HR	RBI	SB
83 NL	.333	2	3	1	1	0	0	0	0	0
85 NL	.204	36	103	14	21	3	1	4	11	3
86 NL	.225	49	138	18	31	4	0	8	21	2
87 NL	.194	53	129	10	25	6	0	3	13	0
88 NL	.208	58	144	13	30	6	0	1	12	2
89 NL	.201	131	368	29	74	12	2	8	44	2
90 NL	.268	143	459	62	123	30	1	12	57	7
91 NL	.196	89	285	36	56	12	0	12	42	5
92 NL	.270	145	485	80	131	32	5	27	109	11
93 NL	.257	147	510	90	131	35	4	24	105	5
94 NL	.300	69	257	43	77	17	1	15	56	4
Life	.243	922	2881	396	700	157	14	114	470	41
3 AVE	.273	130	452	77	123	30	3	24	98	7

CHILI DAVIS

Position: Designated hitter
Team: California Angels
Born: Jan. 17, 1960   Kingston, Jamaica
Height: 6'3"   **Weight:** 210 lbs.
Bats: both   **Throws:** right
Acquired: Signed as a free agent, 12/92

Player Summary	
Fantasy Value	$12 to $15
Card Value	10¢ to 15¢
Will	hit ball hard
Can't	play the field
Expect	patient approach
Don't Expect	stolen bases

Acrimony over player-owner relations had no impact on the booming bat of Chili Davis last summer. He was headed for his second straight 100-RBI campaign when the players walked out. The switch-hitting slugger was also a strong candidate for his first 30-homer season. Unusually patient for a power hitter, Davis took an on-base percentage of .410 into the strike. His patience also paid off in the second-highest batting average of his 14-year career. Davis is slightly more successful against southpaws but also hits right-handers hard. He's a tough out with runners in scoring position and in late-inning pressure situations. Davis doesn't run much anymore and never plays the field, where he is a liability. A two-time All-Star, Davis hit two home runs for the Twins in the 1991 World Series.

Major League Batting Register

	BA	G	AB	R	H	2B	3B	HR	RBI	SB
81 NL	.133	8	15	1	2	0	0	0	0	2
82 NL	.261	154	641	86	167	27	6	19	76	24
83 NL	.233	137	486	54	113	21	2	11	59	10
84 NL	.315	137	499	87	157	21	6	21	81	12
85 NL	.270	136	481	53	130	25	2	13	56	15
86 NL	.278	153	526	71	146	28	3	13	70	16
87 NL	.250	149	500	80	125	22	1	24	76	16
88 NL	.268	158	600	81	161	29	3	21	93	9
89 AL	.271	154	560	81	152	24	1	22	90	3
90 AL	.265	113	412	58	109	17	1	12	58	1
91 AL	.277	153	534	84	148	34	1	29	93	5
92 AL	.288	138	444	63	128	27	2	12	66	4
93 AL	.243	153	573	74	139	32	0	27	112	4
94 AL	.311	108	392	72	122	18	1	26	84	3
Life	.270	1851	6663	945	1799	325	29	250	1014	124
3 AVE	.280	148	523	79	146	28	1	25	99	4

ERIC DAVIS

Position: Outfield
Team: Detroit Tigers
Born: May 29, 1962   Los Angeles, CA
Height: 6'3"   **Weight:** 185 lbs.
Bats: right   **Throws:** right
Acquired: Traded from Dodgers for John DeSilva, 9/93

Player Summary	
Fantasy Value	$6 to $8
Card Value	8¢ to 12¢
Will	play decent defense
Can't	cut his Ks
Expect	his old stroke
Don't Expect	pain-free year

Injuries inevitably interfere with the performance of Eric Davis. In the second game of the 1994 campaign, he suffered a pinched nerve in his neck when he crashed into the center field fence at Fenway Park. Later, he was disabled with a pulled groin muscle. Even when healthy, he seemed far removed from his old 30-30 form. He totaled 20 homers and 35 steals for two clubs in 1993; the last time he reached such lofty levels was 1988. The days of 100 RBI and 50 stolen bases have long since crumbled into the dustbin of history. He fans twice as much as he walks, doesn't bunt his way on base, and can't handle inside heat or outside breaking stuff. Nor is he the player who once won three straight Gold Gloves. He still delivers good range and a good arm in center.

Major League Batting Register

	BA	G	AB	R	H	2B	3B	HR	RBI	SB
84 NL	.224	57	174	33	39	10	1	10	30	10
85 NL	.246	56	122	26	30	3	3	8	18	16
86 NL	.277	132	415	97	115	15	3	27	71	80
87 NL	.293	129	474	120	139	23	4	37	100	50
88 NL	.273	135	472	81	129	18	3	26	93	35
89 NL	.281	131	462	74	130	14	2	34	101	21
90 NL	.260	127	453	84	118	26	2	24	86	21
91 NL	.235	89	285	39	67	10	0	11	33	14
92 NL	.228	76	267	21	61	8	1	5	32	19
93 NL	.234	108	376	57	88	17	0	14	53	33
93 AL	.253	23	75	14	19	1	1	6	15	2
94 AL	.183	37	120	19	22	4	0	3	13	5
Life	.259	1100	3695	665	957	149	20	205	645	306
2 AVE	.234	104	359	46	84	13	1	13	50	27

STORM DAVIS

Position: Pitcher
Team: Detroit Tigers
Born: Dec. 26, 1961   Dallas, TX
Height: 6'4"   **Weight:** 200 lbs.
Bats: right   **Throws:** right
Acquired: Signed as a free agent, 7/93

Player Summary	
Fantasy Value	$1
Card Value	5¢ to 7¢
Will	thrive in role
Can't	halt basestealers
Expect	some control woes
Don't Expect	homers

Style ain't necessarily substance. While the Davis pitching style once reminded scouts of Jim Palmer, the results weren't there. In fact, Davis couldn't even hold a job as a starting pitcher. Moved to middle relief, he seemed to enjoy a midcareer renaissance with Detroit in 1993. Taking to the new role, he compiled a second-half ERA that was just over 3.00. He continued to be one of Detroit's most effective relievers last summer. He averaged more than seven strikeouts and less than seven hits per nine innings, kept the ball in the park, and held hitters to an average just a nose over the Mendoza Line. Though he has control trouble sometimes, Davis is effective when he throws strikes with his fastball, forkball, and curve. He has trouble keeping runners close but fields well.

Major League Pitching Register

	W	L	ERA	G	S	IP	H	ER	BB	SO
82 AL	8	4	3.49	29	0	100.2	96	39	28	67
83 AL	13	7	3.59	34	0	200.1	180	80	64	125
84 AL	14	9	3.12	35	1	225.0	205	78	71	105
85 AL	10	8	4.53	31	0	175.0	172	88	70	93
86 AL	9	12	3.62	25	0	154.0	166	62	49	96
87 NL	2	7	6.18	21	0	62.2	70	43	36	37
87 AL	1	1	3.26	5	0	30.1	28	11	11	28
88 AL	16	7	3.70	33	0	201.2	211	83	91	127
89 AL	19	7	4.36	31	0	169.1	187	82	68	91
90 AL	7	10	4.74	21	0	112.0	129	59	35	62
91 AL	3	9	4.96	51	2	114.1	140	63	46	53
92 AL	7	3	3.43	48	4	89.1	79	34	36	53
93 AL	2	8	5.05	43	4	98.0	93	55	48	73
94 AL	2	4	3.56	35	0	48.0	36	19	34	38
Life	113	96	4.02	442	11	1780.2	1792	796	687	1048
3 AVE	4	6	4.09	47	3	85.1	74	39	44	60

TIM DAVIS

Position: Pitcher
Team: Seattle Mariners
Born: July 14, 1970   Marianna, FL
Height: 5'11"   **Weight:** 165 lbs.
Bats: left   **Throws:** left
Acquired: Sixth-round pick in 6/92 free-agent draft

Player Summary	
Fantasy Value	$2 to $4
Card Value	10¢ to 15¢
Will	improve
Can't	stop lefties
Expect	starting trial
Don't Expect	ragged control

Relief pitchers don't need extensive repertoires to succeed. Since Davis throws five pitches, Seattle decided to switch him from the bullpen to the rotation just before the August player strike started. He throws two different types of fastballs, as well as a curve, a slider, and a changeup. He relies on commanding the strike zone and deceiving the batter. A 10-2 record and 1.85 ERA as a starter for Appleton in 1993 convinced the Mariners that Davis could make the jump from Class-A to the majors. That year, he had 89 strikeouts and 33 walks in 77 ⅔ innings. Though he had some control problems in the majors last year, Davis devoured the on-the-job training. He averaged more than five strikeouts per game, kept the ball in the park, and kept baserunners close. He did yield more hits than innings, however, and needs to show more success stranding inherited runners. In 1991 at Florida State, he was 9-2 with a 2.84 ERA. He played with Team USA in the summer of '92.

Major League Pitching Register

	W	L	ERA	G	S	IP	H	ER	BB	SO
94 AL	2	2	4.01	42	2	49.1	57	22	25	28
Life	2	2	4.01	42	2	49.1	57	22	25	28

ANDRE DAWSON

Position: Designated hitter
Team: Boston Red Sox
Born: July 10, 1954 Miami, FL
Height: 6'3" **Weight:** 195 lbs.
Bats: right **Throws:** right
Acquired: Signed as a free agent, 12/92

Player Summary	
Fantasy Value	$6 to $8
Card Value	15¢ to 25¢
Will	set an example
Can't	use his great arm
Expect	run production
Don't Expect	fielding

Dawson continues to roll along, despite playing in pain. He needs to spend hours stretching before every game and hours icing afterwards. But his example provides fine leadership for his teammates and foes alike. He continued to supply power last year for the Red Sox, chipping in with a .466 slugging average. His on-base percentage, however, was a poor .271, and he drew only nine walks. Those are especially poor numbers for a designated hitter. A certain Hall of Famer, Dawson was a great fielder as well as a fine hitter, but he has lost too much range to be a very effective fielder anymore. Don't be surprised to see him managing in a few years.

Major League Batting Register

		BA	G	AB	R	H	2B	3B	HR	RBI	SB
76	NL	.235	24	85	9	20	4	1	0	7	1
77	NL	.282	139	525	64	148	26	9	19	65	21
78	NL	.253	157	609	84	154	24	8	25	72	28
79	NL	.275	155	639	90	176	24	12	25	92	35
80	NL	.308	151	577	96	178	41	7	17	87	34
81	NL	.302	103	394	71	119	21	3	24	64	26
82	NL	.301	148	608	107	183	37	7	23	83	39
83	NL	.299	159	633	104	189	36	10	32	113	25
84	NL	.248	138	533	73	132	23	6	17	86	13
85	NL	.255	139	529	65	135	27	2	23	91	13
86	NL	.284	130	496	65	141	32	2	20	78	18
87	NL	.287	153	621	90	178	24	2	49	137	11
88	NL	.303	157	591	78	179	31	8	24	79	12
89	NL	.252	118	416	62	105	18	6	21	77	8
90	NL	.310	147	529	72	164	28	5	27	100	16
91	NL	.272	149	563	69	153	21	4	31	104	4
92	NL	.277	143	542	60	150	27	2	22	90	6
93	AL	.273	121	461	44	126	29	1	13	67	2
94	AL	.240	75	292	34	70	18	0	16	48	2
Life		.280	2506	9643	1337	2700	491	95	428	1540	314
3 AVE		.265	123	471	51	125	27	1	19	75	4

JOSE DeLEON

Position: Pitcher
Team: Chicago White Sox
Born: Dec. 20, 1960 Rancho Viejo, Dominican Republic
Height: 6'3" **Weight:** 215 lbs.
Bats: right **Throws:** right
Acquired: Traded from Phillies for Bobby Thigpen, 8/93

Player Summary	
Fantasy Value	$2 to $4
Card Value	5¢ to 7¢
Will	endure in bullpen
Can't	always find strike zone
Expect	low opponents' average
Don't Expect	homers

As a starting pitcher, DeLeon was a scouting enigma—outstanding stuff, losing record. Twice, he lost 19 games. In his only two winning years, DeLeon topped 200 strikeouts. Now a reliever, however, he may have found his niche. He's fared well two years in a row, thanks to his ability to baffle batters with a combination of fastballs, forkballs, curves, and sliders. He's especially effective against right-handed hitters, although lefties struggle against him too. DeLeon in 1994 averaged a strikeout per inning, yielded six and one-half hits per nine innings, and kept the ball in the park. He stranded most of the runners he inherited and didn't allow many stolen bases.

Major League Pitching Register

		W	L	ERA	G	S	IP	H	ER	BB	SO
83	NL	7	3	2.83	15	0	108.0	75	34	47	118
84	NL	7	13	3.74	30	0	192.1	147	80	92	153
85	NL	2	19	4.70	31	3	162.2	138	85	89	149
86	NL	1	3	8.27	9	1	16.1	17	15	17	11
86	AL	4	5	2.96	13	0	79.0	49	26	42	68
87	NL	11	12	4.02	33	0	206.0	177	92	97	153
88	NL	13	10	3.67	34	0	225.1	198	92	86	208
89	NL	16	12	3.05	36	0	244.2	173	83	80	201
90	NL	7	19	4.43	32	0	182.2	168	90	86	164
91	NL	5	9	2.71	28	0	162.2	144	49	61	118
92	NL	2	9	4.37	32	0	117.1	111	57	48	79
93	NL	3	0	3.26	24	0	47.0	39	17	27	34
93	AL	0	0	1.74	11	0	10.1	5	2	3	6
94	AL	3	2	3.36	42	2	67.0	48	25	31	67
Life		81	115	3.69	370	6	1821.1	1489	747	806	1529
3 AVE		3	4	3.72	42	1	89.1	74	37	41	71

CARLOS DELGADO

Position: Catcher; outfield
Team: Toronto Blue Jays
Born: June 25, 1972 Aguadilla, Puerto Rico
Height: 6'3" **Weight:** 220 lbs.
Bats: left **Throws:** right
Acquired: Signed as a free agent, 10/88

Player Summary	
Fantasy Value	$11 to $14
Card Value	50¢ to $1.25
Will	show great power
Can't	supply strong defense
Expect	powerful throwing arm
Don't Expect	more left field

When the Blue Jays saw Delgado hit last spring, they thought he was the second coming of Fred McGriff. Delgado had five homers and a .917 slugging percentage in his first seven games and joined McGriff as the only Jays to homer off the windows of the SkyDome restaurant during the regular season. This wasn't surprising, since Delgado had 55 homers in his last two minor-league seasons and won three loop MVP Awards along with '92 Minor League Player of the Year honors. It also wasn't surprising that he didn't last. After word spread that he could hit the fastball, AL pitchers started feeding him curves and other breaking balls. Delgado, a selective hitter in the minors, began to press and the strikeouts started increasing. Back in Triple-A, he returned to catcher—his normal position—after on-the-job training in left field. He batted .319 with 19 homers, 58 RBI, 42 strikeouts, and 58 bases on balls at Syracuse last year. Defensively, Delgado has always been considered an average catcher in the minors, and he was not prepared to play in a major-league outfield. His best spot could be DH.

Major League Batting Register

	BA	G	AB	R	H	2B	3B	HR	RBI	SB
93 AL	.000	2	1	0	0	0	0	0	0	0
94 AL	.215	43	130	17	28	2	0	9	24	1
Life	.214	45	131	17	28	2	0	9	24	1

JIM DESHAIES

Position: Pitcher
Team: Minnesota Twins
Born: June 23, 1960 Massena, NY
Height: 6'4" **Weight:** 220 lbs.
Bats: left **Throws:** left
Acquired: Signed as a free agent, 1/94

Player Summary	
Fantasy Value	$0
Card Value	5¢ to 7¢
Will	try to keep job
Can't	keep ball in park
Expect	fat ERA
Don't Expect	much improvement

In his second tour with the Twins, Deshaies last summer revived *Home Run Derby*. Not the old TV show, but Deshaies's own version. Whenever he worked, the hitters pretended it was batting practice. Deshaies surrendered 26 home runs, tops in the majors, during the season's first half. He even shortened and quickened his delivery, allowing him to place the ball lower in the strike zone. Though he still throws a fastball, he's lost his old velocity. Deshaies now relies on getting good location with the one-time heater, along with his slider and changeup. He averaged almost four walks per game, but that wasn't bad compared to his nine-inning ratio of 11.74 hits allowed. Since he didn't get many strikeouts (five per game), his defense had to do the work. He does help himself with the glove but doesn't hold runners.

Major League Pitching Register

	W	L	ERA	G	CG	IP	H	ER	BB	SO
84 AL	0	1	11.57	2	0	7.0	14	9	7	5
85 NL	0	0	0.00	2	0	3.0	1	0	0	2
86 NL	12	5	3.25	26	1	144.0	124	52	59	128
87 NL	11	6	4.62	26	1	152.0	149	78	57	104
88 NL	11	14	3.00	31	3	207.0	164	69	72	127
89 NL	15	10	2.91	34	6	225.2	180	73	79	153
90 NL	7	12	3.78	34	2	209.1	186	88	84	119
91 NL	5	12	4.98	28	1	161.0	156	89	72	98
92 NL	4	7	3.28	15	0	96.0	92	35	33	46
93 AL	11	13	4.41	27	1	167.1	159	82	51	80
93 NL	2	2	4.24	5	0	17.0	24	8	6	5
94 AL	6	12	7.39	25	0	130.1	170	107	54	78
Life	84	94	4.09	255	15	1519.2	1419	690	574	945
3 AVE	8	13	5.35	27	0	154.1	171	92	55	80

DELINO DeSHIELDS

Position: Second base
Team: Los Angeles Dodgers
Born: Jan. 15, 1969 Seaford, DE
Height: 6'1" **Weight:** 170 lbs.
Bats: left **Throws:** right
Acquired: Traded from Expos for Pedro Martinez, 11/93

Player Summary	
Fantasy Value	$17 to $20
Card Value	8¢ to 12¢
Will	show patience
Can't	collect extra-base hits
Expect	40 steals
Don't Expect	defensive woes

After flirting with .300 for two straight seasons, DeShields suffered a serious slide last summer. But it wasn't entirely his fault, because he suffered a concussion in a collision and later fouled a ball off his face. He did give the Dodgers more speed at the top of the lineup behind leadoff man Brett Butler. DeShields, a former hacker who once led the NL in strikeouts, is now a contact hitter who walks as often as he fans. Last season, he had 53 strikeouts and 54 bases on balls. DeShields also has a good success ratio as a basestealer, with 40-plus steals four years in a row before the strike-shortened 1994 campaign. He was caught stealing only seven times last year. A spray hitter with quick hands, DeShields doesn't collect many extra-base hits. His speed often turns his walks, bunts, and infield rollers into doubles, however. In the field, he has great range, reactions, and hands. He turns the double play and makes strong, accurate throws. His best years lie ahead of him.

Major League Batting Register

	BA	G	AB	R	H	2B	3B	HR	RBI	SB
90 NL	.289	129	499	69	144	28	6	4	45	42
91 NL	.238	151	563	83	134	15	4	10	51	56
92 NL	.292	135	530	82	155	19	8	7	56	46
93 NL	.295	123	481	75	142	17	7	2	29	43
94 NL	.250	89	320	51	80	11	3	2	33	27
Life	.274	627	2393	360	655	90	28	25	214	214
3 AVE	.280	128	487	76	137	17	6	4	44	42

MIKE DEVEREAUX

Position: Outfield
Team: Baltimore Orioles
Born: April 10, 1963 Casper, WY
Height: 6' **Weight:** 191 lbs.
Bats: right **Throws:** right
Acquired: Traded from Dodgers for Mike Morgan, 3/89

Player Summary	
Fantasy Value	$6 to $8
Card Value	8¢ to 12¢
Will	rebound or lose job
Can't	learn to be patient
Expect	occasional long one
Don't Expect	decline in defense

Sometimes a slump becomes a nightmare. After knocking in 182 combined runs for the Orioles in 1992 and 1993, Devereaux watched his power erode and confidence vanish. For the third straight year, his numbers declined in all departments, with the telling figure a .088 average in late-inning pressure situations through Aug. 11. Impatience at the plate was the main culprit. He fanned more than three times for every walk. He did show spotty power, but he was far off his old form as Baltimore's No. 3 hitter. In fact, only his defense kept Devereaux on the club. He still makes amazing leaps and dives, though his throwing leaves much to be desired. After Dwight Smith joined the team last year, Brady Anderson—usually the left fielder—got lots of playing time in center. It may be too soon to suggest that Devereaux is over the hill. It is not too early, however, to say his 107-RBI performance of 1992 was a career year.

Major League Batting Register

	BA	G	AB	R	H	2B	3B	HR	RBI	SB
87 NL	.222	19	54	7	12	3	0	0	4	3
88 NL	.116	30	43	4	5	1	0	0	2	0
89 AL	.266	122	391	55	104	14	3	8	46	22
90 AL	.240	108	367	48	88	18	1	12	49	13
91 AL	.260	149	608	82	158	27	10	19	59	16
92 AL	.276	156	653	76	180	29	11	24	107	10
93 AL	.250	131	527	72	132	31	3	14	75	3
94 AL	.203	85	301	35	61	8	2	9	33	1
Life	.251	800	2944	379	740	131	30	86	375	68
3 AVE	.248	136	535	66	133	24	6	17	76	5

MARK DEWEY

Position: Pitcher
Team: Pittsburgh Pirates
Born: Jan. 3, 1965 Grand Rapids, MI
Height: 6' **Weight:** 216 lbs.
Bats: right **Throws:** right
Acquired: Claimed from Mets on waivers, 5/93

Player Summary	
Fantasy Value	$1
Card Value	6¢ to 10¢
Will	answer many calls
Can't	notch high K tally
Expect	decent control
Don't Expect	gopher woes

Though he once saved 30 games in a minor-league season, Dewey seems destined to serve as a middle reliever in the majors. A sinker-slider pitcher who also throws a curve and a changeup, he doesn't get many strikeouts. Most outs come on grounders when he keeps the ball down, however. Because he has a resilient arm, Dewey can work often and pitch several innings at a time. Last year, he yielded 10½ hits per nine innings but displayed decent control and kept the ball in the park. In 1993, he did not yield a homer in 21 outings. Dewey does a decent job with inherited runners, fields his position well, and keeps baserunners in check. He's not much of a hitter, however. Originally signed by San Francisco, Dewey pitched with both the Giants and Mets before coming to Pittsburgh. In 1989 with Class-A San Jose, he set a California League single-season record by notching 30 saves. In 1990, Dewey had 13 saves for Double-A Shreveport and six saves for Triple-A Phoenix. The Grand Valley State grad began his pro career in 1987.

Major League Pitching Register

	W	L	ERA	G	S	IP	H	ER	BB	SO
90 NL	1	1	2.78	14	0	22.2	22	7	5	11
92 NL	1	0	4.32	20	0	33.1	37	16	10	24
93 NL	1	2	2.36	21	7	26.2	14	7	10	14
94 NL	2	1	3.68	45	1	51.1	61	21	19	30
Life	5	4	3.43	100	8	134.0	134	51	44	79
2 AVE	2	1	3.88	42	1	52.1	61	23	18	33

ALEX DIAZ

Position: Outfield
Team: Seattle Mariners
Born: Oct. 5, 1968 Brooklyn, NY
Height: 5'11" **Weight:** 180 lbs.
Bats: both **Throws:** right
Acquired: Claimed from Brewers on waivers, 10/94

Player Summary	
Fantasy Value	$1
Card Value	6¢ to 10¢
Will	use speed
Can't	clear fences
Expect	strong defense
Don't Expect	hits vs. lefties

Don't expect Diaz to hit the ball out of the park; speed and defense are his twin trademarks. A speed merchant who twice topped 40 steals in the minors, Diaz gave Milwaukee great range and a strong throwing arm from center field. He also proved he could play second base and the two other outfield positions. Diaz delivered his first big-league homer June 22 when he connected against Baltimore's Ben McDonald in a 9-2 Milwaukee win. A switch-hitter who's better from the left side, Diaz did his best hitting in late-inning pressure situations. After four months, his average in that department stood at .371. To improve his value, he needs to show more patience at the plate. Though he doesn't fan often, he doesn't wait for walks either. The result is an on-base percentage that's not much higher than his batting average. Diaz in 1992 was voted as the Triple-A American Association's Most Exciting Player when he batted .268 with 17 doubles and 42 stolen bases in 106 games for Denver. He was originally the property of the New York Mets.

Major League Batting Register

	BA	G	AB	R	H	2B	3B	HR	RBI	SB
92 AL	.111	22	9	5	1	0	0	0	1	3
93 AL	.319	32	69	9	22	2	0	0	1	5
94 AL	.251	79	187	17	47	5	7	1	17	5
Life	.264	133	265	31	70	7	7	1	19	13

ROB DIBBLE

Position: Pitcher
Team: Cincinnati Reds
Born: Jan. 24, 1964   Bridgeport, CT
Height: 6'4"   **Weight:** 235 lbs.
Bats: left   **Throws:** right
Acquired: First-round pick in secondary phase of 6/83 free-agent draft

Player Summary	
Fantasy Value	$1
Card Value	6¢ to 10¢
Will	seek comeback
Can't	avoid injuries
Expect	great fastball
Don't Expect	work as closer

Dibble's star has been on the descent over the last four years. From 1991 to '93, his save total went down each year while his walk total went up. In addition, his strikeout total has been on a steady decline for several seasons. Last year was a washout. Dibble underwent surgery to repair a damaged rotator cuff and did not pitch. During his recovery, coaches suggested he try throwing from the kneeling position. The idea was to make him throw more overhand, the way a shortstop might when throwing to first. In theory, that might protect the shoulder. Even when healthy, Dibble is often wild, unable to throw his high-powered fastball over the plate. The Dibble slider seems slow by comparison, but it too must find the strike zone. His defense is no help. He is not a good fielder or master of the pickoff. Dibble averaged 13.55 Ks per nine innings in 1991, but those days seem long gone. If he is recovered, though, he could still be a useful pitcher.

Major League Pitching Register

	W	L	ERA	G	S	IP	H	ER	BB	SO
88 NL	1	1	1.82	37	0	59.1	43	12	21	59
89 NL	10	5	2.09	74	2	99.0	62	23	39	141
90 NL	8	3	1.74	68	11	98.0	62	19	34	136
91 NL	3	5	3.17	67	31	82.1	67	29	25	124
92 NL	3	5	3.07	63	25	70.1	48	24	31	110
93 NL	1	4	6.48	45	19	41.2	34	30	42	49
Life	26	23	2.74	354	88	450.2	316	137	192	619
2 AVE	2	5	4.34	54	22	56.0	41	27	37	80

JERRY DiPOTO

Position: Pitcher
Team: New York Mets
Born: May 24, 1968   Jersey City, NJ
Height: 6'2"   **Weight:** 200 lbs.
Bats: right   **Throws:** right
Acquired: Traded from Indians with Dave Mlicki, Paul Byrd, and Jesus Azuaje for Jeromy Burnitz and Joe Roa, 11/94

Player Summary	
Fantasy Value	$2 to $4
Card Value	5¢ to 7¢
Will	return to relief
Can't	rack up Ks
Expect	ground-ball outs
Don't Expect	gopher troubles

After earning the Cleveland closer job with a solid second half in 1993, DiPoto came to spring training last year with high hopes. Instead, he wound up in the hospital for removal of a cancerous thyroid gland. Disabled for many months, DiPoto returned to Cleveland shortly before the players struck in August. The Virginia Commonwealth product spent three minor-league seasons as a starter. He showed flashes of potential during the last two seasons, and there may be a closer spot available for him. A sinker-slider pitcher who tries to keep the ball down, DiPoto gets ground balls instead of strikeouts. He also keeps the ball in the park. He did not surrender a home run in 56⅓ innings as a rookie in 1993. In 1994 at Triple-A Charlotte, he was 3-2 with a 3.15 ERA, 26 strikeouts, 12 walks, and nine saves in 34 innings and 25 games. DiPoto has some problems with control as well as first batters, so he's best used to start an inning rather than to clean up messes. DiPoto fields his position well and does a good job of keeping baserunners close. Few runners challenge him.

Major League Pitching Register

	W	L	ERA	G	S	IP	H	ER	BB	SO
93 AL	4	4	2.40	46	11	56.1	57	15	30	41
94 AL	0	0	8.04	7	0	15.2	26	14	10	9
Life	4	4	3.62	53	11	72.0	83	29	40	50

GARY DiSARCINA

Position: Shortstop
Team: California Angels
Born: Nov. 19, 1967   Malden, MA
Height: 6'1"   **Weight:** 178 lbs.
Bats: right   **Throws:** right
Acquired: Sixth-round pick in 6/88 free-agent draft

Player Summary	
Fantasy Value.	$2 to $4
Card Value	5¢ to 7¢
Will.	hit to all fields
Can't.	generate power
Expect.	decent defense
Don't Expect.	an All-Star

DiSarcina learned the value of patience last year. By reducing his strikeouts and coaxing more walks, he improved both his batting average and on-base percentage. Once a light hitter known strictly for his glove, he suddenly blossomed into a fine all-around shortstop. He still doesn't supply much power but does hit well with runners in scoring position. He's also more potent against left-handers, hitting some 20 points higher against them than righties. DiSarcina uses all fields and tries to hit the ball where it is pitched. In the field, he has good reactions, a strong throwing arm, and very good range. Though he turns the double-play well, DiSarcina still makes occasional errors with careless throws. He is probably best suited for part-time duty. He and his brother Glenn, a shortstop in the White Sox system, attended high school in Billerica, Massachusetts, the hometown of Atlanta pitcher Tom Glavine.

Major League Batting Register

	BA	G	AB	R	H	2B	3B	HR	RBI	SB
89 AL	.000	2	0	0	0	0	0	0	0	0
90 AL	.140	18	57	8	8	1	1	0	0	1
91 AL	.211	18	57	5	12	2	0	0	3	0
92 AL	.247	157	518	48	128	19	0	3	42	9
93 AL	.238	126	416	44	99	20	1	3	45	5
94 AL	.260	112	389	53	101	14	2	3	33	3
Life	.242	433	1437	158	348	56	4	9	123	18
3 AVE	.249	147	494	56	123	20	1	3	44	6

JOHN DOHERTY

Position: Pitcher
Team: Detroit Tigers
Born: June 11, 1967   Bronx, NY
Height: 6'4"   **Weight:** 190 lbs.
Bats: right   **Throws:** right
Acquired: 19th-round pick in 6/89 free-agent draft

Player Summary	
Fantasy Value.	$2 to $4
Card Value	6¢ to 10¢
Will.	yield many hits
Can't	throw ball hard
Expect	ERA to be lower
Don't Expect	strong fielding

After two successful seasons as a Tiger starter, Doherty never got untracked last summer. His control was good but both right- and left-handed hitters feasted on his offerings. Too many ground balls hit off Doherty found their way through the infield, leaving him with a nine-inning average of 12.35 hits at the time of the Aug. 12 strike. Since Doherty doesn't get many strikeouts, he depends upon his defense for help. He needs to cut the free passes; he had as many walks as Ks last year. The Concordia College graduate is a sinker-slider pitcher who also throws a curve and a changeup. When his pitches are up, he gets hammered. He usually handles righties well, but they found him an easy mark last year. Doherty compounds his problems with poor fielding of his own, though he rarely permits runners to steal against him. He did not allow a stolen base over the first four months of last season. Until Sparky Anderson needed him as an emergency starter two years ago, Doherty had spent his entire career in the bullpen.

Major League Pitching Register

	W	L	ERA	G	CG	IP	H	ER	BB	SO
92 AL	7	4	3.88	47	0	116.0	131	50	25	37
93 AL	14	11	4.44	32	3	184.2	205	91	48	63
94 AL	6	7	6.48	18	2	101.1	139	73	26	28
Life	27	22	4.79	97	5	402.0	475	214	99	128
3 AVE	10	8	4.95	35	2	147.1	177	81	37	46

BRIAN DORSETT

Position: Catcher; first base
Team: Cincinnati Reds
Born: April 9, 1961 Terre Haute, IN
Height: 6'4" **Weight:** 222 lbs.
Bats: right **Throws:** right
Acquired: Signed as a free agent, 12/92

Player Summary	
Fantasy Value	$1
Card Value	5¢ to 7¢
Will	show fine arm
Can't	use speed
Expect	big bat vs. lefties
Don't Expect	security

Joe Oliver's ankle problems turned out to be a blessing in disguise for Dorsett. Given his first shot at extended playing time by the Reds, he turned in a fine job while platooning with lefty hitter Eddie Taubensee. Originally signed by Oakland in 1983, Dorsett had cups of coffee with four other clubs before the Reds grabbed him as Triple-A insurance. Little did they realize he'd play an important role on a contending big-league club. A solid hitter against left-hand pitching, Dorsett also helped out on defense, nailing some 40 percent of those who ran on him. He contributed with runners in scoring position, flashed some power, and even showed signs of becoming a selective hitter. He still fans more than he walks but the ratio isn't embarrassing. Dorsett's potential has always been obvious. He had a 20-homer, 100-RBI season in Triple-A as recently as 1992. In 1993 at Triple-A Indianapolis, he batted .299 with 18 homers and 57 RBI in 77 games. He can also fill in at first base.

Major League Batting Register

	BA	G	AB	R	H	2B	3B	HR	RBI	SB
87 AL	.273	5	11	2	3	0	0	1	3	0
88 AL	.091	7	11	0	1	0	0	0	2	0
89 AL	.364	8	22	3	8	1	0	0	4	0
90 AL	.143	14	35	2	5	2	0	0	0	0
91 NL	.083	11	12	0	1	0	0	0	1	0
93 NL	.254	25	63	7	16	4	0	2	12	0
94 NL	.245	76	216	21	53	8	0	5	26	0
Life	.235	146	370	35	87	15	0	8	48	0

DOUG DRABEK

Position: Pitcher
Team: Houston Astros
Born: July 25, 1962 Victoria, TX
Height: 6'1" **Weight:** 185 lbs.
Bats: right **Throws:** right
Acquired: Signed as a free agent, 12/92

Player Summary	
Fantasy Value	$20 to $25
Card Value	8¢ to 12¢
Will	win if ball is down
Can't	keep runners close
Expect	a good bat
Don't Expect	many hits

Determined to rebound from the worst season of his career, Drabek got off to a great start last year. The 1990 NL Cy Young Award winner even inspired talk of a repeat of the honor when he won seven straight games early. The seventh was an 8-0 three-hitter at Atlanta May 24 in which Drabek contributed three hits of his own. He also two-hit the Rockies Aug. 2. When the players struck 10 days later, Drabek was among NL leaders in wins, complete games, and ERA. A control pitcher who averaged seven hits and nearly seven strikeouts per nine innings in 1994, Drabek is equally effective against righties and lefties. He keeps the ball in the park and is a master at working out of jams. A fastball-slider pitcher whose repertoire also includes a curveball and a changeup, he wins when he keeps the ball down, provoking lots of grounders. Though he's a good fielder, Drabek is often a patsy for basestealers.

Major League Pitching Register

	W	L	ERA	G	CG	IP	H	ER	BB	SO
86 AL	7	8	4.10	27	0	131.2	126	60	50	76
87 NL	11	12	3.88	29	1	176.1	165	76	46	120
88 NL	15	7	3.08	33	3	219.1	194	75	50	127
89 NL	14	12	2.80	35	8	244.1	215	76	69	123
90 NL	22	6	2.76	33	9	231.1	190	71	56	131
91 NL	15	14	3.07	35	5	234.2	245	80	62	142
92 NL	15	11	2.77	34	10	256.2	218	79	54	177
93 NL	9	18	3.79	34	7	237.2	242	100	60	157
94 NL	12	6	2.84	23	6	164.2	132	52	45	121
Life	120	94	3.17	283	49	1896.2	1727	669	492	1174
3 AVE	14	12	3.13	33	8	241.2	215	84	59	168

DARREN DREIFORT

Position: Pitcher
Team: Los Angeles Dodgers
Born: May 18, 1972 Wichita, KS
Height: 6'2" **Weight:** 205 lbs.
Bats: right **Throws:** right
Acquired: First-round pick in 6/93 free-agent draft

Player Summary	
Fantasy Value	$8 to $10
Card Value	20¢ to 40¢
Will	throw extreme heat
Can't	bank on experience
Expect	bat to be big help
Don't Expect	control difficulty

In three years at Wichita State, Dreifort had a 26-5 pitching record, a .318 batting average, and 25 homers in 314 at bats. He contributed to two USA national teams, including the 1992 Olympic team, and won College Player of the Year honors and the Golden Spikes Award as the nation's best amateur. The Dodgers didn't hesitate to put him into their bullpen without trying him in the minors first. A sinker-slider pitcher who learned a slow curve from pitching coach Ron Perranoski during 1994 spring training, Dreifort's low-90s heater also has good movement. It looks even faster when contrasted with his late-breaking off-speed pitches. Dreifort has the durable arm and the loose disposition appropriate for relief work. He's especially effective against righties but should intimidate all comers when he learns to use both sides of the plate. Completing that process required some time in the minors last summer. At Double-A San Antonio, he was 3-1 with a 2.80 ERA, 32 Ks, 13 walks, and 36 hits in 35 innings. Dreifort won a game with a pinch-hit single in his first pro at bat.

Major League Pitching Register

	W	L	ERA	G	S	IP	H	ER	BB	SO
94 NL	0	5	6.21	27	6	29.0	45	20	15	22
Life	0	5	6.21	27	6	29.0	45	20	15	22

MARIANO DUNCAN

Position: Second base; third base
Team: Philadelphia Phillies
Born: March 13, 1963 San Pedro de Macoris, Dominican Republic
Height: 6' **Weight:** 185 lbs.
Bats: right **Throws:** right
Acquired: Signed as a free agent, 12/91

Player Summary	
Fantasy Value	$9 to $11
Card Value	6¢ to 10¢
Will	come through in clutch
Can't	supply stellar defense
Expect	higher mark vs. lefties
Don't Expect	many walks

The starting second baseman for the National League All-Stars? Who's kidding whom? The fans made that selection after Duncan had moved to third, leaving second to the left-right platoon of Mickey Morandini and Randy Ready. While Duncan is a decent infielder, he wasn't the best second baseman in the NL last year. Though he hits well in the clutch, Duncan fans four times for every walk, doesn't steal much anymore, and is below average defensively. He hits 40 points higher against lefties than he does against righties and doesn't walk enough to boost his on-base percentage to respectable levels. Of the several positions he plays, third may be Duncan's best. With quick reactions and decent hands, he'll probably make fewer errors than predecessor Dave Hollins. At second, Duncan isn't adept at turning two and has average range.

Major League Batting Register

	BA	G	AB	R	H	2B	3B	HR	RBI	SB
85 NL	.244	142	502	74	137	24	6	6	39	38
86 NL	.229	109	407	47	93	7	0	8	30	48
87 NL	.215	76	261	31	56	8	1	6	18	11
89 NL	.248	94	258	32	64	15	2	3	21	9
90 NL	.306	125	435	67	133	22	11	10	55	13
91 NL	.258	100	333	46	86	7	4	12	40	5
92 NL	.267	142	574	71	153	40	3	8	50	23
93 NL	.282	124	496	68	140	26	4	11	73	6
94 NL	.268	88	347	49	93	22	1	8	48	10
Life	.260	1000	3673	485	955	171	32	72	374	163

SHAWON DUNSTON

Position: Shortstop
Team: Chicago Cubs
Born: March 21, 1963 Brooklyn, NY
Height: 6'1" **Weight:** 175 lbs.
Bats: right **Throws:** right
Acquired: First-round pick in 6/82 free-agent draft

Player Summary	
Fantasy Value.................	$7 to $9
Card Value...................	6¢ to 10¢
Will................	bang a few long hits
Can't...............	show patience at bat
Expect....................	clutch hitting
Don't Expect.........	many stolen bases

After missing nearly two full years with back problems, Dunston reclaimed his old job as shortstop of the Cubs. He played as if he had never left, showing the old pluses and minuses that had become his trademarks. Still an impatient hitter who fans three times more than he walks, Dunston also hits with more authority than many other shortstops. He thrives in late-inning pressure situations, hitting .327 in that department over the first four months of last season. Though his clutch hitting was hardly a surprise, Dunston's poor performance at Wrigley Field and against lefty pitchers were mysteries. There was nothing wrong with his fielding, however. Unveiling the old shotgun arm that made him famous, Dunston convinced NL managers his comeback was complete. In a *Baseball America* poll, they voted that arm the second-strongest infield arm in the NL.

Major League Batting Register

	BA	G	AB	R	H	2B	3B	HR	RBI	SB
85 NL	.260	74	250	40	65	12	4	4	18	11
86 NL	.250	150	581	66	145	37	3	17	68	13
87 NL	.246	95	346	40	85	18	3	5	22	12
88 NL	.249	155	575	69	143	23	6	9	56	30
89 NL	.278	138	471	52	131	20	6	9	60	19
90 NL	.262	146	545	73	143	22	8	17	66	25
91 NL	.260	142	492	59	128	22	7	12	50	21
92 NL	.315	18	73	8	23	3	1	0	2	2
93 NL	.400	7	10	3	4	2	0	0	2	0
94 NL	.278	88	331	38	92	19	0	11	35	3
Life	.261	1013	3674	448	959	178	38	84	379	136

LEN DYKSTRA

Position: Outfield
Team: Philadelphia Phillies
Born: Feb. 10, 1963 Santa Ana, CA
Height: 5'10" **Weight:** 195 lbs.
Bats: left **Throws:** left
Acquired: Traded from Mets with Roger McDowell for Juan Samuel, 6/89

Player Summary	
Fantasy Value..............	$20 to $25
Card Value.................	15¢ to 25¢
Will.................	rattle with speed
Can't..............	make great throws
Expect...........	high on-base average
Don't Expect.........	trouble with lefties

Last May, Dykstra looked like the man who contended for 1993 MVP honors. He was NL Player of the Month with a .392 average, a .504 on-base percentage, a .686 slugging percentage, 25 runs scored, and six stolen bases. But that was before his appendix flared up. Dykstra had it removed June 23, went on the DL, and had trouble finding his form. By the time the strike started, he was struggling against southpaws and not generating much power. He fell from his '93 form, when he led the league in at bats, runs, hits, walks, putouts, and total chances. He also had six homers in postseason play. A healthy Dykstra remains one of baseball's best leadoff men. Even during his skid last year, he walked more than he fanned and fashioned a high on-base percentage. Dykstra averages 30 steals a year and provides strong defense despite a mediocre arm.

Major League Batting Register

	BA	G	AB	R	H	2B	3B	HR	RBI	SB
85 NL	.254	83	236	40	60	9	3	1	19	15
86 NL	.295	147	431	77	127	27	7	8	45	31
87 NL	.285	132	431	86	123	37	3	10	43	27
88 NL	.270	126	429	57	116	19	3	8	33	30
89 NL	.237	146	511	66	121	32	4	7	32	30
90 NL	.325	149	590	106	192	35	3	9	60	33
91 NL	.297	63	246	48	73	13	5	3	12	24
92 NL	.301	85	345	53	104	18	0	6	39	30
93 NL	.305	161	637	143	194	44	6	19	66	37
94 NL	.273	84	315	68	86	26	5	5	24	15
Life	.287	1176	4171	744	1196	260	39	76	373	272
3 AVE	.294	121	475	97	140	33	4	11	46	29

DAMION EASLEY

Position: Second base; third base
Team: California Angels
Born: Nov. 11, 1969 Oakland, CA
Height: 5'11" **Weight:** 155 lbs.
Bats: right **Throws:** right
Acquired: 30th-round pick in 6/88 free-agent draft

Player Summary

Fantasy Value. . . . . $3 to $5
Card Value . . . . 8¢ to 15¢
Will . . . . try to find '93 form
Can't . . . . turn the double play
Expect . . . . better show of speed
Don't Expect . . . . home runs

Easley is still searching for the right position. A minor-league shortstop, he's shuttled between second and third base during his brief tenure in the majors. Last year, he played more than 40 games each at both positions. The jury is also still out on his hitting. One year after posting a .392 on-base percentage, Easley slipped more than 100 points in that department. He struggled against lefties—not even breaking the Mendoza Line—and did not contribute the power the Angels expected, though one-third of his hits went for extra bases. Easley was a basestealer in the minors, topping two-dozen three years in a row. He'll need to reach more often before he can approach those numbers in the big leagues. Easley also needs work on his defense. Despite great range, he makes careless boots and seems to have regressed in the ability he showed in 1993 at turning the double play. He compiled seven errors last year. Easley is young enough that his top priority should be showing his abominable 1994 season was just a fluke.

Major League Batting Register

	BA	G	AB	R	H	2B	3B	HR	RBI	SB
92 AL	.258	47	151	14	39	5	0	1	12	9
93 AL	.313	73	230	33	72	13	2	2	22	6
94 AL	.215	88	316	41	68	16	1	6	30	4
Life	.257	208	697	88	179	34	3	9	64	19
3 AVE	.250	81	275	35	69	14	1	4	25	7

DENNIS ECKERSLEY

Position: Pitcher
Team: Oakland Athletics
Born: Oct. 3, 1954 Oakland, CA
Height: 6'2" **Weight:** 195 lbs.
Bats: right **Throws:** right
Acquired: Traded from Cubs with Dan Rohn for Dave Wilder, Brian Guinn, and Mark Leonette, 4/87

Player Summary

Fantasy Value. . . . . $20 to $25
Card Value . . . . 8¢ to 15¢
Will. . . . . display good control
Can't . . . . retire lefty hitters
Expect . . . . high K count
Don't Expect . . . . 40 saves

Eckersley insisted that age had nothing to do with his slow start last season. Instead, he said that a spring injury—a liner hit him on the thumb—deprived him of his usual amount of 13 exhibition outings. He blew several saves early, then returned to his old reliable form. A sinker-slider sidearmer who also throws a forkball and an occasional curve, Eckersley remained a power pitcher, averaging more than a K per inning. He has struggled against southpaws in recent years, though.

Major League Pitching Register

	W	L	ERA	G	S	IP	H	ER	BB	SO
75 AL	13	7	2.60	34	2	186.2	147	54	90	152
76 AL	13	12	3.43	36	1	199.1	155	76	78	200
77 AL	14	13	3.53	33	0	247.1	214	97	54	191
78 AL	20	8	2.99	35	0	268.1	258	89	71	162
79 AL	17	10	2.99	33	0	246.2	234	82	59	150
80 AL	12	14	4.28	30	0	197.2	188	94	44	121
81 AL	9	8	4.27	23	0	154.0	160	73	35	79
82 AL	13	13	3.73	33	0	224.1	228	93	43	127
83 AL	9	13	5.61	28	0	176.1	223	110	39	77
84 AL	4	4	5.01	9	0	64.2	71	36	13	33
84 NL	10	8	3.03	24	0	160.1	152	54	36	81
85 NL	11	7	3.08	25	0	169.1	145	58	19	117
86 NL	6	11	4.57	33	0	201.0	226	102	43	137
87 AL	6	8	3.03	54	16	115.2	99	39	17	113
88 AL	4	2	2.35	60	45	72.2	52	19	11	70
89 AL	4	0	1.56	51	33	57.2	32	10	3	55
90 AL	4	2	0.61	63	48	73.1	41	5	4	73
91 AL	5	4	2.96	67	43	76.0	60	25	9	87
92 AL	7	1	1.91	69	51	80.0	62	17	11	93
93 AL	2	4	4.16	64	36	67.0	67	31	13	80
94 AL	5	4	4.26	45	19	44.1	49	21	13	47
Life	188	153	3.46	849	294	3082.2	2863	1185	705	2245
3 AVE	5	4	3.33	65	38	70.0	66	26	14	80

81

TOM EDENS

Position: Pitcher
Team: Philadelphia Phillies
Born: June 9, 1961 Ontario, OR
Height: 6'2" **Weight:** 185 lbs.
Bats: right **Throws:** right
Acquired: Traded from Astros for Milt Thompson, 7/94

Player Summary	
Fantasy Value	$0
Card Value	5¢ to 7¢
Will	keep ball in park
Can't	stop basestealers
Expect	curve as out pitch
Don't Expect	closer job

Although Edens averages only a save a year, he's not a bad relief pitcher. Used primarily as a set-up man, he's not supposed to get wins, losses, or saves. A thank-you from his manager will suffice, especially since he is too long in the tooth to win a closer's job now. The rubber-armed right-hander throws a fastball, a forkball, and a big-breaking curveball that serves as his out pitch. In 1994, he averaged three walks and six and one-half strikeouts per game. He yielded just over a hit per inning but kept the ball in the park. Edens strands most inherited runners and fields his position extremely well but has trouble preventing baserunners from stealing. Originally signed by the Royals, Edens launched his pro career at Butte in 1983. He reached the majors with the Mets four years later. He holds a degree in business from Lewis & Clark State College in Idaho and led the baseball team to the NAIA World Series finals in 1983.

Major League Pitching Register

	W	L	ERA	G	S	IP	H	ER	BB	SO
87 NL	0	0	6.75	2	0	8.0	15	6	4	4
90 AL	4	5	4.45	35	2	89.0	89	44	33	40
91 AL	2	2	4.09	8	0	33.0	34	15	10	19
92 AL	6	3	2.83	52	3	76.1	65	24	36	57
93 NL	1	1	3.12	38	0	49.0	47	17	19	21
94 NL	5	1	4.33	42	1	54.0	59	26	18	39
Life	18	12	3.84	177	6	309.1	309	132	120	180
3 AVE	5	2	3.47	50	1	67.0	65	26	27	44

JIM EDMONDS

Position: Outfield
Team: California Angels
Born: June 27, 1970 Fullerton, CA
Height: 6'1" **Weight:** 190 lbs.
Bats: left **Throws:** left
Acquired: Seventh-round pick in 6/88 free-agent draft

Player Summary	
Fantasy Value	$2 to $4
Card Value	8¢ to 15¢
Will	play outfield well
Can't	become big slugger
Expect	hits to all fields
Don't Expect	patience at bat

After six years in the minors, Edmonds advanced to the California varsity last spring and became the regular left fielder shortly after the season started. A line-drive hitter who uses all fields, Edmonds last season did his best hitting with runners in scoring position. He'd be more effective if he were more selective. He fans more than two times for every walk. Though not a slugger, he has the potential to reach double figures in home runs. He has good range in the outfield, where his diving catches caught the scouts' attention in the minors. Edmonds also has an adequate throwing arm. In addition to playing the outfield, he can also play first base. Injuries hampered his progress early in his career, but he remained relatively healthy last season. His approach also improved. He was once criticized for a laid-back attitude that stopped him from playing with an aggressive style his coaches wanted. In 1993, Edmonds batted .315 at Triple-A Vancouver, with nine homers and 74 RBI in 95 games. He batted .313 in 1992 at Double-A Midland and .299 at Triple-A Edmonton.

Major League Batting Register

	BA	G	AB	R	H	2B	3B	HR	RBI	SB
93 AL	.246	18	61	5	15	4	1	0	4	0
94 AL	.273	94	289	35	79	13	1	5	37	4
Life	.269	112	350	40	94	17	2	5	41	4

MARK EICHHORN

Position: Pitcher
Team: Baltimore Orioles
Born: Nov. 21, 1960 San Jose, CA
Height: 6'3" **Weight:** 200 lbs.
Bats: right **Throws:** right
Acquired: Signed as a free agent, 12/93

Player Summary	
Fantasy Value	$4 to $6
Card Value	5¢ to 7¢
Will	throw strikes
Can't	stop runners
Expect	baffling delivery
Don't Expect	homers

When the Orioles signed Eichhorn, the transaction was an agate footnote buried in the sports section. But the pitcher's performance merited much larger type. The veteran set-up man gave the team both innings and production. In June, Eichhorn extended his scoreless innings streak to 16, over a 10-game span. He notched his first save July 4 when he worked four scoreless innings against Seattle. A sidearmer with excellent control of his fastball and changeup, Eichhorn historically struggles against southpaws but beats up on right-handed hitters. The opposite was true last summer, however. One thing remained constant: Almost no one took Eichhorn deep. The pitcher also stranded most inherited runners and fielded his position extremely well. He rarely makes an error. Eichhorn's primary weakness is keeping runners close; his slow delivery hurts.

Major League Pitching Register

	W	L	ERA	G	S	IP	H	ER	BB	SO
82 AL	0	3	5.45	7	0	38.0	40	23	14	16
86 AL	14	6	1.72	69	10	157.0	105	30	45	166
87 AL	10	6	3.17	89	4	127.2	110	45	52	96
88 AL	0	3	4.18	37	1	66.2	79	31	27	28
89 NL	5	5	4.35	45	0	68.1	70	33	19	49
90 AL	2	5	3.08	60	13	84.2	98	29	23	69
91 AL	3	3	1.98	70	1	81.2	63	18	13	49
92 AL	4	4	3.08	65	2	87.2	86	30	25	61
93 AL	3	1	2.72	54	0	72.2	76	22	22	47
94 AL	6	5	2.15	43	1	71.0	62	17	19	35
Life	47	41	2.93	539	32	855.1	789	278	259	616
3 AVE	5	4	2.63	60	1	86.1	83	25	25	52

JIM EISENREICH

Position: Outfield
Team: Philadelphia Phillies
Born: April 18, 1959 St. Cloud, MN
Height: 5'11" **Weight:** 195 lbs.
Bats: left **Throws:** left
Acquired: Signed as a free agent, 1/93

Player Summary	
Fantasy Value	$6 to $8
Card Value	6¢ to 10¢
Will	make good contact
Can't	clear the fences
Expect	solid defense
Don't Expect	high whiff total

Used primarily as a platoon player the last several years, Eisenreich has fattened his average by facing a steady stream of right-handed pitchers. A contact hitter who walks as often as he fans, he does his best hitting with runners in scoring position. He's not much of a home run threat and has never reached double figures in that department. Pitchers who think they can get him out with breaking balls are in for a surprise. On the bases, Eisenreich is no longer a threat to approach his single-season high of 27 steals. When he does try to steal, however, he usually succeeds. He is a good defensive player who seldom makes errors. He has good instincts, good range, a quick release, and an arm that is accurate though not powerful. He plays all three outfield spots but is most often stationed in right. Eisenreich began his pro career in the Minnesota system in 1980.

Major League Batting Register

	BA	G	AB	R	H	2B	3B	HR	RBI	SB
82 AL	.303	34	99	10	30	6	0	2	9	0
83 AL	.286	2	7	1	2	1	0	0	0	0
84 AL	.219	12	32	1	7	1	0	0	3	2
87 AL	.238	44	105	10	25	8	2	4	21	1
88 AL	.218	82	202	26	44	8	1	1	19	9
89 AL	.293	134	475	64	139	33	7	9	59	27
90 AL	.280	142	496	61	139	29	7	5	51	12
91 AL	.301	135	375	47	113	22	3	2	47	5
92 AL	.269	113	353	31	95	13	3	2	28	11
93 NL	.318	153	362	51	115	17	4	7	54	5
94 NL	.300	104	290	42	87	15	4	4	43	6
Life	.285	955	2796	344	796	153	31	36	334	78
3 AVE	.296	138	375	47	111	17	4	5	48	8

CAL ELDRED

Position: Pitcher
Team: Milwaukee Brewers
Born: Nov. 24, 1967 Cedar Rapids, IA
Height: 6'4" **Weight:** 215 lbs.
Bats: right **Throws:** right
Acquired: First-round pick in 6/89 free-agent draft

Player Summary	
Fantasy Value	$15 to $18
Card Value	8¢ to 12¢
Will	try to shrink ERA
Can't	block gopher balls
Expect	improved K totals
Don't Expect	more control woes

Once he harnesses his control, Eldred could become one of baseball's premier starters. Though he yields less than eight hits per nine innings, he surrenders entirely too many walks. He had a nine-inning average of 4.22 by strike time last summer. The former Triple-A American Association strikeout king also forgot how to throw the third strike; his whiff average declined to less than five per game. A workhorse who gives his team innings, Eldred is impressive when all his pitches are working. His 5-1 win over Toronto June 27 was his third straight complete game. On July 30, he outdueled Boston ace Roger Clemens 5-1 at Fenway Park. A fastball-curveball pitcher, Eldred gives up more fly balls than grounders. Too many of those flies sail over the fences, inflating an ERA that's been over 4.00 two years in a row. Eldred also has trouble holding runners close. Otherwise, his defense is more than adequate. He was the AL Rookie Pitcher of the Year in 1992. Eldred played his college ball at the University of Iowa.

Major League Pitching Register

	W	L	ERA	G	CG	IP	H	ER	BB	SO
91 AL	2	0	4.50	3	0	16.0	20	8	6	10
92 AL	11	2	1.79	14	2	100.1	76	20	23	62
93 AL	16	16	4.01	36	8	258.0	232	115	91	180
94 AL	11	11	4.68	25	6	179.0	158	93	84	98
Life	40	29	3.84	78	16	553.1	486	236	204	350
3 AVE	14	11	3.92	28	6	203.0	177	89	77	127

SCOTT ERICKSON

Position: Pitcher
Team: Minnesota Twins
Born: Feb. 2, 1968 Long Beach, CA
Height: 6'4" **Weight:** 220 lbs.
Bats: right **Throws:** right
Acquired: Fourth-round pick in 6/89 free-agent draft

Player Summary	
Fantasy Value	$1
Card Value	8¢ to 12¢
Will	try to come back
Can't	quiet lefty bats
Expect	more hits than frames
Don't Expect	20 wins

Will the real Scott Erickson please stand up? His 6-0 no-hitter against Milwaukee April 27 was the first by a Twin since Dean Chance in 1967. Erickson fanned a career-best 10 while beating Baltimore May 14. Scouts said he improved his velocity and his slider, making his sinking fastball more effective. He also throws a curve and a changeup. He entered the strike with an 8-11 record and 5.44 ERA, however. A genuine baseball enigma, Erickson was a 20-game winner in 1991 and a 19-game loser in 1993. In 1994, he averaged three and one-half walks and six and one-half strikeouts per game but yielded nearly 11 hits per nine innings. The hits wouldn't hurt as much if he could cut the walks in half. The heart of the problem is Erickson's inability to retire left-handed hitters. The pitcher also has problems holding runners, though he improved in that area last year. His attitude suffered; he had so many communication problems with the Minnesota brain trust that he asked to be traded.

Major League Pitching Register

	W	L	ERA	G	CG	IP	H	ER	BB	SO
90 AL	8	4	2.87	19	1	113.0	108	36	51	53
91 AL	20	8	3.18	32	5	204.0	189	72	71	108
92 AL	13	12	3.40	32	5	212.0	197	80	83	101
93 AL	8	19	5.19	34	1	218.2	266	126	71	116
94 AL	8	11	5.44	23	2	144.0	173	87	59	104
Life	57	54	4.05	140	14	891.2	933	401	335	482
3 AVE	11	15	4.67	33	3	211.1	236	110	79	121

ALVARO ESPINOZA

Position: Infield
Team: Cleveland Indians
Born: Feb. 19, 1962 Valencia, Venezuela
Height: 6' **Weight:** 190 lbs.
Bats: right **Throws:** right
Acquired: Signed as a free agent, 4/92

Player Summary	
Fantasy Value	$0
Card Value	5¢ to 7¢
Will	play almost anywhere
Can't	clear outfield fences
Expect	solid bat vs. lefties
Don't Expect	patience at plate

A shortstop by trade, Espinoza served as Cleveland's version of Detroit's supersub, Tony Phillips, last year. The only difference was that Espinoza didn't hit like Phillips. Playing all four infield positions, Espinoza was valuable—especially when shortstop Omar Vizquel was hurt or third baseman Jim Thome was rested against a rough left-hander. Espinoza hits for a solid average against southpaws, though he can't contribute anything approaching Thome's power. When he does hit the ball, Espinoza rarely hits anything more than a single. He makes decent contact but could be far more valuable if he had more patience. Instead, he swings at anything. Last year, he struck out five times more often than he walked. Never a fast runner, Espinoza doesn't have great range at short. He's better at third, where his instincts, hands, and arm are all above average. Espinoza makes strong throws.

Major League Batting Register

	BA	G	AB	R	H	2B	3B	HR	RBI	SB
84 AL	.000	1	0	0	0	0	0	0	0	0
85 AL	.263	32	57	5	15	2	0	0	9	0
86 AL	.214	37	42	4	9	1	0	0	1	0
88 AL	.000	3	0	0	0	0	0	0	0	0
89 AL	.282	146	503	51	142	23	1	0	41	3
90 AL	.224	150	438	31	98	12	2	2	20	1
91 AL	.256	148	480	51	123	23	2	5	33	4
93 AL	.278	129	263	34	73	15	0	4	27	2
94 AL	.238	90	231	27	55	13	0	1	19	1
Life	.255	736	2017	203	515	89	5	12	150	11
2 AVE	.256	128	294	36	75	17	0	3	27	2

TONY EUSEBIO

Position: Catcher
Team: Houston Astros
Born: April 27, 1967 San Jose de Los
  Llamos, Dominican Republic
Height: 6'2" **Weight:** 180 lbs.
Bats: right **Throws:** right
Acquired: Signed as a free agent, 5/85

Player Summary	
Fantasy Value	$1 to $3
Card Value	25¢ to 60¢
Will	slam southpaws
Can't	show selective bat
Expect	strong defense
Don't Expect	many basestealers

Eusebio won a job with a spring training explosion that included a .606 batting average (20-for-33) and a single strikeout. Sharing the catching duties with Scott Servais after the Eddie Taubensee trade, Eusebio murdered left-handers and produced a solid mark with runners in scoring position. He even hit a pair of two-run homers against the Giants June 16. An impatient hitter who in 1993 fanned five times more than he walked, Eusebio did deliver when he connected. One-third of his hits produced extra bases. His batting was not that much of a revelation because of his minor-league record. He batted .324 for Triple-A Tucson in 1993, with one homer, 20 doubles, and 43 RBI in 281 at bats. He also batted .307 with five homers, and 44 RBI in 339 at bats for Double-A Jackson in 1992. He was named to the Texas League All-Star team that year. Defensively, he was a pleasant surprise last summer. He nailed 40 percent of runners trying to steal and did a good job of handling the veteran pitching staff. He previously led two minor leagues in fielding percentage and double plays by a catcher.

Major League Batting Register

	BA	G	AB	R	H	2B	3B	HR	RBI	SB
91 NL	.105	10	19	4	2	1	0	0	0	0
94 NL	.296	55	159	18	47	9	1	5	30	0
Life	.275	65	178	22	49	10	1	5	30	0

STEVE FARR

Position: Pitcher
Team: Boston Red Sox
Born: Dec. 12, 1956 Cheverly, MD
Height: 5'11" **Weight:** 200 lbs.
Bats: right **Throws:** right
Acquired: Traded from Indians with Chris Nabholz for Jeff Russell, 7/94

Player Summary	
Fantasy Value	$1
Card Value	5¢ to 7¢
Will	seek old form
Can't	stifle left-handers
Expect	better K-to-walk ratio
Don't Expect	injury-free year

After topping 20 saves for three straight seasons, Farr stumbled last summer. Plagued by assorted physical problems, he was far off his usual form. Though he usually averages more than two strikeouts for every walk, Farr fell to almost 1-to-1 last year. Lefties lit him up and righties also feasted on his deliveries. When he's right, he holds right-handers to a microscopic average and is equally effective in clutch situations. Although he throws a fastball, a curve, and a slider, he finds the most success when he places the pitches at certain points in and around the strike zone. He's usually good at stranding inherited runners, controlling the running game, and fielding his position. He's not good at staying healthy. Farr has found his name on the disabled list three years in a row.

Major League Pitching Register

	W	L	ERA	G	S	IP	H	ER	BB	SO
84 AL	3	11	4.58	31	1	116.0	106	59	46	83
85 AL	2	1	3.11	16	1	37.2	34	13	20	36
86 AL	8	4	3.13	56	8	109.1	90	38	39	83
87 AL	4	3	4.15	47	1	91.0	97	42	44	88
88 AL	5	4	2.50	62	20	82.2	74	23	30	72
89 AL	2	5	4.12	51	18	63.1	75	29	22	56
90 AL	13	7	1.98	57	1	127.0	99	28	48	94
91 AL	5	5	2.19	60	23	70.0	57	17	20	60
92 AL	2	2	1.56	50	30	52.0	34	9	19	37
93 AL	2	2	4.21	49	25	47.0	44	22	28	39
94 AL	2	1	5.72	30	4	28.1	41	18	18	20
Life	48	45	3.25	509	132	824.1	751	298	334	668
2 AVE	2	2	2.82	50	28	50.0	39	16	24	38

JEFF FASSERO

Position: Pitcher
Team: Montreal Expos
Born: Jan. 5, 1963 Springfield, IL
Height: 6'1" **Weight:** 195 lbs.
Bats: left **Throws:** left
Acquired: Signed as a minor-league free agent, 1/91

Player Summary	
Fantasy Value	$13 to $16
Card Value	6¢ to 10¢
Will	strangle lefties
Can't	keep runners close
Expect	tight ERA
Don't Expect	control trouble

In his first full year as a starter, Fassero found success before injuries intervened. On June 13, he had a no-hitter with two outs in the ninth before he misplayed a Carlos Garcia liner and Jay Bell followed with a home run. A month later, Fassero retired 22 consecutive Dodgers before John Wetteland threw a game-winning homer to Raul Mondesi in the 10th. Fassero tried pitching with a sore elbow and later went on the DL in late July with a strained right oblique muscle. When healthy, he throws strikes with a sinker, a slider, a forkball, and an occasional changeup. Fassero throws any pitch at any time, and his control improved after he became a starter halfway through the 1993 campaign. He now averages two and one-half walks and nearly eight strikeouts per nine innings while yielding less hits than innings pitched. He's especially effective against left-handed hitters. Fassero knows how to bunt and field but needs work on his pickoff move, which is weak for a left-hander.

Major League Pitching Register

	W	L	ERA	G	CG	IP	H	ER	BB	SO
91 NL	2	5	2.44	51	0	55.1	39	15	17	42
92 NL	8	7	2.84	70	0	85.2	81	27	34	63
93 NL	12	5	2.29	56	1	149.2	119	38	54	140
94 NL	8	6	2.99	21	1	138.2	119	46	40	119
Life	30	23	2.64	198	2	429.1	358	126	145	364
3 AVE	10	7	2.71	52	1	143.2	123	43	48	124

JUNIOR FELIX

Position: Outfield
Team: Detroit Tigers
Born: Oct. 3, 1967   Laguna Sabada, Dominican Republic
Height: 5'11"   **Weight:** 165 lbs.
Bats: both   **Throws:** right
Acquired: Signed as a free agent, 1/94

Player Summary	
Fantasy Value	$8 to $10
Card Value	6¢ to 10¢
Will	hit well both ways
Can't	steal successfully
Expect	power bursts
Don't Expect	less whiffs

Having Cecil Fielder as his mentor definitely helped Felix last summer. After coming off the disabled list June 18, Felix went on a 37-for-93 tear that included 10 homers and 28 RBI. He became a .300 hitter for the first time and showed dramatic improvement in the field, where he had been considered a liability. Though he still fans three times more often than he walks, he had a healthy on-base percentage last summer. He also proved, however, that he no longer deserves his one-time billing as a speed-plus-power package. Despite good speed, Felix shows such poor judgement on the bases that he's thrown out far more often than he steals. At least he's eliminated his old rep as a moody player prone to mental lapses. Fined in the past for lack of hustle on the bases and in the outfield, he kept his checkbook balanced last year. He spent most of 1994 as Detroit's everyday right fielder. The Blue Jays discovered Felix at a track meet in 1985 and signed him, though he had not played baseball in years.

Major League Batting Register

	BA	G	AB	R	H	2B	3B	HR	RBI	SB
89 AL	.258	110	415	62	107	14	8	9	46	18
90 AL	.263	127	463	73	122	23	7	15	65	13
91 AL	.283	66	230	32	65	10	2	2	26	7
92 AL	.246	139	509	63	125	22	5	9	72	8
93 NL	.238	57	214	25	51	11	1	7	22	2
94 AL	.306	86	301	54	92	25	1	13	49	1
Life	.264	585	2132	309	562	105	24	55	280	49
3 AVE	.266	106	382	55	102	23	2	11	54	4

FELIX FERMIN

Position: Shortstop; second base
Team: Seattle Mariners
Born: Oct. 9, 1963   Mao Valverde, Dominican Republic
Height: 5'11"   **Weight:** 170 lbs.
Bats: right   **Throws:** right
Acquired: Traded from Indians with Reggie Jefferson and cash for Omar Vizquel, 12/93

Player Summary	
Fantasy Value	$4 to $6
Card Value	5¢ to 7¢
Will	show good glove
Can't	generate power
Expect	clutch hitting
Don't Expect	many strikeouts

A singles hitter who makes good contact, Fermin fanned only once per 36.7 at bats in 1993—the best ratio in the majors. He's adept at bunting or working the hit-and-run play. Because he rarely walks, he does not compile a high on-base percentage—making him an unlikely candidate to hit first or second in the lineup. But he had the highest average of his eight-year career (.317) when the player strike started Aug. 12. Fermin murders left-handed pitchers and produces in the clutch. He doesn't steal much but has enough speed to show good range at short. He also has a strong throwing arm. He spent considerable time at second last summer, where he gave the Mariners better defense than error-prone Rich Amaral. Fermin can turn the double play from both sides of the bag. Originally signed by the Pittsburgh Pirates, Fermin launched his pro career in 1983.

Major League Batting Register

	BA	G	AB	R	H	2B	3B	HR	RBI	SB
87 NL	.250	23	68	6	17	0	0	0	4	0
88 NL	.276	43	87	9	24	0	2	0	2	3
89 AL	.238	156	484	50	115	9	1	0	21	6
90 AL	.256	148	414	47	106	13	2	1	40	3
91 AL	.262	129	424	30	111	13	2	0	31	5
92 AL	.270	79	215	27	58	7	2	0	13	0
93 AL	.262	140	480	48	126	16	2	2	45	4
94 AL	.317	101	379	52	120	21	0	1	35	4
Life	.265	819	2551	269	677	79	11	4	191	25
3 AVE	.287	120	410	49	118	18	1	1	36	3

ALEX FERNANDEZ

Position: Pitcher
Team: Chicago White Sox
Born: Aug. 13, 1969 Miami Beach, FL
Height: 6'1" **Weight:** 205 lbs.
Bats: right **Throws:** right
Acquired: First-round pick in 6/90 free-agent draft

Player Summary	
Fantasy Value	$18 to $21
Card Value	12¢ to 25¢
Will	pile up strikeouts
Can't	keep ball in park
Expect	many fine seasons
Don't Expect	control lapses

After winning the 1990 Golden Spikes Award, Fernandez worked only eight times in the minors before reaching the Sox. Once compared to Tom Seaver, Fernandez floundered for three seasons before becoming an 18-game winner in '93. He continued his winning ways last year, when his 5-0 July helped the Sox take a one-game AL Central lead over Cleveland at the strike deadline. In a seven-hitter against the Indians July 14, Fernandez fanned 12, a career high, and walked only one. He averaged less hits than innings pitched, plus two and one-half walks and six and one-half strikeouts per nine innings. Three of his 11 wins before the strike were shutouts. A fastball-curveball pitcher who also throws a changeup and a slider, Fernandez gets a lot of ground balls. Unfortunately, he also serves up too many gophers, though many come with the bases empty. Right-handed hitters—usually easy prey—gave him a hard time in 1994. Fernandez knows how to hold runners on and field his position.

Major League Pitching Register

	W	L	ERA	G	CG	IP	H	ER	BB	SO
90 AL	5	5	3.80	13	3	87.2	89	37	34	61
91 AL	9	13	4.51	34	2	191.2	186	96	88	145
92 AL	8	11	4.27	29	4	187.2	199	89	50	95
93 AL	18	9	3.13	34	3	247.1	221	86	67	169
94 AL	11	7	3.86	24	4	170.1	163	73	50	122
Life	51	45	3.88	134	16	884.2	858	381	289	592
3 AVE	14	10	3.70	32	4	224.1	217	93	62	145

SID FERNANDEZ

Position: Pitcher
Team: Baltimore Orioles
Born: Oct. 12, 1962 Honolulu, HI
Height: 6'1" **Weight:** 230 lbs.
Bats: left **Throws:** left
Acquired: Signed as a free agent, 11/93

Player Summary	
Fantasy Value	$6 to $8
Card Value	6¢ to 10¢
Will	seek comeback
Can't	stay healthy
Expect	few hits allowed
Don't Expect	gopher problems

Before 1994, the composite average against Sid Fernandez was .204—tied with Nolan Ryan for first all-time by pitchers with 1,500 innings pitched. Unlike Ryan, however, Fernandez has fought weight, knee, and other physical ailments that invariably interfere with his progress. Last year was no exception. He encountered biceps tendinitis during spring training and started the year on the DL. He never got untracked. Lefties found him an easy mark and home run hitters took him deep at every opportunity (27 in 19 starts before the strike). That's not vintage Fernandez. When healthy, he blends a rising fastball with a slow curve and an occasional changeup—throwing all three pitches with good control. Fernandez also yielded less than eight hits per nine innings. He helps himself with his glove but not with baserunners.

Major League Pitching Register

	W	L	ERA	G	CG	IP	H	ER	BB	SO
83 NL	0	1	6.00	2	0	6.0	7	4	7	9
84 NL	6	6	3.50	15	0	90.0	74	35	34	62
85 NL	9	9	2.80	26	3	170.1	108	53	80	180
86 NL	16	6	3.52	32	2	204.1	161	80	91	200
87 NL	12	8	3.81	28	3	156.0	130	66	67	134
88 NL	12	10	3.03	31	1	187.0	127	63	70	189
89 NL	14	5	2.83	35	6	219.1	157	69	75	198
90 NL	9	14	3.46	30	2	179.1	130	69	67	181
91 NL	1	3	2.86	8	0	44.0	36	14	9	31
92 NL	14	11	2.73	32	5	214.2	162	65	67	193
93 NL	5	6	2.93	18	1	119.2	82	39	36	81
94 AL	6	6	5.15	19	2	115.1	109	66	46	95
Life	104	85	3.29	276	25	1706.0	1283	623	649	1553
3 AVE	9	8	3.57	26	3	165.2	133	66	56	136

TONY FERNANDEZ

Position: Third base; shortstop
Team: Cincinnati Reds
Born: June 30, 1962 San Pedro de Macoris, Dominican Republic
Height: 6'2" **Weight:** 175 lbs.
Bats: both **Throws:** right
Acquired: Signed as a free agent, 3/94

Player Summary	
Fantasy Value	$7 to $9
Card Value	6¢ to 10¢
Will	provide strong defense
Can't	be a slugger
Expect	clutch hitting
Don't Expect	happiness

After playing in four All-Star games and winning four Gold Gloves as a shortstop, Fernandez was not happy about moving to third last spring. But the Reds informed him that bumping Barry Larkin from short was not an option. Though he created some waves by carping about his contract and position, Fernandez plugged a vital hole. He hit well from both sides, added unexpected power, and supplied defense that more than compensated for the free-agent loss of Chris Sabo. Fernandez is usually a better left-handed hitter. Nearly a third of his hits go for extra bases, and he's good for 20 swipes. If he catches the infield playing back, he'll bunt his way on. In the field, he has good reactions, excellent range, great hands, and a solid throwing arm.

Major League Batting Register

	BA	G	AB	R	H	2B	3B	HR	RBI	SB
83 AL	.265	15	34	5	9	1	1	0	2	0
84 AL	.270	88	233	29	63	5	3	3	19	5
85 AL	.289	161	564	71	163	31	10	2	51	13
86 AL	.310	163	687	91	213	33	9	10	65	25
87 AL	.322	146	578	90	186	29	8	5	67	32
88 AL	.287	154	648	76	186	41	4	5	70	15
89 AL	.257	140	573	64	147	25	9	11	64	22
90 AL	.276	161	635	84	175	27	17	4	66	26
91 NL	.272	145	558	81	152	27	5	4	38	23
92 NL	.275	155	622	84	171	32	4	4	37	20
93 NL	.225	48	173	20	39	5	2	1	14	6
93 AL	.306	94	353	45	108	18	9	4	50	15
94 NL	.279	104	366	50	102	18	6	8	50	12
Life	.285	1574	6024	790	1714	292	87	61	593	214
3 AVE	.278	148	555	73	154	27	8	7	57	19

MIKE FETTERS

Position: Pitcher
Team: Milwaukee Brewers
Born: Dec. 19, 1964 Van Nuys, CA
Height: 6'4" **Weight:** 212 lbs.
Bats: right **Throws:** right
Acquired: Traded from Angels with Glenn Carter for Chuck Crim, 12/91

Player Summary	
Fantasy Value	$13 to $16
Card Value	6¢ to 10¢
Will	try closer job
Can't	always find zone
Expect	righties to struggle
Don't Expect	gopher woes

Before last season, Fetters had spent five seasons in the thankless job of set-up man. Though he had made 135 relief appearances, he had only three saves to show for his trouble. That changed last summer, when Milwaukee needed a reliable replacement for faltering closer Doug Henry. Fetters filled the bill so well that he had as many saves by Aug. 4 (17) as Henry had managed for all of 1993. Though he occasionally struggled with his control, Fetters averaged eight hits and six strikeouts per nine innings in 1994. He dominated right-handed hitters and was extremely stingy with the home run ball. A sinker-slider pitcher who also uses a curve, a changeup, and a forkball, Fetters gets most of his outs on grounders when he is pitching well. He helps himself by fielding his position well and keeping close tabs on baserunners. The Pepperdine product, proving himself healed from 1993 elbow problems, worked more than 40 times for the third year.

Major League Pitching Register

	W	L	ERA	G	S	IP	H	ER	BB	SO
89 AL	0	0	8.10	1	0	3.1	5	3	1	4
90 AL	1	1	4.12	26	1	67.2	77	31	20	35
91 AL	2	5	4.84	19	0	44.2	53	24	28	24
92 AL	5	1	1.87	50	2	62.2	38	13	24	43
93 AL	3	3	3.34	45	0	59.1	59	22	22	23
94 AL	1	4	2.54	42	17	46.0	41	13	27	31
Life	12	14	3.36	183	20	283.2	273	106	122	160
3 AVE	3	3	2.57	51	9	62.1	52	18	28	37

CECIL FIELDER

Position: First base
Team: Detroit Tigers
Born: Sept. 21, 1963 Los Angeles, CA
Height: 6'3" **Weight:** 255 lbs.
Bats: right **Throws:** right
Acquired: Signed as a free agent, 1/90

Player Summary	
Fantasy Value	$20 to $25
Card Value	12¢ to 25¢
Will	contribute power
Can't	supply strong defense
Expect	another RBI crown
Don't Expect	speed

When the 1994 season began, Fielder had a chance to become the first Tiger with five straight 30-homer seasons and the first since Charlie Gehringer with five straight 100-RBI years. Fielder was en route to both objectives when the players struck. Three days before the walkout, he had a grand slam and six RBI against Milwaukee. In an earlier 9-8 win over the Twins, he homered in the first and 13th innings. A low fastball hitter who likes to pull, Fielder has power to all fields. Although his home run and RBI totals have fallen for three straight seasons, he's still a prodigious run-producer capable of challenging for the RBI crown. He's won it three times, along with a pair of home run titles. Fielder fans twice as much as he walks, has absolutely no speed, and contributes little to the defense. He also hits into oodles of double plays. But that's not surprising for a player who carries extra weight.

Major League Batting Register

	BA	G	AB	R	H	2B	3B	HR	RBI	SB
85 AL	.311	30	74	6	23	4	0	4	16	0
86 AL	.157	34	83	7	13	2	0	4	13	0
87 AL	.269	82	175	30	47	7	1	14	32	0
88 AL	.230	74	174	24	40	6	1	9	23	0
90 AL	.277	159	573	104	159	25	1	51	132	0
91 AL	.261	162	624	102	163	25	0	44	133	0
92 AL	.244	155	594	80	145	22	0	35	124	0
93 AL	.267	154	573	80	153	23	0	30	117	0
94 AL	.259	109	425	67	110	16	2	28	90	0
Life	.259	959	3295	500	853	130	5	219	680	0
3 AVE	.257	154	589	85	151	23	1	35	123	0

CHUCK FINLEY

Position: Pitcher
Team: California Angels
Born: Nov. 26, 1962 Monroe, LA
Height: 6'6" **Weight:** 212 lbs.
Bats: left **Throws:** left
Acquired: First-round pick in 6/85 free-agent draft

Player Summary	
Fantasy Value	$14 to $17
Card Value	8¢ to 12¢
Will	bank on power pitch
Can't	keep ball in park
Expect	at least 15 wins
Don't Expect	a Gold Glove

In four of the five seasons preceding the 1994 campaign, Finley won at least 16 games. He was on pace for similar numbers last year before the strike. Prior to the season, he added a breaking pitch to his fastball-slider repertoire, plus occasional forkballs. He once had control problems but last year averaged about three and one-half walks per nine innings. Finley also fanned more than seven batters per game but yielded less than a hit per inning. He maintained a 2-1 ratio of strikeouts to walks. He sometimes struggles against left-handed hitters, has trouble keeping the ball in the park, and still throws more than his share of wild pitches. He has trouble fielding his position and keeping runners close. But Finley does a fine job of working his way out of jams, coaxing grounders to get out of sticky situations. He's also adept at keeping hits to a minimum with runners in scoring position.

Major League Pitching Register

	W	L	ERA	G	CG	IP	H	ER	BB	SO
86 AL	3	1	3.30	25	0	46.1	40	17	23	37
87 AL	2	7	4.67	35	0	90.2	102	47	43	63
88 AL	9	15	4.17	31	2	194.1	191	90	82	111
89 AL	16	9	2.57	29	9	199.2	171	57	82	156
90 AL	18	9	2.40	32	7	236.0	210	63	81	177
91 AL	18	9	3.80	34	4	227.1	205	96	101	171
92 AL	7	12	3.96	31	4	204.1	212	90	98	124
93 AL	16	14	3.15	35	13	251.1	243	88	82	187
94 AL	10	10	4.32	25	7	183.1	178	88	71	148
Life	99	86	3.50	277	46	1633.1	1552	636	663	1174
3 AVE	12	13	3.81	34	9	238.1	235	101	93	173

STEVE FINLEY

Position: Outfield
Team: Houston Astros
Born: March 12, 1965 Union City, TN
Height: 6'2" **Weight:** 175 lbs.
Bats: left **Throws:** left
Acquired: Traded from Orioles with Pete Harnisch and Curt Schilling for Glenn Davis, 1/91

Player Summary	
Fantasy Value	$15 to $18
Card Value	8¢ to 12¢
Will	take advantage of speed
Can't	always handle lefties
Expect	more triples than homers
Don't Expect	weak throws

Finley has spent the last four years as Houston's regular center fielder. Injuries interfered with his play in 1993 and '94, but he played the complete 162-game schedule in 1992. That was the year he stole a career-best 44 bases. Finley, who holds a degree in physiology from Southern Illinois, is a solid .300 hitter against right-handed pitching. He usually handles lefties fairly well, too, but that was not the case last year. He finally reached double figures in homers last year but had hit more triples than homers four straight years before 1994; playing in the Astrodome makes it easier to hit gappers than dingers. He led the NL with 13 three-baggers in 1993. He's also an accomplished bunter. When healthy, Finley can fly. He has a good success ratio as a basestealer and excellent range in center. His near-perfect positioning, diving catches, and strong throws make him a Gold Glove candidate.

Major League Batting Register

	BA	G	AB	R	H	2B	3B	HR	RBI	SB
89 AL	.249	81	217	35	54	5	2	2	25	17
90 AL	.256	142	464	46	119	16	4	3	37	22
91 AL	.285	159	596	84	170	28	10	8	54	34
92 NL	.292	162	607	84	177	29	13	5	55	44
93 NL	.266	142	545	69	145	15	13	8	44	19
94 NL	.276	94	373	64	103	16	5	11	33	13
Life	.274	780	2802	382	768	109	47	37	248	149
3 AVE	.278	145	559	81	156	22	11	9	48	27

DAVE FLEMING

Position: Pitcher
Team: Seattle Mariners
Born: Nov. 7, 1969 Queens, NY
Height: 6'3" **Weight:** 200 lbs.
Bats: left **Throws:** left
Acquired: Third-round pick in 6/90 free-agent draft

Player Summary	
Fantasy Value	$3 to $5
Card Value	8¢ to 12¢
Will	paint corners
Can't	get hitters with heat
Expect	control to get better
Don't Expect	a dreary year

After winning 29 games in his first full two seasons, Fleming did a belly flop last summer. His usual pinpoint control evaporated, and he couldn't make the big pitch to get out of jams. In the third inning of a scoreless game against New York April 28, Fleming issued five straight walks. He later made a subtle change in his delivery by raising the left arm higher to hide the ball from the hitter better. That enabled him to increase his velocity by throwing more downhill. A sinkerballer who also throws a curveball and a changeup, Fleming relies on location and changing speeds. He allowed five walks per nine innings last year, and until he can cut that number in half, like 1992, he will have troubles. He yields more hits than innings but wins when he has his control. Fleming is more effective against lefties and is good at keeping the ball in the park. He's also adept at fielding his position and keeping baserunners close. The one-time University of Georgia star should have little trouble regrouping.

Major League Pitching Register

	W	L	ERA	G	CG	IP	H	ER	BB	SO
91 AL	1	0	6.62	9	0	17.2	19	13	3	11
92 AL	17	10	3.39	33	7	228.1	225	86	60	112
93 AL	12	5	4.36	26	1	167.1	189	81	67	75
94 AL	7	11	6.46	23	0	117.0	152	84	65	65
Life	37	26	4.48	91	8	530.1	585	264	195	263
3 AVE	13	10	4.58	30	3	187.1	209	95	73	93

DARRIN FLETCHER

Position: Catcher
Team: Montreal Expos
Born: Oct. 3, 1966 Elmhurst, IL
Height: 6'1" **Weight:** 198 lbs.
Bats: left **Throws:** right
Acquired: Traded from Phillies with cash for Barry Jones, 12/91

Player Summary	
Fantasy Value	$5 to $7
Card Value	8¢ to 12¢
Will	produce in clutch
Can't	stop basestealers
Expect	good game-calling
Don't Expect	any speed

Fletcher found a home as Montreal's No. 1 backstop last summer. A rare catcher who makes good contact, he doesn't walk or strike out often. He does his best hitting in late-inning pressure situations and shows surprising power (10 homers in 285 official trips to the plate last year). He would get even more at bats if he could hit lefties at all, batting under .150 against them last year. He's productive against right-handed pitchers, and he formed a fine left-right platoon with Lenny Webster last year. Neither man impressed with his throwing, though. Fletcher had nailed only 23 percent of would-be basestealers by Aug. 12. That was almost twice his 1993 level, however. On the plus side, he is a good game-caller who knows how to block the plate. He can't run at all—few catchers can—and has never stolen a base in the majors. Fletcher's dad was a minor-league pitcher in the 1950s. Drafted by the Cubs, Darrin Fletcher turned pro in 1987.

Major League Batting Register

	BA	G	AB	R	H	2B	3B	HR	RBI	SB
89 NL	.500	5	8	1	4	0	0	1	2	0
90 NL	.130	11	23	3	3	1	0	1	0	0
91 NL	.228	46	136	5	31	8	0	1	12	0
92 NL	.243	83	222	13	54	10	2	2	26	0
93 NL	.255	133	396	33	101	20	1	9	60	0
94 NL	.260	94	285	28	74	18	1	10	57	0
Life	.250	372	1070	83	267	57	4	23	158	0
3 AVE	.254	116	340	28	86	18	1	8	55	0

SCOTT FLETCHER

Position: Second base
Team: Boston Red Sox
Born: July 30, 1958 Fort Walton Beach, FL
Height: 5'11" **Weight:** 173 lbs.
Bats: right **Throws:** right
Acquired: Signed as a free agent, 12/92

Player Summary	
Fantasy Value	$1 to $3
Card Value	6¢ to 10¢
Will	hit or lose his job
Can't	generate much power
Expect	outstanding defense
Don't Expect	too many Ks

Age seemed to be catching up to Fletcher last summer. He barely surfaced above the Mendoza Line before the players walked off the job Aug. 12. In addition, Fletcher failed to hit his weight—which isn't much—in late-inning pressure situations. As a result, the better-hitting Tim Naehring took the job as Boston's regular second baseman. A contact hitter who doesn't walk or strike out very often, Fletcher is strictly a singles guy who sprays the ball around. He's never hit more than five home runs in a season. He's reached double figures in steals five times and still shows good judgement, even though some of his speed is gone. So is some of his range, but he's still a quality second baseman who turns the double play well. Fletcher made only one miscue in his first 53 games last summer.

Major League Batting Register

	BA	G	AB	R	H	2B	3B	HR	RBI	SB
81 NL	.217	19	46	6	10	4	0	0	1	0
82 NL	.167	11	24	4	4	0	0	0	1	1
83 AL	.237	114	262	42	62	16	5	3	31	5
84 AL	.250	149	456	46	114	13	3	3	35	10
85 AL	.256	119	301	38	77	8	1	2	31	5
86 AL	.300	147	530	82	159	34	5	3	50	12
87 AL	.287	156	588	82	169	28	4	5	63	13
88 AL	.276	140	515	59	142	19	4	0	47	8
89 AL	.253	142	546	77	138	25	2	1	43	2
90 AL	.242	151	509	54	123	18	3	4	56	1
91 AL	.206	90	248	14	51	10	1	1	28	0
92 AL	.275	123	386	53	106	18	3	3	51	17
93 AL	.285	121	480	81	137	31	5	5	45	16
94 AL	.227	63	185	31	42	9	1	3	11	8
Life	.263	1545	5076	669	1334	233	37	33	493	98
3 AVE	.268	111	376	59	101	23	3	4	37	15

CLIFF FLOYD

Position: First base; outfield
Team: Montreal Expos
Born: Dec. 5, 1972 Chicago, IL
Height: 6'4" **Weight:** 220 lbs.
Bats: left **Throws:** right
Acquired: First-round pick in 6/91 free-agent draft

Player Summary	
Fantasy Value	$14 to $17
Card Value	30¢ to 50¢
Will	produce in clutch
Can't	show good glove
Expect	speed and power
Don't Expect	McCovey, yet

Though it's still too soon to tell, many scouts insist Floyd will fulfill his immense speed-plus-power potential. Some even say he could be a Willie McCovey with speed. Like McCovey, Floyd is a rangy left-handed hitter who doesn't flinch against left-handed pitching. Last year, he displayed the ability to hit with runners in scoring position and in late-inning pressure situations on the major-league level. Floyd fanned three times more than he walked, but he should become more selective as he learns the pitchers. He had 29 homers, 121 RBI, and 33 steals for three clubs in 1993 (on the Double-A, Triple-A, and big-league levels), when he was named Minor League Player of the Year by *The Sporting News*. *Baseball America* named him the top prospect in the Double-A Eastern League that year. With power to all fields, Floyd could reach double figures in doubles, triples, and home runs. He already did that once in the minors. He's still learning to play first base, so Floyd is best used as an outfielder. Center field is his best position because of his exceptional speed.

Major League Batting Register

	BA	G	AB	R	H	2B	3B	HR	RBI	SB
93 NL	.226	10	31	3	7	0	0	1	2	0
94 NL	.281	100	334	43	94	19	4	4	41	10
Life	.277	110	365	46	101	19	4	5	43	10

JOHN FRANCO

Position: Pitcher
Team: New York Mets
Born: Sept. 17, 1960 Brooklyn, NY
Height: 5'10" **Weight:** 185 lbs.
Bats: left **Throws:** left
Acquired: Traded from Reds with Don Brown for Kip Gross and Randy Myers, 12/89

Player Summary	
Fantasy Value	$20 to $25
Card Value	8¢ to 12¢
Will	assume heavy workload
Can't	worry about his elbow
Expect	best work vs. righties
Don't Expect	gopher problems

Bouncing back from two injury-riddled campaigns, Franco showed last summer that he's still one of baseball's best closers. He saved 30 games for the sixth time while bringing his ERA back to earth. In fact, it was just a shade above the 2.62 career mark he brought into 1994. Franco yielded less hits than innings and averaged seven and one-half strikeouts per game last year. He is stingy with the gopher ball, getting into trouble only when his control isn't sharp. His best pitch—a slow changeup that looks and acts like a screwball—is especially effective against right-handed hitters. Franco also throws a fastball and a slider. He not only fields his position well but keeps a close eye on baserunners. Few challenge him. The St. John's product is a five-time All-Star.

Major League Pitching Register

	W	L	ERA	G	S	IP	H	ER	BB	SO
84 NL	6	2	2.61	54	4	79.1	74	23	36	55
85 NL	12	3	2.18	67	12	99.0	83	24	40	61
86 NL	6	6	2.94	74	29	101.0	90	33	44	84
87 NL	8	5	2.52	68	32	82.0	76	23	27	61
88 NL	6	6	1.57	70	39	86.0	60	15	27	46
89 NL	4	8	3.12	60	32	80.2	77	28	36	60
90 NL	5	3	2.53	55	33	67.2	66	19	21	56
91 NL	5	9	2.93	52	30	55.1	61	18	18	45
92 NL	6	2	1.64	31	15	33.0	24	6	11	20
93 NL	4	3	5.20	35	10	36.1	46	21	19	29
94 NL	1	4	2.70	47	30	50.0	47	15	19	42
Life	63	51	2.63	613	266	770.1	704	225	298	559
3 AVE	4	4	3.10	44	22	46.0	45	16	19	36

JULIO FRANCO

Position: Designated hitter; first base
Team: Chicago White Sox
Born: Aug. 23, 1961   San Pedro de Macoris, Dominican Republic
Height: 6'1"   **Weight:** 185 lbs.
Bats: right   **Throws:** right
Acquired: Signed as a free agent, 12/93

Player Summary	
Fantasy Value	$18 to $21
Card Value	10¢ to 15¢
Will	hit to all fields
Can't	help with defense
Expect	great clutch work
Don't Expect	RBI count to fall

In 12 seasons before 1994, Franco never knocked in more than 92 runs—but he never hit behind Frank Thomas before. Installed as the White Sox DH and cleanup man, Franco collected 48 RBI on his first 47 hits, finishing with 98 in 112 games. He also managed to reach a career peak with 20 homers. A line-drive hitter with a batting crown (in 1991), Franco hits with authority to all fields. He murders left-handed pitchers but does his best hitting in late-inning pressure situations. He's also deadly with runners in scoring position. Slowed by chronic knee problems, the three-time All-Star still steals occasionally and is rarely caught trying. Signed as a shortstop and later switched to second, defense was never his forte. Franco was the 1990 All-Star Game MVP.

Major League Batting Register

	BA	G	AB	R	H	2B	3B	HR	RBI	SB
82 NL	.276	16	29	3	8	1	0	0	3	0
83 AL	.273	149	560	68	153	24	8	8	80	32
84 AL	.286	160	658	82	188	22	5	3	79	19
85 AL	.288	160	636	97	183	33	4	6	90	13
86 AL	.306	149	599	80	183	30	5	10	74	10
87 AL	.319	128	495	86	158	24	3	8	52	32
88 AL	.303	152	613	88	186	23	6	10	54	25
89 AL	.316	150	548	80	173	31	5	13	92	21
90 AL	.296	157	582	96	172	27	1	11	69	31
91 AL	.341	146	589	108	201	27	3	15	78	36
92 AL	.234	35	107	19	25	7	0	2	8	1
93 AL	.289	144	532	85	154	31	3	14	84	9
94 AL	.319	112	433	72	138	19	2	20	98	8
Life	.301	1658	6381	964	1922	299	45	120	861	237
2 AVE	.305	151	571	93	174	29	3	21	111	10

LOU FRAZIER

Position: Outfield; second base
Team: Montreal Expos
Born: Jan. 26, 1965   St. Louis, MO
Height: 6'2"   **Weight:** 175 lbs.
Bats: both   **Throws:** right
Acquired: Signed as a minor-league free agent, 12/92

Player Summary	
Fantasy Value	$3 to $5
Card Value	8¢ to 12¢
Will	hit better left-handed
Can't	clear fences
Expect	great quickness
Don't Expect	fielding woes

A burner who could be the second coming of Otis Nixon, Frazier may even be faster on the steal than Marquis Grissom or Rickey Henderson. Like Nixon, all Frazier needs is a chance. He once stole 162 bases in the minors over a two-year span. Frazier's bat is no longer in question. His mother-in-law had him fitted for glasses after he reported difficulty in seeing the ball at night. A switch-hitter who's better from the left side, he hits over .300 with runners in scoring position and in late-inning pressure situations. He doesn't strike out or walk much and never hits the ball out. He'll bunt his way on, too. Once he reaches, Frazier steals with abandon. When he learns the pitchers, he'll be better—perhaps a league leader. Because of his speed, he has great range in the outfield. From any of the three spots, he's a quick fielder who keeps runners from taking liberties. He can also fill in at second. Frazier was drafted by the Astros in 1986 out of Scottsdale, Arizona, Junior College. He spent three years with Double-A London from 1990 to 1992.

Major League Batting Register

	BA	G	AB	R	H	2B	3B	HR	RBI	SB
93 NL	.286	112	189	27	54	7	1	1	16	17
94 NL	.271	76	140	25	38	3	1	0	14	20
Life	.280	188	329	52	92	10	2	1	30	37

MARVIN FREEMAN

Position: Pitcher
Team: Colorado Rockies
Born: April 10, 1963 Chicago, IL
Height: 6'7" **Weight:** 222 lbs.
Bats: right **Throws:** right
Acquired: Signed as a free agent, 10/93

Player Summary	
Fantasy Value	$7 to $9
Card Value	8¢ to 12¢
Will	retain rotation job
Can't	keep control if rusty
Expect	tight ERA
Don't Expect	high K totals

Freeman always insisted he needed more work to stay sharp. He got it in pitcher-hungry Colorado. Freeman arrived at spring training with three good pitches: a forkball, a slider, and a sinking fastball that produces lots of ground outs. Able to throw strikes from day one, he bolted from the gate with a 3-0 record. He later became the first Rockies' pitcher to beat the Braves. That 7-2 win June 13 ended the club's 16-game losing streak against Atlanta. In seven innings, Freeman fanned three without yielding a walk. No longer "Starvin' Marvin," he found success last year by averaging less than two walks per nine innings while yielding a hit per inning and maintaining a 3-1 ratio of strikeouts to walks. Freeman dominates right-handers and keeps the ball in the park—no mean feat in Colorado. He won't win any awards for defense or holding runners, but his pitching and personality have made him a popular guy.

Major League Pitching Register

	W	L	ERA	G	CG	IP	H	ER	BB	SO
86 NL	2	0	2.25	3	0	16.0	6	4	10	8
88 NL	2	3	6.10	11	0	51.2	55	35	43	37
89 NL	0	0	6.00	1	0	3.0	2	2	5	0
90 NL	1	2	4.31	25	0	48.0	41	23	17	38
91 NL	1	0	3.00	34	0	48.0	37	16	13	34
92 NL	7	5	3.22	58	0	64.1	61	23	29	41
93 NL	2	0	6.08	21	0	23.2	24	16	10	25
94 NL	10	2	2.80	19	0	112.2	113	35	23	67
Life	25	12	3.77	172	0	367.1	339	154	150	250
2 AVE	11	4	2.92	42	0	111.2	110	36	31	68

STEVE FREY

Position: Pitcher
Team: San Francisco Giants
Born: July 29, 1963 Meadowbrook, PA
Height: 5'9" **Weight:** 170 lbs.
Bats: right **Throws:** left
Acquired: Signed as a free agent, 1/94

Player Summary	
Fantasy Value	$1
Card Value	5¢ to 7¢
Will	squelch lefties
Can't	throw with velocity
Expect	50 outings
Don't Expect	great control

Frey's role last season was simple: Face one or two left-handed hitters at a time and get them out. He fared pretty well, holding lefties to a .238 batting average over the first four months. He floundered against right-handers, though, and he yielded an overall average of nearly 11 hits per nine innings—hardly a good ratio for a relief man. Frey's control and ability to keep the ball in the park also left considerable room for improvement. When he falls behind in the count, it usually spells trouble. A curveball specialist who also throws a fastball and a slider, Frey has worked more than 50 games in a season three times. He's never been a big strikeout guy, however, and gets hit hard when he can't keep his curveball down. If he stayed away from issuing bases on balls, though, base hits that he allowed would hurt a lot less. A fine fielder, he keeps close tabs on runners. An original Yankee signee, he pitched for the Expos and Angels before joining the Giants.

Major League Pitching Register

	W	L	ERA	G	S	IP	H	ER	BB	SO
89 NL	3	2	5.48	20	0	21.1	29	13	11	15
90 NL	8	2	2.10	51	9	55.2	44	13	29	29
91 NL	0	1	4.99	31	1	39.2	43	22	23	21
92 AL	4	2	3.57	51	4	45.1	39	18	22	24
93 AL	2	3	2.98	55	13	48.1	41	16	26	22
94 NL	1	0	4.94	44	0	31.0	37	17	15	20
Life	18	10	3.69	252	27	241.1	233	99	126	131
3 AVE	2	2	3.80	56	6	46.1	44	19	23	25

JEFF FRYE

Position: Second base
Team: Texas Rangers
Born: Aug. 31, 1966 Oakland, CA
Height: 5'9" **Weight:** 165 lbs.
Bats: right **Throws:** right
Acquired: 30th-round pick in 6/88 free-agent draft

Player Summary	
Fantasy Value	$2 to $4
Card Value	10¢ to 15¢
Will	make good contact
Can't	produce any power
Expect	gap hits
Don't Expect	defensive trouble

After missing all of 1993 with a serious knee injury, Frye returned with a vengeance last spring. The former minor-league batting king became one of the biggest surprises in Texas. He hit well all season, made good contact, and showed enough patience at the plate to post an on-base percentage of .408 before the players struck. Though he doesn't have much power, Frye does his best hitting in late-inning pressure situations. He also produces with runners in scoring position. His averages against right-handed and left-handed pitchers are virtually equal. Though he's lost some speed because of the injury, Frye remains a good baserunner who usually succeeds when he tries to steal. He's also a premier defensive player who turns the double play well. A first-team NAIA All-American at Southeastern Oklahoma State in 1988, Frye led the Class-A South Atlantic League with a .313 batting average in 1989. He batted .300 at Triple-A Oklahoma City in 1992 and .302 at Double-A Tulsa in '91, and he was named to an All-Star team all three years.

Major League Batting Register

	BA	G	AB	R	H	2B	3B	HR	RBI	SB
92 AL	.256	67	199	24	51	9	1	1	12	1
94 AL	.327	57	205	37	67	20	3	0	18	6
Life	.292	124	404	61	118	29	4	1	30	7
2 AVE	.298	74	244	38	73	19	3	1	19	5

TRAVIS FRYMAN

Position: Third base
Team: Detroit Tigers
Born: March 25, 1969 Lexington, KY
Height: 6'2" **Weight:** 190 lbs.
Bats: right **Throws:** right
Acquired: Third-round pick in 6/87 free-agent draft

Player Summary	
Fantasy Value	$20 to $25
Card Value	20¢ to 35¢
Will	produce lots of power
Can't	curb anxiety at plate
Expect	compact stroke
Don't Expect	defensive woes

Hitting was never a concern for Fryman. He had topped 20 homers and 90 RBI in each of his three full seasons prior to 1994. Fielding was another matter, however. Signed as a shortstop, he broke into the majors at third but returned to short at the start of the 1993 campaign. When his fielding suffered, Tiger manager Sparky Anderson returned Fryman to third. Early last year, Fryman showed the wisdom of that decision. His defense improved so much that he did not make an error between May 2 and June 17. And managers polled by *Baseball America* said he had the AL's second-best infield arm. He probably will not spend much more time playing shortstop. Though he fans three times more than he walks, Fryman feeds off the fastball diet he receives as the hitter preceding Cecil Fielder in the lineup. Fryman is a solid run-producer who gets extra bases on more than one-third of his hits. Because he often swings at the first pitch, breaking balls and high fastballs sometimes give him trouble.

Major League Batting Register

	BA	G	AB	R	H	2B	3B	HR	RBI	SB
90 AL	.297	66	232	32	69	11	1	9	27	3
91 AL	.259	149	557	65	144	36	3	21	91	12
92 AL	.266	161	659	87	175	31	4	20	96	8
93 AL	.300	151	607	98	182	37	5	22	97	9
94 AL	.263	114	464	66	122	34	5	18	85	2
Life	.275	641	2519	348	692	149	18	90	396	34
3 AVE	.276	158	640	93	176	39	5	22	104	7

GARY GAETTI

Position: Third base
Team: Kansas City Royals
Born: Aug. 19, 1958 Centralia, IL
Height: 6' **Weight:** 200 lbs.
Bats: right **Throws:** right
Acquired: Signed as a free agent, 6/93

Player Summary	
Fantasy Value	$6 to $8
Card Value	6¢ to 10¢
Will	display good defense
Can't	show patience at plate
Expect	clutch hitting
Don't Expect	30 homers

Gaetti has been able the past couple of years to salvage a career that looked to be over. After his release from the Angels in 1993, he resurrected his reputation with two strong campaigns for Kansas City. Though he's no longer the 30-homer, 100-RBI guy he once was with Minnesota, Gaetti remains a dangerous clutch hitter. He batted .370 in late-inning pressure situations and .305 with runners in scoring position last year. He's usually a better hitter against left-handed pitchers, though not in 1994. Gaetti's Achilles' heel is impatience at the plate; he fans four times more than he walks. A four-time Gold Glove winner, he still excels in the field. Gaetti is still able to depend upon quick reactions, good hands, and a strong, accurate arm. He's known for starting triple plays.

Major League Batting Register

	BA	G	AB	R	H	2B	3B	HR	RBI	SB
81 AL	.192	9	26	4	5	0	0	2	3	0
82 AL	.230	145	508	59	117	25	4	25	84	0
83 AL	.245	157	584	81	143	30	3	21	78	7
84 AL	.262	162	588	55	154	29	4	5	65	11
85 AL	.246	160	560	71	138	31	0	20	63	13
86 AL	.287	157	596	91	171	34	1	34	108	14
87 AL	.257	154	584	95	150	36	2	31	109	10
88 AL	.301	133	468	66	141	29	2	28	88	7
89 AL	.251	130	498	63	125	11	4	19	75	6
90 AL	.229	154	577	61	132	27	5	16	85	6
91 AL	.246	152	586	58	144	22	1	18	66	5
92 AL	.226	130	456	41	103	13	2	12	48	3
93 AL	.245	102	331	40	81	20	1	14	50	1
94 AL	.287	90	327	53	94	15	3	12	57	0
Life	.254	1835	6689	838	1698	322	32	257	979	83
3 AVE	.254	120	416	52	105	18	2	14	59	1

GREG GAGNE

Position: Shortstop
Team: Kansas City Royals
Born: Nov. 12, 1961 Fall River, MA
Height: 5'11" **Weight:** 172 lbs.
Bats: right **Throws:** right
Acquired: Signed as a free agent, 12/92

Player Summary	
Fantasy Value	$7 to $9
Card Value	6¢ to 10¢
Will	surprise with power
Can't	steal effectively
Expect	possible Gold Glove
Don't Expect	patience at bat

When he joined Kansas City in 1993, Gagne played full time, rarely being lifted for pinch hitters or "rested" against tough righty pitchers, as had been the case with the Twins. Gagne responded by batting with confidence and by playing strong defense. A boot on Opening Day in 1994 ended his club-record streak of 52 consecutive errorless games at short. Though he fans three times more than he walks, Gagne hits with power. He also reaches double figures in steals, but he was thrown out too often last year. He feeds on a fastball diet, but he's susceptible to breaking stuff once he falls behind. Managers polled by *Baseball America* last year named him the AL's No. 2 defensive shortstop (behind Omar Vizquel). Gagne has terrific range, turns the double play, and throws very well.

Major League Batting Register

	BA	G	AB	R	H	2B	3B	HR	RBI	SB
83 AL	.111	10	27	2	3	1	0	0	3	0
84 AL	.000	2	1	0	0	0	0	0	0	0
85 AL	.225	114	293	37	66	15	3	2	23	10
86 AL	.250	156	472	63	118	22	6	12	54	12
87 AL	.265	137	437	68	116	28	7	10	40	6
88 AL	.236	149	461	70	109	20	6	14	48	15
89 AL	.272	149	460	69	125	29	7	9	48	11
90 AL	.235	138	388	38	91	22	3	7	38	8
91 AL	.265	139	408	52	108	23	3	8	42	11
92 AL	.246	146	439	53	108	23	0	7	39	6
93 AL	.280	159	540	66	151	32	3	10	57	10
94 AL	.259	107	375	39	97	23	3	7	51	10
Life	.254	1406	4301	557	1092	238	41	86	443	99
3 AVE	.262	152	502	58	132	29	2	9	56	10

ANDRES GALARRAGA

Position: First base
Team: Colorado Rockies
Born: June 18, 1961 Caracas, Venezuela
Height: 6'3" **Weight:** 235 lbs.
Bats: right **Throws:** right
Acquired: Signed as a free agent, 11/92

Player Summary	
Fantasy Value	$30 to $35
Card Value	15¢ to 30¢
Will	show off-field power
Can't	avoid injuries
Expect	brilliance vs. lefties
Don't Expect	stolen bases

After hitting 103 points above his career average in 1993, Galarraga needed something spectacular for an encore. So he set a National League record with 30 RBI during the month of April. The owner of the game's most open stance reached a career high in homers before a Dave Burba pitch broke his right hand July 28. It's an old story for Galarraga, who missed 41 games with knee and hamstring problems in 1993. When healthy, he is an aggressive hitter who flattens left-handed pitchers, delivers in late-inning pressure situations, and hits with power to all fields. He fanned nine times more than he walked in 1994. Brittle knees and advancing age prevent him from stealing often, but he'll surprise once in awhile. Lack of mobility is also a factor in the field, though Galarraga earned his "Big Cat" nickname for his fancy footwork at first. He is a fine first baseman.

Major League Batting Register

	BA	G	AB	R	H	2B	3B	HR	RBI	SB
85 NL	.187	24	75	9	14	1	0	2	4	1
86 NL	.271	105	321	39	87	13	0	10	42	6
87 NL	.305	147	551	72	168	40	3	13	90	7
88 NL	.302	157	609	99	184	42	8	29	92	13
89 NL	.257	152	572	76	147	30	1	23	85	12
90 NL	.256	155	579	65	148	29	0	20	87	10
91 NL	.219	107	375	34	82	13	2	9	33	5
92 NL	.243	95	325	38	79	14	2	10	39	5
93 NL	.370	120	470	71	174	35	4	22	98	2
94 NL	.319	103	417	77	133	21	0	31	85	8
Life	.283	1165	4294	580	1216	238	20	169	655	69
3 AVE	.319	120	461	72	147	26	2	25	86	6

DAVE GALLAGHER

Position: Outfield; first base
Team: Atlanta Braves
Born: Sept. 20, 1960 Trenton, NJ
Height: 6' **Weight:** 180 lbs.
Bats: right **Throws:** right
Acquired: Traded from Mets for Pete Smith, 11/93

Player Summary	
Fantasy Value	$0
Card Value	5¢ to 7¢
Will	play reserve role
Can't	produce any power
Expect	excellent defense
Don't Expect	any kind of speed

The best part of Gallagher's game is defense. He's a fine reserve outfielder capable of playing any of the three spots, and he can also fill in at first base. Gallagher has good hands and a strong arm, but he needs to compensate for lack of range with proper positioning. He doesn't run well and has only 20 steals in eight seasons. Nor does Gallagher hit with authority. A .272 career hitter before last year, he started to slow down in '94, when he barely poked his head above the Mendoza Line. Not that he didn't receive playing time: For some inexplicable reason, Atlanta manager Bobby Cox decided that Gallagher would be a good left-field platoon partner for rookie slugger Ryan Klesko, who hits left-handed. The move backfired, as Gallagher hit 42 points less against lefties than he did against righties and contributed only seven extra-base hits. At least Gallagher makes contact and walks more than he fans.

Major League Batting Register

	BA	G	AB	R	H	2B	3B	HR	RBI	SB
87 AL	.111	15	36	2	4	1	1	0	1	2
88 AL	.303	101	347	59	105	15	3	5	31	5
89 AL	.266	161	601	74	160	22	2	1	46	5
90 AL	.254	68	126	12	32	4	1	0	7	1
91 AL	.293	90	270	32	79	17	0	1	30	2
92 NL	.240	98	175	20	42	11	1	1	21	4
93 NL	.274	99	201	34	55	12	2	6	28	1
94 NL	.224	89	152	27	34	5	0	2	14	0
Life	.268	721	1908	260	511	87	10	16	178	20
3 AVE	.246	107	197	31	48	10	1	3	23	2

MIKE GALLEGO

Position: Shortstop; second base
Team: New York Yankees
Born: Oct. 31, 1960 Whittier, CA
Height: 5'8" **Weight:** 160 lbs.
Bats: right **Throws:** right
Acquired: Signed as a free agent, 1/92

Player Summary

Fantasy Value	$3 to $5
Card Value	5¢ to 7¢
Will	show some pop
Can't	stay healthy
Expect	decent defense
Don't Expect	hits vs. righties

After showing considerable promise as a hitter during his first two years as the Yankee shortstop, Gallego fell on his face last summer. Overpowered by right-handers, he didn't crack the Mendoza Line with runners in scoring position, and he struggled in late-inning pressure situations. Usually a contact hitter who uses all fields, Gallego may have succumbed to the siren call of the long ball. He hit 10 out of the park in 1993 and might have envisioned himself as a slugger. That's not the idea for him. His role is to move runners up, deliver a few hits, and play good defense. A second baseman by trade, he switched to short when then-teammate Walt Weiss got hurt in 1988. Gallego's range is decent, but his arm isn't great. He is a fine second baseman, however. He has been on the disabled list four times in the last three seasons. He began his pro career at Modesto in 1981.

Major League Batting Register

	BA	G	AB	R	H	2B	3B	HR	RBI	SB
85 AL	.208	76	77	13	16	5	1	1	9	1
86 AL	.270	20	37	2	10	2	0	0	4	0
87 AL	.250	72	124	18	31	6	0	2	14	0
88 AL	.209	129	277	38	58	8	0	2	20	2
89 AL	.252	133	357	45	90	14	2	3	30	7
90 AL	.206	140	389	36	80	13	2	3	34	5
91 AL	.247	159	482	67	119	15	4	12	49	6
92 AL	.254	53	173	24	44	7	1	3	14	0
93 AL	.283	119	403	63	114	20	1	10	54	3
94 AL	.239	89	306	39	73	17	1	6	41	0
Life	.242	990	2625	345	635	107	12	42	269	24
3 AVE	.259	99	336	47	87	17	1	7	42	1

RON GANT

Position: Outfield
Team: Cincinnati Reds
Born: March 2, 1965 Victoria, TX
Height: 6' **Weight:** 172 lbs.
Bats: right **Throws:** right
Acquired: Signed as a free agent, 6/94

Player Summary

Fantasy Value	$19 to $22
Card Value	10¢ to 20¢
Will	stage comeback
Can't	show old speed
Expect	great power
Don't Expect	K reduction

Gant's star, once a shining light in the NL galaxy, began to flicker last February when he suffered a multiple compound fracture of his right leg in a dirt-bike accident. Released by the Braves in March, he eventually signed with the Reds—even though they knew he might not be able to help until 1995. A two-time 30-30 man, Gant may never again run the way he once did. He might be able to duplicate his 1993 career peaks of 36 homers and 117 RBI, however. He also had a career-high 117 strikeouts that year. An aggressive hitter who tries to pull everything, Gant feasts on inside fastballs. He also murders left-handed pitchers. With Gant's basestealing ability now in question, more emphasis will be placed on his erratic defense. He was bad at second base, mediocre in center field, and adequate in left field. Gant's speed used to compensate for his mistakes. What's left of it remains to be seen. His arm is only OK.

Major League Batting Register

	BA	G	AB	R	H	2B	3B	HR	RBI	SB
87 NL	.265	21	83	9	22	4	0	2	9	4
88 NL	.259	146	563	85	146	28	8	19	60	19
89 NL	.177	75	260	26	46	8	3	9	25	9
90 NL	.303	152	575	107	174	34	3	32	84	33
91 NL	.251	154	561	101	141	35	3	32	105	34
92 NL	.259	153	544	74	141	22	6	17	80	32
93 NL	.274	157	606	113	166	27	4	36	117	26
Life	.262	858	3192	515	836	158	27	147	480	157
2 AVE	.262	155	553	88	141	25	5	27	99	29

CARLOS GARCIA

Position: Second base
Team: Pittsburgh Pirates
Born: Oct. 15, 1967 Tachira, Venezuela
Height: 6'1" **Weight:** 185 lbs.
Bats: right **Throws:** right
Acquired: Signed as a free agent, 1/87

Player Summary	
Fantasy Value	$16 to $19
Card Value	8¢ to 12¢
Will	hit left-handers
Can't	show patience
Expect	strong fielding
Don't Expect	top on-base average

Most second basemen are in the lineup for their defense. Garcia is a notable exception. He spent most of last year as Pittsburgh's leadoff man. The experiment may not last, since he doesn't walk enough to compile a solid on-base percentage. He is capable of starting a game with an extra-base hit, though. He fanned four times more than he walked last year but did hit well over .300 against left-handed pitchers and in late-inning pressure situations. He swings the bat with much more authority than his predecessor, Jose Lind. A wrist hitter with good bat speed, Garcia connected for a dozen homers as a 1993 rookie. He also had 13 homers and 70 RBI in Triple-A in 1992. He's stolen 18 bases two years in a row and should add to that total as he gains experience. In the field, he has great range, a strong arm, and a knack for turning the double play. He and Jay Bell formed a fine double-play tandem last summer. Signed as a shortstop, Garcia could eventually return there. He turned pro in 1987.

Major League Batting Register

	BA	G	AB	R	H	2B	3B	HR	RBI	SB
90 NL	.500	4	4	1	2	0	0	0	0	0
91 NL	.250	12	24	2	6	0	2	0	1	0
92 NL	.205	22	39	4	8	1	0	0	4	0
93 NL	.269	141	546	77	147	25	5	12	47	18
94 NL	.277	98	412	49	114	15	2	6	28	18
Life	.270	277	1025	133	277	41	9	18	80	36
2 AVE	.273	140	563	73	154	23	4	10	43	22

MIKE GARDINER

Position: Pitcher
Team: Detroit Tigers
Born: Oct. 19, 1965 Sarnia, Ontario
Height: 6' **Weight:** 200 lbs.
Bats: both **Throws:** right
Acquired: Signed as a free agent, 8/93

Player Summary	
Fantasy Value	$3 to $5
Card Value	5¢ to 7¢
Will	get righties out
Can't	stop gopher balls
Expect	trial as starter
Don't Expect	control problems

Used almost exclusively in relief last year, Gardiner made such a strong impression that he might be tried as a starter in 1995. He yielded less than a hit per inning, showed decent control, and stranded more than 80 percent of the runners he inherited. Deployed in middle relief, he also showed good stamina, working several multi-inning stints. He finished 14 games last year. Though he doesn't get many strikeouts, Gardiner dominates right-handed hitters. He also helps himself by keeping baserunners close and fielding his position. Gardiner does have a problem with throwing too many gopher balls. He needs better location of his pitches to keep the ball in the park. He throws a fastball, a slider, and a curveball. When his pitches are up, they sail out of the park with alarming frequency (10 homers in 58⅔ innings last year). The 1984 Canadian Olympian received a business degree from Indiana State. He started his pro career in 1987.

Major League Pitching Register

	W	L	ERA	G	S	IP	H	ER	BB	SO
90 AL	0	2	10.66	5	0	12.2	22	15	5	6
91 AL	9	10	4.85	22	0	130.0	140	70	47	91
92 AL	4	10	4.75	28	0	130.2	126	69	58	79
93 NL	2	3	5.21	24	0	38.0	40	22	19	21
93 AL	0	0	3.97	10	0	11.1	12	5	7	4
94 AL	2	2	4.14	38	5	58.2	53	27	23	31
Life	17	27	4.91	127	5	381.1	393	208	159	232
3 AVE	3	5	4.59	39	2	87.2	84	45	39	49

MARK GARDNER

Position: Pitcher
Team: Florida Marlins
Born: March 1, 1962   Los Angeles, CA
Height: 6'1"   **Weight:** 190 lbs.
Bats: right   **Throws:** right
Acquired: Signed as a free agent, 1/94

Player Summary

Fantasy Value	$0
Card Value	5¢ to 7¢
Will	win with curve
Can't	keep ball in park
Expect	fine pickoff move
Don't Expect	many Ks

Gardner showed signs last summer of regaining the form he enjoyed when he was in Montreal. He pitched nine no-hit innings during a 1991 game for the Expos and won a career-best 12 games a year later. Last year, he tied a Florida mark with a career-high 10 strikeouts in a 6-1 win against Montreal June 26. He later worked seven and two-thirds scoreless innings after returning from a stint on the disabled list with a groin injury. Not a power pitcher, Gardner is a curveball specialist who also throws a fastball and a changeup. In 1994, he yielded a hit per inning, allowed less than three walks per game, and dominated right-handed hitters. But he's always had problems with the gopher ball. The former Fresno State standout has one of baseball's best pickoff moves. Eleven of the 15 runners who challenged him before strike time didn't make it. Gardner is an average fielder and no great shakes at the plate. He started his pro career at Jamestown in 1985.

Major League Pitching Register

	W	L	ERA	G	CG	IP	H	ER	BB	SO
89 NL	0	3	5.13	7	0	26.1	26	15	11	21
90 NL	7	9	3.42	27	3	152.2	129	58	61	135
91 NL	9	11	3.85	27	0	168.1	139	72	75	107
92 NL	12	10	4.36	33	0	179.2	179	87	60	132
93 AL	4	6	6.19	17	0	91.2	92	63	36	54
94 NL	4	4	4.87	20	0	92.1	97	50	30	57
Life	36	43	4.37	131	3	711.0	662	345	273	506
3 AVE	7	7	4.94	26	0	133.2	136	73	46	89

BRENT GATES

Position: Second base
Team: Oakland Athletics
Born: March 14, 1970   Grand Rapids, MI
Height: 6'1"   **Weight:** 180 lbs.
Bats: both   **Throws:** right
Acquired: First-round pick in 6/91 free-agent draft

Player Summary

Fantasy Value	$12 to $15
Card Value	12¢ to 20¢
Will	show better stick
Can't	clear fences
Expect	line drives
Don't Expect	walks or whiffs

Even before the players strike, Gates was sitting on the sidelines. He was disabled with knee problems on July 16, for the second time. That injury was a major blow to the Athletics, who were just beginning to start a pennant run. When healthy, he is a contact hitter who murders left-handers. He also hit well over .300 in late-inning pressure situations in 1994. Like Paul Molitor and Dave Winfield, Gates is a product of the excellent program at the University of Minnesota. Gates broke many of the college records set by Oakland teammate Terry Steinbach. Gates won't hit many homers or steal many bases, but he will slash line drives to all fields. He once had a 35-game hitting streak in the minors. Gates tied an Oakland club record with eight straight hits last May 23 and 24. He jumped from the Class-A California League—where he batted .321 with 10 homers and 88 RBI in 1992—to Oakland in 1993. In the field, the former college shortstop has great range, soft hands, and a fine arm. He's also improving at turning the double play.

Major League Batting Register

	BA	G	AB	R	H	2B	3B	HR	RBI	SB
93 AL	.290	139	535	64	155	29	2	7	69	7
94 AL	.283	64	233	29	66	11	1	2	24	3
Life	.288	203	768	93	221	40	3	9	93	10
2 AVE	.287	115	432	52	124	22	2	5	51	6

KIRK GIBSON

Position: Designated hitter
Team: Detroit Tigers
Born: May 28, 1957 Pontiac, MI
Height: 6'3" **Weight:** 225 lbs.
Bats: left **Throws:** left
Acquired: Signed as a free agent, 2/93

Player Summary	
Fantasy Value	$8 to $10
Card Value	8¢ to 12¢
Will	deliver clutch hits
Can't	play defense
Expect	run production
Don't Expect	old speed

At his advanced athletic age, Gibson's 1994 power explosion was unexpected. He had not hit so many home runs since winning the National League MVP Award in 1988. Gibson also seemed headed for the first 100-RBI campaign of his career before the player strike started. At that time, his average with runners in scoring position was .363, tops among the Tigers. The Michigan State product and former football All-American is a low fastball hitter with a good batting eye. He draws his share of walks but likes to show off his power. Gibson's brittle knees don't allow him to steal much anymore, but he picks his spots well. An intense competitor, he'll also take an extra base at every opportunity.

Major League Batting Register

	BA	G	AB	R	H	2B	3B	HR	RBI	SB
79 AL	.237	12	38	3	9	3	0	1	4	3
80 AL	.263	51	175	23	46	2	1	9	16	4
81 AL	.328	83	290	41	95	11	3	9	40	17
82 AL	.278	69	266	34	74	16	2	8	35	9
83 AL	.227	128	401	60	91	12	9	15	51	14
84 AL	.282	149	531	92	150	23	10	27	91	29
85 AL	.287	154	581	96	167	37	5	29	97	30
86 AL	.268	119	441	84	118	11	2	28	86	34
87 AL	.277	128	487	95	135	25	3	24	79	26
88 NL	.290	150	542	106	157	28	1	25	76	31
89 NL	.213	71	253	35	54	8	2	9	28	12
90 NL	.260	89	315	59	82	20	0	8	38	26
91 AL	.236	132	462	81	109	17	6	16	55	18
92 AL	.196	16	56	6	11	0	0	2	5	3
93 AL	.261	116	403	62	105	18	6	13	62	15
94 AL	.276	98	330	71	91	17	2	23	72	4
Life	.268	1565	5571	948	1494	248	52	246	835	275
2 AVE	.269	127	434	81	117	21	4	23	82	10

BERNARD GILKEY

Position: Outfield
Team: St. Louis Cardinals
Born: Sept. 24, 1966 St. Louis, MO
Height: 6' **Weight:** 170 lbs.
Bats: right **Throws:** right
Acquired: Signed as a free agent, 8/84

Player Summary	
Fantasy Value	$14 to $17
Card Value	6¢ to 10¢
Will	show his speed
Can't	wait for walks
Expect	better numbers
Don't Expect	great fielding

After topping .300 two straight summers, Gilkey's average fell 50 points in 1994. His power production also tumbled. The highlight of his season came early. He had a two-run, ninth-inning homer in a 6-5 win over the Rockies May 4. An aggressive hitter who fans too often, Gilkey won't wait for walks. As a result, he doesn't have the high on-base percentage one might expect from a man who often leads off. If he coaxed more walks, his value would skyrocket. He could use his great speed to get himself into scoring position—an objective he reached in 1993, when he scored 99 times. Gilkey has proven that he probably would be better off hitting lower in the batting order. Last year, he had inexplicable troubles with right-handers and in late-inning pressure spots. He also had a low success ratio as a basestealer. He was not the same player who twice topped 50 steals in the minors. In the outfield, Gilkey's arm is his best asset. His 19 assists in 1993 led the NL. His overall defense needs polishing, nevertheless.

Major League Batting Register

	BA	G	AB	R	H	2B	3B	HR	RBI	SB
90 NL	.297	18	64	11	19	5	2	1	3	6
91 NL	.216	81	268	28	58	7	2	5	20	14
92 NL	.302	131	384	56	116	19	4	7	43	18
93 NL	.305	137	557	99	170	40	5	16	70	15
94 NL	.253	105	380	52	96	22	1	6	45	15
Life	.278	472	1653	246	459	93	14	35	181	68
3 AVE	.285	139	492	76	140	30	3	10	59	18

JOE GIRARDI

Position: Catcher
Team: Colorado Rockies
Born: Oct. 14, 1964 Peoria, IL
Height: 6' **Weight:** 195 lbs.
Bats: right **Throws:** right
Acquired: First-round pick from Cubs in 11/92 expansion draft

Player Summary	
Fantasy Value.	$4 to $6
Card Value	5¢ to 7¢
Will	execute hit-and-run
Can't	utilize speed
Expect	good defense
Don't Expect	extra bases

One of the most underrated players in the game, Girardi is a solid defensive catcher who also contributes timely hits. He hit well over .300 against left-handed pitching and in late-inning pressure situations last season. Though he fans twice as much as he walks, Girardi makes pretty good contact. He's so good at working the hit-and-run that he often appeared in the No. 2 slot in the Colorado lineup. Basically a singles hitter who doesn't get many extra-base hits, Girardi doesn't add much speed either. As a receiver, he's known for his strong arm, quick release, and ability to block the plate and prevent potential wild pitches. He's also an excellent game-caller. Girardi nailed about 35 percent of baserunners who tried to steal against him last year; he was even more successful throwing in 1993. He is a thinking man's catcher who holds a degree in industrial engineering from Northwestern. He began his pro career at Peoria in 1986.

Major League Batting Register

	BA	G	AB	R	H	2B	3B	HR	RBI	SB
89 NL	.248	59	157	15	39	10	0	1	14	2
90 NL	.270	133	419	36	113	24	2	1	38	8
91 NL	.191	21	47	3	9	2	0	0	6	0
92 NL	.270	91	270	19	73	3	1	1	12	0
93 NL	.290	86	310	35	90	14	5	3	31	6
94 NL	.276	93	330	47	91	9	4	4	34	3
Life	.271	483	1533	155	415	62	12	10	135	19
3 AVE	.279	103	348	40	97	10	4	3	30	3

TOM GLAVINE

Position: Pitcher
Team: Atlanta Braves
Born: March 25, 1966 Concord, MA
Height: 6' **Weight:** 175 lbs.
Bats: left **Throws:** left
Acquired: Second-round pick in 6/84 free-agent draft

Player Summary	
Fantasy Value.	$17 to $20
Card Value	25¢ to 35¢
Will	paint the corners
Can't	always find plate
Expect	20-victory season
Don't Expect	easy first frame

After winning the 1991 Cy Young Award, Glavine has lost more of his magic every year. His ERA has risen in each of the last three years, as his pitches have become more hittable. Last year, his velocity improved but his control was erratic. He threw better breaking stuff than he had the last few years, but he didn't have his usual command. Glavine also seemed to have less confidence in his circle changeup. As a result, he started falling behind in the count and putting pressure on his fastball, slider, and curve. When he's on, Glavine paints the outside corner with the change and throws the heater inside. He fools batters by using the same arm speed with all his pitches. Glavine averaged nearly eight strikeouts per nine innings last year, while yielding a hit per inning. He keeps the ball in the park and helps himself with Gold Glove-caliber fielding and a strong bat. He is an accomplished bunter and baserunner.

Major League Pitching Register

	W	L	ERA	G	CG	IP	H	ER	BB	SO
87 NL	2	4	5.54	9	0	50.1	55	31	33	20
88 NL	7	17	4.56	34	1	195.1	201	99	63	84
89 NL	14	8	3.68	29	6	186.0	172	76	40	90
90 NL	10	12	4.28	33	1	214.1	232	102	78	129
91 NL	20	11	2.55	34	9	246.2	201	70	69	192
92 NL	20	8	2.76	33	7	225.0	197	69	70	129
93 NL	22	6	3.20	36	4	239.1	236	85	90	120
94 NL	13	9	3.97	25	2	165.1	173	73	70	140
Life	108	75	3.58	233	30	1522.1	1467	605	513	904
3 AVE	20	9	3.32	35	5	232.1	226	86	86	149

CHRIS GOMEZ

Position: Shortstop; second base
Team: Detroit Tigers
Born: June 16, 1971 Los Angeles, CA
Height: 6'1" **Weight:** 183 lbs.
Bats: right **Throws:** right
Acquired: Third-round pick in 6/92 free-agent draft

Player Summary	
Fantasy Value	$4 to $6
Card Value	10¢ to 20¢
Will	improve as he matures
Can't	hit right-handers
Expect	strong defense
Don't Expect	patience at bat

As a collegian at Long Beach State, Gomez hit for power with an aluminum bat. As a pro, he used a wooden bat to hit up-the-middle line drives and take the ball to the opposite field. A former All-American with a reputation for defensive excellence, Gomez spent most of last summer switching between shortstop and second base. He played short against right-handed pitchers and second against lefties. Gomez has enough quickness to give him good range at shortstop, and he has a strong throwing arm. He also can play second base if Travis Fryman moves back to shortstop. Gomez connected for his first two homers May 7 against Seattle. Strengthened by an off-season weight-lifting program, Gomez had collected eight home runs by the time the strike started. At his age, there's lots of time for improvement. He needs to become more selective at the plate—fanning twice for every walk in 1994—and be more productive against right-handers. He hammers lefties and hits well with runners in scoring position. He batted .245 with zero homers and 20 RBI in 277 at bats in Triple-A in 1993.

Major League Batting Register

	BA	G	AB	R	H	2B	3B	HR	RBI	SB
93 AL	.250	46	128	11	32	7	1	0	11	2
94 AL	.257	84	296	32	76	19	0	8	53	5
Life	.255	130	424	43	108	26	1	8	64	7

LEO GOMEZ

Position: Third base
Team: Baltimore Orioles
Born: March 2, 1967 Canovanas, Puerto Rico
Height: 6' **Weight:** 202 lbs.
Bats: right **Throws:** right
Acquired: Signed as a free agent, 12/85

Player Summary	
Fantasy Value	$8 to $10
Card Value	5¢ to 7¢
Will	produce in clutch
Can't	add any speed
Expect	extra-base hits
Don't Expect	average over .300

Gomez returned from the dead last summer. After a season-long slump coupled with a wrist injury in '93, he was almost an afterthought at Baltimore's spring training camp. The Orioles even paid big money to free-agent third baseman Chris Sabo. But Gomez got his chance when injuries idled Sabo. Gomez hit so well that Sabo couldn't get his job back. A power hitter who's at his best with runners in scoring position, Gomez thrived in late-inning pressure situations last year. He also hit over .300 against left-handed pitching. He struck out slightly more often than he walked, but he was still selective enough to compile a decent on-base percentage. Nearly half his hits—an astonishing total—resulted in extra bases. This production was incredible after his 1993 disaster. Gomez doesn't run well but he makes all the right moves in the field. He's a solid third baseman with a strong arm. While in the minors, he led his league in assists and double plays. Gomez began his pro career in 1986.

Major League Batting Register

	BA	G	AB	R	H	2B	3B	HR	RBI	SB
90 AL	.231	12	39	3	9	0	0	0	1	0
91 AL	.233	118	391	40	91	17	2	16	45	1
92 AL	.265	137	468	62	124	24	0	17	64	2
93 AL	.197	71	244	30	48	7	0	10	25	0
94 AL	.274	84	285	46	78	20	0	15	56	0
Life	.245	422	1427	181	350	68	2	58	191	3
3 AVE	.253	109	371	52	94	20	0	16	56	1

ALEX GONZALEZ

Position: Shortstop
Team: Toronto Blue Jays
Born: April 8, 1973 Miami, FL
Height: 6′ **Weight:** 182 lbs.
Bats: right **Throws:** right
Acquired: 14th-round pick in 6/91 free-agent draft

Player Summary	
Fantasy Value	$7 to $9
Card Value	15¢ to 20¢
Will	show surprising power
Can't	think about 1993
Expect	use of speed
Don't Expect	patience at plate

Dare we say it? During his brief time in the big leagues last summer, Gonzalez convinced several scouts to compare him with Cincinnati standout Barry Larkin. That's no easy analogy for a 22-year-old who failed his first audition. But Gonzalez has a great arm, above-average speed, and considerable power for a middle infielder. Though he had a few defensive problems last spring—not to mention learning to hit American League pitchers—Gonzalez should stick now that he has a year of Triple-A experience under his belt. His biggest weakness is impatience at the plate. He fans three times more than he walks. He has the potential to become a 20-20 player and Gold Glove shortstop, though. At Triple-A Syracuse last year, he batted .284 with 12 homers, 57 RBI, and 22 doubles in 437 at bats. He was voted the International League's No. 2 prospect by *Baseball America* last year, in between teammates Shawn Green and Carlos Delgado. In 1992, Gonzalez was named the No. 1 prospect in the Double-A Southern League after hitting .289 with 16 homers, 69 RBI, and 29 doubles in 561 at bats.

Major League Batting Register

	BA	G	AB	R	H	2B	3B	HR	RBI	SB
94 AL	.151	15	53	7	8	3	1	0	1	3
Life	.151	15	53	7	8	3	1	0	1	3

JUAN GONZALEZ

Position: Outfield
Team: Texas Rangers
Born: Oct. 16, 1969 Vega Baja, Puerto Rico
Height: 6′3″ **Weight:** 210 lbs.
Bats: right **Throws:** right
Acquired: Signed as a free agent, 5/86

Player Summary	
Fantasy Value	$30 to $35
Card Value	75¢ to $1.25
Will	produce 100 RBI
Can't	lose aching back
Expect	power stroke
Don't Expect	selective bat

The new Texas ballpark did not agree with Gonzalez. After winning consecutive AL home run crowns, he struggled with the spacious left-field dimensions of his new home. Videotapes showed his 1994 swing was longer than usual, resulting in more ground balls. Pressing to justify his seven-year, $45 million contract, Gonzalez worked himself into a funk, sulked, and got into trouble with manager Kevin Kennedy for tardiness and lack of hustle. Dropped from fourth to fifth in the lineup, Gonzalez relaxed and started swinging at better pitches. He had to play through a back injury, bruised shin, and sprained right knee, however. He should try to emulate hero Roberto Clemente, who learned to hit the opposite way at Forbes Field. Gonzalez needs to become more selective, because he fans more than twice for every walk. He does his best hitting against left-handers. In the field, he has good range and a decent throwing arm. He is better in left field than center.

Major League Batting Register

	BA	G	AB	R	H	2B	3B	HR	RBI	SB
89 AL	.150	24	60	6	9	3	0	1	7	0
90 AL	.289	25	90	11	26	7	1	4	12	0
91 AL	.264	142	545	78	144	34	1	27	102	4
92 AL	.260	155	584	77	152	24	2	43	109	0
93 AL	.310	140	536	105	166	33	1	46	118	4
94 AL	.275	107	422	57	116	18	4	19	85	6
Life	.274	593	2237	334	613	119	9	140	433	14
3 AVE	.281	149	571	87	160	27	3	39	116	4

LUIS GONZALEZ

Position: Outfield
Team: Houston Astros
Born: Sept. 3, 1967 Tampa, FL
Height: 6'2" **Weight:** 180 lbs.
Bats: left **Throws:** right
Acquired: Fourth-round pick in 6/88 free-agent draft

Player Summary	
Fantasy Value	$16 to $19
Card Value	8¢ to 12¢
Will	hit with runners on
Can't	always steal
Expect	big second half
Don't Expect	defensive troubles

Once considered a platoon outfielder, Gonzalez became Houston's regular left fielder in 1993 by proving he could hit left-handed pitching. Though he has more power against righties, Gonzalez has learned to wait on the ball longer against lefties. He has a good eye and walks almost as often as he strikes out. He does his best hitting with runners in scoring position, and he had a .429 slugging percentage in 1994. He brings power and speed to the lineup but is not considered a slugger or basestealer. The University of South Alabama product sometimes makes poor decisions on the bases and needs to cut down his ratio of unsuccessful basestealing attempts. Last year, he was caught stealing 13 times. Gonzalez has improved his performance in left, where he was once regarded as a liability after shifting from first base. His speed gives him good range, and he has good reactions—compensating for an arm that is average or a little above. Gonzalez should have many solid seasons ahead of him.

Major League Batting Register

	BA	G	AB	R	H	2B	3B	HR	RBI	SB
90 NL	.190	12	21	1	4	2	0	0	0	0
91 NL	.254	137	473	51	120	28	9	13	69	10
92 NL	.243	122	387	40	94	19	3	10	55	7
93 NL	.300	154	540	82	162	34	3	15	72	20
94 NL	.273	112	392	57	107	29	4	8	67	15
Life	.269	537	1813	231	487	112	19	46	263	52
3 AVE	.275	145	493	67	136	31	4	12	74	16

DWIGHT GOODEN

Position: Pitcher
Team: New York Mets
Born: Nov. 16, 1964 Tampa, FL
Height: 6'3" **Weight:** 210 lbs.
Bats: right **Throws:** right
Acquired: First-round pick in 6/82 free-agent draft

Player Summary	
Fantasy Value	$0
Card Value	8¢ to 12¢
Will	pursue clean image
Can't	shake injury jinx
Expect	a long year
Don't Expect	sympathy

A suspension for substance abuse has placed Gooden's career in limbo. He was exiled last June, for the second time, and he is slated to sit out all of the 1995 season. He has not had a winning year since 1991. Injuries have also interfered with the former Cy Young Award winner's career. Gooden had rotator cuff problems in '91, was disabled twice in '92, and was on the DL with a toe problem last year. He had headaches for four years before he agreed to get glasses and contacts last spring. A fastball-curveball pitcher who changes speeds on both pitches, Gooden no longer has the velocity that produced a 24-4 record and 1.53 ERA in 1985. He still throws strikes and averages almost a K an inning, though. When he's right, few hitters take him deep.

Major League Pitching Register

	W	L	ERA	G	CG	IP	H	ER	BB	SO
84 NL	17	9	2.60	31	7	218.0	161	63	73	276
85 NL	24	4	1.53	35	16	276.2	198	47	69	268
86 NL	17	6	2.84	33	12	250.0	197	79	80	200
87 NL	15	7	3.21	25	7	179.2	162	64	53	148
88 NL	18	9	3.19	34	10	248.1	242	88	57	175
89 NL	9	4	2.89	19	0	118.1	93	38	47	101
90 NL	19	7	3.83	34	2	232.2	229	99	70	223
91 NL	13	7	3.60	27	3	190.0	185	76	56	150
92 NL	10	13	3.67	31	3	206.0	197	84	70	145
93 NL	12	15	3.45	29	7	208.2	188	80	61	149
94 NL	3	4	6.31	7	0	41.1	46	29	15	40
Life	157	85	3.10	305	67	2169.2	1898	747	651	1875
2 AVE	11	14	3.56	30	5	207.1	193	82	66	147

TOM GORDON

Position: Pitcher
Team: Kansas City Royals
Born: Nov. 18, 1967 Sebring, FL
Height: 5'9" **Weight:** 160 lbs.
Bats: right **Throws:** right
Acquired: Sixth-round pick in 6/86 free-agent draft

Player Summary	
Fantasy Value	$7 to $9
Card Value	6¢ to 10¢
Will	coax ground balls
Can't	keep consistency
Expect	runners to steal
Don't Expect	top control

Before 1994, Gordon was a full-time starter only once in five full seasons. The Royals, puzzled by his inability to control his great stuff, couldn't make up their minds what to do with him. Though he yielded less than eight hits and more than seven strikeouts per nine innings in 1994, Gordon remained an enigma. He held opposing hitters to a low average but was overly generous with walks (five per game). He also made more than his share of wild pitches and had enormous difficulty controlling the running game. When he keeps his fine curveball down, Gordon generates numerous ground-ball outs. The pint-sized right-hander, who also throws a fastball and a slider, is most effective against righties. He keeps the ball in the park and helps himself with good defensive ability. But Gordon's slow pace and penchant for creating deep counts drive managers and fielders crazy. He still has the time and talent to stage a breakthrough season.

Major League Pitching Register

	W	L	ERA	G	CG	IP	H	ER	BB	SO
88 AL	0	2	5.17	5	0	15.2	16	9	7	18
89 AL	17	9	3.64	49	1	163.0	122	66	86	153
90 AL	12	11	3.73	32	6	195.1	192	81	99	175
91 AL	9	14	3.87	45	1	158.0	129	68	87	167
92 AL	6	10	4.59	40	0	117.2	116	60	55	98
93 AL	12	6	3.58	48	2	155.2	125	62	77	143
94 AL	11	7	4.35	24	0	155.1	136	75	87	126
Life	67	59	3.94	243	10	960.2	836	421	498	880
3 AVE	11	9	4.16	41	1	163.2	144	76	85	139

JIM GOTT

Position: Pitcher
Team: Los Angeles Dodgers
Born: Aug. 3, 1959 Hollywood, CA
Height: 6'4" **Weight:** 220 lbs.
Bats: right **Throws:** right
Acquired: Signed as a free agent, 12/89

Player Summary	
Fantasy Value	$1
Card Value	5¢ to 7¢
Will	bank on his curve
Can't	shake injury wave
Expect	improving control
Don't Expect	return as starter

When he's healthy, Gott is a workhorse reliever noted for his control, velocity, and willingness to work often. His checkered career record, however, suggests that avoiding ailments has been a major headache. Gott had 34 saves in 1988 and 25 in 1993 but never more than 13 in any other season. He's also missed long stretches because of problems with his rotator cuff (1986), elbow (1989), shoulder (1993), and appendix (1994). He throws a fastball and a slider, but his best pitch is a curve that breaks straight down—giving it the appearance of a forkball. It's especially effective against left-handed hitters. Gott in 1994 notched more than seven strikeouts per nine innings, kept the ball in the park, fielded his position well, and held baserunners close. He has occasional trouble with walks and wild pitches.

Major League Pitching Register

	W	L	ERA	G	S	IP	H	ER	BB	SO
82 AL	5	10	4.43	30	0	136.0	134	67	66	82
83 AL	9	14	4.74	34	0	176.2	195	93	68	121
84 AL	7	6	4.02	35	2	109.2	93	49	49	73
85 NL	7	10	3.88	26	0	148.1	144	64	51	78
86 NL	0	0	7.62	9	1	13.0	16	11	13	9
87 NL	1	2	3.41	55	13	87.0	81	33	40	90
88 NL	6	6	3.49	67	34	77.1	68	30	22	76
89 NL	0	0	0.00	1	0	0.2	1	0	1	1
90 NL	3	5	2.90	50	3	62.0	59	20	34	44
91 NL	4	3	2.96	55	2	76.0	63	25	32	73
92 NL	3	3	2.45	68	6	88.0	72	24	41	75
93 NL	4	8	2.32	62	25	77.2	71	20	17	67
94 NL	5	3	5.94	37	2	36.1	46	24	20	29
Life	54	70	3.80	529	88	1088.2	1043	460	454	818
3 AVE	5	5	3.23	61	11	72.1	69	26	29	61

MARK GRACE

Position: First base
Team: Chicago Cubs
Born: June 28, 1964 Winston-Salem, NC
Height: 6'2" **Weight:** 190 lbs.
Bats: left **Throws:** left
Acquired: 24th-round pick in 6/85 free-agent draft

Player Summary	
Fantasy Value	$12 to $15
Card Value	12¢ to 25¢
Will	hit to all fields
Can't	produce much power
Expect	Gold Glove defense
Don't Expect	good speed

Although he doesn't provide the power associated with his position, Grace compensates in other ways. A career .300 hitter who makes good contact, he walks more often than he fans, rendering a good on-base percentage. He comes through in the clutch. In 1994, he did his best hitting in late-inning pressure situations and hit well over .300 with runners in scoring position. A line-drive hitter who uses all fields, he has good gap power. He's hit more than 30 doubles in a season three times. Clearing the fence is another matter, however. Grace went 179 at bats without a homer during the first half last year and had only three at the All-Star break. He doesn't run much either, thanks to a lack of speed that leads to lots of double plays. Grace can also turn the double play—no mean trick for a first baseman. He knows rival hitters as well as he does rival pitchers, so proper positioning at first is a strong suit. He has great reactions and soft hands.

Major League Batting Register

	BA	G	AB	R	H	2B	3B	HR	RBI	SB
88 NL	.296	134	486	65	144	23	4	7	57	3
89 NL	.314	142	510	74	160	28	3	13	79	14
90 NL	.309	157	589	72	182	32	1	9	82	15
91 NL	.273	160	619	87	169	28	5	8	58	3
92 NL	.307	158	603	72	185	37	5	9	79	6
93 NL	.325	155	594	86	193	39	4	14	98	8
94 NL	.298	106	403	55	120	23	3	6	44	0
Life	.303	1012	3804	511	1153	210	25	66	497	49
3 AVE	.310	154	588	78	182	36	4	10	80	5

JOE GRAHE

Position: Pitcher
Team: California Angels
Born: June 14, 1967 West Palm Beach, FL
Height: 6' **Weight:** 200 lbs.
Bats: right **Throws:** right
Acquired: Second-round pick in 6/89 free-agent draft

Player Summary	
Fantasy Value	$4 to $6
Card Value	6¢ to 10¢
Will	get better save ratio
Can't	ignore runners
Expect	outs on grounders
Don't Expect	many whiffs

Until he blew six saves in 19 chances—an anemic conversion rate of 68 percent—Grahe was California's 1994 closer. He lost the job just before the players struck. He hasn't been able to use the formula that worked so well for him at the University of Miami. A strikeout pitcher there, he started going for grounders once he became a big leaguer. One of the reasons was a frayed rotator cuff that disabled him in 1993. Last year, Grahe was a far cry from the guy who posted a 1.80 relief ERA in 1992. Lefties lit him up and righties hardly retreated when he appeared. By strike time, he had stranded only 35 percent of inherited runners and yielded 14 hits per nine innings. Only his good fielding and ability to hold runners close kept things from being even worse. He needs to place less emphasis on his fastball and more faith in his slider, curve, and change. He simply doesn't have the velocity to succeed without proper pitch location. Grahe also needs to get right-handed batters out consistently.

Major League Pitching Register

	W	L	ERA	G	S	IP	H	ER	BB	SO
90 AL	3	4	4.98	8	0	43.1	51	24	23	25
91 AL	3	7	4.81	18	0	73.0	84	39	33	40
92 AL	5	6	3.52	46	21	94.2	85	37	39	39
93 AL	4	1	2.86	45	11	56.2	54	18	25	31
94 AL	2	5	6.65	40	13	43.1	68	32	18	26
Life	17	23	4.34	157	45	311.0	342	150	138	161
3 AVE	4	5	4.24	49	17	70.2	78	33	30	36

CRAIG GREBECK

Position: Second base; shortstop; third base
Team: Chicago White Sox
Born: Dec. 29, 1964   Johnstown, PA
Height: 5'8"   **Weight:** 160 lbs.
Bats: right   **Throws:** right
Acquired: Signed as a free agent, 8/86

Player Summary	
Fantasy Value	$0
Card Value	5¢ to 7¢
Will	keep utility role
Can't	generate power
Expect	solid late-game bat
Don't Expect	Ks or walks

Although his playing time at second base has declined four years in a row in favor of Joey Cora, Grebeck remains a reserve who is valued for his versatility. Able to play three infield positions, he has served as understudy to Ozzie Guillen, Robin Ventura, and Cora, among others. Grebeck even held his own as a hitter (.281) when given a career-high workload of 107 games in 1991. A little spray hitter who makes good contact, he is extremely tough to fan. He had only five strikeouts in 97 trips by strike time last year. He doesn't walk much either. Grebeck, who feeds off fastballs, was hitting 61 points above his career average when the strike stopped play last summer. He did his best hitting in late-inning pressure situations in 1994. He has occasional power but less-than-average speed for a middle infielder. Though more speed would mean more range, he holds his own at second, short, and third. Grebeck has had some problems turning the double play from second base.

Major League Batting Register

	BA	G	AB	R	H	2B	3B	HR	RBI	SB
90 AL	.168	59	119	7	20	3	1	1	9	0
91 AL	.281	107	224	37	63	16	3	6	31	1
92 AL	.268	88	287	24	77	21	2	3	35	0
93 AL	.226	72	190	25	43	5	0	1	12	1
94 AL	.309	35	97	17	30	5	0	0	5	0
Life	.254	361	917	110	233	50	6	11	92	2
2 AVE	.252	80	239	25	60	13	1	2	24	1

TOMMY GREENE

Position: Pitcher
Team: Philadelphia Phillies
Born: April 6, 1967   Lumberton, NC
Height: 6'5"   **Weight:** 225 lbs.
Bats: right   **Throws:** right
Acquired: Traded from Braves with Dale Murphy for Jeff Parrett, Jim Vatcher, and Victor Rosario, 8/90

Player Summary	
Fantasy Value	$9 to $11
Card Value	6¢ to 10¢
Will	win big if healthy
Can't	favor his shoulder
Expect	help from bat
Don't Expect	detained runners

In two of the last three years, shoulder problems kept Greene sidelined for long stretches. Last season, he needed surgery to repair a small tear in his right rotator cuff. He made only seven starts before the strike. The summer of rest might help. The last time he was idled, he bounced back with a 16-4 season. When healthy, Greene is a power pitcher who supports his fastball with a slider, a curve, and a straight change. In 1993, when he was healthy, he yielded less than eight hits per nine innings, kept the ball in the park, and was equally effective facing righties or lefties. Greene averaged seven and one-half strikeouts per nine innings and two and one-half whiffs per walk that year. At times, he's brilliant. For example, he pitched a 1991 no-hitter and started 8-0 in 1993. Keeping the ball down is the key. Though he doesn't hold runners close, Greene is a fine fielder and one of baseball's best-hitting pitchers. He even has some power.

Major League Pitching Register

	W	L	ERA	G	CG	IP	H	ER	BB	SO
89 NL	1	2	4.10	4	1	26.1	22	12	6	17
90 NL	3	3	5.08	15	0	51.1	50	29	26	21
91 NL	13	7	3.38	36	3	207.2	177	78	66	154
92 NL	3	3	5.32	13	0	64.1	75	38	34	39
93 NL	16	4	3.42	31	7	200.0	175	76	62	167
94 NL	2	0	4.54	7	0	35.2	37	18	22	28
Life	38	19	3.86	106	11	585.1	536	251	216	426
2 AVE	10	4	3.88	22	4	132.1	125	57	48	103

WILLIE GREENE

Position: Third base
Team: Cincinnati Reds
Born: Sept. 23, 1971 Milledgeville, GA
Height: 5'11" **Weight:** 184 lbs.
Bats: left **Throws:** right
Acquired: Traded from Expos with Dave Martinez and Scott Ruskin for John Wetteland and Bill Risley, 12/91

Player Summary	
Fantasy Value	$7 to $9
Card Value	8¢ to 12¢
Will	show enormous power
Can't	reduce whiffs
Expect	instant lineup spot
Don't Expect	many steals

Scouts say he has Gary Sheffield's bat speed, but Greene had to sharpen that bat speed in the minors for another year due to the signing of free agent Tony Fernandez by the Reds in 1994. While Greene has collected four homers during three stints with the Reds, his potential as a power producer has been obvious for years. He's hit around two-dozen home runs in each of the last three years and could increase that total if he shows more patience at the plate. Greene has always posted healthy walk totals but still fans too frequently to please Cincinnati brass. He doesn't steal much but has more speed than most other third basemen. A converted shortstop, he has led several minor leagues in putouts, double plays, and fielding percentage, as well as errors. He was once a first-round draft selection of the Pirates. At Triple-A Indianapolis in 1994, he batted .285 with 23 homers, 80 RBI, and eight stolen bases. He was named the No. 2 prospect in the American Association by *Baseball America*. He batted .267 with 22 homers and 58 RBI at Indy in 1993.

Major League Batting Register

	BA	G	AB	R	H	2B	3B	HR	RBI	SB
92 NL	.269	29	93	10	25	5	2	2	13	0
93 NL	.160	15	50	7	8	1	1	2	5	0
94 NL	.216	16	37	5	8	2	0	0	3	0
Life	.228	60	180	22	41	8	3	4	21	0

MIKE GREENWELL

Position: Outfield
Team: Boston Red Sox
Born: July 18, 1963 Louisville, KY
Height: 6' **Weight:** 200 lbs.
Bats: left **Throws:** right
Acquired: Third-round pick in 6/82 free-agent draft

Player Summary	
Fantasy Value	$12 to $15
Card Value	8¢ to 15¢
Will	hurt southpaws
Can't	be Jim Rice
Expect	more walks than Ks
Don't Expect	great defense

The Sox were spoiled in 1988 by Greenwell when he hit .325 with 22 homers and 119 RBI. Unable to repeat those numbers since, he's been labeled a disappointment. While he has endured more than his share of injuries, people forget he's not a slugger in the Jim Rice mold. In 10 years, Greenwell has reached 20 homers only once. A fastball hitter who sometimes pulls inside curves, he has a line-drive stroke that emphasizes contact over power. He walks more than he fans and hits twice as many doubles as home runs. He doesn't steal much but runs well enough to show some range in left field. Greenwell compensates for an average arm by getting good jumps and getting rid of the ball quickly. He's also mastered the art of playing the tricky caroms at Fenway. If last year's shoulder surgery proves successful, he'll have a strong comeback.

Major League Batting Register

	BA	G	AB	R	H	2B	3B	HR	RBI	SB
85 AL	.323	17	31	7	10	1	0	4	8	1
86 AL	.314	31	35	4	11	2	0	0	4	0
87 AL	.328	125	412	71	135	31	6	19	89	5
88 AL	.325	158	590	86	192	39	8	22	119	16
89 AL	.308	145	578	87	178	36	0	14	95	13
90 AL	.297	159	610	71	181	30	6	14	73	8
91 AL	.300	147	544	76	163	26	6	9	83	15
92 AL	.233	49	180	16	42	2	0	2	18	2
93 AL	.315	146	540	77	170	38	6	13	72	5
94 AL	.269	95	327	60	88	25	1	11	45	2
Life	.304	1072	3847	555	1170	230	33	108	606	67
3 AVE	.285	110	394	59	112	25	2	10	51	3

RUSTY GREER

Position: Outfield; first base
Team: Texas Rangers
Born: Jan. 21, 1969 Fort Rucker, AL
Height: 6′ **Weight:** 190 lbs.
Bats: left **Throws:** left
Acquired: 10th-round pick in 6/90 free-agent draft

Player Summary	
Fantasy Value	$3 to $5
Card Value	8¢ to 15¢
Will	hit righties hard
Can't	vie for Gold Glove
Expect	fine on-base average
Don't Expect	a choker

Though he opened last season in the minors, Greer graduated to the majors with a bang. Called up on May 16, he quickly emerged as a serious contender for AL Rookie of the Year honors. Playing several positions, he became a potent force in the Texas lineup. Blessed with a keen batting eye, he walked as often as he fanned, piling up an on-base percentage of .410 by strike time. His average stopped at .314, with nearly one-third of his hits going for extra bases. Greer ripped right-handed pitching but was at his best in late-inning pressure situations last year. He also topped .300 with runners in scoring position. Greer doesn't steal much but does have enough speed to play a solid center field. His outfield defense still needs polishing, however. He was one of the last squad cuts during 1994 spring training. At Triple-A Oklahoma City last year, he batted .315 with three homers, 12 doubles, and 13 RBI in 111 at bats. Greer was a two-time All-American at the University of Montevallo in Alabama. He batted .291 with 15 homers, 59 RBI, and 10 stolen bases in 1993 at Double-A Tulsa.

Major League Batting Register

	BA	G	AB	R	H	2B	3B	HR	RBI	SB
94 AL	.314	80	277	36	87	16	1	10	46	0
Life	.314	80	277	36	87	16	1	10	46	0

KEN GRIFFEY JR.

Position: Outfield
Team: Seattle Mariners
Born: Nov. 21, 1969 Donora, PA
Height: 6′3″ **Weight:** 195 lbs.
Bats: left **Throws:** left
Acquired: First-round pick in 6/87 free-agent draft

Player Summary	
Fantasy Value	$40 to $45
Card Value	$2 to $4
Will	mount MVP bid
Can't	swing at bad pitches
Expect	All-Star performance
Don't Expect	fielding woes

What can't Junior do? His accomplishments include five All-Star games in six years; an All-Star Game MVP Award; home runs in eight consecutive games; three 100-RBI campaigns; two 40-homer seasons; five straight .300 years; and numerous Gold Gloves. And he won't turn 26 until after the 1995 season. Last year alone, Griffey hit 20 homers in 42 games—matching Mickey Mantle's 1956 start—and inspired talk of a run at Roger Maris's single-season record of 61 in '61. The strike ended that opportunity, but Griffey is young enough to make several more attempts. He hit 56 homers between the 1993 and 1994 All-Star games. His only flaw is a tendency to get overanxious and swing at bad pitches. In the field, his leaps and dives in center are already legendary. He gets great jumps, owns a powerful throwing arm, and rarely makes a boot. Griffey was a *Sports Illustrated* cover boy a record three times last year, even beating the dreaded SI cover jinx.

Major League Batting Register

	BA	G	AB	R	H	2B	3B	HR	RBI	SB
89 AL	.264	127	455	61	120	23	0	16	61	16
90 AL	.300	155	597	91	179	28	7	22	80	16
91 AL	.327	154	548	76	179	42	1	22	100	18
92 AL	.308	142	565	83	174	39	4	27	103	10
93 AL	.309	156	582	113	180	38	3	45	109	17
94 AL	.323	111	433	94	140	24	4	40	90	11
Life	.306	845	3180	518	972	194	19	172	543	88
3 AVE	.314	151	586	109	184	37	4	43	113	14

MARQUIS GRISSOM

Position: Outfield
Team: Montreal Expos
Born: April 17, 1967   Atlanta, GA
Height: 5'11"   **Weight:** 190 lbs.
Bats: right   **Throws:** right
Acquired: Third-round pick in 6/88 free-agent draft

Player Summary	
Fantasy Value	$30 to $35
Card Value	12¢ to 25¢
Will	display dazzling speed
Can't	show patience at plate
Expect	good late-game hitting
Don't Expect	defensive problems

Although his game consists of speed, power, and defense, Grissom could increase his value with more patience at the plate. He fans too frequently for a leadoff man, often hacking at pitches outside the strike zone with runners in scoring position. He was hitting .229 in that department—despite a .288 overall average—when the strike started. After batting in the No. 3 spot, he celebrated his May 28 return to the leadoff spot with a .471 spurt (32-for-68) and scored 29 runs in 20 games. He homered in the All-Star Game and later hit an inside-the-park homer to beat St. Louis 3-2 in 10 innings. He is one of the league's best all-around players, and speed remains his forte. A two-time stolen-base king, Grissom won't hesitate to steal any base at any time. He topped the NL with 11 steals of third in 1993. His speed translates into exceptional range in center, where Grissom is a Gold Glove performer. He has great reactions and a strong, accurate arm.

Major League Batting Register

		BA	G	AB	R	H	2B	3B	HR	RBI	SB
89	NL	.257	26	74	16	19	2	0	1	2	1
90	NL	.257	98	288	42	74	14	2	3	29	22
91	NL	.267	148	558	73	149	23	9	6	39	76
92	NL	.276	159	653	99	180	39	6	14	66	78
93	NL	.298	157	630	104	188	27	2	19	95	53
94	NL	.288	110	475	96	137	25	4	11	45	36
Life		.279	698	2678	430	747	130	23	54	276	266
3 AVE		.287	157	651	113	187	34	5	16	75	61

BUDDY GROOM

Position: Pitcher
Team: Detroit Tigers
Born: July 10, 1965   Dallas, TX
Height: 6'2"   **Weight:** 200 lbs.
Bats: left   **Throws:** left
Acquired: Rule 5 draft pick from White Sox, 12/90

Player Summary	
Fantasy Value	$1
Card Value	8¢ to 15¢
Will	strand runners
Can't	always locate plate
Expect	stints vs. lefties
Don't Expect	gopher balls

After making three return trips to the minors in 1993, Groom set out to carve his niche on the 1994 Tiger staff. He did that by not yielding a single run in his first 11 outings last summer. Used in spot duty against left-handed batters, he gave Detroit some much-needed relief. He yielded less hits than innings pitched, fanned seven and one-half batters per nine innings, and stranded 80 percent of the runners he inherited. Groom needs to improve his control—an average of more than three and one-half walks per game—but does a good job of keeping the ball in the park. He's also adept at keeping baserunners close. For a pitcher who performs primarily against southpaws, he has to concentrate on his performance against left-handed hitters. They hit 40 points higher against him than right-handers did last summer. Although Groom made 10 starts for Detroit in two previous trials, his future remains in relief. He was 9-3 with a 2.74 ERA, 78 strikeouts, and 30 walks in 102 innings and 15 starts at Triple-A Toledo in 1993.

Major League Pitching Register

		W	L	ERA	G	S	IP	H	ER	BB	SO
92	AL	0	5	5.82	12	1	38.2	48	25	22	15
93	AL	0	2	6.14	19	0	36.2	48	25	13	15
94	AL	0	1	3.94	40	1	32.0	31	14	13	27
Life		0	8	5.37	71	2	107.1	127	64	48	57
2 AVE		0	2	4.92	38	1	41.1	46	22	16	27

KEVIN GROSS

Position: Pitcher
Team: Los Angeles Dodgers
Born: June 8, 1961 Downey, CA
Height: 6'5" **Weight:** 215 lbs.
Bats: right **Throws:** right
Acquired: Signed as a free agent, 12/90

Player Summary	
Fantasy Value.	$5 to $7
Card Value	5¢ to 7¢
Will	pitch 200 innings
Can't	scare baserunners
Expect.	solid performance
Don't Expect	mark over .500

Only three times in 12 seasons has Gross won more games than he lost. Last year was one of those years. In fact, he had the best ERA of the five Dodger starters when the players walked out Aug. 12. A durable worker who has topped 200 innings seven times, Gross has had success as a starter and a reliever. He pitched a 1992 no-hitter against the Giants, the same team he deprived of a first-place tie with a 12-1 victory on the last day of the '93 campaign. Gross fanned three times more men than he walked, kept the ball in the park, and threw strikes with a fastball, a changeup, and a hard curve. Because of his high-kicking motion, he has problems holding runners on, but he's a decent fielder. Gross, who has surprising power, is so good with a bat in his hands that he is sometimes asked to pinch-hit.

Major League Pitching Register

	W	L	ERA	G	CG	IP	H	ER	BB	SO
83 NL	4	6	3.56	17	1	96.0	100	38	35	66
84 NL	8	5	4.12	44	1	129.0	140	59	44	84
85 NL	15	13	3.41	38	6	205.2	194	78	81	151
86 NL	12	12	4.02	37	7	241.2	240	108	94	154
87 NL	9	16	4.35	34	3	200.2	205	97	87	110
88 NL	12	14	3.69	33	5	231.2	209	95	89	162
89 NL	11	12	4.38	31	4	201.1	188	98	88	158
90 NL	9	12	4.57	31	2	163.1	171	83	65	111
91 NL	10	11	3.58	46	0	115.2	123	46	50	95
92 NL	8	13	3.17	34	4	204.2	182	72	77	158
93 NL	13	13	4.14	33	3	202.1	224	93	74	150
94 NL	9	7	3.60	25	1	157.1	162	63	43	124
Life	120	134	3.89	403	37	2149.1	2138	930	827	1523
3 AVE	11	12	3.63	34	3	209.1	211	85	71	161

MARK GUBICZA

Position: Pitcher
Team: Kansas City Royals
Born: Aug. 14, 1962 Philadelphia, PA
Height: 6'5" **Weight:** 220 lbs.
Bats: right **Throws:** right
Acquired: Second-round pick in 6/81 free-agent draft

Player Summary	
Fantasy Value.	$3 to $5
Card Value	5¢ to 7¢
Will.	get ground-ball outs
Can't.	stop giving up hits
Expect	good control
Don't Expect	loads of Ks

After spending a year in the bullpen, Gubicza returned to the Royal rotation in 1994. His 6-2 win over Milwaukee May 1 was his first as a starter in two seasons. While he wasn't spectacular the rest of the way, he pitched well enough to retain his starting slot. A control pitcher who in 1994 yielded less than two walks per nine innings, Gubicza relies on location and changing speeds to win. Shoulder problems have sapped the speed out of his fastball, which he now blends with a slider, a curve, and a changeup. He's tried to vary his pregame warmups to shake a severe case of first-inning blues. Gubicza yielded nearly 11 hits per nine innings but managed to keep the ball in the park. When he's right, he gets most of his outs on ground balls. Gubicza plays good defense.

Major League Pitching Register

	W	L	ERA	G	CG	IP	H	ER	BB	SO
84 AL	10	14	4.05	29	4	189.0	172	85	75	111
85 AL	14	10	4.06	29	0	177.1	160	80	77	99
86 AL	12	6	3.64	35	3	180.2	155	73	84	118
87 AL	13	18	3.98	35	10	241.2	231	107	120	166
88 AL	20	8	2.70	35	8	269.2	237	81	83	183
89 AL	15	11	3.04	36	8	255.0	252	86	63	173
90 AL	4	7	4.50	16	2	94.0	101	47	38	71
91 AL	9	12	5.68	26	0	133.0	168	84	42	89
92 AL	7	6	3.72	18	2	111.1	110	46	36	81
93 AL	5	8	4.66	49	0	104.1	128	54	43	80
94 AL	7	9	4.50	22	0	130.0	158	65	26	59
Life	116	109	3.86	330	37	1886.0	1872	808	687	1230
3 AVE	7	9	4.32	33	1	133.1	154	64	39	81

OZZIE GUILLEN

Position: Shortstop
Team: Chicago White Sox
Born: Jan. 20, 1964 Ocumare del Tuy, Venezuela
Height: 5'11" **Weight:** 150 lbs.
Bats: left **Throws:** right
Acquired: Traded from Padres with Tim Lollar, Bill Long, and Luis Salazar for LaMarr Hoyt, Todd Simmons, and Kevin Kristan, 12/84

Player Summary	
Fantasy Value	$7 to $9
Card Value	6¢ to 10¢
Will	display sound defense
Can't	run at former speed
Expect	solid bat vs. righties
Don't Expect	patience at plate

In 1994, for the second year in a row, Guillen produced the best batting average of his career. A spray hitter with little power, he makes good contact but still fans twice as often as he walks because he doesn't show much patience at the plate. Guillen fattens his average by dropping bunts and beating out infield hits. He'll even reach above the strike zone to do his own version of the Baltimore Chop. Guillen is a fastball hitter who hits well against right-handed pitchers. He's hit exactly .300 against righties over the past two seasons. He runs the bases well, but 1992 knee surgery halted his basestealing. In the field, however, his range and reactions remain well above average. The former Gold Glover positions himself well, shows good lateral movement, and turns the double play without thinking.

Major League Batting Register

	BA	G	AB	R	H	2B	3B	HR	RBI	SB
85 AL	.273	150	491	71	134	21	9	1	33	7
86 AL	.250	159	547	58	137	19	4	2	47	8
87 AL	.279	149	560	64	156	22	7	2	51	25
88 AL	.261	156	566	58	148	16	7	0	39	25
89 AL	.253	155	597	63	151	20	8	1	54	36
90 AL	.279	160	516	61	144	21	4	1	58	13
91 AL	.273	154	524	52	143	20	3	3	49	21
92 AL	.200	12	40	5	8	4	0	0	7	1
93 AL	.280	134	457	44	128	23	4	4	50	5
94 AL	.288	100	365	46	105	9	5	1	39	5
Life	.269	1329	4663	522	1254	175	51	15	427	146
2 AVE	.284	137	486	54	138	16	6	3	52	6

BILL GULLICKSON

Position: Pitcher
Team: Detroit Tigers
Born: Feb. 20, 1959 Marshall, MN
Height: 6'3" **Weight:** 200 lbs.
Bats: right **Throws:** right
Acquired: Signed as a free agent, 12/90

Player Summary	
Fantasy Value	$0
Card Value	5¢ to 7¢
Will	seek big comeback
Can't	prevent long ball
Expect	excellent control
Don't Expect	low ERA

Gullickson is a one-time power pitcher struggling to master the fine art of winning with finesse. When he relies on his sinker, his slider, and his curve, he's fairly successful. But he still leans heavily on a fastball no longer worthy of the name. A master of control, Gullickson yielded less than two walks per nine innings last year. He sometimes captures too much of the plate, however—especially with the heater—and batters capitalize with alarming frequency. He allowed 24 gopher balls in 115⅓ innings. Serious shoulder and knee problems, coupled with advanced athletic age, have taken their toll. He averaged five whiffs and 12 hits per nine innings last year. Fortunately for Gullickson, he is a first-rate fielder and owns a fine pickoff move.

Major League Pitching Register

	W	L	ERA	G	CG	IP	H	ER	BB	SO
79 NL	0	0	0.00	1	0	1.0	2	0	0	0
80 NL	10	5	3.00	24	5	141.0	127	47	50	120
81 NL	7	9	2.80	22	3	157.1	142	49	34	115
82 NL	12	14	3.57	34	6	236.2	231	94	61	155
83 NL	17	12	3.75	34	10	242.1	230	101	59	120
84 NL	12	9	3.61	32	3	226.2	230	91	37	100
85 NL	14	12	3.52	29	4	181.1	187	71	47	68
86 NL	15	12	3.38	37	6	244.2	245	92	60	121
87 NL	10	11	4.85	27	3	165.0	172	89	39	89
87 AL	4	2	4.88	8	1	48.0	46	26	11	28
90 NL	10	14	3.82	32	2	193.1	221	82	61	73
91 AL	20	9	3.90	35	4	226.1	256	98	44	91
92 AL	14	13	4.34	34	4	221.2	228	107	50	64
93 AL	13	9	5.37	28	2	159.1	186	95	44	70
94 AL	4	5	5.93	21	1	115.1	156	76	25	65
Life	162	136	3.93	398	54	2560.0	2659	1118	622	1279
3 AVE	11	10	5.12	31	2	181.1	211	103	43	75

114

MARK GUTHRIE

Position: Pitcher
Team: Minnesota Twins
Born: Sept. 22, 1965 Buffalo, NY
Height: 6'4" **Weight:** 202 lbs.
Bats: both **Throws:** left
Acquired: Seventh-round pick in 6/87 free-agent draft

Player Summary	
Fantasy Value $1
Card Value . . . . 5¢ to 7¢
Will. . . . . resume heavy workload
Can't. . . . . halt the hit parade
Expect . . . . progress vs. lefties
Don't Expect . . . . control problems

After a shoulder blood clot shortened his 1993 season, Guthrie returned intact. Though he struggled against right-handed hitters, he showed good control and led the Minnesota staff in appearances. His best outing came June 9, when he worked three and one-third hitless innings against the White Sox. Guthrie was an overall disappointment, however. Southpaws hit .284 against him—136 points higher than they managed one year earlier. As a result, he yielded more than 11 hits per nine innings and blew three of four saves. More than half the hits he surrendered went for extra bases, including eight homers in 51⅓ innings. Guthrie is young enough to regroup if healthy. His repertoire of a forkball, a fastball, and a curveball is adequate for a reliever, and previously he was able to maintain a 3-1 ratio of whiffs to walks. He averaged six and one-half strikeouts per nine innings last year. He helps himself as a fielder and keeps a close eye on baserunners.

Major League Pitching Register

	W	L	ERA	G	S	IP	H	ER	BB	SO
89 AL	2	4	4.55	13	0	57.1	66	29	21	38
90 AL	7	9	3.79	24	0	144.2	154	61	39	101
91 AL	7	5	4.32	41	2	98.0	116	47	41	72
92 AL	2	3	2.88	54	5	75.0	59	24	23	76
93 AL	2	1	4.71	22	0	21.0	20	11	16	15
94 AL	4	2	6.14	50	1	51.1	65	35	18	38
Life	24	24	4.16	204	8	447.1	480	207	158	340
2 AVE	4	3	4.48	62	3	73.1	75	37	24	65

RICKY GUTIERREZ

Position: Shortstop
Team: San Diego Padres
Born: May 23, 1970 Miami, FL
Height: 6'1" **Weight:** 175 lbs.
Bats: right **Throws:** right
Acquired: Traded from Orioles with Erik Schullstrom for Craig Lefferts, 9/92

Player Summary	
Fantasy Value. . . . . $2 to $4
Card Value . . . . 6¢ to 10¢
Will . . . . try to regain job
Can't . . . . hit with much power
Expect. . . . . best bat vs. lefties
Don't Expect . . . . error-free arm

One year after winning the San Diego shortstop job, Gutierrez gave it away. He came to spring camp 17 pounds heavier—the result of a winter weight-lifting program—and struggled both offensively and defensively. After Gutierrez made his 21st error July 9, San Diego manager Jim Riggleman decided he had seen enough. Luis Lopez supplanted Gutierrez at short. Criticized by coaches for his low-key approach to the game, Gutierrez needs to work harder to recapture the promise of his '93 rookie season. He strikes out far too often for a singles hitter and gets caught much too often when he tries to steal. Unless he learns to bunt, beat out infield hits, and draw more walks, he will never add much to the offense. Though he hit five home runs as a rookie, he had only one in three minor-league years prior to that. Breaking balls give him trouble, and he struggles against righties. Gutierrez has soft hands, fine instincts, and great range in the field. His arm is often erratic, as is the case with other young shortstops.

Major League Batting Register

	BA	G	AB	R	H	2B	3B	HR	RBI	SB
93 NL	.251	133	438	76	110	10	5	5	26	4
94 NL	.240	90	275	27	66	11	2	1	28	2
Life	.247	223	713	103	176	21	7	6	54	6
2 AVE	.246	130	413	57	101	13	4	3	33	3

JOSE GUZMAN

Position: Pitcher
Team: Chicago Cubs
Born: April 9, 1963 Santa Isabel, Puerto Rico
Height: 6'3" **Weight:** 198 lbs.
Bats: right **Throws:** right
Acquired: Signed as a free agent, 12/92

Player Summary	
Fantasy Value	$2 to $4
Card Value	5¢ to 7¢
Will	need changeup to win
Can't	keep shoulder intact
Expect	pitch speeds to vary
Don't Expect	top control

For the second time in five seasons, a serious shoulder injury forced Guzman to the sidelines. Counted on to produce double digits in wins for the second year in a row, he instead made the Cubs wonder why they had given him a four-year, $14 million contract. This year, he will need the best season of his career to justify that enormous investment. A sinker-slider pitcher who also throws a curveball, a forkball, and a changeup, he averages about two and one-half strikeouts per walk. Guzman, however, is prone to occasional control problems and throwing too many gopher balls. In addition, he's a streak pitcher who can be either very good or very bad. Only a two-out, ninth-inning single by Otis Nixon separated Guzman from a no-hitter in his first Cub start two years ago, but he hasn't even pitched a shutout since. Runners take advantage of Guzman's leg-lifting delivery, and his defense doesn't help either.

Major League Pitching Register

	W	L	ERA	G	CG	IP	H	ER	BB	SO
85 AL	3	2	2.76	5	0	32.2	27	10	14	24
86 AL	9	15	4.54	29	2	172.1	199	87	60	87
87 AL	14	14	4.67	37	6	208.1	196	108	82	143
88 AL	11	13	3.70	30	6	206.2	180	85	82	157
91 AL	13	7	3.08	25	5	169.2	152	58	84	125
92 AL	16	11	3.66	33	5	224.0	229	91	73	179
93 NL	12	10	4.34	30	2	191.0	188	92	74	163
94 NL	2	2	9.15	4	0	19.2	22	20	13	11
Life	80	74	4.05	193	26	1224.1	1193	551	482	889
2 AVE	14	11	3.97	32	4	208.0	209	92	74	171

JUAN GUZMAN

Position: Pitcher
Team: Toronto Blue Jays
Born: Oct. 28, 1966 Santo Domingo, Dominican Republic
Height: 5'11" **Weight:** 190 lbs.
Bats: right **Throws:** right
Acquired: Traded from Dodgers for Mike Sharperson, 9/87

Player Summary	
Fantasy Value	$8 to $10
Card Value	6¢ to 10¢
Will	improve his record
Can't	win without control
Expect	flame-throwing heat
Don't Expect	more disappointment

Last season was not a good one for the Blue Jays in general nor Guzman in particular. For the second straight year, his ERA climbed in direct proportion to his wavering control. He still managed to win in double figures, however, because Toronto's hitters provided him with the best run support on the staff (six runs per game). After a slow start, he noticed more zip on his fastball in July and began using the pitch more. Not surprisingly, his changeup improved at the same time. Guzman also throws a hard slider with a forkball-style downward break. Sometimes, his pitches break too much. He uncorked 13 wild pitches, tops on the Toronto staff, in 25 starts. Since he also yielded more hits than innings for the first time, while allowing four and one-half walks per nine innings, he had problems. Guzman struggles against southpaws, seldom stops basestealers, and throws his share of gophers. His motion leaves him in poor defensive position. He still has the talent to be a No. 1 starter.

Major League Pitching Register

	W	L	ERA	G	CG	IP	H	ER	BB	SO
91 AL	10	3	2.99	23	1	138.2	98	46	66	123
92 AL	16	5	2.64	28	1	180.2	135	53	72	165
93 AL	14	3	3.99	33	2	221.0	211	98	110	194
94 AL	12	11	5.68	25	2	147.1	165	93	76	124
Life	52	22	3.80	109	6	687.2	609	290	324	606
3 AVE	16	8	4.17	32	2	203.1	193	94	96	178

CHRIS GWYNN

Position: Outfield
Team: Los Angeles Dodgers
Born: Oct. 13, 1964 Los Angeles, CA
Height: 6′ **Weight:** 210 lbs.
Bats: left **Throws:** left
Acquired: Signed as a free agent, 4/94

Player Summary	
Fantasy Value	$0
Card Value	5¢ to 7¢
Will	stroke pinch hits
Can't	deliver any power
Expect	very good contact
Don't Expect	speed

As a fourth outfielder and pinch hitter, Gwynn does little damage to the family name. Like older brother Tony, Chris is a contact hitter who hits line drives to all fields but doesn't have too much power. A low-ball hitter who usually fares better against right-handers, Gwynn proved more potent against lefties last year. At strike time, his average against southpaws was .400—but that's because he was seeing most of his action against righties. Gwynn's average was even better (.421) with runners in scoring position. He rarely walks, fans, steals, or pokes an extra-base hit, but he remains a valuable man off the bench. Gwynn hit an even .300 in 1993 with the Kansas City Royals, when he was given the most at bats of his career. He throws well enough to play right field and runs well enough to play all three outfield spots. A former college All-American from San Diego State, Gwynn was a member of the 1984 U.S. Olympic Team.

Major League Batting Register

	BA	G	AB	R	H	2B	3B	HR	RBI	SB
87 NL	.219	17	32	2	7	1	0	0	2	0
88 NL	.182	12	11	1	2	0	0	0	0	0
89 NL	.235	32	68	8	16	4	1	0	7	1
90 NL	.284	101	141	19	40	2	1	5	22	0
91 NL	.252	94	139	18	35	5	1	5	22	1
92 AL	.286	34	84	10	24	3	2	1	7	0
93 AL	.300	103	287	36	86	14	4	1	25	0
94 NL	.268	58	71	9	19	0	0	3	13	0
Life	.275	451	833	103	229	29	9	15	98	2

TONY GWYNN

Position: Outfield
Team: San Diego Padres
Born: May 9, 1960 Los Angeles, CA
Height: 5′11″ **Weight:** 205 lbs.
Bats: left **Throws:** left
Acquired: Third-round pick in 6/81 free-agent draft

Player Summary	
Fantasy Value	$20 to $25
Card Value	25¢ to 40¢
Will	resume .400 chase
Can't	steal much anymore
Expect	sixth batting title
Don't Expect	great power

Though he won his fifth batting crown last year, Gwynn was stopped in his quest for the majors' first .400 season since 1941. A winter weight-lifting program helped him to launch quickly. On April 25, he netted the eighth five-hit game of his career and tied a San Diego club record with eight straight hits. Able to turn on the ball better and stroke more extra-base hits, Gwynn hit .390 between the 1993 and 1994 All-Star Games. The only NL player who went all the way in last year's game, he scored the winning run in the 10th inning. He has now hit .300 for 12 straight years—the best NL streak since Stan Musial had 16 straight from 1942 to 1958. Gwynn averages two and one-half walks for every strikeout. The five-time Gold Glove winner has a strong arm from right field.

Major League Batting Register

	BA	G	AB	R	H	2B	3B	HR	RBI	SB
82 NL	.289	54	190	33	55	12	2	1	17	8
83 NL	.309	86	304	34	94	12	2	1	37	7
84 NL	.351	158	606	88	213	21	10	5	71	33
85 NL	.317	154	622	90	197	29	5	6	46	14
86 NL	.329	160	642	107	211	33	7	14	59	37
87 NL	.370	157	589	119	218	36	13	7	54	56
88 NL	.313	133	521	64	163	22	5	7	70	26
89 NL	.336	158	604	82	203	27	7	4	62	40
90 NL	.309	141	573	79	177	29	10	4	72	17
91 NL	.317	134	530	69	168	27	11	4	62	8
92 NL	.317	128	520	77	165	27	3	6	41	3
93 NL	.358	122	489	70	175	41	3	7	59	14
94 NL	.394	110	419	79	165	35	1	12	64	5
Life	.333	1695	6609	991	2204	351	79	78	714	268
3 AVE	.358	135	533	86	191	39	2	10	63	8

JOHN HABYAN

Position: Pitcher
Team: St. Louis Cardinals
Born: Jan. 29, 1964 Bayshore, NY
Height: 6'2" **Weight:** 195 lbs.
Bats: right **Throws:** right
Acquired: Signed as a free agent, 1/94

Player Summary	
Fantasy Value	$2 to $4
Card Value	5¢ to 7¢
Will	coax ground outs
Can't	always throw strikes
Expect	lots of relief calls
Don't Expect	gopher troubles

When a set-up man does his job well, he'll have no wins, no losses, and no saves. That's why Habyan's 1994 statistics look so good. He compiled a 1-0 record, one save, and a 3.23 ERA in 52 appearances before the strike. With 12 saves in nine years, he has always shown the ability to do what his manager orders. A sinker-slider pitcher who also throws a curve, Habyan averaged just under a strikeout per inning and just over nine hits per nine innings last year. He had periodic control problems, averaging close to four walks per game, but was effective when his sinker sank, resulting in ground-ball outs. Habyan is most effective against right-handed hitters but stingy with the long ball against everyone. He also strands most of the runners he inherits. Habyan handles the glove well and keeps close watch on potential basestealers. He pitched for the Orioles, the Yankees, and the Royals before St. Louis.

Major League Pitching Register

	W	L	ERA	G	S	IP	H	ER	BB	SO
85 AL	1	0	0.00	2	0	2.2	3	0	0	2
86 AL	1	3	4.44	6	0	26.1	24	13	18	14
87 AL	6	7	4.80	27	1	116.1	110	62	40	64
88 AL	1	0	4.30	7	0	14.2	22	7	4	4
90 AL	0	0	2.08	6	0	8.2	10	2	2	4
91 AL	4	2	2.30	66	2	90.0	73	23	20	70
92 AL	5	6	3.84	56	7	72.2	84	31	21	44
93 AL	2	1	4.15	48	1	56.1	59	26	20	39
94 NL	1	0	3.23	52	1	47.1	50	17	20	46
Life	21	19	3.74	270	12	435.0	435	181	145	287
3 AVE	3	2	3.72	59	3	65.1	71	27	23	49

CHIP HALE

Position: Second base; infield
Team: Minnesota Twins
Born: Dec. 2, 1964 Santa Clara, CA
Height: 5'11" **Weight:** 191 lbs.
Bats: left **Throws:** right
Acquired: 17th-round pick in 6/87 free-agent draft

Player Summary	
Fantasy Value	$1
Card Value	10¢ to 15¢
Will	pinch-hit often
Can't	hit the ball out
Expect	good clutch bat
Don't Expect	patient approach

When Tony Oliva stroked nine straight hits to set a Minnesota club record, he did it in two games. When Hale got eight straight last season, it took two weeks. The problem is that Hale hardly plays. A left-handed hitter who does his best work in late-inning pressure situations (.323), he rarely walks, strikes out, or hits the ball out of the park. Hale slammed lefties in limited action last year but is usually more potent against right-handers. Though he has some speed, he isn't a basestealer. He has glowing minor-league credentials for defensive excellence at second, and he has settled into a niche as an all-purpose reserve and pinch hitter on the major-league level. He played all three bases and the outfield last year while also spending time as a designated hitter. He's best defensively at second, where he led several minor leagues in chances, putouts, assists, and double plays. In '94, however, he spent most of his time at third, where the Twins used him as a lefty platoon partner for Scott Leius.

Major League Batting Register

	BA	G	AB	R	H	2B	3B	HR	RBI	SB
89 AL	.209	28	67	6	14	3	0	0	4	0
90 AL	.000	1	2	0	0	0	0	0	2	0
93 AL	.333	69	186	25	62	6	1	3	27	2
94 AL	.263	67	118	13	31	9	0	1	11	0
Life	.287	165	373	44	107	18	1	4	44	2

DARREN HALL

Position: Pitcher
Team: Toronto Blue Jays
Born: July 14, 1964   Marysville, OH
Height: 6'3"   **Weight:** 205 lbs.
Bats: right   **Throws:** right
Acquired: 28th-round pick in 6/86 free-agent draft

Player Summary	
Fantasy Value	$0
Card Value	10¢ to 15¢
Will	strand runners
Can't	always find zone
Expect	hitters to ache
Don't Expect	many gophers

While struggling in Triple-A in 1993, Hall actually considered retirement. But that was before Syracuse manager Nick Leyva convinced the pitcher to shorten his stride. Suddenly, Hall's pitches started moving, improving both his sinker and slider. As a 30-year-old rookie last summer, he maintained the momentum so well that he supplanted the injured Duane Ward as Toronto's top closer. Hall averaged eight strikeouts, four walks, and just under seven and one-half hits per nine innings. He threw only three gopher balls all year, resulting in three blown saves out of 20 opportunities. Hall was even better at stranding inherited runners—a perfect 12-out-of-12. Hitters had a hard time with his deliveries, and runners rarely challenged. Much more effective against lefties last year, he should improve against righties as he learns the league. With Ward healthy again, Hall will work in front of him—giving Toronto its best set-up man since Mark Eichhorn. Hall had three saves in '94 at Syracuse, and in 1993 he notched 13 saves, 68 Ks, and 31 walks in 79 innings there.

BOB HAMELIN

Position: Designated hitter; first base
Team: Kansas City Royals
Born: Nov. 29, 1967   Elizabeth, NJ
Height: 6'   **Weight:** 235 lbs.
Bats: left   **Throws:** left
Acquired: Second-round pick in 6/88 free-agent draft

Player Summary	
Fantasy Value	$17 to $20
Card Value	15¢ to 30¢
Will	show enormous power
Can't	bring speed to game
Expect	extra-base hits
Don't Expect	a choker

Kansas City fans call him The Hammer. He earned the nickname by becoming the club's top slugger as a 1994 rookie. Hamelin began by hitting .361 with six homers and 21 RBI in April, immediately establishing himself as a legimate cleanup bopper. He shows surprising discipline at the plate, walking almost as much as he strikes out, and did some of his best hitting in late-inning pressure situations (.333 at strike time). Though he hits 30 points higher against right-handers, Hamelin is hardly an automatic out against lefties. There's no question about the American League Rookie of the Year's power. Fifty of his 88 hits last summer went for extra bases. A deadly hitter when he gets ahead in the count, Hamelin has the potential to improve with experience. His progress has been hampered by chronic back problems throughout his career. The Royals considered his bulk and his health when they made him a full-time DH. Besides, he can't match Wally Joyner's ability at first base. In 1993 at Triple-A Omaha, Hamelin batted .259 with 29 homers, 84 RBI, and a loop-best 82 walks.

Major League Pitching Register

	W	L	ERA	G	S	IP	H	ER	BB	SO
94 AL	2	3	3.41	30	17	31.2	26	12	14	28
Life	2	3	3.41	30	17	31.2	26	12	14	28

Major League Batting Register

	BA	G	AB	R	H	2B	3B	HR	RBI	SB
93 AL	.224	16	49	2	11	3	0	2	5	0
94 AL	.282	101	312	64	88	25	1	24	65	4
Life	.274	117	361	66	99	28	1	26	70	4

DARRYL HAMILTON

Position: Outfield
Team: Milwaukee Brewers
Born: Dec. 3, 1964   Baton Rouge, LA
Height: 6'1"   **Weight:** 180 lbs.
Bats: left   **Throws:** right
Acquired: 11th-round pick in 6/86 free-agent draft

Player Summary	
Fantasy Value	$5 to $7
Card Value	6¢ to 10¢
Will	deliver .300 average
Can't	clear outfield fence
Expect	clean bill of health
Don't Expect	defensive woes

Though he changed his throwing mechanics to ease the stress on his elbow, Hamilton still needed season-ending surgery last May. That operation repaired a slight tear in the ulnar collateral ligament of his right elbow. The Brewers were not happy to lose him, because he had been a .310 hitter in two of the three preceding seasons. Though he's never reached double figures in homers, Hamilton contributes speed, defense, and other intangibles. Blessed with a good batting eye, he'll work deep into the count, dropping a bunt if he catches the infield playing back. Hamilton hits well in clutch situations and is at his best with a two-strike count. Once a washout against lefties, he's learned to hit them for a respectable average. When healthy, he is a definite threat to steal (41 in 1992) and a fine defensive outfielder (229 consecutive errorless games). He has the range for center and the arm for right. Hamilton is also a good guy to have in the clubhouse.

Major League Batting Register

	BA	G	AB	R	H	2B	3B	HR	RBI	SB
88 AL	.184	44	103	14	19	4	0	1	11	7
90 AL	.295	89	156	27	46	5	0	1	18	10
91 AL	.311	122	405	64	126	15	6	1	57	16
92 AL	.298	128	470	67	140	19	7	5	62	41
93 AL	.310	135	520	74	161	21	1	9	48	21
94 AL	.262	36	141	23	37	10	1	1	13	3
Life	.295	554	1795	269	529	74	15	18	209	98
2 AVE	.304	132	495	71	151	20	4	7	55	31

JOEY HAMILTON

Position: Pitcher
Team: San Diego Padres
Born: Sept. 9, 1970   Statesboro, GA
Height: 6'4"   **Weight:** 220 lbs.
Bats: right   **Throws:** right
Acquired: First-round pick in 6/91 free-agent draft

Player Summary	
Fantasy Value	$2 to $4
Card Value	10¢ to 15¢
Will	show great poise
Can't	fan many hitters
Expect	double-digit wins
Don't Expect	control lapses

Though he didn't reach the majors until May 24, Hamilton quickly showed poise and confidence beyond his years. A sinker-slider pitcher who throws strikes and knows how to change speeds, he challenges hitters and expects to win. Averaging nearly seven innings per start last year, Hamilton yielded eight hits, five strikeouts, and under two and one-half walks per nine innings. He kept the ball in the park and held baserunners well. He blanked the Reds June 25 for his first big-league shutout. Seven innings of one-run ball against the Phils July 5 lowered his ERA to 1.94. Despite his short stay, Hamilton led San Diego's starters in both victories and earned run average last summer. He went 3-5 with a 2.73 ERA, 32 strikeouts, and 22 walks at Triple-A Las Vegas last year. In 1993, he was 3-2 with a 4.40 ERA at Las Vegas and 4-9 with a 3.97 ERA at Double-A Wichita. The former Georgia Southern University star pitched his team into the College World Series. He has to overcome two roadblocks: a recurrence of the tender shoulder that had plagued him in the past and excessive weight.

Major League Pitching Register

	W	L	ERA	G	CG	IP	H	ER	BB	SO
94 NL	9	6	2.98	16	1	108.2	98	36	29	61
Life	9	6	2.98	16	1	108.2	98	36	29	61

CHRIS HAMMOND

Position: Pitcher
Team: Florida Marlins
Born: Jan. 21, 1966 Atlanta, GA
Height: 6′ **Weight:** 190 lbs.
Bats: left **Throws:** left
Acquired: Traded from Reds for Gary Scott and Hector Carrasco, 3/92

Player Summary	
Fantasy Value.	$2 to $4
Card Value	6¢ to 10¢
Will.	rely on slow change
Can't.	supply strong glove
Expect	first winning year
Don't Expect.	weak hitter

Before lower back problems interfered, Hammond was handling hitters with little difficulty. In May, his best month, he blanked the Phils for his first shutout, then reeled off 22 consecutive scoreless innings, a Florida club record. Though his arsenal includes a fastball, a slider, and a curve, his best pitch is a slow changeup that baffles most batters. He has good control, keeps the ball in the park, and gets most of his outs on ground balls. Though he yields just over a hit per inning, Hammond helps himself with a first-rate pickoff move and a potent bat. He even hits one or two homers per season. He's not much of a fielder, however. A baseball enigma, he has never turned the glowing promise of his minor-league years (he was 15-1 in Triple-A in 1990 and 16-5 in Double-A in '88) into a winning big-league season. Some scouts think he would improve if he used his fastball to offset his slow stuff more often. Failing to challenge the hitters with heat lets them adjust to what's coming.

Major League Pitching Register

	W	L	ERA	G	CG	IP	H	ER	BB	SO
90 NL	0	2	6.35	3	0	11.1	13	8	12	4
91 NL	7	7	4.06	20	0	99.2	92	45	48	50
92 NL	7	10	4.21	28	0	147.1	149	69	55	79
93 NL	11	12	4.66	32	1	191.0	207	99	66	108
94 NL	4	4	3.07	13	1	73.1	79	25	23	40
Life	29	35	4.24	96	2	522.2	540	246	204	281
3 AVE	8	9	4.14	26	1	147.1	156	68	51	81

JEFFREY HAMMONDS

Position: Outfield
Team: Baltimore Orioles
Born: March 5, 1971 Plainfield, NJ
Height: 6′ **Weight:** 195 lbs.
Bats: right **Throws:** right
Acquired: First-round pick in 6/92 free-agent draft

Player Summary	
Fantasy Value.	$13 to $16
Card Value	20¢ to 30¢
Will	show good speed
Can't	wait for walks
Expect	future stardom
Don't Expect.	powerful throws

The first player from the 1992 amateur draft to reach the majors, Hammonds would've arrived sooner if not for serious disc problems that curtailed his '93 campaign. After missing time early last year with a strained right knee, he began to realize his immense potential. He slammed two homers against the Angels July 1 and hit a leadoff ninth-inning homer in an 8-7 win against Oakland eight days later. An aggressive hitter who last year fanned twice as much as he walked, Hammonds should show more selectivity as he gains experience. When he does, he's expected to develop into the speed-plus-power player who started in center field for the 1992 U.S. Olympic team. He is a two-time All-American from Stanford. He batted .311 at Triple-A Rochester last year, with five homers, 23 RBI, and six stolen bases in 151 at bats. Many scouts insist Hammonds has 20-20 potential—perhaps even 30-30 if his power stroke develops. His speed gives him great range in center, but Hammonds hardly has the arm for right. With his bat, who cares?

Major League Batting Register

	BA	G	AB	R	H	2B	3B	HR	RBI	SB
93 AL	.305	33	105	10	32	8	0	3	19	4
94 AL	.296	68	250	45	74	18	2	8	31	5
Life	.299	101	355	55	106	26	2	11	50	9

MIKE HAMPTON

Position: Pitcher
Team: Houston Astros
Born: Sept. 9, 1972 Brooksville, FL
Height: 5'10" **Weight:** 180 lbs.
Bats: right **Throws:** left
Acquired: Traded from Mariners with Mike Felder for Eric Anthony, 12/93

Player Summary	
Fantasy Value................	$1 to $3
Card Value	12¢ to 20¢
Will	induce ground balls
Can't	avoid wild pitches
Expect	more bullpen calls
Don't Expect	dingers

Left-handed pitchers are supposed to handle left-handed hitters—especially in short bullpen stints expressly for that purpose. Hampton unfortunately had problems filling that role last year. Though he made 44 outings, second on the Houston staff, he was lit up at a .324 clip by lefty batters. That was the reason Hampton allowed more hits than innings pitched. A fierce competitor with good composure, he had been pegged for a starter's job by Seattle. The Astros—spotting his arm—demanded his inclusion in the Eric Anthony trade. Hampton throws an above-average fastball, a changeup, and a slurve (a slider-curve hybrid), working both sides of the plate with little difficulty. When his location is good, Hampton gets ground outs. His strikeout ratio, only about five per nine innings last year, was much better in the minors. He walked about three and one-half batters per game, kept the ball in the park, and held runners well. He uncorked too many wild pitches, however. In 1993 at Double-A Jacksonville, he was 6-4 with a 3.71 ERA, 84 strikeouts, and 33 bases on balls in 87⅓ innings.

Major League Pitching Register

	W	L	ERA	G	S	IP	H	ER	BB	SO
93 AL	1	3	9.53	13	1	17.0	28	18	17	8
94 NL	2	1	3.70	44	0	41.1	46	17	16	24
Life	3	4	5.40	57	1	58.1	74	35	33	32

DAVE HANSEN

Position: Third base
Team: Los Angeles Dodgers
Born: Nov. 24, 1968 Long Beach, CA
Height: 6' **Weight:** 180 lbs.
Bats: left **Throws:** right
Acquired: Second-round pick in 6/86 free-agent draft

Player Summary	
Fantasy Value................	$1 to $3
Card Value	5¢ to 7¢
Will	stroke pinch hits
Can't	belt many homers
Expect	strong clutch bat
Don't Expect	lineup return

Hansen had two handicaps last summer: his own pinch-hitting prowess and the unexpected comeback of Tim Wallach. Coming off a year in which he collected a club-record 18 pinch hits, Hansen hardly saw any action in the field. Manager Tommy Lasorda wanted Hansen ready to come off the bench. Before the strike, he played only 36 innings at third base. He did make the most of his 44 at bats. Hansen hit an even .500—that's no typo—at home, in late-inning pressure spots, and against left-handed pitching. Used mostly against righties, he hit "only" .325. An aggressive contact hitter who rarely walks or fans, Hansen is far more productive off the bench; he hit .362 in a reserve role in 1993. Though he's primarily a singles hitter, he hits an occasional home run. He rarely steals a base, however. Though he led several minor leagues in putouts, assists, double plays, and fielding percentage, Hansen has declined defensively, mostly because of back problems. He still wants to try to win a starting job.

Major League Batting Register

	BA	G	AB	R	H	2B	3B	HR	RBI	SB
90 NL	.143	5	7	0	1	0	0	0	1	0
91 NL	.268	53	56	3	15	4	0	1	5	1
92 NL	.214	132	341	30	73	11	0	6	22	0
93 NL	.362	84	105	13	38	3	0	4	30	0
94 NL	.341	40	44	3	15	3	0	0	5	0
Life	.257	314	553	49	142	21	0	11	63	1

ERIK HANSON

Position: Pitcher
Team: Cincinnati Reds
Born: May 18, 1965   Kinnelon, NJ
Height: 6'6"   **Weight:** 210 lbs.
Bats: right   **Throws:** right
Acquired: Traded from Mariners with Bret Boone for Bobby Ayala and Dan Wilson, 11/93

Player Summary	
Fantasy Value	$7 to $9
Card Value	6¢ to 10¢
Will	show great curve
Can't	cut wild pitches
Expect	low gopher total
Don't Expect	stolen bases

Hanson enjoyed mixed success in his first NL season. In his best outing, on June 7, he limited St. Louis to one hit and one walk over eight innings in a 5-0 win. Yet he didn't complete any of his starts and finished the season on the DL after tearing the anterior cruciate ligament of his left knee while fielding a bunt Aug. 2. When healthy, Hanson throws one of the best curveballs in baseball. He also throws a fastball, a changeup, and—against right-handed hitters—a new pitch that is a hybrid of a slider and cut fastball. Hanson had a 5-1 ratio of Ks to walks last year and averaged one and one-half walks per nine innings. He yielded 10 hits per nine innings pitched, in part because he didn't show his usual success against left-handed hitters. Hanson also led the Cincy staff in wild pitches. On the plus side, he kept the ball in the park, stopped half the runners who tried to steal against him, and displayed fine fielding.

Major League Pitching Register

	W	L	ERA	G	CG	IP	H	ER	BB	SO
88 AL	2	3	3.24	6	0	41.2	35	15	12	36
89 AL	9	5	3.18	17	1	113.1	103	40	32	75
90 AL	18	9	3.24	33	5	236.0	205	85	68	211
91 AL	8	8	3.81	27	2	174.2	182	74	56	143
92 AL	8	17	4.82	31	6	186.2	209	100	57	112
93 AL	11	12	3.47	31	7	215.0	215	83	60	163
94 NL	5	5	4.11	22	0	122.2	137	56	23	101
Life	61	59	3.74	167	21	1090.0	1086	453	308	841
3 AVE	9	12	4.10	31	4	191.2	206	87	50	139

PETE HARNISCH

Position: Pitcher
Team: New York Mets
Born: Sept. 23, 1966   Commack, NY
Height: 6'   **Weight:** 207 lbs.
Bats: right   **Throws:** right
Acquired: Traded from Astros for Andy Beckerman, 11/94

Player Summary	
Fantasy Value	$11 to $14
Card Value	6¢ to 10¢
Will	rattle right-handers
Can't	prevent gopher balls
Expect	minimum of 15 wins
Don't Expect	shaky control

Although he entered the 1994 season as the expected ace of the Astros, Harnisch soon yielded the spot to Doug Drabek. A partially torn tendon in his right shoulder prevented Harnisch from showing the same form he had displayed as a 16-game winner in 1993. He tightened his delivery to prevent further damage but still was put on the DL May 27. He returned June 30 and beat the Cubs 5-3 without yielding a walk. He also won his next four decisions. A fastball-slider pitcher whose arsenal also includes a slow curve and tantalizing changeup, Harnisch dominates right-handed hitters. He allowed about three and one-half walks per nine innings in 1994. He's especially tough in clutch situations. When healthy, Harnisch averages two and one-half Ks per walk. A good bunter, he helps himself with his bat and glove but has a poor pickoff move. He stopped only one of 13 runners who tried to steal last year.

Major League Pitching Register

	W	L	ERA	G	CG	IP	H	ER	BB	SO
88 AL	0	2	5.54	2	0	13.0	13	8	9	10
89 AL	5	9	4.62	18	2	103.1	97	53	64	70
90 AL	11	11	4.34	31	3	188.2	189	91	86	122
91 NL	12	9	2.70	33	4	216.2	169	65	83	172
92 NL	9	10	3.70	34	0	206.2	182	85	64	164
93 NL	16	9	2.98	33	5	217.2	171	72	79	185
94 NL	8	5	5.40	17	1	95.0	100	57	39	62
Life	61	55	3.73	168	15	1041.0	921	431	424	785
3 AVE	12	9	3.83	30	2	186.1	165	79	66	145

BRIAN HARPER

Position: Designated hitter; catcher; outfield
Team: Milwaukee Brewers
Born: Oct. 16, 1959 Los Angeles, CA
Height: 6'2" **Weight:** 195 lbs.
Bats: right **Throws:** right
Acquired: Signed as a free agent, 2/94

Player Summary	
Fantasy Value	$3 to $5
Card Value	6¢ to 10¢
Will	stroke line drives
Can't	generate much power
Expect	hits vs. lefties
Don't Expect	time in field

Injuries interfered with Harper's first season in Milwaukee. When a Ken Ryan fastball broke his wrist June 26, Harper had to go on the DL for the second time. When healthy, he hit with authority, batting .512 in late-inning pressure situations, .367 against left-handers, and .304 at home. A fastball hitter who makes good contact, Harper is difficult to strike out. He doesn't walk much either, however. His power is limited, and he is more likely to hit a line-drive into the gaps than he is to clear the fences. He's also a good double-play candidate since his speed is negligible. As a catcher, he is best at blocking the plate and calls a good game. He doesn't throw well and doesn't have great mobility. He'll fill in behind the plate and in left field.

Major League Batting Register

	BA	G	AB	R	H	2B	3B	HR	RBI	SB
79 AL	.000	1	2	0	0	0	0	0	0	0
81 AL	.273	4	11	1	3	0	0	0	1	1
82 NL	.276	20	29	4	8	1	0	2	4	0
83 NL	.221	61	131	16	29	4	1	7	20	0
84 NL	.259	46	112	4	29	4	0	2	11	0
85 NL	.250	43	52	5	13	4	0	0	8	0
86 AL	.139	19	36	2	5	1	0	0	3	0
87 AL	.235	11	17	1	4	1	0	0	3	0
88 AL	.295	60	166	15	49	11	1	3	20	0
89 AL	.325	126	385	43	125	24	0	8	57	2
90 AL	.294	134	479	61	141	42	3	6	54	3
91 AL	.311	123	441	54	137	28	1	10	69	1
92 AL	.307	140	502	58	154	25	0	9	73	0
93 AL	.304	147	530	52	161	26	1	12	73	1
94 AL	.291	64	251	23	73	15	0	4	32	0
Life	.296	999	3144	339	931	186	7	63	428	8
3 AVE	.302	126	462	47	139	24	0	9	64	0

GREG HARRIS

Position: Pitcher
Team: Colorado Rockies
Born: Dec. 1, 1963 Greensboro, NC
Height: 6'2" **Weight:** 190 lbs.
Bats: right **Throws:** right
Acquired: Traded from Padres with Bruce Hurst for Brad Ausmus, Doug Bochtler, and Andy Ashby, 7/93

Player Summary	
Fantasy Value	$1 to $3
Card Value	5¢ to 7¢
Will	bid to salvage job
Can't	stop hanging curve
Expect	control to improve
Don't Expect	patient management

Trying to improve his luck, Harris changed his number twice last summer. It didn't help. A curveball specialist who once strung together three straight low-ERA years for the Padres, Harris struggled in Denver's thin mountain air. Too many hanging curves turned into home runs, giving him the dubious honor of leading the 1994 Rockies in throwing gopher balls (22 in 130 innings). His total in 1993, which he started in San Diego, was 32, most in the NL. He may be young enough to rebound, but his last two years have been a mystery. When he's right, Harris sets hitters up for the curve with a riding fastball, an occasional slider, and a changeup. He used to throw all his pitches with good control, but that was a problem last year too. Harris yielded three and one-half walks and 10½ hits per nine innings as batters compiled an even .300 average against him. He fields his position well but has trouble holding runners.

Major League Pitching Register

	W	L	ERA	G	CG	IP	H	ER	BB	SO
88 NL	2	0	1.50	3	1	18.0	13	3	3	15
89 NL	8	9	2.60	56	0	135.0	106	39	52	106
90 NL	8	8	2.30	73	0	117.1	92	30	49	97
91 NL	9	5	2.23	20	3	133.0	116	33	27	95
92 NL	4	8	4.12	20	1	118.0	113	54	35	66
93 NL	11	17	4.59	35	4	225.1	239	115	69	123
94 NL	3	12	6.65	29	1	130.0	154	96	52	82
Life	45	59	3.80	236	10	876.2	833	370	287	584
3 AVE	6	14	5.20	32	2	175.0	190	101	59	102

LENNY HARRIS

Position: Infield
Team: Cincinnati Reds
Born: Oct. 28, 1964 Miami, FL
Height: 5'10" **Weight:** 195 lbs.
Bats: left **Throws:** right
Acquired: Signed as a free agent, 11/93

Player Summary	
Fantasy Value	$1
Card Value	5¢ to 7¢
Will	hit with men on
Can't	generate power
Expect	pinch hits
Don't Expect	a good glove

Because of his ability to play almost anywhere, plus his expertise in poking pinch hits off the bench, Harris is destined to remain a utility player. He played three infield spots and some outfield for the Reds last year, but he was at his best in the pinch. Harris hit .370 with runners in scoring position en route to the best offensive season of his seven-year career. He was chugging along at .310 when the music stopped Aug. 12. An aggressive hitter who takes his hacks, he seldom walks or hits the ball out of the park. He does make good contact and hits to all fields. Harris has enough speed to steal a base when needed, but he's still a liability in the field. He doesn't have a great arm, can't turn the double play as a second baseman, boots too many balls, and makes too many mental mistakes. Harris is like the reliever who responds well to sudden calls but suffers when given time to ponder an upcoming performance. Give him a bat and he'll hit.

BRYAN HARVEY

Position: Pitcher
Team: Florida Marlins
Born: June 2, 1963 Chattanooga, TN
Height: 6'2" **Weight:** 215 lbs.
Bats: right **Throws:** right
Acquired: First-round pick from Angels in 11/92 expansion draft

Player Summary	
Fantasy Value	$17 to $20
Card Value	10¢ to 15¢
Will	blow batters away
Can't	shake injury jinx
Expect	pinpoint control
Don't Expect	many blown saves

When Harvey was healthy, he was baseball's best closer. In 1993, he had a win and 45 saves for a club that won only 64 games—giving him a hand in a big-league-record 71.9 percent of his team's victories. Two years earlier, while leading the AL with 46 saves, he also had a microscopic ERA. Last year was different. After maintaining his momentum from 1993, Harvey suffered a brief setback when he hurt his elbow April 25. Then he went down for the year when he needed surgery to repair an injured lower abdominal muscle in July. An All-Star in both leagues, Harvey blends high velocity with uncanny control. His low-90s fastball makes his forkball more devastating. When he was sound, he maintained a 5-1 ratio of strikeouts to walks, kept the ball in the park, and averaged more than a strikeout per inning. He rarely blew a save. Though Harvey is not good at defense or holding runners on, few runners reach against him. A comeback is likely.

Major League Batting Register

	BA	G	AB	R	H	2B	3B	HR	RBI	SB
88 NL	.372	16	43	7	16	1	0	0	8	4
89 NL	.236	115	335	36	79	10	1	3	26	14
90 NL	.304	137	431	61	131	16	4	2	29	15
91 NL	.287	145	429	59	123	16	1	3	38	12
92 NL	.271	135	347	28	94	11	0	0	30	19
93 NL	.237	107	160	20	38	6	1	2	11	3
94 NL	.310	66	100	13	31	3	1	0	14	7
Life	.278	721	1845	224	512	63	8	10	156	74
2 AVE	.260	121	254	24	66	9	1	1	21	11

Major League Pitching Register

	W	L	ERA	G	S	IP	H	ER	BB	SO
87 AL	0	0	0.00	3	0	5.0	6	0	2	3
88 AL	7	5	2.13	50	17	76.0	59	18	20	67
89 AL	3	3	3.44	51	25	55.0	36	21	41	78
90 AL	4	4	3.22	54	25	64.1	45	23	35	82
91 AL	2	4	1.60	67	46	78.2	51	14	17	101
92 AL	0	4	2.83	25	13	28.2	22	9	11	34
93 NL	1	5	1.70	59	45	69.0	45	13	13	73
94 NL	0	0	5.23	12	6	10.1	12	6	4	10
Life	17	25	2.42	321	177	387.0	276	104	143	448

BILLY HATCHER

Position: Outfield
Team: Philadelphia Phillies
Born: Oct. 4, 1960 Williams, AZ
Height: 5'9" **Weight:** 185 lbs.
Bats: right **Throws:** right
Acquired: Traded from Red Sox with Paul Quantrill for Wes Chamberlain and Mike Sullivan, 5/94

Player Summary	
Fantasy Value	$3 to $5
Card Value	5¢ to 7¢
Will	swing at first pitch
Can't	clear outfield walls
Expect	impatience at plate
Don't Expect	top fielding

If Hatcher were judged by his World Series record, he'd be a superstar. He holds the single-Series marks for highest batting average (.750) and most consecutive hits (seven), both from the 1990 Cincinnati sweep. Though he's seen considerable service as a leadoff man, he doesn't reach base often enough to be effective in that role. A first-ball, fastball hitter, he walks about as often as Cecil Fielder steals a base. That's too bad, since Hatcher would increase his value by using his speed on the basepaths. A spray hitter, he oddly enough hits right-handers much harder than lefties. He provides better speed and defense than Wes Chamberlain, for whom Hatcher was traded. Hatcher remains little more than an extra outfielder, though.

Major League Batting Register

	BA	G	AB	R	H	2B	3B	HR	RBI	SB
84 NL	.111	8	9	1	1	0	0	0	0	2
85 NL	.245	53	163	24	40	12	1	2	10	2
86 NL	.258	127	419	55	108	15	4	6	36	38
87 NL	.296	141	564	96	167	28	3	11	63	53
88 NL	.268	145	530	79	142	25	4	7	52	32
89 NL	.231	135	481	59	111	19	3	4	51	24
90 NL	.276	139	504	68	139	28	5	5	25	30
91 NL	.262	138	442	45	116	25	3	4	41	11
92 NL	.287	43	94	10	27	3	0	2	10	0
92 AL	.238	75	315	37	75	16	2	1	23	4
93 AL	.287	136	508	71	146	24	3	9	57	14
94 AL	.244	44	164	24	40	9	1	1	18	4
94 NL	.246	43	134	15	33	5	1	2	13	4
Life	.265	1227	4327	584	1145	209	30	54	399	218
3 AVE	.262	126	446	58	117	21	3	5	45	10

CHARLIE HAYES

Position: Third base
Team: Colorado Rockies
Born: May 29, 1965 Hattiesburg, MS
Height: 6' **Weight:** 205 lbs.
Bats: right **Throws:** right
Acquired: First-round pick from Yankees in 11/92 expansion draft

Player Summary	
Fantasy Value	$13 to $16
Card Value	10¢ to 15¢
Will	rip left-handers
Can't	steal too often
Expect	extra-base hits
Don't Expect	bad fielding

After showing offensive improvement for two straight seasons, Hayes was somewhat of a disappointment last summer. His average and power slipped and his defense did not show much improvement—though he toughed out a broken cheek. A fastball hitter who likes to pull, he fanned twice as much as he walked. He usually hits lefties well (.338 in 1993) but dropped in that department last summer. Denver's thin air helped him lead the league with 45 doubles in 1993, but he couldn't maintain that pace last summer. He did manage to top .300 with runners in scoring position, however. A hard swinger, Hayes hits into frequent double plays (25 to top the NL two years ago). He's neither a frequent nor a skilled basestealer but will try on occasion. Hayes has good judgement, range, and hands at third base. Most of his miscues come on rushed throws—especially on bunts. He's led his league in putouts, assists, and fielding percentage at third.

Major League Batting Register

	BA	G	AB	R	H	2B	3B	HR	RBI	SB
88 NL	.091	7	11	0	1	0	0	0	0	0
89 NL	.257	87	304	26	78	15	1	8	43	3
90 NL	.258	152	561	56	145	20	0	10	57	4
91 NL	.230	142	460	34	106	23	1	12	53	3
92 AL	.257	142	509	52	131	19	2	18	66	3
93 NL	.305	157	573	89	175	45	2	25	98	11
94 NL	.288	113	423	46	122	23	4	10	50	3
Life	.267	800	2841	303	758	145	10	83	367	27
3 AVE	.285	153	559	69	159	32	3	19	78	6

SCOTT HEMOND

Position: Catcher; infield
Team: Oakland Athletics
Born: Nov. 18, 1965   Taunton, MA
Height: 6'   **Weight:** 215 lbs.
Bats: right   **Throws:** right
Acquired: Claimed from White Sox on waivers, 3/93

Player Summary	
Fantasy Value	$1 to $3
Card Value	5¢ to 7¢
Will	supply solid defense
Can't	show patience at bat
Expect	extra-base hits
Don't Expect	high average

Able to play everything but the bass fiddle, Hemond has carved a niche for himself in the majors. Though he doesn't hit much, he helps his team by wearing many gloves. Primarily a backup catcher last year, Hemond was also used at first, second, third, and the outfield. He even saw time as an occasional DH. An impatient hitter, Hemond fanned four times more than he walked in '94. He is strong, with one-third of his hits good for extra bases. He has good enough speed to steal some bases. Defense is really his forte. Hemond once led Double-A Southern League third basemen in assists and chances. He is also a solid receiver. He calls a good game, blocks the plate well, prevents wild pitches, and shows a strong arm. His ability to play so many positions may work against him; if he wasn't so versatile, he might be an everyday catcher somewhere. Hemond was a No. 1 draft selection in 1986 out of the University of South Florida, where he was an All-American.

Major League Batting Register

	BA	G	AB	R	H	2B	3B	HR	RBI	SB
89 AL	.000	4	0	2	0	0	0	0	0	0
90 AL	.154	7	13	0	2	0	0	0	1	0
91 AL	.217	23	23	4	5	0	0	0	0	1
92 AL	.225	25	40	8	9	1	0	0	1	1
93 AL	.256	91	215	31	55	16	0	6	26	14
94 AL	.222	91	198	23	44	11	0	3	20	7
Life	.235	241	489	68	115	29	0	9	49	23
2 AVE	.237	110	247	32	58	16	0	5	27	12

DAVE HENDERSON

Position: Outfield
Team: Kansas City Royals
Born: July 21, 1958   Merced, CA
Height: 6'2"   **Weight:** 210 lbs.
Bats: right   **Throws:** right
Acquired: Signed as a free agent, 1/94

Player Summary	
Fantasy Value	$0
Card Value	6¢ to 10¢
Will	seek another season
Can't	hit right-handers
Expect	occasional long one
Don't Expect	any speed

Henderson should be contemplating retirement. Persistent hamstring problems have plagued him for several seasons, and he's far from the 25-homer form that made him an All-Star in 1991. Used as an extra outfielder by the Royals last summer, the former first-round draft choice handled left-handers well and pounded a handful of home runs. He struggled against right-handers, though, and was not productive in late-inning pressure situations. Henderson can still hit the fastball but has trouble with off-speed stuff. He's impatient at the plate, striking out twice as much as he walks. Henderson runs well enough to provide solid defense in the outfield. His best position is center, though he throws well enough to play right as well.

Major League Batting Register

	BA	G	AB	R	H	2B	3B	HR	RBI	SB
81 AL	.167	59	126	17	21	3	0	6	13	2
82 AL	.253	104	324	47	82	17	1	14	48	2
83 AL	.269	137	484	50	130	24	5	17	55	9
84 AL	.280	112	350	42	98	23	0	14	43	5
85 AL	.241	139	502	70	121	28	2	14	68	6
86 AL	.265	139	388	59	103	22	4	15	47	2
87 AL	.234	75	184	30	43	10	0	8	25	1
87 NL	.238	15	21	2	5	2	0	0	1	2
88 AL	.304	146	507	100	154	38	1	24	94	2
89 AL	.250	152	579	77	145	24	3	15	80	8
90 AL	.271	127	450	65	122	28	0	20	63	3
91 AL	.276	150	572	86	158	33	0	25	85	6
92 AL	.143	20	63	1	9	1	0	0	2	0
93 AL	.220	107	382	37	84	19	0	20	53	0
94 AL	.247	56	198	27	49	14	1	5	31	2
Life	.258	1538	5130	710	1324	286	17	197	708	50
2 AVE	.232	93	330	38	77	19	1	14	48	1

RICKEY HENDERSON

Position: Outfield
Team: Oakland Athletics
Born: Dec. 25, 1958 Chicago, IL
Height: 5'10" **Weight:** 190 lbs.
Bats: right **Throws:** left
Acquired: Signed as a free agent, 12/93

Player Summary	
Fantasy Value	$19 to $22
Card Value	20¢ to 30¢
Will	find ways to reach
Can't	make strong throws
Expect	good leadoff power
Don't Expect	swipes crown

Even though his average plunged to a career low last summer, Henderson remained one of the game's top leadoff men. He scored 66 runs, collected 72 walks, and compiled a .411 on-base average. Blessed with a keen batting eye, he walks far more often than he fans, but he's just as capable of hitting homers. On Aug. 7, he hit the 66th leadoff homer of his career—as the first batter Kenny Rogers faced after his perfect game. Henderson's overall effort, however, was disappointing. He failed to hit lefties with his usual authority. Nor did Rickey run well: He slipped to 22 steals, a career low for a man who's led the AL 11 times. Henderson still is hardly ever caught stealing. His speed gives him great range in left field, but he has an inferior arm.

Major League Batting Register

	BA	G	AB	R	H	2B	3B	HR	RBI	SB
79 AL	.274	89	351	49	96	13	3	1	26	33
80 AL	.303	158	591	111	179	22	4	9	53	100
81 AL	.319	108	423	89	135	18	7	6	35	56
82 AL	.267	149	536	119	143	24	4	10	51	130
83 AL	.292	145	513	105	150	25	7	9	48	108
84 AL	.293	142	502	113	147	27	4	16	58	66
85 AL	.314	143	547	146	172	28	5	24	72	80
86 AL	.263	153	608	130	160	31	5	28	74	87
87 AL	.291	95	358	78	104	17	3	17	37	41
88 AL	.305	140	554	118	169	30	2	6	50	93
89 AL	.274	150	541	113	148	26	3	12	57	77
90 AL	.325	136	489	119	159	33	3	28	61	65
91 AL	.268	134	470	105	126	17	1	18	57	58
92 AL	.283	117	396	77	112	18	3	15	46	48
93 AL	.289	134	481	114	139	22	2	21	59	53
94 AL	.260	87	296	66	77	13	0	6	20	22
Life	.289	2080	7656	1652	2216	364	56	226	804	1117
3 AVE	.278	125	431	95	120	19	2	15	44	44

TOM HENKE

Position: Pitcher
Team: St. Louis Cardinals
Born: Dec. 21, 1957 Kansas City, MO
Height: 6'5" **Weight:** 225 lbs.
Bats: right **Throws:** right
Acquired: Signed as a free agent, 12/94

Player Summary	
Fantasy Value	$11 to $14
Card Value	6¢ to 10¢
Will	bank on hard stuff
Can't	fret about gophers
Expect	fine control
Don't Expect	high ERA

After increasing his save totals for two straight seasons, Henke had more than his share of setbacks last summer, for the Rangers. In May, two bulging discs in his back disabled him—the second time that's happened in 10 years—and recurring back problems bothered him even after his return. By the time the players struck Aug. 12, Henke had blown six saves—all by surrendering home runs—in 21 chances. A sinker-slider pitcher who also throws a forkball, he toyed with a sidearm forkball delivery during the spring. Henke in '94 averaged less than eight hits and three walks per nine innings and more than a K per frame. But the batting average against him last year was nearly 30 points higher than in 1993. Henke's slow delivery helps runners, and he is not much of a fielder.

Major League Pitching Register

	W	L	ERA	G	S	IP	H	ER	BB	SO
82 AL	1	0	1.15	8	0	15.2	14	2	8	9
83 AL	1	0	3.38	8	1	16.0	16	6	4	17
84 AL	1	1	6.35	25	2	28.1	36	20	20	25
85 AL	3	3	2.03	28	13	40.0	29	9	8	42
86 AL	9	5	3.35	63	27	91.1	63	34	32	118
87 AL	0	6	2.49	72	34	94.0	62	26	25	128
88 AL	4	4	2.91	52	25	68.0	60	22	24	66
89 AL	8	3	1.92	64	20	89.0	66	19	25	116
90 AL	2	4	2.17	61	32	74.2	58	18	19	75
91 AL	0	2	2.32	49	32	50.1	33	13	11	53
92 AL	3	2	2.26	57	34	55.2	40	14	22	46
93 AL	5	5	2.91	66	40	74.1	55	24	27	79
94 AL	3	6	3.79	37	15	38.0	33	16	12	39
Life	40	41	2.73	590	275	735.1	565	223	237	813
3 AVE	4	5	2.97	58	32	61.1	47	20	22	60

MIKE HENNEMAN

Position: Pitcher
Team: Detroit Tigers
Born: Dec. 11, 1961 St. Charles, MO
Height: 6'4" **Weight:** 205 lbs.
Bats: right **Throws:** right
Acquired: Third-round pick in 6/84 free-agent draft

Player Summary	
Fantasy Value	$7 to $9
Card Value	6¢ to 10¢
Will	seek 20-saves form
Can't	explain 1994 slump
Expect	best work on grass
Don't Expect	great control

After topping 20 saves in five of the six seasons preceding 1994, Henneman earned a reputation as a highly regarded closer. But that was before his control went south, forcing his game to fall apart. At the All-Star break, he had a 6.07 ERA, eight saves in 13 chances, and a 1-3 record—hardly closer credentials. He picked up the pace a bit before the strike a month later but still compiled nine-inning averages of 11 hits, four and one-half walks, and seven strikeouts. In previous years, Henneman mixed a fastball, a slider, and a forkball so well that he got ground outs, yielded less hits than innings, dominated right-handed hitters, and kept the ball in the park. Though not a power pitcher, he maintained a 2-1 ratio of strikeouts to walks and stranded 75 percent of the runners he inherited. It could be that his age, the 600-plus innings, and the seven straight years of 55-plus appearances have caught up to him.

Major League Pitching Register

	W	L	ERA	G	S	IP	H	ER	BB	SO
87 AL	11	3	2.98	55	7	96.2	86	32	30	75
88 AL	9	6	1.87	65	22	91.1	72	19	24	58
89 AL	11	4	3.70	60	8	90.0	84	37	51	69
90 AL	8	6	3.05	69	22	94.1	90	32	33	50
91 AL	10	2	2.88	60	21	84.1	81	27	34	61
92 AL	2	6	3.96	60	24	77.1	75	34	20	58
93 AL	5	3	2.64	63	24	71.2	69	21	32	58
94 AL	1	3	5.19	30	8	34.2	43	20	17	27
Life	57	33	3.12	462	136	640.1	600	222	241	456
3 AVE	3	4	3.78	55	20	65.2	68	28	25	51

BUTCH HENRY

Position: Pitcher
Team: Montreal Expos
Born: Oct. 7, 1968 El Paso, TX
Height: 6'1" **Weight:** 195 lbs.
Bats: left **Throws:** left
Acquired: Traded from Rockies for Kent Bottenfield, 7/93

Player Summary	
Fantasy Value	$1
Card Value	6¢ to 10¢
Will	paint the corners
Can't	avoid gopher balls
Expect	pinpoint control
Don't Expect	many whiffs

A healthy shot of confidence transformed Henry from a hanger-on into a heavyweight. Glad to escape the homer-happy confines of Mile High Stadium, he prospered in Montreal's pitcher-friendly park. For the Expos, he was 1994's version of 1993's Kirk Rueter: He was someone who came out of nowhere to give the team a much-needed lift. A control pitcher who doesn't throw hard, Henry is a sinker-slider specialist who mixes in an occasional curve. He tries to paint the plate, using both corners. He works from the stretch—even with the bases empty. Henry found that a lower arm angle on his delivery made his control even better in 1994. By strike time, he had yielded an average of one and one-half walks per nine innings. Over that same span, he had allowed eight hits while fanning about five and one-half hitters—giving him a ratio of three and one-half strikeouts per walk. Though he throws his share of gopher balls, many come with nobody on. He's not great with a glove or pickoff move, but Henry does help himself with a bat.

Major League Pitching Register

	W	L	ERA	G	CG	IP	H	ER	BB	SO
92 NL	6	9	4.02	28	2	165.2	185	74	41	96
93 NL	3	9	6.12	30	1	103.0	135	70	28	47
94 NL	8	3	2.43	24	0	107.1	97	29	20	70
Life	17	21	4.14	82	3	376.0	417	173	89	213
3 AVE	7	7	3.96	31	1	139.2	152	62	32	81

DOUG HENRY

Position: Pitcher
Team: New York Mets
Born: Dec. 10, 1963 Sacramento, CA
Height: 6'4" **Weight:** 185 lbs.
Bats: right **Throws:** right
Acquired: Traded from Brewers for Javier Gonzalez and a player to be named later, 11/94

· Player Summary ·
Fantasy Value $1
Card Value . . . . 5¢ to 7¢
Will. . . . . search for control
Can't . . . . reclaim closer job
Expect . . . . trouble vs. lefties
Don't Expect. . . . . many saves

Heading into the 1994 campaign, Henry had posted three straight seasons of at least 15 saves. He had worked 122 times over a two-year span and seemed assured of keeping his job as Milwaukee's closer. That was not to be, however. Beset by shoulder tendinitis during spring training, Henry had trouble getting untracked. He struggled, returned to the minors, and eventually returned as a middle reliever. Control, his biggest problem during the second half of 1993, remained elusive for the former Arizona State star. Without command of his fastball, his forkball, or his slider, Henry is mincemeat—especially on the first pitch. Though he yielded a hit per inning and dominated righties, he averaged six and one-half walks per nine innings— leaving him with more walks than strikeouts. Lefties ate him for lunch, and he threw too many gophers. Henry holds runners and fields his position, but his pitching jeopardizes his future. He had a 1.84 ERA and three saves in Triple-A last year.

Major League Pitching Register

	W	L	ERA	G	S	IP	H	ER	BB	SO
91 AL	2	1	1.00	32	15	36.0	16	4	14	28
92 AL	1	4	4.02	68	29	65.0	64	29	24	52
93 AL	4	4	5.56	54	17	55.0	67	34	25	38
94 AL	2	3	4.60	25	0	31.1	32	16	23	20
Life	9	12	3.99	179	61	187.1	179	83	86	138
3 AVE	3	4	4.69	52	15	55.0	59	29	27	39

PAT HENTGEN

Position: Pitcher
Team: Toronto Blue Jays
Born: Nov. 13, 1968 Detroit, MI
Height: 6'2" **Weight:** 200 lbs.
Bats: right **Throws:** right
Acquired: Fifth-round pick in 6/86 free-agent draft

Player Summary
Fantasy Value . . . . $18 to $21
Card Value . . . . 12¢ to 20¢
Will . . . . lead his staff
Can't . . . . prevent homers
Expect . . . . large win total
Don't Expect . . . . high ERA

For the last two seasons, Hentgen was the top winner on the Toronto staff. Last May 3, he fired a 1-0 two-hitter at Kansas City while fanning a club-record 14 hitters. He later ended a 10-game Blue Jay losing streak with a 5-0 three-hitter against Milwaukee June 29. A control pitcher, Hentgen in 1994 yielded three walks and eight hits per nine innings. He overpowered right-handed hitters and averaged seven and one-half strikeouts per game. Hentgen throws a low-90s fastball, an improving curve, a cut fastball, and a changeup. In 24 starts before the strike, he went all the way six times—tops among the Jays and tied for third-best in the AL. Hentgen induces lots of ground balls that turn into double plays, taking him out of jams. That's why opponents don't hit him for a high average with runners in scoring position. Though he's adequate on defense, Hentgen had problems holding runners until last year. Only 11 of the 21 runners who tried to steal against him before Aug. 12 succeeded.

Major League Pitching Register

	W	L	ERA	G	CG	IP	H	ER	BB	SO
91 AL	0	0	2.45	3	0	7.1	5	2	3	3
92 AL	5	2	5.36	28	0	50.1	49	30	32	39
93 AL	19	9	3.87	34	3	216.1	215	93	74	122
94 AL	13	8	3.40	24	6	174.2	158	66	59	147
Life	37	19	3.83	89	9	448.2	427	191	168	311
3 AVE	14	7	3.79	32	4	170.2	162	72	63	123

GIL HEREDIA

Position: Pitcher
Team: Montreal Expos
Born: Oct. 26, 1965 Nogales, AZ
Height: 6'1" **Weight:** 205 lbs.
Bats: right **Throws:** right
Acquired: Traded from Giants for Brett Jenkins, 8/92

Player Summary	
Fantasy Value	$3 to $5
Card Value	12¢ to 20¢
Will	show fine control
Can't	overpower hitters
Expect	many relief calls
Don't Expect	southpaw woes

When Heredia's pitches are working, opposing batters beat the ball into the ground with regularity. A sinker-slider pitcher who banks heavily on his forkball, Heredia doesn't throw hard. He succeeds by pitching to spots. By strike time last year, he had become an important middle man in the Montreal bullpen. Heredia allowed only one and one-half walks per nine innings, giving him a strikeout-to-walk ratio of almost 5-to-1. Though he yielded more hits than innings, Heredia offset that handicap by fanning an average of seven and one-half hitters over a nine-inning span. Used extensively as a starter early in his career, he seems to have found his niche in relief. He's capable of working several innings at a stint and handling both righty and lefty hitters. Though he's not much of a fielder, Heredia showed an improved pickoff move last summer. He doesn't get to hit much but knows what to do at the plate. The former University of Arizona standout once led the Pacific Coast League in ERA.

CARLOS HERNANDEZ

Position: Catcher
Team: Los Angeles Dodgers
Born: May 24, 1967 Bolivar, Venezuela
Height: 5'11" **Weight:** 185 lbs.
Bats: right **Throws:** right
Acquired: Signed as a free agent, 10/84

Player Summary	
Fantasy Value	$0
Card Value	6¢ to 10¢
Will	return as understudy
Can't	generate much power
Expect	hits vs. lefties
Don't Expect	stolen bases

Playing behind Mike Piazza is a thankless job. Hernandez handled the task well over the past two seasons but must have felt frustrated. After all, he had five .300 seasons—including a .345 performance at Triple-A Albuquerque in 1991—during his minor-league tenure. He does not offer Piazza's power, or anything approaching it, however. A first-pitch, fastball hitter who rarely walks or strokes extra-base hits, Hernandez did his best work against left-handed pitchers, batting .300 last year. He struggled against righties and also had trouble clearing the Mendoza Line with runners in scoring position and in late-inning pressure situations. Behind the plate, Hernandez throws well enough to nail about one-third of those who try to steal against him. He calls a good game and is generally regarded as a good handler of pitchers. He led several leagues in chances, putouts, assists, double plays, and errors. Hernandez could find a starting job soon. He started his pro career in 1985.

Major League Pitching Register

	W	L	ERA	G	S	IP	H	ER	BB	SO
91 NL	0	2	3.82	7	0	33.0	27	14	7	13
92 NL	2	3	4.23	20	0	44.2	44	21	20	22
93 NL	4	2	3.92	20	2	57.1	66	25	14	40
94 NL	6	3	3.46	39	0	75.1	85	29	13	62
Life	12	10	3.81	86	2	210.1	222	89	54	137
3 AVE	5	3	3.76	32	1	69.1	77	29	17	50

Major League Batting Register

	BA	G	AB	R	H	2B	3B	HR	RBI	SB
90 NL	.200	10	20	2	4	1	0	0	1	0
91 NL	.214	15	14	1	3	1	0	0	1	1
92 NL	.260	69	173	11	45	4	0	3	17	0
93 NL	.253	50	99	6	25	5	0	2	7	0
94 NL	.219	32	64	6	14	2	0	2	6	0
Life	.246	176	370	26	91	13	0	7	32	1

JEREMY HERNANDEZ

Position: Pitcher
Team: Florida Marlins
Born: July 7, 1966 Burbank, CA
Height: 6'6" **Weight:** 195 lbs.
Bats: right **Throws:** right
Acquired: Traded from Indians for Matt Turner, 4/94

Player Summary	
Fantasy Value.	$7 to $9
Card Value	6¢ to 10¢
Will	bank on forkball
Can't.	stop gopher balls
Expect	late-inning work
Don't Expect	control woes

When he first came to Florida, Hernandez needed some fine-tuning from manager Rene Lachemann. Once Hernandez got it, he clicked. He converted his first nine save opportunities after injury idled top Marlin closer Bryan Harvey April 25. But the injury bug eventually nailed Hernandez too. He went down for the year with two herniated discs in his neck. They have been surgically repaired since. A power pitcher who throws a forkball, a fastball, and a slurve (a slider-curve hybrid), Hernandez fans twice as many hitters as he walks. In 1994, he averaged about six hits per nine innings, induced a lot of ground outs, and yielded about five walks per game. A one-time standout at Cal State Northridge, he strands most of the runners he inherits, keeps baserunners close, and handles the glove well. He's capable of working several innings per stint—an attribute that should make him a great guy to insert for the seventh and eighth. Hernandez also showed last summer that he can do the job of a closer.

ROBERTO HERNANDEZ

Position: Pitcher
Team: Chicago White Sox
Born: Nov. 11, 1964 Santurce, Puerto Rico
Height: 6'4" **Weight:** 220 lbs.
Bats: right **Throws:** right
Acquired: Traded from Angels with Mark Doran for Mark Davis, 8/89

Player Summary	
Fantasy Value.	$30 to $35
Card Value	6¢ to 10¢
Will	return to '93 form
Can't	always keep control
Expect	lots of hard stuff
Don't Expect.	long-ball woes

After saving 38 games for the White Sox in 1993, Hernandez suddenly lost his control, his confidence, and his job. Switched to middle relief for a while, he spent considerable time with new bullpen coach Rick Peterson, a former psychology major and author of a book on the power of positive thinking. When Hernandez is on, he averages more than a strikeout an inning while yielding less hits than innings pitched. Until last year, he had displayed excellent control of his sinking fastball, hard slider, and forkball, averaging about two walks per nine innings. Hernandez keeps the ball in the park, controls the running game well, and fields everything hit his way. Opposing hitters managed only a .228 average against him in '93 and were even less effective in late-inning pressure situations and with runners in scoring position. Hernandez is young enough to learn the error of his ways. He figures to come back strong and should have little trouble regaining his role as No. 1 closer.

Major League Pitching Register

	W	L	ERA	G	S	IP	H	ER	BB	SO
91 NL	0	0	0.00	9	2	14.1	8	0	5	9
92 NL	1	4	4.17	26	1	36.2	39	17	11	25
93 NL	0	2	4.72	21	0	34.1	41	18	7	26
93 AL	6	5	3.14	49	8	77.1	75	27	27	44
94 NL	3	3	2.70	21	9	23.1	16	7	14	13
Life	10	14	3.34	126	20	186.0	179	69	64	117
2 AVE	4	6	3.76	48	5	74.2	78	31	23	48

Major League Pitching Register

	W	L	ERA	G	S	IP	H	ER	BB	SO
91 AL	1	0	7.80	9	0	15.0	18	13	7	6
92 AL	7	3	1.65	43	12	71.0	45	13	20	68
93 AL	3	4	2.29	70	38	78.2	66	20	20	71
94 AL	4	4	4.91	45	14	47.2	44	26	19	50
Life	15	11	3.05	167	64	212.1	173	72	66	195
3 AVE	5	4	2.89	59	23	72.2	58	23	22	70

XAVIER HERNANDEZ

Position: Pitcher
Team: Cincinnati Reds
Born: Aug. 16, 1965 Port Arthur, TX
Height: 6'2" **Weight:** 185 lbs.
Bats: left **Throws:** right
Acquired: Signed as a free agent, 12/94

Player Summary

Fantasy Value	$3 to $5
Card Value	5¢ to 7¢
Will	assume heavy workload
Can't	worry about '94 slump
Expect	great job vs. righties
Don't Expect	return to closing

Hernandez blamed his bad start last year for the Yankees on a mechanical flaw. His shoulder was flying open before his delivery, keeping his fastball high and outside against left-handed hitters. Another problem was an inconsistent forkball, his out pitch. He also throws a slider. He improved his game in July after Yankee pitching coach Billy Connors suggested that Hernandez move from the right side of the pitching rubber to the left. When everything is working, he is a control pitcher who's extremely difficult to hit. In 1993, he had a 4-1 ratio of strikeouts to walks, more strikeouts than innings pitched, and tremendous success against right-handed batters. While struggling with his mechanics last year, Hernandez was banged around. He still fanned more than eight men per nine innings but also averaged nearly 11 hits and five walks over the same span. That cost him his job as the Yankee closer. He holds runners and fields his position well.

Major League Pitching Register

	W	L	ERA	G	S	IP	H	ER	BB	SO
89 AL	1	0	4.76	7	0	22.2	25	12	8	7
90 NL	2	1	4.62	34	0	62.1	60	32	24	24
91 NL	2	7	4.71	32	3	63.0	66	33	32	55
92 NL	9	1	2.11	77	7	111.0	81	26	42	96
93 NL	4	5	2.61	72	9	96.2	75	28	28	101
94 AL	4	4	5.85	31	6	40.0	48	26	21	37
Life	22	18	3.57	253	25	395.2	355	157	155	320
3 AVE	6	4	3.09	64	8	88.1	75	30	33	83

OREL HERSHISER

Position: Pitcher
Team: Los Angeles Dodgers
Born: Sept. 16, 1958 Buffalo, NY
Height: 6'3" **Weight:** 192 lbs.
Bats: right **Throws:** right
Acquired: 17th-round pick in 6/79 free-agent draft

Player Summary

Fantasy Value	$7 to $9
Card Value	8¢ to 12¢
Will	depend upon control
Can't	complete his starts
Expect	experience
Don't Expect	consistency

Since his shoulder was surgically repaired in April 1990, Hershiser has not been the same. He's worked more than 660 innings since the surgery but has not shown the 1988 form that netted him a Cy Young Award and MVP honors in both the NLCS and the World Series. Inconsistency is his problem. After a strong start in 1994, he went 0-4 with a 6.69 ERA over a six-start stretch in June. A sinker-slider pitcher who also throws a changeup and a slow curve, Hershiser relies on changing speeds and pitch location. When he's right, his pitches produce ground balls. He is a control pitcher who allowed less than three walks per nine innings. He has trouble retiring lefties and is also victimized by baserunners. Hershiser has a very strong bat, can bunt, and is an agile fielder.

Major League Pitching Register

	W	L	ERA	G	CG	IP	H	ER	BB	SO
83 NL	0	0	3.38	8	0	8.0	7	3	6	5
84 NL	11	8	2.66	45	8	189.2	160	56	50	150
85 NL	19	3	2.03	36	9	239.2	179	54	68	157
86 NL	14	14	3.85	35	8	231.1	213	99	86	153
87 NL	16	16	3.06	37	10	264.2	247	90	74	190
88 NL	23	8	2.26	35	15	267.0	208	67	73	178
89 NL	15	15	2.31	35	8	256.2	226	66	77	178
90 NL	1	1	4.26	4	0	25.1	26	12	4	16
91 NL	7	2	3.46	21	0	112.0	112	43	32	73
92 NL	10	15	3.67	33	1	210.2	209	86	69	130
93 NL	12	14	3.59	33	5	215.2	201	86	72	141
94 NL	6	6	3.79	21	1	135.1	146	57	42	72
Life	134	102	3.00	343	65	2156.0	1934	719	653	1443
3 AVE	10	12	3.68	32	2	205.2	205	84	67	124

JOE HESKETH

Position: Pitcher
Team: Boston Red Sox
Born: Feb. 15, 1959 Lackawanna, NY
Height: 6'2" **Weight:** 170 lbs.
Bats: left **Throws:** left
Acquired: Signed as a free agent, 7/90

Player Summary	
Fantasy Value	$2 to $4
Card Value	5¢ to 7¢
Will	retire most lefties
Can't	thwart basestealers
Expect	ground-ball outs
Don't Expect	big K count

Before elbow and shoulder problems hampered his performance in midseason, Hesketh proved to be the surprise stopper for the '94 Red Sox. During the first four months, he halted losing streaks of 12, 11, and four games. Far more effective against left-handers, he is a sinker-slider pitcher who coaxes ground balls when his location is good. His control last year (about three and one-half walks per game) was better than it was the year before. Hesketh in '94 yielded about a hit per inning, maintained a 2-1 ratio of strikeouts to walks, and kept the ball in the park. For a lefty, he should enjoy more success in freezing baserunners. He also has occasional problems with his defense. In addition, Hesketh has a history of injuries that makes counting on him risky. He's been used as both a starter and reliever during his tenure in the majors.

Major League Pitching Register

	W	L	ERA	G	CG	IP	H	ER	BB	SO
84 NL	2	2	1.80	11	1	45.0	38	9	15	32
85 NL	10	5	2.49	25	2	155.1	125	43	45	113
86 NL	6	5	5.01	15	0	82.2	92	46	31	67
87 NL	0	0	3.14	18	0	28.2	23	10	15	31
88 NL	4	3	2.85	60	0	72.2	63	23	35	64
89 NL	6	4	5.77	43	0	48.1	54	31	26	44
90 NL	1	2	5.29	33	0	34.0	32	20	14	24
90 AL	0	4	3.51	12	0	25.2	37	10	11	26
91 AL	12	4	3.29	39	0	153.1	142	56	53	104
92 AL	8	9	4.36	30	1	148.2	162	72	58	104
93 AL	3	4	5.06	28	0	53.1	62	30	29	34
94 AL	8	5	4.26	25	0	114.0	117	54	46	83
Life	60	47	3.78	339	4	961.2	947	404	378	726
3 AVE	7	7	4.42	31	0	121.1	130	59	51	85

GREG HIBBARD

Position: Pitcher
Team: Seattle Mariners
Born: Sept. 13, 1964 New Orleans, LA
Height: 6' **Weight:** 190 lbs.
Bats: left **Throws:** left
Acquired: Signed as a free agent, 1/94

Player Summary	
Fantasy Value	$4 to $6
Card Value	6¢ to 10¢
Will	need healthy shoulder
Can't	rely on the strikeout
Expect	southpaws to struggle
Don't Expect	gopher woes

Seattle never got to savor its success at plucking Hibbard off the free-agent market. He suffered a major shoulder injury that kept him idle for virtually all of 1994. The four previous years, he was a starter who won in double figures. Mixing his trademark sinkerball with a curveball, a slider, and a changeup, Hibbard handcuffed left-handed hitters, kept the ball in the park, and got most of his outs on ground balls. He also did his best pitching in clutch situations, holding hitters to a .205 average in that department two years ago. In 1994, however, he allowed opposing batters to compile a .328 batting average and a .484 slugging percentage. Thanks to a tight delivery, Hibbard holds runners extremely well. He rarely even throws to first base. The University of Alabama product is not so staunch on other aspects of defense, however. He needs work on the fundamentals of fielding. Originally signed by the Royals, Hibbard began his pro career in 1986.

Major League Pitching Register

	W	L	ERA	G	CG	IP	H	ER	BB	SO
89 AL	6	7	3.21	23	2	137.1	142	49	41	55
90 AL	14	9	3.16	33	3	211.0	202	74	55	92
91 AL	11	11	4.31	32	5	194.0	196	93	57	71
92 AL	10	7	4.40	31	0	176.0	187	86	57	69
93 NL	15	11	3.96	31	1	191.0	209	84	47	82
94 AL	1	5	6.69	15	0	80.2	115	60	31	39
Life	57	50	4.05	165	11	990.0	1051	446	288	408
3 AVE	9	8	4.77	28	0	160.1	186	85	49	69

BRYAN HICKERSON

Position: Pitcher
Team: Chicago Cubs
Born: Oct. 13, 1963 Bemidji, MN
Height: 6'2" **Weight:** 195 lbs.
Bats: left **Throws:** left
Acquired: Claimed from Giants on waivers, 11/94

Player Summary	
Fantasy Value	$1
Card Value	5¢ to 7¢
Will	search for right role
Can't	prevent homers
Expect	better job vs. lefties
Don't Expect	more control woes

College degrees don't necessarily help. In 1987, Hickerson earned a degree in sports and exercise science from the University of Minnesota. In 1995, he's still trying to find his niche in the majors. For the last two years, he's been a spot starter as well as a middle reliever, often used to retire one or two lefties in key situations for San Francisco. The constant shuffling seems to have hurt. Hickerson had his best year in 1992, when used out of the bullpen in all but one of 61 appearances. A control pitcher who throws a rising fastball, a forkball, and a slider, he was not as sharp as usual last year. He gave up nearly 11 hits and three and one-half walks per nine innings and had trouble keeping the ball in the park. Even lefties—his usual patsies—lit him up. Hickerson allowed half his inherited runners to score and didn't show much as a hitter or fielder, though he froze potential basestealers. He's won some big starts in the past, but it looks as though his best role is in middle relief.

Major League Pitching Register

	W	L	ERA	G	S	IP	H	ER	BB	SO
91 NL	2	2	3.60	17	0	50.0	53	20	17	43
92 NL	5	3	3.09	61	0	87.1	74	30	21	68
93 NL	7	5	4.26	47	0	120.1	137	57	39	69
94 NL	4	8	5.40	28	1	98.1	118	59	38	59
Life	18	18	4.20	153	1	356.0	382	166	115	239
3 AVE	6	6	4.42	49	0	115.1	126	57	38	73

TED HIGUERA

Position: Pitcher
Team: Milwaukee Brewers
Born: Nov. 9, 1958 Los Mochis, Mexico
Height: 5'10" **Weight:** 180 lbs.
Bats: both **Throws:** left
Acquired: Purchased from Juarez of Mexican League, 9/83

Player Summary	
Fantasy Value	$0
Card Value	5¢ to 7¢
Will	need medical miracle
Can't	show old velocity
Expect	best work vs. lefties
Don't Expect	many wins

The Higuera story may not have a happy ending. Though he pitched six strong innings to beat the White Sox 13-4 last April 25, it was his only win of the strike-shortened season. The once-feared fastball was gone, forcing the former power pitcher to rely on the bite of his curve and motion of his changeup. By strike time, he had yielded more than 11 hits and five walks per nine innings and received a demotion to the Brewer bullpen. Though he still did a good job of stifling lefty hitters, Higuera was hit hard by right-handed batters. The one-time master of changing speeds was unable to scrape off the rust from spending 457 days on the disabled list, from 1991 to '93. Of course, that was after Higuera placed his signature on a guaranteed four-year contract worth $13 million. He is one of those guys who just couldn't be helped by rotator cuff surgery (1991). He isn't likely to make much of a comeback in 1995.

Major League Pitching Register

	W	L	ERA	G	CG	IP	H	ER	BB	SO
85 AL	15	8	3.90	32	7	212.1	186	92	63	127
86 AL	20	11	2.79	34	15	248.1	226	77	74	207
87 AL	18	10	3.85	35	14	261.2	236	112	87	240
88 AL	16	9	2.45	31	8	227.1	168	62	59	192
89 AL	9	6	3.46	22	2	135.1	125	52	48	91
90 AL	11	10	3.76	27	4	170.0	167	71	50	129
91 AL	3	2	4.46	7	0	36.1	37	18	10	33
93 AL	1	3	7.20	8	0	30.0	43	24	16	27
94 AL	1	5	7.06	17	0	58.2	74	46	36	35
Life	94	64	3.61	213	50	1380.0	1262	554	443	1081

GLENALLEN HILL

Position: Outfield
Team: Chicago Cubs
Born: March 22, 1965 Santa Cruz, CA
Height: 6'2" **Weight:** 205 lbs.
Bats: right **Throws:** right
Acquired: Traded from Indians for Candy Maldonado, 8/93

Player Summary

Fantasy Value.	$13 to $16
Card Value	5¢ to 7¢
Will	show some power
Can't	play field well
Expect	speed on bases
Don't Expect	great patience

Hill spent the first half of last year platooning in left field with Derrick May, but spent the second half filling in for the slumping Tuffy Rhodes in center. The added playing time agreed with Hill. He narrowly missed his first .300 season. Moreover, he showed signs of developing into the power-plus-speed prospect who collected 15 triples, 21 homers, and 21 steals on the Triple-A level in 1989. A one-time wild swinger at the plate, Hill reduced his whiff-walk ratio from 4-to-1 in 1993 to 2-to-1 last year. He hits both righties and lefties well but could improve his performance in late-inning and clutch situations. Hill could also improve as a baserunner, though he swiped 19 in 25 tries before the strike. Despite his speed, he's not a good defensive outfielder. His arm is neither powerful nor reliable, so left field is probably his best position. Hill rarely gets any assists, but he seldom makes errors.

Major League Batting Register

	BA	G	AB	R	H	2B	3B	HR	RBI	SB
89 AL	.288	19	52	4	15	0	0	1	7	2
90 AL	.231	84	260	47	60	11	3	12	32	8
91 AL	.253	35	99	14	25	5	2	3	11	2
91 AL	.258	72	221	29	57	8	2	8	25	6
92 AL	.241	102	369	38	89	16	1	18	49	9
93 AL	.224	66	174	19	39	7	2	5	25	7
93 NL	.345	31	87	14	30	7	0	10	22	1
94 NL	.297	89	269	48	80	12	1	10	38	19
Life	.258	463	1432	199	370	61	9	64	198	52
3 AVE	.268	108	336	46	90	16	1	16	50	15

KEN HILL

Position: Pitcher
Team: Montreal Expos
Born: Dec. 14, 1965 Lynn, MA
Height: 6'2" **Weight:** 175 lbs.
Bats: right **Throws:** right
Acquired: Traded from Cardinals for Andres Galarraga, 11/91

Player Summary

Fantasy Value.	$20 to $25
Card Value	10¢ to 15¢
Will	exceed 15 wins
Can't	prevent steals
Expect	great forkball
Don't Expect	control lapses

When the music stopped last August, Hill was a surprise Cy Young Award candidate. The NL's first 15-game winner, he and Greg Maddux each had a league-best 16 wins at strike time. Hill's strong start helped him. He had a 7-1 win against the Giants April 27, and it was his first complete game in more than a year. On July 7, Hill's 7-0 win over San Diego—his first shutout of '94—featured eight strikeouts and one walk. A first-time All-Star last year, he proved fully healed from a nagging groin injury that left him with a 9-7 mark for 1993 after a 6-0 start. He walked only two and one-half men per nine innings and dominated righty hitters. Hill also keeps the ball in the park. His arsenal includes a fastball, a curveball, and a forkball that ranks as his No. 1 pitch. He's not afraid to pitch inside—keeping hitters on their toes. He is a good fielder, and he can swing the bat. But Hill's slow delivery is an engraved invitation to basestealers.

Major League Pitching Register

	W	L	ERA	G	CG	IP	H	ER	BB	SO
88 NL	0	1	5.14	4	0	14.0	16	8	6	6
89 NL	7	15	3.80	33	2	196.2	186	83	99	112
90 NL	5	6	5.49	17	1	78.2	79	48	33	58
91 NL	11	10	3.57	30	0	181.1	147	72	67	121
92 NL	16	9	2.68	33	3	218.0	187	65	75	150
93 NL	9	7	3.23	28	2	183.2	163	66	74	90
94 NL	16	5	3.32	23	2	154.2	145	57	44	85
Life	64	53	3.50	168	10	1027.0	923	399	398	622
3 AVE	16	8	3.07	31	3	206.2	185	70	70	120

TREVOR HOFFMAN

Position: Pitcher
Team: San Diego Padres
Born: Oct. 13, 1967 Bellflower, CA
Height: 6'1" **Weight:** 200 lbs.
Bats: right **Throws:** right
Acquired: Traded from Marlins with Jose Martinez and Andres Beruman for Gary Sheffield and Rich Rodriguez, 6/93

Player Summary	
Fantasy Value	$30 to $35
Card Value	6¢ to 10¢
Will	overpower hitters
Can't	use experience
Expect	ineptness by righties
Don't Expect	round-trippers

Hoffman was the most effective pitcher on the San Diego staff last season. In his first 20 outings, he had a 1.71 ERA, eight saves, and 31 strikeouts in 26⅓ innings, getting off to a stalwart beginning. Make no mistake, he is a power pitcher. In addition to a 95-mph fastball, he throws a hard slider and a curve. Before he left the Marlins in 1993, he was also working on a forkball with mentor Bryan Harvey. Hoffman averaged nearly 11 strikeouts per nine innings, held opposing hitters below the Mendoza Line, and rarely allowed anyone to take him deep in 1994. He yielded roughly six hits and three walks per nine innings. He also stranded 70 percent of the runners he inherited. He helps himself with a good bat and a fine glove; he started out his pro career as an infielder. The Reds converted him to a pitcher in 1991, and he saved 20 games his first year on the mound. His brother, Glenn, was a major-league shortstop. Trevor has made big improvements in his pickoff move. He is developing into one of baseball's best closers.

Major League Pitching Register

	W	L	ERA	G	S	IP	H	ER	BB	SO
93 NL	4	6	3.90	67	5	90.0	80	39	39	79
94 NL	4	4	2.57	47	20	56.0	39	16	20	68
Life	8	10	3.39	114	25	146.0	119	55	59	147
2 AVE	5	6	3.28	67	17	84.2	67	31	34	87

CHRIS HOILES

Position: Catcher
Team: Baltimore Orioles
Born: March 20, 1965 Bowling Green, OH
Height: 6' **Weight:** 213 lbs.
Bats: right **Throws:** right
Acquired: Traded from Tigers with Cesar Mejia and Robinson Garces for Fred Lynn, 9/88

Player Summary	
Fantasy Value	$16 to $19
Card Value	8¢ to 12¢
Will	produce power
Can't	run to save his life
Expect	All-Star performance
Don't Expect	big first half

For the second year in a row, Hoiles got off to a slow start. In 1993, he regrouped to finish with a .310 mark. Last year, the strike short-circuited any hope of a similar comeback. He did manage to lift his mark from .233 on July 1 to .247 at the Aug. 12 strike date. He also slugged 19 homers in 99 games. More productive against left-handers, Hoiles hits with power to all fields. He hits more home runs than doubles, but who's complaining? He also shows enough patience to post a surprisingly high on-base percentage (.371 at strike time last year). Catchers who can hit 30 homers are rare, but he could have done it two years in a row (1992 and '93) had injuries not interfered. He runs with the speed of a snail. Behind the plate, Hoiles calls a good game, prevents wild pitches, and nails about one-third of runners who try to steal against him. He's also one of the league's best at blocking the plate. Hoiles is definitely overdue for an All-Star selection.

Major League Batting Register

	BA	G	AB	R	H	2B	3B	HR	RBI	SB
89 AL	.111	6	9	0	1	1	0	0	1	0
90 AL	.190	23	63	7	12	3	0	1	6	0
91 AL	.243	107	341	36	83	15	0	11	31	0
92 AL	.274	96	310	49	85	10	1	20	40	0
93 AL	.310	126	419	80	130	28	0	29	82	1
94 AL	.247	99	332	45	82	10	0	19	53	2
Life	.267	457	1474	217	393	67	1	80	213	3
3 AVE	.276	120	399	64	110	17	0	25	66	1

DAVE HOLLINS

Position: Third base; outfield
Team: Philadelphia Phillies
Born: May 25, 1966 Buffalo, NY
Height: 6'1" **Weight:** 195 lbs.
Bats: both **Throws:** right
Acquired: Rule 5 draft pick from Padres, 12/89

Player Summary	
Fantasy Value	$14 to $17
Card Value	10¢ to 15¢
Will	hit the long ball
Can't	play his position
Expect	patience at bat
Don't Expect	good lefty bat

An extremely intense competitor with a good power stroke, Hollins had his problems last summer. He broke a bone in his left hand during a head-first slide in May, then suffered a broken wrist on the day he returned, July 23. He also vetoed Philadelphia management's plan to move him from third base—where he made 11 errors in the first 40 games—to right field. He would be less detrimental in the outfield. He is a disaster at the hot corner, perhaps because of his hand and wrist injuries. A cross-diamond move to first base seems a possibility. Though he's a better right-handed hitter, Hollins has the ability to hit with opposite-field power from both sides of the plate. He has good knowledge of the strike zone and is willing to wait for walks, though he still strikes out more than 100 times a season. A good run-producer who delivers with runners in scoring position, he had consecutive 93-RBI years in 1992 and 1993. He doesn't steal much but takes extra bases whenever possible.

DARREN HOLMES

Position: Pitcher
Team: Colorado Rockies
Born: April 25, 1966 Asheville, NC
Height: 6' **Weight:** 200 lbs.
Bats: right **Throws:** right
Acquired: First-round pick from Brewers in 11/92 expansion draft

Player Summary	
Fantasy Value	$2 to $4
Card Value	6¢ to 10¢
Will	try for comeback
Can't	always find zone
Expect	reliance on heat
Don't Expect	long-ball woes

Going into the 1994 season, Holmes had hoped to maintain the momentum he created during the second half of 1993. Instead, he endured two stints on the DL with pain in his pitching elbow and had to spend time in the minors for the second year in a row. That was not how he had planned it. He came off the '93 campaign with a 1.08 ERA over his last 22 outings and 22 saves in 23 tries, giving him a team-best 25—not bad for a ballclub that won only 67 games. When he's healthy, he relies on his heater as his No. 1 pitch, blending in a slider and a curve to keep hitters guessing. He usually averages three walks and eight strikeouts per nine innings, keeps the ball in the park, and yields less hits than innings pitched. Holmes dominates right-handed hitters and is tough with runners in scoring position. He also knows how to field and keep baserunners from straying too far. The Holmes we saw last year is not the same hurler who had 31 saves combined in 1992 and '93. Holmes needs to prove himself again.

Major League Batting Register

	BA	G	AB	R	H	2B	3B	HR	RBI	SB
90 NL	.184	72	114	14	21	0	0	5	15	0
91 NL	.298	56	151	18	45	10	2	6	21	1
92 NL	.270	156	586	104	158	28	4	27	93	9
93 NL	.273	143	543	104	148	30	4	18	93	2
94 NL	.222	44	162	28	36	7	1	4	26	1
Life	.262	471	1556	268	408	75	11	60	248	13
3 AVE	.263	120	452	82	119	23	3	17	74	4

Major League Pitching Register

	W	L	ERA	G	S	IP	H	ER	BB	SO
90 NL	0	1	5.19	14	0	17.1	15	10	11	19
91 AL	1	4	4.72	40	3	76.1	90	40	27	59
92 AL	4	4	2.55	41	6	42.1	35	12	11	31
93 NL	3	3	4.05	62	25	66.2	56	30	20	60
94 NL	0	3	6.35	29	3	28.1	35	20	24	33
Life	8	15	4.36	186	37	231.0	231	112	93	202
2 AVE	4	4	3.47	52	16	54.2	46	21	16	46

RICK HONEYCUTT

Position: Pitcher
Team: Texas Rangers
Born: June 29, 1954 Chattanooga, TN
Height: 6'1" **Weight:** 190 lbs.
Bats: left **Throws:** left
Acquired: Signed as a free agent, 11/93

Player Summary	
Fantasy Value	$0
Card Value	5¢ to 7¢
Will	hope to hang on
Can't	get lefties out
Expect	decent control
Don't Expect	major comeback

Is father time catching up with Honeycutt? Although his control was good, he yielded an average of over 13 hits per nine innings—worst on the Texas staff. That was tough to digest for a pitcher who usually allows less hits than innings pitched. Lefties ate him alive last year, compiling a .400-plus batting average. Righties found him an easy mark as well. A sinker-slider pitcher who also throws a cut fastball, Honeycutt had been one of the league's most effective set-up men. He led the AL with 20 holds for Oakland in 1993. Honeycutt is also known for keeping runners close and fielding his position.

Major League Pitching Register

	W	L	ERA	G	S	IP	H	ER	BB	SO
77 AL	0	1	4.34	10	0	29.0	26	14	11	17
78 AL	5	11	4.89	26	0	134.1	150	73	49	50
79 AL	11	12	4.04	33	0	194.0	201	87	67	83
80 AL	10	17	3.94	30	0	203.1	221	89	60	79
81 AL	11	6	3.31	20	0	127.2	120	47	17	40
82 AL	5	17	5.27	30	0	164.0	201	96	54	64
83 AL	14	8	2.42	25	0	174.2	168	47	37	56
83 NL	2	3	5.77	9	0	39.0	46	25	13	18
84 NL	10	9	2.84	29	0	183.2	180	58	51	75
85 NL	8	12	3.42	31	1	142.0	141	54	49	67
86 NL	11	9	3.32	32	0	171.0	164	63	45	100
87 NL	2	12	4.59	27	0	115.2	133	59	45	92
87 AL	1	4	5.32	7	0	23.2	25	14	9	10
88 AL	3	2	3.50	55	7	79.2	74	31	25	47
89 AL	2	2	2.35	64	12	76.2	56	20	26	52
90 AL	2	2	2.70	63	7	63.1	46	19	22	38
91 AL	2	4	3.58	43	0	37.2	37	15	20	26
92 AL	1	4	3.69	54	3	39.0	41	16	10	32
93 AL	1	4	2.81	52	1	41.2	30	13	20	21
94 AL	1	2	7.20	42	1	25.0	37	20	9	18
Life	102	141	3.75	682	32	2065.0	2097	860	639	985
2 AVE	1	4	3.24	53	2	40.1	36	15	15	27

TOM HOWARD

Position: Outfield
Team: Cincinnati Reds
Born: Dec. 11, 1964 Middletown, OH
Height: 6'2" **Weight:** 200 lbs.
Bats: both **Throws:** right
Acquired: Traded from Indians for Randy Milligan, 8/93

Player Summary	
Fantasy Value	$1
Card Value	5¢ to 7¢
Will	serve as swing man
Can't	handle all righties
Expect	speed off bench
Don't Expect	defensive woes

A perfect fourth outfielder, Howard is a switch-hitter who can play all three spots, deliver a pinch hit, drop a bunt, and even hit an occasional long ball. Though he's much more productive from the left side, he'd improve his overall numbers by showing more patience at the plate. He seldom walks, leaving him with a lackluster 3-1 ratio of strikeouts to bases on balls. Howard's value off the bench is demonstrated by his .357 average in late-inning pressure spots last year before the strike. He thrives on low fastballs. Though he once swiped 27 bases in Triple-A, he doesn't steal much anymore. He still has the speed to succeed when he tries. That speed also gives him range that is adequate enough to play center field. Because his throwing arm is better than most other center fielders, Howard also makes a fine fill-in in right. He began his pro career in 1986, and he played for the Padres and Indians before coming to Cincinnati.

Major League Batting Register

	BA	G	AB	R	H	2B	3B	HR	RBI	SB
90 NL	.273	20	44	4	12	2	0	0	0	0
91 NL	.249	106	281	30	70	12	3	4	22	10
92 NL	.333	5	3	1	1	0	0	0	0	0
92 AL	.277	117	358	36	99	15	2	2	32	15
93 AL	.236	74	178	26	42	7	0	3	23	5
93 NL	.277	38	141	22	39	8	3	4	13	5
94 NL	.264	83	178	24	47	11	0	5	24	4
Life	.262	443	1183	143	310	55	8	18	114	39
3 AVE	.266	117	310	40	82	15	2	5	34	10

STEVE HOWE

Position: Pitcher
Team: New York Yankees
Born: March 10, 1958 Pontiac, MI
Height: 5'11" **Weight:** 196 lbs.
Bats: left **Throws:** left
Acquired: Signed as a free agent, 12/92

Player Summary	
Fantasy Value	$8 to $11
Card Value	5¢ to 7¢
Will	stifle lefty hitters
Can't	keep himself healthy
Expect	superb control
Don't Expect	homer problem

Regular work did wonders for Howe last summer. Blending his 92-mph fastball with a slider, a changeup, and a curve gave him a powerful arsenal, as he posted 10-plus saves for the first time since 1983. Seven suspensions for substance abuse plus 12 years of nagging injuries have been factors in Howe's inability to recapture his 1980 Rookie of the Year form. He flourished last year, however, averaging only one and one-half walks and less than six and one-half hits per nine innings, holding hitters to an average below .200, and playing Scrooge with the gopher ball. Howe tends to get stale with long layoffs, and with lots of work he was the most effective pitcher on the Yankee staff. He converted 15 of 19 save opportunities and stranded 68 percent of inherited runners. Howe pitched for the Dodgers, Twins, and Rangers before joining the Yankees.

Major League Pitching Register

	W	L	ERA	G	S	IP	H	ER	BB	SO
80 NL	7	9	2.66	59	17	84.2	83	25	22	39
81 NL	5	3	2.50	41	8	54.0	51	15	18	32
82 NL	7	5	2.08	66	13	99.1	87	23	17	49
83 NL	4	7	1.44	46	18	68.2	55	11	12	52
85 NL	1	1	4.91	19	3	22.0	30	12	5	11
85 AL	2	3	6.16	13	0	19.0	28	13	7	10
87 AL	3	3	4.31	24	1	31.1	33	15	8	19
91 AL	3	1	1.68	37	3	48.1	39	9	7	34
92 AL	3	0	2.45	20	6	22.0	9	6	3	12
93 AL	3	5	4.97	51	4	50.2	58	28	10	19
94 AL	3	0	1.80	40	15	40.0	28	8	7	18
Life	41	37	2.75	416	88	540.0	501	165	116	295
2 AVE	4	3	3.30	54	13	53.1	49	20	10	22

JAY HOWELL

Position: Pitcher
Team: Texas Rangers
Born: Nov. 26, 1955 Miami, FL
Height: 6'3" **Weight:** 205 lbs.
Bats: right **Throws:** right
Acquired: Signed as a free agent, 1/94

Player Summary	
Fantasy Value	$1
Card Value	5¢ to 7¢
Will	seek better numbers
Can't	avoid the long ball
Expect	middle relief roles
Don't Expect	success without curve

A few bad outings can really mess up a guy's ERA. Hit hard early last year, Howell couldn't bring his ERA back to a respectable level before the players walked. He did start throwing strikes again after he rediscovered his patented curve, a pitch that had been vacationing early in the campaign. Though the veteran right-hander also throws a fastball, a slider, and a circle change, the curve is his No. 1 pitch. Even at his age, Howell is a workhorse capable of answering the bell often. He doesn't get many strikeouts but normally yields about a hit per inning and three walks per nine innings. Howell is most effective against right-handed hitters. He keeps a close eye on baserunners, who try to take advantage of his high-kicking windup.

Major League Pitching Register

	W	L	ERA	G	S	IP	H	ER	BB	SO
80 NL	0	0	13.50	5	0	3.1	8	5	0	1
81 NL	2	0	4.84	10	0	22.1	23	12	10	10
82 AL	2	3	7.71	6	0	28.0	42	24	13	21
83 AL	1	5	5.38	19	0	82.0	89	49	35	61
84 AL	9	4	2.69	61	7	103.2	86	31	34	109
85 AL	9	8	2.85	63	29	98.0	98	31	31	68
86 AL	3	6	3.38	38	16	53.1	53	20	23	42
87 AL	3	4	5.89	36	16	44.1	48	29	21	35
88 NL	5	3	2.08	50	21	65.0	44	15	21	70
89 NL	5	3	1.58	56	28	79.2	60	14	22	55
90 NL	5	5	2.18	45	16	66.0	59	16	20	59
91 NL	6	5	3.18	44	16	51.0	39	18	11	40
92 NL	1	3	1.54	41	4	46.2	41	8	18	36
93 NL	3	3	2.31	54	0	58.1	48	15	16	37
94 AL	4	1	5.44	40	2	43.0	44	26	16	22
Life	58	53	3.34	568	155	844.2	782	313	291	666
3 AVE	3	2	3.24	50	2	55.1	50	20	19	35

JOHN HUDEK

Position: Pitcher
Team: Houston Astros
Born: Aug. 8, 1966 Tampa, FL
Height: 6'1" **Weight:** 200 lbs.
Bats: both **Throws:** right
Acquired: Claimed from Tigers on waivers, 7/93

Player Summary	
Fantasy Value.	$18 to $21
Card Value	12¢ to 20¢
Will	blaze ball
Can't	always find plate
Expect	success as closer
Don't Expect	shyness

Hudek didn't bring glittering credentials to Houston's 1994 spring training camp. He had allowed 323 walks in his 427⅔ minor-league innings. But he had won *Baseball America's* honors as Winter League Player of the Year after converting 23 of 24 save opportunities in Venezuela. After making an adjustment in spring training—substituting a leg tuck for his former slide-step delivery—Hudek became a sensation. With three-tenths of a second shaved off his delivery time, his 95-mph fastball seemed even faster. By May, he'd replaced Mitch Williams as the Astro closer. Two months later, Hudek became the first pitcher to make an All-Star team before posting his first big-league win. At the break, he had a 1.97 ERA and 15 saves. For the year, he held opponents to a .174 mark. Though he had some control trouble and threw a few gopher balls, Hudek stranded most runners he inherited, kept the running game in check, and stamped himself as a possible star. The Florida Southern product was with two Triple-A clubs in 1993, going 1-3 with a 5.82 ERA at Toledo and 3-1 with a 3.79 ERA at Tucson.

Major League Pitching Register

	W	L	ERA	G	S	IP	H	ER	BB	SO
94 NL	0	2	2.97	42	16	39.1	24	13	18	39
Life	0	2	2.97	42	16	39.1	24	13	18	39

REX HUDLER

Position: Infield; outfield
Team: California Angels
Born: Sept. 2, 1960 Tempe, AZ
Height: 6' **Weight:** 195 lbs.
Bats: right **Throws:** right
Acquired: Signed as a free agent, 4/94

Player Summary	
Fantasy Value	$1 to $3
Card Value	5¢ to 7¢
Will	play anywhere
Can't	show top power
Expect	hustle at all times
Don't Expect	average over .300

Because of his versatility, Hudler has played professional baseball since 1978. He's played everywhere but pitcher and catcher in the major leagues and still has time to complete the cycle. His .298 average for the Angels last year was a career high, along with the eight homers he delivered in only 124 at bats. He also hit .381 with runners in scoring position and .307 against lefties—making him an ideal pinch hitter when runners reached against southpaws. He still has enough speed to steal on occasion and is fully capable of beating out a drag bunt. Hudler also sweetens his average with infield hits. Second base is his best position, but he's also comfortable in the outfield. "Wonder Dog" is an all-out hustler, making diving catches others wouldn't attempt. Hudler has fans everywhere he has played. He is among the handful of players who made successful returns to the majors after playing in Japan.

Major League Batting Register

	BA	G	AB	R	H	2B	3B	HR	RBI	SB
84 AL	.143	9	7	2	1	1	0	0	0	0
85 AL	.157	20	51	4	8	0	1	0	1	0
86 AL	.000	14	1	1	0	0	0	0	0	1
88 NL	.273	77	216	38	59	14	2	4	14	29
89 NL	.245	92	155	21	38	7	0	6	13	15
90 NL	.282	93	220	31	62	11	2	7	22	18
91 NL	.227	101	207	21	47	10	2	1	15	12
92 NL	.245	61	98	17	24	4	0	3	5	2
94 AL	.298	56	124	17	37	8	0	8	20	2
Life	.256	523	1079	152	276	55	7	29	90	79

MIKE HUFF

Position: Outfield
Team: Toronto Blue Jays
Born: Aug. 11, 1963 Honolulu, HI
Height: 6'1" **Weight:** 190 lbs.
Bats: right **Throws:** right
Acquired: Traded from White Sox for Domingo Martinez, 3/94

Player Summary	
Fantasy Value	$1 to $3
Card Value	5¢ to 7¢
Will	make good contact
Can't	produce much power
Expect	good work in field
Don't Expect	many swipes

When Carlos Delgado flunked his 1994 trial as Toronto's left fielder, Huff stepped in. Acquired as a reserve, the spray-hitting Northwestern graduate finished with the highest average of his brief big-league career. Though he doesn't show much power, Huff makes good contact, walking as much as he strikes out. He hits well against both left-handed and right-handed pitching, delivers with runners in scoring position, and does his best work in late-inning pressure situations. His .304 finish was no surprise to Huff, a five-time .300 hitter in the minors. The Blue Jays were especially pleased with his on-base percentage of .392—a figure that could rise if Huff worked pitchers for more walks. Though he runs well, he rarely steals. Instead, he shows his speed in the outfield, where he's a top-quality defensive player. Because of his great range, Huff is best in center, though he also throws well enough to play right. He could be a late bloomer, getting more playing time in 1995.

Major League Batting Register

	BA	G	AB	R	H	2B	3B	HR	RBI	SB
89 NL	.200	12	25	4	5	1	0	1	2	0
91 AL	.251	102	243	42	61	10	2	3	25	14
92 AL	.209	60	115	13	24	5	0	0	8	1
93 AL	.182	43	44	4	8	2	0	1	6	1
94 AL	.304	80	207	31	63	15	3	3	25	2
Life	.254	297	634	94	161	33	5	8	66	18

TIM HULETT

Position: Second base; third base
Team: Baltimore Orioles
Born: Jan. 12, 1960 Springfield, IL
Height: 6' **Weight:** 185 lbs.
Bats: right **Throws:** right
Acquired: Signed as a free agent, 11/88

Player Summary	
Fantasy Value	$0
Card Value	5¢ to 7¢
Will	remain on bench
Can't	steal too often
Expect	good clutch bat
Don't Expect	top glove

Despite an off-year at the plate in 1994, Hulett remains one of baseball's best utility infielders. He's filled that role in 10 of his 11 big-league seasons, with the sole exception of 1986, when he hit 17 homers as the regular third baseman for the White Sox. Even his '94 slump did not stop him from hitting .300 against left-handed pitching and in late-inning pressure situations. He struggled against righties, though, and fanned twice as much as he walked. A one-time power hitter who lunged for fastballs out of the strike zone, he has cut down on his swing. He rarely runs, has little power, and has limited range, but his ability to play several spots satisfactorily keeps Hulett in the majors. He's best defensively at third base, where he can show off his strong arm, but the South Florida product can also turn the double play from either side of second.

Major League Batting Register

	BA	G	AB	R	H	2B	3B	HR	RBI	SB
83 AL	.200	6	5	0	1	0	0	0	0	1
84 AL	.000	8	7	1	0	0	0	0	0	1
85 AL	.268	141	395	52	106	19	4	5	37	6
86 AL	.231	150	520	53	120	16	5	17	44	4
87 AL	.217	68	240	20	52	10	0	7	28	0
89 AL	.278	33	97	12	27	5	0	3	18	0
90 AL	.255	53	153	16	39	7	1	3	16	1
91 AL	.204	79	206	29	42	9	0	7	18	0
92 AL	.289	57	142	11	41	7	2	2	21	0
93 AL	.300	85	260	40	78	15	0	2	23	1
94 AL	.228	36	92	11	21	2	1	2	15	0
Life	.249	716	2117	245	527	90	13	48	220	14

DAVID HULSE

Position: Outfield
Team: Texas Rangers
Born: Feb. 25, 1968 San Angelo, TX
Height: 5'11" **Weight:** 170 lbs.
Bats: left **Throws:** left
Acquired: 13th-round pick in 6/90 free-agent draft

Player Summary	
Fantasy Value.	$6 to $8
Card Value	6¢ to 10¢
Will	play solid defense
Can't	poke the long ball
Expect	good show of speed
Don't Expect	patience at bat

After opening 1994 as the Texas center fielder and leadoff man, Hulse ran into problems. He encountered vision problems after getting new contact lenses before a road trip that started April 29. The once-selective hitter went into a slump marked by strikeouts and two-pitch at bats. Eventually, the frustrated Rangers returned him to Triple-A Oklahoma City, where he batted .283 with no homers, six RBI, 10 runs, 21 Ks, and six walks in 99 at bats. As a rookie in 1993, he finished his first season with a .290 average. Hulse also walked more often than he fanned that year. He should walk more, but he is a first-pitch fastball hitter who likes to pull the trigger. He swiped 29 bases as a rookie and would've done better if not for a second-half hamstring injury. His speed gives him great range in center, where he grabs balls in the gap and outruns drives others couldn't reach. The arm is only average, however. Hulse needs to show he can hit lefties and work his way on base with walks. Until then, his leadoff status will be in doubt.

Major League Batting Register

	BA	G	AB	R	H	2B	3B	HR	RBI	SB
92 AL	.304	32	92	14	28	4	0	0	2	3
93 AL	.290	114	407	71	118	9	10	1	29	29
94 AL	.255	77	310	58	79	8	4	1	19	18
Life	.278	223	809	143	225	21	14	2	50	50
2 AVE	.272	111	422	76	115	10	8	1	28	27

TODD HUNDLEY

Position: Catcher
Team: New York Mets
Born: May 27, 1969 Martinsville, VA
Height: 5'11" **Weight:** 185 lbs.
Bats: both **Throws:** right
Acquired: Second-round pick in 6/87 free-agent draft

Player Summary	
Fantasy Value.	$5 to $7
Card Value	6¢ to 10¢
Will	show some power
Can't	hit for average
Expect	strong throwing
Don't Expect	many walks

Though it took more than three years, Hundley finally started capitalizing on his immense promise last summer. After letting 27 straight runners steal against him in '93, he nailed seven of the first 15 last year. He had the first two-homer game of his career May 1, giving him five in six games, and hit another pair—one from each side of the plate—June 18. After practicing with a contraption that involved hitting ping-pong balls with a broomstick, Hundley stopped swinging at bad balls. He still fans three times more than he walks and struggles against southpaws. His offensive advancement seemed to give a lift to his defense. By July, his game-calling and throwing had improved dramatically. He nailed 34 percent of potential basestealers last season—a big increase from his 22 percent success rate of 1993. His power, coupled with his improved defense, makes him a valuable young receiver. If he keeps improving, Todd could follow in father Randy's All-Star footsteps.

Major League Batting Register

	BA	G	AB	R	H	2B	3B	HR	RBI	SB
90 NL	.209	36	67	8	14	6	0	0	2	0
91 NL	.133	21	60	5	8	0	1	1	7	0
92 NL	.209	123	358	32	75	17	0	7	32	3
93 NL	.228	130	417	40	95	17	2	11	53	1
94 NL	.237	91	291	45	69	10	1	16	42	2
Life	.219	401	1193	130	261	50	4	35	136	6
3 AVE	.225	127	395	45	89	16	1	14	48	2

BRIAN HUNTER

Position: First base; outfield
Team: Cincinnati Reds
Born: March 4, 1968   El Toro, CA
Height: 6'   **Weight:** 195 lbs.
Bats: right   **Throws:** left
Acquired: Traded from Pirates for Micah Franklin, 7/94

Player Summary	
Fantasy Value	$2 to $4
Card Value	6¢ to 10¢
Will	feast on fastballs
Can't	stop striking out
Expect	pretty good power
Don't Expect	any speed

If he ever masters the strike zone, Hunter could become one of baseball's most productive sluggers. He had a career-high 15 homers in 256 at bats last year but fanned four times more often than he walked. Used against right-handed pitching for the first time, the former Atlanta platoon first baseman produced a respectable .251 average. Unfortunately, he limped home with a .198 mark against lefties—previously regarded as his bread-and-butter. Still, look for him to vie for platoon work in '95. Though Hunter was hardly a great clutch hitter, he did deliver two first-half grand slams in 1994. When he sees a fastball he likes, he generates enormous power with his quick wrists. He's not much of a basestealer, however, and has never been mistaken for Rickey Henderson on the basepaths. Hunter's lack of speed and below-average throwing arm prompted his transfer from left field to first base in 1989. He'll never win a Gold Glove at the new position, where he made five errors in 60 games last summer.

Major League Batting Register

	BA	G	AB	R	H	2B	3B	HR	RBI	SB
91 NL	.251	97	271	32	68	16	1	12	50	0
92 NL	.239	102	238	34	57	13	2	14	41	1
93 NL	.138	37	80	4	11	3	1	0	8	0
94 NL	.234	85	256	34	60	16	1	15	57	0
Life	.232	321	845	104	196	48	5	41	156	1
2 AVE	.236	111	299	41	71	18	2	18	61	1

TIM HYERS

Position: First base
Team: San Diego Padres
Born: Oct. 3, 1971   Atlanta, GA
Height: 6'1"   **Weight:** 195 lbs.
Bats: left   **Throws:** left
Acquired: Rule 5 draft pick from Blue Jays, 12/93

Player Summary	
Fantasy Value	$1
Card Value	12¢ to 20¢
Will	smack line drives
Can't	produce any power
Expect	stalwart fielding
Don't Expect	hits vs. lefties

Last spring, at age 22, Hyers jumped from Double-A to the big leagues as a platoon first baseman. Used almost exclusively against right-handed pitching, he showed a good line-drive stroke and ability to make contact. He seldom walks, strikes out, or hits the ball over the fence. He's still looking for his first big-league homer—even though he batted 118 times last year. Hyers did his best hitting with runners in scoring position but needs to improve his performance in late-inning pressure situations. He has some speed for a first baseman and succeeded on each of his three steal tries last summer. An accomplished fielder, Hyers has led several minor leagues in chances, putouts, assists, double plays, and fielding percentage. Because of his defensive prowess, plus the fact that he's a left-handed line-drive hitter, Hyers has been compared to Mark Grace; the jury is still out. Hyers batted .255 with one homer and five RBI last year in Triple-A. He batted .306 with three homers, 61 RBI, 53 walks, and 51 strikeouts in 487 at bats at Double-A Knoxville in 1993.

Major League Batting Register

	BA	G	AB	R	H	2B	3B	HR	RBI	SB
94 NL	.254	52	118	13	30	3	0	0	7	3
Life	.254	52	118	13	30	3	0	0	7	3

BO JACKSON

Position: Outfield
Team: California Angels
Born: Nov. 30, 1962 Bessemer, AL
Height: 6'1" **Weight:** 235 lbs.
Bats: right **Throws:** right
Acquired: Signed as a free agent, 1/94

Player Summary	
Fantasy Value	$7 to $9
Card Value	15¢ to 20¢
Will	hit big flies
Can't	avoid strikeouts
Expect	at bats vs. lefties
Don't Expect	a Gold Glove

With Chili Davis entrenched as its DH, California's signing of Bo Jackson came as a surprise. But the man with the artificial hip didn't disappoint. Used mostly as a platoon left fielder with lefty-hitting rookie Jim Edmonds, Jackson delivered a career-best .279 average and clubbed 13 homers in 201 at bats. His best game was a five-RBI outburst against the Tigers May 26. He batted .310 with runners in scoring position, but he remains an all-or-nothing hitter who fanned almost four times per walk. He has little trouble with off-speed pitches but has never met a high, inside fastball he didn't like. The one-time 20-20 man can't run much anymore—thanks to the football injury—but is still mobile enough to survive in left field without embarrassing himself. And his powerful throwing arm is as good as ever. Jackson isn't likely to repeat his 30-homer, 100-RBI season of 1989, but he'll still contribute power.

Major League Batting Register

	BA	G	AB	R	H	2B	3B	HR	RBI	SB
86 AL	.207	25	82	9	17	2	1	2	9	3
87 AL	.235	116	396	46	93	17	2	22	53	10
88 AL	.246	124	439	63	108	16	4	25	68	27
89 AL	.256	135	515	86	132	15	6	32	105	26
90 AL	.272	111	405	74	110	16	1	28	78	15
91 AL	.225	23	71	8	16	4	0	3	14	0
93 AL	.232	85	284	32	66	9	0	16	45	0
94 AL	.279	75	201	23	56	7	0	13	43	1
Life	.250	694	2393	341	598	86	14	141	415	82
2 AVE	.255	95	284	32	72	9	0	17	53	1

DANNY JACKSON

Position: Pitcher
Team: St. Louis Cardinals
Born: Jan. 5, 1962 San Antonio, TX
Height: 6' **Weight:** 205 lbs.
Bats: right **Throws:** left
Acquired: Signed as a free agent, 12/94

Player Summary	
Fantasy Value	$10 to $13
Card Value	6¢ to 10¢
Will	top a dozen wins
Can't	stop basestealers
Expect	exceptional slider
Don't Expect	control lapses

Jackson was a beacon in the fog that enveloped Philadelphia last summer. He won nine of his first 10, made the NL All-Stars for the second time, and finished with the second-best season of his 12-year career. The only Phillie starter who avoided the disabled list, Jackson even ranked among the NL's ERA leaders after beating the Cubs 4-2 on June 2. A month later, he completed a streak of 24 consecutive innings without a walk. He yielded a hit per inning and over two walks and six and one-half strikeouts per nine innings. Though the slider is his best pitch, Jackson also sports a fine fastball and a deceptive changeup. He keeps the ball in the park. He sabotages his own efforts with weak defense and a weaker pickoff move—thanks to a high leg kick that slows his delivery.

Major League Pitching Register

	W	L	ERA	G	CG	IP	H	ER	BB	SO
83 AL	1	1	5.21	4	0	19.0	26	11	6	9
84 AL	2	6	4.26	15	1	76.0	84	36	35	40
85 AL	14	12	3.42	32	4	208.0	209	79	76	114
86 AL	11	12	3.20	32	4	185.2	177	66	79	115
87 AL	9	18	4.02	36	11	224.0	219	100	109	152
88 NL	23	8	2.73	35	15	260.2	206	79	71	161
89 NL	6	11	5.60	20	1	115.2	122	72	57	70
90 NL	6	6	3.61	22	0	117.1	119	47	40	76
91 NL	1	5	6.75	17	0	70.2	89	53	48	31
92 NL	8	13	3.84	34	0	201.1	211	86	77	97
93 NL	12	11	3.77	32	2	210.1	214	88	80	120
94 NL	14	6	3.26	25	4	179.1	183	65	46	129
Life	107	109	3.77	304	42	1868.0	1859	782	724	1114
3 AVE	13	11	3.60	34	3	221.1	228	89	74	133

DARRIN JACKSON

Position: Outfield
Team: Chicago White Sox
Born: Aug. 22, 1963   Los Angeles, CA
Height: 6′   **Weight:** 185 lbs.
Bats: right   **Throws:** right
Acquired: Signed as a free agent, 12/93

Player Summary	
Fantasy Value	$11 to $14
Card Value	6¢ to 10¢
Will	use opposite field
Can't	master strike zone
Expect	some show of power
Don't Expect	patience at bat

One year after thyroid problems sapped his strength, the rejuvenated Jackson enjoyed the best season of his nine-year career. A lifetime .245 hitter before '94, he listened when White Sox hitting guru Walt Hriniak told him to hit the ball where it was pitched, rather than trying to pull everything. Finding new ground in the opposite field, Jackson got off to a great start and never wavered. Hitting .317 against lefties and .309 against righties, he finished on the sunny side of .300 for the first time. Though he fanned more than twice for every walk, he made his hits count (.340 in late-inning pressure spots and .346 at the home turf of Comiskey Park). No longer a slugger, Jackson is a better overall hitter. He's a good baserunner whose speed gives him good range in the outfield. Capable of playing center, he also has the arm for right. He led the NL with 18 assists in 1992.

Major League Batting Register

	BA	G	AB	R	H	2B	3B	HR	RBI	SB
85 NL	.091	5	11	0	1	0	0	0	0	0
87 NL	.800	7	5	2	4	1	0	0	0	0
88 NL	.266	100	188	29	50	11	3	6	20	4
89 NL	.218	70	170	17	37	7	0	4	20	1
90 NL	.257	58	113	10	29	3	0	3	9	3
91 NL	.262	122	359	51	94	12	1	21	49	5
92 NL	.249	155	587	72	146	23	5	17	70	14
93 AL	.216	46	176	15	38	8	0	5	19	0
93 NL	.195	31	87	4	17	1	0	1	7	0
94 AL	.312	104	369	43	115	17	3	10	51	7
Life	.257	698	2065	243	531	83	12	67	245	34
3 AVE	.265	126	457	51	121	19	3	12	56	8

MIKE JACKSON

Position: Pitcher
Team: San Francisco Giants
Born: Dec. 22, 1964   Houston, TX
Height: 6′   **Weight:** 185 lbs.
Bats: right   **Throws:** right
Acquired: Traded from Mariners with Bill Swift and Dave Burba for Kevin Mitchell and Mike Remlinger, 12/91

Player Summary	
Fantasy Value	$6 to $8
Card Value	5¢ to 7¢
Will	assume heavy workload
Can't	fret about elbow
Expect	many strikeouts
Don't Expect	righties to reach

After making more than 60 appearances for six straight seasons, the workload finally caught up to Jackson last summer. In June, he encountered elbow tendinitis—perhaps the result of throwing too many sliders. His entire repertoire consists of fastballs and sliders, but he's effective because he throws both pitches with good velocity and location. He had a career-best 1.49 ERA last year and held opposing hitters to a .164 average (.137 by righties and .194 by lefties). Jackson averaged less than five hits, nearly 11 strikeouts, and just over two walks per nine innings last year. He keeps the ball in the park and strands most of the runners he inherits. In a pro career dating back to 1984, he has yielded more hits than innings pitched only once. The former high school infielder is agile with a glove and pays plenty of attention to baserunners. He hasn't forgotten how to hit, either.

Major League Pitching Register

	W	L	ERA	G	S	IP	H	ER	BB	SO
86 NL	0	0	3.38	9	0	13.1	12	5	4	3
87 NL	3	10	4.20	55	1	109.1	88	51	56	93
88 AL	6	5	2.63	62	4	99.1	74	29	43	76
89 AL	4	6	3.17	65	7	99.1	81	35	54	94
90 AL	5	7	4.54	63	3	77.1	64	39	44	69
91 AL	7	7	3.25	72	14	88.2	64	32	34	74
92 NL	6	6	3.73	67	2	82.0	76	34	33	80
93 NL	6	6	3.03	81	1	77.1	58	26	24	70
94 NL	3	2	1.49	36	4	42.1	23	7	11	51
Life	40	49	3.37	510	36	689.0	540	258	303	610
3 AVE	5	5	2.87	66	3	73.1	55	23	24	74

JOHN JAHA

Position: First base
Team: Milwaukee Brewers
Born: May 27, 1966 Portland, OR
Height: 6'1" **Weight:** 195 lbs.
Bats: right **Throws:** right
Acquired: 14th-round pick in 6/84 free-agent draft

Player Summary	
Fantasy Value	$7 to $9
Card Value	6¢ to 10¢
Will	hit for distance
Can't	steal bases
Expect	more patience
Don't Expect	return to minors

In 1993, his first full season in the majors, Jaha gave the Brewers reason for hope with 19 homers and 70 RBI in 153 games. That of course was before the sophomore jinx hit him square in the jaw last summer. He had such severe early problems that he was returned to Triple-A New Orleans with a .228 average July 8. There he batted .403 with two homers and 16 RBI in 62 at bats. Better after his recall, he had moved his mark to .241 before the players walked out Aug. 12. Jaha's problem is discipline—or lack of it. He fanned more than twice as often as he walked in '94; he may be developing into an all-or-nothing slugger. Jaha was a loop MVP in 1989 and '91, led two minor leagues in walks, and in 1991 had a Double-A season that included 30 homers, 134 RBI, and a .344 average. The Brewer brass thinks he can do better on the big-league level. A first-pitch fastball hitter with opposite-field power, Jaha hits lefties well (.283). He hit well in the clutch in '93. Jaha is a good first baseman who ranks among the league leaders in assists.

Major League Batting Register

	BA	G	AB	R	H	2B	3B	HR	RBI	SB
92 AL	.226	47	133	17	30	3	1	2	10	10
93 AL	.264	153	515	78	136	21	0	19	70	13
94 AL	.241	84	291	45	70	14	0	12	39	3
Life	.251	284	939	140	236	38	1	33	119	26
2 AVE	.254	136	462	71	117	20	0	18	62	9

CHRIS JAMES

Position: Outfield
Team: Texas Rangers
Born: Oct. 4, 1962 Rusk, TX
Height: 6'1" **Weight:** 190 lbs.
Bats: right **Throws:** right
Acquired: Traded from Astros for Dave Gandolph, 9/93

Player Summary	
Fantasy Value	$1
Card Value	5¢ to 7¢
Will	serve off bench
Can't	hit right-handers
Expect	occasional power
Don't Expect	great speed

Because he hits left-handers so well, James made a great platoon partner for lefty-hitting rookie Rusty Greer in Texas' right field last year. Against southpaws, James finished at .349—second among the Rangers to little-used infielder Bill Ripken. Though he fans nearly twice as much as he walks, James has a fairly patient approach at the plate. The result last year was an on-base percentage of .361—more than 100 points above his batting average. He also has some power. Usually a capable bench player, he failed to hit his weight with runners in scoring position or in late-inning pressure spots last year. That made him a liability as a pinch hitter, one year after he smacked two pinch-hit homers in an eight-game September stint with Texas. Though he no longer runs well, James has the arm strength and accuracy for right field. He started his pro career in 1982.

Major League Batting Register

	BA	G	AB	R	H	2B	3B	HR	RBI	SB
86 NL	.283	16	46	5	13	3	0	1	5	0
87 NL	.293	115	358	48	105	20	6	17	54	3
88 NL	.242	150	566	57	137	24	1	19	66	7
89 NL	.243	132	482	55	117	17	2	13	65	5
90 AL	.299	140	528	62	158	32	4	12	70	4
91 AL	.238	115	437	31	104	16	2	5	41	3
92 NL	.242	111	248	25	60	10	4	5	32	2
93 NL	.256	65	129	19	33	10	1	6	19	2
93 AL	.355	8	31	5	11	1	0	3	7	0
94 AL	.256	52	133	28	34	8	4	7	19	0
Life	.261	904	2958	335	772	141	24	88	378	26
2 AVE	.255	92	204	25	52	11	3	7	29	2

STAN JAVIER

Position: Outfield
Team: Oakland Athletics
Born: Sept. 1, 1965 San Pedro de Macoris, Dominican Republic
Height: 6' **Weight:** 185 lbs.
Bats: both **Throws:** right
Acquired: Signed as a free agent, 12/93

Player Summary	
Fantasy Value	$11 to $14
Card Value	6¢ to 10¢
Will	rip left-handers
Can't	produce under pressure
Expect	strong defense
Don't Expect	outfield woes

Given 400 at bats in a season for the first time, Javier responded with career highs in home runs, RBI, and stolen bases. He had a career-best 17-game hitting streak in April, two home runs in a game in June, and more homers by June 19 than in the four previous seasons combined. His stolen-base count lent credence to a prediction that he'd swipe 40 if used as a regular. Oakland hitting coach Jim Lefebvre said the main reason for Javier's improvement was better performance with two strikes. That boosted his confidence and allowed him to ignore bad pitches early in the count. A good breaking-ball hitter, he used to be vulnerable to inside heat. Javier finished the season with a .318 average against lefties and a .349 on-base average. Javier is a polished center fielder who throws well and uses his great speed.

Major League Batting Register

	BA	G	AB	R	H	2B	3B	HR	RBI	SB
84 AL	.143	7	7	1	1	0	0	0	0	0
86 AL	.202	59	114	13	23	8	0	0	8	8
87 AL	.185	81	151	22	28	3	1	2	9	3
88 AL	.257	125	397	49	102	13	3	2	35	20
89 AL	.248	112	310	42	77	12	3	1	28	12
90 AL	.242	19	33	4	8	0	2	0	3	0
90 NL	.304	104	276	56	84	9	4	3	24	15
91 AL	.205	121	176	21	36	5	3	1	11	7
92 AL	.249	130	334	42	83	17	1	1	29	29
93 AL	.291	92	237	33	69	10	4	3	28	12
94 AL	.272	109	419	75	114	23	0	10	44	24
Life	.255	959	2454	358	625	100	21	23	219	119
3 AVE	.269	125	387	60	104	20	2	6	40	21

GREGG JEFFERIES

Position: First base
Team: St. Louis Cardinals
Born: Aug. 1, 1967 Burlingame, CA
Height: 5'10" **Weight:** 180 lbs.
Bats: both **Throws:** right
Acquired: Traded from Royals for Felix Jose and Craig Wilson, 2/93

Player Summary	
Fantasy Value	$25 to $30
Card Value	15¢ to 25¢
Will	always make contact
Can't	go for Triple Crown
Expect	speed and power
Don't Expect	poor glove

In two seasons, Jefferies has carved his niche as one of baseball's best all-around players. An exceptional contact hitter who rarely strikes out, he bats from both sides and has power to all fields. He also runs better than any other first baseman in baseball. A 1994 All-Star starter, Jefferies topped .300 against lefties and righties, at home, on the road, and with runners in scoring position. He finished fifth in the league with a .325 average and was among NL leaders with a .391 on-base percentage. Spending half his time in Busch Stadium deflated his power production, but he managed a pair of two-homer games anyway. Though he batted third last year, he could have batted first. He works the count and usually makes contact. Then he drives pitchers crazy on the bases. Jefferies has become a top-fielding first baseman. His transition from third to first recalls a similar move made by Steve Garvey.

Major League Batting Register

	BA	G	AB	R	H	2B	3B	HR	RBI	SB
87 NL	.500	6	6	0	3	1	0	0	2	0
88 NL	.321	29	109	19	35	8	2	6	17	5
89 NL	.258	141	508	72	131	28	2	12	56	21
90 NL	.283	153	604	96	171	40	3	15	68	11
91 NL	.272	136	486	59	132	19	2	9	62	26
92 AL	.285	152	604	66	172	36	3	10	75	19
93 NL	.342	142	544	89	186	24	3	16	83	46
94 NL	.325	103	397	52	129	27	1	12	55	12
Life	.294	862	3258	453	959	183	16	80	418	140
3 AVE	.316	146	569	76	180	33	2	14	78	27

REGGIE JEFFERSON

Position: Designated hitter; first base
Team: Seattle Mariners
Born: Sept. 25, 1968 Tallahassee, FL
Height: 6'4" **Weight:** 210 lbs.
Bats: both **Throws:** left
Acquired: Traded from Indians with Felix Fermin and cash for Omar Vizquel, 12/93

Player Summary	
Fantasy Value	$7 to $9
Card Value	6¢ to 10¢
Will	hit well as lefty
Can't	even hint at speed
Expect	good clutch stroke
Don't Expect	defensive prowess

Jefferson tried something new last spring. Though he is listed as a switch-hitter, he took to batting almost exclusively from the left side—a concerted effort to improve his concentration. The idea seemed to work, since he had a .480 batting average through May 15. Though injuries eventually interfered, he finished with an average 78 points above the .249 mark he produced in 1993. Jefferson hurt right-handers with a .346 mark, hit a rousing .476 with runners in scoring position, and delivered a .351 mark on the road. He also had eight homers in 162 at bats—the best power ratio of his career. Since most pitchers are right-handed, he would certainly receive many at bats in a platoon if he stayed healthy. He's had more injuries than a M*A*S*H rerun over the past five years, however. A better designated hitter than first baseman, he has trouble with throws—not only his own but also low ones from fellow infielders. Lack of speed also limits his mobility around the bag.

Major League Batting Register

	BA	G	AB	R	H	2B	3B	HR	RBI	SB
91 NL	.143	5	7	1	1	0	0	1	1	0
91 AL	.198	26	101	10	20	3	0	2	12	0
92 AL	.337	24	89	8	30	6	2	1	6	0
93 AL	.249	113	366	35	91	11	2	10	34	1
94 AL	.327	63	162	24	53	11	0	8	32	0
Life	.269	231	725	78	195	31	4	22	85	1
2 AVE	.279	101	297	34	83	13	1	11	40	1

HOWARD JOHNSON

Position: Outfield; third base
Team: Colorado Rockies
Born: Nov. 29, 1960 Clearwater, FL
Height: 5'10" **Weight:** 195 lbs.
Bats: both **Throws:** right
Acquired: Signed as a free agent, 11/93

Player Summary	
Fantasy Value	$1 to $3
Card Value	6¢ to 10¢
Will	try new comeback
Can't	stop striking out
Expect	some speed, power
Don't Expect	a 30-30 year

Johnson hasn't been himself since 1991, the last of his three 30-30 seasons. He had shoulder, knee, and wrist injuries in 1992, a broken thumb and viral infection in '93, and the pressure of proving himself to a new club in '94. Though he poked four pinch-hit homers last year, Johnson was pulled from the starting lineup in May. Typically, he seemed to always foul off a fastball before being retired on a pair of curves. Rather than take a pitch to the opposite field, he tried to pull everything. Changeups gave him so much trouble that manager Don Baylor suggested Hojo try batting left-handed against some southpaws. Johnson still has good speed but can't steal unless he reaches more often. Defensively, he's best deployed as a DH. In the National League, he's had problems at short, third, and the outfield.

Major League Batting Register

	BA	G	AB	R	H	2B	3B	HR	RBI	SB
82 AL	.316	54	155	23	49	5	0	4	14	7
83 AL	.212	27	66	11	14	0	0	3	5	0
84 AL	.248	116	355	43	88	14	1	12	50	10
85 NL	.242	126	389	38	94	18	4	11	46	6
86 NL	.245	88	220	30	54	14	0	10	39	8
87 NL	.265	157	554	93	147	22	1	36	99	32
88 NL	.230	148	495	85	114	21	1	24	68	23
89 NL	.287	153	571	104	164	41	3	36	101	41
90 NL	.244	154	590	89	144	37	3	23	90	34
91 NL	.259	156	564	108	146	34	4	38	117	30
92 NL	.223	100	350	48	78	19	0	7	43	22
93 NL	.238	72	235	32	56	8	2	7	26	6
94 NL	.211	93	227	30	48	10	2	10	40	11
Life	.251	1444	4771	734	1196	243	21	221	738	230
3 AVE	.223	101	302	41	67	14	2	9	42	14

LANCE JOHNSON

Position: Outfield
Team: Chicago White Sox
Born: July 7, 1963   Cincinnati, OH
Height: 5'11"   **Weight:** 159 lbs.
Bats: left   **Throws:** left
Acquired: Traded from Cardinals with Ricky Horton for Jose DeLeon, 2/88

Player Summary	
Fantasy Value	$20 to $25
Card Value	6¢ to 10¢
Will	show great speed
Can't	hit the ball out
Expect	three-base hits
Don't Expect	powerful throws

Before Johnson did it in 1994, no player had ever led his league in triples four years in a row. He makes great contact, smacks liners into the gaps, and runs like the wind. He'd make better use of his speed if he worked pitchers for more walks, but he doesn't have the patience. He swings at pitches outside the zone—especially if they're high—and tries to hit them hard. He fattens his average by beating out grounders but also gets extra bases when he hits a hard ground ball down the lines. An opposite-field hitter against lefties, he hits to all fields against righties. With seven homers over the last five years, Johnson has little power. But one of those seven, last July 31, came with the bases loaded. His speed helps on the bases, where he's rarely thrown out stealing. His swiftness also helps in center field. He has great reactions, terrific range, and a quick release that compensates for a popgun arm.

Major League Batting Register

	BA	G	AB	R	H	2B	3B	HR	RBI	SB
87 NL	.220	33	59	4	13	2	1	0	7	6
88 AL	.185	33	124	11	23	4	1	0	6	6
89 AL	.300	50	180	28	54	8	2	0	16	16
90 AL	.285	151	541	76	154	18	9	1	51	36
91 AL	.274	159	588	72	161	14	13	0	49	26
92 AL	.279	157	567	67	158	15	12	3	47	41
93 AL	.311	147	540	75	168	18	14	0	47	35
94 AL	.277	106	412	56	114	11	14	3	54	26
Life	.281	836	3011	389	845	90	66	7	277	192
3 AVE	.288	151	562	74	162	16	15	2	57	38

RANDY JOHNSON

Position: Pitcher
Team: Seattle Mariners
Born: Sept. 10, 1963   Walnut Creek, CA
Height: 6'10"   **Weight:** 225 lbs.
Bats: right   **Throws:** left
Acquired: Traded from Expos with Gene Harris and Brian Holman for Mark Langston and Mike Campbell, 5/89

Player Summary	
Fantasy Value	$20 to $25
Card Value	12¢ to 20¢
Will	blow batters away
Can't	always find plate
Expect	amazing endurance
Don't Expect	many hits

Even the strike didn't stop Johnson from his fourth straight 200-whiff season last summer. The towering southpaw led all big-league starters with an average of 10½ strikeouts per nine innings, held hitters to a .216 average, kept the ball in the park, and enjoyed exceptional success at curtailing the running game. Of his four shutouts, three were thrown consecutively during a 27-inning scoreless streak in June. The final fastball of his 141-pitch effort June 25 was timed at 100 mph. He also throws an exceptional slider and an occasional curve. Goose Gossage, his teammate last year, compared Johnson's slider with Ron Guidry's. AL managers polled by *Baseball America* placed both Johnson's slider and heater at the head of the class. He not only mixes the pitches well but throws them with reasonable accuracy. He has improved his defense and pickoff move.

Major League Pitching Register

	W	L	ERA	G	CG	IP	H	ER	BB	SO
88 NL	3	0	2.42	4	1	26.0	23	7	7	25
89 NL	0	4	6.67	7	0	29.2	29	22	26	26
89 AL	7	9	4.40	22	2	131.0	118	64	70	104
90 AL	14	11	3.65	33	5	219.2	174	89	120	194
91 AL	13	10	3.98	33	2	201.1	151	89	152	228
92 AL	12	14	3.77	31	6	210.1	154	88	144	241
93 AL	19	8	3.24	35	10	255.1	185	92	99	308
94 AL	13	6	3.19	23	9	172.0	132	61	72	204
Life	81	62	3.70	188	35	1245.1	966	512	690	1330
3 AVE	16	10	3.38	33	10	236.1	175	89	115	279

BOBBY JONES

Position: Pitcher
Team: New York Mets
Born: Feb. 10, 1970 Fresno, CA
Height: 6'4" **Weight:** 210 lbs.
Bats: right **Throws:** right
Acquired: First-round pick in 6/91 free-agent draft

Player Summary	
Fantasy Value	$9 to $11
Card Value	15¢ to 25¢
Will	become top starter
Can't	show great velocity
Expect	confidence
Don't Expect	shaky control

Armed with only nine games of big-league experience, Jones became a solid starter for the Mets in 1994. A control pitcher who sets up his changeup with a curve and two types of fastballs (sinking or rising), he seldom gets flustered. If something doesn't work, he finds another way. Relying on location and deception in lieu of power, Jones yielded less hits than innings while walking just over three men per nine innings last year. Though he averaged only four and one-half Ks per game, he kept the ball in the park and fielded his position well. He's more effective against righty hitters. Jones's best game last year was a 1-0 shutout at St. Louis May 7. The 1991 College Pitcher of the Year from Fresno State, he was selected by the Mets with the compensation pick they received when they lost free agent Darryl Strawberry. In 1993 at Triple-A Norfolk, Jones was 12-10 with a 3.63 ERA, 126 Ks, and 32 walks in 166 innings. He was named the Double-A Eastern League's No. 1 prospect in 1992 after a 12-4 year, with a 1.88 ERA, 144 Ks, and 43 walks in 158 innings.

Major League Pitching Register

	W	L	ERA	G	CG	IP	H	ER	BB	SO
93 NL	2	4	3.65	9	0	61.2	61	25	22	35
94 NL	12	7	3.15	24	1	160.0	157	56	56	80
Life	14	11	3.29	33	1	221.2	218	81	78	115
2 AVE	9	7	3.26	21	1	143.1	141	52	50	74

DOUG JONES

Position: Pitcher
Team: Philadelphia Phillies
Born: June 24, 1957 Covina, CA
Height: 6'2" **Weight:** 195 lbs.
Bats: right **Throws:** right
Acquired: Traded from Astros with Jeff Juden for Mitch Williams, 12/93

Player Summary	
Fantasy Value	$17 to $20
Card Value	6¢ to 10¢
Will	quash late fires
Can't	rely on heater
Expect	several changeups
Don't Expect	control trouble

Like the Cleveland Indians in 1991, the Houston Astros gave up on Jones too soon. After he saved 112 games in three years, the Indians released him after a single poor season. He returned to top form with the '92 Astros but was dumped again after slipping a year later. Philadelphia was the beneficiary. A control pitcher who dominates right-handers, Jones depends upon a changeup that he throws at three different speeds. His fastball isn't very fast and is just for show. He averages more than six strikeouts per game. But his biggest assets are his uncanny control (one walk per nine innings last year) and ability to keep the ball in the park (two homers in 54 innings). Though he's topped 50 appearances five times, he struggles when asked to pitch too many innings. He also has occasional problems in the field, though his quick delivery keeps runners close to the bag.

Major League Pitching Register

	W	L	ERA	G	S	IP	H	ER	BB	SO
82 AL	0	0	10.13	4	0	2.2	5	3	1	1
86 AL	1	0	2.50	11	1	18.0	18	5	6	12
87 AL	6	5	3.15	49	8	91.1	101	32	24	87
88 AL	3	4	2.27	51	37	83.1	69	21	16	72
89 AL	7	10	2.34	59	32	80.2	76	21	13	65
90 AL	5	5	2.56	66	43	84.1	66	24	22	55
91 AL	4	8	5.54	36	7	63.1	87	39	17	48
92 NL	11	8	1.85	80	36	111.2	96	23	17	93
93 NL	4	10	4.54	71	26	85.1	102	43	21	66
94 NL	2	4	2.17	47	27	54.0	55	13	6	38
Life	43	54	2.99	474	217	674.2	675	224	143	537
3 AVE	6	8	2.78	72	33	91.1	92	28	15	71

TODD JONES

Position: Pitcher
Team: Houston Astros
Born: April 24, 1968 Marietta, GA
Height: 6'3" **Weight:** 200 lbs.
Bats: left **Throws:** right
Acquired: First-round pick in 6/89 free-agent draft

Player Summary	
Fantasy Value	$8 to $10
Card Value	6¢ to 10¢
Will	answer call often
Can't	get press coverage
Expect	righties to suffer
Don't Expect	return to rotation

Jones tried several roles in his first full big-league season last year. Used mainly as the set-up man for John Hudek, Jones also saw service as a closer. The rubber-armed right-hander wound up as the busiest man in the Houston bullpen. He has an extensive repertoire for a reliever—a sinker, a rising fastball, a curve, and a changeup. He usually throws them for strikes. Jones averaged just over three walks and less than six and one-half hits per nine innings. Especially effective against right-handers (.153 last year), he fanned nearly eight batters per game and rarely let the ball leave the park (three in 72⅔ innings). He also stranded 78 percent of the runners he inherited. Because he throws hard and uses a quick delivery, Jones isn't challenged much by potential basestealers. He's competent in the field. The Jacksonville State product was selected with the pick the Astros received when they lost free agent Nolan Ryan. Formerly a starter, Jones converted to relief in 1992 and notched 25 saves at Double-A Jackson that year.

BRIAN JORDAN

Position: Outfield
Team: St. Louis Cardinals
Born: March 26, 1967 Baltimore, MD
Height: 6'1" **Weight:** 205 lbs.
Bats: right **Throws:** right
Acquired: First-round pick in 6/88 free-agent draft

Player Summary	
Fantasy Value	$14 to $17
Card Value	10¢ to 15¢
Will	seek stroke of '93
Can't	reduce whiff ratio
Expect	more show of speed
Don't Expect	injury-free year

Though blessed with a quick bat, quicker feet, and power potential, Jordan has battled injuries and an overcrowded outfield throughout his career. Last season, he suffered cracked ribs in a July 9 collision with Todd Zeile. The year before, Jordan suffered a shoulder separation. He was even on the disabled list in 1992, his rookie season. The former Atlanta Falcons safety had his best year in '93, when he hammered 10 homers in 67 games and hit .309. Even then, however, he fanned nearly three times more than he walked. Jordan lacks the patience to wait for walks and has trouble with pitchers who change speeds. He shows more power and hits for a higher average against lefties. A fine clutch player in 1993, Jordan struggled in '94. He'll have to improve to regain his reputation as a rising young talent. His speed helps him snare potential gap hits. Though prone to some mistakes, he runs well enough to play center and has a better-than-average arm. Jordan's running ability is neutralized by poor judgement on the basepaths.

Major League Pitching Register

	W	L	ERA	G	S	IP	H	ER	BB	SO
93 NL	1	2	3.13	27	2	37.1	28	13	15	25
94 NL	5	2	2.72	48	5	72.2	52	22	26	63
Life	6	4	2.86	75	7	110.0	80	35	41	88
2 AVE	4	2	2.83	47	5	69.2	51	22	26	57

Major League Batting Register

	BA	G	AB	R	H	2B	3B	HR	RBI	SB
92 NL	.207	55	193	17	40	9	4	5	22	7
93 NL	.309	67	223	33	69	10	6	10	44	6
94 NL	.258	53	178	14	46	8	2	5	15	4
Life	.261	175	594	64	155	27	12	20	81	17
3 AVE	.261	66	222	23	58	10	4	7	29	6

RICKY JORDAN

Position: First base
Team: Philadelphia Phillies
Born: May 26, 1965   Richmond, CA
Height: 6'3"   **Weight:** 210 lbs.
Bats: right   **Throws:** right
Acquired: First-round pick in 6/83 free-agent draft

Player Summary	
Fantasy Value	$7 to $9
Card Value	6¢ to 10¢
Will	hit lefties hard
Can't	wait for walks
Expect	some pinch hits
Don't Expect	strong defense

An aggressive approach, ability to hit left-handers, and clutch production combine to make Jordan one of baseball's best bench players. The caddy for lefty-swinging John Kruk last year, Jordan delivered a .299 mark against left-handed pitchers. He also socked eight homers in 220 at bats, though he averaged more than five strikeouts per walk. Jordan comes off the bench swinging. His 16 pinch hits for the '93 Phillies were instrumental in that club's divisional championship. He hit .302 with runners in scoring position last season. Because he has the speed of a lumbering first baseman, Jordan is no threat to steal. Nor is he a threat to win a Gold Glove Award for his defense. He has limited mobility and doesn't throw well, though his size makes him an inviting target for his infield teammates. Jordan would be a logical choice for a designated-hitter job. When he broke into the majors on July 17, 1988, he homered in his first at bat.

Major League Batting Register

	BA	G	AB	R	H	2B	3B	HR	RBI	SB
88 NL	.308	69	273	41	84	15	1	11	43	1
89 NL	.285	144	523	63	149	22	3	12	75	4
90 NL	.241	92	324	32	78	21	0	5	44	2
91 NL	.272	101	301	38	82	21	3	9	49	0
92 NL	.304	94	276	33	84	19	0	4	34	3
93 NL	.289	90	159	21	46	4	1	5	18	0
94 NL	.282	72	220	29	62	14	2	8	37	0
Life	.282	662	2076	257	585	116	10	54	300	10
3 AVE	.292	95	248	32	72	14	1	7	35	1

FELIX JOSE

Position: Outfield
Team: Kansas City Royals
Born: May 8, 1965   Santo Domingo, Dominican Republic
Height: 6'1"   **Weight:** 190 lbs.
Bats: both   **Throws:** right
Acquired: Traded from Cardinals with Craig Wilson for Gregg Jefferies, 2/93

Player Summary	
Fantasy Value	$16 to $19
Card Value	8¢ to 12¢
Will	hurt lefties
Can't	show much patience
Expect	better use of speed
Don't Expect	weak throws

Free of the shoulder injury that hampered his performance in 1993, Jose finished on the sunny side of .300 for the second time in his career. His best month was June, when he was Kansas City's Player of the Month. A fastball hitter who uses all fields, he brings speed and power into the lineup. He fanned more than twice for every walk in 1994 but got extra bases on more than one-third of his hits. Jose hammered left-handed pitching, hit well over .300 with runners in scoring position, and did his best batting in late-inning pressure situations (.345 last year). He's sometimes over-aggressive on the bases, however, as he was nailed on more than half of his 1994 steal attempts. His speed and strong arm serve him well in right field, where he had seven assists and participated in a pair of double plays. Originally signed by the A's, Jose broke into pro ball in 1984.

Major League Batting Register

	BA	G	AB	R	H	2B	3B	HR	RBI	SB
88 AL	.333	8	6	2	2	1	0	0	1	1
89 AL	.193	20	57	3	11	2	0	0	5	0
90 AL	.264	101	341	42	90	12	0	8	39	8
90 AL	.271	25	85	12	23	4	1	3	13	4
91 NL	.305	154	568	69	173	40	6	8	77	20
92 NL	.295	131	509	62	150	22	3	14	75	28
93 AL	.253	149	499	64	126	24	3	6	43	31
94 AL	.303	99	366	56	111	28	1	11	55	10
Life	.282	687	2431	310	686	133	14	50	308	102
3 AVE	.284	140	508	68	144	28	2	12	65	24

WALLY JOYNER

Position: First base
Team: Kansas City Royals
Born: June 16, 1962   Atlanta, GA
Height: 6'2"   **Weight:** 198 lbs.
Bats: left   **Throws:** left
Acquired: Signed as a free agent, 12/91

Player Summary	
Fantasy Value	$11 to $14
Card Value	10¢ to 15¢
Will	produce in clutch
Can't	clear the fences
Expect	flawless fielding
Don't Expect	weak on-base mark

Though he's no longer the power producer who broke in with back-to-back 100-RBI campaigns, Joyner has become a better all-around hitter. Thanks to tremendous improvement against left-handers, he finished with a career-best .311 mark last summer. He topped .300 against both lefties and righties, hit .315 with runners in scoring position, and batted .356 in late-inning pressure situations. A contact man who walks more than he fans, Joyner hits to all fields while showing most of his power against right-handers. Because he hits line drives and fly balls, he does not hit into many double plays. Joyner has enough speed to steal just a handful of bases. Though he's never won a Gold Glove, he is a terrific fielder who's led AL first baseman in putouts, assists, double plays, and fielding percentage. He makes tough plays look easy. The Brigham Young product began his pro career in 1983.

Major League Batting Register

	BA	G	AB	R	H	2B	3B	HR	RBI	SB
86 AL	.290	154	593	82	172	27	3	22	100	5
87 AL	.285	149	564	100	161	33	1	34	117	8
88 AL	.295	158	597	81	176	31	2	13	85	8
89 AL	.282	159	593	78	167	30	2	16	79	3
90 AL	.268	83	310	35	83	15	0	8	41	2
91 AL	.301	143	551	79	166	34	3	21	96	2
92 AL	.269	149	572	66	154	36	2	9	66	11
93 AL	.292	141	497	83	145	36	3	15	65	5
94 AL	.311	97	363	52	113	20	3	8	57	3
Life	.288	1233	4640	656	1337	262	19	146	706	47
3 AVE	.290	142	527	74	153	33	3	12	70	7

DAVID JUSTICE

Position: Outfield
Team: Atlanta Braves
Born: April 14, 1966   Cincinnati, OH
Height: 6'3"   **Weight:** 200 lbs.
Bats: left   **Throws:** left
Acquired: Fourth-round pick in 6/85 free-agent draft

Player Summary	
Fantasy Value	$20 to $25
Card Value	20¢ to 35¢
Will	reach base often
Can't	depend upon speed
Expect	power vs. righties
Don't Expect	a Gold Glove

Last year, Justice avoided his usual slow start, hit 43 points above his career average, and finished with a higher mark against righties (.326) than lefties (.287). He needed a late surge to reach 19 homers—the first time in five seasons he failed to top 20. Justice probably would've hit 30 had the strike not ended the season on Aug. 12; he's always been a prolific late-season producer. His approach to hitting seemed to be different. He became more of a contact man, showed more patience at the plate, and wound up with 24 more walks than strikeouts—numbers not normally identified with a slugger. Fourth in the league in walks, he ranked second in on-base average (.427)—a terrific figure for a man whose speed is negligible. Justice does his best hitting with runners in scoring position (.386). A hustler with a strong arm, he gets great jumps and makes some spectacular running grabs. He did make 11 errors last year—most on throws that got away.

Major League Batting Register

	BA	G	AB	R	H	2B	3B	HR	RBI	SB
89 NL	.235	16	51	7	12	3	0	1	3	2
90 NL	.282	127	439	76	124	23	2	28	78	11
91 NL	.275	109	396	67	109	25	1	21	87	8
92 NL	.256	144	484	78	124	19	5	21	72	2
93 NL	.270	157	585	90	158	15	4	40	120	3
94 NL	.313	104	352	61	110	16	2	19	59	2
Life	.276	657	2307	379	637	101	14	130	419	28
3 AVE	.279	149	522	85	146	19	4	29	92	3

SCOTT KAMIENIECKI

Position: Pitcher
Team: New York Yankees
Born: April 19, 1964 Mt. Clemens, MI
Height: 6' **Weight:** 195 lbs.
Bats: right **Throws:** right
Acquired: 14th-round pick in 6/86 free-agent draft

Player Summary	
Fantasy Value	$7 to $9
Card Value	5¢ to 7¢
Will	rely on location
Can't	keep ball in park
Expect	best work vs. righties
Don't Expect	many Ks

Though six of his 22 appearances last year came in relief, Kamieniecki shaved some points off his earned run average for the second straight season. Only Jimmy Key had a better ERA among Yankee starters. Not a power pitcher, Kamieniecki relies on changing speeds and finding the right location for his fastball, curveball, slider, and changeup. When all his pitches are working, he gets most of his outs on ground balls. He yielded less hits than innings last year but sometimes struggles with his control. He yielded four and one-half walks per nine innings last year while averaging less than five and one-half strikeouts over the same span. Though much more effective against right-handed hitters, Kamieniecki is no slouch against southpaws, either. He is prone to the gopher ball, however, and that can be a problem if it follows a wild spell. The former Michigan standout is a first-rate fielder who has made dramatic improvements as a pickoff artist in recent seasons. He holds runners well for a right-hander.

Major League Pitching Register

	W	L	ERA	G	CG	IP	H	ER	BB	SO
91 AL	4	4	3.90	9	0	55.1	54	24	22	34
92 AL	6	14	4.36	28	4	188.0	193	91	74	88
93 AL	10	7	4.08	30	2	154.1	163	70	59	72
94 AL	8	6	3.76	22	1	117.1	115	49	59	71
Life	28	31	4.09	89	7	515.0	525	234	214	265
3 AVE	9	10	4.08	30	2	169.1	173	77	72	87

RON KARKOVICE

Position: Catcher
Team: Chicago White Sox
Born: Aug. 8, 1963 Union, NJ
Height: 6'1" **Weight:** 215 lbs.
Bats: right **Throws:** right
Acquired: First-round pick in 6/82 free-agent draft

Player Summary	
Fantasy Value	$5 to $7
Card Value	6¢ to 10¢
Will	show occasional pop
Can't	handle right-handers
Expect	howitzer for an arm
Don't Expect	good bat

Even though Walt Hriniak is supposed to be a genius of hitting, his lessons failed to help Karkovice. The catcher's average fell for the third straight year in 1994, and he was struggling long before knee problems sent him to the sidelines. A much better hitter against left-handers, he spent most of the year platooning with Mike LaValliere. Nearly half of Karkovice's hits went for extra bases, but that's only because he didn't get very many hits. On the other hand, he did reduce the ridiculous 5-1 ratio of strikeouts to walks that plagued him in 1993. It's his defense that keeps him in the lineup. AL managers polled by *Baseball America* last year named him the league's top defensive receiver. In 1993, Karko led the majors by nailing 50 percent of the runners who tried to steal against him (60 percent after the All-Star Game). He's a fine game-caller who prevents wild pitches and blocks the plate well.

Major League Batting Register

	BA	G	AB	R	H	2B	3B	HR	RBI	SB
86 AL	.247	37	97	13	24	7	0	4	13	1
87 AL	.071	39	85	7	6	0	0	2	7	3
88 AL	.174	46	115	10	20	4	0	3	9	4
89 AL	.264	71	182	21	48	9	2	3	24	0
90 AL	.246	68	183	30	45	10	0	6	20	2
91 AL	.246	75	167	25	41	13	0	5	22	0
92 AL	.237	123	342	39	81	12	1	13	50	10
93 AL	.228	128	403	60	92	17	1	20	54	2
94 AL	.213	77	207	33	44	9	1	11	29	0
Life	.225	664	1781	238	401	81	5	67	228	22
3 AVE	.227	120	346	48	78	14	1	16	48	4

ERIC KARROS

Position: First base
Team: Los Angeles Dodgers
Born: Nov. 4, 1967 Hackensack, NJ
Height: 6'4" **Weight:** 205 lbs.
Bats: right **Throws:** right
Acquired: Sixth-round pick in 6/88 free-agent draft

Player Summary	
Fantasy Value	$9 to $11
Card Value	12¢ to 15¢
Will	seek rookie form
Can't	cut Ks
Expect	20 homers
Don't Expect	clutch production

In four seasons in the minors, Karros never hit under .300. In three years in the majors, he's never exceeded .266. Will the real Eric Karros please stand up? The Dodgers wonder whether he will ever evolve from the numbers that earned him the NL Rookie of the Year Award in 1992. Or is he the second coming of Greg Brock? Karros does show occasional power, but in 1994 he fanned twice as much as he walked, resulting in a low on-base average. He also tends to get overanxious at critical times. He hasn't hit his weight in clutch situations for the past two seasons. A dead-pull hitter who rarely goes with the pitch, Karros hits into a lot of double plays. His speed is inferior, and he rarely steals. Nor is Karros a gazelle in the field. He's learned to scoop bad throws, and his defense has improved dramatically in recent years. He also led three minor leagues in putouts and assists. Still, he'll never make anyone forget Steve Garvey. Karros is a UCLA product who started his career in the Pioneer League in 1988.

Major League Batting Register

	BA	G	AB	R	H	2B	3B	HR	RBI	SB
91 NL	.071	14	14	0	1	1	0	0	1	0
92 NL	.257	149	545	63	140	30	1	20	88	2
93 NL	.247	158	619	74	153	27	2	23	80	0
94 NL	.266	111	406	51	108	21	1	14	46	2
Life	.254	432	1584	188	402	79	4	57	215	4
3 AVE	.256	154	579	70	148	29	1	21	78	2

STEVE KARSAY

Position: Pitcher
Team: Oakland Athletics
Born: March 24, 1972 Flushing, NY
Height: 6'3" **Weight:** 205 lbs.
Bats: right **Throws:** right
Acquired: Traded from Blue Jays with Jose Herrera for Rickey Henderson, 7/93

Player Summary	
Fantasy Value	$7 to $9
Card Value	15¢ to 25¢
Will	try to stay sound
Can't	rely on experience
Expect	rotation berth
Don't Expect	control lapses

Karsay pitched only 28 innings last summer before surgeons made arthroscopic repairs on his right elbow. That cost Oakland the services of a man who had been expected to be the No. 4 starter. A fastball-slider pitcher who's still perfecting a breaking ball, Karsay has shown good control during his two brief stints in the majors. He's also indicated that he will allow less hits than innings pitched and maintain about a 2-1 ratio of strikeouts to walks. He has surprising poise and confidence for a pitcher with such limited experience. In four minor-league seasons, he never posted double figures in victories. Karsay was named the No. 4 prospect in the Double-A Southern League in 1993 with an 8-4 record, a 3.59 ERA, 122 strikeouts, and 35 walks in 118 innings. He was the 22nd player taken in the 1990 draft. Karsay fields his position well and keeps close watch on enemy runners. His quick delivery gives his catchers a chance to throw people out. If Karsay is sound after his surgery, he should reclaim his status as one of the most promising young pitchers in the loop.

Major League Pitching Register

	W	L	ERA	G	CG	IP	H	ER	BB	SO
93 AL	3	3	4.04	8	0	49.0	49	22	16	33
94 AL	1	1	2.57	4	1	28.0	26	8	8	15
Life	4	4	3.51	12	1	77.0	75	30	24	48

MIKE KELLY

Position: Outfield
Team: Atlanta Braves
Born: June 2, 1970 Los Angeles, CA
Height: 6'4" **Weight:** 195 lbs.
Bats: right **Throws:** right
Acquired: First-round pick in 6/91 free-agent draft

Player Summary	
Fantasy Value.	$2 to $4
Card Value	15¢ to 30¢
Will	try for 20-20 club
Can't	cut strikeout rate
Expect	solid power stroke
Don't Expect	defensive woes

After spending less than three full seasons in the minors, Kelly acquitted himself well in the majors—despite a minor-league reputation for fanning too frequently. He has already drawn favorable comparisons with Barry Bonds and Eric Davis. In fact, the late Jim Brock, his college coach, said Kelly was more advanced at the same stage of his career than Bonds, another Arizona State product. A multiskilled player, Kelly has already turned the 20-20 trick in the minors. If he ever masters the strike zone—and gets enough playing time—he might blossom into a 30-30 man. He had a .308 average in late-inning pressure spots in '94. His speed gives him great range in center field, his best position. He also has a solid arm. Though he formed a right-left platoon with Ryan Klesko last year, Kelly will eventually play every day. The former All-American was also a College Player of the Year and Golden Spikes Award winner. At Triple-A Richmond last year, he batted .262 with 15 homers, 45 RBI, 32 walks, and 96 strikeouts in 313 at bats. He hit .243 with 19 homers and 58 RBI at Richmond in '93.

Major League Batting Register

	BA	G	AB	R	H	2B	3B	HR	RBI	SB
94 NL	.273	30	77	14	21	10	1	2	9	0
Life	.273	30	77	14	21	10	1	2	9	0

PAT KELLY

Position: Second base
Team: New York Yankees
Born: Oct. 10, 1967 Philadelphia, PA
Height: 6' **Weight:** 180 lbs.
Bats: right **Throws:** right
Acquired: Ninth-round pick in 6/88 free-agent draft

Player Summary	
Fantasy Value.	$7 to $9
Card Value	5¢ to 7¢
Will	play strong defense
Can't	generate much power
Expect	top bat vs. lefties
Don't Expect	high on-base mark

During his first two seasons, Kelly proved so pathetic at the plate that Yankee management questioned his future. Over the last two years, however, he has quieted the critics. Despite leg and hand injuries last year, he hit nearly .300 over the first half before settling for a career-best .280. He even showed some power against left-handers, finishing with a .305 mark against them. Because he's basically a singles hitter, he needs to make better contact to utilize his speed. He twice stole 31 bases in the minors but won't ever approach that total if he doesn't correct the 3-1 ratio of strikeouts to walks that he had in 1994. He lacks the patience to post a decent on-base percentage, though he's a solid RBI man for a No. 9 hitter. A fine bunter who also fattens his average by beating out infield rollers, Kelly may never reach double digits in home runs. Though he struggles in clutch situations, his defense compensates. He has terrific range, a powerful arm, and the ability to make spectacular plays.

Major League Batting Register

	BA	G	AB	R	H	2B	3B	HR	RBI	SB
91 AL	.242	96	298	35	72	12	4	3	23	12
92 AL	.226	106	318	38	72	22	2	7	27	8
93 AL	.273	127	406	49	111	24	1	7	51	14
94 AL	.280	93	286	35	80	21	2	3	41	6
Life	.256	422	1308	157	335	79	9	20	142	40
3 AVE	.262	121	376	45	99	25	2	6	45	10

ROBERTO KELLY

Position: Outfield
Team: Atlanta Braves
Born: Oct. 1, 1964   Panama City, Panama
Height: 6'4"   **Weight:** 185 lbs.
Bats: right   **Throws:** right
Acquired: Traded from Reds with Roger Etheridge for Deion Sanders, 5/94

Player Summary

Fantasy Value	$18 to $21
Card Value	8¢ to 15¢
Will	try to find speed
Can't	wait for walks
Expect	great clutch stick
Don't Expect	poor defense

The Braves spent years trying to land Kelly. They liked his speed-plus-power potential, as well as his defensive ability in center field. An All-Star in both leagues, he has also performed the 20-20 feat in the majors. His stolen base totals have declined four years in a row, however, and he's not the burner he once was. Nor is he suited to the leadoff spot he inherited last summer. He fans twice as much as he walks and lacks the patience to hit at the top of the lineup. The stats suggest he should hit lower. He did his best hitting in 1994 with runners in scoring position (.347) and in late-inning pressure situations (.388). He was also deadly when ahead in the count. Kelly's stats against lefties and righties are virtually equal. He has great range in center and a strong arm. Shoulder injuries had hampered him in the past. His lone problem last year was the strike, stopping him short of a .300 season.

Major League Batting Register

	BA	G	AB	R	H	2B	3B	HR	RBI	SB
87 AL	.269	23	52	12	14	3	0	1	7	9
88 AL	.247	38	77	9	19	4	1	1	7	5
89 AL	.302	137	441	65	133	18	3	9	48	35
90 AL	.285	162	641	85	183	32	4	15	61	42
91 AL	.267	126	486	68	130	22	2	20	69	32
92 AL	.272	152	580	81	158	31	2	10	66	28
93 NL	.319	78	320	44	102	17	3	9	35	21
94 NL	.293	110	434	73	127	23	3	9	45	19
Life	.286	826	3031	437	866	150	18	74	338	191
3 AVE	.290	128	504	76	146	27	3	11	55	25

JEFF KENT

Position: Second base
Team: New York Mets
Born: March 7, 1968   Bellflower, CA
Height: 6'1"   **Weight:** 185 lbs.
Bats: right   **Throws:** right
Acquired: Traded from Blue Jays with Ryan Thompson for David Cone, 8/92

Player Summary

Fantasy Value	$14 to $17
Card Value	12¢ to 20¢
Will	surprise with bat
Can't	reduce whiff rate
Expect	improving defense
Don't Expect	many swipes

After starting the 1994 season like Superman, Kent reclaimed his identity as a steady but not spectacular performer. He hammered two homers in a game April 14, then repeated the feat three days later. But a strained tendon in his right foot bothered him all year; he felt pain when pushing off the foot while batting. Though Kent's batting average has risen for three straight years, his on-base percentage is nothing to brag about. He remains an undisciplined hitter who in '94 fanned nearly four times more than he walked. He's more selective with runners in scoring position, however, achieving a .385 batting average in that department last year. Kent is also a terror against left-handed pitchers (.373 in '94). He has good power and always seems to swing hard. He should increase his power output. Though he can run, he doesn't steal much. His speed gives him good range at second, where he's still mastering the art of defense. He had as many errors as homers in '94. Kent may move to third eventually.

Major League Batting Register

	BA	G	AB	R	H	2B	3B	HR	RBI	SB
92 AL	.240	65	192	36	46	13	1	8	35	2
92 NL	.239	37	113	16	27	8	1	3	15	0
93 NL	.270	140	496	65	134	24	0	21	80	4
94 NL	.292	107	415	53	121	24	5	14	68	1
Life	.270	349	1216	170	328	69	7	46	198	7
3 AVE	.272	131	462	64	126	26	3	17	75	2

JIMMY KEY

Position: Pitcher
Team: New York Yankees
Born: April 22, 1961   Huntsville, AL
Height: 6'1"   **Weight:** 190 lbs.
Bats: right   **Throws:** left
Acquired: Signed as a free agent, 11/92

Player Summary	
Fantasy Value	$20 to $25
Card Value	12¢ to 20¢
Will	vie for Cy Young
Can't	freeze basestealers
Expect	All-Star performance
Don't Expect	control woes

A control pitcher who works fast, Key has good command of a fastball, a curveball, a slider, and a changeup that has improved dramatically recently. In any given game, he never throws the same pitch at the same speed twice. Key compiled an 11-game winning streak, tops in the majors, before starting the 1994 All-Star Game for the American League. It was his fourth All-Star appearance. Before the players struck, Key had become the AL's first 16-game winner and the first Yankee to win 15 in consecutive years since Phil Niekro did it in 1984 and '85. Though he yielded more than a hit per inning, Key won by keeping the ball in the park, stifling left-handed hitters, and allowing less than three walks per nine innings. The Clemson product fields his position well, though he does have problems holding runners close. Key has won 12 or more games for 10 straight years.

Major League Pitching Register

	W	L	ERA	G	CG	IP	H	ER	BB	SO
84 AL	4	5	4.65	63	0	62.0	70	32	32	44
85 AL	14	6	3.00	35	3	212.2	188	71	50	85
86 AL	14	11	3.57	36	4	232.0	222	92	74	141
87 AL	17	8	2.76	36	8	261.0	210	80	66	161
88 AL	12	5	3.29	21	2	131.1	127	48	30	65
89 AL	13	14	3.88	33	5	216.0	226	93	27	118
90 AL	13	7	4.25	27	0	154.2	169	73	22	88
91 AL	16	12	3.05	33	2	209.1	207	71	44	125
92 AL	13	13	3.53	33	4	216.2	205	85	59	117
93 AL	18	6	3.00	34	4	236.2	219	79	43	173
94 AL	17	4	3.27	25	1	168.0	177	61	52	97
Life	151	91	3.36	376	33	2100.1	2020	785	499	1214
3 AVE	18	8	3.26	34	3	230.1	224	83	58	142

DARRYL KILE

Position: Pitcher
Team: Houston Astros
Born: Dec. 2, 1968   Garden Grove, CA
Height: 6'5"   **Weight:** 185 lbs.
Bats: right   **Throws:** right
Acquired: 30th-round pick in 6/87 free-agent draft

Player Summary	
Fantasy Value	$9 to $11
Card Value	8¢ to 12¢
Will	win with control
Can't	always find plate
Expect	world-class curve
Don't Expect	restraint

Consistent control problems hampered Kile's 1994 performance. Battling himself and his mechanics, he was leading the league in walks June 5 before he beat Philadelphia 4-2. He later said that game was the first in which he could concentrate on the hitter. Kile throws a 92-mph fastball, plus a changeup. His out pitch, though, is a curveball with an enormous drop, but he needs to throw it for strikes. When he can't control the curve, he also has trouble controlling his temper. Kile yielded about a hit per inning and six and one-half batters per game last year. His average of five bases on balls per nine innings helped batters compile a .375 on-base average. Those walks prevented him from repeating a 1993 campaign that included 15 wins, an All-Star appearance, and a no-hitter. He also threw 10 wild pitches—more than the rest of the Astro rotation *combined*. When he's right, he gets lots of ground-ball outs. Kile can bunt and field but isn't much of a hitter or pickoff artist.

Major League Pitching Register

	W	L	ERA	G	CG	IP	H	ER	BB	SO
91 NL	7	11	3.69	37	0	153.2	144	63	84	100
92 NL	5	10	3.95	22	2	125.1	124	55	63	90
93 NL	15	8	3.51	32	4	171.2	152	67	69	141
94 NL	9	6	4.57	24	0	147.2	153	75	82	105
Life	36	35	3.91	115	6	598.1	573	260	298	436
3 AVE	11	9	4.06	29	2	168.2	164	76	83	126

JEFF KING

Position: Third base
Team: Pittsburgh Pirates
Born: Dec. 26, 1964   Marion, IN
Height: 6'1"   **Weight:** 180 lbs.
Bats: right   **Throws:** right
Acquired: First-round pick in 6/86 free-agent draft

Player Summary	
Fantasy Value	$9 to $11
Card Value	6¢ to 10¢
Will	hit to all fields
Can't	clear fence often
Expect	better bat vs. lefties
Don't Expect	great speed

After reaching career peaks with a .295 average and 98 RBI in 1993, King couldn't pick up the pace last summer. He struggled against southpaws—after hitting .324 against them the year before—and dropped from .303 with runners in scoring position (1993) to .247. A contact hitter who uses all fields, he is no longer the wild man who once chased high heat and low breaking balls. He now walks almost as often as he fans. He does hit too many ground balls that turn into double plays or easy infield outs. King lacks the speed to fatten his average with infield hits and rarely steals a base (three out of five in 1994). In the field, he has quick reflexes, good hands, and an arm that is reliable though not powerful. He has made dramatic defensive improvement at third in recent seasons. King is a versatile player who in 1992 filled in at each of the other three infield spots. A former All-American from Arkansas, King was the first player taken in the '86 draft.

Major League Batting Register

	BA	G	AB	R	H	2B	3B	HR	RBI	SB
89 NL	.195	75	215	31	42	13	3	5	19	4
90 NL	.245	127	371	46	91	17	1	14	53	3
91 NL	.239	33	109	16	26	1	1	4	18	3
92 NL	.231	130	480	56	111	21	2	14	65	4
93 NL	.295	158	611	82	180	35	3	9	98	8
94 NL	.263	94	339	36	89	23	0	5	42	3
Life	.254	617	2125	267	539	110	10	51	295	25
3 AVE	.265	140	523	63	139	29	2	10	74	5

MIKE KINGERY

Position: Outfield
Team: Colorado Rockies
Born: March 29, 1961   St. James, MN
Height: 6'   **Weight:** 185 lbs.
Bats: left   **Throws:** left
Acquired: Signed as a free agent, 12/93

Player Summary	
Fantasy Value	$3 to $5
Card Value	5¢ to 8¢
Will	handle lefties well
Can't	clear outfield walls
Expect	high on-base average
Don't Expect	great speed

After spending parts of the preceding six seasons in the minors, Kingery proved last spring that perseverance pays off. He won a spot in the Colorado outfield with his steady performance early in the '94 campaign and contributed numerous key hits to the cause. One of the most memorable was a seventh-inning homer July 9 that broke up a no-hitter by Florida's Pat Rapp. It was the only Rocky hit that day. Though he doesn't clear the fences often, Kingery compensates by spraying hits to all fields. Lefties hardly intimidate the left-handed hitter; his 1994 average against southpaws was .378. Kingery also topped .330 against right-handers, at home and on the road. A solid hitter with runners in scoring position, he has good in-the-gap power, with more than one-third of his hits going for extra bases. He doesn't steal much but runs well enough to play center, where he filled in for the injured Ellis Burks. Kingery can also play the corners.

Major League Batting Register

	BA	G	AB	R	H	2B	3B	HR	RBI	SB
86 AL	.258	62	209	25	54	8	5	3	14	7
87 AL	.280	120	354	38	99	25	4	9	52	7
88 AL	.203	57	123	21	25	6	0	1	9	3
89 AL	.224	31	76	14	17	3	0	2	6	1
90 NL	.295	105	207	24	61	7	1	0	24	6
91 NL	.182	91	110	13	20	2	2	0	8	1
92 NL	.107	12	28	3	3	0	0	0	1	0
94 NL	.349	105	301	56	105	27	8	4	41	5
Life	.273	583	1408	194	384	78	20	19	155	30

WAYNE KIRBY

Position: Outfield
Team: Cleveland Indians
Born: Jan. 22, 1964 Williamsburg, VA
Height: 5'11" **Weight:** 185 lbs.
Bats: left **Throws:** right
Acquired: Signed as a free agent, 12/90

Player Summary	
Fantasy Value.	$7 to $9
Card Value	5¢ to 7¢
Will	deliver in clutch
Can't	produce much power
Expect	great throwing arm
Don't Expect.	big hits vs. lefties

One year after leading the AL with 19 assists from right field, Kirby proved more valuable on offense than defense. Used as the lefty platoon partner for rookie Manny Ramirez, Kirby contributed a .293 average, 11 steals in 15 tries, and solid .300-plus marks with runners in scoring position, in late-inning pressure situations, and in road games. While Ramirez struggled in the clutch, Kirby prospered. A singles hitter who makes good contact, Kirby doesn't walk or fan much. Though he's a better hitter against right-handers, he holds his own against left-handers. He thrives on a fastball diet and knows how to take a pitch to the off-field. A good No. 2 hitter, he can bunt, work the hit-and-run, or move runners with a well-placed grounder. He topped 30 steals in the minors six times—most recently in 1992—but uses his speed on defense more than offense. He has great range and a powerful arm in right, though he made only two assists last summer. Kirby started his pro career in 1983.

Major League Batting Register

	BA	G	AB	R	H	2B	3B	HR	RBI	SB
91 AL	.209	21	43	4	9	2	0	0	5	1
92 AL	.167	21	18	9	3	1	0	1	1	0
93 AL	.269	131	458	71	123	19	5	6	60	17
94 AL	.293	78	191	33	56	6	0	5	23	11
Life	.269	251	710	117	191	28	5	12	89	29
2 AVE	.278	120	364	59	101	14	3	7	46	16

RYAN KLESKO

Position: Outfield; first base
Team: Atlanta Braves
Born: June 12, 1971 Westminster, CA
Height: 6'3" **Weight:** 220 lbs.
Bats: left **Throws:** left
Acquired: Fifth-round pick in 6/89 free-agent draft

Player Summary	
Fantasy Value.	$13 to $16
Card Value	20¢ to 35¢
Will	show tremendous power
Can't	rely on speed
Expect	platooning to end
Don't Expect.	solid defense

Cracking a contender's lineup is tough for a rookie, but changing positions makes life doubly difficult. Blocked at first base by Fred McGriff, Klesko was still learning the rudiments of left field when the 1994 season started. His adventures in left reminded some scouts of Greg Luzinski, but so did Klesko's bat. Used almost exclusively against right-handed pitchers—despite Klesko's claim that he hit lefties well in the minors—he finished his first season with a .563 slugging percentage, second only on the Braves to McGriff. As he learns the pitchers, Klesko expects to improve on a strikeout-to-walk ratio of 2-to-1. An intense competitor who tries to coax maximum mileage from his muscular physique, he has a return to first base in his future. As of now, he's determined to make himself into a competent outfielder. A former pitcher, Klesko's strong throwing arm is his biggest asset in the field. In 1993 at Triple-A Richmond, he batted .274 with 22 homers and 74 RBI; he was named the No. 4 prospect in the loop.

Major League Batting Register

	BA	G	AB	R	H	2B	3B	HR	RBI	SB
92 NL	.000	13	14	0	0	0	0	0	1	0
93 NL	.353	22	17	3	6	1	0	2	5	0
94 NL	.278	92	245	42	68	13	3	17	47	1
Life	.268	127	276	45	74	14	3	19	53	1

CHUCK KNOBLAUCH

Position: Second base
Team: Minnesota Twins
Born: July 7, 1968 Houston, TX
Height: 5'9" **Weight:** 175 lbs.
Bats: right **Throws:** right
Acquired: First-round pick in 6/89 free-agent draft

Player Summary	
Fantasy Value	$20 to $25
Card Value	10¢ to 20¢
Will	use opposite field
Can't	produce home runs
Expect	speed and defense
Don't Expect	batting title

A kid who keeps improving, Knoblauch is one of baseball's best second basemen. By standing straighter at the plate and adopting a wider stance, he produced his first .300 season in 1994. He made the All-Star team for the second time, led the majors with 45 doubles, and swiped 35 bases in 41 tries. When he booted a ball July 3, he was four short of Jerry Adair's AL record of 89 consecutive errorless games. Though Knoblauch excels with runners in scoring position, he is so effective at the top of the lineup that he became the Twins' leadoff man April 30. By Memorial Day, he was on pace for 88 doubles, 21 more than Earl Webb's major-league mark. Knoblauch makes contact, walking almost as much as he fans and spraying hits the opposite way. His speed translates into good range at second. The 1991 AL Rookie of the Year also has good instincts, good hands, and a strong enough arm to play short—his position at Texas A&M. A 1994 *Baseball America* poll ranked him No. 2 in the AL on defense at second base.

Major League Batting Register

	BA	G	AB	R	H	2B	3B	HR	RBI	SB
91 AL	.281	151	565	78	159	24	6	1	50	25
92 AL	.297	155	600	104	178	19	6	2	56	34
93 AL	.277	153	602	82	167	27	4	2	41	29
94 AL	.312	109	445	85	139	45	3	5	51	35
Life	.291	568	2212	349	643	115	19	10	198	123
3 AVE	.296	154	610	102	180	36	5	4	56	37

RANDY KNORR

Position: Catcher
Team: Toronto Blue Jays
Born: Nov. 12, 1968 San Gabriel, CA
Height: 6'2" **Weight:** 215 lbs.
Bats: right **Throws:** right
Acquired: 10th-round pick in 6/86 free-agent draft

Player Summary	
Fantasy Value	$1
Card Value	6¢ to 8¢
Will	hit vs. lefties
Can't	run very well
Expect	decent defense
Don't Expect	everyday berth

Though he retained his usual reserve role last summer, Knorr responded well when given the most at bats of his big-league career. He even smashed two home runs in a 9-1 win at Texas July 23. Knorr hit an impressive .333 against left-handed pitchers and finished with a .500 average in late-inning pressure situations, albeit with limited exposure. He does have some pop, evidenced by his three double-digit home run years in the minors. Most recently, in 1992 at Triple-A Syracuse, he batted .272 with 11 homers and 27 RBI in 228 at bats. An over-aggressive hitter who lives for fastballs, Knorr in 1994 averaged three and one-half strikeouts per walk. Like most catchers, his running speed is nonexistent. Before last year, Knorr was known for his ability to nail opposing runners, but he bagged only 23 percent in '94. He did demonstrate good game-calling ability, however. Before the All-Star break, the Jays were 15-7 with him catching but 23-41 without. Juan Guzman specifically requested that Knorr catch his games.

Major League Batting Register

	BA	G	AB	R	H	2B	3B	HR	RBI	SB
91 AL	.000	3	1	0	0	0	0	0	0	0
92 AL	.263	8	19	1	5	0	0	1	2	0
93 AL	.248	39	101	11	25	3	2	4	20	0
94 AL	.242	40	124	20	30	2	0	7	19	0
Life	.245	90	245	32	60	5	2	12	41	0

CHAD KREUTER

Position: Catcher
Team: Detroit Tigers
Born: Aug. 26, 1964 Greenbrae, CA
Height: 6'2" **Weight:** 195 lbs.
Bats: right **Throws:** right
Acquired: Signed as a free agent, 1/92

Player Summary	
Fantasy Value	$2 to $4
Card Value	6¢ to 10¢
Will	try for '93 form
Can't	hit lefties
Expect	strong defense
Don't Expect	many homers

One year after the eruption of his long-dormant bat, Kreuter reverted to his light-hitting ways in 1994. He failed to hit his weight against left-handed pitchers, with runners in scoring position, and in late-inning pressure situations. In fact, he had only one shining moment at the plate: a May 22 home run that cleared the right field roof at Tiger Stadium—territory scaled previously by only 17 hitters. He was able to notch 28 walks and a .327 on-base average. His defense was another story. The Pepperdine College product nailed 20 of the 46 runners who tried to steal against him, a 43 percent success rate that ranked near the top of the league. He calls a good game, prevents wild pitches, and blocks the plate well. If his offense had matched his defense last summer, Mickey Tettleton would have remained a rover, instead of almost splitting games behind the plate with Kreuter. Kreuter's big concern now is to show that 1993 was not a fluke.

Major League Batting Register

	BA	G	AB	R	H	2B	3B	HR	RBI	SB
88 AL	.275	16	51	3	14	2	1	1	5	0
89 AL	.152	87	158	16	24	3	0	5	9	0
90 AL	.045	22	22	2	1	1	0	0	2	0
91 AL	.000	3	4	0	0	0	0	0	0	0
92 AL	.253	67	190	22	48	9	0	2	16	0
93 AL	.286	119	374	59	107	23	3	15	51	2
94 AL	.224	65	170	17	38	8	0	1	19	0
Life	.239	379	969	119	232	46	4	24	102	2
3 AVE	.260	93	268	35	70	14	1	6	31	1

JOHN KRUK

Position: First base
Team: Philadelphia Phillies
Born: Feb. 9, 1961 Charleston, WV
Height: 5'10" **Weight:** 204 lbs.
Bats: left **Throws:** left
Acquired: Traded from Padres with Randy Ready for Chris James, 6/89

Player Summary	
Fantasy Value	$10 to $13
Card Value	10¢ to 20¢
Will	target opposite field
Can't	steal bases
Expect	return to full health
Don't Expect	great power

The feeling persists that Kruk could hit in his sleep. Even in a year when he couldn't stay healthy, he came through the finish line with his average above .300. His physical problems robbed some of his power, but Kruk was more of a line-drive hitter anyway. The three-time All-Star had a cancerous testicle removed during spring training, then later went on the DL with knee trouble—a problem he blamed on the hard artificial turf at Veterans Stadium. Surgeons had to operate on him again. When healthy, he is a dead fastball hitter known for his upright stance, quick wrists, and ability to take the ball the opposite way. He walks more than he fans, giving him a high on-base percentage (.430, second in the NL, in 1993). Though he struggled against southpaws last year, Kruk usually holds his own, and he hurts righties. He's especially potent in the clutch. He's also an above-average fielder at first.

Major League Batting Register

	BA	G	AB	R	H	2B	3B	HR	RBI	SB
86 NL	.309	122	278	33	86	16	2	4	38	2
87 NL	.313	138	447	72	140	14	2	20	91	18
88 NL	.241	120	378	54	91	17	1	9	44	5
89 NL	.300	112	357	53	107	13	6	8	44	3
90 NL	.291	142	443	52	129	25	8	7	67	10
91 NL	.294	152	538	84	158	27	6	21	92	7
92 NL	.323	144	507	86	164	30	4	10	70	3
93 NL	.316	150	535	100	169	33	5	14	85	6
94 NL	.302	75	255	35	77	17	0	5	38	4
Life	.300	1155	3738	569	1121	192	34	98	569	58
3 AVE	.315	133	467	78	147	29	3	10	70	5

MARK LANGSTON

Position: Pitcher
Team: California Angels
Born: Aug. 20, 1960   San Diego, CA
Height: 6'2"   **Weight:** 190 lbs.
Bats: right   **Throws:** left
Acquired: Signed as a free agent, 12/89

Player Summary	
Fantasy Value	$10 to $13
Card Value	10¢ to 20¢
Will	win big with help
Can't	keep ball in park
Expect	lots of strikeouts
Don't Expect	top control

The 1994 campaign was not a good one for Langston. He had April surgery on his left elbow for the removal of bone chips and didn't return to full strength for several months. The three-time strikeout king had entered the season determined to reduce his number of pitches per game. He knew he had lost some velocity off his fastball—a fact that often became obvious in the late innings. He couldn't overcome the combination of surgery, poor run support (4.33), and the Aug. 12 player strike, as his five-year streak of double-digit wins came to an end. Langston did finish fourth in the AL with more than eight strikeouts per nine innings. His repertoire includes a heater, a curveball, a slider, and a changeup. He is especially effective against lefties. A multiple Gold Glove winner, Langston also has a good pickoff move.

Major League Pitching Register

	W	L	ERA	G	CG	IP	H	ER	BB	SO
84 AL	17	10	3.40	35	5	225.0	188	85	118	204
85 AL	7	14	5.47	24	2	126.2	122	77	91	72
86 AL	12	14	4.85	37	9	239.1	234	129	123	245
87 AL	19	13	3.84	35	14	272.0	242	116	114	262
88 AL	15	11	3.34	35	9	261.1	222	97	110	235
89 AL	4	5	3.56	10	2	73.1	60	29	19	60
89 NL	12	9	2.39	24	6	176.2	138	47	93	175
90 AL	10	17	4.40	33	5	223.0	215	109	104	195
91 AL	19	8	3.00	34	7	246.1	190	82	96	183
92 AL	13	14	3.66	32	9	229.0	206	93	74	174
93 AL	16	11	3.20	35	7	256.1	220	91	85	196
94 AL	7	8	4.68	18	2	119.1	121	62	54	109
Life	151	134	3.74	352	77	2448.1	2158	1017	1081	2110
3 AVE	13	12	3.74	31	6	218.1	199	90	78	175

RAY LANKFORD

Position: Outfield
Team: St. Louis Cardinals
Born: June 5, 1967   Modesto, CA
Height: 5'11"   **Weight:** 180 lbs.
Bats: left   **Throws:** left
Acquired: Third-round pick in 6/87 free-agent draft

Player Summary	
Fantasy Value	$18 to $21
Card Value	10¢ to 15¢
Will	show good speed
Can't	hit left-handers
Expect	solid power bat
Don't Expect	fielding trouble

Though he avoided the nasty injuries that plagued him in 1993, Lankford remained a mystery to the Cardinals. He was only a shadow of the player who produced 20 home runs, 42 stolen bases, and a league-best 438 outfield putouts in 1992. His biggest problem is an inability to hit left-handers. He not only failed to hit his weight against lefties but also sank under the Mendoza Line in late-inning pressure situations. By midsummer, the Cardinals were lifting him for switch-hitting Gerald Young against some southpaws. Though Lankford tied Todd Zeile with a team-high 19 homers, he also led the club with 113 strikeouts—giving him a 2-1 ratio of whiffs to walks. It was the fourth straight year he finished above the century mark in strikeouts. Unless he can regain his reputation as a basestealer (86 stolen bases total in 1991 and '92), Lankford could become a platoon player. He is a strong defensive center fielder, but that will not be enough to keep him in the lineup every day.

Major League Batting Register

	BA	G	AB	R	H	2B	3B	HR	RBI	SB
90 NL	.286	39	126	12	36	10	1	3	12	8
91 NL	.251	151	566	83	142	23	15	9	69	44
92 NL	.293	153	598	87	175	40	6	20	86	42
93 NL	.238	127	407	64	97	17	3	7	45	14
94 NL	.267	109	416	89	111	25	5	19	57	11
Life	.265	579	2113	335	561	115	30	58	269	119
3 AVE	.269	145	530	92	143	31	5	18	70	24

MIKE LANSING

Position: Second base
Team: Montreal Expos
Born: April 3, 1968 Rawlins, WY
Height: 6′ **Weight:** 175 lbs.
Bats: right **Throws:** right
Acquired: Purchased from Miami of the
Florida State League, 9/91

Player Summary	
Fantasy Value	$7 to $9
Card Value	6¢ to 10¢
Will	make decent contact
Can't	generate much power
Expect	better use of speed
Don't Expect	bad bat vs. lefties

Though his offense suffered slightly last summer, Lansing escaped the sophomore jinx unscathed. He succeeded the traded Delino DeShields as Montreal's regular second baseman, and Lansing also filled in more than a dozen times each at short and third. In addition, he provided a steady bat from the No. 8 hole. A good contact man who walks almost as often as he fans, Lansing can bunt, work the hit-and-run, and deliver line drives to all fields. He'll even clear the fences occasionally, though most of his extra-base hits (20-plus per year) are doubles. He has enough speed to top 20 steals per year but sometimes takes too many chances. His speed helps in the field, where he has excellent range, quick reactions, and a fine throwing arm. He can also turn two from either side of second base. The constant position-changing may be hurting his defense, however. Lansing made 10 errors in 82 games at second. The Wichita State product led the NCAA in runs scored in 1989 and was chosen in 1990 in the sixth round by the independent Miami Miracle.

Major League Batting Register

	BA	G	AB	R	H	2B	3B	HR	RBI	SB
93 NL	.287	141	491	64	141	29	1	3	45	23
94 NL	.266	106	394	44	105	21	2	5	35	12
Life	.278	247	885	108	246	50	3	8	80	35
2 AVE	.276	145	523	63	144	29	2	5	47	20

BARRY LARKIN

Position: Shortstop
Team: Cincinnati Reds
Born: April 28, 1964 Cincinnati, OH
Height: 6′ **Weight:** 185 lbs.
Bats: right **Throws:** right
Acquired: First-round pick in 6/85 free-agent
draft

Player Summary	
Fantasy Value	$25 to $30
Card Value	15¢ to 25¢
Will	seek 20-20
Can't	avoid injuries
Expect	All-Star play
Don't Expect	too many Ks

Though the player strike stopped his five-year streak of .300 seasons, Larkin retained his reputation as the NL's best at his position. After struggling for two months, he compiled a 19-game hitting streak in June. Fans voted him the All-Star starting shortstop for the second straight year. His eighth-inning homer against John Burkett beat the Giants 2-1 June 21. Ten days before the strike, Larkin had two homers and a double in a 9-7 win against San Francisco. A contact hitter who walks more than he fans, he loves fastballs and uses all fields. He has enough power to get extra bases on nearly one-third of his hits. The former Michigan All-American swiped 26 out of 28 bases last year (a .929 success ratio) and hit a solid .323 with runners in scoring position. Larkin's defense may transcend his offense. His reactions, hands, and arm are excellent, and his range at shortstop is easily the best in the NL.

Major League Batting Register

	BA	G	AB	R	H	2B	3B	HR	RBI	SB
86 NL	.283	41	159	27	45	4	3	3	19	8
87 NL	.244	125	439	64	107	16	2	12	43	21
88 NL	.296	151	588	91	174	32	5	12	56	40
89 NL	.342	97	325	47	111	14	4	4	36	10
90 NL	.301	158	614	85	185	25	6	7	67	30
91 NL	.302	123	464	88	140	27	4	20	69	24
92 NL	.304	140	533	76	162	32	6	12	78	15
93 NL	.315	100	384	57	121	20	3	8	51	14
94 NL	.279	110	427	78	119	23	5	9	52	26
Life	.296	1045	3933	613	1164	193	38	87	471	188
3 AVE	.297	132	506	81	150	28	5	11	67	22

MIKE LaVALLIERE

Position: Catcher
Team: Chicago White Sox
Born: Aug. 18, 1960 Charlotte, NC
Height: 5'9" **Weight:** 210 lbs.
Bats: left **Throws:** right
Acquired: Signed as a free agent, 5/93

Player Summary	
Fantasy Value	$0
Card Value	5¢ to 7¢
Will	produce in clutch
Can't	reach the fences
Expect	good contact bat
Don't Expect	any speed

Throughout his 11-year career in the majors, LaValliere has been most highly regarded for his defensive skills. Despite his rotund physique, the one-time Philadelphia draftee won a Gold Glove in 1987 and earned a berth on the NL All-Star team selected by *The Sporting News* a year later. At the plate, he is a singles hitter who makes good contact, walking more often than he fans. All his hits are legitimate, since he has no hope of fattening his average on rollers that remain in the infield. Though usually more effective against right-handed pitchers, he hit lefties at a .304 clip last year. He saved his best hitting for late-inning pressure situations, with a .350 average. LaValliere calls good games, blocks the plate well, prevents wild pitches, and owns a strong arm. He has played in four League Championship Series.

Major League Batting Register

	BA	G	AB	R	H	2B	3B	HR	RBI	SB
84 NL	.000	6	7	0	0	0	0	0	0	0
85 NL	.147	12	34	2	5	1	0	0	6	0
86 NL	.234	110	303	18	71	10	2	3	30	0
87 NL	.300	121	340	33	102	19	0	1	36	0
88 NL	.261	120	352	24	92	18	0	2	47	3
89 NL	.316	68	190	15	60	10	0	2	23	0
90 NL	.258	96	279	27	72	15	0	3	31	0
91 NL	.289	108	336	25	97	11	2	3	41	2
92 NL	.256	95	293	22	75	13	1	2	29	0
93 NL	.200	1	5	0	1	0	0	0	0	0
93 AL	.258	37	97	6	25	2	0	0	8	0
94 AL	.281	59	139	6	39	4	0	1	24	0
Life	.269	833	2375	178	639	103	5	17	275	5

MANNY LEE

Position: Shortstop; second base
Team: Texas Rangers
Born: June 17, 1965 San Pedro de Macoris, Dominican Republic
Height: 5'9" **Weight:** 161 lbs.
Bats: both **Throws:** right
Acquired: Signed as a free agent, 12/92

Player Summary	
Fantasy Value	$3 to $5
Card Value	5¢ to 7¢
Will	use opposite field
Can't	produce much power
Expect	pretty solid glove
Don't Expect	great on-base mark

A switch-hitter who's better from the right side, Lee loves to spray singles to the opposite field. Though not known for his power, he delivered in the clutch last summer by hitting .337 with runners in scoring position and .304 in late-inning pressure situations. Those are great numbers for a man deployed at the bottom of the lineup. Lee would be more valuable if he learned to wait for his pitch. He struck out three times more than he walked in 1994. An aggressive hitter with little patience, he hits better with the count in his favor. He has the speed to bunt for base hits but more often uses the bunt in sacrifice situations. Usually a sound defensive shortstop, Lee made only seven miscues in 128 games in 1992, but he had 13 in 85 games last year. He has sound instincts, good hands, and superb range. Lee also has a quick release that compensates for a fair arm.

Major League Batting Register

	BA	G	AB	R	H	2B	3B	HR	RBI	SB
85 AL	.200	64	40	9	8	0	0	0	0	1
86 AL	.205	35	78	8	16	0	1	1	7	0
87 AL	.256	56	121	14	31	2	3	1	11	2
88 AL	.291	116	381	38	111	16	3	2	38	3
89 AL	.260	99	300	27	78	9	2	3	34	4
90 AL	.243	117	391	45	95	12	4	6	41	3
91 AL	.234	138	445	41	104	18	3	0	29	7
92 AL	.263	128	396	49	104	10	1	3	39	6
93 AL	.220	73	205	31	45	3	1	1	12	2
94 AL	.278	95	335	41	93	18	2	2	38	3
Life	.254	921	2692	303	685	88	20	19	249	31
3 AVE	.261	112	358	46	93	13	2	2	35	4

PHIL LEFTWICH

Position: Pitcher
Team: California Angels
Born: May 19, 1969 Lynchburg, VA
Height: 6'5" **Weight:** 205 lbs.
Bats: right **Throws:** right
Acquired: Second-round pick in 6/90 free-agent draft

Player Summary	
Fantasy Value	$1
Card Value	12¢ to 20¢
Will	go for grounders
Can't	avoid homers
Expect	improved changeup
Don't Expect	ERA to stay high

The sophomore jinx hit Leftwich hard last summer, never mind that his run support was the weakest on the Angel staff at just under four runs a game. A sinker-slider pitcher with a still-developing changeup, he usually has good location, allowing about three and one-third walks per nine innings in '94. He yielded more than 10 hits per nine innings, however, and had trouble keeping the ball in the park. Not a power pitcher, he didn't even come close to posting a 2-1 ratio of strikeouts to walks. Instead, too many of the ground balls he yielded eluded the gloves of Angel infielders. The Radford University star keeps a close watch on runners but sometimes has problems fielding. Leftwich has the size, strength, and potential to blossom into a big-league standout. He fanned 163 batters in 173 innings in 1991 at Class-A Quad City but has yet to recapture that form in the big leagues. Leftwich launched his pro career with an 8-2 record and a 1.86 ERA for Class-A Boise in 1990. At Triple-A Vancouver in 1993, he was 7-7 with a 4.64 ERA, 102 strikeouts, and 45 walks in 126 frames.

Major League Pitching Register

	W	L	ERA	G	CG	IP	H	ER	BB	SO
93 AL	4	6	3.79	12	1	80.2	81	34	27	31
94 AL	5	10	5.68	20	1	114.0	127	72	42	67
Life	9	16	4.90	32	2	194.2	208	106	69	98
2 AVE	6	10	5.05	20	1	120.1	130	68	43	63

AL LEITER

Position: Pitcher
Team: Toronto Blue Jays
Born: Oct. 23, 1965 Toms River, NJ
Height: 6'3" **Weight:** 215 lbs.
Bats: left **Throws:** left
Acquired: Traded from Yankees for Jesse Barfield, 4/89

Player Summary	
Fantasy Value	$1 to $3
Card Value	5¢ to 7¢
Will	keep ball in park
Can't	locate home plate
Expect	high whiff totals
Don't Expect	double-digit wins

After pitching effectively out of the Toronto bullpen during the second half of 1993, Leiter returned to the rotation last season. The move may have weakened both areas. Unable to throw strikes with his fastball, cut fastball, or curve, he averaged more than five walks per nine innings. When he tried to compensate by catching the fat part of the plate, the hitters were ready. Leiter wound up surrendering more than 10 hits per nine innings, though he did have good success at keeping the ball in the park. He pitched effectively against lefties. His tendency toward wildness hurts, nonetheless. Though he ranked fifth in innings among Toronto starters last year, he was first in balks, with five, and second in wild pitches, with seven. He keeps baserunners at bay but doesn't help himself with his fielding. With his injury woes behind him, Leiter is long past the potential stage. Now is the time to produce.

Major League Pitching Register

	W	L	ERA	G	CG	IP	H	ER	BB	SO
87 AL	2	2	6.35	4	0	22.2	24	16	15	28
88 AL	4	4	3.92	14	0	57.1	49	25	33	60
89 AL	1	2	5.67	5	0	33.1	32	21	23	26
90 AL	0	0	0.00	4	0	6.1	1	0	2	5
91 AL	0	0	27.00	3	0	1.2	3	5	5	1
92 AL	0	0	9.00	1	0	1.0	1	1	2	0
93 AL	9	6	4.11	34	0	105.0	93	48	56	66
94 AL	6	7	5.08	20	1	111.2	125	63	65	100
Life	22	21	4.75	85	2	339.0	328	179	201	286
2 AVE	9	8	4.69	31	1	131.1	135	68	74	103

MARK LEITER

Position: Pitcher
Team: California Angels
Born: April 13, 1963   Joliet, IL
Height: 6'3"   **Weight:** 210 lbs.
Bats: right   **Throws:** right
Acquired: Signed as a free agent, 4/94

Player Summary

Fantasy Value	$1
Card Value	5¢ to 7¢
Will	strand baserunners
Can't	prevent home runs
Expect	best work from pen
Don't Expect	runners to steal

Though he had spent most of his career as a starter, Leiter proved to be a valuable member of the Angel bullpen last summer. He stranded 21 of the 24 runners he inherited, an 87.5 percent success rate, and was extremely effective against right-handed hitters (.236). He worked a career-high 40 times, with all but seven coming in relief, while maintaining a 2-1 ratio of strikeouts to walks. He yielded just over a hit per inning, and three and one-third walks and about six and one-half strikeouts per nine innings. Keeping the ball in the park was a bit of a problem, however. Though shoulder problems have hampered his performance in the past, Leiter seemed sound last summer. He throws a fastball, a slider, and a changeup with a three-quarters delivery that is deceiving to right-handers. He bears down with runners in scoring position and keeps a close eye on potential basestealers. A quick delivery helps. The Leiter glove doesn't; like his brother, Al, Mark is not a very good fielder.

Major League Pitching Register

	W	L	ERA	G	S	IP	H	ER	BB	SO
90 AL	1	1	6.84	8	0	26.1	33	20	9	21
91 AL	9	7	4.21	38	1	134.2	125	63	50	103
92 AL	8	5	4.18	35	0	112.0	116	52	43	75
93 AL	6	6	4.72	27	0	106.2	111	56	44	70
94 AL	4	7	4.72	40	2	95.1	99	50	35	71
Life	28	26	4.57	148	3	475.0	484	241	181	340
3 AVE	7	7	4.55	39	1	117.1	122	59	45	82

SCOTT LEIUS

Position: Third base
Team: Minnesota Twins
Born: Sept. 24, 1965   Yonkers, NY
Height: 6'3"   **Weight:** 185 lbs.
Bats: right   **Throws:** right
Acquired: 13th-round pick in 6/86 free-agent draft

Player Summary

Fantasy Value	$3 to $5
Card Value	5¢ to 7¢
Will	produce some power
Can't	steal all the time
Expect	improvement vs. lefties
Don't Expect	high on-base mark

Suddenly, last summer, Leius became a long-ball threat. After hitting eight home runs in 633 at bats during his first three seasons in the majors, the Concordia College product collected 14 in 350 at bats last year. Though he hit 12 points under his previous career average in 1994, Leius also reached double digits in home runs for the first time in a pro career that began in 1986. It wasn't his best season—that came in 1991, when he hit .286 and made such good contact that he had almost as many walks as strikeouts. The '94 power production was welcome, however, because third base is generally regarded as a power position. His output would have been even better if he had shown his usual form against left-handers, whom he hit at a .314 clip in 1992. Though he seldom steals, Leius runs well enough to have decent mobility around the third-base bag. He has good instincts, good hands, and the same strong throwing arm he had when he signed as a shortstop.

Major League Batting Register

	BA	G	AB	R	H	2B	3B	HR	RBI	SB
90 AL	.240	14	25	4	6	1	0	1	4	0
91 AL	.286	109	199	35	57	7	2	5	20	5
92 AL	.249	129	409	50	102	18	2	2	35	6
93 AL	.167	10	18	4	3	0	0	0	2	0
94 AL	.246	97	350	57	86	16	1	14	49	2
Life	.254	359	1001	150	254	42	5	22	110	13
2 AVE	.247	133	451	65	112	20	2	11	52	4

MARK LEMKE

Position: Second base
Team: Atlanta Braves
Born: Aug. 13, 1965 Utica, NY
Height: 5'9" **Weight:** 167 lbs.
Bats: both **Throws:** right
Acquired: 27th-round pick in 6/83 free-agent draft

Player Summary

Fantasy Value	$3 to $5
Card Value	6¢ to 10¢
Will	turn the double play
Can't	produce homers
Expect	solid hitting
Don't Expect	good speed

Boosting his average for the fourth time in five years, Lemke established himself as a fine No. 8 hitter. A switch-hitter who hit .294 against both lefties and righties, he used to be much better right-handed. He has worked hard to improve the other way, though, and has apparently succeeded. A contact hitter with an inside-out swing against lefties, Lemke has little speed and only occasional power. Despite his heroics in the 1991 World Series, he's not much of a clutch hitter. He seldom steals and hits into frequent double plays. Though he's a fine full-count hitter, Lemke would be more valuable if he showed more patience at the plate. He walks as much as he fans but doesn't do either with frequency. Lemke rarely produces when given the green light on a 3-1 count. He's a dependable fielder, despite his lack of height and speed. He turns two better than anyone, positions himself well, and has good reactions, soft hands, and a decent arm.

Major League Batting Register

	BA	G	AB	R	H	2B	3B	HR	RBI	SB
88 NL	.224	16	58	8	13	4	0	0	2	0
89 NL	.182	14	55	4	10	2	1	2	10	0
90 NL	.226	102	239	22	54	13	0	0	21	0
91 NL	.234	136	269	36	63	11	2	2	23	1
92 NL	.227	155	427	38	97	7	4	6	26	0
93 NL	.252	151	493	52	124	19	2	7	49	1
94 NL	.294	104	350	40	103	15	0	3	31	0
Life	.245	678	1891	200	464	71	9	20	162	2
3 AVE	.259	151	471	49	122	16	2	6	40	0

DARREN LEWIS

Position: Outfield
Team: San Francisco Giants
Born: Aug. 28, 1967 Berkeley, CA
Height: 6' **Weight:** 175 lbs.
Bats: right **Throws:** right
Acquired: Traded from Athletics with Pedro Pena for Ernest Riles, 12/90

Player Summary

Fantasy Value	$13 to $16
Card Value	6¢ to 10¢
Will	bunt for base hits
Can't	produce much power
Expect	Gold Glove defense
Don't Expect	tons of walks

If he ever learns to hit, Lewis will become one of baseball's most effective leadoff men. Though he's swiped 76 bases over the last two years, he would've stolen many more had he reached base more frequently. He walks more than he strikes out, but he could take more bases on balls to utilize his speed. Lewis is an aggressive hitter who likes to take his hacks. Since he has little power, the usual result is a flurry of singles up the middle. Like Brett Butler, Lewis is a skilled bunter who will beat out infield rollers or deliver timely sacrifices. He and Butler tied for the NL lead with nine triples each last year. Lewis's speed also helps him in center field, where he has made exactly two errors in a career that has spanned 446 games. He holds major-league records for consecutive errorless games and chances by an outfielder. His range and reactions are so impeccable that his leaps and dives seem almost ordinary in comparison. He took home his first Gold Glove in 1994.

Major League Batting Register

	BA	G	AB	R	H	2B	3B	HR	RBI	SB
90 AL	.229	25	35	4	8	0	0	0	1	2
91 NL	.248	72	222	41	55	5	3	1	15	13
92 NL	.231	100	320	38	74	8	1	1	18	28
93 NL	.253	136	522	84	132	17	7	2	48	46
94 NL	.257	114	451	70	116	15	9	4	29	30
Life	.248	447	1550	237	385	45	20	8	111	119
3 AVE	.250	132	492	74	123	15	7	3	36	39

RICHIE LEWIS

Position: Pitcher
Team: Florida Marlins
Born: Jan. 25, 1966 Muncie, IN
Height: 5'10" **Weight:** 175 lbs.
Bats: right **Throws:** right
Acquired: Second-round pick from Orioles in 11/92 expansion draft

Player Summary

Fantasy Value $0
Card Value .... 5¢ to 7¢
Will............... use overhand curve
Can't .... find strike zone
Expect .... heavy workload
Don't Expect .... woes with righties

A severe case of the sophomore jinx followed Lewis's fine freshman season for Florida. Though he pitched effectively against right-handers (.224) and stranded two-thirds of the runners he inherited, he battled control problems throughout the season. He averaged seven and one-half strikeouts per nine innings, but, unfortunately, he yielded close to six and one-half walks and led the Marlin bullpen with 10 wild pitches—thanks to an overhand curveball that breaks in the dirt with alarming frequency. Also deploying a high-80s fastball in a secondary role, Lewis has always had control trouble, but he has never had such a hard time with left-handed hitters. They ate him alive last year, batting .353. Lewis yielded more than 10 hits per nine innings, threw too many home run balls, and went 0-for-8 in nailing baserunners who tried to steal against him. The former Florida State hurler led the Marlin bullpen in relief wins and innings in 1993 and appearances last year. Continued control trouble will discontinue that.

Major League Pitching Register

	W	L	ERA	G	S	IP	H	ER	BB	SO
92 AL	1	1	10.80	2	0	6.2	13	8	7	4
93 NL	6	3	3.26	57	0	77.1	68	28	43	65
94 NL	1	4	5.67	45	0	54.0	62	34	38	45
Life	8	8	4.57	104	0	138.0	143	70	88	114
2 AVE	4	4	4.45	60	0	77.1	78	38	48	64

JIM LEYRITZ

Position: Catcher; designated hitter; first base
Team: New York Yankees
Born: Dec. 27, 1963 Lakewood, OH
Height: 6' **Weight:** 190 lbs.
Bats: right **Throws:** right
Acquired: Signed as a free agent, 8/85

Player Summary

Fantasy Value................. $5 to $7
Card Value .... 6¢ to 10¢
Will..................... hit to all fields
Can't .... steal many bases
Expect .... occasional power
Don't Expect .... fine defense

A valuable bench player, Leyritz can fill in at various positions, poke an important pinch hit, or serve as designated hitter. Don Mattingly's caddy at first base for several seasons, Leyritz outhomered the Yankee captain 17-6 while seeing considerably less playing time last summer. A good clutch hitter, Leyritz had a 1993 batting average of .394 with two outs and runners in scoring position. He didn't fare so well under pressure last summer but still delivered a career high in home runs. Oddly, he fares better against right-handed pitching than against left-handers. Being a role player and not a starter doesn't sit well with him; Leyritz caused controversy by complaining about a lack of playing time during a 10-game Yankee winning streak last year. He doesn't add anything as a basestealer or fielder, although he does own a strong enough arm for both catching and right field. Leyritz is not a great receiver, however, and nailed 24 percent of the runners who tried to steal against him last year.

Major League Batting Register

	BA	G	AB	R	H	2B	3B	HR	RBI	SB
90 AL	.257	92	303	28	78	13	1	5	25	2
91 AL	.182	32	77	8	14	3	0	0	4	0
92 AL	.257	63	144	17	37	6	0	7	26	0
93 AL	.309	95	259	43	80	14	0	14	53	0
94 AL	.265	75	249	47	66	12	0	17	58	0
Life	.266	357	1032	143	275	48	1	43	166	2
2 AVE	.284	100	305	55	86	15	0	19	67	0

JON LIEBER

Position: Pitcher
Team: Pittsburgh Pirates
Born: April 2, 1970   Council Bluffs, IA
Height: 6'3"   **Weight:** 220 lbs.
Bats: left   **Throws:** right
Acquired: Traded from Royals with Dan Miceli for Stan Belinda, 7/93

Player Summary	
Fantasy Value. . . . . $6 to $8
Card Value . . . . 8¢ to 12¢
Will. . . . . depend on sinker
Can't. . . . . quiet lefty bats
Expect . . . . pinpoint control
Don't Expect . . . . expanded ERA

Lieber arrived in the majors last spring with poise and confidence beyond his years. A control artist whose best pitch is a sinking fastball, he also throws a sharp-breaking slider and a rising fastball that stops the radar gun at 92 mph. He yielded three hits in eight innings for his first big-league win, 6-0 over Montreal May 21—getting 13 outs on grounders, seven on fly balls, and four on Ks. He had eight whiffs and no walks during his first complete-game win, 8-2 over Houston July 14. Like a veteran, Lieber seems able to wiggle his way out of jams. Though he yielded more than a hit per inning last year, he averaged nearly six Ks and just over two walks per nine innings—a whiff-walk ratio of just under 3-to-1. He dominated righty hitters (.224) and froze baserunners with an unusually fine pickoff move. He proved last year that he is completely recovered from the shoulder tendinitis that plagued him late in 1993. That year the South Alabama product went 9-3 with a 2.67 ERA for Class-A Wilmington, 2-1 with a 6.86 ERA for Double-A Memphis, and 4-2 with a 3.97 ERA for Double-A Carolina.

Major League Pitching Register

	W	L	ERA	G	CG	IP	H	ER	BB	SO
94 NL	6	7	3.73	17	1	108.2	116	45	25	71
Life	6	7	3.73	17	1	108.2	116	45	25	71

DEREK LILLIQUIST

Position: Pitcher
Team: Atlanta Braves
Born: Feb. 20, 1966   Winter Park, FL
Height: 6'   **Weight:** 214 lbs.
Bats: left   **Throws:** left
Acquired: Claimed from Indians on waivers, 11/94

Player Summary	
Fantasy Value. . . . . $3 to $5
Card Value . . . . 5¢ to 7¢
Will . . . . dominate lefties
Can't. . . . . wait to hit
Expect . . . . return to old form
Don't Expect . . . . wildness

If he pitched exclusively against lefties, Lilliquist would be one of the game's top relievers. The former Georgia All-American held left-handed hitters to a .205 average last year. But that's where the good statistics stopped. After two solid years as Cleveland's No. 1 closer, Lilliquist lost his grip on the job. The reasons were obvious: He yielded nearly 10½ hits per nine innings while averaging only four and one-half strikeouts over the same span. While he averaged less than two and one-half walks per game, he needed to cut that further still. He also had trouble keeping the ball in the park. Because he used to start, Lilliquist has an extensive repertoire, including a fastball, a curveball, a slider, and a changeup. He's always had good control, sometimes posting a 3-1 ratio of strikeouts to walks. A fine athlete, Lilliquist was probably the best hitting pitcher hidden by the DH rule the last few years; he once hit two home runs in a game for the Braves.

Major League Pitching Register

	W	L	ERA	G	S	IP	H	ER	BB	SO
89 NL	8	10	3.97	32	0	165.2	202	73	34	79
90 NL	5	11	5.31	30	0	122.0	136	72	42	63
91 NL	0	2	8.79	6	0	14.1	25	14	4	7
92 AL	5	3	1.75	71	6	61.2	39	12	18	47
93 AL	4	4	2.25	56	10	64.0	64	16	19	40
94 AL	1	3	4.91	36	1	29.1	34	16	8	15
Life	23	33	4.00	229	17	457.0	500	203	125	251
2 AVE	5	4	2.01	64	8	63.1	52	14	19	44

JOSE LIND

Position: Second base
Team: Kansas City Royals
Born: May 1, 1964 Toabaja, Puerto Rico
Height: 5'11" **Weight:** 170 lbs.
Bats: right **Throws:** right
Acquired: Traded from Pirates for Dennis Moeller and Joel Johnston, 11/92

Player Summary	
Fantasy Value	$1
Card Value	5¢ to 7¢
Will	hack at everything
Can't	hit ball over wall
Expect	infield acrobatics
Don't Expect	top on-base mark

In 1992, just before he was swapped across league lines, Lind interrupted Ryne Sandberg's string of nine consecutive Gold Gloves. Even with Roberto Alomar in the same league, Lind's leaps, dives, stops, and exceptional range have become legendary in two short years. The 1994 arrival of shortstop Greg Gagne gave Lind a steady double-play partner. Lind has led both leagues in fielding percentage at second base. Because he's so good in the field, anything he does with the bat is a bonus. He surprised last year with a .316 average in late-inning pressure situations, a .293 mark with runners in scoring position, and his first home run in three years. Placed at the bottom of the lineup because of his low on-base percentage, Lind is an aggressive hitter who makes contact but rarely walks. He hits lots of opposite-field singles but will also drop occasional bunts, especially in sacrifice situations.

Major League Batting Register

	BA	G	AB	R	H	2B	3B	HR	RBI	SB
87 NL	.322	35	143	21	46	8	4	0	11	2
88 NL	.262	154	611	82	160	24	4	2	49	15
89 NL	.232	153	578	52	134	21	3	2	48	15
90 NL	.261	152	514	46	134	28	5	1	48	8
91 NL	.265	150	502	53	133	16	6	3	54	7
92 NL	.235	135	468	38	110	14	1	0	39	3
93 AL	.248	136	431	33	107	13	2	0	37	3
94 AL	.269	85	290	34	78	16	2	1	31	9
Life	.255	1000	3537	359	902	140	27	9	317	62
3 AVE	.250	130	436	40	109	17	2	0	40	6

PAT LISTACH

Position: Second base; shortstop; outfield
Team: Milwaukee Brewers
Born: Sept. 12, 1967 Natchitoches, LA
Height: 5'9" **Weight:** 170 lbs.
Bats: both **Throws:** right
Acquired: Fifth-round pick in 6/88 free-agent draft

Player Summary	
Fantasy Value	$5 to $7
Card Value	8¢ to 15¢
Will	seek old form
Can't	avoid strikeouts
Expect	50 stolen bases
Don't Expect	power

The sophomore jinx usually lasts for a single season. Listach may insist it lasts for two. He's had nothing but trouble since winning the American League's Rookie of the Year Award in 1992. In addition to hamstring and back problems, plus bouts with pneumonia and a viral infection, he suffered knee problems that kept him sidelined for a large chunk of the 1993 campaign. When the same knee acted up again last year after just 54 at bats, he submitted to surgery. Listach is expected to return to full strength. He's just not sure where he'll play. Signed as a shortstop, he's done a good job at second and shown enough speed to play a solid center field. A natural right-handed hitter who loves lefty pitching, the switch-hitting Listach sends singles to all fields, fattens his average with bunts and infield hits, and hits well in the clutch. He needs to reduce his strikeout-to-walk ratio, however, and make contact to better take advantage of his speed. In the field, Listach has great range at shortstop and second and a strong throwing arm.

Major League Batting Register

	BA	G	AB	R	H	2B	3B	HR	RBI	SB
92 AL	.290	149	579	93	168	19	6	1	47	54
93 AL	.244	98	356	50	87	15	1	3	30	18
94 AL	.296	16	54	8	16	3	0	0	2	2
Life	.274	263	989	151	271	37	7	4	79	74
2 AVE	.273	124	468	72	128	17	4	2	39	36

SCOTT LIVINGSTONE

Position: Third base
Team: San Diego Padres
Born: July 15, 1965 Dallas, TX
Height: 6' **Weight:** 190 lbs.
Bats: left **Throws:** right
Acquired: Traded from Tigers for Gene Harris, 5/94

Player Summary	
Fantasy Value	. . . . $1
Card Value	. . . . 5¢ to 7¢
Will	. . . . produce under pressure
Can't	. . . . find old power
Expect	. . . . a platoon job
Don't Expect	. . . . top bat vs. lefties

The stats tell the story: Livingstone hit .280 against right-handed pitchers last year but only .167 against left-handers. Sitting him against southpaws was a good idea for San Diego, since right-handed hitter Craig Shipley proved a perfect platoon partner. All Shipley did was demolish lefties at a .383 clip. Livingstone's star has dimmed in each of his three full seasons. He gets fewer at bats every year and doesn't show any sign of the power he displayed while winning All-America honors at Texas A&M. A line-drive hitter who uses the whole field, Livingstone used to be known for his ability to make contact. He's so anxious to produce given his limited playing time, though, that he now hacks at anything. The result was a strikeout-to-walk ratio of nearly 4-to-1 last year. At least he produced in late-inning pressure situations (.292). Livingstone neither runs nor fields very well, although he has a strong throwing arm. No wonder he was used as a designated hitter in college.

Major League Batting Register

	BA	G	AB	R	H	2B	3B	HR	RBI	SB
91 AL	.291	44	127	19	37	5	0	2	11	2
92 AL	.282	117	354	43	100	21	0	4	46	1
93 AL	.293	98	304	39	89	10	2	2	39	1
94 AL	.217	15	23	0	5	1	0	0	1	0
94 NL	.272	57	180	11	49	12	1	2	10	2
Life	.283	331	988	112	280	49	3	10	107	6
3 AVE	.281	105	315	32	88	16	1	3	33	2

GRAEME LLOYD

Position: Pitcher
Team: Milwaukee Brewers
Born: April 9, 1967 Victoria, Australia
Height: 6'7" **Weight:** 215 lbs.
Bats: left **Throws:** left
Acquired: Traded from Phillies for John Trisler, 12/92

Player Summary	
Fantasy Value	. . . . $1 to $3
Card Value	. . . . 5¢ to 7¢
Will	. . . . get ground outs
Can't	. . . . handle righties
Expect	. . . . middle-relief role
Don't Expect	. . . . control woes

The busiest member of the Milwaukee bullpen last summer, Lloyd couples good control with the ability to retire left-handed hitters. A sinkerballer who gets batters to hit ground balls, he maintained a 2-1 ratio of strikeouts to walks and kept the ball in the park last summer. He has frequent problems with right-handed hitters, whose .294 average against him in '94 was 72 points higher than the mark compiled by left-handed batters. As a result, Lloyd's ERA rose from its 1993 rookie level of 2.83 to an unsightly 5.17. He also yielded slightly more than a hit per inning and averaged nearly six strikeouts per nine innings. He has trouble keeping inherited runners from scoring, stranding only about 53 percent in 1994—down from 70 percent in '93. The towering Australian helps himself with a fine pickoff move and is adequate in the field. He began his pro career in 1988 in the Toronto system. Lloyd was a closer in the minors, notching 14 saves at Double-A Knoxville in '92 and 24 saves at Class-A Dunedin in 1991.

Major League Pitching Register

	W	L	ERA	G	S	IP	H	ER	BB	SO
93 AL	3	4	2.83	55	0	63.2	64	20	13	31
94 AL	2	3	5.17	43	3	47.0	49	27	15	31
Life	5	7	3.82	98	3	110.2	113	47	28	62
2 AVE	3	4	4.02	58	2	65.1	67	29	17	37

KENNY LOFTON

Position: Outfield
Team: Cleveland Indians
Born: May 31, 1967 East Chicago, IN
Height: 6' **Weight:** 180 lbs.
Bats: left **Throws:** left
Acquired: Traded from Astros with Dave Rohde for Willie Blair and Eddie Taubensee, 12/91

Player Summary	
Fantasy Value.	$40 to $45
Card Value	25¢ to 50¢
Will.	show superb glove
Can't.	hide new power
Expect.	world-class speed
Don't Expect	weak arm

In three short seasons, Lofton has established himself as a new version of Rickey Henderson. Like Henderson, Lofton is an ideal leadoff man capable of completely taking over a game with his speed. He not only led the league in steals for the third straight year in 1994 but also finished first in base hits. Twelve of those hits were homers—a career high. A patient hitter who walks as much as he fans, Lofton topped the .320 mark against lefties, righties, at home, on the road, and with runners in scoring position. He stole 60 bases in 72 tries (an .833 success average) and made the AL All-Star team for the first time. Lofton can bury the opposition with a bunt or a blast. He placed 35 bunts into play in 1993 and then began the '94 season by winning two April games with extra-inning homers. His leaps, dives, and dashes in center are nightly highlight-film features. The former point guard at Arizona has a strong throwing arm and notched 13 assists last year. He makes few miscues.

Major League Batting Register

	BA	G	AB	R	H	2B	3B	HR	RBI	SB
91 NL	.203	20	74	9	15	1	0	0	0	2
92 AL	.285	148	576	96	164	15	8	5	42	66
93 AL	.325	148	569	116	185	28	8	1	42	70
94 AL	.349	112	459	105	160	32	9	12	57	60
Life	.312	428	1678	326	524	76	25	18	141	198
3 AVE	.321	151	597	120	191	29	10	8	55	74

JAVIER LOPEZ

Position: Catcher
Team: Atlanta Braves
Born: Nov. 5, 1970 Ponce, Puerto Rico
Height: 6'3" **Weight:** 185 lbs.
Bats: right **Throws:** right
Acquired: Signed as a free agent, 11/87

Player Summary	
Fantasy Value.	$10 to $13
Card Value	20¢ to 35¢
Will.	produce some power
Can't.	reduce whiff ratio
Expect.	average to improve
Don't Expect.	a Gold Glove

The talent is there but the kid is still learning. That was the verdict on Lopez after he got his first extended audition at the big-league level. Though he showed some power, his bat cooled after a hot start, and he wound up with anemic averages with runners in scoring position, in late-inning pressure situations, and against left-handed pitching. Since Lopez is a natural pull hitter, lefties are likely to pay for that unexpected early success. An aggressive hitter who needs to show more patience, he fanned four times more than he walked. He batted .305 with 17 homers and 74 RBI in Triple-A in 1993, and .321 with 16 homers and 60 RBI in Double-A in '92. He has the potential to make considerable improvement on his first-year mark of .245. That will happen as he masters the art of hitting to the opposite field. Lopez has better-than-average speed for a catcher but isn't likely to steal much. He should, however, become more adept at nailing opposing basestealers. His offense is still ahead of his defense, but Lopez is working hard to improve.

Major League Batting Register

	BA	G	AB	R	H	2B	3B	HR	RBI	SB
92 NL	.375	9	16	3	6	2	0	0	2	0
93 NL	.375	8	16	1	6	1	1	1	2	0
94 NL	.245	80	277	27	68	9	0	13	35	0
Life	.259	97	309	31	80	12	1	14	39	0

LUIS LOPEZ

Position: Shortstop; second base
Team: San Diego Padres
Born: Sept. 4, 1970 Cidra, Puerto Rico
Height: 5'11" **Weight:** 175 lbs.
Bats: both **Throws:** right
Acquired: Signed as a free agent, 9/87

Player Summary	
Fantasy Value	$1 to $3
Card Value	8¢ to 15¢
Will	make some contact
Can't	hit big flies
Expect	utility role
Don't Expect	top on-base mark

During his six-year tenure in the minors, Lopez not only hit .300 three times but led several leagues in chances, putouts, assists, and double plays by a shortstop. He also led three leagues in errors, however, and once made a whopping 74 in 127 games. He combines great range, bad hands, and an erratic throwing arm. He made 14 boots in 43 games at short last summer and handled himself better when tried at second (29 games) or third (five games). A switch-hitter who's far better from the right side (.333 in '94), Lopez is a singles hitter who makes fair contact. His on-base percentage was low because he walked as often as it snows in San Diego. Lopez held his own with runners in scoring position but needs to improve in late-inning pressure situations. He has decent speed but is not much of a basestealer. A stopgap for the disappointing Ricky Gutierrez last season, Lopez probably has a big-league future as a utility man. Playing every day isn't likely. Last year, he batted .204 at Triple-A Las Vegas, but in only 49 at bats. He hit .305 at Las Vegas in 1993 and had 36 doubles.

Major League Batting Register

	BA	G	AB	R	H	2B	3B	HR	RBI	SB
93 NL	.116	17	43	1	5	1	0	0	1	0
94 NL	.277	77	235	29	65	16	1	2	20	3
Life	.252	94	278	30	70	17	1	2	21	3

MIKE MACFARLANE

Position: Catcher
Team: Kansas City Royals
Born: April 12, 1964 Stockton, CA
Height: 6'1" **Weight:** 200 lbs.
Bats: right **Throws:** right
Acquired: Fourth-round pick in 6/85 free-agent draft

Player Summary	
Fantasy Value	$10 to $13
Card Value	6¢ to 10¢
Will	hit some homers
Can't	nab baserunners
Expect	extra-base hits
Don't Expect	great glove

Although Macfarlane's .255 batting average didn't light up the league last year, his ratio of extra-base hits was worth writing home about. The Santa Clara product collected extra bases on a whopping 43 percent of his hits. A fastball hitter who crowds the plate, he likes to pull the ball, especially when it's pitched inside. He occasionally goes to the opposite field against left-handers. A good 3-2 hitter, Macfarlane hit well with runners in scoring position two years ago (.293) but slipped in that category last summer. He fanned twice as much as he walked. He seldom steals a base, and provides defense that can only be described as mediocre. In 1994, he nailed only 23 percent of the runners who tried to steal against him—his worst total in three years. Macfarlane calls a decent game, prevents wild pitches, and blocks the plate well. Nonetheless, his hitting and defense were better in 1993 than in '94.

Major League Batting Register

	BA	G	AB	R	H	2B	3B	HR	RBI	SB
87 AL	.211	8	19	0	4	1	0	0	3	0
88 AL	.265	70	211	25	56	15	0	4	26	0
89 AL	.223	69	157	13	35	6	0	2	19	0
90 AL	.255	124	400	37	102	24	4	6	58	1
91 AL	.277	84	267	34	74	18	2	13	41	1
92 AL	.234	129	402	51	94	28	3	17	48	1
93 AL	.273	117	388	55	106	27	0	20	67	2
94 AL	.255	92	314	53	80	17	3	14	47	1
Life	.255	693	2158	268	551	136	12	76	309	6
3 AVE	.254	125	411	60	104	26	2	19	60	1

SHANE MACK

Position: Outfield
Team: Minnesota Twins
Born: Dec. 7, 1963 Los Angeles, CA
Height: 6′ **Weight:** 190 lbs.
Bats: right **Throws:** right
Acquired: Drafted from Padres, 12/89

Player Summary	
Fantasy Value	$19 to $22
Card Value	8¢ to 12¢
Will	blast lefty pitchers
Can't	make powerful throws
Expect	fine on-base average
Don't Expect	end to injuries

After starting last year on the DL because he couldn't throw, Mack made a triumphant return in May. The surgery that repaired his slight rotator cuff tear actually made him a better hitter. Unable to hold his hands up the way he once did, Mack was forced to shorten his swing. The result was more bat speed and a career-best .333 average—without any loss of power. Playing with a swollen left hand, a painful right thigh, and the healing shoulder, Mack murdered left-handed pitching (.418) while topping .300 against right-handers, at home, on the road, and with runners in scoring position. Though he had only 303 at bats, he ranked second among the Twins with 15 homers. The former UCLA All-American and U.S. Olympian runs well enough to steal more than a dozen bases per year. That speed helps Mack snare potential gap hits in the outfield, where he's best in center or left. Because of his shoulder, Mack no longer throws well enough to play right.

Major League Batting Register

	BA	G	AB	R	H	2B	3B	HR	RBI	SB
87 AL	.239	105	238	28	57	11	3	4	25	4
88 NL	.244	56	119	13	29	3	0	0	12	5
90 AL	.326	125	313	50	102	10	4	8	44	13
91 AL	.310	143	442	79	137	27	8	18	74	13
92 AL	.315	156	600	101	189	31	6	16	75	26
93 AL	.276	128	503	66	139	30	4	10	61	15
94 AL	.333	81	303	55	101	21	2	15	61	4
Life	.299	794	2518	392	754	133	27	71	352	80
3 AVE	.307	133	510	81	157	30	4	16	74	16

GREG MADDUX

Position: Pitcher
Team: Atlanta Braves
Born: April 14, 1966 San Angelo, TX
Height: 6′ **Weight:** 170 lbs.
Bats: right **Throws:** right
Acquired: Signed as a free agent, 12/92

Player Summary	
Fantasy Value	$30 to $35
Card Value	25¢ to 35¢
Will	dominate all comers
Can't	change demeanor
Expect	Cy Young bid
Don't Expect	many homers

Despite the strike, 1994 was a fine year for Maddux. He not only made his first All-Star start but became the first pitcher ever to win the Cy Young Award three years in a row. There was little need to vote: Maddux led the league in ERA, complete games, and innings pitched, tied for first in shutouts and wins, and placed third in strikeouts. Opposing hitters combined for a .207 average and managed just four home runs in 202 innings. He fanned five times more batters than he walked, averaging one and one-third walks and almost seven strikeouts per nine innings. He yielded less than seven hits per game. Maddux had command of a varied repertoire that includes a sinker, a slider, a cut fastball, a curve, and a circle change. He's always ahead in the count. A thinking man's pitcher who never gets rattled, Maddux is noted for his ability to work out of jams. He is a good hitter, and he's won multiple Gold Gloves.

Major League Pitching Register

	W	L	ERA	G	CG	IP	H	ER	BB	SO
86 NL	2	4	5.52	6	1	31.0	44	19	11	20
87 NL	6	14	5.61	30	1	155.2	181	97	74	101
88 NL	18	8	3.18	34	9	249.0	230	88	81	140
89 NL	19	12	2.95	35	7	238.1	222	78	82	135
90 NL	15	15	3.46	35	8	237.0	242	91	71	144
91 NL	15	11	3.35	37	7	263.0	232	98	66	198
92 NL	20	11	2.18	35	9	268.0	201	65	70	199
93 NL	20	10	2.36	36	8	267.0	228	70	52	197
94 NL	16	6	1.56	25	10	202.0	150	35	31	156
Life	131	91	3.02	273	60	1911.0	1730	641	538	1290
3 AVE	21	10	2.02	35	10	273.0	213	61	55	205

MIKE MADDUX

Position: Pitcher
Team: New York Mets
Born: Aug. 27, 1961 Dayton, OH
Height: 6'2" **Weight:** 180 lbs.
Bats: right **Throws:** right
Acquired: Traded from Padres for Roger Mason and Mike Freitas, 12/92

Player Summary	
Fantasy Value	$1 to $3
Card Value	5¢ to 7¢
Will	remain in relief
Can't	stop gophers
Expect	ERA to be better
Don't Expect	control woes

The older brother of Greg Maddux, Mike cannot match his younger brother's ability. Though he has a similar repertoire—a fastball, a slider, a curve, and a changeup—Mike doesn't have the command, control, or mastery of his sibling. A middle reliever throughout his nine-year career, Maddux has maintained a strikeout-to-walk ratio of 2-to-1. Relying heavily on the curveball and slider, he tries to keep the ball down, hoping to get ground outs. In 1994, he yielded about a hit per inning while averaging slightly more than two and one-half walks per nine innings. He's much more effective against right-handed hitters. He fields his position well, but he has trouble keeping runners close. Though he retired more than 70 percent of the runners he inherited, Maddux had trouble keeping the ball in the park, which hurt him last year. Mike probably has seen his better days.

Major League Pitching Register

	W	L	ERA	G	S	IP	H	ER	BB	SO
86 NL	3	7	5.42	16	0	78.0	88	47	34	44
87 NL	2	0	2.65	7	0	17.0	17	5	5	15
88 NL	4	3	3.76	25	0	88.2	91	37	34	59
89 NL	1	3	5.15	16	1	43.2	52	25	14	26
90 NL	0	1	6.53	11	0	20.2	24	15	4	11
91 NL	7	2	2.46	64	5	98.2	78	27	27	57
92 NL	2	2	2.37	50	5	79.2	71	21	24	60
93 NL	3	8	3.60	58	5	75.0	67	30	27	57
94 NL	2	1	5.11	27	2	44.0	45	25	13	32
Life	24	27	3.83	274	18	545.1	533	232	182	361
3 AVE	3	4	3.58	49	4	72.1	67	29	23	54

DAVE MAGADAN

Position: Third base; first base
Team: Florida Marlins
Born: Sept. 30, 1962 Tampa, FL
Height: 6'3" **Weight:** 195 lbs.
Bats: left **Throws:** right
Acquired: Traded from Mariners for Jeff Darwin and cash, 11/93

Player Summary	
Fantasy Value	$1
Card Value	5¢ to 7¢
Will	make good contact
Can't	provide home runs
Expect	good pressure bat
Don't Expect	great glove

One of baseball's best contact hitters, Magadan regularly walks more often than he strikes out but rarely hits the ball out of the park. A good two-strike hitter, he slices singles to the opposite field and builds up a good on-base percentage by showing patience at the plate. Though he's usually more productive against right-handed pitchers, Magadan always manages to get his bat on the ball—especially in clutch situations. He shares his philosophy of hitting with his more famous cousin, Lou Piniella. Magadan even played for Piniella in Seattle a few years ago. Magadan shows good contact, little power, and no speed. He has little range or mobility but good reactions, good hands, and a good throwing arm. The former University of Alabama All-American is probably better at first base, where he's adept at saving potential errors and starting the 3-6-3 double play.

Major League Batting Register

	BA	G	AB	R	H	2B	3B	HR	RBI	SB
86 NL	.444	10	18	3	8	0	0	0	3	0
87 NL	.318	85	192	21	61	13	1	3	24	0
88 NL	.277	112	314	39	87	15	0	1	35	0
89 NL	.286	127	374	47	107	22	3	4	41	1
90 NL	.328	144	451	74	148	28	6	6	72	2
91 NL	.258	124	418	58	108	23	0	4	51	1
92 NL	.283	99	321	33	91	9	1	3	28	1
93 NL	.286	66	227	22	65	12	0	4	29	0
93 AL	.259	71	228	27	59	11	0	1	21	2
94 NL	.275	74	211	30	58	7	0	1	17	0
Life	.289	912	2754	354	792	140	11	27	321	7
3 AVE	.276	113	358	41	99	14	0	3	34	1

JOE MAGRANE

Position: Pitcher
Team: California Angels
Born: July 2, 1964 Des Moines, IA
Height: 6'6" **Weight:** 230 lbs.
Bats: right **Throws:** left
Acquired: Signed as a free agent, 8/93

Player Summary	
Fantasy Value	$0
Card Value	5¢ to 7¢
Will	seek huge comeback
Can't	stop power hitters
Expect	control to improve
Don't Expect	rotation return

Has the end come for Magrane? One year after indicating his elbow problems were over, he plunged headfirst into the worst of his seven big-league summers. Yielding nearly 11 hits and more than six walks per nine innings, he emerged with only two wins and an earned run average that could only be described as embarrassing. He couldn't retire lefties and couldn't keep the ball in the park. When right, Magrane shows good control of a fastball, a slider, a curve, and a forkball. He doesn't throw with his presurgery velocity but tries to get by with location. Last year, however, nothing seemed to work. The University of Arizona product sabotaged a good pickoff move with a slow, high-kicking delivery and continued to struggle in the field because of an awkward follow-through. Because he's a lefty with size and experience, Magrane may get one more shot. But his chances of returning to the rotation seem remote.

Major League Pitching Register

	W	L	ERA	G	CG	IP	H	ER	BB	SO
87 NL	9	7	3.54	27	4	170.1	157	67	60	101
88 NL	5	9	2.18	24	4	165.1	133	40	51	100
89 NL	18	9	2.91	34	9	234.2	219	76	72	127
90 NL	10	17	3.59	31	3	203.1	204	81	59	100
92 NL	1	2	4.02	5	0	31.1	34	14	15	20
93 NL	8	10	4.97	22	0	116.0	127	64	37	38
93 AL	3	2	3.94	8	0	48.0	48	21	21	24
94 AL	2	6	7.30	20	1	74.0	89	60	51	33
Life	56	62	3.65	171	21	1043.0	1011	423	366	543
2 AVE	7	10	5.69	29	1	134.0	150	85	65	54

PAT MAHOMES

Position: Pitcher
Team: Minnesota Twins
Born: Aug. 9, 1970 Bryan, TX
Height: 6'4" **Weight:** 210 lbs.
Bats: right **Throws:** right
Acquired: Sixth-round pick in 6/88 free-agent draft

Player Summary	
Fantasy Value	$6 to $8
Card Value	10¢ to 15¢
Will	mix pitches better
Can't	locate home plate
Expect	a hit per inning
Don't Expect	many whiffs

For Mahomes, the road to stardom leads right through the strike zone. After getting off to a slow start in '94, he learned the value of throwing his slider and his curveball more often to complement a fastball that exceeds 90 mph. Though his velocity was down a bit last summer, his location was vastly improved. Throwing strikes more consistently, as well as mixing his pitches better, allowed Mahomes to keep more batters off balance. As a result, he won more games than any Minnesota pitcher except Kevin Tapani. Though Mahomes yielded only a hit per inning, he had trouble with left-handers and struggled to keep the ball in the park. He walked more men than he fanned and averaged less than four strikeouts per nine innings—stats he'll have to change. Mahomes does a fine job of keeping runners close. He also helps himself with his fielding. He led two minor leagues in ERA, but he also led two leagues in walks. In 1993 at Triple-A Portland, he was 11-4 with a 3.03 ERA, 94 strikeouts, and 54 walks in 155⅔ innings.

Major League Pitching Register

	W	L	ERA	G	CG	IP	H	ER	BB	SO
92 AL	3	4	5.04	14	0	69.2	73	39	37	44
93 AL	1	5	7.71	12	0	37.1	47	32	16	23
94 AL	9	5	4.72	21	0	120.0	121	63	62	53
Life	13	14	5.31	47	0	227.0	241	134	115	120
2 AVE	8	6	4.82	22	0	119.1	122	64	62	59

CANDY MALDONADO

Position: Outfield; designated hitter
Team: Cleveland Indians
Born: Sept. 5, 1960 Humacao, Puerto Rico
Height: 6' **Weight:** 195 lbs.
Bats: right **Throws:** right
Acquired: Traded from Cubs for Glenallen Hill, 8/93

Player Summary	
Fantasy Value	$1
Card Value	6¢ to 10¢
Will	provide some power
Can't	play solid defense
Expect	pinch-hitting role
Don't Expect	better days

If not for last year's player strike, Maldonado—at the right place at the right time—might have played for his seventh divisional champion in 14 years. Cleveland's great run last year was hardly fueled by his bat, however. Though he hit .286 at Jacobs Field, the Candy Man barely hit his weight when road games were included. Despite three previous 20-homer campaigns, he has looked like a shadow of his former self the last couple of years. He fans too much, walks too little, and doesn't deliver his old power against left-handed pitchers. That hurts, since Maldonado is little more than a platoon player who can't run or supply good defense. He has a strong, wild arm but is often guilty of bad judgement in the field.

Major League Batting Register

	BA	G	AB	R	H	2B	3B	HR	RBI	SB
81 NL	.083	11	12	0	1	0	0	0	0	0
82 NL	.000	6	4	0	0	0	0	0	0	0
83 NL	.194	42	62	5	12	1	1	1	6	0
84 NL	.268	116	254	25	68	14	0	5	28	0
85 NL	.225	121	213	20	48	7	1	5	19	1
86 NL	.252	133	405	49	102	31	3	18	85	4
87 NL	.292	118	442	69	129	28	4	20	85	8
88 NL	.255	142	499	53	127	23	1	12	68	6
89 NL	.217	129	345	39	75	23	0	9	41	4
90 AL	.273	155	590	76	161	32	2	22	95	3
91 AL	.250	86	288	37	72	15	0	12	48	4
92 AL	.272	137	489	64	133	25	4	20	66	2
93 NL	.186	70	140	8	26	5	0	3	15	0
93 AL	.247	28	81	11	20	2	0	5	20	0
94 AL	.196	42	92	14	18	5	1	5	12	1
Life	.253	1336	3916	470	992	211	17	137	588	33
2 AVE	.252	118	355	42	90	16	2	14	51	1

KIRT MANWARING

Position: Catcher
Team: San Francisco Giants
Born: July 15, 1965 Elmira, NY
Height: 5'11" **Weight:** 190 lbs.
Bats: right **Throws:** right
Acquired: Second-round pick in 6/86 free-agent draft

Player Summary	
Fantasy Value	$2 to $4
Card Value	6¢ to 10¢
Will	supply solid defense
Can't	provide the home run
Expect	cannon arm
Don't Expect	big on-base mark

One of baseball's best defensive catchers, Manwaring amazed the baseball world with a career-peak .275 batting average in 1993. Scouts were ready to chuck his good-fielder, no-hitter label until they watched him in 1994. The label is back. After topping .300 against lefties two years in a row, Manwaring batted only .200 against southpaws last summer. His batting average was four points above his career mark. A singles hitter who goes up the middle against right-handers but the opposite way against lefties, Manwaring fans twice as much as he walks. He rarely gets an extra-base hit or steals a base, but he's terrific at preventing others from stealing. He nailed 44 percent in 1992 and 42 percent in '93 before slipping to a still respectable 35 percent last year. A good game-caller, Manwaring snares potential wild pitches, blocks the plate well, and uses his soft hands to convert foul tips into strikeouts.

Major League Batting Register

	BA	G	AB	R	H	2B	3B	HR	RBI	SB
87 NL	.143	6	7	0	1	0	0	0	0	0
88 NL	.250	40	116	12	29	7	0	1	15	0
89 NL	.210	85	200	14	42	4	2	0	18	2
90 NL	.154	8	13	0	2	0	1	0	1	0
91 NL	.225	67	178	16	40	9	0	0	19	1
92 NL	.244	109	349	24	85	10	5	4	26	2
93 NL	.275	130	432	48	119	15	1	5	49	1
94 NL	.250	97	316	30	79	17	1	1	29	1
Life	.246	542	1611	144	397	62	10	11	157	7
3 AVE	.257	125	409	38	105	16	2	3	39	1

JOSIAS MANZANILLO

Position: Pitcher
Team: New York Mets
Born: Oct. 16, 1967   San Pedro de Macoris, Dominican Republic
Height: 6′   **Weight:** 190 lbs.
Bats: right   **Throws:** right
Acquired: Traded from Brewers for Wayne Housie, 6/93

Player Summary	
Fantasy Value	$7 to $9
Card Value	10¢ to 15¢
Will	dominate righties
Can't	hit like brother
Expect	very good control
Don't Expect	poise to sag

Like brother Ravelo, Josias Manzanillo spent almost all of his 10-year pro career in the minors before reaching the majors to stay in 1994. The experience paid off. Manzanillo became the Mets' best reliever, pitching so well that some thought was given to trying him as a closer, even though the Mets had John Franco. Manzanillo held right-handers to a .146 average, yielded less than six and one-half hits per nine innings, showed fine control, and kept the ball in the park. He also averaged more than a strikeout per inning. An enthusiastic player who sprints from the mound to the dugout, Manzanillo throws a fastball, a slider, and a changeup. He was timed at 94 mph July 1, then ran up a scoreless streak of 18⅔ innings. He has such confidence in his stuff that he's not afraid to challenge the hitters. He's also a good clubhouse guy. Though he can't match his brother as a hitter, Manzanillo has such a good pickoff move that he did not yield a stolen base in '94. He's also a fine fielder. He was a starter for Triple-A Norfolk in 1993.

Major League Pitching Register

	W	L	ERA	G	S	IP	H	ER	BB	SO
91 AL	0	0	18.00	1	0	1.0	2	2	3	1
93 AL	1	1	9.53	10	1	17.0	22	18	10	10
93 NL	0	0	3.00	6	0	12.0	8	4	9	11
94 NL	3	2	2.66	37	2	47.1	34	14	13	48
Life	4	3	4.42	54	3	77.1	66	38	35	70

RAVELO MANZANILLO

Position: Pitcher
Team: Pittsburgh Pirates
Born: Oct. 17, 1963   San Pedro de Macoris, Dominican Republic
Height: 5′10″   **Weight:** 190 lbs.
Bats: left   **Throws:** left
Acquired: Signed as a minor-league free agent, 1/94

Player Summary	
Fantasy Value	$0
Card Value	12¢ to 15¢
Will	strand baserunners
Can't	locate home plate
Expect	expertise with bat
Don't Expect	more balk woes

After a 10-year pro odyssey that included stops from Veracruz to Taiwan, Manzanillo made his mark in the majors last summer. He became the busiest member of the Pittsburgh bullpen and the most effective Pirate pitcher against left-handers (.177). Manzanillo stranded 75 percent of the runners he inherited, kept the ball in the park, and yielded less than a hit per inning. He also averaged more than seven strikeouts per nine innings. But his efforts were sabotaged by control troubles that left him with more walks than strikeouts. Manzanillo keeps the running game in check but needs to refine a pickoff move that resulted in a staff-high five balks. Manzanillo should have some kind of major-league future—if he masters the art of throwing strikes. He has one advantage: an ability to hit. A pinch hitter in the minors, Manzanillo singled in his first major-league at bat. He played first base and center field, batting cleanup, when he wasn't pitching in the Dominican Summer League. His brother Josias pitched for the Mets last season. Ravelo pitched in Taiwan in 1992.

Major League Pitching Register

	W	L	ERA	G	S	IP	H	ER	BB	SO
94 NL	4	2	4.14	46	1	50.0	45	23	42	39
Life	4	2	4.14	46	1	50.0	45	23	42	39

AL MARTIN

Position: Outfield
Team: Pittsburgh Pirates
Born: Nov. 24, 1967   West Covina, CA
Height: 6'2"   **Weight:** 210 lbs.
Bats: left   **Throws:** left
Acquired: Signed as a free agent, 11/91

Player Summary	
Fantasy Value	$13 to $16
Card Value	10¢ to 15¢
Will	show good patience
Can't	hit lefty pitching
Expect	20-20 performance
Don't Expect	great glove

Suffocated by southpaws as a 1993 rookie, Martin spent most of last summer in a platoon role, playing almost exclusively against right-handers. The result was a better batting average and less power production, albeit with far fewer at bats. The former free swinger showed dramatic improvement in the patience department, compiling a .367 on-base percentage that led the Pirate regulars. He showed both power and speed, plus a good clutch bat (.314 in late-inning pressure situations). A product of the fine USC baseball program, Martin hits with power to all fields. He runs well enough to develop into a 20-20 player, but he does not always take advantage of his speed in the outfield. Even though he is often hidden in left field, he still needs considerable work on his defense. His reactions, charging ability, and throwing arm all below average. He played some center field last year for the injured Andy Van Slyke. Martin was a first baseman when drafted by Atlanta in '85. His uncle is former Raider linebacker Rod Martin.

Major League Batting Register

	BA	G	AB	R	H	2B	3B	HR	RBI	SB
92 NL	.167	12	12	1	2	0	1	0	2	0
93 NL	.281	143	480	85	135	26	8	18	64	16
94 NL	.286	82	276	48	79	12	4	9	33	15
Life	.281	237	768	134	216	38	13	27	99	31
2 AVE	.283	129	434	76	123	21	7	15	55	19

DAVE MARTINEZ

Position: Outfield
Team: San Francisco Giants
Born: Sept. 26, 1964   New York, NY
Height: 5'10"   **Weight:** 170 lbs.
Bats: left   **Throws:** left
Acquired: Signed as a free agent, 12/92

Player Summary	
Fantasy Value	$3 to $5
Card Value	5¢ to 7¢
Will	stay ready on bench
Can't	generate much power
Expect	fine defensive game
Don't Expect	walks or Ks

Because of his versatility, fielding skill, and ability to make contact, Martinez is an ideal player to have on the bench. Good enough to play all three outfield spots, as well as first base, he also makes a fine pinch hitter because he rarely strikes out. An aggressive hitter who doesn't walk much, Martinez plays almost exclusively against right-handed pitchers. He hits line drives to all fields but rarely gets extra-base hits. Nor does he steal much, though he twice topped 20 earlier in his career. He prefers to save his speed for the outfield, where center may be his best position. His range, reactions, and hands are good, though his throwing arm is not always accurate. The one-time minor-league batting champ was originally the property of the Cubs. He has also played for the Reds and Expos. Although he has spent nine years in the majors, Martinez has played in 140 games in a season only once.

Major League Batting Register

	BA	G	AB	R	H	2B	3B	HR	RBI	SB
86 NL	.139	53	108	13	15	1	1	1	7	4
87 NL	.292	142	459	70	134	18	8	8	36	16
88 NL	.255	138	447	51	114	13	6	6	46	23
89 NL	.274	126	361	41	99	16	7	3	27	23
90 NL	.279	118	391	60	109	13	5	11	39	13
91 NL	.295	124	396	47	117	18	5	7	42	16
92 NL	.254	135	393	47	100	20	5	3	31	12
93 NL	.241	91	241	28	58	12	1	5	27	6
94 NL	.247	97	235	23	58	9	3	4	27	3
Life	.265	1024	3031	380	804	120	41	48	282	116
3 AVE	.248	121	322	36	80	15	3	5	32	7

DENNIS MARTINEZ

Position: Pitcher
Team: Cleveland Indians
Born: May 14, 1955 Granada, Nicaragua
Height: 6'1" **Weight:** 180 lbs.
Bats: right **Throws:** right
Acquired: Signed as a free agent, 12/93

Player Summary	
Fantasy Value	$15 to $18
Card Value	8¢ to 12¢
Will	show good control
Can't	stop basestealers
Expect	double-digit wins
Don't Expect	many gophers

"Age is a question of mind over matter. If you don't mind, it doesn't matter." Martinez was living proof of Satchel Paige's quote last year by becoming Cleveland's No. 1 starter at the ripe old age of 38. A control pitcher, Martinez yields less than a hit per inning and keeps the ball in the park. He's especially tough on righties, though lefties don't like facing Martinez either. Three of his seven complete games last summer were shutouts. A three-time All-Star who once pitched a perfect game, Martinez has good command of a fastball, a slider, and a changeup. He's also a fine fielder.

Major League Pitching Register

	W	L	ERA	G	CG	IP	H	ER	BB	SO
76 AL	1	2	2.60	4	1	27.2	23	8	8	18
77 AL	14	7	4.10	42	5	166.2	157	76	64	107
78 AL	16	11	3.52	40	15	276.1	257	108	93	142
79 AL	15	16	3.66	40	18	292.1	279	119	78	132
80 AL	6	4	3.97	25	2	99.2	103	44	44	42
81 AL	14	5	3.32	25	9	179.0	173	66	62	88
82 AL	16	12	4.21	40	10	252.0	262	118	87	111
83 AL	7	16	5.53	32	4	153.0	209	94	45	71
84 AL	6	9	5.02	34	7	141.2	145	79	37	77
85 AL	13	11	5.15	33	3	180.0	203	103	63	68
86 AL	0	0	6.75	4	0	6.2	11	5	2	2
86 NL	3	6	4.59	19	1	98.0	103	50	28	63
87 NL	11	4	3.30	22	2	144.2	133	53	40	84
88 NL	15	13	2.72	34	9	235.1	215	71	55	120
89 NL	16	7	3.18	34	5	232.0	227	82	49	142
90 NL	10	11	2.95	32	7	226.0	191	74	49	156
91 NL	14	11	2.39	31	9	222.0	187	59	62	123
92 NL	16	11	2.47	32	6	226.1	172	62	60	147
93 NL	15	9	3.85	35	2	224.2	211	96	64	138
94 AL	11	6	3.52	24	7	176.2	166	69	44	92
Life	219	171	3.63	582	117	3560.2	3427	1436	1034	1923
3 AVE	15	9	3.28	34	6	233.2	206	85	62	138

EDGAR MARTINEZ

Position: Third base
Team: Seattle Mariners
Born: Jan. 2, 1963 New York, NY
Height: 5'11" **Weight:** 175 lbs.
Bats: right **Throws:** right
Acquired: Signed as a free agent, 12/82

Player Summary	
Fantasy Value	$15 to $18
Card Value	8¢ to 12¢
Will	destroy southpaws
Can't	shake injury jinx
Expect	high on-base mark
Don't Expect	a Gold Glove

Since winning the 1992 AL hitting crown, Martinez has had one operation and five stints on the DL. Putting his hamstring and shoulder problems behind him last summer, he started to show the form that produced three straight .300 seasons from 1990 to '92. One of baseball's best contact hitters when healthy, he walks more than he fans, devours left-handed pitching, and produces under pressure. Because he's willing to wait for his pitch, he maintains a high on-base percentage. He uses all fields but also has enough power to collect extra bases on more than one-third of his hits. The 1992 American League leader with 46 doubles, Martinez can hit a dozen homers per season. He doesn't steal much, despite decent speed. At third, he has fine range, keen instincts, and good hands. He threw better before the shoulder surgery. A product of American College in Puerto Rico, Martinez was an All-Star in 1992.

Major League Batting Register

	BA	G	AB	R	H	2B	3B	HR	RBI	SB
87 AL	.372	13	43	6	16	5	2	0	5	0
88 AL	.281	14	32	0	9	4	0	0	5	0
89 AL	.240	65	171	20	41	5	0	2	20	2
90 AL	.302	144	487	71	147	27	2	11	49	1
91 AL	.307	150	544	98	167	35	1	14	52	0
92 AL	.343	135	528	100	181	46	3	18	73	14
93 AL	.237	42	135	20	32	7	0	4	13	0
94 AL	.285	89	326	47	93	23	1	13	51	6
Life	.303	652	2266	362	686	152	9	62	268	23
2 AVE	.316	130	494	83	156	39	2	18	72	11

PEDRO MARTINEZ

Position: Pitcher
Team: San Diego Padres
Born: Sept. 29, 1968 Santo Domingo, Dominican Republic
Height: 6'2" **Weight:** 185 lbs.
Bats: right **Throws:** left
Acquired: Signed as a free agent, 9/86

Player Summary	
Fantasy Value	$4 to $6
Card Value	6¢ to 10¢
Will	strand runners
Can't	always find zone
Expect	low ERA
Don't Expect	stolen bases

The other Pedro Martinez gets all the press, but this one deserves credit too. He was the busiest Padre pitcher last season and one of the most effective. While the sophomore jinx was felling second-year players like dominoes, Martinez went about his business. He held hitters to a low .210 batting average, kept the ball in the park, and stranded 75 percent of the runners he inherited. So what if his control was shaky? Martinez, who mixes a fastball with a screwball, is a left-hander who thrives on a heavy workload. In 48 games last year, he worked 68⅓ relief innings, leading the Padres in both departments. He yielded less than seven hits and had nearly seven Ks per nine innings. He's also good at catching potential basestealers, nailing eight of 11 last year. Martinez is a fine fielder and bunter but isn't much of a hitter. A starter during seven years in the minors, he switched to relief with the Padres in 1993. In 1993 at Triple-A Las Vegas, he was 3-5 with a 4.72 ERA, 65 Ks, and 20 walks in 88 innings. He was 11-7 with a 2.99 ERA at Double-A Wichita in 1992.

Major League Pitching Register

	W	L	ERA	G	S	IP	H	ER	BB	SO
93 NL	3	1	2.43	32	0	37.0	23	10	13	32
94 NL	3	2	2.90	48	3	68.1	52	22	49	52
Life	6	3	2.73	80	3	105.1	75	32	62	84
2 AVE	4	2	2.77	50	2	66.1	48	20	41	53

PEDRO MARTINEZ

Position: Pitcher
Team: Montreal Expos
Born: July 25, 1971 Manoguayabo, Dominican Republic
Height: 5'11" **Weight:** 170 lbs.
Bats: right **Throws:** right
Acquired: Traded from Dodgers for Delino DeShields, 11/93

Player Summary	
Fantasy Value	$17 to $20
Card Value	12¢ to 20¢
Will	rack up strikeouts
Can't	shake headhunter rep
Expect	righties to suffer
Don't Expect	gopher woes

After languishing in the Dodger bullpen during his rookie year, Martinez muscled his way into Montreal's rotation. The move was a success, although he developed a reputation as a headhunter. In his first six starts at home, nine players were ejected. Several ejections came April 13, when he hit Reggie Sanders with an 0-2 pitch after retiring 23 consecutive batters; Sanders charged the mound. Though he has good control, Martinez is noted for pitching inside. He yields less than three walks and a little more than seven hits per nine innings while averaging almost a strikeout an inning. Martinez throws a 95-mph fastball, a circle change, and a curve that still needs refining. He dominates right-handed hitters (.182) and is very stingy with the gopher ball. Martinez knows what to do with a glove but has trouble stopping baserunners. He doesn't hit like his older brother Ramon, but perhaps he will over time. Pedro is far from the finished product. Swapping Delino DeShields for Martinez might have been a master stroke of genius.

Major League Pitching Register

	W	L	ERA	G	CG	IP	H	ER	BB	SO
92 NL	0	1	2.25	2	0	8.0	6	2	1	8
93 NL	10	5	2.61	65	0	107.0	76	31	57	119
94 NL	11	5	3.42	24	1	144.2	115	55	45	142
Life	21	11	3.05	91	1	259.2	197	88	103	269
2 AVE	13	6	3.14	49	1	155.1	119	54	60	160

RAMON MARTINEZ

Position: Pitcher
Team: Los Angeles Dodgers
Born: March 22, 1968   Santo Domingo, Dominican Republic
Height: 6'4"   **Weight:** 173 lbs.
Bats: right   **Throws:** right
Acquired: Signed as a free agent, 9/84

Player Summary

Fantasy Value	$10 to $13
Card Value	8¢ to 12¢
Will	help himself at bat
Can't	maintain consistency
Expect	flashes of brilliance
Don't Expect	many hits

After struggling for two seasons, Martinez flashed his old form at various times last summer. Three of his four complete games were shutouts—two of them in succession. Martinez yielded less hits than innings pitched for the seventh straight year, allowed less than three walks per nine innings, and showed surprising effectiveness against left-handed hitters. The wiry right-hander showed the most life on his rising fastball since his 20-6 campaign of 1990. He mixes the heater with a changeup (his best pitch) and an excellent curveball. When he throws strikes, he gets most outs on ground balls—a pronounced change for a man who once fanned 18 in a game and 223 in a season. An agile athlete, Martinez runs well, handles the glove with little trouble, and dares baserunners to test him (he nailed seven of 10 last year). He's also one of the game's best-hitting pitchers. With five multihit games, Martinez finished at .273 in 1994.

Major League Pitching Register

	W	L	ERA	G	CG	IP	H	ER	BB	SO
88 NL	1	3	3.79	9	0	35.2	27	15	22	23
89 NL	6	4	3.19	15	2	98.2	79	35	41	89
90 NL	20	6	2.92	33	12	234.1	191	76	67	223
91 NL	17	13	3.27	33	6	220.1	190	80	69	150
92 NL	8	11	4.00	25	1	150.2	141	67	69	101
93 NL	10	12	3.44	32	4	211.2	202	81	104	127
94 NL	12	7	3.97	24	4	170.0	160	75	56	119
Life	74	56	3.44	171	29	1121.1	990	429	428	832
3 AVE	12	11	3.79	30	4	200.1	189	85	84	132

TINO MARTINEZ

Position: First base
Team: Seattle Mariners
Born: Dec. 7, 1967   Tampa, FL
Height: 6'2"   **Weight:** 205 lbs.
Bats: left   **Throws:** left
Acquired: First-round pick in 6/88 free-agent draft

Player Summary

Fantasy Value	$10 to $13
Card Value	6¢ to 10¢
Will	provide some punch
Can't	reduce strikeouts
Expect	hits vs. righties
Don't Expect	fielding woes

In three-plus major-league seasons, Martinez is still trying to justify his press clippings. An All-American at the University of Tampa, he also played on the 1988 U.S. Olympic team. He was named the Minor League Player of the Year in 1990 and won the MVP Award in the Pacific Coast League in '91. But after flunking two early trials, he had to share his position with Pete O'Brien in 1992. Martinez has good power—especially against right-handed pitchers—but would be much more valuable if he showed some discipline at the plate. His ratio of strikeouts to walks reached its worst level (nearly 2-to-1) last season. Martinez did his best hitting (.314) in late-inning pressure situations. He doesn't run well but supplies strong defense at first. He led two minor leagues in chances, putouts, and fielding percentage. He's adept at charging bunts, digging out bad throws, and starting the 3-6-3 double play. His .997 fielding percentage ranked second in the AL in 1993.

Major League Batting Register

	BA	G	AB	R	H	2B	3B	HR	RBI	SB
90 AL	.221	24	68	4	15	4	0	0	5	0
91 AL	.205	36	112	11	23	2	0	4	9	0
92 AL	.257	136	460	53	118	19	2	16	66	2
93 AL	.265	109	408	48	108	25	1	17	60	0
94 AL	.261	97	329	42	86	21	0	20	61	1
Life	.254	402	1377	158	350	71	3	57	201	3
3 AVE	.261	127	444	53	116	25	1	20	71	1

ROGER MASON

Position: Pitcher
Team: New York Mets
Born: Sept. 18, 1958 Bellaire, MI
Height: 6'6" **Weight:** 220 lbs.
Bats: right **Throws:** right
Acquired: Purchased from Phillies, 4/94

Player Summary	
Fantasy Value	$1 to $3
Card Value	5¢ to 7¢
Will	rely on forkball
Can't	avoid home runs
Expect	ground outs
Don't Expect	perfect control

Although Mason has made more than a half-dozen stops during his nine-year odyssey through the majors, he's a capable middle reliever when he gets his forkball over. He has a 0.00 ERA over seven appearances in League Championship Series action and a 1.17 ERA in four World Series games. Mason had his moments last year, when he yielded under a hit per inning and walked less than four hitters per nine innings. With less than five strikeouts over the same span, however, he needed help from his defense. He didn't always get it. The lanky right-hander, who also throws a fastball and a slider, threw too many home run balls (eight in 60 innings) and allowed too many steals (eight in nine attempts). His success in stranding inherited runners also left something to be desired. But Mason's ERA was his best in three years. If only his batting average would do so well: He can't hit or bunt.

Major League Pitching Register

	W	L	ERA	G	S	IP	H	ER	BB	SO
84 AL	1	1	4.50	5	1	22.0	23	11	10	15
85 NL	1	3	2.12	5	0	29.2	28	7	11	26
86 NL	3	4	4.80	11	0	60.0	56	32	30	43
87 NL	1	1	4.50	5	0	26.0	30	13	10	18
89 NL	0	0	20.25	2	0	1.1	2	3	2	3
91 NL	3	2	3.03	24	3	29.2	21	10	6	21
92 NL	5	7	4.09	65	8	88.0	80	40	33	56
93 NL	5	12	4.06	68	0	99.2	90	45	34	71
94 NL	3	5	3.75	47	1	60.0	55	25	25	33
Life	22	35	4.02	232	13	416.1	385	186	161	286
3 AVE	5	9	3.98	66	3	90.2	82	40	34	58

DON MATTINGLY

Position: First base
Team: New York Yankees
Born: April 20, 1961 Evansville, IN
Height: 6' **Weight:** 192 lbs.
Bats: left **Throws:** left
Acquired: 19th-round pick in 6/79 free-agent draft

Player Summary	
Fantasy Value	$9 to $11
Card Value	25¢ to 40¢
Will	always make contact
Can't	recapture old power
Expect	Gold Glove fielding
Don't Expect	poor clutch play

Lingering back and wrist injuries have made Mattingly a mere shadow of his former self. A six-time All-Star who also won a batting crown and an MVP Award, he can no longer turn on a pitch with power. Instead, he hits like a leadoff man, slapping opposite-field singles and driving balls into the gaps. One of baseball's best contact hitters, Mattingly walked nearly three times for every strikeout and hit both lefties and righties well. In 1994, he hit .340 with runners in scoring position. No threat to steal, Mattingly is a great threat to steal hits with stellar defense. He won his first Gold Glove in 1985 and has dominated since. He was named the AL's top defensive first baseman in a *Baseball America* poll. He charges and throws well. The Yankee captain got his 2,000th hit on July 23.

Major League Batting Register

	BA	G	AB	R	H	2B	3B	HR	RBI	SB
82 AL	.167	7	12	0	2	0	0	0	1	0
83 AL	.283	91	279	34	79	15	4	4	32	0
84 AL	.343	153	603	91	207	44	2	23	110	1
85 AL	.324	159	652	107	211	48	3	35	145	2
86 AL	.352	162	677	117	238	53	2	31	113	0
87 AL	.327	141	569	93	186	38	2	30	115	1
88 AL	.311	144	599	94	186	37	0	18	88	1
89 AL	.303	158	631	79	191	37	2	23	113	3
90 AL	.256	102	394	40	101	16	0	5	42	1
91 AL	.288	152	587	64	169	35	0	9	68	2
92 AL	.287	157	640	89	184	40	0	14	86	3
93 AL	.291	134	530	78	154	27	2	17	86	0
94 AL	.304	97	372	62	113	20	1	6	51	0
Life	.309	1657	6545	948	2021	410	18	215	1050	14
3 AVE	.293	143	565	85	166	32	1	13	81	1

DERRICK MAY

Position: Outfield
Team: Chicago Cubs
Born: July 14, 1968 Rochester, NY
Height: 6'4" **Weight:** 205 lbs.
Bats: left **Throws:** right
Acquired: First-round pick in 6/86 free-agent draft

Player Summary	
Fantasy Value	$8 to $10
Card Value	8¢ to 12¢
Will	make contact
Can't	shake shoulder woes
Expect	line drives
Don't Expect	top on-base mark

The potential is there. Two years ago, he struggled against left-handed pitchers. Last year, he hit them well (.313) but had trouble with righties. If May ever gets his act together, he may yet realize his promise. It was after advice from his father, former big leaguer Dave, that Derrick collected eight hits and eight RBI in three games last year. Pop told Derrick to go into a more pronounced crouch at home plate. May makes good contact, walking almost as much as he fans, but doesn't show enough patience to rack up a high on-base percentage. The owner of a line-drive stroke with in-the-gap power, he uses all fields against righties but pulls against lefties. He did his best hitting with runners in scoring position in 1994, compiling a .308 average. He's a decent runner but not a prolific basestealer. Despite shoulder problems that have plagued him for two years and robbed him of some arm strength, May is a competent left fielder who had four assists in 1994. He made only one error.

Major League Batting Register

	BA	G	AB	R	H	2B	3B	HR	RBI	SB
90 NL	.246	17	61	8	15	3	0	1	11	1
91 NL	.227	15	22	4	5	2	0	1	3	0
92 NL	.274	124	351	33	96	11	0	8	45	5
93 NL	.295	128	465	62	137	25	2	10	77	10
94 NL	.284	100	345	43	98	19	2	8	51	3
Life	.282	384	1244	150	351	60	4	28	187	19
3 AVE	.285	131	434	52	124	21	2	10	65	6

BRENT MAYNE

Position: Catcher
Team: Kansas City Royals
Born: April 19, 1968 Loma Linda, CA
Height: 6'1" **Weight:** 190 lbs.
Bats: left **Throws:** right
Acquired: First-round pick in 6/89 free-agent draft

Player Summary	
Fantasy Value	$1
Card Value	5¢ to 8¢
Will	produce under pressure
Can't	reach fences
Expect	strong defense
Don't Expect	great bat

Remember the Mayne? With Mike Macfarlane getting most of the playing time last summer, Kansas City's backup catcher had to make the most of his opportunities. Mayne did hit his first career grand slam May 5, helping K.C. top Toronto, 11-9. He hit only one other homer and now has seven in five big-league seasons. Though not known for his bat, he did hit well under pressure. Last year, he finished with a .343 average with runners in scoring position and a .360 mark in late-inning pressure situations. Lefty-hitting catchers are great platoon material, but he was a .250 hitter against both lefties and righties. Mayne fans twice as much as he walks. He'll steal a handful of times per year. The Cal State-Fullerton product is in the majors primarily for his defensive prowess. Though he's had trouble throwing for the past two years (29 percent of basestealers nailed in '94), Mayne is a good game-caller who prevents wild pitches, blocks the plate well, and knows how to handle pitchers.

Major League Batting Register

	BA	G	AB	R	H	2B	3B	HR	RBI	SB
90 AL	.231	5	13	2	3	0	0	0	1	0
91 AL	.251	85	231	22	58	8	0	3	31	2
92 AL	.225	82	213	16	48	10	0	0	18	0
93 AL	.254	71	205	22	52	9	1	2	22	3
94 AL	.257	46	144	19	37	5	1	2	20	1
Life	.246	289	806	81	198	32	2	7	92	6
2 AVE	.239	77	209	19	50	10	1	1	20	2

DAVID McCARTY

Position: First base
Team: Minnesota Twins
Born: Nov. 23, 1969 Houston, TX
Height: 6'5" **Weight:** 215 lbs.
Bats: right **Throws:** left
Acquired: First-round pick in 6/91 free-agent draft

Player Summary	
Fantasy Value. . . . . $3 to $5
Card Value . . . . 12¢ to 20¢
Will . . . . seek old power
Can't. hit curveball
Expect . . . . impatient brass
Don't Expect . . . . many walks

After two strong seasons in the upper minors, McCarty seemed ready to deliver on his immense promise last summer. But the former Stanford star stumbled backward instead—even getting an unexpected ticket to Triple-A. At Salt Lake, he batted .253 with three homers and 19 RBI. Preoccupied with finding his former power stroke, McCarty not only fanned at an alarming rate but ran into fielding problems too. Though he finished with a .260 average, he hit only one home run while striking out five times more than he walked. He was only a shadow of the player who hit .385 with eight homers in 143 at bats for Triple-A Portland in 1993. He has the size and strength of a slugger but hasn't learned how to pull or hit the curve. His long fly balls to center field are nothing but instant outs. If he doesn't deliver soon, he could jeopardize a future that projected him as Kent Hrbek's heir apparent at first base. McCarty handles himself well defensively despite a lack of speed. In 1992 at Double-A Orlando, he batted .271 with 18 homers and 79 RBI.

Major League Batting Register

	BA	G	AB	R	H	2B	3B	HR	RBI	SB
93 AL	.214	98	350	36	75	15	2	2	21	2
94 AL	.260	44	131	21	34	8	2	1	12	2
Life	.227	142	481	57	109	23	4	3	33	4

KIRK McCASKILL

Position: Pitcher
Team: Chicago White Sox
Born: April 9, 1961 Kapuskasing, Ontario
Height: 6'1" **Weight:** 196 lbs.
Bats: right **Throws:** right
Acquired: Signed as a free agent, 12/91

Player Summary	
Fantasy Value. . . . . $3 to $5
Card Value . . . . 5¢ to 7¢
Will . . . . depend upon change
Can't. . . . . avoid gopher balls
Expect . . . . good pickoff move
Don't Expect . . . . starting role

McCaskill was almost a forgotten man in the White Sox bullpen last summer. Though he finished with his best earned run average since 1990, his innings pitched declined to a career-low 52⅔ frames. He's been used less in each of the last two seasons. Once a top starter for the Angels, he moved to the bullpen in 1993 after losing his effectiveness. He had trouble keeping his curve, once his No. 1 pitch, in the strike zone. McCaskill, who also throws a fastball, a slider, and a very good changeup, showed better control last year. He averaged more than three and one-half walks per nine innings. McCaskill led the Chicago bullpen in gopher balls, though. He also struggled against right-handed hitters—usually his favorite patsies. The former All-America hockey player from the University of Vermont helps his own cause with fine defense and a first-rate pickoff move.

Major League Pitching Register

	W	L	ERA	G	S	IP	H	ER	BB	SO
85 AL	12	12	4.70	30	0	189.2	189	99	64	102
86 AL	17	10	3.36	34	0	246.1	207	92	92	202
87 AL	4	6	5.67	14	0	74.2	84	47	34	56
88 AL	8	6	4.31	23	0	146.1	155	70	61	98
89 AL	15	10	2.93	32	0	212.0	202	69	59	107
90 AL	12	11	3.25	29	0	174.1	161	63	72	78
91 AL	10	19	4.26	30	0	177.2	193	84	66	71
92 AL	12	13	4.18	34	0	209.0	193	97	95	109
93 AL	4	8	5.23	30	2	113.2	144	66	36	65
94 AL	1	4	3.42	40	3	52.2	51	20	22	37
Life	95	99	3.99	296	5	1596.1	1579	707	601	925
3 AVE	6	9	4.34	40	2	132.2	136	64	54	75

BEN McDONALD

Position: Pitcher
Team: Baltimore Orioles
Born: Nov. 24, 1967 Baton Rouge, LA
Height: 6'7" **Weight:** 212 lbs.
Bats: right **Throws:** right
Acquired: First-round pick in 6/89 free-agent draft

Player Summary	
Fantasy Value	$16 to $19
Card Value	10¢ to 20¢
Will	display diverse arsenal
Can't	freeze running game
Expect	ground outs
Don't Expect	gopher woes

When he finds consistency, McDonald will rank as one of baseball's best pitchers. He was AL Pitcher of the Month last April with a 5-0 record and 2.65 ERA. He won his next two decisions, becoming the first Oriole ever to start a year 7-0, but then he went 3-5 with a 5.18 ERA. A durable performer, McDonald made 80 straight starts before missing one due to a groin injury June 2. He yielded less than a hit per inning and three walks per game but fanned under five and one-half per nine innings. To get the ground balls he needs, McDonald has to have good location of his two curves, a straight changeup, a combination cut fastball-slider, and a forkball. Once easy prey for home runs, he has learned to reduce the gopher count by keeping the ball down. He did that so well on Aug. 5 that he notched his second career one-hitter, beating Milwaukee 4-0. The former Louisiana State All-American is a good fielder. He keeps an eye on runners, but his slow delivery gives them a jump.

Major League Pitching Register

	W	L	ERA	G	CG	IP	H	ER	BB	SO
89 AL	1	0	8.59	6	0	7.1	8	7	4	3
90 AL	8	5	2.43	21	3	118.2	88	32	35	65
91 AL	6	8	4.84	21	1	126.1	126	68	43	85
92 AL	13	13	4.24	35	4	227.0	213	107	74	158
93 AL	13	14	3.39	34	7	220.1	185	83	86	171
94 AL	14	7	4.06	24	5	157.1	151	71	54	94
Life	55	47	3.86	141	20	857.0	771	368	296	576
3 AVE	15	12	3.90	34	6	223.1	204	97	79	154

JACK McDOWELL

Position: Pitcher
Team: New York Yankees
Born: Jan. 16, 1966 Van Nuys, CA
Height: 6'5" **Weight:** 179 lbs.
Bats: right **Throws:** right
Acquired: Traded from White Sox for Keith Heberling and a player to be named later, 12/94

Player Summary	
Fantasy Value	$18 to $21
Card Value	10¢ to 20¢
Will	escape most jams
Can't	stop basestealers
Expect	route-going wins
Don't Expect	long losing skid

One year after winning the Cy Young Award, McDowell struggled to stay over the .500 mark. He dropped seven of his first nine, then recovered in time for a strong finish before the strike. In his last 10 games, he went 7-2 with a 1.81 ERA. McDowell's 3-0 win against Detroit July 20 was his 46th complete game and 10th career shutout. He made his in-season turnaround when he began throwing better pitches and working his way out of jams. A forkball master, he also uses a fine fastball and an occasional curve, while creating changeups with off-speed forkballs. Though he yielded more hits than innings in '94, McDowell has such sharp control that he keeps baserunners to a minimum. He walked two per game last year. He is also stingy with the gopher ball. The former Stanford standout is a first-rate fielder with a fine pickoff move but had trouble holding runners, with 18 of 23 who tried to steal against him successful.

Major League Pitching Register

	W	L	ERA	G	CG	IP	H	ER	BB	SO
87 AL	3	0	1.93	4	0	28.0	16	6	6	15
88 AL	5	10	3.97	26	1	158.2	147	70	68	84
90 AL	14	9	3.82	33	4	205.0	189	87	77	165
91 AL	17	10	3.41	35	15	253.2	212	96	82	191
92 AL	20	10	3.18	34	13	260.2	247	92	75	178
93 AL	22	10	3.37	34	10	256.2	261	96	69	158
94 AL	10	9	3.73	25	6	181.0	185	75	42	127
Life	91	58	3.50	191	49	1343.2	1258	522	419	918
3 AVE	19	11	3.42	34	10	257.1	257	98	68	172

ODDIBE McDOWELL

Position: Outfield
Team: Texas Rangers
Born: Aug. 25, 1962 Hollywood, FL
Height: 5'9" **Weight:** 165 lbs.
Bats: left **Throws:** left
Acquired: Signed as a free agent, 7/93

Player Summary
Fantasy Value	$2 to $4
Card Value	5¢ to 7¢
Will	make use of speed
Can't	find former power
Expect	good clutch stick
Don't Expect	fine arm

Though he spent the three preceding seasons exclusively in the minors, McDowell made it back to the majors last year after a solid showing at the Rangers' training camp. He finished at .262—10 points higher than his career major-league mark over six years. The former Arizona State All-American can still run. He swiped 14 bases in 16 tries. He also surprised with his prodigious performance under pressure. He batted .342 with runners in scoring position and .364 in key late-inning spots. Usually a better hitter against righties, McDowell was better against lefties last year (in limited playing time). He hit .308 against southpaws, whom he had hit at a .230 clip before. He didn't show as much power as he had in the past. Instead, he focused on getting on base. For a leadoff man, McDowell has to be less aggressive and more patient. The opposite approach applies in center, where he makes up for an inadequate arm with outstanding range.

Major League Batting Register
	BA	G	AB	R	H	2B	3B	HR	RBI	SB
85 AL	.239	111	406	63	97	14	5	18	42	25
86 AL	.266	154	572	105	152	24	7	18	49	33
87 AL	.241	128	407	65	98	26	4	14	52	24
88 AL	.247	120	437	55	108	19	5	6	37	33
89 AL	.222	69	239	33	53	5	2	3	22	12
89 NL	.304	76	280	56	85	18	4	7	24	15
90 NL	.243	113	305	47	74	14	0	7	25	13
94 AL	.262	59	183	34	48	5	1	1	15	14
Life	.253	830	2829	458	715	125	28	74	266	169

ROGER McDOWELL

Position: Pitcher
Team: Los Angeles Dodgers
Born: Dec. 21, 1960 Cincinnati, OH
Height: 6'1" **Weight:** 185 lbs.
Bats: right **Throws:** right
Acquired: Traded from Phillies for Mike Hartley and Braulio Castillo, 7/91

Player Summary
Fantasy Value	$0
Card Value	5¢ to 7¢
Will	seek comeback
Can't	always find plate
Expect	reliance on sinker
Don't Expect	a huge ERA

McDowell used to be a lot better at the bullpen game. He's fashioned four 20-save seasons in 10 years and had a 3.07 career ERA before dissolving last summer. Too many innings may have taken their toll. Heading into 1994, he had topped 50 appearances nine years in a row. Last year, the sinker didn't sink and the slider often broke outside the strike zone. As a result, McDowell yielded nearly 11 hits per nine innings and walked almost five over that same span. He also had trouble with inherited runners. He has now allowed more hits than innings pitched for three years in a row and four out of the last five. He surrendered a second-half average of .330 in 1993 and was only slightly better last summer (.303). He also finished with the worst ERA of his career (5.23). McDowell helps himself with his fielding, his pickoff move, and even his ability to hit.

Major League Pitching Register
	W	L	ERA	G	S	IP	H	ER	BB	SO
85 NL	6	5	2.83	62	17	127.1	108	40	37	70
86 NL	14	9	3.02	75	22	128.0	107	43	42	65
87 NL	7	5	4.16	56	25	88.2	95	41	28	32
88 NL	5	5	2.63	62	16	89.0	80	26	31	46
89 NL	4	8	1.96	69	23	92.0	79	20	38	47
90 NL	6	8	3.86	72	22	86.1	92	37	35	39
91 NL	9	9	2.93	71	10	101.1	100	33	48	50
92 NL	6	10	4.09	65	14	83.2	103	38	42	50
93 NL	5	3	2.25	54	2	68.0	76	17	30	27
94 NL	0	3	5.23	32	0	41.1	50	24	22	29
Life	62	65	3.17	618	151	905.2	890	319	353	455
3 AVE	4	6	3.81	55	5	70.1	83	30	34	39

CHUCK McELROY

Position: Pitcher
Team: Cincinnati Reds
Born: Oct. 1, 1967 Galveston, TX
Height: 6′ **Weight:** 195 lbs.
Bats: left **Throws:** left
Acquired: Traded from Cubs for Larry Luebbers, Mike Anderson, and Darron Cox, 12/93

Player Summary	
Fantasy Value	$6 to $8
Card Value	5¢ to 7¢
Will	assume big workload
Can't	strand runners
Expect	few walks
Don't Expect	stolen bases

The trade to Cincinnati worked wonders for McElroy last year. He pitched so well out of the bullpen that he was actually considered for the NL All-Star team. Showing much better control than he did the previous year, he yielded only about two and one-third walks per nine innings and averaged almost six strikeouts over that same span. The hard-throwing southpaw yielded less hits than innings, kept the ball in the park, and topped 50 appearances for the third time in four years. Stranding inherited runners posed problems for McElroy, however. Nearly half of them scored—seemingly a holdover of the first-batter woes he suffered in 1993. He has good command of a fastball, a forkball, and a slider. He also has an outstanding pickoff move that resulted in an 0-for-5 showing by baserunners who challenged him. An agile athlete, McElroy fields his position well. He's also been known to deliver a hit on one of those rare occasions when he bats.

Major League Pitching Register

	W	L	ERA	G	S	IP	H	ER	BB	SO
89 NL	0	0	1.74	11	0	10.1	12	2	4	8
90 NL	0	1	7.71	16	0	14.0	24	12	10	16
91 NL	6	2	1.95	71	3	101.1	73	22	57	92
92 NL	4	7	3.55	72	6	83.2	73	33	51	83
93 NL	2	2	4.56	49	0	47.1	51	24	25	31
94 NL	1	2	2.34	52	5	57.2	52	15	15	38
Life	13	14	3.09	271	14	314.1	285	108	162	268
3 AVE	2	4	3.31	65	4	70.2	66	26	32	56

WILLIE McGEE

Position: Outfield
Team: San Francisco Giants
Born: Nov. 2, 1958 San Francisco, CA
Height: 6′1″ **Weight:** 195 lbs.
Bats: both **Throws:** right
Acquired: Signed as a free agent, 12/90

Player Summary	
Fantasy Value	$5 to $7
Card Value	6¢ to 10¢
Will	seek medical miracle
Can't	reduce K rate
Expect	clutch hitting
Don't Expect	patience at plate

Though he still runs well and delivers in the clutch, McGee is far from the player who won two batting titles and an MVP Award. He was idled last June with a torn Achilles tendon. When healthy, he is a slap hitter with occasional to-the-gaps power. He lacks the patience to lead off and is too prone to striking out; he fans more than twice as much as he walks. A switch-hitter who hits for a better average right-handed but shows more power left-handed, McGee tends to produce in streaks. Red-hot the first half of 1993 (.338), he compiled a .241 average the rest of the way. Even at his age, McGee has enough speed to steal in double digits, stay out of double plays, and take an extra base. Though his range is fine in right field, his arm is not. He had to move to make room for Darren Lewis.

Major League Batting Register

	BA	G	AB	R	H	2B	3B	HR	RBI	SB
82 NL	.296	123	422	43	125	12	8	4	56	24
83 NL	.286	147	601	75	172	22	8	5	75	39
84 NL	.291	145	571	82	166	19	11	6	50	43
85 NL	.353	152	612	114	216	26	18	10	82	56
86 NL	.256	124	497	65	127	22	7	7	48	19
87 NL	.285	153	620	76	177	37	11	11	105	16
88 NL	.292	137	562	73	164	24	6	3	50	41
89 NL	.236	58	199	23	47	10	2	3	17	8
90 NL	.335	125	501	76	168	32	5	3	62	28
90 AL	.274	29	113	23	31	3	2	0	15	3
91 NL	.312	131	497	67	155	30	3	4	43	17
92 NL	.297	138	474	56	141	20	2	1	36	13
93 NL	.301	130	475	53	143	28	1	4	46	10
94 NL	.282	45	156	19	44	3	0	5	23	3
Life	.298	1637	6300	845	1876	288	84	66	708	320
3 AVE	.296	110	390	45	115	17	1	4	38	9

FRED McGRIFF

Position: First base
Team: Atlanta Braves
Born: Oct. 31, 1963   Tampa, FL
Height: 6'3"   **Weight:** 215 lbs.
Bats: left   **Throws:** left
Acquired: Traded from Padres for Melvin Nieves, Donnie Elliott, and Vince Moore, 7/93

Player Summary

Fantasy Value	$35 to $40
Card Value	20¢ to 30¢
Will	get clutch hits
Can't	steal too often
Expect	gargantuan power
Don't Expect	drought vs. lefties

Though the strike stopped McGriff's bid for a fourth straight 100-RBI campaign, it didn't halt his quest for his seventh consecutive 30-homer season—a feat accomplished by only eight others. Few sluggers are much more consistent or more feared by opposing pitchers. He hits well over .300 against right-handers, with runners in scoring position, and in late-inning pressure situations. He also holds his own against southpaws (.293 last year). His two-run, pinch-hit homer off Lee Smith tied the 1994 All-Star Game in the ninth inning and earned McGriff MVP honors. A prototype cleanup hitter, he is willing to take a walk or swing at a pitch early in the count. When he's hot, he can carry a club, as he proved with the 1993 Braves. He will even steal a handful of bases a year. And while he is not Sid Bream, McGriff is an adequate fielder, and his size makes him a towering target.

Major League Batting Register

	BA	G	AB	R	H	2B	3B	HR	RBI	SB
86 AL	.200	3	5	1	1	0	0	0	0	0
87 AL	.247	107	295	58	73	16	0	20	43	3
88 AL	.282	154	536	100	151	35	4	34	82	6
89 AL	.269	161	551	98	148	27	3	36	92	7
90 AL	.300	153	557	91	167	21	1	35	88	5
91 NL	.278	153	528	84	147	19	1	31	106	4
92 NL	.286	152	531	79	152	30	4	35	104	8
93 NL	.291	151	557	111	162	29	2	37	101	5
94 NL	.318	113	424	81	135	25	1	34	94	7
Life	.285	1147	3984	703	1136	202	16	262	710	45
3 AVE	.299	154	562	101	168	31	2	40	112	8

TERRY McGRIFF

Position: Catcher
Team: St. Louis Cardinals
Born: Sept. 23, 1963   Fort Pierce, FL
Height: 6'2"   **Weight:** 195 lbs.
Bats: right   **Throws:** right
Acquired: Signed as a minor-league free agent, 10/93

Player Summary

Fantasy Value	$0
Card Value	5¢ to 7¢
Will	show fair defense
Can't	duplicate Fred's power
Expect	top work vs. lefties
Don't Expect	everyday play

Don't let the last name fool you. While he is related to Fred (they're cousins), Terry is strictly a singles hitter. He has managed only three big-league homers in 326 at bats, spread over parts of six seasons. For a man who plays sparingly, he shows patience at the plate and makes good contact. Last year, in fact, McGriff walked more often than he struck out. He hit for a decent average (.250) against left-handed pitching and held his own with runners in scoring position. Several solid seasons in the upper minors suggest he might become a good batter if given enough playing time. In 1993, he led the Triple-A Pacific Coast League with a .426 on-base percentage. No threat to steal, he is a hazard to rivals who try. He gunned down 32 percent last season. Though he'll never be mistaken for Tom Pagnozzi or Kirt Manwaring, McGriff is a solid defensive receiver who led several leagues in chances, putouts, assists, double plays, and fielding. Terry is also related to Florida's Charles Johnson.

Major League Batting Register

	BA	G	AB	R	H	2B	3B	HR	RBI	SB
87 NL	.225	34	89	6	20	3	0	2	11	0
88 NL	.198	35	96	9	19	3	0	1	4	1
89 NL	.273	6	11	1	3	0	0	0	2	0
90 NL	.000	6	9	0	0	0	0	0	0	0
93 NL	.000	3	7	0	0	0	0	0	0	0
94 NL	.219	42	114	10	25	6	0	0	13	0
Life	.206	126	326	26	67	12	0	3	30	1

MARK McGWIRE

Position: First base
Team: Oakland Athletics
Born: Oct. 1, 1963 Pomona, CA
Height: 6'5" **Weight:** 225 lbs.
Bats: right **Throws:** right
Acquired: First-round pick in 6/84 free-agent draft

Player Summary	
Fantasy Value	$17 to $20
Card Value	12¢ to 25¢
Will	seek full recovery
Can't	count on speed
Expect	run production
Don't Expect	low on-base mark

McGwire thought off-season surgery repaired the left heel injury that sliced four and one-half months off his 1993 season. He was wrong. After he hit nine homers in his first 84 at bats of '94, the heel problem erupted again. The result was a season that ended after just 135 at bats. McGwire hopes to return fully healthy in 1995. When sound, he's one of the game's most prolific sluggers. Though he strikes out frequently, he's also a very selective hitter who once led the American League with 110 walks. In recent years, he's shortened his swing to reach inside pitches and adjusted his stance for outside pitches. He hit under the .200 mark against left-handed pitchers last year, which was a big surprise. Slow even before the heel injury, McGwire seldom steals. He moves well at first base, however, where he won a Gold Glove in 1990. The former Olympian has quick reactions, soft hands, and a good arm.

Major League Batting Register

	BA	G	AB	R	H	2B	3B	HR	RBI	SB
86 AL	.189	18	53	10	10	1	0	3	9	0
87 AL	.289	151	557	97	161	28	4	49	118	1
88 AL	.260	155	550	87	143	22	1	32	99	0
89 AL	.231	143	490	74	113	17	0	33	95	1
90 AL	.235	156	523	87	123	16	0	39	108	2
91 AL	.201	154	483	62	97	22	0	22	75	2
92 AL	.268	139	467	87	125	22	0	42	104	0
93 AL	.333	27	84	16	28	6	0	9	24	0
94 AL	.252	47	135	26	34	3	0	9	25	0
Life	.250	990	3342	546	834	137	5	238	657	6

MARK McLEMORE

Position: Second base
Team: Texas Rangers
Born: Oct. 4, 1964 San Diego, CA
Height: 5'11" **Weight:** 195 lbs.
Bats: both **Throws:** right
Acquired: Signed as a free agent, 12/94

Player Summary	
Fantasy Value	$7 to $9
Card Value	5¢ to 7¢
Will	display good speed
Can't	hit the long ball
Expect	patient at bats
Don't Expect	hits vs. lefties

A switch-hitter who's far better against right-handers, McLemore spent most of last year in a second-base platoon for the Orioles. McLemore welcomed the return to his natural position after spending most of the previous season in right field. He bats like a second baseman. He is a singles hitter who makes good contact, sprays hits to all fields, bunts on occasion, and likes to use his speed. He swiped 20 bases in 25 tries last summer. Deployed as the No. 9 hitter most of last summer, McLemore was like a second leadoff man. His on-base percentage, swelled by the fact that he walks as often as he fans, was a solid .354. His negatives are an inability to hit lefties and a tendency to hit into double plays. At second base, McLemore has fine range and good reactions. Though he didn't match the defense of recent O's second sackers Bill Ripken and Harold Reynolds, McLemore compensated with his bat.

Major League Batting Register

	BA	G	AB	R	H	2B	3B	HR	RBI	SB
86 AL	.000	5	4	0	0	0	0	0	0	0
87 AL	.236	138	433	61	102	13	3	3	41	25
88 AL	.240	77	233	38	56	11	2	2	16	13
89 AL	.243	32	103	12	25	3	1	0	14	6
90 AL	.150	28	60	6	9	2	0	0	2	1
91 NL	.148	21	61	6	9	1	0	0	2	0
92 AL	.246	101	228	40	56	7	2	0	27	11
93 AL	.284	148	581	81	165	27	5	4	72	21
94 AL	.257	104	343	44	88	11	1	3	29	20
Life	.249	654	2046	288	510	75	14	12	203	97
3 AVE	.267	132	431	61	115	16	3	3	47	20

GREG McMICHAEL

Position: Pitcher
Team: Atlanta Braves
Born: Dec. 1, 1966 Knoxville, TN
Height: 6'3" **Weight:** 215 lbs.
Bats: right **Throws:** right
Acquired: Signed as a minor-league free agent, 4/91

Player Summary	
Fantasy Value	$18 to $21
Card Value	6¢ to 10¢
Will	vary changeup's break
Can't	win without location
Expect	middle relief
Don't Expect	control woes

Between the 1993 and 1994 All-Star Games, McMichael recorded 37 saves, tied for third in the majors. But he wasn't the same pitcher in '94 that he was the year before. His magic vanished, as opposing hitters raised their average against him from .206 in 1993 to .280 last year. Both righties and lefties seemed to have figured out the secret of his changeup, a pitch McMichael can break in several different directions. When he throws strikes, he can blend the change with a fastball and a slider—pitches that look quicker when compared to the slow change. McMichael couldn't maintain his 1993 ratio of three whiffs per walk and averaged nearly three passes per nine innings last year. He also yielded more than 10 hits over that same stretch. Though he threw only one home run ball, it resulted in one of his 10 blown saves. McMichael helps himself with his fielding and keeps baserunners close. Because he was so erratic last year, his future should lie in middle relief. Mostly a starter in the minors, he saved five games in five years before '93.

Major League Pitching Register

	W	L	ERA	G	S	IP	H	ER	BB	SO
93 NL	2	3	2.06	74	19	91.2	68	21	29	89
94 NL	4	6	3.84	51	21	58.2	66	25	19	47
Life	6	9	2.75	125	40	150.1	134	46	48	136
2 AVE	4	6	2.90	73	24	86.2	80	28	28	78

BRIAN McRAE

Position: Outfield
Team: Kansas City Royals
Born: Aug. 27, 1967 Bradenton, FL
Height: 6' **Weight:** 180 lbs.
Bats: both **Throws:** right
Acquired: First-round pick in 6/85 free-agent draft

Player Summary	
Fantasy Value	$16 to $19
Card Value	8¢ to 12¢
Will	set table well
Can't	throw bullets
Expect	blinding speed
Don't Expect	many home runs

Dad's message finally got through last season. Brian McRae, responding to the pleas of his father, Hal, showed good patience at the plate for the first time. It wasn't enough to save dad's job as Kansas City's manager, but it was enough to give Brian the best on-base percentage of his career (.359). He had his first five-hit game (four singles and a double), against Boston May 31. Though he has gap power, McRae fattens his average with bunts and infield hits. He put 47 bunts into play, second in the AL, in 1993. A switch-hitter who's better right-handed, he batted almost 50 points higher against southpaws than against right-handers in 1994. He swiped a career-best 28 bases on 36 tries last year and could have reached 40 over a full season. McRae's speed and hustling, aggressive style serve him well in center, where his leaps and dives have become legendary in four-plus seasons. McRae's arm isn't the greatest but his speed compensates; he gets to balls others only dream of reaching.

Major League Batting Register

	BA	G	AB	R	H	2B	3B	HR	RBI	SB
90 AL	.286	46	168	21	48	8	3	2	23	4
91 AL	.261	152	629	86	164	28	9	8	64	20
92 AL	.223	149	533	63	119	23	5	4	52	18
93 AL	.282	153	627	78	177	28	9	12	69	23
94 AL	.273	114	436	71	119	22	6	4	40	28
Life	.262	614	2393	319	627	109	32	30	248	93
3 AVE	.261	154	591	80	155	27	7	7	59	27

KEVIN McREYNOLDS

Position: Outfield
Team: New York Mets
Born: Oct. 16, 1959 Little Rock, AR
Height: 6'1" **Weight:** 215 lbs.
Bats: right **Throws:** right
Acquired: Traded from Royals for Vince Coleman and cash, 1/94

Player Summary	
Fantasy Value	$1
Card Value	5¢ to 7¢
Will	hit with runners on
Can't	steal anymore
Expect	hits vs. lefties
Don't Expect	old power

After watching his RBI totals decline for six straight seasons, it's hard to believe McReynolds once had a five-year streak of 20-plus homers and 80-plus RBI. Troubled by chronic back pain over the last six years, he seems to spend more time on the disabled list than the active roster. He was idled three times over the first four months last year, thanks to a bulging disc in his neck, cartilage damage to his right knee, and other ills. McReynolds has the same stance and swing that he used during his heyday in the late 1980s, but his bat speed has declined. He still hits well with runners in scoring position (.303 last year) and is more productive against left-handed pitchers. He's also better in front of the home crowd. He had led NL outfielders in chances, assists, and double plays, but those days are history.

Major League Batting Register

	BA	G	AB	R	H	2B	HR	RBI	SB
83 NL	.221	39	140	15	31	3	1	4	14	2
84 NL	.278	147	525	68	146	26	6	20	75	3
85 NL	.234	152	564	61	132	24	4	15	75	4
86 NL	.287	158	560	89	161	31	6	26	96	8
87 NL	.276	151	590	86	163	32	5	29	95	14
88 NL	.288	147	552	82	159	30	2	27	99	21
89 NL	.272	148	545	74	148	25	3	22	85	15
90 NL	.269	147	521	75	140	23	1	24	82	9
91 NL	.259	143	522	65	135	32	1	16	74	6
92 AL	.247	109	373	45	92	25	0	13	49	7
93 AL	.245	110	351	44	86	22	4	11	42	2
94 AL	.256	51	180	23	46	11	2	4	21	2
Life	.265	1502	5423	727	1439	284	35	211	807	93
3 AVE	.248	97	326	40	81	21	2	10	40	4

RUSTY MEACHAM

Position: Pitcher
Team: Kansas City Royals
Born: Jan. 27, 1968 Stuart, FL
Height: 6'2" **Weight:** 175 lbs.
Bats: right **Throws:** right
Acquired: Claimed from Tigers on waivers, 10/91

Player Summary	
Fantasy Value	$3 to $5
Card Value	6¢ to 8¢
Will	check hitters
Can't	supply defense
Expect	fine K-walk ratio
Don't Expect	control woes

After spending the second half of '93 on the shelf recovering from a ligament tear in his pitching elbow, Meacham reclaimed his spot in the Kansas City bullpen last summer. He even compiled a string of 22⅓ consecutive scoreless innings before giving up a run July 2. A control pitcher who yielded a hit per inning but only two walks per game last year, Meacham maintained a 3-1 ratio of strikeouts to walks. He averaged more than six strikeouts per nine innings. He throws a fastball, a slider, a curve, and a forkball. He tries to keep the ball down but surrendered an uncharacteristic seven homers last year. Though he's done well against lefties in the past, Meacham was more effective against righthanders last summer. He's always effective against potential basestealers, who are so confused by his various speeds and motions that they rarely challenge him. A quick worker with a quick delivery, Meacham isn't so quick when it comes to his own defense. As a fielder, he's mediocre at best.

Major League Pitching Register

	W	L	ERA	G	S	IP	H	ER	BB	SO
91 AL	2	1	5.20	10	0	27.2	35	16	11	14
92 AL	10	4	2.74	64	2	101.2	88	31	21	64
93 AL	2	2	5.57	15	0	21.0	31	13	5	13
94 AL	3	3	3.73	36	4	50.2	51	21	12	36
Life	17	10	3.63	125	6	201.0	205	81	49	127
2 AVE	7	4	3.15	57	4	86.2	80	30	19	57

PAT MEARES

Position: Shortstop
Team: Minnesota Twins
Born: Sept. 6, 1968 Salina, KS
Height: 6' **Weight:** 185 lbs.
Bats: right **Throws:** right
Acquired: 12th-round pick in 6/90 free-agent draft

Player Summary	
Fantasy Value	$2 to $4
Card Value	6¢ to 10¢
Will	hit righties best
Can't	provide power
Expect	adequate fielding
Don't Expect	many walks

After a shaky start, Meares avoided the sophomore jinx last season. He hit a respectable .266 and provided solid defense at short. Meares, who doesn't do anything but lift weights during the off-season, blamed his slow start on the rough Kansas winter. He made six of his 13 errors in April and started slowly at the plate. A singles hitter who uses all fields, he is much better against right-handed pitchers. He yielded to Jeff Reboulet (.302 vs. lefties) against most southpaws last summer. Meares would be more valuable if he reduced a strikeout-to-walk ratio that was nearly 3-to-1 in 1994. He stole five bases in six tries and could do better if he reached more often. Not known for his power, Meares has hit only two big-league homers—both in the same game against Baltimore last June 19. For a No. 9 hitter, he swings a good bat with runners in scoring position (.283). The former college center fielder has good range and a strong—but not always accurate—arm at shortstop. Meares was a member of the Wichita State team that won the 1989 College World Series.

Major League Batting Register

	BA	G	AB	R	H	2B	3B	HR	RBI	SB
93 AL	.251	111	346	33	87	14	3	0	33	4
94 AL	.266	80	229	29	61	12	1	2	24	5
Life	.257	191	575	62	148	26	4	2	57	9
2 AVE	.259	112	334	37	86	15	2	1	33	6

ORLANDO MERCED

Position: First base; outfield
Team: Pittsburgh Pirates
Born: Nov. 2, 1966 San Juan, Puerto Rico
Height: 5'11" **Weight:** 170 lbs.
Bats: left **Throws:** right
Acquired: Signed as a free agent, 2/85

Player Summary	
Fantasy Value	$8 to $10
Card Value	6¢ to 10¢
Will	make contact
Can't	hammer homers
Expect	opposite-field hits
Don't Expect	batting title

Some guys hit better when the chips are down, and Merced is certainly one of them. He hit .346 in late-inning pressure situations last year. His overall batting average was 74 points lower. A line-drive hitter with gap power, he needs to maintain his momentum over a full season. For the second straight year, he was a hot starter who fizzled. He also continued a four-year pattern of alternating good and bad years. Merced has matured as a hitter, showing patience at the plate and hitting the ball wherever it's pitched. He uses all fields against right-handers but takes the ball up the middle against lefties. The former switch-hitter, once an easy out for lefties, actually did better against southpaws last year (.281) than against righties (.269). He hits almost all of his home runs against right-handers. Merced doesn't add much speed to a game. He steals a handful of bases a year. His fielding has declined, and he is not considered an adequate outfielder. He is better at first base.

Major League Batting Register

	BA	G	AB	R	H	2B	3B	HR	RBI	SB
90 NL	.208	25	24	3	5	1	0	0	0	0
91 NL	.275	120	411	83	113	17	2	10	50	8
92 NL	.247	134	405	50	100	28	5	6	60	5
93 NL	.313	137	447	68	140	26	4	8	70	3
94 NL	.272	108	386	48	105	21	3	9	51	4
Life	.277	524	1673	252	463	93	14	33	231	20
3 AVE	.278	141	465	62	129	28	4	9	67	5

KENT MERCKER

Position: Pitcher
Team: Atlanta Braves
Born: Feb. 1, 1968   Dublin, OH
Height: 6'2"   **Weight:** 195 lbs.
Bats: left   **Throws:** left
Acquired: First-round pick in 6/86 free-agent draft

Player Summary

Fantasy Value	$9 to $11
Card Value	6¢ to 10¢
Will	intimidate hitters
Can't	always stay sharp
Expect	low-hit games
Don't Expect	return to pen

The No. 5 Atlanta starter when 1994 began, Mercker emerged as the second-most effective member of the rotation. He no-hit the Dodgers in his first start, held lefties to a .206 average, and yielded just over seven hits per nine innings. He averaged almost a strikeout an inning—the rotation's best—and just over three and one-half walks per nine innings. Mercker might have done even better if not for his irregular schedule. Off-days and rainouts cost him several starts, limiting him to a total of 17. He won nine, four more than he had ever won in five previous years as a reliever. His previous control problems were corrected by regular work. He said he learned how to set up hitters by charting games for three-time Cy Young Award winner Greg Maddux. Mercker mixes an exceptional fastball with a slider, a curve, and a changeup that was much improved last year. The hard-throwing lefty keeps runners close and fields his position well but can't hit a lick.

Major League Pitching Register

	W	L	ERA	G	CG	IP	H	ER	BB	SO
89 NL	0	0	12.46	2	0	4.1	8	6	6	4
90 NL	4	7	3.17	36	0	48.1	43	17	24	39
91 NL	5	3	2.58	50	0	73.1	56	21	35	62
92 NL	3	2	3.42	53	0	68.1	51	26	35	49
93 NL	3	1	2.86	43	0	66.0	52	21	36	59
94 NL	9	4	3.45	20	2	112.1	90	43	45	111
Life	24	17	3.24	204	2	372.2	300	134	181	324
3 AVE	6	3	3.31	41	1	97.1	77	36	45	88

JOSE MESA

Position: Pitcher
Team: Cleveland Indians
Born: May 22, 1966   Azua, Dominican Republic
Height: 6'3"   **Weight:** 222 lbs.
Bats: right   **Throws:** right
Acquired: Traded from Orioles for Kyle Washington, 7/92

Player Summary

Fantasy Value	$4 to $6
Card Value	5¢ to 7¢
Will	welcome workload
Can't	retire southpaws
Expect	high K ratio
Don't Expect	big fly woes

Could all those coaches and managers have been wrong? Prior to 1994, Mesa was strictly a starting pitcher. All but three of his 98 appearances were starts but most weren't successful (27-40 lifetime record and 5.03 ERA). Last year, however, Cleveland moved him to the bullpen, and the pitcher responded with his best year. A control artist who throws hard, Mesa mixes a sinking fastball with a slider, a curve, and an occasional forkball. He averaged two and one-half strikeouts per walk, less hits than innings, and just over three walks per game in 1994. He dominated right-handed hitters (.244) and was extremely tough to take deep (three home runs in 73 innings). When he's on, he gets a lot of grounders, and he had a nine-inning average of over seven and one-half strikeouts last year. He also eats up innings, topping the Tribe in appearances last year. Mesa has a good pickoff move for a righty and quick reactions in the field.

Major League Pitching Register

	W	L	ERA	G	S	IP	H	ER	BB	SO
87 AL	1	3	6.03	6	0	31.1	38	21	15	17
90 AL	3	2	3.86	7	0	46.2	37	20	27	24
91 AL	6	11	5.97	23	0	123.2	151	82	62	64
92 AL	7	12	4.54	28	0	160.2	169	82	70	62
93 AL	10	12	4.92	34	0	208.2	232	114	62	118
94 AL	7	5	3.82	51	2	73.0	71	31	26	63
Life	34	45	4.89	149	2	644.0	698	350	262	348
3 AVE	9	10	4.57	45	1	157.1	167	80	56	90

MATT MIESKE

Position: Outfield
Team: Milwaukee Brewers
Born: Feb. 13, 1968 Midland, MI
Height: 6′ **Weight:** 185 lbs.
Bats: right **Throws:** right
Acquired: Traded from Padres with Ricky Bones and Jose Valentin for Gary Sheffield and Geoff Kellogg, 3/92

Player Summary	
Fantasy Value	$6 to $8
Card Value	15¢ to 30¢
Will	improve his power
Can't	reduce strikeouts
Expect	20-20 bid
Don't Expect	high on-base mark

The potential is obvious. At various stages of his tenure in the minors, Mieske led his league in hits, doubles, home runs, RBI, batting, total bases, on-base percentage, chances, putouts, and assists. No wonder the Brewers wanted him included in the package for Gary Sheffield. Though Mieske didn't make an immediate splash when he finally reached the majors last year, he showed enough power, speed, and defensive skill to be considered a future comer. He hit lefties at a .299 clip and had no problems in late-inning pressure spots (.278). But he fanned three times for every walk—perhaps because of anxiety—and failed to produce a good on-base mark. Mieske did manage 10 homers and should do better once he masters the major-league strike zone. He twice topped 25 steals in the minors and might develop into a 20-20 man. He throws well enough for right (seven assists in 80 games) and has good range. An Academic All-American from Western Michigan, Mieske batted .260 with eight homers and 22 RBI in 219 at bats at Triple-A New Orleans in 1993.

Major League Batting Register

	BA	G	AB	R	H	2B	3B	HR	RBI	SB
93 AL	.241	23	58	9	14	0	0	3	7	0
94 AL	.259	84	259	39	67	13	1	10	38	3
Life	.256	107	317	48	81	13	1	13	45	3

RANDY MILLIGAN

Position: First base
Team: Montreal Expos
Born: Nov. 27, 1961 San Diego, CA
Height: 6′2″ **Weight:** 225 lbs.
Bats: right **Throws:** right
Acquired: Traded from Indians for Brian Barnes, 12/93

Player Summary	
Fantasy Value	$1
Card Value	5¢ to 7¢
Will	wait for walks
Can't	provide top defense
Expect	pinch-hitting duty
Don't Expect	hits vs. righties

Although he's played sparingly in recent seasons, Milligan maintains his reputation as a solid bench player who can poke a late pinch hit, spell an overworked first baseman, and provide a good clubhouse presence. An extremely selective hitter who's willing to wait for a walk, he always has an on-base percentage much higher than his batting average. There was a 105-point difference last year, for example. Milligan's main thing is battering left-handed pitching—especially in key situations. His 1993 numbers included a .383 mark against lefties and a .315 average with runners in scoring position. He is always a threat to hit a round-tripper. In recent years, however, he's been more content to poke an RBI single with runners on or work out a walk with the bases empty. Milligan hasn't stolen a base in four years and won't start now. He's adequate in the field.

Major League Batting Register

	BA	G	AB	R	H	2B	3B	HR	RBI	SB
87 NL	.000	3	1	0	0	0	0	0	0	0
88 NL	.220	40	82	10	18	5	0	3	8	1
89 AL	.268	124	365	56	98	23	5	12	45	9
90 AL	.265	109	362	64	96	20	1	20	60	6
91 AL	.263	141	483	57	127	17	2	16	70	0
92 AL	.240	137	462	71	111	21	1	11	53	0
93 NL	.274	83	234	30	64	11	1	6	29	0
93 AL	.426	19	47	7	20	7	0	0	7	0
94 NL	.232	47	82	10	19	2	0	2	12	0
Life	.261	703	2118	305	553	106	10	70	284	16
2 AVE	.262	120	372	54	98	20	1	9	45	0

ALAN MILLS

Position: Pitcher
Team: Baltimore Orioles
Born: Oct. 18, 1966 Lakeland, FL
Height: 6'1" **Weight:** 190 lbs.
Bats: both **Throws:** right
Acquired: Traded from Yankees for Francisco de la Rosa and Mike Carper, 2/92

Player Summary	
Fantasy Value	$5 to $7
Card Value	5¢ to 7¢
Will	strand runners
Can't	always find zone
Expect	high velocity
Don't Expect	righties to hit

The ERA wasn't great, but Mills had his magic moments in the Baltimore bullpen last summer. He stranded 33 of the 41 runners he inherited (an 80.5 percent success rate), held right-handed hitters to a .226 average, yielded less hits than innings pitched, and averaged nearly a strikeout per inning. In addition, he was the busiest member of the Oriole staff with 47 appearances. His ERA ballooned to a career worst, however, because of erratic control. He allowed more than four and one-half walks per nine innings. When he allowed bases on balls, he started to have trouble. He also gave up seven gopher balls and allowed left-handers to bat .292. A fastball-slider pitcher who needs an off-speed delivery so he can confuse batters better, Mills throws everything hard. He has no trouble fielding shots that come back at him, and he's adept at controlling the running game. Only three men stole against him in 1994. An Angel draftee, Mills broke into the majors with the Yankees.

Major League Pitching Register

	W	L	ERA	G	S	IP	H	ER	BB	SO
90 AL	1	5	4.10	36	0	41.2	48	19	33	24
91 AL	1	1	4.41	6	0	16.1	16	8	8	11
92 AL	10	4	2.61	35	2	103.1	78	30	54	60
93 AL	5	4	3.23	45	4	100.1	80	36	51	68
94 AL	3	3	5.16	47	2	45.1	43	26	24	44
Life	20	17	3.49	169	8	307.0	265	119	170	207
3 AVE	6	4	3.45	49	3	89.1	73	34	46	63

ANGEL MIRANDA

Position: Pitcher
Team: Milwaukee Brewers
Born: Nov. 9, 1969 Arecibo, Puerto Rico
Height: 6'1" **Weight:** 190 lbs.
Bats: left **Throws:** left
Acquired: Signed as a free agent, 3/87

Player Summary	
Fantasy Value	$5 to $7
Card Value	6¢ to 8¢
Will	quiet lefty bats
Can't	locate the plate
Expect	screwball use
Don't Expect	low whiff totals

Though used mostly in relief during his minor-league tenure, Miranda made a fine debut as a rookie starter with the 1993 Brewers. He might have maintained that momentum if imperative knee surgery hadn't slowed his progress. Miranda did return in time to make eight starts last summer but wasn't as sharp as he had been the year before. A screwball specialist who also throws a lively fastball, he is much more difficult on left-handed batters (.208 in 1994). He yielded less than eight hits per nine innings but ran into trouble when his control wasn't sharp. Though he was a strikeout pitcher in the minors, Miranda averaged only about four and one-half strikeouts per nine innings last year. That should improve as he returns to full strength. He's not a great fielder and needs work on his pickoff move. All nine batters who challenged him last year stole successfully. Miranda should have a bright future ahead of him if he can find home plate consistently. He moved to a starter's role in 1992 at Triple-A Denver and went 6-12 with a 4.77 ERA. He saved 24 games for Class-A Stockton in 1990.

Major League Pitching Register

	W	L	ERA	G	CG	IP	H	ER	BB	SO
93 AL	4	5	3.30	22	2	120.0	100	44	52	88
94 AL	2	5	5.28	8	1	46.0	39	27	27	24
Life	6	10	3.85	30	3	166.0	139	71	79	112

KEVIN MITCHELL

Position: Outfield
Team: Cincinnati Reds
Born: Jan. 13, 1962   San Diego, CA
Height: 5'11"   **Weight:** 244 lbs.
Bats: right   **Throws:** right
Acquired: Traded from Mariners for Norm Charlton, 11/92

Player Summary	
Fantasy Value	$20 to $25
Card Value	12¢ to 20¢
Will	flaunt huge power
Can't	show OK glove
Expect	run production
Don't Expect	low on-base mark

Though dogged by injuries and controversies throughout his career, Mitchell has always used his bat to silence his critics. The guy can flat-out hit. He not only slugged 30 homers in 310 at bats last summer but topped .300 against lefties (.346), righties (.319), at home (.347), on the road (.300), with runners in scoring position (.326), and in late-inning pressure spots (.302). Had the strike not shortened the season, Mitchell might have exceeded the career-peak 47 homers of his 1989 MVP season. When he's willing and able to play, he can carry a ballclub. He loves fastballs but hits anything—with power to all fields. Some of his home runs seem to be launched rather than hit. He doesn't run well on the basepaths or in left field, but he surprised last year with nine assists, two double plays, and only four errors. A shift to first base is a strong possibility.

Major League Batting Register

	BA	G	AB	R	H	2B	3B	HR	RBI	SB
84 NL	.214	7	14	0	3	0	0	0	1	0
86 NL	.277	108	328	51	91	22	2	12	43	3
87 NL	.280	131	328	68	130	20	2	22	70	9
88 NL	.251	148	505	60	127	25	7	19	80	5
89 NL	.291	154	543	100	158	34	6	47	125	3
90 NL	.290	140	524	90	152	24	2	35	93	4
91 NL	.256	113	371	52	95	13	1	27	69	2
92 AL	.286	99	360	48	103	24	0	9	67	0
93 NL	.341	93	323	56	110	21	3	19	64	1
94 NL	.326	95	310	57	101	18	1	30	77	2
Life	.286	1088	3742	582	1070	201	24	220	689	29
3 AVE	.317	109	373	61	118	23	1	23	80	1

PAUL MOLITOR

Position: Designated hitter; infield
Team: Toronto Blue Jays
Born: Aug. 22, 1956   St. Paul, MN
Height: 6'   **Weight:** 185 lbs.
Bats: right   **Throws:** right
Acquired: Signed as a free agent, 12/92

Player Summary	
Fantasy Value	$25 to $30
Card Value	20¢ to 30¢
Will	reach base often
Can't	wait to swing bat
Expect	speed plus power
Don't Expect	declining output

Last year, Molitor finished second in the league in hits, sixth in batting, seventh in runs, and tied for ninth in on-base percentage. A contact hitter who walks more than he fans, Molitor mixes power and speed. Almost one-third of his hits go for extra bases, and he picks his spots so well as a basestealer that he succeeded all 20 times he tried last year. The University of Minnesota product hit .326 against righties and .391 against lefties. Toronto deployed him almost exclusively as a DH. Yet Molitor signed as a shortstop and has played almost everywhere. He's been an AL All-Star seven times, including the last four in a row. The future Hall of Famer needs just 353 hits to join the 3,000-hit club.

Major League Batting Register

	BA	G	AB	R	H	2B	3B	HR	RBI	SB
78 AL	.273	125	521	73	142	26	4	6	45	30
79 AL	.322	140	584	88	188	27	16	9	62	33
80 AL	.304	111	450	81	137	29	2	9	37	34
81 AL	.267	64	251	45	67	11	0	2	19	10
82 AL	.302	160	666	136	201	26	8	19	71	41
83 AL	.270	152	608	95	164	28	6	15	47	41
84 AL	.217	13	46	3	10	1	0	0	6	1
85 AL	.297	140	576	93	171	28	3	10	48	21
86 AL	.281	105	437	62	123	24	6	9	55	20
87 AL	.353	118	465	114	164	41	5	16	75	45
88 AL	.312	154	609	115	190	34	6	13	60	41
89 AL	.315	155	615	84	194	35	4	11	56	27
90 AL	.285	103	418	64	119	27	6	12	45	18
91 AL	.325	158	665	133	216	32	13	17	75	19
92 AL	.320	158	609	89	195	36	7	12	89	31
93 AL	.332	160	636	121	211	37	5	22	111	22
94 AL	.341	115	454	86	155	30	4	14	75	20
Life	.307	2131	8610	1482	2647	472	95	196	976	454
3 AVE	.331	160	628	110	208	38	6	18	102	27

RAUL MONDESI

Position: Outfield
Team: Los Angeles Dodgers
Born: March 12, 1971 San Cristobal, Dominican Republic
Height: 5'11" **Weight:** 202 lbs.
Bats: right **Throws:** right
Acquired: Signed as a free agent, 6/88

Player Summary	
Fantasy Value	$17 to $20
Card Value	30¢ to 70¢
Will	impress with arm
Can't	reduce K ratio
Expect	20-20 showing
Don't Expect	patience at bat

A five-tool player, Mondesi made a shambles of the 1994 NL Rookie of the Year voting. He showed power, speed, and the ability to produce with runners in scoring position (.363). But his major contribution was his play in right field, where he had 15 assists in 109 games. A natural center fielder who moved because of his arm, he throws no harder than Mark Whiten but gets to the ball faster, releases it faster, and makes more accurate pegs. If Mondesi has a flaw, it's his over-aggressive style at the plate and on the bases. An impatient hitter, he fanned four times more than he walked last year, hurting his on-base percentage and reducing his steal opportunities. He's also an impetuous basestealer who's thrown out almost half the time he tries. Mondesi should improve as he gains experience. The Dodgers loved his homer that beat Houston 1-0 on May 11, and his 10th-inning shot that beat John Wetteland 2-1 July 5. They also loved his two 14-game hitting streaks during the season's first half. At Triple-A Albuquerque in 1993, he batted .280 with 12 homers and 65 RBI.

Major League Batting Register

	BA	G	AB	R	H	2B	3B	HR	RBI	SB
93 NL	.291	42	86	13	25	3	1	4	10	4
94 NL	.306	112	434	63	133	27	8	16	56	11
Life	.304	154	520	76	158	30	9	20	66	15

JEFF MONTGOMERY

Position: Pitcher
Team: Kansas City Royals
Born: Jan. 7, 1962 Wellston, OH
Height: 5'11" **Weight:** 180 lbs.
Bats: right **Throws:** right
Acquired: Traded from Reds for Van Snider, 2/88

Player Summary	
Fantasy Value	$35 to $40
Card Value	8¢ to 12¢
Will	save 30 if sound
Can't	nail all lefties
Expect	lighter workload
Don't Expect	control woes

Montgomery would just as soon forget 1994. Plagued by bursitis in his right shoulder, he yielded more hits than innings pitched, walked more than three batters per game, and stranded only 66.7 percent of the runners he inherited. Though he converted 27 of 32 save chances, his three-year string of 30-plus saves crashed to a stop. A power pitcher who throws a fastball, a slider, a curve, and a changeup, he did manage to average more than 10 strikeouts per nine innings. But lefties hit him at a .302 clip and he finished with the second-worst ERA of his eight-year career. Too many innings may have taken their toll. Unlike most other closers, Montgomery's outings usually involved multiple innings. He pitched 90 frames three straight seasons. He should rebound in 1995 if he stays healthy. He helps his own cause with good fielding and a fine pickoff move.

Major League Pitching Register

	W	L	ERA	G	S	IP	H	ER	BB	SO
87 NL	2	2	6.52	14	0	19.1	25	14	9	13
88 AL	7	2	3.45	45	1	62.2	54	24	30	47
89 AL	7	3	1.37	63	18	92.0	66	14	25	94
90 AL	6	5	2.39	73	24	94.1	81	25	34	94
91 AL	4	4	2.90	67	33	90.0	83	29	28	77
92 AL	1	6	2.18	65	39	82.2	61	20	27	69
93 AL	7	5	2.27	69	45	87.1	65	22	23	66
94 AL	2	3	4.03	42	27	44.2	48	20	15	50
Life	36	30	2.64	438	187	573.0	483	168	191	510
3 AVE	4	5	2.71	64	41	77.2	65	23	24	68

MIKE MOORE

Position: Pitcher
Team: Detroit Tigers
Born: Nov. 26, 1959 Eakly, OK
Height: 6'4" **Weight:** 205 lbs.
Bats: right **Throws:** right
Acquired: Signed as a free agent, 12/92

Player Summary

Fantasy Value	$0
Card Value	5¢ to 7¢
Will	fight for spot
Can't	notch Ks
Expect	gopher woes
Don't Expect	ERA to drop

Moore seems to be sinking into baseball oblivion. His ERA has risen three years in a row, his control has disappeared, and he's become a favorite patsy for homer-happy sluggers. Though he allowed less hits than innings in 1994, he yielded more walks than strikeouts. His 10 wild pitches last season topped the Tigers. He has good command of only two pitches—a curve and a changeup—but has to come in with a fat fastball when he falls behind. Since his fastball is only slightly faster than Charlie Hough's, that doesn't help. Moore tries to keep hitters honest by blending in a slider and a forkball but has trouble throwing them for strikes. He holds lefties and righties to respectable averages, but his combination of walks and homers is deadly. He fields his position and holds runners but has a slow delivery.

Major League Pitching Register

	W	L	ERA	G	CG	IP	H	ER	BB	SO
82 AL	7	14	5.36	28	1	144.1	159	86	79	73
83 AL	6	8	4.71	22	3	128.0	130	67	60	108
84 AL	7	17	4.97	34	6	212.0	236	117	85	158
85 AL	17	10	3.46	35	14	247.0	230	95	70	155
86 AL	11	13	4.30	38	11	266.0	279	127	94	146
87 AL	9	19	4.71	33	12	231.0	268	121	84	115
88 AL	9	15	3.78	37	9	228.2	196	96	63	182
89 AL	19	11	2.61	35	6	241.2	193	70	83	172
90 AL	13	15	4.65	33	3	199.1	204	103	84	73
91 AL	17	8	2.96	33	3	210.0	176	69	105	153
92 AL	17	12	4.12	36	2	223.0	229	102	103	117
93 AL	13	9	5.22	36	4	213.2	227	124	89	89
94 AL	11	10	5.42	25	4	154.1	152	93	89	62
Life	156	161	4.23	425	78	2699.0	2679	1270	1088	1603
3 AVE	15	12	4.91	36	4	218.1	223	119	106	98

MICKEY MORANDINI

Position: Second base
Team: Philadelphia Phillies
Born: April 22, 1966 Kittanning, PA
Height: 5'11" **Weight:** 170 lbs.
Bats: left **Throws:** right
Acquired: Fifth-round pick in 6/88 free-agent draft

Player Summary

Fantasy Value	$4 to $6
Card Value	6¢ to 10¢
Will	supply strong defense
Can't	hit left-handers
Expect	speed to hike average
Don't Expect	great power

A terrific platoon player, Morandini hits right-handed pitching hard (.305 last year) but struggles against southpaws (.235). He began last year as Mariano Duncan's lefty platoon partner but finished it as the southpaw alter ego of Randy Ready. A contact hitter who walks as much as he fans, Morandini reached a career peak in batting average by making a dramatic reduction in his strikeout rate. Though he sprays singles to all fields and has occasional gap power, he fattens his average with infield chops, rollers, and bunts. He surprised last year by hitting .313 with runners in scoring position. Morandini has enough speed to take extra bases, race from first to third, and compile a good success rate as a base-stealer. A fine defensive player, he's the only second baseman ever to make an unassisted triple play during the regular season. He also had a 74-game errorless streak. The 1988 Olympian mixes quick reactions, excellent range, and good hands with a strong and accurate arm.

Major League Batting Register

	BA	G	AB	R	H	2B	3B	HR	RBI	SB
90 NL	.241	25	79	9	19	4	0	1	3	3
91 NL	.249	98	325	38	81	11	4	1	20	13
92 NL	.265	127	422	47	112	8	8	3	30	8
93 NL	.247	120	425	57	105	19	9	3	33	13
94 NL	.292	87	274	40	80	16	5	2	26	10
Life	.260	457	1525	191	397	58	26	10	112	47
3 AVE	.267	123	411	53	110	17	8	3	33	12

MIKE MORGAN

Position: Pitcher
Team: Chicago Cubs
Born: Oct. 8, 1959 Tulare, CA
Height: 6'2" **Weight:** 215 lbs.
Bats: right **Throws:** right
Acquired: Signed as a free agent, 12/91

Player Summary	
Fantasy Value	$1
Card Value	6¢ to 10¢
Will	assume big workload
Can't	worry about '94
Expect	comeback season
Don't Expect	help at bat

A double-digit winner in six previous seasons, Morgan spent most of 1994 playing catch-up. He got off to a bad start, endured two first-half stints on the disabled list, and experimented with a circle change and a palmball. When the players walked on Aug. 12, Morgan was out with a sore back. His ego had to be sore too. His statistics were unsettling for someone supposed to be the staff ace. A sinker-slider pitcher who also throws a forkball, Morgan is widely known for his ability to get ground-ball outs. When he was healthy, he yielded a hit per inning, walked three per game, and kept the ball in the park. A fierce competitor, he will pitch through nagging injuries and give his team innings. Morgan serves as a fifth infielder with his quick moves. He also has a fine pickoff move.

Major League Pitching Register

	W	L	ERA	G	CG	IP	H	ER	BB	SO
78 AL	0	3	7.30	3	1	12.1	19	10	8	0
79 AL	2	10	5.94	13	2	77.1	102	51	50	17
82 AL	7	11	4.37	30	2	150.1	167	73	67	71
83 AL	0	3	5.16	16	0	45.1	48	26	21	22
85 AL	1	1	12.00	2	0	6.0	11	8	5	2
86 AL	11	17	4.53	37	9	216.1	243	109	86	116
87 AL	12	17	4.65	34	8	207.0	245	107	53	85
88 AL	1	6	5.43	22	2	71.1	70	43	23	29
89 NL	8	11	2.53	40	0	152.2	130	43	33	72
90 NL	11	15	3.75	33	6	211.0	216	88	60	106
91 NL	14	10	2.78	34	5	236.1	197	73	61	140
92 NL	16	8	2.55	34	6	240.0	203	68	79	123
93 NL	10	15	4.03	32	1	207.2	206	93	74	111
94 NL	2	10	6.69	15	1	80.2	111	60	35	57
Life	95	137	4.01	345	43	1914.1	1968	852	655	951
3 AVE	10	12	3.94	29	3	187.2	188	82	67	105

HAL MORRIS

Position: First base
Team: Cincinnati Reds
Born: April 9, 1965 Fort Rucker, AL
Height: 6'4" **Weight:** 215 lbs.
Bats: left **Throws:** left
Acquired: Traded from Yankees with Rodney Imes for Tim Leary and Van Snider, 12/89

Player Summary	
Fantasy Value	$15 to $18
Card Value	8¢ to 12¢
Will	murder right-handers
Can't	steal lots of bases
Expect	slicing line drives
Don't Expect	great power

Before he can win a batting title, Morris must reduce a tendency to strike out twice for every walk. His .385 on-base percentage last year would have soared well over .400 had he walked more frequently. Nor does he make contact often enough for a man not regarded as a slugger. Morris has reached double digits in home runs only twice and is three times more likely to hit a double than he is to hit the ball out of the park. He hits line drives to all fields but struggles against southpaws (.255). That was the main reason the Reds acquired Brian Hunter as his occasional right-handed platoon partner. Morris moves around in the batter's box, and Reds manager Davey Johnson didn't interfere last year. The result was the second-best average of Morris's career. He steals a few bases but is not much of a baserunner. He's much better in the field, where he's overcome a reputation as a liability. He reacts quickly to balls hit down the line.

Major League Batting Register

	BA	G	AB	R	H	2B	3B	HR	RBI	SB
88 AL	.100	15	20	1	2	0	0	0	0	0
89 AL	.278	15	18	2	5	0	0	0	4	0
90 NL	.340	107	309	50	105	22	3	7	36	9
91 NL	.318	136	478	72	152	33	1	14	59	10
92 NL	.271	115	395	41	107	21	3	6	53	6
93 NL	.317	101	379	48	120	18	0	7	49	2
94 NL	.335	112	436	60	146	30	4	10	78	6
Life	.313	601	2035	274	637	124	11	44	279	33
3 AVE	.312	125	463	58	144	27	3	9	71	5

JAMES MOUTON

Position: Outfield
Team: Houston Astros
Born: Dec. 29, 1968   Denver, CO
Height: 5'9"   **Weight:** 175 lbs.
Bats: right   **Throws:** right
Acquired: Seventh-round pick in 6/91 free-agent draft

Player Summary

Fantasy Value	$9 to $11
Card Value	20¢ to 30¢
Will	show dazzling speed
Can't	produce under pressure
Expect	better K ratio
Don't Expect	great power

A little guy with big-time speed, Mouton moved from second base to right field to meet Houston's needs. He took over as leadoff man. Though Mouton showed an affinity for the new position, his offense didn't cooperate. He fanned so frequently (three times for every walk) that he found himself back at Triple-A Tucson. There he batted .412 in 17 at bats. The Mouton story doesn't stop there. He left a good impression with 24 steals in 29 tries and a .315 batting average against left-handed pitchers. Before he can return, however, he needs to improve against righties (.208), with runners in scoring position (.171), and in late-inning pressure situations (.143). With his world-class speed, Mouton won't be down long. He led several minor leagues in hits, runs, doubles, and stolen bases, once stealing 110 times in two years. He made a smooth transition from second, where he was a butcher, to right, where he showed top range and a good arm. He had five assists, two double plays, and three miscues in 80 games. In 1993 at Tucson, he batted .315 with 16 homers, 92 RBI, and 126 runs scored.

Major League Batting Register

	BA	G	AB	R	H	2B	3B	HR	RBI	SB
94 NL	.245	99	310	43	76	11	0	2	16	24
Life	.245	99	310	43	76	11	0	2	16	24

JAMIE MOYER

Position: Pitcher
Team: Baltimore Orioles
Born: Nov. 18, 1962   Sellersville, PA
Height: 6'   **Weight:** 170 lbs.
Bats: left   **Throws:** left
Acquired: Signed as a minor-league free agent, 12/92

Player Summary

Fantasy Value	$5 to $7
Card Value	5¢ to 7¢
Will	fight for job
Can't	avoid gophers
Expect	fine control
Don't Expect	complete games

Moyer's poor showing last season strongly suggests that 1993 was his career year. That campaign included a 10-3 finish and 20 consecutive scoreless innings. He reverted to more typical form in 1994. His 4.77 ERA wasn't far from the 4.36 career mark he had taken into the season. He yielded more hits than innings for the eighth time, and he failed to complete any of his 23 starts. While Moyer's control was good (he allowed just over two walks per game), he threw too many home run balls and let opponents rip him for a .271 average—highest allowed by any Oriole starter. A fastball-slider pitcher who also throws a slow curve and a straight change, Moyer needs location to succeed. He fanned just over five hitters per nine innings last year. Only adequate in the field, Moyer also needs more work in holding runners. Seven of 10 stole successfully against him in 1994.

Major League Pitching Register

	W	L	ERA	G	CG	IP	H	ER	BB	SO
86 NL	7	4	5.05	16	1	87.1	107	49	42	45
87 NL	12	15	5.10	35	1	201.0	210	114	97	147
88 NL	9	15	3.48	34	3	202.0	212	78	55	121
89 AL	4	9	4.86	15	1	76.0	84	41	33	44
90 AL	2	6	4.66	33	1	102.1	115	53	39	58
91 NL	0	5	5.74	8	0	31.1	38	20	16	20
93 AL	12	9	3.43	25	3	152.0	154	58	38	90
94 AL	5	7	4.77	23	0	149.0	158	79	38	87
Life	51	70	4.42	189	10	1001.0	1078	492	358	612
2 AVE	10	9	4.21	29	2	181.0	188	85	46	106

TERRY MULHOLLAND

Position: Pitcher
Team: New York Yankees
Born: March 9, 1963 Uniontown, PA
Height: 6'3" **Weight:** 200 lbs.
Bats: right **Throws:** left
Acquired: Traded from Phillies with Jeff Patterson for Bobby Munoz, Kevin Jordan, and Ryan Karp, 2/94

Player Summary	
Fantasy Value	$7 to $9
Card Value	6¢ to 10¢
Will	seek comeback
Can't	worry about gophers
Expect	strikes
Don't Expect	stolen bases

He threw a no-hitter, started an All-Star Game, and had a three-year run as a No. 1 starter. So why couldn't this martial arts advocate and Steve Carlton disciple maintain his magic? Yankee pitching coach Billy Connors said Mulholland's mind meandered. He lacked concentration, couldn't keep the ball down, and became a nibbler, negating his usual aggressive style. He met with predictable results: Lefties lit him up with a .338 mark—122 points higher than the year before—and righties were at .297, a 50-point hike. His control deteriorated from pinpoint (almost two walks per game in 1993) to decent (over two and one-half in 1994), and the home runs flew at an alarming pace (a career-worst 24 in 120⅔ innings). The sinkerballer also throws a slider and a changeup. His celebrated pick-off move didn't go south. The only AL baserunner with the audacity to challenge Mulholland was caught in the act.

Major League Pitching Register

	W	L	ERA	G	CG	IP	H	ER	BB	SO
86 NL	1	7	4.94	15	0	54.2	51	30	35	27
88 NL	2	1	3.72	9	2	46.0	50	19	7	18
89 NL	4	7	4.92	25	2	115.1	137	63	36	66
90 NL	9	10	3.34	33	6	180.2	172	67	42	75
91 NL	16	13	3.61	34	8	232.0	231	93	49	142
92 NL	13	11	3.81	32	12	229.0	227	97	46	125
93 NL	12	9	3.25	29	7	191.0	177	69	40	116
94 AL	6	7	6.49	24	2	120.2	150	87	37	72
Life	63	65	4.04	201	39	1169.1	1195	525	292	641
3 AVE	11	10	4.40	32	7	196.1	205	96	46	114

BOBBY MUNOZ

Position: Pitcher
Team: Philadelphia Phillies
Born: March 3, 1968 Rio Piedras, Puerto Rico
Height: 6'7" **Weight:** 237 lbs.
Bats: right **Throws:** right
Acquired: Traded from Yankees with Kevin Jordan and Ryan Karp for Terry Mulholland and Jeff Patterson, 2/94

Player Summary	
Fantasy Value	$9 to $11
Card Value	6¢ to 8¢
Will	keep rotation job
Can't	rack up Ks
Expect	help from bat
Don't Expect	fuzzy control

When the Phillies first saw Munoz, he was a reliever with such erratic control that he had to return to the minors. After regular work restored his confidence, he became a quality starter with a booming bat. A starter in the minors for years, he became the closer at Triple-A Columbus in 1993, notching 10 saves. Munoz couldn't keep his control with the Yankees, making him expendable. The Phillies became the beneficiaries. Stepping in when injuries felled Curt Schilling and Tommy Greene, Munoz was magnificent. In a two-hitter at Florida July 27, he went all the way for the first time, didn't walk a man, and retired the last 23 batters. Philadelphia's most effective starter, Munoz in 1994 yielded less hits than innings, kept the ball in the park, and averaged three walks and five strikeouts per game. The sinker-slider pitcher, who also throws a curve, gets many grounders. Munoz needs work on his fielding and pick-off move, but his bat is a bonus. He hit a three-run homer off Kent Mercker June 25 en route to a .206 finish.

Major League Pitching Register

	W	L	ERA	G	CG	IP	H	ER	BB	SO
93 AL	3	3	5.32	38	0	45.2	48	27	26	33
94 NL	7	5	2.67	21	1	104.1	101	31	35	59
Life	10	8	3.48	59	1	150.0	149	58	61	92
2 AVE	6	5	3.30	34	1	96.2	95	35	38	58

MIKE MUNOZ

Position: Pitcher
Team: Colorado Rockies
Born: July 12, 1965   Baldwin Park, CA
Height: 6'2"   **Weight:** 200 lbs.
Bats: left   **Throws:** left
Acquired: Signed as a minor-league free agent, 5/93

Player Summary

Fantasy Value	$0
Card Value	5¢ to 7¢
Will	strand runners
Can't	locate plate
Expect	low average
Don't Expect	little work

Until his elbow flared up in late July, Munoz was Colorado's top reliever. At the time of his injury, he was leading the team with 53 appearances and a 2.82 ERA. A screwball specialist who also has a fastball, Munoz stranded more than 75 percent of the runners he inherited, held hitters to a .223 average, and kept the ball in the park. Though he averaged more than six strikeouts and just over seven hits per nine innings, he was not without his faults. Tops on the list was erratic control—a chronic problem that curtailed his previous tenure with the Tigers. With 32 strikeouts and 31 walks last year, Munoz had a ratio that baffled both his manager and pitching coach. At least he helped himself with his fielding and pick-off move. Of the four runners who ran on him last year, only two succeeded. A durable pitcher who has topped 40 appearances seven times in his pro career, Munoz still could have a good future, but he has to throw strikes.

Major League Pitching Register

	W	L	ERA	G	S	IP	H	ER	BB	SO
89 NL	0	0	16.88	3	0	2.2	5	5	2	3
90 NL	0	1	3.18	8	0	5.2	6	2	3	2
91 NL	0	0	9.64	6	0	9.1	14	10	5	3
92 AL	1	2	3.00	65	2	48.0	44	16	25	23
93 AL	0	1	6.00	8	0	3.0	4	2	6	1
93 NL	2	1	4.50	21	0	18.0	21	9	9	16
94 NL	4	2	3.74	57	1	45.2	37	19	31	32
Life	7	7	4.28	168	3	132.1	131	63	81	80
2 AVE	3	2	3.43	73	2	56.1	48	21	34	34

PEDRO MUNOZ

Position: Outfield; first base
Team: Minnesota Twins
Born: Sept. 19, 1968   Ponce, Puerto Rico
Height: 5'11"   **Weight:** 170 lbs.
Bats: right   **Throws:** right
Acquired: Traded from Blue Jays with Nelson Liriano for John Candelaria, 7/90

Player Summary

Fantasy Value	$9 to $10
Card Value	8¢ to 15¢
Will	get extra bases
Can't	inject speed
Expect	better contact
Don't Expect	many walks

Munoz showed dramatic improvement in his hitting last season. Although he still fanned more than three times for every walk, he fanned 30 fewer times than the previous year. He made better contact, boosting his average to a career-best .295. Munoz hit well against both righties (.301) and lefties (.284) while collecting extra bases on more than one-third of his hits. He might have done better if he hadn't split playing time with lefty Alex Cole. When Cole played center, Shane Mack shifted to left, pushing Munoz onto the bench. Munoz had played right in the past but couldn't dislodge Kirby Puckett in 1994. Munoz notched double-digit stolen bases in the minors, but knee surgery has sapped his speed. Though he still runs well enough to play left field, he spent time working out at first base last year to prepare for the retirement of Kent Hrbek. Though he lacks Hrbek's height, Munoz (if he can play first) could receive a chance to fill the power vacuum left by Hrbek.

Major League Batting Register

	BA	G	AB	R	H	2B	3B	HR	RBI	SB
90 AL	.271	22	85	13	23	4	1	0	5	3
91 AL	.283	51	138	15	39	7	1	7	26	3
92 AL	.270	127	418	44	113	16	3	12	71	4
93 AL	.233	104	326	34	76	11	1	13	38	1
94 AL	.295	75	244	35	72	15	2	11	36	0
Life	.267	379	1211	141	323	53	8	43	176	11
3 AVE	.267	112	363	42	97	16	2	13	53	2

ROB MURPHY

Position: Pitcher
Team: New York Yankees
Born: May 26, 1960 Miami, FL
Height: 6'2" **Weight:** 215 lbs.
Bats: left **Throws:** left
Acquired: Claimed from Cardinals on waivers, 8/94

Player Summary	
Fantasy Value	$0
Card Value	5¢ to 7¢
Will	tackle big workload
Can't	prevent homers
Expect	decent control
Don't Expect	former heat

A rubber-armed southpaw who has topped 70 appearances four times, Murphy has never made a start during a big-league career that has lasted 10 seasons. Often used to retire one or two left-handed hitters, he has good control of a fastball, a slider, and a forkball. Though he can't match the velocity of his younger days, he still strands 75 percent of the runners he inherits. Signed by the Reds out of the University of Florida, Murphy has made a career for himself in middle relief. He's never posted double digits in saves. He yielded less than three walks and eight hits per nine innings last year while averaging more than five and one-half strikeouts over the same stretch. He throws his share of gopher balls but doesn't let anyone steal against him; both men who tried last year were erased. He's adequate in the field.

Major League Pitching Register

	W	L	ERA	G	S	IP	H	ER	BB	SO
85 NL	0	0	6.00	2	0	3.0	2	2	2	1
86 NL	6	0	0.72	34	1	50.1	26	4	21	36
87 NL	8	5	3.04	87	3	100.2	91	34	32	99
88 NL	0	6	3.08	76	3	84.2	69	29	38	74
89 AL	5	7	2.74	74	9	105.0	97	32	41	107
90 AL	0	6	6.32	68	7	57.0	85	40	32	54
91 AL	0	1	3.00	57	4	48.0	47	16	19	34
92 NL	3	1	4.04	59	0	55.2	56	25	21	42
93 NL	5	7	4.87	73	1	64.2	73	35	20	41
94 NL	4	3	3.79	50	2	40.1	35	17	13	25
94 AL	0	0	16.20	3	0	1.2	3	3	0	0
Life	31	36	3.49	583	30	611.0	584	237	239	513
3 AVE	5	4	4.42	69	1	59.3	61	29	20	39

EDDIE MURRAY

Position: Designated hitter; first base
Team: Cleveland Indians
Born: Feb. 24, 1956 Los Angeles, CA
Height: 6'2" **Weight:** 224 lbs.
Bats: both **Throws:** right
Acquired: Signed as a free agent, 12/93

Player Summary	
Fantasy Value	$8 to $10
Card Value	15¢ to 25¢
Will	knock in runs
Can't	pursue Gold Glove
Expect	power
Don't Expect	patience

In his first year as Cleveland's DH, Murray suffered such serious knee and thumb injuries that he finished with a career low in RBI. It was only the second time that his final count dipped below 80. He did manage to reach a career milestone on April 21, however, when he hit home runs from the left side and right side in the same game for the 11th time—breaking Mickey Mantle's record. Murray can still swing the bat—especially with runners in scoring position (.331 last year). He's deadly when batting with the bases loaded. His strike-zone judgement seems to be waning with age, however. His mobility and fielding skills have also deteriorated.

Major League Batting Register

	BA	G	AB	R	H	2B	3B	HR	RBI	SB
77 AL	.283	160	611	81	173	29	2	27	88	0
78 AL	.285	161	610	85	174	32	3	27	95	6
79 AL	.295	159	606	90	179	30	2	25	99	10
80 AL	.300	158	621	100	186	36	2	32	116	7
81 AL	.294	99	378	57	111	21	2	22	78	2
82 AL	.316	151	550	87	174	30	1	32	110	7
83 AL	.306	156	582	115	178	30	3	33	111	5
84 AL	.306	162	588	97	180	26	3	29	110	10
85 AL	.297	156	583	111	173	37	1	31	124	5
86 AL	.305	137	495	61	151	25	1	17	84	3
87 AL	.277	160	618	89	171	28	3	30	91	1
88 AL	.284	161	603	75	171	27	2	28	84	5
89 NL	.247	160	594	66	147	29	1	20	88	7
90 NL	.330	155	558	96	184	22	3	26	95	8
91 NL	.260	153	576	69	150	23	1	19	96	10
92 NL	.261	156	551	64	144	37	2	16	93	4
93 NL	.285	154	610	77	174	28	1	27	100	2
94 AL	.254	108	433	57	110	21	1	17	76	8
Life	.288	2706	10167	1477	2930	511	34	458	1738	100
3 AVE	.267	154	590	74	158	32	1	22	100	6

MIKE MUSSINA

Position: Pitcher
Team: Baltimore Orioles
Born: Dec. 8, 1968 Williamsport, PA
Height: 6′ **Weight:** 182 lbs.
Bats: right **Throws:** right
Acquired: First-round pick in 6/90 free-agent draft

Player Summary

Fantasy Value	$20 to $25
Card Value	20¢ to 35¢
Will	out-think hitters
Can't	waste any pitches
Expect	20-win season
Don't Expect	control lapses

One of baseball's rising young stars, Mussina has produced an average of 16 victories over his three full seasons. A thinking man's hurler who throws strikes with five pitches, he averages two and one-half strikeouts for every walk. The former Stanford star applies his economics degree when he's on the hill, rarely wasting a pitch. Mussina allowed about two walks and eight and one-third hits per nine innings last year. He keeps batters guessing with a repertoire that includes two fastballs plus a slider, a knuckle-curve, and a superb change of pace. He'll throw any pitch at any point in the count. Equally effective against righties and lefties, Mussina is particularly tough in pressure situations. He helps himself with an outstanding pickoff move and fine fielding. It's no accident that he owns the best winning percentage among active pitchers. An AL All-Star in each of the last three seasons, Mussina seems to be improving with experience, and he has a brilliant future.

GREG MYERS

Position: Catcher
Team: California Angels
Born: April 14, 1966 Riverside, CA
Height: 6′2″ **Weight:** 206 lbs.
Bats: left **Throws:** right
Acquired: Traded from Blue Jays with Rob Ducey for Mark Eichhorn, 7/92

Player Summary

Fantasy Value	$1
Card Value	5¢ to 7¢
Will	respond in clutch
Can't	win fielding award
Expect	power vs. righties
Don't Expect	extended work

The 1994 platoon partner for rookie Chris Turner, Myers failed to hold up his end of the bargain. He hit only .229 against right-handed pitchers, lifting his overall mark to .246 because he hit so well against south-paws (.333). That wasn't unusual for the veteran, who also tattooed lefties the year before (.333) after struggling against them previously. Overpowered by some south-paws, Myers manages to save his entire home run output for right-handers. He hit just two out of the park last year but had seven, one short of his career high, when given more playing time in 1993. He would be more valuable if he didn't fan nearly three times per walk. He produced in late-inning pressure spots (.316) and hit above his norm with runners in scoring position (.250). Though not highly regarded as a catcher, Myers nailed 46 percent of the would-be basestealers who tested him last year. He's not a great game-caller or handler of pitchers.

Major League Pitching Register

	W	L	ERA	G	CG	IP	H	ER	BB	SO
91 AL	4	5	2.87	12	2	87.2	77	28	21	52
92 AL	18	5	2.54	32	8	241.0	212	68	48	130
93 AL	14	6	4.46	25	3	167.2	163	83	44	117
94 AL	16	5	3.06	24	3	176.1	163	60	42	99
Life	52	21	3.20	93	16	672.2	615	239	155	398
3 AVE	18	6	3.23	30	5	219.1	202	79	50	129

Major League Batting Register

	BA	G	AB	R	H	2B	3B	HR	RBI	SB
87 AL	.111	7	9	1	1	0	0	0	0	0
89 AL	.114	17	44	0	5	2	0	0	1	0
90 AL	.236	87	250	33	59	7	1	5	22	0
91 AL	.262	107	309	25	81	22	0	8	36	0
92 AL	.231	30	78	4	18	7	0	1	13	0
93 AL	.255	108	290	27	74	10	0	7	40	3
94 AL	.246	45	126	10	31	6	0	2	8	0
Life	.243	401	1106	100	269	54	1	23	120	3

RANDY MYERS

Position: Pitcher
Team: Chicago Cubs
Born: Sept. 19, 1962 Vancouver, WA
Height: 6'1" **Weight:** 210 lbs.
Bats: left **Throws:** left
Acquired: Signed as a free agent, 12/92

Player Summary	
Fantasy Value.	$30 to $35
Card Value	8¢ to 12¢
Will	destroy lefties
Can't.	achieve without work
Expect	improved K rate
Don't Expect.	old heat

Lack of work may have hurt Myers last year. After saving an NL-record 53 games in 1993, he threw only 40⅓ innings in 38 outings, both career lows. The Cubs gave him little to save. Though he continued to tie up left-handed hitters (who compiled a .138 average), he converted only 21 of 26 save chances, stranded just 61 percent of runners, and didn't show the same control or strikeout ratio he had during his record run. After averaging about 10 Ks per nine innings in '93, Myers last year managed just about seven a game. Though he fanned twice the number he walked, that was only half his 1993 rate. Righties ripped him at a .288 clip—helping to explain his five losses. It's obvious that Myers isn't going to maintain his once-feared velocity. He augments his fastball and slider with a curve developed only recently. He helps himself with his fielding and pickoff move.

Major League Pitching Register

	W	L	ERA	G	S	IP	H	ER	BB	SO
85 NL	0	0	0.00	1	0	2.0	0	0	1	2
86 NL	0	0	4.22	10	0	10.2	11	5	9	13
87 NL	3	6	3.96	54	6	75.0	61	33	30	92
88 NL	7	3	1.72	55	26	68.0	45	13	17	69
89 NL	7	4	2.35	65	24	84.1	62	22	40	88
90 NL	4	6	2.08	66	31	86.2	59	20	38	98
91 NL	6	13	3.55	58	6	132.0	116	52	80	108
92 NL	3	6	4.29	66	38	79.2	84	38	34	66
93 NL	2	4	3.11	73	53	75.1	65	26	26	86
94 NL	1	5	3.79	38	21	40.1	40	17	16	32
Life	33	47	3.11	486	205	654.0	543	226	291	654
3 AVE	2	6	3.74	64	40	70.1	68	29	28	66

CHRIS NABHOLZ

Position: Pitcher
Team: Boston Red Sox
Born: Jan. 5, 1967 Harrisburg, PA
Height: 6'5" **Weight:** 210 lbs.
Bats: left **Throws:** left
Acquired: Traded from Indians with Steve Farr for Jeff Russell, 7/94

Player Summary	
Fantasy Value	$0
Card Value	5¢ to 7¢
Will	win with sinker
Can't	find plate
Expect	success on grass
Don't Expect	tolerance

After spending four years in the Montreal rotation, Nabholz found his first exposure to AL hitters unsettling. A sinkerballer who's usually effective on grass, he had trouble with his delivery, confidence, and control. A strained upper back also hampered the transition. Because he's not a power pitcher, Nabholz needs command of his four-pitch repertoire. In addition to the sinker, he throws a straight fastball, a curve, and a changeup. Last year, he couldn't throw strikes with any of them. He yielded almost six and one-half walks per game and threw six wild pitches in 53 innings. Such erratic control forced Nabholz to overcompensate. When he caught too much of the plate, the hitters were ready. Opponents hit .318 against him. He should have been much more effective against lefties (.333) than righties (.315), but he wasn't. The result was a nine-inning yield of about 11 hits and an unsightly 7.64 ERA. Walks lead to big innings—often early in the game—and could cost Nabholz his job.

Major League Pitching Register

	W	L	ERA	G	CG	IP	H	ER	BB	SO
90 NL	6	2	2.83	11	1	70.0	43	22	32	53
91 NL	8	7	3.63	24	1	153.2	134	62	57	99
92 NL	11	12	3.32	32	1	195.0	176	72	74	130
93 NL	9	8	4.09	26	1	116.2	100	53	63	74
94 AL	3	5	7.64	14	0	53.0	67	45	38	28
Life	37	34	3.89	107	4	588.1	520	254	264	384
3 AVE	7	7	3.98	22	1	109.1	103	48	50	70

TIM NAEHRING

Position: Infield
Team: Boston Red Sox
Born: Feb. 1, 1967 Cincinnati, OH
Height: 6'2" **Weight:** 190 lbs.
Bats: right **Throws:** right
Acquired: Eighth-round pick in 6/88 free-agent draft

Player Summary	
Fantasy Value	$8 to $10
Card Value	6¢ to 10¢
Will	produce in clutch
Can't	shake injuries
Expect	surprising pop
Don't Expect	speed

A versatile performer who played all four infield spots for the 1994 BoSox, Naehring finished the season as the club's second baseman. He's battled back, shoulder, wrist, and ankle injuries in recent years, but showed last summer he could produce if given the chance. Naehring in 1994 hit .300 with runners in scoring position and socked seven homers and 18 doubles in 297 at bats. He netted extra bases on almost one-third of his hits. Though he fanned nearly twice for every walk, he's patient enough to compile a solid on-base percentage. He hits the ball up the middle against right-handers but to the off-field against lefties. He's not much of a runner, but he has quick reactions and good hands in the field. He positions himself well and turns the double play, though not as well as predecessor Scott Fletcher. Naehring makes the long throws from the left side but seems determined to succeed at second. Management likes the Miami of Ohio product's combative nature and line-drive stroke.

Major League Batting Register

	BA	G	AB	R	H	2B	3B	HR	RBI	SB
90 AL	.271	24	85	10	23	6	0	2	12	0
91 AL	.109	20	55	1	6	1	0	0	3	0
92 AL	.231	72	186	12	43	8	0	3	14	0
93 AL	.331	39	127	14	42	10	0	1	17	1
94 AL	.276	80	297	41	82	18	1	7	42	1
Life	.261	235	750	78	196	43	1	13	88	2
2 AVE	.262	92	302	35	79	17	1	6	37	1

CHARLES NAGY

Position: Pitcher
Team: Cleveland Indians
Born: May 5, 1967 Bridgeport, CT
Height: 6'3" **Weight:** 200 lbs.
Bats: left **Throws:** right
Acquired: First-round pick in 6/88 free-agent draft

Player Summary	
Fantasy Value	$15 to $18
Card Value	8¢ to 12¢
Will	be No. 1 starter
Can't	worry about shoulder
Expect	200 innings
Don't Expect	control woes

After losing most of 1993 with arthroscopic shoulder surgery, Nagy recaptured the fine form he had displayed as a 17-game winner in 1992. Only Dennis Martinez was more effective among the five Cleveland starters last year. Nagy is a control pitcher who coaxes grounders with a sinker, a forkball, a curve, and a changeup. He allowed a hit per inning and two and one-half walks per game. He also maintained a strikeout-to-walk ratio of better than 2-to-1. Righties hit him hard in 1994, however, compiling a .306 average. Nagy keeps the ball in the park and helps himself with his glove. He had trouble freezing potential basestealers last year even though he owns an exceptional pickoff move for a right-hander. He nailed 15 would-be thieves in '92. Now that he's returned to full strength, the former University of Connecticut standout should be able to top 200 innings pitched for the third time in his brief career. Nagy was a member of the 1988 U.S. Olympic Team. He broke into pro ball in 1989.

Major League Pitching Register

	W	L	ERA	G	CG	IP	H	ER	BB	SO
90 AL	2	4	5.91	9	0	45.2	58	30	21	26
91 AL	10	15	4.13	33	6	211.1	228	97	66	109
92 AL	17	10	2.96	33	10	252.0	245	83	57	169
93 AL	2	6	6.29	9	1	48.2	66	34	13	30
94 AL	10	8	3.45	23	3	169.1	175	65	48	108
Life	41	43	3.83	107	20	727.0	772	309	205	442
2 AVE	16	11	3.20	33	7	245.1	246	87	62	161

JAIME NAVARRO

Position: Pitcher
Team: Milwaukee Brewers
Born: March 27, 1967 Bayamon, Puerto Rico
Height: 6'4" **Weight:** 210 lbs.
Bats: right **Throws:** right
Acquired: Third-round pick in 6/87 free-agent draft

Player Summary	
Fantasy Value	$0
Card Value	5¢ to 7¢
Will	show OK control
Can't	get lefties out
Expect	many ground outs
Don't Expect	decent fielding

After winning 32 total games in 1991 and '92, Navarro lost his magic. His ERA rose for two straight years, and he pitched so poorly that he lost the spot in the rotation he had held since 1989. Weight and shoulder problems contributed to his demise, but he was also guilty of tipping his pitches, according to his godfather, Cleveland hitting coach Jose Morales. Navarro's control was OK last year (three and one-half walks per nine innings), but opposing batters lit him up at a .314 clip, including a .344 mark by left-handers. Not a power pitcher, he relies on locating his fastball, his slider, and his changeup. When he's on, he gets lots of ground balls. He gave up too many gopher balls—usually when he caught too much of the plate with his mediocre fastball. To try to escape his slump, Navarro has tinkered with his motion over the last couple of years. He now throws more overhand. He doesn't help himself with his fielding or his pickoff move.

Major League Pitching Register

	W	L	ERA	G	CG	IP	H	ER	BB	SO
89 AL	7	8	3.12	19	1	109.2	119	38	32	56
90 AL	8	7	4.46	32	3	149.1	176	74	41	75
91 AL	15	12	3.92	34	10	234.0	237	102	73	114
92 AL	17	11	3.33	34	5	246.0	224	91	64	100
93 AL	11	12	5.33	35	5	214.1	254	127	73	114
94 AL	4	9	6.62	29	0	89.2	115	66	35	65
Life	62	59	4.30	183	24	1043.0	1125	498	318	524
3 AVE	11	12	4.77	37	3	195.1	213	104	62	102

DENNY NEAGLE

Position: Pitcher
Team: Pittsburgh Pirates
Born: Sept. 13, 1968 Prince Georges County, MD
Height: 6'4" **Weight:** 209 lbs.
Bats: left **Throws:** left
Acquired: Traded from Twins for John Smiley and Midre Cummings, 3/92

Player Summary	
Fantasy Value	$2 to $4
Card Value	5¢ to 7¢
Will	help with bat
Can't	win without location
Expect	lower ERA
Don't Expect	luck vs. lefties

Sometimes, statistics don't jive. In 1994, Neagle yielded less hits than innings pitched while averaging eight strikeouts and just over three walks per nine innings. Opposing batters hit him at a .259 clip, and left-handed batters hit him at a .279 clip. So how did Neagle wind up with the worst ERA in the Pirate rotation? Greg Maddux wonders; on April 30, Neagle beat the Cy Young winner 2-1. Barry Bonds wonders; on June 9, Neagle picked Bonds off twice while fanning nine Giants for another victory. Though his velocity is only average, Neagle wins by blending his fastball with a curveball, a slider, and a changeup. When he has good location, he's tough to beat. The University of Minnesota product maintained a 3-1 ratio of strikeouts to walks last summer. He fields his position well and often helps himself with the bat. At one stretch last year, he went 8-for-23 (.348). Neagle hit his first home run on July 25. If he yielded fewer homers to others, his record would improve.

Major League Pitching Register

	W	L	ERA	G	CG	IP	H	ER	BB	SO
91 AL	0	1	4.05	7	0	20.0	28	9	7	14
92 NL	4	6	4.48	55	0	86.1	81	43	43	77
93 NL	3	5	5.31	50	0	81.1	82	48	37	73
94 NL	9	10	5.12	24	2	137.0	135	78	49	122
Life	16	22	4.93	136	2	324.2	326	178	136	286
3 AVE	7	8	5.01	46	1	120.1	118	67	50	107

TROY NEEL

Position: First base; designated hitter
Team: Oakland Athletics
Born: Sept. 14, 1965 Freeport, TX
Height: 6'4" **Weight:** 210 lbs.
Bats: left **Throws:** right
Acquired: Traded from Indians for Larry Arndt, 1/91

Player Summary	
Fantasy Value	$10 to $13
Card Value	8¢ to 12¢
Will	slam southpaws
Can't	produce under pressure
Expect	power production
Don't Expect	dynamic defense

Like Barry Bonds and Fred McGriff, Neel is a member of an elite group of left-handed sluggers who love to face left-handed pitchers. In both of his big-league seasons, Neel has produced far better batting averages against southpaws. He ripped them at a .350 clip last year, lifting his overall mark to a somewhat-disappointing .266. A broken bone in his right hand cost him three weeks in June and contributed to the 24-point fall off his 1993 average. Neel's biggest problem is a tendency to strike out twice for every walk. He still shows enough patience, however, to build an on-base percentage nearly 100 points higher than his batting average. He also batted .300 at home last year. The former Texas A&M standout has power to all fields; he notched a few 20-homer years in the minors. He needs to become more productive in clutch situations. He's not a Gold Glove candidate. Though he's played both first and the outfield, Neel's best position is DH. He spent most of 1994 subbing for the injured Mark McGwire at first base.

Major League Batting Register

	BA	G	AB	R	H	2B	3B	HR	RBI	SB
92 AL	.264	24	53	8	14	3	0	3	9	0
93 AL	.290	123	427	59	124	21	0	19	63	3
94 AL	.266	83	278	43	74	13	0	15	48	2
Life	.280	230	758	110	212	37	0	37	120	5
2 AVE	.279	120	409	60	114	20	0	20	65	3

ROBB NEN

Position: Pitcher
Team: Florida Marlins
Born: Nov. 28, 1969 San Pedro, CA
Height: 6'4" **Weight:** 200 lbs.
Bats: right **Throws:** right
Acquired: Traded from Rangers with Kurt Miller for Cris Carpenter, 7/93

Player Summary	
Fantasy Value	$25 to $30
Card Value	12¢ to 20¢
Will	handcuff hitters
Can't	maintain pace
Expect	high K count
Don't Expect	blown saves

When Bryan Harvey was sidelined last July for abdominal surgery, the Marlins feared their once-formidable bullpen would require federal aid. But that was before Nen stepped to the fore. Armed with a 97-mph fastball, a fine curveball, and a recently-perfected slider, the kid proved nothing short of sensational. Converting all 15 save opportunities, he stranded 27 of 28 inherited runners (a 96 percent success rate); held hitters to a .222 average; and showed poise, control, and command far beyond his years. Scouts couldn't believe the Nen they saw last year was the same one who suffered recent shoulder problems that made it tough for him to throw strikes. In fact, he didn't receive much work as he pitched in only six games in 1991 and four games in 1992. Last year's statistics are there, however. He had more than a strikeout per inning, about two and one-half walks per game, and just over seven hits over the same span. He keeps runners close and fields his position but doesn't hit much. The way he pitches, though, who cares?

Major League Pitching Register

	W	L	ERA	G	S	IP	H	ER	BB	SO
93 AL	1	1	6.35	9	0	22.2	28	16	26	12
93 NL	1	0	7.02	15	0	33.1	35	26	20	27
94 NL	5	5	2.95	44	15	58.0	46	19	17	60
Life	7	6	4.82	68	15	114.0	109	61	63	99
2 AVE	5	4	4.49	43	11	68.2	64	34	35	62

DAVID NIED

Position: Pitcher
Team: Colorado Rockies
Born: Dec. 22, 1968 Dallas, TX
Height: 6'2" **Weight:** 185 lbs.
Bats: right **Throws:** right
Acquired: First-round pick from Braves in 11/92 expansion draft

Player Summary	
Fantasy Value	$2 to $4
Card Value	10¢ to 20¢
Will	improve
Can't	handle all lefties
Expect	better whiff-walk ratio
Don't Expect	control lapses

After spending most of 1993 on the disabled list with a torn elbow ligament, Nied last year started to justify his selection as the No. 1 pick in the 1992 expansion draft. He threw the first nine-inning shutout in Colorado history June 21 and raised his record to 8-4 with a route-going 2-1 win against Florida July 7. Like other Rocky hurlers, he pitched better away from Mile High Stadium. He mixes a fastball, a curveball, and a changeup, usually with decent control. He allowed less than three and one-half walks per game last year. He yielded more than 10 hits per nine innings, however, and threw his share of gopher balls. He also pitched more effectively against right-handed hitters. His progress was slowed last summer by a June rib injury. Nied had some personal hardships to overcome, and he did by adopting a more mature approach. The team's transfer to Coors Field should help him as well as the other Colorado pitchers. He can hit and field, but his pickoff move needs work. He also throws too many wild pitches.

DAVE NILSSON

Position: Catcher
Team: Milwaukee Brewers
Born: Dec. 14, 1969 Queensland, Australia
Height: 6'3" **Weight:** 185 lbs.
Bats: left **Throws:** right
Acquired: Signed as free agent, 2/87

Player Summary	
Fantasy Value	$10 to $13
Card Value	8¢ to 12¢
Will	punish right-handers
Can't	erase basestealers
Expect	run production
Don't Expect	a choker

The Nilsson ratings are coming in, and they're getting better. For the third straight season, the receiver from Australia boosted his batting average. He did it by beating up on right-handed pitchers (.289) and producing in late-inning pressure situations (.300). He also reached double digits in homers for the first time in a professional career that started in 1987. Swinging harder to reach the fences cost Nilsson his previous reputation as a contact man who walked as much as he fanned. Last year, he had nearly two whiffs for every walk, but he also had 69 RBI in 397 at bats—a ratio that is very respectable. In fact, nobody on the Milwaukee roster knocked in more runs. On the minus side, Nilsson's throwing left much to be desired. He nailed a woeful 15 percent of the runners who tried to steal against him, down from 23 percent in '93 and 36 percent in '92. Platoon partner Dave Valle's defense was so much better that Nilsson played 43 games as a DH. Nilsson needs to improve his work behind the plate, and do it quickly.

Major League Pitching Register

	W	L	ERA	G	CG	IP	H	ER	BB	SO
92 NL	3	0	1.17	6	0	23.0	10	3	5	19
93 NL	5	9	5.17	16	1	87.0	99	50	42	46
94 NL	9	7	4.80	22	2	122.0	137	65	47	74
Life	17	16	4.58	44	3	232.0	246	118	94	139
2 AVE	9	9	4.92	23	2	129.0	146	71	54	75

Major League Batting Register

	BA	G	AB	R	H	2B	3B	HR	RBI	SB
92 AL	.232	51	164	15	38	8	0	4	25	2
93 AL	.257	100	296	35	76	10	2	7	40	3
94 AL	.275	109	397	51	109	28	3	12	69	1
Life	.260	260	857	101	223	46	5	23	134	6
3 AVE	.262	102	340	41	89	19	2	9	54	2

OTIS NIXON

Position: Outfield
Team: Texas Rangers
Born: Jan. 9, 1959 Evergreen, NC
Height: 6'2" **Weight:** 180 lbs.
Bats: both **Throws:** right
Acquired: Traded from Red Sox with Luis Ortiz for Jose Canseco, 12/94

Player Summary	
Fantasy Value	$25 to $30
Card Value	6¢ to 10¢
Will	set the table
Can't	provide power
Expect	40 steals
Don't Expect	powerful throws

Nixon gave the Sox what they wanted: speed at the top of the lineup and strong defense in center. A switch-hitter who's better left-handed, he ripped righties for a .290 mark last year. He hit .289 with runners in scoring position. He also managed 42 steals, third in the league and more than any previous Red Sox except Tris Speaker and Tommy Harper. Nailed 10 times, Nixon had a success rate of 80.8 percent. He would have done even better if not for back spasms. Although he strikes out more frequently than a singles hitter should, he also shows patience, enabling him to walk enough to post a decent on-base percentage (.360 last year). He compiles computerized notes on opposing pitchers and catchers. With his exceptional range, he makes few errors in center.

Major League Batting Register

	BA	G	AB	R	H	2B	3B	HR	RBI	SB
83 AL	.143	13	14	2	2	0	0	0	0	2
84 AL	.154	49	91	16	14	0	0	0	1	12
85 AL	.235	104	162	34	38	4	0	3	9	20
86 AL	.263	105	95	33	25	4	1	0	8	23
87 AL	.059	19	17	2	1	0	0	0	1	2
88 NL	.244	90	271	47	66	8	2	0	15	46
89 NL	.217	126	258	41	56	7	2	0	21	37
90 NL	.251	119	231	46	58	6	2	1	20	50
91 NL	.297	124	401	81	119	10	1	0	26	72
92 NL	.294	120	456	79	134	14	2	2	22	41
93 NL	.269	134	461	77	124	12	3	1	24	47
94 AL	.274	103	398	60	109	15	1	0	25	42
Life	.261	1106	2855	518	746	80	14	7	172	394
3 AVE	.279	133	493	80	137	16	2	1	27	49

MATT NOKES

Position: Catcher; designated hitter
Team: Baltimore Orioles
Born: Oct. 31, 1963 San Diego, CA
Height: 6'1" **Weight:** 185 lbs.
Bats: left **Throws:** right
Acquired: Signed as a free agent, 12/94

Player Summary	
Fantasy Value	$1 to $3
Card Value	5¢ to 7¢
Will	supply lefty power
Can't	show patience
Expect	bench warmth
Don't Expect	great arm

Nokes can't get rid of the good-hit, no-field tag that follows him around like a lost puppy. Even last year, when his playing time was limited by surgery to repair a broken bone in his right hand, he displayed outstanding power but poor defense (80 percent of those who tried to steal on him succeeded) for the Yankees. An impatient hitter, he fanned twice per walk. He usually struggles against lefties, but that was not the case in 1994. His .500 mark against southpaws, combined with his .261 mark against righties, yielded an overall average of .291, a career high (albeit with limited playing time). Nokes hasn't stolen a base in three years. He has stolen at least one pitcher's heart, however. He was behind the plate for Jim Abbott's 1993 no-hitter. Nokes handles pitchers well and calls a good game but isn't about to win a Gold Glove.

Major League Batting Register

	BA	G	AB	R	H	2B	3B	HR	RBI	SB
85 NL	.208	19	53	3	11	2	0	2	5	0
86 AL	.333	7	24	2	8	1	0	1	2	0
87 AL	.289	135	461	69	133	14	2	32	87	2
88 AL	.251	122	382	53	96	18	0	16	53	0
89 AL	.250	87	268	15	67	10	0	9	39	1
90 AL	.248	136	351	33	87	9	1	11	40	2
91 AL	.268	135	456	52	122	20	0	24	77	3
92 AL	.224	121	384	42	86	9	1	22	59	0
93 AL	.249	76	217	25	54	8	0	10	35	0
94 AL	.291	28	79	11	23	3	0	7	19	0
Life	.257	866	2675	305	687	94	4	134	416	8
2 AVE	.233	99	301	34	70	9	1	16	47	0

CHARLIE O'BRIEN

Position: Catcher
Team: Atlanta Braves
Born: May 1, 1961 Tulsa, OK
Height: 6'2" **Weight:** 190 lbs.
Bats: right **Throws:** right
Acquired: Signed as a free agent, 11/93

Player Summary	
Fantasy Value	$0
Card Value	5¢ to 7¢
Will	play strong defense
Can't	provide speed
Expect	hits vs. lefties
Don't Expect	many starts

Though he spent most of 1994 on the bench, O'Brien was one of Atlanta's unsung heroes. A defensive whiz, he tutored Javy Lopez, a heralded rookie whose glove has yet to match his bat. O'Brien was also the kid's caddy, especially against lefthanders. The veteran hit .306 against lefties and .325 with runners in scoring position. He also hit as many home runs as he had in the four previous seasons *combined*. He did it in just 152 at bats, his fewest since 1988. Before hitting .255 for the 1993 Mets, he had been a .205 career hitter. He didn't even hit his weight in 1990 or '91. He made such good contact that the Mets sometimes hit him in the No. 2 hole. That was unusual, since he clogs up the bases. He's a terrific receiver, however, and pitchers rave about his game-calling. He's nailed more than 40 percent of the runners who have tried to steal against him during his career.

Major League Batting Register

	BA	G	AB	R	H	2B	3B	HR	RBI	SB
85 AL	.273	16	11	3	3	1	0	0	1	0
87 AL	.200	10	35	2	7	3	1	0	0	0
88 AL	.220	40	118	12	26	6	0	2	9	0
89 AL	.234	62	188	22	44	10	0	6	35	0
90 AL	.186	46	145	11	27	7	2	0	11	0
90 NL	.162	28	68	6	11	3	0	0	9	0
91 NL	.185	69	168	16	31	6	0	2	14	0
92 NL	.212	68	156	15	33	12	0	2	13	0
93 NL	.255	67	188	15	48	11	0	4	23	1
94 NL	.243	51	152	24	37	11	0	8	28	0
Life	.217	457	1229	126	267	70	3	24	143	1
3 AVE	.239	69	186	21	44	13	0	6	25	0

JOSE OFFERMAN

Position: Shortstop
Team: Los Angeles Dodgers
Born: Nov. 8, 1968 San Pedro de Macoris, Dominican Republic
Height: 6' **Weight:** 160 lbs.
Bats: both **Throws:** right
Acquired: Signed as a free agent, 7/86

Player Summary	
Fantasy Value	$4 to $6
Card Value	5¢ to 7¢
Will	show speed
Can't	generate power
Expect	strong arm
Don't Expect	a Gold Glove

When he was hitting, Offerman was considered an above-average offensive shortstop whose defense might develop over time. When he stopped hitting last year, the Dodgers grew tired of waiting. The 1990 Minor League Player of the Year displayed a bad attitude, hit for a .210 batting average, and committed a total of 90 errors in two and one-half years. Offerman has the tools to do much, much better. A good bunter and outstanding baserunner, he's also been a selective hitter, willing to walk and use his speed. Offerman had a .346 on-base percentage in 1993. He also knocked in 62 runs while hitting second most of the year. He never got untracked last year, however, and his frustration culminated in a shouting match with Tommy Lasorda before Offerman's dispatch to the minors. Instead of sulking, he got his act together, hitting .330 in 224 at bats at Triple-A Albuquerque. He is still young enough to bounce back, if he hustles, concentrates, and doesn't argue.

Major League Batting Register

	BA	G	AB	R	H	2B	3B	HR	RBI	SB
90 NL	.155	29	58	7	9	0	0	1	7	1
91 NL	.195	52	113	10	22	2	0	0	3	3
92 NL	.260	149	534	67	139	20	8	1	30	23
93 NL	.269	158	590	77	159	21	6	1	62	30
94 NL	.210	72	243	27	51	8	4	1	25	2
Life	.247	460	1538	188	380	51	18	4	127	59
3 AVE	.252	136	489	61	123	17	7	1	42	19

JOHN OLERUD

Position: First base
Team: Toronto Blue Jays
Born: Aug. 5, 1968   Seattle, WA
Height: 6'5"   **Weight:** 205 lbs.
Bats: left   **Throws:** left
Acquired: Third-round pick in 6/89 free-agent draft

Player Summary	
Fantasy Value	$18 to $21
Card Value	20¢ to 30¢
Will	hit to all fields
Can't	cover big turf
Expect	clutch bat
Don't Expect	stolen bases

One year after winning the American League batting crown, Olerud returned to earth last summer. Pitchers teased him by keeping the ball out of the strike zone, and the frustrated Olerud started swinging at too many bad pitches. He still walked more than he fanned, but he wasn't close to his 1993 ratio of two walks per whiff. He was also quite ordinary against left-handed pitchers (.264) and good but not great (.312 instead of .396) against righties. As a result, the former Washington State star watched his on-base average drop by 80 points and his dinger total dwindle to half its 1993 level. Make no mistake: He is still an outstanding hitter. Last year he did his best work with runners in scoring position (.357) and in late-inning pressure spots (.320). He hits the ball where it is pitched and has no trouble with off-speed stuff. He doesn't have the speed to steal or cover much ground at first. But Olerud has fine instincts, soft hands, and a strong arm.

Major League Batting Register

	BA	G	AB	R	H	2B	3B	HR	RBI	SB
89 AL	.375	6	8	2	3	0	0	0	0	0
90 AL	.265	111	358	43	95	15	1	14	48	0
91 AL	.256	139	454	64	116	30	1	17	68	0
92 AL	.284	138	458	68	130	28	0	16	66	1
93 AL	.363	158	551	109	200	54	2	24	107	0
94 AL	.297	108	384	47	114	29	2	12	67	1
Life	.297	660	2213	333	658	156	6	83	356	2
3 AVE	.317	149	517	81	164	41	2	19	89	1

OMAR OLIVARES

Position: Pitcher
Team: St. Louis Cardinals
Born: July 6, 1967   Mayaguez, Puerto Rico
Height: 6'1"   **Weight:** 193 lbs.
Bats: right   **Throws:** right
Acquired: Traded from Padres for Alex Cole and Steve Peters, 2/90

Player Summary	
Fantasy Value	$0
Card Value	7¢ to 10¢
Will	help with bat
Can't	cope with lefties
Expect	many sinkers
Don't Expect	many Ks

After winning 11 games as a rookie for the 1991 Cardinals, Olivares has watched his ERA rise for three straight seasons. He lost his spot in the starting rotation and even had to return to the minors. A tendency to rush his delivery resulted in a higher-than-usual kick and fouled up his mechanics. At Louisville last year, he compiled a 2-1 record with a 4.37 ERA in nine games. A sinker-slider pitcher who also throws a fork-ball, Olivares runs into problems when the sinker doesn't sink or when it sinks out of the strike zone. Lefties ripped him last year, and he yielded more than 10 hits and four and one-half walks per nine innings. Since he didn't get many strikeouts (only about three per game), those numbers didn't earn passing grades. Olivares also has problems keeping the ball in the park and throws more than his share of wild pitches. On the plus side, he is an excellent hitter whose .214 average ranked eighth among NL hurlers last year. A capable fielder, he has a decent pickoff move for a righty.

Major League Pitching Register

	W	L	ERA	G	CG	IP	H	ER	BB	SO
90 NL	1	1	2.92	9	0	49.1	45	16	17	20
91 NL	11	7	3.71	28	0	167.1	148	69	61	91
92 NL	9	9	3.84	32	1	197.0	189	84	63	124
93 NL	5	3	4.17	58	0	118.2	134	55	54	63
94 NL	3	4	5.74	14	1	73.2	84	47	37	26
Life	29	24	4.02	141	2	606.0	600	271	232	324
3 AVE	6	6	4.40	37	1	139.2	147	68	56	75

JOE OLIVER

Position: Catcher
Team: Cincinnati Reds
Born: July 24, 1965 Memphis, TN
Height: 6'3" **Weight:** 210 lbs.
Bats: right **Throws:** right
Acquired: Second-round pick in 6/83 free-agent draft

Player Summary	
Fantasy Value	$4 to $6
Card Value	6¢ to 10¢
Will	hit southpaws
Can't	show speed
Expect	clutch stick
Don't Expect	defensive woes

After establishing a reputation as one of baseball's most durable receivers, Oliver ran into a brick wall last April. Idled after just 19 at bats by an inflammation in his left ankle, the power-hitting catcher missed the remainder of the strike-shortened year. He should be back at full strength this summer. A healthy Oliver loves to pull low fastballs but goes with the pitch on off-speed serves, often sending them up the middle or the opposite way. An aggressive hitter with little patience, he fans four times more often than he walks. But he's a much better hitter with runners in scoring position and in late-inning pressure spots. He's also more productive against left-handers. Like most catchers, Oliver can't run. He's just as likely to hit into a double play as he is to smack one out of the park. He does have a good throwing arm, however, and is a fine game-caller and handler of pitchers. He's led the NL in chances, putouts, and fielding percentage.

Major League Batting Register

	BA	G	AB	R	H	2B	3B	HR	RBI	SB
89 NL	.272	49	151	13	41	8	0	3	23	0
90 NL	.231	121	364	34	84	23	0	8	52	1
91 NL	.216	94	269	21	58	11	0	11	41	0
92 NL	.270	143	485	42	131	25	1	10	57	2
93 NL	.239	139	482	40	115	28	0	14	75	0
94 NL	.211	6	19	1	4	0	0	1	5	0
Life	.245	552	1770	151	433	95	1	47	253	3
2 AVE	.254	141	484	41	123	27	1	12	66	1

GREGG OLSON

Position: Pitcher
Team: Atlanta Braves
Born: Oct. 11, 1966 Omaha, NE
Height: 6'4" **Weight:** 210 lbs.
Bats: right **Throws:** right
Acquired: Signed as a free agent, 2/94

Player Summary	
Fantasy Value	$1 to $3
Card Value	6¢ to 10¢
Will	count on curve
Can't	win with bad elbow
Expect	one last shot
Don't Expect	30 saves

The elbow problems that shortened Olson's 1993 campaign continued to cause problems last season. The Braves, believing the torn ligament would heal, brought him to spring training then let him work his way into shape at Triple-A Richmond. Rushed to fill the gaping bullpen void in Atlanta, Olson didn't deliver, twisting his future into a giant question mark. Though he's only 28, his career may have ended prematurely from the strain of throwing too many curve-balls. Healthy, he was a power pitcher who mixed the curve—his best pitch—with a fastball and a slider to average a strikeout an inning. He averaged nearly three whiffs per walk, rarely surrendered a home run, and dominated left-handed batters. Olson's star might have burned out early. He worked at least 50 times for five straight seasons before 1994. Olson's fielding and pickoff move have posed problems for him in the past, but pitching is his only concern at the moment.

Major League Pitching Register

	W	L	ERA	G	S	IP	H	ER	BB	SO
88 AL	1	1	3.27	10	0	11.0	10	4	10	9
89 AL	5	2	1.69	64	27	85.0	57	16	46	90
90 AL	6	5	2.42	64	37	74.1	57	20	31	74
91 AL	4	6	3.18	72	31	73.2	74	26	29	72
92 AL	1	5	2.05	60	36	61.1	46	14	24	58
93 AL	0	2	1.60	50	29	45.0	37	8	18	44
94 AL	0	2	9.20	16	1	14.2	19	15	13	10
Life	17	23	2.54	336	161	365.0	300	103	171	357
2 AVE	1	4	1.86	55	33	53.1	42	11	21	51

PAUL O'NEILL

Position: Outfield
Team: New York Yankees
Born: Feb. 25, 1963 Columbus, OH
Height: 6'4" **Weight:** 210 lbs.
Bats: left **Throws:** left
Acquired: Traded from Reds with Joe DeBerry for Roberto Kelly, 11/92

Player Summary

Fantasy Value	$19 to $22
Card Value	10¢ to 15¢
Will	produce under pressure
Can't	win Triple Crown
Expect	strong arm
Don't Expect	platooning

O'Neill's sudden success against southpaws last summer led to the batting title. His .380 mark against right-handers wasn't nearly as shocking as his .305 mark against lefties. O'Neill had hit so poorly against southpaws (.219 over five previous seasons) that he was often rested against them. Last year, that wasn't necessary. The Otterbein College product hit .385 with runners in scoring position and .426 in late-inning pressure situations. He even knocked Don Mattingly out of the No. 3 batting hole. A patient hitter who walks more than he fans, O'Neill finished with a .460 on-base mark, second to Frank Thomas in the majors. O'Neill's .603 slugging percentage placed fourth in the AL. He made just one error in right but had only six assists because few runners dared to challenge his powerful arm.

Major League Batting Register

	BA	G	AB	R	H	2B	3B	HR	RBI	SB
85 NL	.333	5	12	1	4	1	0	0	1	0
86 NL	.000	3	2	0	0	0	0	0	0	0
87 NL	.256	84	160	24	41	14	1	7	28	2
88 NL	.252	145	485	58	122	25	3	16	73	8
89 NL	.276	117	428	49	118	24	2	15	74	20
90 NL	.270	145	503	59	136	28	0	16	78	13
91 NL	.256	152	532	71	136	36	0	28	91	12
92 NL	.246	148	496	59	122	19	1	14	66	6
93 AL	.311	141	498	71	155	34	1	20	75	2
94 AL	.359	103	368	68	132	25	1	21	83	5
Life	.277	1043	3484	460	966	206	9	137	569	68
3 AVE	.306	145	504	75	154	29	1	21	86	5

STEVE ONTIVEROS

Position: Pitcher
Team: Oakland Athletics
Born: March 5, 1961 Tularosa, NM
Height: 6' **Weight:** 190 lbs.
Bats: right **Throws:** right
Acquired: Signed as a free agent, 1/94

Player Summary

Fantasy Value	$10 to $13
Card Value	6¢ to 8¢
Will	keep ball down
Can't	blow hitters away
Expect	good control
Don't Expect	injury-free year

Ontiveros finally stayed healthy enough in 1994 to throw a significant amount of innings. In doing so, he became the most dependable of Oakland's starting hurlers, keeping the Athletics in almost every game he pitched. He led the AL with a 2.65 ERA. Ontiveros has suffered from a myriad of elbow injuries, beginning in 1985, and was shelved for most of the 1988 to 1992 seasons. He had two reconstructive surgeries during this time, including the "Tommy John" procedure. However, a minor-league comeback in 1993 led Oakland to sign Ontiveros, and he won a job in spring training. The veteran finesse pitcher survives by changing speeds, putting the ball low, and keeping the ball in play. Never overpowering even when healthy, he doesn't strike many hitters out. He doesn't walk many either, however, and allowed only seven homers in '94. It's unlikely that Ontiveros has conquered his injury problems, but when healthy, he can pitch.

Major League Pitching Register

	W	L	ERA	G	CG	IP	H	ER	BB	SO
85 AL	1	3	1.93	39	0	74.2	45	16	19	36
86 AL	2	2	4.71	46	0	72.2	72	38	25	54
87 AL	10	8	4.00	35	2	150.2	141	67	50	97
88 AL	3	4	4.61	10	0	54.2	57	28	21	30
89 AL	2	1	3.82	6	0	30.2	34	13	15	12
90 NL	0	0	2.70	5	0	10.0	9	3	3	6
93 AL	0	2	1.00	14	0	18.0	18	2	6	13
94 AL	6	4	2.65	27	2	115.1	93	34	26	56
Life	24	24	3.43	182	4	526.2	469	201	165	304

JESSE OROSCO

Position: Pitcher
Team: Milwaukee Brewers
Born: April 21, 1957 Santa Barbara, CA
Height: 6'2" **Weight:** 185 lbs.
Bats: right **Throws:** left
Acquired: Purchased from Indians, 12/91

Player Summary	
Fantasy Value	$0
Card Value	5¢ to 7¢
Will	hang around
Can't	afford walks
Expect	off-speed pitches
Don't Expect	saves

After three straight excellent seasons, Orosco slumped seriously in 1994. His control, exceptional since 1990, deserted him last season, and his ERA shot up. Continuing a trend that began in 1992, the veteran left-hander held right-handers in check (just .195 in 1994) but was battered unmercifully by left-handers. Brewers manager Phil Garner has stopped using Orosco against tough lefty hitters, opting for Graeme Lloyd instead. Orosco is also an uncommonly easy left-hander to run on, as opponents stole eight bases in eight attempts against him last season. Part of this is due to his reliance on screwballs and changeups. He is close to slipping out of the majors for good, and unless he irons out his problems, he'll be no more than a 10th pitcher.

Major League Pitching Register

	W	L	ERA	G	S	IP	H	ER	BB	SO
79 NL	1	2	4.89	18	0	35.0	33	19	22	22
81 NL	0	1	1.56	8	1	17.1	13	3	6	18
82 NL	4	10	2.72	54	4	109.1	92	33	40	89
83 NL	13	7	1.47	62	17	110.0	76	18	38	84
84 NL	10	6	2.59	60	31	87.0	58	25	34	85
85 NL	8	6	2.73	54	17	79.0	66	24	34	68
86 NL	8	6	2.33	58	21	81.0	64	21	35	62
87 NL	3	9	4.44	58	16	77.0	78	38	31	78
88 NL	3	2	2.72	55	9	53.0	41	16	30	43
89 AL	3	4	2.08	69	3	78.0	54	18	26	79
90 AL	5	4	3.90	55	2	64.2	58	28	38	55
91 AL	2	0	3.74	47	0	45.2	52	19	15	36
92 AL	3	1	3.23	59	1	39.0	33	14	13	40
93 AL	3	5	3.18	57	8	56.2	47	20	17	67
94 AL	3	1	5.08	40	0	39.0	32	22	26	36
Life	69	64	2.95	754	130	971.2	797	318	405	862
3 AVE	3	2	3.88	57	3	50.1	42	22	22	53

JOE ORSULAK

Position: Outfield
Team: New York Mets
Born: May 31, 1962 Glen Ridge, NJ
Height: 6'1" **Weight:** 196 lbs.
Bats: left **Throws:** left
Acquired: Signed as a free agent, 12/92

Player Summary	
Fantasy Value	$5 to $7
Card Value	5¢ to 7¢
Will	come off bench
Can't	show much speed
Expect	good defense
Don't Expect	top on-base mark

Always a valuable reserve, Orsulak filled in capably at the outfield corners for the Mets in 1994. He throws well (racking up eight assists in limited 1994 action), has good range, and can even play center in a pinch. His primary value, in fact, is probably on defense; the veteran flychaser has never been a serious offensive threat. Orsulak is a proven average hitter and makes good contact, but has never had much extra-base power and seldom walks. He hit just .214 against left-handed pitchers in 1994. In younger days, he stole as many as 24 bases a season, but he has lost almost all of his speed. The popular Orsulak missed some time in 1994 to be with his wife, who is suffering from a serious illness, but returned before the strike in August. Despite opportunities to play regularly with Pittsburgh and Baltimore, Orsulak has found his niche coming off the bench.

Major League Batting Register

	BA	G	AB	R	H	2B	3B	HR	RBI	SB
83 NL	.182	7	11	0	2	0	0	0	1	0
84 NL	.254	32	67	12	17	1	2	0	3	3
85 NL	.300	121	397	54	119	14	6	0	21	24
86 NL	.249	138	401	60	100	19	6	2	19	24
88 NL	.288	125	379	48	109	21	3	8	27	9
89 AL	.285	123	390	59	111	22	5	7	55	5
90 AL	.269	124	413	49	111	14	3	11	57	6
91 AL	.278	143	486	57	135	22	1	5	43	6
92 AL	.289	117	391	45	113	18	3	4	39	5
93 NL	.284	134	409	59	116	15	4	8	35	5
94 NL	.260	96	292	39	76	3	0	8	42	4
Life	.278	1160	3636	482	1009	149	33	53	342	91
3 AVE	.277	129	404	53	112	12	2	8	44	5

DONOVAN OSBORNE

Position: Pitcher
Team: St. Louis Cardinals
Born: June 21, 1969 Roseville, CA
Height: 6'2" **Weight:** 195 lbs.
Bats: both **Throws:** left
Acquired: First-round pick in 6/90 free-agent draft

Player Summary

Fantasy Value.	$5 to $7
Card Value.	6¢ to 10¢
Will	try to rebound
Can't.	retire all righties
Expect	fine control
Don't Expect	top second half

With 21 wins in his first two seasons, Osborne had established himself as a fast-developing young southpaw. But that was before he developed such severe tendinitis in his pitching shoulder that he needed corrective surgery. Sidelined for the entire 1994 season, he must now prove himself sound before he can return to his previous career path. When healthy, the former UNLV strikeout king has good control of his fastball, slider, and changeup. He averaged two strikeouts per walk, yielded fewer hits than innings pitched, and decimated left-handed hitters before the injury. His season-long stamina was uncertain before the injury, however, since he had fast starts but slow finishes in both of his two big-league summers. Now his endurance is profoundly in doubt. Though his defense needs work, Osborne already has a fine pickoff move. He also helps himself with his offense and offers speed on the bases; he's appeared three times as a pinch runner. He was a college All-America selection in 1989, a year before he was drafted.

Major League Pitching Register

	W	L	ERA	G	CG	IP	H	ER	BB	SO
92 NL	11	9	3.77	34	0	179.0	193	75	38	104
93 NL	10	7	3.76	26	1	155.2	153	65	47	83
Life	21	16	3.76	60	1	334.2	346	140	85	187
2 AVE	11	8	3.76	30	1	167.1	173	70	43	94

SPIKE OWEN

Position: Third base; infield
Team: California Angels
Born: April 19, 1961 Cleburne, TX
Height: 5'10" **Weight:** 170 lbs.
Bats: both **Throws:** right
Acquired: Traded from Yankees for Jose Musset, 12/93

Player Summary

Fantasy Value.	$1 to $3
Card Value.	5¢ to 7¢
Will	use many gloves
Can't.	show much speed
Expect.	declining range
Don't Expect	a bat crown

Rebounding from a poor 1993 with the Yankees, in which his production slipped to new lows, Owen found a home at third base in Anaheim. The veteran hit .319 against right-handers in 1994 and adjusted well to his new position. His range at shortstop had declined over the years, but he fared well at the hot corner, showing steady hands and a decent arm. While Owen has little speed or power, he still contributed in the No. 2 spot, posting his highest career batting average and taking 49 walks for a .418 on-base percentage. While these lofty numbers are likely to decline in 1995, he did help the Angels and has salvaged much of his reputation. This summer is the final year of Owen's big contract, and it will be interesting to see if he can keep up his surprising surge.

Major League Batting Register

	BA	G	AB	R	H	2B	3B	HR	RBI	SB
83 AL	.196	80	306	36	60	11	3	2	21	10
84 AL	.245	152	530	67	130	18	8	3	43	16
85 AL	.259	118	352	41	91	10	6	6	37	11
86 AL	.231	154	528	67	122	24	7	1	45	4
87 AL	.259	132	437	50	113	17	7	2	48	11
88 AL	.249	89	257	40	64	14	1	5	18	0
89 NL	.233	142	437	52	102	17	4	6	41	3
90 NL	.234	149	453	55	106	24	5	5	35	8
91 NL	.255	139	424	39	108	22	8	3	26	2
92 NL	.269	122	386	52	104	16	3	7	40	9
93 AL	.234	103	334	41	78	16	2	2	20	3
94 AL	.310	82	268	30	83	17	2	3	37	2
Life	.246	1462	4712	570	1161	206	56	45	411	79
3 AVE	.272	114	366	45	100	19	3	4	37	5

TOM PAGNOZZI

Position: Catcher
Team: St. Louis Cardinals
Born: July 30, 1962 Tucson, AZ
Height: 6'1" **Weight:** 190 lbs.
Bats: right **Throws:** right
Acquired: Eighth-round pick in 6/83 free-agent draft

Player Summary	
Fantasy Value	$5 to $7
Card Value	6¢ to 10¢
Will	hit left-handers
Can't	make headlines
Expect	consistency
Don't Expect	defensive lapses

Pagnozzi is lost in the crowd of NL catchers, but ranks with the best of them. Lacking a cannon arm or booming bat, the Redbird receiver instead features agility behind the plate and a quick throwing release. He also makes some offensive contributions. The Cardinals suffered a difficult 1994, due in part to nagging injuries that limited Pagnozzi's effectiveness. He began the year on the disabled list with torn cartilage in his left knee, which kept him sidelined until May 5. After his rehabilitation, he battered lefties at a .333 clip and showed a bit of power. He hits for a decent average every year and, when healthy, makes good contact at the plate. He walked enough to notch a .327 on-base percentage. Pagnozzi also tossed out a superb 25 of 50 runners attempting to steal on him in 1994. Despite his lack of headline-type abilities, he has won two Gold Gloves and is regarded as one of the NL's better backstops.

Major League Batting Register

	BA	G	AB	R	H	2B	3B	HR	RBI	SB
87 NL	.188	27	48	8	9	1	0	2	9	1
88 NL	.282	81	195	17	55	9	0	0	15	0
89 NL	.150	52	80	3	12	2	0	0	3	0
90 NL	.277	69	220	20	61	15	0	2	23	1
91 NL	.264	140	459	38	121	24	5	2	57	9
92 NL	.249	139	485	33	121	26	3	7	44	2
93 NL	.258	92	330	31	85	15	1	7	41	1
94 NL	.272	70	243	21	66	12	1	7	40	0
Life	.257	670	2060	171	530	104	10	27	232	14
3 AVE	.258	110	386	31	100	19	2	8	47	1

LANCE PAINTER

Position: Pitcher
Team: Colorado Rockies
Born: July 21, 1967 Bedford, England
Height: 6'1" **Weight:** 194 lbs.
Bats: left **Throws:** left
Acquired: Second-round pick from Padres in 11/92 expansion draft

Player Summary	
Fantasy Value	$0
Card Value	7¢ to 10¢
Will	get another chance
Can't	blow hitters away
Expect	decent starts
Don't Expect	a Cy Young

Painter began and finished the 1994 season at Triple-A. In between, the well-regarded young left-hander made 14 starts with the big club. Although he showed flashes of brilliance, he had plenty of trouble with big-league hitters. Working in the cozy confines of Mile High Stadium is difficult for any young pitcher, but Painter compounded his troubles by struggling with his control. He has shown fine command while working in the minor leagues and throws with reasonably good velocity. However, he is not ready; opponents hit .302 against Painter in 1994, and he allowed nine homers. He is also easy to run on, and struggled despite receiving almost seven runs of support per start. Painter's talents will afford him several more chances to crack the Rockies' rotation, and eventually he should be a useful No. 3 starter. At Triple-A Colorado Springs last summer, he was 4-3 with a 4.79 ERA, 59 strikeouts, and 28 walks in 71 innings. He was 9-7 with a 4.30 ERA, 91 Ks, and 44 walks in 138 frames at Colorado Springs in 1993. He went 10-5 with a 3.53 ERA at Double-A Wichita in '92.

Major League Pitching Register

	W	L	ERA	G	CG	IP	H	ER	BB	SO
93 NL	2	2	6.00	10	1	39.0	52	26	9	16
94 NL	4	6	6.11	15	0	73.2	91	50	26	41
Life	6	8	6.07	25	1	112.2	143	76	35	57

VICENTE PALACIOS

Position: Pitcher
Team: St. Louis Cardinals
Born: July 19, 1963 Mataloma, Mexico
Height: 6'3" **Weight:** 175 lbs.
Bats: right **Throws:** right
Acquired: Signed as a free agent, 12/93

Player Summary	
Fantasy Value	$1
Card Value	5¢ to 7¢
Will	show good stuff
Can't	catch a break
Expect	variety of roles
Don't Expect	saves

After Palacios spent the 1993 season as a short reliever for Yucatan and Aguascalientes in the Mexican League—where he notched 20 saves and had almost a K an inning—the former Pirate answered the Cardinals' call to shore up their thin pitching. The veteran right-hander still has excellent velocity and decent control, but he suffered a tough 1994 season. He began the year in the rotation, and continued to spot start and long relieve over the course of the campaign. His 3-8 record is deceiving; he posted by far the best ERA of any member of the Cardinal rotation. In addition, much of his troubles can be blamed on his teammates, who provided him with a measly three runs of support per start. Palacios allowed 16 home runs last year, but opponents hit just .246 against him. He pitched better as the season progressed, and he looks like he has earned a spot at the major-league level. It's surprising that a pitcher with his stuff was unwanted for an entire season.

Major League Pitching Register

	W	L	ERA	G	CG	IP	H	ER	BB	SO
87 NL	2	1	4.30	6	0	29.1	27	14	9	13
88 NL	1	2	6.66	7	0	24.1	28	18	15	15
90 NL	0	0	0.00	7	0	15.0	4	0	2	8
91 NL	6	3	3.75	36	0	81.2	69	34	38	64
92 NL	3	2	4.25	20	0	53.0	56	25	27	33
94 NL	3	8	4.44	31	1	117.2	104	58	43	95
Life	15	16	4.18	107	2	321.0	288	149	134	228
2 AVE	4	7	4.39	32	1	109.1	101	53	44	83

DONN PALL

Position: Pitcher
Team: Chicago Cubs
Born: Jan. 11, 1962 Chicago, IL
Height: 6'1" **Weight:** 180 lbs.
Bats: right **Throws:** right
Acquired: Signed as a free agent, 8/94

Player Summary	
Fantasy Value	$2 to $4
Card Value	5¢ to 7¢
Will	baffle
Can't	afford a slump
Expect	good control
Don't Expect	more work

Pall survives on the fringes. A right-hander who lacks great stuff, he relies on control and a good attitude in order to stick around. The Yankees signed him last winter, and he toiled for them in middle relief. Despite a decent performance with the Bronx Bombers, in which he showed his customary fine control, he never broke out of the 11th-pitcher role and was released in late July. Pall returned to his hometown and joined the Cubs' troubled bullpen shortly before the strike. He had pitched five and one-half years with the crosstown White Sox before moving to the Phillies in mid-1993. His best pitch is a split-finger fastball that dips sharply out of the strike zone. His other pitches are average at best. He had a 2-1 ratio of Ks to walks last year. A key member of the Players Association, Pall is good enough to hang around a few more seasons, but he will probably fill out several more change-of-address forms.

Major League Pitching Register

	W	L	ERA	G	S	IP	H	ER	BB	SO
88 AL	0	2	3.45	17	0	28.2	39	11	8	16
89 AL	4	5	3.31	53	6	87.0	90	32	19	58
90 AL	3	5	3.32	56	2	76.0	63	28	24	39
91 AL	7	2	2.41	51	0	71.0	59	19	20	40
92 AL	5	2	4.93	39	1	73.0	79	40	27	27
93 AL	2	3	3.22	39	1	58.2	62	21	11	29
93 NL	1	0	2.55	8	0	17.2	15	5	3	11
94 AL	1	2	3.60	26	0	35.0	43	14	9	21
94 NL	0	0	4.50	2	0	4.0	8	2	1	2
Life	23	21	3.43	291	10	451.0	458	172	122	243
3 AVE	3	3	3.90	42	1	68.1	76	30	18	33

RAFAEL PALMEIRO

Position: First base
Team: Baltimore Orioles
Born: Sept. 24, 1964 Havana, Cuba
Height: 6′ **Weight:** 180 lbs.
Bats: left **Throws:** left
Acquired: Signed as a free agent, 12/93

Player Summary	
Fantasy Value	$25 to $30
Card Value	15¢ to 25¢
Will	deliver the goods
Can't	win pennant alone
Expect	success vs. lefties
Don't Expect	defensive acclaim

The multimillion-dollar free agent brought high expectations with him to Baltimore. Palmeiro, undaunted, did his best to fulfill them in his first season as an Oriole, putting together another excellent all-around campaign. Once regarded as a slow-footed, defensively suspect platoon player in his days with the Cubs, Palmeiro has erased those knocks. He is a smart if not speedy baserunner, swiping seven bases in 10 tries last season. Defensively, he made just four errors at first base in 1994 and showed decent range. Raffy once struggled against lefties, but last year he battered them at a .352 clip. He hits well in every situational breakdown and walks as often as he strikes out. He has a smooth swing and decent power. He has evolved into a top-line offensive player, the best Oriole first baseman since Eddie Murray in the mid-1980s. Palmeiro should enjoy several more productive seasons.

Major League Batting Register

	BA	G	AB	R	H	2B	3B	HR	RBI	SB
86 NL	.247	22	73	9	18	4	0	3	12	1
87 NL	.276	84	221	32	61	15	1	14	30	2
88 NL	.307	152	580	75	178	41	5	8	53	12
89 AL	.275	156	559	76	154	23	4	8	64	4
90 AL	.319	154	598	72	191	35	6	14	89	3
91 AL	.322	159	631	115	203	49	3	26	88	4
92 AL	.268	159	608	84	163	27	4	22	85	2
93 AL	.295	160	597	124	176	40	2	37	105	22
94 AL	.319	111	436	82	139	32	0	23	76	7
Life	.298	1157	4303	669	1283	266	25	155	602	57
3 AVE	.294	158	606	108	178	37	2	30	99	11

DEAN PALMER

Position: Third base
Team: Texas Rangers
Born: Dec. 27, 1968 Tallahassee, FL
Height: 6′1″ **Weight:** 190 lbs.
Bats: right **Throws:** right
Acquired: Third-round pick in 6/86 free-agent draft

Player Summary	
Fantasy Value	$14 to $17
Card Value	10¢ to 15¢
Will	whiff often
Can't	afford errors
Expect	good power
Don't Expect	stolen bases

Palmer, the Rangers' strong young third sacker, failed to develop in 1994. In fact, instead of becoming the Matt Williams-type of slugger that Texas fans hoped he would be, Palmer sank dangerously close to replacement-level performance both at the plate and in the field. He fanned 89 times and walked just 26, making his on-base percentage a dismal .302. In addition, his power production was far below expected levels. Palmer compiled a .464 slugging percentage in 1994. He has little speed and has not hit well with men in scoring position during his career. He does a good job against left-handers. There is still time for him to improve, but he needs to learn the strike zone. In the field, Palmer made 22 errors, which led all AL players at any position, but he did show good range at third. He has a strong if occasionally inaccurate arm. While Palmer is an average player at this point, he has the potential to make consistent contact at the plate and could become a top-line performer.

Major League Batting Register

	BA	G	AB	R	H	2B	3B	HR	RBI	SB
89 AL	.105	16	19	0	2	2	0	0	1	0
91 AL	.187	81	268	38	50	9	2	15	37	0
92 AL	.229	152	541	74	124	25	0	26	72	10
93 AL	.245	148	519	88	127	31	2	33	96	11
94 AL	.246	93	342	50	84	14	2	19	59	3
Life	.229	490	1689	250	387	81	6	93	265	24
3 AVE	.240	144	514	77	123	25	2	29	84	8

DEREK PARKS

Position: Catcher
Team: Minnesota Twins
Born: Sept. 29, 1968 Covina, CA
Height: 6′ **Weight:** 217 lbs.
Bats: right **Throws:** right
Acquired: First-round pick in 6/86 free-agent draft

Player Summary	
Fantasy Value	$1
Card Value	6¢ to 10¢
Will	show defensive skill
Can't	provide offense
Expect	one more chance
Don't Expect	long career

Parks continues to disappoint as a major leaguer. The former first-round draft pick has a fine arm and reasonable agility behind the plate, and he tossed out 36 percent of enemy basestealers in 1994. Parks, however, simply has not been able to master the science of hitting. It took three years for him to get the hang of Triple-A hurlers, and he shows no signs of figuring out big-league pitching. He fanned 20 times in just 89 at bats in 1994 and showed no ability to hit for average or power. He took just four walks in 1994, and his on-base percentage was an anemic .242. Of course, he wasn't much worse as a hitter than Twins' starting receiver Matt Walbeck, but Parks has now been playing professionally for nine seasons without much advancement as an offensive player. The worst stat is that he batted only .211 against left-handers, so he wasn't even a candidate for platoon status. He did bat .313 with 17 homers and 71 RBI in 1993 at Triple-A Portland. This summer may be his last chance to prove that he will be anything more than a defensive replacement.

Major League Batting Register

	BA	G	AB	R	H	2B	3B	HR	RBI	SB
92 AL	.333	7	6	1	2	0	0	0	0	0
93 AL	.200	7	20	3	4	0	0	0	1	0
94 AL	.191	31	89	6	17	6	0	1	9	0
Life	.200	45	115	10	23	6	0	1	10	0

LANCE PARRISH

Position: Catcher
Team: Pittsburgh Pirates
Born: June 15, 1956 Clarion, PA
Height: 6′3″ **Weight:** 224 lbs.
Bats: right **Throws:** right
Acquired: Signed as a free agent, 4/94

Player Summary	
Fantasy Value	$0
Card Value	5¢ to 7¢
Will	try to stick around
Can't	add any speed
Expect	decent performance
Don't Expect	starting job

After being dumped by Cleveland in mid-1993, Parrish took the rest of the summer off. He gained an invitation to Detroit's 1994 spring camp and began the year in Triple-A. However, the Pirates expressed interest in him and signed him on April 30. Serving as Don Slaught's backup, Parrish did a good job, arresting some of his previous decline both at the dish and behind it. He threw out 33 percent of baserunners trying to steal, was reasonably agile defensively, and hit well in a protected role. Once a free-swinger, he drew 18 walks and fanned just 28 times in 1994. He ranks 10th on the all-time games-caught list, and Parrish may have shown enough skill to hang on for a while. He is a possible Hall of Famer.

Major League Batting Register

	BA	G	AB	R	H	2B	3B	HR	RBI	SB
77 AL	.196	12	46	10	9	2	0	3	7	0
78 AL	.219	85	288	37	63	11	3	14	41	0
79 AL	.276	143	493	65	136	26	3	19	65	6
80 AL	.286	144	553	79	158	34	6	24	82	6
81 AL	.244	96	348	39	85	18	2	10	46	2
82 AL	.284	133	486	75	138	19	2	32	87	3
83 AL	.269	155	605	80	163	42	3	27	114	1
84 AL	.237	147	578	75	137	16	2	33	98	2
85 AL	.273	140	549	64	150	27	1	28	98	2
86 AL	.257	91	327	53	84	6	1	22	62	0
87 NL	.245	130	466	42	114	21	0	17	67	0
88 NL	.215	123	424	44	91	17	2	15	60	0
89 AL	.238	124	433	48	103	12	1	17	50	1
90 AL	.268	133	470	54	126	14	0	24	70	2
91 AL	.216	119	402	38	87	12	0	19	51	0
92 AL	.233	93	275	26	64	13	1	12	32	1
93 AL	.200	10	20	2	4	1	0	1	2	1
94 NL	.270	40	126	10	34	5	0	3	16	1
Life	.253	1918	6889	841	1746	296	27	320	1048	28

223

BOB PATTERSON

Position: Pitcher
Team: California Angels
Born: May 16, 1959 Jacksonville, FL
Height: 6'2" **Weight:** 192 lbs.
Bats: right **Throws:** left
Acquired: Signed as a minor-league free
agent, 1/94

Player Summary	
Fantasy Value	$0
Card Value	5¢ to 7¢
Will	stay in bullpen
Can't	expand his role
Expect	work vs. lefties
Don't Expect	unemployment

Once part of a successful "closer by committee" for Jim Leyland's Pirates, Patterson found himself an itinerant laborer in 1994. After a disappointing 1993 campaign in which his performance declined dramatically as a member of the Rangers, Patterson signed in January 1994 with California. He won a big-league job after coming to spring training as a nonroster invitee. Serving as a left-handed middleman, he held opposing batters to a .229 average, best on the club. Unfortunately, he allowed six homers in just 42 innings and had some control problems. Patterson lacks a great fastball, surviving by changing speeds and keeping the ball near the plate. He did strand 74 percent of his inherited runners. He should be able to stick around for another couple of seasons at this level. He's never going to play a key role on a contending team, but he has enjoyed a fine career from modest beginnings.

Major League Pitching Register

	W	L	ERA	G	S	IP	H	ER	BB	SO
85 NL	0	0	24.75	3	0	4.0	13	11	3	1
86 NL	2	3	4.95	11	0	36.1	49	20	5	20
87 NL	1	4	6.70	15	0	43.0	49	32	22	27
89 NL	4	3	4.05	12	1	26.2	23	12	8	20
90 NL	8	5	2.95	55	5	94.2	88	31	21	70
91 NL	4	3	4.11	54	2	65.2	67	30	15	57
92 NL	6	3	2.92	60	9	64.2	59	21	23	43
93 AL	2	4	4.78	52	1	52.2	59	28	11	46
94 AL	2	3	4.07	47	1	42.0	35	19	15	30
Life	29	28	4.27	309	19	429.2	442	204	123	314
3 AVE	4	4	3.86	59	4	58.1	56	25	18	44

ROGER PAVLIK

Position: Pitcher
Team: Texas Rangers
Born: Oct. 4, 1967 Houston, TX
Height: 6'3" **Weight:** 220 lbs.
Bats: right **Throws:** right
Acquired: Second-round pick in 2/86 free-
agent draft

Player Summary	
Fantasy Value	$3 to $5
Card Value	8¢ to 12¢
Will	work his way back
Can't	afford walks
Expect	good velocity
Don't Expect	total health

Pavlik, a potentially dominating right-hander, has fine velocity and baffling movement on his pitches. Unfortunately, injuries derailed him in 1994. He made three separate trips to the disabled list due to an aching right shoulder, which has bothered him his entire career. Pavlik began the 1994 season unable to pitch due to a rotator cuff injury, which some blame on his unorthodox cross-body delivery. He didn't appear with the Rangers until May 14, and he hadn't fully recovered yet. Pavlik was sidelined again in June and July. He didn't pitch well for most of the season when he was healthy, failing to win a game from May 31 to July 29. Batters compiled a .300 batting average and a .493 slugging average against him last year. He did start to pitch better in the time leading up to the strike, lending the Rangers hope that their gifted but injury-prone hurler can once again contribute in 1995. Pavlick tallied about five walks and five and one-half Ks per nine innings in 1994; he needs to cut his walk rate in half.

Major League Pitching Register

	W	L	ERA	G	CG	IP	H	ER	BB	SO
92 AL	4	4	4.21	13	1	62.0	66	29	34	45
93 AL	12	6	3.41	26	2	166.1	151	63	80	131
94 AL	2	5	7.69	11	0	50.1	61	43	30	31
Life	18	15	4.36	50	3	278.2	278	135	144	207
2 AVE	8	5	3.63	20	2	114.1	109	46	57	88

GERONIMO PENA

Position: Second base
Team: St. Louis Cardinals
Born: March 29, 1967   Distrito Nacional, Dominican Republic
Height: 6'1"   **Weight:** 170 lbs.
Bats: both   **Throws:** right
Acquired: Signed as a free agent, 12/84

Player Summary	
Fantasy Value	$7 to $9
Card Value	6¢ to 10¢
Will	show good bat
Can't	hit righties
Expect	frequent injuries
Don't Expect	great glove

Joe Torre tossed the Cardinals' second base job up in the air in 1994, but neither Pena nor Luis Alicea could catch it. However, Pena showed flashes of brilliance offensively and defensively and had claimed the spot by July. Unfortunately, a John Wetteland pitch broke Pena's left elbow on August 2, ending the second sacker's season. The injury-prone Pena has hot streaks and slumps every year, but he always comes out on the good side of the ledger. He had received an undeserved reputation as a poor gloveman and is an underrated fielder. He also has good power and drew 24 walks last season for a .344 on-base percentage. He hit left-handers at a .280 clip last year, but he struggled a little against right-handers, batting .239. Pena does strike out a lot, whiffing 54 times in '94. Before his injury, he had driven in at least one run in seven straight games. A good baserunner, he swiped nine bases in 10 tries. One of these years, Pena is going to stay healthy and put it all together.

Major League Batting Register

	BA	G	AB	R	H	2B	3B	HR	RBI	SB
90 NL	.244	18	45	5	11	2	0	0	2	1
91 NL	.243	104	185	38	45	8	3	5	17	15
92 NL	.305	62	203	31	62	12	1	7	31	13
93 NL	.256	74	254	34	65	19	2	5	30	13
94 NL	.254	83	213	33	54	13	1	11	34	9
Life	.263	341	900	141	237	54	7	28	114	51
3 AVE	.268	84	252	37	68	16	1	9	36	13

TONY PENA

Position: Catcher
Team: Cleveland Indians
Born: June 4, 1957   Monte Cristi, Dominican Republic
Height: 6'   **Weight:** 185 lbs.
Bats: right   **Throws:** right
Acquired: Signed as a minor-league free agent, 2/94

Player Summary	
Fantasy Value	$1
Card Value	6¢ to 10¢
Will	handle pitchers
Can't	play every day
Expect	success against lefties
Don't Expect	any speed

No team would offer Pena a guaranteed contract for 1994, or even place him on their 40-man roster. However, the Indians decided to take a flier, and he turned in a surprisingly good performance. Pena batted .352 against left-handed pitching. He also showed surprising power and made excellent contact at the plate, whiffing just 11 times and taking nine walks. In addition to chipping in with the bat in 1994, Pena continued to contribute on defense. He called games well, still threw effectively, and was valued for the wisdom and strong work ethic he brings to the young ballclub. Pena tossed out 31 percent of enemy basestealers last season.

Major League Batting Register

	BA	G	AB	R	H	2B	3B	HR	RBI	SB
80 NL	.429	8	21	1	9	1	1	0	1	0
81 NL	.300	66	210	16	63	9	1	2	17	1
82 NL	.296	138	497	53	147	28	4	11	63	2
83 NL	.301	151	542	51	163	22	3	15	70	6
84 NL	.286	147	546	77	156	27	2	15	78	12
85 NL	.249	147	546	53	136	27	2	10	59	12
86 NL	.288	144	510	56	147	26	2	10	52	9
87 NL	.214	116	384	40	82	13	4	5	44	6
88 NL	.263	149	505	55	133	23	1	10	51	6
89 NL	.259	141	424	36	110	17	2	4	37	5
90 AL	.263	143	491	62	129	19	1	7	56	8
91 AL	.231	141	464	45	107	23	2	5	48	8
92 AL	.241	133	410	39	99	21	1	1	38	3
93 AL	.181	126	304	20	55	11	0	4	19	1
94 AL	.295	40	112	18	33	8	1	2	10	0
Life	.263	1790	5966	622	1569	275	27	101	643	79
2 AVE	.216	130	357	30	77	16	1	3	29	2

TERRY PENDLETON

Position: Third base
Team: Atlanta Braves
Born: July 16, 1960   Los Angeles, CA
Height: 5'9"   **Weight:** 195 lbs.
Bats: both   **Throws:** right
Acquired: Signed as a free agent, 12/90

Player Summary	
Fantasy Value	$7 to $9
Card Value	10¢ to 15¢
Will	rehabilitate
Can't	turn back clock
Expect	a starting job
Don't Expect	stolen bases

In 1994, the popular Pendleton suffered his worst big-league season in several years. Hobbled by nagging knee injuries and disabled for a month by a strained lower back, he now must work to confirm himself as a top player. Jose Oliva's emergence puts a limit on Pendleton's time in Atlanta. If the switch-hitter is healthy, he should be able to rebound in 1995. However, it appears that the former Cardinal has entered a declining phase. He has lost both running speed and bat speed, and he has neither the power nor strike-zone judgement to survive if he doesn't hit for a high average. In 1994, he fanned 57 times while drawing just 12 walks and batted .241 versus right-handed pitchers. Pendleton has always had quick reflexes and a good arm, and he remains an asset with the glove. The gutsy veteran may have another comeback left in him, and he carries a winning reputation.

Major League Batting Register

	BA	G	AB	R	H	2B	3B	HR	RBI	SB
84 NL	.324	67	262	37	85	16	3	1	33	20
85 NL	.240	149	559	56	134	16	3	5	69	17
86 NL	.239	159	578	56	138	26	5	1	59	24
87 NL	.286	159	583	82	167	29	4	12	96	19
88 NL	.253	110	391	44	99	20	2	6	53	3
89 NL	.264	162	613	83	162	28	5	13	74	9
90 NL	.230	121	447	46	103	20	2	6	58	7
91 NL	.319	153	586	94	187	34	8	22	86	10
92 NL	.311	160	640	98	199	39	1	21	105	5
93 NL	.272	161	633	81	172	33	1	17	84	5
94 NL	.252	77	309	25	78	18	3	7	30	2
Life	.272	1478	5601	702	1524	279	37	111	747	121
3 AVE	.281	143	569	71	160	32	2	16	77	4

EDUARDO PEREZ

Position: Third base
Team: California Angels
Born: Sept. 11, 1969   Cincinnati, OH
Height: 6'4"   **Weight:** 215 lbs.
Bats: right   **Throws:** right
Acquired: First-round pick in 6/91 free-agent draft

Player Summary	
Fantasy Value	$6 to $8
Card Value	12¢ to 20¢
Will	return to bigs
Can't	add speed
Expect	third base job
Don't Expect	25 homers

Perez began 1994 as California's starting first baseman. However, he didn't add much offensively or defensively and was sent to Triple-A Vancouver on June 3, after Marcel Lachemann replaced Buck Rodgers as the Angels' manager. The new brain trust decided that Perez's future is at third base, not first, and that he needed to work on all facets of the game. At this point, it's still hard to get excited about him. He doesn't have the hitting ability, speed, or plate patience to be an impact player—and his power and glovework are average at best. In the majors last year, he fanned 29 times and walked just 12. His on-base percentage was just .275 and his slugging percentage only .380. He should improve on those numbers in the future. He batted .297 with seven homers, 38 RBI, 34 walks, and 53 strikeouts in 219 at bats at Vancouver last year. Perez has fine physical attributes but needs to get on his horse soon if he's to have a long major-league career. In 1993 at Vancouver, Perez batted .306 with 12 home runs, 70 RBI, 28 bases on balls, and 83 strikeouts in 363 at bats.

Major League Batting Register

	BA	G	AB	R	H	2B	3B	HR	RBI	SB
93 AL	.250	52	180	16	45	6	2	4	30	5
94 AL	.209	38	129	10	27	7	0	5	16	3
Life	.233	90	309	26	72	13	2	9	46	8

MELIDO PEREZ

Position: Pitcher
Team: New York Yankees
Born: Feb. 15, 1966   San Cristobal, Dominican Republic
Height: 6'4"   **Weight:** 210 lbs.
Bats: right   **Throws:** right
Acquired: Traded from White Sox with Domingo Jean and Bob Wickman for Steve Sax, 1/92

Player Summary	
Fantasy Value	$9 to $11
Card Value	6¢ to 10¢
Will	throw the splitter
Can't	pitch 250 innings
Expect	strikeouts
Don't Expect	pinpoint control

The streaky Perez rebounded to post a fine record in 1994. He was hampered the year before by a sore shoulder, but he recovered in fine form. Perez's bread and butter is his split-finger fastball, which won him a July 1994 *Sporting News* poll as the AL's best practitioner of the pitch. The reedy right-hander also throws a hard slider, a fastball with good velocity, and a decent curve. However, his strikeouts-per-inning rate was down in 1994, and this may be cause for concern. He may have been overworked in 1992, and he has pitched just one complete game in the last two years. In 1994, he allowed 16 homers, but opponents hit just .238. He also held enemy batters to a .311 on-base average and a .394 slugging percentage. Perez is not easy to run on, and he fields his position very well. He has always been colorful and animated, but he seems to have toned down his antics.

Major League Pitching Register

		W	L	ERA	G	CG	IP	H	ER	BB	SO
87	AL	1	1	7.84	3	0	10.1	18	9	5	5
88	AL	12	10	3.79	32	3	197.0	186	83	72	138
89	AL	11	14	5.01	31	2	183.1	187	102	90	141
90	AL	13	14	4.61	35	3	197.0	177	101	86	161
91	AL	8	7	3.12	49	0	135.2	111	47	52	128
92	AL	13	16	2.87	33	10	247.2	212	79	93	218
93	AL	6	14	5.19	25	0	163.0	173	94	64	148
94	AL	9	4	4.10	22	1	151.1	134	69	58	109
Life		73	80	4.09	230	19	1285.1	1198	584	520	1048
3 AVE		11	12	3.90	30	4	208.1	191	90	80	173

MIKE PEREZ

Position: Pitcher
Team: St. Louis Cardinals
Born: Oct. 19, 1964   Yauco, Puerto Rico
Height: 6'   **Weight:** 187 lbs.
Bats: right   **Throws:** right
Acquired: 12th-round pick in 6/86 free-agent draft

Player Summary	
Fantasy Value	$2 to $4
Card Value	6¢ to 10¢
Will	look for comeback
Can't	win closer job
Expect	recovery if healthy
Don't Expect	many walks

Perez struggled mightily when finally allowed to close games for the Cardinals in 1994. He took over for Lee Smith late in 1993, but Perez eventually lost the job last season to Rene Arocha. Despite registering 12 saves, Perez allowed opponents to compile a .391 batting average. His performance worsened as the season went on, and he had allowed nearly a run an inning before the Cardinals sent him to Triple-A Louisville on July 16. Injuries were the main reason for Perez's poor performance. He missed two weeks in April and May with a pulled muscle in his right shoulder, and the injury flared up again in June. In fact, Perez did not pitch after being sent to Louisville. With an extended period of recovery, he has a good chance to come back healthy in 1995. He has a fine fastball and has always had excellent control. Unfortunately, his chance to be a closer in St. Louis is probably gone, but he'll be kept around in the Cardinals' bullpen due to the team's dearth of good pitching.

Major League Pitching Register

		W	L	ERA	G	S	IP	H	ER	BB	SO
90	NL	1	0	3.95	13	1	13.2	12	6	3	5
91	NL	0	2	5.82	14	0	17.0	19	11	7	7
92	NL	9	3	1.84	77	0	93.0	70	19	32	46
93	NL	7	2	2.48	65	7	72.2	65	20	20	58
94	NL	2	3	8.71	36	12	31.0	52	30	10	20
Life		19	10	3.40	205	20	227.1	218	86	72	136
3 AVE		6	3	3.49	64	8	70.1	69	27	22	44

YORKIS PEREZ

Position: Pitcher
Team: Florida Marlins
Born: Sept. 30, 1967   Bajos de Haina, Dominican Republic
Height: 6′   **Weight:** 180 lbs.
Bats: left   **Throws:** left
Acquired: Signed as a minor-league free agent, 12/93

Player Summary	
Fantasy Value	$3 to $5
Card Value	10¢ to 15¢
Will	strike out hitters
Can't	be a starter
Expect	appearances
Don't Expect	many saves

Given the way management bemoans the quality of today's major-league pitching, it's odd that a left-handed pitcher with Perez's stuff couldn't find a team who would take a chance on him. Finally, in 1994, the Marlins called on the younger brother of Melido and Pascual to fill a hole in their bullpen. Yorkis did a fine job, fanning a man an inning and limiting opponents to a .220 batting average. He also walked just 14 and held hitters to a .291 on-base percentage. Despite missing two weeks in June with a strained shoulder, Perez still tied for second on the Marlins in appearances. He has always averaged nearly a strikeout per inning during his pro career. He began his pro career in 1983 in the Minnesota organization, signing at 15 years of age. He has been a reliever almost exclusively since 1989. In 1993 at Double-A Harrisburg, he was 4-2 with a 3.45 ERA and three saves. He was 0-1 with a 3.60 ERA and five saves at Triple-A Ottawa. Perez has now pitched professionally in the United States, Canada, Japan, and the Dominican Republic. His travels may finally be over.

Major League Pitching Register

	W	L	ERA	G	S	IP	H	ER	BB	SO
91 NL	1	0	2.08	3	0	4.1	2	1	2	3
94 NL	3	0	3.54	44	0	40.2	33	16	14	41
Life	4	0	3.40	47	0	45.0	35	17	16	44

TONY PHILLIPS

Position: Outfield
Team: Detroit Tigers
Born: April 15, 1959   Atlanta, GA
Height: 5′10″   **Weight:** 175 lbs.
Bats: both   **Throws:** right
Acquired: Signed as a free agent, 12/89

Player Summary	
Fantasy Value	$15 to $18
Card Value	6¢ to 10¢
Will	play every day
Can't	add much defense
Expect	jawing with umpires
Don't Expect	low on-base mark

Once a fringe player with few offensive skills, Phillips has remade his image over a 13-year big-league tenure. He reached a career high in home runs in 1994 and cleared .275 for the fourth straight season. He is one of the AL's best leadoff men, drawing 95 walks (third best in the league) for a .409 on-base percentage. Phillips isn't fast, but last year he stole 13 bases in 18 tries. After splitting time between second and the outfield in 1993, he moved full-time to left field in 1994. He has decent range, but his arm is not strong. Another debit on Phillips's ledger is his tendency to argue with umpires, sometimes to the detriment of his team. It is this intensity, however, that has helped make him the player he is. Phillips is also a link to baseball's past: He is the last active major leaguer traded for Willie Montanez.

Major League Batting Register

	BA	G	AB	R	H	2B	3B	HR	RBI	SB
82 AL	.210	40	81	11	17	2	2	0	8	2
83 AL	.248	148	412	54	102	12	3	4	35	16
84 AL	.266	154	451	62	120	24	3	4	37	10
85 AL	.280	42	161	23	45	12	2	4	17	3
86 AL	.256	118	441	76	113	14	5	5	52	15
87 AL	.240	111	379	48	91	20	0	10	46	7
88 AL	.203	79	212	32	43	8	4	2	17	0
89 AL	.262	143	451	48	118	15	6	4	47	3
90 AL	.251	152	573	97	144	23	5	8	55	19
91 AL	.284	146	564	87	160	28	4	17	72	10
92 AL	.276	159	606	114	167	32	3	10	64	12
93 AL	.313	151	566	113	177	27	0	7	57	16
94 AL	.281	114	438	91	123	19	3	19	61	13
Life	.266	1557	5335	856	1420	236	40	94	568	126
3 AVE	.289	157	596	118	172	29	2	15	69	15

MIKE PIAZZA

Position: Catcher
Team: Los Angeles Dodgers
Born: Sept. 4, 1968 Norristown, PA
Height: 6'3" **Weight:** 197 lbs.
Bats: right **Throws:** right
Acquired: 62nd-round pick in 6/88 free-agent draft

Player Summary	
Fantasy Value	$25 to $30
Card Value	75¢ to $1.50
Will	swing a big bat
Can't	play stellar defense
Expect	more walks
Don't Expect	stolen bases

Piazza was not highly regarded as a prospect, but he worked long and hard to become one of the best hitters in the world. His efforts continue to pay off, as he enjoyed an MVP-type 1994 season. The Dodger receiver combines a quick bat with a booming power stroke. He hit .351 against left-handers in 1994 and fanned just 65 times, a fine total for a power hitter. He has little speed and walked just 33 times last year, but still notched a .370 on-base percentage. His 35 rookie homers beat Matt Nokes's 1987 rookie record for a catcher by seven dingers. Piazza doesn't have great defensive skills but has plenty of time to develop. He threw out just one quarter of basestealers in 1994 and made 10 errors. Piazza is quick behind the plate but still has trouble blocking pitches. He is a hard worker and will improve. A hockey fan and aspiring heavy metal guitarist, he slugged a 477-foot home run at Florida on June 6 and was the NL's Co-Player of the Month for May, when he hit .386 with 24 RBI. He will have more months like that in the years to come.

HIPOLITO PICHARDO

Position: Pitcher
Team: Kansas City Royals
Born: Aug. 22, 1969 Jicome Esperanza, Dominican Republic
Height: 6'1" **Weight:** 185 lbs.
Bats: right **Throws:** right
Acquired: Signed as a free agent, 12/87

Player Summary	
Fantasy Value	$3 to $5
Card Value	5¢ to 7¢
Will	work in middle
Can't	expand his role
Expect	ground balls
Don't Expect	strikeouts

Despite intermittent success as a starter in 1992 and 1993, Pichardo was moved to the bullpen last season. Working in middle-relief and setup roles, he doesn't have overpowering stuff and is most effective when he throws his sinker and keeps his fastball down. Unfortunately, his control is just mediocre, and too often his pitches rise. AL hitters can tee off on Pichardo when he's up in the strike zone, and they batted .309 against him in 1994. He was able to notch more than four and one-half strikeouts per nine innings last summer, and he allowed just over three walks per game. If Pichardo could cut his walk ratio in half, he could be a useful starter. He was able to notch three saves last season, but blew three as well. He is unlikely to ever be a closer. He simply doesn't have the stuff on his pitches to do the job. While Pichardo is a useful pitcher to have on a staff, he's not going to be anything more than a middle reliever unless he can get his pitches to behave. Pichardo has a decent move to first but is just a mediocre fielder.

Major League Batting Register

	BA	G	AB	R	H	2B	3B	HR	RBI	SB
92 NL	.232	21	69	5	16	3	0	1	7	0
93 NL	.318	149	547	81	174	24	2	35	112	3
94 NL	.319	107	405	64	129	18	0	24	92	1
Life	.312	277	1021	150	319	45	2	60	211	4
2 AVE	.318	150	559	86	178	25	1	34	121	2

Major League Pitching Register

	W	L	ERA	G	S	IP	H	ER	BB	SO
92 AL	9	6	3.95	31	0	143.2	148	63	49	59
93 AL	7	8	4.04	30	0	165.0	183	74	53	70
94 AL	5	3	4.92	45	3	67.2	82	37	24	36
Life	21	17	4.16	106	3	376.1	413	174	126	165
3 AVE	8	6	4.21	41	1	134.2	149	63	45	60

PHIL PLANTIER

Position: Outfield
Team: San Diego Padres
Born: Jan. 27, 1969 Manchester, NH
Height: 5'11" **Weight:** 195 lbs.
Bats: left **Throws:** right
Acquired: Traded from Red Sox for Jose Melendez, 12/92

Player Summary	
Fantasy Value	$11 to $14
Card Value	10¢ to 15¢
Will	hit for distance
Can't	run well
Expect	low batting average
Don't Expect	a Gold Glove

Once again in 1994, Plantier showed the big power that brought him to the majors. The former Red Sox outfielder slugged 13 home runs before June 1 for the Padres and seemed headed for a monster season. Unfortunately, nagging injuries to his right elbow and hip, exacerbated by his left-handed uppercut swing, brought his average and power production to a crashing halt. He slumped dramatically through the last three months of the season and was benched by then-Pads manager Jim Riggleman. In addition to his injury problems, Plantier also continues to have problems making contact. He fanned 91 times in 1994. He also hit a weak .152 against left-handed pitchers. He walked 36 times, but his on-base percentage was just .302. In the outfield, he's mediocre at best. Plantier threw out five runners, and he has a good arm. He has little speed or range, however. If his defense doesn't improve, he may have to become a designated hitter. He still has plenty of promise.

Major League Batting Register

	BA	G	AB	R	H	2B	3B	HR	RBI	SB
90 AL	.133	14	15	1	2	1	0	0	3	0
91 AL	.331	53	148	27	49	7	1	11	35	1
92 AL	.246	108	349	46	86	19	0	7	30	2
93 NL	.240	138	462	67	111	20	1	34	100	4
94 NL	.220	96	341	44	75	21	0	18	41	3
Life	.246	409	1315	185	323	68	2	70	209	10
3 AVE	.234	127	430	58	101	23	0	22	63	3

DAN PLESAC

Position: Pitcher
Team: Pittsburgh Pirates
Born: Feb. 4, 1962 Gary, IN
Height: 6'5" **Weight:** 215 lbs.
Bats: left **Throws:** left
Acquired: Signed as a free agent, 11/94

Player Summary	
Fantasy Value	$0
Card Value	5¢ to 7¢
Will	appear often
Can't	get righties out
Expect	strikeouts
Don't Expect	many walks

After a horrible 1993 season, Plesac rebounded in 1994. An off-season conditioning program strengthened his arm and gave him back some of his old velocity. He averaged nearly a strikeout per inning. Unfortunately, the Cubs' poor starting pitching forced Plesac to appear far too frequently. He was eighth in the NL in games pitched and slumped seriously in the second half. In late June, his ERA was a tidy 3.20, and opponents were batting just .231. By the end of the year, his ERA had leapt by a run and one-half, and hitters had solved him at a .279 clip. Right-handers, in particular, feasted on his pitches. Plesac does have fine control and good velocity, but, unfortunately, he allowed nine home runs. He pitched too often last season and will probably never again be a closer as he was for the Brewers. Plesac, though, is still able to help a ballclub at his present level of performance.

Major League Pitching Register

	W	L	ERA	G	S	IP	H	ER	BB	SO
86 AL	10	7	2.97	51	14	91.0	81	30	29	75
87 AL	5	6	2.61	57	23	79.1	63	23	23	89
88 AL	1	2	2.41	50	30	52.1	46	14	12	52
89 AL	3	4	2.35	52	33	61.1	47	16	17	52
90 AL	3	7	4.43	66	24	69.0	67	34	31	65
91 AL	2	7	4.29	45	8	92.1	92	44	39	61
92 AL	5	4	2.96	44	1	79.0	64	26	35	54
93 NL	2	1	4.74	57	0	62.2	74	33	21	47
94 NL	2	3	4.61	54	1	54.2	61	28	13	53
Life	33	41	3.48	476	134	641.2	595	248	220	548
3 AVE	3	3	4.05	59	1	72.2	75	33	25	59

ERIC PLUNK

Position: Pitcher
Team: Cleveland Indians
Born: Sept. 3, 1963 Wilmington, CA
Height: 6'6" **Weight:** 220 lbs.
Bats: right **Throws:** right
Acquired: Signed as a free agent, 4/92

Player Summary	
Fantasy Value	$7 to $9
Card Value	5¢ to 7¢
Will	throw hard
Can't	get respect
Expect	control troubles
Don't Expect	20 saves

Even after 1993, when Plunk cut down on his walks and overpowered AL hitters, he didn't get much respect from Indians manager Mike Hargrove. Even after Steve Farr and Jeff Russell failed in the closer's role in 1994, Hargrove refused to give Plunk an extended audition as the go-to guy. To be fair to Hargrove, Plunk blew four of seven save opportunities last year and struggled a bit with his control. Opponents hit just .233 with only three home runs against his overpowering fastball, however. He fanned over a man an inning and held right-handed hitters to a .171 mark. Plunk is fairly easy to run on and tossed seven wild pitches last year. Still, he is certainly a valuable part of anybody's bullpen and might expand his role someday to include closing out games if a manager takes a liking to him. Plunk has improved mightily since his early days with the Athletics and Yankees, especially since he improved his control.

LUIS POLONIA

Position: Outfield
Team: New York Yankees
Born: Oct. 12, 1964 Santiago City, Dominican Republic
Height: 5'8" **Weight:** 150 lbs.
Bats: left **Throws:** left
Acquired: Signed as a free agent, 12/93

Player Summary	
Fantasy Value	$18 to $21
Card Value	6¢ to 10¢
Will	hit right-handers
Can't	play defense
Expect	high average
Don't Expect	any power

A smart manager recognizes his players' strengths and neutralizes their weaknesses. Yankee skipper Buck Showalter realized that Polonia simply cannot hit left-handers, and limited Polonia's at bats so that he would face as few southpaws as possible. The result was increased productivity from New York's left-field slot. Polonia enjoyed a good season in a platoon role. While he doesn't walk enough to be a true leadoff man (just 37 times in 1994), he struck out just 36 times and will always hit for a high average against right-handers. His on-base percentage last year was a lofty .383. However, Polonia has his rough spots: He has absolutely no power and was thrown out stealing 12 times last year. While his defense has improved over the years—he notched nine assists in 1994—he still makes far too many defensive mistakes. He has mediocre range. It appears the Yankees did well by signing Polonia.

Major League Pitching Register

	W	L	ERA	G	S	IP	H	ER	BB	SO
86 AL	4	7	5.31	26	0	120.1	91	71	102	98
87 AL	4	6	4.74	32	2	95.0	91	50	62	90
88 AL	7	2	3.00	49	5	78.0	62	26	39	79
89 AL	8	6	3.28	50	1	104.1	82	38	64	85
90 AL	6	3	2.72	47	0	72.2	58	22	43	67
91 AL	2	5	4.76	43	0	111.2	128	59	62	103
92 AL	9	6	3.64	58	4	71.2	61	29	38	50
93 AL	4	5	2.79	70	15	71.0	61	22	30	77
94 AL	7	2	2.54	41	3	71.0	61	20	37	73
Life	51	42	3.81	416	30	795.2	695	337	477	722
3 AVE	8	5	2.94	62	8	81.1	69	26	40	77

Major League Batting Register

	BA	G	AB	R	H	2B	3B	HR	RBI	SB
87 AL	.287	125	435	78	125	16	10	4	49	29
88 AL	.292	84	288	51	84	11	4	2	27	24
89 AL	.286	59	206	31	59	6	4	1	17	13
89 AL	.313	66	227	39	71	11	2	2	29	9
90 AL	.335	120	403	52	135	7	9	2	35	21
91 AL	.296	150	604	92	179	28	8	2	50	48
92 AL	.286	149	577	83	165	17	4	0	35	51
93 AL	.271	152	576	75	156	17	6	1	32	55
94 AL	.311	95	350	62	109	21	6	1	36	20
Life	.295	1000	3666	563	1083	134	53	15	310	270
3 AVE	.288	145	549	82	158	21	6	1	39	45

MARK PORTUGAL

Position: Pitcher
Team: San Francisco Giants
Born: Oct. 30, 1962 Los Angeles, CA
Height: 6' **Weight:** 190 lbs.
Bats: right **Throws:** right
Acquired: Signed as a free agent, 11/93

Player Summary	
Fantasy Value	$8 to $10
Card Value	8¢ to 12¢
Will	stay in rotation
Can't	overpower hitters
Expect	good control
Don't Expect	complete games

Portugal left the Astros late in 1993 and inked a pretty substantial three-year deal with the Giants. Despite injuries, he did a good job for his new team. He improved his control dramatically and held hitters to a .260 average. Portugal allowed 17 homers, but he walked fewer than three men per game to limit the damage. Unfortunately, he missed two weeks in June with a groin pull and was lost for the year when he tore a knee ligament Aug. 5. The right-hander, now with his third big-league team, has come back from serious injuries over the last few years, including shoulder tendinitis and elbow surgery in 1992. Not particularly durable, Portugal has completed just one game in each of the last five seasons. However, San Francisco is happy to have his innings. In addition to his good work on the mound, he kicks in at the plate; Portugal hit .354 with five doubles and a triple in 1994.

Major League Pitching Register

	W	L	ERA	G	CG	IP	H	ER	BB	SO
85 AL	1	3	5.55	6	0	24.1	24	15	14	12
86 AL	6	10	4.31	27	3	112.2	112	54	50	67
87 AL	1	3	7.77	13	0	44.0	58	38	24	28
88 AL	3	3	4.53	26	0	57.2	60	29	17	31
89 NL	7	1	2.75	20	2	108.0	91	33	37	86
90 NL	11	10	3.62	32	1	196.2	187	79	67	136
91 NL	10	12	4.49	32	1	168.1	163	84	59	120
92 NL	6	3	2.66	18	1	101.1	76	30	41	62
93 NL	18	4	2.77	33	1	208.0	194	64	77	131
94 NL	10	8	3.93	21	1	137.1	135	60	45	87
Life	73	57	3.78	228	10	1158.1	1100	486	431	760
3 AVE	13	6	3.20	27	1	167.1	153	60	60	105

TODD PRATT

Position: Catcher
Team: Philadelphia Phillies
Born: Feb. 9, 1967 Bellevue, NE
Height: 6'3" **Weight:** 225 lbs.
Bats: right **Throws:** right
Acquired: Rule 5 draft pick from Red Sox, 12/91

Player Summary	
Fantasy Value	$0
Card Value	7¢ to 10¢
Will	be a backup
Can't	make contact
Expect	good throwing
Don't Expect	Daulton power

When Darren Daulton was put on the disabled list June 28, the Phillies could have made Pratt their full-time starter. Instead the team brought Mike Lieberthal up from Triple-A and split starting duty between the two receivers until the strike. Pratt is reasonably agile behind the plate and tossed out half of the runners who tried to steal against him in 1994. He also calls a good game and did not commit an error in his 250 innings of catching. That's all fine, but his offense was very poor. Slumping from a good 1993 season, he fanned 29 times in just 102 at bats last summer. He hit just .235 against left-handers. He has some patience at the plate, drawing 12 walks last season, but it so poorly that his on-base percentage was a paltry .281. He did compile batting averages over .300 in both Double-A and Triple-A in 1992. Pratt is capable of some improvement at the plate but will never hit for enough power or average to be a starter. It's more likely that the former Red Sox prospect will be a backup for more than one team in his career.

Major League Batting Register

	BA	G	AB	R	H	2B	3B	HR	RBI	SB
92 NL	.283	16	46	6	13	1	0	2	10	0
93 NL	.287	33	87	8	25	6	0	5	13	0
94 NL	.196	28	102	10	20	6	1	2	9	0
Life	.247	77	235	24	58	13	1	9	32	0

KIRBY PUCKETT

Position: Outfield
Team: Minnesota Twins
Born: March 14, 1961   Chicago, IL
Height: 5'9"   **Weight:** 220 lbs.
Bats: right   **Throws:** right
Acquired: First-round pick in 6/82 free-agent draft

Player Summary	
Fantasy Value	$25 to $30
Card Value	30¢ to 50¢
Will	show good arm
Can't	win alone
Expect	extra bases
Don't Expect	many walks

The lovable Puckett enjoyed another outstanding season in 1994. As incredible as it seems, he is losing something to age. He can't run much anymore, doesn't have great range, and is no longer a strong pull hitter. However, Puckett has made adjustments and is still one of the top players in baseball. He makes excellent contact, fanning only 47 times last season, and drives the ball the opposite way. He slugged .540 for the 1994 season. He walked just 22 times, but his on-base percentage was still .362. His league-leading RBI total is even more impressive when you consider that he plays for a team that finished just sixth in the AL in runs scored. Puckett throws well from right field, nailing 12 baserunners last year, and he plays as hard as he can every day. He collected his 2,000th career hit last April 8 against Oakland.

Major League Batting Register

	BA	G	AB	R	H	2B	3B	HR	RBI	SB
84 AL	.296	128	557	63	165	12	5	0	31	14
85 AL	.288	161	691	80	199	29	13	4	74	21
86 AL	.328	161	680	119	223	37	6	31	96	20
87 AL	.332	157	624	96	207	32	5	28	99	12
88 AL	.356	158	657	109	234	42	5	24	121	6
89 AL	.339	159	635	75	215	45	4	9	85	11
90 AL	.298	146	551	82	164	40	3	12	80	5
91 AL	.319	152	611	92	195	29	6	15	89	11
92 AL	.329	160	639	104	210	38	4	19	110	17
93 AL	.296	156	622	89	184	39	3	22	89	8
94 AL	.317	108	439	79	139	32	3	20	112	6
Life	.318	1646	6706	988	2135	375	57	184	986	131
3 AVE	.314	156	626	101	197	41	4	23	119	11

CARLOS PULIDO

Position: Pitcher
Team: Minnesota Twins
Born: Aug. 5, 1971   Caracas, Venezuela
Height: 6'   **Weight:** 190 lbs.
Bats: left   **Throws:** left
Acquired: Signed as a free agent, 2/89

Player Summary	
Fantasy Value	$0
Card Value	12¢ to 20¢
Will	attempt control
Can't	be a starter
Expect	time at Triple-A
Don't Expect	instant success

Desperate for left-handed starting pitchers, Minnesota began 1994 with rookie Pulido in their rotation. He was 10-6 with a 4.19 ERA at Triple-A Portland in 1993, but he had made just 27 professional starts. With fellow portsider Jim Deshaies struggling and no other options, the Twins bit the bullet and used Pulido. He was not ready for the majors and struggled from the outset of the 1994 campaign before finally being sent to the bullpen in July. Not a power pitcher, he made his mark by showing good location in each of his minor-league stops. Unfortunately, he had serious control problems in Minnesota last year. In addition to giving up over four walks a game, he allowed 25 doubles and 17 homers in just 84 innings, as opponents slugged .524. Pulido does have a good pickoff move, and left-handers batted just .222 against him, implying that he may have a future as a short man. He was, in fact, a reliever until 1993 and served as a successful closer at Class-A ball in 1991, notching 17 saves at Visalia. He was 10-6 with a 4.19 ERA, 79 Ks, and 45 walks in 146 innings at Triple-A Portland in 1993.

Major League Pitching Register

	W	L	ERA	G	CG	IP	H	ER	BB	SO
94 AL	3	7	5.98	19	0	84.1	87	56	40	32
Life	3	7	5.98	19	0	84.1	87	56	40	32

PAUL QUANTRILL

Position: Pitcher
Team: Philadelphia Phillies
Born: Nov. 3, 1968   London, Ontario, Canada
Height: 6'1"   **Weight:** 185 lbs.
Bats: left   **Throws:** right
Acquired: Traded from Red Sox with Billy Hatcher for Wes Chamberlain and Mike Sullivan, 5/94

Player Summary	
Fantasy Value. . . . . $3 to $5
Card Value . . . . 8¢ to 15¢
Will . . . . throw strikes
Can't. . . . . overpower anybody
Expect . . . . bullpen time
Don't Expect . . . . a marquee role

Quantrill pitched well for the Red Sox in 1993 and was on his way to another good campaign for Beantown in 1994. In 23 innings with Boston, he allowed just five walks. However, he was dealt to Philadelphia in May and immediately had trouble adjusting to his new league. Quantrill was lit up by NL hitters at a .331 clip and failed to show the good control he'd always had with the Red Sox. Not only did he walk 10 men in his 30 innings with the Phillies, he also allowed 10 doubles and three home runs. Philadelphia responded by sending Quantrill to Triple-A Scranton in order to teach him another pitch. There, he was 3-3 with a 3.47 ERA, 36 strikeouts, and only six bases on balls in 57 innings. Once a starter, he washed out in that role and works best in middle relief. When he's on, he uses a steady diet of sinkers and sliders to induce ground balls. He has always had success stranding inherited runners. If Quantrill regains his control, he could be useful to the Phillies in 1995 as a righty set-up man.

Major League Pitching Register

	W	L	ERA	G	S	IP	H	ER	BB	SO
92 AL	2	3	2.19	27	1	49.1	55	12	15	24
93 AL	6	12	3.91	49	1	138.0	151	60	44	66
94 AL	1	1	3.52	17	0	23.0	25	9	5	15
94 NL	2	2	6.00	18	1	30.0	39	20	10	13
Life	11	18	3.78	111	3	240.1	270	101	74	118
3 AVE	4	6	3.88	42	1	87.0	99	38	27	43

TIM RAINES

Position: Outfield
Team: Chicago White Sox
Born: Sept. 16, 1959   Sanford, FL
Height: 5'8"   **Weight:** 186 lbs.
Bats: both   **Throws:** right
Acquired: Traded from Expos with Jeff Carter and Mario Brito for Barry Jones and Ivan Calderon, 12/90

Player Summary	
Fantasy Value. . . . . $9 to $11
Card Value . . . . 8¢ to 15¢
Will . . . . get walks
Can't . . . . steal big bags
Expect. . . . . improved average
Don't Expect . . . . top health

Battling aches and pains, Raines turned in another good season in 1994. Despite a sore thumb which affected his swing, he continued to show excellent on-base skills and good power. Raines didn't have a top batting average but coaxed 61 walks (and fanned just 43 times) for a .365 on-base percentage. He finished second on the Sox in runs scored and stole 13 bases without being caught. However, it's not clear whether Raines will be a regular for many more years. He is clearly losing bat speed and is increasingly susceptible to injuries. Never an exceptional outfielder, his range has declined dramatically. Raines is a possible Hall of Famer.

Major League Batting Register

	BA	G	AB	R	H	2B	3B	HR	RBI	SB
79 NL	.000	6	0	3	0	0	0	0	0	2
80 NL	.050	15	20	5	1	0	0	0	0	5
81 NL	.304	88	313	61	95	13	7	5	37	71
82 NL	.277	156	647	90	179	32	8	4	43	78
83 NL	.298	156	615	133	183	32	8	11	71	90
84 NL	.309	160	622	106	192	38	9	8	60	75
85 NL	.320	150	575	115	184	30	13	11	41	70
86 NL	.334	151	580	91	194	35	10	9	62	70
87 NL	.330	139	530	123	175	34	8	18	68	50
88 NL	.270	109	429	66	116	19	7	12	48	33
89 NL	.286	145	517	76	148	29	6	9	60	41
90 NL	.287	130	457	65	131	11	5	9	62	49
91 AL	.268	155	609	102	163	20	6	5	50	51
92 AL	.294	144	551	102	162	22	9	7	54	45
93 AL	.306	115	415	75	127	16	4	16	54	21
94 AL	.266	101	384	80	102	15	5	10	52	13
Life	.296	1920	7264	1293	2152	346	105	134	762	764
3 AVE	.287	134	502	97	144	20	7	12	60	28

MANNY RAMIREZ

Position: Outfield
Team: Cleveland Indians
Born: May 30, 1972 Santo Domingo, Dominican Republic
Height: 6′ **Weight:** 190 lbs.
Bats: right **Throws:** right
Acquired: First-round pick in 6/91 free-agent draft

Player Summary	
Fantasy Value	$13 to $16
Card Value	30¢ to 60¢
Will	show power
Can't	make contact
Expect	decent defense
Don't Expect	blinding speed

Ramirez's fine rookie campaign helped the Indians' rise in 1994. He showed terrific power, especially against left-handed pitchers, and he has the potential to grow into an impact player. The New York City native made Cleveland's Opening Day roster and became the everyday right fielder, pushing 1993 regular Wayne Kirby to the bench. Ramirez started hot, smashing eight homers by mid-May. Once pitchers got the book on him, though, he went into a slump. He struggled all year against right-handers, batting just .205, but solved lefties at a .361 clip. He should get more consistent as his career proceeds. Ramirez also needs to work on making better contact; he fanned 72 times in 1994. However, he cut down on his swing as the season went on and picked up the pace in late July. Ramirez walked 42 times in his rookie year, an excellent total for a young power hitter, and compiled a .357 on-base percentage. He throws well, notching seven assists in 1994, though he can improve his fielding. In 1993, Ramirez was named the *Baseball America* Minor League Player of the Year.

Major League Batting Register

	BA	G	AB	R	H	2B	3B	HR	RBI	SB
93 AL	.170	22	53	5	9	1	0	2	5	0
94 AL	.269	91	290	51	78	22	0	17	60	4
Life	.254	113	343	56	87	23	0	19	65	4

PAT RAPP

Position: Pitcher
Team: Florida Marlins
Born: July 13, 1967 Jennings, LA
Height: 6′3″ **Weight:** 205 lbs.
Bats: right **Throws:** right
Acquired: First-round pick from Giants in 11/92 expansion draft

Player Summary	
Fantasy Value	$1 to $3
Card Value	6¢ to 10¢
Will	be durable
Can't	stay consistent
Expect	control troubles
Don't Expect	high K totals

Two starts Rapp made within 10 days in 1994 sum up his season perfectly. He blanked the Rockies July 22 on just three hits and three walks, while fanning eight. Then, on Aug. 1, he lost to the Cubs, allowing six walks in four innings, striking out just one, flinging a wild pitch, and hitting a batter. Rapp had some outstanding stretches last season, and he ended with a fine earned run average, but much of his performance was mediocre. Like other young Marlins hurlers, Rapp throws reasonably hard—relying on a hard sinkerball—but he has poor command. He walked nearly five men per game in 1994 and registered a poor strikeout-to-innings ratio. He is a ground-ball pitcher, but often he makes mistakes high in the strike zone. Those mistakes turned into 13 homers last season. Left-handers compiled a .316 batting average off Rapp in 1994, but righties could only manage a .213 mark. He is durable and has a fine pickoff move. Rapp is promising, but he can't progress without some improvement in control.

Major League Pitching Register

	W	L	ERA	G	CG	IP	H	ER	BB	SO
92 NL	0	2	7.20	3	0	10.0	8	8	6	3
93 NL	4	6	4.02	16	1	94.0	101	42	39	57
94 NL	7	8	3.85	24	2	133.1	132	57	69	75
Life	11	16	4.06	43	3	237.1	241	107	114	135
2 AVE	7	9	3.91	25	2	141.1	143	61	68	81

JEFF REBOULET

Position: Infield
Team: Minnesota Twins
Born: April 30, 1964 Dayton, OH
Height: 6′ **Weight:** 169 lbs.
Bats: right **Throws:** right
Acquired: 10th-round pick in 6/86 free-agent draft

Player Summary	
Fantasy Value	$0
Card Value	7¢ to 10¢
Will	fill in
Can't	show speed
Expect	success against lefties
Don't Expect	an everyday job

The utility infielder nicknamed "Inspector Clouseau" shocked everyone in baseball with a power binge in June. A .392 stretch late in the month helped to elevate Reboulet's statistics to a .321 average and a .482 slugging percentage. Of course, he cooled off as the campaign progressed. He really has never hit much during his nine-year pro career. However, Tom Kelly ended up using Reboulet at all four infield positions, in the outfield, and even at designated hitter in 1994. Any offense is a bonus from the reliable Reboulet, who is in the majors mostly for his glove and versatility. He has a steady glove and decent range at all infield spots. He has little speed and strikes out far too often, but did take 18 walks in 1994 for a .327 on-base percentage. He has hit over .300 against left-handers over the last two seasons. Reboulet has done far more in the majors than his poor minor-league record gave indication that he would. His best batting averages were a .287 mark in Class-A in 1986 and .286 at Triple-A in 1992.

Major League Batting Register

	BA	G	AB	R	H	2B	3B	HR	RBI	SB
92 AL	.190	73	137	15	26	7	1	1	16	3
93 AL	.258	109	240	33	62	8	0	1	15	5
94 AL	.259	74	189	28	49	11	1	3	23	0
Life	.242	256	566	76	137	26	2	5	54	8
2 AVE	.259	107	253	36	66	12	1	3	24	3

JODY REED

Position: Second base
Team: Milwaukee Brewers
Born: July 26, 1962 Tampa, FL
Height: 5′9″ **Weight:** 165 lbs.
Bats: right **Throws:** right
Acquired: Signed as a minor-league free agent, 2/94

Player Summary	
Fantasy Value	$4 to $6
Card Value	6¢ to 10¢
Will	hit consistently
Can't	get acclaim
Expect	fine glovework
Don't Expect	extra-base hits

Reed was offered a multiyear deal from the Dodgers last winter, but he held out for more money. Los Angeles then traded for Delino DeShields, leaving Reed in the cold. The former Red Sox second sacker (and shortstop) was forced to sign with Milwaukee for much less than the Dodgers had offered. Despite this indignity, Reed played well for his new team. He led AL second basemen in assists and putouts, committed just three errors, and often made spectacular stops. He lacks speed, but he has a quick first step and plays hitters intelligently. He also kicked in on offense last year, drawing 57 walks for a .362 on-base percentage. Reed has negligible power and no speed, but he rarely strikes out. For some reason, he hit just .218 against lefties in 1994, a mark 80 points below his previous career rate. A generally consistent player, Reed has enjoyed a fine career. He is probably out of surprises, however.

Major League Batting Register

	BA	G	AB	R	H	2B	3B	HR	RBI	SB
87 AL	.300	9	30	4	9	1	1	0	8	1
88 AL	.293	109	338	60	99	23	1	1	28	1
89 AL	.288	146	524	76	151	42	2	3	40	4
90 AL	.289	155	598	70	173	45	0	5	51	4
91 AL	.283	153	618	87	175	42	2	5	60	6
92 AL	.247	143	550	64	136	27	1	3	40	7
93 NL	.276	132	445	48	123	21	2	2	31	1
94 AL	.271	108	399	48	108	22	0	2	37	5
Life	.278	955	3502	457	974	223	9	21	295	29
3 AVE	.264	142	519	60	137	26	1	3	41	5

236

STEVE REED

Position: Pitcher
Team: Colorado Rockies
Born: March 11, 1966 Los Angeles, CA
Height: 6'2" **Weight:** 202 lbs.
Bats: right **Throws:** right
Acquired: Third-round pick from Giants in 11/92 expansion draft

Player Summary	
Fantasy Value	$0
Card Value	6¢ to 8¢
Will	work often
Can't	be a closer
Expect	good control
Don't Expect	big fastball

For the past two years, the Rockies have had one of the best relievers in baseball pitching for them—half the time. More than any other Rockies pitcher, Reed suffers terribly in his home park. His ERA was 5.94 in Denver with opponents hitting .358; on the road, Reed held the opposition to a .248 average with a sparkling 1.76 ERA. The previous season, his ERA at Mile High was 6.39 and his road mark just 1.60. Rockies manager Don Baylor called on the submarining right-hander often in 1994, leading Reed to pace the major leagues with 61 appearances. Unfortunately, he had trouble coming into games with runners aboard, allowing well over half of his inherited runners to score. The former Giant has good control but below-average velocity. He was tagged for nine homers and blew seven of 10 save opportunities. Reed, who also had some elbow problems in July, probably won't be sad to see the Rockies move into brand-new Coors Field. In 1992, he saved 43 games while pitching in the minor leagues, notching 23 in Double-A and 20 in Triple-A.

Major League Pitching Register

	W	L	ERA	G	S	IP	H	ER	BB	SO
92 NL	1	0	2.30	18	0	15.2	13	4	3	11
93 NL	9	5	4.48	64	3	84.1	80	42	30	51
94 NL	3	2	3.94	61	3	64.0	79	28	26	51
Life	13	7	4.06	143	6	164.0	172	74	59	113
2 AVE	7	4	4.20	75	4	87.1	96	41	33	61

CARLOS REYES

Position: Pitcher
Team: Oakland Athletics
Born: April 4, 1969 Miami, FL
Height: 6'1" **Weight:** 190 lbs.
Bats: both **Throws:** right
Acquired: Rule 5 draft pick from Braves, 12/93

Player Summary	
Fantasy Value	$3 to $5
Card Value	10¢ to 15¢
Will	fan hitters
Can't	have major role
Expect	control woes
Don't Expect	many saves

Oakland drafted Reyes from Atlanta last winter knowing they would have to keep him on the roster all year or return him to the Braves. The Athletics used him in a swing role, shuttling him between middle relief and spot starting, and the rookie acquitted himself decently. The four-year pro had only made three career starts prior to 1994, working as a middle reliever in the prospect-heavy Atlanta system. However, Reyes showed a good, moving fastball. He fanned nearly seven men per game in his rookie season. Unfortunately, he also had his difficulties adjusting to the majors. With only 29 innings of Triple-A work under his belt, that was to be expected. He had serious control problems and allowed 20 doubles and 10 homers in his 78 innings. Opponents hit just .242 but slugged .427. With some work, the young righty could be a productive major-league pitcher in one of many roles—starter, short reliever, or swing man. At Double-A Greenville in 1993, Reyes was 8-1 with a 2.06 ERA, 57 strikeouts, 24 walks, and two saves in 70 innings and 30 appearances.

Major League Pitching Register

	W	L	ERA	G	S	IP	H	ER	BB	SO
94 AL	0	3	4.15	27	1	78.0	71	36	44	57
Life	0	3	4.15	27	1	78.0	71	36	44	57

HAROLD REYNOLDS

Position: Second base
Team: California Angels
Born: Nov. 26, 1960 Eugene, OR
Height: 5'11" **Weight:** 165 lbs.
Bats: both **Throws:** right
Acquired: Traded from Padres for Hilly Hathaway, 3/94

Player Summary	
Fantasy Value	$0
Card Value	6¢ to 10¢
Will	carry good glove
Can't	provide offense
Expect	some speed
Don't Expect	everyday duty

Reynolds came over to the Angels in the spring, but he did little for his new team. Not only did he hit for his lowest average since 1986, he drove in just 11 runs and posted a meager .310 on-base percentage. In the past, he used his great speed to contribute to the attack. In 1994, he was caught stealing seven times and hit only one triple. The former Gold Glover did show fine defensive skills last summer, registering good range numbers and committing just one error. However, he hit the bench when Marcel Lachemann took California's managerial reins, registering only 33 at bats after July 1. It appears that Reynolds's time as a regular is over. Expensive veterans on the bench are a luxury, and Reynolds hasn't been productive for several years, so he will have to scrape for work.

Major League Batting Register

	BA	G	AB	R	H	2B	3B	HR	RBI	SB
83 AL	.203	20	59	8	12	4	1	0	1	0
84 AL	.300	10	10	3	3	0	0	0	0	1
85 AL	.144	67	104	15	15	3	1	0	6	3
86 AL	.222	126	445	46	99	19	4	1	24	30
87 AL	.275	160	530	73	146	31	8	1	35	60
88 AL	.283	158	598	61	169	26	11	4	41	35
89 AL	.300	153	613	87	184	24	9	0	43	25
90 AL	.252	160	642	100	162	36	5	5	55	31
91 AL	.254	161	631	95	160	34	6	3	57	28
92 AL	.247	140	458	55	113	23	3	3	33	15
93 AL	.252	145	485	64	122	20	4	4	47	12
94 AL	.232	74	207	33	48	10	1	0	11	10
Life	.258	1374	4782	640	1233	230	53	21	353	250
3 AVE	.245	130	412	55	101	19	3	2	32	14

SHANE REYNOLDS

Position: Pitcher
Team: Houston Astros
Born: March 26, 1968 Bastrop, LA
Height: 6'3" **Weight:** 210 lbs.
Bats: right **Throws:** right
Acquired: Third-round pick in 6/89 free-agent draft

Player Summary	
Fantasy Value	$10 to $13
Card Value	8¢ to 12¢
Will	throw strikes
Can't	retire lefties
Expect	future success
Don't Expect	relief duties

The only reason Reynolds isn't already well-known is that the Astros haven't yet decided what to do with him. While he doesn't own an overpowering heater, he throws three pitches very well and has better control than almost anyone in the big leagues. Rookie hurlers with 5-to-1 strikeout-to-walk ratios don't pop up every day. Reynolds is one of the rare ones. Bouncing between long relief and the rotation, he fanned nearly a man per inning and walked fewer than two per contest last year. The only trouble that Reynolds had in 1994 was with left-handers, who batted .304 against him. He allowed 10 home runs as a result of being around the plate constantly, but with nobody on base, the homers did little damage. It's likely that Reynolds will move into the Astros' rotation on a full-time basis. He was far more successful as a starting pitcher than as a reliever in 1994. In 1993 at Triple-A Tucson, he was 10-6 with a 3.62 ERA, 106 Ks, and 21 walks in 139 innings. He was 9-8 with a 3.68 ERA, 106 strikeouts, and 34 walks for Tucson in 1992. He pitched for the University of Texas.

Major League Pitching Register

	W	L	ERA	G	S	IP	H	ER	BB	SO
92 NL	1	3	7.11	8	0	25.1	42	20	6	10
93 NL	0	0	0.82	5	0	11.0	11	1	6	10
94 NL	8	5	3.05	33	0	124.0	128	42	21	110
Life	9	8	3.54	46	0	160.1	181	63	33	130

ARMANDO REYNOSO

Position: Pitcher
Team: Colorado Rockies
Born: May 1, 1966 San Luis Potosi, Mexico
Height: 6′ **Weight:** 186 lbs.
Bats: right **Throws:** right
Acquired: Third-round pick from Braves in 11/92 expansion draft

Player Summary	
Fantasy Value.	$1 to $3
Card Value	8¢ to 12¢
Will	get many chances
Can't	count on durability
Expect	good control
Don't Expect	many strikeouts

Reynoso was the Rockies' best pitcher in 1993. He didn't even start the year with the club but, in the end, was invaluable. His performance was outstanding, especially when you consider that he worked half his games in Mile High Stadium. However, Reynoso's season was ruined by a right knee injury and, more seriously, a torn ligament in his pitching elbow. After surgery in late May, he missed the remainder of the season. He will attempt to come back in 1995, but he will probably be worked on a very lenient schedule. Although Reynoso couldn't crack the peerless Braves' rotation, he is still good enough to rate as at least a No. 3 starter on many teams. He's not by any means a strikeout pitcher, but he has good control. Reynoso also generally keeps the ball low, and this is the key to success in Denver. In 1994, he had a bit of control trouble, but if he's healthy this year, Reynoso should once again be a dependable performer. He won't be brought back too quickly. He led the Triple-A International League with a 2.61 ERA in 1991.

Major League Pitching Register

	W	L	ERA	G	CG	IP	H	ER	BB	SO
91 NL	2	1	6.17	6	0	23.1	26	16	10	10
92 NL	1	0	4.70	3	0	7.2	11	4	2	2
93 NL	12	11	4.00	30	4	189.0	206	84	63	117
94 NL	3	4	4.82	9	1	52.1	54	28	22	25
Life	18	16	4.36	48	5	272.1	297	132	97	154

ARTHUR RHODES

Position: Pitcher
Team: Baltimore Orioles
Born: Oct. 24, 1969 Waco, TX
Height: 6′2″ **Weight:** 206 lbs.
Bats: left **Throws:** left
Acquired: Second-round pick in 6/88 free-agent draft

Player Summary	
Fantasy Value.	$5 to $7
Card Value	10¢ to 15¢
Will	fan hitters
Can't	master control
Expect	fine curveball
Don't Expect	more demotions

The Orioles still haven't figured out how to cultivate Rhodes. He began the year with Baltimore, juggled good and bad games, was injured in May, was then demoted to Triple-A, recalled in June, sent back to the minors a week later, recalled again in late July, and sent back to Triple-A during the strike. Previously, the Baltimore brain trust had said Rhodes would pitch all year at Rochester. He racked up a 6-3 record with a 2.75 ERA in Triple-A, fanning nearly a man an inning. Unfortunately, he struggled in Baltimore. Poor 1994 performances from other Oriole lefties indicate that Rhodes will likely be in the rotation this season. In limited 1994 duty with the big club, he still tossed three complete games, including two shutouts just before the strike. A power pitcher all the way, he has a fine fastball, a big curve, and a sharp-breaking slider. He did allow seven home runs, often laying pitches over the plate when behind in the count. A small improvement in control will mean big success for Rhodes.

Major League Pitching Register

	W	L	ERA	G	CG	IP	H	ER	BB	SO
91 AL	0	3	8.00	8	0	36.0	47	32	23	23
92 AL	7	5	3.63	15	2	94.1	87	38	38	77
93 AL	5	6	6.51	17	0	85.2	91	62	49	49
94 AL	3	5	5.81	10	3	52.2	51	34	30	47
Life	15	19	5.56	50	5	268.2	276	166	140	196
2 AVE	6	6	5.00	16	1	90.2	89	50	44	63

TUFFY RHODES

Position: Outfield
Team: Chicago Cubs
Born: Aug. 21, 1968 Cincinnati, OH
Height: 6′ **Weight:** 195 lbs.
Bats: left **Throws:** left
Acquired: Traded to Royals for Paul
Assenmacher, 7/93; Royals sent
Assenmacher to Yankees for John Habyan
to complete three-way trade.

Player Summary	
Fantasy Value	$4 to $6
Card Value	6¢ to 10¢
Will	show some power
Can't	keep regular job
Expect	defensive woes
Don't Expect	high average

The Cubs gave Rhodes the leadoff and
center field jobs last season, hoping he
could repeat the 30-homer performance he
had Triple-A in 1993. He started 1994 with
a bang, bashing three mammoth homers
on Opening Day at Wrigley Field off Doc
Gooden. Rhodes was the first player in NL
history to notch three round-trippers on the
season's inaugural day. He hit .290 in April,
but from there it was downhill for the former
Astro flychaser. NL pitchers figured him out
quickly, working him inside and high, and
Rhodes's numbers began to sag. While he
drew 33 walks in 1994, his .318 on-base
percentage was abysmal for a leadoff hitter, and Rhodes lost that job in June. He
also fanned 64 times and was caught stealing four times. Rhodes fared well in Wrigley
Field; he hit just .207 on the road and,
oddly, only .225 against right-handers. In
addition, he showed poor defensive skills in
center field, with five errors and only three
assists.

Major League Batting Register

	BA	G	AB	R	H	2B	3B	HR	RBI	SB
90 NL	.244	38	86	12	21	6	1	1	3	4
91 NL	.213	44	136	7	29	3	1	1	12	2
92 NL	.000	5	4	0	0	0	0	0	0	0
93 NL	.278	20	54	12	15	2	1	3	7	2
94 NL	.234	95	269	39	63	17	0	8	19	6
Life	.233	202	549	70	128	28	3	13	41	14

JOSE RIJO

Position: Pitcher
Team: Cincinnati Reds
Born: May 13, 1965 San Cristobal,
Dominican Republic
Height: 6′2″ **Weight:** 210 lbs.
Bats: right **Throws:** right
Acquired: Traded from Athletics with Tim
Birtsas for Dave Parker, 12/87

Player Summary	
Fantasy Value	$20 to $25
Card Value	10¢ to 15¢
Will	throw tough slider
Can't	get a break
Expect	great velocity
Don't Expect	control woes

Rijo has been a consistently excellent
moundsman since coming to the Reds.
Last summer, in a *Sporting News* poll, NL
hitters chose his slider as the league's best
(in an almost-unanimous vote). Rijo also
has a superior fastball, good control, and a
knack for the strikeout pitch. He finished
second in the league in punchouts in 1994
after pacing the NL the season before. He
uses a big windup to generate some of his
velocity, and therefore he is easy to run on.
However, he allows few baserunners and
doesn't walk batters much. Rijo is also a respectable hitter, improving over the years.
Ending the year on a high note, he fanned
12 Dodgers and allowed just four hits in his
last start Aug. 11, but lost 2-0. This was a
typical Rijo outing; he had the worst run
support of any Cincinnati starter in 1994.

Major League Pitching Register

	W	L	ERA	G	CG	IP	H	ER	BB	SO
84 AL	2	8	4.76	24	0	62.1	74	33	33	47
85 AL	6	4	3.53	12	0	63.2	57	25	28	65
86 AL	9	11	4.65	39	4	193.2	172	100	108	176
87 AL	2	7	5.90	21	1	82.1	106	54	41	67
88 NL	13	8	2.39	49	0	162.0	120	43	63	160
89 NL	7	6	2.84	19	1	111.0	101	35	48	86
90 NL	14	8	2.70	29	7	197.0	151	59	78	152
91 NL	15	6	2.51	30	3	204.1	165	57	55	172
92 NL	15	10	2.56	33	2	211.0	185	60	44	171
93 NL	14	9	2.48	36	2	257.1	218	71	62	227
94 NL	9	6	3.08	26	2	172.1	177	59	52	171
Life	106	83	3.12	318	22	1717.0	1526	596	612	1494
3 AVE	14	9	2.71	35	2	237.1	217	71	60	213

CAL RIPKEN

Position: Shortstop
Team: Baltimore Orioles
Born: Aug. 24, 1960   Havre de Grace, MD
Height: 6'4"   **Weight:** 220 lbs.
Bats: right   **Throws:** right
Acquired: Second-round pick in 6/78 free-agent draft

Player Summary	
Fantasy Value	$15 to $18
Card Value	35¢ to 60¢
Will	hit anything
Can't	steal bases
Expect	steady defense
Don't Expect	days off

The hard-working Ripken played in his 2,000th straight contest last Aug. 1 in Minnesota, and now it appears a cinch that he will break Lou Gehrig's consecutive-games-played mark. Ripken got rid of some bad habits at the plate, shortened his stroke, and, as a result, enjoyed his best offensive performance in three seasons. Though he didn't hit for his old-time power, he batted over .300 against both lefties and righties, at home and on the road. He walked just 32 times last year, but his on-base percentage was still .364. Ripken makes good contact, fanning only 52 times in 1994, and is a good hit-and-run man. He has never had much speed, but he remains a dependable shortstop. Ripken's seven errors in 1994 are impressively low.

Major League Batting Register

	BA	G	AB	R	H	2B	3B	HR	RBI	SB
81 AL	.128	23	39	1	5	0	0	0	0	0
82 AL	.264	160	598	90	158	32	5	28	93	3
83 AL	.318	162	663	121	211	47	2	27	102	0
84 AL	.304	162	641	103	195	37	7	27	86	2
85 AL	.282	161	642	116	181	32	5	26	110	2
86 AL	.282	162	627	98	177	35	1	25	81	4
87 AL	.252	162	624	97	157	28	3	27	98	3
88 AL	.264	161	575	87	152	25	1	23	81	2
89 AL	.257	162	646	80	166	30	0	21	93	3
90 AL	.250	161	600	78	150	28	4	21	84	3
91 AL	.323	162	650	99	210	46	5	34	114	6
92 AL	.251	162	637	73	160	29	1	14	72	4
93 AL	.257	162	641	87	165	26	3	24	90	1
94 AL	.315	112	444	71	140	19	3	13	75	1
Life	.277	2074	6027	1201	2227	414	40	310	1179	34
3 AVE	.274	161	634	87	174	27	3	19	89	2

BILL RISLEY

Position: Pitcher
Team: Seattle Mariners
Born: May 29, 1967   Chicago, IL
Height: 6'2"   **Weight:** 215 lbs.
Bats: right   **Throws:** right
Acquired: Claimed on waivers from Expos, 3/94

Player Summary	
Fantasy Value	$5 to $7
Card Value	7¢ to 10¢
Will	get strikeouts
Can't	be wild again
Expect	some home runs
Don't Expect	many hits

All Risley ever needed was a chance to pitch, but he was buried in Montreal's deep minor-league system. Actually, there are many experts who feel that the Expos were trying to hide him. Finally, Montreal was forced to waive the fireballer, and he found himself in the Mariners bullpen. The man previously called "Wild Bill" tamed his control, and everyone involved reaped the benefits. Risley, working in the middle for Seattle, fanned more than a man an inning and showed spectacular control. Opponents compiled a minuscule .170 batting average against the overpowering right-hander, with just a .246 on-base percentage. Risley stranded 70 percent of his inherited runners. He also allowed seven home runs, the result of good control and amazing velocity. He missed a few days at midseason with a shoulder strain, but he came back strong. He was the surprise find of 1994 and looks to have a bright future in Seattle. The downside is that he blew all three of his save chances in 1994. He may not be ready to move into a closer's role this summer.

Major League Pitching Register

	W	L	ERA	G	S	IP	H	ER	BB	SO
92 NL	1	0	1.80	1	0	5.0	4	1	1	2
93 NL	0	0	6.00	2	0	3.0	2	2	2	2
94 AL	9	6	3.44	37	0	52.1	31	20	19	61
Life	10	6	3.43	40	0	60.1	37	23	22	65

KEVIN RITZ

Position: Pitcher
Team: Colorado Rockies
Born: June 8, 1965 Eatontown, NJ
Height: 6'4" **Weight:** 220 lbs.
Bats: right **Throws:** right
Acquired: Second-round pick from Tigers in 11/92 expansion draft

Player Summary	
Fantasy Value	$0
Card Value	5¢ to 7¢
Will	get his chances
Can't	show consistency
Expect	good velocity
Don't Expect	walk-free games

Ritz had a few good starts in 1994, but he showed no consistency. He didn't make the Rockies staff in spring 1993 and chose free agency instead of being sent down to Triple-A. Cleveland was going to sign him, but the Indians backed off when medical tests showed elbow damage. Colorado then paid for Ritz's "Tommy John" surgery, which shelved him for a year. He recovered in 1994 with his velocity intact, but he still has no idea where his pitches are going. Ritz went an impressive 5-0 in Triple-A, joined Colorado's battered staff, and won his first big-league game in nearly two years last May 30. Unfortunately, good outings for Ritz were few and far between. He walked over four men a game, allowed right-handers a .331 average, tossed six wild pitches, and had a 6.64 ERA on the road. The former Tiger has little chance to ever be dependable, but he has a fine arm and will get plenty of chances. Colorado's desperation brought him back to the majors and may put Ritz in the rotation in 1995.

Major League Pitching Register

	W	L	ERA	G	CG	IP	H	ER	BB	SO
89 AL	4	6	4.38	12	1	74.0	75	36	44	56
90 AL	0	4	11.05	4	0	7.1	14	9	14	3
91 AL	0	3	11.74	11	0	15.1	17	20	22	9
92 AL	2	5	5.60	23	0	80.1	88	50	44	57
94 NL	5	6	5.62	15	0	73.2	88	46	35	53
Life	11	24	5.78	65	1	250.2	282	161	159	178
2 AVE	5	7	5.61	22	0	91.2	106	57	47	66

BEN RIVERA

Position: Pitcher
Team: Philadelphia Phillies
Born: Jan. 11, 1969 San Pedro de Macoris, Dominican Republic
Height: 6'6" **Weight:** 230 lbs.
Bats: right **Throws:** right
Acquired: Traded from Braves for Donnie Elliott, 5/92

Player Summary	
Fantasy Value	$0
Card Value	6¢ to 10¢
Will	bring heat
Can't	afford wildness
Expect	frequent starts
Don't Expect	ground balls

Rivera won Philadelphia's No. 4 starter job in spring training, but he slumped as the season began. He pitched very poorly and had lost an amazing amount of velocity. Even though Rivera said nothing was physically wrong, some felt he was missing as much as 10 mph from his fastball. After a poor game in early May, he was moved to middle relief and shortly afterward placed on the disabled list with a strained right rotator cuff. Rivera rested until late July but was not effective when he returned. At least he appeared to be throwing hard, and he will try to return strong in 1995. Rivera is a power pitcher with mediocre control at best. Opponents in 1994 notched almost five and one-quarter walks per nine innings against Rivera. He allowed seven home runs in his limited appearances last year, and opponents compiled a .274 batting average. For some reason, even though he's a fly-ball pitcher, Rivera's career ERA is markedly worse on artificial turf. The Phillies, with an injury-plagued staff, are counting on Rivera this year.

Major League Pitching Register

	W	L	ERA	G	CG	IP	H	ER	BB	SO
92 NL	7	4	3.07	28	4	117.1	99	40	45	77
93 NL	13	9	5.02	30	1	163.0	175	91	85	123
94 NL	3	4	6.87	9	0	38.0	40	29	22	19
Life	23	17	4.52	67	5	318.1	314	160	152	219
2 AVE	10	7	4.21	29	3	140.1	137	66	65	100

KEVIN ROBERSON

Position: Outfield
Team: Chicago Cubs
Born: Jan. 29, 1968 Decatur, IL
Height: 6'4" **Weight:** 210 lbs.
Bats: both **Throws:** right
Acquired: 15th-round pick in 6/88 free-agent draft

Player Summary	
Fantasy Value	$1 to $3
Card Value	6¢ to 8¢
Will	chase bad pitches
Can't	count on job
Expect	good power
Don't Expect	top defense

The Cubs called on Roberson often in 1994, but he was seldom in the starting lineup. The switch-hitting outfielder was their best pinch hitter, going 9-for-35 in the role, including three doubles and three home runs (tying a team record). Unfortunately, his season ended earlier than expected. After a tough at bat July 4 against Colorado, he punched a wall and broke his hand. Roberson has more than just a physical recovery to work on, however. He continues to struggle unsuccessfully with the strike zone. Although the powerful Roberson compiled a .509 slugging percentage in 1994, he drew just two walks and fanned 14 times. His on-base percentage was an unacceptable .271. In addition, he batted just .209 against left-handers, despite homering off them three times. He's had success batting against Triple-A pitching, but has been inept in the big leagues. Roberson has only average defensive skills and little running speed. He won't hold a starting job in the majors without patching up the holes in his offense.

Major League Batting Register

	BA	G	AB	R	H	2B	3B	HR	RBI	SB
93 NL	.189	62	180	23	34	4	1	9	27	0
94 NL	.218	44	55	8	12	4	0	4	9	0
Life	.196	106	235	31	46	8	1	13	36	0

BIP ROBERTS

Position: Second base; third base
Team: San Diego Padres
Born: Oct. 27, 1963 Berkeley, CA
Height: 5'7" **Weight:** 165 lbs.
Bats: both **Throws:** right
Acquired: Signed as a free agent, 1/94

Player Summary	
Fantasy Value	$16 to $19
Card Value	6¢ to 10¢
Will	get on base
Can't	find power stroke
Expect	decent speed
Don't Expect	a Gold Glove

The once and future Padre leadoff man began 1994 in a funk. Beset by emotional problems, Roberts slumped terribly at bat. By mid-May, he was hitting just .207 and left the team for a few days when his migraine headaches became intolerable. However, shortly afterward Roberts turned things around and ended up having a good season. He hit for his usual fine average, stole some bases, and showed far more durability than he had when he was with the Reds in 1993. Unfortunately, Roberts must improve in order to be the All-Star he feels he should be. He walked just 39 times last season, hit for negligible power, and didn't run as much as he might have. He needs to do more than hit singles to be an impact player. Roberts doesn't struggle from either side of the plate. He plays a decent second base and third base. Since his prime skill is reaching base, Roberts would almost certainly be a more helpful player with a good team.

Major League Batting Register

	BA	G	AB	R	H	2B	3B	HR	RBI	SB
86 NL	.253	101	241	34	61	5	2	1	12	14
88 NL	.333	5	9	1	3	0	0	0	0	0
89 NL	.301	117	329	81	99	15	8	3	25	21
90 NL	.309	149	556	104	172	36	3	9	44	46
91 NL	.281	117	424	66	119	13	3	3	32	26
92 NL	.323	147	532	92	172	34	6	4	45	44
93 NL	.240	83	292	46	70	13	0	1	18	26
94 NL	.320	105	403	52	129	15	5	2	31	21
Life	.296	824	2786	476	825	131	27	23	207	198
3 AVE	.304	126	464	70	141	23	4	3	36	33

CARLOS RODRIGUEZ

Position: Shortstop
Team: Boston Red Sox
Born: Nov. 1, 1967 Mexico City, Mexico
Height: 5'9" **Weight:** 160 lbs.
Bats: both **Throws:** right
Acquired: Signed as a minor-league free agent, 10/93

Player Summary	
Fantasy Value	$0
Card Value	6¢ to 8¢
Will	show strong glove
Can't	run well
Expect	utility role
Don't Expect	any power

Formerly a prospect in the Yankees' organization, Rodriguez was purchased by New York from the Mexico City Tigers in 1986. He joined the Boston system last winter. He was not known for his bat, owning only three professional home runs entering 1994, but instead for his fine range and arm at shortstop. Carlos, one of four unrelated players named "Rodriguez" playing in '94 with the Triple-A Pawtucket PawSox, started out hot. He connected for two dingers and a .315 average before receiving the call to Boston on May 5. He hit surprisingly well with the Red Sox, fanning only 13 times and walking 11 for a .330 on-base percentage. He also compiled a batting average over .300 against left-handers. He is tough to strike out. He has little speed or power, and he probably can't keep his average at his 1994 level, but he did quite well in his Boston trial. Rodriguez hadn't done nearly so well in a 1991 stint with New York. While he doesn't project as a regular, Rodriguez fields with enough skill to stick as a utility infielder.

HENRY RODRIGUEZ

Position: Outfield
Team: Los Angeles Dodgers
Born: Nov. 8, 1967 Santo Domingo, Dominican Republic
Height: 6'1" **Weight:** 210 lbs.
Bats: left **Throws:** left
Acquired: Signed as a free agent, 7/85

Player Summary	
Fantasy Value	$6 to $8
Card Value	6¢ to 10¢
Will	take big swing
Can't	get on base
Expect	platoon role
Don't Expect	great defense

At the end of May, Rodriguez was hitting .336 and causing Dodger fans to believe that their left fielder had turned a corner. Unfortunately, it was not to be. His average cooled off considerably, as NL pitchers continued to exploit his absolute lack of strike-zone judgement. By year's end, his on-base percentage had dropped to a poor .307 as a result of drawing just 17 walks. Rodriguez also fanned 58 times. In addition, he failed to deliver the power that he had shown during his pro career. Although he had a .405 slugging percentage, it was not enough for a mediocre defensive outfielder with no on-base skills and little speed. Dodger manager Tommy Lasorda firmly believed Rodriguez was a platoon player, giving him just 20 at bats against left-handed pitchers over the last two seasons. (Oddly, he did go 5-for-14 with two homers versus portsiders in 1994.) Perhaps Rodriguez could survive as a platoon designated hitter, but until he improves his strike-zone judgement and his defense, he appears miscast as an everyday player.

Major League Batting Register

	BA	G	AB	R	H	2B	3B	HR	RBI	SB
92 NL	.219	53	146	11	32	7	0	3	14	0
93 NL	.222	76	176	20	39	10	0	8	23	1
94 NL	.268	104	306	33	82	14	2	8	49	0
Life	.244	233	628	64	153	31	2	19	86	1
2 AVE	.255	111	304	33	77	15	1	10	46	1

Major League Batting Register

	BA	G	AB	R	H	2B	3B	HR	RBI	SB
91 AL	.189	15	37	1	7	0	0	0	2	0
94 AL	.287	57	174	15	50	14	1	1	13	1
Life	.270	72	211	16	57	14	1	1	15	1

IVAN RODRIGUEZ

Position: Catcher
Team: Texas Rangers
Born: Nov. 30, 1971 Vega Baja, Puerto Rico
Height: 5'9" **Weight:** 205 lbs.
Bats: right **Throws:** right
Acquired: Signed as a free agent, 7/88

Player Summary	
Fantasy Value	$15 to $18
Card Value	20¢ to 30¢
Will	excel all around
Can't	run on him
Expect	improvement
Don't Expect	defensive woes

No questions remain about "Pudge" Rodriguez's ability, in the field or at bat. He has the best raw defensive skills of any AL catcher, and his arm is second only to that of Ron Karkovice. Rodriguez handles his pitchers well and calls a good game. He has also gained a great deal of growth as a hitter in his short career. He made excellent contact in 1994, fanning only 42 times, and took 31 walks on his way to a fine .360 on-base percentage. The power has arrived as well, as he reached a career high in home runs. His power should just increase with time. While he doesn't have blazing speed, he runs as well as any catcher and doesn't make many baserunning mistakes. The few knocks on Rodriguez concern his attitude. There had been some who viewed him as selfish and immature, or too intense. With time, these concerns should fade. Already a three-time All-Star and a Gold Glove winner, Rodriguez has already eclipsed the best performances of the man he was once seen as a "protégé" of—Benito Santiago.

RICH RODRIGUEZ

Position: Pitcher
Team: St. Louis Cardinals
Born: March 1, 1963 Los Angeles, CA
Height: 6' **Weight:** 200 lbs.
Bats: left **Throws:** left
Acquired: Claimed on waivers from Marlins, 3/94

Player Summary	
Fantasy Value	$1
Card Value	5¢ to 7¢
Will	appear often
Can't	blow hitters away
Expect	work in middle
Don't Expect	perfect control

Rodriguez was sent from San Diego to Florida in the 1993 Gary Sheffield deal. The Marlins waived Rodriguez last spring, however, and the desperate Cardinals immediately snatched him up for their depleted bullpen. The veteran reliever turned in a good, but atypical, season in 1994. In the past, Rodriguez had trouble with left-handed hitters but mastered righties. In 1994, he held fellow portsiders to a .183 mark and one home run, but right-handers hit .300 (55 points above their career mark against Rodriguez). He led the team in appearances, but he often faced just a hitter or two. Rodriguez improved his location somewhat last year and struck out more hitters than usual. He relies on off-speed pitches rather than a big fastball, and probably wouldn't have a job in the show if he didn't throw with his left hand. He walked almost four batters per nine innings last summer, which is an unacceptable ratio for someone who doesn't have outstanding stuff. He has a decent pickoff move.

Major League Batting Register

	BA	G	AB	R	H	2B	3B	HR	RBI	SB
91 AL	.264	88	280	24	74	16	0	3	27	0
92 AL	.260	123	420	39	109	16	1	8	37	0
93 AL	.273	137	473	56	129	28	4	10	66	8
94 AL	.298	99	363	56	108	19	1	16	57	6
Life	.273	447	1536	175	420	79	6	37	187	14
3 AVE	.278	133	468	58	130	24	2	14	61	5

Major League Pitching Register

	W	L	ERA	G	S	IP	H	ER	BB	SO
90 NL	1	1	2.83	32	1	47.2	52	15	16	22
91 NL	3	1	3.26	64	0	80.0	66	29	44	40
92 NL	6	3	2.37	61	0	91.0	77	24	29	64
93 NL	2	4	3.79	70	3	76.0	73	32	33	43
94 NL	3	5	4.03	56	0	60.1	62	27	26	43
Life	15	14	3.22	283	4	355.0	330	127	148	212
3 AVE	4	5	3.36	70	1	84.0	79	31	33	56

KENNY ROGERS

Position: Pitcher
Team: Texas Rangers
Born: Nov. 10, 1964   Savannah, GA
Height: 6'1"   **Weight:** 205 lbs.
Bats: left   **Throws:** left
Acquired: 39th-round pick in 6/82 free-agent draft

Player Summary	
Fantasy Value	$11 to $14
Card Value	6¢ to 10¢
Will	cash in
Can't	keep ball in park
Expect	good heat
Don't Expect	return to pen

Rogers threw the 14th perfect game in baseball history last July 28, shutting down California at The Ballpark in Arlington. The gem served notice that Rogers has become one of baseball's better left-handed starters. He continues to work on his control problems, slicing his walks per game from the three that he compiled in 1993 to just over two and one-half in 1994. He was able to accomplish this without sacrificing the good fastball and fine movement that get him strikeouts. However, he still has trouble getting ahead in the count and pays for it in extra-base hits. Rogers allowed a whopping 38 doubles and 24 dingers last year, which contributed to his somewhat high earned run average. He did improve against right-handers in 1994, holding them to a .252 mark, but slumped against fellow lefties, who hit .311. The very durable lefty finished tied for fourth in the league with six complete games and has matured since being converted from relief in 1992.

Major League Pitching Register

	W	L	ERA	G	CG	IP	H	ER	BB	SO
89 AL	3	4	2.93	73	0	73.2	60	24	42	63
90 AL	10	6	3.13	69	0	97.2	93	34	42	74
91 AL	10	10	5.42	63	0	109.2	121	66	61	73
92 AL	3	6	3.09	81	0	78.2	80	27	26	70
93 AL	16	10	4.10	35	5	208.1	210	95	71	140
94 AL	11	8	4.46	24	6	167.1	169	83	52	120
Life	53	44	4.03	345	11	735.1	733	329	294	540
3 AVE	11	9	4.11	50	4	174.1	176	80	57	126

MEL ROJAS

Position: Pitcher
Team: Montreal Expos
Born: Dec. 10, 1968   Haina, Dominican Republic
Height: 5'11"   **Weight:** 195 lbs.
Bats: right   **Throws:** right
Acquired: Signed as a free agent, 11/85

Player Summary	
Fantasy Value	$10 to $13
Card Value	6¢ to 10¢
Will	search for role
Can't	allow homers
Expect	some saves
Don't Expect	many walks

Rojas pitched very well in 1994, looking almost nothing like the pitcher who struggled in 1993. He fanned a man an inning, cut down his walks considerably, and overpowered both left-handed (.226) and right-handed (.228) hitters. However, Rojas wasn't perfect. He had some rough stretches and allowed 11 homers last year. Fortunately, few men were on base for the blasts. Rojas also took the closer reins for a spell, saving games when John Wetteland went on the disabled list in April. When Wetteland returned, Rojas unhappily went back to his set-up role. The two pitchers work well together: The Expos were 14-0 in the last 14 games the two pitched in. Rojas has an outstanding fastball and a baffling forkball. And he is durable. He has enough talent to close games for most teams in the majors, and he possesses the makeup for late relief. There should be plenty of teams who show interest in him. The Expos are likely to hang on to both Rojas and Wetteland for as long as they can, though.

Major League Pitching Register

	W	L	ERA	G	S	IP	H	ER	BB	SO
90 NL	3	1	3.60	23	1	40.0	34	16	24	26
91 NL	3	3	3.75	37	6	48.0	42	20	13	37
92 NL	7	1	1.43	68	10	100.2	71	16	34	70
93 NL	5	8	2.95	66	10	88.1	80	29	30	48
94 NL	3	2	3.32	58	16	84.0	71	31	21	84
Life	21	15	2.79	252	43	361.0	298	112	122	265
3 AVE	5	4	2.60	72	14	102.1	84	30	31	79

JOHN ROPER

Position: Pitcher
Team: Cincinnati Reds
Born: Nov. 21, 1971   Moore County, NC
Height: 6′   **Weight:** 170 lbs.
Bats: right   **Throws:** right
Acquired: 12th-round pick in 6/90 free-agent draft

Player Summary

Fantasy Value	$6 to $8
Card Value	8¢ to 12¢
Will	struggle with control
Can't	dominate
Expect	success vs. righties
Don't Expect	many strikeouts

Roper has a truckload of potential, but he is struggling to put his talent to work in the majors. He throws reasonably hard, but he relies on a knuckle-curve hybrid rather than an overwhelming fastball. He doesn't strike many hitters out. Roper was 7-0 with a 2.17 ERA at Triple-A Indianapolis before his 1994 call-up to Cincinnati, but even at Triple-A, he fanned just 33 in 58 innings. He posted a fine 6-2 record in his 15 Cincinnati starts. He still has skeletons in the closet, however. Left-handers hit .321 against Roper with an amazing 10 homers last year. The slightly built righty hasn't yet mastered his control and is very easy to run on. Roper's success was partially due to the six and one-half runs of support per game he received from his Reds teammates. He did have some fine starts, and he held right-handed hitters to a minuscule .201 average. If he can get his pitches to move in on lefties, Roper has a chance to be a productive starter. In 1993 at Indianapolis, he was 3-3 with a 4.47 ERA. He was 10-9 with a 4.03 ERA at Double-A Chattanooga in 1992.

Major League Pitching Register

	W	L	ERA	G	CG	IP	H	ER	BB	SO
93 NL	2	5	5.63	16	0	80.0	92	50	36	54
94 NL	6	2	4.50	16	0	92.0	90	46	30	51
Life	8	7	5.02	32	0	172.0	182	96	66	105
2 AVE	5	4	4.93	19	0	105.0	109	57	39	63

RICH ROWLAND

Position: Catcher
Team: Boston Red Sox
Born: Feb. 25, 1967   Cloverdale, CA
Height: 6′1″   **Weight:** 215 lbs.
Bats: right   **Throws:** right
Acquired: Traded from Tigers for John Flaherty, 4/94

Player Summary

Fantasy Value	$1
Card Value	5¢ to 7¢
Will	show good power
Can't	hit for average
Expect	OK throwing
Don't Expect	regular duty

When Rowland was swapped for fellow backup receiver John Flaherty last spring, the move didn't make headlines. It was simply a case of two organizations giving up on midlevel catching prospects, exchanging Flaherty's defense for Rowland's bat. Despite a mediocre season, Rowland did wrest away the Red Sox's backup job from Dave Valle, forcing the veteran to be traded to Milwaukee. Rowland has excellent home-run pop, hitting five dingers against right-handed pitchers and four against lefties. Oddly, he hit just .189 on the road, but he connected for six of his home runs in away games. One reason Rowland won't ever be a regular catcher is his inability to make consistent contact. He fanned 35 times last year, and walked just 11. His on-base percentage was a miserable .295. He doesn't add speed or defense. In 1994, he threw out 36 percent of baserunners trying to steal, but he showed little mobility behind the dish and committed six errors. Besides home runs, Rowland offers little.

Major League Batting Register

	BA	G	AB	R	H	2B	3B	HR	RBI	SB
90 AL	.158	7	19	3	3	1	0	0	0	0
91 AL	.250	4	4	0	1	0	0	0	1	0
92 AL	.214	6	14	2	3	0	0	0	4	0
93 AL	.217	21	46	2	10	3	0	4	0	
94 AL	.229	46	118	14	27	3	0	9	20	0
Life	.219	84	201	21	44	7	0	9	25	0

KIRK RUETER

Position: Pitcher
Team: Montreal Expos
Born: Dec. 1, 1970 Nashville, IL
Height: 6'3" **Weight:** 190 lbs.
Bats: left **Throws:** left
Acquired: 19th-round pick in 6/91 free-agent draft

Player Summary

Fantasy Value	$1 to $3
Card Value	10¢ to 15¢
Will	stifle lefties
Can't	overwhelm with heat
Expect	good control
Don't Expect	1993 repeat

Rueter's 1994 won-lost record is misleading. He didn't really pitch well, and he would have had a substandard mark if the Expos hadn't scored well over six runs per game while he was on the mound. He has underwhelming stuff. He has to move the ball around and trick hitters to be effective. Unfortunately, he allowed well over a hit per inning last year, and opponents compiled a .442 slugging percentage. Left-handers are almost helpless against Rueter, hitting just .213 last year, but righties tagged him for a .316 average and 10 home runs. He does have excellent control, allowing only two and one-quarter walks per nine innings. The way that batters hit him, he should even cut the number of walks allowed even down from that, though. His stuff is so mediocre that he lives on the edge even when he's effective. Most successful finesse pitchers induce ground balls, but he has not shown that ability. Few pitchers who don't either get strikeouts or ground-ball outs have long careers. Rueter may have to return to the minors to refine his game.

Major League Pitching Register

	W	L	ERA	G	CG	IP	H	ER	BB	SO
93 NL	8	0	2.73	14	1	85.2	85	26	18	31
94 NL	7	3	5.17	20	0	92.1	106	53	23	50
Life	15	3	3.99	34	1	178.0	191	79	41	81
2 AVE	9	2	4.20	21	1	107.2	117	50	25	51

BRUCE RUFFIN

Position: Pitcher
Team: Colorado Rockies
Born: Oct. 4, 1963 Lubbock, TX
Height: 6'2" **Weight:** 213 lbs.
Bats: both **Throws:** left
Acquired: Signed as a free agent, 12/92

Player Summary

Fantasy Value	$10 to $13
Card Value	5¢ to 7¢
Will	appear frequently
Can't	show great control
Expect	strikeouts
Don't Expect	a starter

Ruffin, a middle reliever in 1993, stepped into a breach and assumed closing duties for Colorado last season. He has always thrown extremely hard and gets enough ground balls to be successful. The former Phillie and Brewer converted 16 of 21 save opportunities in 1994, despite a slump in June and July. Although he notched a poor 5.11 ERA in cozy Mile High Stadium, he allowed just two home runs at home and only six on the season. Part of Ruffin's 1994 success was due to a slight improvement in control, but he still gave nearly five free passes per game. That is an excessively high number, especially for the thin air of Denver. However, he also fanned a spectacular number of hitters. Another reason for Ruffin's effectiveness was that he held right-handers to a .244 average. Because of his lack of control, he's not ideally suited to closing duties, but he has more value in that role than he did as a starter.

Major League Pitching Register

	W	L	ERA	G	S	IP	H	ER	BB	SO
86 NL	9	4	2.46	21	0	146.1	138	40	44	70
87 NL	11	14	4.35	35	0	204.2	236	99	73	93
88 NL	6	10	4.43	55	3	144.1	151	71	80	82
89 NL	6	10	4.44	24	0	125.2	152	62	62	70
90 NL	6	13	5.38	32	0	149.0	178	89	62	79
91 NL	4	7	3.78	31	0	119.0	125	50	38	85
92 AL	1	6	6.67	25	0	58.0	66	43	41	45
93 NL	6	5	3.87	59	2	139.2	145	60	69	126
94 NL	4	5	4.04	56	16	55.2	55	25	30	65
Life	53	74	4.25	338	21	1142.1	1246	539	499	715
3 AVE	4	6	4.51	54	8	91.2	96	46	51	88

JOHNNY RUFFIN

Position: Pitcher
Team: Cincinnati Reds
Born: July 29, 1971 Butler, AL
Height: 6'3" **Weight:** 170 lbs.
Bats: right **Throws:** right
Acquired: Traded from White Sox with Jeff Pierce for Tim Belcher, 7/93

Player Summary	
Fantasy Value	$7 to $9
Card Value	6¢ to 10¢
Will	expand his role
Can't	keep ball in park
Expect	fastballs
Don't Expect	return to farm

Ruffin, stolen from the White Sox late in 1993, showed he belonged in the big leagues in 1994. Cincinnati skipper Davey Johnson used the hard-throwing youngster mostly in long-relief situations, allowing him to learn how to pitch big-league hitters with a minimal amount of pressure. Ruffin owns an excellent fastball. The Reds see him as a key part of the future of their pitching staff. He may even be moved to the starting rotation if he can master an off-speed pitch, but he also could be part of a closer-by-committee. Ruffin's control is merely adequate right now, and he allowed seven home runs and three triples in just 70 innings last year. He did overpower hitters last year, who batted just .223, and especially tamed right-handers, who hit just .212. He has not proved himself to be a solid citizen: His summer in 1994 was marred by a run-in with the law, and he has to perform community service as his punishment. In 1993 at Triple-A, he went 4-5 with a 3.11 ERA, 75 strikeouts, 18 bases on balls, and two saves in 67 innings pitched.

Major League Pitching Register

	W	L	ERA	G	S	IP	H	ER	BB	SO
93 NL	2	1	3.58	21	2	37.2	36	15	11	30
94 NL	7	2	3.09	51	1	70.0	57	24	27	44
Life	9	3	3.26	72	3	107.2	93	39	38	74
2 AVE	6	2	3.22	46	2	68.1	58	24	25	46

JEFF RUSSELL

Position: Pitcher
Team: Cleveland Indians
Born: Sept. 2, 1961 Cincinnati, OH
Height: 6'3" **Weight:** 210 lbs.
Bats: right **Throws:** right
Acquired: Traded from Red Sox for Steve Farr and Chris Nabholz, 7/94

Player Summary	
Fantasy Value	$20 to $25
Card Value	6¢ to 10¢
Will	work late frames
Can't	stay healthy
Expect	success vs. righties
Don't Expect	30 saves

Russell had all sorts of problems in 1994. He saved 12 of 15 games with the Red Sox, but all was not well on or off the diamond. He argued with Boston GM Dan Duquette about personnel moves, and Russell also suffered several horrid outings. He had an ERA over 5.00 at the end of June and was being booed constantly. Few were surprised when he was dealt to the Indians July 1. Unfortunately, the trade didn't help either Cleveland or Russell; the veteran reliever blew three of his eight save chances, continued to have control problems, and appeared to have lost much of his stuff. He allowed left-handers to bat over .300 and surrendered five home runs in his short tenure. He wasn't entirely healthy last year, and he has had some elbow problems in the past. Russell may not be able to shoulder even the light load he has been given.

Major League Pitching Register

	W	L	ERA	G	S	IP	H	ER	BB	SO
83 NL	4	5	3.03	10	0	68.1	58	23	22	40
84 NL	6	18	4.26	33	0	181.2	186	86	65	101
85 AL	3	6	7.55	13	0	62.0	85	52	27	44
86 AL	5	2	3.40	37	2	82.0	74	31	31	54
87 AL	5	4	4.44	52	3	97.1	109	48	52	56
88 AL	10	9	3.82	34	0	188.2	183	80	66	88
89 AL	6	4	1.98	71	38	72.2	45	16	24	77
90 AL	1	5	4.26	27	10	25.1	23	12	16	16
91 AL	6	4	3.29	68	30	79.1	71	29	26	52
92 AL	4	3	1.63	59	30	66.1	55	12	25	48
93 AL	1	4	2.70	51	33	46.2	39	14	14	45
94 AL	1	6	5.09	42	17	40.2	43	23	16	28
Life	52	70	3.79	497	163	1011.0	971	426	384	649
3 AVE	2	5	3.09	56	29	56.3	52	19	21	44

KEN RYAN

Position: Pitcher
Team: Boston Red Sox
Born: Oct. 24, 1968 Pawtucket, RI
Height: 6'3" **Weight:** 215 lbs.
Bats: right **Throws:** right
Acquired: Signed as a free agent, 6/86

Player Summary	
Fantasy Value	$10 to $13
Card Value	8¢ to 12¢
Will	work inside
Can't	afford weight gain
Expect	20 saves
Don't Expect	home runs

Ryan's emergence allowed the Red Sox to kiss disgruntled closer Jeff Russell good-bye last July. In fact, Ryan was one of the AL's better relievers in 1994. The New England native throws very hard and runs the ball low and inside. This was the reason that he was able to keep the ball in the park, allowing just one home run last year. Ryan held opponents to a .256 batting average and converted 13 of his 16 save opportunities. Neither lefties nor righties could hit him. In addition, the big right-hander stranded all of his inherited baserunners in 1994. He has had control trouble in the past, but last season he cut his walks down to about three per nine innings. That was nearly half the number of walks per game that he allowed in 1993. In 1992 at Double-A New Britain, he notched a 1.95 ERA and 22 saves. He added seven more saves at Triple-A Pawtucket that year. He's still new to relief pitching. If he can stay trim (a concern) and healthy, and if he can continue to improve on his control, Ryan will be one of the AL's better closers.

Major League Pitching Register

	W	L	ERA	G	S	IP	H	ER	BB	SO
92 AL	0	0	6.43	7	1	7.0	4	5	5	5
93 AL	7	2	3.60	47	1	50.0	43	20	29	49
94 AL	2	3	2.44	42	13	48.0	46	13	17	32
Life	9	5	3.26	96	15	105.0	93	38	51	86
2 AVE	5	3	2.93	53	10	59.0	54	19	26	47

BRET SABERHAGEN

Position: Pitcher
Team: New York Mets
Born: April 11, 1964 Chicago Heights, IL
Height: 6'1" **Weight:** 190 lbs.
Bats: right **Throws:** right
Acquired: Traded from Royals with Bill Pecota for Kevin McReynolds, Gregg Jefferies, and Keith Miller, 12/91

Player Summary	
Fantasy Value	$20 to $25
Card Value	8¢ to 15¢
Will	win if healthy
Can't	carry team alone
Expect	great stuff
Don't Expect	any walks

Saberhagen last summer broke the "odd year-even year" curse with an excellent performance. His control, always excellent, bordered on the unbelievable in 1994. He had more wins than walks, and Saberhagen amassed one of the lowest full-season base-on-balls totals ever. He is a truly dominating hurler, the owner of a terrific fastball and a very good curve. Opponents hit .254 against Saberhagen last year with an anemic .271 on-base percentage. He's always around the plate, which explains his 13 home runs allowed in 1994. Perhaps Saberhagen's best game of last year came on July 15, when he threw 10 scoreless innings with 11 Ks and no walks against San Diego. He captured his final seven decisions on the season and responded quite well to the No. 1 starter's role.

Major League Pitching Register

	W	L	ERA	G	CG	IP	H	ER	BB	SO
84 AL	10	11	3.48	38	2	157.2	138	61	36	73
85 AL	20	6	2.87	32	10	235.1	211	75	38	158
86 AL	7	12	4.15	30	4	156.0	165	72	29	112
87 AL	18	10	3.36	33	15	257.0	246	96	53	163
88 AL	14	16	3.80	35	9	260.2	271	110	59	171
89 AL	23	6	2.16	36	12	262.1	209	63	43	193
90 AL	5	9	3.27	20	5	135.0	146	49	28	87
91 AL	13	8	3.07	28	7	196.1	165	67	45	136
92 NL	3	5	3.50	17	1	97.2	84	38	27	81
93 NL	7	7	3.29	19	4	139.1	131	51	17	93
94 NL	14	4	2.74	24	4	177.1	169	54	13	143
Life	134	94	3.19	312	73	2074.2	1935	736	388	1410
3 AVE	10	6	3.05	23	4	162.1	151	55	21	125

CHRIS SABO

Position: Third base; outfield
Team: Baltimore Orioles
Born: Jan. 19, 1962   Detroit, MI
Height: 6′   **Weight:** 185 lbs.
Bats: right   **Throws:** right
Acquired: Signed as a free agent, 1/94

Player Summary	
Fantasy Value	$9 to $11
Card Value	8¢ to 12¢
Will	hit for power
Can't	run anymore
Expect	good effort
Don't Expect	top on-base mark

Sabo came aboard the Orioles' pennant express expecting to start at third base, but after a poor first month, he was benched for Leo Gomez. Sabo's bad start was compounded by the hot bat of Gomez, a favorite of Baltimore owner Peter Angelos. An everyday player from the day he came to the big leagues, Sabo complained about the lack of duty. Then-Baltimore manager Johnny Oates tried to placate Sabo by playing him in the outfield, but that was a disaster. Ultimately Sabo settled, none too happily, into a part-time role. Injuries and age have robbed him of most of his speed, but he still has decent power. "Spuds" was able to compile a .465 slugging percentage last season. He rarely walks, and last year his on-base percentage was just .320. He hit .278 against left-handers in 1994, suggesting that he has time left in a platoon role. Sabo has mediocre range but a strong arm at third base, and he seems to have lost some ability with the glove.

Major League Batting Register

	BA	G	AB	R	H	2B	3B	HR	RBI	SB
88 NL	.271	137	538	74	146	40	2	11	44	46
89 NL	.260	82	304	40	79	21	1	6	29	14
90 NL	.270	148	567	95	153	38	2	25	71	25
91 NL	.301	153	582	91	175	35	3	26	88	19
92 NL	.244	96	344	42	84	19	3	12	43	4
93 NL	.259	148	552	86	143	33	2	21	82	6
94 AL	.256	68	258	41	66	15	3	11	42	1
Life	.269	832	3145	469	846	201	16	112	399	115
3 AVE	.254	113	420	62	107	24	3	16	61	4

TIM SALMON

Position: Outfield
Team: California Angels
Born: Aug. 24, 1968   Long Beach, CA
Height: 6′3″   **Weight:** 220 lbs.
Bats: right   **Throws:** right
Acquired: Third-round pick in 6/89 free-agent draft

Player Summary	
Fantasy Value	$25 to $30
Card Value	20¢ to 35¢
Will	club homers
Can't	be a superstar
Expect	outfield assists
Don't Expect	stolen bases

Obviously, Salmon has never heard of the "sophomore jinx," because his second big-league season was nearly as good as his 1993 Rookie of the Year campaign. Despite missing time in July and August with a pulled hamstring, he posted fine power numbers, compiling a .531 slugging percentage. He also hit for a fine average, and he did well in late-inning pressure situations. Salmon does strike out quite a bit, whiffing 102 times in 1994, but he also drew 54 walks for an excellent .382 on-base percentage. Oddly, he has hit right-handers far better than lefties in his first two seasons. He has little running speed. Defensively, he made eight errors last year, but he showed a strong arm from right field, nailing nine baserunners. Salmon's range in right field is merely adequate. In 1992, he was the Triple-A Pacific Coast League's MVP and *Baseball America's* Minor League Player of the Year. He is being asked to carry the Angels. He may not have the overall skills needed to shoulder the load, and he needs more help from his teammates.

Major League Batting Register

	BA	G	AB	R	H	2B	3B	HR	RBI	SB
92 AL	.177	23	79	8	14	1	0	2	6	1
93 AL	.283	142	515	93	146	35	1	31	95	5
94 AL	.287	100	373	67	107	18	2	23	70	1
Life	.276	265	967	168	267	54	3	56	171	7
2 AVE	.285	141	520	94	148	30	2	32	97	3

JUAN SAMUEL

Position: Outfield; infield
Team: Detroit Tigers
Born: Dec. 9, 1960 San Pedro de Macoris, Dominican Republic
Height: 5'11" **Weight:** 180 lbs.
Bats: right **Throws:** right
Acquired: Signed as a free agent, 2/94

Player Summary	
Fantasy Value	$1
Card Value	5¢ to 7¢
Will	fill in
Can't	show old speed
Expect	some power
Don't Expect	starting job

Samuel worked hard in 1994 to arrest some of the decline he had experienced in the past several seasons. Accepting a utility role with Sparky Anderson's squad, the well-traveled Samuel played in the outfield, at DH, and at second and first last year. He hit .333 against right-handers and showed excellent power, leading the Tigers with a .559 slugging percentage. Samuel fit in well both on and off the field in Detroit, as his attitude was enthusiastic even though he wasn't given an everyday job. While he is a smarter baserunner than in his early days, he has lost most of his once-blinding speed and won't be stealing 72 bases anytime soon. Samuel will never again be a regular in the majors, but he saved his endangered career in 1994.

Major League Batting Register

	BA	G	AB	R	H	2B	3B	HR	RBI	SB
83 NL	.277	18	65	14	18	1	2	2	5	3
84 NL	.272	160	701	105	191	36	19	15	69	72
85 NL	.264	161	663	101	175	31	13	19	74	53
86 NL	.266	145	591	90	157	36	12	16	78	42
87 NL	.272	160	655	113	178	37	15	28	100	35
88 NL	.243	157	629	68	153	32	9	12	67	33
89 NL	.235	137	532	69	125	16	2	11	48	42
90 NL	.242	143	492	62	119	24	3	13	52	38
91 NL	.271	153	594	74	161	22	6	12	58	23
92 NL	.262	47	122	7	32	3	1	0	15	2
92 AL	.284	29	102	15	29	5	3	0	8	6
93 AL	.230	103	261	31	60	10	4	4	26	9
94 AL	.309	59	136	32	42	9	5	5	21	5
Life	.260	1472	5543	781	1440	262	94	137	621	363
2 AVE	.249	90	243	27	61	9	4	2	25	9

REY SANCHEZ

Position: Second base; shortstop
Team: Chicago Cubs
Born: Oct. 15, 1967 Rio Piedras, Puerto Rico
Height: 5'9" **Weight:** 170 lbs.
Bats: right **Throws:** right
Acquired: Traded from Rangers for Bryan House, 1/90

Player Summary	
Fantasy Value	$3 to $5
Card Value	5¢ to 7¢
Will	make contact
Can't	hit for power
Expect	fine glovework
Don't Expect	speed

Sanchez filled in admirably for Shawon Dunston in 1993, but Dunston moved him back to the bench last spring. Ryne Sandberg's surprise retirement during the season, however, gave Sanchez another shot at everyday duty, and the one-time Ranger prospect took full advantage. He showed excellent range at second base, as he had at shortstop, and made many tremendous plays. He fields well enough right now to start in the majors, and there was actually negligible drop-off in fielding at the keystone sack from Sandberg to Sanchez. Sanchez is also improving at bat. He hits for decent average and makes excellent contact (fanning just 29 times last year). However, he has no speed, little power, and took only 20 walks in 1994. In 1993, Sanchez hit well in the first half before fading late. Last season, he was more consistent throughout the year. He has no clear patterns yet against left-handers or right-handers. If Sanchez can take a few more walks and hit near .300, he will be a fine regular.

Major League Batting Register

	BA	G	AB	R	H	2B	3B	HR	RBI	SB
91 NL	.261	13	23	1	6	0	0	0	2	0
92 NL	.251	74	255	24	64	14	3	1	19	2
93 NL	.282	105	344	35	97	11	2	0	28	1
94 NL	.285	96	291	26	83	13	1	0	24	2
Life	.274	288	913	86	250	38	6	1	73	5
3 AVE	.275	105	336	32	93	14	2	0	27	2

DEION SANDERS

Position: Outfield
Team: Cincinnati Reds
Born: Aug. 9, 1967 Fort Myers, FL
Height: 6'1" **Weight:** 195 lbs.
Bats: left **Throws:** left
Acquired: Traded from Braves for Roberto Kelly, 5/94

Player Summary

Fantasy Value	$20 to $25
Card Value	25¢ to 35¢
Will	be in limelight
Can't	play great defense
Expect	stolen bases
Don't Expect	top on-base mark

Sanders moved his multisport traveling show from "America's Team" to "Marge's Mascots" last May, at least in baseball. He infused the Reds with some pep, but he still hasn't learned to get on base enough to be a top-flight leadoff man. His mediocre on-base percentage of .342 resulted from just 32 walks. However, Sanders's great speed will continue to keep him at the top of the order. He stole bases at a 70 percent success rate last year. He hit .301 against right-handed pitching, but he continued to struggle with lefties, who held him to a .233 mark. He struck out too much, whiffing 63 times in 1994, and did not display his previous power. In center field, Sanders has decent range but a poor arm, with which he nailed just two enemy baserunners. The prominent Sanders was arrested last August after an altercation with a Cincinnati policeman. He took advantage of the strike to test the limits of the NFL's salary cap with the 49ers.

Major League Batting Register

	BA	G	AB	R	H	2B	3B	HR	RBI	SB
89 AL	.234	14	47	7	11	2	0	2	7	1
90 AL	.158	57	133	24	21	2	2	3	9	8
91 NL	.191	54	110	16	21	1	2	4	13	11
92 NL	.304	97	303	54	92	6	14	8	28	26
93 NL	.276	95	272	42	75	18	6	6	28	19
94 NL	.283	92	375	58	106	17	4	4	28	38
Life	.263	409	1240	201	326	46	28	27	113	103
3 AVE	.287	107	368	59	105	16	9	7	32	33

REGGIE SANDERS

Position: Outfield
Team: Cincinnati Reds
Born: Dec. 1, 1967 Florence, SC
Height: 6'1" **Weight:** 180 lbs.
Bats: right **Throws:** right
Acquired: Seventh-round pick in 6/87 free-agent draft

Player Summary

Fantasy Value	$20 to $25
Card Value	10¢ to 20¢
Will	play every day
Can't	afford strikeouts
Expect	speed and power
Don't Expect	cleanup

Sanders had a surprisingly difficult 1994. After hitting in the fifth slot for most of the season, his inability to make consistent contact forced Reds manager Davey Johnson to drop Sanders down to the sixth or seventh spot. The gifted right fielder fanned a league-leading 114 times last year. When he did put the bat on the ball, he showed fine extra-base power, slugging .480. He also has fine speed (stealing bases last year at a 70 percent success rate), but he drew just 41 walks for a middling .332 on-base percentage. The aggressive outfielder also was suspended five games for charging Montreal's Pedro Martinez after being hit by a pitch in April. Sanders was converted from shortstop to the outfield in the minors. He has good range, improving instincts, and a powerful arm. His 12 outfield assists in 1994 ranked second to Raul Mondesi in the league. At his present level, Sanders is a quality regular. With improved strike-zone judgement, he'd be one of the league's most complete packages.

Major League Batting Register

	BA	G	AB	R	H	2B	3B	HR	RBI	SB
91 NL	.200	9	40	6	8	0	0	1	3	1
92 NL	.270	116	385	62	104	26	6	12	36	16
93 NL	.274	138	496	90	136	16	4	20	83	27
94 NL	.262	107	400	66	105	20	8	17	62	21
Life	.267	370	1321	224	353	62	18	50	184	65
3 AVE	.269	135	481	82	129	23	7	19	69	24

SCOTT SANDERS

Position: Pitcher
Team: San Diego Padres
Born: March 25, 1969 Hannibal, MO
Height: 6'4" **Weight:** 215 lbs.
Bats: right **Throws:** right
Acquired: Second-round pick in 6/90 free-agent draft

Player Summary

Fantasy Value	$5 to $7
Card Value	8¢ to 12¢
Will	be in rotation
Can't	afford control woes
Expect	good stuff
Don't Expect	righties to hit

Sanders is blessed with a fine moving fastball and a terrific changeup. Even while compiling a dismal won-lost record in 1994, he held opponents to a .245 batting average. Right-handers, in particular, were helpless, batting just .188. Sanders also fanned nearly a man per inning in Padres garb. Unfortunately, he was undermined in 1994 by poor control. The former shortstop walked nearly four men per game, tossed 10 wild pitches (tied for highest in the league), and often worked from behind in the count. Sanders has dominated in the past, pacing the Triple-A Pacific Coast League in strikeouts in 1993. He seems to be just a slight refinement in control away from becoming a fine starting pitcher. He needs to make that adjustment soon, but the Padres are likely to stick with him, given a lack of alternatives. Hopefully, he'll stay in the sports pages and off the police blotter; he and teammate Derek Bell were arrested in New York last April. At Triple-A Las Vegas in 1993, Sanders was 5-10 with a 4.96 ERA, a loop-high 161 strikeouts, and 62 walks in 152⅓ innings.

Major League Pitching Register

	W	L	ERA	G	CG	IP	H	ER	BB	SO
93 NL	3	3	4.13	9	0	52.1	54	24	23	37
94 NL	4	8	4.78	23	0	111.0	103	59	48	109
Life	7	11	4.57	32	0	163.1	157	83	71	146

SCOTT SANDERSON

Position: Pitcher
Team: Chicago White Sox
Born: July 22, 1956 Dearborn, MI
Height: 6'5" **Weight:** 192 lbs.
Bats: right **Throws:** right
Acquired: Signed as a minor-league free agent, 3/94

Player Summary

Fantasy Value	$0
Card Value	5¢ to 7¢
Will	get strikes
Can't	throw hard
Expect	many home runs
Don't Expect	star role

Sanderson has now stayed healthy for six straight seasons. That is remarkable for a pitcher who was once a disabled-list regular. However, he has lost his stuff and may not be of much help to any ballclub. He never walks anyone, but he allowed an amazing 20 home runs last year. Oddly, he gave up 10 gophers each to both left-handers and right-handers. While Sanderson had a few good starts in 1994 for the White Sox, his fine record is due to nearly seven runs per game of support from his teammates. He was unhappy about being sent to the bullpen when the White Sox called up Scott Ruffcorn in July.

Major League Pitching Register

	W	L	ERA	G	CG	IP	H	ER	BB	SO
78 NL	4	2	2.51	10	1	61.0	52	17	21	50
79 NL	9	8	3.43	34	5	168.0	148	64	54	138
80 NL	16	11	3.11	33	7	211.1	206	73	56	125
81 NL	9	7	2.95	22	4	137.1	122	45	31	77
82 NL	12	12	3.46	32	7	224.0	212	86	58	158
83 NL	6	7	4.65	18	0	81.1	98	42	20	55
84 NL	8	5	3.14	24	3	140.2	140	49	24	76
85 NL	5	6	3.12	19	2	121.0	100	42	27	80
86 NL	9	11	4.19	37	1	169.2	165	79	37	124
87 NL	8	9	4.29	32	0	144.2	156	69	50	106
88 NL	1	2	5.28	11	0	15.1	13	9	3	6
89 NL	11	9	3.94	37	2	146.1	155	64	31	86
90 AL	17	11	3.88	34	2	206.1	205	89	66	128
91 AL	16	10	3.81	34	2	208.0	200	88	29	130
92 AL	12	11	4.93	33	2	193.1	220	106	64	104
93 AL	7	11	4.46	21	4	135.1	153	67	27	66
93 NL	4	2	3.51	11	0	48.2	48	19	7	36
94 AL	8	4	5.09	18	1	92.0	110	52	12	36
Life	162	138	3.81	460	43	2504.1	2503	1060	617	1581
3 AVE	11	10	4.71	30	2	169.1	192	88	38	86

BENITO SANTIAGO

Position: Catcher
Team: Florida Marlins
Born: March 9, 1965 Ponce, Puerto Rico
Height: 6'1" **Weight:** 185 lbs.
Bats: right **Throws:** right
Acquired: Signed as a free agent, 12/92

Player Summary	
Fantasy Value	$7 to $9
Card Value	8¢ to 12¢
Will	hit left-handers
Can't	show speed
Expect	cannon arm
Don't Expect	on-base ability

Santiago enjoyed a good campaign, for a change, in 1994. Staying healthy the entire season, he hit for his best average since 1987, added some power, and once again showed excellent defensive skills. Santiago batted a fine .340 against left-handers last year and hit .329 with men in scoring position. While he has trouble with right-handers, batting just .245 against them in 1994, he did club them for eight of his home runs. Santiago has poor on-base skills, walking just 25 times last year, and his once-excellent speed has vanished. The NL Rookie of the Year in 1987, Santiago had been struggling for years. He contributed from behind the plate as usual, tossing out nearly half of enemy basestealers. He also continued to show good agility, especially before knuckleballer Charlie Hough retired. Santiago calls a good game and still is one of the better defensive catchers in baseball.

Major League Batting Register

	BA	G	AB	R	H	2B	3B	HR	RBI	SB
86 NL	.290	17	62	10	18	2	0	3	6	0
87 NL	.300	146	546	64	164	33	2	18	79	21
88 NL	.248	139	492	49	122	22	2	10	46	15
89 NL	.236	129	462	50	109	16	3	16	62	11
90 NL	.270	100	344	42	93	8	5	11	53	5
91 NL	.267	152	580	60	155	22	3	17	87	8
92 NL	.251	106	386	37	97	21	0	10	42	2
93 NL	.230	139	469	49	108	19	6	13	50	10
94 NL	.273	101	337	35	92	14	2	11	41	1
Life	.260	1029	3678	396	958	157	23	109	466	73
3 AVE	.252	129	443	45	112	20	3	13	50	4

BOB SCANLAN

Position: Pitcher
Team: Milwaukee Brewers
Born: Aug. 9, 1966 Los Angeles, CA
Height: 6'7" **Weight:** 215 lbs.
Bats: right **Throws:** right
Acquired: Traded from Cubs for Rafael Novoa and Mike Carter, 12/93

Player Summary	
Fantasy Value	$1 to $3
Card Value	5¢ to 7¢
Will	work often
Can't	nail down a role
Expect	extra-base hits
Don't Expect	many saves

Brewers manager Phil Garner couldn't figure out what to do with Scanlan. The big right-hander began 1994 in the bullpen, and he worked both middle and late relief but failed to impress much. He was moved to the rotation in June and made eight starts, but he didn't set the world afire in that spot either. Scanlan throws hard, but he doesn't have a good off-speed pitch and lacks much movement on his fastball. He has never been much of a strikeout pitcher, and in fact, Scanlan fanned just 11 men in his last 27 innings last season. His control improved upon leaving tiny Wrigley Field, but Scanlan kept feeding gophers, allowing 11 home runs last season. He also allowed 21 doubles. He gave up less than two and one-half bases on balls and more than 10 hits per nine innings in 1994. He lacks a good pickoff move and does not field his position well. Despite a good arm, Scanlan appears to be a middle reliever at best. He just doesn't have the stuff to be a closer, nor the repertoire to be a starter.

Major League Pitching Register

	W	L	ERA	G	S	IP	H	ER	BB	SO
91 NL	7	8	3.89	40	1	111.0	114	48	40	44
92 NL	3	6	2.89	69	14	87.1	76	28	30	42
93 NL	4	5	4.54	70	0	75.1	79	38	28	44
94 AL	2	6	4.11	30	2	103.0	117	47	28	65
Life	16	25	3.85	209	17	376.2	386	161	126	195
3 AVE	3	6	3.87	60	6	102.1	107	44	32	59

CURT SCHILLING

Position: Pitcher
Team: Philadelphia Phillies
Born: Nov. 14, 1966 Anchorage, AK
Height: 6'4" **Weight:** 215 lbs.
Bats: right **Throws:** right
Acquired: Traded from Astros for Jason Grimsley, 4/92

Player Summary	
Fantasy Value	$10 to $13
Card Value	6¢ to 10¢
Will	allow homers
Can't	afford walks
Expect	a comeback
Don't Expect	durability

Schilling suffered a disastrous season last summer. He pitched very poorly for the first month of the season before going on the disabled list with a bone spur in his pitching elbow. The injury shut Schilling down for the year. He was also bothered by torn cartilage in his left knee, which hampered his delivery. The player voted MVP of the 1993 National League Championship Series is expected to come back at close to full strength in 1995, but he will surely not be able to throw with his old velocity right away. When healthy, Schilling has outstanding control and fans three times the men he walks. Last year, he couldn't put the ball where he wanted it and as a result allowed nine home runs and 10 doubles in his 55 innings. Right-handers hit .303 off Schilling in 1994, a full 60 points higher than their career mark against him. The Phillies are depending on a healthy Schilling in 1995, but he seems to have become injury-prone.

Major League Pitching Register

	W	L	ERA	G	CG	IP	H	ER	BB	SO
88 AL	0	3	9.82	4	0	14.2	22	16	10	4
89 AL	0	1	6.23	5	0	8.2	10	6	3	6
90 AL	1	2	2.54	35	0	46.0	38	13	19	32
91 NL	3	5	3.81	56	0	75.2	79	32	39	71
92 NL	14	11	2.35	42	10	226.1	165	59	59	147
93 NL	16	7	4.02	34	7	235.1	234	105	57	186
94 NL	2	8	4.48	13	1	82.1	87	41	28	58
Life	36	37	3.55	189	18	689.0	635	272	215	504
3 AVE	11	10	3.46	31	6	192.1	174	74	52	138

DICK SCHOFIELD

Position: Shortstop
Team: Toronto Blue Jays
Born: Nov. 21, 1962 Springfield, IL
Height: 5'10" **Weight:** 179 lbs.
Bats: right **Throws:** right
Acquired: Signed as a free agent, 1/93

Player Summary	
Fantasy Value	$1
Card Value	5¢ to 7¢
Will	play hard
Can't	provide punch
Expect	steady defense
Don't Expect	great play

The Jays were counting on young Alex Gonzalez to play shortstop in 1994. Unfortunately, he proved unready for major-league pitching, and veteran Schofield saw most of the action. Considered just an insurance policy, Schofield performed decently both in the field and at bat. He is a steady defender with decent range and a good arm. He had been considered a heck of a fielder when he was with the Angels a few years ago. Despite showing some power earlier in his career, he is not much of a threat now. He was caught stealing as often as he was successful last year and has little extra-base punch. Schofield did draw 34 walks last season and compiled a .332 on-base percentage. He hits equally against righties and lefties. Schofield recovered fully from the broken leg that shelved him in 1993.

Major League Batting Register

	BA	G	AB	R	H	2B	3B	HR	RBI	SB
83 AL	.204	21	54	4	11	2	0	3	4	0
84 AL	.192	140	400	39	77	10	3	4	21	5
85 AL	.219	147	438	50	96	19	3	8	41	11
86 AL	.249	139	458	67	114	17	6	13	57	23
87 AL	.251	134	479	52	120	17	3	9	46	19
88 AL	.239	155	527	61	126	11	6	6	34	20
89 AL	.228	91	302	42	69	11	2	4	26	9
90 AL	.255	99	310	41	79	8	1	1	18	3
91 AL	.225	134	427	44	96	9	3	0	31	8
92 AL	.333	1	3	0	1	0	0	0	0	0
92 NL	.205	142	420	52	86	18	2	4	36	11
93 AL	.191	36	110	11	21	1	2	0	5	3
94 AL	.255	95	325	38	83	14	1	4	32	7
Life	.230	1334	4253	501	979	137	32	56	351	119
2 AVE	.232	138	440	53	102	19	2	5	41	10

PETE SCHOUREK

Position: Pitcher
Team: Cincinnati Reds
Born: May 10, 1969   Austin, TX
Height: 6'5"   **Weight:** 205 lbs.
Bats: left   **Throws:** left
Acquired: Claimed on waivers from Mets, 4/94

Player Summary	
Fantasy Value.	$3 to $5
Card Value	5¢ to 7¢
Will	get starts
Can't	keep ball in park
Expect	OK control
Don't Expect	ERA title

The Reds claimed Schourek off waivers in early April and stuck him in the bullpen. He worked ineffectively in long relief until early July, when he was moved into the injured Tim Pugh's rotation spot. At that time, the Cincinnati brain trust convinced Schourek to throw overhand instead of using the three-quarters motion that he had previously employed. Suddenly, Schourek put together a hot streak. Never a strikeout pitcher in the past, he fanned 37 men in six effective starts leading up to the strike. There is still room for Schourek to improve, however. This was his first good major-league stretch, and even in 1994 he allowed fellow left-handers to compile a .433 batting average. Oddly, he held righties to an outstanding .244. The former Met is a fly-ball pitcher, and allowed 11 dingers last season. If he doesn't put too many people on with walks, though, he can survive some home runs. He allowed a little more than three bases on balls per nine innings last year. Schourek could be very valuable this year.

TIM SCOTT

Position: Pitcher
Team: Montreal Expos
Born: Nov. 16, 1966   Hanford, CA
Height: 6'2"   **Weight:** 205 lbs.
Bats: right   **Throws:** right
Acquired: Traded from Padres for Archi Cianfrocco, 6/93

Player Summary	
Fantasy Value.	$1 to $3
Card Value	6¢ to 10¢
Will	work in middle
Can't	win closer's job
Expect	success vs. lefties
Don't Expect	home runs

Only the Shadow knows. Scott has enjoyed two successful years in the Expo bullpen, although it's hard to see why. His talents and the results he produces require explanation. First of all, he's a fly-ball pitcher, but he did not allow a single home run last season after giving up just four in 1993. Next, for the second straight year, the right-handed Scott held left-handers to under a .200 average, although he allowed fellow righties to hit over .310. Third, he is very easy to run on (opponents stole 12 bases in 14 tries with Scott pitching in 1994) but still stranded 90 percent of his inherited baserunners. These indeed are mysteries, but as long as he can produce, the Expos will be glad to have him. He doesn't own an overpowering fastball, but he has decent control, allowing three walks per nine innings in 1994. So far, he has done the job. Scott has no chance of expanding his role in an outstanding Montreal bullpen, but he is a fine middle reliever who does a good job walking a tightrope.

Major League Pitching Register

	W	L	ERA	G	S	IP	H	ER	BB	SO
91 NL	5	4	4.27	35	2	86.1	82	41	43	67
92 NL	6	8	3.64	22	0	136.0	137	55	44	60
93 NL	5	12	5.96	41	0	128.1	168	85	45	72
94 NL	7	2	4.09	22	0	81.1	90	37	29	69
Life	23	26	4.54	120	2	432.0	477	218	161	268
3 AVE	7	8	4.56	31	0	126.1	144	64	43	76

Major League Pitching Register

	W	L	ERA	G	S	IP	H	ER	BB	SO
91 NL	0	0	9.00	2	0	1.0	2	1	0	1
92 NL	4	1	5.26	34	0	37.2	39	22	21	30
93 NL	7	2	3.01	56	1	71.2	69	24	34	65
94 NL	5	2	2.70	40	1	53.1	51	16	18	37
Life	16	5	3.46	132	2	163.2	161	63	73	133
3 AVE	6	2	3.34	49	1	61.2	60	23	27	49

DAVID SEGUI

Position: First base; outfield
Team: New York Mets
Born: July 19, 1966   Kansas City, KS
Height: 6'1"   **Weight:** 202 lbs.
Bats: both   **Throws:** left
Acquired: Traded from Orioles for Kevin Baez and Tom Wegmann, 3/94

Player Summary	
Fantasy Value	$2 to $4
Card Value	5¢ to 7¢
Will	show fine glove
Can't	hit left-handers
Expect	platoon duty
Don't Expect	many strikeouts

The Orioles had no room for Segui after signing Rafael Palmeiro and dumped his salary in spring training. The Mets installed Segui as their starting first baseman, and he hit .275 over the first three weeks of the season. Unfortunately, he cooled off shortly afterward, and he ended the season platooning with Rico Brogna. With a bat, Segui does several things, but none of them particularly well. He has fair power, makes good contact, and draws a few walks (43 strikeouts and 33 walks last season). Last season he hit right-handers at around a .260 clip. However, he has no speed, can't hit left-handers at all, and doesn't do enough of anything to justify an everyday job. He compiled a .190 batting average against southpaws last season, and his slugging percentage stood at the .387 level. Segui's excellent glove at first base and his ability to play the outfield give him value beyond his mediocre offense. He has enough value that he will at least be on a major-league roster in 1995.

Major League Batting Register

	BA	G	AB	R	H	2B	3B	HR	RBI	SB
90 AL	.244	40	123	14	30	7	0	2	15	0
91 AL	.278	86	212	15	59	7	0	2	22	1
92 AL	.233	115	189	21	44	9	0	1	17	1
93 AL	.273	146	450	54	123	27	0	10	60	2
94 NL	.241	92	336	46	81	17	1	10	43	0
Life	.257	479	1310	150	337	67	1	25	157	4
3 AVE	.253	130	371	47	94	20	0	8	46	1

KEVIN SEITZER

Position: Infield
Team: Milwaukee Brewers
Born: March 26, 1962   Springfield, IL
Height: 5'11"   **Weight:** 180 lbs.
Bats: right   **Throws:** right
Acquired: Signed as a free agent, 7/93

Player Summary	
Fantasy Value	$7 to $9
Card Value	6¢ to 10¢
Will	put bat on ball
Can't	play much defense
Expect	good average
Don't Expect	stolen bases

The former Royal and Athletic played an unexpected marquee role for the Brew Crew in 1994, leading the team in batting average and pacing them with a .375 on-base percentage as well. Seitzer made excellent contact, hit right-handers at a .325 clip in 1994, and batted .343 on the road. Unfortunately, he seems to have lost most of the other skills he had in Kansas City. He doesn't walk much anymore (drawing just 30 passes last season), owns only fleeting power, and no longer steals bases. He compiled a .453 slugging average and a .375 on-base percentage last year. In addition, Seitzer's defense at third has deteriorated to an unacceptable level. In fact, he was moved to first base when teammate John Jaha was demoted in midseason. Seitzer is a fine example of a moderately talented player who is simply filling a role until better, younger players come along. In Milwaukee, he's one of the team's stars.

Major League Batting Register

	BA	G	AB	R	H	2B	3B	HR	RBI	SB
86 AL	.323	28	96	16	31	4	1	2	11	0
87 AL	.323	161	641	105	207	33	8	15	83	12
88 AL	.304	149	559	90	170	32	5	5	60	10
89 AL	.281	160	597	78	168	17	2	4	48	17
90 AL	.275	158	622	91	171	31	5	6	38	7
91 AL	.265	85	234	28	62	11	3	1	25	4
92 AL	.270	148	540	74	146	35	1	5	71	13
93 AL	.269	120	417	45	112	16	2	11	57	7
94 AL	.314	80	309	44	97	24	2	5	49	2
Life	.290	1089	4015	571	1164	203	29	54	442	72
3 AVE	.283	127	464	60	132	28	2	8	66	8

AARON SELE

Position: Pitcher
Team: Boston Red Sox
Born: June 25, 1970 Golden Valley, MN
Height: 6'5" **Weight:** 205 lbs.
Bats: right **Throws:** right
Acquired: First-round pick in 6/91 free-agent draft

Player Summary	
Fantasy Value	$14 to $17
Card Value	20¢ to 30¢
Will	get righties out
Can't	keep ball in park
Expect	strikeouts
Don't Expect	zero walks

Although Sele had some problems in his sophomore season, the Red Sox love him. He has a fine mix of pitches, including a low-running fastball, a fine curve, and a changeup. When he's right, Sele induces hitters to pound the ball into the ground. He was murder on right-handers last year, holding them to a .227 average. However, lefties were able to compile a .300 batting average and generate excellent power against him. He's hittable when his pitches sail high, and he is still trying to gain his control. He walked nearly four men per game last season—about the same level that he did in 1993—and allowed 13 home runs. Despite his youth, Sele is a key part of the Sox staff, finishing second on the team in strikeouts, innings pitched, and ERA in 1994. He has a good pickoff move and is mobile off the mound. Until last May, he had never allowed more than three earned runs in a game in the majors. In 1993, he was 8-2 with a 2.19 ERA at Triple-A Pawtucket before getting his ticket to Fenway. The young right-hander has an outstanding future.

Major League Pitching Register

	W	L	ERA	G	CG	IP	H	ER	BB	SO
93 AL	7	2	2.74	18	0	111.2	100	34	48	93
94 AL	8	7	3.83	22	2	143.1	140	61	60	105
Life	15	9	3.35	40	2	255.0	240	95	108	198
2 AVE	9	6	3.44	24	1	156.2	149	60	66	120

SCOTT SERVAIS

Position: Catcher
Team: Houston Astros
Born: June 4, 1967 LaCrosse, WI
Height: 6'2" **Weight:** 195 lbs.
Bats: right **Throws:** right
Acquired: Third-round pick in 6/88 free-agent draft

Player Summary	
Fantasy Value	$1
Card Value	5¢ to 7¢
Will	call a good game
Can't	throw well
Expect	some home runs
Don't Expect	top average

Servais has very clear strengths and short-comings. Defensively, he calls an excellent game and has always been above average at digging pitches out of the dirt. He committed two errors in 627 innings behind the dish last season. Unfortunately, he does not throw well, nailing fewer than 30 percent of enemy baserunners in 1994. He also has his strong and weak points on offense. He does hit left-handers well, batting .254 last year. However, the trade of platoon partner Eddie Taubensee to Cincinnati last April spelled more duty against right-handers for Servais, and they held him to a weak .174. Servais has fair power, but he swings from the heels and doesn't make contact on a consistent basis. He fanned 44 times last year and drew just 10 walks. His on-base percentage was .235. And he wasn't able to make up for his lack of on-base acumen with extra-base hits, compiling just a .371 slugging percentage. If Servais plays against righties this year, he will again post subpar numbers.

Major League Batting Register

	BA	G	AB	R	H	2B	3B	HR	RBI	SB
91 NL	.162	16	37	0	6	3	0	0	6	0
92 NL	.239	77	205	12	49	9	0	0	15	0
93 NL	.244	85	258	24	63	11	0	11	32	0
94 NL	.195	78	251	27	49	15	1	9	41	0
Life	.222	256	751	63	167	38	1	20	94	0
3 AVE	.222	91	272	25	60	14	0	8	35	0

GARY SHEFFIELD

Position: Outfield
Team: Florida Marlins
Born: Nov. 18, 1968 Tampa, FL
Height: 5'11" **Weight:** 190 lbs.
Bats: right **Throws:** right
Acquired: Traded from Padres with Rich Rodriguez for Trevor Hoffman, Andres Berumen, and Jose Martinez, 6/93

Player Summary	
Fantasy Value	$20 to $25
Card Value	20¢ to 30¢
Will	make contact
Can't	stay healthy
Expect	big power
Don't Expect	low average

Sheffield didn't complain when the Marlins shifted him to right field last season. In fact, he worked hard to master his new position—maybe too hard. Diving for a ball on May 9, Sheffield injured his left shoulder and missed four weeks. The injury took a huge bite out of the Marlins' lineup and out of Sheffield's final statistics. The former Brewer and Padre again showed tremendous power in 1994, walked a career-high 51 times (for a .380 on-base percentage), and had just 50 strikeouts. Oddly, Sheffield hit only .212 against left-handers in 1994 after pounding them at a .350 clip the year before. He was able to compile a batting average that was well over .300 against right-handers last season, however. Sheffield has fair speed but is a smart baserunner. He registered seven assists from right field in 1994, but he still needs to improve. Sheffield seems to be on track to post big numbers again.

Major League Batting Register

	BA	G	AB	R	H	2B	3B	HR	RBI	SB
88 AL	.237	24	80	12	19	1	0	4	12	3
89 AL	.247	95	368	34	91	18	0	5	32	10
90 AL	.294	125	487	67	143	30	1	10	67	25
91 AL	.194	50	175	25	34	12	2	2	22	5
92 NL	.330	146	557	87	184	34	3	33	100	5
93 NL	.294	140	494	67	145	20	5	20	73	17
94 NL	.276	87	322	61	89	16	1	27	78	12
Life	.284	667	2483	353	705	131	12	101	384	77
3 AVE	.302	136	502	80	151	26	3	30	94	13

CRAIG SHIPLEY

Position: Infield
Team: San Diego Padres
Born: Jan. 7, 1963 Sydney, Australia
Height: 6'1" **Weight:** 190 lbs.
Bats: right **Throws:** right
Acquired: Signed as a minor-league free agent, 12/90

Player Summary	
Fantasy Value	$1 to $3
Card Value	5¢ to 7¢
Will	Impress with glove
Can't	show much power
Expect	aggressive hitting
Don't Expect	stolen bases

Shipley had a big season off the bench in 1994. In his fourth season with San Diego, he finally began to contribute with the bat as well as the glove. In fact, Shipley hit so well that by the end of last season he was a platoon third baseman, starting against left-handers. While his performance was very good, Shipley still has gaping holes in his game. He lacks adequate power, took just nine bases on balls last season (while fanning 28 times), and was caught stealing as often as he succeeded. If he doesn't hit .300 or over, he won't help the Padres much. He is in the majors because of his versatility, attitude, and defensive ability. Shipley can play third base and second base skillfully and shortstop competently, and he never complains about his role. Last summer probably was his career year, but he could still be productive. The Padres are bad enough that he might luck into a starting job in 1995, but he likely doesn't have enough ability to keep it.

Major League Batting Register

	BA	G	AB	R	H	2B	3B	HR	RBI	SB
86 NL	.111	12	27	3	3	1	0	0	4	0
87 NL	.257	26	35	3	9	1	0	0	2	0
89 NL	.143	4	7	3	1	0	0	0	0	0
91 NL	.275	37	91	6	25	3	0	1	6	0
92 NL	.248	52	105	7	26	6	0	0	7	1
93 NL	.235	105	230	25	54	9	0	4	22	12
94 NL	.333	81	240	32	80	14	4	4	30	6
Life	.269	317	735	79	198	34	4	9	71	19
2 AVE	.293	110	284	35	83	14	3	5	32	10

TERRY SHUMPERT

Position: Second base; third base
Team: Boston Red Sox
Born: Aug. 16, 1966 Paducah, KY
Height: 5'11" **Weight:** 185 lbs.
Bats: right **Throws:** right
Acquired: Traded from Royals for a player to be named later, 12/94

Player Summary	
Fantasy Value	$4 to $6
Card Value	5¢ to 8¢
Will	try to win job
Can't	get on base
Expect	good speed
Don't Expect	15 homers

Shumpert was the Royals' regular second baseman in 1991, but he played so badly that his career in the big leagues, at least in Kansas City, appeared to be over. He hit .300 with 14 homers, 59 RBI, and a league-best 36 stolen bases at Triple-A Omaha in 1993, however, and resurrected his career with the big club in 1994. When Jose Lind was lost for two weeks in May with chicken pox, Shumpert hit well enough to draw rave notices from then-Kansas City manager Hal McRae. Shumpert showed better-than-expected power, especially against left-handers (five home runs in 54 at bats), and stole 18 bases in 21 attempts in 1994. While he has improved offensively, he still has some things to work on. He drew only 13 walks last season while whiffing 39 times. His on-base percentage was .289. With a glove on, he adds plenty of value. He has excellent range and can play third as well as second. Shumpert will probably stick as a utility player, and the former University of Kentucky star may soon contend for a starting job.

Major League Batting Register

	BA	G	AB	R	H	2B	3B	HR	RBI	SB
90 AL	.275	32	91	7	25	6	1	0	8	3
91 AL	.217	144	369	45	80	16	4	5	34	17
92 AL	.149	36	94	6	14	5	1	1	11	2
93 AL	.100	8	10	0	1	0	0	0	0	1
94 AL	.240	64	183	28	44	6	2	8	24	18
Life	.220	284	747	86	164	33	8	14	77	41

RUBEN SIERRA

Position: Outfield
Team: Oakland Athletics
Born: Oct. 6, 1965 Rio Piedras, Puerto Rico
Height: 6'1" **Weight:** 200 lbs.
Bats: both **Throws:** right
Acquired: Traded from Rangers with Bobby Witt and Jeff Russell for Jose Canseco, 8/92

Player Summary	
Fantasy Value	$20 to $25
Card Value	15¢ to 25¢
Will	bash left-handers
Can't	curb errors
Expect	show of power
Don't Expect	much speed

Sierra was the Athletics' 1994 All-Star representative, but he starred in only one measure—runs batted in. His career is levelling due to his impatience at the plate and inability to hit right-handers. The former Ranger did show adequate, but not overwhelming, power in 1994, compiling a .484 slugging percentage. He also hit .327 against lefties. However, Sierra batted a poor .233 against right-handers, the third straight year his average declined against northpaws. He regularly wastes at bats by swinging at awful pitches, and he drew only 23 walks last season. Sierra's once-good speed has faded. In 1994, he was caught stealing five of 13 tries. In the outfield, he used his strong arm to nail eight men in 1994, but he still can't master the fundamentals. His nine errors led all AL outfielders last year. Despite acceptable power totals, Sierra may never live up to his huge promise.

Major League Batting Register

	BA	G	AB	R	H	2B	3B	HR	RBI	SB
86 AL	.264	113	382	50	101	13	10	16	55	7
87 AL	.263	158	643	97	169	35	4	30	109	16
88 AL	.254	156	615	77	156	32	2	23	91	18
89 AL	.306	162	634	101	194	35	14	29	119	8
90 AL	.280	159	608	70	170	37	2	16	96	9
91 AL	.307	161	661	110	203	44	5	25	116	16
92 AL	.278	151	601	83	167	34	7	17	87	14
93 AL	.233	158	630	77	147	23	5	22	101	25
94 AL	.268	110	426	71	114	21	1	23	92	8
Life	.273	1328	5200	736	1421	274	50	201	866	121
3 AVE	.259	155	610	87	158	29	4	24	106	17

DON SLAUGHT

Position: Catcher
Team: Pittsburgh Pirates
Born: Sept. 11, 1958   Long Beach, CA
Height: 6'1"   **Weight:** 190 lbs.
Bats: right   **Throws:** right
Acquired: Traded from Yankees for Willie Smith and Jeff Robinson, 12/89

Player Summary	
Fantasy Value	$4 to $6
Card Value	6¢ to 10¢
Will	get base hits
Can't	outrun a tortoise
Expect	contact
Don't Expect	everyday duty

The venerable Slaught can still chip in with the bat. His offensive game is extremely consistent, although he had an uncharacteristic power surge in 1993. Now with his fourth major-league club, he hit a mighty .367 against left-handers in 1994 and has amassed a career average near .300 against them. He also stands in well against righties and walks about as often as he fans. In fact, Slaught took a career-high 34 free passes last year and compiled a terrific .381 on-base percentage. This increased patience may be a danger signal, however, as Slaught may be losing some bat speed. The veteran receiver may slump at the plate in 1995. He is a fair defensive catcher who calls a fine game. He lacks throwing ability and is one of baseball's slowest runners.

Major League Batting Register

	BA	G	AB	R	H	2B	3B	HR	RBI	SB
82 AL	.278	43	115	14	32	6	0	3	8	0
83 AL	.312	83	276	21	86	13	4	0	28	3
84 AL	.264	124	409	48	108	27	4	4	42	0
85 AL	.280	102	343	34	96	17	4	8	35	5
86 AL	.264	95	314	39	83	17	1	13	46	3
87 AL	.224	95	237	25	53	15	2	8	16	0
88 AL	.283	97	322	33	91	25	1	9	43	1
89 AL	.251	117	350	34	88	21	3	5	38	1
90 NL	.300	84	230	27	69	18	3	4	29	0
91 NL	.295	77	220	19	65	17	1	1	29	1
92 NL	.345	87	255	26	88	17	3	4	37	2
93 NL	.300	116	377	34	113	19	2	10	55	2
94 NL	.287	76	240	21	69	7	0	2	21	0
Life	.282	1196	3688	375	1041	219	28	71	427	18
3 AVE	.307	103	323	30	99	15	2	6	41	1

HEATHCLIFF SLOCUMB

Position: Pitcher
Team: Philadelphia Phillies
Born: June 7, 1966   Jamaica, NY
Height: 6'3"   **Weight:** 220 lbs.
Bats: right   **Throws:** right
Acquired: Traded from Indians for Ruben Amaro, 11/93

Player Summary	
Fantasy Value	$1
Card Value	5¢ to 7¢
Will	throw low smoke
Can't	save games
Expect	relief duty
Don't Expect	perfect control

Philadelphia GM Lee Thomas pulled off another fine trade when he acquired Slocumb. While the hard-throwing former Cub and Indian isn't likely to expand his role past that of middle reliever, he can pitch. Slocumb's style is to keep the ball low. Very low, in fact; he did not allow a triple or a home run in 1994. The only black mark on his ledger is his control. In keeping the ball low, he walked nearly three and one-half men per game last year and uncorked nine wild pitches—an amazing total for a relief pitcher. Opponents compiled a .328 on-base average. He blew all five of his save opportunities and allowed nearly half of his inherited runners to score last year. He has saved as many as 22 games in one season in the minor leagues. Slocumb has terrific raw velocity and fanned over seven men per nine innings in 1994. With his arm, he'll get plenty of time to improve, and he isn't a bad pitcher right now. If he cuts his bases on balls, though, he will move up to the terrific category.

Major League Pitching Register

	W	L	ERA	G	S	IP	H	ER	BB	SO
91 NL	2	1	3.45	52	1	62.2	53	24	30	34
92 NL	0	3	6.50	30	1	36.0	52	26	21	27
93 NL	1	0	3.38	10	0	10.2	7	4	4	4
93 AL	3	1	4.28	20	0	27.1	28	13	16	18
94 NL	5	1	2.86	52	0	72.1	75	23	28	58
Life	11	6	3.88	164	2	209.0	215	90	99	141
3 AVE	4	2	3.86	44	0	58.1	64	25	27	44

JOHN SMILEY

Position: Pitcher
Team: Cincinnati Reds
Born: March 17, 1965 Phoenixville, PA
Height: 6'4" **Weight:** 215 lbs.
Bats: left **Throws:** left
Acquired: Signed as a free agent, 11/92

Player Summary	
Fantasy Value.	$10 to $13
Card Value	6¢ to 10¢
Will	throw strikes
Can't	hold baserunners
Expect	home runs
Don't Expect.	great heater

Less than one year after undergoing arthroscopic elbow surgery, Smiley returned to form in 1994. He was able to throw his sharp-breaking curve for strikes consistently and showed an adequate fastball as well. Smiley's control is as good as almost anyone's in baseball when he's on, and last year he walked just over two men per game. He did allow 18 home runs last year, but he held opponents to a fine .320 on-base percentage, so few of those gophers were incapacitating. Left-handed hitters batted just .248 against Smiley. The former Pirate and Twin did struggle with righties, allowing them 15 home runs and a .280 average. The lanky lefty is quite easy to run on and adds nothing as a hitter. Smiley's Reds teammates helped him out, supplying him with nearly six runs per game of support last season. Although he remained injury-free in 1994, the Reds must again be careful not to overwork Smiley this year.

Major League Pitching Register

	W	L	ERA	G	CG	IP	H	ER	BB	SO
86 NL	1	0	3.86	12	0	11.2	4	5	4	9
87 NL	5	5	5.76	63	0	75.0	69	48	50	58
88 NL	13	11	3.25	34	5	205.0	185	74	46	129
89 NL	12	8	2.81	28	8	205.1	174	64	49	123
90 NL	9	10	4.64	26	2	149.1	161	77	36	86
91 NL	20	8	3.08	33	2	207.2	194	71	44	129
92 AL	16	9	3.21	34	5	241.0	205	86	65	163
93 NL	3	9	5.62	18	2	105.2	117	66	31	60
94 NL	11	10	3.86	24	1	158.2	169	68	37	112
Life	90	70	3.70	272	25	1359.1	1278	559	362	869
3 AVE	11	11	3.91	29	3	190.2	187	83	49	127

DWIGHT SMITH

Position: Outfield
Team: Baltimore Orioles
Born: Nov. 8, 1963 Tallahassee, FL
Height: 5'11" **Weight:** 175 lbs.
Bats: left **Throws:** right
Acquired: Traded from Angels for Basilio Ortiz, 7/94

Player Summary	
Fantasy Value.	$4 to $6
Card Value	5¢ to 7¢
Will	show power
Can't.	run much
Expect	hits vs. righties
Don't Expect	adequate defense

After playing somewhat regularly in 1993 with the Cubs, Smith split his time last year between California and Baltimore. The likeable and popular Smith is a poor defensive player, has unexceptional speed, and owns just over 100 career at bats against left-handers. Why, then, is Smith a major leaguer? Because he has good power and a lifetime average of nearly .300 against righties. He is simply a pure hitter, and his lumber was made for the American League. His slugging percentage last year was an excellent .459. That was almost his fielding average as well in 1994; Smith made an amazing seven errors in limited outfield play and registered only two assists. He no longer is a dangerous baserunner, and he needs to work on making better contact. He fanned 37 times last year. A disciplined hitter at times, he drew just 12 walks in 1994. Smith is a valuable reserve, but only if he is used in situations where he can utilize his strengths.

Major League Batting Register

	BA	G	AB	R	H	2B	3B	HR	RBI	SB
89 NL	.324	109	343	52	111	19	6	9	52	9
90 NL	.262	117	290	34	76	15	0	6	27	11
91 NL	.228	90	167	16	38	7	2	3	21	2
92 NL	.276	109	217	28	60	10	3	3	24	9
93 NL	.300	111	310	51	93	17	5	11	35	8
94 AL	.281	73	196	31	55	7	2	8	30	2
Life	.284	609	1523	212	433	75	18	40	189	41
3 AVE	.287	108	268	41	77	12	4	8	34	7

LEE SMITH

Position: Pitcher
Team: California Angels
Born: Dec. 4, 1957 Jamestown, LA
Height: 6'6" **Weight:** 269 lbs.
Bats: right **Throws:** right
Acquired: Signed as a free agent, 12/94

Player Summary	
Fantasy Value	$20 to $25
Card Value	10¢ to 15¢
Will	get saves
Can't	keep ball in park
Expect	fine control
Don't Expect	big heat

Smith, the all-time leader in saves, was one hot pitcher the first two months of 1994. Then-Baltimore manager Johnny Oates gave Smith plenty of easy save opportunities, often bringing him in at the start of the ninth, and Smith converted. As of May 29, he had 20 saves in 21 tries, a tiny 0.95 ERA, 20 strikeouts, and just three walks. From that point on, "Big Lee" slumped. Left-handers hit .306 against him in 1994, and opponents connected for six homers. He no longer has the fearsome fastball he did in the 1980s, but he works with an effective arsenal of off-speed deliveries. Last season, Smith converted 33 of 39 save chances, but he can no longer carry a heavy load by himself.

Major League Pitching Register

		W	L	ERA	G	S	IP	H	ER	BB	SO
80	NL	2	0	2.91	18	0	21.2	21	7	14	17
81	NL	3	6	3.51	40	1	66.2	57	26	31	50
82	NL	2	5	2.69	72	17	117.0	105	35	37	99
83	NL	4	10	1.65	66	29	103.1	70	19	41	91
84	NL	9	7	3.65	69	33	101.0	98	41	35	86
85	NL	7	4	3.04	65	33	97.2	87	33	32	112
86	NL	9	9	3.09	66	31	90.1	69	31	42	93
87	NL	4	10	3.12	62	36	83.2	84	29	32	96
88	AL	4	5	2.80	64	29	83.2	72	26	37	96
89	AL	6	1	3.57	64	25	70.2	53	28	33	96
90	AL	2	1	1.88	11	4	14.1	13	3	9	17
90	NL	3	4	2.10	53	27	68.2	58	16	20	70
91	NL	6	3	2.34	67	47	73.0	70	19	13	67
92	NL	4	9	3.12	70	43	75.0	62	26	26	60
93	NL	2	4	4.50	55	43	50.0	49	25	9	49
93	AL	0	0	0.00	8	3	8.0	4	0	5	11
94	AL	1	4	3.29	41	33	38.1	34	14	11	42
Life		68	82	2.93	891	434	1163.0	1006	378	427	1152
3 AVE		2	6	3.40	64	45	62.0	54	24	18	60

OZZIE SMITH

Position: Shortstop
Team: St. Louis Cardinals
Born: Dec. 26, 1954 Mobile, AL
Height: 5'10" **Weight:** 168 lbs.
Bats: both **Throws:** right
Acquired: Traded from Padres for Garry Templeton, 2/82

Player Summary	
Fantasy Value	$4 to $6
Card Value	20¢ to 30¢
Will	make contact
Can't	show old range
Expect	decent average
Don't Expect	power or speed

Smith continued his decline at bat and in the field in 1994. Ozzie still makes good contact, fanning just 26 times last year, but the ball doesn't travel very far. Smith has never had much power, and he no longer hits for a high average. He drew 38 walks last year for a mediocre .326 on-base percentage. The sure Hall of Famer is still a steady, dependable defender and has a fine throwing release, but he lacks his former great speed and amazing range. Last summer, Smith provided one of the All-Star Game's memorable moments. Appearing in his 13th midsummer classic, the tiny shortstop nearly bashed a homer off big Randy Johnson.

Major League Batting Register

		BA	G	AB	R	H	2B	3B	HR	RBI	SB
78	NL	.258	159	590	69	152	17	6	1	46	40
79	NL	.211	156	587	77	124	18	6	0	27	28
80	NL	.230	158	609	67	140	18	5	0	35	57
81	NL	.222	110	450	53	100	11	2	0	21	22
82	NL	.248	140	488	58	121	24	1	2	43	25
83	NL	.243	159	552	69	134	30	6	3	50	34
84	NL	.257	124	412	53	106	20	5	1	44	35
85	NL	.276	158	537	70	148	22	3	6	54	31
86	NL	.280	153	514	67	144	19	4	0	54	31
87	NL	.303	158	600	104	182	40	4	0	75	43
88	NL	.270	153	575	80	155	27	1	3	51	57
89	NL	.273	155	593	82	162	30	8	2	50	29
90	NL	.254	143	512	61	130	21	1	1	50	32
91	NL	.285	150	550	96	157	30	3	3	50	35
92	NL	.295	132	518	73	153	20	2	0	31	43
93	NL	.288	141	545	75	157	22	6	1	53	21
94	NL	.262	98	381	51	100	18	3	3	30	6
Life		.262	2447	9013	1205	2365	387	66	26	764	569
3 AVE		.282	137	533	73	150	22	4	2	42	24

PETE SMITH

Position: Pitcher
Team: Cincinnati Reds
Born: Feb. 27, 1966 Weymouth, MA
Height: 6'2" **Weight:** 200 lbs.
Bats: right **Throws:** right
Acquired: Signed as a free agent, 12/94

Player Summary	
Fantasy Value	$0
Card Value	6¢ to 10¢
Will	get chances
Can't	afford walks
Expect	plenty of homers
Don't Expect	old velocity

Smith's career has been destroyed by injuries. For the second straight season, shoulder tendinitis hampered his performance and forced him to the disabled list. Four out of the last five years, Smith has been shelved by shoulder miseries. Of course, he was pitching so badly at the time of the last injury that the Mets were happy to rest him. Smith couldn't find the plate consistently and allowed a monstrous 25 home runs as opponents slugged .505. Lefties hit over .300 against him in 1994, and right-handers batted .270. His ERA was the second-worst in the NL for pitchers who notched over 100 innings. He compiled just over four strikeouts and just less than three walks per nine innings last year. Once a hard thrower with a sharp curve, Smith can no longer throw hard or with good movement as a result of his frequent injuries. He has to do two things to keep a major-league job: stay healthy and improve his location.

Major League Pitching Register

	W	L	ERA	G	CG	IP	H	ER	BB	SO
87 NL	1	2	4.83	6	0	31.2	39	17	14	11
88 NL	7	15	3.69	32	5	195.1	183	80	88	124
89 NL	5	14	4.75	28	1	142.0	144	75	57	115
90 NL	5	6	4.79	13	3	77.0	77	41	24	56
91 NL	1	3	5.06	14	0	48.0	48	27	22	29
92 NL	7	0	2.05	12	2	79.0	63	18	28	43
93 NL	4	8	4.37	20	0	90.2	92	44	36	53
94 NL	4	10	5.55	21	1	131.1	145	81	42	62
Life	34	58	4.34	146	12	795.0	791	383	311	493
3 AVE	6	7	4.47	21	1	118.1	120	59	41	61

ZANE SMITH

Position: Pitcher
Team: Pittsburgh Pirates
Born: Dec. 28, 1960 Madison, WI
Height: 6'1" **Weight:** 205 lbs.
Bats: left **Throws:** left
Acquired: Traded from Expos for Moises Alou, Scott Ruskin, and Willie Greene, 8/90

Player Summary	
Fantasy Value	$8 to $10
Card Value	5¢ to 7¢
Will	stifle left-handers
Can't	dominate with Ks
Expect	success if healthy
Don't Expect	poor control

Smith endured a poor team, constant trade rumors, and some shoulder woes to post another fine season in Pittsburgh. The baffling lefty is one of baseball's most pronounced finesse pitchers, inducing as many ground-ball outs as anyone in the game. He throws a hard sinker that stays low in the strike zone, and, more often than not, opponents beat the elusive pitch into the dirt. Few hitters strike out against him, but even fewer draw walks. He allowed under two walks per nine innings in 1994. Smith held left-handers to just a .217 mark last year. His .279 mark against righties is adequate as long as he shows good control. His long, slow delivery makes him a very easy target for basestealers. In addition, when he gets his pitches up in the strike zone, Smith is easy to hit. Opponents tagged him for 17 home runs last year.

Major League Pitching Register

	W	L	ERA	G	CG	IP	H	ER	BB	SO
84 NL	1	0	2.25	3	0	20.0	16	5	13	16
85 NL	9	10	3.80	42	2	147.0	135	62	80	85
86 NL	8	16	4.05	38	3	204.2	209	92	105	139
87 NL	15	10	4.09	36	9	242.0	245	110	91	130
88 NL	5	10	4.30	23	3	140.1	159	67	44	59
89 NL	1	13	3.49	48	0	147.0	141	57	52	93
90 NL	12	9	2.55	33	4	215.1	196	61	50	130
91 NL	16	10	3.20	35	6	228.0	234	81	29	120
92 NL	8	8	3.06	23	4	141.0	138	48	19	56
93 NL	3	7	4.55	14	1	83.0	97	42	22	32
94 NL	10	8	3.27	25	2	157.0	162	57	34	57
Life	88	101	3.56	320	34	1725.1	1732	682	539	917
3 AVE	8	9	3.44	24	3	148.0	154	57	30	56

JOHN SMOLTZ

Position: Pitcher
Team: Atlanta Braves
Born: May 15, 1967   Detroit, MI
Height: 6'3"   **Weight:** 185 lbs.
Bats: right   **Throws:** right
Acquired: Traded from Tigers for Doyle Alexander, 8/87

Player Summary	
Fantasy Value	$11 to $14
Card Value	12¢ to 20¢
Will	attempt comeback
Can't	show pinpoint control
Expect	great arsenal
Don't Expect	20 wins

A *Sporting News* poll last July showed that NL hitters feel Smoltz has the fourth-best fastball, third-best splitter, and second-best slider in the loop. However, control problems and inconsistency have kept him from harnessing his awesome talent. He held batters to just a .239 average last summer, and right-handers could only muster a .209 mark. Unfortunately, while he walks fewer men than he once did, Smoltz still has trouble getting the ball where he wants it. He gave up 15 homers, allowed a little over three walks per nine innings, and fired seven wild pitches in 1994. He has always been streaky, and he did not win in his final six starts last season. In addition, he received fewer than four runs per game of support. Smoltz's frustrating season was capped by rumors that he'd be moved to short relief and, finally, news that he would undergo off-season surgery to remove a bone spur from his pitching elbow.

Major League Pitching Register

	W	L	ERA	G	CG	IP	H	ER	BB	SO
88 NL	2	7	5.48	12	0	64.0	74	39	33	37
89 NL	12	11	2.94	29	5	208.0	160	68	72	168
90 NL	14	11	3.85	34	6	231.1	206	99	90	170
91 NL	14	13	3.80	36	5	229.2	206	97	77	148
92 NL	15	12	2.85	35	9	246.2	206	78	80	215
93 NL	15	11	3.62	35	3	243.2	208	98	100	208
94 NL	6	10	4.14	21	1	134.2	120	62	48	113
Life	78	75	3.59	202	29	1358.0	1180	541	500	1059
3 AVE	13	12	3.49	33	4	226.2	194	88	83	194

J.T. SNOW

Position: First base
Team: California Angels
Born: Feb. 26, 1968   Long Beach, CA
Height: 6'2"   **Weight:** 202 lbs.
Bats: both   **Throws:** left
Acquired: Traded from Yankees with Jerry Nielsen and Russ Springer for Jim Abbott, 12/92

Player Summary	
Fantasy Value	$2 to $4
Card Value	10¢ to 15¢
Will	play fine defense
Can't	get bat in gear
Expect	another chance
Don't Expect	20 homers

Snow's second major-league season was even more disappointing than his first. He began the season at Triple-A Vancouver, hitting .294 with seven homers before the Angels recalled him June 3. However, he again suffered a disappointing performance at the big-league level. Snow at least had a hot streak in his rookie year, but in 1994 he was flat from start to finish and against all types of pitchers. Snow showed little power, compiling a .345 slugging percentage. He hit just .226 against lefties and .216 versus right-handers, fanned 48 times, and drew just 19 walks. His on-base percentage was an awful .289, and he showed no speed. Reversing his 1993 trend, Snow hit well in Anaheim last season but very poorly on the road. Despite good seasons at Double-A and Triple-A as a Yankee farmhand, Snow hasn't shown any ability to adjust to major-league pitching and may never be a productive regular. He is an excellent defensive first baseman, and he certainly will be given several more chances in California due to his relative youth.

Major League Batting Register

	BA	G	AB	R	H	2B	3B	HR	RBI	SB
92 AL	.143	7	14	1	2	1	0	0	2	0
93 AL	.241	129	419	60	101	18	2	16	57	3
94 AL	.220	61	223	22	49	4	0	8	30	0
Life	.232	197	656	83	152	23	2	24	89	3
2 AVE	.232	107	367	45	85	12	1	14	50	2

CORY SNYDER

Position: Outfield; third base
Team: Los Angeles Dodgers
Born: Nov. 11, 1962 Inglewood, CA
Height: 6'3" **Weight:** 206 lbs.
Bats: right **Throws:** right
Acquired: Signed as a free agent, 12/92

Player Summary	
Fantasy Value	$1
Card Value	5¢ to 7¢
Will	hint at power
Can't	get on base
Expect	strikeouts
Don't Expect	regular duty

Snyder, once seen as a rising star with Cleveland, has instead become a multiposition reserve. The booming home run bat is gone, but he has saved his career by becoming versatile. He has a good arm (although he made several throwing errors last season), he hustles, and he is willing to play anywhere Dodger manager Tommy Lasorda asks him. In 1994, Snyder saw action at first, second, third, shortstop, and in the outfield. Despite good raw power and an ability to hit left-handers, he has far too many weaknesses to play regularly. He has always had trouble making contact, and in 1994 fanned 47 times while taking just 14 walks. Snyder's career on-base percentage is under .300. He does not run well and has a career batting average under .240 against right-handed pitchers. Often seen in the past as uncoachable, Snyder now seems to fit in well as a professional bench player.

Major League Batting Register

	BA	G	AB	R	H	2B	3B	HR	RBI	SB
86 AL	.272	103	416	58	113	21	1	24	69	2
87 AL	.236	157	577	74	136	24	2	33	82	5
88 AL	.272	142	511	71	139	24	3	26	75	5
89 AL	.215	132	489	49	105	17	0	18	59	6
90 AL	.233	123	438	46	102	27	3	14	55	1
91 AL	.175	71	166	14	29	4	1	3	17	0
92 NL	.269	124	390	48	105	22	2	14	57	4
93 NL	.266	143	516	61	137	33	1	11	56	4
94 NL	.235	73	153	18	36	6	0	6	18	1
Life	.247	1068	3656	439	902	178	13	149	488	28
3 AVE	.261	123	374	45	98	21	1	11	46	3

LUIS SOJO

Position: Second base
Team: Seattle Mariners
Born: Jan. 3, 1966 Barquisimeto, Venezuela
Height: 5'11" **Weight:** 175 lbs.
Bats: right **Throws:** right
Acquired: Signed as a minor-league free agent, 1/94

Player Summary	
Fantasy Value	$1
Card Value	5¢ to 7¢
Will	swing at anything
Can't	be a starter
Expect	some power
Don't Expect	speed

Sojo's size and build would lead one to believe he is a singles-hitting, speedy, defensive-minded player. One would be wrong. Sojo (nicknamed "So slow" by some wags in Seattle) has a steady glove, but he commands surprisingly little range. He was one of several players who lost Seattle's starting second base job last season. However, he does some things well. While he has no speed, he doesn't make many mistakes on the bases, and he has good power for a middle infielder. Oddly, 15 of his 17 career home runs have come against fellow right-handers, although he hits for a good average against left-handers (.333 in 1994). Sojo would be even more valuable if he could get on base regularly, but he rarely takes a base on balls. He took just eight free passes last season while striking out 25 times, compiling a .308 on-base average. Sojo probably won't be a major-league starter again, and because he lacks much value defensively, he will see significant action only for an understocked team.

Major League Batting Register

	BA	G	AB	R	H	2B	3B	HR	RBI	SB
90 AL	.225	33	80	14	18	3	0	1	9	1
91 AL	.258	113	364	38	94	14	1	3	20	4
92 AL	.272	106	368	37	100	12	3	7	43	7
93 AL	.170	19	47	5	8	2	0	0	6	0
94 AL	.277	63	213	32	59	9	2	6	22	2
Life	.260	334	1072	126	279	40	6	17	100	14
2 AVE	.274	97	334	41	92	12	3	8	37	5

PAUL SORRENTO

Position: First base
Team: Cleveland Indians
Born: Nov. 17, 1965   Somerville, MA
Height: 6'2"   **Weight:** 220 lbs.
Bats: left   **Throws:** right
Acquired: Traded from Twins for Oscar Munoz and Curt Leskanic, 3/92

Player Summary	
Fantasy Value	$9 to $11
Card Value	5¢ to 7¢
Will	perform capably
Can't	win Gold Glove
Expect	little running
Don't Expect	an All-Star

Until recently an example of one of the many adequate major-league hitters rotting away in other team's systems, Sorrento has done pretty well since being liberated from the Twins. He played regularly at first base for the Indians last season, sitting only against tough lefties. He did hit .270 with three homers off portsiders in 1994, however. Most of Sorrento's power comes against right-handers. The burly first sacker takes a normal amount of free passes (34 times last season) and strikes out twice as often as he walks. He compiled a .345 on-base percentage last summer. Spanking-new Jacobs Field certainly helped Sorrento, who hit .312 at home last year. He has absolutely no speed and adds little on defense. At his 1994 playing level, Sorrento is only an ordinary first baseman and must either hit for more power or get on base more to be an above-average first sacker. He has, however, ensured himself of at least platoon play for several years.

Major League Batting Register

	BA	G	AB	R	H	2B	3B	HR	RBI	SB
89 AL	.238	14	21	2	5	0	0	0	1	0
90 AL	.207	41	121	11	25	4	1	5	13	1
91 AL	.255	26	47	6	12	2	0	4	13	0
92 AL	.269	140	458	52	123	24	1	18	60	0
93 AL	.257	148	463	75	119	26	1	18	65	3
94 AL	.280	95	322	43	90	14	0	14	62	0
Life	.261	464	1432	189	374	70	3	59	214	4
3 AVE	.268	141	458	63	123	23	1	19	71	1

SAMMY SOSA

Position: Outfield
Team: Chicago Cubs
Born: Oct. 10, 1968   San Pedro de Macoris, Dominican Republic
Height: 6'   **Weight:** 175 lbs.
Bats: right   **Throws:** right
Acquired: Traded from White Sox with Ken Patterson for George Bell, 3/92

Player Summary	
Fantasy Value	$30 to $35
Card Value	10¢ to 15¢
Will	frustrate
Can't	master fundamentals
Expect	power and speed
Don't Expect	patience at bat

The dynamic Sosa led the Cubs in home runs, RBI, and batting average last year. If one judges a player by Triple Crown stats, he is one of the major league's best hitters. He slugged .545 for the season and battered lefties for a .336 average and nine homers in just 113 at bats. Unfortunately, Sosa is deficient in other phases of the game—most importantly, he cannot lay off lousy pitches. He whiffed 92 times last year and drew only 25 walks, compiling a mediocre .339 on-base percentage. Sosa hasn't figured out how to use his speed, either. He was thrown out stealing 13 times last year, and his poor decisions ran the Cubs out of many innings. Chicago management doesn't think Sosa can play center field. He has a powerful arm in right, but his throws are rarely accurate, and he habitually overthrows cutoff men. Last year, he made seven errors and four assists. As a raw package of talent, Sosa is nearly peerless. As a baseball player, he is frustrating.

Major League Batting Register

	BA	G	AB	R	H	2B	3B	HR	RBI	SB
89 AL	.257	58	183	27	47	8	0	4	13	7
90 AL	.233	153	532	72	124	26	10	15	70	32
91 AL	.203	116	316	39	64	10	1	10	33	13
92 NL	.260	67	262	41	68	7	2	8	25	15
93 NL	.261	159	598	92	156	25	5	33	93	36
94 NL	.300	105	426	59	128	17	6	25	70	22
Life	.253	658	2317	330	587	93	24	95	304	125
3 AVE	.277	125	487	72	135	19	5	25	72	27

BILL SPIERS

Position: Infield
Team: New York Mets
Born: June 5, 1966 Orangeburg, SC
Height: 6'2" **Weight:** 190 lbs.
Bats: left **Throws:** right
Acquired: Claimed from Brewers on waivers, 10/94

Player Summary	
Fantasy Value	$1 to $3
Card Value	5¢ to 7¢
Will	hit vs. right-handers
Can't	reach base often
Expect	steady glovework
Don't Expect	extra-base hits

Since enjoying a fine 1991 campaign, Spiers has been neither lucky nor good. Back surgery administered in 1992 has slowed him down considerably, and he hasn't hit or fielded well enough when healthy to warrant playing time. After losing the Milwaukee shortstop job last summer to Jose Valentin, Spiers spent his time at third base, where he showed a dependable glove but little else. He is no longer quick enough to play the middle infield positions regularly, and he won't chip in enough offense to play every day at any spot. Spiers does hit right-handers well, batting .279 against them last year. He was caught stealing just once, also. Unfortunately, that's all he offers at bat. He has no power, is helpless against left-handers (just over .200 lifetime, .114 in 1994), struck out one in every five at bats last year, rarely walks, and totaled a subpar .316 on-base percentage. All that Spiers can do now is try to hang on to a job as a utility man.

Major League Batting Register

	BA	G	AB	R	H	2B	3B	HR	RBI	SB
89 AL	.255	114	345	44	88	9	3	4	33	10
90 AL	.242	112	363	44	88	15	3	2	36	11
91 AL	.283	133	414	71	117	13	6	8	54	14
92 AL	.313	12	16	2	5	2	0	0	2	1
93 AL	.238	113	340	43	81	8	4	2	36	9
94 AL	.252	73	214	27	54	10	1	0	17	7
Life	.256	557	1692	231	433	57	17	16	178	52
2 AVE	.245	108	321	41	79	11	3	1	30	9

ED SPRAGUE

Position: Third base
Team: Toronto Blue Jays
Born: July 25, 1967 Castro Valley, CA
Height: 6'2" **Weight:** 215 lbs.
Bats: right **Throws:** right
Acquired: First-round pick in 6/88 free-agent draft

Player Summary	
Fantasy Value	$7 to $9
Card Value	6¢ to 10¢
Will	play hard
Can't	make contact
Expect	adequate defense
Don't Expect	stolen bases

After showing some promise in 1993, Sprague came back to have a poor 1994 season. Pitchers exploited his lack of strike-zone command to disastrous effect. His production in all offensive phases deteriorated to intolerable levels. He looked bad on breaking pitches and couldn't pull the trigger on fastballs. Sprague whiffed 95 times and walked just 23, notching a miserable .296 on-base percentage. He showed no basestealing ability and didn't hit for nearly enough power to mitigate his poor batting average. He had a .373 slugging percentage. Sprague hit .288 against left-handers, but just .220 against righties. He was mired near .200 at the All-Star break. If he were Brooks Robinson at third, some of this might be forgiven. Sprague is not Gold Glove material at the hot corner, however. The former catcher has a strong arm and chases pop flies well, but he lacks range. He did an acceptable job at third in 1993, but he regressed last year. Sprague should come back to an average level this summer.

Major League Batting Register

	BA	G	AB	R	H	2B	3B	HR	RBI	SB
91 AL	.275	61	160	17	44	7	0	4	20	0
92 AL	.234	22	47	6	11	2	0	1	7	0
93 AL	.260	150	546	50	142	31	1	12	73	1
94 AL	.240	109	405	38	97	19	1	11	44	1
Life	.254	342	1158	111	294	59	2	28	144	2
2 AVE	.250	152	558	52	139	29	1	14	67	1

MIKE STANLEY

Position: Catcher
Team: New York Yankees
Born: June 25, 1963 Fort Lauderdale, FL
Height: 6' **Weight:** 190 lbs.
Bats: right **Throws:** right
Acquired: Signed as a free agent, 1/92

Player Summary	
Fantasy Value	$13 to $15
Card Value	6¢ to 10¢
Will	hit with power
Can't	dominate defensively
Expect	patience at bat
Don't Expect	speed

Stanley experienced a slow start in 1994, but the veteran receiver had a fine second half. Taken as a whole, he put together a strong offensive season, one almost as good as his spectacular 1993 performance. Stanley's improvement can be traced to his increased proficiency against right-handed pitchers. After slumping against them for most of his career, he hit .304 in 1993 and .290 last year. The former Ranger is also extremely patient at the plate, working the count in his favor and accepting walks if they're offered. Stanley took 39 free passes in 1994 and notched a fine .384 on-base percentage. He has a quick bat and tremendous power, which he used to slug .545 last season. In addition to his hitting talent, he also chips in on defense. Although he lacks agility or a mighty arm, he calls a good game and handles his pitchers well. He threw out over 40 percent of runners trying to steal in 1994.

Major League Batting Register

	BA	G	AB	R	H	2B	3B	HR	RBI	SB
86 AL	.333	15	30	4	10	3	0	1	1	1
87 AL	.273	78	216	34	59	8	1	6	37	3
88 AL	.229	94	249	21	57	8	0	3	27	0
89 AL	.246	67	122	9	30	3	1	1	11	1
90 AL	.249	103	189	21	47	8	1	2	19	1
91 AL	.249	95	181	25	45	13	1	3	25	0
92 AL	.249	68	173	24	43	7	0	8	27	0
93 AL	.305	130	423	70	129	17	1	26	84	1
94 AL	.300	82	290	54	87	20	0	17	57	0
Life	.271	732	1873	262	507	87	5	67	288	7
3 AVE	.293	105	335	57	98	17	0	19	64	0

MIKE STANTON

Position: Pitcher
Team: Atlanta Braves
Born: June 2, 1967 Houston, TX
Height: 6'1" **Weight:** 190 lbs.
Bats: left **Throws:** left
Acquired: 13th-round pick in 6/87 free-agent draft

Player Summary	
Fantasy Value	$3 to $5
Card Value	5¢ to 7¢
Will	stop lefties
Can't	locate zone
Expect	appearances
Don't Expect	huge success

One of the guilty-by-association members of the maligned Braves bullpen, Stanton continues to show terrific raw stuff that he can't control. He throws very hard and mixes in a good slider, but he lacks an off-speed pitch and too often bounces pitches into the dirt. He walked over five men per nine innings last year and allowed over half of his inherited runners to score. Watching that kind of performance, Atlanta manager Bobby Cox hardly enjoyed bringing Stanton in with men on base. However, Stanton does have overpowering stuff, holding hitters to a .248 mark in 1994 and allowing just four doubles and two home runs. In 1993, he began the year as the Braves' closer, but he lost the job to Greg McMichael. Last season, Stanton had only four save opportunities, and he converted three of them. While Stanton dominated left-handers last year (.200), he has the ability and the makeup of someone who is more than a one-out guy.

Major League Pitching Register

	W	L	ERA	G	S	IP	H	ER	BB	SO
89 NL	0	1	1.50	20	7	24.0	17	4	8	27
90 NL	0	3	18.00	7	2	7.0	16	14	4	7
91 NL	5	5	2.88	74	7	78.0	62	25	21	54
92 NL	5	4	4.10	65	8	63.2	59	29	20	44
93 NL	4	6	4.67	63	27	52.0	51	27	29	43
94 NL	3	1	3.55	49	3	45.2	41	18	26	35
Life	17	20	3.90	278	54	270.1	246	117	108	210
3 AVE	4	4	4.07	66	13	59.2	56	27	29	45

TERRY STEINBACH

Position: Catcher
Team: Oakland Athletics
Born: March 2, 1962   New Ulm, MN
Height: 6'1"   **Weight:** 195 lbs.
Bats: right   **Throws:** right
Acquired: Ninth-round pick in 6/83 free-agent draft

Player Summary	
Fantasy Value...............	$10 to $13
Card Value	6¢ to 10¢
Will...................	play aggressively
Can't...............	dazzle with speed
Expect..................	.280 average
Don't Expect.............	a Gold Glove

Steinbach, the AL's player representative and the heart and soul of the Athletics, had another good year in 1994. He is a consistent offensive and defensive performer who contributes something on the field every day. Steinbach is well-respected for his knowledge of hitters and game-calling, and he nailed 44 percent of enemy basestealers last season. He does lack some mobility behind the plate. At bat, Steinbach has developed power over his career; he reached double-digit homers for the third straight time in 1994. While he doesn't often walk (just 26 times last year), Steinbach murders left-handers and smokes line drives all over the diamond. He does strike out a fair amount. Over his career, he has batted over .270 both on grass and turf. After being knocked out of action with a broken wrist in August 1993, Steinbach recovered and stayed healthy last season.

Major League Batting Register

	BA	G	AB	R	H	2B	3B	HR	RBI	SB
86 AL	.333	6	15	3	5	0	0	2	4	0
87 AL	.284	122	391	66	111	16	3	16	56	1
88 AL	.265	104	351	42	93	19	1	9	51	3
89 AL	.273	130	454	37	124	13	1	7	42	1
90 AL	.251	114	379	32	95	15	2	9	57	0
91 AL	.274	129	456	50	125	31	1	6	67	2
92 AL	.279	128	438	48	122	20	1	12	53	2
93 AL	.285	104	389	47	111	19	1	10	43	3
94 AL	.285	103	369	51	105	21	2	11	57	2
Life	.275	940	3242	376	891	154	12	82	430	14
3 AVE	.283	126	449	56	127	23	2	12	59	3

DAVE STEVENS

Position: Pitcher
Team: Minnesota Twins
Born: March 4, 1970   Fullerton, CA
Height: 6'3"   **Weight:** 210 lbs.
Bats: right   **Throws:** right
Acquired: Traded from Cubs with Matt Walbeck for Willie Banks, 11/93

Player Summary	
Fantasy Value.................	$4 to $6
Card Value	8¢ to 12¢
Will................	show fine stuff
Can't...............	master strike zone
Expect..................	opportunities
Don't Expect.............	many saves

Young hard throwers will always get the seats in the front of the bus. Stevens has a tremendous fastball and a great sinker, and the Twins worked hard to get him. He went 5-0 with a 1.01 ERA in 27 innings while at Triple-A Salt Lake City before the Twins called him up May 20 for his first big-league action. While Stevens threw well, he experienced the same control troubles in Minnesota that he had in the minors. He fell behind the count early and often, and, as a result, he allowed opponents to compile a .302 batting average, 10 doubles, and six home runs in 45 innings. He also walked as many as he fanned. Stevens did strand 14 of 17 inherited runners. Shoulder woes disabled Stevens just before the strike, and, when healed, he headed back to Triple-A to stay sharp. In 1993 at Double-A Orlando, he was 6-1 with a 4.22 ERA, 49 strikeouts, and 35 walks in 70 innings. He was 4-0 with a 4.19 ERA, 29 strikeouts, and 14 walks in 34 innings that year at Triple-A Iowa. If he can rein in his control a bit, Stevens could be an overpowering reliever. For now, he's a project who might need some more time on the farm.

Major League Pitching Register

	W	L	ERA	G	S	IP	H	ER	BB	SO
94 AL	5	2	6.80	24	0	45.0	55	34	23	24
Life	5	2	6.80	24	0	45.0	55	34	23	24

DAVE STEWART

Position: Pitcher
Team: Toronto Blue Jays
Born: Feb. 1, 1957 Oakland, CA
Height: 6'2" **Weight:** 200 lbs.
Bats: right **Throws:** right
Acquired: Signed as a free agent, 12/92

Player Summary	
Fantasy Value	$0
Card Value	8¢ to 12¢
Will	issue walks
Can't	show old velocity
Expect	spirit
Don't Expect	an ERA crown

Stewart again took his regular turn on a depleted Toronto staff in 1994, but he was hit very hard and ended the year hinting that he might retire. One of baseball's best hurlers of the 1980s, he is still a power pitcher, but age and poor control have taken much of the gas out of his tank. He has lost enough off his fastball that AL hitters have battered him three out of the last four seasons. Stewart's ERA last year was one of the AL's highest, and he completed just one game. Now with his fifth big-league team, Stew is still struggling with his control, walking over four men per game in 1994. Unless Stewart can start to retire batters consistently, he's got no future.

Major League Pitching Register

	W	L	ERA	G	CG	IP	H	ER	BB	SO
78 NL	0	0	0.00	1	0	2.0	1	0	0	1
81 NL	4	3	2.49	32	0	43.1	40	12	14	29
82 NL	9	8	3.81	45	0	146.1	137	62	49	80
83 NL	5	2	2.96	46	0	76.0	67	25	33	54
83 AL	5	2	2.14	8	2	59.0	50	14	17	24
84 AL	7	14	4.73	32	3	192.1	193	101	87	119
85 AL	0	6	5.42	42	0	81.1	86	49	37	64
85 NL	0	0	6.23	4	0	4.1	5	3	4	2
86 NL	0	0	6.57	8	0	12.1	15	9	4	9
86 AL	9	5	3.74	29	4	149.1	137	62	65	102
87 AL	20	13	3.68	37	8	261.1	224	107	105	205
88 AL	21	12	3.23	37	14	275.2	240	99	110	192
89 AL	21	9	3.32	36	8	257.2	260	95	69	155
90 AL	22	11	2.56	36	11	267.0	226	76	83	166
91 AL	11	11	5.18	35	2	226.0	245	130	105	144
92 AL	12	10	3.66	31	2	199.1	175	81	79	130
93 AL	12	8	4.44	26	0	162.0	146	80	72	96
94 AL	7	8	5.87	22	1	133.1	151	87	62	111
Life	165	122	3.86	507	55	2548.2	2398	1092	995	1683
3 AVE	11	10	4.65	29	1	183.1	178	95	79	127

KELLY STINNETT

Position: Catcher
Team: New York Mets
Born: Feb. 14, 1970 Lawton, OK
Height: 5'11" **Weight:** 195 lbs.
Bats: right **Throws:** right
Acquired: Rule 5 draft pick from Indians, 12/93

Player Summary	
Fantasy Value	$0
Card Value	12¢ to 20¢
Will	serve as backup
Can't	stop working
Expect	decent speed
Don't Expect	much power

Stinnett beat out a host of competitors for the Mets' backup catching job last spring. In his first major-league season, the former Cleveland prospect acquitted himself well defensively and chipped in a little with his bat. A hard-working, hustling approach also made him a favorite with Mets manager Dallas Green. Stinnett hit .284 against right-handers, but oddly batted just .224 versus lefties—which makes platooning him with lefty Todd Hundley somewhat problematic. Stinnett doesn't hit for much power, owning only 30 professional homers in five seasons, and he compiled just a .360 slugging percentage last year. However, Stinnett is faster than most catchers and swiped two bases without being caught in 1994. Behind the plate, he is an aggressive, agile athlete with a strong arm but an imperfect release. He tossed out 35 percent of enemy basestealers last season. That ratio should improve as he gains experience. Even in the minors, Stinnett only once played over 100 games, and it's unlikely he'll ever play regularly in the bigs. He did show enough to last as a reserve.

Major League Batting Register

	BA	G	AB	R	H	2B	3B	HR	RBI	SB
94 NL	.253	47	150	20	38	6	2	2	14	2
Life	.253	47	150	20	38	6	2	2	14	2

KEVIN STOCKER

Position: Shortstop
Team: Philadelphia Phillies
Born: Feb. 13, 1970 Spokane, WA
Height: 6'1" **Weight:** 178 lbs.
Bats: both **Throws:** right
Acquired: Second-round pick in 6/91 free-agent draft

Player Summary	
Fantasy Value	$4 to $6
Card Value	10¢ to 20¢
Will	play every day
Can't	afford to slip
Expect	top on-base mark
Don't Expect	a Gold Glove

He was bound to fall back to earth, but at least he had a parachute. Stocker couldn't sustain the unreal pace he established in 1993, when he helped to deliver a pennant to Philadelphia. His second season wasn't bad, nevertheless. He has negligible power, but he took 44 walks last year and fanned just 41 times. Stocker's on-base average in 1994 was an excellent .383, and he may have a future as a No. 2 batter. In order to move up, he will have to run more. He has fairly good speed, stealing 64 bases in his three minor-league seasons. Another place Stocker must improve is in the field. He moves gracefully at his position and has better-than-average range, but he has had trouble with routine plays on the big-league level and doesn't throw especially well. He had been named the best defensive shortstop in the Florida State League in 1992, so the promise is there. Stocker is still learning how to play. If Stocker, a former University of Washington star, can smooth out the rough spots, he could become a fine player.

Major League Batting Register

	BA	G	AB	R	H	2B	3B	HR	RBI	SB
93 NL	.324	70	259	46	84	12	3	2	31	5
94 NL	.273	82	271	38	74	11	2	2	28	2
Life	.298	152	530	84	158	23	5	4	59	7
2 AVE	.294	93	320	50	94	14	3	2	35	4

TODD STOTTLEMYRE

Position: Pitcher
Team: Toronto Blue Jays
Born: May 20, 1965 Sunnyside, WA
Height: 6'3" **Weight:** 190 lbs.
Bats: left **Throws:** right
Acquired: First-round pick in secondary phase of 6/85 free-agent draft

Player Summary	
Fantasy Value	$4 to $6
Card Value	5¢ to 7¢
Will	throw high and tight
Can't	blow hitters away
Expect	home runs
Don't Expect	a big season

Although the defending world champion Jays slumped seriously last year, Stottlemyre pitched slightly better in 1994 than he did the previous two seasons. Better control was the main reason for the lanky righty's improvement, as he walked just over three men per game and fanned nearly seven. He does not have great raw stuff, however, and AL hitters still compiled a .276 batting average with 31 doubles and 19 home runs against him. When an opponent does connect off Stottlemyre, the hitter should be wide awake the next time up. The Toronto hurler has been known to throw inside, and he has embroiled his squad in beanball wars. Despite his occasional forays outside the strike zone, Stottlemyre threw no wild pitches in 1994. He does not hold runners well. His 7-7 record is exactly as one could have predicted, considering he notched a 4.22 ERA and received over four runs per game in support. Right now, Stottlemyre is average.

Major League Pitching Register

	W	L	ERA	G	CG	IP	H	ER	BB	SO
88 AL	4	8	5.69	28	0	98.0	109	62	46	67
89 AL	7	7	3.88	27	0	127.2	137	55	44	63
90 AL	13	17	4.34	33	4	203.0	214	98	69	115
91 AL	15	8	3.78	34	1	219.0	194	92	75	116
92 AL	12	11	4.50	28	6	174.0	175	87	63	98
93 AL	11	12	4.84	30	1	176.2	204	95	69	98
94 AL	7	7	4.22	26	3	140.2	149	66	48	105
Life	69	70	4.39	206	15	1139.0	1182	555	414	662
3 AVE	11	11	4.51	32	4	182.2	196	92	67	115

DOUG STRANGE

Position: Second base; third base
Team: Texas Rangers
Born: April 13, 1964 Greenville, SC
Height: 6'2" **Weight:** 170 lbs.
Bats: both **Throws:** right
Acquired: Signed as a free agent, 1/93

Player Summary	
Fantasy Value	$1 to $3
Card Value	5¢ to 7¢
Will	play hard
Can't	dazzle with bat
Expect	several jobs
Don't Expect	everyday duty

Strange has little claim on a regular job. He hasn't shown exceptional batting average, power, speed, or on-base ability in his major-league career. He also doesn't amaze with the glove. Due to the Rangers' lack of other options, he played every day in 1993, but last year he shared time with Jeff Frye. Strange does not hit left-handers well (just .065 in 1994), and the righty-hitting Frye's emergence means Strange won't even play against southpaws anyway. Strange hit only .236 against right-handers last year, drew just 15 walks, and had a poor .268 on-base percentage. He also fanned 38 times and was caught stealing three of four tries. He's not going to last in even half-time duty without showing the same kind of production he did in 1993. He lacks the range to be a top defensive second baseman; he can also play third. Part of the reason for Strange's decline may be the Rangers' move from Arlington Stadium; after hitting nearly .300 there in 1993, he batted under .220 at The Ballpark in Arlington last season.

Major League Batting Register

	BA	G	AB	R	H	2B	3B	HR	RBI	SB
89 AL	.214	64	196	16	42	4	1	1	14	3
91 NL	.444	3	9	0	4	1	0	0	1	1
92 NL	.160	52	94	7	15	1	0	1	5	1
93 AL	.256	145	484	58	124	29	0	7	60	6
94 AL	.212	73	226	26	48	12	1	5	26	1
Life	.231	337	1009	107	233	47	2	14	106	12
2 AVE	.239	124	401	47	96	23	1	7	48	4

DARRYL STRAWBERRY

Position: Outfield
Team: San Francisco Giants
Born: March 12, 1962 Los Angeles, CA
Height: 6'6" **Weight:** 215 lbs.
Bats: left **Throws:** left
Acquired: Signed as a free agent, 6/94

Player Summary	
Fantasy Value	$5 to $7
Card Value	5¢ to 7¢
Will	drive in runs
Can't	show old speed
Expect	lefty woes
Don't Expect	great impact

Strawberry could have been one of the great ones. The troubled slugger entered a substance-abuse program last April. After his rehabilitation ended in May, the Dodgers (who had dealt with this before) released him. San Francisco snapped Strawberry up shortly afterward and sent him to Triple-A. After a hot streak at Phoenix, Strawberry hit the show July 6. He slumped for a time but had some big hits as well. The question now is whether Strawberry will be a productive player in the future. In 1994, he did not show above-average power and seemed to have lost some bat speed. He drew 19 walks for a .363 on-base percentage but fanned 22 times. Left-handers held him to a .207 mark. No longer blessed with his old speed and defensive ability, Strawberry can only contribute if he keeps his bat, back, and psyche fully healthy.

Major League Batting Register

	BA	G	AB	R	H	2B	3B	HR	RBI	SB
83 NL	.257	122	420	63	108	15	7	26	74	19
84 NL	.251	147	522	75	131	27	4	26	97	27
85 NL	.277	111	393	78	109	15	4	29	79	26
86 NL	.259	136	475	76	123	27	5	27	93	28
87 NL	.284	154	532	108	151	32	5	39	104	36
88 NL	.269	153	543	101	146	27	3	39	101	29
89 NL	.225	134	476	69	107	26	1	29	77	11
90 NL	.277	152	542	92	150	18	1	37	108	15
91 NL	.265	139	505	86	134	22	4	28	99	10
92 NL	.237	43	156	20	37	8	0	5	25	3
93 NL	.140	32	100	12	14	2	0	5	12	1
94 NL	.239	29	92	13	22	3	1	4	17	0
Life	.259	1352	4756	793	1232	222	35	294	886	205

B.J. SURHOFF

Position: Outfield; infield
Team: Milwaukee Brewers
Born: Aug. 4, 1964 Bronx, NY
Height: 6'1" **Weight:** 200 lbs.
Bats: left **Throws:** right
Acquired: First-round pick in 6/85 free-agent draft

Player Summary

Fantasy Value	$7 to $9
Card Value	6¢ to 10¢
Will	make contact
Can't	show old speed
Expect	good average
Don't Expect	20 homers

Most of Surhoff's 1994 season was lost to injuries. Projected to be the Brewers' starting right fielder, he instead began the year on the disabled list, after shoulder surgery. He first saw action April 16 but was sidelined again four days later with a strained abdomen. The injury kept him out until May 23. On July 7, he was shelved for the remainder of the season when the abdomen injury returned. This is unfortunate, because in between, Surhoff was having his best offensive year. Usually, he doesn't do much besides hit around .270. Last year, however, Surhoff showed power, drew 16 walks, and fanned just 14 times. His on-base percentage was .336, and his slugging percentage a fine .485. In 1994, he batted a splendid .328 against lefties. He has a career mark over .280 against his fellow portsiders. He no longer has much speed. Surhoff may see action at third and first, as well as right field, this year.

Major League Batting Register

	BA	G	AB	R	H	2B	3B	HR	RBI	SB
87 AL	.299	115	395	50	118	22	3	7	68	11
88 AL	.245	139	493	47	121	21	0	5	38	21
89 AL	.248	126	436	42	108	17	4	5	55	14
90 AL	.276	135	474	55	131	21	4	6	59	18
91 AL	.289	143	505	57	146	19	4	5	68	5
92 AL	.252	139	480	63	121	19	1	4	62	14
93 AL	.274	148	552	66	151	38	3	7	79	12
94 AL	.261	40	134	20	35	11	2	5	22	0
Life	.268	985	3469	400	931	168	21	44	451	95
2 AVE	.264	144	516	65	136	29	2	6	71	13

BILL SWIFT

Position: Pitcher
Team: San Francisco Giants
Born: Oct. 27, 1961 South Portland, ME
Height: 6' **Weight:** 180 lbs.
Bats: right **Throws:** right
Acquired: Traded from Mariners with Mike Jackson and Dave Burba for Kevin Mitchell and Mike Remlinger, 12/91

Player Summary

Fantasy Value	$10 to $13
Card Value	6¢ to 10¢
Will	pitch effectively
Can't	bank on health
Expect	sinkers
Don't Expect	many walks

Injuries, the bane of Swift's career, struck again in 1994. Twice he was shelved with inflamed muscles on his right side (near the arm). In between his trips to the disabled list, each of which lasted nearly a month, Swift pitched typically well. He has fine control and one of baseball's nastiest sinkers. Most hitters can do little more than beat Swift's deliveries into the ground. Rarely do his pitches sail. He tossed just two wild pitches and allowed only 10 homers in 1994. Opponents usually collect a decent amount of singles against Swift, but few walks or extra-base hits. He has good control, allowing two and one-half bases on balls per nine innings last summer. Opponents compiled just a .313 on-base percentage in 1994. If he could only stay healthy, he'd be one of the game's best pitchers. Unfortunately, it appears that Swift will never be able to shoulder a heavy load.

Major League Pitching Register

	W	L	ERA	G	CG	IP	H	ER	BB	SO
85 AL	6	10	4.77	23	0	120.2	131	64	48	55
86 AL	2	9	5.46	29	1	115.1	148	70	55	55
88 AL	8	12	4.59	38	6	174.2	199	89	65	47
89 AL	7	3	4.43	37	0	130.0	140	64	38	45
90 AL	6	4	2.39	55	0	128.0	135	34	21	42
91 AL	1	2	1.99	71	0	90.1	74	20	26	48
92 NL	10	4	2.08	30	3	164.2	144	38	43	77
93 NL	21	8	2.82	34	1	232.2	195	73	55	157
94 NL	8	7	3.38	17	0	109.1	109	41	31	62
Life	69	59	3.51	334	11	1265.2	1275	493	382	588
3 AVE	14	7	2.75	29	1	183.2	164	56	47	107

GREG SWINDELL

Position: Pitcher
Team: Houston Astros
Born: Jan. 2, 1965   Fort Worth, TX
Height: 6'3"   **Weight:** 225 lbs.
Bats: both   **Throws:** left
Acquired: Signed as a free agent, 12/92

Player Summary	
Fantasy Value	$8 to $10
Card Value	8¢ to 12¢
Will	allow homers
Can't	be a staff ace
Expect	great control
Don't Expect	stumped lefties

Nine years into his career, Swindell is still more potential than pitcher. He's never lived up to expectations, and he has failed to overcome his problems. Despite enormous physical talent, Swindell is now a third starter at best. Since coming to Houston, he has had more trouble than one would expect from a good hurler moving into the pitcher-friendly Astrodome. He does have outstanding location, allowing just one and one-half walks per game last year, but he has lost some velocity on his fastball. He gave up 36 doubles and 20 homers in 1994, and he continues to have serious problems with left-handers, who batted well over .300. In addition, some in Houston feel Swindell is overweight. On the positive side, he always takes his turn, holds runners on base very well, and has one of the NL's best sliders. When he puts the ball where he wants it, he is usually effective.

Major League Pitching Register

	W	L	ERA	G	CG	IP	H	ER	BB	SO
86 AL	5	2	4.23	9	1	61.2	57	29	15	46
87 AL	3	8	5.10	16	4	102.1	112	58	37	97
88 AL	18	14	3.20	33	12	242.0	234	86	45	180
89 AL	13	6	3.37	28	5	184.1	170	69	51	129
90 AL	12	9	4.40	34	3	214.2	245	105	47	135
91 AL	9	16	3.48	33	7	238.0	241	92	31	169
92 NL	12	8	2.70	31	5	213.2	210	64	41	138
93 NL	12	13	4.16	31	1	190.1	215	88	40	124
94 NL	9	4	4.37	24	1	148.1	175	72	26	74
Life	92	85	3.74	239	39	1595.1	1659	663	333	1092
3 AVE	12	11	3.72	32	2	204.1	224	84	39	122

KEVIN TAPANI

Position: Pitcher
Team: Minnesota Twins
Born: Feb. 18, 1964   Des Moines, IA
Height: 6'   **Weight:** 180 lbs.
Bats: right   **Throws:** right
Acquired: Traded from Mets with David West, Jack Savage, Rick Aguilera, and Tim Drummond for Loy McBride and Frank Viola, 7/89

Player Summary	
Fantasy Value	$9 to $11
Card Value	8¢ to 12¢
Will	show fine control
Can't	unfurl heat
Expect	plenty of doubles
Don't Expect	an ERA title

After a rough April, Tapani won seven straight starts in May and June on his way to a good season. He didn't notch a great ERA, but he did a fine job working in a hitters' park during a hitters' year. The former Met is durable, works quickly, and keeps the ball near the plate. He seldom walks batters, allowing just two and one-quarter bases on balls per nine innings last summer. He threw only one wild pitch in 1994. He must change speeds and work the corners to be successful. Tapani usually can place the ball where he wants it, but he lacks raw velocity, and as a result allows his share of extra-base hits. In 1994, AL hitters rapped out 44 doubles and 13 homers against Tapani. He led all Twins starters in innings pitched, ERA, and complete games, and he was the unquestioned leader of the staff. While he is far from being a star, Tapani is a dependable hurler.

Major League Pitching Register

	W	L	ERA	G	CG	IP	H	ER	BB	SO
89 NL	0	0	3.68	3	0	7.1	5	3	4	2
89 AL	2	2	3.86	5	0	32.2	34	14	8	21
90 AL	12	8	4.07	28	1	159.1	164	72	29	101
91 AL	16	9	2.99	34	4	244.0	225	81	40	135
92 AL	16	11	3.97	34	4	220.0	226	97	48	138
93 AL	12	15	4.43	36	3	225.2	243	111	57	150
94 AL	11	7	4.62	24	4	156.0	181	80	39	91
Life	69	52	3.94	164	16	1045.0	1078	458	225	638
3 AVE	14	12	4.34	35	4	222.1	241	107	53	139

TONY TARASCO

Position: Outfield
Team: Atlanta Braves
Born: Dec. 9, 1970 New York, NY
Height: 6'1" **Weight:** 205 lbs.
Bats: left **Throws:** right
Acquired: 15th-round pick in 6/88 free-agent draft

Player Summary	
Fantasy Value	$5 to $7
Card Value	12¢ to 20¢
Will	hit right-handers
Can't	develop on bench
Expect	more playing time
Don't Expect	top on-base mark

Tarasco's skills are the kind scouts love. He has a quick bat, decent speed, a good line-drive stroke, a strong arm, and good range. Unfortunately, his baseball acumen has not yet caught up to his physical attributes. Tarasco shows little ability to work the strike zone, and as a result, he rarely received good pitches to drive as a rookie in 1994. He walked just nine times and fanned 17 last year. His on-base average was .313. In the minors, he hardly had problems making contact and rarely walked. The Braves are hoping Tarasco will develop power, but his pro high in homers is 15. He notched that mark at Triple-A Richmond in 1993 in 370 at bats. He also hit .330 with 53 RBI that year, and he was named the No. 6 prospect in the International League. At Double-A Greenville in 1992, he had 15 four-baggers in 489 at bats. He was viewed as a platoon player by Atlanta manager Bobby Cox, and the young center fielder faced left-handers just 19 times in his rookie season. Tarasco will never develop by seeing as little action as he did in 1994. He needs to play every day—somewhere.

Major League Batting Register

	BA	G	AB	R	H	2B	3B	HR	RBI	SB
93 NL	.229	24	35	6	8	2	0	0	2	0
94 NL	.273	87	132	16	36	6	0	5	19	5
Life	.263	111	167	22	44	8	0	5	21	5

DANNY TARTABULL

Position: Designated hitter
Team: New York Yankees
Born: Oct. 30, 1962 San Juan, Puerto Rico
Height: 6'1" **Weight:** 205 lbs.
Bats: right **Throws:** right
Acquired: Signed as a free agent, 1/92

Player Summary	
Fantasy Value	$15 to $18
Card Value	10¢ to 15¢
Will	provide offense
Can't	help elsewhere
Expect	hits vs. righties
Don't Expect	congeniality

Despite a high profile and a strong bat, Tartabull isn't paying the freight. Once a second baseman with Seattle, then an outfielder in Kansas City, Tartabull now rarely does anything but DH. His bat is poor defensively and does not run well. His bat has always carried him. Unfortunately, Tartabull cannot solve right-handers or hit well at Yankee Stadium, and he is now just an ordinary designated hitter. He has awesome power, as evidenced by the .484 slugging percentage that he compiled in 1994, but he hit only .219 against right-handers and .246 in home games. He drew 66 walks and was on base at a .360 clip, but he whiffed 111 times, fourth-highest in the American League. He did stay healthy all season and rebounded strongly against left-handers, hitting .339 against them last year after slumping in 1993. Questions concerning Tartabull's attitude persist.

Major League Batting Register

	BA	G	AB	R	H	2B	3B	HR	RBI	SB
84 AL	.300	10	20	3	6	1	0	2	7	0
85 AL	.328	19	61	8	20	7	1	1	7	1
86 AL	.270	137	511	76	138	25	6	25	96	4
87 AL	.309	158	582	95	180	27	3	34	101	9
88 AL	.274	146	507	80	139	38	3	26	102	8
89 AL	.268	133	441	54	118	22	0	18	62	4
90 AL	.268	88	313	41	84	19	0	15	60	1
91 AL	.316	132	484	78	153	35	3	31	100	6
92 AL	.266	123	421	72	112	19	0	25	85	2
93 AL	.250	138	513	87	128	33	2	31	102	0
94 AL	.256	104	399	68	102	24	1	19	67	1
Life	.278	1188	4252	662	1180	250	19	227	789	36
3 AVE	.256	136	499	85	128	29	1	28	94	1

EDDIE TAUBENSEE

Position: Catcher
Team: Cincinnati Reds
Born: Oct. 31, 1968 Beeville, TX
Height: 6'4" **Weight:** 205 lbs.
Bats: left **Throws:** right
Acquired: Traded from Astros for Ross Powell and Marty Lister, 4/94

Player Summary	
Fantasy Value	$3 to $5
Card Value	5¢ to 7¢
Will	hit right-handers
Can't	start strong
Expect	some power
Don't Expect	great throwing

Houston may already regret trading Taubensee. Their remaining catchers didn't do much, and the Reds seemed happy with their new acquisition. Cincinnati apparently never expected Taubensee to be an everyday player, and the ballclub instead concentrated on letting him do what he can. He rarely begins the season well, and last year was hitting just over .200 in early June. However, he turns on the juice when the weather heats up, and he finished 1994 with a .291 batting average and seven homers against right-handers. He usually strikes out twice as often as he walks. Last year, he took 15 walks for a .333 on-base percentage. While Taubensee probably cannot be a success with everyday duty, he does just fine in a platoon role. Defensively, he has excellent arm strength but a poor release. In 1994, he threw out fewer than 30 percent of enemy basestealers. Taubensee is respected for his pitcher-handling ability, and he is still young enough to develop a little more in every phase of his game.

Major League Batting Register

	BA	G	AB	R	H	2B	3B	HR	RBI	SB
91 AL	.242	26	66	5	16	2	1	0	8	0
92 NL	.222	104	297	23	66	15	0	5	28	2
93 NL	.250	94	288	26	72	11	1	9	42	1
94 NL	.283	66	187	29	53	8	2	8	21	2
Life	.247	290	838	83	207	36	4	22	99	5
3 AVE	.251	97	283	30	71	12	1	8	33	2

MICKEY TETTLETON

Position: Catcher; first base
Team: Detroit Tigers
Born: Sept. 19, 1960 Oklahoma City, OK
Height: 6'2" **Weight:** 212 lbs.
Bats: both **Throws:** right
Acquired: Traded from Orioles for Jeff Robinson, 1/91

Player Summary	
Fantasy Value	$14 to $17
Card Value	8¢ to 12¢
Will	hit homers
Can't	add any speed
Expect	several jobs
Don't Expect	high bat mark

Tettleton has long been a capable offensive player who combines power with plate discipline. However, his penchant for taking pitches until he sees one he likes reached almost comic proportions in 1994. He either fanned or walked in nearly half of his plate appearances last year, taking 97 free passes and striking out 98 times. This increase in non-contact at bats is troublesome, but for now he is productive. He registered a now-customary mediocre batting average last year but still showed typical extra-base power, slugging .463. His on-base percentage of .419 was sixth-best in the AL. Sparky Anderson used Tettleton mostly at catcher in 1994 but also inserted him at first base, designated hitter, and the outfield. His game-calling and agility behind the dish are poor, and he threw out a paltry 17 percent of basestealers last season.

Major League Batting Register

	BA	G	AB	R	H	2B	3B	HR	RBI	SB
84 AL	.263	33	76	10	20	2	1	1	5	0
85 AL	.251	78	211	23	53	12	0	3	15	2
86 AL	.204	90	211	26	43	9	0	10	35	7
87 AL	.194	82	211	19	41	3	0	8	26	1
88 AL	.261	86	283	31	74	11	1	11	37	0
89 AL	.258	117	411	72	106	21	2	26	65	3
90 AL	.223	135	444	68	99	21	2	15	51	2
91 AL	.263	154	501	85	132	17	2	31	89	3
92 AL	.238	157	525	82	125	25	0	32	83	0
93 AL	.245	152	522	79	128	25	4	32	110	3
94 AL	.248	107	339	57	84	18	2	17	51	0
Life	.242	1191	3734	552	905	164	14	186	567	21
3 AVE	.244	153	508	80	124	25	2	29	88	1

BOB TEWKSBURY

Position: Pitcher
Team: St. Louis Cardinals
Born: Nov. 30, 1960 Concord, NH
Height: 6'4" **Weight:** 208 lbs.
Bats: right **Throws:** right
Acquired: Signed as a free agent, 12/88

Player Summary	
Fantasy Value	$6 to $8
Card Value	6¢ to 10¢
Will	endure streaks
Can't	afford extra bases
Expect	fine location
Don't Expect	top fastballs

"Streaky" describes Tewksbury accurately. He had a horrid first half of 1993, but he saved that season with a fine stretch. Last year, he reversed the pattern, starting out 7-0 with a 3.38 ERA in his first eight starts. He had fanned 35 and walked just nine in 61 innings. However, he went 1-7 in his next eight appearances, and he allowed 42 runs over 44 innings (an 8.59 ERA). The soft-tossing Tewksbury then settled into a consistent, but ineffective, groove for the rest of the season. His repertoire includes several pitches, but none of them incorporates above-average movement or velocity. Tewksbury wins by changing speeds, keeping hitters off balance, and maintaining his usually outstanding location. He rarely walks anybody, and last year was no exception. Every mistake he made last year seemed to fly away, though. Opponents slugged 42 doubles and 19 homers in 1994.

Major League Pitching Register

	W	L	ERA	G	CG	IP	H	ER	BB	SO
86 AL	9	5	3.31	23	2	130.1	144	48	31	49
87 AL	1	4	6.75	8	0	33.1	47	25	7	12
87 NL	0	4	6.50	7	0	18.0	32	13	13	10
88 NL	0	0	8.10	1	0	3.1	6	3	2	1
89 NL	1	0	3.30	7	1	30.0	25	11	10	17
90 NL	10	9	3.47	28	3	145.1	151	56	15	50
91 NL	11	12	3.25	30	3	191.0	206	69	38	75
92 NL	16	5	2.16	33	5	233.0	217	56	20	91
93 NL	17	10	3.83	32	2	213.2	258	91	20	97
94 NL	12	10	5.32	24	4	155.2	190	92	22	79
Life	77	59	3.62	193	20	1153.2	1276	464	178	481
3 AVE	17	10	3.74	33	4	221.2	248	92	24	100

FRANK THOMAS

Position: First base
Team: Chicago White Sox
Born: May 27, 1968 Columbus, GA
Height: 6'5" **Weight:** 257 lbs.
Bats: right **Throws:** right
Acquired: First-round pick in 6/89 free-agent draft

Player Summary	
Fantasy Value	$35 to $40
Card Value	$2 to $4
Will	clear 35 homers
Can't	add defense
Expect	high on-base average
Don't Expect	many problems

Thomas will be a Triple Crown contender for years to come. He enjoyed a Jimmie Foxx-like season in 1994, combining awesome power, a high average, and matchless strike-zone judgement on his way to his second straight MVP Award. "The Big Hurt" paced the American League in slugging percentage, on-base percentage, walks, and runs scored. He finished second in homers and third in doubles and batting average. He batted a stunning .385 against left-handers and .342 versus righties, as well as hitting .385 at home and .327 on the road. Thomas saw some action at designated hitter last season, and some feel he won't be playing much first base in another year or so. This might not be a bad idea, since Thomas has mediocre range, average hands, and a poor throwing arm. Of course, if he could play Gold Glove-caliber first base, he might be the best first baseman who ever lived. Without fielding ability, he may just have to settle for being the best offensive first baseman ever.

Major League Batting Register

	BA	G	AB	R	H	2B	3B	HR	RBI	SB
90 AL	.330	60	191	39	63	11	3	7	31	0
91 AL	.318	158	559	104	178	31	2	32	109	1
92 AL	.323	160	573	108	185	46	2	24	115	6
93 AL	.317	153	549	106	174	36	0	41	128	4
94 AL	.353	113	399	106	141	34	1	38	101	2
Life	.326	644	2271	463	741	158	8	142	484	13
3 AVE	.331	157	561	121	186	43	1	40	128	4

JIM THOME

Position: Third base
Team: Cleveland Indians
Born: Aug. 27, 1970 Peoria, IL
Height: 6'4" **Weight:** 220 lbs.
Bats: left **Throws:** right
Acquired: 13th-round pick in 6/89 free-agent draft

Player Summary	
Fantasy Value	$10 to $13
Card Value	20¢ to 30¢
Will	bash right-handers
Can't	make contact
Expect	walks
Don't Expect	great glove

Indians manager Mike Hargrove deserves credit for sticking with Thome through the young third baseman's rough 1994 start. The big lefty hitter began poorly, and at the end of May he was hitting just .228, although he had smacked six home runs. However, Thome picked up the pace and by season's end was one of the Tribe's most productive players. He belted three long home runs against the White Sox at Jacobs Field July 22, and he finished second on the team in dingers. He also drew 46 walks and had a .359 on-base percentage. Thome is far from perfect, however. He fanned 84 times in 1994 and hit a poor .167 against left-handers. He also made 15 errors at third base. Many miscues came on wild throws or muffs of easy plays, although he has fine reflexes and made his share of outstanding stops. He really isn't that far from being an average big-league hot corner man. It is possible that Thome will move permanently to first base in a year or two, allowing him to concentrate more on his strong point—offense.

Major League Batting Register

	BA	G	AB	R	H	2B	3B	HR	RBI	SB
91 AL	.255	27	98	7	25	4	2	1	9	1
92 AL	.205	40	117	8	24	3	1	2	12	2
93 AL	.266	47	154	28	41	11	0	7	22	2
94 AL	.268	98	321	58	86	20	1	20	52	3
Life	.255	212	690	101	176	38	4	30	95	8
2 AVE	.267	93	303	55	81	20	1	18	48	3

MILT THOMPSON

Position: Outfield
Team: Houston Astros
Born: Jan. 5, 1959 Washington, DC
Height: 5'11" **Weight:** 190 lbs.
Bats: left **Throws:** right
Acquired: Traded from Phillies for Tom Edens, 7/94

Player Summary	
Fantasy Value	$3 to $5
Card Value	5¢ to 7¢
Will	hit right-handers
Can't	add much power
Expect	good speed
Don't Expect	regular duty

While Thompson is far from exceptional, he does those things that he's expected to do well. Last year, he hit .288 against right-handers, stole nine bases in 11 tries, drew 24 walks, and notched a .346 on-base percentage. He also showed good range in the outfield and didn't commit an error all season. All these things make Thompson a fine bench player, but his weaknesses—an inability to solve lefties, an almost complete lack of power, and a poor throwing arm—limit him. The Astros acquired him to platoon with Kevin Bass when James Mouton lost his grip on the right-field job. Thompson served well as a regular for several seasons with the Cardinals and Phillies in the 1980s, and he has been a very consistent hitter during his career. He should be good for a couple more seasons of part-time duty.

Major League Batting Register

	BA	G	AB	R	H	2B	3B	HR	RBI	SB
84 NL	.303	25	99	16	30	1	0	2	4	14
85 NL	.302	73	182	17	55	7	2	0	6	9
86 NL	.251	96	299	38	75	7	1	6	23	19
87 NL	.302	150	527	86	159	26	9	7	43	46
88 NL	.288	122	378	53	109	16	2	2	33	17
89 NL	.290	155	545	60	158	28	8	4	68	27
90 NL	.218	135	418	42	91	14	7	6	30	25
91 NL	.307	115	326	55	100	16	5	6	34	16
92 NL	.293	109	208	31	61	9	1	4	17	18
93 NL	.262	129	340	42	89	14	2	4	44	9
94 NL	.274	96	241	34	66	7	0	4	33	9
Life	.279	1205	3563	474	993	145	37	45	335	209
3 AVE	.274	124	296	40	81	11	1	5	36	13

ROBBY THOMPSON

Position: Second base
Team: San Francisco Giants
Born: May 10, 1962   West Palm Beach, FL
Height: 5'11"   **Weight:** 173 lbs.
Bats: right   **Throws:** right
Acquired: First-round pick in secondary phase of 6/83 free-agent draft

Player Summary

Fantasy Value	$8 to $10
Card Value	8¢ to 12¢
Will	play solid defense
Can't	add much speed
Expect	good power
Don't Expect	perfect health

After signing a lucrative three-year free-agent deal last winter, Thompson turned around and had his most nightmarish campaign. The Giants were counting on their All-Star second sacker to help carry them to a division title, but Thompson couldn't stay in the lineup. Usually a consistent month-to-month performer, he began the season poorly and was hitting just .202 with one home run when he was sidelined with a strained right shoulder May 9. He could not make good contact—fanning 32 times in 1994—and was especially helpless against right-handers. Thompson was reactivated June 25 but was put back on the disabled list on July 5 when an examination revealed a torn tendon in his right rotator cuff. The resulting surgery ended Thompson's lost season. He is expected back in 1995, but his history of injuries is worrisome. When healthy, he hits well, draws a few walks, and is regarded as a top fielder.

Major League Batting Register

	BA	G	AB	R	H	2B	3B	HR	RBI	SB
86 NL	.271	149	549	73	149	27	3	7	47	12
87 NL	.262	132	420	62	110	26	5	10	44	16
88 NL	.264	138	477	66	126	24	6	7	48	14
89 NL	.241	148	547	91	132	26	11	13	50	12
90 NL	.245	144	498	67	122	22	3	15	56	14
91 NL	.262	144	492	74	129	24	5	19	48	14
92 NL	.260	128	443	54	115	25	1	14	49	5
93 NL	.312	128	494	85	154	30	2	19	65	10
94 NL	.209	35	129	13	27	8	2	2	7	3
Life	.263	1146	4049	585	1064	212	38	106	414	100
2 AVE	.287	128	469	70	135	28	2	17	57	8

RYAN THOMPSON

Position: Outfield
Team: New York Mets
Born: Nov. 4, 1967   Chestertown, MD
Height: 6'3"   **Weight:** 200 lbs.
Bats: right   **Throws:** right
Acquired: Traded from Blue Jays with Jeff Kent for David Cone, 8/92

Player Summary

Fantasy Value	$6 to $8
Card Value	6¢ to 10¢
Will	go downtown
Can't	grasp his ability
Expect	stellar defense
Don't Expect	top on-base mark

Thompson continued last year to exhibit exciting strengths and fatal weaknesses both on offense and defense. He has superior speed and outstanding range as a center fielder, and last year he regularly made highlight-film plays for the Mets. Unfortunately, he has a very poor arm, notching just five assists in 1994. At bat, Thompson has the same frustrating blend of good and bad. He sports a quick bat and has fine raw power. He still doesn't know the strike zone from the Magna Carta, however. Thompson is unable to resist breaking pitches in the dirt, and he fanned a whopping 94 times last year. He also hit just .218 against right-handers and an amazing .134 in home games. Taking only 28 walks, he registered a poor .301 on-base percentage, which helped to flatten his fine wheels. In addition, he failed when given the opportunity to use his speed to augment his offense, making plenty of mistakes on the basepaths. The Mets have tried him in several different lineup spots and found him wanting. Thompson is running out of time.

Major League Batting Register

	BA	G	AB	R	H	2B	3B	HR	RBI	SB
92 NL	.222	30	108	15	24	7	1	3	10	2
93 NL	.250	80	288	34	72	19	2	11	26	2
94 NL	.225	98	334	39	75	14	1	18	59	1
Life	.234	208	730	88	171	40	4	32	95	5
2 AVE	.234	109	379	44	89	19	2	18	55	2

LEE TINSLEY

Position: Outfield
Team: Boston Red Sox
Born: March 4, 1969 Shelbyville, KY
Height: 5'10" **Weight:** 185 lbs.
Bats: both **Throws:** right
Acquired: Traded from Mariners for a player to be named later, 3/94

Player Summary	
Fantasy Value	$2 to $4
Card Value	5¢ to 7¢
Will	run like the wind
Can't	hit for power
Expect	patience at bat
Don't Expect	a bat crown

While Tinsley is probably never going to hit for a high enough average to play regularly in the majors, he does some things well. He is very fast, three times swiping over 40 bases in a season during his pro career. He was not once caught stealing with the Red Sox in 1994. A first-round pick by Oakland in 1987, Tinsley was a very poor hitter for his first several pro seasons, but he has done much better as he has moved up the minor-league ladder. This improvement culminated when he notched a .302 mark at Triple-A Calgary in 1993. He also will take the walk, drawing 19 free passes last year. Unfortunately, his on-base percentage was just .315 due to his poor batting average. Tinsley has little power, and he whiffed 36 times in 1994. Despite his switch-hitting ability, he didn't enjoy a distinct advantage from either side. Boston used the speedster in left field and center field last year, and Tinsley showed excellent range. He does not have a strong arm. While he will never be a top-notch player, he could hang around for several years. Tinsley is still young enough to improve at the dish.

SALOMON TORRES

Position: Pitcher
Team: San Francisco Giants
Born: March 11, 1972 San Pedro de Macoris, Dominican Republic
Height: 5'11" **Weight:** 165 lbs.
Bats: right **Throws:** right
Acquired: Signed as a free agent, 9/89

Player Summary	
Fantasy Value	$2 to $4
Card Value	10¢ to 15¢
Will	impress with repertoire
Can't	keep ball in park
Expect	strikeouts
Don't Expect	command

A storied minor-league career advanced Torres to the major leagues, but he may not be ready for the high level of scrutiny or competition. After a fine performance down the stretch for San Francisco in 1993, he did not get out of the gate last year. After falling to a 2-6 record on June 19, Torres went AWOL. He turned up in the Dominican Republic, apparently experiencing a serious personal crisis: Torres was reportedly agonizing over the twin demands of his profession and his spirituality. He returned to the Giants four days after leaving, but he immediately jumped into hot water by beaning Charlie Hayes in Denver. The Giants finally shipped Torres to Triple-A on July 3. At Phoenix, he continued to struggle. He has an outstanding mix of pitches, including a tremendous curve, but he cannot afford the wildness and inconsistency he showed last year. Left-handers hit .325 against Torres in 1994 after batting only .169 the previous year. Opponents rapped 10 homers against him last year. The young right-hander may need time in the minors to regain his confidence.

Major League Batting Register

	BA	G	AB	R	H	2B	3B	HR	RBI	SB
93 AL	.158	11	19	2	3	1	0	1	2	0
94 AL	.222	78	144	27	32	4	0	2	14	13
Life	.215	89	163	29	35	5	0	3	16	13

Major League Pitching Register

	W	L	ERA	G	CG	IP	H	ER	BB	SO
93 NL	3	5	4.03	8	0	44.2	37	20	27	23
94 NL	2	8	5.44	16	1	84.1	95	51	34	42
Life	5	13	4.95	24	1	129.0	132	71	61	65

STEVE TRACHSEL

Position: Pitcher
Team: Chicago Cubs
Born: Oct. 31, 1970   Oxnard, CA
Height: 6'4"   **Weight:** 205 lbs.
Bats: right   **Throws:** right
Acquired: Eighth-round pick in 6/91 free-agent draft

Player Summary	
Fantasy Value	$9 to $11
Card Value	20¢ to 35¢
Will	mix pitches
Can't	dominate with heat
Expect	some home runs
Don't Expect	control woes

The largely unheralded Trachsel doesn't have an overpowering pitch. What he does have, however, is a good repertoire, including a fastball, an overhand curve, a good slider, and a changeup. He also possesses a shrewd attitude. As a raw rookie, he showed the poise that Cub fans had been missing since Greg Maddux left town. Despite his youth, Trachsel became the staff ace almost immediately. He is able and unafraid to throw strikes, and he began 1994 as a strikeout machine, ranking among the league leaders for the first month. Trachsel does allow plenty of homers, giving up 19 in 1994. His fastball rides in on left-handed hitters (who batted just .212), but sometimes the heater stays fat to right-handers, who batted .268 with 13 of those round-trippers. As a disappointing Cub campaign rolled on, Trachsel refused to give in, taking the ball every time. When the Cubs put him on the DL in July with a blister, he was vocal in his opposition to the move. After the strike, the Cubs sent him to Triple-A to give him more work. He could be a 20-game winner sometime in the future.

Major League Pitching Register

	W	L	ERA	G	CG	IP	H	ER	BB	SO
93 NL	0	2	4.58	3	0	19.2	16	10	3	14
94 NL	9	7	3.21	22	1	146.0	133	52	54	108
Life	9	9	3.37	25	1	165.2	149	62	57	122

ALAN TRAMMELL

Position: Shortstop
Team: Detroit Tigers
Born: Feb. 21, 1958   Garden Grove, CA
Height: 6'   **Weight:** 185 lbs.
Bats: right   **Throws:** right
Acquired: Second-round pick in 6/76 free-agent draft

Player Summary	
Fantasy Value	$5 to $7
Card Value	10¢ to 15¢
Will	hit left-handers
Can't	amaze with defense
Expect	Hall of Fame debate
Don't Expect	much more

No longer able to play every day due to physical problems and age, Trammell still rapped left-handers at a .297 clip in 1994 and showed his trademark power stroke. Once a stellar defensive player, he committed 10 errors in limited 1994 action and spent much of his time watching his heir apparent, Chris Gomez, play. Trammell never was flashy, but was one of the best shortstops of the 1980s. His career, while impressive, has often been interrupted by a string of injuries. Many will argue that Trammell deserves a trip to Cooperstown. He has made six All-Star teams, won four Gold Gloves, and was named the 1984 World Series MVP.

Major League Batting Register

	BA	G	AB	R	H	2B	3B	HR	RBI	SB
77 AL	.186	19	43	6	8	0	0	0	0	0
78 AL	.268	139	448	49	120	14	6	2	34	3
79 AL	.276	142	460	68	127	11	4	6	50	17
80 AL	.300	146	560	107	168	21	5	9	65	12
81 AL	.258	105	392	52	101	15	3	2	31	10
82 AL	.258	157	489	66	126	34	3	9	57	19
83 AL	.319	142	505	83	161	31	2	14	66	30
84 AL	.314	139	555	85	174	34	5	14	69	19
85 AL	.258	149	605	79	156	21	7	13	57	14
86 AL	.277	151	574	107	159	33	7	21	75	25
87 AL	.343	151	597	109	205	34	3	28	105	21
88 AL	.311	128	466	73	145	24	1	15	69	7
89 AL	.243	121	449	54	109	20	3	5	43	10
90 AL	.304	146	559	71	170	37	1	14	89	12
91 AL	.248	101	375	57	93	20	0	9	55	11
92 AL	.275	29	102	11	28	7	1	1	11	2
93 AL	.329	112	401	72	132	25	3	12	60	12
94 AL	.267	76	292	38	78	17	1	8	28	3
Life	.287	2153	7872	1187	2260	398	55	182	964	227
2 AVE	.298	110	406	63	121	24	2	12	50	8

CHRIS TURNER

Position: Catcher
Team: California Angels
Born: March 23, 1969   Bowling Green, KY
Height: 6'1"   **Weight:** 190 lbs.
Bats: right   **Throws:** right
Acquired: Seventh-round pick in 6/91 free-agent draft

Player Summary	
Fantasy Value $1
Card Value . . . . 7¢ to 10¢
Will . . . . develop offense
Can't . . . . hit right-handers
Expect. . . . . improved defense
Don't Expect . . . . big homers

Turner has only played pro ball four seasons, and he has already seen significant action in the majors. Originally an outfielder (and freshman All-American) at Western Kentucky, he did not catch until he was a senior. The Angels drafted him and moved him along because they like his game-calling ability and arm, although his throwing mechanics are poor. He nailed only 26 percent of enemy baserunners in 1994, but he was much better in that category than he had been in his first season. While Turner does not offer much at the plate now, he is expected to improve. He batted .262 against left-handers last year and stole three bases without being caught. Right-handers held him to just a .215 mark. After beginning the season with California, he was sent down to Triple-A with a miserable .138 average on June 29. He was recalled July 3, and two days later he returned to the lineup with a bang. Turner went 5-for-5 and stole home against Boston and fared well from that point on. He had some trouble making contact last year, fanning 29 times and drawing just 10 walks.

ISMAEL VALDES

Position: Pitcher
Team: Los Angeles Dodgers
Born: Aug. 21, 1973   Victoria, Mexico
Height: 6'3"   **Weight:** 183 lbs.
Bats: right   **Throws:** right
Acquired: Signed as a free agent, 6/91

Player Summary	
Fantasy Value $0
Card Value . . . . 10¢ to 15¢
Will . . . . notch strikeouts
Can't . . . . be closer yet
Expect. . . . . expanded role
Don't Expect . . . . righties to hit

The Dodgers' bullpen was so poor last year that the big-league club raided its farm system early and often for relievers. On June 11, Los Angeles again reached into its hat, and this time pulled out a rabbit. With only 19 games of pro experience prior to 1994, Valdes began the year as a starter at Double-A San Antonio. He posted a 3.38 ERA with 55 strikeouts and eight walks in 54 innings before being promoted to Triple-A Albuquerque. There, he posted a 3-0 record, with a 2.77 ERA, 24 strikeouts, and six walks in 26 innings. The Dodgers had seen enough, and brought him to the show. The young righty appeared entirely ready for the big leagues, holding opponents to a .206 mark. Fellow right-handers were especially helpless, hitting just .154. Valdes has a wide assortment of pitches and good velocity. He fanned a man per inning and allowed only two home runs in 1994. The Dodgers sent Valdes back to Triple-A in order to stay sharp during the strike, an indication of how much they value their talented rookie. Despite working in the middle last season, Valdes will play a larger role in 1995.

Major League Batting Register

	BA	G	AB	R	H	2B	3B	HR	RBI	SB
93 AL	.280	25	75	9	21	5	0	1	13	1
94 AL	.242	58	149	23	36	7	1	1	12	3
Life	.254	83	224	32	57	12	1	2	25	4

Major League Pitching Register

	W	L	ERA	G	S	IP	H	ER	BB	SO
94 NL	3	1	3.18	21	0	28.1	21	10	10	28
Life	3	1	3.18	21	0	28.1	21	10	10	28

JOHN VALENTIN

Position: Shortstop
Team: Boston Red Sox
Born: Feb. 18, 1967 Mineola, NY
Height: 6′ **Weight:** 170 lbs.
Bats: right **Throws:** right
Acquired: Fifth-round pick in 6/88 free-agent draft

Player Summary	
Fantasy Value	$10 to $13
Card Value	8¢ to 12¢
Will	show good range
Can't	steal bases
Expect	extra-base hits
Don't Expect	a bat title

His infield mates—Mo Vaughn, Tim Naehring, and Scott Cooper—get more ink, but Boston's unsung shortstop deserves recognition. Valentin did an excellent job in 1994, despite missing over a month due to surgery to repair torn cartilage in his right knee. Batting .282 with minimal power before the injury, he cranked up the offense after he returned. He showed power, finishing second on the Red Sox in slugging percentage. His .316 batting average was a personal best. One reason Valentin had never hit for high average was an inability to solve left-handers. Last summer, however, he batted over .320 against them. The strong shortstop is also quite patient at the dish, taking 42 walks for a .400 on-base percentage. He halved his strikeouts, too, fanning just 38 times last year. Valentin does not have great speed, but he is quick enough to play a good shortstop. He possessed fine range to the left and the right. He also has a strong, though occasionally inaccurate, arm. Valentin's array of talents could make him an All-Star.

JOSE VALENTIN

Position: Shortstop
Team: Milwaukee Brewers
Born: Oct. 12, 1969 Manati, Puerto Rico
Height: 5′10″ **Weight:** 175 lbs.
Bats: both **Throws:** right
Acquired: Traded from Padres with Ricky Bones and Matt Mieske for Gary Sheffield and Geoff Kellogg, 3/92

Player Summary	
Fantasy Value	$7 to $9
Card Value	10¢ to 15¢
Will	impress defensively
Can't	solve left-handers
Expect	some power
Don't Expect	great average

Amidst the wreckage that was the Brewers' 1994 season, there were a few signs of life. Valentin, who began the year as a reserve infielder, got a chance to start at shortstop after injuries sidelined Pat Listach. As a newcomer, Valentin showed excellent range and a strong arm at shortstop, although he committed 20 errors. His concentration could be better, as most of his boots came on easy plays. However, he is already one of the AL's better defensive shortstops. Offensively, he ranks up there with the better young shortstops, too. While Valentin's batting average is consistent with what he did in the minors (between .250 to .260), he has also shown excellent power throughout his pro career. Left-handers held him to just a .135 mark last year, however. He also is a patient hitter and took 38 walks last year for a .330 on-base percentage. Two of Valentin's home runs last year were grand slams, and he finished third on the club in RBI despite hitting ninth in the order. Valentin has a good grasp on the shortstop job.

Major League Batting Register

	BA	G	AB	R	H	2B	3B	HR	RBI	SB
92 AL	.276	58	185	21	51	13	0	5	25	1
93 AL	.278	144	468	50	130	40	3	11	66	3
94 AL	.316	84	301	53	95	26	2	9	49	3
Life	.289	286	954	124	276	79	5	25	140	7
3 AVE	.292	107	359	49	105	30	2	10	53	3

Major League Batting Register

	BA	G	AB	R	H	2B	3B	HR	RBI	SB
92 AL	.000	4	3	1	0	0	0	0	1	0
93 AL	.245	19	53	10	13	1	2	1	7	1
94 AL	.239	97	285	47	68	19	0	11	46	12
Life	.238	120	341	58	81	20	2	12	54	13

WILLIAM VanLANDINGHAM

Position: Pitcher
Team: San Francisco Giants
Born: July 16, 1970   Columbia, TN
Height: 6'2"   **Weight:** 210 lbs.
Bats: right   **Throws:** right
Acquired: Fifth-round pick in 6/91 free-agent draft

Player Summary	
Fantasy Value	$5 to $7
Card Value	15¢ to 25¢
Will	halt right-handers
Can't	thread the needle
Expect	fine repertoire
Don't Expect	polished package

Last season at Double-A Shreveport, Van-Landingham posted a 4-3 record, a 2.81 ERA, and 45 strikeouts in eight starts. He was recalled to San Francisco last May 18 when Rich Monteleone was disabled. Van-Landingham immediately moved into the Giants' rotation and made an impressive debut. The hard-throwing rookie has good movement on all of his pitches, but the specialty of his arsenal is a fine overhand curve. VanLandingham's impact was felt most in July, when he was 4-0 with a 2.31 ERA. The right-hander took to Candlestick Park, posting a 2.76 ERA at home. He also held opponents to a .215 batting average, and right-handers hit just .205. His only problem was control; VanLandingham walked close to five men per game. However, even struggling with location, he threw just three wild pitches and kept the ball low. He allowed just four homers in the majors last season. Assuming he improves his game even a little, VanLandingham is staff ace material. The former University of Kentucky star was 14-8 with a 5.12 ERA at Class-A San Jose in 1993.

Major League Pitching Register

	W	L	ERA	G	CG	IP	H	ER	BB	SO
94 NL	8	2	3.54	16	0	84.0	70	33	43	56
Life	8	2	3.54	16	0	84.0	70	33	43	56

TODD VAN POPPEL

Position: Pitcher
Team: Oakland Athletics
Born: Dec. 9, 1971   Hinsdale, IL
Height: 6'5"   **Weight:** 210 lbs.
Bats: right   **Throws:** right
Acquired: First-round pick in 6/90 free-agent draft

Player Summary	
Fantasy Value	$1
Card Value	12¢ to 15¢
Will	throw smoke
Can't	find plate
Expect	further work
Don't Expect	more muddling

The Athletics would have been pleased if Van Poppel could have spent 1994 working out his serious control troubles in the minors. However, earlier roster shenanigans meant that the fireballing young right-hander was out of options, and he could not have been sent down without being exposed to waivers. Therefore, Van Poppel was forced to stay with the Athletics. As he did in 1993, he threw extremely hard but was not able to control his pitches. Opponents had just a .250 batting average, and right-handed hitters could only manage a .231 mark. However, he tied for the AL lead in walks despite pitching just 116⅔ innings. In addition, when Van Poppel can't get the ball over, he pays for it, allowing 20 home runs last year. Despite the highest run support (with over five runs per game) of the Oakland starters, he could not pitch well enough to win. The Athletics have to find a way to help Van Poppel harness his considerable stuff. He was the High School Player of the Year in 1990, but he has not had consistent success as a pro.

Major League Pitching Register

	W	L	ERA	G	CG	IP	H	ER	BB	SO
91 AL	0	0	9.64	1	0	4.2	7	5	2	6
93 AL	6	6	5.04	16	0	84.0	76	47	62	47
94 AL	7	10	6.09	23	0	116.2	108	79	89	83
Life	13	16	5.74	40	0	205.1	191	131	153	136
2 AVE	8	10	5.74	24	0	124.1	114	79	94	82

ANDY VAN SLYKE

Position: Outfield
Team: Pittsburgh Pirates
Born: Dec. 21, 1960 Utica, NY
Height: 6'2" **Weight:** 195 lbs.
Bats: left **Throws:** right
Acquired: Traded from Cardinals with Mike Dunne and Mike LaValliere for Tony Pena, 4/87

Player Summary

Fantasy Value.	$12 to $15
Card Value	10¢ to 15¢
Will	attempt comeback
Can't	hit with old power
Expect	flashy defense
Don't Expect.	blinding speed

The always-entertaining but injury-marred Van Slyke had a miserable 1994 season. In addition to suffering his worst batting average in five years and losing most of his power, he almost appeared disinterested. The lefty batter stayed off the DL all season, but lingering back problems may have contributed to his poor performance. He is losing bat speed. He drew 52 walks for a .340 on-base percentage while fanning 74 times. Hampered early in his career by ineffectiveness against lefties, Van Slyke now hits equally against righties or lefties. Last year that meant equally poorly. He did steal seven bases without being caught last year, and he had nine assists in center field. Although he makes highlight-film catches, he doesn't have great range.

Major League Batting Register

	BA	G	AB	R	H	2B	3B	HR	RBI	SB
83 NL	.262	101	309	51	81	15	5	8	38	21
84 NL	.244	137	361	45	88	16	4	7	50	28
85 NL	.259	146	424	61	110	25	6	13	55	34
86 NL	.270	137	418	48	113	23	7	13	61	21
87 NL	.293	157	564	93	165	36	11	21	82	34
88 NL	.288	154	587	101	169	23	15	25	100	30
89 NL	.237	130	476	64	113	18	9	9	53	16
90 NL	.284	136	493	67	140	26	6	17	77	14
91 NL	.265	138	491	87	130	24	7	17	83	10
92 NL	.324	154	614	103	199	45	12	14	89	12
93 NL	.310	83	323	42	100	13	4	8	50	11
94 NL	.246	105	374	41	92	18	3	6	30	7
Life	.276	1578	5434	803	1500	282	89	158	768	238
3 AVE	.293	128	488	68	143	28	7	10	60	11

GREG VAUGHN

Position: Outfield; designated hitter
Team: Milwaukee Brewers
Born: July 3, 1965 Sacramento, CA
Height: 6' **Weight:** 193 lbs.
Bats: right **Throws:** right
Acquired: Fourth-round pick in 6/86 free-agent draft

Player Summary

Fantasy Value.	$19 to $22
Card Value	10¢ to 15¢
Will	show fine power
Can't.	run much
Expect	time at DH
Don't Expect	strong throws

Only on the Brewers—an aging squad filled with iron gloves—could Vaughn have played 81 games in the outfield last year. He is recovering from recent rotator-cuff surgery and is hobbled by bone spurs in both knees. Not a particularly strong thrower to begin with, Vaughn could not uncork at full velocity after the surgery. He no longer runs the bases or plays the outfield as well as he once did. By the end of the season, his shoulder had given out, and his bat died. He anticipated further surgery. Despite these problems, Vaughn did lead the Brewers in homers and extra-base hits. After tattooing left-handers in 1993, he fell to .266 against them last year. Fortunately, Vaughn stands in well against righties. A favorite of Brewer fans (who have dubbed left field "Vaughn's Valley"), he hit .292 at County Stadium. He is a patient hitter and took 51 walks last year for a .345 on-base percentage. His employers would do everyone a service by allowing him to be a full-time DH.

Major League Batting Register

	BA	G	AB	R	H	2B	3B	HR	RBI	SB
89 AL	.265	38	113	18	30	3	0	5	23	4
90 AL	.220	120	382	51	84	26	2	17	61	7
91 AL	.244	145	542	81	132	24	5	27	98	2
92 AL	.228	141	501	77	114	18	2	23	78	15
93 AL	.267	154	569	97	152	28	2	30	97	10
94 AL	.254	95	370	59	94	24	1	19	55	9
Life	.245	693	2477	383	606	123	12	121	412	47
3 AVE	.250	143	530	86	133	27	2	27	84	13

MO VAUGHN

Position: First base
Team: Boston Red Sox
Born: Dec. 15, 1967 Norwalk, CT
Height: 6'1" **Weight:** 225 lbs.
Bats: left **Throws:** right
Acquired: First-round pick in 6/89 free-agent draft

Player Summary	
Fantasy Value.	$30 to $35
Card Value	10¢ to 15¢
Will.	hit home runs
Can't	field for beans
Expect	high on-base mark
Don't Expect	stolen bases

By now, most of the doubters have been silenced. Early in his career, Vaughn was seen as, at best, a platoon player who was able to take advantage of cozy Fenway Park. However, he has improved every year, and in 1994, Vaughn continued to show why he is more than capable of playing every day. He batted .310 against both left-handers and right-handers, with good power against each. He led the Red Sox with a .576 slugging percentage and took 57 walks on his way to an excellent .408 on-base percentage. A likeable guy, Vaughn also hit .318 with fine power on the road, as opposed to .302 in Boston last year. However, there is still room for improvement. He fanned 112 times last year, the third-highest total in the AL. The former All-American at Seton Hall has always been a poor defensive first baseman, and last year he made 10 errors while showing mediocre range. He is also slow and a poor baserunner. A move to designated hitter might come soon, but at whatever position, Vaughn has earned the right to play.

Major League Batting Register

	BA	G	AB	R	H	2B	3B	HR	RBI	SB
91 AL	.260	74	219	21	57	12	0	4	32	2
92 AL	.234	113	355	42	83	16	2	13	57	3
93 AL	.297	152	539	86	160	34	1	29	101	4
94 AL	.310	111	394	65	122	25	1	26	82	4
Life	.280	450	1507	214	422	87	4	72	272	13
3 AVE	.286	140	483	73	138	28	1	26	91	4

RANDY VELARDE

Position: Infield
Team: New York Yankees
Born: Nov. 24, 1962 Midland, TX
Height: 6' **Weight:** 192 lbs.
Bats: right **Throws:** right
Acquired: Traded from White Sox with Pete Filson for Scott Nielsen and Mike Soper, 1/87

Player Summary	
Fantasy Value.	$6 to $8
Card Value	5¢ to 7¢
Will	wield strong bat
Can't	win Gold Glove
Expect	several jobs
Don't Expect	on-base mastery

Velarde spent several years riding the Yankee pine, but he has proven he can play in the majors. In 1994, his free-agent season, he again showed a strong bat and the ability to wear several gloves. Although he usually has problems with right-handers, last year Velarde hit nearly .280 against both lefties and righties. He also batted .318 in road games, over 70 points above his previous career mark. He is not an overly patient hitter, but he did accept 29 walks last year for a .338 on-base percentage. He fanned 61 times. Yankee manager Buck Showalter used Velarde 49 times last season at shortstop but also worked him in at third base, second base, and the outfield. Although Velarde does not have great speed, he is competent defensively at all positions. It is odd that he has not seen time as a DH, though the Yanks have had strong batters on their roster.

Major League Batting Register

	BA	G	AB	R	H	2B	3B	HR	RBI	SB
87 AL	.182	8	22	1	4	0	0	0	1	0
88 AL	.174	48	115	18	20	6	0	5	12	1
89 AL	.340	33	100	12	34	4	2	2	11	0
90 AL	.210	95	229	21	48	6	2	5	19	0
91 AL	.245	80	184	19	45	11	1	1	15	3
92 AL	.272	121	412	57	112	24	1	7	46	7
93 AL	.301	85	226	28	68	13	2	7	24	2
94 AL	.279	77	280	47	78	16	1	9	34	4
Life	.261	547	1568	203	409	80	9	36	162	17
3 AVE	.281	105	344	50	97	20	1	9	39	5

ROBIN VENTURA

Position: Third base
Team: Chicago White Sox
Born: July 14, 1967 Santa Maria, CA
Height: 6'1" **Weight:** 198 lbs.
Bats: left **Throws:** right
Acquired: First-round pick in 6/88 free-agent draft

Player Summary	
Fantasy Value	$17 to $20
Card Value	12¢ to 20¢
Will	reach base often
Can't	carry an offense
Expect	good glove
Don't Expect	flashes of speed

While he will probably never put up tremendous power figures, Ventura does his part to drive in runs, batting .306 with men in scoring position last year. He also reached base often, notching an on-base percentage of .373 as a result of 61 walks. Relieved of cleanup duty last year by Julio Franco, Ventura responded to that eased pressure by adjusting his swing to make better contact. He fanned just 69 times, an excellent total considering his power and patience. He does not take overt advantage of his home park as some ChiSox sluggers do, and in fact, he posted a better average and power numbers in road games. Often helpless against left-handers, he hit .270 against them last year, though with little power. He is one of the slowest ChiSox, but he doesn't make many baserunning mistakes. As a defender, Ventura finished second among AL third basemen in putouts in 1994. He is a fine fielder, having won multiple Gold Glove Awards.

Major League Batting Register

	BA	G	AB	R	H	2B	3B	HR	RBI	SB
89 AL	.178	16	45	5	8	3	0	0	7	0
90 AL	.249	150	493	48	123	17	1	5	54	1
91 AL	.284	157	606	92	172	25	1	23	100	2
92 AL	.282	157	592	85	167	38	1	16	93	2
93 AL	.262	157	554	85	145	27	1	22	94	1
94 AL	.282	109	401	57	113	15	1	18	78	3
Life	.271	746	2691	372	728	125	5	84	426	9
3 AVE	.275	156	570	83	157	29	1	21	99	2

DAVE VERES

Position: Pitcher
Team: Houston Astros
Born: Oct. 19, 1966 Montgomery, AL
Height: 6'2" **Weight:** 195 lbs.
Bats: right **Throws:** right
Acquired: Signed as a minor-league free agent, 5/92

Player Summary	
Fantasy Value	$0
Card Value	7¢ to 10¢
Will	get his Ks
Can't	count his chickens
Expect	good repertoire
Don't Expect	glamour role

In 1994, Veres began the season at Triple-A Tucson, where he had been a spot starter in 1993. He allowed just two earned runs in his first 20 innings before being promoted to the big leagues on May 9. He throws a good mix of pitches and has been a dominating strikeout pitcher in the minors. What kept Veres from the majors was poor control, but his location was good in Houston. Opponents hit just four home runs off the rookie and batted just .247, with an anemic .280 on-base percentage. However, he did allow over half of his inherited runners to score last season. A fine example of the multitude of talented players in the high minors, Veres made the most of his break and should break camp with the big club this season. He probably won't ever play a key role, though, and next year he could be a few bad outings away from a return ticket to Triple-A. Veres attended Mt. Hood Community College in Oregon and was drafted by Oakland in 1986. Four years later he rose to Triple-A, and the Dodgers traded for him in 1991. However, he was released soon afterward, and the Astros inked him.

Major League Pitching Register

	W	L	ERA	G	S	IP	H	ER	BB	SO
94 NL	3	3	2.41	32	1	41.0	39	11	7	28
Life	3	3	2.41	32	1	41.0	39	11	7	28

FERNANDO VINA

Position: Infield
Team: New York Mets
Born: April 16, 1969   Sacramento, CA
Height: 5'9"   **Weight:** 170 lbs.
Bats: left   **Throws:** right
Acquired: Purchased from Mariners, 6/93

Player Summary	
Fantasy Value $0	
Card Value . . . . 12¢ to 20¢	
Will . . . . show speed	
Can't . . . . amaze with glove	
Expect. . . . . hustle and grit	
Don't Expect . . . . home run power	

Selected by Seattle in the Rule 5 draft in December 1992, Vina saw limited action with the Mariners before being sold back to the Mets. The diminutive infielder spent the rest of 1993 at Triple-A Norfolk, hitting just .230. He had a strong spring in 1994, though, and impressed New York manager Dallas Green with his attitude and versatility. Vina played second base, shortstop, third base, and left field in 1994. He spent some time leading off when Jose Vizcaino was injured. Despite not showing on-base skills in his minor-league days, he compiled a .372 on-base percentage. He has good speed but is still learning how to use it. Since he hasn't got much power, he will have to hit for average to be a quality everyday player. His defense is best at second and shortstop, but it is not of Gold Glove caliber anywhere. Vina is still young enough to be a regular at some point, and he could step into a bigger role in someone's middle infield soon. New York thought enough of Vina to send him to Triple-A during the strike in order to keep him sharp. There he batted only .176, though.

Major League Batting Register

	BA	G	AB	R	H	2B	3B	HR	RBI	SB
93 AL	.222	24	45	5	10	2	0	0	2	6
94 NL	.250	79	124	20	31	6	0	0	6	3
Life	.243	103	169	25	41	8	0	0	8	9

FRANK VIOLA

Position: Pitcher
Team: Boston Red Sox
Born: April 19, 1960   Hempstead, NY
Height: 6'4"   **Weight:** 210 lbs.
Bats: left   **Throws:** left
Acquired: Signed as a free agent, 12/92

Player Summary	
Fantasy Value $1	
Card Value . . . . 8¢ to 12¢	
Will . . . . change speeds	
Can't. . . . . afford poor control	
Expect . . . . success vs. lefties	
Don't Expect. . . . . heavy workload	

Viola suffered a career-threatening injury last May 3. Hurling for the BoSox, he uncorked a pitch against Seattle, blew out his elbow, and left the field in terrible pain. He underwent his second elbow surgery in two years, this one performed by Dr. Frank Jobe. Viola spent the rest of 1994 resting his arm and exercising to stay in shape. While a healthy Viola would be able to help almost every major-league team's rotation, his fragile elbow may not be ready to handle that responsibility. He has lost much of his old velocity, and he now counts on control and mixing his pitches to be effective. Viola's location, once peerless, has been just mediocre over the past three seasons. When he is at his best, he throws a baffling changeup and is not afraid to brush hitters off the plate.

Major League Pitching Register

	W	L	ERA	G	CG	IP	H	ER	BB	SO
82 AL	4	10	5.21	22	3	126.0	152	73	38	84
83 AL	7	15	5.49	35	4	210.0	242	128	92	127
84 AL	18	12	3.21	35	10	257.2	225	92	73	149
85 AL	18	14	4.09	36	9	250.2	262	114	68	135
86 AL	16	13	4.51	37	7	245.2	257	123	83	191
87 AL	17	10	2.90	36	7	251.2	230	81	66	197
88 AL	24	7	2.64	35	7	255.1	236	75	54	193
89 AL	8	12	3.79	24	7	175.2	171	74	47	138
89 NL	5	5	3.38	12	2	85.1	75	32	27	73
90 NL	20	12	2.67	35	7	249.2	227	74	60	182
91 NL	13	15	3.97	35	3	231.1	259	102	54	132
92 AL	13	12	3.44	35	6	238.0	214	91	89	121
93 AL	11	8	3.14	29	2	183.2	180	64	72	91
94 AL	1	1	4.65	6	0	31.0	34	16	17	9
Life	175	146	3.67	412	74	2791.2	2764	1139	840	1822
2 AVE	12	10	3.31	32	4	211.1	197	78	81	106

JOSE VIZCAINO

Position: Shortstop
Team: New York Mets
Born: March 26, 1968 Paleneque, Dominican Republic
Height: 6'1" **Weight:** 180 lbs.
Bats: both **Throws:** right
Acquired: Traded from Cubs for Anthony Young and Ottis Smith, 3/94

Player Summary	
Fantasy Value	$3 to $5
Card Value	6¢ to 10¢
Will	hit left-handers
Can't	steal bases
Expect	aggressive defense
Don't Expect	extra-base hits

Pushed out of a starting role with the Cubs, Vizcaino took the shortstop—and leadoff—jobs in New York. The onetime Dodger prospect can certainly run an infield. He charges grounders well and has good range, especially up the middle. Despite lacking outstanding arm strength, he does throw accurately. Unfortunately, Vizcaino is no leadoff man. Though he began the year hot, batting .350 through April 17, he soon chilled considerably. Drawing just 33 walks (eight in those hot two weeks), he registered a .310 on-base percentage, which is subpar for a leadoff hitter. In addition, someone must have told him that leadoff men are required by law to steal bases. He's always had a very poor stolen-base percentage, and he was caught a remarkable 11 times in 12 attempts in 1994. He did hit .280 against left-handers and .283 on the road. He lacks power against righties. Vizcaino should bat eighth and take advantage of his defense.

Major League Batting Register

	BA	G	AB	R	H	2B	3B	HR	RBI	SB
89 NL	.200	7	10	2	2	0	0	0	0	0
90 NL	.275	37	51	3	14	1	1	0	2	1
91 NL	.262	93	145	7	38	5	0	0	10	2
92 NL	.225	86	285	25	64	10	4	1	17	3
93 NL	.287	151	551	74	158	19	4	4	54	12
94 NL	.256	103	410	47	105	13	3	3	33	1
Life	.262	477	1452	158	381	48	12	8	116	19
3 AVE	.262	127	471	55	123	16	4	3	39	5

OMAR VIZQUEL

Position: Shortstop
Team: Cleveland Indians
Born: April 24, 1967 Caracas, Venezuela
Height: 5'9" **Weight:** 165 lbs.
Bats: both **Throws:** right
Acquired: Traded from Mariners for Reggie Jefferson and Felix Fermin, 12/93

Player Summary	
Fantasy Value	$6 to $8
Card Value	6¢ to 10¢
Will	impress defensively
Can't	hit left-handers
Expect	good contact
Don't Expect	much power

Shipping Vizquel to Cleveland was just one of the deals that hurt Seattle's chances in 1994. But that transaction proved just dandy for Cleveland manager Mike Hargrove. The still young Vizquel plays outstanding defense, combining a decent throwing arm with fine range, quick footwork, and soft hands. Unfortunately, his ability to turn the double play caused him to miss almost two months of action in 1994. Texas's Ivan Rodriguez took the diminutive shortstop out with what some called a "dirty" slide, severely spraining a ligament in Vizquel's knee. The play came during a heated series in April, and Vizquel didn't return until June. He hit very well upon returning and finished with fine totals. He swiped 13 bases in 17 tries, hit .304 against right-handers, and made excellent contact, fanning just 23 times. He took just 23 walks last year, fashioning a mediocre .325 on-base percentage, and he continues to have trouble with left-handers.

Major League Batting Register

	BA	G	AB	R	H	2B	3B	HR	RBI	SB
89 AL	.220	143	387	45	85	7	3	1	20	1
90 AL	.247	81	255	19	63	3	2	2	18	4
91 AL	.230	142	426	42	98	16	4	1	41	7
92 AL	.294	136	483	49	142	20	4	0	21	15
93 AL	.255	158	560	68	143	14	2	2	31	12
94 AL	.273	69	286	39	78	10	1	1	33	13
Life	.254	729	2397	262	609	70	16	7	164	52
3 AVE	.273	130	482	57	132	16	2	1	33	15

PAUL WAGNER

Position: Pitcher
Team: Pittsburgh Pirates
Born: Nov. 14, 1967 Milwaukee, WI
Height: 6'1" **Weight:** 185 lbs.
Bats: right **Throws:** right
Acquired: 13th-round pick in 6/89 free-agent draft

Player Summary	
Fantasy Value	$2 to $4
Card Value	6¢ to 10¢
Will	show impressive arm
Can't	master his pitches
Expect	ground balls
Don't Expect	bullpen time

Wagner backslid in 1994 following an impressive rookie campaign. Wildness and inconsistency plagued him all year and landed him into the bullpen before the strike. He allowed 16 first-inning runs in his first 16 starts, and he walked nearly four men per game. He has proven to be easy to run on, and last summer he didn't get much help from his catchers. He also pitched poorly in night games and compiled a ghastly 5.47 ERA on the road. His control was much better at home, suggesting a possible problem with confidence or focus. Wagner's arm is outstanding, and he still has tremendous potential. Even during his difficult 1994 season, he kept the ball low, allowing only seven homers. A power pitcher, Wagner succeeds with ground balls and strikeouts. If he can manage left-handers better (they hit .312 last year), he will be effective. He also needs to reduce the three and three-quarters walks per nine innings he allowed in 1994. Despite his past problems, Wagner will probably start in 1995.

Major League Pitching Register

	W	L	ERA	G	CG	IP	H	ER	BB	SO
92 NL	2	0	0.69	6	0	13.0	9	1	5	5
93 NL	8	8	4.27	44	1	141.1	143	67	42	114
94 NL	7	8	4.59	29	1	119.2	136	61	50	86
Life	17	16	4.24	79	2	274.0	288	129	97	205
2 AVE	9	10	4.44	42	1	154.2	167	76	56	118

MATT WALBECK

Position: Catcher
Team: Minnesota Twins
Born: Oct. 2, 1969 Sacramento, CA
Height: 5'11" **Weight:** 190 lbs.
Bats: both **Throws:** right
Acquired: Traded from Cubs with Dave Stevens for Willie Banks, 11/93

Player Summary	
Fantasy Value	$1
Card Value	6¢ to 10¢
Will	nail runners
Can't	hit right-handers
Expect	improved average
Don't Expect	many home runs

Despite doing some things well last year, Walbeck really struggled overall. The Twins gave the rookie the full-time catching job after saying goodbye to free agent Brian Harper, and Walbeck appeared over his head. A standout minor-league defender, Walbeck has a fine arm and a quick release, and he was unfazed by American League runners. He tossed out 40 percent of potential basestealers in 1994. However, he needs some work in game-calling, and he has not yet proven capable of managing Twins pitchers. Walbeck also needs help managing enemy pitchers, who held him well in check last year. He hit .254 against left-handers, only .194 versus righties, and just over .200 both at home and on the road. Although he did make good contact, striking out only 37 times, he took just 17 walks and registered a pathetic .246 on-base percentage. Walbeck does not have much extra-base power, but he did pound a grand slam May 4 at Milwaukee to help sink the Brewers. In 1993 at Triple-A Iowa, he batted .281 with six homers and 43 RBI. He hit .301 at Double-A Charlotte in 1992.

Major League Batting Register

	BA	G	AB	R	H	2B	3B	HR	RBI	SB
93 NL	.200	11	30	2	6	2	0	1	6	0
94 AL	.204	97	338	31	69	12	0	5	35	1
Life	.204	108	368	33	75	14	0	6	41	1

LARRY WALKER

Position: Outfield; first base
Team: Montreal Expos
Born: Dec. 1, 1966 Maple Ridge, British Columbia
Height: 6'3" **Weight:** 215 lbs.
Bats: left **Throws:** right
Acquired: Signed as a free agent, 11/84

Player Summary	
Fantasy Value	$25 to $30
Card Value	15¢ to 25¢
Will	make big money
Can't	throw like old
Expect	extra-base power
Don't Expect	on-base woes

Despite an aching shoulder, which he is hoping to fix with rotator-cuff surgery, Walker last summer finished second on the Expos in batting average and slugging percentage (.567). He also tied with Craig Biggio for the league lead in doubles. Walker was a large part of the team-wide offensive explosion in June, hitting .333 with six homers and 24 RBI for the month. He took 47 walks last year and compiled a terrific .394 on-base percentage. He batted .310 or higher against both lefties and righties, at home and away. Walker also hit .367 at night, but just .217 in day games. His .330 mark against left-handers was one of the league's best. Blessed with surprising speed for his size, he is a fine baserunner and stole 15 bases in 20 tries in 1994. In right field, the sore-shouldered Walker had just five assists and made nine errors—including a live-ball souvenir give away on national TV. If his shoulder does not recover, he can shift to first base.

Major League Batting Register

	BA	G	AB	R	H	2B	3B	HR	RBI	SB
89 NL	.170	20	47	4	8	0	0	0	4	1
90 NL	.241	133	419	59	101	18	3	19	51	21
91 NL	.290	137	487	59	141	30	2	16	64	14
92 NL	.301	143	528	85	159	31	4	23	93	18
93 NL	.265	138	490	85	130	24	5	22	86	29
94 NL	.322	103	395	76	127	44	2	19	86	15
Life	.281	674	2366	368	666	147	16	99	384	98
3 AVE	.297	142	525	92	156	39	4	24	100	23

TIM WALLACH

Position: Third base
Team: Los Angeles Dodgers
Born: Sept. 14, 1957 Huntington Park, CA
Height: 6'3" **Weight:** 202 lbs.
Bats: right **Throws:** right
Acquired: Traded from Expos for Tim Barker, 11/92

Player Summary	
Fantasy Value	$6 to $8
Card Value	6¢ to 10¢
Will	hit for power
Can't	outrun a piano
Expect	fine defense
Don't Expect	MVP season

Wallach's comeback in 1994 was one of the year's most unlikely stories. After three straight subpar seasons, the former Expo All-Star finished second on the Los Angeles squad in home runs, RBI, and doubles. He also came in third with 46 walks and fourth in batting average. Wallach hit his most homers in seven seasons. He has no speed and still strikes out too much, whiffing 80 times last year. Although Wallach hit just .235 at Dodger Stadium, he whaled NL pitchers for a .317 average and 16 homers on the road. After batting .194 against left-handed pitchers in 1993, Wallach improved to .279 last season. The two-time Gold Glove winner is still one of the league's best fielders at third base, possessing good range and a strong arm.

Major League Batting Register

	BA	G	AB	R	H	2B	3B	HR	RBI	SB
80 NL	.182	5	11	1	2	0	0	1	2	0
81 NL	.236	71	212	19	50	9	1	4	13	0
82 NL	.268	158	596	89	160	31	3	28	97	6
83 NL	.269	156	581	54	156	33	3	19	70	0
84 NL	.246	160	582	55	143	25	4	18	72	3
85 NL	.260	155	569	70	148	36	3	22	81	9
86 NL	.233	134	480	50	112	22	1	18	71	8
87 NL	.298	153	593	89	177	42	4	26	123	9
88 NL	.257	159	592	52	152	32	5	12	69	2
89 NL	.277	154	573	76	159	42	0	13	77	3
90 NL	.296	161	626	69	185	37	5	21	98	6
91 NL	.225	151	577	60	130	22	1	13	73	2
92 NL	.223	150	537	53	120	29	1	9	59	2
93 NL	.222	133	477	42	106	19	1	12	62	0
94 NL	.280	113	414	68	116	21	1	23	78	0
Life	.258	2013	7420	847	1916	400	33	239	1045	50
3 AVE	.244	147	532	64	130	26	1	18	77	1

DUANE WARD

Position: Pitcher
Team: Toronto Blue Jays
Born: May 28, 1964   Parkview, NM
Height: 6'4"   **Weight:** 215 lbs.
Bats: right   **Throws:** right
Acquired: Traded from Braves for Doyle Alexander, 7/86

Player Summary	
Fantasy Value	$19 to $22
Card Value	8¢ to 12¢
Will	seek return
Can't	be overworked
Expect	save opportunities
Don't Expect	perfect control

The Blue Jays, almost to a man, called Ward's season-long unavailability the biggest blow to their chances of repeating as world champions. After a spectacular 1993 season, in which he showed why enemy hitters regard him as one of baseball's best closers, Ward went into spring training with a tender shoulder. At first, it was simply thought to be soreness. After the season began, the injury was called a cartilage tear. Finally, he was diagnosed with a torn rotator cuff and underwent season-ending surgery. He is expected back for 1995, but he will almost certainly not return to form right away. Ward has excellent velocity on his pitches and owns an explosive, late-breaking sinker that many say is the best in the game. He is a dominating strikeout pitcher but occasionally has control woes. There is no telling how much durability or raw stuff Ward will have on his return.

Major League Pitching Register

	W	L	ERA	G	S	IP	H	ER	BB	SO
86 NL	0	1	7.31	10	0	16.0	22	13	8	8
86 AL	0	1	13.50	2	0	2.0	3	3	4	1
87 AL	1	0	6.94	12	0	11.2	14	9	12	10
88 AL	9	3	3.30	64	15	111.2	101	41	60	91
89 AL	4	10	3.77	66	15	114.2	94	48	58	122
90 AL	2	8	3.45	73	11	127.2	101	49	42	112
91 AL	7	6	2.77	81	23	107.1	80	33	33	132
92 AL	7	4	1.95	79	12	101.1	76	22	39	103
93 AL	2	3	2.13	71	45	71.2	49	17	25	97
Life	32	36	3.19	458	121	664.0	540	235	281	676
2 AVE	5	4	2.03	75	29	87.0	63	20	32	100

TURNER WARD

Position: Outfield
Team: Milwaukee Brewers
Born: April 11, 1965   Orlando, FL
Height: 6'2"   **Weight:** 185 lbs.
Bats: both   **Throws:** right
Acquired: Claimed on waivers from Blue Jays, 11/93

Player Summary	
Fantasy Value	$1 to $3
Card Value	5¢ to 7¢
Will	draw some walks
Can't	provide punch
Expect	fine defense
Don't Expect	full-time play

Signed as a reserve, Ward instead became a starter when injuries hobbled the Brewers last spring. The former Indian and Blue Jay began the year with a bang, hitting .307 with 18 walks and four homers in April. Shortly afterward, however, he slid dramatically as AL pitchers remembered how they had gotten him out during previous seasons. He ended the year going 21 for his last 143 (.147), looking nothing like a big-league regular. Left-handers held Ward to a .198 mark last year, far below his previous average from the right side of the dish. He also hit just .211 on the road. He had some positives, swiping six bases in eight tries and taking 52 walks. Unfortunately, Ward's low average led to a paltry .328 on-base percentage. Despite an overall lack of hitting skill, he still has some positive attributes. He has good range and can play all three outfield spots. Although his arm is just fair, Ward made his share of thrilling catches in 1994, and he was good enough to be a defensive replacement.

Major League Batting Register

	BA	G	AB	R	H	2B	3B	HR	RBI	SB
90 AL	.348	14	46	10	16	2	1	1	10	3
91 AL	.239	48	113	12	27	7	0	0	7	0
92 AL	.345	18	29	7	10	3	0	1	3	0
93 AL	.192	72	167	20	32	4	2	4	28	3
94 AL	.232	102	367	55	85	15	2	9	45	6
Life	.235	254	722	104	170	31	5	15	93	12
2 AVE	.222	108	342	49	76	13	2	8	46	6

ALLEN WATSON

Position: Pitcher
Team: St. Louis Cardinals
Born: Nov. 18, 1970   Jamaica, NY
Height: 6'3"   **Weight:** 190 lbs.
Bats: left   **Throws:** left
Acquired: First-round pick in 6/91 free-agent draft

Player Summary	
Fantasy Value	$3 to $5
Card Value	10¢ to 15¢
Will	show good stuff
Can't	hold runners
Expect	success vs. lefties
Don't Expect	great control

Formerly a college All-American at the New York Institute of Technology, Watson cut through the minor leagues like a buzz saw in butter. Unfortunately, his control has been poor since coming to the majors. Not only did he walk over four men per game last season, he also was forced to lay mediocre fastballs over the plate when behind in the count. As a result, hitters tagged him for 15 homers and 34 doubles. For a left-hander, Watson is easy to run on, allowing opponents to swipe 17 bases in 22 tries. He was able to accomplish some goals in 1994, though. He held left-handed hitters to a paltry .227 mark (righties tagged him at .300) and showed he is unafraid to pitch inside. However, this aggressiveness led to an incident May 22 when Watson, tagged for three homers in an inning, then plunked Orestes Destrade. A brawl ensued, and Watson served an eight-game suspension. Despite good stuff, he may need more time at Triple-A to work on his location. At Triple-A Louisville in 1993, he was 5-4 with a 2.91 ERA, 86 Ks, and 31 walks in 120⅔ innings.

Major League Pitching Register

	W	L	ERA	G	CG	IP	H	ER	BB	SO
93 NL	6	7	4.60	16	0	86.0	90	44	28	49
94 NL	6	5	5.52	22	0	115.2	130	71	53	74
Life	12	12	5.13	38	0	201.2	220	115	81	123
2 AVE	7	7	5.21	23	0	124.1	137	72	51	77

DAVID WEATHERS

Position: Pitcher
Team: Florida Marlins
Born: Sept. 25, 1969   Lawrenceburg, TN
Height: 6'3"   **Weight:** 205 lbs.
Bats: right   **Throws:** right
Acquired: Second-round pick from Blue Jays in 11/92 expansion draft

Player Summary	
Fantasy Value	$2 to $4
Card Value	6¢ to 10¢
Will	be durable
Can't	afford wildness
Expect	sinkers, sliders
Don't Expect	great velocity

Weathers landed a rotation spot in Florida last season. He has only an average fastball, but, when effective, he moves the ball around low in the strike zone. He started the season quite well, and, as late as mid-June, he had a fine 3.21 ERA and 7-5 record. Even then, though, he wasn't striking many people out and was walking too many for comfort. Soon, NL hitters began to pound Weathers, who lost seven of his last eight decisions and was tagged for 46 earned runs in his last 42 innings (a 9.78 ERA). Poor control certainly contributed to Weathers's problems; he fired seven wild pitches and got far too many mistake pitches high in the strike zone, allowing 13 home runs. Opponents batted .306 against him, and left-handers especially tagged him. Weathers didn't give up, however. He led the Marlins in innings and took the ball every time that it was his turn. With improved control, he could start in the big leagues, though the same could be said about many Triple-A hurlers. In 1993, he was 11-4 with a 3.83 ERA at Triple-A Edmonton.

Major League Pitching Register

	W	L	ERA	G	CG	IP	H	ER	BB	SO
91 AL	1	0	4.91	15	0	14.2	15	8	17	13
92 AL	0	0	8.10	2	0	3.1	5	3	2	3
93 AL	2	3	5.12	14	0	45.2	57	26	13	34
94 NL	8	12	5.27	24	0	135.0	166	79	59	72
Life	11	15	5.26	55	0	198.2	243	116	91	122

LENNY WEBSTER

Position: Catcher
Team: Montreal Expos
Born: Feb. 10, 1965 New Orleans, LA
Height: 5'9" **Weight:** 195 lbs.
Bats: right **Throws:** right
Acquired: Traded from Twins for a player to be named later, 3/94

Player Summary	
Fantasy Value	$1
Card Value	6¢ to 8¢
Will	get on base
Can't	throw with skill
Expect	some pop
Don't Expect	starting job

Webster has now hit over .270 in all but one of his big-league seasons. Dealt to the Expos in spring training, the former Twin enjoyed a fine campaign as one of Felipe Alou's capable crew of reserves. Webster hit for good power and a high average. He also drew 16 walks. His slugging percentage was .448, and he totaled a .370 on-base average. Although he has power against both righties and lefties, he hits for a much higher average against southpaws. Last year, he compiled a .303 batting average against southpaws, and he hit .306 at home. Even when playing well, Webster has never encouraged anyone to think of him as everyday material. This is based mainly on his average glovework. Webster has decent defensive tools, but he is not spectacularly mobile and threw out only 28 percent of potential basestealers in 1994. He is said to call a fairly good game, however, and the struggling Twins certainly could have used him last season.

Major League Batting Register

	BA	G	AB	R	H	2B	3B	HR	RBI	SB
89 AL	.300	14	20	3	6	2	0	0	1	0
90 AL	.333	2	6	1	2	1	0	0	0	0
91 AL	.294	18	34	7	10	1	0	3	8	0
92 AL	.280	53	118	10	33	10	1	1	13	0
93 AL	.198	49	106	14	21	2	0	1	8	1
94 NL	.273	57	143	13	39	10	0	5	23	0
Life	.260	193	427	48	111	26	1	10	53	1

BILL WEGMAN

Position: Pitcher
Team: Milwaukee Brewers
Born: Dec. 19, 1962 Cincinnati, OH
Height: 6'5" **Weight:** 220 lbs.
Bats: right **Throws:** right
Acquired: Fifth-round pick in 6/81 free-agent draft

Player Summary	
Fantasy Value	$4 to $6
Card Value	5¢ to 7¢
Will	throw strikes
Can't	break glass
Expect	mix of pitches
Don't Expect	consistent success

Wegman, an occasionally effective finesse pitcher, is also an exasperating one. He has poor velocity and must change speeds and fool hitters to succeed. If his control isn't nearly perfect, he gets creamed. He has enjoyed good seasons, but he has never been even close to establishing consistency. In addition, frequent injuries make Wegman even harder to count on. In danger of being released during a poor spring, he was taken north largely because of his contract. Despite missing time with an abdominal strain, Wegman pitched well, and as of July 4, was 6-0 with a 3.50 ERA. However, he then fell apart and was bombed to the tune of a 6.18 ERA over the rest of the season. Opponents hit .303 against Wegman in 1994, connecting for 29 doubles and 14 dingers. He did allow just over two walks per nine innings. He will almost certainly be a starter this year if healthy.

Major League Pitching Register

	W	L	ERA	G	CG	IP	H	ER	BB	SO
85 AL	2	0	3.57	3	0	17.2	17	7	3	6
86 AL	5	12	5.13	35	2	198.1	217	113	43	82
87 AL	12	11	4.24	34	7	225.0	229	106	53	102
88 AL	13	13	4.12	32	4	199.0	207	91	20	84
89 AL	2	6	6.71	11	0	51.0	69	38	21	27
90 AL	2	2	4.85	8	1	29.2	37	16	6	20
91 AL	15	7	2.84	28	7	193.1	176	61	40	89
92 AL	13	14	3.20	35	7	261.2	251	93	55	127
93 AL	4	14	4.48	20	5	120.2	135	60	34	50
94 AL	8	4	4.51	19	0	115.2	140	58	26	59
Life	76	83	4.10	225	33	1412.0	1478	643	331	646
3 AVE	9	11	3.87	27	4	181.2	194	78	42	87

WALT WEISS

Position: Shortstop
Team: Colorado Rockies
Born: Nov. 28, 1963 Tuxedo, NY
Height: 6′ **Weight:** 175 lbs.
Bats: both **Throws:** right
Acquired: Signed as a free agent, 1/94

Player Summary	
Fantasy Value	$4 to $6
Card Value	6¢ to 10¢
Will	take walks
Can't	add blazing speed
Expect	dependable defense
Don't Expect	any power

Weiss has made the rounds of the newest major-league teams. He spent 1993 as Florida's first full-time shortstop then moved to Colorado for 1994. He has stayed healthy the last two years, a surprise given his injury problems when he was with Oakland. However, even while physically able, Weiss did not contribute much to the Rockies' attack. He has no real power and cannot compensate in other offensive areas. Weiss has never been a good base thief, and he was caught stealing seven times last year. He hit just .229 against right-handed pitching and only .239 in road games. One thing Weiss does very well is take the walk; he drew 56 in 1994, but a .251 batting average makes for a mediocre .336 on-base percentage. He walks as often as he strikes out, and fanned 58 times last year. Much of his reputation is based on defense, and he makes his share of fine plays. However, his arm and range are just average.

Major League Batting Register

	BA	G	AB	R	H	2B	3B	HR	RBI	SB
87 AL	.462	16	26	3	12	4	0	0	1	1
88 AL	.250	147	452	44	113	17	3	3	39	4
89 AL	.233	84	236	30	55	11	0	3	21	6
90 AL	.265	138	445	50	118	17	1	2	35	9
91 AL	.226	40	133	15	30	6	1	0	13	6
92 AL	.212	103	316	36	67	5	2	0	21	6
93 NL	.266	158	500	50	133	14	2	1	39	7
94 NL	.251	110	423	58	106	11	4	1	32	12
Life	.250	796	2531	286	634	85	13	10	201	51
3 AVE	.247	139	471	56	116	11	3	1	35	10

BOB WELCH

Position: Pitcher
Team: Oakland Athletics
Born: Nov. 3, 1956 Detroit, MI
Height: 6′3″ **Weight:** 198 lbs.
Bats: right **Throws:** right
Acquired: Traded from Dodgers with Matt Young for Alfredo Griffin and Jay Howell, 12/87

Player Summary	
Fantasy Value	$0
Card Value	6¢ to 10¢
Will	try to hang on
Can't	get the ball over
Expect	one more try
Don't Expect	a fat contract

The oft-injured and declining Welch fell out of the rotation last year and may never return. Once a dominating power pitcher with a fine curveball, he now relies almost entirely on off-speed pitches. He certainly threw with fine movement last season, and he fooled some hitters, but too often couldn't get near home plate. When behind in the count, he lacks the raw stuff to succeed. After beginning 1994 with an 0-5 record and a 9.53 ERA in eight starts, Welch was banished to the pen and finished out the season in long relief. He pitched slightly better afterward, notching a 4.67 ERA.

Major League Pitching Register

	W	L	ERA	G	CG	IP	H	ER	BB	SO
78 NL	7	4	2.02	23	4	111.1	92	25	26	66
79 NL	5	6	3.98	25	1	81.1	82	36	32	64
80 NL	14	9	3.29	32	3	213.2	190	78	79	141
81 NL	9	5	3.44	23	2	141.1	141	54	41	88
82 NL	16	11	3.36	36	9	235.2	199	88	81	176
83 NL	15	12	2.65	31	4	204.0	164	60	72	156
84 NL	13	13	3.78	31	3	178.2	191	75	58	126
85 NL	14	4	2.31	23	8	167.1	141	43	35	96
86 NL	7	13	3.28	33	7	235.2	227	86	55	183
87 NL	15	9	3.22	35	6	251.2	204	90	86	196
88 AL	17	9	3.64	36	4	244.2	237	99	81	158
89 AL	17	8	3.00	33	1	209.2	191	70	78	137
90 AL	27	6	2.95	35	2	238.0	214	78	77	127
91 AL	12	13	4.58	35	7	220.0	220	112	91	101
92 AL	11	7	3.27	20	0	123.2	114	45	43	47
93 AL	9	11	5.29	30	0	166.2	208	98	56	63
94 AL	3	6	7.08	25	0	68.2	75	54	43	44
Life	211	146	3.47	506	61	3092.0	2894	1191	1034	1969
3 AVE	8	9	5.09	28	0	128.2	144	73	53	57

DAVID WELLS

Position: Pitcher
Team: Detroit Tigers
Born: May 20, 1963 Torrance, CA
Height: 6'4" **Weight:** 225 lbs.
Bats: left **Throws:** left
Acquired: Signed as a free agent, 4/93

Player Summary	
Fantasy Value	$6 to $8
Card Value	5¢ to 7¢
Will	pour it in
Can't	get respect
Expect	some home runs
Don't Expect	perfect health

Wells was the top pitcher on a poor Detroit pitching staff in 1994. He still received no acknowledgment. Despite missing two months last year due to injury, Wells finished second on the club in strikeouts, led all Tiger starters in ERA (by a wide margin), and again showed excellent control. The former Blue Jay hurler made just three starts, allowing 11 runs in 18 innings, before an inflamed left elbow forced him to the sidelines from April 16 until June 4. After rest and a rehabilitation assignment, Wells returned to the rotation and posted a 3.66 ERA. He has always had fine location, and keeps the ball low. Opponents hit 13 home runs last year, a good total considering Wells pitches in a hitter's park. He held opponents to a .260 batting average and just a .302 on-base percentage in 1994. One of his problems has been staying healthy. Four times in his career, he has missed significant time with arm ailments.

DAVID WEST

Position: Pitcher
Team: Philadelphia Phillies
Born: Sept. 1, 1964 Memphis, TN
Height: 6'6" **Weight:** 230 lbs.
Bats: left **Throws:** left
Acquired: Traded from Twins for Mike Hartley, 12/92

Player Summary	
Fantasy Value	$2 to $4
Card Value	5¢ to 7¢
Will	overpower hitters
Can't	find plate
Expect	high K totals
Don't Expect	static runners

Opposing batters could manage just a .205 average against West last year, but he was still saddled with a 4-10 record. The fire-balling lefty began the season in his customary middle-relief role, setting up closer Doug Jones. West walked 18 men in his first 19 innings, however, and was 0-4 with a 5.12 ERA in late May. At that point, he hardly deserved a promotion, but injuries to other Phillies' starters forced him into the rotation. He pitched four scoreless frames against St. Louis May 24, then six shutout innings against Houston five days later to pick up a win. West remained a starter for the rest of the season. He compiled a fine 3.16 ERA in the role and improved—but did not master—his awful control. He throws hard and high, fanning nearly a hitter per inning, but he walks far too many and fired nine wild pitches in 1994. Opponents tagged West for seven homers and ran on him almost at will.

Major League Pitching Register

	W	L	ERA	G	CG	IP	H	ER	BB	SO
87 AL	4	3	3.99	18	0	29.1	37	13	12	32
88 AL	3	5	4.62	41	0	64.1	65	33	31	56
89 AL	7	4	2.40	54	0	86.1	66	23	28	78
90 AL	11	6	3.14	43	0	189.0	165	66	45	115
91 AL	15	10	3.72	40	2	198.1	188	82	49	106
92 AL	7	9	5.40	41	0	120.0	138	72	36	62
93 AL	11	9	4.19	32	0	187.0	183	87	42	139
94 AL	5	7	3.96	16	5	111.1	113	49	24	71
Life	63	53	3.88	285	7	985.2	955	425	267	659
3 AVE	8	9	4.42	32	2	154.0	160	76	37	100

Major League Pitching Register

	W	L	ERA	G	S	IP	H	ER	BB	SO
88 NL	1	0	3.00	2	0	6.0	6	2	3	3
89 NL	0	2	7.40	11	0	24.1	25	20	14	19
89 AL	3	2	6.41	10	0	39.1	48	28	19	31
90 AL	7	9	5.10	29	0	146.1	142	83	78	92
91 AL	4	4	4.54	15	0	71.1	66	36	28	52
92 AL	1	3	6.99	9	0	28.1	32	22	20	19
93 NL	6	4	2.92	76	3	86.1	60	28	51	87
94 NL	4	10	3.55	31	0	99.0	74	39	61	83
Life	26	34	4.63	183	3	501.0	453	258	274	386
2 AVE	6	9	3.31	60	2	113.1	82	41	68	102

JOHN WETTELAND

Position: Pitcher
Team: Montreal Expos
Born: Aug. 21, 1968 San Mateo, CA
Height: 6'2" **Weight:** 195 lbs.
Bats: right **Throws:** right
Acquired: Traded from Reds with Bill Risley for Dave Martinez, Scott Ruskin, and Willie Greene, 12/91

Player Summary	
Fantasy Value...............	$40 to $45
Card Value	10¢ to 15¢
Will......................	register Ks
Can't.................	show control
Expect....................	top velocity
Don't Expect...............	many hits

Wetteland had an odd but effective 1994 season. While the dominating fireballer wasn't quite up to the amazing standard he set in 1993, he was a key player in the Expos' title drive. His season didn't begin very well. Wetteland blew six of his first 12 save chances, and he didn't pitch from April 18 to May 3 because of a strained right hamstring. When he returned, he reclaimed his position from Mel Rojas by saving eight games in June and eight more in July. In the latter month, Wetteland allowed just two earned runs in 16 innings. He gets most of his outs on fly balls and strikeouts. He throws his fastball and slider with such velocity that opponents could only connect for five homers and a .202 batting average last year. Wetteland had an 0.49 ERA on grass fields and a 1.57 ERA in road games. Oddly, he struggled to a 4.30 home ERA in 1994. If he can iron out his occasional inconsistency, Wetteland could be the best reliever in baseball.

Major League Pitching Register

	W	L	ERA	G	S	IP	H	ER	BB	SO
89 NL	5	8	3.77	31	1	102.2	81	43	34	96
90 NL	2	4	4.81	22	0	43.0	44	23	17	36
91 NL	1	0	0.00	6	0	9.0	5	0	3	9
92 NL	4	4	2.92	67	37	83.1	64	27	36	99
93 NL	9	3	1.37	70	43	85.1	58	13	28	113
94 NL	4	6	2.83	52	25	63.2	46	20	21	68
Life	25	25	2.93	248	106	387.0	298	126	139	421
3 AVE	6	5	2.37	70	38	86.2	62	23	31	103

LOU WHITAKER

Position: Second base
Team: Detroit Tigers
Born: May 12, 1957 Brooklyn, NY
Height: 5'11" **Weight:** 185 lbs.
Bats: left **Throws:** right
Acquired: Fifth-round pick in 6/75 free-agent draft

Player Summary	
Fantasy Value...............	$9 to $11
Card Value	10¢ to 15¢
Will.................	mash right-handers
Can't.................	add much speed
Expect.........	high on-base mark
Don't Expect	great glove

Whitaker has become a very good platoon player, battering right-handed pitching, drawing walks, and showing excellent power. The former All-Star no longer plays much against southpaws. However, he's in there every day against righties. He solved northpaws at a .304 clip with 11 homers in 1994. Usually batting second in the Tiger lineup, Whitaker walks nearly as often as he strikes out, taking 41 free passes last year and whiffing 47 times. Defensively, Whitaker's skills are beginning to erode. His hands are no longer sure, and his range is declining somewhat. He is posting career numbers that some feel merit a trip to Cooperstown.

Major League Batting Register

	BA	G	AB	R	H	2B	3B	HR	RBI	SB
77 AL	.250	11	32	5	8	1	0	0	2	2
78 AL	.285	139	484	71	138	12	7	3	58	7
79 AL	.286	127	423	75	121	14	8	3	42	20
80 AL	.233	145	477	68	111	19	1	1	45	8
81 AL	.263	109	335	48	88	14	4	5	36	5
82 AL	.286	152	560	76	160	22	8	15	65	11
83 AL	.320	161	643	94	206	40	6	12	72	17
84 AL	.289	143	558	90	161	25	1	13	56	6
85 AL	.279	152	609	102	170	29	8	21	73	6
86 AL	.269	144	584	95	157	26	6	20	73	13
87 AL	.265	149	604	110	160	38	6	16	59	13
88 AL	.275	115	403	54	111	18	2	12	55	2
89 AL	.251	148	509	77	128	21	1	28	85	6
90 AL	.237	132	472	75	112	22	2	18	60	8
91 AL	.279	138	470	94	131	26	2	23	78	4
92 AL	.278	130	453	77	126	26	0	19	71	6
93 AL	.290	119	383	72	111	32	1	9	67	3
94 AL	.301	92	322	67	97	21	2	12	43	2
Life	.276	2306	8321	1350	2296	406	65	230	1040	139
3 AVE	.290	126	430	81	125	29	1	15	66	4

DEVON WHITE

Position: Outfield
Team: Toronto Blue Jays
Born: Dec. 29, 1962 Kingston, Jamaica
Height: 6'2" **Weight:** 178 lbs.
Bats: both **Throws:** right
Acquired: Traded from Angels with Willie Fraser and Marcus Moore for Junior Felix, Luis Sojo, and Ken Rivers, 12/90

Player Summary	
Fantasy Value	$15 to $18
Card Value	10¢ to 15¢
Will	show good power
Can't	disregard speed
Expect	excellent defense
Don't Expect	leadoff skill

White's decline was one reason the Blue Jays did not repeat in 1994. He did not run nor hit the way Toronto needed him to. Part of this decline was due to knee and Achilles tendon problems that limited White's baserunning speed and range in center field. He has many Gold Gloves lining his shelves. Unfortunately, he also had problems putting bat on ball. His strikeout-to-walk ratio increased to 4-to-1 last season. Despite a good batting average, White's on-base percentage was just .313, poor for a leadoff hitter. He was fourth on the club in runs scored, also well below average for a top-of-the-order man. White does have good power and hit .306 against left-handers in 1994. If he can regain his speed, his baserunning, offense, and outstanding play in center field will again make him a top player.

Major League Batting Register

	BA	G	AB	R	H	2B	3B	HR	RBI	SB
85 AL	.143	21	7	7	1	0	0	0	0	3
86 AL	.235	29	51	8	12	1	1	1	3	6
87 AL	.263	159	639	103	168	33	5	24	87	32
88 AL	.259	122	455	76	118	22	2	11	51	17
89 AL	.245	156	636	86	156	18	13	12	56	44
90 AL	.217	125	443	57	96	17	3	11	44	21
91 AL	.282	156	642	110	181	40	10	17	60	33
92 AL	.248	153	641	98	159	26	7	17	60	37
93 AL	.273	146	598	116	163	42	6	15	52	34
94 AL	.270	100	403	67	109	24	6	13	49	11
Life	.258	1167	4515	728	1163	223	53	121	462	238
3 AVE	.263	147	602	103	159	34	7	17	60	29

RICK WHITE

Position: Pitcher
Team: Pittsburgh Pirates
Born: Dec. 23, 1968 Springfield, OH
Height: 6'4" **Weight:** 215 lbs.
Bats: right **Throws:** right
Acquired: 15th-round pick in 6/90 free-agent draft

Player Summary	
Fantasy Value	$3 to $5
Card Value	10¢ to 15¢
Will	survive on control
Can't	overpower hitters
Expect	some starts
Don't Expect	closing duties

While not being on anybody's list of top prospects, White spent all of 1994 with the Pirates despite having just seven games of Triple-A experience. He had been a starter in the minors, and he made his mark with excellent control. White's velocity is just average, but he changes speeds well. In 1993 at Double-A Carolina, White was 4-3 with a 3.50 ERA and just 12 walks in 69 innings before earning a brief promotion to Triple-A Buffalo. Despite his past in the starting rotation, Jim Leyland saw a gap in his bullpen and made White his late-inning reliever. White responded well; by May 1, he had registered five saves in six tries and owned an 0.71 ERA in 13 innings. From that point, however, he had a rough ride. A series of bad outings, in which he did not find the plate consistently, forced White from the closer's job. He later made five starts for the Bucs. For the season, opponents socked nine home runs against White, and fellow right-handers clipped him for a .293 average. He has a future in Pittsburgh, but without great raw stuff, he must throw with the location he had in the bushes.

Major League Pitching Register

	W	L	ERA	G	S	IP	H	ER	BB	SO
94 NL	4	5	3.82	43	6	75.1	79	32	17	38
Life	4	5	3.82	43	6	75.1	79	32	17	38

RONDELL WHITE

Position: Outfield
Team: Montreal Expos
Born: Feb. 23, 1972 Milledgeville, GA
Height: 6'1" **Weight:** 205 lbs.
Bats: right **Throws:** right
Acquired: First-round pick in 6/90 free-agent draft

Player Summary

Fantasy Value	$10 to $13
Card Value	10¢ to 15¢
Will	be on base
Can't	show strong arm
Expect	extra-base hits
Don't Expect	bench time

White, regarded for several seasons as one of baseball's best prospects, hit well both at Triple-A and in the majors in 1994. He began the year on the Expos' roster after hitting .329 during spring training, but he could find no place to play. He was sent down to Triple-A Ottawa April 19 in order to see everyday action. Due to an injury to Marquis Grissom, White was recalled for five days in May, then shipped back to Triple-A. He returned to Montreal for good June 17, and he will probably never spend another day in the minors. At Ottawa in 1994, White hit .272 with seven homers and nine stolen bases. With the big club, he showed fine extra-base power, took nine walks (for a .358 on-base percentage), and indicated that he was ready to assume full-time duty. It is likely that White will be a regular in 1995. There are some things he should work on, however; last year he did strike out 18 times and hit just .246 at night. Despite quickness and good range, he is not a stellar outfielder. He also lacks a quality arm. He has fine speed, but he has not yet learned to use it.

Major League Batting Register

	BA	G	AB	R	H	2B	3B	HR	RBI	SB
93 NL	.260	23	73	9	19	3	1	2	15	1
94 NL	.278	40	97	16	27	10	1	2	13	1
Life	.271	63	170	25	46	13	2	4	28	2

MARK WHITEN

Position: Outfield
Team: St. Louis Cardinals
Born: Nov. 25, 1966 Pensacola, FL
Height: 6'3" **Weight:** 215 lbs.
Bats: both **Throws:** right
Acquired: Traded from Indians for Mark Clark, 3/93

Player Summary

Fantasy Value	$16 to $19
Card Value	8¢ to 12¢
Will	show power
Can't	erase mistakes
Expect	a rifle arm
Don't Expect	contact hitting

Whiten hit for his highest average ever in 1994, totaling marks over .290 against both lefties and righties. He also showed the raw power he has become known for. Whiten's 14 homers were third-best on the Cardinals, and his .453 slugging percentage and .364 on-base percentage were career highs. He is far from a refined talent, nevertheless. He fanned 75 times last year, more than he regularly does, and his 37 walks were fewer than usual. Whiten has fine speed, but has never been able to use it effectively as a baserunner. He was caught stealing five out of 15 times in 1994. Defensively, the strong St. Louis right fielder last year proved that he has one of baseball's best arms, nailing nine enemies on the basepaths. Unfortunately, he also made nine errors. His range is just adequate, he does not charge base hits well, and sometimes Whiten's throws sail off target. Despite occasionally being frustrating, Whiten has raw talent that generates encouragement. His four-homer, 12-RBI game in 1993 is proof of that.

Major League Batting Register

	BA	G	AB	R	H	2B	3B	HR	RBI	SB
90 AL	.273	33	88	12	24	1	1	2	7	2
91 AL	.243	116	407	46	99	18	7	9	45	4
92 AL	.254	148	508	73	129	19	4	9	43	16
93 NL	.253	152	562	81	142	13	4	25	99	15
94 NL	.293	92	334	57	98	18	2	14	53	10
Life	.259	541	1899	269	492	69	18	59	247	47
3 AVE	.266	143	514	78	136	19	4	18	72	15

MATT WHITESIDE

Position: Pitcher
Team: Texas Rangers
Born: Aug. 8, 1967 Charleston, MO
Height: 6′ **Weight:** 195 lbs.
Bats: right **Throws:** right
Acquired: 25th-round pick in 6/90 free-agent draft

Player Summary

Fantasy Value	$0
Card Value	6¢ to 8¢
Will	pitch often
Can't	succeed on road
Expect	many sliders
Don't Expect	perfect control

Despite a fine arm, Whiteside still has not found the key to major-league effectiveness. He misses with his slider far too often, walks a myriad of hitters, and has not been able to establish a reliable repertoire. The Rangers front office would like him to seize the closer's job soon. Unfortunately, Whiteside hasn't earned his chance yet. Most of the reliever's problems come in games away from Texas. In 1993, his home ERA was 3.23, and his road mark 5.56. Last year, the split was even worse. Whiteside's home ERA was a respectable 3.89, but his road mark was a ghastly 7.45. He also did not pitch well in day games or on artificial turf. Opponents smacked him around at a .286 clip last year and drew well over four walks per nine innings. That was unacceptable considering that he notched only about five and one-half strike-outs per game. He only allowed six home runs last year, but he gave up over a hit per inning. Whiteside will get opportunities, but he needs to establish some consistency soon.

BOB WICKMAN

Position: Pitcher
Team: New York Yankees
Born: Feb. 6, 1969 Green Bay, WI
Height: 6′1″ **Weight:** 212 lbs.
Bats: right **Throws:** right
Acquired: Traded from White Sox with Melido Perez and Domingo Jean for Steve Sax, 1/92

Player Summary

Fantasy Value	$7 to $9
Card Value	8¢ to 12¢
Will	humble righties
Can't	overpower anybody
Expect	shifting roles
Don't Expect	30 saves

Wickman is missing part of the index finger on his right hand. This seeming disadvantage actually helps the Yankee hurler, as he gets an intense breaking motion both on his slider and on what otherwise would be a below-average fastball. When he is accurate low in the strike zone, Wickman can win. He spent the entire 1994 season in the Yankee bullpen. He began the year as a long man, then got some save opportunities when Xavier Hernandez blew his chance at the closer's job. While Wickman did notch six saves, his future will probably be as an all-purpose pitcher who can start in a pinch, close games if needed, and do a fine job as a setup man and long reliever. Wickman held right-handers to just a .201 average last year and cut down his walks dramatically, allowing less than three and one-half per nine innings. Opponents notched a .287 on-base percentage. He also allowed only three home runs. If he continues to pitch well, Wickman will be another reason that the Sax trade is already a great deal for the Yanks.

Major League Pitching Register

	W	L	ERA	G	S	IP	H	ER	BB	SO
92 AL	1	1	1.93	20	4	28.0	26	6	11	13
93 AL	2	1	4.32	60	1	73.0	78	35	23	39
94 AL	2	2	5.02	47	1	61.0	68	34	28	37
Life	5	4	4.17	127	6	162.0	172	75	62	89
2 AVE	2	2	4.69	63	1	79.0	87	41	31	46

Major League Pitching Register

	W	L	ERA	G	S	IP	H	ER	BB	SO
92 AL	6	1	4.11	8	0	50.1	51	23	20	21
93 AL	14	4	4.63	41	4	140.0	156	72	69	70
94 AL	5	4	3.09	53	6	70.0	54	24	27	56
Life	25	9	4.11	102	10	260.1	261	119	116	147
2 AVE	11	5	3.99	58	6	119.0	116	53	54	74

RICK WILKINS

Position: Catcher
Team: Chicago Cubs
Born: July 4, 1967 Jacksonville, FL
Height: 6'2" **Weight:** 210 lbs.
Bats: left **Throws:** right
Acquired: 23rd-round pick in 6/86 free-agent draft

Player Summary
Fantasy Value	$8 to $10
Card Value	6¢ to 10¢
Will	contribute on defense
Can't	solve left-handers
Expect	power, walks
Don't Expect	1993 repeat

Will the real Rick Wilkins please stand up? Is he the high-average, big-power team leader who was perhaps the Cubs' best player in 1993? Or is he the strikeout-prone, puzzled-looking man who best represented the poor 1994 Chicago club? The answer probably lies in between the offensive numbers of the two seasons. Few expected Wilkins to repeat his 1993 average, but even fewer thought he'd be hitting .214 with four homers at the All-Star break. Despite a late surge, he had a tremendously disappointing year. He fanned 86 times and hit just .154 against lefties. Wilkins did take 40 walks, but his on-base percentage was still a substandard .317. Most of the trouble stems from adjustments pitchers made last off-season. Wilkins saw far fewer fastballs in 1994 than he had in the past, and he could not adjust to a steady diet of off-speed pitches. Luckily for Cubs pitchers, his defensive game did not suffer. An agile, intelligent catcher, Wilkins threw out 37 percent of enemy basestealers in 1994.

BERNIE WILLIAMS

Position: Outfield
Team: New York Yankees
Born: Sept. 13, 1968 San Juan, Puerto Rico
Height: 6'2" **Weight:** 200 lbs.
Bats: both **Throws:** right
Acquired: Signed as a free agent, 9/85

Player Summary
Fantasy Value	$15 to $18
Card Value	6¢ to 10¢
Will	be on base
Can't	utilize speed
Expect	success vs. lefties
Don't Expect	great defense

With some of the load taken off his back, Williams had an outstanding season for the Yankees in 1994. Allowed to be just one of the team's big guns, he batted .312 with eight homers in road games and led New York in runs scored despite hitting in the seventh spot. Against left-handed pitchers, he hit .366 with half of his home runs in just 145 at bats, after batting .325 against them in 1993. If he can just learn to use his speed on the bases, Williams will be an even more valuable player. He still makes baserunning mistakes and was thrown out nine times last year trying to steal. In center field, he notched seven assists but showed only average range. Tried and found wanting earlier in his career as a top-of-the-order man, Williams hit .357 last season when leading off an inning. He also drew 61 walks while cutting his strikeouts almost in half, fanning just 54 times. His on-base percentage was an outstanding .384. Sooner or later, Williams might just end up back in the leadoff spot.

Major League Batting Register
	BA	G	AB	R	H	2B	3B	HR	RBI	SB
91 NL	.222	86	203	21	45	9	0	6	22	3
92 NL	.270	83	244	20	66	9	1	8	22	0
93 NL	.303	136	446	78	135	23	1	30	73	2
94 NL	.227	100	313	44	71	25	2	7	39	4
Life	.263	405	1206	163	317	66	4	51	156	9
3 AVE	.266	120	377	53	100	22	2	16	50	3

Major League Batting Register
	BA	G	AB	R	H	2B	3B	HR	RBI	SB
91 AL	.237	85	320	43	76	19	4	3	34	10
92 AL	.280	62	261	39	73	14	2	5	26	7
93 AL	.268	139	567	67	152	31	4	12	68	9
94 AL	.289	108	408	80	118	29	1	12	57	16
Life	.269	394	1556	229	419	93	11	32	185	42
3 AVE	.279	118	468	73	130	29	2	11	58	13

BRIAN WILLIAMS

Position: Pitcher
Team: Houston Astros
Born: Feb. 15, 1969 Lancaster, SC
Height: 6'2" **Weight:** 195 lbs.
Bats: right **Throws:** right
Acquired: First-round pick in 6/90 free-agent draft

Player Summary	
Fantasy Value	$0
Card Value	6¢ to 10¢
Will	work anywhere
Can't	get lefties out
Expect	control troubles
Don't Expect	complete games

The lanky Williams served as the Astros' swingman last year, making 13 starts and seven relief appearances. He began the campaign suffering from severe control problems, walking 14 in his first 18 innings before being shipped to Triple-A Tucson May 9. Two weeks later, after compiling a 2-0 mark in three starts, Williams was re-called to Houston. He stayed with the big club until being put on the DL with back spasms Aug. 1. The injury shelved Williams for the rest of the season. Unfortunately, he couldn't solve NL hitters when healthy. Opponents batted .343 with nine home runs, and left-handers rapped Williams at an amazing .397 clip. He allowed nearly five walks per game, and he still has not completed any of his 36 starts. He lacks overpowering velocity, but his off-speed pitches move well. If he can improve his control, he could be an effective starter. It's more likely, however, that he will try to work out his problems from the bullpen. Williams was a star at the University of South Carolina.

GERALD WILLIAMS

Position: Outfield
Team: New York Yankees
Born: Aug. 10, 1966 New Orleans, LA
Height: 6'2" **Weight:** 190 lbs.
Bats: right **Throws:** right
Acquired: 14th-round pick in 6/87 free-agent draft

Player Summary	
Fantasy Value	$1
Card Value	6¢ to 10¢
Will	seek regular duty
Can't	waste much time
Expect	extra-base power
Don't Expect	on-base prowess

"Ice" played it cool in 1994. Despite seeing only sporadic duty, Williams spent the whole season on the Yankees' roster and played well when asked. This alone must have made him happy. In 1993, he racked up the frequent-flier miles, spending four separate stints with the Yankees. Last year, he hit .333 against AL right-handers and .277 versus lefties. He showed outstanding power, slugging a mighty .523 for the year. Williams, however, needs to improve his strike-zone judgement and learn to use his speed if he intends to be a major-league regular. He was thrown out three of four times trying to steal last year, and he drew only four walks while fanning 17 times. Despite a good batting average, Williams's on-base percentage was a mediocre .319. He was often used as a late-inning defensive replacement for iron-gloved Luis Polonia, and Williams could return in that role in 1995. Should he show improvement with the stick, he might get a shot at regular duty. That's hardly a given, nonetheless, and Williams is a little old to be a prospect.

Major League Pitching Register

	W	L	ERA	G	CG	IP	H	ER	BB	SO
91 NL	0	1	3.75	2	0	12.0	11	5	4	4
92 NL	7	6	3.92	16	0	96.1	92	42	42	54
93 NL	4	4	4.83	42	0	82.0	76	44	38	56
94 NL	6	5	5.74	20	0	78.1	112	50	41	49
Life	17	16	4.72	80	0	268.2	291	141	125	163
3 AVE	6	6	4.88	29	0	96.1	109	52	46	60

Major League Batting Register

	BA	G	AB	R	H	2B	3B	HR	RBI	SB
92 AL	.296	15	27	7	8	2	0	3	6	2
93 AL	.149	42	67	11	10	2	3	0	6	2
94 AL	.291	57	86	19	25	8	0	4	13	1
Life	.239	114	180	37	43	12	3	7	25	5

MATT WILLIAMS

Position: Third base
Team: San Francisco Giants
Born: Nov. 28, 1965 Bishop, CA
Height: 6'2" **Weight:** 216 lbs.
Bats: right **Throws:** right
Acquired: First-round pick in 6/86 free-agent draft

Player Summary	
Fantasy Value	$30 to $35
Card Value	15¢ to 25¢
Will	show good glove
Can't	run well
Expect	home runs
Don't Expect	Roger Maris

Posting his second straight strong campaign, Williams led the major leagues in home runs last year. He showed consistent power in every month. He hit 10 home runs in April, nine in May, 10 in June, 11 in July, and three in August before the strike halted his chance to break Roger Maris's all-time mark. Williams once again battered left-handed pitchers in 1994, hitting .297 with an astounding 16 home runs in just 104 at bats. Williams did his job last year, producing plenty of home runs and RBI, but his doubles count did drop dramatically. He still rarely takes a base on balls. He walked just 33 times last year, fanned 87, and sported a .319 on-base percentage. Despite 12 errors last season (seven after the All-Star break), the former shortstop is still considered by many as one of the game's best defensive third basemen. He lacks speed, but has a strong arm and good reflexes. He has won several Gold Gloves.

Major League Batting Register

	BA	G	AB	R	H	2B	3B	HR	RBI	SB
87 NL	.188	84	245	28	46	9	2	8	21	4
88 NL	.205	52	156	17	32	6	1	8	19	0
89 NL	.202	84	292	31	59	18	1	18	50	1
90 NL	.277	159	617	87	171	27	2	33	122	7
91 NL	.268	157	589	72	158	24	5	34	98	5
92 NL	.227	146	529	58	120	13	5	20	66	7
93 NL	.294	145	579	105	170	33	4	38	110	1
94 NL	.267	112	445	74	119	16	3	43	96	1
Life	.253	939	3452	472	875	146	23	202	582	26
3 AVE	.264	150	578	89	153	23	4	40	104	3

MITCH WILLIAMS

Position: Pitcher
Team: California Angels
Born: Nov. 17, 1964 Santa Ana, CA
Height: 6'4" **Weight:** 205 lbs.
Bats: left **Throws:** left
Acquired: Signed as a free agent, 12/94

Player Summary	
Fantasy Value	$0
Card Value	5¢ to 7¢
Will	be Wild Thing
Can't	close immediately
Expect	a hard road
Don't Expect	complete health

Williams had a lost 1994. After serving up Joe Carter's World Series-winning home run in 1993, Williams, then a Phillie, braved a media blitz and offered no excuses. But having to deal with the public was another thing, and he was shipped to Houston for reliever Doug Jones. Close to his Texas home for the '94 campaign, Williams still wasn't able to have a successful season. Losing all semblance of control, he allowed over 10½ bases on balls per nine innings, blew two saves, and compiled an embarrassing ERA. He was waived by the Astros, and he declared that he did not want to pitch for another team. Williams had a change of heart during the off-season. A left-hander, he was able to receive another opportunity to prove himself. He did hold lefty hitters to a .148 batting average last year, so if nothing else, Williams could be used against tough southpaws. He leaves himself in a terrible fielding position after delivering a pitch.

Major League Pitching Register

	W	L	ERA	G	S	IP	H	ER	BB	SO
86 AL	8	6	3.58	80	8	98.0	69	39	79	90
87 AL	8	6	3.23	85	6	108.2	63	39	94	129
88 AL	2	7	4.63	67	18	68.0	48	35	47	61
89 NL	4	4	2.76	76	36	81.2	71	25	52	67
90 NL	1	8	3.93	59	16	66.1	60	29	50	55
91 NL	12	5	2.34	69	30	88.1	56	23	62	84
92 NL	5	8	3.78	66	29	81.0	69	34	64	74
93 NL	3	7	3.34	65	43	62.0	56	23	44	60
94 NL	1	4	7.65	25	6	20.0	21	17	24	21
Life	44	55	3.53	592	192	674.0	513	264	516	641
2 AVE	4	8	3.59	66	36	72.0	63	29	54	67

DAN WILSON

Position: Catcher
Team: Seattle Mariners
Born: March 25, 1969   Arlington Heights, IL
Height: 6'3"   **Weight:** 190 lbs.
Bats: right   **Throws:** right
Acquired: Traded from Reds with Bobby Ayala for Bret Boone and Erik Hanson, 11/93

Player Summary	
Fantasy Value	$1
Card Value	6¢ to 10¢
Will	play regularly
Can't	hit for power
Expect	good defense
Don't Expect	on-base ability

Wilson's defensive skills are undisputed. His managers have always prized the youngster's game-calling ability, outstanding agility, and pure receiving skills. In addition, despite an inexperienced and a wild Mariners staff that didn't hold baserunners well, Wilson threw out nearly 40 percent of enemy basestealers in 1994. He lacks a strong arm but has a good release. Unfortunately, Wilson gave the Mariners little with the bat. He has only 16 career home runs in five professional seasons, and he has only once hit over .262. Last year, in his first trial as a big-league regular, Wilson was the least-effective member of a mediocre Seattle offense. He slugged just .312 and drew only 10 walks to register a pathetic .244 on-base percentage. He did not make good contact, whiffing 57 times, and he showed no baserunning speed. In home games, Wilson batted just .179. If he can continue to play good defense, he may be able to buy enough time to improve his batting skill. He is likely to end up as a backup, however.

Major League Batting Register

	BA	G	AB	R	H	2B	3B	HR	RBI	SB
92 NL	.360	12	25	2	9	1	0	0	3	0
93 NL	.224	36	76	6	17	3	0	0	8	0
94 AL	.216	91	282	24	61	14	2	3	27	1
Life	.227	139	383	32	87	18	2	3	38	1

DAVE WINFIELD

Position: Designated hitter
Team: Cleveland Indians
Born: Oct. 3, 1951   St. Paul, MN
Height: 6'6"   **Weight:** 245 lbs.
Bats: right   **Throws:** right
Acquired: Traded from Twins for Russ Swan, 8/94

Player Summary	
Fantasy Value	$5 to $7
Card Value	20¢ to 30¢
Will	hit mistakes
Can't	show old athleticism
Expect	some power
Don't Expect	high average

The Indians acquired Winfield during the strike, hoping he could add some punch to the Tribe. Unfortunately, he never suited up for the Tribe. In Minnesota, he again showed decent extra-base power, but batted just .225 against righties after enjoying success against them in 1993. Formerly a standout baserunner and defensive player, Winfield is no longer mobile enough to steal bases or man the outfield regularly. If used mostly against left-handers, he could be a terrific player. At this point, platoon duty is probably all the future Hall of Famer will get.

Major League Batting Register

	BA	G	AB	R	H	2B	3B	HR	RBI	SB
73 NL	.277	56	141	9	39	4	1	3	12	0
74 NL	.265	145	498	57	132	18	4	20	75	9
75 NL	.267	143	509	74	136	20	2	15	76	23
76 NL	.283	137	492	81	139	4	13	69	26
77 NL	.275	157	615	104	169	29	7	25	92	16
78 NL	.308	158	587	88	181	30	5	24	97	21
79 NL	.308	159	597	97	184	27	10	34	118	15
80 NL	.276	162	558	89	154	25	6	20	87	23
81 AL	.294	105	388	52	114	25	1	13	68	11
82 AL	.280	140	539	84	151	24	8	37	106	5
83 AL	.283	152	598	99	169	26	8	32	116	15
84 AL	.340	141	567	106	193	34	4	19	100	6
85 AL	.275	155	633	105	174	34	6	26	114	19
86 AL	.262	154	565	90	148	31	5	24	104	6
87 AL	.275	156	575	83	158	22	1	27	97	5
88 AL	.322	149	559	96	180	37	2	25	107	9
90 AL	.267	132	475	70	127	21	2	21	78	0
91 AL	.262	150	568	75	149	27	4	28	86	7
92 AL	.290	156	583	92	169	33	3	26	108	2
93 AL	.271	143	547	72	148	27	2	21	76	2
94 AL	.252	77	294	35	74	15	3	10	43	2
Life	.284	2927	10888	1658	3088	535	88	463	1829	222
3 AVE	.273	136	515	71	140	27	3	20	82	2

BOBBY WITT

Position: Pitcher
Team: Oakland Athletics
Born: May 11, 1964 Arlington, VA
Height: 6'2" **Weight:** 205 lbs.
Bats: right **Throws:** right
Acquired: Traded from Rangers with Ruben Sierra and Jeff Russell for Jose Canseco, 8/92

Player Summary	
Fantasy Value	$4 to $6
Card Value	6¢ to 10¢
Will	show impressive stuff
Can't	master his control
Expect	30 starts
Don't Expect	stolen bases

Witt endured another on-again, off-again campaign in 1994. The talented but erratic hurler still throws an outstanding fastball and a fine slider, but he has no consistent off-speed pitch. Following a strong 1993 season, he slumped again last year. By mid-June, Witt was 4-7 with a 6.15 ERA, walking five men per game before unexpectedly heating up. On June 23, he tossed a one-hit shutout against Kansas City, fanning 14 and walking none. The only baserunner reached on a disputed infield single. Witt then fired shutouts in his next two starts, lowering his ERA to 4.69. Unfortunately, he pulled a muscle in his side during his next start, and from that point to the strike he allowed 14 earned runs in 20 innings. Witt still has problems getting ahead in the count, and he allowed 22 home runs last year as opponents batted .283. He has a fine pickoff move.

Major League Pitching Register

	W	L	ERA	G	CG	IP	H	ER	BB	SO
86 AL	11	9	5.48	31	0	157.2	130	96	143	174
87 AL	8	10	4.91	26	1	143.0	114	78	140	160
88 AL	8	10	3.92	22	13	174.1	134	76	101	148
89 AL	12	13	5.14	31	5	194.1	182	111	114	166
90 AL	17	10	3.36	33	7	222.0	197	83	110	221
91 AL	3	7	6.09	17	1	88.2	84	60	74	82
92 AL	10	14	4.29	31	0	193.0	183	92	114	125
93 AL	14	13	4.21	35	5	220.0	226	103	91	131
94 AL	8	10	5.04	24	5	135.2	151	76	70	111
Life	91	96	4.56	250	37	1528.2	1401	775	957	1318
3 AVE	12	14	4.50	33	4	201.2	207	101	101	137

MARK WOHLERS

Position: Pitcher
Team: Atlanta Braves
Born: Jan. 23, 1970 Holyoke, MA
Height: 6'4" **Weight:** 207 lbs.
Bats: right **Throws:** right
Acquired: 10th-round pick in 6/88 free-agent draft

Player Summary	
Fantasy Value	$3 to $5
Card Value	6¢ to 10¢
Will	utilize fastball
Can't	afford control woes
Expect	short relief
Don't Expect	many home runs

Throughout his seven-year pro career, Wohlers has been plagued by poor control, which ruined him last season as he walked nearly six men per nine innings. The lanky fireballer still has dominating stuff, as opponents hit only one home run against him in 1994. In addition, right-handers could manage just a .224 average against Wohlers. Unfortunately, pitch after pitch bounced into the dirt or wide of the plate, and the Braves paid the price. Wohlers appeared to lose his concentration on the mound, baserunners ran wild against him, and 17 of his 41 inherited runners scored. By the end of the season, Bobby Cox didn't know what to do with his wild reliever. Wohlers has an arm too good to waste on middle relief, but he may have to go back to Triple-A to regain his confidence. The Braves still have high hopes that he can become the late-inning closer they crave. Unless he can put the ball where it's supposed to go, however, Wohlers won't be trusted with many save opportunities.

Major League Pitching Register

	W	L	ERA	G	S	IP	H	ER	BB	SO
91 NL	3	1	3.20	17	2	19.2	17	7	13	13
92 NL	1	2	2.55	32	4	35.1	28	10	14	17
93 NL	6	2	4.50	46	0	48.0	37	24	22	45
94 NL	7	2	4.59	51	1	51.0	51	26	33	58
Life	17	7	3.92	146	7	154.0	133	67	82	133
3 AVE	6	2	4.10	50	2	52.0	46	24	27	48

TODD WORRELL

Position: Pitcher
Team: Los Angeles Dodgers
Born: Sept. 26, 1959 Arcadia, CA
Height: 6'5" **Weight:** 222 lbs.
Bats: right **Throws:** right
Acquired: Signed as a free agent, 12/92

Player Summary	
Fantasy Value	$6 to $8
Card Value	6¢ to 10¢
Will	try to stay healthy
Can't	carry the load
Expect	strikeouts
Don't Expect	30 saves

The entire Dodger bullpen had problems in 1994, and Worrell represented the crew quite well. He blew eight of 19 save opportunities, allowed nine of 14 inherited runners to score, and could not keep runners close. Oddly enough, he pitched very well in the first three months. His real problems came in July and August, as he allowed 15 runs in his last 18 innings. The veteran fireballer also was troubled by a pulled ribcage muscle, which caused him to miss two weeks of duty in May. For the year, he held enemy hitters to a .236 batting average, was stingy with the base on balls, and gave up just four home runs. Righty batters hit .254 against him, though. Worrell no longer throws as hard as he used to, but he still fanned over a man per inning last season. He has worked hard to rehabilitate from the serious elbow injury that sidelined him for two years, but injuries and inconsistency have kept Worrell from his former star status.

Major League Pitching Register

	W	L	ERA	G	S	IP	H	ER	BB	SO
85 NL	3	0	2.91	17	5	21.2	17	7	7	17
86 NL	9	10	2.08	74	36	103.2	86	24	41	73
87 NL	8	6	2.66	75	33	94.2	86	28	34	92
88 NL	5	9	3.00	68	32	90.0	69	30	34	78
89 NL	3	5	2.96	47	20	51.2	42	17	26	41
92 NL	5	3	2.11	67	3	64.0	45	15	25	64
93 NL	1	1	6.05	35	5	38.2	46	26	11	31
94 NL	6	5	4.29	38	11	42.0	37	20	12	44
Life	40	39	2.97	421	145	506.1	428	167	190	440
3 AVE	5	4	3.85	52	8	54.1	48	23	18	52

ERIC YOUNG

Position: Outfield
Team: Colorado Rockies
Born: May 18, 1967 Jacksonville, FL
Height: 5'9" **Weight:** 180 lbs.
Bats: right **Throws:** right
Acquired: First-round pick from Dodgers in 11/92 expansion draft

Player Summary	
Fantasy Value	$14 to $17
Card Value	6¢ to 10¢
Will	show good speed
Can't	win regular job
Expect	defensive struggles
Don't Expect	road success

As he did the season before, Young puffed up his 1994 statistics by taking advantage of cozy Mile High Stadium. He hit extremely well in Colorado but poorly everyplace else. In home games, he batted .309, drew 22 walks to register an outstanding .414 on-base percentage, and slugged six home runs. His performance on the road featured just one home run, a .217 batting average, and a mediocre .339 on-base percentage. Despite showing good power in Denver, Young is not much of an offensive threat. He struck out just 17 times last year but hit only .215 against left-handed pitching. He has exemplary speed and steals bases well, succeeding in 18 of 25 tries in 1994. He has too many holes in his game to be a consistent leadoff hitter, though. In addition, Young lacks exceptional range or a strong arm, and he cannot seem to hold a job in the outfield. He has also failed previous trials at second base. While Young has not proven that he is developed enough to play every day, he does enough things to merit a job coming off the bench.

Major League Batting Register

	BA	G	AB	R	H	2B	3B	HR	RBI	SB
92 NL	.258	49	132	9	34	1	0	1	11	6
93 NL	.269	144	490	82	132	16	8	3	42	42
94 NL	.272	90	228	37	62	13	1	7	30	18
Life	.268	283	850	128	228	30	9	11	83	66
2 AVE	.270	135	406	67	110	17	5	6	42	34

KEVIN YOUNG

Position: First base; third base
Team: Pittsburgh Pirates
Born: June 16, 1969 Alpena, MI
Height: 6'2" **Weight:** 213 lbs.
Bats: right **Throws:** right
Acquired: Seventh-round pick in 6/90 free-agent draft

Player Summary	
Fantasy Value	$3 to $5
Card Value	8¢ to 12¢
Will	play strong defense
Can't	crush home runs
Expect	some comeback
Don't Expect	future stardom

Nearly everyone in the Pirates' organization loves Young's swing, but the big infielder has not shown that he can hit major-league pitching. He began 1994 platooning at first base with Brian Hunter, but Young hit just .192 with 21 strikeouts in 52 at bats before being sent down to Triple-A Buffalo on May 10. He hit .327 there and was recalled on May 25. Again, he could not produce in Pittsburgh. Reluctantly, the Bucs sent Young out again July 11, where he spent the rest of the season. While back in Triple-A, Young returned to his original position, third base, but slumped at bat. He was rushed through the minors and has not yet shown the speed, patience, or average-hitting ability that got him to Pittsburgh. (He was named the top prospect in the Triple-A American Association in 1992.) He took just eight walks last year, compiling a miserable .258 on-base percentage, and batted only .118 against left-handers. The slick-fielding Young may need a full season back on the farm before he can lay claim to a major-league roster spot.

Major League Batting Register

	BA	G	AB	R	H	2B	3B	HR	RBI	SB
92 NL	.571	10	7	2	4	0	0	0	4	1
93 NL	.236	141	449	38	106	24	3	6	47	2
94 NL	.205	59	122	15	25	7	2	1	11	0
Life	.234	210	578	55	135	31	5	7	62	3

TODD ZEILE

Position: Third base
Team: St. Louis Cardinals
Born: Sept. 9, 1965 Van Nuys, CA
Height: 6'1" **Weight:** 190 lbs.
Bats: right **Throws:** right
Acquired: Third-round pick in 6/86 free-agent draft

Player Summary	
Fantasy Value	$14 to $17
Card Value	8¢ to 12¢
Will	provide offense
Can't	win a Gold Glove
Expect	15 home runs
Don't Expect	stolen bases

Many observers hold Zeile as responsible as any Cardinal for the team's poor 1994 season. On the surface, this seems odd. He led the club in RBI, tied with Ray Lankford for the team's top spot in home runs, finished second in walks and runs scored, and had a decent batting average. One reason for the unhappiness with Zeile's performance may stem from his yearly tendency to do his best hitting in July and August. He did not play well early in the 1994 season, and he only got his burners turned on as the team fell out of the pennant race. At the All-Star break, Zeile was hitting just .250 with 11 home runs. He enjoyed a late surge but could not help the team get out of its hole. He took 52 walks last year and fanned just 56 times. His on-base percentage was .348. He hit .299 against left-handers. A catcher in the minor leagues, he moved to third in the bigs and has improved his defense. Zeile lacks exceptional range, but he has a fine arm and made just 12 errors last summer.

Major League Batting Register

	BA	G	AB	R	H	2B	3B	HR	RBI	SB
89 NL	.256	28	82	7	21	3	1	1	8	0
90 NL	.244	144	495	62	121	25	3	15	57	2
91 NL	.280	155	565	76	158	36	3	11	81	17
92 NL	.257	126	439	51	113	18	4	7	48	7
93 NL	.277	157	571	82	158	36	1	17	103	5
94 NL	.267	113	415	62	111	25	1	19	75	1
Life	.266	723	2567	340	682	143	13	70	372	32
3 AVE	.268	147	532	73	142	30	2	17	86	4

BOB ABREU

Position: Outfield
Team: Houston Astros
Born: March 11, 1974 Aragua, Venezuela
Height: 6′ **Weight:** 160 lbs.
Bats: left **Throws:** right
Acquired: Signed as a nondrafted free agent, 8/90

Player Summary	
Fantasy Value $0
Card Value . . . . 12¢ to 20¢
Will . . . . hit triples
Can't. . . . . pull everything
Expect . . . . slugging
Don't Expect . . . . great glove

Ever since signing at the age of 16, Abreu has shown an ability to hit. If all goes according to plan, his success will only increase as he gets to be as old as his competition. Abreu left his mark on the Double-A Texas League last year, beginning when he hit a home run on Opening Night. By the time the season ended, he had reached career highs in batting average, home runs, RBI, and doubles. He also stole in double figures for the fourth time in as many pro seasons. He has achieved all this despite having to battle a language barrier, but he's even making strides in that direction. Abreu is a serviceable, though not spectacular player in the field. His niche in the big leagues will involve being a tough out from the left side of the plate; he also may develop an incredible power stroke by the time he graces the big leagues. His speed will not put him in a class with burners, but he won't be in over his head on the Astrodome surface, either. At Osceola of the Class-A Florida State League in 1993, Abreu set a franchise record with 17 triples.

Professional Batting Register

	BA	G	AB	R	H	2B	3B	HR	RBI	SB
91 R	.301	56	183	21	55	7	3	0	20	10
92 A	.292	135	480	81	140	21	4	8	48	15
93 A	.283	129	474	62	134	21	17	5	55	10
94 AA	.303	118	400	61	121	25	9	16	73	12

JUAN ACEVEDO

Position: Pitcher
Team: Colorado Rockies
Born: May 5, 1970 Juarez, Mexico
Height: 6′2″ **Weight:** 195 lbs.
Bats: right **Throws:** right
Acquired: 14th-round pick in 6/93 free-agent draft

Player Summary	
Fantasy Value $1
Card Value . . . . 15¢ to 20¢
Will. . . . . advance quickly
Can't. . . . . get ink
Expect . . . . shutouts
Don't Expect . . . . bad outings

Entering their very first draft, the Rockies wanted to be extra thorough. Maybe that's how they found such a strong prospect in the 14th round. Acevedo has developed more quickly than many in the Colorado organization who were selected ahead of him, and at his current pace he could be in the majors to stay before very long. Last year while playing for New Haven of the Double-A Eastern League, he boasted a 9-3 mark with a 2.89 ERA at midsummer. He made the All-Star squad, though his appearance in the game didn't go all that well. He allowed three hits and three earned runs in one inning but did not get the decision. Acevedo's regular-season outings were much more productive. He won his ninth straight decision on July 2, beating Portland 9-1. At the time, he ranked among the top Colorado farmhands in strikeouts. He also fired a three-hit shutout to trigger a New Haven streak in which the team went 45 innings without allowing an earned run. Acevedo held Eastern League hitters to a .219 batting average. League managers named him the No. 4 prospect in a poll by *Baseball America*.

Professional Pitching Register

	W	L	ERA	G	CG	IP	H	ER	BB	SO
92 A	3	4	5.54	13	1	66.2	79	41	34	40
93 A	9	8	4.40	27	1	118.2	119	58	58	107
94 AA	17	6	2.37	26	5	174.2	142	46	38	161

WILLIE ADAMS

Position: Pitcher
Team: Oakland Athletics
Born: Oct. 8, 1972 Gallup, NM
Height: 6'7" **Weight:** 215 lbs.
Bats: right **Throws:** right
Acquired: Second-round pick in 6/93 free-agent draft

Player Summary	
Fantasy Value	$0
Card Value	50¢ to 70¢
Will	advance quickly
Can't	lose stamina
Expect	split-finger pitch
Don't Expect	overpowering stuff

Dave Stewart rendered excellent service to the Athletics during his years in Oakland, and he may wind up helping them for years to come in the person of Willie Adams. Stewart's move to Toronto gave Oakland a compensation pick after the first round of the 1993 draft, and the A's used it to grab this right-hander out of Stanford. Adams might have gone even sooner in the draft, but fatigue took some velocity off his pitches toward the end of the 1993 season. Still, when the Athletics made Adams the 36th overall pick, they saw him as someone who had the potential to advance quickly, and he has not disappointed them. He outgrew the Class-A California League in the first several weeks of 1994, and he was soon with Oakland's Double-A affiliate in Huntsville, where he got people out. His size and stats might indicate he's overpowering, but that's not necessarily the case. His strikeout-to-walk ratio in Double-A demonstrates that he has to get ahead of hitters to be effective. Adams has been compared in style to another young right-hander—Mets prospect Bobby Jones.

EDGARDO ALFONZO

Position: Second base; infield
Team: New York Mets
Born: Aug. 11, 1973 Station Teresa, Venezuela
Height: 5'11" **Weight:** 174 lbs.
Bats: right **Throws:** right
Acquired: Signed as a free agent, 2/91

Player Summary	
Fantasy Value	$0
Card Value	15¢ to 25¢
Will	put ball in play
Can't	wow 'em with glove
Expect	extra-base sock
Don't Expect	shortstop

Alfonzo was once a candidate to play shortstop for the Mets, but that apparently has changed with the rapid development of prospect Rey Ordonez. Thus Alfonzo, just 20 when he opened last season in Double-A ball, is now being looked at as a potential second baseman, and that switch may be permanent. Of course, there are problems there, too, because he has Jeff Kent above him at the major-league level. It is too soon to worry about that. Alfonzo has had some defensive troubles on his way up the ladder while playing shortstop (26 errors in 1992, and 29 miscues in 1993) and that could hurt. But he also has prowess with the bat, as shown in 1993 when he hit 11 homers and drove in 86 runs in the Class-A Florida State League, a very tough circuit for power. He makes good contact and will take a walk. Last year, he notched 64 bases on balls and 55 strikeouts. He can steal bases, though his percentage is not always the best. Even so, Alfonzo must sharpen his glove, because the Mets are trying to upgrade their defense. His brother Ed is in the Baltimore system.

Professional Pitching Register

	W	L	ERA	G	CG	IP	H	ER	BB	SO
93 A	0	2	3.38	5	0	18.2	21	7	8	22
94 A	7	1	3.38	11	0	45.1	41	17	10	42
94 AA	4	3	4.30	10	0	60.2	58	29	23	33

Professional Batting Register

	BA	G	AB	R	H	2B	3B	HR	RBI	SB
91 R	.331	54	175	29	58	8	4	0	27	6
92 A	.349	78	303	41	106	13	5	1	44	7
93 A	.294	128	494	75	145	18	3	11	86	26
94 AA	.293	127	498	89	146	34	2	15	75	14

JERMAINE ALLENSWORTH

Position: Outfield
Team: Pittsburgh Pirates
Born: Jan. 11, 1972   Anderson, IN
Height: 5'11"   **Weight:** 180 lbs.
Bats: right   **Throws:** right
Acquired: First-round pick in 6/93 free-agent draft

Player Summary	
Fantasy Value	$0
Card Value	30¢ to 50¢
Will	get hit by pitches
Can't	swing at bad balls
Expect	solid tools
Don't Expect	exceptional arm

Allensworth is part of a recent early-round bounty that the Pirates hope will make them contenders in the near future. In 1992, the Bucs had two picks apiece in the first and second rounds. In 1993, they had three first-rounders. Allensworth was the second of those three, coming as compensation for the loss of free agent Doug Drabek. After making his debut in short-season Class-A in 1993, Allensworth jumped to Double-A ball, where he opened the 1994 season as center fielder for Carolina of the Southern League. He has the makings of a leadoff man and has shown a knack for getting hit by pitches. His stolen base total is very disappointing for someone with his speed. It will be a rare thing for him to hit the ball out of the park, though he could collect his share of doubles. He will have to improve his strikeout-to-walk ratio to remain at the top of the order. He had 39 bases on balls and 79 strikeouts last year. Out of Purdue, Allensworth is already 23 years old, so he doesn't have a whole lot of time to climb. He'll have to show a lot more in Double-A ball to take the next step.

Professional Batting Register

	BA	G	AB	R	H	2B	3B	HR	RBI	SB
93 A	.308	67	263	44	81	16	4	1	32	18
94 AA	.241	118	452	63	109	26	8	1	34	16

GARRET ANDERSON

Position: Outfield
Team: California Angels
Born: June 30, 1972   Los Angeles, CA
Height: 6'3"   **Weight:** 190 lbs.
Bats: left   **Throws:** left
Acquired: Fourth-round pick in 6/90 free-agent draft

Player Summary	
Fantasy Value	$1
Card Value	20¢ to 30¢
Will	hit line drives
Can't	play center nor right
Expect	hitting streaks
Don't Expect	power

Anderson starred in Southern California years ago, and he could be doing it again soon. Last time, he was leading Kennedy High School to the 1989 Los Angeles city title. Next time, he'll be playing left field and smacking line drives for the Angels. The reason? He can hit. Anderson was assigned to the Triple-A Pacific Coast League for the second straight season in 1994, and once again he knocked the pitchers around. He hit in 27 straight games from May 19 to June 17. As he approached the campaign's midpoint (and his 22nd birthday), he was hitting well over .300 and played in the Triple-A All-Star Game. His offensive game is not without flaws. So far he hasn't shown home run power or the ability to steal bases. As far as defensive play goes, Anderson might be an adequate left fielder who has some speed, but that will not be his distinguishing point. He has also spent some time at first base, where his height makes him a good target for infield throws.

Professional Batting Register

	BA	G	AB	R	H	2B	3B	HR	RBI	SB
90 R	.213	32	127	5	27	2	0	0	14	3
90 A	.253	25	83	11	21	3	1	1	8	0
91 A	.260	105	392	40	102	22	2	2	42	5
92 A	.323	81	322	46	104	15	2	1	62	1
92 AA	.274	39	146	16	40	5	0	2	19	2
93 AAA	.293	124	467	57	137	34	4	4	71	3
94 AAA	.321	123	505	75	162	42	6	12	102	3
94 AL	.385	5	13	0	5	0	0	0	1	0

SHANE ANDREWS

Position: Third base
Team: Montreal Expos
Born: Aug. 28, 1971 Dallas, TX
Height: 6'1" **Weight:** 215 lbs.
Bats: right **Throws:** right
Acquired: First-round pick in 6/90 free-agent draft

Player Summary	
Fantasy Value	$1
Card Value	15¢ to 25¢
Will	be streaky
Can't	eliminate errors
Expect	power
Don't Expect	speed

Andrews is a power-hitting third baseman who has a future if he can make contact with the ball—both with his bat and glove. The issue at the plate is strikeouts; he fanned 173 times in 453 at bats three years ago in Class-A ball. However, when promoted to Double-A, he trimmed the strikeouts by 55. He had a few more strikeouts last year, but he also was able to notch more walks. He may never be a contact hitter, but if he works on it, the K total should be acceptable. As far as defense, in 1993 Andrews finished second among Eastern League third basemen in total chances. But his fielding percentage was only .927. He got off to a slow start in Triple-A in 1994, making two errors and going 1-for-12 at the dish. But he went on a 20-for-52 tear with 16 RBI. Then he went into a 2-for-24 slump with 10 strikeouts. Perhaps even more significantly, at one point he was batting .371 against lefties and .200 against righties. Obviously, there is more than one hole in his game. Power has allure, and Andrews keeps putting up pretty impressive slugging stats.

Professional Batting Register

	BA	G	AB	R	H	2B	3B	HR	RBI	SB
90 R	.242	56	190	31	46	7	1	3	24	11
91 A	.208	105	356	46	74	16	7	11	49	5
92 A	.230	136	453	76	104	18	1	25	87	8
93 AA	.260	124	442	77	115	29	2	18	70	10
94 AAA	.254	137	460	79	117	25	2	16	85	6

MATT APANA

Position: Pitcher
Team: Seattle Mariners
Born: Jan. 16, 1971 Newport Beach, CA
Height: 6'1" **Weight:** 190 lbs.
Bats: right **Throws:** right
Acquired: 22nd-round pick in 6/93 free-agent draft

Player Summary	
Fantasy Value	$0
Card Value	15¢ to 25¢
Will	be promoted
Can't	rush development
Expect	few hits
Don't Expect	few walks

Matthew Kaleolani Apana is a resident of Hawaii who made life anything but a paradise for opposing hitters. A graduate of Roosevelt High School in Honolulu, where he received all-state honors in baseball, Apana was the Pitcher of the Year in the Class-A California League last year. Playing for the Riverside Pilots, he ranked among the top Seattle farmhands in victories, strikeouts, and earned run average. He held Cal League hitters to a .232 batting average. He was especially tough in the second half, going 5-1 with a 2.07 ERA in his first nine starts after the All-Star Game. He fired a three-hitter, striking out nine and walking none, in a 1-0 victory on July 6. He was named to the California League All-Star team. Apana attended the University of Hawaii and received second-team WAC Scholar-Athlete honors as a freshman. As a junior, he was named his team's outstanding pitcher. In his first year of pro ball, he went five innings and combined with two relievers on a no-hitter. The Mariners might be tempted to rush him, but he had only one good year so far as a pro, and patience would serve them better.

Professional Pitching Register

	W	L	ERA	G	CG	IP	H	ER	BB	SO
93 A	5	3	4.43	14	0	61.0	50	30	43	59
94 A	14	4	2.83	26	3	165.1	142	52	70	137

JAMIE ARNOLD

Position: Pitcher
Team: Atlanta Braves
Born: March 24, 1974 Dearborn, MI
Height: 6'2" **Weight:** 185 lbs.
Bats: right **Throws:** right
Acquired: First-round pick in 6/92 free-agent draft

Player Summary	
Fantasy Value	$0
Card Value	15¢ to 25¢
Will	throw hard
Can't	lose confidence
Expect	improved control
Don't Expect	consistency

Arnold is arriving a little less quickly than his pitches do, but then again, that's easy to do when you throw around 93 mph. He is moving through Atlanta's organization one level at a time, which is just as well. With the pitching depth at the major-league level in Atlanta, there is no urgency in the organization. In 1994, Arnold graduated to high Class-A ball, where he made the Carolina League All-Star team. Through his 21 starts with Durham, he went 6-7 with a 5.10 ERA. He walked 61 in his first 118 innings. That may be simply a matter of developing the confidence to throw strikes. The 21st overall pick in 1992, Arnold has a live arm but doesn't yet have the location of a top prospect. He allowed almost five bases on balls per nine innings last year, a ratio that led directly to his high ERA. He should cut that ratio at least in half. He also allowed 26 homers in his 145 innings pitched. He is young enough to win at the high Class-A level this year, move on to Double-A in 1996, and be a big-league pitcher by 1997—if he is able to master the strike zone.

MATT ARRANDALE

Position: Pitcher
Team: St. Louis Cardinals
Born: Dec. 14, 1970 St. Louis, MO
Height: 6' **Weight:** 165 lbs.
Bats: right **Throws:** right
Acquired: 35th-round pick in 6/93 free-agent draft

Player Summary	
Fantasy Value	$0
Card Value	15¢ to 20¢
Will	throw strikes
Can't	overpower hitters
Expect	a Cards fan
Don't Expect	13-0 again

Like Bob Tewksbury has been doing for years with the St. Louis Cardinals, Arrandale last year showed what a pitcher can accomplish simply by throwing the ball over the plate. He just edged out fellow farmhand Alan Benes for the victory crown in the organization, garnering 18 wins (albeit all on the Class-A level) to Benes's 17 (from Class-A to Triple-A). Arrandale allowed only 32 walks last year, and he also struck out roughly five men to every one he walked, a ratio that should serve him well as he progresses. A St. Louis native, he grew up rooting for the Cardinals, and cheered when they won the 1982 World Series. He throws a fastball, a slider, and a changeup. He used his three pitches well enough to race off to a 13-0 start in the South Atlantic League last year. He made the loop's All-Star team. His one and one-half walks per nine innings in the Sally League is all the more amazing when considering his eight Ks per game. Later he was promoted to St. Petersburg of the Florida State League. The University of Illinois product should start 1995 in the Double-A Texas League.

Professional Pitching Register

	W	L	ERA	G	CG	IP	H	ER	BB	SO
92 R	0	1	4.05	7	0	20.0	16	9	6	22
93 A	8	9	3.12	27	1	164.1	142	57	56	124
94 A	7	7	4.66	25	0	145.0	144	75	79	91

Professional Pitching Register

	W	L	ERA	G	CG	IP	H	ER	BB	SO
93 A	4	4	4.03	14	0	82.2	85	37	17	64
94 A	18	7	2.25	28	5	192.1	177	48	32	150

IVAN ARTEAGA

Position: Pitcher
Team: Colorado Rockies
Born: July 20, 1972 Puerto Cabello, Venezuela
Height: 6'2" **Weight:** 220 lbs.
Bats: left **Throws:** right
Acquired: Traded from Expos with Rod Pedraza for Freddie Benavides, 1/92

Player Summary	
Fantasy Value $0
Card Value . . . . 20¢ to 30¢
Will . . . . need a third pitch
Can't . . . . rely on curve
Expect . . . . a strong arm
Don't Expect . . . . polish

One tactic for an expansion team—especially one that plays in thin mountain air—is to pick up some pitching in every deal. That's what happened when the Rockies sent infielder Freddie Benavides to the Expos for hurlers Rod Pedraza and Arteaga. It was another turn in what has been an unusual career for Arteaga, who grew up a fan of slugger Andres Galarraga. Arteaga was a first baseman when signed by the Expos as a nondrafted free agent in 1989. He didn't make it as a hitter, but he showed such a strong arm that he was converted to pitcher. In his first year on the mound, he led the Dominican League with a 1.91 ERA. He had 60 strikeouts and 45 walks that year. He attended the Florida Instructional League in 1992 and opened enough eyes to be placed on the Montreal roster. In 1993, Arteaga spent most of the season in the Class-A Midwest League, where he turned in a fine ERA. Upon being acquired by Colorado, he was assigned to Double-A, where he was the youngest New Haven pitcher. Arteaga started 24 of 27 games last year, but he may be in a relief role in the future.

Professional Pitching Register

	W	L	ERA	G	CG	IP	H	ER	BB	SO
93 A	6	8	3.42	24	2	142.0	137	54	56	121
94 AA	8	9	3.48	27	2	150.0	123	58	70	101

BILLY ASHLEY

Position: Outfield
Team: Los Angeles Dodgers
Born: July 11, 1970 Taylor, MI
Height: 6'7" **Weight:** 230 lbs.
Bats: right **Throws:** right
Acquired: Third-round pick in 6/88 free-agent draft

Player Summary	
Fantasy Value . . . . $1 to $3
Card Value . . . . 15¢ to 20¢
Will . . . . hit it long
Can't . . . . get on base
Expect . . . . double plays
Don't Expect . . . . great glove

Ashley has tasted a few cups of coffee with Los Angeles, but he hasn't been able to establish anything at the big-league level. So he did the next-best thing—go back to Triple-A Albuquerque and do the best he could. For the Dukes in 1994, he hit .345 with 37 homers and 105 RBI. Trouble is, there are a few obstacles for him. One, he pays for his power with a high strikeout total. Two, he's not an exceptional defensive player. Three, the Dodgers seem to have their share of prospects in the outfield, especially Roger Cedeno and Todd Hollandsworth. Finally, Ashley is a little old for prospect status. However, he can hit the ball a long way and drive in runs, and there's always use for that. *Baseball America* tabbed him its top power prospect in 1993 and the No. 2 prospect in the PCL in 1994. He made the Triple-A All-Star team as well last year. With his power, he could be in the bigs for a long time.

Professional Batting Register

	BA	G	AB	R	H	2B	3B	HR	RBI	SB
88 R	.154	9	26	3	4	0	0	0	0	1
89 R	.238	48	160	23	38	6	2	1	19	9
90 A	.218	99	331	48	72	13	1	9	40	17
91 A	.252	61	206	18	52	11	2	7	42	9
92 AA	.279	101	380	60	106	23	1	24	66	13
92 AAA	.211	25	95	11	20	7	0	2	10	1
92 NL	.221	29	95	6	21	5	0	2	6	0
93 AAA	.297	125	482	88	143	31	4	26	100	6
93 NL	.243	14	37	0	9	0	0	0	0	0
94 AAA	.345	107	388	93	134	19	4	37	105	6
94 NL	.333	2	6	0	2	1	0	0	0	0

KYM ASHWORTH

Position: Pitcher
Team: Los Angeles Dodgers
Born: July 31, 1976 Millicent, Australia
Height: 6'2" **Weight:** 175 lbs.
Bats: left **Throws:** left
Acquired: Signed as a nondrafted free agent,
  12/92

Player Summary	
Fantasy Value	$0
Card Value	15¢ to 25¢
Will	hit right spots
Can't	overpower batters
Expect	fine breaking ball
Don't Expect	bewilderment

Ashworth may be the most exciting prospect among the increasing number of players coming from Down Under. A mere look at his age and where he's been competing—the high Class-A California League at 17—mark him as a hot talent to follow. He made his North American debut with Great Falls of the rookie Pioneer League when he was just 16. *Baseball America* named him the circuit's best major-league prospect after a 3-3 season in which his combined walks and hits were less than his innings pitched. As the 1994 campaign began, Ashworth was the youngest player on a full-season roster. He was rocked in his California League debut, but in his next outing, he allowed only one hit through five innings. He finally got his first no-hitter on July 4. Ashworth's fastball is nothing special, but he throws a wonderful curve and a fine changeup. He also seems to have the intangibles, and he should get stronger as his body matures. The Dodgers have two fine options for 1995; Ashworth could be allowed another year in the Cal League, or he could move up to the Double-A Texas League.

Professional Pitching Register

	W	L	ERA	G	CG	IP	H	ER	BB	SO
93 R	3	3	2.44	11	0	59.0	43	16	14	52
94 A	6	7	3.95	24	1	127.2	112	56	69	109
94 AA	0	1	4.50	1	0	4.0	5	2	0	6

RICH AUDE

Position: First base
Team: Pittsburgh Pirates
Born: July 13, 1971 Van Nuys, CA
Height: 6'5" **Weight:** 220 lbs.
Bats: right **Throws:** right
Acquired: Second-round pick in 6/89 free-
  agent draft

Player Summary	
Fantasy Value	$0
Card Value	20¢ to 30¢
Will	draw a walk
Can't	return to third
Expect	decent contact
Don't Expect	Dwight Evans

Aude (pronounced AW-day) seemed to slip a little bit last year after a very solid 1993 campaign. Only his double total was exceptional; maybe his heroics in the previous year made pitchers more wary of him. He has shown the ability to hit the ball out of the park and drive in his share of runs. He was named the American Association's top defensive first baseman in a *Baseball America* poll, and he also plays some outfield. Out of Chatsworth, California, High School, which produced former Red Sox standout Dwight Evans, Aude spent four years in the Pittsburgh farm system without distinction. However, in 1993, he emerged to hit 22 homers with 93 RBI while getting promoted twice. His RBI total led all Pirates farmhands, and he made the Double-A Southern League All-Star team. He also got his first look at the bigs, and got his first hit off the Cardinals' Tom Urbani. Aude can still use help with the breaking ball and with situational hitting.

Professional Batting Register

	BA	G	AB	R	H	2B	3B	HR	RBI	SB
89 R	.216	24	88	13	19	3	0	0	7	2
90 A	.234	128	475	48	111	23	1	6	61	4
91 A	.265	103	366	45	97	12	2	3	43	4
92 A	.286	122	447	63	128	26	4	9	60	11
92 AA	.200	6	20	4	4	1	0	2	3	0
93 AA	.289	120	422	66	122	25	3	18	73	8
93 AAA	.375	21	64	17	24	9	0	4	16	0
93 NL	.115	13	26	1	3	1	0	0	4	0
94 AAA	.281	138	520	66	146	38	4	15	79	9

JAMES BALDWIN

Position: Pitcher
Team: Chicago White Sox
Born: July 15, 1971 Southern Pines, NC
Height: 6'3" **Weight:** 210 lbs.
Bats: right **Throws:** right
Acquired: Fourth-round pick in 6/90 free-agent draft

Player Summary	
Fantasy Value	$2 to $4
Card Value	30¢ to 50¢
Will	field well
Can't	get behind
Expect	presence
Don't Expect	top curve

Baldwin's game is power, and many a batter has seen it firsthand. In fact, he entered the 1994 season having averaged more than eight and one-half strikeouts per nine innings. He has a changeup and a curveball just good enough to round out his repertoire, but Baldwin will be relying on his fastball to establish himself in the majors. He was named the White Sox's top prospect by *Baseball America* as last season began, but he didn't look it in his first six starts, going only 2-2 with a 4.70 ERA. However, he righted himself and wound up the month of May with four straight wins. Baldwin's strength is shown by the fact he was sought by many schools as a fullback. He also played baseball and basketball in high school and pitched against the Reds' John Roper. Baldwin will have to improve on his strikeout-to-walk ratio, but there's no adjustment needed on his powerful arm. He was named the No. 1 prospect in the Triple-A American Association last year.

Professional Pitching Register

	W	L	ERA	G	CG	IP	H	ER	BB	SO
90 R	1	6	4.10	9	0	37.1	32	17	18	32
91 R	3	1	2.12	6	0	34.0	16	8	16	48
91 A	1	4	5.30	7	1	37.1	40	22	27	23
92 A	10	7	2.52	27	2	175.1	149	49	52	176
93 AA	8	5	2.25	17	4	120.0	94	30	43	107
93 AAA	5	4	2.61	10	1	69.0	43	20	36	61
94 AAA	12	6	3.72	26	2	162.0	144	67	83	156

TRAVIS BAPTIST

Position: Pitcher
Team: Toronto Blue Jays
Born: Dec. 30, 1971 Forest Grove, OR
Height: 6' **Weight:** 175 lbs.
Bats: both **Throws:** left
Acquired: 46th-round pick in 6/90 free-agent draft

Player Summary	
Fantasy Value	$0
Card Value	20¢ to 30¢
Will	throw strikes
Can't	lose more time
Expect	progress
Don't Expect	46th-round tools

An injury-filled 1993 interrupted a drive toward the majors for this talented lefty. Baptist, who had led the minors with a 1.45 ERA in 1992, made only seven starts for Knoxville of the Double-A Southern League in 1993. But the Blue Jays think so much of him that when 1994 rolled around, they promoted him to Triple-A anyway. He has so much talent that he did a nice job with the adjustment. One reason for Baptist's success is his ability to throw strikes. In his exceptional '92 campaign, he walked only 22 in 118 innings. He allowed only two and one-half walks per game last year. Baptist comes out of Hillsboro High School in Oregon, where he twice earned first-team all-state honors. He was chosen Senior Babe Ruth World Series MVP in 1989. Despite his low draft position, he made a solid entrance into pro ball in 1991, going 4-4 in 14 starts. His next year was even better, as he led the Sally League in opponents' batting average (.192) and fewest baserunners per nine innings, at just over eight. Baptist has time to progress.

Professional Pitching Register

	W	L	ERA	G	CG	IP	H	ER	BB	SO
91 R	4	4	4.11	14	1	85.1	100	39	22	48
92 A	11	2	1.45	19	2	118.0	81	19	22	97
93 AA	1	3	4.09	7	0	33.0	37	15	7	24
94 AAA	8	8	4.55	24	1	122.2	145	62	33	42

BRIAN BARBER

Position: Pitcher
Team: St. Louis Cardinals
Born: March 4, 1973 Hamilton, OH
Height: 6'1" **Weight:** 175 lbs.
Bats: right **Throws:** right
Acquired: First-round pick in 6/91 free-agent draft

Player Summary	
Fantasy Value $0
Card Value . . . . 15¢ to 20¢
Will . . . . pitch in majors
Can't . . . . move too quickly
Expect . . . . 90-mph heat
Don't Expect . . . . pinpoint control

Just when it seemed Barber was zooming toward the majors last year, he got a taste of adversity. First he suffered a groin pull, and he didn't get his first victory of the season until May 25. Later in the year he was demoted from Triple-A Louisville to Double-A Arkansas. Maybe the detour will work out for the best, because Barber still has some work to do. His control, for instance, could be a little better. He also slumped in the second half of 1993, demonstrating that his endurance might use some enhancing. He is on the slender side. Barber came to the Cards via a compensation pick earned when the Mets signed free agent Vince Coleman. The 22nd overall pick, Barber owned a 26-2 mark in high school, including 11-0 in his senior year. In two years as a pro, he advanced through three levels of Class-A. Barber reached Double-A in 1993, and his almost eight strikeouts per nine innings ranked him fourth among Texas League starters. Barber appears to be on track, when his age is taken into account.

Professional Pitching Register

	W	L	ERA	G	CG	IP	H	ER	BB	SO
91 R	4	6	5.40	14	0	73.1	62	44	38	84
92 A	8	9	3.40	27	1	164.0	138	62	70	158
93 AA	9	8	4.02	24	1	143.1	154	64	56	126
93 AAA	0	1	4.76	1	0	5.2	4	3	4	5
94 AA	1	3	3.25	6	0	36.0	31	13	16	54
94 AAA	4	7	5.38	19	0	85.1	79	51	46	95

MARC BARCELO

Position: Pitcher
Team: Minnesota Twins
Born: Jan. 10, 1972 Van Nuys, CA
Height: 6'3" **Weight:** 210 lbs.
Bats: right **Throws:** right
Acquired: First-round pick in 6/93 free-agent draft

Player Summary	
Fantasy Value $0
Card Value . . . . 15¢ to 25¢
Will . . . . prevent base hits
Can't . . . . increase Ks
Expect . . . . good control
Don't Expect . . . . inexperience

Minnesota owned four picks before the second round of the 1993 draft, and Barcelo became the second of those four. Specifically, he came in a selection that the Twins acquired as compensation for the loss of free agent John Smiley. It was the 33rd overall pick in the grab bag, and so far it seems as if the Twins made good on it. After turning pro, Barcelo impressed in seven appearances in the Florida State League, showing an extensive repertoire and outstanding tenacity. He earned a promotion to Double-A Nashville in '93. That's where he started the 1994 campaign, and he prospered, going 3-0 with a 2.60 ERA in his first five starts. Barcelo was named a Double-A All-Star, though he did not appear in the game. He ranked among the top Twins' farmhands in ERA and strikeouts. He was also named the No. 6 prospect in the loop last year by *Baseball America*. Barcelo comes out of Arizona State, a high-profile program where he received a lot of experience. That should make his climb to the majors all the more rapid, especially if he keeps pitching the way he has so far.

Professional Pitching Register

	W	L	ERA	G	CG	IP	H	ER	BB	SO
93 A	1	1	2.74	7	0	23.0	18	7	4	24
93 AA	1	0	3.86	2	0	9.1	9	4	5	5
94 AA	11	6	2.65	29	4	183.1	167	54	45	153

KIMERA BARTEE

Position: Outfield
Team: Baltimore Orioles
Born: July 21, 1972   Omaha, NE
Height: 6′   **Weight:** 175 lbs.
Bats: both   **Throws:** right
Acquired: 14th-round pick in 6/93 free-agent draft

Player Summary	
Fantasy Value	$0
Card Value	15¢ to 20¢
Will	score runs
Can't	make contact
Expect	threat on bases
Don't Expect	a dead weight

For a player in only his second year of pro ball, Bartee looked like an old pro. He was among the top basestealers in the Orioles' organization. He was also named to the Class-A Carolina League's postseason All-Star squad and earned the No. 9 slot among league prospects, according to *Baseball America*. Nicknamed "Brick," Bartee is anything but a dead weight. He has more than enough speed to play center field, and he does a good job of getting around the bases. Last year, he led Frederick by a wide margin in runs scored. In 1993, he had flashed the same speed in the Appalachian League, topping the circuit with 27 steals and finishing in a tie for second with 52 runs scored. He also utilizes his speed when he's on base. Bartee comes out of Creighton University. A member of the College World Series squad in 1991, he also was tabbed for the 1992 Missouri Valley All-Tournament team. The chief flaw in his game is a tendency to strike out—he had 117 last year. If he can close the gap between his walks and Ks, his steals will soar, and he can become that speedy leadoff hitter that every team in baseball is looking for.

Professional Batting Register

	BA	G	AB	R	H	2B	3B	HR	RBI	SB
93 R	.246	66	264	59	65	15	2	4	37	27
94 A	.292	130	514	97	150	22	4	10	57	44

TONY BATISTA

Position: Shortstop; infield
Team: Oakland Athletics
Born: Dec. 9, 1973   Puerto Plata, Dominican Republic
Height: 6′   **Weight:** 167 lbs.
Bats: right   **Throws:** right
Acquired: Signed as a nondrafted free agent, 6/92

Player Summary	
Fantasy Value	$0
Card Value	10¢ to 15¢
Will	show strong arm
Can't	K so much
Expect	good glove
Don't Expect	contact hitting

Signed by Juan Marichal, Batista made the Class-A California League All-Star team in 1994 at the age of 20. He was recognized as one of the top defensive shortstops, with one of the best arms, in the league. He also showed an ability to hit the ball out of the park now and then, quite a feat for someone of such a slight build. (When he was signed, he weighed 145 pounds.) He was able to notch a .459 slugging percentage. When he fills out a little more, he could still see a relative increase in power. Batista also needs to sharpen his ability to make contact with the ball. He had 108 strikeouts last year. Upon signing, Batista played in his native country in 1991, then in Arizona for two seasons. He got a brief look at the Triple-A Pacific Coast League in 1993, an indication the A's think well of him. He has played some second base, and versatility could be a factor in his advancement. He must contend with the fact that Fausto Cruz is ahead of him in the farm system. All the tools seem to be there for Batista to make the bigs eventually.

Professional Batting Register

	BA	G	AB	R	H	2B	3B	HR	RBI	SB
92 R	.246	45	167	32	41	6	2	0	22	1
93 R	.327	24	104	21	34	6	2	2	17	6
93 AAA	.167	4	12	1	2	1	0	0	1	0
94 A	.281	119	466	91	131	26	3	17	68	7

DANNY BAUTISTA

Position: Outfield
Team: Detroit Tigers
Born: May 24, 1972   Santo Domingo, Dominican Republic
Height: 5'11"   **Weight:** 170 lbs.
Bats: right   **Throws:** right
Acquired: Signed as a free agent, 6/89

Player Summary	
Fantasy Value	$4 to $6
Card Value	15¢ to 25¢
Will	bring speed
Can't	be 20-20 man
Expect	center field
Don't Expect	Rico Carty

Bautista is one of the top prospects in a Tigers organization that is beginning to make a transition toward a younger look. He broke into the majors late in 1993 at the age of 21, and began to get more playing time in 1994. But a broken right middle finger in June took away some of his momentum. Still, there should be plenty of time for this center fielder to make his mark. Bautista has shown flashes of excellence in many phases of the game, though he undoubtedly is not a polished player yet. His lack of walks (nine last year, 33 in 1993) indicate that. But he could be formidable when he puts it all together. For example, he logged 17 assists in 1992 while in the Class-A South Atlantic League. In 1993 at Double-A, he posted a career-high 28 stolen bases. He's also beginning to hit with some power, though his size wouldn't necessarily indicate that. Bautista's idol when growing up was former major leaguer Rico Carty. His stepfather, Jesus De La Rosa, appeared briefly for the Astros in 1975.

Professional Batting Register

	BA	G	AB	R	H	2B	3B	HR	RBI	SB
90 R	.274	27	95	9	26	3	0	2	12	2
91 A	.192	69	234	21	45	6	4	1	30	7
92 A	.269	121	453	59	122	22	0	5	52	18
93 AA	.285	117	424	55	121	21	1	6	48	28
93 AL	.311	17	61	6	19	3	0	1	9	3
94 AAA	.255	27	98	7	25	7	0	2	14	2
94 AL	.232	31	99	12	23	4	1	4	15	1

TREY BEAMON

Position: Outfield
Team: Pittsburgh Pirates
Born: Feb. 11, 1974   Dallas, TX
Height: 6'3"   **Weight:** 195 lbs.
Bats: left   **Throws:** right
Acquired: Second-round pick in 6/92 free-agent draft

Player Summary	
Fantasy Value	$0
Card Value	15¢ to 20¢
Will	hit for average
Can't	show power yet
Expect	disciplined at bats
Don't Expect	center field

Beamon came out of William T. White High School in Dallas as part of a plentiful 1992 draft for the Pirates. It looks like his pick, the 61st overall that year, may be one of the most exciting ones Pittsburgh made. He's athletic, he's improving, and he was the youngest player on the Double-A Carolina roster at the start of the 1994 campaign (he later ceded that distinction to fellow farmhand Jason Kendall). Beamon played in the loop's All-Star Game and impressed with his bat, going 2-for-3 with a triple and scoring two runs. He was named the No. 1 prospect in the league last year. He has a package of skills that could enable him to contend for a big-league batting title someday. Beamon neither walks nor strikes out a great deal, notching 33 bases on balls and 53 Ks in 1994. He probably will continue to have more triples than home runs as he progresses. His baserunning could use some refining. He got off to a fast start in Double-A, logging nine two-hit games in his first 14 outings. On defense, Beamon seems headed for left field at this point.

Professional Batting Register

	BA	G	AB	R	H	2B	3B	HR	RBI	SB
92 R	.308	13	39	9	12	1	0	1	6	0
92 A	.290	19	69	15	20	5	0	3	9	4
93 A	.271	104	373	64	101	18	6	0	45	19
94 AA	.323	112	434	69	140	18	9	5	47	24

RICH BECKER

Position: Outfield
Team: Minnesota Twins
Born: Feb. 1, 1972 Aurora, IL
Height: 5'10" **Weight:** 180 lbs.
Bats: both **Throws:** left
Acquired: Third-round pick in 6/90 free-agent draft

Player Summary	
Fantasy Value	$5 to $7
Card Value	15¢ to 30¢
Will	bring five tools
Can't	keep getting hurt
Expect	walks
Don't Expect	old speed

Knee problems have kept Becker from taking full advantage of a couple of chances he received with the Twins. First he tore up his knee sliding into second base shortly after joining Minnesota late in 1993. He underwent surgery to repair torn cartilage, and he was ready to start the '94 campaign. However, he suffered another injury and missed more time. When he finally returned to action, it was on a rehab assignment in the minors. He got back into the lineup for Triple-A Salt Lake City on May 20 and broke up a perfect game bid with a seventh-inning single off Colorado Springs' Kevin Ritz. The Twins hope that Becker's knee trouble will not be a chronic thing, because he is an exciting prospect. He can run, hit, throw, play defense, and belt the ball out of the park. He compiled a .433 slugging percentage and a .401 on-base average at Salt Lake City in 1994. He has the potential to steal 20 bases and hit 20 homers in a season, while playing an above-average center field.

Professional Batting Register

	BA	G	AB	R	H	2B	3B	HR	RBI	SB
90 R	.289	56	194	54	56	5	1	6	24	18
91 A	.267	130	494	100	132	38	3	13	53	19
92 A	.316	136	506	118	160	37	2	15	82	29
93 AA	.287	138	516	93	148	25	7	15	66	29
93 AL	.286	3	7	3	2	2	0	0	0	1
94 AAA	.316	71	282	64	89	21	3	2	38	7
94 AL	.265	28	98	12	26	3	0	1	8	6

DAVID BELL

Position: Third base; infield
Team: Cleveland Indians
Born: Sept. 14, 1972 Cincinnati, OH
Height: 5'10" **Weight:** 175 lbs.
Bats: right **Throws:** right
Acquired: Seventh-round pick in 6/90 free-agent draft

Player Summary	
Fantasy Value	$0
Card Value	15¢ to 25¢
Will	show versatility
Can't	unseat Jim Thome
Expect	contact
Don't Expect	30 homers

Bell is the son of former Ranger and Indian Buddy Bell and the grandson of ex-big leaguer Gus Bell. David also has a brother, Mike, who was drafted by Texas in 1993. David has made a step-by-step climb through the Cleveland chain, improving his offensive stats. He received *Baseball America*'s nod as the Double-A Eastern League's 10th-best prospect in 1993, even though he was the youngest player in the league. Last year, he was named the Triple-A International League's No. 9 prospect. But he may face an obstacle in third baseman Jim Thome, who is just establishing himself at the major-league level. However, Bell may be able to find a niche through versatility; he can play shortstop and second base as well as third base. At the plate, David resembles his father, showing a bit of home run power without giving up contact. He notched a .457 slugging average last year. He won't tear up the basepaths. In '94, Bell hit grand slams on consecutive days against Pawtucket on April 28 and Ottawa on April 29.

Professional Batting Register

	BA	G	AB	R	H	2B	3B	HR	RBI	SB
90 R	.235	42	153	22	36	6	2	0	15	3
91 A	.230	136	491	47	113	24	1	5	63	3
92 A	.252	123	464	52	117	17	2	6	47	2
93 AA	.292	129	483	69	141	20	2	9	60	3
94 AAA	.293	134	481	66	141	17	4	18	88	2

MIKE BELL

Position: Third base
Team: Texas Rangers
Born: Dec. 7, 1974   Cincinnati, OH
Height: 6'2"   **Weight:** 185 lbs.
Bats: right   **Throws:** right
Acquired: Second-round pick in 6/93 free-agent draft

Player Summary	
Fantasy Value	$0
Card Value	20¢ to 30¢
Will	know how to play
Can't	catch ball yet
Expect	size and speed
Don't Expect	walks

So far in his pro career, Bell looks like he was born to play baseball, which, in a sense, he was. After all, the bloodlines are there—with his father Buddy, his grandfather Gus, and his brother David all pro players. Mike, however, may have more size—and speed—than any of them. He struck out 76 times last year, which is not a bad number but an increase from 1993. He also was caught stealing 12 times. He was the 30th overall choice in 1993 via a compensation pick awarded for the Cubs' signing of Jose Guzman. The selection was an especially important one for the Rangers, since it was their first of 1993; they had lost their first-rounder in signing free agent Tom Henke. Bell, so far, has made their choice look awfully good. He made the Class-A South Atlantic League All-Star squad last year. It was a bittersweet experience, as he had severe defensive problems in the game. It was the second straight year he made an All-Star team, having done so in the Gulf Coast League in 1993. A third baseman like his father and brother, he must upgrade his glove while gradually expanding his production.

Professional Batting Register

	BA	G	AB	R	H	2B	3B	HR	RBI	SB
93 R	.317	60	230	48	73	13	6	3	34	9
94 A	.263	120	475	58	125	22	6	6	58	16

ALAN BENES

Position: Pitcher
Team: St. Louis Cardinals
Born: Jan. 21, 1972   Evansville, IN
Height: 6'5"   **Weight:** 215 lbs.
Bats: right   **Throws:** right
Acquired: First-round pick in 6/93 free-agent draft

Player Summary	
Fantasy Value	$1 to $3
Card Value	40¢ to 60¢
Will	be a competitor
Can't	master mechanics
Expect	curve, change
Don't Expect	Andy's heat

When Andy Benes was selected first overall in the 1988 draft, he came with the reputation for throwing a 100-mph fastball. No such buildup came with Alan Benes, though he is Andy's little brother and himself a first-round pick (16th overall). None of this baggage seemed to bother Alan in his first look at full-season ball. He was the Opening Day pitcher for Savannah of the Class-A South Atlantic League. Within weeks, he was boosted to St. Petersburg of the Florida State League (where he was named the No. 3 prospect in the loop). It didn't stop there, taking the next step to Double-A Arkansas of the Texas League, where after 13 starts he impressed enough managers to be named the No. 2 prospect in the league in a poll conducted by *Baseball America*. He even had a couple of starts at Triple-A Louisville. He finished among the ERA, victory, and strikeout leaders in the St. Louis chain. Out of Creighton University, Benes throws a fastball, a curveball, and a changeup. If he keeps using them the way he has, then Alan will join his brother in the bigs.

Professional Pitching Register

	W	L	ERA	G	CG	IP	H	ER	BB	SO
93 A	0	4	3.65	7	0	37.0	39	15	14	29
94 A	9	1	1.58	15	0	102.2	76	18	22	93
94 AA	7	2	2.98	13	1	87.2	58	29	26	75
94 AAA	1	0	2.93	2	1	15.1	10	5	4	16

ARMANDO BENITEZ

Position: Pitcher
Team: Baltimore Orioles
Born: Nov. 3, 1972 Ramon Santana, Dominican Republic
Height: 6'4" **Weight:** 220 lbs.
Bats: right **Throws:** right
Acquired: Signed as a nondrafted free agent, 4/90

Player Summary	
Fantasy Value	$6 to $8
Card Value	20¢ to 30¢
Will	strike people out
Can't	administer changeup
Expect	95-mph heat
Don't Expect	another Lee Smith

Benitez certainly did not look like the Orioles' closer of the future in the early stages of last season. Even though he had seven saves in 20 outings, his ERA over the same span was 6.85, and he allowed 23 walks in 24 innings. Then he began putting it together at one point in June, going 3-0 with no earned runs to win Double-A Eastern League Pitcher of the Week honors. It was the type of dominating performance that Benitez is capable of giving. He was named the No. 1 prospect by league managers last year in *Baseball America*. His size and the velocity on his pitches invite some comparisons to veteran closer Lee Smith. Benitez can simply take a batter out of a game; even during his bad stretch last year he was averaging well over a strikeout per inning. He has been a reliever for virtually all his pro career, having made three starts in 1991. He picked up 18 saves over two levels of Class-A ball in 1993, averaging 15 strikeouts per nine innings, best in the minors. He had over 13 Ks per nine innings last year.

Professional Pitching Register

	W	L	ERA	G	S	IP	H	ER	BB	SO
91 R	3	2	2.72	14	0	36.1	35	11	11	33
92 R	1	2	4.31	25	5	31.1	35	15	23	37
93 A	8	1	1.34	52	18	67.0	38	10	23	112
94 AA	8	4	3.14	53	16	71.2	41	25	39	106
94 AL	0	0	0.90	3	0	10.0	8	1	4	14

HIRAM BOCACHICA

Position: Shortstop
Team: Montreal Expos
Born: March 4, 1976 Ponce, Puerto Rico
Height: 5'11" **Weight:** 170 lbs.
Bats: right **Throws:** right
Acquired: First-round pick in 6/94 free-agent draft

Player Summary	
Fantasy Value	$0
Card Value	15¢ to 25¢
Will	make plays
Can't	push the bigs
Expect	doubles hitter
Don't Expect	instant power

With the 21st overall pick last June, the Expos had their worst draft position since 1982, when they ceded their spot to the Cubs. For that reason, the selection of Bocachica was an especially important one. He is a shortstop with a good glove and an ability to run. You can't rule out power for him, either. *Baseball America* had rated Bocachica the 22nd best prospect available, and the 10th-best position player. The publication also saw him as the second-best defensive player and the third-best athlete among high schoolers. He has the reputation of having a great arm. Of course, it will take some time to see how it works out. Bocachica is nowhere near being ready for the big leagues. But the Expos like his instincts, and they think he may be able to steal bases. The first order of business was to sign him, because he had an offer to play at Louisiana State University. That turned out not to be a problem, as they inked him for a bonus reported to be around $635,000. At short-season Class-A ball, he showed pretty good power, slugging at a .423 clip. He was named the No. 8 prospect in the Gulf Coast League last year.

Professional Batting Register

	BA	G	AB	R	H	2B	3B	HR	RBI	SB
94 R	.280	43	168	31	47	9	0	5	16	11

JOSH BOOTY

Position: Shortstop
Team: Florida Marlins
Born: April 29, 1975 Starkville, MS
Height: 6'3" **Weight:** 215 lbs.
Bats: right **Throws:** left
Acquired: First-round pick in 6/94 free-agent draft

Player Summary	
Fantasy Value	$0
Card Value	15¢ to 20¢
Will	draw walks
Can't	ponder football
Expect	power
Don't Expect	a shortstop

Sometimes taking the best available athlete involves assuming some risks. For instance, when the Marlins used the fifth overall pick to take Booty, they knew they were competing with the Louisiana State University football program for his services. But they felt they had to take a chance at acquiring his talent, so they made the move, even though they had lost 1993 second-rounder John Lynch to the NFL. This time they won the gamble, signing Booty to a record $1.6 million bonus. The signing came early enough to let Booty get his feet wet in pro ball in 1994. So what made him so irresistible? He earned national honors as a quarterback at Evangel Christian Academy in Shreveport, Louisiana. He also was named to *Baseball America*'s All-High School team. He has great size, fine quickness, an outstanding arm, and superior leadership. Hamstring problems and mononucleosis finished his 1994 season, though he was able to get 14 pro games in before shutting down. He has quite a bit of size for a shortstop, so don't be surprised to see a position switch. He'll have some work to do in 1995.

Professional Batting Register

	BA	G	AB	R	H	2B	3B	HR	RBI	SB
94 R	.222	10	36	5	8	0	0	1	2	1
94 A	.250	4	16	1	4	1	0	0	1	0

MIKE BOVEE

Position: Pitcher
Team: Kansas City Royals
Born: Aug. 21, 1973 San Diego, CA
Height: 5'10" **Weight:** 200 lbs.
Bats: right **Throws:** right
Acquired: Sixth-round pick in 6/91 free-agent draft

Player Summary	
Fantasy Value	$0
Card Value	15¢ to 25¢
Will	throw it over
Can't	get taller
Expect	sharp control
Don't Expect	Wilmington in '95

Bovee was part of an outstanding rotation that helped the Wilmington Blue Rocks stampede the Class-A Carolina League's Northern Division in the first half last year. What makes him especially interesting is his age. While teammate and fellow All-Star Bart Evans, for example, pitched the entire campaign at the age of 23, Bovee only turned 21 during the latter part of the season. This makes his performance all the more impressive. Twice in a three-week span he was named the league's Pitcher of the Week. He began the season with 13 straight scoreless innings. Most important of all, he did something in 1994 that he had not done in his three previous seasons—win. He held Carolina League batters to a .236 average, and he allowed only about one and one-half bases on balls per nine innings. The only downside to all this is Bovee's size; right-handers under 6' tall often have a tough time getting noticed. Then again, the Royals were content with 5'9" Tom Gordon. Bovee may be able to compensate with good to excellent control.

Professional Pitching Register

	W	L	ERA	G	CG	IP	H	ER	BB	SO
91 R	3	1	2.04	11	0	61.2	52	14	12	76
92 A	9	10	3.56	28	1	149.1	143	59	41	120
93 A	5	9	4.21	20	2	109.0	118	51	30	111
94 A	13	4	2.65	28	0	169.2	149	50	32	154

TERRY BRADSHAW

Position: Outfield
Team: St. Louis Cardinals
Born: Feb. 3, 1969   Franklin, VA
Height: 6'   **Weight:** 180 lbs.
Bats: left   **Throws:** right
Acquired: Ninth-round pick in 6/90 free-agent draft

Player Summary	
Fantasy Value	$0
Card Value	15¢ to 20¢
Will	run
Can't	worry about knee
Expect	advancement
Don't Expect	many homers

This namesake of the former NFL quarterback might already be in the majors had he not suffered a severe knee injury in the Winter Instructional League after the 1991 season. The injury came after Bradshaw had delivered a 65-steal year, and it knocked him out for the entire 1992 campaign. Bradshaw resumed his career in 1993, making the Class-A Florida State League All-Star team and tying for second in the league in runs and walks. Bradshaw continued his development in 1994 at Double-A, being named the Texas League's best hitting prospect, best defensive outfielder, and most exciting player by *Baseball America*. He was also named the No. 4 prospect in the loop. However, his basestealing pace slowed. Bradshaw played baseball, football, and basketball in high school. He was a shortstop at Norfolk State University, but he was converted to an outfielder by the Cardinals. With their outfield so crowded, the Cards have a nice problem on their hands, as Bradshaw has the tools that make him a possibility for the majors.

TARRICK BROCK

Position: Outfield
Team: Detroit Tigers
Born: Dec. 25, 1973   Goleta, CA
Height: 6'3"   **Weight:** 170 lbs.
Bats: left   **Throws:** left
Acquired: Third-round pick in 6/91 free-agent draft

Player Summary	
Fantasy Value	$0
Card Value	20¢ to 30¢
Will	steal bases
Can't	K so often
Expect	late bloomer
Don't Expect	some runs

After three years of getting used to pro ball, this Christmas Day arrival finally began to unwrap his talents in 1994. Playing in the Class-A Florida State League for the first time, Brock made the midseason All-Star team. Just about the time he was named to the squad, he was tied for the minor-league lead with 11 triples; that was as many as he had collected his entire pro career. He got off to a .423 start in '94, then survived a brutal stretch during which he went 1-for-20, including a 1-for-10 showing in a 20-inning game. Later in the summer, he was bumped up to Double-A Trenton, though he was not at all ready for that league. Brock's slow career start can be explained in part by his extremely young age. He was only 17½ when he first reported to Bristol of the rookie Appalachian League in 1991. He then spent two years in the Class-A South Atlantic League. His chances of advancing depend on him being able to use his speed. Until 1994, the best part of his game was stealing bases. But to steal bases, he must improve his strikeout-to-walk ratio.

Professional Batting Register

	BA	G	AB	R	H	2B	3B	HR	RBI	SB
90 A	.234	68	235	37	55	5	1	3	13	15
91 A	.237	132	443	91	105	17	1	7	42	65
93 A	.291	125	461	84	134	25	6	5	51	43
94 AA	.280	114	425	65	119	25	8	10	52	1	3
94 AAA	.250	22	80	16	20	4	0	4	8	5

Professional Batting Register

	BA	G	AB	R	H	2B	3B	HR	RBI	SB
91 R	.266	55	177	26	47	7	3	1	13	14
92 A	.218	100	271	35	59	5	4	0	17	15
93 A	.215	116	427	60	92	8	4	3	47	25
94 A	.233	86	331	43	77	17	14	2	32	15
94 AA	.139	34	115	12	16	1	4	2	11	3

WES BROOKS

Position: Pitcher
Team: Boston Red Sox
Born: Jan. 11, 1972 Belleville, IL
Height: 6'3" **Weight:** 200 lbs.
Bats: right **Throws:** right
Acquired: 23rd-round pick in 6/92 free-agent draft

Player Summary	
Fantasy Value	$0
Card Value	20¢ to 30¢
Will	take the ball
Can't	dazzle with stats
Expect	strikeouts
Don't Expect	greatness

Brooks has the look of a workhorse starter who can provide innings without putting up spectacular numbers. Over his three-year pro career, he has never shown an eye-popping ratio between hits and innings pitched. Nor will his strikeout totals ever lead the league, though he did rank among the top Red Sox farmhands in that department. He just keeps making starts and picking up decisions, while moving through the farm system. Brooks was a three-year letterman in basketball at Lebanon High School in Illinois, from where he graduated in 1990. But he was not drafted until two years later, when he attended Belleville Area College. Brooks pitched in the Florida Instructional League in 1992. In 1993, he led the Florida State League with three shutouts. Upon joining Lynchburg of the Carolina League in 1994, he won his first two starts, allowing only eight hits in 11 innings. He fanned 10 in a four-hit shutout on April 23. He allowed almost three and one-half bases on balls per nine innings last year, but if he is going to allow opposing hitters to bat .262, Brooks will have to cut his walks.

KEVIN BROWN

Position: Catcher
Team: Texas Rangers
Born: April 21, 1973 Valparaiso, IN
Height: 6'1" **Weight:** 205 lbs.
Bats: right **Throws:** right
Acquired: Second-round pick in 6/94 free-agent draft

Player Summary	
Fantasy Value	$0
Card Value	15¢ to 25¢
Will	throw out runners
Can't	swing at bad pitches
Expect	legitimate power
Don't Expect	a quick ascent

The Rangers, who had a Kevin Brown on their pitching staff when the 1994 season began, decided they would one day have one behind the plate, too. And in some ways, the younger Brown enjoyed a better season than his namesake did. He came out of the University of Southern Indiana, where he belted 13 homers while hitting nearly .400. He showed some power in the short-season New York-Penn League, not exactly a hitter's paradise. He did have some problem making contact, as his .246 average and 86 strikeouts indicate. But that can be corrected with determination. Brown was taken with the 56th overall pick—the Rangers were the final squad to get a selection in the draft. He was rated the 42nd best pick and the fifth-highest catcher by *Baseball America*. He is strong at throwing out baserunners, and he is a hard worker. After signing, Brown started quickly, putting together back-to-back three-hit games in late June. With Ivan Rodriguez ahead of him at the big-league level, Brown need not be in any particular hurry to get to Texas. This year should find him in Class-A ball.

Professional Pitching Register

	W	L	ERA	G	CG	IP	H	ER	BB	SO
92 R	3	5	3.53	14	1	71.1	78	28	21	57
93 A	8	5	3.89	19	4	127.1	124	55	42	85
94 A	12	12	4.80	28	4	172.2	176	92	64	117

Professional Batting Register

	BA	G	AB	R	H	2B	3B	HR	RBI	SB
94 A	.246	68	232	33	57	19	1	6	32	0

MATT BRUNSON

Position: Shortstop
Team: Detroit Tigers
Born: Sept. 2, 1974 Denver, CO
Height: 5'11" **Weight:** 165 lbs.
Bats: both **Throws:** right
Acquired: First-round pick in 6/93 free-agent draft

Player Summary	
Fantasy Value	$0
Card Value	15¢ to 20¢
Will	reach base
Can't	abandon his game
Expect	big speed
Don't Expect	big power

The Tigers liked Brunson's speed when they made him the ninth overall pick in the draft, and he showed why in his first professional season. Brunson needed only half a campaign to reach the 30-steal mark, and eventually got over 50, quite a feat considering he was having his troubles at the plate. He helped offset a low batting average with a knack for drawing walks. In fact, he had a .367 on-base average in 103 South Atlantic League games last year. That put him in position to run the bases. He was named the No. 8 prospect in the circuit by *Baseball America* last year, despite a .216 batting average. He received a promotion from the Class-A Sally League to the Class-A Florida State League late in the season. He is the son of former NFL wide receiver Larry Brunson, so athletic ability is in his bloodlines. *Baseball America* rated Matt the fastest high schooler in the 1993 draft. The downside was that Brunson signed late, so he didn't get his feet wet in pro ball until he attended the Instructional League in the fall. There he impressed the coaches with his approach. He will have to impress the Tigers with his ability to hit, too.

Professional Batting Register

	BA	G	AB	R	H	2B	3B	HR	RBI	SB
94 A	.212	114	387	79	82	9	1	1	31	53

BRIAN BUCHANAN

Position: Outfield
Team: New York Yankees
Born: July 21, 1973 Miami, FL
Height: 6'4" **Weight:** 215 lbs.
Bats: right **Throws:** right
Acquired: First-round pick in 6/94 free-agent draft

Player Summary	
Fantasy Value	$0
Card Value	15¢ to 20¢
Will	hit ball hard
Can't	be a Gold Glover
Expect	decent speed
Don't Expect	return to first

Buchanan comes out of the University of Virginia, where he played both first base and the outfield and set records with his bat. Last year, he hit .396 with 22 homers and 66 RBI for the Cavaliers, prompting the Yankees to make him the 24th overall pick. He was signed and sent to Oneonta of the short-season New York-Penn League, where he had some problems at the plate. In his first 100 at bats, Buchanan produced just three homers and 17 RBI. Such problems are not unusual for power hitters coming from college ball. He did finish with a .367 slugging percentage. He also notched 24 walks and had a .335 on-base average. Right now, of more importance is the decision the Yankees have made regarding Buchanan's position. He played the outfield in Oneonta, and that's where the Yankees say he will stay. He has the athletic ability to play both outfield corners. *Baseball America* tabbed him as the best college power hitter in the draft. In taking a college player, the Yankees changed their approach. They had opted for a high school athlete with their first selection for six consecutive seasons.

Professional Batting Register

	BA	G	AB	R	H	2B	3B	HR	RBI	SB
94 A	.226	50	177	28	40	9	2	4	26	5

DARREN BURTON

Position: Outfield
Team: Kansas City Royals
Born: Sept. 16, 1972 Somerset, KY
Height: 6'1" **Weight:** 185 lbs.
Bats: both **Throws:** right
Acquired: Fifth-round pick in 6/90 free-agent draft

Player Summary	
Fantasy Value	$0
Card Value	15¢ to 25¢
Will	cover ground
Can't	hit 15 homers
Expect	emotion
Don't Expect	Kansas City

Burton has been viewed as a possible five-tool talent, but his first year above the Class-A level brought disappointment. Halfway through the season, he had shown a dropoff in average, home runs, and stolen bases. His relatively tender age of 21 may help account for that. Burton has been associated with two winners during his five-year apprenticeship in the Royals' chain. In 1992, he helped Baseball City reach the championship round of the Class-A Florida State League playoffs. One year later, his Class-A Wilmington squad went to the title series of the Carolina League. In his high school career, he played for three straight state championship clubs. To take the final two steps to the majors, he will have to put the ball on the ground to make the best possible use of his wheels. He also needs to draw more walks; he had only a .316 on-base percentage last year. He had better quicken the pace. With Brian McRae looming above him in the Royals' organization, Burton will have to put up better numbers if he wants to create a spot for himself.

JOHN CARTER

Position: Pitcher
Team: Cleveland Indians
Born: Feb. 16, 1972 Chicago, IL
Height: 6'1" **Weight:** 195 lbs.
Bats: right **Throws:** right
Acquired: Traded from Pirates with Tony Mitchell for Alex Cole, 7/92

Player Summary	
Fantasy Value	$0
Card Value	15¢ to 25¢
Will	throw in 90s
Can't	center on heat
Expect	a changeup
Don't Expect	great stuff

In days gone by, Cleveland couldn't even fill its major-league pitching staff adequately, much less stockpile prospects in the minors. That, however, has begun to change, and Carter is a prime example. He came over from Pittsburgh with Tony Mitchell for Alex Cole on July 4, 1992. Carter's career seemed to take off shortly thereafter. A hard thrower who features a breaking ball and a change, Carter blossomed in 1993, leading the Class-A South Atlantic League and the Cleveland organization with 17 victories. He was named winner of the Bob Feller Award, given to Cleveland's top minor leaguer. He was originally picked in the 38th round of the 1990 draft by the Pirates and actually pitched well for them. He worked a total of 61⅔ innings over three stops, allowing only 21 walks. Control is a strong point, as he showed at Double-A in 1994, allowing three and one-half walks per nine innings. Look for Carter to start the 1995 campaign in Triple-A, and if he succeeds, he may challenge for a big-league job by the end of the season.

Professional Batting Register

	BA	G	AB	R	H	2B	3B	HR	RBI	SB
90 R	.207	15	58	10	12	0	1	0	2	6
91 A	.269	134	531	78	143	32	6	2	51	38
92 A	.246	123	431	54	106	15	6	4	36	16
93 A	.277	134	549	82	152	23	5	10	45	30
94 AA	.255	97	373	55	95	12	3	3	37	10

Professional Pitching Register

	W	L	ERA	G	CG	IP	H	ER	BB	SO
91 R	5	4	3.29	10	0	41.0	42	15	13	28
92 A	4	7	3.77	17	3	83.2	70	35	40	58
93 A	17	7	2.79	29	1	180.1	147	56	48	134
94 AA	9	6	4.33	22	3	131.0	134	63	53	73

RAUL CASANOVA

Position: Catcher
Team: San Diego Padres
Born: Aug. 23, 1972 Humacao, Puerto Rico
Height: 5'11" **Weight:** 190 lbs.
Bats: right **Throws:** right
Acquired: Traded from Mets with Wally Whitehurst and D.J. Dozier for Tony Fernandez, 12/92

Player Summary	
Fantasy Value	$0
Card Value	12¢ to 20¢
Will	light it up
Can't	explain emergence
Expect	extra-base hits
Don't Expect	poor glove

After four years without distinguishing himself at the dish in the minors, Casanova emerged last year as one of the most feared hitters in any farm system. In fact, he was named the most dangerous hitter in the Class-A California League after narrowly missing the Triple Crown in the San Diego organization. He led in batting average and RBI, while finishing second to Mel Nieves in home runs. Casanova made the Cal League's postseason All-Star squad and was named the No. 6 prospect in the league by *Baseball America*. He was particularly tough in the second half, hitting close to .400 during some stretches. He was the league's Player of the Month for July, hitting .468 with six homers and 31 RBI. He did all this despite a stint on the DL with tendinitis in the wrist. While most good-hitting catchers have problems with the glove, Casanova is a fine backstopper. As impressive as his season was, he faces a battle in the system with fellow catcher Sean Mulligan.

Professional Batting Register

	BA	G	AB	R	H	2B	3B	HR	RBI	SB
90 R	.077	23	65	4	5	0	0	0	1	0
91 R	.217	37	129	19	28	4	2	0	9	3
92 R	.270	42	137	25	37	9	1	4	27	3
92 A	.167	5	18	2	3	0	0	0	1	0
93 A	.256	76	227	32	58	12	0	6	30	0
94 A	.340	123	471	83	160	27	2	23	120	1

RAMON CASTRO

Position: Catcher
Team: Houston Astros
Born: March 1, 1976 Vega Baja, Puerto Rico
Height: 6'3" **Weight:** 195 lbs.
Bats: right **Throws:** right
Acquired: First-round pick in 6/94 free-agent draft

Player Summary	
Fantasy Value	$0
Card Value	15¢ to 20¢
Will	show power
Can't	climb quickly
Expect	strong arm
Don't Expect	polish

Castro was the first of three selections the Astros made in the opening round of the draft (one was a supplemental pick). The 17th overall pick, he was a high schooler in Vega Baja, Puerto Rico, same hometown as the Rangers' Ivan Rodriguez and Juan Gonzalez. The Astros would love for Castro to have Rodriguez's arm and Gonzalez's power, but that obviously would be too much to ask. Still, Castro's two main attributes seem to be power potential and a strong throwing arm, the right ingredients for a catching prospect. Castro was rated the second-best prospect in Puerto Rico by *Baseball America*, ranking only behind Hiram Bocachica, who wound up being taken by the Expos later in the first round. Castro was quickly signed to a bonus reported at $450,000, and was assigned to Houston's rookie-league club in Kissimmee. There he did everything that was expected of him. He hit for average, had some homers, and worked on his defense. He compiled a .407 slugging percentage and a .373 on-base average. He was named the No. 10 prospect in the loop. As with other young catchers, Castro will need plenty of time to develop into a pro.

Professional Batting Register

	BA	G	AB	R	H	2B	3B	HR	RBI	SB
94 R	.276	37	123	17	34	7	0	3	14	5

FRANK CATALANOTTO

Position: Second base
Team: Detroit Tigers
Born: April 27, 1974 Smithtown, NY
Height: 6′ **Weight:** 170 lbs.
Bats: left **Throws:** right
Acquired: 10th-round pick in 6/92 free-agent draft

Player Summary	
Fantasy Value	$0
Card Value	15¢ to 20¢
Will	pepper the gaps
Can't	rule out power
Expect	an achiever
Don't Expect	great tools

Catalanotto won some attention last year by very nearly capturing the batting title in the Class-A South Atlantic League. Playing for Fayetteville, he finished second behind Hickory's Ben Boulware. However, Catalanotto still went home with a berth on the postseason All-Star team. It was a breakthrough season after parts of two years spent with Bristol of the rookie Appalachian League. He looks like he could hit for average, though for the moment he does not appear able to match Lou Whitaker in the power department. Instead, Catalanotto relies on contact, hitting line drives, and sending the ball into the gaps. He struck out only 54 times last year, while compiling 37 bases on balls. He could develop more power as he fills out, though he doesn't figure as much of a basestealer. What Catalanotto may have more than anything is an aptitude for improvement. He doesn't bring first-round tools, but he has raised the level of his play to succeed against tougher competition. The next step would logically take him to the Class-A Florida State League.

ROGER CEDENO

Position: Outfield
Team: Los Angeles Dodgers
Born: Aug. 16, 1974 Valencia, Venezuela
Height: 6′1″ **Weight:** 165 lbs.
Bats: both **Throws:** right
Acquired: Signed as a free agent, 3/91

Player Summary	
Fantasy Value	$0
Card Value	25¢ to 40¢
Will	play center field
Can't	get caught on bases
Expect	a prodigy
Don't Expect	many Ks

Cedeno is among the top prospects in all the minor leagues, having torn up the Triple-A Pacific Coast League at the age of 19. It was his third straight outstanding season in pro ball, and it placed him right on target to succeed Brett Butler in center field, perhaps as soon as this year. PCL managers named Cedeno the No. 5 prospect in the loop last year. A switch-hitter with speed, he has been compiling stellar stats and awards ever since he began playing in North America. He made the 1992 All-Star team in the rookie Pioneer League, leading the circuit with 40 stolen bases. One year later, he became the youngest player in the Double-A Texas League since Bobby Tolan in 1964. That year, Cedeno had a 17-game hitting streak, a high for San Antonio. He tied for the league lead with his eight triples and was fifth with 28 steals. So far, his success rate at stealing bases has not been particularly high, and he'll have to improve in that area. He seems to have improved his batting eye and discipline, as his strikeouts declined in 1994; he had 57 Ks and 51 walks.

Professional Batting Register

	BA	G	AB	R	H	2B	3B	HR	RBI	SB
92 R	.200	21	50	6	10	2	0	0	4	0
93 R	.307	55	199	37	61	9	5	3	22	3
94 A	.325	119	458	72	149	24	8	3	56	4

Professional Batting Register

	BA	G	AB	R	H	2B	3B	HR	RBI	SB
92 R	.316	69	256	60	81	6	5	2	27	40
93 AA	.288	122	465	70	134	12	8	4	30	28
93 AAA	.222	6	18	1	4	1	1	0	3	0
94 AAA	.321	104	383	84	123	18	5	4	49	30

McKAY CHRISTIANSEN

Position: Outfield
Team: California Angels
Born: Aug. 14, 1975 Upland, CA
Height: 6'5" **Weight:** 195 lbs.
Bats: right **Throws:** right
Acquired: First-round pick in 6/94 free-agent draft

Player Summary	
Fantasy Value	$0
Card Value	15¢ to 25¢
Will	be filed away
Can't	hit with power
Expect	speed
Don't Expect	strong instincts

Christiansen represents a coup for the Angels, who gambled that they could sign this speedster even after he flatly stated he would not play baseball. His family had warned all 28 clubs that he wanted to play football at Brigham Young and serve a Mormon mission. The Angels, however, changed his mind with a bonus reported at $700,000, plus an agreement that he could postpone his baseball career until 1996. This is an unusual move for California, which in the recent past has been a organization that looked for college players who provide a more immediate return. So, the good news is that the Angels collected one of the top talents in the draft. The bad news is that they must file him away, and not even think about him for another year. What attracted the Angels was Christiansen's speed, among the best in the draft. He also has an arm strong enough to make him a potential center fielder. The risk is that he's not playing enough baseball to learn how to fully use all that speed. But the Angels won their gamble on the signing, and they may have found a player. Now Christiansen has to develop for the Halos.

No minor-league experience

SCOTT CHRISTMAN

Position: Pitcher
Team: Chicago White Sox
Born: Dec. 3, 1971 Miami, AZ
Height: 6'3" **Weight:** 190 lbs.
Bats: left **Throws:** left
Acquired: First-round pick in 6/93 free-agent draft

Player Summary	
Fantasy Value	$0
Card Value	15¢ to 25¢
Will	keep getting better
Can't	judge him on wins
Expect	first-round talent
Don't Expect	quick progress

If you went by wins and losses alone, you'd have to say that Christman didn't fare too well in his first extended stay in Class-A ball. But a closer look at his stats indicates he didn't pitch badly at all. He no doubt would benefit by pitching ahead in the count more often, but in general the White Sox seem to be on track with their plan for the man taken 17th overall in 1993. He allowed a .261 batting average and about three and one-half walks per nine innings last year. Christman attended Oregon State and went 14-1 with a 2.20 ERA in 1993. He was named a *Collegiate Baseball* first-team All-American, and Pacific-10 Conference Player of the Year. His win total left him one short of the conference record set by Washington State's John Olerud. Upon signing, Christman played in the rookie and Class-A levels. He spent a month on the disabled list while with Sarasota of the Florida State League, which helps account for the fact he only pitched a total of 21⅔ innings. Chicago's wealth of talent in the minors means he can develop slowly. While Christman doesn't have great velocity, he throws strikes.

Professional Pitching Register

	W	L	ERA	G	CG	IP	H	ER	BB	SO
93 R	0	0	0.00	4	0	11.1	3	0	4	15
93 A	0	1	0.87	2	0	10.1	5	1	5	6
94 A	6	11	3.80	20	2	116.0	116	49	44	94

JEFF CIRILLO

Position: Third base
Team: Milwaukee Brewers
Born: Sept. 23, 1969 Pasadena, CA
Height: 6'2" **Weight:** 190 lbs.
Bats: right **Throws:** right
Acquired: 11th-round pick in 6/91 free-agent draft

Player Summary	
Fantasy Value	$0
Card Value	20¢ to 30¢
Will	put ball in play
Can't	forget power
Expect	reliability
Don't Expect	stolen bases

Cirillo made it to the big leagues last year and quickly learned about the highs and lows there. He got off to a slow start, going 3-for-28, but he delivered a game-winning, two-run double in a 6-4 victory over the Twins on the first day back after the All-Star break. He also produced a big hit the next night in another win. Cirillo was coming off a highly successful 1993 campaign in which he batted .319 with 73 RBI while splitting time between Double-A and Triple-A ball. He flashed more power in '94 than he had in the past, sporting a .530 slugging percentage at Triple-A. Cirillo will make consistent contact. He also had a .386 on-base average in the minors in 1994. A communications major at Southern Cal, Cirillo was a two-time All-Pac-10 selection. He entered pro ball in 1991, making the All-Star team in the Pioneer League. He established himself in Class-A ball in 1992, finishing second in the Midwest League with a .417 on-base percentage. Cirillo should make a strong bid to open the season in the majors.

Professional Batting Register

	BA	G	AB	R	H	2B	3B	HR	RBI	SB
91 R	.350	70	286	60	100	16	2	10	51	3
92 A	.301	133	468	67	141	28	3	9	76	21
93 AA	.341	67	249	53	85	16	2	9	41	2
93 AAA	.293	58	215	31	63	13	2	3	32	2
94 AAA	.309	61	236	45	73	18	2	10	46	4
94 AL	.238	39	126	17	30	9	0	3	12	0

TONY CLARK

Position: First base; designated hitter
Team: Detroit Tigers
Born: June 15, 1972 Newton, KS
Height: 6'7" **Weight:** 240 lbs.
Bats: both **Throws:** right
Acquired: First-round pick in 6/90 free-agent draft

Player Summary	
Fantasy Value	$1 to $3
Card Value	20¢ to 30¢
Will	drive the ball
Can't	steal bases
Expect	a DH
Don't Expect	contact

After four unproductive seasons, Clark finally began to show why the Tigers made him the second overall pick in the 1990 grab bag. Playing for Trenton of the Double-A Eastern League, he outshone all other Tiger farmhands in home runs and RBI at last year's All-Star break. Included was a six-game stretch over which he cracked four home runs. He compiled a .500-plus slugging average at Trenton, and he was named to the postseason All-Star squad as the designated hitter. He was eventually promoted to Triple-A Toledo. It must have been a welcome sight for the Tigers, who had seen him collect only 275 at bats in his first four pro seasons. He played rookie ball in Bristol in 1990, batting just 73 times. After missing all of the 1991 campaign, he appeared in only 27 games in 1992, but showed a hint of his potential. Clark experienced wrist and back problems while with Lakeland of the Class-A Florida State League in 1993. Clark will have to deliver lots of power because speed is not his forte. He played hoops at the University of Arizona and San Diego State University.

Professional Batting Register

	BA	G	AB	R	H	2B	3B	HR	RBI	SB
90 R	.164	25	73	2	12	2	0	1	8	0
92 A	.306	27	85	12	26	9	0	5	17	1
93 A	.265	36	117	14	31	4	1	1	22	0
94 AA	.279	107	394	50	110	25	0	21	86	0
94 AAA	.261	25	92	10	24	4	0	2	13	2

BRAD CLONTZ

Position: Pitcher
Team: Atlanta Braves
Born: April 25, 1971 Stuart, VA
Height: 6'1" **Weight:** 180 lbs.
Bats: right **Throws:** right
Acquired: 10th-round pick in 6/92 free-agent draft

Player Summary

Fantasy Value	$0
Card Value	12¢ to 20¢
Will	close games
Can't	start
Expect	ball to sink
Don't Expect	great stuff

Considering some of their problems in the bullpen last year, the Braves no doubt wished Clontz had been ready for the majors. But it was only his third year of pro ball, and he spent it getting people out in Double-A. He even pitched the last inning of the Double-A All-Star Game, allowing no hits and striking out one as the NL farmhands played out a 10-4 loss. It was one of the few times Clontz failed to get a save. As July turned to August, he had nearly tripled his previous career high in saves. In mid-June, he received *USA TODAY Baseball Weekly's* nod as Minor League Player of the Week; by then, he had already collected 20 saves. He also won postseason honors as the Pitcher of the Year in the Southern League. He is not a wild closer, allowing two and one-half walks per nine innings last year at both Double-A and Triple-A combined. A sidearmer out of Virginia Tech, Clontz has been a reliever throughout his pro career. He averaged a K per inning last season, but he's just as apt to get an out on the ground.

Professional Pitching Register

	W	L	ERA	G	S	IP	H	ER	BB	SO
92 R	0	0	1.59	4	1	5.2	3	1	2	7
92 A	2	1	3.91	17	2	23.0	19	10	10	18
93 A	1	7	2.75	51	10	75.1	69	23	26	79
94 AA	1	2	1.20	39	27	45.0	32	6	10	49
94 AAA	0	0	2.10	24	11	25.2	19	6	9	21

MARTY CORDOVA

Position: Outfield
Team: Minnesota Twins
Born: July 10, 1969 Las Vegas, NV
Height: 6'2" **Weight:** 205 lbs.
Bats: right **Throws:** right
Acquired: 10th-round pick in 6/89 free-agent draft

Player Summary

Fantasy Value	$1 to $3
Card Value	15¢ to 25¢
Will	hit for average
Can't	crack the lineup
Expect	some speed
Don't Expect	another MVP

Cordova hurt any chance of making the big club last year when he suffered a broken wrist during spring training. He did his best to make up for it, though, by going to Salt Lake City of the Triple-A Pacific Coast League and having an outstanding year. As the season moved past the midpoint, Cordova's average was above the .370 mark. He settled into a .358 groove. He also had a .592 slugging percentage. Now the question is whether he can come anywhere near his stats during the 1992 campaign, when he was named the Most Valuable Player in the Class-A California League. He also was tabbed as the Twins' Minor League Player of the Year and was voted by league managers as the best batting prospect. Cordova attended Orange Coast Junior College. His coach there was Mike Mayne, father of major-league catcher Brent Mayne. While Cordova has to find a way into a crowded Minnesota outfield, there is no doubt that he can hit. And while he may not have had the best tools in the PCL, he certainly can help the Twins.

Professional Batting Register

	BA	G	AB	R	H	2B	3B	HR	RBI	SB
89 R	.284	38	148	32	42	2	3	8	29	2
90 A	.216	81	269	35	58	7	5	7	25	6
91 A	.212	71	189	31	40	6	1	7	19	2
92 A	.341	134	513	103	175	31	6	28	131	13
93 AA	.250	138	508	83	127	30	5	19	77	10
94 AAA	.358	103	385	69	138	25	4	19	66	17

CRAIG COUNSELL

Position: Shortstop; second base
Team: Colorado Rockies
Born: Aug. 21, 1970   South Bend, IN
Height: 6'   **Weight:** 177 lbs.
Bats: left   **Throws:** right
Acquired: 11th-round pick in 6/92 free-agent draft

Player Summary	
Fantasy Value	$0
Card Value	15¢ to 25¢
Will	be on base
Can't	lose batting eye
Expect	some speed
Don't Expect	15 homers

Counsell has been zooming through the Colorado farm system. After he got acquainted with the pro game in 1992, the Rockies assigned him to the Class-A California League for the '93 campaign, and he responded with some eye-opening offense. He walked 27 times more than he struck out and collected 34 extra-base hits. Counsell was even more impressive in 1994 when boosted to New Haven of the Double-A Eastern League, a circuit that often separates the hitters from the pretenders. He shrugged off a fractured foot that sidelined him from Opening Day to May 13, and proceeded to go to work. Once again he showed a fine batting eye and some extra-base power. He actually improved his slugging percentage from .380 in Class-A to .403 in Double-A. He needs to work on defense, and second base may be his ultimate position. The Notre Dame product could fit in well in Colorado, where his extra-base power should translate into some long-ball damage. Look for him in Triple-A to start 1995, and maybe Denver later in the year.

Professional Batting Register

	BA	G	AB	R	H	2B	3B	HR	RBI	SB
92 A	.246	18	61	11	15	6	1	0	8	1
93 A	.280	131	471	79	132	26	3	5	59	14
94 AA	.280	83	300	47	84	20	1	5	37	4

JOHN COURTRIGHT

Position: Pitcher
Team: Cincinnati Reds
Born: May 30, 1970   Marion, OH
Height: 6'2"   **Weight:** 185 lbs.
Bats: left   **Throws:** left
Acquired: Eighth-round pick in 6/91 free-agent draft

Player Summary	
Fantasy Value	$0
Card Value	15¢ to 25¢
Will	rack up innings
Can't	seem to finish
Expect	few hits
Don't Expect	15 wins

Courtright has overcome an injury to march up the ladder in the Reds' organization. For the last two seasons, however, he has been a bit of a mystery man who can deliver innings and ratios but not an inspiring winning percentage. In 1993 at Double-A Chattanooga, he made 27 starts and compiled a 3.50 ERA, but only won five games. Last year at Triple-A Indianapolis, he won only four of his first 11 starts, even though he had a trim 3.43 ERA and walked only 21 men in 66 innings. He allowed Triple-A hitters to compile a .269 batting average and almost three walks per nine innings last year. Courtright was born and grew up in Ohio, but he attended college at Duke. Upon being drafted, he made one start in rookie ball before being sidelined by tendinitis in his elbow. When he returned, Courtright enjoyed a fine 1992 campaign in the Class-A South Atlantic League, ranking seventh in the circuit with a 3.50 ERA. In 1993, he was eighth in the Southern League in ERA. If Courtright is going to make it in the big leagues, he'll have to win.

Professional Pitching Register

	W	L	ERA	G	CG	IP	H	ER	BB	SO
91 R	1	0	0.00	1	0	6.0	2	0	1	4
92 A	10	5	2.50	27	1	173.0	147	48	55	147
93 AA	5	11	3.50	27	1	175.0	179	68	70	96
94 AA	1	2	5.40	4	0	21.2	19	13	14	12
94 AAA	9	10	3.55	24	2	142.0	144	56	46	73

FELIPE CRESPO

Position: Third base; infield
Team: Toronto Blue Jays
Born: March 5, 1973 Caguas, Puerto Rico
Height: 5'11" **Weight:** 190 lbs.
Bats: both **Throws:** right
Acquired: Third-round pick in 6/90 free-agent draft

Player Summary	
Fantasy Value	$0
Card Value	20¢ to 30¢
Will	steal bases
Can't	deliver regular power
Expect	doubles
Don't Expect	return to second

Crespo is another of those fantastic athletes the Blue Jays always seem to find. He is a switch-hitter, runs well enough to steal in double figures, and may be able to hit the ball out of the park every once in a while. He came into pro ball as a second baseman, but he has spent the last two years at third. Last year, his fourth in the pro ranks, Crespo played Double-A ball in Knoxville and turned in his finest season, tying or passing career highs in runs, doubles, steals, homers, and RBI before August. The most impressive stat may have been his doubles total, which stamps him as owning bona fide extra-base power. He also had 57 bases on balls, but unfortunately his strikeout total increased to 95, more than double any total he has had before. Crespo, out of Notre Dame High School in Puerto Rico, made his North American pro debut playing for Medicine Hat of the rookie Pioneer League. He tied for 10th in the league with a .478 slugging percentage, led second basemen with 97 putouts, and paced the team with a .310 average.

Professional Batting Register

	BA	G	AB	R	H	2B	3B	HR	RBI	SB
91 R	.310	49	184	40	57	11	4	4	31	6
92 A	.281	81	263	43	74	14	3	1	29	7
93 A	.299	96	345	51	103	16	8	6	39	18
94 AA	.269	129	502	74	135	30	4	8	49	20

FAUSTO CRUZ

Position: Shortstop; infield
Team: Oakland Athletics
Born: May 1, 1972 Monte Cristi, Dominican Republic
Height: 5'10" **Weight:** 165 lbs.
Bats: right **Throws:** right
Acquired: Signed as a free agent, 1/90

Player Summary	
Fantasy Value	$0
Card Value	15¢ to 25¢
Will	play everywhere
Can't	hit for power
Expect	singles, doubles
Don't Expect	stolen bases

Cruz was one of the reasons the A's were able to trade away shortstop prospect Kurt Abbott. Cruz is a versatile defensive player who can hit, and he has adjusted well to a quick rise through the farm system. He played briefly for the A's last year, appearing at second base, third base, and shortstop, but he was sent down when the strike hit. He showed enough stick to compile a .422 slugging percentage last year at Triple-A Tacoma. He also had a .377 on-base average. Signed by Juan Marichal, Cruz showed his ability in his first pro season. He led rookie Arizona League shortstops with a .941 fielding average. By 1992, Cruz was established enough to make the midseason All-Star squad in the Class-A California League. In 1993, he began the season at Modesto but shot up two levels, playing third base, shortstop, second base, and even left field at one point or another. He is mostly a singles and doubles hitter who will get on base. He is not a base-stealer.

Professional Batting Register

	BA	G	AB	R	H	2B	3B	HR	RBI	SB
91 R	.278	52	180	38	50	2	1	2	36	3
91 A	.207	18	58	9	12	1	0	0	0	1
92 A	.319	127	489	86	156	22	11	9	90	8
93 A	.236	43	165	21	39	3	0	1	20	6
93 AA	.335	63	251	45	84	15	2	3	31	2
93 AAA	.243	21	74	13	18	2	1	0	6	3
94 AAA	.321	65	218	27	70	19	0	1	17	2
94 AL	.107	17	28	2	3	0	0	0	0	0

MIDRE CUMMINGS

Position: Outfield
Team: Pittsburgh Pirates
Born: Oct. 14, 1971 St. Croix, Virgin Islands
Height: 6′ **Weight:** 196 lbs.
Bats: left **Throws:** right
Acquired: Traded from Twins with Denny Neagle for John Smiley, 3/92

Player Summary	
Fantasy Value	$4 to $6
Card Value	20¢ to 30¢
Will	hit for average
Can't	belt many homers
Expect	a center fielder
Don't Expect	stolen bases

Cummings could very well be the Pirates' starting center fielder in 1995, but he won't have much time to establish himself. That's because the Pirates have some talent pushing him from underneath, particularly in the person of Jermaine Allensworth. However, Cummings can't do anything about that except play his own game. That game consists mainly of an ability to hit for average. He was hitting well over .300 when summoned to the Pirates in the middle of last summer. He already has one batting title on his resume, in the Class-A Midwest League in 1991. Cummings followed that campaign with the best overall season of his career, hitting .305 with 14 homers and 23 steals for Salem of the Class-A Carolina League. He was the No. 8 prospect in the Triple-A American Association in 1993. In 1994, however, he failed to break through in the big leagues and didn't deliver as much power as the Pirates would have liked, either. His stolen base totals have fallen off since 1991.

Professional Batting Register

	BA	G	AB	R	H	2B	3B	HR	RBI	SB
90 R	.316	47	177	28	56	3	4	5	28	14
91 A	.322	106	382	59	123	20	4	4	54	28
92 A	.305	113	420	55	128	21	5	14	75	23
93 AA	.295	63	237	33	70	17	2	6	26	5
93 AAA	.276	60	232	36	64	12	1	9	21	5
93 NL	.111	13	36	5	4	1	0	0	3	0
94 AAA	.311	49	183	23	57	12	4	2	22	5
94 NL	.244	24	86	11	21	4	0	1	12	0

WILL CUNNANE

Position: Pitcher
Team: Florida Marlins
Born: April 24, 1974 Suffern, NY
Height: 6′2″ **Weight:** 175 lbs.
Bats: right **Throws:** right
Acquired: Signed as a nondrafted free agent, 8/92

Player Summary	
Fantasy Value	$0
Card Value	12¢ to 20¢
Will	stay in rotation
Can't	push him
Expect	strikes
Don't Expect	same ERA

Cunnane established himself as a prospect last year, earning an honorable mention designation on *USA TODAY Baseball Weekly's* list of the year's top players. Working both as a starter and reliever for Class-A Kane County, he led the Midwest League (and the minor leagues) in ERA. Circuit managers named him the No. 8 prospect in the loop in a poll conducted by *Baseball America*. As an added bonus, he was assigned to Florida's Instructional League team during the off-season. And he's just turning 21 years old. Cunnane comes out of Clarktown North High School in New York. He broke into pro ball in 1993, finishing third in strikeouts in the rookie Gulf Coast League. Last year he made his mark again, being switched from the bullpen to the rotation. He won three straight starts from June 8 to 28, including a one-hitter. He was named Pitcher of the Week twice in a row. Later, he tossed two straight shutouts. At one point, he amassed a 27-inning scoreless streak. Next year should find him in the high Class-A Florida State League, which has the bonus of being close to the parent club's watchful eyes.

Professional Pitching Register

	W	L	ERA	G	CG	IP	H	ER	BB	SO
93 R	3	3	2.70	16	0	66.2	75	20	8	64
94 A	11	3	1.43	32	4	138.2	110	22	23	106

JOHNNY DAMON

Position: Outfield
Team: Kansas City Royals
Born: Nov. 5, 1973 Fort Riley, KS
Height: 6′ **Weight:** 175 lbs.
Bats: left **Throws:** left
Acquired: Second-round pick in 6/92 free-agent draft

Player Summary	
Fantasy Value	$0
Card Value	40¢ to 60¢
Will	lead off
Can't	be too aggressive
Expect	good range
Don't Expect	bigs in '95

Damon is an electrifying player who combines speed with the ability to hit for average. He also is starting to show a power stroke, and he may be one of the top leadoff men in the game. The 35th overall pick in the draft, Damon comes out of Dr. Phillips High in Orlando, Florida, where he was named to the 1992 *USA TODAY* High School All-America team. In his first pro season, Damon led the rookie Gulf Coast League in batting average, runs, triples, total bases, slugging percentage, and on-base percentage. Promoted to the Class-A Midwest League in 1993, Damon made the All-Star squad and led the Kansas City farm system with 59 steals. He took another step in 1994, as he was one of the top hitters and fielders in the Class-A Carolina League. He made the loop's All-Star squad and was named the No. 1 prospect in the league by *Baseball America*. An aggressive player, he will strike out, but he doesn't mind taking a walk. He has obviously accomplished all he can at the Class-A level, and now the only question is where the Royals will assign Damon for 1995.

Professional Batting Register

	BA	G	AB	R	H	2B	3B	HR	RBI	SB
92 R	.349	50	192	58	67	12	9	4	24	23
92 A	.000	1	0	0	0	0	0	0	0	0
93 A	.290	127	511	82	148	25	13	5	50	59
94 A	.316	119	472	96	149	25	13	6	75	44

VIC DARENSBOURG

Position: Pitcher
Team: Florida Marlins
Born: Nov. 13, 1970 Los Angeles, CA
Height: 5′10″ **Weight:** 165 lbs.
Bats: left **Throws:** left
Acquired: Signed as a nondrafted free agent, 6/92

Player Summary	
Fantasy Value	$0
Card Value	20¢ to 30¢
Will	get good look
Can't	walk people
Expect	starting spot
Don't Expect	many hits

Darensbourg entered the 1994 season as one of the candidates to be the Marlins' closer of the future. But the Marlins switched him to the starting rotation, and he fared well at their Double-A affiliate in Portland of the Eastern League. He had opened the campaign with 13 appearances out of the bullpen, collecting four saves. After joining the rotation, he posted a victory in only his second start. By the end of the year, he had a winning record and a fair ERA. He allowed three and one-half walks per game and a .264 batting average last year, however; two stats that he will have to shave. His signing is due to the persistence of the Marlin scouting staff. Signed by scout Dejon Watson out of Lewis and Clark, Darensbourg impressed in his first pro season, appearing in eight Gulf Coast League games and compiling an 0.64 ERA. He continued his startling development in 1993, when he was named the Marlins' Minor League Pitcher of the Year, and he was picked for the Class-A Midwest League's postseason All-Star team. Look for him to open this season in Triple-A.

Professional Pitching Register

	W	L	ERA	G	CG	IP	H	ER	BB	SO
92 R	2	1	0.64	8	0	42.0	28	3	11	37
93 A	9	1	2.12	47	0	72.1	58	17	28	90
94 AA	10	7	3.81	34	1	149.0	146	63	60	103

RUSS DAVIS

Position: Third base
Team: New York Yankees
Born: Sept. 13, 1969 Birmingham, AL
Height: 6′ **Weight:** 170 lbs.
Bats: right **Throws:** right
Acquired: 29th-round pick in 6/88 free-agent draft

Player Summary	
Fantasy Value	$1
Card Value	25¢ to 35¢
Will	get a shot
Can't	lead loop in errors
Expect	homers, doubles
Don't Expect	a burner

Davis was leading the Triple-A International League in home runs last year when a pitch from Charlotte's John Farrell broke his right wrist and ended his season. Maybe there's a silver lining, and that pitch could have been Davis's last one in the minors. He certainly deserves to go up after two fine seasons, but he's been stuck behind Yankee third baseman Wade Boggs. Davis for the last two years has been named the No. 7 prospect in the IL by *Baseball America*. He has now spent seven years in the minors, and he had his best season in 1993, hitting 26 homers and driving in 83 runs for New York's Triple-A affiliate in Columbus. But he also led IL third basemen with 25 errors. In addition, he has trouble making contact and doesn't steal bases. In 1990, he led the Carolina League with 37 doubles. He topped Double-A Eastern League third basemen with 83 putouts, 205 assists, and 314 total chances in 1991, and was named the EL's Player of the Year in 1992.

Professional Batting Register

	BA	G	AB	R	H	2B	3B	HR	RBI	SB
88 R	.230	58	213	33	49	11	3	2	30	6
89 A	.248	113	383	41	95	12	6	9	64	6
90 A	.249	137	510	55	127	37	3	16	71	3
91 AA	.218	135	473	57	103	23	3	8	58	3
92 AA	.285	132	491	77	140	23	4	22	71	3
93 AAA	.255	113	424	63	108	24	1	26	83	1
94 AAA	.276	117	416	76	115	30	2	25	69	3
94 AL	.143	4	14	0	2	0	0	0	1	0

TOMMY DAVIS

Position: Third base; first base
Team: Baltimore Orioles
Born: May 21, 1973 Mobile, AL
Height: 6′1″ **Weight:** 200 lbs.
Bats: right **Throws:** right
Acquired: Second-round pick in 6/94 free-agent draft

Player Summary	
Fantasy Value	$0
Card Value	20¢ to 30¢
Will	go the other way
Can't	let Ks pile up
Expect	bat speed
Don't Expect	Brooks Robinson

Baltimore owned no first-round pick last year, and the team had to wait nearly until the end of the second go-round before grabbing some talent. For that reason, the selection of Davis is an especially important one. He has experience both at first and third base. He did not prove himself to be a standout at either position before the draft, however. His potential rests instead with a bat that was deemed one of the best in college ball last year. At the University of Southern Mississippi, Davis hit over .400 and piled on the extra-base hits. *Baseball America* saw him as the second-best power hitter among draft-eligible college players. Upon signing, Davis landed in the Class-A South Atlantic League, where he had a rough start. He picked up just one RBI in his first 15 at bats, and was hitting only .180 after 50 official trips. Sometimes it is harder for a power-hitting college player to make the adjustment to pro ball immediately. By the end of the year, his production was more than respectable, however. A jump to the Class-A Carolina League is a distinct possibility for Davis in 1995.

Professional Batting Register

	BA	G	AB	R	H	2B	3B	HR	RBI	SB
94 A	.273	61	216	35	59	10	1	5	35	2

JOHN DETTMER

Position: Pitcher
Team: Texas Rangers
Born: March 4, 1970 Centerville, IL
Height: 6' **Weight:** 185 lbs.
Bats: right **Throws:** right
Acquired: 11th-round pick in 6/92 free-agent draft

Player Summary	
Fantasy Value	$0
Card Value	15¢ to 20¢
Will	improve numbers
Can't	be rushed
Expect	winning pitcher
Don't Expect	Double-A stats

History is filled with pitchers who have been rushed to the big leagues. Some have made it, some haven't. It remains to be seen where Dettmer winds up after taking a very fast track to the majors. He lost his first five decisions with the Rangers last year, allowing eight homers in his first 45 innings. It was not exactly what the Rangers had hoped for when they called him up, but you could hardly blame Dettmer. The University of Missouri product had spent the 1993 season in Class-A ball. He led the Class-A Florida State League in victories that year, made the All-Star team, and was named the FSL Pitcher of Month for both July and August. Promoted to Double-A in 1994, Dettmer dominated. With victories on May 10 and 15, he was named the Texas League Pitcher of the Week. He followed that up with a four-hitter, raising his record to 6-1. Soon after, he got the call to Triple-A, and then to the majors. Dettmer could challenge for a big-league spot this spring. He needs just a little time to realize that good pitches can get good hitters out.

EINAR DIAZ

Position: Catcher
Team: Cleveland Indians
Born: Dec. 28, 1972 Chiriqui, Panama
Height: 5'10" **Weight:** 165 lbs.
Bats: right **Throws:** right
Acquired: Signed as a nondrafted free agent, 10/90

Player Summary	
Fantasy Value	$0
Card Value	15¢ to 25¢
Will	throw out runners
Can't	lose contact
Expect	modest production
Don't Expect	return to third

An intriguing long-term project, Diaz has only been catching for two years. Even though it's understood he needs lots of time to get to the majors, the results thus far have been good. Diaz came into pro ball as a third baseman in 1992, but he was switched after two seasons. He immediately made an impact defensively in 1993, throwing out 48 percent of the runners who tested him and leading the rookie Appalachian League catchers with 54 assists. Diaz continued his fine work in the Class-A South Atlantic League in 1994, getting outstanding grades for his defensive play. Although he doesn't have the normal size for a backstopper, he seems to have the glove. The question is whether Diaz will hit enough to make an impact, and he does have one interesting trademark. In 1993, he led all short-season players in fewest strikeouts per plate appearance. He was just as tenacious in 1994, while improving his power production. He notched a .432 slugging percentage last year and was named the No. 7 prospect in the Sally League by *Baseball America*.

Professional Pitching Register

	W	L	ERA	G	CG	IP	H	ER	BB	SO
92 A	10	1	2.02	15	3	98.0	74	22	17	102
93 A	16	3	2.15	27	5	163.0	132	39	33	128
94 AA	6	1	2.41	10	2	74.2	57	20	12	65
94 AAA	3	2	5.63	8	1	46.1	59	29	11	26
94 AL	0	6	4.33	11	0	54.0	63	26	20	27

Professional Batting Register

	BA	G	AB	R	H	2B	3B	HR	RBI	SB
92 R	.208	52	178	19	37	3	0	1	14	2
93 R	.299	60	231	40	69	15	3	5	33	7
93 A	.000	1	5	0	0	0	0	0	0	0
94 A	.279	120	491	67	137	23	2	16	71	4

RAY DURHAM

Position: Second base
Team: Chicago White Sox
Born: Nov. 30, 1971 Charlotte, NC
Height: 5'8" **Weight:** 170 lbs.
Bats: both **Throws:** right
Acquired: Fifth-round pick in 6/90 free-agent draft

Player Summary	
Fantasy Value	$2 to $4
Card Value	15¢ to 25¢
Will	hit for average
Can't	make 30 errors
Expect	occasional power
Don't Expect	top theft rate

Durham showed a television audience what he could do in the Triple-A All-Star Game last summer, leading off and playing second base for the American League farmhands. He went 3-for-3 and scored a run in an 8-5 loss. He may not be in Triple-A much longer, as the path seems headed for Chicago. Durham, who is called both "Sugar" Ray and "Bull" Durham, has shown an ability to hit for average. He was named the No. 4 prospect in the American Association last year by *Baseball America*. He can also steal bases, though his percentage hasn't been the best. He sometimes has trouble making contact, and he must be careful not to give up too many at bats in pursuit of the long ball. The biggest potential obstacle may be his glove. In 1993 at the Double-A level, Durham made 30 errors. He has fine range, however. A third baseman and shortstop in high school, he played on a "state select" team. He was also an honorable mention All-America defensive back.

Professional Batting Register

	BA	G	AB	R	H	2B	3B	HR	RBI	SB
90 R	.276	35	116	18	32	3	3	0	13	23
91 R	.304	6	23	3	7	1	0	0	4	5
91 A	.254	39	142	29	36	2	7	0	17	12
92 R	.538	5	13	3	7	2	0	0	2	1
92 A	.272	57	202	37	55	6	3	0	7	28
93 AA	.271	137	528	83	143	22	10	3	37	39
94 AAA	.296	133	527	89	156	33	12	16	66	34

SCOTT ELARTON

Position: Pitcher
Team: Houston Astros
Born: Feb. 23, 1976 Lamar, CO
Height: 6'8" **Weight:** 220 lbs.
Bats: right **Throws:** right
Acquired: First-round pick in 6/94 free-agent draft

Player Summary	
Fantasy Value	$0
Card Value	20¢ to 25¢
Will	throw in mid-90s
Can't	play shortstop
Expect	intelligence
Don't Expect	0.00 ERA

Not many players make the impact in their pro debut that Elarton did last year. Taken with the 25th overall pick, he was the second opening-round Astro selection, following catcher Ramon Castro, who went 17th. Elarton might have gone even higher except for a commitment to Stanford that scared some teams away. He was sent to Houston's farm club in the rookie Gulf Coast League, and he made five starts without allowing a run. At the end of the season, he was named the No. 2 prospect in the loop by *Baseball America*. That performance earned him a promotion to Quad City of the Class-A Midwest League, where he combined with Jamie Walker on a one-hitter. Elarton proved that he could compete at that level. Naturally, not everything will go that well, but the fact remains that Elarton has a range of talents. He throws in the mid-90s, and he already has the makings of a complete repertoire. He is athletic enough to have hit .600 and play shortstop at Lamar High in Colorado. He also was class valedictorian. That intelligence should serve him well when it comes to make the inevitable adjustments.

Professional Pitching Register

	W	L	ERA	G	CG	IP	H	ER	BB	SO
94 R	4	0	0.00	5	0	28.0	9	0	5	28
94 A	4	1	3.29	9	0	54.2	42	20	18	42

BART EVANS

Position: Pitcher
Team: Kansas City Royals
Born: Dec. 30, 1970 Springfield, MO
Height: 6'1" **Weight:** 190 lbs.
Bats: right **Throws:** right
Acquired: Ninth-round pick in 6/92 free-agent draft

Player Summary	
Fantasy Value	$0
Card Value	15¢ to 20¢
Will	overpower hitters
Can't	throw too much
Expect	K per inning
Don't Expect	Class-A

Evans spent his third year in pro ball and improved on the excellent showing he had in the Class-A Midwest League the previous season. In 1994, he made the Class-A Carolina League All-Star team and helped Wilmington dominate the Northern Division in the first half. A strikeout artist who can compete with anyone in the Kansas City chain in overpowering hitters, Evans also showed remarkable consistency. He went the entire first half without allowing more than three runs in a start, and at the break, he led the league with a 1.95 ERA. At one point he was second among minor-league starters, allowing a .172 batting average. In a May 2 outing, Evans struck out 11 in just six innings to pick up a victory. He fanned 18 in just nine innings in his first two starts but did not pick up a decision in either case. He was ranked as the No. 5 prospect in the loop last year by *Baseball America*, and he was tabbed the league's top pitcher. The key to his improvement has been throwing strikes. A graduate of Mansfield High School in Missouri, Evans attended Southwest Missouri State. Expect him to jump to Double-A in 1995.

Professional Pitching Register

	W	L	ERA	G	CG	IP	H	ER	BB	SO
92 A	1	1	6.23	13	0	26.0	17	18	31	39
93 A	10	4	4.36	27	0	99.0	95	48	60	120
94 A	10	3	2.98	26	0	145.0	107	48	61	145

CARL EVERETT

Position: Outfield
Team: New York Mets
Born: June 3, 1971 Tampa, FL
Height: 6' **Weight:** 190 lbs.
Bats: both **Throws:** right
Acquired: Traded form Marlins for Quilvio Veres, 11/94

Player Summary	
Fantasy Value	$1 to $3
Card Value	15¢ to 20¢
Will	combine power, speed
Can't	make contact
Expect	nice tools
Don't Expect	Gary Sheffield

This is probably the most important year in Everett's career. He has served his apprenticeship in the minors and must now show whether he can help a big-league ballclub. Everett arrived in Florida as the first pick in the second round of the expansion draft (the 27th overall selection). He played center field for part of last year's Triple-A All-Star Game, going 0-for-2 for the National League farmhands. He was summoned to the majors shortly before the strike. Everett is a speed demon, who also delivers good extra-base power. Last year, he had a .505 slugging percentage at Edmonton in the Triple-A Pacific Coast League. In 1993, while playing at three different levels, he had 25 doubles, 10 triples, and 16 homers, with 37 steals. He also fanned 127 times, however, which defeats his whole game. If he does not put the ball in play, he can't run. Everett went to the same high school that produced Doc Gooden and Gary Sheffield.

Professional Batting Register

	BA	G	AB	R	H	2B	3B	HR	RBI	SB
90 R	.259	48	185	28	48	8	5	1	14	15
91 A	.271	123	468	96	127	18	0	4	40	28
92 A	.239	52	205	37	49	8	2	6	9	12
93 A	.289	59	253	48	73	12	6	10	52	24
93 AAA	.309	35	136	28	42	13	4	6	16	12
93 NL	.105	11	19	0	2	0	0	0	0	1
94 AAA	.336	78	321	63	108	17	2	11	47	16
94 NL	.216	16	51	7	11	1	0	2	6	4

RIKKERT FANEYTE

Position: Outfield
Team: San Francisco Giants
Born: May 31, 1969   Amsterdam, Netherlands
Height: 6'1"   **Weight:** 170 lbs.
Bats: right   **Throws:** right
Acquired: 16th-round pick in 6/90 free-agent draft

Player Summary	
Fantasy Value	$0
Card Value	20¢ to 30¢
Will	throw folks out
Can't	be intimidated
Expect	all-around game
Don't Expect	center field

Faneyte has already become only the third native of the Netherlands to play in the majors, following in the footsteps of Bert Blyleven and Win Remmerswaal. The question is what happens to Faneyte's career now. Although he has hit well in the minors, he has not done so in brief trips to the majors. Also, he is a center fielder, but he would never dislodge Giants defensive star Darren Lewis. And remember, Barry Bonds is in left. That leaves right field, provided Faneyte can hit big-league pitching. He was leading the Giants' minor-league system in batting when promoted to the bigs in the first half of the 1994 season. He comes out of Miami Dade South Junior College in Florida, where he was a teammate of White Sox hurler Alex Fernandez. Faneyte made the Class-A California League All-Star team in only his second year of pro ball, and he received a call to the majors one year later. When he is at his best, Faneyte will hit for a solid average, deliver some pop, and steal an occasional base.

Professional Batting Register

	BA	G	AB	R	H	2B	3B	HR	RBI	SB
91 A	.255	107	384	73	98	14	7	6	52	18
92 A	.263	94	342	69	90	13	2	9	43	17
93 AAA	.312	115	426	71	133	23	2	11	71	15
93 NL	.133	7	15	2	2	0	0	0	0	0
94 AAA	.334	94	365	62	122	17	6	6	57	15
94 NL	.115	19	26	1	3	3	0	0	4	0

MARK FARRIS

Position: Third base
Team: Pittsburgh Pirates
Born: Feb. 9, 1975   Harlingen, TX
Height: 6'2"   **Weight:** 190 lbs.
Bats: left   **Throws:** right
Acquired: First-round pick in 6/94 free-agent draft

Player Summary	
Fantasy Value	$0
Card Value	15¢ to 25¢
Will	take some time
Can't	play short
Expect	some walks
Don't Expect	instant power

Farris attended Angleton High School in Texas, where he quarterbacked the football team with such distinction that he could have attended Texas A&M on scholarship. But the Pirates took a chance with the 11th overall pick in the 1994 draft, and the Bucs signed him for a bonus reported at over $800,000. Farris was assigned to Welland of the short-season New York-Penn League, where, after his first 15 games, he was leading the club with a .314 average. He was named the No. 6 prospect in the league by *Baseball America*. He showed his hitting ability in a two-game sequence against Jamestown, when he went 7-for-8. Farris is an infielder who is seen by the Pirates as having the potential to function in the middle of the order, even though he hit just three homers during the '94 high school season and only two in his first 213 pro at bats. As far as defense is concerned, Farris played shortstop in high school and some as a pro, but he is big for the position. He seems headed for a job at third base or perhaps the outfield. The fact that the Pirates got him signed quickly and into the lineup can only help his development.

Professional Batting Register

	BA	G	AB	R	H	2B	3B	HR	RBI	SB
94 A	.249	59	213	18	53	7	1	2	19	2

RICK FORNEY

Position: Pitcher
Team: Baltimore Orioles
Born: Oct. 24, 1971   Annapolis, MD
Height: 6'4"   **Weight:** 210 lbs.
Bats: right   **Throws:** right
Acquired: 26th-round pick in 6/91 free-agent draft

Player Summary	
Fantasy Value	. . . . $0
Card Value	. . . . 15¢ to 25¢
Will	. . . . take the ball
Can't	. . . . rely on runs
Expect	. . . . decisions
Don't Expect	. . . . No. 1 spot

Forney showed the ability to win in three of his four pro seasons, with the one curious exception being in 1992, when he won only three times in 20 appearances, including 18 starts. He even managed to accumulate victories last year, even though his ERA and hits-allowed total soared. For example, he went 3-0 in four June starts, even though his ERA over those games was 5.76. One thing that really helped him is that he allowed just three walks per nine innings last year. Maybe Forney is one of those pitchers who just knows how to win. It is possible that things will catch up to him in 1995, however, if he gets to Triple-A. Forney was about to take a scholarship to the University of South Carolina-Aiken when he was drafted by the Orioles. He reported to the rookie Gulf Coast League and wound up tying for the loop lead in wins. Despite his 3-6 mark in 1992, he made the Class-A Midwest League All-Star team. He excelled in 1993 when he got to the Carolina League, leading the loop with 14 wins and finishing fourth with a 2.78 ERA. His 179 strikeouts led the Birds' farm system.

MICAH FRANKLIN

Position: Outfield
Team: Pittsburgh Pirates
Born: May 25, 1972   San Francisco, CA
Height: 6'   **Weight:** 190 lbs.
Bats: both   **Throws:** right
Acquired: Traded from Reds for Brian Hunter, 10/94

Player Summary	
Fantasy Value	. . . . $0
Card Value	. . . . 20¢ to 30¢
Will	. . . . hit it out
Can't	. . . . live on mistakes
Expect	. . . . high-round tools
Don't Expect	. . . . patient hitter

Franklin's career was nearly over as soon as it began. The Mets' third choice in the 1990 draft, he displayed attitude problems that got him released in less than two years. But Franklin turned things around in the Reds' chain, and the Pirates liked what they saw so much that they nabbed him in a trade. He began the season in the Class-A Carolina League and was leading the minors in homers when he received a promotion to Double-A, even though his power totals were somewhat inflated by the home field. After homering in both ends of a doubleheader, he was named the Southern League Player of the Week June 10. Despite his turnaround, Franklin still has a long way to go. He needs better knowledge of the strike zone and more patience at the plate. He must get used to the fact that as he moves up, pitchers won't make the same mistakes that he's hitting for home runs now. Still, he's done enough that the Pirates must give him a long look, and even if he doesn't make it, he deserves credit for his progress.

Professional Pitching Register

	W	L	ERA	G	CG	IP	H	ER	BB	SO
91 R	7	0	2.19	12	2	65.2	48	16	10	51
92 A	3	6	2.48	20	2	123.1	114	34	26	104
93 A	14	8	2.78	27	2	165.0	156	51	64	175
93 AA	0	0	1.29	1	0	7.0	1	1	1	4
94 AA	13	8	4.62	28	4	165.2	168	85	58	125

Professional Batting Register

	BA	G	AB	R	H	2B	3B	HR	RBI	SB
90 R	.259	39	158	29	41	10	3	7	25	5
91 A	.259	65	247	45	64	8	2	2	22	16
92 R	.335	75	251	58	84	13	2	11	60	18
93 A	.257	122	412	66	106	15	5	20	74	6
94 A	.300	42	150	44	45	7	0	21	44	7
94 AA	.276	79	279	46	77	17	0	10	40	2

RYAN FRANKLIN

Position: Pitcher
Team: Seattle Mariners
Born: March 5, 1973 Ft. Smith, AR
Height: 6'3" **Weight:** 165 lbs.
Bats: right **Throws:** right
Acquired: 23rd-round draft pick in 6/92 free-agent draft

Player Summary	
Fantasy Value	$0
Card Value	15¢ to 25¢
Will	need seasoning
Can't	think it's easy
Expect	leanness
Don't Expect	a 12-0 mark

If the strike had not hit last year, there's no telling where Franklin might have gone by the end of the season. As it was, he rocketed through three levels of minor-league ball, finally reaching the Mariners' top farm team in Calgary of the Pacific Coast League. It was quite a journey for a 23rd-round pick just two years removed from the draft. He began the season with Appleton of the Class-A Midwest League, and he succeeded there, going 9-6 with a 3.13 ERA, 102 strikeouts, and just 23 bases on balls in 118 innings. In one highlight, he struck out 12 batters in eight innings on June 16. He was promoted to Riverside of the Class-A California League, where he went 4-2 with a 3.06 ERA. Later came another promotion, this time all the way to Calgary. He was able to look so good in part because he allowed only one and one-half walks per nine innings last year. Franklin was drafted by the Blue Jays in 1991 but did not sign, instead attending Seminole Junior College in Oklahoma. The Mariners drafted him in 1992, but he returned to Seminole in '93 and went 12-0 with a 2.99 ERA.

Professional Pitching Register

	W	L	ERA	G	CG	IP	H	ER	BB	SO
93 A	5	3	2.92	15	1	74.0	72	24	27	55
94 A	13	8	3.11	26	6	179.2	166	62	31	137
94 AAA	0	0	7.94	1	0	5.2	9	5	1	2

KARIM GARCIA

Position: Outfield
Team: Los Angeles Dodgers
Born: Oct. 29, 1975 Cuidad Obregon, Mexico
Height: 6' **Weight:** 172 lbs.
Bats: left **Throws:** left
Acquired: Signed as a free agent, 7/92

Player Summary	
Fantasy Value	$0
Card Value	25¢ to 35¢
Will	mash ball
Can't	play in bigs yet
Expect	slugging
Don't Expect	stolen bases

Garcia grabs attention because of the way he holds his own against much older competition. He played in the California League at age 17, and last year he made the Class-A Florida State League All-Star team at 18. His success in these situations indicates that it's just a matter of time before he fits in somewhere in the Los Angeles lineup. He appears to have legitimate home run power, and a high percentage of his hits go for extra bases. He notched a .511 slugging percentage last year. Don't be surprised to see Garcia reach double figures in doubles, triples, and homers while driving in runs. One example of his powerful style came early in the season, when Garcia was named FSL Player of the Week. He went 9-for-30, with one double, two triples, three homers, and six RBI. In the first half, his 12 homers placed him third in the league. He was the All-Star right fielder for the loop last year, and league managers tabbed him as the No. 9 prospect in the FSL in a poll by *Baseball America*. He is listed at 6' but could grow even a little more. Signed by Mike Brito, Garcia attended Preparatoria Abierta in Mexico.

Professional Batting Register

	BA	G	AB	R	H	2B	3B	HR	RBI	SB
93 A	.241	123	460	61	111	20	9	19	54	5
94 A	.265	121	452	72	120	28	10	21	84	8

NOMAR GARCIAPARRA

Position: Shortstop
Team: Boston Red Sox
Born: July 23, 1973   Whittier, CA
Height: 6'   **Weight:** 162 lbs.
Bats: right   **Throws:** right
Acquired: First-round pick in 6/94 free-agent draft

Player Summary	
Fantasy Value	$0
Card Value	15¢ to 25¢
Will	make plays
Can't	burn basepaths
Expect	a great athlete
Don't Expect	Barry Larkin

Garciaparra gained a great deal of experience in his amateur career, playing for the U.S. Olympic Team in 1992 and then becoming an All-American for a Georgia Tech squad that reached the College World Series final in 1994. Now it's time for him to move into even better company. The Red Sox showed what they thought of Garciaparra, making him the 12th overall selection in last year's draft. He is an exceptional athlete—one of the best in the entire draft—with outstanding defensive skills. His coach at Georgia Tech, Danny Hall, has favorably compared Garciaparra to Reds shortstop Barry Larkin. Garciaparra was the most advanced defensive player in the draft, and he could probably compete at the major-league level now. At the plate, he doesn't project as a monster. He did have a few good games with Sarasota of the Class-A Florida State League after signing, and he notched a .419 slugging percentage. The Red Sox hope he can drive pitches into the gaps. He won't be a burner on the bases, but his all-around athletic ability should be welcomed by a team in need of it. Garciaparra could see big-league duty as soon as late 1995.

CADE GASPAR

Position: Pitcher
Team: Detroit Tigers
Born: Aug. 21, 1973   Mission Viejo, CA
Height: 6'3"   **Weight:** 185 lbs.
Bats: right   **Throws:** right
Acquired: First-round pick in 6/94 free-agent draft

Player Summary	
Fantasy Value	$0
Card Value	15¢ to 25¢
Will	throw breaking ball
Can't	leap to majors
Expect	fresh arm
Don't Expect	experience

Gaspar was one of three sons of former major leaguers to be taken in the first round in 1994. His father, Rod, was an infielder who played for the 1969 Miracle Mets. But the Tigers don't think it would take a miracle for the younger Gaspar to help them. They exercised their first pick, 18th overall in the draft, to take this Pepperdine product. He went a little lower than expected, and only time will tell if the Tigers got a bargain. He supposedly scared some clubs away because of his asking price. Reports of his fastball range all the way from average to 93 mph, which is quite a range of opinions. He also is said to have a breaking ball that could compare with any in the draft and a fine curveball. Gaspar was signed and sent to Lakeland of the Class-A Florida State League, where he hurled two scoreless innings in his debut. He had some ups and downs after that. For instance, he absorbed a three-homer shelling on Aug. 11, but then he turned in five strong innings five nights later. He held FSL hitters to a .248 batting average and kept his walks at a respectable level. Gaspar is probably only a year or so away from Detroit.

Professional Batting Register

	BA	G	AB	R	H	2B	3B	HR	RBI	SB
94 A	.295	28	105	20	31	8	1	1	16	5

Professional Pitching Register

	W	L	ERA	G	CG	IP	H	ER	BB	SO
94 A	1	3	5.58	8	0	30.2	28	19	8	25

JASON GIAMBI

Position: Third base
Team: Oakland Athletics
Born: Jan. 8, 1971   West Covina, CA
Height: 6'2"   **Weight:** 200 lbs.
Bats: left   **Throws:** right
Acquired: Second-round pick in 6/92 free-
agent draft

Player Summary

Fantasy Value	$0
Card Value	15¢ to 25¢
Will	play third
Can't	find stability
Expect	another shuttle
Don't Expect	an A's starter

No one could blame Giambi if he never got into a groove in 1994. He began the season on the disabled list, then moved up and down between the Double-A Southern League and the Triple-A Pacific Coast League. Somewhat curiously, but good for his career, Giambi hit better in the higher league than he did in Double-A. He started the month of August by going 13-for-33 with 12 RBI. The exposure to a higher level of competition can only improve his chances at the big club in 1995. He notched a .500 slugging average at Tacoma, and he walked as much as he struck out in both leagues. Out of Long Beach State, Giambi made the 1992 U.S. Olympic Team, but not without a hitch. He was cut after the trials and then brought back, and wound up hitting .308. Giambi had previously gained experience in international play with the 1991 Pan Am team, when he hit .340. He began making his mark in the pros in 1993, when he was named to the California League All-Star team. A third baseman, Giambi also has some experience at first. He should be in the bigs by late '95.

Professional Batting Register

	BA	G	AB	R	H	2B	3B	HR	RBI	SB
92 A	.317	13	41	9	13	3	0	3	13	1
93 A	.291	89	313	72	91	16	2	12	60	2
94 AA	.223	56	193	31	43	9	0	6	30	0
94 AAA	.318	52	176	28	56	20	0	4	38	1

STEVE GIBRALTER

Position: Outfield
Team: Cincinnati Reds
Born: Oct. 9, 1972   Dallas, TX
Height: 6'   **Weight:** 185 lbs.
Bats: right   **Throws:** right
Acquired: Sixth-round pick in 6/90 free-agent
draft

Player Summary

Fantasy Value	$0
Card Value	15¢ to 25¢
Will	cover outfield
Can't	linger in Double-A
Expect	more development
Don't Expect	another MVP

Gibralter has been having trouble breaking through Double-A ever since his awesome 1992 campaign with Cedar Rapids of the Class-A Midwest League. That was the year he captured the league MVP Award and led the circuit in homers and RBI. He also was named the league's best defensive outfielder. Gibralter's production slid sharply when he was boosted to Double-A, however. Even though he led the Southern League with 334 total chances and 319 putouts, he could not match that excellence at the plate. He played in the Arizona Fall League but was sidelined by a problem with his right shoulder. Gibralter spent the 1994 season trying to reestablish his bat and had some impressive moments. In early July, he was named Southern League Player of the Week for going 11-for-25 with one homer and eight RBI. By the end of the season, he had a .435 slugging average and a .345 on-base percentage. It's important to remember that Gibralter is only 22. He still can't afford to waste time getting to Triple-A, though. The Reds, impressed by his glove, will see that he advances.

Professional Batting Register

	BA	G	AB	R	H	2B	3B	HR	RBI	SB
90 R	.259	52	174	26	45	11	3	4	27	9
91 A	.267	140	544	72	145	36	7	6	71	11
92 A	.306	137	529	92	162	32	3	19	99	12
93 AA	.237	132	477	65	113	25	3	11	47	7
94 AA	.270	133	460	71	124	28	3	14	63	10

BENJI GIL

Position: Shortstop
Team: Texas Rangers
Born: Oct. 6, 1972 Tijuana, Mexico
Height: 6'2" **Weight:** 182 lbs.
Bats: right **Throws:** right
Acquired: First-round pick in 6/91 free-agent draft

Player Summary	
Fantasy Value	$1
Card Value	12¢ to 15¢
Will	get another shot
Can't	swing for fences
Expect	great arm
Don't Expect	high average

Gil was the 19th player taken in the 1991 draft, and less than two years later he was in the majors. It was a fast trip, probably too fast. He opened the 1993 campaign with the Rangers and was the majors' youngest player at the time. His first big-league hit came off Boston's Roger Clemens, but Gil couldn't do much against the other pitchers, and he was farmed after 29 at bats. In his second stint he fared even worse, so more seasoning was in order. He spent the majority of his time in 1993 at Double-A Tulsa, and he was named the No. 5 prospect in the Texas League that year. Now that he's had that seasoning—last year in Triple A—the question is whether he'll step forward and be the Rangers' shortstop in 1995. It may all depend on whether he hits. As his 1994 stats indicate, Gil can hit the ball out of the park, but not enough to justify his many strikeouts. He should try to better use his speed. Then again, with the sluggers in Texas' lineup, Gil doesn't have to be a huge factor at the plate. A good glove, with some productive at bats, would do.

Professional Batting Register

	BA	G	AB	R	H	2B	3B	HR	RBI	SB
91 R	.287	32	129	25	37	4	3	2	15	9
92 A	.274	132	482	75	132	21	1	9	55	26
93 AA	.275	101	342	45	94	9	1	17	59	20
93 AL	.123	22	57	3	7	0	0	0	2	1
94 AAA	.248	139	487	62	121	20	6	10	55	14

WAYNE GOMES

Position: Pitcher
Team: Philadelphia Phillies
Born: Jan. 15, 1973 Hampton, VA
Height: 6'2" **Weight:** 215 lbs.
Bats: right **Throws:** right
Acquired: First-round pick in 6/93 free-agent draft

Player Summary	
Fantasy Value	$0
Card Value	20¢ to 30¢
Will	bring heat
Can't	get ahead
Expect	big curve
Don't Expect	boring outings

The Phillies certainly could have used a top-flight Gomes last year, with all the pitching problems they endured, but he wasn't ready for prime time. However, it would be wrong to minimize his talent with just a look at his stat line. Virtually all of Gomes's problems came from a lack of control. Not only was his walk total astronomical, but he was always pitching behind in the count and had to come in with a fat pitch. When he starts throwing strikes more consistently, people will better appreciate the positive side of his stats. He should be able to maintain a fine hits-to-innings ratio and a tidy strikeout total. In 1993, he was used as a reliever, and that is where his future will probably lie—if he can cut his walks. The fourth overall pick in the draft, Gomes came out of Old Dominion University, where he struck out 55 in only 26⅔ innings in 1993. He was named first-team All-Colonial Athletic Association. *Collegiate Baseball* named him a first-team freshman All-American in 1991. He has a 93-mph fastball, a big curve, and a tough slider. To get more honors, Gomes will have to learn to throw strikes early and often.

Professional Pitching Register

	W	L	ERA	G	S	IP	H	ER	BB	SO
93 A	1	0	1.20	14	4	15.0	5	2	17	24
94 A	6	8	4.74	23	1	104.1	85	55	82	102

CURTIS GOODWIN

Position: Outfield
Team: Baltimore Orioles
Born: Sept. 30, 1972 Oakland, CA
Height: 5'11" **Weight:** 180 lbs.
Bats: left **Throws:** left
Acquired: 12th-round pick in 6/91 free-agent draft

Player Summary	
Fantasy Value	$0
Card Value	30¢ to 50¢
Will	cover ground
Can't	give up at bats
Expect	strength
Don't Expect	big homers

After three years in the lower levels of the minors, Goodwin jumped to Double-A ball and did it with style. He was judged to be the fastest runner, best baserunner, and most exciting player in the Double-A Eastern League by *Baseball America*. He was also named the loop's No. 9 prospect. This came one year after Goodwin had been named the top prospect in the Class-A Carolina League. So far, he has shown the ability to hit for a solid average, steal bases, score runs, and cover ground in the outfield. His extra-base hits will come mainly on speed, and he's already reached double figures in triples in a season. Goodwin must still work on his stolen-base percentage and keep sharpening his selection at the plate. He struck out almost 200 times combined in 1992 and 1993, and that's counterproductive for a player with his speed. Last year, he cut his Ks down to 78 and notched 40 walks. Goodwin comes from an athletic family. His brother Jay attended the University of Washington and was a walk-on fullback for the Huskies' national title team in 1991.

RICK GORECKI

Position: Pitcher
Team: Los Angeles Dodgers
Born: Aug. 27, 1973 Evergreen Park, IL
Height: 6'3" **Weight:** 167 lbs.
Bats: right **Throws:** right
Acquired: 19th-round pick in 6/91 free-agent draft

Player Summary	
Fantasy Value	$0
Card Value	15¢ to 25¢
Will	throw breaking ball
Can't	pitch behind
Expect	dedication
Don't Expect	1994 again

Quite often, the way a player faces adversity can tell you more about him than a stat sheet or a radar gun. Such was the case with Gorecki, who had to battle injury to establish himself at the Triple-A level last year. At one point, he was 3-6 with a 6.55 ERA. He went on the disabled list, and when he returned, he began working those numbers toward respectability. Before long, he had improved his record to 8-6 and pulled the ERA down to 5.07. His hit and walk totals weren't where he wanted them to be, but he was a 21-year-old pitching in a hitter's league. His experience can only mean good things. Gorecki comes out of Oak Forest High School in Illinois and was named the *Chicago Sun-Times* High School Baseball Player of the Year. His signature pitch is an outstanding breaking ball. Judging by how many walks he gives up, he'll have to throw it when he's behind in the count. Gorecki has time to work on his control, but he gave up more than five bases on balls per nine innings last year. He'll need to cut that ratio quite a bit.

Professional Batting Register

	BA	G	AB	R	H	2B	3B	HR	RBI	SB
91 R	.258	48	151	32	39	5	0	0	9	26
92 A	.282	134	542	85	153	7	5	1	42	52
93 A	.281	138	555	98	156	15	10	2	42	61
94 AA	.286	142	597	105	171	18	8	2	37	59

Professional Pitching Register

	W	L	ERA	G	CG	IP	H	ER	BB	SO
91 R	0	3	4.41	13	0	51.0	44	25	27	56
92 A	11	7	4.05	25	0	129.0	122	58	90	115
93 AA	6	9	3.35	26	1	156.0	136	58	62	118
94 AAA	8	6	5.07	22	0	103.0	119	58	60	73

JEFF GRANGER

Position: Pitcher
Team: Kansas City Royals
Born: Dec. 16, 1971   San Pedro, CA
Height: 6'4"   **Weight:** 200 lbs.
Bats: right   **Throws:** left
Acquired: First-round pick in 6/93 free-agent draft

Player Summary	
Fantasy Value	$0
Card Value	20¢ to 30¢
Will	return to bigs
Can't	let walks pile up
Expect	No. 1 spot
Don't Expect	Roy Branch

Granger came as the fifth overall pick in the draft, and he was the Royals' highest selection since they tabbed Roy Branch fifth in 1971. Branch made it to the majors eight years later—for two games with Seattle. There's every reason to believe this pick will turn out better than that one did. In fact, Granger made his major-league debut less than four months after getting picked, becoming the second man from the '93 draft to take that step. Granger had some ups and downs while pitching at Double-A Memphis in 1994. Southern League hitters compiled a .283 batting average against him, and he allowed almost four walks per nine innings. He is a strong all-around athlete who played four sports in high school. He compiled a 42-game hitting streak as a senior, the second-longest in national high school history. He was also Texas A&M's starting quarterback for eight games in 1992. In baseball, he was a first-team All-Southwest Conference and All-America selection, as well as a finalist for the '93 Golden Spikes Award given to the top amateur baseball player.

Professional Pitching Register

	W	L	ERA	G	CG	IP	H	ER	BB	SO
93 A	3	3	3.00	8	0	36.0	28	12	10	56
93 AL	0	0	27.00	1	0	1.0	3	3	2	1
94 AA	7	7	3.87	25	0	139.2	155	60	61	112
94 AL	0	1	6.75	2	0	9.1	13	7	6	3

SHAWN GREEN

Position: Outfield
Team: Toronto Blue Jays
Born: Nov. 10, 1972   Des Plaines, IL
Height: 6'4"   **Weight:** 190 lbs.
Bats: left   **Throws:** left
Acquired: First-round pick in 6/91 free-agent draft

Player Summary	
Fantasy Value	$3 to $5
Card Value	30¢ to 50¢
Will	run and throw
Can't	rule out power
Expect	good citizen
Don't Expect	John Olerud

Green is a multitool talent who could be making his impact in the majors very quickly. He is an outstanding hitter whose swing has prompted comparisons to John Olerud. Green won the Triple-A International League batting title last year, and he also showed the makings of some fine power as well, garnering a .510 slugging percentage. He cut his strikeouts from 73 in 1993 to 62 last year. Green came out of Tustin High in California, where his 147 hits as a senior tied the California Interscholastic Federation record. He was also named to the 1991 *USA TODAY* All-USA High School Team. Upon turning pro, he stole his first 13 bases without getting caught. In 1993, a broken right thumb limited him to only 99 minor-league games, though he showed speed and hitting ability. Green needs to work on his defense, though he owns a fine throwing arm. He turned down a scholarship to Stanford, and he donated part of his signing bonus to a charity that provides breakfasts to needy children in Toronto. He should earn a job with the Blue Jays in 1995.

Professional Batting Register

	BA	G	AB	R	H	2B	3B	HR	RBI	SB
92 A	.273	110	417	44	114	21	3	1	49	22
93 AA	.283	99	360	40	102	14	2	4	34	4
93 AL	.000	3	6	0	0	0	0	0	0	0
94 AAA	.344	109	433	82	149	27	3	13	61	19
94 AL	.091	14	33	1	3	1	0	0	1	1

TODD GREENE

Position: Catcher
Team: California Angels
Born: May 8, 1971 Augusta, GA
Height: 5'9" **Weight:** 195 lbs.
Bats: right **Throws:** right
Acquired: 12th-round pick in 6/93 free-agent draft

Player Summary	
Fantasy Value	$0
Card Value	70¢ to $1
Will	crush the ball
Can't	let runners go
Expect	tough transition
Don't Expect	Gold Glove

Last year, Greene undertook a difficult switch from the outfield to behind the plate, but the way he hit, he may be able to work his way into the lineup at either position. He had about 10 more home runs than anyone else in the Class-A California League last year. Three of them came in one game, on Aug. 20, tying a league record. He also notched a pretty fair .584 slugging percentage. He was named league MVP and Rookie of the Year, and *Baseball America* tabbed him as the loop's No. 9 prospect. It was his second straight MVP Award in as many pro seasons, as he was tabbed for that honor in the Northwest League in 1993, as an outfielder. The Angels switched Greene to catcher and sent him to the Cal League, where he had the problems you'd might expect in the early days of the transition. He allowed 15 stolen bases in 18 attempts and permitted eight passed balls in his first nine games. Not long after that, he was twice named Cal League Player of the Week and earned a spot in the All-Star Game. He allowed 44 passed balls by season's end. Greene has a bright future, but it may not be behind the dish.

Professional Batting Register

	BA	G	AB	R	H	2B	3B	HR	RBI	SB
93 A	.269	76	305	55	82	15	3	15	71	4
94 A	.302	133	524	98	158	39	2	35	124	10

BEN GRIEVE

Position: Outfield
Team: Oakland Athletics
Born: May 4, 1976 Arlington, TX
Height: 6'4" **Weight:** 185 lbs.
Bats: left **Throws:** right
Acquired: First-round pick in 6/94 free-agent draft

Player Summary	
Fantasy Value	$0
Card Value	25¢ to 35¢
Will	hit home runs
Can't	play center
Expect	ability
Don't Expect	a burner

Grieve is the son of former major leaguer Tom Grieve, who was the general manager of the Texas Rangers. When Ben was taken second overall by Oakland, Tom and Ben became the first father-son duo to have gone in the initial round. Out of Martin High in Texas, the younger Grieve owns a beautiful swing that he has already put to good use in pro ball. He has been compared to both John Olerud and Paul O'Neill, but Grieve could wind up having more power than either one. He has a fine arm and should find himself in right field, especially since he doesn't have the speed for center. Because of his background, he already knows some things that most other draft picks must learn. Grieve quickly signed and was assigned to Southern Oregon. Within weeks, he was named Northwest League Player of the Week. He displayed fine power, notching a .464 slugging percentage, and a fine batting eye, walking more than he struck out and touting a .456 on-base average. He was named to the postseason All-Star squad. *Baseball America* named him the No. 1 prospect in the loop. Grieve could grow into a player that his dad would have paid big bucks for.

Professional Batting Register

	BA	G	AB	R	H	2B	3B	HR	RBI	SB
94 A	.329	72	252	44	83	13	0	7	50	2

RYAN HANCOCK

Position: Pitcher
Team: California Angels
Born: Nov. 11, 1971   Santa Clara, CA
Height: 6'2" **Weight:** 215 lbs.
Bats: right **Throws:** right
Acquired: Second-round pick in 6/93 free-agent draft

Player Summary	
Fantasy Value $0
Card Value . . . . 20¢ to 30¢
Will . . . . throw in high 80s
Can't . . . . worry about knee
Expect . . . . composure
Don't Expect . . . . a tight slider

Hancock assembled a successful season in 1994, but numbers are only part of it. More important was the fact that his surgically repaired knee held up under the test of a full season. He hurt it while playing quarterback for Brigham Young University, and he had to undergo reconstructive surgery in November 1992. Even though he only pitched 18 innings the following spring, the Angels still thought enough of him to make him their second-round pick. He reported to Boise of the Northwest League, where he made three starts. That's why '94 loomed so large, and he passed the test with flying colors. He won Cal League Pitcher of the Week honors, and he showed the fine control and nice velocity that attracted the Halos in the first place. Among his victories was a two-hit shutout in which he faced only 28 batters and retired the last nine. Hancock held Cal League hitters to a .253 batting average. He later received a promotion to California's Double-A team in Midland. Hancock can throw in the high 80s to low 90s, and he has a breaking pitch. He also has a commanding presence on the mound.

Professional Pitching Register

	W	L	ERA	G	CG	IP	H	ER	BB	SO
93 A	1	0	3.31	3	0	16.1	14	6	8	18
94 A	9	6	3.79	18	3	116.1	113	49	36	95
94 AA	3	4	5.81	8	0	48.0	63	31	11	35

LaTROY HAWKINS

Position: Pitcher
Team: Minnesota Twins
Born: Dec. 21, 1972   Gary, IN
Height: 6'5" **Weight:** 195 lbs.
Bats: right **Throws:** right
Acquired: Seventh-round pick in 6/91 free-agent draft

Player Summary	
Fantasy Value $1
Card Value . . . . 60¢ to $1
Will . . . . win
Can't . . . . be Satchel
Expect . . . . big repertoire
Don't Expect . . . . the bullpen

Hawkins is quite likely the best starting pitching prospect in the Twins' organization—and possibly in all of baseball. Nicknamed "Satchel" after Hall of Famer Satchel Paige, Hawkins has risen quickly in the last two years. His fastball is average or above, but it has movement. He complements it with a slider and a curve, and he can also deliver a changeup. Hawkins blossomed in 1993, after a slump in which he went to the bullpen. He wound up being named the Twins' Minor League Player of the Year. He opened the 1994 season with Fort Myers of the Class-A Florida State League and went on a tear, at one point going 20⅓ innings without allowing a run. He was quickly promoted to Double-A Nashville and didn't suffer a defeat until May 23. By then, he had impeccable credentials for being named to the Double-A All-Star team. *Baseball America* named him the No. 2 prospect in the league. He didn't linger very long in Double-A, as a promotion to Triple-A followed. Hawkins should be in the majors before too long.

Professional Pitching Register

	W	L	ERA	G	CG	IP	H	ER	BB	SO
91 R	4	3	4.75	11	0	55.0	62	29	26	47
92 R	3	3	3.29	11	2	63.0	57	23	21	71
93 A	15	5	2.06	26	4	157.1	110	36	41	179
94 A	4	0	2.33	6	1	38.2	32	10	6	36
94 AA	9	2	2.33	11	1	73.1	50	19	28	53
94 AAA	5	4	4.08	12	1	81.2	92	37	33	37

JIMMY HAYNES

Position: Pitcher
Team: Baltimore Orioles
Born: Sept. 5, 1972 LaGrange, GA
Height: 6'4" **Weight:** 185 lbs.
Bats: right **Throws:** right
Acquired: Seventh-round pick in 6/91 free-agent draft

Player Summary	
Fantasy Value	$0
Card Value	20¢ to 30¢
Will	have quality starts
Can't	rush delivery
Expect	coachability
Don't Expect	Double-A

The Orioles have cultivated a tradition of developing their own pitchers, and Haynes looks like he could become part of that line. Pitching for Bowie of the Eastern League last year, Haynes made the Double-A All-Star team, though he did not pitch in the game because he had been promoted to Triple-A Rochester. At the time, he was leading the Eastern League with 108 strikeouts. He eventually led the loop with 177 strikeouts, and he was named the circuit's No. 7 prospect by *Baseball America*. Haynes finished the season ranked with the best in the Orioles' system in victories, ERA, and strikeouts. He comes out of Troup County High School in Georgia, where he hit a grand slam in his final game. In 1992, he was the Oriole organization's Pitcher of the Month for August. In 1993, he made the Carolina League's midseason All-Star team. At one point, he notched seven straight wins, including a two-hit victory over Kinston. His Triple-A experience puts him into position to contend for a berth in the big club's starting rotation in 1995.

Professional Pitching Register

	W	L	ERA	G	CG	IP	H	ER	BB	SO
91 R	3	2	1.60	14	1	62.0	44	11	21	67
92 A	7	11	2.56	24	4	144.0	131	41	45	141
93 A	12	8	3.03	27	2	172.1	139	58	61	174
94 AA	13	8	2.90	25	5	173.2	154	56	46	177
94 AAA	1	0	6.75	3	0	13.1	20	10	6	14

KEITH HEBERLING

Position: Pitcher
Team: Chicago White Sox
Born: Sept. 21, 1972 Greenwich, CT
Height: 6'3" **Weight:** 192 lbs.
Bats: left **Throws:** left
Acquired: Traded from Yankees with a player to be named later for Jack McDowell, 12/94

Player Summary	
Fantasy Value	$0
Card Value	15¢ to 25¢
Will	have pressure
Can't	forget draft spot
Expect	strikeouts
Don't Expect	astonishment

Imagine being drafted by the New York Yankees in the 46th round. Then imagine having two strong seasons in Class-A ball and being a principal in a trade for a Cy Young Award winner and one of the best starters in the game. Heberling's stock has risen so much since being drafted in the 46th round of the 1992 draft (he didn't sign until May 30, 1993) that he was one of two talents that the White Sox sought for Jack McDowell. Heberling is a strong physical specimen who played baseball and swam at Vero Beach High School in Florida. In just two pro seasons, he has dominated hitters, quickly moving through the system. In 1993, he compiled a 1.76 ERA in 97 frames, best of all Yankee minor leaguers for that many innings pitched. In 1994, he had an impressive season at Tampa in the Class-A Florida State League. Although he didn't overpower FSL batters, he did show fine control, notching less than two and one-half walks per game. He made the loop's All-Star team, and he received a promotion to the Double-A Eastern League. Heberling should return to Double-A in 1995.

Professional Pitching Register

	W	L	ERA	G	CG	IP	H	ER	BB	SO
93 A	10	2	1.76	15	0	97.0	67	19	26	101
94 A	11	7	2.92	22	1	138.2	149	45	37	121
94 AA	1	3	5.66	6	1	35.0	44	22	6	21

RODNEY HENDERSON

Position: Pitcher
Team: Montreal Expos
Born: March 11, 1971 Greensburg, KY
Height: 6'4" **Weight:** 193 lbs.
Bats: right **Throws:** right
Acquired: Second-round pick in 6/92 free-agent draft

Player Summary	
Fantasy Value	$0
Card Value	25¢ to 35¢
Will	get straightened out
Can't	blame car crash
Expect	a live arm
Don't Expect	boring innings

After a spectacular 1993 campaign, Henderson experienced problems last year when he got his first taste of Triple-A ball. A starter for all his pro career, he was sent to the bullpen after a particularly rough stretch in which he allowed 14 runs in five innings. He responded with a save against Columbus on Aug. 3, the first of his career. He showed last year that his arm remains live, but he lost some of the control that he had been refining. Out of the University of Kentucky, Henderson lost virtually a year of development to injury. In 1992, with just one pro appearance in the books, he was involved in a car crash and suffered two fractured vertebrae and a broken pitching wrist. He bounced back with a spectacular 1993 campaign, going a combined 17-7 with 152 strikeouts. Even though he was promoted to Double-A in early August, he still finished fourth in the Florida State League in victories and third in shutouts. Expect him to straighten out his problems at the Triple-A level in 1995.

Professional Pitching Register

	W	L	ERA	G	CG	IP	H	ER	BB	SO
92 A	0	0	6.00	1	0	3.0	2	2	5	2
93 A	12	7	2.90	22	1	143.0	110	46	44	127
93 AA	5	0	1.82	5	0	29.2	20	6	15	25
94 AA	2	0	1.50	2	0	12.0	5	2	4	16
94 AAA	6	9	4.62	23	0	122.2	123	63	67	100
94 NL	0	1	9.45	3	0	6.2	9	7	7	3

DUSTIN HERMANSON

Position: Pitcher
Team: San Diego Padres
Born: Dec. 21, 1972 Springfield, OH
Height: 6'2" **Weight:** 185 lbs.
Bats: right **Throws:** right
Acquired: First-round pick in 6/94 free-agent draft

Player Summary	
Fantasy Value	$1
Card Value	15¢ to 25¢
Will	close games
Can't	rule out bigs
Expect	a good slider
Don't Expect	a starter

Hermanson was the third overall pick in the 1994 draft, and the Padres can have no complaints about their choice. Hermanson quickly signed for a bonus reported to be about $960,000 and reported to the Double-A Texas League. There he picked up eight saves in 16 appearances while compiling an 0.43 ERA. That pretty much settled any question about which role he will fill as a pro. He was named the No. 3 prospect in the league, and he received a promotion to Triple-A Las Vegas. Hermanson comes out of Kent State, where his numbers weren't all that impressive. But he has a superior fastball and a good slider. *Baseball America* ranked him second in velocity among all college draft candidates, with only Paul Wilson, the top pick, considered faster. Hermanson pitched for the U.S. National Team in 1993, picking up seven saves and posting an ERA under 1.00. He was taken in the low rounds by Pittsburgh in a previous draft, but he elected to go to college. The Padres could choose to bring Hermanson to the big leagues if he has a good spring, but he probably should get some more pro experience at Triple-A.

Professional Pitching Register

	W	L	ERA	G	S	IP	H	ER	BB	SO
94 AA	1	0	0.43	16	8	21.0	13	1	6	30
94 AAA	0	0	6.14	7	3	7.1	6	5	5	6

JOSE HERRERA

Position: Outfield
Team: Oakland Athletics
Born: Aug. 30, 1972 Santo Domingo, Dominican Republic
Height: 6′ **Weight:** 165 lbs.
Bats: left **Throws:** left
Acquired: Traded from Blue Jays with Steve Karsay for Rickey Henderson, 8/93

Player Summary	
Fantasy Value	$0
Card Value	20¢ to 30¢
Will	show speed
Can't	get caught so much
Expect	assists
Don't Expect	25 homers

Herrera came to the Athletics to complete a deal in which Rickey Henderson went to the Blue Jays for pitching prospect Steve Karsay. It was a good example of how to rebuild an organization. The Athletics now have two prospects, and they got Henderson back the next year. Last year, Herrera's first full season in the Oakland chain, was spent with Modesto of the Class-A California League, where he hit for a solid average while showing some power. He also has speed to burn and is a fine defensive outfielder. Cal League managers voted Herrera the league's No. 1 prospect in a poll by *Baseball America*. Originally signed by Toronto as an undrafted free agent, Herrera played one year in the Dominican Republic. In 1992, he was MVP in the rookie Pioneer League. When the trade came, Herrera was having a fine season with Hagerstown of the South Atlantic League. He stole 37 bases in 1993, but needed 56 tries to do it—an area to improve. Look for Herrera in the Double-A Southern League in 1995.

Professional Batting Register

	BA	G	AB	R	H	2B	3B	HR	RBI	SB
91 R	.245	40	143	21	35	5	1	1	11	6
91 A	.333	3	9	3	3	1	0	0	2	0
92 R	.272	72	265	45	72	9	2	0	21	32
93 A	.313	99	402	61	126	22	5	5	42	37
94 A	.286	103	370	59	106	20	3	11	56	21

RICHARD HIDALGO

Position: Outfield
Team: Houston Astros
Born: July 2, 1975 Caracas, Venezuela
Height: 6′2″ **Weight:** 175 lbs.
Bats: right **Throws:** right
Acquired: Signed as a nondrafted free agent, 7/91

Player Summary	
Fantasy Value	$0
Card Value	15¢ to 25¢
Will	hit doubles
Can't	rule out power
Expect	good fielding
Don't Expect	Clemente's arm

Hidalgo is being moved through the Houston farm system at what seems to be a deliberate pace, even though his play might warrant more rapid promotions. However, the Astros face no particular urgency with the big-league club doing well and other outfielders ahead of Hidalgo in the organization. Besides, he will only turn 20 in July, giving him plenty of time. No one can quarrel with what he has accomplished; he seems to put up superlative stats wherever he goes. Last year he challenged the Class-A Midwest League record for doubles in a season. At one point in August, he owned more doubles than any two of his Quad City teammates combined. Hidalgo also hit for average and battled for the RBI title among Houston farmhands. He was named the No. 4 prospect in the loop by *Baseball America*. He doesn't have a great strikeout-to-walk ratio, but he can improve on that as he progresses. Long and lean, he has inspired comparisons to Hall of Fame outfielder Roberto Clemente. Hidalgo had 30 assists in 1993, and it is a mystery why people kept running on him.

Professional Batting Register

	BA	G	AB	R	H	2B	3B	HR	RBI	SB
92 R	.310	51	184	20	57	7	3	1	27	14
93 A	.270	111	403	49	109	23	3	10	55	21
94 A	.292	124	476	68	139	47	6	12	76	12

TODD HOLLANDSWORTH

Position: Outfield
Team: Los Angeles Dodgers
Born: April 20, 1973 Dayton, OH
Height: 6'2" **Weight:** 193 lbs.
Bats: left **Throws:** left
Acquired: Third-round pick in 6/91 free-agent draft

Player Summary	
Fantasy Value	$0
Card Value	30¢ to 50¢
Will	be a slugger
Can't	give up at bats
Expect	starts
Don't Expect	top swipe percentage

In 1991, the Dodgers did not pick until the third round. The ballclub made an astute selection when they got the chance. Despite being one of the youngest players in each of the pro leagues that he has played in, Hollandsworth has assembled a resume that seems to point him directly to the majors. Last year at age 21, for instance, he played at Triple-A and showed both power and speed. He exercised better strike-zone judgement and compiled a .343 on-base average. He also had a career-best .479 slugging percentage. Sometimes, the Pacific Coast League can inflate power stats, but Hollandsworth has delivered the long ball at all four pro stops. In 1993, he finished in the Texas League's to p 10 in triples, homers, extra-base hits, and slugging percentage. One year earlier, he led Bakersfield of the Class-A California League in doubles, triples, homers, RBI, and stolen bases. He needs to work on his stolen-base percentage and defense, though he has an adequate arm. Look for Hollandsworth in the Dodger outfield sometime in 1995.

Professional Batting Register

	BA	G	AB	R	H	2B	3B	HR	RBI	SB
91 R	.313	6	16	1	5	0	0	0	0	0
91 A	.236	56	203	34	48	5	1	8	33	11
92 A	.258	119	430	70	111	23	5	13	58	27
93 AA	.251	126	474	57	119	24	9	17	63	24
94 AAA	.285	132	505	80	144	31	5	19	91	15

DAMON HOLLINS

Position: Outfield
Team: Atlanta Braves
Born: June 12, 1974 Fairfield, CA
Height: 5'11" **Weight:** 210 lbs.
Bats: right **Throws:** left
Acquired: Fourth-round pick in 6/92 free-agent draft

Player Summary	
Fantasy Value	$0
Card Value	20¢ to 30¢
Will	produce runs
Can't	swing at bad balls
Expect	compact build
Don't Expect	low strikeouts

In the last decade, Atlanta has produced a series of outfielders who could drive the ball out of the "Launching Pad." One day soon, Hollins's name may be on that list. He is moving through the farm system, hiking his power and production every year. Last year, he played for Durham of the Class-A Carolina League and made the All-Star team. He started the season with a .220 average in his first 12 games, but he began to hit in May. By July, he led Atlanta's minor leaguers in RBI and was among the top home run hitters. In a four-game stretch from June 25 to 28, Hollins homered three times, and at one point he had nine homers over a span of 19 contests. He was named the No. 7 prospect in the loop by *Baseball America*. His big drawback last year was that his strikeout count shot way up. In the field, Hollins has the range to cover center, and he can throw well enough to play right. That makes for pleasant options. He was named the rookie Appalachian League's No. 1 prospect after a strong 1993 season. If he keeps producing the way that he has, Hollins should get a shot at Double-A Greenville in 1995.

Professional Batting Register

	BA	G	AB	R	H	2B	3B	HR	RBI	SB
92 R	.229	49	179	35	41	12	1	1	15	15
93 R	.321	62	240	37	77	15	2	7	51	10
94 A	.270	131	485	76	131	28	0	23	88	12

BRIAN HUNTER

Position: Outfield
Team: Houston Astros
Born: March 5, 1971 Portland, OR
Height: 6'4" **Weight:** 180 lbs.
Bats: right **Throws:** right
Acquired: Second-round pick in 6/89 free-agent draft

Player Summary	
Fantasy Value	$5 to $7
Card Value	30¢ to 50¢
Will	hit triples
Can't	think about homers
Expect	high average
Don't Expect	great eye

Hunter's exceptional season in Triple-A last year demonstrates that he has strong potential to hit for average and steal bases in the majors. He could even add a bit of power and run production, although you have to be a little wary of Pacific Coast League numbers. He made some needed progress on his strikeout-to-walk ratio. In his first five pro seasons, Hunter seldom came close to walking more often than he struck out. Last year, he had 52 strikeouts and 52 bases on balls. He was named the PCL's No. 1 prospect by *Baseball America*, a year after that publication touted him the Texas League's No. 2 prospect. He scored the winning run in last year's Triple-A All-Star Game. With this ability to improve, he reminds people of San Diego's Tony Gwynn. Hunter made his big-league debut on June 27, 1994, and picked up a hit and a stolen base. He led the PCL in batting, hits, stolen bases, and runs scored. Imagine what kind of runs Hunter could score getting on base ahead of Jeff Bagwell.

Professional Batting Register

	BA	G	AB	R	H	2B	3B	HR	RBI	SB
89 R	.170	51	206	15	35	2	0	0	13	12
90 A	.250	127	444	84	111	14	6	0	16	45
91 A	.240	118	392	51	94	15	3	1	30	32
92 A	.299	131	489	62	146	18	9	1	62	39
93 AA	.294	133	523	84	154	22	5	10	52	35
94 AAA	.372	128	513	113	191	28	9	10	51	49
94 NL	.250	6	24	2	6	1	0	0	0	2

TORII HUNTER

Position: Outfield
Team: Minnesota Twins
Born: July 18, 1975 Pine Bluff, AR
Height: 6'2" **Weight:** 200 lbs.
Bats: right **Throws:** right
Acquired: First-round pick in 6/93 free-agent draft

Player Summary	
Fantasy Value	$0
Card Value	20¢ to 30¢
Will	hold his own
Can't	overswing
Expect	slow start
Don't Expect	center field

At age 19, Hunter was thrown in with some pretty strong competition in the Class-A Midwest League, and he came out of it looking just as promising as he did the day the Twins made him the 20th overall pick. He was Fort Wayne's hottest hitter in August with a .316 average, which can only bode well for this year. He displayed some power, notching a slugging percentage of over .400 last summer. While he struck out 80 times—a number that is somewhat worrisome—he accumulated 25 walks and had an on-base percentage over .340. Hunter came to the Twins with the pick they acquired as compensation for the loss of pitcher John Smiley. While he is a long way from achieving the star status that Smiley did, Hunter has the talent to make an impact. He has size, strength, and a fine throwing arm. Drafted out of Pine Bluff, Arkansas, High School, Hunter had planned to go to the University of Arkansas, but he signed instead with the Twins. With Rich Becker a possibility for center field, Hunter figures to wind up in left or right. If he continues to progress at bat, either position would suit the Twins just fine.

Professional Batting Register

	BA	G	AB	R	H	2B	3B	HR	RBI	SB
93 R	.190	28	100	6	19	3	0	0	8	4
94 A	.293	91	335	57	98	17	1	10	50	8

JIMMY HURST

Position: Outfield
Team: Chicago White Sox
Born: March 1, 1972 Druid City, AL
Height: 6'6" **Weight:** 215 lbs.
Bats: right **Throws:** right
Acquired: 12th-round pick in 6/90 free-agent draft

Player Summary	
Fantasy Value	$0
Card Value	12¢ to 20¢
Will	mash the ball
Can't	rival Thomas
Expect	honors
Don't Expect	majors in '95

If Frank Thomas is "The Big Hurt," what is Hurst? After all, he is an inch taller than Thomas, though quite a bit lighter than Thomas's 257 pounds. No matter what you call him, Hurst looks like he might do some damage in the major leagues some day. He certainly did so with Prince William of the Class-A Carolina League last year, ranking among the top White Sox farmhands in home runs and RBI. He also took an impressive 72 bases on balls. He was named to the CL postseason All-Star squad and tabbed by the circuit's No. 2 prospect by *Baseball America*. It was the third straight year that Hurst claimed some honor or another. In 1993, he was named the No. 7 prospect in the Midwest League by *Baseball America*. And the year before that, he led Class-A Utica with six home runs. Out of Three Rivers Junior College in Missouri, Hurst still has a way to go before he's within a phone call of a major-league job. He needs to work on his defense and baserunning, but he is making progress. Expect to see Hurst hitting the ball out of Double-A ballparks in 1995.

Professional Batting Register

	BA	G	AB	R	H	2B	3B	HR	RBI	SB
91 R	.256	36	121	14	31	4	0	0	12	6
92 A	.227	68	220	31	50	8	5	6	35	11
93 A	.244	123	464	79	113	26	0	20	79	15
94 A	.277	127	455	90	126	31	6	25	91	15

JASON ISRINGHAUSEN

Position: Pitcher
Team: New York Mets
Born: Sept. 7, 1972 Brighton, IL
Height: 6'3" **Weight:** 196 lbs.
Bats: right **Throws:** right
Acquired: 44th-round pick in 6/91 free-agent draft

Player Summary	
Fantasy Value	$0
Card Value	20¢ to 30¢
Will	blow hitters away
Can't	top his control
Expect	a knuckle-curve
Don't Expect	many hits

Isringhausen was a key ingredient for a Double-A Binghamton staff that the Mets hope will soon be starting to make an impression in New York. He was joined in Double-A by Bill Pulsipher and Chris Roberts. Isringhausen arrived with little of the fanfare that accompanied his teammates; he even played outfield in junior college. He has a pure power arm, however, and is capable of blowing hitters away. He can throw more than 90 miles an hour and complements the heat with a breaking ball. He also owns a potentially devastating pitch in the knuckle-curve, but he is still working to gain command of that delivery. Isringhausen spent half of the season in the Class-A Florida State League and was named to the FSL postseason All-Star squad. He grew up as a Cardinals fan and says he hated the Mets. He did admire another power pitcher, Nolan Ryan, though. Right now Isringhausen needs more seasoning, but the Mets are happy with his progress and think he could arrive quickly. He may receive a call-up sometime in 1995, with a shot at the rotation in '96.

Professional Pitching Register

	W	L	ERA	G	CG	IP	H	ER	BB	SO
92 R	6	5	3.74	13	1	65.0	58	27	29	49
93 A	7	4	3.29	15	2	90.1	68	33	28	104
94 A	6	4	2.23	14	6	101.0	76	25	27	59
94 AA	5	4	3.02	14	2	92.1	78	31	23	69

DAMIAN JACKSON

Position: Shortstop
Team: Cleveland Indians
Born: Aug. 16, 1973 Los Angeles, CA
Height: 5'10" **Weight:** 160 lbs.
Bats: right **Throws:** right
Acquired: 44th-round pick in 6/91 free-agent draft

Player Summary	
Fantasy Value	$0
Card Value	20¢ to 30¢
Will	get on base
Can't	figure draft spot
Expect	good range
Don't Expect	an easy out

Baseball is sprinkled with stories of players who have excelled despite being acquired low in the draft, and Jackson may be the next big one. When you look at his stats and resume, you wonder what the scouts were thinking when they left him until the 44th round. Even though he was the youngest player on the squad, Jackson was the starting shortstop for the American League farmhands in the Double-A All-Star Game last year, going 1-for-4 from the leadoff position. His appearance in that showcase reflects an athlete who keeps getting better as the competition grows more intense. He was voted the best defensive shortstop and the No. 10 prospect in the Eastern League last year. Jackson needs to cut down on his strikeouts and put the ball in play. He has never stolen fewer than 26 bases in his three pro seasons, showing off his exceptional speed. He can drop a bunt and turn it into a base hit, and he will drive in an occasional run. He led all shortstops in the rookie Appalachian League with a .933 fielding average in 1993, and he was also tops in assists and total chances.

Professional Batting Register

	BA	G	AB	R	H	2B	3B	HR	RBI	SB
92 R	.248	62	226	32	56	12	1	0	23	29
93 A	.269	108	350	70	94	19	3	6	45	26
94 AA	.269	138	531	85	143	29	5	5	46	37

JASON JACOME

Position: Pitcher
Team: New York Mets
Born: Nov. 24, 1970 Tulsa, OK
Height: 6'1" **Weight:** 175 lbs.
Bats: left **Throws:** left
Acquired: 12th-round pick in 6/91 free-agent draft

Player Summary	
Fantasy Value	$1
Card Value	15¢ to 25¢
Will	pitch with men on
Can't	replace Gooden
Expect	low ERA
Don't Expect	orderly games

Jacome gave up two runs in his first major-league inning, but he made up for it by hurling a shutout over the Dodgers in just his second big-league appearance. It was a performance all the more appreciated because it came shortly after Doc Gooden received a 60-day suspension. Jacome (pronounced Hock-O-Me) had turned in a fine season at Triple-A Norfolk before his call-up. He allowed fewer than three walks per nine innings, and he finished the year with the third-best ERA in the International League. He quickly impressed the Mets with his ability to pitch out of trouble. He was a Junior College All-American at Pima County College. In his first year of pro ball, he finished with the third-best ERA among short-season Met farmhands. One year later, he again ranked among the top New York hopefuls, despite getting boosted to a higher level early in the season. Jacome's goatee gives him extra incentive to stay in the big leagues—the Mets won't let their farmhands wear facial hair.

Professional Pitching Register

	W	L	ERA	G	CG	IP	H	ER	BB	SO
91 R	5	4	1.63	12	3	55.1	35	10	13	48
92 A	10	8	2.26	25	6	167.0	138	42	45	115
93 A	6	3	3.08	14	2	99.1	106	34	23	66
93 AA	8	4	3.21	14	0	87.0	85	31	38	56
94 AAA	8	6	2.84	19	4	126.2	138	40	42	80
94 NL	4	3	2.67	8	1	54.0	54	16	17	30

DEREK JETER

Position: Shortstop
Team: New York Yankees
Born: June 26, 1974 Pequannock, NJ
Height: 6'3" **Weight:** 175 lbs.
Bats: right **Throws:** right
Acquired: First-round pick in 6/92 free-agent draft

Player Summary	
Fantasy Value	$4 to $6
Card Value	35¢ to 50¢
Will	star at shortstop
Can't	avoid buildup
Expect	a cannon
Don't Expect	attitude

Jeter has the potential to be an electrifying performer for the Yankees, and he should be a fixture at his position well into the next decade. He is an outstanding hitter with good defensive ability, a fine arm, plus intangibles that can make him a star. At the same time, he is a soft-spoken individual who will probably keep a low profile to cope with the glare of New York's spotlight. That quality could serve him well, because last year's strike brought him some extra attention, and a buildup awaits him in the Big Apple. Last year he started the season with Class-A Tampa, made the Florida State League All-Star Team, and was named the loop's No. 1 prospect by *Baseball America*, which also named him the No. 3 prospect in the Double-A Eastern League in '94. That publication also touted him as the Minor League Player of the Year. Jeter was the No. 2 prospect in the Class-A South Atlantic League in '93, according to *Baseball America*. The sixth overall pick in 1992, he was the first high schooler selected.

Professional Batting Register

	BA	G	AB	R	H	2B	3B	HR	RBI	SB
92 R	.202	47	173	19	35	9	1	3	25	2
92 A	.243	11	37	4	9	0	0	1	4	0
93 A	.295	128	515	85	152	14	11	5	71	18
94 A	.329	69	292	61	96	13	8	0	39	28
94 AA	.377	34	122	17	46	7	2	2	13	12
94 AAA	.349	35	126	25	44	7	1	3	16	10

CHARLES JOHNSON

Position: Catcher
Team: Florida Marlins
Born: July 20, 1971 Ft. Pierce, FL
Height: 6'2" **Weight:** 215 lbs.
Bats: right **Throws:** right
Acquired: First-round pick in 6/92 free-agent draft

Player Summary	
Fantasy Value	$5 to $7
Card Value	30¢ to 50¢
Will	show power
Can't	top him for suspense
Expect	a cornerstone
Don't Expect	stolen bases

Johnson was the first player the Marlins ever took in the amateur draft, and he already has become the club's first draftee to reach the majors. Now it may not be long before he makes an impact. Johnson spent most of last year with Portland of the Double-A Eastern League. He hiked his home run total considerably over the previous season. That feat is especially impressive because there's a perception that if you can hit in the EL, you can hit anywhere. He also notched a .524 slugging percentage. He was touted as the No. 2 prospect in the league by *Baseball America*. Johnson was originally drafted by the Expos in the first round in 1989, but did not sign. The Marlins then took him 28th overall in '92, with the same man—Gary Hughes—doing the scouting. Johnson kept the Marlins in suspense, and was the last of the 1992 first-rounders to sign. His father is a math teacher and baseball coach at Ft. Pierce Westwood High School. His mother is a city accountant. He comes out of the University of Miami, where he was a two-time Golden Spikes Award finalist. Look for Johnson to be in Florida in 1995.

Professional Batting Register

	BA	G	AB	R	H	2B	3B	HR	RBI	SB
93 A	.275	135	488	74	134	29	5	19	94	9
94 AA	.264	132	443	64	117	29	1	28	80	4
94 NL	.455	4	11	5	5	1	0	1	4	0

MARK JOHNSON

Position: Catcher
Team: Chicago White Sox
Born: Sept. 12, 1975 Wheat Ridge, CO
Height: 6′ **Weight:** 185 lbs.
Bats: left **Throws:** right
Acquired: First-round pick in 6/94 free-agent draft

Player Summary	
Fantasy Value	$0
Card Value	15¢ to 25¢
Will	make the throws
Can't	forget offense
Expect	intensity
Don't Expect	big slugging

Johnson was the fourth catcher selected in last year's draft, coming after Paul Konerko (Los Angeles), Jason Varitek (Seattle), and Ramon Castro (Houston). A competitor, Johnson would love to prove that the order was incorrect. He has developed a reputation as an excellent receiver, and he likes to show off his strong arm. Having a good-glove designation is fine as long as it doesn't mean being typecast as a defensive backstop with no stick. He hit for average and power at Warner Robins High in Georgia. He also showed a good eye at the plate during his first pro season, at the White Sox affiliate in the rookie Gulf Coast League. He drew 14 walks and had 15 strikeouts last year, and he was able to compile a .365 on-base percentage. Of course, lefty-hitting catchers are at a premium. His 32 games played aren't enough to draw any conclusions; the real test will come in his first full season. A good athlete, he wrestled and played basketball, in addition to baseball. Johnson signed for a bonus reported at a little more than $500,000.

CHIPPER JONES

Position: Outfield; infield
Team: Atlanta Braves
Born: April 24, 1972 DeLand, FL
Height: 6′3″ **Weight:** 195 lbs.
Bats: both **Throws:** right
Acquired: First-round pick in 6/90 free-agent draft

Player Summary	
Fantasy Value	$6 to $8
Card Value	15¢ to 20¢
Will	play left field
Can't	assume he's sound
Expect	a top talent
Don't Expect	old speed

We list Jones's position as outfield, even though he came up as a shortstop. That's because he had earned a berth in left field before last spring's devastating knee injury. Atlanta manager Bobby Cox also said he had decided to have Jones hitting third in the batting order. Those plans changed when the one-time first overall pick tore a ligament while straining to beat out a grounder. Now the obvious question is whether he can come back and be anything close to what he was. As of late summer, Jones sounded confident that the rehab process had gone well. When healthy, he is a run-producer who will hit for average and pile up extra-base hits. He has never stolen fewer than 23 bases in a full season, but he might have lost some speed. A top-fielding shortstop, he has more than enough range and arm for left field. He had been one of the most highly touted players in the minor leagues. In 1993, Jones was named Rookie of the Year in the International League and was the loop's No. 2 prospect.

Professional Batting Register

	BA	G	AB	R	H	2B	3B	HR	RBI	SB
90 R	.229	44	140	20	32	1	1	1	18	5
91 A	.326	136	473	104	154	24	11	15	98	40
92 A	.277	70	264	43	73	22	1	4	31	10
92 AA	.346	67	266	43	92	17	11	9	42	14
93 AAA	.325	139	536	97	174	31	12	13	89	23
93 NL	.667	8	3	2	2	1	0	0	0	0

Professional Batting Register

	BA	G	AB	R	H	2B	3B	HR	RBI	SB
94 R	.241	32	87	10	21	5	0	0	14	1

KEVIN JORDAN

Position: Second base
Team: Philadelphia Phillies
Born: Oct. 9, 1969 San Francisco, CA
Height: 6'1" **Weight:** 185 lbs.
Bats: right **Throws:** right
Acquired: Traded from Yankees with Bobby Munoz and Ryan Karp for Terry Mulholland and Jeff Patterson, 2/94

Player Summary	
Fantasy Value	$0
Card Value	15¢ to 25¢
Will	hit for extra bases
Can't	wait longer
Expect	solid offense
Don't Expect	top quickness

Jordan is a second baseman who was trapped in the Yankee farm system behind Pat Kelly. Jordan got new life when he came to the Philadelphia chain with pitcher Ryan Karp in the deal that sent pitcher Terry Mulholland to New York. But it wasn't the best of years for Jordan. He opened by going 4-for-20 for Triple-A Scranton before getting his average up to .290 by the end of the season. In mid-1994, he suffered a broken fibula and missed almost two months. All things considered, his numbers weren't bad. Jordan attended the University of Nebraska and was a third-team All-American in 1990. The Yankees drafted him in the 20th round in June of 1990, and he was named to the Topps Short Class-A/Rookie League All-Star squad. He moved up the ladder, making All-Star teams in both the Class-A Florida State League and the Class-A Carolina League. In 1993, he led the Double-A Eastern League with 234 total bases and 53 extra-base hits. Whether the injury robbed Jordan of some quickness for Philadelphia's artificial turf is a question.

Professional Batting Register

	BA	G	AB	R	H	2B	3B	HR	RBI	SB
90 A	.333	73	276	47	92	13	7	4	54	19
91 A	.272	121	448	61	122	25	5	4	53	14
92 A	.311	112	438	67	136	29	8	8	63	6
93 AA	.283	135	513	87	145	33	4	16	87	8
94 AAA	.290	81	314	44	91	22	1	12	57	0

GREG KEAGLE

Position: Pitcher
Team: San Diego Padres
Born: June 28, 1971 Corning, NY
Height: 6'1" **Weight:** 185 lbs.
Bats: right **Throws:** right
Acquired: Sixth-round pick in 6/93 free-agent draft

Player Summary	
Fantasy Value	$0
Card Value	12¢ to 20¢
Will	go in streaks
Can't	be dazzled
Expect	a normal year
Don't Expect	10 straight wins

It looks like the Padres came up with something special when they tabbed this Keagle. After making a respectable pro debut in 1993, he followed up with a spectacular season at Rancho Cucamonga in the Class-A California League last year. He opened with 10 straight victories, before the string was snapped when he lasted just two and one-third innings in a start against Riverside. His heroics earned him a boost to Wichita of the Double-A Texas League, where he proceeded to go 0-for-July. Keagle finally broke the slide with eight innings of four-hit ball on Aug. 3. He wound up making both the midseason and postseason All-Star squads in the Cal League. While his success in Class-A was nice, of more importance was the trouble he found while moving up to Double-A. Was it the percentages catching up with him, the normal adjustments to a higher level, or did he top out? The Padres should get some answers in 1995, when Keagle should return to Double-A. For now, the San Diego brass should enjoy the very interesting selection out of Florida International University.

Professional Pitching Register

	W	L	ERA	G	CG	IP	H	ER	BB	SO
93 A	3	3	3.25	15	1	83.0	80	30	40	77
94 A	11	1	2.05	14	1	92.0	62	21	41	91
94 AA	3	9	6.27	13	0	70.1	84	49	32	57

JASON KENDALL

Position: Catcher
Team: Pittsburgh Pirates
Born: June 26, 1974   San Diego, CA
Height: 6′   **Weight:** 180 lbs.
Bats: right   **Throws:** right
Acquired: First-round pick in 6/92 free-agent draft

Player Summary	
Fantasy Value	$0
Card Value	15¢ to 20¢
Will	make contact
Can't	throw out runners
Expect	solid average
Don't Expect	big power

Kendall came as part of the bountiful early draft that also yielded Trey Beamon and Danny Clyburn. But Kendall was the first of them all, coming with the 23rd overall selection. He is the son of Fred Kendall, a former major-league catcher, and the bloodlines are evident in some of Jason's work behind the plate. On the other hand, he has had trouble throwing out runners for the past two years, and that element of his game must improve or he won't progress much further. Last season was a success in other respects, however. Playing for Class-A Salem, Kendall enjoyed his best offensive season in the pros so far, hitting for average and starting to deliver some sock. He also showed an uncanny knack for contact for someone his age, ranking among the toughest hitters to fan. He had only 21 whiffs in 371 at bats, and he notched 47 walks to register a .406 on-base percentage. He made the Carolina League All-Star team. In his high school days, Kendall assembled a 43-game hitting streak, tying a national record.

BROOKS KIESCHNICK

Position: Outfield
Team: Chicago Cubs
Born: June 6, 1972   Robstown, TX
Height: 6′4″   **Weight:** 228 lbs.
Bats: left   **Throws:** right
Acquired: First-round pick in 6/93 free-agent draft

Player Summary	
Fantasy Value.	$2 to $4
Card Value	35¢ to 50¢
Will	run well
Can't	field well
Expect	streaks
Don't Expect	huge RBI tally

Kieschnick had some problems in his second year of pro ball. Playing for Orlando of the Double-A Southern League, he hit for a respectable average, and he had a .438 slugging percentage and a .332 on-base average. But he had trouble driving in runs. For instance, he hit in 14 straight games from May 14 to 28, but had no homers and just one RBI over that span. He went on another streak from June 9 to 21, hitting in nine of 10 games. But none of it seemed to add up to great run production. This was not what the Cubs had in mind when they took Kieschnick with the 10th pick in the '93 draft. At the time, he was considered one of the top pure hitters in the nation. Out of the University of Texas, he led the country in a variety of offensive categories and was the first two-time winner of the Dick Howser Trophy as the best college baseball player. There have been some reservations about his ability as an outfielder, but he has the arm to play right field. What the Cubs really want to see, however, is Kieschnick hitting the way he has in the past.

Professional Batting Register

	BA	G	AB	R	H	2B	3B	HR	RBI	SB
92 R	.252	34	111	7	28	2	0	0	10	2
93 A	.276	102	366	43	101	17	4	1	40	8
94 A	.318	101	371	68	118	19	2	7	66	14
94 AA	.234	13	47	6	11	2	0	0	6	0

Professional Batting Register

	BA	G	AB	R	H	2B	3B	HR	RBI	SB
93 R	.222	3	9	0	2	1	0	0	0	0
93 A	.182	6	22	1	4	2	0	0	2	0
93 AA	.341	25	91	12	31	8	0	2	10	1
94 AA	.282	126	468	57	132	25	3	14	55	3

DARON KIRKREIT

Position: Pitcher
Team: Cleveland Indians
Born: Aug. 7, 1972 Anaheim, CA
Height: 6'6" **Weight:** 225 lbs.
Bats: right **Throws:** right
Acquired: First-round pick in 6/93 free-agent draft

Player Summary	
Fantasy Value	$0
Card Value	25¢ to 35¢
Will	make his starts
Can't	jump right in
Expect	Double-A
Don't Expect	a pushover

Some players can step right in and make an impact. Others need time to adjust. Based on what happened in 1994, Kirkreit belongs in the latter group. He lost his first five starts with Kinston, but rebounded to become one of the Carolina League's top starters. Through 10 starts, Kirkreit had allowed a batting average of .195, second-stingiest total in the circuit. He made the All-Star team and even pushed his record above .500. League managers tabbed Kirkreit as the No. 4 prospect in a poll by *Baseball America*. Promoted to Double-A, he once again had some problems at the start. A first-team All-American and a member of the U.S. Olympic team in 1992, Kirkreit is out of the University of California at Riverside. He owns school records with 112 strikeouts in a season and a 2.61 career ERA. He has a fastball that can reach 93 mph, and he is composed on the mound. After breaking into pro ball with Watertown of the New York-Penn League, he attended the Florida Instructional League. Kirkreit is the resilient type who will make the majors in time.

Professional Pitching Register

	W	L	ERA	G	CG	IP	H	ER	BB	SO
93 A	4	1	2.23	7	1	36.1	33	9	11	44
94 A	8	7	2.68	20	4	127.2	92	38	40	116
94 AA	3	5	6.22	9	0	46.1	53	32	25	54

STEVE KLINE

Position: Pitcher
Team: Cleveland Indians
Born: Aug. 22, 1972 Sunbury, PA
Height: 6'2" **Weight:** 200 lbs.
Bats: both **Throws:** left
Acquired: Eighth-round pick in 6/93 free-agent draft

Player Summary	
Fantasy Value	$0
Card Value	10¢ to 15¢
Will	take the ball
Can't	stay in Class-A
Expect	good fielder
Don't Expect	low hit ratio

Cleveland can only hope that Kline will offer more seasons just like the one he registered in 1994. Just one year out of the draft, the big lefty may have been the most dominant pitcher in the chain. He ranked among the organization's best in victories, strikeouts, and ERA. Kline worked in the Class-A South Atlantic League, striking out nearly five times as many batters as he walked. He tied the Columbus club record for most victories in a single season. He needs to work on his hits-per-inning ratio, and his ERA was a little high. He comes out of West Virginia University, where he was the Atlantic 10 Conference's Pitcher of the Year in 1993. After the draft, Kline went to Burlington of the rookie Appalachian League, and he was later promoted to Watertown of the New York-Penn League. He put an exclamation point on that season with a shutout in his last start. Kline stayed at the low Class-A level the whole '94 season; he should be making a little more rapid advancement. His 1995 assignment should tell a lot about his future.

Professional Pitching Register

	W	L	ERA	G	CG	IP	H	ER	BB	SO
93 R	1	1	4.91	2	0	7.1	11	4	2	4
93 A	5	4	3.19	13	2	79.0	77	28	12	45
94 A	18	5	3.01	28	2	185.2	175	62	36	174

SCOTT KLINGENBECK

Position: Pitcher
Team: Baltimore Orioles
Born: Feb. 3, 1971 Cincinnati, OH
Height: 6'2" **Weight:** 205 lbs.
Bats: right **Throws:** right
Acquired: Fifth-round pick in 6/92 free-agent draft

Player Summary	
Fantasy Value	$0
Card Value	25¢ to 35¢
Will	be in rotation
Can't	stop base hits
Expect	a competitor
Don't Expect	command woes

Before the 1994 season, the Orioles were saying Klingenbeck had a chance to reach Triple-A by the end of the season. He exceeded that guess, making his major-league debut on June 2. Filling in for the injured Ben McDonald, Klingenbeck went seven innings in an 11-5 triumph over the Tigers. He later spent some time on the disabled list, but it wasn't a bad season for him. He had a pretty good K-to-walk ratio while pitching at Double-A Bowie in the Eastern League. EL batters compiled a .267 batting average against him, however, and his ERA was unacceptable. A star at Ohio State, Klingenbeck had been drafted by the Tigers in the 50th round in 1989, but he passed on signing in favor of school. He was named the Big Ten Freshman of the Year in 1990 and was a second-team All-American as a sophomore. He played for Team USA for two seasons, including the 1991 campaign with Jeffrey Hammonds and Jay Powell, who both later became Baltimore first-rounders. It may not be much longer before Klingenbeck is a member of the Orioles' starting rotation.

Professional Pitching Register

	W	L	ERA	G	CG	IP	H	ER	BB	SO
92 A	3	4	2.63	11	0	68.1	50	20	28	64
93 A	13	4	2.98	23	0	139.0	151	46	35	146
94 AA	7	5	3.63	25	3	143.2	151	58	37	120
94 AL	1	0	3.86	1	0	7.0	6	3	4	5

PAUL KONERKO

Position: Catcher
Team: Los Angeles Dodgers
Born: March 5, 1976 Providence, RI
Height: 6'2" **Weight:** 195 lbs.
Bats: right **Throws:** right
Acquired: First-round pick in 6/94 free-agent draft

Player Summary	
Fantasy Value	$0
Card Value	15¢ to 25¢
Will	hit extra bases
Can't	run well
Expect	long development
Don't Expect	great glove, yet

Even though the Dodgers would seem to be set for years with Mike Piazza behind the plate, they used their first 1994 draft pick on a catcher with power. With the 13th overall choice, they selected Konerko out of Chaparral High School in Scottsdale, Arizona. It was the second time in three years they spent their top pick on a receiver, having gone for Ryan Luzinski in '92. With Piazza at the major-league level and Luzinski in the pipeline, the Dodgers may be watching Konerko's bat to see where it takes his career. So far it has taken him to the attention of the scouts. He hit over .500 with power in his senior year of high school, and he could have gone to a big college program. Instead, he signed for a bonus reported at $775,000 and was sent to Yakima of the short-season Northwest League. Not long afterward, he hit a grand slam, and later in the summer he won Player of the Week honors. He finished the season with a .432 slugging percentage and a .379 on-base percentage, showing both a good batting eye and pretty fair power. He was named the No. 2 prospect in the league by *Baseball America*. The question is whether his defense can match his bat.

Professional Batting Register

	BA	G	AB	R	H	2B	3B	HR	RBI	SB
94 A	.288	67	257	25	74	15	2	6	58	1

ANDY LARKIN

Position: Pitcher
Team: Florida Marlins
Born: June 27, 1974   Chelan, WA
Height: 6'4"   **Weight:** 175 lbs.
Bats: right   **Throws:** right
Acquired: 25th-round pick in 6/92 free-agent draft

Player Summary	
Fantasy Value	$0
Card Value	15¢ to 25¢
Will	throw strikes
Can't	stay healthy
Expect	quality starts
Don't Expect	a sound elbow

Larkin made Marlins history by hurling the organization's first no-hitter. It came on July 25, 1993, in the New York-Penn League, when Larkin shut down Welland to give Elmira a 6-0 win. Later, he went 3-1 in August to be named the organization's Pitcher of the Month. He tied for the lead among short-season pitchers with 12 hit batsmen, indicating a willingness to come inside. Last year he graduated to some fairly advanced competition at the Class-A Midwest League, where he pitched well without his record reflecting it. He won three starts from April 20 to May 1, striking out 23 and allowing only one walk in 21 innings. Larkin fanned 11 against West Michigan on June 6. A strained elbow put him on the disabled list. Despite the time off, he ranked among the organization's leaders in strikeouts. He held ML hitters to a .238 average, and he posted an impressive strikeout-to-walk ratio. Larkin's fastball isn't the quickest, but he is getting the job done. He can throw strikes all day, and he has won some points for his demeanor. He should be headed to high Class-A.

MATT LAWTON

Position: Outfield
Team: Minnesota Twins
Born: Nov. 3, 1971   Gulfport, MS
Height: 5'10"   **Weight:** 180 lbs.
Bats: left   **Throws:** right
Acquired: 13th-round pick in 6/91 free-agent draft

Player Summary	
Fantasy Value	$0
Card Value	20¢ to 30¢
Will	set the table
Can't	hit 15 homers
Expect	high on-base mark
Don't Expect	poor baserunning

Lawton is developing beautifully as he moves through the Twins' system, showing the ability to run and hit for average. Playing for Fort Myers, he was one of the top players in the Class-A Florida State League. He made the All-Star team, and collected three hits in the game. He was also selected to the postseason All-Star squad. Out of Gulf Coast Junior College, Lawton led Fort Myers in July with a .314 average. One July 15, he went 6-for-6 with a double and a triple. At one point in early August, he was leading the league in on-base percentage, and he was third in hits and stolen bases. Lawton was the best baserunner in the Twins' system. Home runs aren't his forte, but he did hit nine in 340 at bats in the Class-A Midwest League in 1993, and it's not out of the question that he could hit a few in the Metrodome. He is willing to take a walk. He accumulated 80 bases on balls last year (for a .407 on-base average), and in 1993 at Ft. Wayne in the Midwest League, he had 65 walks (and a .410 on-base average). Lawton could develop into an effective table-setter in the big leagues.

Professional Pitching Register

	W	L	ERA	G	CG	IP	H	ER	BB	SO
92 R	1	2	5.23	14	0	41.1	41	24	19	20
93 A	5	7	2.97	14	4	88.0	74	29	23	89
94 A	9	7	2.83	21	3	140.0	125	44	27	125

Professional Batting Register

	BA	G	AB	R	H	2B	3B	HR	RBI	SB
92 R	.260	53	173	39	45	8	3	2	26	20
93 A	.285	111	340	50	97	21	3	9	38	23
94 A	.300	122	446	79	134	30	1	7	51	42

MIKE LIEBERTHAL

Position: Catcher
Team: Philadelphia Phillies
Born: Jan. 18, 1972 Glendale, CA
Height: 6′ **Weight:** 179 lbs.
Bats: right **Throws:** right
Acquired: First-round pick in 6/90 free-agent draft

Player Summary	
Fantasy Value	$0
Card Value	7¢ to 10¢
Will	bring solid glove
Can't	overtake Daulton
Expect	strong arm
Don't Expect	power

Lieberthal received his first chance to play in the big leagues when All-Star catcher Darren Daulton went down with an injury last June. Daulton is signed through the 1997 season, and that doesn't leave much room for Lieberthal, the third overall pick in the 1990 draft. That places him in the same situation many other prospects have faced—keep working and try not to worry about things you can't control. So far, he has built an impressive resume, making All-Star teams in the Class-A South Atlantic League and Double-A Eastern League. In 1992, *Baseball America* rated Lieberthal the EL's best defensive catcher and No. 9 prospect. He has shown that he has a great arm during his time in the minor leagues. He also is a good game-caller. The downside is that he doesn't project as even an offensively average major-league catcher. He does a good job of putting the ball in play, and he will take a base on balls. His club will likely be satisfied if he can hit .250 and drive in some key runs.

JOSE LIMA

Position: Pitcher
Team: Detroit Tigers
Born: Sept. 30, 1972 Santiago, Dominican Republic
Height: 6′2″ **Weight:** 170 lbs.
Bats: right **Throws:** right
Acquired: Signed as a free agent, 11/89

Player Summary	
Fantasy Value	$1
Card Value	10¢ to 15¢
Will	show flashes
Can't	seem to win
Expect	solid stuff
Don't Expect	more no-hitters

The strike gave minor leaguers a chance in the spotlight, and Lima certainly shined. Working for the Triple-A Toledo Mud Hens, Lima hurled a no-hitter against the Pawtucket Red Sox on Aug. 17. He missed a perfect game when he walked Eric Wedge to lead off the eighth inning. Lima struck out 13 in the game. Now the problem is to get more consistency out of Lima. In five years, the .500 mark has been elusive for him. He has not reached double figures in wins, even though he has been a starter for most of his career. All his ratios are in order, and in 1992 he led Detroit's minor-league system with 137 strikeouts, so the stuff is there. His control slipped a little last year, as he allowed three and one-half bases on balls per nine innings. In 1993 at Double-A London, he allowed only three walks per game. Perhaps Lima is making pitches at the wrong time. The openings are there in the majors if he can put things together. With his live arm and ability to get strikeouts, Lima may best be suited for a relief role, eventually.

Professional Batting Register

	BA	G	AB	R	H	2B	3B	HR	RBI	SB
90 R	.228	49	184	26	42	9	0	4	22	2
91 A	.302	88	295	41	89	19	0	0	38	1
92 AA	.285	86	309	30	88	16	1	2	37	4
92 AAA	.200	16	45	4	9	1	0	0	4	0
93 AAA	.262	112	382	35	100	17	0	7	40	2
94 AAA	.233	84	296	23	69	16	0	1	32	1
94 NL	.266	24	79	6	21	3	1	1	5	0

Professional Pitching Register

	W	L	ERA	G	CG	IP	H	ER	BB	SO
90 R	3	8	5.02	14	1	75.1	89	42	22	64
91 A	1	4	6.08	22	0	62.2	69	42	27	65
92 A	5	11	3.16	25	5	151.0	132	53	21	137
93 AA	8	13	4.07	27	2	177.0	160	80	59	138
94 AAA	7	9	3.60	23	3	142.1	124	57	48	117
94 AL	0	1	13.50	3	0	6.2	11	10	3	7

CARLTON LOEWER

Position: Pitcher
Team: Philadelphia Phillies
Born: Sept. 21, 1973   Eunice, LA
Height: 6'6"   **Weight:** 204 lbs.
Bats: both   **Throws:** right
Acquired: First-round pick in 6/94 free-agent draft

Player Summary	
Fantasy Value	$0
Card Value	15¢ to 25¢
Will	throw three pitches
Can't	throw strikes
Expect	a fine changeup
Don't Expect	consistency

You often hear horror stories about college athletes not attending class, but in this case the Phillies are glad that their mound hopeful didn't start lugging the books. Loewer, taken as the 23rd overall pick, did not come to contract terms with the Phils until Aug. 23. He had returned to Mississippi State one day earlier, but he did not report to class. Had he done so, he could not have signed with Philadelphia, according to major-league baseball draft rules. Instead, the Phils and Loewer completed the deal. The Phillies sent him to the Florida Instructional League for the fall, but he did not sign in time for any minor-league duty. Loewer has good size. In college he threw three pitches: a fastball that approaches 90 mph, a curveball, and a changeup. But all of his ability did not add up to great stats in college, which probably cost him several slots in the draft. He compiled only a 7-5 record with a 4.63 ERA last year. His biggest problem was control; he walked 53 in 103 innings. The Phillies made this selection on tools, not stats. After being drafted, Loewer collected some innings in the Cape Cod League before coming to terms with Philadelphia.

No minor-league experience

TERRENCE LONG

Position: Outfield; first base
Team: New York Mets
Born: Feb. 29, 1976   Montgomery, AL
Height: 6'1"   **Weight:** 180 lbs.
Bats: left   **Throws:** left
Acquired: First-round pick in 6/94 free-agent draft

Player Summary	
Fantasy Value	$0
Card Value	12¢ to 15¢
Will	show speed, power
Can't	climb quickly
Expect	outfield or first
Don't Expect	quiet buildup

Many high school power hitters have a difficult adjustment to wood bats. Such was not the case with Long, who hit 12 homers in 215 at bats for Kingsport in the rookie Appalachian League. He also displayed a fairly good batting eye. He accumulated 32 walks to notch an on-base average over .330. Long did have an unacceptable 52 strikeouts. Still, it was a promising beginning for a young man who will certainly create some excitement in New York if he can keep it up. Appy League skippers tabbed Long as the No. 4 prospect in the loop, according to a poll by *Baseball America*. Out of Stanhope Elmore High School in Alabama, he arrived as the 20th overall pick, the second of the Mets' two first-rounders. He played both first base and the outfield last year, but it looks like he'll stay in the outfield. He has the speed for the corners, but his arm is best suited to left field. Long was tabbed by *Baseball America* as the second-best pure hitter among high schoolers. He signed for a bonus reported at around $500,000, and Long got right to work on making the choice look good. The Mets are probably looking at him to arrive no earlier than late 1997.

Professional Batting Register

	BA	G	AB	R	H	2B	3B	HR	RBI	SB
94 R	.233	60	215	39	50	9	2	12	39	9

ALBIE LOPEZ

Position: Pitcher
Team: Cleveland Indians
Born: Aug. 18, 1971 Mesa, AZ
Height: 6'2" **Weight:** 210 lbs.
Bats: right **Throws:** right
Acquired: 20th-round pick in 6/91 free-agent draft

Player Summary	
Fantasy Value	$0
Card Value	25¢ to 35¢
Will	vie for rotation
Can't	stay in Triple-A
Expect	a basic arsenal
Don't Expect	wildness

Lopez has spent brief parts of two seasons in the majors, and soon he may be ready to stay. It certainly seems as if he has accomplished all he can in the minors. Last year he was one of the top pitchers in the organization. During one stretch, he went 7-1 in 10 games, and shortly thereafter he was promoted to Cleveland. A starting pitcher virtually all his career, Lopez throws a fastball, a curve, and a changeup, all with good control. He allowed only about two and one-half walks per nine innings last year at Triple-A Charlotte. He comes out of Westwood High School in Mesa, Arizona, and attended Mesa Junior College. In 1992, his second year of pro ball, he was third in the Cleveland organization in strikeouts, fourth in wins, and fifth in ERA. He began the 1993 season in Double-A, and on July 6 received the first of his call-ups. He was named a Double-A midyear All-Star and to the Eastern League's postseason squad. He was also named the No. 6 prospect in the EL that year.

Professional Pitching Register

	W	L	ERA	G	CG	IP	H	ER	BB	SO
91 R	4	5	3.44	13	0	73.1	61	28	23	81
92 A	12	4	3.13	26	2	161.0	136	56	59	161
93 AA	9	4	3.11	16	2	110.0	79	38	47	80
93 AAA	1	0	2.25	3	0	12.0	8	3	2	7
93 AL	3	1	6.16	9	0	49.2	49	34	32	25
94 AAA	13	3	3.94	22	3	144.0	136	63	42	105
94 AL	1	2	4.24	4	1	17.0	20	8	6	18

MARK LORETTA

Position: Shortstop
Team: Milwaukee Brewers
Born: Aug. 14, 1971 Santa Monica, CA
Height: 6' **Weight:** 175 lbs.
Bats: right **Throws:** left
Acquired: Seventh-round pick in 6/93 free-agent draft

Player Summary	
Fantasy Value	$0
Card Value	15¢ to 25¢
Will	make plays
Can't	swing for fences
Expect	contact hitting
Don't Expect	great range

Almost immediately after being drafted, Loretta began making a bid to be the Brewers' shortstop of the future. At two stops in 1993—rookie league and Class-A—he impressed sufficiently to be sent to Double-A to start the 1994 season. Loretta took well to his El Paso assignment, being named to the Double-A All-Star team. At one point early in El Paso's season, he doubled in four straight games. That kind of output might be the exception, however, because extra-base hits don't figure to be Loretta's specialty. He is an above-average defensive shortstop who will have to deliver productive at bats to make up for a lack of power. Later in the year Loretta was promoted to Triple-A New Orleans, but he had a tough time adjusting at the plate. He did finally hit a home run, his first one in more than 350 at bats. Loretta will work a walk and doesn't strike out too much, and that should help him as he goes higher. He had 27 bases on balls and 33 strikeouts last year in Double-A. He should get a call to the bigs in '95 if he succeeds at Triple-A.

Professional Batting Register

	BA	G	AB	R	H	2B	3B	HR	RBI	SB
93 R	.321	6	28	5	9	1	0	1	8	0
93 A	.363	53	201	36	73	4	1	4	31	8
94 AA	.315	77	302	50	95	13	6	0	38	8
94 AAA	.210	43	138	16	29	7	0	1	14	2

ANDREW LORRAINE

Position: Pitcher
Team: California Angels
Born: Aug. 11, 1972 Los Angeles, CA
Height: 6'3" **Weight:** 195 lbs.
Bats: left **Throws:** left
Acquired: Fourth-round pick in 6/93 free-agent draft

Player Summary	
Fantasy Value	$1
Card Value	15¢ to 25¢
Will	get another shot
Can't	throw gopher ball
Expect	good makeup
Don't Expect	a 10.61 ERA

Angel scouts did their work on Lorraine, who was in the majors just 14 months after being drafted. Chances are he'll never forget the circumstances, either. He went 0-2 with a 10.61 ERA, allowing seven home runs and a .683 slugging percentage. Shortly after that, the lefty was sent down just before the strike started. Back in Vancouver, he extended his Triple-A Pacific Coast League winning streak to six games with victories over Tacoma and Edmonton. Lorraine was not overly successful at Stanford, but he had size and ability, and the Halos took a chance. He made an impact in pro ball, hurling complete games in three of his six starts in the Northwest League. The Angels thought so much of him that they jumped him all the way to Triple-A in 1994. He pitched two innings in the Triple-A All-Star Game. *Baseball America* named him the best pitching prospect and the No. 3 prospect overall in the PCL. He has a four-pitch repertoire. Lorraine allowed just over two bases on balls per nine innings in Triple-A last year. He had better leave the gopher ball behind—he allowed 13 homers in 1994.

Professional Pitching Register

	W	L	ERA	G	CG	IP	H	ER	BB	SO
93 A	4	1	1.29	6	3	42.0	33	6	6	39
94 AAA	12	4	3.42	22	4	142.0	156	54	34	90
94 AL	0	2	10.61	4	0	18.2	30	22	11	10

MATT LUKE

Position: Outfield; first base
Team: New York Yankees
Born: Feb. 26, 1971 Long Beach, CA
Height: 6'5" **Weight:** 225 lbs.
Bats: left **Throws:** left
Acquired: Eighth-round pick in 6/92 free-agent draft

Player Summary	
Fantasy Value	$0
Card Value	15¢ to 20¢
Will	reach seats
Can't	stall at Double-A
Expect	some speed
Don't Expect	all or nothing

Luke offers the prospect of left-handed power in Yankee Stadium, if his numbers in 1994 are any indication. Splitting the season between Tampa of the Florida State League and Albany of the Eastern League, he ranked among the top Yankee farmhands both in homers and RBI. He had some rough spots along the way, including a stretch on the disabled list early in the season, but he managed to be named to the midseason FSL All-Star team. He homered in four straight games June 7 to 10 to be named FSL Player of the Week. He had 28 bases on balls and 27 strikeouts in the FSL, showing a good batting eye for a big man. He also had 28 walks at Albany. Luke went on an August tear in Double-A, during which he hit well over .300. Even with his size, he has enough quickness to steal an occasional base. Luke went to the University of California and twice earned All-Pac-10 honors. In 1992, he paced the New York-Penn League with seven triples. He led all Yankee minor leaguers with 157 hits in 1993, and five came when he hit for the cycle against Asheville.

Professional Batting Register

	BA	G	AB	R	H	2B	3B	HR	RBI	SB
92 A	.247	69	271	30	67	11	7	2	34	4
93 A	.286	135	549	83	157	37	5	21	91	11
94 A	.306	57	222	52	68	11	2	16	42	4
94 AA	.284	63	236	34	67	11	2	8	40	6

JOSE MALAVE

Position: Outfield
Team: Boston Red Sox
Born: May 31, 1971 Cumana, Venezuela
Height: 6'2" **Weight:** 195 lbs.
Bats: right **Throws:** right
Acquired: Signed as a nondrafted free agent, 8/89

Player Summary	
Fantasy Value	$1
Card Value	30¢ to 40¢
Will	show power
Can't	think about hand
Expect	Triple-A
Don't Expect	durability

Malave bounced back from a broken hand to make an All-Star team for the third straight year. He was selected to the Double-A squad and at 23 was the youngest outfielder among the American League standouts. Around the time of the game, he was cruising along with 14 homers and 56 RBI, and was leading the Eastern League with 47 extra-base hits. Malave was named the No. 7 prospect in the EL by *Baseball America*. He notched a .563 slugging percentage and a .369 on-base percentage last year. One year earlier, Malave was also headed for a good year, but he was hit on the right hand by a Paul Shuey pitch and sidelined for the season. By then, however, Malave had already established himself as a player to watch. Playing for Lynchburg of the Carolina League, Malave ranked among the leaders in Boston's farm system in batting average, home runs, and RBI. He made the All-Star team, going 2-for-3 with a home run and an RBI. He had also made an All-Star team in 1992, when *Baseball America* named him to its final New York-Penn League squad.

Professional Batting Register

	BA	G	AB	R	H	2B	3B	HR	RBI	SB
90 A	.138	13	29	4	4	1	0	0	3	1
91 R	.322	37	146	24	47	4	2	2	28	6
92 A	.311	73	293	45	91	9	1	12	46	8
93 A	.301	82	312	42	94	27	1	8	54	2
94 AA	.299	122	465	87	139	37	7	24	92	4

ANGEL MARTINEZ

Position: Catcher
Team: Toronto Blue Jays
Born: Oct. 3, 1972 Santo Domingo, Dominican Republic
Height: 6'4" **Weight:** 200 lbs.
Bats: left **Throws:** right
Acquired: Signed as a nondrafted free agent, 1/90

Player Summary	
Fantasy Value	$0
Card Value	15¢ to 25¢
Will	throw out runners
Can't	expose throwing hand
Expect	wild swings
Don't Expect	Delgado's power

Not too long ago, the Blue Jays had a catching prospect make the All-Star team in the Class-A Florida State League. His name was Carlos Delgado, and he's already reached the majors. Now it's Martinez, who made the FSL All-Star team last year. The similarities end there. He does not figure to hit with the power that Delgado can, but Martinez will compensate by being a better man with the glove. His arm has gained attention. He threw out 47.5 percent of the runners who tested him in the Class-A South Atlantic League in 1993. A year before that, he cut down 49.4 percent in the Pioneer League. He could be a serviceable offensive player, if he improves his batting eye and makes contact. He had 22 walks and 79 strikeouts last year, and he notched a .310 on-base percentage. FSL skippers tabbed him the loop's No. 8 prospect in a poll by *Baseball America*. Martinez missed a chunk of the '93 season with a fractured right hand suffered when he was struck by a foul tip.

Professional Batting Register

	BA	G	AB	R	H	2B	3B	HR	RBI	SB
91 R	.173	34	98	8	17	1	0	2	16	0
91 A	.184	12	38	3	7	1	0	0	3	0
92 R	.252	57	206	27	52	15	0	4	39	0
92 A	.200	4	15	4	3	1	0	2	4	0
93 A	.263	94	338	41	89	16	1	9	46	1
94 A	.260	122	450	50	117	14	6	7	52	1

FELIX MARTINEZ

Position: Shortstop
Team: Kansas City Royals
Born: May 18, 1974   Nagua, Dominican Republic
Height: 6′   **Weight:** 170 lbs.
Bats: both   **Throws:** right
Acquired: Signed as a nondrafted free agent, 3/93

Player Summary	
Fantasy Value	$0
Card Value	15¢ to 25¢
Will	switch-hit
Can't	overswing
Expect	nice speed
Don't Expect	a gap hitter

You can tell a lot about Martinez's chances by examining what he's done in pro ball, where he's done it, and at what age he's done it. He entered the tough Class-A Carolina League when he was only 19 years old and established himself as a force. *Baseball America* gave him the nod as the league's top shortstop arm, and he has a soft pair of hands. He also was more than respectable at the plate. He accumulated a .343 slugging percentage and a .322 on-base percentage. He also ran well enough to steal in double figures for the second time in as many pro seasons. In short, Martinez looks like the kind of player who could fit in well on the large artificial surface at Royals Stadium. His switch-hitting adds an element of versatility, and his speed and arm will help make the field a little smaller. Martinez has been a quick learner who played winter ball in his native country after the 1993 season. He projects as a singles hitter who must keep his swing short to avoid strikeouts. That was his biggest problem in 1994. Martinez accumulated 91 strikeouts, a figure which is much too high. He might add some punch as he fills out.

Professional Batting Register

	BA	G	AB	R	H	2B	3B	HR	RBI	SB
93 R	.255	57	165	23	42	5	1	0	12	22
94 A	.268	117	400	65	107	16	4	2	43	19

RAY McDAVID

Position: Outfield
Team: San Diego Padres
Born: July 20, 1971   San Diego, CA
Height: 6′3″   **Weight:** 200 lbs.
Bats: left   **Throws:** right
Acquired: Ninth-round pick in 6/89 free-agent draft

Player Summary	
Fantasy Value	$2 to $4
Card Value	20¢ to 30¢
Will	bring tools
Can't	drive in runs
Expect	occasional flashes
Don't Expect	impact

McDavid's arrival has been eagerly awaited ever since he tore up the Class-A California League in 1992. Trouble is, that's the last time he made any real noise. Even in the Pacific Coast League, a hitter's paradise, he didn't pile up power numbers last year. He accumulated a .429 slugging percentage, which isn't bad but not what the Pads had hoped. McDavid has a good eye and will take a walk. His .370 on-base average came courtesy of his 67 bases on balls. So, even though McDavid looks like a supremely gifted athlete, it's time to wonder what kind of impact he might make in the majors. McDavid was a star basketball and football player in high school. To illustrate his athletic ability, consider that he did not even play baseball in his senior year in high school, but he still was able to make the team at Arizona Western College and get the Padres' attention. He blossomed in 1992, leading the California League in home run frequency. McDavid moved up to the Texas League in 1993, and declined in runs, doubles, homers, RBI, and steals.

Professional Batting Register

	BA	G	AB	R	H	2B	3B	HR	RBI	SB
90 R	.146	13	41	4	6	0	2	0	1	3
91 A	.247	127	425	93	105	16	9	10	45	60
92 A	.276	123	428	94	118	22	5	24	94	43
93 AA	.270	126	441	65	119	18	5	11	55	33
94 AAA	.271	128	476	85	129	24	6	13	62	24
94 NL	.250	9	28	2	7	1	0	0	2	1

RYAN McGUIRE

Position: First base
Team: Boston Red Sox
Born: Nov. 23, 1971 Wilson, NC
Height: 6'2" **Weight:** 210 lbs.
Bats: left **Throws:** left
Acquired: Third-round pick in 6/93 free-agent draft

Player Summary	
Fantasy Value	$0
Card Value	60¢ to 80¢
Will	make noise at bat
Can't	start poorly
Expect	average, power
Don't Expect	Vaughn's replacement

At first glance, McGuire's numbers say he didn't have a very strong 1994 campaign. However, he had a robust second half, hitting close to .300. A patient hitter, he also showed fine gap power. He had 77 strikeouts last year and 79 bases on balls. He was able to accumulate a .371 on-base average. The only problem is the perception of McGuire's role. He's a big, strong lefty-swinging first baseman who can reach the right-field seats at Fenway. But his .393 slugging percentage in 1994 is not what the BoSox were expecting. They are looking for huge power. McGuire was drafted out of UCLA, where he enjoyed a spectacular '93 campaign. He led the NCAA Division I with 26 homers and finished second with 91 RBI. He also led his team with a .376 batting average. After being drafted, he was sent to the Class-A Florida State League and made some noise. McGuire remains a top Red Sox prospect, though they'd like to see him start faster in '95; he needs to have a big year in Double-A. The Red Sox have Mo Vaughn, but it doesn't hurt to have depth in the organization.

Professional Batting Register

	BA	G	AB	R	H	2B	3B	HR	RBI	SB
93 A	.324	58	213	23	69	12	2	4	38	2
94 A	.272	137	489	70	133	29	0	10	73	10

JOSE MERCEDES

Position: Pitcher
Team: Milwaukee Brewers
Born: March 5, 1971 El Seibo, Dominican Republic
Height: 6'1" **Weight:** 180 lbs.
Bats: right **Throws:** right
Acquired: Rule 5 draft pick from Orioles, 12/93

Player Summary	
Fantasy Value	$1
Card Value	8¢ to 12¢
Will	be a reliever
Can't	get in trouble
Expect	some gopher balls
Don't Expect	many hits

The Brewers made a shrewd move when they plucked Mercedes out of the Baltimore farm system after what was statistically a mediocre season. However, the Brewers made a major adjustment, converting him from a starter to a reliever, and that made all the difference. Mercedes made his major-league debut on May 31, 1994, going five and one-third scoreless innings against Texas. Mercedes was originally signed by the Orioles in 1989, and he spent two seasons in the Dominican Summer League. He opened the 1992 season in rookie ball, and was promoted to the Midwest League in July. He jumped another level in 1993, and got some experience when he pitched (and lost) game three of the Eastern League playoff semifinals. He did get three starts last year at Triple-A New Orleans, but he will probably stay in the bullpen in the show. In his first several big-league outings, Mercedes managed to keep his ERA down despite walking more than he struck out, allowing one-third of the batters he faced to reach base.

Professional Pitching Register

	W	L	ERA	G	S	IP	H	ER	BB	SO
92 R	2	3	1.78	8	0	35.1	31	7	13	21
92 A	3	2	2.66	8	0	47.1	40	14	15	45
93 AA	6	8	4.78	26	0	147.0	170	78	65	75
94 AA	2	0	4.66	3	0	9.2	13	5	4	8
94 AAA	0	0	4.91	3	0	18.1	19	10	8	7
94 AL	2	0	2.32	19	0	31.0	22	8	16	11

RALPH MILLIARD

Position: Infield
Team: Florida Marlins
Born: Dec. 30, 1973 Willemstad, Curacao
Height: 5'11" **Weight:** 170 lbs.
Bats: right **Throws:** right
Acquired: Signed as a nondrafted free agent, 8/93

Player Summary	
Fantasy Value	$0
Card Value	10¢ to 15¢
Will	hit doubles
Can't	be a slugger
Expect	discipline
Don't Expect	a shortstop

It isn't every day that you see a prospect who was born in Curacao, but somehow Milliard got on a road that he hopes will take him to Miami. Milliard, who lives in Soest, Netherlands, played his first full season of minor-league ball last year, and he made quite an impression. Not only did he make the Class-A Midwest League All-Star team, but he went 1-for-2 in the game. An infielder whose future is probably at second, Milliard ranked among the top hitters in the Florida chain for much of the season. He also displayed a knack for collecting doubles. He showed some surprising power for a middle infielder. After not homering in 192 at bats in 1993, he knocked eight round-trippers last year. His batting eye also seemed to improve. He accumulated 68 bases on balls. Milliard played for the Netherlands Junior National Team in 1989 and 1990, and for the national squad in 1991. Signed by European scout Tim Schmidt, Milliard reported to rookie ball in 1993. He led Gulf Coast League second basemen in putouts, assists, total chances, and fielding percentage. He only struck out once every 13½ plate appearances.

Professional Batting Register

	BA	G	AB	R	H	2B	3B	HR	RBI	SB
93 R	.234	53	192	35	45	15	0	0	25	11
94 A	.297	133	515	97	153	34	2	8	67	10

DOUG MILLION

Position: Pitcher
Team: Colorado Rockies
Born: Oct. 13, 1975 Ft. Thomas, KY
Height: 6'4" **Weight:** 175 lbs.
Bats: left **Throws:** left
Acquired: First-round pick in 6/94 free-agent draft

Player Summary	
Fantasy Value	$0
Card Value	15¢ to 25¢
Will	show live heat
Can't	hang curve
Expect	strikeouts
Don't Expect	Denver in '95

Million failed to live up to his name after being drafted, signing for $900,000. But time is on his side. If he pitches the way the scouts feel he can, his middle name might one day be "Multi." The seventh overall pick, Million comes out of Sarasota High School in Florida, bringing outstanding control and a breaking ball that gets your attention. His ability was too much for the first batters to face him in the pros. Assigned to rookie ball in the Arizona League, Million made three starts and struck out 19 men in 12 innings while walking only three. After being promoted to Bend of the short-season Northwest League, he fanned 20 in his first 14 innings. He held Class-A batters to a .227 average, which is impressive for such a young hurler pitching against many players who are college-age. The strikeouts were nothing new, as he had fanned more than one and one-half batters per inning as a prep. He was named *Baseball America*'s High School Player of the Year last year. Such dominance won't continue as he moves up. That's where an ability to pitch will come in handy, and indications are that he has it.

Professional Pitching Register

	W	L	ERA	G	CG	IP	H	ER	BB	SO
94 R	1	0	1.50	3	0	12.0	8	2	3	19
94 A	5	3	2.34	10	0	57.2	50	15	21	75

CHAD MOTTOLA

Position: Outfield
Team: Cincinnati Reds
Born: Oct. 15, 1971 Augusta, GA
Height: 6'3" **Weight:** 220 lbs.
Bats: right **Throws:** right
Acquired: First-round pick in 6/92 free-agent draft

Player Summary	
Fantasy Value	$0
Card Value	30¢ to 40¢
Will	show an arm
Can't	get injured again
Expect	rebound in '95
Don't Expect	a burner

In looking at Mottola's chances, it might be best to throw out last year. That's probably what he'd like to do, because he hardly ever got started. In the midst of a 3-for-22 slump in early May, Mottola fouled a ball off his foot and was placed on the disabled list. Returning on May 28, he experienced a power shortage, collecting only three extra-base hits in his first 17 games back. Mottola went three months—from April 22 to July 23—without hitting a home run. Things did pick up later, as he raised his average 28 points over 17 games spanning July and August. He finished with a .346 slugging percentage and a poor .294 on-base average. For all the problems, Mottola remains a talent; he threw out two runners trying to score on Opening Night. His stolen base totals have been modest. Out of the University of Central Florida, Mottola led the Class-A Carolina League in RBI in 1993. That production was absent last year, and the Reds may keep him in Double-A long enough to see if it returns. While it may be too early to say that it is a make-or-break year for him, Mottola needs to rebound.

Professional Batting Register

	BA	G	AB	R	H	2B	3B	HR	RBI	SB
92 R	.286	57	213	53	61	8	3	12	37	12
93 A	.280	137	493	76	138	25	3	21	91	13
94 AA	.241	118	402	44	97	19	1	7	41	9

PHIL NEVIN

Position: Third base; outfield
Team: Houston Astros
Born: Jan. 19, 1971 Fullerton, CA
Height: 6'2" **Weight:** 180 lbs.
Bats: right **Throws:** right
Acquired: First-round pick in 6/92 free-agent draft

Player Summary	
Fantasy Value	$0
Card Value	30¢ to 50¢
Will	hit bigs in '95
Can't	show speed
Expect	line drives
Don't Expect	No. 1 impact

The first overall pick in the draft, Nevin has spent two years in Triple-A, putting up respectable, though not spectacular, numbers. He had a .393 slugging percentage and a .343 on-base average at Tucson last year, though both were down from his 1993 showing at Tucson. He had a .413 slugging percentage and a .359 on-base average that year and was named the No. 7 prospect in the PCL by *Baseball America*. He can play both third base and left field. Nevin is a fine fielder at third base, with good range and a solid arm. He looks like he could fit in well on the Astrodome's artificial surface, because he's more of a line-drive hitter than a home run man. He's not much of a basestealer. After being picked in the draft, he elected to play for the U.S. Olympic Team in Barcelona. When he returned, he attended the Instructional League. Nevin batted .402 with 22 homers for the Cal State-Fullerton team that was runner-up in the 1992 College World Series. He also lettered three years as a kicker in football, being named best freshman kicker in the country by *The Sporting News* in 1989.

Professional Batting Register

	BA	G	AB	R	H	2B	3B	HR	RBI	SB
93 AAA	.286	123	448	67	128	21	3	10	93	8
94 AAA	.263	118	445	67	117	20	1	12	79	3

MARC NEWFIELD

Position: Outfield
Team: Seattle Mariners
Born: Oct. 19, 1972 Sacramento, CA
Height: 6'4" **Weight:** 205 lbs.
Bats: right **Throws:** right
Acquired: First-round pick in 6/90 free-agent draft

Player Summary	
Fantasy Value.................	$4 to $6
Card Value	15¢ to 20¢
Will.........................	stick this year
Can't.......................	rule out first
Expect	tape-measure shots
Don't Expect	Ken Griffey Jr.

The Mariners have displayed some magnificent talent in their outfield in recent years, and they may be adding even more in 1995. Newfield is a big, strong power hitter who could have some fun in the cozy Kingdome. He's seen action in the majors in each of the last two years, and this could be the season when he sticks. He played most of 1994 at Triple-A Calgary, excelling in all three Triple Crown categories. He also put up a .593 slugging percentage and a .413 on-base average. He struck out only 58 times last year. He was named the No. 6 prospect in the Pacific Coast League by *Baseball America*. The sixth overall pick in the 1990 grab bag, Newfield put his talent on display in his first pro game, hitting a 500-foot home run. He was later named to the Arizona League All-Star team. He also made the All-Star squad in 1991, this time in the Cal League. Newfield encountered foot problems and underwent surgery in 1992. A fast start in Double-A in 1993 earned him a call-up to the majors.

Professional Batting Register

	BA	G	AB	R	H	2B	3B	HR	RBI	SB
90 R	.313	51	192	34	60	13	2	6	38	4
91 A	.300	125	440	64	132	22	3	11	68	12
91 AA	.231	6	26	4	6	3	0	0	2	0
92 AA	.247	45	162	15	40	12	0	4	19	0
93 AA	.307	91	336	48	103	18	0	19	51	1
93 AL	.227	22	66	5	15	3	0	1	7	0
94 AAA	.349	107	430	89	150	44	2	19	83	0
94 AL	.184	12	38	3	7	1	0	1	4	0

MELVIN NIEVES

Position: Outfield
Team: San Diego Padres
Born: Dec. 28, 1971 San Juan, Puerto Rico
Height: 6'2" **Weight:** 210 lbs.
Bats: both **Throws:** right
Acquired: Traded from Braves with Vince Moore and Donnie Elliott for Fred McGriff, 7/93

Player Summary	
Fantasy Value.................	$2 to $4
Card Value	15¢ to 20¢
Will	be solid
Can't	match McGriff
Expect	streaks
Don't Expect	All-Star status

After seven years of pro ball, Nieves finally looks as if he's ready to make a contribution in the major leagues. At least the Padres hope so, because he may be the most significant return on a deal in which they sent slugger Fred McGriff to Atlanta. Nieves probably won't be another Mc-Griff—there aren't many of them—but he does project as a regular outfielder who can hit for both average and power. He put up good numbers at Las Vegas of the Pacific Coast League last year, notching a .564 slugging percentage and a .403 batting average. Those numbers include a slump during which he hit only .200 with four homers from the All-Star break through Aug. 16. Fans should expect streaks like that from Nieves. He had 138 Ks last year, a strikeout ratio that he needs to cut. Nieves was originally signed by Atlanta as a free agent in 1988 at the age of 16.

Professional Batting Register

	BA	G	AB	R	H	2B	3B	HR	RBI	SB
88 R	.170	56	176	16	30	6	0	1	12	5
89 R	.277	64	231	43	64	16	3	9	46	6
90 A	.283	126	459	60	130	24	7	9	59	10
91 A	.264	64	201	31	53	11	0	9	25	3
92 A	.302	31	106	18	32	9	1	8	32	4
92 AA	.283	100	350	61	99	23	5	18	76	6
92 NL	.211	12	19	0	4	1	0	0	1	0
93 AAA	.289	121	432	69	125	20	4	17	60	6
93 NL	.191	19	47	4	9	0	0	2	3	0
94 AAA	.308	111	406	81	125	17	6	25	92	1
94 NL	.263	10	19	2	5	1	0	1	4	0

C.J. NITKOWSKI

Position: Pitcher
Team: Cincinnati Reds
Born: March 9, 1973 Suffren, NY
Height: 6'2" **Weight:** 185 lbs.
Bats: left **Throws:** left
Acquired: First-round pick in 6/94 free-agent draft

Player Summary	
Fantasy Value	$0
Card Value	20¢ to 30¢
Will	throw knuckle-curve
Can't	hit 90
Expect	majors quickly
Don't Expect	wildness

Nitkowski made the transition from college ball to Double-A with minimal problems. He even had a possible shot at the majors before the strike hit. He comes out of St. John's, which has produced, among others, Frank Viola and John Franco. No one knows whether Nitkowski's career can match theirs, but he looks like someone who can pitch in the majors. He has only a modest fastball, but he is able to bring a slider and a changeup. His ace in the hole, though, is a knuckle-curve that could be a devastating pitch if used correctly in combination with the other pitches. He used his whole arsenal to go 5-4 with a 1.59 ERA for St. John's, en route to being the top prospect from the Northeast. After being taken ninth overall in the draft, Nitkowski signed for an estimated $650,000 and was assigned to Chattanooga of the Double-A Southern League. In his pro debut, he lasted only two and two-thirds innings, but things got better. He had a 6-3 record with a 3.50 ERA. However, his control was not exceptional, as he walked 40 in his 74⅔ innings, or almost five per game. A location-oriented left-hander, Nitkowski is going to have to throw strikes.

TROT NIXON

Position: Outfield
Team: Boston Red Sox
Born: April 11, 1974 Durham, NC
Height: 6'2" **Weight:** 196 lbs.
Bats: left **Throws:** left
Acquired: First-round pick in 6/93 free-agent draft

Player Summary	
Fantasy Value	$0
Card Value	70¢ to $1
Will	hit the ball
Can't	play with bad back
Expect	conservative pace
Don't Expect	any pitching

Nixon was enjoying an All-Star season in his first pro campaign when he went on the disabled list with a lower back problem. Back pains are never good news, so the Red Sox will only feel relieved when they see the seventh overall pick in the '93 draft return to action. When healthy, Nixon is one of the game's top prospects. He has the potential for tremendous offensive production, as shown by his final season at New Hanover High School in Wilmington, North Carolina. He hit .519 with 12 homers and 56 RBI to help secure the 4-A state title. Of course, his 12-0 pitching record with a 0.40 ERA had something to do with that, too. He didn't sign with Boston until the end of the season in 1993, so his first exposure to pro ball was in the Florida Instructional League that year. Nixon hit .366 with 13 RBI in 24 games in his first pro action. He also established himself in full-season Class-A in 1994, making the All-Star team in the Carolina League. He had a .428 slugging percentage and a .357 on-base average. He walked 44 times and struck out 53 times. CL skippers labelled him the No. 6 project in the loop, according to a poll in *Baseball America*.

Professional Pitching Register

	W	L	ERA	G	CG	IP	H	ER	BB	SO
94 AA	6	3	3.50	14	0	74.2	61	29	40	60

Professional Batting Register

	BA	G	AB	R	H	2B	3B	HR	RBI	SB
94 A	.246	71	264	33	65	12	0	12	43	10

SERGIO NUNEZ

Position: Second base
Team: Kansas City Royals
Born: Jan. 3, 1975 Santo Domingo, Dominican Republic
Height: 5′11″ **Weight:** 155 lbs.
Bats: right **Throws:** right
Acquired: Signed as a nondrafted free agent, 11/91

Player Summary	
Fantasy Value	. . . . $0
Card Value	. . . . 10¢ to 15¢
Will	. . . . hit .300
Can't	. . . . show pop
Expect	. . . . great instincts
Don't Expect	. . . . a shortstop

Nunez turned in the kind of season that can keep a farm director warm through the winter cold. Nunez's exploits in short-season ball raised such expectations that his play in 1995 should be well worth watching. Playing in the rookie Gulf Coast League in '94, Nunez won the batting title by 35 points over his nearest pursuer while helping the Royals dominate the Western Division. Though he was a shortstop before coming into pro baseball, he played second base last year and made the All-Star team there. He averaged more than a run per game, and he walked more than twice as often as he struck out. His five home runs tied him for the team lead and raised the chance of real power once he puts on more muscle. A superior fielder, he also showed speed on the basepaths. Gulf Coast League managers named Nunez the No. 1 prospect in the loop, according to *Baseball America*. It was his first season in pro ball in the United States, but he played for two years at Salcedo in the Dominican Summer League—which is a rookie level. He batted over .300 both years. A hike to full-season Class-A ball seems certain. The only question is whether it will be high or low Class-A.

Professional Batting Register

	BA	G	AB	R	H	2B	3B	HR	RBI	SB
94 R	.397	59	232	64	92	9	7	5	24	37

ALEX OCHOA

Position: Outfield
Team: Baltimore Orioles
Born: March 29, 1972 Miami Lakes, FL
Height: 6′ **Weight:** 185 lbs.
Bats: right **Throws:** right
Acquired: Third-round pick in 6/91 free-agent draft

Player Summary	
Fantasy Value	. . . . $0
Card Value	. . . . 25¢ to 35¢
Will	. . . . advance in '95
Can't	. . . . hit 25 homers
Expect	. . . . great arm
Don't Expect	. . . . Double-A

Ochoa is a multitalented prospect who can run, hit with power, and throw. He has been moving deliberately through the farm system, and he should be within a phone call of the majors in 1995. Playing at Bowie of the Double-A Eastern League last year, Ochoa showed a good eye at the plate, hit the ball out of the park, and stole some bases. He had a .437 slugging percentage and a .355 on-base average. On June 5, he and teammate Brent Miller each homered twice in the fourth inning against Harrisburg. Ochoa's arm was rated best among outfielders in the league by *Baseball America*. That publication also named him the No. 8 prospect in the loop. It was his fourth straight solid year in the pros, and came after an award-winning season. In 1993, Ochoa captured the Brooks Robinson Award given to the best hitter in the organization. He was also selected to the Carolina League's All-Star team. He was named the CL's No. 2 prospect by *Baseball America* that year. Later, he was sent to Bowie for the playoffs, but went 0-for-6.

Professional Batting Register

	BA	G	AB	R	H	2B	3B	HR	RBI	SB
91 R	.307	53	179	26	55	8	3	1	30	11
92 A	.295	133	499	65	147	22	7	1	59	31
93 A	.276	137	532	84	147	29	5	13	90	34
94 AA	.301	134	519	77	156	25	2	14	82	28

JOSE OLIVA

Position: Third base; infield
Team: Atlanta Braves
Born: March 3, 1971   San Pedro de Macoris, Dominican Republic
Height: 6'3"   **Weight:** 215 lbs.
Bats: right   **Throws:** right
Acquired: Traded from Rangers for Charlie Leibrandt and Pat Gomez, 12/92

Player Summary	
Fantasy Value	$1
Card Value	30¢ to 40¢
Will	go on streaks
Can't	make contact
Expect	solid fielding
Don't Expect	consistency

It appears that Oliva is a front-runner to capture the third base job for the Atlanta Braves in 1995 from Terry Pendleton. While he hasn't performed in the same spotlight that Pendleton has, Oliva can also offer some gifts. He is a power hitter who can drive in runs. He had a .493 slugging percentage last year with Triple-A Richmond, netting 64 RBI in 99 games. *Baseball America* named him the No. 4 prospect in the Triple-A International League last year. He spent 1993 with Richmond. There he showed how streaky he can be; 28 of his 65 RBI came in seven games; he produced 37 RBI in the other 118 contests. Much of that inconsistency can be blamed on strikeouts. During his career he has fanned more than three times as often as he has walked. He had 92 Ks and 25 walks last year at Triple-A. He was named Best Defensive Third Baseman in the Double-A Texas League in 1992.

Professional Batting Register

	BA	G	AB	R	H	2B	3B	HR	RBI	SB
88 R	.214	27	70	5	15	3	0	1	11	0
89 R	.211	41	114	18	24	2	3	4	13	4
90 A	.209	120	387	43	81	25	1	10	52	9
91 A	.240	108	383	55	92	17	4	14	59	9
91 R	.091	3	11	0	1	1	0	0	1	0
92 AA	.270	124	445	57	120	28	6	16	75	3
93 AAA	.235	125	412	63	97	20	6	21	65	1
94 AAA	.253	99	371	52	94	17	0	24	64	2
94 NL	.288	19	59	6	17	5	0	6	11	0

REY ORDONEZ

Position: Shortstop
Team: New York Mets
Born: Jan. 11, 1972   Havana, Cuba
Height: 5'10"   **Weight:** 170 lbs.
Bats: both   **Throws:** right
Acquired: Drafted from St. Paul, 10/93

Player Summary	
Fantasy Value	$0
Card Value	15¢ to 25¢
Will	make plays
Can't	drive the ball
Expect	fielding honors
Don't Expect	top baserunning

Years ago, the Mets made history when they won a lottery for the rights to Tom Seaver. Now they may have hit the jackpot again, this time with a shortstop. No one is saying that Ordonez will make the Hall of Fame like Seaver did, but he has already made quite an impact in the Mets' farm system. Teammates and instructors say that Ordonez is already a major-league shortstop in the field. He has a fine arm and unbelievable range. Ordonez defected from the Cuban National Team while it was in Buffalo in the summer of 1993. He went to play for St. Paul in the Northern League. Then the Mets won his rights in a lottery, drafted him, and assigned him to the Class-A Florida State League, where he made the All-Star team. *Baseball America* tabbed him as the No. 2 prospect in the FSL last year, behind Yankee shortstop prospect Derek Jeter. Ordonez earned a promotion to Double-A, and he did a pretty good job there. His bat is considered to be behind his glove, but he didn't hit all that badly in '94. He had 14 walks in 328 plate appearances at Class-A last summer. If he can deliver productive at bats, he has a future.

Professional Batting Register

	BA	G	AB	R	H	2B	3B	HR	RBI	SB
93 I	.283	15	60	10	17	4	0	0	7	3
94 A	.309	79	314	47	97	21	2	2	40	11
94 AA	.262	48	191	22	50	10	2	1	20	4

ANTONIO OSUNA

Position: Pitcher
Team: Los Angeles Dodgers
Born: April 12, 1973 Sinaloa, Mexico
Height: 5'11" **Weight:** 160 lbs.
Bats: right **Throws:** right
Acquired: Signed as a free agent, 6/91

Player Summary	
Fantasy Value	$5 to $7
Card Value	15¢ to 20¢
Will	flash 90-mph heat
Can't	get over tendinitis
Expect	a closer
Don't Expect	a repertoire

Osuna has a chance to be a closer in the major leagues one day soon. He missed much of the 1994 season with soreness in his shoulder, but he still managed to have an impressive year. Upon returning from the injury, he became the closer for the San Antonio Missions of the Double-A Texas League. He then was promoted to Albuquerque of the Triple-A Pacific Coast League, where he filled the same role. He is an extremely hard thrower, with a fastball that dents the radar gun in the 90s. He also has a little curveball, but his game is mostly heat. He is shorter than most coaches prefer their pitchers to be, but if he can succeed, it'll be no problem. In his first 46 innings last year at Double-A, he allowed only 19 hits while striking out 53. He pitched for Mexico City (a Triple-A level club) in 1993 and was 16-7 with a 3.57 ERA, 139 strikeouts, 70 walks, and five saves in 166⅔ innings. In 1993 while pitching in the Mexican Winter League, he struck out 15 consecutive batters to set a circuit record. Despite the time he missed, Osuna shot to the top of the saves list among Dodger farmhands last year.

Professional Pitching Register

	W	L	ERA	G	S	IP	H	ER	BB	SO
91 R	0	0	0.82	8	4	11.0	8	1	0	13
91 A	0	2	3.20	13	5	25.1	18	9	8	39
93 A	0	2	4.91	14	2	18.1	19	10	5	20
94 AA	1	2	0.98	35	19	46.0	19	5	18	53
94 AAA	0	0	0.00	6	4	6.0	5	0	1	8

WILLIS OTANEZ

Position: Third base
Team: Los Angeles Dodgers
Born: April 19, 1973 Cotui, Dominican Republic
Height: 5'11" **Weight:** 150 lbs.
Bats: right **Throws:** right
Acquired: Signed as a free agent, 2/90

Player Summary	
Fantasy Value	$0
Card Value	15¢ to 20¢
Will	hit homers
Can't	be written off
Expect	great arm
Don't Expect	average size

Otanez generates a tremendous amount of power from what is a relatively small frame. A third baseman who was tabbed as having the best infield arm in the Class-A California League in 1993 by *Baseball America*, he followed that performance with an All-Star campaign in '94. He tore up the Florida State League, which is not easy to do. He led the FSL with 14 homers and 46 RBI in the first half and had two hits in the All-Star Game. In the first game after the break, he homered to help power a rout. On July 25, his 13th-inning single gave Vero Beach a win. At the time, he was leading the FSL with 18 homers, almost as many homers as he had achieved in his first four years of pro ball (20). He had a slugging percentage over .500 and an on-base average over .350. That brings us to the downside: Otanez has now spent five years in the lower levels of the minors. He was signed at 17 and played in the Dominican Republic in 1990. He was only 21 years old last year, however, so he is on track. Otanez in 1994 had the breakthrough season necessary to propel him forward.

Professional Batting Register

	BA	G	AB	R	H	2B	3B	HR	RBI	SB
91 R	.288	58	222	38	64	9	2	6	39	3
92 A	.221	117	390	27	86	18	0	3	27	2
93 A	.262	95	325	34	85	11	2	10	39	1
94 A	.277	131	476	77	132	27	1	19	72	4

CHAN HO PARK

Position: Pitcher
Team: Los Angeles Dodgers
Born: June 30, 1973 Kong Ju City, Korea
Height: 6'2" **Weight:** 185 lbs.
Bats: right **Throws:** right
Acquired: Signed as a free agent, 1/94

Player Summary

Fantasy Value	$1 to $3
Card Value	50¢ to 75¢
Will	bring heat
Can't	justify hype
Expect	ability
Don't Expect	consistency

One of the biggest stories in 1994 spring training was Chan Ho Park, the phenom who pitched for the Korean National Team as a youngster and who signed for a big bonus to pitch for a marquee team. He fires a 92-plus mph fastball, and that attracted a lot of notice from the national press in spring training. What really attracted attention was that the Korean press followed him around and the fact that Makoto Suzuki had generated similar notice with the Mariners. Park moved to L.A. to start the season, then reality hit. Showing that he was not a major-league pitcher yet, he was sent down to Double-A San Antonio, where he showed great ability for someone who had never pitched pro ball. He held Texas League hitters to a .241 batting average, although he allowed over five walks per nine innings. He still was named the No. 10 prospect in the loop by *Baseball America*. He has a four-pitch arsenal, and he showed that he can really bring it. He pitched in international competition for Korea, and that experience helped him when he was facing tough times in Double-A. Park will have to learn to be more consistent and throw more strikes, but he has the ability.

Professional Pitching Register

	W	L	ERA	G	CG	IP	H	ER	BB	SO
94 AA	5	7	3.55	20	0	101.1	91	40	57	100
94 NL	0	0	11.25	2	0	4.0	5	5	5	6

TROY PERCIVAL

Position: Pitcher
Team: California Angels
Born: Aug. 9, 1969 Fontana, CA
Height: 6'3" **Weight:** 200 lbs.
Bats: right **Throws:** right
Acquired: Sixth-round pick in 6/90 free-agent draft

Player Summary

Fantasy Value	$0
Card Value	15¢ to 25¢
Will	offer good stuff
Can't	start over
Expect	interest
Don't Expect	a closer, yet

Percival has the kind of arm that keeps attracting interest. He has had physical problems that have kept him from realizing his potential, but teams still are impressed with his huge fastball. Therefore, even though he's not a phenom anymore, Percival could still make the majors. Drafted as a catcher, he hit only .200 in his first pro season but showed an incredible throwing ability, leading to the conversion to pitcher. His work at Class-A Boise in 1991 proved the decision was correct, and he seemed to be headed toward a fine career. But in 1992, Percival missed time with an inflamed elbow, and later that season had bursitis. He began the 1993 season on California's 40-man roster, but underwent elbow surgery on June 4 to remove calcium deposits of the medial collateral ligament. Back in action in '94, he had trouble stopping hitters. He did have 73 strikeouts in 61 innings and allowed only 29 walks. If he can somehow find a way to get ahead of the hitters and get more of them out, he could still be a useful reliever.

Professional Pitching Register

	W	L	ERA	G	S	IP	H	ER	BB	SO
91 A	2	0	1.41	28	12	38.1	23	6	18	63
92 A	1	1	5.06	11	2	10.2	6	6	8	16
92 AA	3	0	2.37	20	5	19.0	18	5	11	24
93 AAA	0	1	6.27	18	4	18.2	24	13	13	19
94 AAA	2	6	4.13	49	15	61.0	63	28	29	73

NEIFI PEREZ

Position: Shortstop; second base
Team: Colorado Rockies
Born: Feb. 2, 1975   Villa Mella, Dominican Republic
Height: 6'   **Weight:** 165 lbs.
Bats: both   **Throws:** right
Acquired: Signed as a nondrafted free agent, 10/92

Player Summary	
Fantasy Value	$0
Card Value	15¢ to 20¢
Will	play second or short
Can't	K so often
Expect	good range
Don't Expect	quick arrival

Perez has already made baseball history as the first man in the 52-year history of the California League to pull an unassisted triple play. It happened May 9 when he was playing shortstop for Central Valley. He caught a line drive by Miguel Castro, stepped on second to double off Mike Kinney, then tagged out Matt Schwenke. The Rockies are hoping, however, that Perez saves most of his history for the big-league level. He has good running speed to complement his switch-hitting. This quickness gives him good range in the field. Perez can play either shortstop or second base. He has good range and a fine arm, and time will tell where his future lies. His speed has not produced success on the bases, however. He'll have to work on his base-stealing percentage, but he must start by getting more walks to get his speed on base. Perez got off to a terrible start at the plate in the Cal League and finished with a .284 on-base average last year, which is not very good. Perez did play in the league at age 19, and while he wasn't a great hitter, he did hold his own at the plate. Another year at Class-A ball will help him.

Professional Batting Register

	BA	G	AB	R	H	2B	3B	HR	RBI	SB
93 A	.260	75	296	35	77	11	4	3	32	19
94 A	.239	134	506	64	121	16	7	1	35	9

ROBERTO PETAGINE

Position: First base
Team: Houston Astros
Born: June 7, 1971   Nueva Esparita, Venezuela
Height: 6'1"   **Weight:** 172 lbs.
Bats: left   **Throws:** left
Acquired: Signed as a nondrafted free agent, 2/90

Player Summary	
Fantasy Value	$0
Card Value	30¢ to 40¢
Will	get on base
Can't	oust Jeff Bagwell
Expect	high average
Don't Expect	wild swings

Petagine received his first taste of the major leagues in 1994, and he had a productive year in Triple-A. It's difficult to say what the Houston organization has in store for him, with Jeff Bagwell firmly entrenched at first base. Petagine reinforced his hitting credentials in 1994 while with Tucson of the Pacific Coast League, but had his season interrupted by injury. He had back-to-back three-hit games in April, and was batting .333 when he suffered a broken hand. He came off the disabled list and went 2-for-4 in a game against Albuquerque. Petagine should yield a high on-base percentage. He brought home a .399 on-base mark in 1994. He usually walks and strikes out at the same rate, though last year he slipped in that area, notching 20 more Ks than bases on balls. He did have a .514 slugging percentage. In 1993, he won the MVP Award in the Texas League, hitting .399 with runners in scoring position en route to becoming the first player in Jackson franchise history to win the TL batting title.

Professional Batting Register

	BA	G	AB	R	H	2B	3B	HR	RBI	SB
90 R	.289	55	187	35	54	5	4	2	24	9
91 A	.259	124	432	72	112	24	1	12	58	7
92 A	.293	86	307	52	90	22	4	7	49	3
92 AA	.300	21	70	8	21	4	0	4	12	1
93 AA	.334	128	437	73	146	36	2	15	90	6
94 AAA	.316	65	247	53	78	19	0	10	44	3
94 NL	.000	8	7	0	0	0	0	0	0	0

JAYSON PETERSON

Position: Pitcher
Team: Chicago Cubs
Born: Nov. 2, 1975 Denver, CO
Height: 6'4" **Weight:** 185 lbs.
Bats: both **Throws:** right
Acquired: First-round pick in 6/94 free-agent draft

Player Summary	
Fantasy Value	$0
Card Value	15¢ to 25¢
Will	get better
Can't	walk as many
Expect	big curve
Don't Expect	the bigs, yet

Anyone familiar with the Cubs and their home park knows that the team is always looking for pitching. With that in mind, they went out and took Peterson with the 15th overall pick. He is a tall, slim right-hander who brings tremendous velocity and a fine breaking ball. At East High School in Denver last year, Peterson went 7-0 in seven games, with 82 strikeouts in 42 innings. Peterson's stats with Huntington of the rookie Appalachian League showed that he has a great deal of learning to do. His 1-5 record and 5.03 ERA were a wake-up call. Most of his problems came from a failure to throw the ball over the plate; he allowed almost seven and one-half bases on balls per nine innings. He also had nine wild pitches last year. Batters lit him up at a .294 clip. He'll be all right as soon as he learns that strikes are the secret no matter what the level. Wanting to throw strikes and being able to throw them are two different things, though. Through all of his problems last summer, Appy League managers named Peterson the No. 9 prospect in the circuit, according to *Baseball America*.

JOSE PETT

Position: Pitcher
Team: Toronto Blue Jays
Born: Jan. 8, 1976 Sao Paulo, Brazil
Height: 6'6" **Weight:** 195 lbs.
Bats: right **Throws:** right
Acquired: Signed as a free agent, 7/92

Player Summary	
Fantasy Value	$0
Card Value	20¢ to 30¢
Will	attract attention
Can't	stay healthy
Expect	strikes
Don't Expect	polish

The Blue Jays needed money and hard work to sign Jose Pett. Now it appears they will need patience to develop him. Pett, a phenom who was the center of a bidding war in 1992, pitched his second pro season last year, and showed that he still has a ways to go. After working in extended spring training, he reported to Dunedin of the Class-A Florida State League, where in his first outing he gave up 11 hits in four innings. He finally got his first complete pro game on July 19, but lost 3-2 to West Palm Beach. He allowed less than two bases on balls per nine innings last year, and that is one huge reason for hope. Although FSL hitters were able to compile a .289 average, Pett proved he belonged in the loop. He was 18 years old, and other top pitchers in that league were 21 or 22. As an amateur, Pett attracted attention from five big-league clubs, but the Blue Jays prevailed with a $700,000 offer. With a Brazil-Canada tax agreement, Pett had to pay no income taxes. He brought the promise of a 90-mph fastball, though he did have some arm trouble in 1993. Still, he's one to keep an eye on.

Professional Pitching Register

	W	L	ERA	G	CG	IP	H	ER	BB	SO
94 R	1	5	5.03	9	0	39.1	45	22	32	32

Professional Pitching Register

	W	L	ERA	G	CG	IP	H	ER	BB	SO
93 R	1	1	3.60	4	0	10.0	10	4	3	7
94 A	4	8	3.77	15	1	90.2	103	38	20	49

ANDY PETTITTE

Position: Pitcher
Team: New York Yankees
Born: June 15, 1972 Baton Rouge, LA
Height: 6'5" **Weight:** 220 lbs.
Bats: left **Throws:** left
Acquired: Signed as a free agent, 5/91

Player Summary	
Fantasy Value	$0
Card Value	20¢ to 30¢
Will	throw strikes
Can't	go nine
Expect	good fielding
Don't Expect	many walks

Pettitte pitched so well last year that he is a candidate to join New York's rotation in 1995. He was drafted by the Yankees with their 22nd pick in the 1990 draft, but he declined to turn pro. He then signed as a free agent in May 1991. Since then, he has climbed surely through the farm system, and was at Columbus of the Triple-A International League. Pettitte throws a fastball in the 90s and complements it with a curveball and a changeup. Blessed with lots of size and strength, he can also throw strikes all day, a plus for anyone, especially a young left-hander. He doesn't figure to go the route that often; entering 1994 he only had pitched six complete games in 66 career starts. Pettitte began the 1994 season with Albany in Double-A, and owned a 2.71 ERA when promoted to Columbus. He finished among the victory and ERA leaders in the Yankee system. He held Double-A hitters to a .220 batting average, and Triple-A hitters batted .272 against him. He showed outstanding control, and he made the pitches when he had to.

Professional Pitching Register

	W	L	ERA	G	CG	IP	H	ER	BB	SO
91 R	4	1	0.98	6	0	36.2	16	4	8	51
91 A	2	2	2.18	6	1	33.0	33	8	16	32
92 A	10	4	2.20	27	2	168.0	141	41	55	130
93 A	11	9	3.04	26	2	159.2	146	54	47	129
93 AA	1	0	3.60	1	0	5.0	5	2	2	6
94 AA	7	2	2.71	11	0	73.0	60	22	18	50
94 AAA	7	2	2.98	16	3	96.2	101	32	21	61

J.R. PHILLIPS

Position: First base
Team: San Francisco Giants
Born: April 29, 1970 West Covina, CA
Height: 6'1" **Weight:** 185 lbs.
Bats: left **Throws:** left
Acquired: Claimed from Angels on waivers, 12/92

Player Summary	
Fantasy Value	$2 to $4
Card Value	20¢ to 30¢
Will	play first
Can't	show speed
Expect	extra-base hits
Don't Expect	Will Clark

The chance was there for Phillips to seize the first-base job vacated by Will Clark. But Phillips was unable to do so, and thus spent the year back in Triple-A. He didn't waste his time there, hitting for average and power in the Pacific Coast League. He had an outstanding .631 slugging percentage and a .382 on-base average last year. Phillips was originally selected by California in the third round of the 1988 June draft. He began his pro career in Bend, playing both first base and the outfield. He didn't get out of Class-A until 1992, when he played in the Texas League All-Star Game. When the Angels signed Chili Davis as a free agent and took Phillips off their 40-man roster, San Francisco grabbed him on a waiver claim. He played the 1993 season at Triple-A and set career highs in doubles, homers, and RBI. He was named both to the Triple-A All-Star team and the PCL's postseason squad.

Professional Batting Register

	BA	G	AB	R	H	2B	3B	HR	RBI	SB
88 A	.190	56	210	24	40	8	0	4	23	3
89 A	.192	125	442	41	85	29	1	8	50	3
90 A	.198	46	162	14	32	4	1	1	15	3
90 A	.196	116	399	44	78	10	1	11	49	4
91 A	.248	130	471	64	117	22	2	20	70	15
92 AA	.237	127	497	58	118	32	4	14	77	5
93 AAA	.263	134	506	80	133	35	2	27	94	7
93 NL	.313	11	16	1	5	1	1	1	4	0
94 AAA	.300	95	360	69	108	28	5	27	79	4
94 NL	.132	15	38	1	5	0	0	1	3	1

JIM PITTSLEY

Position: Pitcher
Team: Kansas City Royals
Born: April 3, 1974 Du Bois, PA
Height: 6'7" **Weight:** 215 lbs.
Bats: right **Throws:** right
Acquired: First-round pick in 6/92 free-agent draft

Player Summary	
Fantasy Value	$0
Card Value	15¢ to 25¢
Will	throw three pitches
Can't	be rushed
Expect	good instincts
Don't Expect	top changeup

Pittsley proved himself in the Class-A Carolina League last year, making the All-Star team, a development that bodes well for the Royals. His fast start got attention. Through April 27, he was leading the league with a 1.29 ERA (he finished the year fourth), and he went on to pile up a ton of strikeouts. He also allowed less than two and one-half bases on balls per nine innings last year. His work might seem to have merited a midseason boost, but at the age of 20, he was probably in the right spot. League managers tabbed him as the No. 3 prospect in the loop, according to a poll in *Baseball America*. In 1993, Pittsley pitched in the Midwest League, though he missed a chunk of the season with a cyst on his back. Pittsley was the 17th overall pick in the 1992 grab bag, coming out of Du Bois High School. He had been named a first-team *USA TODAY* High School All-American and led his squad to runner-up in the state tourney. He has a fastball, a curveball, and a still-developing changeup. Pittsley should get to Double-A in '95, and he may start moving faster if he succeeds.

Professional Pitching Register

	W	L	ERA	G	CG	IP	H	ER	BB	SO
92 R	4	1	3.32	9	0	43.1	27	16	15	47
92 A	0	0	0.00	1	0	3.0	2	0	1	4
93 A	5	5	4.26	15	2	80.1	76	38	32	87
94 A	11	5	3.17	27	1	161.2	154	57	42	171

DANTE POWELL

Position: Outfield
Team: San Francisco Giants
Born: Aug. 25, 1973 Long Beach, CA
Height: 6'2" **Weight:** 185 lbs.
Bats: right **Throws:** right
Acquired: First-round pick in 6/94 free-agent draft

Player Summary	
Fantasy Value	$0
Card Value	25¢ to 35¢
Will	cover ground
Can't	cut Ks
Expect	athleticism
Don't Expect	top concentration

If there were any questions about Powell's bat entering the draft, he did his best to eradicate them in his first few weeks as a pro. Playing for Everett of the Northwest League, Powell was hitting .326 with 11 stolen bases after just 86 at bats. At one point, he hit in 19 of 24 games. His stay in the rookie short-season league included more than a few highlights. In his pro debut, he collected two singles, a steal, and an RBI. On Aug. 1, he hit a grand slam to beat Spokane. On Aug. 15 against Bellingham, he went 6-for-7 with three doubles. He finished the season with a .503 slugging percentage and a .389 on-base average. He was older than the rest of his competition, though, and that has to be taken into account. Powell comes out of Cal State-Fullerton, where he served as a leadoff man. The Giants made him the 22nd overall pick in the draft, and signed him for a bonus reported at just over $500,000. But there had been doubts about his bat, especially in view of his weak showing in the College World Series. But the early returns from pro ball indicate that Powell may have a great deal to offer.

Professional Batting Register

	BA	G	AB	R	H	2B	3B	HR	RBI	SB
94 A	.314	42	169	31	53	15	2	5	25	27

ARQUIMEDEZ POZO

Position: Second base
Team: Seattle Mariners
Born: Aug. 24, 1973 Santo Domingo, Dominican Republic
Height: 5'10" **Weight:** 160 lbs.
Bats: right **Throws:** right
Acquired: Signed as a free agent, 8/90

Player Summary	
Fantasy Value	$0
Card Value	15¢ to 25¢
Will	hit doubles
Can't	duplicate '93
Expect	high on-base mark
Don't Expect	great defense

Pozo moved up a notch last year and kept pounding away at what is rapidly becoming his trademark—doubles. For the second straight year, he excelled in that department, although his total fell somewhat. The drop can be attributed in part to an early-season injury that landed Pozo on the disabled list. Otherwise, he might have approached his 1993 total of 44, which led not only the California League but all of the minor leagues. He was named the No. 4 prospect in the Cal League that year by *Baseball America*. Pozo's ability led the Mariners to clear a spot for him at Double-A by moving Ruben Santana from second base to third. Pozo was able to notch 32 walks and post a .341 on-base average. He also had a .456 slugging percentage. He comes out of the Mariners' Dominican Summer League team in Santo Domingo. After a 1992 season in which he hit 20 doubles in 348 at bats, Pozo went to Riverside in '93 and became the team MVP. That year he was named to the Class-A All-Star team and was the Cal League Rookie of the Year. One concern is the 24 errors he made in '93, but only two came after July 30.

Professional Batting Register

	BA	G	AB	R	H	2B	3B	HR	RBI	SB
92 A	.261	93	348	70	100	20	4	10	40	22
93 A	.342	127	515	98	176	44	6	13	83	10
94 AA	.289	119	447	70	129	31	1	14	54	11

BILL PULSIPHER

Position: Pitcher
Team: New York Mets
Born: Oct. 9, 1973 Ft. Benning, GA
Height: 6'4" **Weight:** 195 lbs.
Bats: left **Throws:** left
Acquired: Second-round pick in 6/91 free-agent draft

Player Summary	
Fantasy Value	$3 to $5
Card Value	30¢ to 50¢
Will	move up in '95
Can't	lose temper
Expect	good stuff
Don't Expect	total command

The Mets have quickly rebuilt their pitching staff with the likes of Bobby Jones and Jason Jacome, and Pulsipher may be the next man to step up from within the organization. A big man, Pulsipher can throw in the 90s, and he has a changeup and a curve that he can throw for strikes. His ball has quite a bit of movement. Pulsipher pitched for New York's Double-A team in the Eastern League in 1994, and was one of the top hurlers there; *Baseball America* named him the No. 5 prospect in the league. He was the starting pitcher for the National League farmhands in the Double-A All-Star Game, and he worked one scoreless inning, allowing a hit and two walks. He has taken steps to mature on the mound, curbing his temper and resisting the temptation to try to blow away each hitter he faces. He could still improve his command of the strike zone. He allowed almost four bases on balls per nine innings last year. He held EL hitters to a .239 batting average, so those walks didn't sting as much. In 1993, he dominated Florida State League batters and was named the loop's No. 3 prospect by *Baseball America*.

Professional Pitching Register

	W	L	ERA	G	CG	IP	H	ER	BB	SO
92 A	6	3	2.84	14	0	95.0	88	30	56	83
93 A	9	6	2.24	19	4	139.2	97	34	51	131
94 AA	14	9	3.22	28	5	201.0	179	72	89	171

JOE RANDA

Position: Third base
Team: Kansas City Royals
Born: Dec. 18, 1969 Milwaukee, WI
Height: 5'11" **Weight:** 190 lbs.
Bats: right **Throws:** right
Acquired: 11th-round pick in 6/91 free-agent draft

Player Summary

Fantasy Value	$3 to $5
Card Value	15¢ to 25¢
Will	play third
Can't	hit 20 homers
Expect	solid offense
Don't Expect	George Brett

Randa looms as a top candidate to be the next Royals' third baseman. He began hitting almost the minute he stepped into pro ball, and for the most part has kept up his impressive play. His work last year at Triple-A indicates that he's on track to compete for a roster spot in spring training. He showed a fine batting eye, notching 30 bases on balls and an on-base percentage over .320. He also displayed a little power. He is a good fielder with an amply strong arm. Randa was assigned to the Arizona Fall League, and he impressed the Royals brass there. As a senior in high school, he helped his team win the Wisconsin baseball crown. Randa's first look at pro ball came with Eugene of the Northwest League, where he took MVP honors. He led in hits, total bases, on-base percentage, and fielding percentage among third basemen. In 1992, he was voted to the midseason Midwest League All-Star Game, then received another promotion, this time to Baseball City of the Florida State League. Randa reached Double-A in 1993, and there won more All-Star mention.

Professional Batting Register

	BA	G	AB	R	H	2B	3B	HR	RBI	SB
91 A	.338	72	275	53	93	20	2	11	59	6
92 A	.290	123	455	77	132	20	0	6	55	10
93 AA	.295	131	505	74	149	31	5	11	72	8
94 AAA	.275	127	455	65	125	27	2	10	51	5

POKEY REESE

Position: Shortstop; second base
Team: Cincinnati Reds
Born: June 10, 1973 Columbia, SC
Height: 5'11" **Weight:** 180 lbs.
Bats: right **Throws:** right
Acquired: First-round pick in 6/91 free-agent draft

Player Summary

Fantasy Value	$0
Card Value	20¢ to 30¢
Will	make majors
Can't	supplant Barry Larkin
Expect	an acrobat
Don't Expect	Ozzie Smith

Reese is a talented fielder who can play either middle infield position. Trouble is, he has Barry Larkin and Bret Boone looming ahead of him. In 1994, Reese went out and had a career season, one in which he added power to his game. Playing at Chattanooga of the Double-A Southern League, he doubled his previous high in home runs, and he notched a .407 slugging percentage. Along with a career-best .269 batting average, he garnered 43 walks to post a .336 on-base average. He also posted career bests in stolen bases and doubles. *Baseball America* named him the No. 3 prospect in the loop last year, and he was named the shortstop on the postseason All-Star team. Reese's fielding has never been the question, although he has been known to have trouble with his throws. His moves in the field, however, have led to comparisons to Ozzie Smith. Reese underwent surgery on his throwing elbow late in 1992, then he injured his hand early in 1993. He was signed as a shortstop, but he has played some second base. Reese will find a way into the majors.

Professional Batting Register

	BA	G	AB	R	H	2B	3B	HR	RBI	SB
91 R	.238	62	231	30	55	8	3	3	27	10
92 A	.268	106	380	50	102	19	3	6	53	19
93 AA	.212	102	345	35	73	17	4	3	37	8
94 AA	.269	134	484	77	130	23	4	12	49	21

EDGAR RENTERIA

Position: Shortstop
Team: Florida Marlins
Born: Aug. 7, 1975 Barranquilla, Colombia
Height: 6'1" **Weight:** 172 lbs.
Bats: right **Throws:** right
Acquired: Signed as a nondrafted free agent, 1/92

Player Summary

Fantasy Value	$0
Card Value	15¢ to 20¢
Will	make plays
Can't	hit for power
Expect	contact hitting
Don't Expect	Tony Fernandez

The Marlins scout extensively in Latin American countries. Renteria could become the fruit of this effort, though he may not arrive in the majors for another year or so. He is a skilled shortstop who has drawn comparisons to Tony Fernandez. Renteria has great range and a better-than-average arm. Right now his bat is a huge question, though he did hold his own in the Class-A Florida State League last year. He hits with virtually no punch, but at least he puts the ball in play. He posted a .307 on-base average, drawing 35 walks. He also cut his strikeouts from 94 in 1993 to 56 last year. Renteria's growth is impressive considering he was 18 years old for much of the season and was playing against older competition. His older brother, Edinson, is also in the Florida organization. Edgar was named by *Baseball America* as the third-best prospect in the rookie Gulf Coast League in 1992. If he has the same kind of success in Double-A that he did in the FSL, look for him to make an appearance in the majors late this year. A starting job in Florida by 1996 is a possibility.

Professional Batting Register

	BA	G	AB	R	H	2B	3B	HR	RBI	SB
92 R	.288	43	163	25	47	8	1	0	9	10
93 A	.203	116	384	40	78	8	0	1	35	7
94 A	.253	128	439	46	111	15	1	0	36	6

RUBEN RIVERA

Position: Outfield
Team: New York Yankees
Born: Nov. 14, 1973 Chorrera, Panama
Height: 6'3" **Weight:** 170 lbs.
Bats: right **Throws:** right
Acquired: Signed as a nondrafted free agent, 12/90

Player Summary

Fantasy Value	$0
Card Value	60¢ to 80¢
Will	drive it to right
Can't	miss him
Expect	20-20 stats
Don't Expect	lethargy

Rivera has become one of the most compelling prospects in the Yankee system, and he could develop into a star in New York. He has power, speed, an athlete's physique, and style. He might one day be a 20-20 man in the majors. He tore apart the Class-A South Atlantic League in 1994, winning the circuit's Most Valuable Player Award and showing up well in all three Triple Crown categories. *Baseball America* named him the Sally League's No. 1 prospect. He got a promotion to the Florida State League last year and had success there. Rivera can drive the ball to the opposite field with power, and pull high majestic drives to left field. On the bases, he runs with personality and will slide headfirst into a base. Rivera spent the 1993 season in Oneonta and was named to the New York-Penn League All-Star team. He led the league with three outfield double plays, was second with a .568 slugging percentage, tied for second with six triples, and was fourth with 13 homers. He was the loop's MVP and was named to the Topps Class A/Rookie All-Star team. Look for him either in high Class-A or Double-A in 1995.

Professional Batting Register

	BA	G	AB	R	H	2B	3B	HR	RBI	SB
92 R	.273	53	194	37	53	10	3	1	20	21
93 A	.276	55	199	45	55	7	6	13	47	12
94 A	.281	139	534	101	150	28	6	33	101	48

SID ROBERSON

Position: Pitcher
Team: Milwaukee Brewers
Born: Sept. 7, 1971   Jacksonville, FL
Height: 5'9"   **Weight:** 170 lbs.
Bats: left   **Throws:** left
Acquired: 29th-round pick in 6/92 free-agent draft

Player Summary	
Fantasy Value	$0
Card Value	15¢ to 20¢
Will	use repertoire
Can't	ignore him
Expect	shrewdness
Don't Expect	few hits

You hardly need a degree in accounting to know that Roberson's numbers are pointing him firmly toward a shot at the major leagues. But Roberson is studying accounting anyway, and thus is well prepared for a career no matter how far he travels in baseball. He was named the Double-A Texas League's outstanding pitcher last year, helping El Paso dominate the regular season and the playoffs. He went seven and two-thirds strong innings in the opening game of the final series, igniting the Diablos to a four-game sweep. Roberson kept up on his studies all the while, flying back to the University of Florida for classes. He led the league in wins and the Milwaukee minor leaguers in ERA despite pitching in a park where hitters prosper. He allowed more hits than innings pitched, but didn't get damaged, in part because he doesn't give up many walks. Roberson allowed less than two and one-half walks per nine innings. He also had two and one-half strikeouts per free pass, so he can sit a hitter down. He's the proverbial crafty left-hander. Roberson could appear in the majors sometime in 1995.

CHRIS ROBERTS

Position: Pitcher
Team: New York Mets
Born: June 25, 1971   Green Cove Springs, FL
Height: 6'1"   **Weight:** 185 lbs.
Bats: right   **Throws:** left
Acquired: First-round pick in 6/92 free-agent draft

Player Summary	
Fantasy Value	$0
Card Value	30¢ to 50¢
Will	have changeup
Can't	throw wild pitches
Expect	better control
Don't Expect	overpowering stuff

Roberts was part of a fine staff that helped Binghamton to a first-place finish in the Eastern League's Northern Division last year. The 18th overall pick in the draft, he was the club's second selection in 1992. The Mets had gained the pick as compensation for the loss of left-hander Frank Viola. The comparison to Viola is not perfect, but Roberts does project as one of those crafty lefties who keeps batters off balance, particularly with a changeup. Roberts also has a functional fastball and an outstanding curveball. Out of Florida State, he was a fill-in player on the U.S. Olympic Team in 1992. In 1993, he was named to the Florida State League's postseason All-Star squad. In 1994, he had some trouble with his control, which is his bread and butter. While he held EL hitters to a .250 batting average—about the mark he gave up to FSL hitters the year before—he also allowed almost four bases on balls per nine innings. That led directly to the increase in ERA. He also uncorked 12 wild pitches. Yet, he still had a satisfactory year. The next step for Roberts is probably Triple-A.

Professional Pitching Register

	W	L	ERA	G	CG	IP	H	ER	BB	SO
92 R	4	4	3.46	9	1	65.0	68	25	18	65
93 A	12	8	2.60	24	6	166.0	157	48	34	87
94 AA	15	8	2.83	25	8	181.1	190	57	48	119

Professional Pitching Register

	W	L	ERA	G	CG	IP	H	ER	BB	SO
93 A	13	5	2.75	25	3	173.1	162	53	36	111
94 AA	13	8	3.29	27	2	175.1	164	64	77	128

ALEX RODRIGUEZ

Position: Shortstop
Team: Seattle Mariners
Born: July 27, 1975   New York, NY
Height: 6'3"   **Weight:** 190 lbs.
Bats: right   **Throws:** right
Acquired: First-round pick in 6/93 free-agent draft

Player Summary	
Fantasy Value	$7 to $9
Card Value	$1.50 to $2.00
Will	cover ground
Can't	develop overnight
Expect	a drawing card
Don't Expect	Barry Larkin, yet

The first overall pick in the draft, Rodriguez made it to the majors only about 13 months after being taken. He was just 18 years old at the time—and it showed. He was not able to give the Mariners enough quality at bats. But that in no way diminishes what he has to offer. He dominated in 65 games at Appleton in the Class-A Midwest League, notching a .605 slugging percentage and a .379 on-base average while winning All-Star honors and a nod from *Baseball America* as the loop's best prospect. Rodriguez was a first-team prep All-American as a senior at Westminster Christian High School in Miami. He was a finalist for the Golden Spikes Award, given annually to the nation's top amateur baseball player. He was also named USA Junior Baseball Player of the Year. In 1993, he became the first high school player ever invited to try out for the U.S. National Team. He was hit in the cheek by a throw while sitting in the dugout on July 28. The Mariners must give Rodriguez time to develop confidence in his hitting. His glove is now above average by major-league standards.

FRANKIE RODRIGUEZ

Position: Pitcher
Team: Boston Red Sox
Born: Dec. 11, 1972   Brooklyn, NY
Height: 6'   **Weight:** 175 lbs.
Bats: right   **Throws:** right
Acquired: Second-round pick in 6/90 free-agent draft

Player Summary	
Fantasy Value	$1
Card Value	15¢ to 25¢
Will	throw hard
Can't	return to short
Expect	complete games
Don't Expect	discipline

Rodriguez has enough talent that he could probably have reached the majors either as a pitcher or position player. However, after the 1991 season, he switched over to pitching full-time, and now he could be arriving at Fenway Park very soon. Rodriguez had a losing record last year at Pawtucket of the Triple-A International League, but he was pitching at that high level at age 21. He displayed his live arm, and he allowed almost three walks per nine innings. Out of Eastern District High School in Brooklyn, Rodriguez was Boston's first pick in the draft, and the 41st selection overall. The Red Sox owned the pick as compensation for the departure of free agent Nick Esasky. Rodriguez did not sign immediately, instead attending Howard Junior College in Texas. He was the 1991 Junior College Player of the Year as a pitcher and shortstop. He not only hit .464, but he also clinched a national title with a 17-strikeout outing against Manatee Junior College. Rodriguez has an excellent arm, throwing a slider and a fastball. He also throws sidearm now and then to keep right-handed batters honest.

Professional Batting Register

	BA	G	AB	R	H	2B	3B	HR	RBI	SB
94 A	.319	65	248	49	79	17	6	14	55	16
94 AA	.288	17	59	7	17	4	1	1	8	2
94 AAA	.311	32	119	22	37	7	4	6	21	2
94 AL	.204	17	54	4	11	0	0	0	2	3

Professional Pitching Register

	W	L	ERA	G	CG	IP	H	ER	BB	SO
92 A	12	7	3.09	25	1	148.2	125	11	65	129
93 AA	7	11	3.74	28	4	170.2	147	71	78	151
94 AAA	8	13	3.92	28	8	186.0	182	81	60	160

JOE ROSELLI

Position: Pitcher
Team: San Francisco Giants
Born: May 28, 1972 Burbank, CA
Height: 6'1" **Weight:** 170 lbs.
Bats: right **Throws:** left
Acquired: Fifth-round pick in 6/90 free-agent draft

Player Summary

Fantasy Value	$0
Card Value	15¢ to 25¢
Will	throw a slider
Can't	ignore arm woes
Expect	good control
Don't Expect	polished curveball

Roselli appeared to have bounced back from a lost 1993 in which he underwent surgery to remove an obstruction in his pitching shoulder. For a while he looked like the ace who was named the Class-A California League Pitcher of the Year in 1992. Then he went on the disabled list with elbow problems, raising questions about his health. He's got a major-league fastball and a fine slider, and he is working on his curve. He'd also like to get a bit more movement on his fastball. He held Double-A Texas League hitters to a .206 batting average last year, and he allowed only one and one-half bases on balls per nine innings. *Baseball America* tabbed him as the No. 8 prospect in the loop. Roselli's athletic ability can be seen by the fact he starred at quarterback in high school and was recruited by several programs. In 1992, he wound up on *Baseball America*'s Class-A All-Star team, and was named the Cal League's top pitching prospect. But a year after that, he tried to pitch through the pain, and was shut down after four outings.

Professional Pitching Register

	W	L	ERA	G	CG	IP	H	ER	BB	SO
90 A	4	4	4.71	15	0	78.1	87	41	29	90
91 A	8	7	3.10	22	2	153.2	144	53	49	127
92 A	11	4	2.41	22	4	149.2	145	40	46	111
93 AA	0	1	3.13	4	0	23.0	22	8	7	19
94 AA	7	2	1.89	14	2	90.2	67	19	17	54
94 AAA	1	8	4.94	13	0	74.2	96	41	15	35

SCOTT RUFFCORN

Position: Pitcher
Team: Chicago White Sox
Born: Dec. 29, 1969 New Braunfels, TX
Height: 6'4" **Weight:** 210 lbs.
Bats: right **Throws:** right
Acquired: First-round pick in 6/91 free-agent draft

Player Summary

Fantasy Value	$2 to $4
Card Value	20¢ to 30¢
Will	be a starter
Can't	hold him back
Expect	90-mph heat
Don't Expect	a top changeup

Ruffcorn had his best season to date in 1994, dominating the American Association and making the Triple-A All-Star team. League managers named him the No. 3 prospect in the loop, according to a poll in *Baseball America*. In fact, he probably would have been a major-league starter for many franchises, but the White Sox were pretty well stocked. That shouldn't prevent him from claiming a starting job in '95, as he has accomplished all he can in the minors. Ruffcorn was the 25th overall selection in the draft after a 7-1 campaign in his junior year at Baylor. He had been the team's MVP as a sophomore. In his second year as a pro, he blossomed, winning MVP honors at Sarasota of the Class-A Florida State League. He got his first taste of the majors in 1993, making his debut on June 19 against California. He was named to the Double-A Southern League's postseason All-Star squad in '93. Ruffcorn has pretty good control, he throws a fastball in the 90s, and he has a slurve (a slider-curve hybrid).

Professional Pitching Register

	W	L	ERA	G	CG	IP	H	ER	BB	SO
91 R	0	0	3.18	4	0	11.1	8	4	5	15
91 A	1	3	3.92	9	0	43.2	35	19	25	45
92 A	14	5	2.19	25	2	160.1	122	39	39	140
93 AA	9	4	2.73	20	3	135.0	108	41	52	141
93 AAA	2	2	2.80	7	1	45.0	30	14	8	44
93 AL	2	8	8.10	3	0	10.0	9	9	10	2
94 AL	0	2	12.79	2	0	6.1	15	9	5	3
94 AAA	15	3	2.72	24	3	165.2	139	50	40	144

JULIO SANTANA

Position: Pitcher
Team: Texas Rangers
Born: Jan. 20, 1973 San Pedro de Macoris, Dominican Republic
Height: 6' **Weight:** 175 lbs.
Bats: right **Throws:** right
Acquired: Signed as a nondrafted free agent, 2/90

Player Summary	
Fantasy Value.	$2 to $4
Card Value	15¢ to 25¢
Will	get people out
Can't	change role
Expect	Triple-A
Don't Expect	experience

Santana made quite a move in 1994, beginning the season in the Class-A South Atlantic League and moving up to Double-A ball. Through it all, he kept his effectiveness, and challenged for the lead among Ranger minor leaguers in ERA, strikeouts, and wins. Santana, who throws an exceptional fastball, a curveball, and a changeup, is a converted shortstop who hit .247 over three seasons in the Dominican Republic. He moved to the mound in 1992, when he allowed three earned runs in eight and one-third innings. His first full year as a pitcher came in 1993, when he led the Gulf Coast League in appearances and posted a 1.38 ERA. Santana underwent still another change in 1994, this time moving from the bullpen into the starting rotation. He had stretches of wildness, but he didn't allow much damage when he threw the ball over the plate. He was named the No. 3 prospect in the Sally League by *Baseball America* and was the loop's only pitcher on the top 10 list. A nephew of former major leaguer Rico Carty, Santana needs only more experience before he arrives.

Professional Pitching Register

	W	L	ERA	G	CG	IP	H	ER	BB	SO
93 R	4	1	1.38	26	0	39.0	31	6	7	50
94 A	6	7	2.46	16	0	91.1	65	25	44	103
94 AA	7	2	2.90	11	2	71.1	50	23	41	45

DAN SERAFINI

Position: Pitcher
Team: Minnesota Twins
Born: Jan. 25, 1974 San Francisco, CA
Height: 6'1" **Weight:** 185 lbs.
Bats: both **Throws:** left
Acquired: First-round pick in 6/92 free-agent draft

Player Summary	
Fantasy Value	$0
Card Value . . . . 15¢ to 25¢
Will . . . . strike people out
Can't . . . . get hurt again
Expect . . . . inconsistency
Don't Expect . . . . a fast developer

Not even an injury and a month without a win could keep Serafini from turning in a respectable season for Fort Myers in the Class-A Florida State League last year. A left-hander taken 26th overall in 1992, Serafini did not make his first start of 1994 until May 8, when he went five innings to beat West Palm Beach. He went without a victory from June 15 until he hurled a three-hitter on July 16. That triumph kicked off a streak over which Serafini went 5-1 with a 2.06 ERA. That stretch obviously reflects what the Twins thought he could do when they drafted him. The important thing is that Serafini took another step up the organizational ladder, and he could be positioned for a shot at Double-A in 1995. He notched nearly a K per inning. He also dropped his walk tally from 1993. He allowed about three and three-quarters walks per nine innings last year (down from more than five per game in 1993), but he will have to trim that rate even further. That is something common to young left-handers, of course. And Serafini was 20 years old in the FSL. The stuff for success is there.

Professional Pitching Register

	W	L	ERA	G	CG	IP	H	ER	BB	SO
92 R	1	0	3.64	8	0	29.2	27	12	15	33
93 A	10	8	3.65	27	1	140.2	117	57	83	147
94 A	9	9	4.61	23	2	136.2	149	70	57	130

JACOB SHUMATE

Position: Pitcher
Team: Atlanta Braves
Born: Jan. 22, 1976 Florence, SC
Height: 6'1" **Weight:** 175 lbs.
Bats: right **Throws:** right
Acquired: First-round pick in 6/94 free-agent draft

Player Summary	
Fantasy Value	$0
Card Value	20¢ to 30¢
Will	need time
Can't	pitch behind
Expect	a live arm
Don't Expect	control

Atlanta did not get a selection until the 66th pick in 1993 but had a first-rounder last year, and the team went close to home to find him. With the 27th overall choice, the organization tabbed Shumate out of Hartsville High School in South Carolina and signed him for a bonus reported at $430,000. Shumate, who starred in both football and baseball in high school, throws a lively fastball in the low to mid-90s and owns a breaking ball. Most observers felt that he had one of the best arms among high school pitchers in the draft. Before he can move up the ladder to the bigs, Shumate must learn to throw strikes. After walking 55 in 65 innings in high school last year, he reported to Danville of the Appalachian League, where he issued 30 bases on balls in his first 14 innings. He ended up with 52 walks in 31⅔ innings, which is more than 14½ walks per nine innings. That doesn't even include the number of times he pitched behind in the count. He also had 15 wild pitches and eight hit batsmen. Shumate did show a live arm, and he struck out a batter per inning. Now it's up to the organization to refine all this talent.

Professional Pitching Register

	W	L	ERA	G	CG	IP	H	ER	BB	SO
94 R	0	4	8.24	12	0	31.2	30	29	52	29

JOSE SILVA

Position: Pitcher
Team: Toronto Blue Jays
Born: Dec. 19, 1973 Tijuana, Mexico
Height: 6'5" **Weight:** 180 lbs.
Bats: right **Throws:** right
Acquired: Ninth-round pick in 6/91 free-agent draft

Player Summary	
Fantasy Value	$0
Card Value	15¢ to 25¢
Will	try to rebound
Can't	afford a '94 repeat
Expect	top stuff
Don't Expect	panic

If Silva remains a top prospect, you couldn't tell it from his stats last year. He was one of the top-rated prospects in the Toronto system entering 1994, and one season shouldn't undo that. But what a season it was. He was the Opening Day pitcher for Dunedin of the Class-A Florida State League. Hampered by control problems, though, he did not pitch particularly well. FSL hitters compiled a .265 average, and he allowed about five walks per game. Despite that, he received a promotion to Knoxville of the Double-A Southern League. He showed some flashes, but they were outnumbered by the negatives. He did cut his rate of bases on balls per nine innings down to three when he moved up to Double-A. Southern League managers were impressed with his 90-plus mph fastball and his age (20), and they named him the No. 8 prospect in the circuit in a poll by *Baseball America*. Silva broke into pro ball in 1992, when he led the rookie Gulf Coast League in strikeouts per nine innings. In his last four starts that year, he compiled a 1.13 ERA in 24 innings.

Professional Pitching Register

	W	L	ERA	G	CG	IP	H	ER	BB	SO
92 R	6	4	2.28	12	0	59.1	42	15	18	78
93 A	12	5	2.52	24	0	142.2	103	40	62	161
94 A	0	2	3.77	8	0	43.0	41	18	24	41
94 AA	4	8	4.14	16	1	91.1	89	42	31	71

CHRIS SMITH

Position: Third base; shortstop
Team: California Angels
Born: Jan. 14, 1974   Vallejo, CA
Height: 5'11"   **Weight:** 180 lbs.
Bats: right   **Throws:** right
Acquired: Second-round pick in 6/92 free-agent draft

Player Summary

Fantasy Value	$0
Card Value	15¢ to 20¢
Will	hit breaking ball
Can't	belt 20 homers
Expect	promotion
Don't Expect	seasoning

Smith played last season in the Double-A Texas League, a stringent test for him at the age of 20. In fact, when the campaign began he was the youngest man on the Midland roster by two years. Smith has now played three seasons in pro ball, and even though his statistics aren't eye-popping, he seems right on track. He was a rock in Class-A in 1993, and last year he responded with the same steady game. One highlight came on June 16, when he delivered a two-run single in the 15th inning. His home run total is not nearly what you'd like out of a third baseman, but the run production was there even if the long ball was not. He was able to compile a .342 slugging percentage last year. He also had 34 bases on balls and a .322 on-base average. Smith attended high school in Vallejo, California. After he was drafted, he went to Boise of the Northwest League. In 1993, Smith started the season in the Midwest League, did well, and received a midseason promotion to the California League, and wound up with 60 RBI in 110 games. He'll probably move to Triple-A in 1995.

Professional Batting Register

	BA	G	AB	R	H	2B	3B	HR	RBI	SB
92 A	.217	53	189	20	41	12	3	1	27	2
93 A	.279	40	154	27	43	7	2	2	21	3
93 A	.260	110	400	56	107	18	4	7	60	4
94 AA	.261	110	421	61	110	17	4	3	56	2

MATT SMITH

Position: First base; outfield; pitcher
Team: Kansas City Royals
Born: June 2, 1976   San Francisco, CA
Height: 6'4"   **Weight:** 225 lbs.
Bats: left   **Throws:** left
Acquired: First-round pick in 6/94 free-agent draft

Player Summary

Fantasy Value	$0
Card Value	15¢ to 20¢
Will	have great arm
Can't	rule out pitching
Expect	middle of lineup
Don't Expect	center fielder

Many players serve as both pitchers and position players in high school, but few of them can be drafted as either one. Smith was. Seen by *Baseball America* as the 15th-rated pitcher in the draft, Smith was coveted by the Royals as a hitter. They made him the 16th overall pick, and the 10th position player taken. Then they had to sign him away from the opportunity to attend Stanford to play football—which they did for a bonus reported at $1 million. What attracted the Royals was the lure of left-handed power. With his size, Smith could cut down the distances in Royals Stadium. He played first base at Grants Pass High School, but he might also do well enough in left field. Smith did not immediately show his power upon turning pro. At Fort Myers of the rookie Gulf Coast League, he hit no homers in his first 49 at bats, though five of his 13 hits went for extra bases. He ended up with a .376 slugging percentage and a .325 on-base average. If things don't work out at the plate, he could conceivably return to pitching. Smith started two games in the Gulf Coast League, pitching four innings, striking out two, and walking none.

Professional Batting Register

	BA	G	AB	R	H	2B	3B	HR	RBI	SB
94 R	.238	32	101	13	24	5	3	1	12	1

SHANNON STEWART

Position: Outfield
Team: Toronto Blue Jays
Born: Feb. 25, 1974 Cincinnati, OH
Height: 6'1" **Weight:** 185 lbs.
Bats: right **Throws:** right
Acquired: First-round pick in 6/92 free-agent draft

Player Summary	
Fantasy Value	$0
Card Value	20¢ to 30¢
Will	cover ground
Can't	keep getting hurt
Expect	run production
Don't Expect	top arm

Stewart impressed in Toronto's training camp last spring. Assigned to Hagerstown of the Class-A South Atlantic League, Stewart opened the season in a slump, however, then went on the disabled list in June with a dislocated shoulder. In between, he managed to show why he was the 19th overall pick in the '92 draft. He hit for average, added enough extra-base punch to make things interesting, and stole bases. At one point early in the year, Stewart went on a 25-for-57 tear that included a 5-for-6 game against Macon April 26. He finished the 1994 campaign with 23 bases on balls and a .386 on-base average, a key stat for him. The more he is on base, the more he can utilize his speed. He also had a .467 slugging percentage. Sally League managers tabbed him as the No. 6 prospect in the loop, according to a poll by *Baseball America*. Stewart comes out of Southridge High School, where he lettered in baseball, football, and track. He made the All-Dade County baseball team as a senior. His track experience is part of what makes him such an intriguing prospect.

Professional Batting Register

	BA	G	AB	R	H	2B	3B	HR	RBI	SB
92 R	.233	50	172	44	40	1	0	1	11	32
93 A	.279	75	301	53	84	15	2	3	29	25
94 A	.324	56	225	39	73	10	5	4	25	39

CHRIS STYNES

Position: Second base; infield
Team: Toronto Blue Jays
Born: Jan. 19, 1973 Queens, NY
Height: 5'9" **Weight:** 170 lbs.
Bats: right **Throws:** right
Acquired: Third-round pick in 6/91 free-agent draft

Player Summary	
Fantasy Value	$0
Card Value	12¢ to 20¢
Will	make contact
Can't	hit 20 homers
Expect	versatility
Don't Expect	Robby Alomar

Stynes plays second base in the Blue Jays' farm system at the heels of Roberto Alomar, which must be somewhat akin to being in the same writing class as William Shakespeare. But that didn't stop Stynes from turning in an All-Star year in the Double-A Southern League in 1994. He not only made the postseason All-Star team, but he created some interesting stats with his ability to make contact. He collected more than twice as many RBI (79) as strikeouts (36). He also had nearly as many doubles (32) and stolen bases (28) as whiffs. He finished second in the loop in batting. Such offensive skill can only serve him well as he tries to find a niche in the majors. Stynes has shown a gift for extra-base hits ever since coming into pro ball. In 1991, he tied for second in the rookie Gulf Coast League with 15 doubles. A year later, he was second in the Class-A South Atlantic League in the same category. Stynes is a good fielder with adequate range. He has played third base and shortstop as well as second in his pro career, so this versatility will be his ticket.

Professional Batting Register

	BA	G	AB	R	H	2B	3B	HR	RBI	SB
91 R	.306	57	219	29	67	15	1	4	39	10
92 A	.284	127	489	67	139	36	0	7	46	28
93 A	.304	123	496	72	151	28	5	7	48	19
94 AA	.317	136	545	79	173	32	4	8	79	28

SCOTT SULLIVAN

Position: Pitcher
Team: Cincinnati Reds
Born: March 3, 1971 Tuscaloosa, AL
Height: 6'4" **Weight:** 210 lbs.
Bats: right **Throws:** right
Acquired: Second-round pick in 6/93 free-agent draft

Player Summary	
Fantasy Value	$0
Card Value	15¢ to 20¢
Will	close
Can't	rule out Reds
Expect	mound presence
Don't Expect	subtlety

Just one year removed from the draft, Sullivan made his mark in Double-A ball, looking not a bit out of place. He had success both as a starter and reliever. Out of Auburn University, he began the season in Chattanooga's starting rotation. On May 3, he fanned 12 over seven innings and allowed only one unearned run. Through June 8, he was leading the Southern League with eight wins, and was also the top strikeout man in Clncinnati's farm system. With an eye toward his powerful arm, the Lookouts moved Sullivan to the closer role. Through his first 12 outings coming out of the bullpen, he had four saves and a 2.28 ERA, averaging more than a strikeout per inning. As the season neared its end, Sullivan was challenging for the team lead in saves, despite his late start. He allowed almost three walks per nine innings, however, and he needs to prune that ratio a bit. Still, it was Sullivan's second straight positive season. In 1993, he overpowered hitters in the Pioneer League. While he probably will move to Triple-A as a closer, he could be in the Cincinnati bullpen as early as this season.

JEFF SUPPAN

Position: Pitcher
Team: Boston Red Sox
Born: Jan. 2, 1975 Oklahoma City, OK
Height: 6'2" **Weight:** 210 lbs.
Bats: right **Throws:** right
Acquired: Second-round pick in 6/93 free-agent draft

Player Summary	
Fantasy Value	$0
Card Value	30¢ to 40¢
Will	throw curve
Can't	prevail without control
Expect	a competitor
Don't Expect	blazing heat

Suppan may have been the best minor-league pitcher in the Red Sox system last year. That's really saying something, considering he got off to a poor start and did not pitch his first gem until a two-hit shutout on June 1. Working for Sarasota of the Class-A Florida State League, Suppan at one point was 0-5. Within a few weeks after that, however, he had soared to the top of the strikeout chart for Red Sox farmhands. Not long after that, he joined the leaders in victories as well. In midsummer, Suppan ripped off six straight wins. He also set a Red Sox FSL record for strikeouts in a season. This all speaks well for his ability to respond to adversity and to make adjustments. FSL hitters compiled a .236 batting average against him last year. He also showed control, allowing two and one-half bases on balls per nine innings. *Baseball America* named him the No. 10 prospect in the league. Suppan broke into pro ball with some impressive work in the rookie Gulf Coast League in '93. After the season, he attended the Florida Instructional League and did superbly. At his tender age, he might stay in Class-A ball for a while.

Professional Pitching Register

	W	L	ERA	G	S	IP	H	ER	BB	SO
93 R	5	0	1.67	18	3	54.0	33	10	25	79
94 AA	11	7	3.41	34	7	121.1	101	46	40	111

Professional Pitching Register

	W	L	ERA	G	CG	IP	H	ER	BB	SO
93 R	4	3	2.18	10	2	57.2	52	14	16	64
94 A	13	7	3.26	27	4	174.0	153	63	50	173

MAC SUZUKI

Position: Pitcher
Team: Seattle Mariners
Born: May 31, 1975   Kobe, Japan
Height: 6'3"   **Weight:** 195 lbs.
Bats: right   **Throws:** right
Acquired: Signed as a free agent, 9/93

Player Summary	
Fantasy Value	$0
Card Value	30¢ to 50¢
Will	need a role
Can't	lose another year
Expect	great tools
Don't Expect	durability

Suzuki's season hardly even got started in 1994. Assigned to Jacksonville of the Double-A Southern League, he developed a sore shoulder, came back and pitched for a while, then experienced tenderness in his elbow. Thus, he's barely any closer to the majors than he was at this time last year, except now there are concerns about his health and durability. He did pitch fairly well before the injury, however. Suzuki, who had never pitched in the professional leagues in Japan, instead got started with Salinas of the Class-A California League in 1992, hurling one shutout inning on the final day of the season. He worked mostly as a reliever for independent San Bernardino of the Cal League in 1993. After going 0-1 with a 6.11 ERA in his first 12 appearances, Suzuki established himself in June, when he went 2-0 with a 2.05 ERA. In July, he was moved into the closer role. He wound up the season allowing an opposing batting average of .205. He was named the No. 6 prospect in the loop that year by *Baseball America*. The M's plan to move him from the bullpen to the starting rotation.

JULIAN TAVAREZ

Position: Pitcher
Team: Cleveland Indians
Born: May 22, 1973   Santiago, Dominican Republic
Height: 6'2"   **Weight:** 165 lbs.
Bats: right   **Throws:** right
Acquired: Signed as a nondrafted free agent, 3/90

Player Summary	
Fantasy Value	$2 to $4
Card Value	25¢ to 35¢
Will	keep ball low
Can't	stay in minors
Expect	fine stuff
Don't Expect	a flop

Tavarez is one of the game's top pitching prospects. He has been a winner throughout his career, and he has grown increasingly dominant as he climbs through the Cleveland farm system. Last year, he pitched for Charlotte of the Triple-A International League and was singled out by *Baseball America* for owning the top breaking pitch in the circuit; that publication also tabbed him as the IL's top pitching prospect and the No. 5 prospect overall. He was also named to the Triple-A All-Star Team. He consistently gets the ball over the plate, allowing just over two bases on balls per nine innings last year. Tavarez has already seen action in the majors, getting there at the age of 20. He made his big-league debut on Aug. 7, 1993, against Baltimore. He had begun that season in Kinston of the Class-A Carolina League, where he was named the Player of the Year. He also made the midseason and postseason All-Star squads. Besides the fine breaking ball, Tavarez can also throw the fastball.

Professional Pitching Register

	W	L	ERA	G	S	IP	H	ER	BB	SO
92 A	0	0	0.00	1	0	1.0	0	0	0	1
93 A	4	4	3.68	48	12	80.2	59	33	56	87
94 AA	1	0	2.84	8	1	12.2	15	4	6	10

Professional Pitching Register

	W	L	ERA	G	CG	IP	H	ER	BB	SO
92 R	6	3	2.68	14	2	87.1	86	26	12	69
93 A	11	5	2.42	18	2	119.0	102	32	28	107
93 AA	2	1	0.95	3	1	19.0	14	2	1	11
93 AL	2	2	6.57	8	0	37.0	53	27	13	19
94 AL	0	1	21.60	1	0	1.2	6	4	1	0
94 AAA	15	6	3.48	26	2	176.0	167	68	43	102

BRIEN TAYLOR

Position: Pitcher
Team: New York Yankees
Born: Dec. 26, 1971 Beaufort, NC
Height: 6'3" **Weight:** 195 lbs.
Bats: left **Throws:** left
Acquired: First-round pick in 6/91 free-agent draft

Player Summary	
Fantasy Value $0
Card Value . . . . 25¢ to 35¢
Will . . . . be questionable
Can't . . . . rely on talent
Expect . . . . slow timetable
Don't Expect . . . . 99-mph heat

Taylor's interesting career so far has been followed closely by Yankee fans, even though he hasn't come close to throwing a pitch in the big leagues. As the top overall pick in 1991, he signed only after some vigorous bargaining that resulted in a huge bonus. He pitched well in his first two pro seasons. He was the Double-A Eastern League's No. 4 prospect in 1993, according to *Baseball America*, even though he allowed more than five and one-half bases on balls per nine innings. Then, in the off-season between 1993 and '94, he was involved in a fight and injured his shoulder. It required reconstructive surgery, which was performed by Dr. Frank Jobe. The injury put Taylor out for the entire '94 season, and now the Yankees can only hope he regains as much as possible of that 99-mph fastball. He also had a curveball that reminded some people of Doc Gooden's. Taylor graduated from East Carteret High School, where he compiled a 29-6 record with a 1.25 ERA with 476 Ks in 239⅓ innings. But now his challenges will be tougher, and the Yankees are anxious to see the state of Taylor's arm.

Professional Pitching Register

	W	L	ERA	G	S	IP	H	ER	BB	SO
92 A	6	8	2.57	27	0	161.1	122	46	66	187
93 AA	13	7	3.48	27	1	163.0	127	63	102	150

AMAURY TELEMACO

Position: Pitcher
Team: Chicago Cubs
Born: Jan. 19, 1974 Higuey, Dominican Republic
Height: 6'3" **Weight:** 210 lbs.
Bats: right **Throws:** right
Acquired: Signed as a free agent, 5/91

Player Summary	
Fantasy Value $0
Card Value . . . . 15¢ to 20¢
Will . . . . throw slider
Can't . . . . concede inside
Expect . . . . strikeouts
Don't Expect . . . . a perfect change

Telemaco had a successful season in 1994, one year after he made the All-Star team in the Class-A Midwest League. He is shaping up as one of Chicago's better pitching prospects, and he could improve with some refining of his off-speed stuff. Telemaco started well last year in the Class-A Florida State League, allowing only seven hits in his first 13 innings. He won his first five starts for Daytona, posting an ERA of 2.86, and owned five of the staff's 12 wins after 32 games. Through June 1, he was tied for the FSL lead with seven wins and was fourth with 59 strikeouts. He held FSL hitters to a .221 batting average, and he allowed only two and one-half bases on balls per nine innings. On June 7, he was promoted to Double-A Orlando, and three days later he tossed seven and two-thirds scoreless innings in his debut. Telemaco didn't collect many victories in the Southern League, but that wasn't necessarily his fault. He threw the ball over the plate and had an acceptable ratio of hits to innings. He'll likely start 1995 in Double-A.

Professional Pitching Register

	W	L	ERA	G	CG	IP	H	ER	BB	SO
92 R	3	5	4.01	12	2	76.1	71	34	17	93
92 A	0	1	7.94	2	0	5.2	9	5	5	5
93 A	8	11	3.45	23	3	143.2	129	55	54	133
94 A	7	3	3.40	11	2	76.2	62	29	23	59
94 AA	3	5	3.45	12	2	62.2	56	24	20	49

JASON THOMPSON

Position: First base
Team: San Diego Padres
Born: June 13, 1971   Orlando, FL
Height: 6'4"   **Weight:** 205 lbs.
Bats: left   **Throws:** left
Acquired: Ninth-round pick in 6/93 free-agent draft

Player Summary	
Fantasy Value	$0
Card Value	10¢ to 15¢
Will	be in lineup
Can't	overswing
Expect	a physical specimen
Don't Expect	stolen bases

San Diego lost good players during a massive cost-cutting effort in recent years. But if the farm system replenishes the Pads with talent like Thompson, the process will have been a success. He began last season with Rancho Cucamonga and was named the Class-A California League Player of the Month for May with a .343 average, 10 doubles, four homers, and 26 RBI. Through the early part of June, he was leading the league in batting average, RBI, hits, doubles, slugging percentage, extra-base hits, and runs. Shortly thereafter, he was promoted to Double-A ball. He did not enjoy the same success at the higher level, and his strikeout pace increased substantially. He still produced enough runs to give the Padres hope, though. Thompson has the classic look of a first baseman. He throws left-handed and has size and power. He also is a fine gloveman. California League skippers named Thompson the No. 8 prospect in the loop in a poll conducted by *Baseball America*. In 1993, the University of Arizona product led the short-season Class-A Northwest League with 556 total chances and 507 putouts.

Professional Batting Register

	BA	G	AB	R	H	2B	3B	HR	RBI	SB
93 A	.300	66	240	36	72	25	1	7	38	3
94 A	.360	68	253	57	91	19	2	13	63	1
94 AA	.260	63	215	35	56	17	2	8	46	0

MICHAEL TUCKER

Position: Outfield
Team: Kansas City Royals
Born: June 25, 1971   South Boston, VA
Height: 6'2"   **Weight:** 185 lbs.
Bats: left   **Throws:** right
Acquired: First-round pick in 6/92 free-agent draft

Player Summary	
Fantasy Value	$2 to $4
Card Value	40¢ to 60¢
Will	generate runs
Can't	star at second
Expect	decent power
Don't Expect	lots of steals

Tucker is an all-around offensive player who is strong enough to hit the ball out of Royals Stadium and quick enough to prosper on the artificial turf. He has played quite a bit of second base and could fill in there in an emergency, but he is more likely to be in the outfield. He had an outstanding year for Triple-A Omaha, being one of four Royals to reach 20 home runs. He was among the top run producers in the Kansas City system and finished with a .468 slugging percentage. He also garnered 69 bases on balls and a .366 on-base average. American Association skippers called him the No. 7 prospect in the loop last year, in a poll by *Baseball America*. Tucker attended Longwood College, where he was named a Division II first-team All-American in 1991. He was tabbed for the all-tournament team at the Division II championships. Tucker went on to play for the United States Olympic squad in Barcelona in 1992, hitting .291 and leading the team with 28 steals. He won't produce many stolen bases as a pro, but he has speed. It will help in the outfield of Royals Stadium, where you can expect to see Tucker soon.

Professional Batting Register

	BA	G	AB	R	H	2B	3B	HR	RBI	SB
93 A	.305	61	239	42	73	14	2	6	44	12
93 AA	.279	72	244	38	68	7	4	9	35	12
94 AAA	.276	132	485	75	134	16	7	21	77	11

TIM UNROE

Position: Third base; first base
Team: Milwaukee Brewers
Born: Oct. 7, 1970   Round Lake Beach, IL
Height: 6'3"   **Weight:** 200 lbs.
Bats: right   **Throws:** right
Acquired: 28th-round pick in 6/92 free-agent draft

Player Summary	
Fantasy Value	$0
Card Value	15¢ to 20¢
Will	hit doubles
Can't	repeat '94
Expect	utility role
Don't Expect	hot corner job

It looks like the Brewers may have filled two positions when they made their first-round pick last June. Not only did they cull third baseman Antone Williamson with the fourth overall pick, but, in order to accomodate him, they switched Unroe from third to first base at Double-A El Paso when Williamson joined the team. Now Unroe becomes a very intriguing prospect because he has played more than one position. And he can hit. Unroe's stock has never been higher. He won MVP honors in the Double-A Texas League and helped El Paso to the title. Unroe made the Double-A All-Star Team and hit a long home run in the game. He was second in the league with 47 RBI in the first half. He went 15-for-30 with 10 RBI to win Player of the Week honors for June 20-26. He went 5-for-6 in an August game. Unroe looks like he will have extra-base power without necessarily hitting a lot of homers. Out of Lewis University, he was solid in his first two pro years. His next assignment should be at Triple-A, though the Brewers may just bring Unroe up to the majors at the beginning of the season.

Professional Batting Register

	BA	G	AB	R	H	2B	3B	HR	RBI	SB
92 R	.278	74	266	61	74	13	2	16	58	3
93 A	.251	108	382	57	96	21	6	12	63	9
94 AA	.310	126	474	97	147	36	7	15	103	14

UGIE URBINA

Position: Pitcher
Team: Montreal Expos
Born: Feb. 15, 1974   Caracas, Venezuela
Height: 6'2"   **Weight:** 184 lbs.
Bats: right   **Throws:** right
Acquired: Signed as a nondrafted free agent, 11/90

Player Summary	
Fantasy Value	$0
Card Value	15¢ to 20¢
Will	hang in there
Can't	forget shoulder woes
Expect	wild pitches
Don't Expect	trepidation

Urbina rebounded from personal tragedy and injury to blaze his way through the Eastern League last year, and soon the Expos may have to think about making room for him in the rotation. He experienced some shoulder problems early in the season, then had to deal with the death of his father less than two months into the campaign. After a leave of absence, Urbina returned in the middle of June and began putting his season back together. He hurled five hitless innings at New Britain on June 16, then defeated the Red Sox again in his next start. He allowed just over three walks per nine innings, and EL hitters compiled just a .218 batting average against him. All this is even more impressive when you consider that he was the youngest man in the league when the season began. It was the second straight outstanding season for Urbina, who went a combined 14-6 in 1993. He held Midwest League hitters to a .200 batting average that year. Urbina showed toughness in 1994, and that can only help him as he takes the final couple of steps.

Professional Pitching Register

	W	L	ERA	G	CG	IP	H	ER	BB	SO
91 R	3	3	2.29	10	3	63.0	58	16	10	51
92 A	7	13	3.22	24	5	142.1	111	51	54	100
93 A	10	1	1.99	16	4	108.1	78	24	36	107
93 AA	4	5	3.99	11	3	70.0	66	31	32	45
94 AA	9	3	3.28	21	0	120.2	96	44	43	86

MARC VALDES

Position: Pitcher
Team: Florida Marlins
Born: Dec. 20, 1971 Dayton, OH
Height: 6′ **Weight:** 187 lbs.
Bats: right **Throws:** right
Acquired: First-round pick in 6/93 free-agent draft

Player Summary	
Fantasy Value $0
Card Value . . . . 10¢ to 15¢
Will . . . . throw slider
Can't. throw in 90s
Expect . . . . sinking fastball
Don't Expect . . . . complete games

Few things can please a scouting staff more than to see a first-round pick go out and pitch like one. That's what happened in Valdes's case last year. In his first full pro season, he began in the Midwest League and pitched his way into Double-A, helping New Haven reach the Eastern League playoffs. At Class-A Kane County in 1994, he allowed less than two and one-half bases on balls per nine innings and less hits than innings pitched. Proving that those stats were no fluke, in the second half of the season he held Double-A batters to less hits than innings, although his walks per game ratio inched up to three and one-half. Along the way, he showed himself to be one of Florida's top pitching prospects, with a very real chance of reaching the majors in 1995. His ball has a nice sinking action, and he throws a slider. Valdes pitched for the University of Florida and tried out for the U.S. Olympic Team in 1992, only to be cut on the last day. Valdes finished his school career as UF's all-time leader with 31 victories and 351 Ks. He ranked sixth all-time in complete games.

Professional Pitching Register

	W	L	ERA	G	CG	IP	H	ER	BB	SO
93 A	0	2	5.59	3	0	9.2	8	6	7	15
94 A	7	4	2.95	11	2	76.1	62	25	21	68
94 AA	8	4	2.55	15	0	99.0	77	28	39	70

BEN VanRYN

Position: Pitcher
Team: Cincinnati Reds
Born: Aug. 9, 1971 Fort Wayne, IN
Height: 6′5″ **Weight:** 185 lbs.
Bats: left **Throws:** left
Acquired: Traded from Dodgers for William Brunson, 12/94

Player Summary	
Fantasy Value $0
Card Value . . . . 15¢ to 25¢
Will . . . . be back
Can't . . . . find consistency
Expect. . . . . slider
Don't Expect . . . . a collapse

After being named the Double-A Texas League's Pitcher of the Year (and No. 1 prospect by *Baseball America*) in 1993, VanRyn probably never imagined that he would have had to go back to that league. He certainly seemed headed for the majors on a fast track. And after winning his first four starts in Triple-A ball, the only man in the Pacific Coast League to do so last year, he had to be thinking about the majors. Suddenly, however, VanRyn got a lesson in the percentages of the game. He went 0-1 with a 9.59 ERA in his next eight appearances and was sent back to San Antonio. There he stabilized nicely, finishing with some nice stats, and the next time he comes up he'll have more experience. He allowed more than four walks per nine innings in the PCL. VanRyn had been drafted by the Expos in the 37th round in 1990 and was hit hard in the low minors in 1991. After a trade to the Dodgers' system, he led Vero Beach of the Florida State League in wins.

Professional Pitching Register

	W	L	ERA	G	CG	IP	H	ER	BB	SO
90 R	5	3	1.74	10	0	51.2	44	10	15	58
91 A	5	16	5.49	26	1	141.2	159	97	73	100
92 A	10	7	3.20	26	1	137.2	125	49	54	108
93 AA	14	4	2.21	21	1	134.1	118	33	37	144
93 AAA	1	4	10.73	6	0	24.1	35	29	17	9
94 AAA	4	1	6.39	12	0	50.2	75	36	24	44
94 AA	8	3	2.99	17	0	102.1	93	34	35	72

JOE VITIELLO

Position: First base
Team: Kansas City Royals
Born: April 11, 1970 Cambridge, MA
Height: 6'2" **Weight:** 215 lbs.
Bats: right **Throws:** right
Acquired: First-round pick in 6/91 free-agent draft

Player Summary	
Fantasy Value	$1 to $3
Card Value	20¢ to 30¢
Will	play somewhere
Can't	hurt knee again
Expect	power
Don't Expect	durability

Vitiello could hardly have enjoyed a more successful year in Triple-A than he did. He captured Rookie of the Year honors while playing for Kansas City's affiliate in the American Association. He was also named the AA's first baseman on the postseason All-Star team, beating out Pirate prospect Rich Aude. Vitiello's season ended with a knee injury, something to keep an eye on. He had suffered a subluxation of the left knee sliding into second base during the 1993 campaign. He had a .526 slugging percentage last year and walked 56 times for a .440 on-base mark. He also cut his strikeout frequency. Vitiello was the seventh player chosen overall in the 1991 draft and was named by *Baseball America* the top power-hitting prospect in college that year. He showed it immediately, hitting six homers in just 64 at bats for Eugene of the Northwest League. In 1992, Vitiello played in the Florida State League and managed eight homers in a tough circuit to hit four-baggers. He has also played some outfield. If he keeps up the production, he'll find a spot somewhere.

Professional Batting Register

	BA	G	AB	R	H	2B	3B	HR	RBI	SB
91 A	.328	19	64	16	21	2	0	6	21	1
91 AA	.219	36	128	15	28	4	1	0	18	0
92 A	.285	115	400	52	114	16	1	8	65	0
93 AA	.288	117	413	62	119	25	2	15	66	2
94 AAA	.344	98	352	46	121	28	3	10	61	3

TERRELL WADE

Position: Pitcher
Team: Atlanta Braves
Born: Jan. 25, 1973 Rembert, SC
Height: 6'3" **Weight:** 205 lbs.
Bats: left **Throws:** left
Acquired: Signed as a nondrafted free agent, 6/91

Player Summary	
Fantasy Value	$0
Card Value	$1.00 to $1.50
Will	strike folks out
Can't	throw too much
Expect	a big-loop starter
Don't Expect	complete games

Wade is now just a phone call away from the major leagues, an astonishingly rapid climb for someone who was not even drafted. He began 1994 at Atlanta's Double-A affiliate in Greenville, and by the end of the season he was helping Richmond win the Triple-A International League's Western Division. He was named the No. 5 prospect in the Double-A Southern League last year by *Baseball America*. Wade can be over-powering, and he figures to strike out his share. He had a K an inning at both Double-A and Triple-A last year. But he'll also walk a few, so he'll be throwing a lot of pitches. For example, on May 15, Wade pitched five hitless innings; at that point, he was near the Southern League lead in both strikeouts and walks. Wade turned in two unimpressive seasons in 1991 and '92. But in 1993, he was the organization's top minor-league pitcher. Wade turned in the top strikeout game in the minor leagues that year, with 18. *Baseball America* tabbed him as the Class-A South Atlantic League's No. 1 prospect.

Professional Pitching Register

	W	L	ERA	G	CG	IP	H	ER	BB	SO
91 R	2	0	6.26	10	0	23.0	29	16	15	22
92 R	1	4	6.44	13	0	50.1	59	36	42	54
93 A	10	3	2.17	19	0	116.1	83	28	54	168
93 AA	1	1	3.21	8	1	42.0	32	15	29	40
94 AA	9	3	3.83	21	0	105.2	87	45	58	105
94 AAA	2	2	2.63	4	0	24.0	23	7	15	26

BILLY WAGNER

Position: Pitcher
Team: Houston Astros
Born: June 25, 1971   Tannersville, VA
Height: 5'11"   **Weight:** 180 lbs.
Bats: left   **Throws:** left
Acquired: First-round pick in 6/93 free-agent draft

Player Summary	
Fantasy Value	$0
Card Value	50¢ to 70¢
Will	overpower hitters
Can't	forget to win
Expect	too many walks
Don't Expect	one-pitch outs

Wagner looked every bit like a first-round pick last year, showing devastating stuff while pitching for Quad City of the Class-A Midwest League. However, while his strike-out total, ERA, and hits-per-inning ratio were superb, he didn't have the wins to show for it. Some of that came from subpar control, and some from poor support. On April 13, he allowed just one hit over five and one-third innings but lost 2-1. A couple of weeks later, he struck out 14 over six innings but received no decision. He fired a four-hitter, fanning 15, in a victory on May 29. At that point, he led his club with 76 strikeouts. Through June 8, he led all minor-league pitchers in batting-average against at .150, and he finished at .188. He also led the minors in strikeouts last year. He was named to the All-Star team and pitched one inning. Midwest League managers named Wagner as the No. 2 prospect in the loop last year, according to a poll by *Baseball America*. Out of Ferrum College, he compiled a three-year mark of 17-3. A 1993 All-America selection, Wagner set NCAA records for single-season strikeouts per nine innings.

Professional Pitching Register

	W	L	ERA	G	CG	IP	H	ER	BB	SO
93 A	1	3	4.08	7	0	28.2	25	13	25	31
94 A	8	9	3.29	26	2	153.0	99	56	91	204

BRET WAGNER

Position: Pitcher
Team: St. Louis Cardinals
Born: April 17, 1973   New Cumberland, PA
Height: 6'   **Weight:** 190 lbs.
Bats: left   **Throws:** left
Acquired: First-round pick in 6/94 free-agent draft

Player Summary	
Fantasy Value	$0
Card Value	15¢ to 25¢
Will	need a role
Can't	rely on heat
Expect	a promotion
Don't Expect	quick progress

In 1993, the Cardinals drafted Alan Benes, a hard-throwing college pitcher who adapted quickly to pro ball. They hope the same formula works for Wagner, who was taken with the 19th overall pick. But whereas Benes looks like a starter through and through, there was some thought that Wagner might go to the bullpen; he did some closing in college. That was not the case in his early days in pro ball, as he went into the rotation with New Jersey of the New York-Penn League, and again when boosted to Savannah of the South Atlantic League. If his work in Savannah is any indication, he has a future in the rotation. He held Sally League hitters to a .175 batting average through his seven starts there, and he gave up less than one and one-half bases on balls per nine innings. Wagner comes out of Wake Forest University, and his most outstanding characteristic is the control he shows as a young lefty. Wagner, a good hitter, was the ninth pitcher drafted. He signed for a bonus reported at more than $500,000. His next step should be high Class-A. The question is whether Wagner will pitch next year as a starter or reliever.

Professional Pitching Register

	W	L	ERA	G	CG	IP	H	ER	BB	SO
94 A	4	2	2.09	10	0	56.1	37	13	10	53

TODD WALKER

Position: Second base; infield
Team: Minnesota Twins
Born: May 25, 1973 Bakersfield, CA
Height: 6' **Weight:** 170 lbs.
Bats: left **Throws:** right
Acquired: First-round pick in 6/94 free-agent draft

Player Summary	
Fantasy Value	$0
Card Value	15¢ to 25¢
Will	make contact
Can't	forget glove
Expect	slugging
Don't Expect	a future at second

When the Twins drafted Walker with the eighth overall pick last year, they felt they were getting the best hitter available. His performance in his first pro season can only reinforce that opinion. After signing, Walker reported to Fort Myers of the Class-A Florida State League and began doing the same things he did at Louisiana State. He hit for average, hit the ball out of the park, got on base, and made contact. He took 32 bases on balls (and had a .406 on-base average) while striking out only 15 times. He also notched a .532 slugging percentage. He went 9-for-23 with a double, three homers, and six RBI in his first six games. Walker hit a two-run homer in the eighth inning on Aug. 8 to provide a 3-2 victory over Vero Beach. By the end of August, he was the team's home run leader. Florida State League skippers named him the No. 7 prospect in the loop, according to a poll by *Baseball America*. The cozy Metrodome should only accentuate Walker's gifts. The downside is Walker's glove, which is not considered any more than average. He has been a second baseman, but Walker may have the hot corner in his future.

JOHN WASDIN

Position: Pitcher
Team: Oakland Athletics
Born: Aug. 5, 1972 Fort Belvoir, VA
Height: 6'2" **Weight:** 190 lbs.
Bats: right **Throws:** right
Acquired: First-round pick in 6/93 free-agent draft

Player Summary	
Fantasy Value	$0
Card Value	30¢ to 40¢
Will	work inside
Can't	overpower hitters
Expect	command
Don't Expect	a choker

Wasdin has so far ranked among the most impressive of the 1993 first-rounders. Last year he began in the Class-A Cal League, then worked his way up to the Double-A Southern League, where he pitched with consistency and purpose. His stuff is not exceptional, but he has a way of going about his business. At one point early in the campaign, Wasdin was named Pitcher of the Week in the Cal League. He was 3-1 when he got the call to join Huntsville of the Southern League. He promptly hurled a 2-1 victory over Chattanooga for his first win. He held SL hitters to a .236 batting average and had less than two bases on balls per nine innings. He was named the No. 4 prospect in the Southern League by *Baseball America*. Wasdin comes out of Godby High School in Tallahassee, Florida, where he was the team MVP in both his junior and senior years. He was drafted by the Yankees in the 42nd round, but instead went to Florida State. He appeared in the College World Series as a freshman and compiled a 10-1 mark as a junior. He was the 25th overall pick in 1993.

Professional Batting Register

	BA	G	AB	R	H	2B	3B	HR	RBI	SB
94 A	.304	46	171	29	52	5	2	10	34	6

Professional Pitching Register

	W	L	ERA	G	CG	IP	H	ER	BB	SO
93 R	0	0	3.00	1	0	3.0	3	1	0	1
93 A	2	6	2.37	12	0	64.2	49	17	13	51
94 A	3	1	1.69	6	0	26.2	17	5	5	30
94 AA	12	3	3.43	21	0	141.2	126	54	29	108

PAT WATKINS

Position: Outfield
Team: Cincinnati Reds
Born: Sept. 2, 1972 Raleigh, NC
Height: 6'2" **Weight:** 185 lbs.
Bats: right **Throws:** right
Acquired: First-round pick in 6/93 free-agent draft

Player Summary	
Fantasy Value	$0
Card Value	15¢ to 25¢
Will	cover ground
Can't	rule out 30-30
Expect	center field
Don't Expect	a slugger's Ks

Watkins is one of the biggest surprises to have come out of the '93 draft. The Reds suspected they were getting a good athlete, of course, but even they might not have guessed they'd get the power they did from Watkins. He became a 25-25 man, ranking among the organization's leaders in both home runs and stolen bases. The Winston-Salem ballpark was a big part of the reason for the power explosion—nine players on the Spirits' roster reached double figures in homers—but you still can't quibble with Watkins' production. He fashioned a .510 slugging percentage. He struck out 84 times, but he accumulated 62 walks and had a .369 on-base average. He was named to the Class-A Carolina League's postseason All-Star team. He was also named the No. 8 prospect in the loop by *Baseball America*. He was the 32nd overall choice in the draft, taken with a pick awarded as compensation for the loss of free agent Greg Swindell. Out of East Carolina University, Watkins is a fine gloveman. He has the speed for center field and the arm for right. Watkins has earned a shot at Double-A; will his power hold up in a bigger park, though?

CASEY WHITTEN

Position: Pitcher
Team: Cleveland Indians
Born: May 23, 1972 Evansville, IN
Height: 6' **Weight:** 175 lbs.
Bats: left **Throws:** left
Acquired: Second-round pick in 6/93 free-agent draft

Player Summary	
Fantasy Value	$0
Card Value	20¢ to 30¢
Will	gather Ks
Can't	always find plate
Expect	a deliberate rise
Don't Expect	many hits

Whitten spent last season in the Class-A Carolina League, serving as one of Kinston's top starting pitchers. His won-lost record was not spectacular, but he posted a solid hits-to-innings ratio and averaged just about a strikeout per inning. It wasn't a bad performance considering he didn't get his first win until May 6. He was one of the top strikeout artists in the Cleveland chain. Whitten held CL hitters to a .228 batting average. He allowed more than three and one-half bases on balls per nine innings, a rate that he needs to slice. He attended Indiana State University and captured All-Missouri Valley Conference and third-team All-America laurels. He came out of the draft and reported to Watertown, and finished sixth in the New York-Penn League with a 2.42 ERA. He was also named the lefty on the league's All-Star team. During one stretch, he went 4-0 with a 1.38 ERA, allowing only 23 hits in 32⅔ innings. After the season, Whitten went to the Instructional League, where he fanned 15 in 12 innings. Like many young lefties, he must sharpen his control. Whitten will start the 1995 season in Double-A.

Professional Batting Register

	BA	G	AB	R	H	2B	3B	HR	RBI	SB
93 R	.238	66	235	46	63	10	3	6	30	15
94 A	.290	132	524	107	152	24	5	27	83	31

Professional Pitching Register

	W	L	ERA	G	CG	IP	H	ER	BB	SO
93 A	6	3	2.42	14	0	81.2	75	22	18	81
94 A	9	10	4.28	27	0	153.1	127	73	64	148

GLENN WILLIAMS

Position: Shortstop
Team: Atlanta Braves
Born: July 18, 1977 Gosford, Australia
Height: 6'2" **Weight:** 170 lbs.
Bats: both **Throws:** right
Acquired: Signed as a nondrafted free agent, 7/93

Player Summary	
Fantasy Value	$0
Card Value	15¢ to 25¢
Will	hit more
Can't	judge him yet
Expect	slow promotions
Don't Expect	Chipper Jones

Like Jose Pett, Williams created a stir by signing at a young age from a country not usually known as a baseball export center. But whereas Pett comes from Brazil and signed with the Blue Jays, Williams hails from Down Under and is hoping to make his name with Atlanta. In fact, he has a chance to be the most significant player ever developed in his country. Williams got his feet wet in North America last year at the lowest levels of the minor leagues, not bad considering he just turned 17 last July. He played both in the rookie Gulf Coast League and the rookie Appalachian League. Even though his stats weren't the best, you have to consider all the circumstances, including his age and the fact that he was so far from home. He did better in the Appy League than in the Gulf Coast League. He had a .253 batting average in the Appy League, with a .344 on-base percentage. Appy League skippers tabbed Williams as the No. 1 prospect in the circuit, according to a poll in *Baseball America*. He enjoyed a solid August, indicating that he was not overmatched. Williams received some additional pro experience playing in the Australian Winter League.

KEITH WILLIAMS

Position: Outfield
Team: San Francisco Giants
Born: April 21, 1972 Bedford, PA
Height: 6' **Weight:** 190 lbs.
Bats: right **Throws:** right
Acquired: Seventh-round pick in 6/93 free-agent draft

Player Summary	
Fantasy Value	$0
Card Value	15¢ to 20¢
Will	play left
Can't	steal bunches
Expect	good batting eye
Don't Expect	Barry Bonds

The Giants are well fixed in the outfield right now, but they won't be forever. When an opening comes up, Williams could be the man to fill it. He has played two years of pro ball and been a superior player each time. In fact, he was named to *Baseball America*'s short-season All-Star team for his work in the Northwest League in 1993. That publication also named him the No. 3 prospect in the circuit that year. Last year, he was one of the top home run hitters and RBI men in the San Francisco farm system. Playing for San Jose of the Class-A California League, he hit 10 home runs with a .377 average during the month of August. He led his squad in doubles, homers, RBI, and runs, and he was second in triples. And for all his power, he struck out only about 100 times, not great but something a team can live with from a slugger. His slugging percentage was over the .500 mark, and he walked 60 times to push his on-base average over the .370 level. In there every day, Williams was the only San Jose batter to reach 500 at bats. The Clemson product is a good fielder who has the speed to play center and enough arm to be stationed in right.

Professional Batting Register

	BA	G	AB	R	H	2B	3B	HR	RBI	SB
94 R	.226	48	168	19	38	4	0	3	16	6

Professional Batting Register

	BA	G	AB	R	H	2B	3B	HR	RBI	SB
93 A	.302	75	288	57	87	21	5	12	49	21
94 A	.300	128	504	91	151	30	8	21	97	4

ANTONE WILLIAMSON

Position: Third base
Team: Milwaukee Brewers
Born: July 18, 1973 Torrance, CA
Height: 6'1" **Weight:** 185 lbs.
Bats: left **Throws:** right
Acquired: First-round pick in 6/94 free-agent draft

Player Summary	
Fantasy Value	$0
Card Value	25¢ to 35¢
Will	hit homers
Can't	rule out bunt
Expect	expertise with lumber
Don't Expect	a Gold Glove

Williamson has developed a reputation as having one of the best swings coming into the pro game. The Brewers see him as someone who can play third base and provide run production, possibly within a year. Out of Arizona State, he created quite a sensation at the College World Series, batting over .500 and being named to the all-tournament team. He collected three of his team's seven hits in the game that knocked them out of the tourney. Williamson was named to the college All-America team by *Baseball America* and was the publication's choice as the second-best pure hitter among college players in the draft. He signed for a bonus just under $900,000, then reported to the rookie Pioneer League. After just six games, he was promoted to the Class-A California League, where in his first game he showed his plate skills with a seventh-inning homer that tied the score and a game-winning ninth-inning squeeze. His defense does not draw the same raves, but the Brewers think it will do. Williamson will begin the year in Double-A, if not higher, and should be in Milwaukee by the end of the season.

Professional Batting Register

	BA	G	AB	R	H	2B	3B	HR	RBI	SB
94 R	.423	6	26	5	11	2	1	0	4	0
94 A	.224	23	85	6	19	4	0	3	13	0
94 AA	.250	14	48	8	12	3	0	1	9	0

ENRIQUE WILSON

Position: Shortstop
Team: Cleveland Indians
Born: July 27, 1975 Santo Domingo, Dominican Republic
Height: 5'11" **Weight:** 160 lbs.
Bats: both **Throws:** right
Acquired: Traded from Twins for Shawn Bryant, 2/94

Player Summary	
Fantasy Value	$0
Card Value	12¢ to 20¢
Will	hit doubles
Can't	worry about the road
Expect	a great glove
Don't Expect	a slap hitter

Wilson was a pleasant surprise after being acquired in a little-noticed deal before the season. Signed as a free agent by the Twins in December of 1992, Wilson had spent two solid years in their organization. In fact, he was second in the rookie Appalachian League in home run frequency in 1993, hitting one every 15 at bats. Cleveland traded pitcher Shawn Bryant to the Twins, and Wilson was chosen as the player to be named later. He was assigned to the Class-A South Atlantic League, where he hit for average, and reached double figures in triples, home runs, and stolen bases. A shortstop, he can complement his quickness and good hands with an ability to switch-hit. Wilson hit his first home run in the Cleveland organization on April 13 in a 5-3 victory. He fared much better at home than on the road, hitting .452 in his first 10 home games and only .188 over the same span on the road. At one point in June, he led the league in hits. By the end of the season, South Atlantic League skippers tabbed Wilson as the loop's No. 2 prospect in *Baseball America*.

Professional Batting Register

	BA	G	AB	R	H	2B	3B	HR	RBI	SB
92 R	.341	13	44	12	15	1	0	0	8	3
93 R	.289	58	197	42	57	8	4	13	50	5
94 A	.279	133	512	82	143	28	12	10	72	21

NIGEL WILSON

Position: Outfield
Team: Florida Marlins
Born: Jan. 12, 1970 Oshawa, Ontario
Height: 6'1" **Weight:** 185 lbs.
Bats: left **Throws:** left
Acquired: First-round pick from Blue Jays in 11/92 expansion draft

Player Summary	
Fantasy Value	$1
Card Value	12¢ to 15¢
Will	face crucial year
Can't	wait much longer
Expect	decreased speed
Don't Expect	run producer

Wilson arrived in the Florida organization amid lots of fanfare as the club's first pick of the expansion draft. But time is running out on his prospect status, as he has turned 25 with a club acquiring new talent all the time. Last year in the Pacific Coast League, Wilson got off to a poor start, then went on the disabled list with a sprained ankle. As a result, he didn't put up much in the way of totals. Still, in '94 he had a .369 on-base average and a .506 slugging percentage. It was the third straight season that he had a slugging average over .500. Wilson was originally signed by the Blue Jays as a non-drafted free agent in 1987, after he was a member of the Canadian National team. His best season in the Toronto chain came in 1992, when he led the Southern League with 34 doubles and was named to the postseason All-Star team. There is absolutely no reason for Wilson to play another game in the minor leagues. All that is left for him to do is go to Florida and hit big-league pitching.

Professional Batting Register

	BA	G	AB	R	H	2B	3B	HR	RBI	SB
88 A	.204	40	103	12	21	1	2	2	11	8
89 A	.217	42	161	17	35	5	2	4	18	8
90 A	.273	110	440	77	120	23	9	16	62	22
91 A	.301	119	455	64	137	18	13	12	55	27
92 AA	.274	137	521	85	143	34	7	26	69	13
93 AAA	.292	96	370	66	108	26	7	17	68	8
93 NL	.000	7	16	0	0	0	0	0	0	0
94 AAA	.309	87	314	50	97	24	1	12	62	2

PAUL WILSON

Position: Pitcher
Team: New York Mets
Born: March 28, 1973 Orlando, FL
Height: 6'5" **Weight:** 217 lbs.
Bats: right **Throws:** right
Acquired: First-round pick in 6/94 free-agent draft

Player Summary	
Fantasy Value	$0
Card Value	15¢ to 20¢
Will	come at you
Can't	be distracted
Expect	top command
Don't Expect	a bust

As the first player taken in the 1994 draft, Wilson will find it very hard to escape scrutiny. Some players never adjust to this; others don't seem to mind. It remains to be seen how Wilson handles it. There is little doubt about his stuff. He has a high velocity fastball with ample movement to it. His slider and changeup are both plus pitches. His control is also above average, and he has received high grades for his attitude. After being signed to a bonus of about $1.55 million, Wilson reported to the rookie Gulf Coast League and then graduated to the Class-A Florida State League. The Mets held him under a pitch limit. He did not win a game in the pros, but he showed the tremendous velocity that earned him the first-selection status. His command of his pitches seemed to waver in the FSL. The Mets sent him to the Instructional League to work on his control. Wilson comes out of Florida State, where he pitched the Seminoles into the College World Series. Among his games was a 16-strikeout effort against Charleston. Wilson will probably start the 1995 season in Double-A, but he might not be beating the bushes by the end of the season.

Professional Pitching Register

	W	L	ERA	G	CG	IP	H	ER	BB	SO
94 R	0	2	3.00	3	0	12.0	8	4	4	13
94 A	0	5	5.06	8	0	37.1	32	21	17	37

JAY WITASICK

Position: Pitcher
Team: St. Louis Cardinals
Born: Aug. 28, 1972 Baltimore, MD
Height: 6'4" **Weight:** 205 lbs.
Bats: right **Throws:** right
Acquired: Second-round pick in 6/93 free-agent draft

Player Summary	
Fantasy Value	$0
Card Value	15¢ to 25¢
Will	be question mark
Can't	worry about back
Expect	strikeouts
Don't Expect	lots of contact

Witasick was one of the top pitchers in the St. Louis system until a back injury cut him down in midseason. He was leading all of minor-league ball with 141 strikeouts when he was forced to the sidelines. As another indication of his dominance, Witasick had allowed an opponents' batting average of .135 through May 24. Then, on June 18, he fanned 13 in six and two-thirds innings. In his next start, he again struck out 13, stretching his winning streak to six. At that point, Witasick was leading the Midwest League with 127 strikeouts and was fifth in ERA at 2.25. Then his fortunes began to change. A 5-3 loss to Clinton on July 9 broke his winning streak, and shortly thereafter Witasick went on the disabled list. Even with his season cut short, he still ranked among the organization's leaders in strikeouts and ERA. He walked less than three and one-half batters per nine innings last year. ML skippers put him as the No. 3 prospect in the loop, according to a poll by *Baseball America*. He also was named to the postseason All-Star team. Obviously, the biggest issue now is Witasick's health and whether he can come back throwing the way he did in 1994.

KEVIN WITT

Position: Shortstop; infield
Team: Toronto Blue Jays
Born: Jan. 5, 1976 High Point, NC
Height: 6'4" **Weight:** 185 lbs.
Bats: left **Throws:** right
Acquired: First-round pick in 6/94 free-agent draft

Player Summary	
Fantasy Value	$0
Card Value	15¢ to 25¢
Will	show tools
Can't	zoom through system
Expect	a choice bat
Don't Expect	a shortstop

With a talent like Alex Gonzalez knocking on the door, you'd think the last thing the Blue Jays needed was a shortstop. But not only did they tab Witt with their first pick, they picked three other high school shortstops in the top seven rounds. *Baseball America* ranked Witt as the 39th prospect entering the draft. The Blue Jays took him 28th overall, closing out the first round. He comes out of Jacksonville, Florida, where he hit close to .500 last year. He turned out to be a quick sign and was dispatched to Medicine Hat of the Pioneer League. One highlight came when he hit a game-winning, leadoff homer in the 11th inning on Aug. 4. With his size, power would not be a surprise. He ended the season with a .416 slugging percentage. He struck out 52 times, a rate that he needs to trim. He also garnered 15 bases on balls and had a .300 on-base average. It would also not be a surprise to see him at another position. He has the arm and the hands for shortstop, though he might not have the range. The Blue Jays may let Witt develop at shortstop and switch him to third base only when it is necessary.

Professional Pitching Register

	W	L	ERA	G	CG	IP	H	ER	BB	SO
94 A	10	4	2.32	18	2	112.1	74	29	42	141

Professional Batting Register

	BA	G	AB	R	H	2B	3B	HR	RBI	SB
94 R	.255	60	243	37	62	10	4	7	36	4

BRAD WOODALL

Position: Pitcher
Team: Atlanta Braves
Born: June 25, 1969 Atlanta, GA
Height: 6′ **Weight:** 175 lbs.
Bats: both **Throws:** left
Acquired: Signed as a free agent, 6/91

Player Summary
```
Fantasy Value. . . . . . . . . . . . . . . . . $1 to $3
Card Value . . . . . . . . . . . . . . . . 12¢ to 15¢
Will . . . . . . . . . . . . . . . . . . . . stay in Atlanta
Can't . . . . . . . . . . . . . . . . . rule out bullpen
Expect. . . . . . . . . . . . . . . . . . . . a changeup
Don't Expect. . . . . . . . . . . . . . . . . a fizzle
```

NL clubs would say that the last thing Atlanta needs is more pitching, but that's exactly what may be on the way. *Baseball America* chose Woodall as the No. 10 prospect in the Triple-A International League. That publication also tabbed him as having the best control in the circuit. He was the winning pitcher in the Triple-A All-Star Game, tossing two perfect innings. He had entered the break in style, hurling a shutout and earning Player of the Week honors from *USA TODAY Baseball Weekly*. He was named to the postseason All-Star team and was the loop's Most Valuable Pitcher. While he has a below-average fastball, he paints the corners, changes speeds, and throws strikes. He allowed less than two and one-half bases on balls per nine innings. Out of the University of North Carolina, Woodall has only been a starting pitcher for two years. In fact, he served as closer when he broke into pro ball, picking up 15 saves in two stops.

Professional Pitching Register
	W	L	ERA	G	CG	IP	H	ER	BB	SO
91 R	4	1	1.37	28	0	39.1	29	6	19	57
91 A	0	0	2.45	4	0	7.1	4	2	4	14
92 A	1	2	2.13	24	0	42.1	30	10	11	51
92 AA	3	4	3.20	21	0	39.1	26	14	17	45
93 A	3	1	3.00	6	1	30.0	21	10	6	27
93 AA	2	4	3.38	8	1	53.1	43	20	24	38
93 AAA	5	3	4.21	10	0	57.2	59	27	16	45
94 AAA	15	6	2.42	27	4	185.2	159	50	49	137
94 NL	0	1	4.50	1	0	6.0	5	3	2	2

JARET WRIGHT

Position: Pitcher
Team: Cleveland Indians
Born: Dec. 29, 1975 Anaheim, CA
Height: 6′2″ **Weight:** 218 lbs.
Bats: right **Throws:** right
Acquired: First-round pick in 6/94 free-agent draft

Player Summary
```
Fantasy Value . . . . . . . . . . . . . . . . . . . . . $0
Card Value . . . . . . . . . . . . . . . . 15¢ to 25¢
Will . . . . . . . . . . . . . . . . . . sink his fastball
Can't . . . . . . . . . . . . . . . . . . rely on name
Expect . . . . . . . . . . . . . . . . a breaking ball
Don't Expect . . . . . . . . . . . pinpoint control
```

Wright grew up in the shadow of Anaheim Stadium, but if all goes the way it should, he'll be returning as an enemy. The son of former big-league pitcher Clyde Wright, Jaret was taken with the 10th overall pick, and was only the second high school pitcher tabbed in '94. The younger Wright comes out of Katella High School in Anaheim, where he struck out 111 in 82 innings. According to *Baseball America*, he owned the best velocity of any high schooler in the draft. He adds a sinking action to his fastball and can also throw a breaking ball. He is taller and heftier than his father was, and he looks like a power pitcher. After a somewhat lengthy negotiation, Wright signed and was sent to Burlington of the rookie Appalachian League. In his pro debut, he threw in the 90s consistently. Wright compiled a 6.48 ERA in his first three starts, but the important thing is that he got his feet wet. The Appy League managers still tabbed him as the No. 3 prospect in the loop and top pitching prospect, according to *Baseball America*. This year, Wright will probably report to a low Class-A league. There is no need to rush him through the system.

Professional Pitching Register
	W	L	ERA	G	CG	IP	H	ER	BB	SO
94 R	0	1	5.40	4	0	13.1	13	8	9	16

Team Overviews

You'll find an overview of the 28 major-league organizations in this section. Because there were no final pennant races in 1994, this section is arranged alphabetically, starting with the AL East, followed by the AL Central, the AL West, the NL East, the NL Central, and the NL West.

The teams are ordered as follows: Baltimore Orioles, Boston Red Sox, Detroit Tigers, New York Yankees, and Toronto Blue Jays in the AL East; Chicago White Sox, Cleveland Indians, Kansas City Royals, Milwaukee Brewers, and Minnesota Twins in the AL Central; California Angels, Oakland Athletics, Seattle Mariners, and Texas Rangers in the AL West; Atlanta Braves, Florida Marlins, Montreal Expos, New York Mets, and Philadelphia Phillies in the NL East; Chicago Cubs, Cincinnati Reds, Houston Astros, Pittsburgh Pirates, and St. Louis Cardinals in the NL Central; and Colorado Rockies, Los Angeles Dodgers, San Diego Padres, and San Francisco Giants in the NL West.

Each team overview begins with an analysis of that club's key players (not all of each ballclub's players are mentioned); the team's 1994 season is examined as well. The manager section includes the skipper's overall record, including each major-league ballclub he has managed, his overall record with his current team, and his record in 1994. The abbreviations for managers are: **W** = wins; **L** = losses; **PCT** = winning percentage. The executives listed comprise the ownership and front-office baseball structure for each organization.

The "Five-Year Finishes" show in what place each organization finished in its division in the last five years. If two or more clubs were tied for a position—such as the Baltimore Orioles and the Detroit Tigers, who tied for third in the 1993 AL East—each ballclub gets a "T" designation; the Orioles and the Tigers received a T3. Each team's overall five-year record is included; the "Rank" compares the five-year record against the other 27 major-league organizations. The ballparks that the franchise has occupied, plus the years that it was there, are shown. If more than one ballpark is listed for a given year, the franchise occupied both parks during that season. The seating capacity and the dimensions of the present ballpark are included, as is the team's address. A brief history of each organization is presented with an emphasis on how each franchise has done over the last 15 to 20 years.

BALTIMORE ORIOLES
63-49 .563 6½ GB Manager: Johnny Oates

After spending big bucks in the off-season to procure a pennant, the Orioles fell just short of their goal by the time the strike hit in August. Newcomers Rafael Palmeiro, Lee Smith, Sid Fernandez, and Chris Sabo were expected to provide the additional talent that manager Johnny Oates needed to take the O's to the top. It didn't happen, and Oates lost his job. Baltimore boasted two of the best-looking young starters in the AL, with Mike Mussina (16-5, 3.06 ERA) cementing his reputation as one of the league's top hurlers and Ben McDonald (14-7, 4.06) fulfilling some of the promise he showed as the top pick in the 1989 draft. Jamie Moyer (5-7, 4.77), Fernandez (6-6, 5.15), and Arthur Rhodes (3-5, 5.81) filled out a rotation that was a big part of the O's disappointing outcome. Smith led the league with 33

saves, anchoring a bullpen that included Mark Eichhorn (6-5, 2.15), Alan Mills (3-3, 5.16), and Mark Williamson (3-1, 4.01). Palmeiro again showed a fine bat (.319, 23 homers, 76 RBI, 82 runs scored) and led the offense. The iron man, Cal Ripken, also put up outstanding numbers (.315, 13, 75) while playing in every game. Outfielder Brady Anderson (.263, 78 runs) provided a solid bat, while Jeff Hammonds (.296) proved to be one of the most exciting youngsters in the game. Second baseman Mark McLemore (.257) and catcher Chris Hoiles (.247, 19, 53) ebbed somewhat after big 1993 seasons. Also contributing to the Orioles' attack was DH Harold Baines (.294, 16, 54) and third basemen Leo Gomez (.274, 15, 56) and Sabo (.256, 11, 42). Outfielder Mike Devereaux (.203) turned in a poor season.

Manager Phil Regan	W	L	PCT
Major-league record	—	—	—
with Orioles	—	—	—
1994 record	—	—	—

Coaches: Elrod Hendricks, Mike Flanagan, Lee May, Al Bumbry, Chuck Cottier, Steve Boros

Five-Year Finishes

90	91	92	93	94
5	6	3	T3	2

Five-Year Record: 380-379; .501
Rank: 6th in AL; 11th in ML

Chief Executive Officer: Peter Angelos
GM: Roland Hemond
Assistant GM: Frank Robinson
Director of Player Development: Syd Thrift
Director of Scouting: Gary Nickels

Address
Oriole Park at Camden Yards
333 West Camden Street
Baltimore, MD 21201

Ballparks

Milwaukee: Lloyd Street Grounds 1901. **St. Louis:** Sportsman's Park 1902-1953. **Baltimore:** Memorial Stadium 1954-1991; Oriole Park at Camden Yards 1992-present
Capacity: 48,000

1994 Attendance: 2,535,359
Surface: natural grass
Left field fence: 333 feet
Center field fence: 400 feet
Right field fence: 318 feet
Left-center fence: 410 feet
Right-center fence: 373 feet

Team History

For nearly 45 years, futility in American League baseball had a home in St. Louis. The Browns, founded in 1902, wallowed at the bottom of the standings until 1944. Winning the pennant in 1944, they lost the Series to the crosstown Cardinals. The franchise began anew in 1954, moving to Baltimore. By developing a very productive farm system, the Orioles became pennant contenders by the 1960s. A first-ever World Series win came to the franchise in 1966, and the Orioles went on to become a force to

be dealt with, challenging for top honors for three consecutive years (1969 to '71). Boasting the talents of such players as Brooks and Frank Robinson, Boog Powell, Jim Palmer, and Cal Ripken Jr., and manager Earl Weaver, the Orioles are noted for unity and strong fundamentals. They have won seven division titles, six pennants, and three world titles (1966, 1970, and '83). They stumbled out of the blocks in 1984, but by 1989 they had recovered, going from last place to one game out of first.

411

BOSTON RED SOX

54-61 .470 17 GB Manager: Butch Hobson

Lacking top talent, the Red Sox turned in another middling season before the strike. This mediocre effort in scouting and actual playing caused turnover in the front office. General manager Dan Duquette at the end of the season fired skipper Butch Hobson and started to realign the franchise. His first order of business should be to improve an offense that finished near the bottom of the league in runs scored. First baseman Mo Vaughn (.310, 26 homers, 82 RBI) was the only real sharp point in an otherwise dull attack. The outfield provided speed with Otis Nixon (.274, 60 runs scored, 42 stolen bases) and hitting with Mike Greenwell (.269, 11, 45). Third baseman Scott Cooper (.282, 13, 53) had his moments. Tom Brunansky (.234, 10, 34) and Wes Chamberlain (.256) showed some pop in right field. Young shortstop John Valentin (.316) and second baseman Tim Naehring (.276, 7, 42) gave BoSox fans hope for a solid middle infield. Designated hitter Andre Dawson (.240, 16, 48) started to show his age. Roger Clemens (9-7, 2.85 ERA, 168 strikeouts), as always, headed up the starting rotation. Young gun Aaron Sele (8-7, 3.83) showed promise, while Joe Hesketh (8-5, 4.26) and Danny Darwin (7-5, 6.30) provided innings. Steve Farr (four saves) figured to lead the bullpen, but young Ken Ryan wrested the closer job away and notched 13 saves. The rest of the relief staff was in disarray.

Manager			
Kevin Kennedy	W	L	PCT
Major-league record	138	138	.500
with Red Sox	—	—	—
1994 record (with Rangers)	52	62	.456

Coaches: Mike Easler, Frank White, Tim Johnson, Herm Starrette, Dave Oliver

Ballparks

Huntington Avenue Grounds
1901-1911; Fenway Park
1912-present
Capacity: 33,925
1994 Attendance: 1,775,826
Surface: natural grass

Left field fence: 315 feet
Center field fence: 390 feet
Right field fence: 302 feet
Left-center fence: 379 feet
Right-center fence: 380 feet

Five-Year Finishes

90	91	92	93	94
1	T2	7	5	4

Five-Year Record: 379-384, .497
Rank: 7th in AL; 13th in ML

President: John L. Harrington
Owner and General Partner: Haywood C. Sullivan
Executive VP: Lou Gorman
GM: Dan Duquette
VP, Baseball Development: Edward M. Kasko
Director of Scouting: W. Wayne Britton
Director of Minor League Operations: Edward P. Kenney

Address
Fenway Park
4 Yawkey Way
Boston, MA 02215

Team History

Long-suffering Beantown fans wish they could be transported back to the early 1900s, when the BoSox were winners—five pennants, four world titles. But after selling Babe Ruth to the Yankees in 1920, the franchise fell fast. The Sox rebounded in the 1940s and 1950s, but didn't bounce back quite enough, save a pennant in '46. The arrival of young blood in the 1960s helped elevate the team to a pennant in '67. Not until 1975, and the influx of more youngsters, did the sagging Sox get another lift. They stretched out a run at a world championship in '75, only to lose to the Reds in game seven. Again in 1986, exceptional talent brought the BoSox a pennant, but not even the likes of Wade Boggs and Roger Clemens could overcome what seems to be the perpetual close-but-no-cigar syndrome. The Red Sox also won division championships in 1988 and '90 but failed to move past the Athletics in the ALCS each time.

DETROIT TIGERS

53-62 .465 18 GB Manager: Sparky Anderson

The Tigers outscored all but two teams in 1994, but with a poor 5.38 team ERA, Detroit had no chance to compete for a division title. Manager Sparky Anderson continues to accumulate more wins and now stands below just Connie Mack, John McGraw, and Bucky Harris on the all-time list. Anderson last year relied on big bats such as first baseman Cecil Fielder (.259, 28 homers, 90 RBI), third baseman Travis Fryman (.263, 18, 85), and catcher-utility player Mickey Tettleton (.248, 17, 51). Former utility man Tony Phillips played mostly in left field and turned in a fine year (.281, 19, 61, 91 runs scored). Lou Whitaker (.301, 12, 43) and Alan Trammell (.267, 8, 28) again by and large formed the keystone combination, as they have done for about every year since 1978. Chris Gomez (.257, 8, 53) capably supported the duo. There were some problems in center field, with Eric Davis getting hurt, but Juan Samuel and Milt Cuyler filled in adequately. Junior Felix played well in right field, but Chad Kreuter was disappointing behind the plate. Speaking of disappointing, the Detroit starting rotation was pummelled last year. David Wells (5-7, 3.56 ERA) had the best season. Tim Belcher (7-15, 5.89), Mike Moore (11-10, 5.42), Bill Gullickson (4-5, 5.93), and John Doherty (6-7, 6.48) received five runs of support a game or more, but still they could not have successful seasons. Joe Boever, Buddy Groom, Mike Gardiner, and Storm Davis had OK seasons in the bullpen, but former closer Mike Henneman (1-3, 5.19 ERA, eight saves, five blown saves) seems to have lost it.

Manager			
Sparky Anderson	W	L	PCT
Major-league record	2134	1750	.549
with Tigers	1271	1164	.522
1994 record	53	62	.465

Coaches: Larry Herndon, Gene Roof, Dick Tracewski, Billy Consolo, Ralph Treuel, Jeff Jones

Five-Year Finishes

90	91	92	93	94
3	T2	6	T3	5

Five-Year Record: 376-387; .493
Rank: 9th in AL; T16th in ML

Owner, Chairman of the Board: Mike Ilitch
GM: Jerry Walker
Assistant GM: Gary Vitto
Senior Director, Scouting: Joe Klein
Director, Minor League Operations: Dave Miller
Director, Field Operations: John Lipon

Address
Tiger Stadium
Detroit, MI 48216

Ballparks

Bennett Park 1901-1911; Tiger Stadium 1912-present
Capacity: 52,416
1994 Attendance: 1,184,783
Surface: natural grass

Left field fence: 340 feet
Center field fence: 440 feet
Right field fence: 325 feet
Left-center fence: 365 feet
Right-center fence: 375 feet

Team History

With a winning percentage of over .500, the Tigers have been perennial contenders since their inception in 1901. They have finished last only six times and have never had more than four consecutive losing seasons. The franchise has won 11 titles and brought world championships to the Motor City in 1935, 1945, 1968, and 1984. The Tigers brought a feisty manager aboard in mid-1979. Sparky Anderson provided a mature, seasoned presence, shaping the Detroit club into a formidable force in less than five years. The Tigers were a mighty power in '84, boasting big arms on offense and defense. The next two years, however, they dipped down to third in their division. In 1987, they roared back to win the AL East, but fell short of making the Series. In 1989, they bottomed out, finishing last in their division. The Tigers have found offense but are still looking for pitching in the 1990s.

NEW YORK YANKEES

70-43 .619 0 GB Manager: Buck Showalter

The unofficial American League champions, the New York Yankees combined a superior and deep offense, a solid starting rotation, and good fielding to produce the best won-lost margin in the loop. Manager Buck Showalter focused on teamwork and dependability, and the Bronx Bombers were staunch the entire year. The offense led the league with a .290 batting average, due in part to batting champion Paul O'Neill (.359, 21 homers, 83 RBI). O'Neill looked like he was going to make a run at .400 early before he settled into his .359 groove. Third baseman Wade Boggs (.342) also showed that he could still hit for a high average, while first baseman and captain Don Mattingly (.304) provided more than just inspiration, although he was still denied postseason play.

Others contributing with the lumber were Bernie Williams (.289, 80 runs scored), Luis Polonia (.311), Danny Tartabull (.256, 19, 67), Mike Stanley (.300, 17, 57), and Jim Leyritz (.265, 17, 58). Pat Kelly and Mike Gallego provided solid keystone play. Jimmy Key (17-4, 3.27 ERA) had a fantastic season. Jim Abbott (9-8, 4.55), Scott Kamieniecki (8-6, 3.76), and Melido Perez (9-4, 4.10) joined Key in forming a solid rotation. Terry Mulholland (6-7, 6.49) had an off year, however. Left-hander Steve Howe notched 15 saves and a 1.80 ERA to take command of the closer's job. Bob Wickman was the workhorse from the right side, but the rest of the bullpen—Xavier Hernandez, Paul Gibson, and Sterling Hitchcock—had some troubles.

Manager			
Buck Showalter	W	L	PCT
Major-league record	234	203	.536
with Yankees	234	203	.536
1994 record	70	43	.619

Coaches: Clete Boyer, Tony Cloninger, Mark Connor, Rick Down, Ed Napoleon, Brian Butterfield, Willie Randolph, Billy Connors

Five-Year Finishes

90	91	92	93	94
7	5	T4	2	1

Five-Year Record: 372-389; .489
Rank: 10th in AL; 18th in ML

Principal Owner: George M. Steinbrenner
VP, GM: Gene Michael
VP, Player Development and Scouting: Bill Livesey
Assistant GM, Baseball Operations: Tim McCleary
Coordinator of Scouting: Kevin Elfering
Director of Minor League Operations: Mitch Lukevics

Address
Yankee Stadium
Bronx, NY 10451

Ballparks

American League Park 1901-1902; Hilltop Park 1903-1912; Polo Grounds 1913-1922; Shea Stadium 1974-1975; Yankee Stadium 1923-1973, 1976-present
Capacity: 57,545

1994 Attendance: 1,675,557
Surface: natural grass
Left field fence: 318 feet
Center field fence: 408 feet
Right field fence: 314 feet
Left-center fence: 399 feet
Right-center fence: 385 feet

Team History

Easily baseball's showcase franchise, the Yankees have won a record 22 world championships and have fielded some of the game's greatest teams, players, and managers. The 1927 "Murderer's Row" unit featured immortals Babe Ruth and Lou Gehrig, while Hall of Famers like Joe DiMaggio, Yogi Berra, and Whitey Ford dotted the rosters in the 1930s, 1940s, and 1950s. The 1977 and '78 championship squads boasted Reggie Jackson and

Catfish Hunter. The 1980s saw the Yankees twist in the wind. Owner George Steinbrenner had Billy Martin on a revolving door when it came to the skipper position. During Steinbrenner's first 17 years as owner, there were 17 different managers. By 1990, the once-legendary Yankees were at the bottom of their division. In 1991 and '92, they had stepped up to fifth, and finished second in 1993. In 1994, the Bombers had the best record in the AL.

TORONTO BLUE JAYS

55-60 .478 16 GB Manager: Cito Gaston

In 1993, Toronto used offensive firepower to pick up the slack for a pedestrian pitching staff and win a world championship. Again in '94 Toronto had an ordinary mound squad, but when its offense sank into mediocrity, the club became, well, mediocre. GM Pat Gillick, in his last season before retirement, counted on youngsters such as Carlos Delgado (.215, nine homers, 24 RBI), Alex Gonzalez (.151), and Shawn Green (.091) to provide new talent for manager Cito Gaston, and the kids just weren't ready. Eventually, they will be. Meanwhile, the ageless Paul Molitor (.341, 14, 75) continued to amaze with a drive toward the Hall of Fame. Robby Alomar (.306, eight, 38, 78 runs scored) remained perhaps the best second baseman in baseball. Right fielder Joe Carter (.271, 27, 103) started out hot and again put up fine numbers. Devon White (.270) is still a fine center fielder, while first sacker John Olerud (.297), although not equalling 1993's numbers, had a pretty good year. Mike Huff (.304) was the biggest surprise of the season. Ed Sprague struggled a bit at third, Dick Schofield filled in at shortstop, and Pat Borders again received much of the catching chores. Staff pitching ace Juan Guzman (12-11, 5.68 ERA, 124 strike-outs) seems to have lost some of his control. Pat Hentgen turned in another pretty good season (13-8, 3.40). Todd Stottlemyre, Dave Stewart, and Al Leiter all had problems in the rotation. Duane Ward, 1993's closer, was hurt all season, so the closer duties fell on minor-league veteran but major-league rookie Darren Hall, who acquitted himself quite nicely (17 saves). Tony Castillo and Woody Williams also had good years in the bullpen.

Manager			
Cito Gaston	W	L	PCT
Major-league record	473	369	.562
with Blue Jays	473	369	.562
1994 record	55	60	.478
Coaches: Bob Bailor, Galen Cisco, Larry Hisle, John Sullivan, Gene Tenace, Nick Leyva, Dennis Holmberg			

Ballparks

Exhibition Stadium 1977-1989;
  SkyDome 1989-present
Capacity: 50,516
1994 Attendance: 2,907,933
Surface: artificial turf
Retractable Dome

Left field fence: 328 feet
Center field fence: 400 feet
Right field fence: 328 feet
Left-center fence: 375 feet
Right-center fence: 375 feet

Five-Year Finishes

90	91	92	93	94
2	1	1	1	3

Five-Year Record: 423-340; .554
Rank: 2nd in AL; 3rd in ML

Chairman: P.N.T. Widdrington
President & CEO: Paul Beeston
GM: Gord Ash
VP, Baseball: Bob Mattick
VP, Baseball: Al LaMacchia
Director, Development: Mel Queen
Director, Scouting: Bob Engle

Address
1 Blue Jays Way
Suite 3200, SkyDome
Toronto, Ontario M5V 1J1

Team History

Unlike their 1977 expansion sibling, Seattle, the Blue Jays have enjoyed growing success over the years. Toronto asserted itself in the early 1980s and became a contender. The Jays won the 1985 AL East crown but choked away the '87 title, losing their last seven games. In 1989, the Blue Jays moved from Exhibition Stadium to the SkyDome. It was that same year that Cito Gaston took over as skipper. They rebounded to win a division title again in '89, but that was as far as the Blue Jays progressed. The following season was disappointing for the Jays, as after much effort, they failed to sew up their division on the final day of regular-season play. The team, developing a reputation for choking, put an end to that in 1992 by becoming world champions, winning the fall classic in six games over Atlanta. The Blue Jays again took a trophy through customs in 1993 by beating the Phillies in six.

CHICAGO WHITE SOX

67-46 .593 0 GB Manager: Gene Lamont

Manager Gene Lamont's ChiSox powered their way to the top of the new AL Central division, beating out Cleveland by one game before the strike. The South Siders were led by a starting staff that was rivaled by few others in baseball. Black Jack McDowell (10-9, 3.73 ERA, 127 strikeouts) started the season incredibly slow before picking it up at the end. Jason Bere (12-2, 3.81) caught everyone's attention as a comer. Wilson Alvarez (12-8, 3.45) proved to be one of the better young pitchers in the game, Alex Fernandez (11-7, 3.86) started to come into his own, and even Scott Sanderson contributed. While the bullpen wasn't quite up to the rotation's standards, it played OK by and large. Roberto Hernandez saved 14 games, but his stats were well off his 1993 pace. Paul Assenmacher, Jose DeLeon, Kirk McCaskill, and Dennis Cook all performed well. While the

White Sox had the best pitching in the American League, notching a 3.96 ERA, they are the "Hitless Wonders" no longer. Of course, when you have the "Big Hurt," you have an offense. Two-time MVP Frank Thomas (.353, 38 homers, 101 RBI, 109 walks, 106 runs scored) led the league in both on-base average and slugging percentage. Julio Franco (.319, 20, 98) showed an incredibly powerful stick as a DH, protecting Thomas. Left fielder Tim Raines (.266, 80 runs scored) again turned in a solid season, third baseman Robin Ventura continued to hit effectively (.282, 18, 78), and right fielder Darrin Jackson (.312) was a fine surprise. Lance Johnson, Ozzie Guillen, and Joey Cora provided fine defense and were valuable hitters as well. Ron Karkovice was the best defensive catcher in baseball last year.

Manager			
Gene Lamont	W	L	PCT
Major-league record	247	190	.565
with White Sox	247	190	.565
1994 record	67	46	.593

Coaches: Terry Bevington, Jackie Brown, Walt Hriniak, Doug Mansolino, Joe Nossek, Dewey Robinson

Five-Year Finishes

90	91	92	93	94
2	2	3	1	1

Five-Year Record: 428-332; .563
Rank: 1st in AL; 1st in ML

Chairman: Jerry Reinsdorf
Vice Chairman: Eddie Einhorn
Executive VP: Howard Pizer
Senior VP, Major League Operations: Ron Schueler
Senior VP, Baseball: Jack Gould
VP, Scouting & Minor League Operations: Larry Monroe

Address
Comiskey Park
333 W. 35th Street
Chicago, IL 60616

Ballparks

South Side Park 1901-1910;
  Comiskey Park 1910-1990;
  Comiskey Park II 1991-
  present
Capacity: 44,321
1994 Attendance: 1,697,398

Surface: natural grass
Left field fence: 347 feet
Center field fence: 400 feet
Right field fence: 347 feet
Left-center fence: 375 feet
Right-center fence: 375 feet

Team History

Although the Sox' 91-year history has been a roller-coaster ride, no one could ever call it boring. They won the AL pennant in their first year (1901) and captured world championships in 1906 and 1917. While baseball got a black eye when the infamous "Black Sox" scandal hit after the 1919 World Series, the Sox found themselves stripped of their stars. A drought began after this unfortunate event and the ChiSox didn't win another pennant for 40 years. In 1959,

under the ownership of Bill Veeck, the Sox experienced a resurgence and won their division title. The Sox also claimed AL West titles in 1983 and 1993. They had the best record in the new AL Central in 1994, and they finished second in their division in 1990 and 1991. The Sox also got a new home in 1991, located just across the street from where the old Comiskey Park stood.

CLEVELAND INDIANS

66-47 .584 1 GB Manager: Mike Hargrove

Although the Indians fell just short to the White Sox in the race for the new AL Central pennant, the Clevelanders would have under the expanded playoffs earned their first postseason berth since 1954 had the strike not quashed those dreams. It was a dream season, nonetheless, for the Tribe. Manager Mike Hargrove's ballclub moved into the new and beautiful Jacobs Field and, with an offense that led the league with 679 runs scored, contended from Opening Day. Left fielder Albert Belle had a corker of a season (.357, 36 homers, 101 RBI). Center fielder Kenny Lofton—.349 average and league highs with 160 hits and 60 stolen bases—became recognized as one of the best players in the game. Second baseman Carlos Baerga (.314, 19, 80) remains one of the best

at his position. DH Eddie Murray (.254, 17, 76), third baseman Jim Thome (20 homers), first sacker Paul Sorrento (62 RBI), catcher Sandy Alomar (14 homers), and rookie right fielder Manny Ramirez (.269, 17, 60) helped propel the offense. Shortstop Omar Vizquel won his second Gold Glove. The Tribe had some pitching too, led by Dennis Martinez (11-6, 3.52 ERA) and Charles Nagy (10-8, 3.45 ERA). The season surprise was Mark Clark, who had an 11-3 record with a 3.82 ERA before going out with an injury. Jeff Russell had a poor season, notching 17 saves, six losses, and six blown saves to go with his 5.09 ERA. Jose Mesa and Eric Plunk each turned in good seasons in relief, however.

Manager			
Mike Hargrove	**W**	**L**	**PCT**
Major-league record	250	272	.479
with Indians	250	272	.479
1994 record	66	47	.584

Coaches: Buddy Bell, Ken Bolek, Luis Isaac, Charlie Manuel, Dave Nelson, Jeff Newman, Mark Wiley

Five-Year Finishes

90	91	92	93	94
4	7	T4	6	2

Five-Year Record: 352-409; .463

Rank: 13th in AL; 24th in ML

Chairman of the Board & CEO:
Richard E. Jacobs

Vice Chairman of the Board: David H. Jacobs

VP, Baseball Operations: John Hart

Director, Player Development: Dan O'Dowd

Director, Scouting: Mickey White

Address
2401 Ontario Street
Cleveland, OH 44115

Ballparks

League Park 1901-1946;
  Cleveland Stadium 1932-1993; Jacobs Field 1994-present
Capacity: 42,400
1994 Attendance: 1,995,174

Surface: natural grass
Left field fence: 325 feet
Center field fence: 405 feet
Right field fence: 325 feet
Left-center fence: 370 feet
Right-center fence: 375 feet

Team History

Fans of the Indians can testify to the fact that baseball can break your heart. In their earlier days, the Tribe was an AL power. Cleveland won the AL pennant in 1920 and again in '48, taking the World Series trophy both times. Six years later, it set a league record for wins (111), en route to the 1954 pennant. Since that time, there has been little to cheer about. Frustration has been the constant companion of the Indians. From 1969 to 1992, the Tribe finished in

last place in the AL East eight times and second to last 10 times. In 1990, Cleveland finished fourth in the AL East. Reality set in again in 1991, as the Indians plummeted to 105 losses, a new team record. Showing a little muscle in 1992, they bounced back to a fourth-place finish. The Indians moved into Jacobs Field in 1994 and finished second in the new AL Central.

KANSAS CITY ROYALS

64-51 .557 4 GB Manager: Hal McRae

While Kansas City wasn't quite able to contend last year, the Royals at least got back to doing what the franchise had been known for in its glory years. Finishing second in the league in team ERA, the Royals also led the loop in stolen bases. While it wasn't enough to save manager Hal McRae's job, pitching and speed did provide some excitement at Royals Stadium. Cy Young Award winner David Cone led the pitching staff back to glory. The right-hander put together a 16-5 record with a 2.94 ERA, 132 strikeouts, and 54 bases on balls. Tom Gordon (11-7, 4.35), Kevin Appier (7-6, 3.83), and Mark Gubicza (7-9, 4.50)—themselves all righties—also had good seasons. Closer Jeff Montgomery, on the other hand, had a few

problems (2-3, 4.03 ERA, 27 saves). Billy Brewer, Hipolito Pichardo, Stan Belinda, Mike Magnate, and Rusty Meacham were also featured in a bountiful pen. Vince Coleman (.240, 50 swipes) finished second in the league in stolen bases, and he combined with Brian McRae (.273, 28 steals) and Felix Jose (.303, 11 homers, 55 RBI) to give the Royals a speedy outfield. Rookie of the Year Bob Hamelin (.282, 24, 65) got most of his at bats as a designated hitter and provided pop. Third baseman Gary Gaetti (.287, 12, 57) continued his comeback with the bat and the glove, while first baseman Wally Joyner (.311, eight, 57) was steady. Second baseman Jose Lind and shortstop Greg Gagne provided solid defense up the middle.

Manager Bob Boone	W	L	PCT
Major-league record	—	—	—
with Royals	—	—	—
1994 record	—	—	—

Coaches: Glenn Ezell, Bruce Kison, Jamie Quirk, Greg Luzinski, Mitchell Page, Jeff Cox

Five-Year Finishes

90	91	92	93	94
6	6	T5	3	3

Five-Year Record: 377-385; .495
Rank: 8th in AL; T14th in ML

Executive VP & GM: Herk Robinson
VP of Baseball Operations: George Brett
Assistant GM: Jay Hinrichs
Director of Scouting: Art Stewart
Director of Minor League Operations: Bob Hegman

Address
1 Royal Way
Kansas City, MO 64129

Ballparks

Municipal Stadium 1969-1972; Royals Stadium 1973-present
Capacity: 40,625
1994 Attendance: 1,400,494
Surface: artificial turf

Left field fence: 330 feet
Center field fence: 410 feet
Right field fence: 330 feet
Left-center fence: 385 feet
Right-center fence: 385 feet

Team History

The Kansas City Royals came into existence in 1968 to fill a void left by the departed A's. In no time at all, the Royals began to make themselves known. Moving quickly to the top of the AL West, they won divisional titles from 1976 through '78, led by George Brett. The team took its first pennant in 1980. In 1984, they took another AL West crown. They went on to win a world championship in 1985, overcoming 3-1

deficits in the playoffs and World Series. The Royals continued to show their strength from 1986 through '89 by remaining in second or third place in their division. In 1990, however, they plummeted to sixth in the AL West. This fast, hard tumble came as a surprise to all, and the drought lasted a few years. The Royals had solid seasons in 1993 and '94, however.

MILWAUKEE BREWERS
53-62 .461 15 GB Manager: Phil Garner

MIlwaukee was known more during 1994 for owner Bud Selig's high-profile work as acting commissioner than it was for its team's play—probably a good thing. As the strike drama unfolded, there was Selig as the owners' point man, taking the hard line. The Brewers hit the skids early, sliding through a 14-game losing streak in late May that effectively ended their chances of a pennant and consigned them to the bottom of the AL Central. It helped somewhat that the slide was injury-related (Darryl Hamilton and Pat Listach were out) and that the team went 36-34 after the bad period. But Milwaukee still lacked enough power and pitching to contend, even if everyone was healthy. Third baseman Kevin Seitzer (.314, 49 RBI) was a steady contributor, although he missed 35 games because of an injury. Left fielder Greg Vaughn (.254, 19 HRs, 55 RBI), catcher Dave Nilsson (.275, 12, 69), and rookie outfielder Matt Mieske (.259, 10, 38) provided some pop. John Jaha (.241, 12, 39) showed some promise at first base. Second baseman Jody Reed and shortstop Jose Valentin formed the keystone combo. Turner Ward played center field, and Brian Harper (.291) was the DH. All-Star Ricky Bones (10-9, 3.43 ERA) developed into a dependable starter, while Cal Eldred (11-11, 4.68) rebounded late in the year to join Bill Wegman (8-4, 4.51) as serviceable starters. Closer Mike Fetters (17 saves, 2.54) was consistent. Graeme Lloyd, Bob Scanlan, and Jesse Orosco staffed an unreliable bullpen.

Manager Phil Garner	W	L	PCT
Major-league record	214	225	.488
with Brewers	214	225	.488
1994 record	53	62	.461

Coaches: Bill Castro, Gene Clines, Duffy Dyer, Tim Foli, Don Rowe

Five-Year Finishes

90	91	92	93	94
6	4	2	7	5

Five-Year Record: 371-392; .486
Rank: 11th in AL; 20th in ML

President, CEO: Bud Selig
Senior VP, Baseball Operations: Sal Bando
Senior VP: Harry Dalton
Assistant VP, Baseball Operations: Bruce Manno
Scouting Director: Ken Califano

Address
P.O. Box 3099
Milwaukee, WI 53201

Ballparks

Seattle: Sicks Stadium 1969
Milwaukee: County Stadium 1970-present
Capacity: 53,192
1994 Attendance: 1,268,397
Surface: natural grass

Left field fence: 362 feet
Center field fence: 402 feet
Right field fence: 362 feet
Left-center fence: 392 feet
Right-center fence: 392 feet

Team History

After a one-season stint as the last-place, first-year Seattle Pilots, this franchise brought baseball back to Milwaukee in 1970. The Brewers floundered in the AL East for much of the next decade. By 1978, however, they posted their first winning season, finishing third. The Brew Crew really came alive in the early 1980s, due largely to multitalented Robin Yount. The Brewers won the second-half crown in strike-shortened 1981. In 1982, they took their only AL pennant, not coincidentally during Yount's MVP, All-Star, and Gold Glove season. They took the Cardinals all the way to seven games in a futile bid for the world championship in '82. The brightest moment for the franchise in 1987 was their sprint out of the gate. The Brewers got off to a record-tying start of 13 consecutive wins. They hit the skids shortly thereafter, losing 12 games in a row. This decline continued until 1992, when they finished the season second in their division. In 1993, however, the bottom dropped out once again with the loss of Paul Molitor, and the Brewers suffered another last-place finish again in 1994.

MINNESOTA TWINS

53-60 .469 14 GB Manager: Tom Kelly

In a season filled with disappointments on the field, perhaps the biggest frustration felt by the Twins and their fans during 1994 was the inability to give long-time first baseman and local hero Kent Hrbek a proper send-off. The popular Hrbek retired after the season, and because of the strike, was unable to be properly feted. It shouldn't surprise observers that the Hrbek (.270, 10 HRs, 53 RBI) retirement went wrong, since mostly everything else involving the club was off during the '94 season. Minnesota's awful pitching (5.68 ERA) was the worst in the American League, a statistic exacerbated by a drop-off in run production. Kirby Puckett could not be faulted for any of the problems. The hitting machine was again a catalyst (.317, 20, 112) and was on pace to drive in nearly 160

runs when play stopped. Dynamic second baseman Chuck Knoblauch (.312, 51 RBI, 45 doubles) was on pace to break the major-league doubles record of 67. Shane Mack (.333, 15, 61) had another strong season, and center fielder Alex Cole (.296, 29 stolen bases) teamed with Knoblauch to give the team some speed at the top of the lineup. Dave Winfield was the designated hitter, while Scott Leius looked pretty good at third. The pitching was dreadful, even though Scott Erickson (8-11, 5.44 ERA) threw a no-hitter against Milwaukee. Starters Kevin Tapani (11-7, 4.62) and Scott Mahomes (9-5, 4.73) won when the Twins scored plenty of runs. Closer Rick Aguilera (23 saves) was solid, though the rest of the bullpen was rotten.

Manager			
Tom Kelly	W	L	PCT
Major-league record	651	619	.513
with Twins	651	619	.513
1994 record	53	60	.469

Coaches: Terry Crowley, Ron Gardenhire, Rick Stelmaszek, Dick Such, Wayne Terwilliger

Five-Year Finishes

90	91	92	93	94
7	1	2	T5	4

Five-Year Record: 383-378; .503
Rank: 4th in AL; 9th in ML

Owner: Carl R. Pohlad
Chairman of the Board: Howard T. Fox, Jr.
President: Jerry Bell
Executive VP, GM: Terry Ryan
VP: Billy Smith
Director of Minor Leagues: Jim Rantz
Director of Scouting: Mike Radcliff

Address
501 Chicago Avenue South
Minneapolis, MN 55145

Ballparks

Washington: American League Park 1901-1910; Griffith Stadium 1911-1960.
Minnesota: Metropolitan Stadium 1961-1981; Hubert H. Humphrey Metrodome 1982-present
Capacity: 55,883

1994 Attendance: 1,398,565
Surface: artificial turf
Stationary Dome
Left field fence: 343 feet
Center field fence: 408 feet
Right field fence: 327 feet
Left-center fence: 385 feet
Right-center fence: 367 feet

Team History

As the Washington Senators, this franchise mixed a few highs—three pennants and a 1924 world championship—with years of deep lows. After a move to the Twin Cities in 1960, the team won the 1965 pennant but slid out of contention for most of the next two decades. Perhaps all they needed was to be sheltered from the elements. The team moved indoors and captured the World Series in '87 with a young squad of sluggers. In 1990, the Twins finished

last in their division. Then, as if a magic wand had been waved over the Metrodome, they came back with a vengeance in '91. The Twins posted a regular-season record of 95-67, won the pennant, and went seven games in the World Series, overcoming Atlanta for all the marbles. The Twins finished second in their division in 1992, then tied for fifth in 1993, and placed fourth in 1994.

CALIFORNIA ANGELS

47-68 .409 5½ GB Managers: Buck Rodgers (16-23); Marcel Lachemann (31-45)

Since the Angels finished dead last in the wretched AL West, it's a good thing they did something during the 1994 season that was a first. By hiring Marcel Lachemann on May 17 to replace Buck Rodgers, California allowed brothers to be managing together in the big leagues for the first time since the turn of the century. Marcel had been pitching coach for his brother Rene with the Marlins. Of course, one look at the Angel team ERA (5.42, third-worst in AL), and one would question Lachemann's credentials as a pitching coach. Before the strike intervened, the Angels were on pace to lose a club-record 97 games, and the crowds at the Big A had become so surly that Angels players actually welcomed road trips, a sentiment indicated by their dreadful 23-40 home record. California's run production came primarily from DH Chili Davis (.311, 26 HRs, 84 RBI) and second-year sensation right fielder Tim Salmon (.287, 23, 70). Left fielder Bo Jackson (.279, 13, 43) didn't run too well but could still hit. Chad Curtis (.256, 11, 50) continued to show some promise in center field. J.T. Snow (.220) showed limitations at first. Damion Easley, Gary DiSarcina, Harold Reynolds, and Spike Owens staffed the infield. Chuck Finley (10-10, 4.32 ERA) led an improving pitching staff that included Brian Anderson (7-5, 5.22), Mark Langston (7-8, 4.68), and impressive second-year man Phil Leftwich. The bullpen had troubles. Joe Grahe (6.65, 13 saves) was the closer, while Mark Leiter, Bob Patterson, and others struggled.

Manager **Marcel Lachemann**	W	L	PCT
Major-league record	31	45	.408
with Angels	31	45	.408
1994 record	31	45	.408

Coaches: Rod Carew, Chuck Hernandez, Bobby Knoop, Rick Burleson, Rick Lachemann, Joe Maddon

Five-Year Finishes

90	91	92	93	94
4	7	T5	T5	4

Five-Year Record: 351-412; .460
Rank: 14th in AL; 25th in ML

Chairman of the Board: Gene Autry
President & CEO: Richard Brown
Executive VP: Jackie Autry
VP & GM: Bill Bavasi
Assistant GM: Tim Mead
Coordinator of Scouting Operations: Tim Kelly
Director, Player Development: Joe Maddon

Address
P.O. Box 2000
Anaheim, CA 92803

Ballparks

Los Angeles: Wrigley Field 1961; Dodger Stadium 1962-65. **Anaheim:** Anaheim Stadium 1966-present
Capacity: 64,593
1994 Attendance: 1,512,622

Surface: natural grass
Left field fence: 370 feet
Center field fence: 404 feet
Right field fence: 370 feet
Left-center fence: 386 feet
Right-center fence: 386 feet

Team History

Cowboy singer Gene Autry gave birth to the Angels in Los Angeles in 1961. His Halos, however, have yet to ride off into the sunset with an American League pennant—much less a world championship—slung over their shoulders. Although California managed to finish third in 1964, they faltered for the next 14 years. They spent freely when the era of free agency began in the mid-1970s. This strategy seemed to pay off for them a few years later. In 1979, they won a divisional title, using a strong corps of veteran free agents. The Angels did manage to repeat the feat in 1982 and '86, but have yet to progress beyond that point. The loss in 1986 was perhaps the most painful of all as the team was only one pitch away from clinching the pennant when fate stepped in. The Halos once again walked off empty-handed, losing this time to Boston.

OAKLAND ATHLETICS
51-63 .447 1 GB Manager: Tony LaRussa

After stumbling to a 19-43 start, the A's put on a tremendous charge and almost claimed the AL West title—not a great accomplishment, though. Manager Tony LaRussa deserved credit for keeping the young team together and competing with it, and A's fans were relieved in mid-October when LaRussa agreed to stay in the Bay Area for at least another season. Owner Walter Haas has put the franchise on the market and expressed desire to sell to a Bay Area group, though nothing could be guaranteed. The A's were last in the league with a .260 team batting average. Among the more valuable assets on the team was unheralded designated hitter Geronimo Berroa (.306, 13 HRs, 65 RBI), who led the team's regulars in hitting. Catcher Terry Steinbach (.285, 11, 57) was again solid, and center fielder Stan Javier (.272, 10, 44) continued to prove himself a good big leaguer. Ruben Sierra (.268, 23, 92) rebounded from an off 1993, but first baseman Mark McGwire (heel) continued to struggle with injuries. Left fielder Rickey Henderson (.260, 66 runs) is still a fine leadoff hitter. Brent Gates (.283) showed promise at second base, while shortstop Mike Bordick and third sacker Scott Brosius were adequate. The pitching rotation was led by veteran Steve Ontiveros (6-4, 2.65 ERA) who won the AL's ERA title. Ron Darling (10-11, 4.50) resurrected his flagging career somewhat, but Bobby Witt (8-10, 5.04) and Todd Van Poppel (7-10, 6.09) were unreliable. Journeyman set-up guy Billy Taylor was a stalwart all year in the pen, but Dennis Eckersley (4.26, 19 saves) struggled for the first time in years.

Manager			
Tony LaRussa	W	L	PCT
Major-league record	1253	1106	.531
with Athletics	731	599	.550
1994 record	51	63	.447

Coaches: Dave Duncan, Art Kusnyer, Jim Lefebvre, Dave McKay, Tommie Reynolds

Five-Year Finishes

90	91	92	93	94
1	4	1	7	2

Five-Year Record: 402-360; .528
Rank: 3rd in AL; 6th in ML

Owner/Managing General Partner:
Walter A. Haas, Jr.
Chairman & CEO: Walter J. Haas
President & GM: Sandy Alderson
Assistant GM: Billy Beane
Director of Baseball Administration:
Pamela Pitts
Director of Player Development:
Keith Lieppman
Director of Scouting: Dick Bogard

Address
Oakland-Alameda County Coliseum
Oakland, CA 94621

Ballparks

Philadelphia: Columbia Park 1901-1908; Shibe Park 1909-1954 . **Kansas City:** Municipal Stadium 1955-1967. **Oakland:** Oakland-Alameda County Coliseum 1968-present
Capacity: 47,313

1994 Attendance: 1,242,692
Surface: natural grass
Left field fence: 330 feet
Center field fence: 400 feet
Right field fence: 330 feet
Left-center fence: 375 feet
Right-center fence: 375 feet

Team History

The Athletics have had a colorful existence. Formed in 1901 in Philadelphia, the A's captured world championships in 1910, 1911, '13, '29, and '30, before embarking on a dismal period that saw the franchise move to Kansas City. Then in 1968, Charlie Finley had a plan. He wanted to move his team to Oakland, make it a success, and sell lots of tickets. His Oakland dream became a reality and the winning began—just not in front of as large an audience as had been hoped. Three straight world titles came from 1972 to '74. After winning the division championship in the strike-affected '81 season, area businesses took over the reins. Packing the team with power and talent, the A's won pennants from 1988 to '90, with a world championship in 1989. Topping their division in '92, Oakland went from first to worst in 1993.

SEATTLE MARINERS
49-63 2 GB Manager: Lou Piniella

After winning 82 games in 1993, the Mariners were poised for a breakthrough season last year. But they were not able to overcome a slow start, an unbalanced offense, and poor starting pitching, and Seattle finished third in a weak AL West. Manager Lou Piniella was able to count on center fielder Ken Griffey Jr. (.323, 40 homers, 90 RBI, 94 runs scored) to generate quite a bit of heat at the plate. Junior was supported by right fielder Jay Buhner (.279, 21, 68) and first baseman Tino Martinez (.261, 20, 61). Even with these three bats, the M's still finished ninth in the AL in runs scored. Third baseman Edgar Martinez (.285, 13, 51), back from injury, had a fair season. Eric Anthony (.237, 10, 30)

didn't quite live up to his promise. Corner man Mike Blowers (.289, nine, 49) and DH Reggie Jefferson (.327, eight, 32) contributed to the offense, however. Felix Fermin batted .317 and displayed fine defense at shortstop. Randy Johnson (13-6, 3.19 ERA) continued to rule the AL strikeout department. He led the loop with 204 Ks last year. Unfortunately, he didn't have much help in the rotation. Chris Bosio (4-10, 4.32) was injury-prone, Dave Fleming (7-11, 6.46) struggled, and Greg Hibbard (1-5, 6.69) and Roger Salkeld (2-5, 7.17) were just plain bad. Goose Gossage and Bill Risley led the bullpen, setting up new closer Bobby Ayala, who had 18 saves last year.

Manager

Lou Piniella	W	L	PCT
Major-league record	610	567	.518
with Mariners	131	143	.478
1994 record	49	63	.438

Coaches: Lee Elia, Bobby Cuellar, Ken Griffey Sr., John McLaren, Sam Mejias, Sam Perlozzo, Matt Sinatro

Five-Year Finishes

90	91	92	93	94
5	5	7	4	3

Five-Year Record: 355-405; .467
Rank: 12th in AL; 22nd in ML

CEO: John Ellis
President & Chief Operating Officer: Chuck Armstrong
VP, Baseball Operations: Woody Woodward
Director of Baseball Administration: Lee Pelekoudas
Farm Director: Jim Beattie
Coordinator of Minor League Instruction: Jim Skaalen

Address
411 First Avenue South
Seattle, WA 98104

Ballpark

Kingdome 1977-present
Capacity: 58,823
1994 Attendance: 1,103,798
Surface: artificial turf
Stationary Dome

Left field fence: 331 feet
Center field fence: 405 feet
Right field fence: 312 feet
Left-center fence: 389 feet
Right-center fence: 349 feet

Team History

When the Seattle Pilots flew out of the Pacific Northwest, Seattle was a little more than miffed to be stranded. Demanding a team to call their own, they were awarded the 1977 expansion franchise, the Seattle Mariners. The highest position the Mariners had achieved before '94 in the American League West standings was fourth place. They had only reached fourth place three times—first in 1982, and again in 1987 and 1993. In 1989, they claimed their first-ever All-Star selection, Ken Griffey Jr. The

Mariners posted their first winning season in 1991. In 1992, the Seattle franchise saw a complete reversal of the previous season's efforts, finishing in the cellar again. But in 1993, Sweet Lou Piniella arrived with much fanfare. If you count the Rangers' division title in '94, the Mariners are the only current AL team to never to win a division championship or a pennant. The Mariners so far have brought little joy to fans in the Pacific Northwest.

TEXAS RANGERS

52-62 .456 0 GB Manager: Kevin Kennedy

For what it's worth, the Rangers went into the strike as the leaders of the AL West, though they were 10 games under .500. A brand new ballpark (named "The Ballpark") and a division "title" couldn't save GM Tom Grieve's or manager Kevin Kennedy's jobs, and general partner George Bush got a new job in the Lone Star State, governor. Only the sorry staff in Minnesota (5.68 ERA) could save the Ranger pitchers (5.45 ERA) the ignominy of having the worst ERA in the AL. Kevin Brown (7-9, 4.82 ERA) and Kenny Rogers (11-8, 4.46) actually pitched OK, indicating that the rest of the hurlers are in a mess. Roger Pavlik (7.69), Hector Fajardo (6.91), and Bruce Hurst (7.11) were among the starters who let opponents' runs flow. Tom Henke headed up the relief corps,

garnering 15 saves and a 3.79 ERA. Rookie Darren Oliver (4-0, 3.42, two saves) was also solid. The Texas offense was able to generate some runs, but not enough to get the club to .500. DH Jose Canseco (.282, 31 HRs, 90 RBI) came back from elbow surgery to provide power. First baseman Will Clark (.329, 13, 80) had a fine season, while left fielder Juan Gonzalez (.275, 19, 85) overcame a slow start to post top numbers. Third baseman Dean Palmer (.246, 19, 59) showed pop, and catcher Pudge Rodriguez (.298, 16, 57) continues to be the league's best young backstop. Rusty Greer, Chris James, and Oddibe McDowell adequately staffed the outfield, while shortstop Manny Lee brandished a good glove.

Manager			
Johnny Oates	**W**	**L**	**PCT**
Major-league record with Rangers	291	270	.519
	—	—	—
1994 record (with Orioles)	63	49	.563
Coaches: Dick Bosman, Larry Hardy, Jerry Narron, Rudy Jaramillo, Bucky Dent, Ed Napoleon			

Five-Year Finishes

90	91	92	93	94
3	3	4	2	1

Five-Year Record: 383-379; .503
Rank: 5th in AL; 10th in ML

General Partner: Rusty Rose
President: Tom Schieffer
GM: Doug Melvin
Assistant GM, Personnel: Sandy Johnson
Director, Minor Leagues: Reid Nichols

Address
P.O. Box 90111
Arlington, TX 76004

Ballparks

Washington: Griffith Stadium 1961; Robert F. Kennedy Stadium 1962-1971. **Texas:** Arlington Stadium 1972-1993; The Ballpark in Arlington 1994-present
Capacity: 48,100

1994 Attendance: 2,502,538
Surface: natural grass
Left field fence: 332 feet
Center field fence: 400 feet
Right field fence: 325 feet
Left-center fence: 388 feet
Right-center fence: 379 feet

Team History

What can you expect from a team that began as the reincarnation of the Washington Senators? In the three decades since its inception in 1961 in the nation's capital, this franchise has won only the incomplete 1994 AL West title and has rarely managed to sneak above .500. They circled the wagons in 1972 and headed west for Arlington. Racked by instability, the Rangers have become an exercise in futility. Billy Martin, taking a stab at making something happen, took the team as far as second place in 1974.

The team had been worked so hard, though, that by mid-1975 they fizzled out. In 1977, four different managers attempted to take over the helm. The fourth one, Billy Hunter, drove the team to a club-record 94 wins. Since the move in '72 until 1993, the team reached second place in the AL West six times. Looking to build a strong tradition in their new stadium, the Rangers had the best record in the AL West in 1994.

ATLANTA BRAVES

68-46 .596 6 GB Manager: Bobby Cox

The second-best ballclub in the National League in 1994, the Braves would have gone to the playoffs under the new wild-card system set up by the owners had there been a postseason. A strong, deep, and very talented team, Atlanta had pitching, defense, and power in spades. Manager Bobby Cox was able to give the ball to the league's best starting rotation, again led by Cy Young Award winner Greg Maddux (16-6, 1.56 ERA, 156 strikeouts), who is the game's most dominating hurler. Tom Glavine (13-9, 3.97) and Steve Avery (8-3, 4.04) are fine hurlers who didn't pitch to their high standards. Kent Mercker (9-4, 3.45) made the switch to the rotation in fine fashion. John Smoltz (6-10, 4.14) had a down season. Greg McMichael filled the closer role, notching 21 saves but also

blowing 10. Mark Wohlers (4.59), Mike Stanton (3.55), and Steve Bedrosian (3.33) helped out in the pen. The Atlanta offense topped the league with 137 homers, led by the "Crime Dog," Fred McGriff (.318, 34 homers, 94 RBI). Right fielder David Justice (.313, 19, 59) was sizzling toward the end of the season. Atlanta traded Deion Sanders, a lefty-hitting center fielder, to Cincinnati for righty-hitting Roberto Kelly (.293, 73 runs scored). Rookies Ryan Klesko (.278, 17, 47), Tony Tarasco, and Mike Kelly shared left field with Dave Gallagher. Second baseman Mark Lemke (.294) had a fine year at bat, but third sacker Terry Pendleton and shortstop Jeff Blauser suffered off years at the plate. Javier Lopez (13 homers) and Charlie O'Brien shared catcher duties.

Manager

Bobby Cox	W	L	PCT
Major-league record	1025	908	.530
with Braves	670	616	.521
1994 record	68	46	.596

Coaches: Jim Beauchamp, Pat Corrales, Clarence Jones, Ned Yost, Leo Mazzone, Jimy Williams

Ballparks

Boston: South End Grounds 1871-1914; Braves Field 1914-1952. **Milwaukee:** County Stadium 1953-1965. **Atlanta:** Fulton County Stadium 1966-present
Capacity: 52,709

1994 Attendance: 2,539,240
Surface: natural grass
Left field fence: 330 feet
Center field fence: 402 feet
Right field fence: 330 feet
Left-center fence: 385 feet
Right-center fence: 385 feet

Five-Year Finishes

90	91	92	93	94
6	1	1	1	2

Five-Year Record: 429-333; .563
Rank: 1st in NL; 2nd in ML

Chairman of the Board: William C. Bartholomay
President: Stanley H. Kasten
Senior VP & Assistant to the President: Henry L. Aaron
Executive VP & GM: John Schuerholz
Assistant GM: Dean Taylor
Director of Scouting & Player Development: Chuck LaMar

Address
P.O. Box 4064
Atlanta, GA 30302

Team History

The Braves began in the National Association in 1871 as the Boston Red Stockings. After winning four NA pennants and joining the National League in 1876, the Braves flourished and dominated the NL in the 1890s (winning five pennants). Money woes (brought on in part by the AL's Red Sox) caused five decades of misery to follow, broken only by the "Miracle Braves" of 1914 and the pennant winners of 1948. Boston loved the Red Sox, so the Braves moved to Milwaukee in 1953. The Spahn- and Aaron-led club won a world championship in '57

and a pennant in '58. The Braves were the first club to shift twice, moving to Atlanta in 1966. Division championships in 1969 and 1982 brightened otherwise dismal years for the club down South. The worst club in the league in 1990, the Braves won three straight NL West pennants. The team drove to the World Series in 1991, losing to the Twins, and in 1992, losing to the Blue Jays. After winning 104 games in 1993, Atlanta stumbled to the Phillies in the NLCS. The Braves finished second in 1994.

FLORIDA MARLINS
51-64 .443 23½ GB Manager: Rene Lachemann

The Marlins moved up a notch in the standings in 1994—through no doing of their own. National League realignment created a five-team Eastern Division, and the Marlins finished fifth, one better than last year's sixth-place showing. Florida posted a much better winning percentage—.443—than 1993's .395, and it began the long journey from inaugural-season excitement to real contention. Some highlights in 1994 included the feats of long-balling outfielder Jeff Conine (.319, 18 HRs, 82 RBI) and catcher Benito Santiago (.273, 11, 41), who made a remarkable comeback from consecutive poor seasons. Gary Sheffield (.276, 27, 78) adapted well to the outfield after playing third base much of his career. Second baseman Bret Barberie (.301) had a big year, and shortstop Kurt Abbott

(.249) flashed potential. Center fielder Chuck Carr (.263, 32 stolen bases) provided speed at the top of the lineup. First baseman Orestes Destrade was replaced by promising rookie Greg Colbrunn. The pitching staff was a blend of highs and lows. Outstanding closer Bryan Harvey's elbow wouldn't let him throw a single pitch, but second-year pitcher Robb Nen was 15-for-15 in save opportunities. Richie Lewis and Yorkis Perez also saw action out of the bullpen. Chris Hammond (4-4, 3.07 ERA) started the year well but was shelved by injuries. Youngsters Pat Rapp (7-8, 3.85) and Dave Weathers (8-12, 5.27) pitched relatively well. Mark Gardner (4-4, 4.87) also filled a spot. Aging knuckleballer Charlie Hough (5-9, 5.15) was finally forced to hang it up.

Manager			
Rene Lachemann	W	L	PCT
Major-league record	322	436	.425
with Marlins	115	162	.415
1994 record	51	64	.443

Coaches: Vada Pinson, Doug Rader, Larry Rothschild, Cookie Rojas, Jose Morales, Rick Williams

Two-Year Finishes

93	94
6	5

Two-Year Record: 115-162, .415
Rank: 14th in NL; 28th in ML

Chairman: H. Wayne Huizenga
Executive VP & GM: Dave Dombrowski
Assistant GM: Frank Wren
Director of Scouting: Gary Hughes
Director of Player Development: John Boles

Address
100 N.E. Third Avenue
Third Floor
Fort Lauderdale, FL 33301

Ballpark

Joe Robbie Stadium 1993-present
Capacity: 48,000
1994 Attendance: 1,937,467
Surface: natural grass

Left field fence: 334 feet
Center field fence: 410 feet
Right field fence: 345 feet
Left-center fence: 380 feet
Right-center fence: 380 feet

Team History

In 1989, the NL started a search for two teams to increase the loop's number of franchises from 12 to 14, matching the AL. The next year, Blockbuster millionaire H. Wayne Huizenga purchased half of Joe Robbie Stadium, intending to fill the facility with 81 baseball games a year. His ownership group was chosen over several others in the South Florida area, and on June 10, 1990, the Marlins, along with the Rockies, were chosen as the two new NL franchises to play in the 1993 season. Carl Berger and Dave Dombrowski were initially hired to start the organization, with Rene Lachemann as the first manager. Florida then picked up Nigel Wilson as their first pick in the expansion draft. By signing such high-priced veterans as Benito Santiago and Gary Sheffield, the Marlins have shown that they are not afraid to spend money to bring talent to the Sunshine State.

426

MONTREAL EXPOS
74-40 .649 0 GB Manager: Felipe Alou

The Expos played exciting baseball in 1994, rushing to the major league's best overall record and ending a string of runner-up finishes with an NL East crown in the strike-aborted season. But it's not like anybody in Quebec was really paying attention. The Expos may have been thrilling on the field, but the town's laid-back population spent much of the baseball season counting the days until the Canadiens would begin play again. It wasn't until July that the Expos "faithful" began showing up at Stade Olympique and supporting their team. No wonder the Montreal brass has worked so hard in recent years to keep their payroll low. That the Expos had a superior team is a testament to the front office and skipper Felipe Alou. Montreal had many strengths, beginning with a lineup that was extremely productive and continuing on through a deep, stingy pitching staff. Outfielder Moises Alou (.339, 22 HRs, 78 RBI) continued his climb toward stardom, as did shortstop Wil Cordero (.294). Outfielders Larry Walker (.322, 19, 86) and Marquis Grissom (.288, 36 stolen bases) were among the best at their positions. First baseman Cliff Floyd (.281) is an exciting prospect. Third baseman Sean Berry and second baseman Mike Lansing were solid, and catcher Darrin Fletcher (.260, 11, 57) emerged as a steady everyday backstop. Few pitchers were better than Ken Hill (16-5, 3.32 ERA). Pedro Martinez (11-5, 3.42) and Jeff Fassero (8-6, 2.99) helped give the Expos one of the best rotations in the league, while Kirk Rueter and Butch Henry also contributed. Closers John Wetteland (25 saves) and Mel Rojas (16 saves) had solid numbers. The fine bullpen included Jeff Shaw and Gil Heredia.

Manager

Felipe Alou	W	L	PCT
Major-league record	238	183	.565
with Expos	238	183	.565
1994 record	74	40	.649

Coaches: Tommy Harper, Tim Johnson, Joe Kerrigan, Jerry Manuel, Luis Pujols, Jim Tracy

Ballparks

Jarry Park 1969-1976; Stade Olympique 1977-present
Capacity: 46,500
1994 Attendance: 1,276,250
Retractable Dome
Surface: artificial turf

Left field fence: 325 feet
Center field fence: 404 feet
Right field fence: 325 feet
Left-center fence: 375 feet
Right-center fence: 375 feet

Five-Year Finishes

90	91	92	93	94
3	6	2	2	1

Five-Year Record: 411-350; .540
Rank: 3rd in NL; 5th in ML

President & General Partner: Claude Brochu
VP, Baseball Operations: Bill Stoneman
Director, Scouting: Kevin Malone
Director, Minor League Field Operations: Herm Starrette
Director, Minor League Operations: Kent Qualls

Address
P.O. Box 500, Station M
Montreal, Quebec
H1V 3P2 Canada

Team History

Named for the city's world exposition in the late 1960s, the Expos have given fans very few highlights until recently. Their humble beginnings in tiny Jarry Park were matched by equally modest performances. The Expos did not contend for the NL East title until 1973, when their fourth-place finish betrayed the fact that they were only three and one-half games out of first. The franchise did not come close again until 1979, finishing second by two games to the eventual world champion Pirates.

Success did not wait quite so long to make another appearance; the Expos captured the division crown in 1981. From 1982 through 1989, the Expos never went above the third rung in the NL East, and in 1991, they wound up dead last in the division. Montreal built a fine farm system and has leaned on youngsters to provide talent. In 1992 and '93, the team finished second in the NL East. In 1994, the Expos had the best record in baseball.

NEW YORK METS

55-58 .487 18½ GB Manager: Dallas Green

It's all perspective. The Mets had a successful season in 1994, even though they were three games under .500. Manager Dallas Green helped to instill some badly needed order to a franchise that was in chaos following a 59-103 1993 season. Much of the improvement came with a consistent pitching staff, led not by Doc Gooden (who was suspended in June for a drug-abuse relapse), but rather Bret Saberhagen. Pitching 177 innings, Saberhagen allowed an amazing 13 bases on balls. He was 14-4 with a 2.74 ERA. Young Bobby Jones (12-7, 3.15 ERA) was impressive in his rookie year. Another rookie, Jason Jacome (4-3, 2.67) displayed promise. Gooden, Pete Smith, and others filled out the rotation. John Franco (a loop-best 30 saves) had another All-Star season.

Roger Mason, Josias Manzanillo, and Doug Linton also served well in the bullpen. Bobby Bonilla might have been the biggest monetary loser because of the strike, but he turned in a fine season (.290, 20 homers, 67 RBI) before walking the picket line. He acquitted himself satisfactorily at third base. Second baseman Jeff Kent (.292, 14, 68) started the season on fire before cooling. Late trades provided first basemen Dave Segui (.241, 10, 43) and Rico Brogna (.351, seven, 20), and shortstop Jose Vizcaino (.256, 47 runs scored). Todd Hundley (.260, 16, 42) and Kelly Stinnett shared the catcher duties. Center fielder Ryan Thompson (.225, 18, 59) showed power. Joe Orsulak, Kevin McReynolds, and others stocked the outfield corners.

Manager Dallas Green	W	L	PCT
Major-league record	326	331	.496
with Mets	101	136	.426
1994 record	55	58	.487

Coaches: Mike Cubbage, Tom McCraw, Frank Howard, Greg Pavlick, Steve Swisher, Bobby Wine

Five-Year Finishes

90	91	92	93	94
2	5	5	7	3

Five-Year Record: 354-406; .466
Rank: 11th in NL; 23rd in ML

Chairman of the Board: Nelson Doubleday
President & CEO: Fred Wilpon
GM: Joe McIlvaine
Senior VP—Consultant: J. Frank Cashen
Assistant VP, Baseball Operations: Gerald Hunsicker
Director of Minor Leagues: Steve Phillips

Address
126th Street & Roosevelt Avenue
Flushing, NY 11368

Ballparks

Polo Grounds 1962-63; Shea Stadium 1964-present
Capacity: 55,601
1994 Attendance: 1,151,471
Surface: natural grass

Left field fence: 338 feet
Center field fence: 410 feet
Right field fence: 338 feet
Left-center fence: 371 feet
Right-center fence: 371 feet

Team History

The 30-year history of the Big Apple's "other" franchise has been filled with meteoric highs and laughable lows. New York debuted in 1962 and lost 120 games, but the Miracle Mets stunned the baseball world in 1969 with a storybook World Series title. New York won another pennant in 1973 but was inept until a mid-1980s renaissance. The Mets struggled through the first four years of the decade, finishing last or next to last. They became contenders in '84

under new manager Davey Johnson. Another second-place finish was in order in 1985, as they closed the gap, finishing only three games out of first. Adding clutch hitting and a fine offensive lineup to their sterling pitching staff, the Mets won it all in '86, bringing home their second world championship trophy. Another division title would be theirs in 1988, but they have yet to duplicate the success enjoyed in the mid-1980s.

PHILADELPHIA PHILLIES
54-61 .470 20½ GB Manager: Jim Fregosi

The "Barbarians at the Gate" were shut out last year. After storming into the playoffs in 1993, the Phillies in '94 lost some thunder, generally because of injuries. Manager Jim Fregosi was not able to count on the same kind of run production; the Phils tied for last in the NL with 80 homers last year. First baseman John Kruk had a variety of health problems, the most serious being his battle with testicular cancer. He still batted .302 with five homers and 38 RBI. Catcher Darren Daulton (.300, 15 homers, 56 RBI) had a great year before his injury. The team spark plug, Lenny Dykstra (.273, 68 runs scored) didn't perform up to his high standards. Left fielder Pete Incaviglia (.273, 13, 32) provided power but not much else. Jim Eisenreich (.300, four, 43), Billy Hatcher, and rookie Tony Longmire also saw time in the outfield. Mariano Duncan (.268, eight, 48) played all four infield positions. First baseman Ricky Jordan (.282, eight, 37), second baseman Mickey Morandini (.292), third baseman Dave Hollins, and shortstop Kevin Stocker (.273) all contributed. Danny Jackson (14-6, 3.26 ERA, 129 strikeouts) reclaimed his status as a top pitcher. Bobby Munoz (7-5, 2.67 ERA) was acquired from the Yanks in the Terry Mulholland trade and pitched well. Curt Schilling, however, had his problems (2-8, 4.48). Ben Rivera (3-4, 6.87) was woeful. Doug Jones was swapped for Mitch Williams and had a strong season, notching 27 saves. Heathcliff Slocumb (5-1, 2.86), David West, and Tom Edens also contributed in the bullpen.

Manager Jim Fregosi	W	L	PCT
Major-league record	749	767	.494
with Phillies	295	293	.502
1994 record	54	61	.470

Coaches: Larry Bowa, Denis Menke, Johnny Podres, Mel Roberts, Mike Ryan, John Vuckovich

Five-Year Finishes

90	91	92	93	94
T4	T3	6	1	4

Five-Year Record: 376-387; .493
Rank: 8th in NL; T16th in ML

President, CEO, and General Partner: Bill Giles
Executive VP and COO: David Montgomery
Senior VP, GM: Lee Thomas
Director, Player Development: Del Unser
Director, Scouting: Mike Arbuckle

Address
P.O. Box 7575
Philadelphia, PA 19101

Ballparks

Philadelphia Base Ball Grounds 1887-1894; Baker Bowl 1895-1938; Shibe Park/Connie Mack Stadium 1938-1970; Veterans Stadium 1971-present
Capacity: 62,382

1994 Attendance: 2,290,971
Surface: artificial turf
Left field fence: 330 feet
Center field fence: 408 feet
Right field fence: 330 feet
Left-center fence: 371 feet
Right-center fence: 371 feet

Team History

The Phillies have won just one world championship in 108 years. The 1915 pennant winners lost in the Series to Boston, while the 1950 NL champion "Whiz Kids" were dropped by the Yankees. The Phils won the NL East from 1976 to '78 but didn't reach the Series until 1980, when they finally won. They waited a record 97 years as a franchise to gain their first world championship. A 1983 World Series appearance was not so fruitful, as they managed to win only one game against the Orioles. The rest of the '80s were an abysmal plight for Philly players and fans. Only once did they grab second place in the NL East ('86), and that year they were over 20 games behind the first place Mets. Winding up the decade with two successive last-place finishes, the outlook was grim. In 1992, they finished in last place, only to turn it around and win the NL pennant in 1993 with a bunch of gruff, fun-loving ballplayers, before falling to the Blue Jays.

CHICAGO CUBS

49-64 .434 16½ GB Tom Trebelhorn

The Cubs begin another new era in 1995. The team began anew at the beginning of the '94 season, hiring Tom Trebelhorn to be its skipper. After another poor year, though, Trebelhorn and GM Larry Himes were both given the old heave-ho. More importantly, however, All-Star fixture Ryne Sandberg retired during the season, leaving a gaping hole both at second base and in the clubhouse. Although Chicago's longtime defect, pitching, again was a problem, the envisioned scoring never materialized. Sammy Sosa (.300, 25 homers, 75 RBI) continued to post strong numbers at the plate, while fellow outfielders Derrick May (.284, eight, 51) and Glenallen Hill (.297, 10, 38) wielded some lumber. Tuffy Rhodes hit three homers on Opening Day and finished the season with eight. First baseman Mark Grace (.298, six, 44) rebounded from a slow start. Shawon Dunston (.278) came back from injury to reclaim the shortstop job, Rey Sanchez (.285) filled in for Sandberg at second, and Steve Buechele (14 HRs) played third. Catcher Rick Wilkins had a bad year. Steve Trachsel (9-7, 3.21 ERA) became the ace of the staff in his rookie year. Willie Banks (8-12, 5.40) had his ups and downs, and Kevin Foster (3-4, 2.89) posted some encouraging starts. Anthony Young (4-6, 3.92) and Mike Morgan (2-10, 6.69) battled injury and ineffectiveness. Randy Myers (3.79 ERA) notched 21 saves. Jose Bautista, Dan Plesac, Chuck Crim, Dave Otto, and Jim Bullinger occupied an adequate bullpen.

Manager			
Jim Riggleman	W	L	PCT
Major-league record	112	179	.385
with Cubs	—	—	—
1994 record (with Padres)	47	70	.402

Coaches: Tony Muser, Marv Foley, Billy Williams, Ferguson Jenkins, Dave Bialas, Dan Radison

Five-Year Finishes

90	91	92	93	94
T4	T3	4	4	5

Five-Year Record: 365-394; .481
Rank: 10th in NL; 21st in ML

Chairman of the Board: Stanton R. Cook
President: Andy McPhail
GM: Ed Lynch
Director, Minor Leagues: Jim Hendry

Address
1060 W. Addison Street
Chicago, IL 60613

Ballparks

Union Base-Ball Grounds, 23rd Street Grounds, LakeFront Park, South Side Park pre-1916; Wrigley Field 1916-present
Capacity: 38,756
1994 Attendance: 1,845,208

Surface: natural grass
Left field fence: 355 feet
Center field fence: 400 feet
Right field fence: 353 feet
Left-center fence: 368 feet
Right-center fence: 368 feet

Team History

The Cubs are notorious for having baseball's longest championship drought. Born the White Stockings in 1870, the franchise dominated National League play during the late 1800s. Chicago won the 1906 pennant and featured the likes of double-play combo Joe Tinker, Johnny Evers, and Frank Chance, as well as pitcher Three Finger Brown. They captured world championships in 1907 and 1908, beating the Tigers both times. Despite seven National League pennants from 1910 to '45, the Cubs couldn't win another Series. It was about this time that the Cubs began to acquire their reputation for being perpetual also-rans. There were only three winning seasons from 1940 through 1966, and the Cubs finished dead last six times. Chicago has never won another pennant, though they did take the NL East in 1984 and 1989. Night games came to Wrigley Field in 1988.

CINCINNATI REDS
66-48 .579 0 GB Manager: Davey Johnson

In the 1994 version of the "Marge Schott Follies," the Reds' owner continued to light up in smoke-free Riverfront Stadium while her team battled its way to the top of the Central. Cincinnati overcame Schott's abrasive ways thanks to one of baseball's best offenses, a deep bench, and a solid bullpen. Given an entire year to run the team, manager Davey Johnson delivered, leading the Reds to a quick start and holding off the charging Astros before the strike intervened. Johnson and GM Jim Bowden spent much of the year hearing rumors that Schott would fire them. The owner was incensed that Bowden had allowed the team's payroll to balloon to $43 million. First baseman Hal Morris (.335, 10 homers, 78 RBI), outfielder Kevin Mitchell (.326, 30, 77), and second baseman Bret Boone (.320, 12, 68) delighted fans. The early-season arrival of Deion Sanders (.283) made headlines, but so did shortstop Barry Larkin's (.279) struggles. Tony Fernandez (.279) filled in well at third, while in right field, Reggie Sanders (.262, 17, 62) had an average year. The catcher duties were handled by Brian Dorsett and Eddie Taubensee. Neither free agent Ron Gant nor reliever Rob Dibble played, while catcher Joe Oliver appeared in only six games before hitting the DL. Jose Rijo (9-6, 3.08 ERA, 171 Ks) was again the ace of the pitching staff, while John Smiley (11-10, 3.86), Erik Hanson (5-5, 4.11), Pete Schourek (7-2, 4.09), and John Roper (6-2) had solid years. Jeff Brantley (2.48, 15 saves) filled the closer's role. The fine bullpen was also staffed by Chuck McElroy, Johnny Ruffin, and Hector Carrasco.

Manager			
Davey Johnson	W	L	PCT
Major-league record	714	530	.574
with Reds	119	103	.536
1994 record	66	48	.579

Coaches: Don Gullett, Grant Jackson, Ray Knight, Joel Youngblood, Hal McRae

Five-Year Finishes

90	91	92	93	94
1	5	2	5	1

Five-Year Record: 394-368; .517
Rank: 4th in NL; 7th in ML

President & CEO: Marge Schott
GM: Jim Bowden
Director of Scouting: Julian Mock
Director of Player Development: Sheldon Bender
Special Assistant to the GM: Gene Bennett

Address
100 Riverfront Stadium
Cincinnati, OH 45202

Ballparks

Lincoln Park Grounds 1876;
Avenue Grounds 1876-1879;
Bank Street Grounds 1880;
League Park 1890-1901;
Palace of the Fans 1902-1911;
Crosley Field 1912-1970;
Riverfront Stadium 1970-present

Capacity: 52,952
1994 Attendance: 1,897,681
Surface: artificial turf
Left field fence: 330 feet
Center field fence: 404 feet
Right field fence: 330 feet
Left-center fence: 375 feet
Right-center fence: 375 feet

Team History

Baseball's first professional team has enjoyed recent history much more than its earlier decades. The Reds won the tainted 1919 World Series but didn't top the baseball world again until 1939. A 1961 pennant was followed by the emergence of the "Big Red Machine." During the 1970s, this powerhouse organization finished in first place six times, won four National League pennants, and captured the 1975 and '76 World Series. The 1980s were not as kind to the franchise. To add to their woes, manager Pete Rose was shrouded in controversy over alleged gambling while involved with the team. In 1990, they proved they had put the scandal behind them, rebounding from a fifth-place finish the year before, bolting all the way to first. That would be the year they won it all, sweeping Oakland in the Series and bringing another world championship crown to Cincinnati. Since then, the team drifted before finishing first in the new NL Central in 1994.

HOUSTON ASTROS

66-49 .574 ½ GB Manager: Terry Collins

By finishing a scant half-game behind Cincinnati in the initial Central Division derby, the Astros were left with an off-season filled with frustration. Any fan could point to one game as the one that would have given new manager Terry Collins's team a division championship, albeit a strike-induced, meaningless one. The best thing about being an Astro fan in 1994 was watching Jeff Bagwell play. He was magnificent at first base. Before suffering a broken hand on Aug. 10, the NL's MVP (.368, 39 HRs, 116 RBI) was having a Triple Crown kind of year, establishing himself as a superstar. Second baseman Craig Biggio (.318, 44 doubles) was pretty solid himself and could have challenged the league doubles record if the strike hadn't intervened. Other offensive highlights were provided by third baseman Ken Caminiti (.283, 18, 75) and

center fielder Steve Finley (.276, 11, 64 runs scored). Left fielder Luis Gonzalez (.273, eight, 67) and right fielders James Mouton (.245), a rookie, and Kevin Bass (.310) staffed the outfield. Shortstop duties were handled by Andujar Cedeno. The pitching staff had its problems, particularly among the starters. Doug Drabek (12-6, 2.84) rebounded from an off year in '93, but Greg Swindell (8-9, 4.37), Darryl Kile (9-6, 4.57), and Pete Harnisch (8-5, 5.40) weren't very consistent and needed to be bailed out by Houston's big bats. The Astros' ill-fated two-month Mitch Williams experiment provided enough gastric upset for a full season. Rookie John Hudek (16 saves) took over for Williams and received some support from set-up men Todd Jones (5-2, 2.72), Shane Reynolds (8-5, 3.05), Mike Hampton, and Dave Veres.

Manager Terry Collins	W	L	PCT
Major-league record	66	49	.574
with Astros	66	49	.574
1994 record	66	49	.574

Coaches: Matt Galante, Steve Henderson, Jesse Barfield, Julio Linares, Mel Stottlemyre

Ballparks

Colt Stadium 1962-64; The Astrodome: 1965-present
Capacity: 53,821
1994 Attendance: 1,561,136
Surface: artificial turf
Stationary Dome

Left field fence: 330 feet
Center field fence: 400 feet
Right field fence: 330 feet
Left-center fence: 380 feet
Right-center fence: 380 feet

Five-Year Finishes

90	91	92	93	94
4	6	4	3	2

Five-Year Record: 372-391; .488
Rank: 9th in NL; 19th in ML

Chairman, CEO: Drayton McLane Jr.
GM: Bob Watson
Director of Player Administration: Tim Helimuth
Director of Baseball Administration: Barry Waters
Director of Minor League Operations: Fred Nelson
Director of Scouting: Dan O'Brien

Address
The Astrodome
P.O. Box 288
Houston, TX 77001

Team History

Baseball purists may curse the arrival of baseball in Texas. After three years outdoors as the Colt .45s, the franchise became the first to play indoors. In an attempt to beat the heat, the Astrodome was built in 1965. However, growing real grass indoors presented a problem. Astro-Turf arrived the next year. Houston's play, however, hasn't been nearly so innovative. Although they contended for most of the 1970s, the Astros did not win their first division title

until 1980. In strike-split '81, Houston won the second half of the season but lost to the Dodgers in postseason play. The 'Stros didn't see another division title until 1986 but failed in their attempt for a pennant when the Mets prevailed four games to two. After finishing dead last in 1991, the Astros depended on youth to rebound to a .500 finish in '92 and a third-place finish in '93. In 1994, Houston was a half game from first in the NL Central when the strike hit.

PITTSBURGH PIRATES
53-61 .465 13 GB Manager: Jim Leyland

There was nothing even remotely resembling the Pirate teams that had won three-straight NL East crowns from 1990 to '92 taking the field at Three Rivers Stadium in 1994. Even colorful outfielder Andy Van Slyke, one of the few remaining reminders of the team's early 1990s success stumbled to an awful (.246, six homers, 30 RBI) season. There were few highlights in Pittsburgh during the 1994 season. The Pirates scored the fewest runs of any NL team (466), had an unimpressive 4.64 team ERA, showed little team speed, and delivered inadequate defense. While management complained about the difficulties of succeeding as a small-market team, the Pirate on-field contingent did little to give fans reason to buy tickets. About the best move Pittsburgh made in 1994 was holding on to manager Jim Leyland, who certainly couldn't be blamed for the team's poor season. Among the brighter lights in a dim season were outfielders Dave Clark (.296, 10, 40) and Al Martin (.286, 9, 33), first baseman-outfielder Orlando Merced (51 RBI), catcher Don Slaught (.288), shortstop Jay Bell (.276, 9, 45), and second baseman Carlos Garcia (.277, 18 stolen bases). Third baseman Jeff King (42 RBI) didn't duplicate his 1993 run production, though outfielder Midre Cummings appears promising. Starters Zane Smith (10-8, 3.27 ERA) and Jon Lieber (6-7, 3.73) had strong years, while youngsters Paul Wagner (7-8, 4.59), Steve Cooke (4-11, 5.02), and Denny Neagle (9-10, 5.12) struggled. The bullpen was filled by Ricky White, Ravelo Manzanillo, Mark Dewey, and others.

Manager Jim Leyland	W	L	PCT
Major-league record	723	688	.512
with Pirates	723	688	.512
1994 record	53	61	.465
Coaches: Rich Donnelly, Milt May, Ray Miller, Tommy Sandt, Spin Williams			

Ballparks

Exposition Park 1891-1909;
    Forbes Field 1909-1970;
    Three Rivers Stadium 1970-present
Capacity: 47,972
1994 Attendance: 1,222,517

Surface: artificial turf
Left field fence: 335 feet
Center field fence: 400 feet
Right field fence: 335 feet
Left-center fence: 375 feet
Right-center fence: 375 feet

Five-Year Finishes

90	91	92	93	94
1	1	1	3	5

Five-Year Record: 417-345; .547
Rank: 2nd in NL; 4th in ML

Chairman of the Executive
    Committee: Vincent A. Sami
President, CEO: Mark Sauer
GM: Cam Bonifay
Director of Minor League
    Operations: Chet Montgomery
Director of Scouting: Paul Tinnell
Director of Baseball Administation:
    John Sirignano

Address
P.O. Box 7000
Pittsburgh, PA 15212

Team History

From the early 1900s, Pirate fans have enjoyed much success. Pittsburgh won five pennants from 1900 through '30 and two World Series (1909 and '25). After sagging throughout the 1940s and 1950s, the Bucs stunned the Yankees in the 1960 fall classic. They captured the 1971 Series as well and were on top again in 1979. The 1970s were a joyous time to be a Pirate fan. The Bucs finished first or second in the NL East nine out of 10 years. As the 1980s unfolded, that joy turned to pain. Instead of being a perennial contender, the highest level of success the Pirates attained was two trips to second in the division. Not happy to just slip one or two rungs, the Bucs spent three consecutive years (1984 through '86) in dead last. The 1990s have been good, however. From 1990 through 1992, the Pirates won the division title each year. In 1993 and '94, they wavered but exhibited some promising young talent.

ST. LOUIS CARDINALS

53-61 .465 13 GB Manager: Joe Torre

Even though the season ended abruptly on Aug. 12, the Cardinals still held a Fan Appreciation Day in late September. Of course, if the Cards had really cared about their fans, they would have played better than they did during the 1994 season. Management made GM Dal Maxvill the scapegoat, firing him after the strike. But Maxvill sure didn't post a 5.14 ERA, like the Cardinal pitching staff did, and Maxvill didn't score only 535 runs, among the lowest in the majors. With few exceptions, the players who were so steady the year before stumbled in 1994. Even staff ace Bob Tewksbury (12-10, 5.32 ERA) was well off his usual production. Of course, when compared to such starters as Allen Watson (6-5, 5.52), Omar Olivares (3-4, 5.74), and Rheal Cormier (3-2, 5.45), Tewksbury was Cy Young material. Vicente Palacios

(3-8, 4.44) resurrected his career, but Rick Sutcliffe could not bounce back. Rene Arocha had 11 saves and Mike Perez had 12, but they along with Rich Rodriguez, John Habyan, Rob Murphy, and Bryan Eversgard really struggled. First baseman Gregg Jefferies (.325, 12 homers, 55 RBI) led the offense. He received help from outfielders Mark Whiten (.293, 14, 53) and Ray Lankford (.267, 19, 57), and third baseman Todd Zeile (.267, 19, 75). Ageless shortstop Ozzie Smith reached the 100-hit mark for the 17th straight season and committed only eight errors. Outfielders Bernard Gilkey and Brian Jordan failed to live up to their potential. Geronimo Pena and Luis Alicea shared second base, while catcher Tom Pagnozzi again had a fine season behind the plate.

Manager			
Joe Torre	W	L	PCT
Major-league record	875	976	.473
with Cardinals	352	337	.511
1994 record	53	61	.465

Coaches: Jose Cardenal, Chris Chambliss, Gaylen Pitts, Mark Riggins, Bob Gibson, Red Schoendienst, John Costello

Five-Year Finishes

90	91	92	93	94
6	2	3	3	4

Five-Year Record: 377-385; .495
Rank: 7th in NL; T14th in ML

Chairman of the Board: August Busch III
Vice Chairman: Fred L. Kuhlmann
President, CEO: Mark Lamping
GM: Walt Jocketty
Director of Player Development: Mike Jorgensen
Director of Scouting: Marty Maier
Director of Personnel: Jerry Walker

Address
250 Stadium Plaza
St. Louis, MO 63102

Ballparks

Robison Field 1893-1920; Sportsman's Park 1920-1966; Busch Stadium 1966-present
Capacity: 56,627
1994 Attendance: 1,866,544

Surface: artificial turf
Left field fence: 330 feet
Center field fence: 402 feet
Right field fence: 330 feet
Left-center fence: 375 feet
Right-center fence: 375 feet

Team History

Born in 1884, the St. Louis Cardinals won six world championships from 1926 through '46, thanks mostly to Branch Rickey's fine farm system. St. Louis was back on top in 1964 and '67. The 1970s were thin on excitement for Cardinal fans, but then the tide turned. In strike-split '81, the Cards had the best winning percentage overall, but did not get to progress into postseason play due to the method of determining regular-season winners. They continued on in

earnest in '82, winning the division, the pennant, and then took the World Series trophy after emerging victorious over Milwaukee. The St. Louis team migrated to the lower half of the standings for the next few years, but got right back in the thick of things in '85. They won pennants in 1985 and again in 1987. Known more for speed on the basepaths rather than long-ball prowess, the Cardinals usually have been in the hunt during the 1990s.

COLORADO ROCKIES
53-64 .453 6½ GB Manager: Don Baylor

The Rockies have quickly moved from expansion ineptitude to respectability. The question, then, becomes, is the organization improving too rapidly to build from the bottom? Out of the Rockies who saw significant action last year, only Eric Young, David Nied, and Lance Painter were 26 years old or younger as of Opening Day 1994. Manager Don Baylor's charges scored runs and gave up a lot of runs, finishing last in the league in runs allowed and team ERA. Some feel that the new Coors Field, opening in 1995, will be a little more pitcher friendly. Marvin Freeman (10-2, 2.80 ERA) was the staff ace. Nied (9-7, 4.80) displayed the arm that made him the No. 1 pick in the expansion draft, and he should develop into the No. 1 starter. Greg Harris (6.65 ERA), Mike Harkey (5.79), and Kevin Ritz (5.62) all had problems. Bruce Ruffin notched 16 saves, preserving his career. Steve Reed and Mike Munoz pitched well in relief. Andres Galarraga (.319, 31 homers, 85 RBI) was again outstanding at first base, and Charlie Hayes (.288, 10, 50) handled the hot corner ably. Nelson Liriano and Walt Weiss were a steady keystone combo. Dante Bichette (.304, 27, 95) terrorized NL pitching and played a fine right field. Ellis Burks (.322, 13, 24) got bit by the injury bug but was capably replaced by Mike Kingery (.349). Howard Johnson (.211) lost left field to the speedy Young (.272). Joe Girardi (.276) was a capable catcher.

Manager

Don Baylor	W	L	PCT
Major-league record	120	159	.430
with Rockies	120	159	.430
1994 record	53	64	.453

Coaches: Larry Bearnarth, Ron Hassey, Amos Otis, Jerry Royster, Don Zimmer, Art Howe

Two-Year Finishes

93	94
6	3

Two-Year Record: 120-159; .430
Rank: 13th in NL; 27th in ML

Chairman, CEO: Jerry McMorris
Executive VP, Baseball Operations: John McHale, Jr.
Senior VP, GM: Bob Gebhard
VP, Player Personnel: Dick Balderson
Director of Scouting: Pat Daugherty

Address
Coors Field
2001 Blake Street
Denver, CO 80205-2010

Ballparks

Mile High Stadium 1993-94;
Coors Field 1995
Capacity: 50,000
1994 Attendance: 3,281,511
Surface: natural grass

Left field fence: 347 feet
Center field fence: 415 feet
Right field fence: 350 feet
Left-center fence: 390 feet
Right-center fence: 375 feet

Team History

In 1990, the NL chose the Rockies (along with the Marlins) as the most recent expansion franchises, to increase the number of teams in the loop from 12 to 14. Before beginning play in 1993, the Rockies chose former Twins front-office man Bob Gebhard as the GM. He in turn chose former slugger and batting coach Don Baylor as the team's first manager. Baylor and Co. selected David Nied as the first pick in the expansion draft, and the team also picked up first baseman Andres Galarraga, who became the first player in expansion history to win a batting title by hitting .370. This did not go unnoticed, as a record 4,483,270 patrons watched the Rockies in their initial season. While the owners figured baseball would go over big, they had no idea how hungry area fans were for the major leagues. The Rockies improved substantially in 1994.

LOS ANGELES DODGERS

58-56 .509 0 GB Manager: Tommy Lasorda

The Dodgers were the only team to finish over .500 in the NL West in 1994, so they came away with the title. Manager Tommy Lasorda relied on some old friends—good starting pitchers and Rookies of the Year—to help cover any rough spots that Los Angeles may have had on its roster. The starting rotation pitched many innings to cover for a bullpen that struggled. Ramon Martinez (12-7, 3.97 ERA, 170 innings) may not be the power pitcher he once was, but he was able to do the job. Kevin Gross (9-7, 3.60, 157 innings) had a fine year. Tom Candiotti (7-7, 4.12), Pedro Astacio (6-8, 4.29), and crowd favorite Orel Hershiser (6-6, 3.79) each provided more than 135 (usually quality) innings. Three veteran righty relievers—Todd Worrell (4.29, 11 saves), Jim Gott (5.94), and

Roger McDowell (5.23)—had less-than-stellar seasons. Omar Daal and Ismael Valdes, however, provided hope for the future. Hope is something the Dodger organization excels in. Raul Mondesi (.306, 16 homers, 56 RBI, 15 assists from right field) handily won the '94 NL Rookie of the Year Award. He joined the '93 prize winner, catcher Mike Piazza (.319, 24, 92), who had a monster year. First baseman Eric Karros (.266, 14, 46) won the prize in 1992 but was unspectacular in '94. Delino DeShields (.250, 51 runs scored) proved to be a fine second baseman, while third baseman Tim Wallach (.280, 23, 78) revived his career. Brett Butler (.314, 79 runs scored) was a top center fielder.

Manager

Tommy Lasorda	W	L	PCT
Major-league record	1480	1338	.525
with Dodgers	1480	1338	.525
1994 record	58	56	.509

Coaches: Mark Cresse, Dave Wallace, Manny Mota, Joe Ferguson, Bill Russell, Reggie Smith, Ben Hines

Five-Year Finishes

90	91	92	93	94
2	2	6	4	1

Five-Year Record: 381-381; .500
Rank: 6th in NL; 12th in ML

President: Peter O'Malley
VP: Fred Claire
Director, Minor League Operations: Charlie Blaney
Director, Scouting: Terry Reynolds

Address
1000 Elysian Park Avenue
Los Angeles, CA 90012

Ballparks

Brooklyn: Union Grounds, 1876; Washington Park 1891-1897; Ebbetts Field 1913-1957. **Los Angeles:** Memorial Coliseum 1958-1961; Dodger Stadium 1962-present
Capacity: 56,000

1994 Attendance: 2,279,421
Surface: natural grass
Left field fence: 330 feet
Center field fence: 395 feet
Right field fence: 330 feet
Left-center fence: 385 feet
Right-center fence: 385 feet

Team History

The National League's most successful franchise got its start in Brooklyn in 1884, named for the borough's Trolley Dodgers. Flatbush fans suffered until "next year" finally brought a world championship in 1955. They cried two years later when Walter O'Malley moved the team to LA, where the Dodgers won World Series in 1959, 1963, 1965, 1981, and 1988. In 1989, the team from tinseltown finished fourth in their division. They took some steps in the right direction during 1990, regaining second

place in the division, but finishing five games behind the eventual world champion Reds that season. Spirits were high in '91, but the mighty Dodgers fell apart down the stretch. LA finished '91 only one game behind the Braves. After coming so close, the '92 season was an extra-painful reality, though the Dodgers rebounded in 1993. The Dodgers "won" the NL West title in 1994, being the only team in the division to finish above .500.

SAN DIEGO PADRES
47-70 .402 12½ GB Manager: Jim Riggleman

The most exciting baseball news in San Diego was Tony Gwynn's run at .400, which ended with his .394 batting average on Aug. 12. The worst team in baseball, the Padres at least showed a few signs of improving. Manager Jim Riggleman, looking around, decided that Chicago was a better place to be and signed on with former Padre front-office man and new Cub GM Ed Lynch. The Padres immediately promoted third base coach Bruce Bochy. The Pads displayed a promising starting rotation, led by one of the league's top young pitchers, Andy Benes (6-14, 3.86 ERA, a loop-best 189 Ks). Andy Ashby (6-11, 3.40) and Scott Sanders (4-8, 4.78) pitched better than their won-lost records indicated. Joey Hamilton (9-6,

2.98) emerged as a top rookie. Closer Trevor Hoffman (4-4, 2.57, 20 saves) starred in the bullpen, and he was set up well by young lefty Pedro Martinez (3-2, 2.90). Jeff Tabaka, Tim Mauser, and Donnie Elliott also had good years in relief. Center fielder Derek Bell (.311, 14 homers, 54 RBI) and left fielder Phil Plantier (.240, 18, 41) continued to hit the ball. Second baseman Bip Roberts (.320, 52 runs) was a fine leadoff batter. Ricky Gutierrez (.240) and Luis Lopez (.277) shared the shortstop slot. At catcher, Brad Ausmus was solid. Craig Shipley (.333), Scott Livingstone, and Archi Cianfrocco shared third base. Eddie Williams (.331, 11, 42) played well at first, while Phil Clark was disappointing.

Manager			
Bruce Bochy	**W**	**L**	**PCT**
Major-league record	—	—	—
with Padres	—	—	—
1994 record	—	—	—

Coaches: Rob Picciolo, Merv Rettenmund, Dan Warthen, Sonny Siebert, Graig Nettles, Davey Lopes, Ty Waller

Five-Year Finishes

90	91	92	93	94
5	3	3	7	4

Five-Year Record: 349-416; .456
Rank: 12th in NL; 26th in ML

Chairman, Managing Partner: Tom Werner
President: Dick Freeman
GM: Randy Smith
Assistant VP, Baseball Operations & Assistant GM: John Barr
Director, Scouting: Reggie Waller

Address
P.O. Box 2000
San Deigo, CA 92112

Ballpark

Jack Murphy Stadium 1969-present
Capacity: 59,700
1994 Attendance: 953,857
Surface: natural grass

Left field fence: 327 feet
Center field fence: 405 feet
Right field fence: 327 feet
Left-center fence: 370 feet
Right-center fence: 370 feet

Team History

A product of the 1969 expansion with Montreal, the Padres struggled below .500 for their first 15 seasons. Their first winning year—1984—they also became pennant winners. Taking three out of five games in the NLCS, the Padres put away the Cubs and faced the formidable force that was the Detroit Tigers. Unfortunately for San Diego fans, the dream season ended in short order with the Tigers snuffing out any world championship hopes the Padres had in only five games. The rest of the 1980s featured middle-division finishes. One little glimmer came in 1989, when the Padres finished second in their division, just three games behind the eventual pennant-winning Giants. Injuries hit the San Diego team hard in 1990, and it was evidenced in their next-to-last-place finish. The Pads rebounded somewhat in 1991 and '92, but in 1993 fell to the bottom as the team unloaded its high-priced veterans and went with youth. It stayed on the bottom in '94.

SAN FRANCISCO GIANTS
55-60 .478 3½ GB Manager: Dusty Baker

One year after winning 103 games, San Francisco in 1994 had some troubles that it couldn't overcome. Manager Dusty Baker's Giants had the league's second-best offense in 1993, but they were one of the worst in 1994, scoring 504 runs, 10th in the league. Losing Will Clark to free agency and Robby Thompson and Willie McGee to injury led to the scoring drought. Third baseman Matt Williams (.267, 43 homers, 96 RBI) led the league in dingers and was chasing the ghost of Roger Maris before the strike. Barry Bonds (.312, 37, 81) wanted to chase a fourth MVP title before his slow start. Imagine the offense without those two. Darryl Strawberry (.239) provided a small boost after he signed in June. Todd Benzinger (.265, nine, 31) didn't come close to filling Clark's shoes at first base. Thompson (.209) was replaced by

John Patterson (.238) at second. Shortstop Royce Clayton (.236), center fielder Darren Lewis (.257, 70 runs), and right fielder Dave Martinez (.247) were solid complementary players. Kirt Manwaring (.250) struggled at bat but displayed his fine glove. Bill Swift (8-7, 3.38 ERA) had some injury problems but pitched well when healthy. Another top pitcher from the '93 squad, John Burkett, had a proficient season but a lackluster won-lost record (6-8, 3.62). Mark Portugal (10-8, 3.93) and rookie William VanLandingham (8-2, 3.54) keyed a solid starting rotation. Rod Beck notched 28 saves and had no blown saves, bringing home a 2.77 ERA. Mike Jackson had a 1.49 ERA and four saves. Dave Burba, Steve Frey, Bryan Hickerson, and Rich Monteleone had their troubles in the pen.

Manager Dusty Baker	W	L	PCT
Major-league record	158	119	.570
with Giants	158	119	.570
1994 record	55	60	.478

Coaches: Bobby Bonds, Bob Brenly, Wendell Kim, Bob Lillis, Dick Pole, Denny Sommers

Five-Year Finishes

90	91	92	93	94
3	4	5	2	2

Five-Year Record: 390-373; .511
Rank: 5th in NL; 8th in ML

Managing General Partner: Peter Magowan
Senior VP and GM: Bob Quinn
Executive VP: Larry Baer
VP, Scouting and Player Personnel: Brian Sabean
VP, Baseball Administration: Tony Siegle
Coordinator of Scouting: Bob Hartsfield

Address
Candlestick Park
San Francisco, CA 94124

Ballparks

New York: Polo Grounds 1883-1888, 1891-1957; St. George Cricket Grounds 1889-1890. **San Francisco:** Seals Stadium 1958-1959; Candlestick Park 1960-present
Capacity: 62,000

1994 Attendance: 1,704,614
Surface: natural grass
Left field fence: 335 feet
Center field fence: 400 feet
Right field fence: 328 feet
Left-center fence: 365 feet
Right-center fence: 365 feet

Team History

Few dispute the economic reasons for moving this proud franchise west from New York, but many believe the Giants were never the same after coming to San Francisco. The Giants dominated the NL before 1900, and they won 15 pennants and five world championships from 1904 to '54. Led by Willie Mays, Willie McCovey, and Juan Marichal, the Giants enjoyed 14 consecutive winning seasons after their 1958 move, but won only two more pennants—

1962 and 1989. In the latter World Series, they lost to the world-shaking Athletics. The Giants also won their division in 1987, but lost the pennant to the Cardinals. When the 1990s began, San Francisco fans had little to cheer about. After almost moving out of the Bay Area, the Giants in 1993 returned to lose by one game against the Braves in one of the greatest pennant battles of all time. The '94 Giants slipped back to mediocrity.

Hall of Fame

Profiles of the players, managers, umpires, and executives who have been inducted into the National Baseball Hall of Fame and Museum comprise this section. The profiles are presented in alphabetical order. At the end of each profile is a date in parentheses; this is the year the member was enshrined into the Hall.

In preparation for baseball's centennial in 1939, a National Baseball Museum was proposed, first as a matter of civic pride, and later as a memorial for the greatest of those who have ever played the game.

While the rules governing election to the Hall of Fame have varied in specifics over the years, in general the criteria have remained the same. One must be named on 75 percent of ballots cast by members of the Baseball Writers' Association of America. To be eligible, players must have played for at least 10 years. The players have to be retired for at least five years but not more than 20 years. A player is eligible for 15 years in the BBWAA vote.

If the player is not named on 75 percent of the ballots in 15 years, his name becomes eligible for consideration by the Committee on Baseball Veterans. This committee also considers managers, umpires, and executives for induction to Cooperstown. The same 75 percent rule applies. Anyone on baseball's permanently ineligible list is excluded from consideration.

The Committee on the Negro Leagues was added to the selection process in 1971. This board considered players who had 10 years of service in the pre-1946 Negro Leagues, and also those who made the major leagues. The Negro League board dissolved into the Veterans' Committee in 1977.

HANK AARON
Outfielder (1954-1976) Aaron is baseball's all-time leader in home runs with 755 and in RBI with 2,297. During a 23-year career with the Braves and the Brewers, "Hammerin' Hank" stood out as one of the game's most complete and consistent performers. He was the NL MVP in 1957 when he hit .322 with 44 home runs and 132 RBI. Aaron hit 40 home runs or more eight times and totaled over 100 RBI 11 times. (1982)

GROVER ALEXANDER
Pitcher (1911-1930) Despite his battles against alcohol and epilepsy, Alexander's 373 wins are tied for the NL record. With Philadelphia in 1916, he recorded a major-league record 16 shutouts on his way to a 33-12 record. "Pete" led the senior loop in wins six times, ERA five times, and shutouts seven times. His 90 shutouts are second on the all-time list. (1938)

WALTER ALSTON
Manager (1954-1976) In 23 years as manager of the Dodgers, all under one-year contracts, Alston led the club to seven pennants and four world championships. Under his patient leadership, the Dodgers made pitching and defense a winning combination. His career record is 2,040-1,613—a .558 winning percentage. (1983)

CAP ANSON

First baseman (1871-1897); manager (1879-1898) A baseball pioneer, as player, manager, and part-owner of NL Chicago, "Pop" Anson was the game's most influential figure in the 19th century. He hit .300 or better in 20 consecutive seasons and won five pennants. However, in 1887, his racist views led him to intimidate organized baseball into banning blacks. (1939)

LUIS APARICIO

Shortstop (1956-1973) No man played more games at shortstop—2,581—than Aparicio. The swift, sure-handed infielder played a vital role in championship seasons for the White Sox in 1959 and the Orioles in 1966. The winner of nine Gold Gloves, Aparicio led the AL in stolen bases nine times en route to 506 career thefts. (1984)

LUKE APPLING

Shortstop (1930-1943; 1945-1950) Known better for his bat than his glove, Appling nonetheless played shortstop for the White Sox for 20 years. "Old Aches and Pains" led the AL in batting twice, finishing with a .310 career average. He finished his career with 1,116 RBI and 1,319 runs scored. In 1936, he hit .388 with 128 RBI, despite hitting only six home runs. (1964)

EARL AVERILL

Outfielder (1929-1941) The only outfielder selected to the first six All-Star games, Averill didn't turn pro until age 23, and didn't make the major leagues, with Cleveland, until age 26. In his first 10 seasons he was one of the game's best sluggers. In a 1933 doubleheader, he hit four home runs, three consecutively. Averill had more than 90 RBI in nine seasons. A congenital back condition cut his career short. (1975)

FRANK BAKER

Third baseman (1908-1922) Despite never hitting more than 12 home runs in a season, during baseball's dead-ball era Baker was a slugger supreme. He led the AL in home runs from 1911 to 1914. Two 1911 World Series home runs earned him his "Home Run" nickname. In six World Series with the A's and Yankees, he hit .363. (1955)

DAVE BANCROFT

Shortstop (1915-1930) One of the best fielding shortstops of all time, Bancroft set a major-league record in 1922 when he handled 984 chances. A heady ballplayer, "Beauty" was named captain of the Giants in 1920 and led them to three straight pennants. He batted over .300 five times. (1971)

ERNIE BANKS

Shortstop; first baseman (1953-1971) Banks combined unbridled enthusiasm with remarkable talent to become one of the most popular players of his era. As a shortstop he won back-to-back NL MVP awards in 1958 and 1959 and a Gold Glove in 1960, before switching to first base. Despite his 512 career home runs, the Cubs did not win a pennant during his tenure. "Mr. Cub" had 2,583 lifetime hits and 1,636 RBI. (1977)

AL BARLICK

Umpire (1940-1971) A respected arbiter, Barlick worked in Jackie Robinson's first game. Barlick umpired in seven All-Star contests and in seven World Series. (1989)

ED BARROW

Executive In 1918, BoSox manager Barrow transferred Babe Ruth from the mound to the outfield. Barrow followed Ruth to the Yankees. "Cousin Ed" was in charge of the Bronx Bombers from 1920 to 1947. (1953)

JAKE BECKLEY

First baseman (1888-1907) Beckley played more games at first base than anyone else. He had 2,930 hits, 1,600 runs, and 1,575 RBI. His handle-bar mustache made him a fan favorite. "St. Jacob's" 243 career triples are fourth all time. (1971)

COOL PAPA BELL

Outfielder (1922-1946) Perhaps the fastest man to ever play the game, Bell starred as an outfielder in the Negro Leagues for more than two decades. Satchel Paige claimed Bell was so fast he could switch off the light and leap into bed before the room got dark. Often credited with scoring from second on a sacrifice fly, Bell hit .392 against organized major-league competition. (1974)

JOHNNY BENCH

Catcher (1967-1983) Upon his arrival in the big leagues in 1967, Bench was heralded as baseball's best defensive catcher. After his NL MVP year in 1970 at age 22, with 45 home runs and 148 RBI, he was baseball's best catcher, period. He won his second MVP in 1972. With Bench behind the plate, the Reds won four pennants and two World Series. In the 1976 World Series, he hit .533. He had 389 homers and 1,376 RBI. (1989)

CHIEF BENDER

Pitcher (1903-1917; 1925) An alumnus of the Carlisle Indian School, the half-Chippewa Bender overcame bigotry to become one of the Philadelphia A's most valued members. He had a career 212-127 record, and he won six World Series games. He led the AL in winning percentage three times, including a 17-3 mark in 1914. (1953)

YOGI BERRA

Catcher (1946-1965) If championships are the best measure of success, then Berra stands second to no one. His 14 World Series appearances, 75 Series games played, and 71 Series hits are all records. A three-time MVP, the Yankee hit 20 homers in 10 consecutive seasons. Known as well for his way with words, Berra will be remembered for the oft-quoted "It's never over till it's over." He had 1,430 lifetime RBI to go with his 358 home runs. (1972)

JIM BOTTOMLEY

First baseman (1922-1937) One of the first products of the famous Cardinals' farm system, Bottomley was named NL MVP in 1928 for hitting .325 and 31 homers, and driving in 136 runs. On September 16, 1924, "Sunny Jim" knocked in 12 runs with six hits against Brooklyn. He batted .310 lifetime with 1,422 runs batted in. (1974)

LOU BOUDREAU

Shortstop (1938-1952); manager (1942-1950; 1952-1957; 1960) Boudreau was one of the game's great shortstops. He was named Cleveland's player-manager at age 24. In 1948, he led the club to the AL pennant, hitting .355, scoring 116 runs, while driving in 106, capturing the AL MVP Award. He led AL shortstops in fielding eight times. As a manager, he won 1,162 games. (1970)

ROGER BRESNAHAN

Catcher (1897; 1900-1915) The first catcher elected to the Hall of Fame, Bresnahan is most famous for pioneering the use of shin guards and batting helmets. Bresnahan hit .350 and stole 34 bases with the Giants in 1903. (1945)

LOU BROCK

Outfielder (1961-1979) Brock's career totals of 938 stolen bases and 3,023 hits, coupled with a .293 batting average, gained him admittance to the Hall. In 1974, at age 35, he stole 118 bases. He excelled in three World Series for the Cardinals, hitting .391 and scoring 16 runs. Brock reached 200 hits four times. (1985)

DAN BROUTHERS
First baseman (1879-1896; 1904) Baseball's premier 19th century slugger, Brouthers toiled for 11 different clubs, in three major leagues, for 19 seasons. He was the first man to win back-to-back batting titles, in 1882 and 1883. He batted over .300 in 16 consecutive seasons, reaching .374 in 1883. (1945)

THREE FINGER BROWN
Pitcher (1903-1916) A farm accident in a corn grinder mutilated Brown's right hand, severing most of his index finger, mangling his middle finger, and paralyzing his little finger. The injuries, however, gave his pitches a natural sink and curve. Pitching with the Cubs, between 1904 and 1910 Brown's highest ERA was 1.86, helping Chicago to four pennants. He had a career 239-129 record, with a 2.06 ERA and 55 shutouts. (1948)

MORGAN BULKELEY
NL President (1876) In 1876, Bulkeley was named the first President of the new National League. He served one year without distinction and resigned. (1937)

JESSE BURKETT
Outfielder (1890-1905) In the 1890s, the left-handed-hitting Burkett hit over .400 two times. A fine baserunner and bunter, the third-strike foul-bunt rule was created due to Burkett's prowess at the art. "Crab" won three batting titles. He scored 1,720 runs, drew 1,029 walks, and notched 2,850 base hits in his 16-year career. (1946)

ROY CAMPANELLA
Catcher (1948-1957) Campanella, one of the great athletes of his time, had a .312

average, 41 homers, 103 runs scored, and 142 RBI in 1953—amazing marks for a backstop. In 1951, 1953, and 1955 the Dodger catcher was named the NL's MVP. He led his team to five pennants in 10 years. A 1958 automobile accident left Campanella paralyzed, and his struggle to remain active served as an inspiration. (1969)

ROD CAREW
First baseman; second baseman (1967-1985) An infielder with Minnesota and California, Carew was one of baseball's premiere singles hitters, notching 3,053 hits and a lifetime .328 batting average. He topped .300 in 15 consecutive seasons on his way to seven batting titles, a mark surpassed only by Ty Cobb's 12. Carew's 1977 MVP year consisted of a .388 batting average, 239 hits, 128 runs scored, and 100 RBI. (1991)

MAX CAREY
Outfielder (1910-1929) A tremendous defensive center fielder, primarily with Pittsburgh, Carey swiped 738 bases. In 1925, despite two broken ribs, "Scoops" batted .458 in the World Series as the Pirates defeated Washington. In game seven, his four hits and three runs scored beat the great Walter Johnson. Carey scored 1,545 runs and had 2,665 base hits in his 20-year career. (1961)

STEVE CARLTON
Pitcher (1965-1988) "Lefty" set a major-league record with four Cy Young Awards (1972, '77, '80, and '82), won 329 games with a career 3.22 ERA, and finished second to Nolan Ryan on the all-time strike-out list with 4,136. In 1972, Carlton went 27-10 for a Phillies team that won just 59 games, accounting for a modern record 45.8 percent of his club's wins. He was devout in his work habits and in his refusal to speak to the press. (1994)

ALEXANDER CARTWRIGHT

Executive On September 23, 1845, Alexander Cartwright formed the Knickerbocker Base Ball Club and formalized a set of 20 rules that gave baseball its basic shape. While Cartwright's involvement with the game lasted only a few years, he is the man most responsible for the game that is played, and loved, today. (1938)

HENRY CHADWICK

Writer-Statistician While Alexander Cartwright is baseball's inventor, Chadwick is the first man to chronicle the game. The only sportswriter enshrined in the Hall itself, Chadwick published guides and instructional booklets that helped popularize the game, and his method of scoring led to the game's wealth of statistics. (1938)

FRANK CHANCE

First baseman (1898-1914) Anchor of the Cubs' "Tinker-to-Evers-to-Chance" double-play combo, Chance helped Chicago win four pennants. While he was hardly a dominant player, he nevertheless hit .296 during his career and hit .310 in Series play. Chance's career was cut short by repeated beanings, which eventually left him deaf in one ear. "The Peerless Leader" managed the Cubs for seven years. (1946)

HAPPY CHANDLER

Commissioner (1945-1951) The former governor and U.S. senator from Kentucky, Chandler succeeded Judge Kenesaw Mountain Landis as the second commissioner of baseball. Despite the opposition of most baseball owners, Chandler backed Branch Rickey's signing of Jackie Robinson and prevented a player strike by threatening to ban any striking player for life. Preferring a "yes-man," the owners voted Chandler out in 1951. (1982)

OSCAR CHARLESTON

Outfielder (1915-1941) Blessed with speed and power in abundance, center fielder Charleston is thought by many to be greatest of all Negro League players. Superb defensively, on offense he could both steal a base and hit a home run. In 1932, he became player-manager of the Pittsburgh Crawfords, whose lineup, including Charleston, featured five Hall of Famers. The team went 99-36 that year, and Charleston hit .363. (1976)

JACK CHESBRO

Pitcher (1899-1909) Chesbro's 41 victories in 454⅔ innings in 1904 stand as one of the game's more remarkable single-season achievements. A master of the spitball, his wild pitch in the next to the last game of the 1904 season against Boston, however, cost New York the AL pennant. "Happy Jack" led his league in winning percentage in three seasons. (1946)

FRED CLARKE

Outfielder (1894-1911; 1913-1915); manager (1897-1915) For 19 of his 21 big league seasons, Clarke was a manager as well as a player, all for the NL Louisville-Pittsburgh franchise. As a player, he hit .312 with 2,672 base hits and 1,619 runs scored. As manager he won one World Series, in 1909, and four pennants, including three in a row from 1901 to 1903. "Cap" was 1,602-1,881 as a manager. (1945)

JOHN CLARKSON

Pitcher (1882-1894) Clarkson excelled during the years when the pitching distance was 50 feet. Six times he hurled more than 400 innings, twice more than 600. In 1885 with the White Stockings, he went 53-16. With the Beaneaters in 1889, Clarkson's record was 49-19 in 73 appearances. Winner of 328 career games, he had 485 complete games and led the NL in strikeouts three times. (1963)

ROBERTO CLEMENTE

Outfielder (1955-1972) Clemente won four NL batting titles and also possessed one of the strongest outfield arms in baseball history. Intensely proud of his Puerto Rican heritage, it was not until the 1971 World Series, when Clemente led Pittsburgh to victory with a .414 average, that he began to receive his due. In 13 of his 18 seasons he hit .300 or better, topping the .350 mark three times. On New Year's Eve, 1972, Clemente died in a plane crash bringing supplies to earthquake-ravaged Nicaragua. Clemente was the first Hispanic elected to the Hall of Fame. (1973)

TY COBB

Outfielder (1905-1928) The first man elected to the Hall of Fame, Cobb received more votes than any of his counterparts. Intense beyond belief, the daring Cobb epitomized the "scientific" style of play that dominated baseball in the first quarter of the 20th century. In 22 of his 24 seasons Cobb hit over .320, and his lifetime .366 average is still the all-time best. He led the AL in batting average 10 seasons. The "Georgia Peach's" 2,246 runs scored are the most in history, while his 4,189 hits and 891 stolen bases rank second and fourth, respectively. (1936)

MICKEY COCHRANE

Catcher (1925-1937) An exceptional defensive catcher and dangerous hitter, Cochrane led the Athletics and Tigers to five pennants, including two as Detroit manager. "Black Mike" cracked the .300 mark in eight seasons, and his lifetime .320 batting average is the highest of any catcher. Mickey was twice AL MVP. In 1937, Cochrane was beaned by Yankee pitcher

Bump Hadley and suffered a fractured skull, ending his career at the age of 34. (1947)

EDDIE COLLINS

Second baseman (1906-1930) As Connie Mack's on-field manager, Collins led the Athletics to four pennants in five years. Traded to the White Sox, he helped that club to two more. An accomplished all-around ballplayer, Collins smacked 3,312 hits for a career average of .333, yet led the AL in batting only once. A consummate basestealer, he ranks sixth on the all-time list with 744 career swipes. "Cocky" scored 1,821 runs and drove in 1,300 runs in his 25-year career. (1939)

JIMMY COLLINS

Third baseman (1895-1908) Collins revolutionized the third base position by moving around, charging in, and fielding bunts bare-handed. Playing primarily for both the Boston Beaneaters in the National League and the Boston Pilgrims in the AL, Collins hit a robust .294, topping the .300 mark five times and the 100 RBI mark twice. (1945)

EARLE COMBS

Outfielder (1924-1935) While Babe Ruth and Lou Gehrig cleaned up at the plate, Combs set the table. As the leadoff man and center fielder for the Yankees, Combs scored 100 or more runs in eight straight seasons. "The Kentucky Colonel" had a lifetime .325 average and scored 1,186 runs. A collision with an outfield fence in 1934 forced his retirement a year later. (1970)

CHARLES COMISKEY

Executive Comiskey parlayed modest field success into managerial brilliance, later becoming the first former player to be sole owner of a major-league franchise, the White Sox. The "Old Roman" assisted Ban Johnson in the formation of the American League. Some historians feel that his parsimonious spending habits indirectly led to the 1919 "Black Sox" scandal. (1939)

JOCKO CONLAN

Umpire (1941-1964) Conlan started umpiring by accident. In a 1935 minor-league game, when one of the regular umpires was overcome by the heat, Conlan was rushed in to pinch-ump. He umpired in six World Series and six All-Star Games. (1974)

TOMMY CONNOLLY

Umpire (1898-1931) Connolly became an NL umpire in 1898. Frustrated with the circuit, he signed with the AL in 1901. Thirty years later he was named chief of AL umpires. Connolly and Bill Klem became the first umpires named to the Hall of Fame. Connolly umpired in eight World Series, including the first, in 1903. (1953)

ROGER CONNOR

First baseman (1880-1897) Until Babe Ruth broke the mark in 1921, Connor held the lifetime record for home runs with 138. A career .317 hitter, the Giant first baseman was a bona fide dead-ball era slugger, smacking 233 triples, fifth all time. In his first game with the Giants in 1883, he hit such an impressive shot that the fans passed the hat and bought him a gold watch. He scored 1,620 runs and had 1,322 RBI in his career. (1976)

STAN COVELESKI

Pitcher (1912; 1916-1928) A coal miner at age 13, Coveleski didn't reach the majors to stay until 1916, at age 27. The spitball artist had his best years with Cleveland from 1918 to 1921, winning 20 games or more each season. Coveleski won 215 games, while his brother Harry won 81. Stan lost only 142 games and retired with a lifetime 2.89 ERA. (1969)

SAM CRAWFORD

Outfielder (1899-1917) Crawford played outfield for Detroit alongside Ty Cobb. The powerful Crawford is baseball's all-time leader in triples with 309, having smashed at least 10 in every full season he played. A native of Wahoo, Nebraska, "Wahoo Sam" retired only 39 hits shy of 3,000. He hit .309 lifetime, with 1,391 runs scored and 1,525 RBI. He later returned to baseball as an umpire in the Pacific Coast League. (1957)

JOE CRONIN

Shortstop (1926-1945); manager (1933-1947); AL President (1959-1973) For 50 years, Cronin excelled as a player, manager, and executive. A hard-hitting shortstop, in 1934 the Red Sox purchased him from Washington for a record $225,000. Cronin was a .301 career batter, and he had 1,233 runs scored and 1,424 RBI to go with his 515 doubles. As a manager, Cronin led the Senators to a pennant in 1933 and the Red Sox to one in 1946. From 1959 to 1973, he served as AL President. (1956)

CANDY CUMMINGS

Pitcher (1872-1877) Baseball's legendary inventor of the curveball, Cummings allegedly discovered the pitch while tossing clam shells as a youngster. Despite standing 5'9" and never weighing more than 120 pounds, he won 146 games from 1872 to 1877. (1939)

KIKI CUYLER

Outfielder (1921-1938) Pronounced "Cuy-Cuy," Kiki Cuyler hit a robust .354 as a Pirate rookie in 1924 and was heralded as "the next Ty Cobb." Kiki hit over .300 10 times and topped the .350 mark four times. He accumulated 2,299 hits for a lifetime mark of .321. He had 1,295 runs, 1,065 RBI, and 328 stolen bases during his career. (1968)

RAY DANDRIDGE
Third baseman (1933-1950) Dandridge excelled at third base in the Negro and Mexican Leagues, hitting for power and average while fielding with precision. He accumulated a .347 average against white big-league pitching. In 1949, he signed with the Giants and tore apart the American Association for Minneapolis, but at age 36 never received a call to the majors. (1987)

DIZZY DEAN
Pitcher (1930-1941; 1947) Baseball's most colorful pitcher, Dean threw smoke, spoke in homespun hyperbole, and by age 26 had won 134 games for the Cardinals. After breaking his toe in the 1937 All-Star Game, Dean altered his pitching motion, hurt his arm, and never approached his previous record. He had a 150-83 career record with a 3.02 ERA. Dizzy was the last NL pitcher to notch 30 wins in a season when he went 30-7 in 1934. (1953)

ED DELAHANTY
Outfielder (1888-1903) One of five brothers to play in the majors, Delahanty was perhaps baseball's premier hitter of the 1890s. He hit .400 three times, and his .346 career mark is fourth all time. He lived as hard as he played. In 1903, Delahanty was suspended for drinking. En route to his home, "Big Ed" (age 35) was kicked off a train, fell into the Niagara River, and was swept over the falls to his death. (1945)

BILL DICKEY
Catcher (1928-1943; 1946) Catcher of 100 or more games for 13 consecutive seasons, in 1936 Dickey hit .362, still a record for the position. He accumulated a .313 batting average and 1,209 RBI in his career. During his 17 years, the Yankees won nine pennants and captured eight world championships. Dickey is also credited with developing the receiving skills of Yogi Berra. (1954)

MARTIN DIHIGO
Pitcher; infielder; outfielder (1923-1945) The first Cuban elected to the Hall, Dihigo starred as a pitcher, infielder, and outfielder in Negro and Caribbean baseball. Winner of more than 250 games from the mound, he hit over .400 three times. He was one of the most versatile players in the game's history; he was able to play all of the infield positions, as well as being one of the best hurlers in history. (1977)

JOE DiMAGGIO
Outfielder (1936-1942; 1946-1951) "Joltin' Joe" led the Yankees to nine pennants while making 13 All-Star teams in 13 seasons. A three-time MVP, the quiet, graceful center fielder is often credited with being the best player of his generation. In 1941, "The Yankee Clipper" hit in a record 56 consecutive games. He led the AL in batting average twice, slugging average twice, triples once, home runs twice, runs scored once, and RBI twice. He retired with a .325 batting average, 361 home runs, 1,390 runs scored, and 1,537 RBI. (1955)

BOBBY DOERR
Second baseman (1937-1944; 1946-1951) Doerr was known for his reliable defensive play and potent bat. For 14 seasons he was one of the best second basemen in baseball, spending his entire career with the Red Sox, and never playing a game at another position. In 1944, Doerr led the AL in slugging at .528. He had a career .288 average, 223 homers, and 1,247 RBI. (1986)

DON DRYSDALE
Pitcher (1956-1969) In the early 1960s, Drysdale and teammate Sandy Koufax

gave the Dodgers baseball's best pitching tandem. The intimidating Drysdale led the NL in Ks three times. He was 25-9 with a 2.83 ERA and a league-best 232 strikeouts in 1962, winning the Cy Young Award. In 1968, "Big D" hurled six shutouts in a row on his way to 58 consecutive scoreless innings. He was 209-166 with a 2.95 ERA and 2,486 strikeouts. (1984)

HUGH DUFFY
Outfielder (1888-1906) In 1894, the diminutive Duffy hit .440 for NL Boston, the highest mark ever recorded under current rules. He also captured the Triple Crown that year, with 18 homers and 145 RBI. He compiled a career .324 average, 1,551 runs, and 1,299 RBI. After his retirement, Duffy continued in baseball another 48 seasons. (1945)

LEO DUROCHER
Manager (1939-1946; 1948-1955; 1966-1973) A shortstop for 17 years in the bigs, "Leo the Lip" as manager compiled a 2,008-1,709 record and a .570 winning percentage. In 1951, he piloted the Giants to the "Miracle at Coogan's Bluff" and reached three World Series overall, winning the championship in 1954. In 1947, he was suspended for one year for conduct detrimental to baseball. (1994)

BILLY EVANS
Umpire (1906-1927) Evans was a sportswriter and then did what many writers thought they could do better—be an umpire. He was one of the best, working six Series. (1973)

JOHNNY EVERS
Second baseman (1902-1917; 1922; 1929) Perhaps the best of the "Tinker-to-Evers-to-Chance" double-play combination, second baseman Evers relied on a steady glove and just enough hitting to help lead his club to five pennants in 16 seasons. Although he played most of his career with the Cubs, in 1914 he was the NL MVP with the "Miracle" Boston Braves. "The Trojan" had 919 runs and 324 stolen bases. (1946)

BUCK EWING
Catcher (1880-1897) Connie Mack called Ewing "the greatest catcher of all time." He eclipsed the .300 mark in 10 seasons, including a string of eight straight times. Ewing had a lifetime .303 batting average and scored 1,129 runs. (1939)

RED FABER
Pitcher (1914-1933) One of the last spitball pitchers, Faber spent his entire 20-year career with the White Sox, posting a 254-213 record. An illness and injury in 1919 left him untouched by the "Black Sox" scandal. He led the AL in ERA and in complete games twice. Faber posted a career 3.15 ERA in 4,086⅔ innings, with 273 complete games. (1964)

BOB FELLER
Pitcher (1936-1941; 1945-1956) Phenom Feller left the farm at age 17 and struck out 15 in his first official big-league appearance. Amazingly, he was signed by a Cleveland scout for one dollar and an autographed baseball. Feller's fastball, once timed at over 98 mph, may have been the fastest of all time. "Rapid Robert" led the AL seven times in strikeouts, six seasons in wins, and four times in shutouts. Feller won 266 games, all for Cleveland, with three no-hitters. (1962)

RICK FERRELL
Catcher (1929-1947) One of the few players inducted primarily for his defense, Ferrell nonetheless hit .300 four times. He was a career .281 hitter and drew 931 walks. With the Red Sox, for four seasons Ferrell teamed with brother Wes. (1984)

ROLLIE FINGERS
Pitcher (1968-1985) The earliest to be used in a "closer" role, Fingers was the first pitcher to reach 300 saves. He was the fireman for the champion Athletics in the early 1970s, then led the NL in saves with San Diego. In 1981 with the Brewers, he won the MVP and Cy Young awards. He had 341 career saves. (1992)

ELMER FLICK
Outfielder (1898-1910) A speedy outfielder for the Phillies and Indians, in 1905 Flick won the AL batting crown with an average of .308. In the spring of 1907, Detroit thought so much of Flick it offered Ty Cobb in trade but was turned down. That season Flick hit .302 in his last full season; Cobb hit .350 in his first. Flick had a .313 career batting average. (1963)

WHITEY FORD
Pitcher (1950; 1953-1967) Ford's winning percentage of .690 is the best of any 20th-century pitcher. The Yankee pitcher led the AL in wins three times and ERA twice. Ford holds eight World Series pitching records, including wins (10) and strikeouts (94). His 25-4 record in 1961 earned him the Cy Young Award. "The Chairman of the Board" was 236-106 with a 2.75 ERA and 156 complete games. (1974)

RUBE FOSTER
Executive; pitcher As a star pitcher for a number of early black teams, and later as the first president of the Negro National League, Foster earned the title "Father of Black Baseball." Foster's efforts in organizing the NNL gave black baseball needed stability. He in effect saved the Negro League and made it popular. (1981)

JIMMIE FOXX
First baseman (1925-1942; 1944-1945) For 12 consecutive seasons with the Athletics and Red Sox, Foxx slammed 30 or more home runs and knocked in more than 100 runs. In 1933, Foxx hit .356, swatted 48 homers, and knocked in 163 RBI to win the Triple Crown. A three-time MVP, "Double X" had a lifetime slugging average of .609, fourth all time. Foxx had 534 career homers, 1,922 RBI, and a .325 average. (1951)

FORD FRICK
NL President (1934-1951); Commissioner (1951-1965) Frick was named NL President in 1934. In 1951, he was elected commissioner. He helped establish the Hall of Fame, supported Branch Rickey's signing of Jackie Robinson, and presided over baseball's busiest period of expansion. (1970)

FRANKIE FRISCH
Second baseman (1919-1937) A member of more NL pennant winners than any other player, Frisch played in four fall classics with the Giants and four with the Cardinals. He cracked the .300 mark 13 times, scored 100 runs seven times, and was the 1931 NL MVP. As player-manager, "The Fordham Flash" led the "Gashouse Gang" to the title in 1934. He scored 1,532 career runs and hit .316. (1947)

PUD GALVIN
Pitcher (1875; 1879-1892) Nicknamed "Pud" because he made pudding out of hitters, Galvin was pitcher supreme for NL Buffalo in the 1880s. On his way to 364 career victories, Galvin pitched more than 400 innings nine times, and won 46 games in both 1883 and 1884. "Gentle Jeems" is tied for 10th on the all-time list with 58 shutouts, and is second all time with 646 complete games and $6,000\frac{1}{3}$ innings. (1965)

LOU GEHRIG
First baseman (1923-1939) "The Iron Horse," Gehrig played in a record 2,130

consecutive games for the Yankees. Gehrig knocked 46 home runs and set the AL record for RBI with 184 in 1931. He had more than 40 home runs in five seasons, more than 150 RBI in seven seasons, and a .600 slugging percentage in nine seasons. "Columbia Lou" had a .632 career slugging percentage, a .340 batting average, 493 home runs, 1,995 RBI, and 1,888 runs scored. Although fatally ill with amyotrophic lateral sclerosis, in 1939 he bid farewell to 61,000 fans at Yankee Stadium by saying "Today I consider myself the luckiest man on the face of the earth." The waiting period for the Hall was waived, and Gehrig was admitted. (1939)

CHARLIE GEHRINGER

Second baseman (1924-1942) His efficient play at second base for the Tigers earned Gehringer the appellation "The Mechanical Man." He regularly led the league in fielding and hit over .300 in 13 of 16 seasons. He logged over 100 RBI and had 200 or more hits in seven seasons. In 1937, his loop-high .371 average made him AL MVP. He had a career .320 batting average, 2,839 hits, 1,774 runs scored, and 1,427 RBI. (1949)

BOB GIBSON

Pitcher (1959-1975) In 1968, Gibson had the second-lowest ERA in modern NL history, a stingy 1.12, while winning both Cy Young and MVP honors. He also won the Cy Young Award in 1970. In the 1967 World Series, he led St. Louis to victory over Boston, winning three times while giving up only 14 hits. Gibson's speed and control resulted in 251 career wins. "Hoot" had a career 2.91 ERA, 3,117 Ks, and 255 complete games. (1981)

JOSH GIBSON

Catcher (1930-1946) For 16 seasons Gibson reigned as the Negro Leagues' supreme slugger, perhaps smacking near-

ly 1,000 home runs and as many as 90 in a single season. The powerful catcher was often called the black Babe Ruth; in another time, Ruth may have been referred to as the poor man's Josh Gibson. One of the most dedicated players ever, Gibson would play 200 games over a single year. In 1947, with Jackie Robinson on the verge of breaking the big-league color line, Gibson, only age 36, died of a brain hemorrhage. (1972)

WARREN GILES

NL President (1951-1969) Giles started as president of minor league Moline in 1919 and ended 50 years later as president of the NL. During his tenure, he oversaw the transfer of the Giants and Dodgers to California, and the addition of four expansion franchises. (1979)

LEFTY GOMEZ

Pitcher (1930-1943) Gomez's sense of humor was matched only by his skill on the mound. A 20-game winner four times for the Yankees, Gomez went undefeated in six World Series decisions. He led the AL in Ks three times and in ERA twice. His secret to success? Quipped Lefty, "Clean living and a fast outfield." "Goofy" was 189-102 with a 3.34 ERA. (1972)

GOOSE GOSLIN

Outfielder (1921-1938) The best hitter ever to play for the Senators, Goslin led Washington to its only three appearances in the World Series. He slugged three home runs in both the 1924 and 1925 fall classics. Goose had 100 RBI or more and batted over .300 in 11 seasons. He had 1,609 RBI, 2,735 hits, and a .316 average. (1968)

HANK GREENBERG

First baseman (1930; 1933-1941; 1945-1947) Despite playing only nine full seasons, Greenberg smacked 331 home

449

runs and captured AL MVP honors in 1935 and 1940 for the Tigers. He lost three years to World War II, but came back in 1946 to lead the AL in homers and RBI. He had league- and career-high totals of 58 dingers (1938) and 183 RBI (1937). "Hammerin' Hank" had a career .313 batting average, a .605 slugging percentage, and 1,276 RBI. (1956)

CLARK GRIFFITH

Manager (1901-1920) A leading pitcher of the 1890s, Griffith won 20 games six straight seasons. Over a 20-year period the cagey "Old Fox" managed the White Sox, Yankees, Reds, and Senators. He had a 1,491-1,367 record and won but one pennant. He was also president of the Senators from 1920 to 1955. (1946)

BURLEIGH GRIMES

Pitcher (1916-1934) In 1934, Grimes threw the last legal spitter in baseball history. Over the preceding 19 seasons, he won 270 games with seven teams. One of a handful of pitchers allowed to throw the spitter after its ban in 1920, Grimes was the most successful. "Ol' Stubblebeard" won more than 20 games five times. (1964)

LEFTY GROVE

Pitcher (1925-1941) In an era dominated by hitting, the lefthanded Grove was almost unhittable, winning 20 games or more seven straight seasons with Connie Mack's Philadelphia A's, including a remarkable 31-4 mark in 1931. That year, "Mose" was the AL MVP. On his way to 300 wins, he led the AL in strikeouts seven times, in ERA nine times, in complete games three times, and in winning percentage five times. (1947)

CHICK HAFEY

Outfielder (1924-1937) Hafey's misfortune was to play before the advent of the batting helmet. Several beanings and a chronic sinus condition affected his vision, forcing him to wear glasses in an effort to correct the damage. Nevertheless, Chick hit over .300 in nine seasons and captured the NL title in 1931 with a .349 mark. He was known for his rifle arm and his line drives. Ill health and vision problems, however, forced the career .317 batter to retire. (1971)

JESSE HAINES

Pitcher (1918; 1920-1937) Knuckleballer Haines didn't make the big leagues for good until he was 26 years old. However, he stuck around until he was 45, winning 20 games three times and finishing with 210 victories for the Cardinals, including a no-hitter against the Braves in 1924. In 1927, he racked up a 24-10 record, leading the NL with 25 complete games and six shutouts. "Pop" had 209 complete games. (1970)

BILLY HAMILTON

Outfielder (1888-1901) While playing with Philadelphia and Boston in the NL, "Sliding Billy" ran into the records. He was credited with 912 stolen bases, although for most of his career a runner received credit for a base theft by advancing an extra base on a hit. He had a lifetime .344 batting average. In 1894, his ability on the bases let him score a record 196 times. (1961)

WILL HARRIDGE

AL President (1931-1959) Harridge stayed out of the limelight and quietly led the league. An early supporter of the All-Star Game and night baseball, Harridge insisted on order. (1972)

BUCKY HARRIS

Manager (1924-1943; 1947-1948; 1950-1956) An above average second baseman for the Senators, Harris was a natural leader who had his greatest success as manager. In his first season as player-manager in 1924, he led the Senators to their only world championship. He went on to manage another 28 seasons with five other clubs, going 2,157-2,218. Harris was a respected strategist. (1975)

GABBY HARTNETT

Catcher (1922-1941) In his time, Hartnett was likely the NL's best catcher. A fine defensive catcher, his best season was 1930, when he hit .339 with 37 home runs and 122 RBI. He was an All-Star from 1933 through 1938. In the 1934 game, he was the backstop when Ruth, Gehrig, Foxx, Simmons, and Cronin were put away in order. He hit .344 as the NL MVP in 1935. His late-season, ninth-inning "homer in the gloaming" against Pittsburgh won the 1938 pennant for the Cubs. He had a .297 career batting average, with 236 homers and 1,179 RBI. (1955)

HARRY HEILMANN

Outfielder (1914; 1916-1930; 1932) In the four seasons that Heilmann won the AL batting crown, his lowest average was .393. He batted over .300 in 12 seasons and hit an amazing .403 in 1923. Playing mostly for Detroit, the slow-footed outfielder (nicknamed "Slug") wielded a line-drive bat that resulted in 2,660 hits, including 542 doubles, for a .342 batting average. (1952)

BILLY HERMAN

Second baseman (1931-1943; 1946-1947) A 10-time All-Star, Herman's 227 hits and 57 doubles in 1935 were tops in the NL. The best defensive second baseman in the loop, he hit .300 or better eight times in his career. After playing most of his career for the Cubs, in 1941 he was traded to Brooklyn. Herman had a career .304 batting average and 486 doubles. (1975)

HARRY HOOPER

Outfielder (1909-1925) A right field star, Hooper's arm was legendary (he averaged 20 assists a year) as he teamed with Duffy Lewis and Tris Speaker to give the BoSox the best outfield of the era. A lifetime .281 hitter, Hooper scored 1,429 runs. (1971)

ROGERS HORNSBY

Second baseman (1915-1937) Perhaps the greatest right-handed hitter of all time, Hornsby's career .358 average is second only to Ty Cobb's .366. "Rajah's" .424 mark in 1924 is the best of the century. His greatest success came with the Cardinals; from 1920 to 1925 he collected six straight batting titles, as well as two Triple Crowns. Hornsby's fierce demeanor made him one of the most disliked players of his time. (1942)

WAITE HOYT

Pitcher (1918-1938) The Yankee pitching ace of the 1920s, Hoyt won 20 games only twice, but compiled a 6-4 record in the World Series with a 1.83 ERA. In 1927, "Schoolboy" led the AL in wins (22), and ERA (2.63). He won in double figures 12 seasons and had a career 237-182 record. He was one of the first ex-ballplayers to work in broadcasting. (1969)

CAL HUBBARD

Umpire (1936-1951; 1954-1962) Hubbard is the only man in the baseball, college football, and pro football Halls of Fame. When he retired from football he became an AL umpire. (1976)

CARL HUBBELL

Pitcher (1928-1943) Hubbell used the screwball to notch 253 career wins and a 2.98 ERA, all for the Giants. From 1933 to 1937, he posted five straight 20-win seasons, and was NL MVP in '33 and '36.

"King Carl" led the NL in wins three times, ERA three times, and in strikeouts once. In the 1934 All-Star Game, the left-handed "Meal Ticket" struck out five straight Hall-of-Famers—Babe Ruth, Lou Gehrig, Jimmie Foxx, Al Simmons, and Joe Cronin. (1947)

MILLER HUGGINS

Manager (1913-1929) Huggins was the Yankee manager of the 1920s. Standing only 5′6″, he was the one man able to temper the boisterous Babe Ruth. "The Mighty Mite's" 1927 Yankees team is widely considered the best of all time. "Hug" was 1,413-1,134 in his career, including five seasons with mediocre Cardinal clubs. He won six pennants and three Series in his 12 years with the Yankees. (1964)

CATFISH HUNTER

Pitcher (1965-1979) Given his nickname by A's owner Charlie Finley, Hunter went directly from high school to the major leagues. Beginning in 1971, Catfish won more than 20 games five straight seasons and earned the Cy Young Award in 1974 with a 25-12 record. After three A's world championships (1972 to 1974), Hunter signed with the Yankees for $3.75 million in 1975, then the biggest contract in baseball history. He had a 224-166 career record with a 3.26 ERA and 2,012 strikeouts. (1987)

MONTE IRVIN

Outfielder (Negro Leagues 1939-1943; 1945-1948; NL 1949-1956) Despite twice leading the Negro National League in hitting, it was 1949 before the 30-year-old Irvin was signed by the Giants. He began his Negro League career in 1939, and he also played in the Mexican League, where he won a Triple Crown in 1940. In eight NL seasons, he hit .293, leading the league in RBI with 121 in 1951. (1973)

REGGIE JACKSON

Outfielder (1967-1987) "The Straw that Stirs the Drink," Jackson was a publicity hog, a prolific slugger, a superior outfielder, and most of all, a big winner. He played on 11 division winners and five world champions. "Mr. October's" finest moment came in game six of the 1977 Series, when he smacked three homers. The four-time home run king had 563 homers and 1,702 RBI, but he also compiled more Ks (2,597) than any other player. (1993)

TRAVIS JACKSON

Shortstop (1922-1936) A solid defensive shortstop for the Giants of the 1920s and 1930s, Jackson helped the club to four pennants. "Stonewall" also batted over .300 in six seasons. He accumulated a career average of .291. (1982)

FERGUSON JENKINS

Pitcher (1965-1983) After being traded from the Phillies to the Cubs in early 1966, Jenkins embarked on a string of six consecutive 20-plus win seasons. He won only 14 games in 1973 and was traded to Texas, where he won the 1974 Cy Young Award with a 25-12 record. One of the game's most durable pitchers, Jenkins had a career 284-226 record, with a 3.34 ERA and 3,192 Ks. (1991)

HUGHIE JENNINGS

Shortstop (1891-1903; 1907; 1909; 1912; 1918); manager (1907-1920; 1924) From 1894 to 1897 as shortstop of NL Baltimore, Jennings led the club to pennants. In his five years with Baltimore, he never hit below .328 and was a lifetime .311 hitter. He was 1,163-984 as a manager. (1945)

BAN JOHNSON

AL President (1901-1927) The founder of the American League, Johnson was arguably the most powerful man in baseball during the first quarter of the 20th century. When the minor Western League folded in 1893, Johnson revived it. He put it on solid footing and made it a major league in 1901. The "Black Sox" scandal of 1920 undermined his power, however, and led to the commissioner system, leading to Johnson's retirement in 1927. (1937)

JUDY JOHNSON

Third baseman (1919-1936) The greatest third baseman in Negro League history, Johnson combined steady defensive play with stellar batting performances. A line-drive hitter, Johnson hit .390 and .406 in two of his seasons with the Philadelphia Hilldales, leading them to two black World Series appearances. In later years, Judy scouted for the A's and Phillies. (1975)

WALTER JOHNSON

Pitcher (1907-1927) One of the first five men elected to the Hall, Johnson's legendary fastball and pinpoint control enabled him to win 417 games (second on the all-time list) with the usually inferior Senators. In his 20-year career, "The Big Train" led the AL in strikeouts 12 times, shutouts seven times, and in victories six times. Johnson's 110 shutouts are the most in history. "Barney's" 2.17 career ERA is eighth lowest, his 531 complete games rank fourth, and his 5,915 innings pitched are the third most in baseball. (1936)

ADDIE JOSS

Pitcher (1902-1910) In only nine seasons with Cleveland, Joss won 160 games with a winning percentage of .623 and an ERA of 1.89 (second all time). He struck out 920 batters and walked only 364 in 2,327 innings pitched. In 1911, he died of tubercular meningitis at age 31. The Hall's usual 10-year career requirement was waived for Joss. (1978)

AL KALINE

Outfielder (1953-1974) As a 20-year-old outfielder with Detroit in 1955, Kaline won the batting title, with a .340 average, to become the youngest batting champion ever. Although he never duplicated that figure, he played in 18 All-Star games, won 11 Gold Gloves, and accumulated 3,007 hits. He also belted 498 doubles, 399 home runs, and 1,583 RBI, with 1,622 runs scored and 1,277 walks. (1980)

TIM KEEFE

Pitcher (1880-1893) In only 14 seasons, Keefe won 342 games, one of six 19th century pitchers to top the 300 mark. Remarkably, after overhand pitching was legalized in 1884, Keefe continued to pitch—and win—underhanded. "Sir Timothy" pioneered the use of the changeup to notch a career 2.62 ERA with 554 complete games. (1964)

WEE WILLIE KEELER

Outfielder (1892-1910) Keeler said, "I hit 'em where they ain't." Utilizing his good speed and batting skills, he developed the "Baltimore chop" to bounce the ball over and between infielders. From 1894 to 1901, he collected a major-league record 200 hits each season. He had 2,932 career hits, 1,719 runs, and a .341 batting average. In 1897, he hit in 44 consecutive games. That same year he notched a personal best .424 batting average. (1939)

GEORGE KELL

Third baseman (1943-1957) An excellent third baseman and career .306 hitter, Kell excelled for five different clubs in the 1940s and 1950s. In 1949, he edged out Ted Williams for his only batting crown, hitting .3429 to Williams's .3427. Kell scored a lifetime 881 runs and drove in 870 runs. (1983)

JOE KELLEY

Outfielder (1891-1906; 1908) Kelley played for the great Baltimore teams of the 1890s and later went on to star with Brooklyn and Cincinnati. He batted over .300 for 11 straight years. In 1894, he hit .393 and went 9-for-9 in a doubleheader. Kelley had a lifetime .317 average, with 194 triples, and 1,424 runs scored. (1971)

GEORGE KELLY

First baseman (1915-1917; 1919-1930; 1932) After failing in his first three seasons in the bigs, Kelly came into his own for the Giants in 1919. From 1921 to 1926, Kelly hit over .300 and averaged 108 RBI, helping the Giants capture four pennants. He was a .297 hitter and totaled 1,020 RBI. (1973)

KING KELLY

Outfielder; catcher (1878-1893) Baseball's first celebrity, Kelly was the subject of the popular song, "Slide, Kelly, Slide" and recited "Casey At The Bat" on stage. On the field, he perfected the hit-and-run and developed the hook and head-first slides. He hit .308 lifetime and scored 1,357 runs. (1945)

HARMON KILLEBREW

First baseman; third baseman (1954-1975) Killebrew hit 573 home runs; only Babe Ruth hit more in AL history. Killebrew led the league in homers six times, each time hitting more than 40. "Killer" had 40 or more homers in eight different seasons. The 1969 AL MVP also drove in more than 100 RBI in nine years, pacing the AL three times. He hit only .256 lifetime but had 1,559 bases on balls. (1984)

RALPH KINER

Outfielder (1946-1955) Joining Pittsburgh after World War II, in his first seven seasons Kiner led or tied for the NL lead in

homers. He had 369 lifetime dingers, 1,015 RBI, and 1,011 bases on balls in 10 years. Kiner has enjoyed a second career as a broadcaster for the Mets. (1975)

CHUCK KLEIN

Outfielder (1928-1944) Playing five and one-half seasons in Philadelphia's cozy Baker Bowl, Klein led the NL in homers four times and never hit below .337. He was the 1932 NL MVP and won the Triple Crown in 1933 (.368 average, 28 homers, 120 RBI). Klein set an all-time record for outfield assists with 44 in 1930. He had a lifetime .320 batting average, 300 homers, and 1,201 RBI. (1980)

BILL KLEM

Umpire (1905-1941) Baseball's best-known umpire, Klem revolutionized the position, and is credited with being the first to employ hand signals and don a chest protector. He worked a record 18 World Series, and he was the umpire at the first All-Star Game in 1933. (1953)

SANDY KOUFAX

Pitcher (1955-1966) Koufax had two careers. His best record in his first six years was an 11-11 mark. But, between 1961 and 1966, the lefty led the NL in wins and shutouts three times each and Ks four times. Koufax paced the Dodgers to pennants in '63, '65, and '66 while winning the Cy Young Award each year. His 25-5 record in 1963 earned him the NL MVP. Pitching in excruciating pain due to arthritis, Koufax led the NL in ERA his final five seasons, culminating with a 1.73 mark while going 27-9 in 1966. He had a 165-87 record with a 2.76 career ERA and 2,396 strikeouts to only 817 walks. (1972)

NAP LAJOIE

Second baseman (1896-1916) One of the best righty batters in history, Lajoie was the best second baseman of his era and became the first man at his position to be elected to the Hall. A graceful fielder, he hit over .300 16 times in his career. He won the Triple Crown in 1901, the American League's debut season; he batted .426 with 14 homers and 125 RBI. His presence gave the AL respect. Lajoie had a career .338 average, 3,242 hits, and 657 doubles. (1937)

KENESAW MOUNTAIN LANDIS

Commissioner (1920-1944) Baseball's first commissioner, Landis left his job as a federal judge in 1920 to take complete control of the major leagues. In cleaning up the "Black Sox" scandal, he restored the public's confidence in the integrity of baseball. His rule was law, and nobody dared challenge his authority. A champion of player rights, he unsuccessfully tried to halt the farm system—one of the few battles he ever lost. (1944)

TONY LAZZERI

Second baseman (1926-1939) The second baseman on the "Murderer's Row" Yankee teams of the 1920s and '30s, Lazzeri combined power, high average, and slick fielding. A career .292 hitter who socked 178 homers, "Poosh 'Em Up" topped the .300 mark five times and hit .354 in 1929. (1991)

BOB LEMON

Pitcher (1941-1942; 1946-1958) Lemon made the big leagues as a third baseman, but he made the Hall of Fame as a pitcher. Switched to pitching during World War II, Lemon won 20 games for the Indians seven times from 1948 to 1956. He led the AL in wins three times and in complete games five times. He had a career 207-128 record for a .618 winning percentage. As manager, he led the Yankees to a championship in 1978. (1976)

BUCK LEONARD

First baseman (1934-1948) In the Negro Leagues, Walter Leonard played Lou Gehrig to teammate Josh Gibson's Babe Ruth. Leonard played for the Homestead Grays and helped lead them to nine consecutive pennants. He was a left-handed power hitter and clutch RBI man who hit for a high average. He twice led the NNL in hitting, peaking at .410 in 1947. In 1952, at age 45, Leonard turned down an offer from Bill Veeck to play for the St. Louis Browns. (1972)

FREDDIE LINDSTROM

Third baseman (1924-1936) Lindstrom survived two bad-hop grounders in the, '24 World Series to top the .300 mark seven times, including a .379 average in 1930. A year later an injury led to a switch to the outfield. He batted .311 lifetime, with 301 doubles and 895 runs scored. (1976)

POP LLOYD

Shortstop (1905-1932) The finest shortstop in Negro baseball, Lloyd's stellar performance in a 1909 exhibition series against Ty Cobb's Tigers so embarrassed Cobb he vowed never to play blacks again. In 1928, despite being age 44, Lloyd led the Negro National League in batting with an eye-popping .564 average. From his time in Cuba, his nickname was *"El Cuchara,"* which means "scoop" in Spanish. (1977)

ERNIE LOMBARDI

Catcher (1931-1947) Called "Schnozz" because of his enormous nose, Lombardi was a slow, awkward-looking catcher who could hit a ton. He surpassed the .300 mark 10 times. In 1938, his league-leading .342 average with Cincinnati earned him the NL MVP Award. Five years later with the Braves, Lombardi again led the league with a .330 average, becoming the only catcher to do so twice. He hit .306 lifetime, with 990 RBI. (1986)

AL LOPEZ

Catcher (1928; 1930-1947); manager (1951-1965; 1968-1969) A workhorse behind the plate, Lopez held the major-league record for games caught until 1987. He turned manager in 1951, and in 1954 led Cleveland to 111 wins. In 1959, he won another pennant with the White Sox. He drove his 17 teams to a 1,410-1,004 record for a .584 winning percentage. Usually losing the pennant to the Yankees, Lopez's clubs finished second in the AL 10 times. (1977)

TED LYONS

Pitcher (1923-1942; 1946) Lyons had the misfortune of pitching for some bad White Sox teams. He won 260 games lifetime, with 356 complete games. He led the AL in shutouts twice and wins twice. In 1942, he led the AL with a 2.10 ERA. At age 42, he served three years in World War II, then returned to baseball for one last season. (1955)

CONNIE MACK

Manager (1894-1896; 1901-1950) As player, manager, and owner, Mack had a career that spanned an incredible eight decades. Manager of the Athletics from 1901 to 1950, Mack built then tore apart several championship clubs. His first dynasty was from 1910 to 1914, when the Athletics won four pennants and three world championships. He sold off many of those players and finished in last place from 1915 to 1921. His second dynasty was the 1929 to 1931 clubs—three pennants and two world champs. He was 3,731-3,948 in his 53 years as a manager. (1937)

LARRY MacPHAIL

Executive As an executive with the Reds, Dodgers, and Yankees, MacPhail played a part in virtually every baseball development between the wars. He brought air travel and lights to the major leagues in 1935, and radio broadcasts to Brooklyn in 1938. (1978)

MICKEY MANTLE

Outfielder (1951-1968) Named after Mickey Cochrane, Mantle was taught to switch hit and became baseball's leading switch-hitter. Succeeding Joe DiMaggio as Yankee center fielder, all Mantle did was match Joe's three MVP Awards (1956, 1957, 1962). "The Commerce Comet" hit .353 with 52 homers and 130 RBI to win the Triple Crown in 1956. He led the AL in home runs four times, RBI once, runs scored six times, and walks five times. If not for a series of knee injuries, Mantle may have been the best of all time. He had the most all-time World Series homers, RBI, and runs. He possessed a .298 batting average, 536 homers, 1,509 RBI, 1,677 runs scored, and 1,733 walks. (1974)

HEINIE MANUSH

Outfielder (1923-1939) Often overlooked, Manush was one of the best hitters during his era. Topping the .300 mark 11 times, he compiled a career average of .330. Playing for the Tigers, Browns, Senators, Braves, Pirates, and Dodgers, he led his league in hits twice. Manush notched 1,183 career RBI and 1,287 runs. (1964)

RABBIT MARANVILLE

Shortstop (1912-1933; 1935) A top defensive shortstop and consummate showman, Maranville was the kind of player that did the little things to make his team better. A superior fielder, he ranks first among all shortstops in putouts (5,139). Maranville collected 2,605 hits and scored 1,255 runs. (1954)

JUAN MARICHAL

Pitcher (1960-1975) In the mid-1960s, the Giants' Marichal was one of the best and most consistent pitchers in the game. His patented high leg kick masked a multitude of pitches. A six-time 20-game winner, Marichal somehow failed to win the Cy Young Award. His 243 career wins more than made up for that omission. He led the league in shutouts and in complete games twice. "The Dominican Dandy" had a career 243-142 record, a 2.89 ERA, 2,303 Ks, and 52 shutouts. (1983)

RUBE MARQUARD
Pitcher (1908-1925) In 1912, Marquard won his first 19 decisions for the Giants on his way to a 26-11 record. Although he won 23 games the following season, he never again matched his earlier play. Marquard had a 201-177 career record with 197 complete games. (1971)

EDDIE MATHEWS
Third baseman (1952-1968) Mathews combined with Hank Aaron to form one of the best power combos ever. For 14 consecutive years, Mathews hit 23 or more home runs, hitting 40 or more four times. A steady defensive player, he was an All-Star nine times. He led the NL in bases on balls in four seasons to retire with a total of 1,444. He also tallied 512 career homers, 1,453 RBI, and 1,509 runs scored. (1978)

CHRISTY MATHEWSON
Pitcher (1900-1916) As the most popular player in his day, Mathewson dispelled the notion at the time that ballplayers need be crude and uneducated. "Big Six" was also perhaps the game's best pitcher. For 12 consecutive seasons he won 20 or more games for the Giants, as his trademark "fadeaway," a screwball, baffled a generation of batters. In the 1905 World Series, he hurled three shutouts in six days. He led the NL in ERA in five seasons, in Ks five times, and in shutouts four times. "Matty" had a 373-188 career record, with a 2.13 ERA and 79 shutouts. (1936)

WILLIE MAYS
Outfielder (1951-1952; 1954-1973) Mays could do everything: hit, field, and run. While the Giant center fielder's 660 home runs rank third all time, his magnificent over-the-shoulder catch of Vic Wertz's blast to center field in the 1954 World Series has become the standard against which all other catches are compared. "The Say Hey Kid" led the NL in slugging percentage five times, homers and stolen bases four times, triples three times, and runs scored twice. He had 3,283 career hits, a .302 batting average, a .557 slugging percentage, 1,903 RBI, and 2,062 runs scored. (1979)

JOE McCARTHY
Manager (1926-1946; 1948-1950) In 24 years as manager, McCarthy collected seven world championships and nine pennants. His 2,125-1,333 record gives him an all-time best .615 winning percentage. Most of his success came with the Yankees, where he won four straight World Series from 1936 to 1939. After winning the NL pennant with the Cubs in 1929, McCarthy piloted the Yankees to a pennant in 1932 to become the first manager to win a pennant in both leagues. (1957)

TOMMY McCARTHY
Outfielder (1884-1896) McCarthy made a lasting mark by perfecting the fly-ball trap in order to throw out the lead runner of a double play, leading to the infield fly rule. Although known for his defense, in 1890 he hit a robust .350. He was a career .292 hitter and topped .300 four times. (1946)

WILLIE McCOVEY
First baseman (1959-1980) Willie McCovey joined Giants teammate Willie Mays to give NL pitchers the willies. McCovey smashed 30 or more home runs seven times, leading the NL in dingers three times and in RBI twice. In 1969,

"Stretch" was NL MVP with a .320 average, 45 homers, and 126 RBI. That same year he drew a record 45 intentional walks. In 1970, McCovey homered in all 12 parks, a rare feat. "Big Mac" notched 521 homers, 1,555 RBI, 1,229 runs scored, and 1,345 walks. (1986)

JOE McGINNITY

Pitcher (1899-1908) While McGinnity's nickname "Iron Man" was derived from his off-season occupation in a foundry, it well described his mound efforts. For nine straight years he pitched 300-plus innings, topping 400 twice and leading the league four times. He had a career 246-142 record with a 2.66 ERA and 314 complete games. He then pitched another 17 seasons in the minors. (1946)

BILL McGOWAN

Umpire (1925-1954) McGowan earned his "No. 1" nickname in the AL because of his renown for accuracy. Chosen to work in eight World Series, he also worked four All-Star games, including the first in 1933. (1992)

JOHN McGRAW

Manager (1899; 1901-1932) As third baseman for Baltimore in the 1890s, McGraw was talented enough to make the Hall on his merits as a player. As the Giants manager from 1902 to 1932, he dominated baseball during its "scientific" era, and successfully made the transition to the power game of the 1920s. Despite capturing 10 pennants, "Little Napoleon" won the World Series only three times. A manager for 33 years, McGraw racked up 2,784 victories in 4,801 games, both second on the all-time list to Connie Mack. (1937)

BILL McKECHNIE

Manager (1915; 1922-1926; 1928-1946) McKechnie may have been the best-liked manager ever while winning pennants with three different teams. "The Deacon's" best effort, though, might have been with the fifth-place 1937 Braves, enough to win the Manager of the Year award. He won two world championships and was 1,896-1,723 in 25 years. (1962)

JOE MEDWICK

Outfielder (1932-1948) Medwick provided the power to light up the 1930s Cardinals' "Gashouse Gang." He led the NL in RBI three consecutive years and in hits twice. In 1937, "Ducky" (a nickname he loathed) batted .374 with 31 homers and 154 RBI to capture the Triple Crown. "Muscles" was a brawler who had a career .324 average, 1,383 RBI, and 540 doubles. In the 1934 World Series against Detroit, he was ordered from the field for his own safety. (1968)

JOHNNY MIZE

First baseman (1936-1942; 1946-1953) Despite losing three prime years to World War II, Mize still connected for 359 home runs, primarily with the Cardinals and Giants. He led the NL in homers four times and RBI three times. Sold to the Yankees in 1949, Mize played in five World Series, hitting three home runs in the 1952 classic. "The Big Cat" batted .312 lifetime, slugged .562, and drove in 1,337 runs. (1981)

JOE MORGAN

Second baseman (1963-1984) Where Morgan played, championships followed. After leading Cincinnati's "Big Red Machine" of the mid-1970s to two World Series victories, Morgan led the 1980 Astros to a division title. He then helped Philadelphia capture the pennant in 1983. "Little Joe" won back-to-back NL MVP Awards in 1975 and '76. Only 5'7", he had 268 career homers, 689 stolen bases, 1,133 RBI, 1,650 runs, and 1,865 walks. (1990)

STAN MUSIAL
Outfielder; first baseman (1941-1944; 1946-1963) Originally signed as a pitcher, Musial hurt his arm and transferred to the outfield. Joining the Cardinals in 1941, Musial batted .426 in 12 games, and he went on to lead the NL seven times in batting average. NL MVP in 1943, '46, and '48, he used his "corkscrew" batting stance to hit over .310 for 16 seasons in a row. When he retired in 1963, "Stan the Man" held more than 50 major-league and NL records. He had a career .331 batting average, 3,630 base hits (fourth all time), 725 doubles (third), 475 home runs, 1,951 RBI, and 1,949 runs scored. (1969)

HAL NEWHOUSER
Pitcher (1939-1955) The only pitcher to win back-to-back MVPs (in 1944 and '45), Newhouser was a Detroit native who pitched 15 seasons for the Tigers. Slighted by some as a wartime wonder, he had 275 Ks and a 26-9 record in 1946, and a 21-12 record in 1948. He had 207 career wins. (1992)

KID NICHOLS
Pitcher (1890-1901; 1904-1906) Ranked sixth all time in wins with 361, Nichols starred in the 1890s for Boston, leading them to five NL pennants. Winner of 30 games seven times, Nichols finished what he started. In his 501 Boston starts, he was relieved only 25 times. He had a lifetime 361-208 record and a 2.95 ERA. (1949)

JIM O'ROURKE
Outfielder (1872-1893; 1904) In 1876, O'Rourke collected the first base hit in NL history, one of 2,304 he'd gather for his career. A lifetime .310 hitter, O'Rourke's manner of speaking earned him the nickname "Orator Jim." (1945)

MEL OTT
Outfielder (1926-1947) Despite his small stature (5'9", 170 pounds), this Giant outfielder stands as a colossus among the game's sluggers. Ott's unique leg kick enabled him to generate the power for 511 home runs, the first man in NL history to hit 500. He led the NL in homers six times, but in RBI only once. When he retired in 1947, he held the NL career mark for homers, runs scored (1,859), RBI (1,860), and walks (1,708). "Master Melvin" retired with a .304 average. (1951)

SATCHEL PAIGE
Pitcher (Negro Leagues 1926-1947; 1950; AL 1948-1949; 1951-1953; 1965) The first African-American ever elected to the Hall of Fame, Paige was the Negro Leagues' greatest drawing card. He started pitching for the Birmingham Black Barons in 1926 at age 20. His blazing fastball and effervescent personality made him a legend by age 30. He made his greatest mark on the game by pitching for the Kansas City Monarchs in the 1940s. In 1948, at age 42, he made his major-league debut and helped Cleveland to the AL pennant. (1971)

JIM PALMER
Pitcher (1965-1967; 1969-1984) Ace of Baltimore's powerful teams of the 1970s, Palmer won 20 games eight times on his way to three Cy Young Awards and 268 career wins. He led the AL in ERA twice and in innings pitched four times. He had a career 2.86 ERA, 2,212 Ks, and 1,311 walks in 3,948 innings pitched. (1990)

HERB PENNOCK
Pitcher (1912-1917; 1919-1934) Pennock finessed his way through 22 seasons to earn 240 wins. He had his greatest success with the Yankees of the 1920s, for whom he went 5-0 in World Series play.

"The Knight of Kennett Square" won in double figures for 13 seasons and completed 247 of his 420 career starts. (1948)

GAYLORD PERRY
Pitcher (1962-1983) Though he won 314 games, struck out 3,534 batters, and registered a 3.11 ERA during a 22-year career, Perry was best known for throwing—or not throwing—a spitball. He won 20 games five times in his career. He won the AL Cy Young in 1972 and the NL Cy Young in 1978, making him the only pitcher in history to have won the award in both leagues. (1991)

EDDIE PLANK
Pitcher (1901-1917) A late bloomer, Plank didn't reach Connie Mack's A's until age 26. No matter, the left-hander blossomed to win 326 games. He won at least 20 games in eight seasons, with four in a row from 1902 to 1905. "Gettysburg Eddie" compiled 69 career shutouts (fifth all time) and a 2.35 ERA. (1946)

OLD HOSS RADBOURN
Pitcher (1880-1891) In 1884, Radbourn won 59 games for NL Providence, still an all-time record, notching a 1.38 ERA and 679 innings pitched. In only 12 seasons he chalked up 309 wins and a 2.67 ERA. Old Hoss's 489 career complete games are eighth on the all-time list. (1939)

PEE WEE REESE
Shortstop (1940-1942; 1946-1958) Reese led the Dodgers to seven pennants between 1941 and 1956. One of the top fielding shortstops during the 1940s and 1950s, Pee Wee was an All-Star from 1947 to 1954. He scored 1,338 runs in his career, leading the NL in 1947 with 132. When Branch Rickey signed Jackie Robinson, it was Reese, a Southerner, who led the Dodgers to accept Robinson as a teammate. (1984)

SAM RICE
Outfielder (1915-1934) Rice, a fleet 150-pounder, smacked 2,987 hits on his way to a .322 career average for Washington. He led the AL in hits twice and had 200 or more base hits six times. He scored 1,514 career runs and stole 351 bases. A master of bat control, Rice struck out only nine times in 616 at bats in 1929. (1963)

BRANCH RICKEY
Executive Rickey invented the farm system and built NL dynasties in St. Louis and Brooklyn. When he joined the Cardinals in 1919 as president and field manager, the franchise could not compete with richer clubs. "The Mahatma" began to buy minor-league clubs from which the Cards could obtain talent. By 1941, St. Louis had 32 minor-league affiliates. He moved to Brooklyn in 1942. Rickey integrated the major leagues in 1947, winning his biggest fight when he signed Jackie Robinson. (1967)

EPPA RIXEY
Pitcher (1912-1917; 1919-1933) Rixey was a very good pitcher for some not very good teams, winning 266 games while losing 251. A master of control, Rixey won in double figures in 14 seasons and won 20 games four times. In 1922, he went a league-leading 25-13 for Cincinnati. (1963)

PHIL RIZZUTO
Shortstop (1941-1942; 1946-1956) "Scooter" played Yankee shortstop for 13 years and went to the World Series in nine of them. Just 5'6", he won the AL MVP Award in 1950 with a .324 average, 200 hits, and 125 runs scored. He was selected for the All-Star Game five times. He embarked on a long broadcasting career after his playing days. (1994)

ROBIN ROBERTS

Pitcher (1948-1966) Despite a penchant for throwing the gopher ball, Roberts won 20 games for six consecutive seasons from 1950 to 1955. He topped the NL in wins four straight years, and in innings and complete games five times each. He also led the NL two years in a row in Ks. In 1952, he went 28-7 for the Phillies. Roberts was 286-245 with a 3.41 ERA. (1976)

BROOKS ROBINSON

Third baseman (1955-1977) One of the greatest fielding third basemen ever, Robinson won the Gold Glove 16 times in 23 seasons. The AL MVP in 1964, Brooks turned in a .317 average, 28 homers, and a league-leading 118 RBI. He sparkled in postseason play, posting a .348 average in 18 ALCS games. In the 1970 World Series, he led the Orioles over the Reds, hitting .429 and turning in one spectacular fielding play after another, earning him MVP honors for the Series. "Hoover" had 268 career homers, 1,357 RBI, and 1,232 runs. (1983)

FRANK ROBINSON

Outfielder (1956-1976) Robinson was the first player to be selected MVP in both leagues. He was named NL Rookie of the Year in 1956 and the loop's MVP in 1961, when he paced the NL with a .611 slugging average and led the Reds to a pennant. Traded to Baltimore after the '65 season, Frank responded in '66 by hitting .316, slugging 49 home runs, and knocking in 122 runs to win the Triple Crown. He hit 30 homers in 11 seasons, and his 586 career homers rank fourth on the all-time list. He also had 1,812 career runs batted in and 1,829 runs scored. Named manager of the Indians in 1975, Robinson was the first African-American to manage a major-league team. (1982)

JACKIE ROBINSON

Second baseman (1947-1956) The first African-American to play major-league baseball since 1884, Robinson succeeded under almost unbearable pressure to secure the black player a permanent place in the game. He endured numerous racial slights, even from his own teammates, without yielding his dignity, while leading the Dodgers to six pennants. A tremendous athlete, Robinson was a four-sport star at UCLA and also served in the Army during World War II. As a 28-year-old rookie for Brooklyn in 1947, Robinson's aggressive base-running and hitting earned him Rookie of the Year honors. Two years later, in 1949, he led the NL with a .342 average and was named NL MVP. He had a career .311 batting average. (1962)

WILBERT ROBINSON

Manager (1902; 1914-1931) A catching star for Baltimore in the 1890s, Robinson coached under the Giants' John McGraw before becoming Brooklyn's manager in 1914. "Uncle Robbie" won pennants in 1916 and 1920 but never won a World Series. He had a career 1,399-1,398 record. (1945)

EDD ROUSH

Outfielder (1913-1929; 1931) One of the great defensive outfielders, Roush swung his 48-ounce bat with enough authority to attain two NL batting titles and a .323 lifetime average. In his 10 years in Cincinnati, he never hit lower than .321. He had 1,099 career runs and 981 RBI. Roush habitually held out of spring training. (1962)

RED RUFFING

Pitcher (1924-1942; 1945-1947) In six seasons with the Red Sox, Ruffing couldn't win, going 39-96 from 1924 to 1930 and leading the AL in losses twice.

After he was traded to the Yankees, he couldn't lose, with a career 273-225 record and a 7-2 mark in 10 World Series games. He won 20 games each season from 1936 to 1939. (1967)

AMOS RUSIE
Pitcher (1889-1895; 1897-1898; 1901) Rusie's fastball forced the rule makers to move the mound from 45 feet to 60 feet 6 inches. From 1890 to 1895, the Giants pitcher led the NL in Ks five times, yet he had about one walk for every K. "The Hoosier Thunderbolt" had eight 20-win seasons and 245 career victories. (1977)

BABE RUTH
Outfielder; pitcher (1914-1935) George Herman Ruth is arguably the greatest player of all time. A man of gargantuan appetites and ability, the Babe's mystique has transcended the sport of baseball and has become ingrained in American mythology. Starting his career as a pitcher with Boston, he was one of the best in the AL. In 1916, the Babe led the AL with a 1.75 ERA while going 23-12. He had 24 wins in '17 with a loop-high 35 complete games. Converted to the outfield part-time in 1918, he led the AL in homers with 11. After he was sold to the Yankees in 1920, he became a full-time flycatcher, and all but invented the home run, slugging 714 for his career, including a then-record 60 in 1927. He led the AL in homers 12 seasons, RBI six seasons, slugging percentage 12 times, and bases on balls 11 times. He had a career .342 batting average, .690 slugging average (first all time), 506 doubles, 2,213 RBI (second all time), 2,174 runs (second all time), and 2,056 walks (first all time). (1936)

RAY SCHALK
Catcher (1912-1929) Although Schalk's career average was .253, few complained when he was elected to the Hall. A superb catcher, Ray's game was defense. In 1920, he caught four 20-game winners for the White Sox, and four no-hitters, more than any other catcher. He holds the AL record for assists by a catcher (1,811). (1955)

RED SCHOENDIENST
Second baseman (1945-1963) Schoendienst teamed with shortstop Marty Marion to form one of baseball's best-ever double-play combinations. Red could also hit, reaching a career-high .342 in 1953. He had 2,449 career hits and 1,223 runs scored. (1989)

TOM SEAVER
Pitcher (1967-1986) In 1992, Seaver was named on a record 98.8 percent of the ballots for enshrinement, indicating his stature among fans. A three-time Cy Young winner (1969, '73, and '75), he also finished second twice and third once. "Tom Terrific" led the Mets to a miracle world championship in 1969. He won 311 games and struck out 3,640 batters, and his .603 winning percentage was the best of any 300-game winner since Lefty Grove retired in 1941. (1992)

JOE SEWELL
Shortstop (1920-1933) Sewell replaced Ray Chapman in the Cleveland lineup following Chapman's tragic death in 1920. One of the game's best shortstops, Sewell struck out 114 times in 7,132 at bats. He had 1,141 runs and 1,051 RBI. (1977)

AL SIMMONS
Outfielder (1924-1941; 1943-1944) An unlikely looking hitter due to his "foot in the bucket" batting stance, Simmons was a leading slugger of his era. From 1929 to 1931, he helped the Athletics to three consecutive pennants, winning batting titles in both 1930 and 1931 with averages of .381 and .390. "Bucketfoot Al" batted over .300

in the first 11 seasons of his career, racking up 2,927 hits and a career .334 batting average. (1953)

GEORGE SISLER
First baseman (1915-1922; 1924-1930)
Like Babe Ruth, Sisler's hitting was too good to be on a pitcher's schedule. He was switched to first base full-time in 1916 for the Browns and became one of the best, defensively. At bat he was simply unbelievable, hitting .407, .371, and .420 from 1920 to 1922. In 1920, "Gorgeous George" collected 257 base hits, still the all-time record. A sinus infection that affected his vision sidelined him in 1923. He returned to play seven more seasons. (1939)

ENOS SLAUGHTER
Outfielder (1938-1942; 1946-1959)
Slaughter would do anything in order to win, using hustle to make up for any shortcomings in talent. His mad dash from first to home on a double won the 1946 World Series for the Cardinals. "Country" led the NL in base hits in 1942 before going to war; he led the league in RBI when he came back. (1985)

DUKE SNIDER
Outfielder (1947-1964) Known as the "Duke of Flatbush" to his Brooklyn fans, Snider was one of a trio of Hall of Fame center fielders in New York during the 1950s. The others were named Willie Mays and Mickey Mantle. Snider hit 40 homers from 1953 to 1957. He had 407 career homers, 1,333 RBI, and 1,259 runs scored. (1980)

WARREN SPAHN
Pitcher (1942; 1946-1965) Baseball's winningest left-hander, Spahn didn't even stick in the majors until age 25. With the Braves, he won 20 games or more in 13 seasons, tying the major-league record.

He led the league in wins eight times, complete games nine times, and strikeouts four times. He won the Cy Young Award in 1957. Spahn retired with 363 wins (fifth all time), 245 losses, a 3.09 ERA, 382 complete games, and 63 shutouts (sixth all time) in 5,243⅔ innings pitched. (1973)

AL SPALDING
Pitcher (1871-1878); executive A star pitcher in the 1870s, Spalding started a sporting goods company and took over NL Chicago. As a pitcher, he had a .796 career winning percentage. He helped write the new NL's constitution and was inducted as an executive. (1939)

TRIS SPEAKER
Outfielder (1907-1928) The best center fielder of his time, Speaker played close enough to the infield to take pick-off throws at second. "The Grey Eagle" hit over .300 in 18 seasons and topped .375 six times on his way to a career .345 mark (fifth all time). Traded from Boston to Cleveland in 1916, he won his only batting title, at .386. "Spoke" had a record 792 career doubles and 3,514 hits (fifth all time). (1937)

WILLIE STARGELL
Outfielder; first baseman (1962-1982)
One of the strongest players ever, Stargell made tape-measure homers common. He had 13 consecutive years of 20 or more home runs, pacing the NL in 1971 and 1973. He was named season, NLCS, and World Series MVP in 1979, when he led the world champion Bucs. He had 475 career homers and 1,540 RBI. (1988)

CASEY STENGEL
Manager (1934-1936; 1938-1943; 1949-1960; 1962-1965) As manager of Brooklyn and Boston, Stengel earned a reputation as an entertaining, if not very effective, skipper. His creative use of the lan-

guage, dubbed "Stengelese," made him a fan favorite. Named Yankee manager in 1949, "The Old Professor" won 10 pennants in 12 years, plus seven world championships. He had a career 1,905-1,842 record. (1966)

BILL TERRY

First baseman (1923-1936) A career .341 hitter, Terry was the last National Leaguer to hit over .400, batting .401 in 1930 with 254 hits. "Memphis Bill" had more than 100 RBI from 1927 to 1932. Showing long-ball power when he wanted, Terry smashed 28 homers in 1932. Generally, though, his strengths were doubles and triples. He took over as Giant manager in 1932 and led the team to three pennants. (1954)

SAM THOMPSON

Outfielder (1885-1898; 1906) Thompson was a home run hitter in an era when the talent was not appreciated. He had his greatest success with the Phillies in the 1890s, where in 1894, he hit .407. "Big Sam" led the NL in hits three times, and in homers and RBI twice each. He had 127 career homers, with a .331 average and 1,299 RBI. (1974)

JOE TINKER

Shortstop (1902-1916) Interestingly, Tinker, Johnny Evers, and Frank Chance were all elected to the Hall in the same year. Shortstop Tinker was a fielding whiz who keyed the success of that double-play combo. Although not a great hitter, he stole 336 career bases to augment his .263 average. (1946)

PIE TRAYNOR

Third baseman (1920-1935; 1937) Traynor earned his way into the Hall of Fame as the best fielding third baseman of his era. A career .320 hitter for Pittsburgh, he hit .300 or better 10 times and had more than 100 RBI seven times. Pie had 1,273 career RBI and 1,183 runs. (1948)

DAZZY VANCE

Pitcher (1915; 1918; 1922-1935) As a 31-year-old rookie with Brooklyn in 1922, Vance won 18 games. Two years later his mark of 28-6 earned him league MVP honors. Armed with an incredible fastball, he led the major leagues in Ks each of his first seven seasons and paced the NL in ERA three times. Dazzy had a career 197-140 record. (1955)

ARKY VAUGHAN

Shortstop (1932-1943; 1947-1948) One of the game's best hitting shortstops, only twice in 14 seasons did Vaughan fail to hit .300. In 1935, his .385 average for Pittsburgh led the NL. Arky notched a career .406 on-base percentage, .318 batting average, 1,173 runs, and 926 RBI. He led the NL in putouts and assists three times. (1985)

BILL VEECK

Executive One of baseball's most colorful showmen, Veeck integrated the AL by signing Larry Doby with the Indians. He owned three AL teams—Cleveland, St. Louis, and Chicago. He sent midget Eddie Gaedel up to bat for the Browns, and as the chief of the White Sox, introduced baseball's first exploding scoreboard. (1991)

RUBE WADDELL

Pitcher (1897; 1899-1910) Waddell threw hard and lived even harder. In the AL's first six seasons, Rube was the circuit's best left-hander, under the watchful eye of Connie Mack, winning 20 games four straight years and leading the league in Ks six consecutive years. An eccentric, Waddell couldn't confine himself to baseball. He had a career 193-143 record with 2,316 Ks. (1946)

HONUS WAGNER

Shortstop (1897-1917) One of the game's first five inductees to the Hall of Fame, Wagner hit over .300 15 consecutive seasons. Bowlegged and awkward looking, Wagner possessed tremendous speed and range afield. For his 21-year career, he had 722 stolen bases and a .327 batting average, highest of any shortstop. Honus led the NL in batting eight times, slugging six times, RBI five times, runs scored twice, and doubles seven times. "The Flying Dutchman" had 3,415 career hits, 640 doubles, 252 triples, 1,732 RBI, 1,736 runs scored, and 963 walks. Some consider Wagner the greatest of all time. (1936)

BOBBY WALLACE

Shortstop (1894-1918) The first AL shortstop elected to the Hall, Wallace made his mark with the glove, leading the league in putouts three times and assists four times. He had 6.1 chances per game lifetime. (1953)

ED WALSH

Pitcher (1904-1917) Perhaps no other pitcher threw the spitball as successfully as Walsh. While his arm gave out after only seven full seasons as a starter, he recorded nearly 170 of his career 195 wins during that span. In 1908, he pitched 464 innings for the White Sox on his way to 40 victories. He led the AL in games pitched five times, innings pitched four times, and strikeouts twice. "Big Ed" had a career 195-126 record with a 1.82 ERA, the lowest of all time. (1946)

LLOYD WANER

Outfielder (1927-1942; 1944-1945) "Little Poison," to older brother Paul's "Big Poison," Lloyd Waner used his speed to cover the vast Forbes Field outfield, leading the NL in putouts four times. In 1927, Waner's rookie year, the little lead-off man hit 198 one-baggers. Waner had a .316 career batting average, 2,459 hits, and 1,201 runs scored. (1967)

PAUL WANER

Outfielder (1926-1945) "Big Poison" didn't settle for hitting singles like his little brother; 905 of Paul Waner's 3,152 career hits were for extra bases. He led the NL in hitting four times, peaking at .380 in 1927, when he led Pittsburgh to the pennant and was named league MVP. Waner retired with a .333 batting average, 605 doubles, 1,627 runs scored, and 1,309 RBI. (1952)

MONTE WARD

Pitcher; shortstop (1878-1894) Perhaps no figure in baseball had distinguished himself in so many areas as did Ward. As a pitcher for Providence, he led the NL in ERA in 1878 and in wins in 1879. Switched to shortstop in 1885, he became the best in the league for New York. Unhappy with the reserve clause, in 1890 he helped form the Players' League. Becoming a manager, he led the Giants to a championship in 1894. (1964)

GEORGE WEISS

Executive As farm director and general manager of the Yankees from 1932-1960, Weiss deserves much of the credit for creating the Yankee dynasty. He built the farm system to 21 teams, then became general manager and dealt from strength, constantly picking up precisely the player the Yankees needed in exchange for prospects plucked from the system he created. (1971)

MICKEY WELCH

Pitcher (1880-1892) The third man to win 300 games, Welch starred in the 1880s for Troy and New York of the NL. In 1885 he won 17 consecutive decisions on his way to 44 wins for the year. "Smiling Mickey" won at least 20 games nine times, with four seasons of more than 30. He had a career 307-210 record with a 2.71 ERA. (1973)

ZACK WHEAT

Outfielder (1909-1927) The Dodgers' first star, Wheat played left field in Ebbets Field for 18 seasons. A line-drive hitter, he topped the .300 mark in 14 seasons, including an NL-best .335 in 1918. He had a career .317 average, 2,884 hits, 1,248 RBI, 1,289 runs scored, and 205 stolen bases. (1959)

HOYT WILHELM

Pitcher (1952-1972) Wilhelm was the first pitcher elected to the Hall solely on his merits as a reliever. A knuckleballer, he toiled for nine teams, pitching in a record 1,070 games and winning 124 in relief. He started only 52 games in his 21-year career, compiling 227 saves and a 2.52 ERA. "Snacks" pitched five consecutive seasons (1964 to 1968) with an ERA under 2.00. (1985)

BILLY WILLIAMS

Outfielder (1959-1976) Williams's much admired swing produced 426 career homers and a .290 batting average. The NL Rookie of the Year in 1961, he had at least 20 home runs and 84 RBI in 13 consecutive seasons. His two best seasons were in 1970 and 1972. In 1970, Billy hit .322 with 42 homers, a league-best 137 runs scored, and 129 RBI. He led the NL with a .333 batting average and a .606 slugging average, with 37 homers and 122 RBI in 1972. Playing most of his career for the Cubs, between 1963 and 1970 Williams played in an NL-record 1,117 consecutive games. (1987)

TED WILLIAMS

Outfielder (1939-1942; 1946-1960) Williams's one desire was to walk down the street and have people say, "There goes the greatest hitter that ever lived." Arguably, he was. Despite missing nearly five years to the military, the Red Sox left fielder won two MVP Awards, six batting and four home run titles, and two Triple Crowns. "The Splendid Splinter" batted over .316 in each of his 19 seasons except one. In 1941, "The Kid" hit a .406 mark. He's the last player to attain that plateau. He had 30 or more homers in eight seasons, 20 or more in 16 seasons. "Teddy Ballgame" has the sixth highest career batting average (.344), the second highest slugging average (.634), the second most bases on balls (2,019), No. 10 for home runs (521), and No. 11 for RBI (1,839). (1966)

HACK WILSON

Outfielder (1923-1934) From 1926 to 1930, the muscular, midgetlike Wilson was one of the game's greatest sluggers. In 1930, the Cub outfielder hit an NL-record 56 homers and knocked in a major-league record 190 runs. He led the NL in homers four times and in RBI twice. Liquor, however, was Wilson's downfall, and by the end of 1934, he was out of baseball. (1979)

GEORGE WRIGHT

Shortstop (1871-1882) The star shortstop for the original Cincinnati Red Stockings team that went undefeated for the entire 1869 season, Wright played through the 1882 season. He then helped start the Union Association in 1884. Later in life he served on baseball's Centennial Commission, and was instrumental in the creation of the National Baseball Hall of Fame. (1937)

HARRY WRIGHT

Manager (1871-1893) Harry Wright, the older brother of George, was player-manager of the Cincinnati Red Stockings (the first overtly all-professional team), which

Harry led to some 130 consecutive victories. He helped start the National Association in 1871, and later managed a number of NL teams, going 225-60 in the National Association and 1,000-825 in the National League. (1953)

EARLY WYNN
Pitcher (1939; 1941-1944; 1946-1963) Wynn was traded to Cleveland in 1949 and became a big winner. He won 20 games for the Indians four times and had eight consecutive winning seasons. Traded to the White Sox after the '57 season, "Gus" led Chicago to the pennant in 1959 by winning 22 games, plus the Cy Young Award. He had a 300-244 career record and a 3.54 ERA. (1972)

CARL YASTRZEMSKI
Outfielder (1961-1983) Spending his entire 23-year career with the Red Sox, Yastrzemski was the first AL player to collect over 3,000 hits and 400 home runs. "Yaz" will always be remembered for one remarkable season—1967, the year of The Impossible Dream. He won the Triple Crown and during a most remarkable September that season, he single-handedly won the pennant for Boston. Taking over left field for Ted Williams, "Captain Carl" won batting titles in 1963, '67, and '68. He had 3,419 career hits, a .285 average, 646 doubles, 452 home runs, 1,844 RBI, 1,816 runs scored, and 1,845 walks. (1989)

TOM YAWKEY
Executive Yawkey is one of the few inducted to the Hall who neither played, coached, umpired, nor served as a general manager. In 1933, at age 30, he received his inheritance and bought the Red Sox for $1.5 million. Boston at that time was a doormat and Fenway Park was falling apart. Over the next 44 seasons he spent lavishly on the club and the stadium, doling out another $1.5 million for renovations alone. (1980)

CY YOUNG
Pitcher (1890-1911) Young won 511 games, which is 94 victories more than runner-up Walter Johnson. In a career that bridged three decades and several eras of play, Cy was consistently superb. Blessed with speed, control, stamina, and just about every quality a successful pitcher needs, Young won 20 or more games 15 times, including nine seasons in a row from 1891 to 1899. He led his league in victories four times, and in ERA, winning percentage, and strikeouts twice each. Cy is also first on the complete-game list with 749 and innings pitched list with 7,356⅔. When they decided to give an award to the season's top pitcher, they named it after Young. (1937)

ROSS YOUNGS
Outfielder (1917-1926) Youngs was a star on four straight pennant winners for John McGraw's Giants in the early 1920s. On the verge of greatness, in 1925 Youngs's skills deserted him. Diagnosed with Bright's disease, a terminal kidney disorder, Youngs gamely played one more season and died in 1927. He had a .322 career batting average with 1,491 hits and 812 runs scored. (1972)

Awards and Highlights

Baseball's top achievements and tributes are listed in this section. The all-time career leaders in several batting and pitching categories are included (with players active in 1994 in **bold**), as well as the leaders among active players. The all-time single-season leaders are next. The Most Valuable Players, the Cy Young Award winners, and the Rookies of the Year follow. Fielding excellence is acknowledged with the Gold Glove Award winners. Finally, the winners and losers of the World Series and the National League and American League Championship Series are listed.

ALL-TIME LEADERS

BATTING AVERAGE
1. Ty Cobb .... .366
2. Rogers Hornsby .... .358
3. Joe Jackson .... .356
4. Ed Delahanty .... .346
5. Tris Speaker .... .345
6. Ted Williams .... .344
7. Billy Hamilton .... .344
8. Dan Brouthers .... .342
9. Babe Ruth .... .342
10. Harry Heilmann .... .342
11. Pete Browning .... .341
12. Willie Keeler .... .341
13. Bill Terry .... .341
14. George Sisler .... .340
15. Lou Gehrig .... .340
16. Jesse Burkett .... .338
17. Nap Lajoie .... .338
18. Riggs Stephenson .... .336
19. **Wade Boggs** .... **.335**
20. Al Simmons .... .334

HITS
1. Pete Rose 4,256
2. Ty Cobb 4,189
3. Hank Aaron 3,771
4. Stan Musial 3,630
5. Tris Speaker 3,514
6. Carl Yastrzemski 3,419
7. Honus Wagner 3,415
   Cap Anson 3,415
9. Eddie Collins 3,312
10. Willie Mays 3,283
11. Nap Lajoie 3,242
12. George Brett 3,154
13. Paul Waner 3,152
14. Robin Yount 3,142
15. **Dave Winfield** **3,088**
16. Rod Carew 3,053

17. Lou Brock 3,023
18. Al Kaline 3,007
19. Roberto Clemente 3,000
20. Sam Rice 2,987

DOUBLES
1. Tris Speaker 792
2. Pete Rose 746
3. Stan Musial 725
4. Ty Cobb 724
5. George Brett 665
6. Nap Lajoie 657
7. Carl Yastrzemski 646
8. Honus Wagner 640
9. Hank Aaron 624
10. Paul Waner 605
11. Robin Yount 583
12. Cap Anson 582
13. Charlie Gehringer 574
14. Harry Heilmann 542
15. Rogers Hornsby 541
16. Joe Medwick 540
17. Al Simmons 539
18. **Dave Winfield** **535**
19. Lou Gehrig 534
20. Al Oliver 529

TRIPLES
1. Sam Crawford 309
2. Ty Cobb 295
3. Honus Wagner 252
4. Jake Beckley 243
5. Roger Connor 233
6. Tris Speaker 222
7. Fred Clarke 220
8. Dan Brouthers 205
9. Joe Kelley 194
10. Paul Waner 191
11. Bid McPhee 188
12. Eddie Collins 186

13. Ed Delahanty 185
14. Sam Rice 184
15. Edd Roush 182
    Jesse Burkett 182
17. Ed Konetchy 181
18. Buck Ewing 178
19. Stan Musial 177
    Rabbit Maranville 177

HOME RUNS
1. Hank Aaron 755
2. Babe Ruth 714
3. Willie Mays 660
4. Frank Robinson 586
5. Harmon Killebrew 573
6. Reggie Jackson 563
7. Mike Schmidt 548
8. Mickey Mantle 536
9. Jimmie Foxx 534
10. Ted Williams 521
    Willie McCovey 521
12. Eddie Mathews 512
    Ernie Banks 512
14. Mel Ott 511
15. Lou Gehrig 493
16. Willie Stargell 475
    Stan Musial 475
18. **Dave Winfield** **463**
19. **Eddie Murray** **458**
20. Carl Yastrzemski 452

RUNS BATTED IN
1. Hank Aaron 2,297
2. Babe Ruth 2,213
3. Lou Gehrig 1,995
4. Cap Anson 1,981
5. Stan Musial 1,951
6. Ty Cobb 1,937
7. Jimmie Foxx 1,922
8. Willie Mays 1,903

468

9. Mel Ott.....................1,860
10. Carl Yastrzemski 1,844
11. Ted Williams..............1,839
12. **Dave Winfield**..........**1,829**
13. Al Simmons................1,827
14. Frank Robinson.........1,812
15. **Eddie Murray**............**1,738**
16. Honus Wagner 1,732
17. Reggie Jackson 1,702
18. Tony Perez.................1,652
19. Ernie Banks...............1,636
20. Goose Goslin 1,609

SLUGGING AVERAGE
1. Babe Ruth 690
2. Ted Williams 634
3. Lou Gehrig 632
4. Jimmie Foxx 609
5. Hank Greenberg..........605
6. Joe DiMaggio 579
7. Rogers Hornsby............577
8. Johnny Mize 562
9. Stan Musial...................559
10. Willie Mays 557
11. Mickey Mantle 557
12. Hank Aaron 555
13. Ralph Kiner..................548
14. Hack Wilson 545
15. Chuck Klein 543
16. **Fred McGriff**...............**.541**
17. Duke Snider 540
18. Frank Robinson 537
19. **Barry Bonds**..............**.537**
20. Al Simmons 535

ON-BASE PERCENTAGE
1. Ted Williams 483
2. Babe Ruth 474
3. John McGraw 465
4. Billy Hamilton................455
5. Lou Gehrig 447
6. Rogers Hornsby............434
7. Ty Cobb 433
8. Jimmie Foxx 428
9. **Wade Boggs**...............**.428**
10. Tris Speaker................428
11. Ferris Fain 425
12. Eddie Collins 424
13. Dan Brouthers 423
14. Joe Jackson 423
15. Max Bishop..................423
16. Mickey Mantle 423
17. Mickey Cochrane.........419
18. Stan Musial..................418
19. Cupid Childs................416
20. Jesse Burkett...............415

STOLEN BASES
1. **Rickey Henderson** ..**1,117**
2. Lou Brock 938
3. Billy Hamilton................912
4. Ty Cobb 892
5. **Tim Raines** **764**
6. Eddie Collins 744
7. Arlie Latham 739
8. Max Carey 738
9. Honus Wagner 722
10. **Vince Coleman**..........**698**
11. Joe Morgan 689
12. **Willie Wilson** **668**
13. Tom Brown 657
14. Bert Campaneris 649
15. George Davis 616
16. Dummy Hoy 594
17. Maury Wills..................586
18. George Van Haltren 583
19. Hugh Duffy 574
20. **Ozzie Smith** **569**

RUNS SCORED
1. Ty Cobb 2,246
2. Babe Ruth 2,174
   Hank Aaron 2,174
4. Pete Rose..................2,165
5. Willie Mays 2,062
6. Cap Anson 1,996
7. Stan Musial................1,949
8. Lou Gehrig 1,888
9. Tris Speaker...............1,882
10. Mel Ott......................1,859
11. Frank Robinson 1,829
12. Eddie Collins 1,821
13. Carl Yastrzemski 1,816
14. Ted Williams 1,798
15. Charlie Gehringer........1,774
16. Jimmie Foxx 1,751
17. Honus Wagner 1,736
18. Jim O'Rourke...............1,732
19. Jesse Burkett..............1,720
20. Willie Keeler 1,719

BASES ON BALLS
1. Babe Ruth 2,056
2. Ted Williams..............2,019
3. Joe Morgan 1,865
4. Carl Yastrzemski 1,845
5. Mickey Mantle 1,733
6. Mel Ott......................1,708
7. Eddie Yost 1,614
8. Darrell Evans 1,605
9. Stan Musial 1,599
10. Pete Rose 1,566
11. Harmon Killebrew 1,559

12. Lou Gehrig..................1,508
13. Mike Schmidt...............1,507
14. Eddie Collins 1,499
15. **Rickey Henderson** ..**1,478**

GAMES PLAYED
1. Pete Rose..................3,562
2. Carl Yastrzemski 3,308
3. Hank Aaron 3,298
4. Ty Cobb 3,035
5. Stan Musial................3,026
6. Willie Mays 2,992
7. Rusty Staub................2,951
8. **Dave Winfield**..........**2,927**
9. Brooks Robinson.........2,896
10. Robin Yount................2,856
11. Al Kaline.....................2,834
12. Eddie Collins 2,826
13. Reggie Jackson 2,820
14. Frank Robinson 2,808
15. Honus Wagner 2,792
16. Tris Speaker................2,789
17. Tony Perez..................2,777
18. Mel Ott.......................2,730
19. George Brett...............2,707
20. **Eddie Murray**...........**2,706**

WINS
1. Cy Young....................511
2. Walter Johnson 417
3. Christy Mathewson......373
   Grover Alexander 373
5. Pud Galvin..................364
6. Warren Spahn 363
7. Kid Nichols 361
8. Tim Keefe 342
9. Steve Carlton 329
10. John Clarkson 328
11. Eddie Plank 326
12. Don Sutton 324
    Nolan Ryan.................324
14. Phil Niekro 318
15. Gaylord Perry 314
16. Tom Seaver................311
17. Old Hoss Radbourn.....309
18. Mickey Welch 307
19. Early Wynn 300
    Lefty Grove 300

WINNING PERCENTAGE
1. Al Spalding 796
2. Dave Foutz 690
3. Whitey Ford 690
4. Bob Caruthers 688
5. Lefty Grove 680
6. Vic Raschi 667

7. Larry Corcoran .... .665
8. Christy Mathewson .... .665
9. Sam Leever .... .660
10. Sal Maglie .... .657
11. Dick McBride .... .656
12. Sandy Koufax .... .655
13. Johnny Allen .... .654
14. Ron Guidry .... .651
15. Lefty Gomez .... .649
16. **Roger Clemens** .... .649
17. **Dwight Gooden** .... .649
18. John Clarkson .... .648
19. Three Finger Brown .. .648
20. Dizzy Dean .... .644

EARNED RUN AVERAGE
1. Ed Walsh 1.82
2. Addie Joss 1.89
3. Three Finger Brown ... 2.06
4. John Ward 2.10
5. Christy Mathewson 2.13
6. Al Spalding 2.14
7. Rube Waddell 2.16
8. Walter Johnson 2.17
9. Orval Overall 2.23
10. Will White 2.28
11. Ed Reulbach 2.28
12. Jim Scott 2.30
13. Tommy Bond 2.31
14. Eddie Plank 2.35
15. Larry Corcoran 2.36
16. George McQuillan 2.38
17. Eddie Cicotte 2.38
18. Ed Killian 2.38
19. Doc White 2.39
20. George Bradley 2.42

STRIKEOUTS
1. Nolan Ryan 5,714
2. Steve Carlton 4,136
3. Bert Blyleven 3,701
4. Tom Seaver 3,640
5. Don Sutton 3,574
6. Gaylord Perry 3,534
7. Walter Johnson 3,509
8. Phil Niekro 3,342
9. Fergie Jenkins 3,192
10. Bob Gibson 3,117
11. Jim Bunning 2,855
12. Mickey Lolich 2,832
13. Cy Young 2,803
14. Frank Tanana 2,773
15. Warren Spahn 2,583
16. Bob Feller 2,581
17. Jerry Koosman 2,556
18. Tim Keefe 2,543

19. Christy Mathewson ... 2,502
20. Don Drysdale 2,486

SAVES
1. **Lee Smith** **434**
2. **Jeff Reardon** **367**
3. Rollie Fingers 341
4. **Rich Gossage** **310**
5. Bruce Sutter 300
6. **Dennis Eckersley** **294**
7. **Tom Henke** **275**
8. **John Franco** **266**
9. **Dave Righetti** **252**
10. Dan Quisenberry 244
11. Sparky Lyle 238
12. Hoyt Wilhelm 227
13. Gene Garber 218
14. **Doug Jones** **217**
15. Dave Smith 216
16. **Randy Myers** **205**
17. **Bobby Thigpen** **201**
18. Roy Face 193
19. **Mitch Williams** **192**
20. Mike Marshall 188

COMPLETE GAMES
1. Cy Young 749
2. Pud Galvin 646
3. Tim Keefe 554
4. Kid Nichols 531
    Walter Johnson 531
6. Mickey Welch 525
    Bobby Mathews 525
8. Old Hoss Radbourn ... 489
9. John Clarkson 485
10. Tony Mullane 468
11. Jim McCormick 466
12. Gus Weyhing 448
13. Grover Alexander 437
14. Christy Mathewson 434
15. Jack Powell 422
16. Eddie Plank 410
17. Will White 394
18. Amos Rusie 392
19. Vic Willis 388
20. Tommy Bond 386

SHUTOUTS
1. Walter Johnson 110
2. Grover Alexander 90
3. Christy Mathewson 79
4. Cy Young 76
5. Eddie Plank 69
6. Warren Spahn 63
7. Tom Seaver 61
    Nolan Ryan 61

9. Bert Blyleven 60
10. Don Sutton 58
    Pud Galvin 58
12. Ed Walsh 57
13. Bob Gibson 56
14. Steve Carlton 55
    Three Finger Brown ... 55

GAMES PITCHED
1. Hoyt Wilhelm 1,070
2. Kent Tekulve 1,050
3. **Rich Gossage** 1,002
4. Lindy McDaniel 987
5. Rollie Fingers 944
6. Gene Garber 931
7. Cy Young 906
8. Sparky Lyle 899
9. Jim Kaat 898
10. **Lee Smith** 891
11. **Jeff Reardon** 880
12. Don McMahon 874
13. Phil Niekro 864
14. **Charlie Hough** 858
15. **Dennis Eckersley** 849
16. Roy Face 848
17. Tug McGraw 824
18. Nolan Ryan 807
19. Walter Johnson 802
20. Gaylord Perry 777

INNINGS PITCHED
1. Cy Young 7,356.2
2. Pud Galvin 6,003.1
3. Walter Johnson 5,915.0
4. Phil Niekro 5,404.1
5. Nolan Ryan 5,386.0
6. Gaylord Perry 5,350.1
7. Don Sutton 5,282.1
8. Warren Spahn 5,243.2
9. Steve Carlton 5,217.1
10. Grover Alexander 5,190.0
11. Kid Nichols 5,056.1
12. Tim Keefe 5,047.1
13. Bert Blyleven 4,970.0
14. Bobby Mathews 4,956.1
15. Mickey Welch 4,802.0
16. Tom Seaver 4,782.2
17. C. Mathewson 4,780.2
18. Tommy John 4,710.1
19. Robin Roberts 4,688.2
20. Early Wynn 4,564.0

GAMES STARTED
1. Cy Young 815
2. Nolan Ryan 773
3. Don Sutton 756

4. Phil Niekro 716
5. Steve Carlton 709
6. Tommy John..............700
7. Gaylord Perry 690
8. Pud Galvin 689
9. Bert Blyleven 685
10. Walter Johnson 666
11. Warren Spahn 665

12. Tom Seaver................647
13. Jim Kaat 625
14. Frank Tanana 616
15. Early Wynn 612

RATIO OF BASERUNNERS
1. Addie Joss 8.71
2. Ed Walsh 9.00

3. John Ward 9.40
4. Christy Mathewson.....9.53
5. Walter Johnson 9.55
6. Three Finger Brown...9.59
7. George Bradley 9.00
8. Babe Adams.............9.83
9. Tommy Bond 9.83
10. Juan Marichal 9.91

ACTIVE LEADERS

HITS
1. Dave Winfield 3,088
2. Eddie Murray 2,930
3. Andre Dawson...........2,700
4. Paul Molitor 2,647
5. Wade Boggs 2,392
6. Ozzie Smith 2,365
7. Lou Whitaker 2,296
8. Alan Trammell 2,260
9. Cal Ripken...............2,227
10. Rickey Henderson......2,216

8. Don Mattingly 1,050
9. Lance Parrish 1,048
10. Tim Wallach...............1,045

GAMES PLAYED
1. Dave Winfield 2,927
2. Eddie Murray 2,706
3. Andre Dawson...........2,506
4. Ozzie Smith 2,447
5. Lou Whitaker 2,306
6. Willie Wilson 2,154
7. Alan Trammell 2,153
8. Paul Molitor 2,131
9. Rickey Henderson......2,080
10. Cal Ripken...............2,074

HOME RUNS
1. Dave Winfield 463
2. Eddie Murray 458
3. Andre Dawson............428
4. Lance Parrish 320
5. Cal Ripken...............310
6. Joe Carter................302
7. Darryl Strawberry 294
8. Kent Hrbek 293
9. Harold Baines............277
10. Jose Canseco............276

WINS
1. Jack Morris 254
2. Dennis Martinez 219
3. Charlie Hough 216
4. Bob Welch 211
5. Dennis Eckersley........188
6. Frank Viola 175
7. Roger Clemens 172
8. Rick Sutcliffe.............171
9. Dave Stewart.............165
10. Scott Sanderson.........162
    Bill Gullickson 162

RUNS BATTED IN
1. Dave Winfield 1,829
2. Eddie Murray 1,738
3. Andre Dawson...........1,540
4. Harold Baines............1,198
5. Cal Ripken...............1,179
6. Joe Carter................1,097
7. Kent Hrbek 1,086

GAMES PITCHED
1. Rich Gossage............1,002
2. Lee Smith 891

3. Jeff Reardon................880
4. Charlie Hough 858
5. Dennis Eckersley........849
6. Jesse Orosco 754
7. Dave Righetti.............708
8. Steve Bedrosian.........703
9. Larry Andersen...........699
10. Craig Lefferts............696

STRIKEOUTS
1. Jack Morris 2,478
2. Charlie Hough 2,362
3. Dennis Eckersley........2,245
4. Roger Clemens 2,201
5. Mark Langston...........2,110
6. Bob Welch 1,969
7. Dennis Martinez 1,923
8. Dwight Gooden...........1,875
9. F. Valenzuela 1,861
10. Frank Viola 1,822

SAVES
1. Lee Smith 434
2. Jeff Reardon..............367
3. Rich Gossage 310
4. Dennis Eckersley........294
5. Tom Henke 275
6. John Franco 266
7. Dave Righetti.............252
8. Doug Jones 217
9. Randy Myers 205
10. Bobby Thigpen 201

SINGLE-SEASON LEADERS (Since 1900)

BATTING AVERAGE	BA	YEAR		BA	YEAR
1. Rogers Hornsby STL (NL)	.424	1924	11. Rogers Hornsby STL (NL)	.401	1922
2. Nap Lajoie PHI (AL)	.422	1901	12. Bill Terry NY (NL)	.401	1930
3. George Sisler STL (AL)	.420	1922	13. Ty Cobb DET	.401	1922
4. Ty Cobb DET	.420	1911	14. Lefty O'Doul PHI (NL)	.398	1929
5. Ty Cobb DET	.410	1912	15. Harry Heilmann DET	.398	1927
6. Joe Jackson CLE	.408	1911	16. Rogers Hornsby STL (NL)	.397	1921
7. George Sisler STL (AL)	.407	1920	17. Joe Jackson CLE	.395	1912
8. Ted Williams BOS (AL)	.406	1941	18. Tony Gwynn SD	.394	1994
9. Rogers Hornsby STL (NL)	.403	1925	19. Harry Heilmann DET	.394	1921
10. Harry Heilmann DET	.403	1923	20. Babe Ruth NY (AL)	.393	1923

HITS

	H	YEAR
1. George Sisler STL (AL)	257	1920
2. Lefty O'Doul PHI (NL)	254	1929
Bill Terry NY (NL)	254	1930
4. Al Simmons PHI (AL)	253	1925
5. Rogers Hornsby STL (NL)	250	1922
Chuck Klein PHI (NL)	250	1930
7. Ty Cobb DET	248	1911
8. George Sisler STL (AL)	246	1922
9. Heinie Manush STL (AL)	241	1928
Babe Herman BKN	241	1930
11. Wade Boggs BOS	240	1985
12. Rod Carew MIN	239	1977
13. Don Mattingly NY (AL)	238	1986
14. Harry Heilmann DET	237	1921
Paul Waner PIT	237	1927
Joe Medwick STL (NL)	237	1937
17. Jack Tobin STL (AL)	236	1921
18. Rogers Hornsby STL (NL)	235	1921
19. Lloyd Waner PIT	234	1929
Kirby Puckett MIN	234	1988

DOUBLES

	2B	YEAR
1. Earl Webb BOS (AL)	67	1931
2. George Burns CLE	64	1926
Joe Medwick STL (NL)	64	1936
4. Hank Greenberg DET	63	1934
5. Paul Waner PIT	62	1932
6. Charlie Gehringer DET	60	1936
7. Tris Speaker CLE	59	1923
Chuck Klein PHI (NL)	59	1930
9. Billy Herman CHI (NL)	57	1935
Billy Herman CHI (NL)	57	1936

TRIPLES

	3B	YEAR
1. Owen Wilson PIT	36	1912
2. Joe Jackson CLE	26	1912
Sam Crawford DET	26	1914
Kiki Cuyler PIT	26	1925
5. Sam Crawford DET	25	1903
Larry Doyle NY (NL)	25	1911
Tommy Long STL (NL)	25	1915
8. Ty Cobb DET	24	1911
9. Sam Crawford CIN	23	1902
Ty Cobb DET	23	1912
Sam Crawford DET	23	1913
Ty Cobb DET	23	1917
Earle Combs NY (AL)	23	1927
Adam Comorosky PIT	23	1930
Dale Mitchell CLE	23	1949

HOME RUNS

	HR	YEAR
1. Roger Maris NY (AL)	61	1961
2. Babe Ruth NY (AL)	60	1927
3. Babe Ruth NY (AL)	59	1921
4. Jimmie Foxx PHI (AL)	58	1932
Hank Greenberg DET	58	1938
6. Hack Wilson CHI (NL)	56	1930
7. Babe Ruth NY (AL)	54	1920
Babe Ruth NY (AL)	54	1928
Ralph Kiner PIT	54	1949
Mickey Mantle NY (AL)	54	1961
11. Mickey Mantle NY (AL)	52	1956
Willie Mays SF	52	1965
George Foster CIN	52	1977
14. Ralph Kiner PIT	51	1947
Johnny Mize NY (NL)	51	1947
Willie Mays NY (NL)	51	1955
Cecil Fielder DET	51	1990
18. Jimmie Foxx BOS (AL)	50	1938
19. Babe Ruth NY (AL)	49	1930
Lou Gehrig NY (AL)	49	1934
Lou Gehrig NY (AL)	49	1936
Ted Kluszewski CIN	49	1954
Willie Mays SF	49	1962
Harmon Killebrew MIN	49	1964
Frank Robinson BAL	49	1966
Harmon Killebrew MIN	49	1969
Andre Dawson CHI (NL)	49	1987
Mark McGwire OAK	49	1987

HOME RUN PERCENTAGE

	HR%	YEAR
1. Babe Ruth NY (AL)	11.8	1920
2. Babe Ruth NY (AL)	11.1	1927
3. Babe Ruth NY (AL)	10.9	1921
4. Mickey Mantle NY (AL)	10.5	1961
5. Hank Greenberg DET	10.4	1938
6. Roger Maris NY (AL)	10.3	1961
7. Babe Ruth NY (AL)	10.1	1928
8. Jimmie Foxx PHI (AL)	9.9	1932
9. Ralph Kiner PIT	9.8	1949
10. Mickey Mantle NY (AL)	9.8	1956
11. Jeff Bagwell HOU	9.8	1994
12. Kevin Mitchell CIN	9.7	1994
13. Matt Williams SF	9.7	1994
14. Hack Wilson CHI (NL)	9.6	1930
15. Frank Thomas CHI (AL)	9.5	1994
16. Babe Ruth NY (AL)	9.5	1926
Hank Aaron ATL	9.5	1971
18. Jim Gentile BAL	9.5	1961
19. Barry Bonds SF	9.5	1994
20. Babe Ruth NY (AL)	9.5	1930

RUNS BATTED IN

	RBI	YEAR
1. Hack Wilson CHI (NL)	190	1930
2. Lou Gehrig NY (AL)	184	1931
3. Hank Greenberg DET	183	1937
4. Lou Gehrig NY (AL)	175	1927
Jimmie Foxx BOS (AL)	175	1938
6. Lou Gehrig NY (AL)	174	1930
7. Babe Ruth NY (AL)	171	1921
8. Chuck Klein PHI (NL)	170	1930
Hank Greenberg DET	170	1935

10. Jimmie Foxx PHI (AL)	169	1932
11. Joe DiMaggio NY (AL)	167	1937
12. Al Simmons PHI (AL)	165	1930
Lou Gehrig NY (AL)	165	1934
14. Babe Ruth NY (AL)	164	1927
15. Babe Ruth NY (AL)	163	1931
Jimmie Foxx PHI (AL)	163	1933
17. Hal Trosky CLE	162	1936
18. Hack Wilson CHI (NL)	159	1929
Lou Gehrig NY (AL)	159	1937
Vern Stephens BOS (AL)	159	1949
Ted Williams BOS (AL)	159	1949

SLUGGING AVERAGE

	SA	YEAR
1. Babe Ruth NY (AL)	.847	1920
2. Babe Ruth NY (AL)	.846	1921
3. Babe Ruth NY (AL)	.772	1927
4. Lou Gehrig NY (AL)	.765	1927
5. Babe Ruth NY (AL)	.764	1923
6. Rogers Hornsby STL (NL)	.756	1925
7. Jeff Bagwell HOU	.750	1994
8. Jimmie Foxx PHI (AL)	.749	1932
9. Babe Ruth NY (AL)	.739	1924
10. Babe Ruth NY (AL)	.737	1926
11. Ted Williams BOS (AL)	.735	1941
12. Babe Ruth NY (AL)	.732	1930
13. Ted Williams BOS	.731	1957
14. Frank Thomas CHI (AL)	.729	1994
15. Hack Wilson CHI (NL)	.723	1930
16. Rogers Hornsby STL (NL)	.722	1922
17. Lou Gehrig NY (AL)	.721	1930
18. Albert Belle CLE	.714	1994
19. Babe Ruth NY (AL)	.709	1928
20. Al Simmons PHI (AL)	.708	1930

TOTAL BASES

	TB	YEAR
1. Babe Ruth NY (AL)	457	1921
2. Rogers Hornsby STL (NL)	450	1922
3. Lou Gehrig NY (AL)	447	1927
4. Chuck Klein PHI (NL)	445	1930
5. Jimmie Foxx PHI (AL)	438	1932
6. Stan Musial STL (NL)	429	1948
7. Hack Wilson CHI (NL)	423	1930
8. Chuck Klein PHI (NL)	420	1932
9. Lou Gehrig NY (AL)	419	1930
10. Joe DiMaggio NY (AL)	418	1937
11. Babe Ruth NY (AL)	417	1927
12. Babe Herman BKN	416	1930
13. Lou Gehrig NY (AL)	410	1931
14. Rogers Hornsby CHI (NL)	409	1929
Lou Gehrig NY (AL)	409	1934
16. Joe Medwick STL (NL)	406	1937
Jim Rice BOS	406	1978
18. Chuck Klein PHI (NL)	405	1929
Hal Trosky CLE	405	1936
20. Jimmie Foxx PHI (AL)	403	1933
Lou Gehrig NY (AL)	403	1936

BASES ON BALLS

	BB	YEAR
1. Babe Ruth NY (AL)	170	1923
2. Ted Williams BOS (AL)	162	1947
Ted Williams BOS (AL)	162	1949
4. Ted Williams BOS (AL)	156	1946
5. Eddie Yost WAS	151	1956
6. Eddie Joost PHI (AL)	149	1949
7. Babe Ruth NY (AL)	148	1920
Eddie Stanky BKN	148	1945
Jimmy Wynn HOU	148	1969
10. Jimmy Sheckard CHI (AL)	147	1911
11. Mickey Mantle NY (AL)	146	1957
12. Ted Williams BOS (AL)	145	1941
Ted Williams BOS (AL)	145	1942
Harmon Killebrew MIN	145	1969
15. Babe Ruth NY (AL)	144	1921
Babe Ruth NY (AL)	144	1926
Eddie Stanky NY (NL)	144	1950
Ted Williams BOS (AL)	144	1951

RUNS SCORED

	RS	YEAR
1. Babe Ruth NY (AL)	177	1921
2. Lou Gehrig NY (AL)	167	1936
3. Babe Ruth NY (AL)	163	1928
Lou Gehrig NY (AL)	163	1931
5. Babe Ruth NY (AL)	158	1920
Babe Ruth NY (AL)	158	1927
Chuck Klein PHI (NL)	158	1930
8. Rogers Hornsby CHI (NL)	156	1929
9. Kiki Cuyler CHI (NL)	155	1930
10. Lefty O'Doul PHI (NL)	152	1929
Woody English CHI (NL)	152	1930
Al Simmons PHI (AL)	152	1930
Chuck Klein PHI (NL)	152	1932
14. Babe Ruth NY (AL)	151	1923
Jimmie Foxx PHI (AL)	151	1932
Joe DiMaggio NY (AL)	151	1937
17. Babe Ruth NY (AL)	150	1930
Ted Williams BOS (AL)	150	1949
19. Lou Gehrig NY (AL)	149	1927
Babe Ruth NY (AL)	149	1931

STOLEN BASES

	SB	YEAR
1. Rickey Henderson OAK	130	1982
2. Lou Brock STL	118	1974
3. Vince Coleman STL	110	1985
4. Vince Coleman STL	109	1987
5. Rickey Henderson OAK	108	1983
6. Vince Coleman STL	107	1986
7. Maury Wills LA	104	1962
8. Rickey Henderson OAK	100	1980
9. Ron LeFlore MON	97	1980
10. Ty Cobb DET	96	1915
Omar Moreno PIT	96	1980
12. Maury Wills LA	94	1965
13. Rickey Henderson NY (AL)	93	1988

14.	Tim Raines MON	90	1983
15.	Clyde Milan WAS	88	1912
16.	Rickey Henderson NY (AL)	87	1986
17.	Ty Cobb DET	83	1911
	Willie Wilson KC	83	1979
19.	Eddie Collins PHI (AL)	81	1910
	Bob Bescher CIN	81	1911
	Vince Coleman STL	81	1988

WINS

		W	YEAR
1.	Jack Chesbro NY (NL)	41	1904
2.	Ed Walsh CHI (AL)	40	1908
3.	Christy Mathewson NY (NL)	37	1908
4.	Walter Johnson WAS	36	1913
5.	Joe McGinnity NY (NL)	35	1904
6.	Smoky Joe Wood BOS (AL)	34	1912
7.	Cy Young BOS (AL)	33	1901
	Christy Mathewson NY (NL)	33	1904
	Grover Alexander PHI (NL)	33	1916
10.	Cy Young BOS (AL)	32	1902
	Walter Johnson WAS	32	1912
12.	Joe McGinnity NY (NL)	31	1903
	Christy Mathewson NY (NL)	31	1905
	Jack Coombs PHI (AL)	31	1910
	Grover Alexander PHI (NL)	31	1915
	Jim Bagby CLE	31	1920
	Lefty Grove PHI (AL)	31	1931
	Denny McLain DET	31	1968
19.	Christy Mathewson NY (NL)	30	1903
	Grover Alexander PHI (NL)	30	1917
	Dizzy Dean STL (NL)	30	1934

WINNING PERCENTAGE

		W%	YEAR
1.	Roy Face PIT	.947	1959
2.	Rick Sutcliffe CHI (NL)	.941	1984
3.	Johnny Allen CLE	.938	1937
4.	Ron Guidry NY (AL)	.893	1978
5.	Freddie Fitzsimmons BKN	.889	1940
6.	Lefty Grove PHI (AL)	.886	1931
7.	Bob Stanley BOS	.882	1978
8.	Preacher Roe BKN	.880	1951
9.	Tom Seaver CIN	.875	1981
10.	Smoky Joe Wood BOS (AL)	.872	1912
11.	David Cone NY (NL)	.870	1988
12.	Orel Hershiser LA	.864	1985
13.	Wild Bill Donovan DET	.862	1907
	Whitey Ford NY (AL)	.862	1961
15.	Dwight Gooden NY (NL)	.857	1985
	Roger Clemens BOS	.857	1986

EARNED RUN AVERAGE

		ERA	YEAR
1.	Dutch Leonard BOS (AL)	1.01	1914
2.	Three Finger Brown CHI (NL)	1.04	1906
3.	Walter Johnson WAS	1.09	1913
4.	Bob Gibson STL	1.12	1968
5.	Christy Mathewson NY (NL)	1.14	1909
6.	Jack Pfiester CHI (NL)	1.15	1907
7.	Addie Joss CLE	1.16	1908
8.	Carl Lundgren CHI (NL)	1.17	1907
9.	Grover Alexander PHI (NL)	1.22	1915
10.	Cy Young BOS (AL)	1.26	1908
11.	Ed Walsh CHI (AL)	1.27	1910
12.	Walter Johnson WAS	1.27	1918
13.	Christy Mathewson NY (NL)	1.27	1905
14.	Jack Coombs PHI (AL)	1.30	1910
15.	Three Finger Brown CHI (NL)	1.31	1909

STRIKEOUTS

		SO	YEAR
1.	Nolan Ryan CAL	383	1973
2.	Sandy Koufax LA	382	1965
3.	Nolan Ryan CAL	367	1974
4.	Rube Waddell PHI (AL)	349	1904
5.	Bob Feller CLE	348	1946
6.	Nolan Ryan CAL	341	1977
7.	Nolan Ryan CAL	329	1972
8.	Nolan Ryan CAL	327	1976
9.	Sam McDowell CLE	325	1965
10.	Sandy Koufax LA	317	1966
11.	Walter Johnson WAS	313	1910
	J.R. Richard HOU	313	1979
13.	Steve Carlton PHI	310	1972
14.	Mickey Lolich DET	308	1971
	Randy Johnson SEA	308	1993

SAVES

		SV	YEAR
1.	Bobby Thigpen CHI (AL)	57	1990
2.	Randy Myers CHI (NL)	53	1993
3.	Dennis Eckersley OAK	51	1992
4.	Dennis Eckersley OAK	48	1990
	Rod Beck SF	48	1993
6.	Lee Smith STL	47	1991
7.	Dave Righetti NY (AL)	46	1986
	Bryan Harvey CAL	46	1991
9.	Dan Quisenberry KC	45	1983
	Bruce Sutter STL	45	1984
	Dennis Eckersley OAK	45	1988
	Bryan Harvey FLA	45	1993
	Jeff Montgomery KC	45	1993
	Duane Ward TOR	45	1993
15.	Dan Quisenberry KC	44	1984
	Mark Davis SD	44	1989

SHUTOUTS

		ShO	YEAR
1.	Grover Alexander PHI (NL)	16	1916
2.	Jack Coombs PHI (AL)	13	1910
	Bob Gibson STL	13	1968
4.	Christy Mathewson NY (NL)	12	1908
	Grover Alexander PHI (NL)	12	1915
6.	Ed Walsh CHI (AL)	11	1908
	Walter Johnson WAS	11	1913
	Sandy Koufax LA (NL)	11	1963
	Dean Chance LA (AL)	11	1964

COMPLETE GAMES	CG	YEAR
1. Jack Chesbro NY (NL)	48	1904
2. Vic Willis BOS (NL)	45	1902
3. Joe McGinnity NY (NL)	44	1903
4. George Mullin DET	42	1904
Ed Walsh CHI (AL)	42	1908
6. Noodles Hahn CIN	41	1901
Cy Young BOS (AL)	41	1902
Irv Young BOS (NL)	41	1905
9. Cy Young BOS (AL)	40	1904

GAMES PITCHED	GP	YEAR
1. Mike Marshall LA	106	1974
2. Kent Tekulve PIT	94	1979
3. Mike Marshall MON	92	1973
4. Kent Tekulve PIT	91	1978
5. Wayne Granger CIN	90	1969
Mike Marshall MIN	90	1979
Kent Tekulve PHI	90	1987

8. Mark Eichhorn TOR	89	1987
9. Wilbur Wood CHI (AL)	88	1968
10. Rob Murphy CIN	87	1987

INNINGS PITCHED	IP	YEAR
1. Ed Walsh CHI (AL)	464.0	1908
2. Jack Chesbro NY (NL)	454.2	1904
3. Joe McGinnity NY (NL)	434.0	1903
4. Ed Walsh CHI (AL)	422.1	1907
5. Vic Willis BOS (NL)	410.0	1902
6. Joe McGinnity NY (NL)	408.0	1904
7. Ed Walsh CHI (AL)	393.0	1912
8. Dave Davenport STL (FL)	392.2	1915
9. Christy Mathewson NY (NL)	390.2	1908
10. Jack Powell NY (NL)	390.1	1904

MOST VALUABLE PLAYERS

NATIONAL LEAGUE

CHALMERS
1911 Wildfire Schulte CHI (OF)
1912 Larry Doyle NY (2B)
1913 Jake Daubert BKN (1B)
1914 Johnny Evers BOS (2B)
1915-21 No Selection

LEAGUE
1922-23 No Selection
1924 Dazzy Vance BKN (P)
1925 Rogers Hornsby STL (2B)
1926 Bob O'Farrell STL (C)
1927 Paul Waner PIT (OF)
1928 Jim Bottomley STL (1B)
1929 Rogers Hornsby CHI (2B)
1930 No Selection

BASEBALL WRITERS ASSOCIATION OF AMERICA
1931 Frankie Frisch STL (2B)
1932 Chuck Klein PHI (OF)
1933 Carl Hubbell NY (P)
1934 Dizzy Dean STL (P)
1935 Gabby Hartnett CHI (C)
1936 Carl Hubbell NY (P)
1937 Joe Medwick STL (OF)
1938 Ernie Lombardi CIN (C)
1939 Bucky Walters CIN (P)
1940 Frank McCormick CIN (1B)
1941 Dolph Camilli BKN (1B)
1942 Mort Cooper STL (P)

1943 Stan Musial STL (OF)
1944 Marty Marion STL (SS)
1945 Phil Cavarretta CHI (1B)
1946 Stan Musial STL (1B)
1947 Bob Elliott BOS (3B)
1948 Stan Musial STL (OF)
1949 Jackie Robinson BKN (2B)
1950 Jim Konstanty PHI (P)
1951 Roy Campanella BKN (C)
1952 Hank Sauer CHI (OF)
1953 Roy Campanella BKN (C)
1954 Willie Mays NY (OF)
1955 Roy Campanella BKN (C)
1956 Don Newcombe BKN (P)
1957 Hank Aaron MIL (OF)
1958 Ernie Banks CHI (SS)
1959 Ernie Banks CHI (SS)
1960 Dick Groat PIT (SS)
1961 Frank Robinson CIN (OF)
1962 Maury Wills LA (SS)
1963 Sandy Koufax LA (P)
1964 Ken Boyer STL (3B)
1965 Willie Mays SF (OF)
1966 Roberto Clemente PIT (OF)
1967 Orlando Cepeda STL (1B)
1968 Bob Gibson STL (P)
1969 Willie McCovey SF (1B)
1970 Johnny Bench CIN (C)
1971 Joe Torre STL (3B)
1972 Johnny Bench CIN (C)
1973 Pete Rose CIN (OF)

1974 Steve Garvey LA (1B)
1975 Joe Morgan CIN (2B)
1976 Joe Morgan CIN (2B)
1977 George Foster CIN (OF)
1978 Dave Parker PIT (OF)
1979 Keith Hernandez STL (1B)
Willie Stargell PIT (1B)
1980 Mike Schmidt PHI (3B)
1981 Mike Schmidt PHI (3B)
1982 Dale Murphy ATL (OF)
1983 Dale Murphy ATL (OF)
1984 Ryne Sandberg CHI (2B)
1985 Willie McGee STL (OF)
1986 Mike Schmidt PHI (3B)
1987 Andre Dawson CHI (OF)
1988 Kirk Gibson LA (OF)
1989 Kevin Mitchell SF (OF)
1990 Barry Bonds PIT (OF)
1991 Terry Pendleton ATL (3B)
1992 Barry Bonds PIT (OF)
1993 Barry Bonds SF (OF)
1994 Jeff Bagwell HOU (1B)

AMERICAN LEAGUE

CHALMERS
1911 Ty Cobb DET (OF)
1912 Tris Speaker BOS (OF)
1913 Walter Johnson WAS (P)
1914 Eddie Collins PHI (2B)
1915-21 No Selection

LEAGUE
1922 George Sisler STL (1B)
1923 Babe Ruth NY (OF)
1924 Walter Johnson WAS (P)
1925 Roger Peckinpaugh WAS (SS)
1926 George Burns CLE (1B)
1927 Lou Gehrig NY (1B)
1928 Mickey Cochrane PHI (C)
1929-30 No Selection

BASEBALL WRITERS ASSOCIATION OF AMERICA
1931 Lefty Grove PHI (P)
1932 Jimmie Foxx PHI (1B)
1933 Jimmie Foxx PHI (1B)
1934 Mickey Cochrane DET (C)
1935 Hank Greenberg DET (1B)
1936 Lou Gehrig NY (1B)
1937 Charlie Gehringer DET (2B)
1938 Jimmie Foxx BOS (1B)
1939 Joe DiMaggio NY (OF)
1940 Hank Greenberg DET (1B)
1941 Joe DiMaggio NY (OF)
1942 Joe Gordon NY (2B)

1943 Spud Chandler NY (P)
1944 Hal Newhouser DET (P)
1945 Hal Newhouser DET (P)
1946 Ted Williams BOS (OF)
1947 Joe DiMaggio NY (OF)
1948 Lou Boudreau CLE (SS)
1949 Ted Williams BOS (OF)
1950 Phil Rizzuto NY (SS)
1951 Yogi Berra NY (C)
1952 Bobby Shantz PHI (P)
1953 Al Rosen CLE (3B)
1954 Yogi Berra NY (C)
1955 Yogi Berra NY (C)
1956 Mickey Mantle NY (OF)
1957 Mickey Mantle NY (OF)
1958 Jackie Jensen BOS (OF)
1959 Nellie Fox CHI (2B)
1960 Roger Maris NY (OF)
1961 Roger Maris NY (OF)
1962 Mickey Mantle NY (OF)
1963 Elston Howard NY (C)
1964 Brooks Robinson BAL (3B)
1965 Zoilo Versalles MIN (SS)
1966 Frank Robinson BAL (OF)
1967 Carl Yastrzemski BOS (OF)
1968 Denny McLain DET (P)

1969 Harmon Killebrew MIN (3B)
1970 Boog Powell BAL (1B)
1971 Vida Blue OAK (P)
1972 Richie Allen CHI (1B)
1973 Reggie Jackson OAK (OF)
1974 Jeff Burroughs TEX (OF)
1975 Fred Lynn BOS (OF)
1976 Thurman Munson NY (C)
1977 Rod Carew MIN (1B)
1978 Jim Rice BOS (OF)
1979 Don Baylor CAL (DH)
1980 George Brett KC (3B)
1981 Rollie Fingers MIL (P)
1982 Robin Yount MIL (SS)
1983 Cal Ripken BAL (SS)
1984 Willie Hernandez DET (P)
1985 Don Mattingly NY (1B)
1986 Roger Clemens BOS (P)
1987 George Bell TOR (OF)
1988 Jose Canseco OAK (OF)
1989 Robin Yount MIL (OF)
1990 Rickey Henderson OAK (OF)
1991 Cal Ripken BAL (SS)
1992 Dennis Eckersley OAK (P)
1993 Frank Thomas CHI (1B)
1994 Frank Thomas CHI (1B)

CY YOUNG AWARD WINNERS (ONE SELECTION 1956-66)

NATIONAL LEAGUE
1956 Don Newcombe BKN (RH)
1957 Warren Spahn MIL (LH)
1960 Vern Law PIT (RH)
1962 Don Drysdale LA (RH)
1963 Sandy Koufax LA (LH)
1965 Sandy Koufax LA (LH)
1966 Sandy Koufax LA (LH)
1967 Mike McCormick SF (LH)
1968 Bob Gibson STL (RH)
1969 Tom Seaver NY (RH)
1970 Bob Gibson STL (RH)
1971 Ferguson Jenkins CHI (RH)
1972 Steve Carlton PHI (LH)
1973 Tom Seaver NY (RH)
1974 Mike Marshall LA (RH)
1975 Tom Seaver NY (RH)
1976 Randy Jones SD (LH)
1977 Steve Carlton PHI (LH)
1978 Gaylord Perry SD (RH)
1979 Bruce Sutter CHI (RH)

1980 Steve Carlton PHI (LH)
1981 Fernando Valenzuela LA (LH)
1982 Steve Carlton PHI (LH)
1983 John Denny PHI (RH)
1984 Rick Sutcliffe CHI (RH)
1985 Dwight Gooden NY (RH)
1986 Mike Scott HOU (RH)
1987 Steve Bedrosian PHI (RH)
1988 Orel Hershiser LA (RH)
1989 Mark Davis SD (LH)
1990 Doug Drabek PIT (RH)
1991 Tom Glavine ATL (LH)
1992 Greg Maddux CHI (RH)
1993 Greg Maddux ATL (RH)
1994 Greg Maddux ATL (RH)

AMERICAN LEAGUE
1958 Bob Turley NY (RH)
1959 Early Wynn CHI (RH)
1961 Whitey Ford NY (LH)
1964 Dean Chance LA (RH)
1967 Jim Lonborg BOS (RH)

1968 Denny McLain DET (RH)
1969 Mike Cuellar BAL (LH)
    Denny McLain DET (RH)
1970 Jim Perry MIN (RH)
1971 Vida Blue OAK (LH)
1972 Gaylord Perry CLE (RH)
1973 Jim Palmer BAL (RH)
1974 Jim (Catfish) Hunter OAK (RH)
1975 Jim Palmer BAL (RH)
1976 Jim Palmer BAL (RH)
1977 Sparky Lyle NY (LH)
1978 Ron Guidry NY (LH)
1979 Mike Flanagan BAL (LH)
1980 Steve Stone BAL (RH)
1981 Rollie Fingers MIL (RH)
1982 Pete Vuckovich MIL (RH)
1983 LaMarr Hoyt CHI (RH)
1984 Willie Hernandez DET (LH)
1985 Bret Saberhagen KC (RH)
1986 Roger Clemens BOS (RH)

1987 Roger Clemens
BOS (RH)
1988 Frank Viola MIN (LH)
1989 Bret Saberhagen
KC (RH)

1990 Bob Welch OAK (RH)
1991 Roger Clemens
BOS (RH)
1992 Dennis Eckersley
OAK (RH)

1993 Jack McDowell CHI (RH)
1994 David Cone KC (RH)

ROOKIE OF THE YEAR (ONE SELECTION 1947-48)

NATIONAL LEAGUE
1947 Jackie Robinson
BKN (1B)
1948 Alvin Dark BOS (SS)
1949 Don Newcombe BKN (P)
1950 Sam Jethroe BOS (OF)
1951 Willie Mays NY (OF)
1952 Joe Black BKN (P)
1953 Junior Gilliam BKN (2B)
1954 Wally Moon STL (OF)
1955 Bill Virdon STL (OF)
1956 Frank Robinson CIN (OF)
1957 Jack Sanford PHI (P)
1958 Orlando Cepeda SF (1B)
1959 Willie McCovey SF (1B)
1960 Frank Howard LA (OF)
1961 Billy Williams CHI (OF)
1962 Ken Hubbs CHI (2B)
1963 Pete Rose CIN (2B)
1964 Richie Allen PHI (3B)
1965 Jim Lefebvre LA (2B)
1966 Tommy Helms CIN (2B)
1967 Tom Seaver NY (P)
1968 Johnny Bench CIN (C)
1969 Ted Sizemore LA (2B)
1970 Carl Morton MON (P)
1971 Earl Williams ATL (C)
1972 Jon Matlack NY (P)
1973 Gary Matthews SF (OF)
1974 Bake McBride STL (OF)
1975 Jon Montefusco SF (P)
1976 Pat Zachry CIN (P)
Butch Metzger SD (P)
1977 Andre Dawson MON (OF)
1978 Bob Horner ATL (3B)

1979 Rick Sutcliffe LA (P)
1980 Steve Howe LA (P)
1981 Fernando Valenzuela
LA (P)
1982 Steve Sax LA (2B)
1983 Darryl Strawberry
NY (OF)
1984 Dwight Gooden NY (P)
1985 Vince Coleman STL (OF)
1986 Todd Worrell STL (P)
1987 Benito Santiago SD (C)
1988 Chris Sabo CIN (3B)
1989 Jerome Walton CHI (OF)
1990 Dave Justice ATL (OF)
1991 Jeff Bagwell HOU (1B)
1992 Eric Karros LA (1B)
1993 Mike Piazza LA (C)
1994 Raul Mondesi LA (OF)

AMERICAN LEAGUE
1949 Roy Sievers STL (OF)
1950 Walt Dropo BOS (1B)
1951 Gil McDougald NY (3B)
1952 Harry Byrd PHI (P)
1953 Harvey Kuenn DET (SS)
1954 Bob Grim NY (P)
1955 Herb Score CLE (P)
1956 Luis Aparicio CHI (SS)
1957 Tony Kubek NY (SS)
1958 Albie Pearson WAS (OF)
1959 Bob Allison WAS (OF)
1960 Ron Hansen BAL (SS)
1961 Don Schwall BOS (P)
1962 Tom Tresh NY (SS)
1963 Gary Peters CHI (P)

1964 Tony Oliva MIN (OF)
1965 Curt Blefary BAL (OF)
1966 Tommie Agee CHI (OF)
1967 Rod Carew MIN (2B)
1968 Stan Bahnsen NY (P)
1969 Lou Piniella KC (OF)
1970 Thurman Munson NY (C)
1971 Chris Chambliss CLE (1B)
1972 Carlton Fisk BOS (C)
1973 Al Bumbry BAL (OF)
1974 Mike Hargrove TEX (1B)
1975 Fred Lynn BOS (OF)
1976 Mark Fidrych DET (P)
1977 Eddie Murray BAL (DH)
1978 Lou Whitaker DET (2B)
1979 Alfredo Griffin TOR (SS)
John Castino MIN (3B)
1980 Joe Charboneau
CLE (OF)
1981 Dave Righetti NY (P)
1982 Cal Ripken BAL (SS)
1983 Ron Kittle CHI (OF)
1984 Alvin Davis SEA (1B)
1985 Ozzie Guillen CHI (SS)
1986 Jose Canseco OAK (OF)
1987 Mark McGwire OAK (1B)
1988 Walt Weiss OAK (SS)
1989 Gregg Olson BAL (P)
1990 Sandy Alomar CLE (C)
1991 Chuck Knoblauch
MIN (2B)
1992 Pat Listach MIL (SS)
1993 Tim Salmon CAL (OF)
1994 Bob Hamelin KC (DH)

GOLD GLOVE AWARD WINNERS

COMBINED SELECTION-1957
P   Bobby Shantz NY (AL)
C   Sherm Lollar CHI (AL)
1B Gil Hodges BKN
2B Nellie Fox CHI (AL)
3B Frank Malzone BOS
SS Roy McMillan CIN
LF Minnie Minoso CHI (AL)
CF Willie Mays NY (NL)
RF Al Kaline DET

Pitchers/NL
1958 Harvey Haddix CIN
1959-60 Harvey Haddix PIT
1961 Bobby Shantz PIT
1962-63 Bobby Shantz STL
1964 Bobby Shantz PHI
1965-73 Bob Gibson STL
1974-75 Andy Messersmith LA
1976-77 Jim Kaat PHI
1978-80 Phil Niekro ATL

1981 Steve Carlton PHI
1982-83 Phil Niekro ATL
1984 Joaquin Andujar STL
1985 Rick Reuschel PIT
1986 Fernando Valenzuela LA
1987 Rick Reuschel SF
1988 Orel Hershiser LA
1989 Ron Darling NY
1990-92 Greg Maddux CHI
1993-94 Greg Maddux ATL

Pitchers/AL

1958-60 Bobby Shantz NY
1961 Frank Lary DET
1962-72 Jim Kaat MIN
1973 Jim Kaat MIN, CHI
1974-75 Jim Kaat CHI
1976-79 Jim Palmer BAL
1980-81 Mike Norris OAK
1982-86 Ron Guidry NY
1987-88 Mark Langston SEA
1989 Bret Saberhagen KC
1990 Mike Boddicker BOS
1991-94 Mark Langston CAL

Catchers/NL

1958-60 Del Crandall MIL
1961 Johnny Roseboro LA
1962 Del Crandall MIL
1963-64 Johnny Edwards CIN
1965 Joe Torre MIL
1966 Johnny Roseboro LA
1967 Randy Hundley CHI
1968-77 Johnny Bench CIN
1978-79 Bob Boone PHI
1980-82 Gary Carter MON
1983-85 Tony Pena PIT
1986 Jody Davis CHI
1987 Mike LaValliere PIT
1988-90 Benito Santiago SD
1991-92 Tom Pagnozzi STL
1993 Kurt Manwaring SF
1994 Tom Pagnozzi STL

Catchers/AL

1958-59 Sherm Lollar CHI
1960 Earl Battey WAS
1961-62 Earl Battey MIN
1963-64 Elston Howard NY
1965-69 Bill Freehan DET
1970-71 Ray Fosse CLE
1972 Carlton Fisk BOS
1973-75 Thurman Munson NY
1976-81 Jim Sundberg TEX
1982 Bob Boone CAL
1983-85 Lance Parrish DET
1986-88 Bob Boone CAL
1989 Bob Boone KC
1990 Sandy Alomar CLE
1991 Tony Pena BOS
1992-94 Ivan Rodriguez TEX

First Basemen/NL

1958-59 Gil Hodges LA
1960-65 Bill White STL
1966 Bill White PHI
1967-72 Wes Parker LA

1973 Mike Jorgenson MON
1974-77 Steve Garvey LA
1978-82 Keith Hernandez STL
1983 Keith Hernandez STL, NY
1984-88 Keith Hernandez NY
1989-90 Andres Galarraga MON
1991 Will Clark SF
1992-93 Mark Grace CHI
1994 Jeff Bagwell HOU

First Basemen/AL

1958-61 Vic Power CLE
1962-63 Vic Power MIN
1964 Vic Power LA
1965-66 Joe Pepitone NY
1967-68 George Scott BOS
1969 Joe Pepitone NY
1970 Jim Spencer CAL
1971 George Scott BOS
1972-76 George Scott MIL
1977 Jim Spencer CHI
1978 Chris Chambliss NY
1979-80 Cecil Cooper MIL
1981 Mike Squires CHI
1982-84 Eddie Murray BAL
1985-89 Don Mattingly NY
1990 Mark McGwire OAK
1991-94 Don Mattingly NY

Second Basemen/NL

1958 Bill Mazeroski PIT
1959 Charlie Neal LA
1960-61 Bill Mazeroski PIT
1962 Ken Hubbs CHI
1963-67 Bill Mazeroski PIT
1968 Glenn Beckert CHI
1969 Felix Millan ATL
1970-71 Tommy Helms CIN
1972 Felix Millan ATL
1973-77 Joe Morgan CIN
1978 Davey Lopes LA
1979 Manny Trillo PHI
1980 Doug Flynn NY
1981-82 Manny Trillo PHI
1983-91 Ryne Sandberg CHI
1992 Jose Lind PIT
1993 Robby Thompson SF
1994 Craig Biggio HOU

Second Basemen/AL

1958 Frank Bolling DET
1959-60 Nellie Fox CHI
1961-65 Bobby Richardson NY
1966-68 Bobby Knoop CAL
1969-71 Dave Johnson BAL

1972 Doug Griffin BOS
1973-76 Bobby Grich BAL
1977-82 Frank White KC
1983-85 Lou Whitaker DET
1986-87 Frank White KC
1988-90 Harold Reynolds SEA
1991-94 Roberto Alomar TOR

Third Basemen/NL

1958-61 Ken Boyer STL
1962 Jim Davenport SF
1963 Ken Boyer STL
1964-68 Ron Santo CHI
1969 Clete Boyer ATL
1970-74 Doug Rader HOU
1975 Ken Reitz STL
1976-84 Mike Schmidt PHI
1985 Tim Wallach MON
1986 Mike Schmidt PHI
1987 Terry Pendleton STL
1988 Tim Wallach MON
1989 Terry Pendleton STL
1990 Tim Wallach MON
1991 Matt Williams SF
1992 Terry Pendleton ATL
1993-94 Matt Williams SF

Third Basemen/AL

1958-59 Frank Malzone BOS
1960-75 Brooks Robinson BAL
1976 Aurelio Rodriguez DET
1977-78 Graig Nettles NY
1979-84 Buddy Bell TEX
1985 George Brett KC
1986-89 Gary Gaetti MIN
1990 Kelly Gruber TOR
1991-93 Robin Ventura CHI
1994 Wade Boggs NY

Shortstops/NL

1958-59 Roy McMillan CIN
1960 Ernie Banks CHI
1961-62 Maury Wills LA
1963 Bobby Wine PHI
1964 Ruben Amaro PHI
1965 Leo Cardenas CIN
1966-67 Gene Alley PIT
1968 Dal Maxvill STL
1969-70 Don Kessinger CHI
1971 Bud Harrelson NY
1972 Larry Bowa PHI
1973 Roger Metzger HOU
1974-77 Dave Concepcion CIN
1978 Larry Bowa PHI
1979 Dave Concepcion CIN
1980-81 Ozzie Smith SD

1982-92 Ozzie Smith STL
1993 Jay Bell PIT
1994 Barry Larkin CIN

Shortstops/AL
1958-62 Luis Aparicio CHI
1963 Zoilo Versalles MIN
1964 Luis Aparicio BAL
1965 Zoilo Versalles MIN

1966 Luis Aparicio BAL
1967 Jim Fregosi CAL
1968 Luis Aparicio CHI
1969 Mark Belanger BAL
1970 Luis Aparicio CHI
1971 Mark Belanger BAL
1972 Eddie Brinkman DET
1973-78 Mark Belanger BAL
1979 Rick Burleson BOS

1980-81 Alan Trammell DET
1982 Robin Yount MIL
1983-84 Alan Trammell DET
1985 Alfredo Griffin OAK
1986-89 Tony Fernandez TOR
1990 Ozzie Guillen CHI
1991-92 Cal Ripken BAL
1993 Omar Vizquel SEA
1994 Omar Vizquel CLE

Outfielders/NL
1958
Frank Robinson CIN (LF)
Willie Mays SF (CF)
Hank Aaron MIL (RF)

1959
Jackie Brant SF (LF)
Willie Mays SF (CF)
Hank Aaron MIL (RF)

1960
Wally Moon LA (LF)
Willie Mays SF (CF)
Hank Aaron MIL (RF)

1961
Willie Mays SF
Roberto Clemente PIT
Vada Pinson CIN

1962
Willie Mays SF
Roberto Clemente PIT
Bill Virdon PIT

1963-68
Willie Mays SF
Roberto Clemente PIT
Curt Flood STL

1969
Roberto Clemente PIT
Curt Flood STL
Pete Rose CIN

1970
Roberto Clemente PIT
Tommy Agee NY
Pete Rose CIN

1971
Roberto Clemente PIT
Bobby Bonds SF
Willie Davis LA

1972
Roberto Clemente PIT
Cesar Cedeno HOU
Willie Davis LA

1973
Bobby Bonds SF
Cesar Cedeno HOU
Willie Davis LA

1974
Cesar Cedeno HOU
Cesar Geronimo CIN
Bobby Bonds SF

1975-76
Cesar Cedeno HOU
Cesar Geronimo CIN
Garry Maddox PHI

1977
Cesar Geronimo CIN
Garry Maddox PHI
Dave Parker PIT

1978
Garry Maddox PHI
Dave Parker PIT
Ellis Valentine MON

1979
Garry Maddox PHI
Dave Parker PIT
Dave Winfield SD

1980
Andre Dawson MON
Garry Maddox PHI
Dave Winfield SD

1981
Andre Dawson MON
Garry Maddox PHI
Dusty Baker LA

1982
Andre Dawson MON
Dale Murphy ATL
Garry Maddox PHI

1983
Andre Dawson MON
Dale Murphy ATL
Willie McGee STL

1984
Dale Murphy ATL
Bob Dernier CHI
Andre Dawson MON

1985
Willie McGee STL
Andre Dawson MON
Dale Murphy ATL

1986
Dale Murphy ATL
Willie McGee STL
Tony Gwynn SD

1987
Eric Davis CIN
Tony Gwynn SD
Andre Dawson CHI

1988
Andre Dawson CHI
Eric Davis CIN
Andy Van Slyke PIT

1989
Eric Davis CIN
Tony Gwynn SD
Andy Van Slyke PIT

1990-91
Barry Bonds PIT
Tony Gwynn SD
Andy Van Slyke PIT

1992
Barry Bonds PIT
Larry Walker MON
Andy Van Slyke PIT

1993
Barry Bonds SF
Marquis Grissom MON
Larry Walker MON

1994
Barry Bonds SF
Marquis Grissom MON
Darren Lewis SF

Outfielders/AL
1958
Norm Siebern NY (LF)
Jimmy Piersall BOS (CF)
Al Kaline DET (RF)

1959
Minnie Minoso CLE (LF)
Al Kaline DET (CF)
Jackie Jensen BOS (RF)

1960
Minnie Minoso CHI (LF)
Jim Landis CHI (CF)
Roger Maris NY (RF)

1961
Al Kaline DET
Jimmy Piersall CLE
Jim Landis CHI

1962
Jim Landis CHI
Mickey Mantle NY
Al Kaline DET

1963
Al Kaline DET
Carl Yastrzemski BOS
Jim Landis CHI

1964
Al Kaline DET
Jim Landis CHI
Vic Davalillo CLE

1965
Al Kaline DET
Tom Tresh NY
Carl Yastrzemski BOS

1966
Al Kaline DET
Tommy Agee CHI
Tony Oliva MIN

1967
Carl Yastrzemski BOS
Paul Blair BAL
Al Kaline DET

1968
Mickey Stanley DET
Carl Yastrzemski BOS
Reggie Smith BOS

1969
Paul Blair BAL
Mickey Stanley DET
Carl Yastrzemski BOS

1970
Mickey Stanley DET
Paul Blair BAL
Ken Berry CHI

1971
Paul Blair BAL
Amos Otis KC
Carl Yastrzemski BOS

1972
Paul Blair BAL
Bobby Murcer NY
Ken Berry CAL

1973
Paul Blair BAL
Amos Otis KC
Mickey Stanley DET

1974
Paul Blair BAL
Amos Otis KC
Joe Rudi OAK

1975
Paul Blair BAL
Joe Rudi OAK
Fred Lynn BOS

1976
Joe Rudi OAK
Dwight Evans BOS
Rick Manning CLE

1977
Juan Beniquez TEX
Carl Yastrzemski BOS
Al Cowens KC

1978
Fred Lynn BOS
Dwight Evans BOS
Rick Miller CAL

1979
Dwight Evans BOS
Sixto Lezcano MIL
Fred Lynn BOS

1980
Fred Lynn BOS
Dwayne Murphy OAK
Willie Wilson KC

1981
Dwayne Murphy OAK
Dwight Evans BOS
Rickey Henderson OAK

1982-84
Dwight Evans BOS
Dave Winfield NY
Dwayne Murphy OAK

1985
Gary Pettis CAL
Dave Winfield NY
Dwight Evans BOS
Dwayne Murphy OAK

1986
Jesse Barfield TOR
Kirby Puckett MIN
Gary Pettis CAL

1987
Jesse Barfield TOR
Kirby Puckett MIN
Dave Winfield NY

1988
Devon White CAL
Gary Pettis CAL
Kirby Puckett MIN

1989
Devon White CAL
Gary Pettis DET
Kirby Puckett MIN

1990
Ken Griffey Jr. SEA
Ellis Burks BOS
Gary Pettis TEX

1991-92
Ken Griffey Jr. SEA
Devon White TOR
Kirby Puckett MIN

1993-94
Ken Griffey Jr. SEA
Kenny Lofton CLE
Devon White TOR

THE WORLD SERIES 1903-94

YEAR	WINNER	SERIES	LOSER	YEAR	WINNER	SERIES	LOSER
1903	BOS Pilgrims	5-3	PIT Pirates (NL)	1931	STL Cardinals (NL)	4-3	PHI Athletics (AL)
1904	NO SERIES			1932	NY Yankees (AL)	4-0	CHI Cubs (NL)
1905	NY Giants (NL)	4-1	PHI Athletics (AL)	1933	NY Giants (NL)	4-1	WAS Senators (AL)
1906	CHI White Sox (AL)	4-2	CHI Cubs (NL)	1934	STL Cardinals (NL)	4-3	DET Tigers (AL)
1907	CHI Cubs (NL)	4-0	DET Tigers (AL)	1935	DET Tigers (AL)	4-2	CHI Cubs (NL)
1908	CHI Cubs (NL)	4-1	DET Tigers (AL)	1936	NY Yankees (AL)	4-2	NY Giants (NL)
1909	PIT Pirates (NL)	4-3	DET Tigers (AL)	1937	NY Yankees (AL)	4-1	NY Giants (NL)
1910	PHI Athletics (AL)	4-1	CHI Cubs (NL)	1938	NY Yankees (AL)	4-0	CHI Cubs (NL)
1911	PHI Athletics (AL)	4-2	NY Giants (NL)	1939	NY Yankees (AL)	4-0	CIN Reds (NL)
1912	BOS Red Sox (AL)	4-3	NY Giants (NL)	1940	CIN Reds (NL)	4-3	DET Tigers (AL)
1913	PHI Athletics (AL)	4-1	NY Giants (NL)	1941	NY Yankees (AL)	4-1	BKN Dodgers (NL)
1914	BOS Braves (NL)	4-0	PHI Athletics (AL)	1942	STL Cardinals (NL)	4-1	NY Yankees (AL)
1915	BOS Red Sox (AL)	4-1	PHI Phillies (NL)	1943	NY Yankees (AL)	4-1	STL Cardinals (NL)
1916	BOS Red Sox (AL)	4-1	BKN Robins (NL)	1944	STL Cardinals (NL)	4-2	STL Browns (AL)
1917	CHI White Sox (AL)	4-2	NY Giants (NL)	1945	DET Tigers (AL)	4-3	CHI Cubs (NL)
1918	BOS Red Sox (AL)	4-2	CHI Cubs (NL)	1946	STL Cardinals (NL)	4-3	BOS Red Sox (AL)
1919	CIN Reds (NL)	5-3	CHI White Sox (AL)	1947	NY Yankees (AL)	4-3	BKN Dodgers (NL)
1920	CLE Indians (AL)	5-2	BKN Robins (NL)	1948	CLE Indians (AL)	4-2	BOS Braves (NL)
1921	NY Giants (NL)	5-3	NY Yankees (AL)	1949	NY Yankees (AL)	4-1	BKN Dodgers (NL)
1922	NY Giants (NL)	4-0	NY Yankees (AL)	1950	NY Yankees (AL)	4-0	PHI Phillies (NL)
1923	NY Yankees (AL)	4-2	NY Giants (NL)	1951	NY Yankees (AL)	4-2	NY Giants (NL)
1924	WAS Senators (AL)	4-3	NY Giants (NL)	1952	NY Yankees (AL)	4-3	BKN Dodgers (NL)
1925	PIT Pirates (NL)	4-3	WAS Senators (AL)	1953	NY Yankees (AL)	4-2	BKN Dodgers (NL)
1926	STL Cardinals (NL)	4-3	NY Yankees (AL)	1954	NY Giants (NL)	4-0	CLE Indians (AL)
1927	NY Yankees (AL)	4-0	PIT Pirates (NL)	1955	BKN Dodgers (NL)	4-3	NY Yankees (AL)
1928	NY Yankees (AL)	4-0	STL Cardinals (NL)	1956	NY Yankees (AL)	4-3	BKN Dodgers (NL)
1929	PHI Athletics (AL)	4-1	CHI Cubs (NL)	1957	MIL Braves (NL)	4-3	NY Yankees (AL)
1930	PHI Athletics (AL)	4-2	STL Cardinals (NL)	1958	NY Yankees (AL)	4-3	MIL Braves (NL)

YEAR	WINNER	SERIES	LOSER
1959	LA Dodgers (NL)	4-2	CHI White Sox (AL)
1960	PIT Pirates (NL)	4-3	NY Yankees (AL)
1961	NY Yankees (AL)	4-1	CIN Reds (NL)
1962	NY Yankees (AL)	4-3	SF Giants (NL)
1963	LA Dodgers (NL)	4-0	NY Yankees (AL)
1964	STL Cardinals (NL)	4-3	NY Yankees (AL)
1965	LA Dodgers (NL)	4-3	MIN Twins (AL)
1966	BAL Orioles (AL)	4-0	LA Dodgers (NL)
1967	STL Cardinals (NL)	4-3	BOS Red Sox (AL)
1968	DET Tigers (AL)	4-3	STL Cardinals (NL)
1969	NY Mets (NL)	4-1	BAL Orioles (AL)
1970	BAL Orioles (AL)	4-1	CIN Reds (NL)
1971	PIT Pirates (NL)	4-3	BAL Orioles (AL)
1972	OAK Athletics (AL)	4-3	CIN Reds (NL)
1973	OAK Athletics (AL)	4-3	NY Mets (NL)
1974	OAK Athletics (AL)	4-1	LA Dodgers (NL)
1975	CIN Reds (NL)	4-3	BOS Red Sox (AL)
1976	CIN Reds (NL)	4-0	NY Yankees (AL)
1977	NY Yankees (AL)	4-2	LA Dodgers (NL)
1978	NY Yankees (AL)	4-2	LA Dodgers (NL)
1979	PIT Pirates (NL)	4-3	BAL Orioles (AL)
1980	PHI Phillies (NL)	4-2	KC Royals (AL)
1981	LA Dodgers (NL)	4-2	NY Yankees (AL)
1982	STL Cardinals (NL)	4-3	MIL Brewers (AL)
1983	BAL Orioles (AL)	4-1	PHI Phillies (NL)
1984	DET Tigers (AL)	4-1	SD Padres (NL)
1985	KC Royals (AL)	4-3	STL Cardinals (NL)
1986	NY Mets (NL)	4-3	BOS Red Sox (AL)
1987	MIN Twins (AL)	4-3	STL Cardinals (NL)
1988	LA Dodgers (NL)	4-1	OAK Athletics (AL)
1989	OAK Athletics (AL)	4-0	SF Giants (NL)
1990	CIN Reds (NL)	4-0	OAK Athletics (AL)
1991	MIN Twins (AL)	4-3	ATL Braves (NL)
1992	TOR Blue Jays (AL)	4-2	ATL Braves (NL)
1993	TOR Blue Jays (AL)	4-2	PHI Phillies (NL)
1994	NO SERIES		

LEAGUE CHAMPIONSHIP SERIES 1969-1994

NLCS

YEAR	WINNER	SERIES	LOSER
1969	NY Mets (E)	3-0	ATL Braves (W)
1970	CIN Reds (W)	3-0	PIT Pirates (E)
1971	PIT Pirates (E)	3-1	SF Giants (W)
1972	CIN Reds (W)	3-2	PIT Pirates (E)
1973	NY Mets (E)	3-2	CIN Reds (W)
1974	LA Dodgers (W)	3-1	PIT Pirates (E)
1975	CIN Reds (W)	3-0	PIT Pirates (E)
1976	CIN Reds (W)	3-0	PHI Phillies (E)
1977	LA Dodgers (W)	3-1	PHI Phillies (E)
1978	LA Dodgers (W)	3-1	PHI Phillies (E)
1979	PIT Pirates (W)	3-1	CIN Reds (W)
1980	PHI Phillies (E)	3-2	HOU Astros (W)
1981	NL EAST PLAYOFF		
	MON Expos	3-2	PHI Phillies
	NL WEST PLAYOFF		
	LA Dodgers	3-2	HOU Astros
	LCS		
	LA Dodgers (W)	3-2	MON Expos (E)
1982	STL Cardinals (E)	3-0	ATL Braves (W)
1983	PHI Phillies (E)	3-1	LA Dodgers (W)
1984	SD Padres (W)	3-2	CHI Cubs (E)
1985	STL Cardinals (E)	4-2	LA Dodgers (W)
1986	NY Mets (E)	4-2	HOU Astros (W)
1987	STL Cardinals (E)	4-3	SF Giants (W)
1988	LA Dodgers (W)	4-3	NY Mets (E)
1989	SF Giants (W)	4-1	CHI Cubs (E)
1990	CIN Reds (W)	4-2	PIT Pirates (E)
1991	ATL Braves (W)	4-3	PIT Pirates (E)
1992	ATL Braves (W)	4-3	PIT Pirates (E)
1993	PHI Phillies (E)	4-2	ATL Braves (W)
1994	NO SERIES		

ALCS

YEAR	WINNER	SERIES	LOSER
1969	BAL Orioles (E)	3-0	MIN Twins (W)
1970	BAL Orioles (E)	3-0	MIN Twins (W)
1971	BAL Orioles (E)	3-0	OAK Athletics (W)
1972	OAK Athletics (W)	3-2	DET Tigers (E)
1973	OAK Athletics (W)	3-2	BAL Orioles (E)
1974	OAK Athletics (W)	3-1	BAL Orioles (E)
1975	BOS Red Sox (E)	3-0	OAK Athletics (W)
1976	NY Yankees (E)	3-2	KC Royals (W)
1977	NY Yankees (E)	3-2	KC Royals (W)
1978	NY Yankees (E)	3-1	KC Royals (W)
1979	BAL Orioles (E)	3-1	CAL Angels (W)
1980	KC Royals (W)	3-0	NY Yankees (E)
1981	AL EAST PLAYOFF		
	NY Yankees	3-2	MIL Brewers
	AL WEST PLAYOFF		
	OAK Athletics	3-0	KC Royals
	LCS		
	NY Yankees (E)	3-0	OAK Athletics (W)
1982	MIL Brewers (E)	3-2	CAL Angels (W)
1983	BAL Orioles (E)	3-1	CHI White Sox (W)
1984	DET Tigers (E)	3-0	KC Royals (W)
1985	KC Royals (W)	4-3	TOR Blue Jays (E)
1986	BOS Red Sox (E)	4-3	CAL Angels (W)
1987	MIN Twins (W)	4-1	DET Tigers (E)
1988	OAK Athletics (W)	4-0	BOS Red Sox (E)
1989	OAK Athletics (W)	4-1	TOR Blue Jays (E)
1990	OAK Athletics (W)	4-0	BOS Red Sox (E)
1991	MIN Twins (W)	4-2	TOR Blue Jays (E)
1992	TOR Blue Jays (E)	4-2	OAK Athletics (W)
1993	TOR Blue Jays (E)	4-2	CHI White Sox (W)
1994	NO SERIES		

Yearly Team and Individual Leaders

In this section, you will find how each National League and American League organization did in each season since 1900. Included also are each league's individual leaders in batting and pitching for each year.

Above the team names is a standard won-lost line. The abbreviations are: **W** = wins; **L** = losses; **PCT** = winning percentage; **GB** = games the team finished behind the league winner or the division winner; **R** = runs scored by the team; **OR** = runs scored by the team's opponents; **BA** = team batting average; **FA** = team fielding average; **ERA** = team earned run average. The league's total runs, opponents runs, batting average, fielding average, and earned run average are shown totaled below the columns. The team that won the World Series received a star (★), the team that won the LCS but not the fall classic received a bullet (●).

The year's individual leaders in each league follow, beginning with hitters' categories—batting average, hits, doubles, triples, home runs, runs batted in, slugging average, stolen bases, and runs scored. Pitchers' categories follow—wins, winning percentage, earned run average, strikeouts, saves, complete games, shutouts, games pitched, and innings pitched. Most of these categories will have the top three leaders in the league. When two or more players tied for a position, it is indicated. If there are two who were far and away the leaders in any one category, and many who either tied or were among the ordinary, only two players are listed. There have been many agreed-upon changes in the leaders among baseball researchers, however, and this publication tries to reflect changes if there is verification. Several changes occur because wins or saves were credited to the wrong pitcher, or at bats were credited to the wrong batter. Some occurred, however, because of changes to minimum requirements necessary for consideration, and this publication was updated to reflect those changes.

1900 NL

	W	L	PCT	GB	R	OR	BA	FA	ERA
BROOKLYN	82	54	.603	—	816	722	.293	.948	3.89
PITTSBURGH	79	60	.568	4.5	733	612	.272	.945	3.06
PHILADELPHIA	75	63	.543	8	810	791	.290	.945	4.12
BOSTON	66	72	.478	17	778	739	.283	.953	3.72
CHICAGO	65	75	.464	19	635	751	.260	.933	3.23
ST. LOUIS	65	75	.464	19	743	747	.291	.943	3.75
CINCINNATI	62	77	.446	21.5	702	745	.266	.945	3.83
NEW YORK	60	78	.435	23	713	823	.279	.928	3.96
					5930	5930	.279	.942	3.69

BATTING AVERAGE
Honus Wagner PIT..... .381
Elmer Flick PHI .... .367
Jesse Burkett STL ...... .363

HITS
W. Keeler BKN............ 204
Jesse Burkett STL 203
Honus Wagner PIT 201

DOUBLES
Honus Wagner PIT 45
Nap Lajoie PHI.............. 33
two tied at 32

TRIPLES
Honus Wagner PIT 22
P. Hickman NY 17
Joe Kelley BKN............. 17

HOME RUNS
Herman Long BOS 12
Elmer Flick PHI 11
Mike Donlin STL 10

RUNS BATTED IN
Elmer Flick PHI 110
Ed Delahanty PHI 109
Honus Wagner PIT 100

SLUGGING AVERAGE
Honus Wagner PIT .... .573
Elmer Flick PHI .... .545
Nap Lajoie PHI............ .510

STOLEN BASES
Patsy Donovan STL...... 45
Van Haltren NY 45
Jimmy Barrett CIN 44

RUNS SCORED
Roy Thomas PHI 134
Jimmy Slagle PHI 115
two tied at 114

WINS
Joe McGinnity BKN...... 29
four tied at..................... 20

WINNING PERCENTAGE
Jesse Tannehill PIT .... .769
Joe McGinnity BKN..... .763
Chick Fraser PHI .... .615

EARNED RUN AVERAGE
Rube Waddell PIT...... 2.37
Ned Garvin CHI 2.41
Jack Taylor CHI 2.55

STRIKEOUTS
Rube Waddell PIT....... 130
Noodles Hahn CIN...... 127
Cy Young STL 115

SAVES
Frank Kitson BKN 4
Bill Bernhard PHI............ 2
five tied at 1

COMPLETE GAMES
Pink Hawley NY 34
Bill Dinneen BOS.......... 33
four tied at..................... 32

SHUTOUTS
four tied at....................... 4

GAMES PITCHED
Bill Carrick NY.............. 45
Joe McGinnity BKN....... 44
Ed Scott CIN 43

INNINGS PITCHED
Joe McGinnity BKN..... 347
Bill Carrick NY............. 342
Pink Hawley NY 329

1901 AL

	W	L	PCT	GB	R	OR	BA	FA	ERA
CHICAGO	83	53	.610	—	819	631	.276	.941	2.98
BOSTON	79	57	.581	4	759	608	.279	.943	3.04
DETROIT	74	61	.548	8.5	741	694	.279	.930	3.30
PHILADELPHIA	74	62	.544	9	805	761	.288	.942	4.00
BALTIMORE	68	65	.511	13.5	760	750	.294	.926	3.73
WASHINGTON	61	73	.455	21	678	767	.269	.943	4.09
CLEVELAND	55	82	.401	28.5	663	827	.271	.942	4.12
MILWAUKEE	48	89	.350	35.5	641	828	.261	.934	4.06
					5866	5866	.277	.938	3.66

BATTING AVERAGE
Nap Lajoie PHI............ .422
Mike Donlin BAL .... .347
Buck Freeman BOS... .345

HITS
Nap Lajoie PHI............ 229
John Anderson MIL..... 190
Jimmy Collins BOS 187

DOUBLES
Nap Lajoie PHI............ 48
John Anderson MIL..... 46
Jimmy Collins BOS 42

TRIPLES
Jimmy Williams BAL 21
Bill Keister BAL 21
Sam Mertes CHI 17

HOME RUNS
Nap Lajoie PHI............ 13
Buck Freeman BOS...... 12
Mike Grady WAS 9

RUNS BATTED IN
Nap Lajoie PHI............ 125
Buck Freeman BOS.... 114
John Anderson MIL....... 99

SLUGGING AVERAGE
Nap Lajoie PHI............ .635
Buck Freeman BOS... .527
Socks Seybold PHI .... .499

STOLEN BASES
Frank Isbell CHI 52
Sam Mertes CHI 46
two tied at 38

RUNS SCORED
Nap Lajoie PHI............ 145
Fielder Jones CHI 120
Jimmy Williams BAL ... 113

WINS
Cy Young BOS 33
Joe McGinnity BAL 26
Clark Griffith CHI............ 24

WINNING PERCENTAGE
Clark Griffith CHI......... .774
Cy Young BOS .... .767
Nixie Callahan CHI .... .652

EARNED RUN AVERAGE
Cy Young BOS 1.62
Nixie Callahan CHI 2.42
Joe Yeager DET 2.61

STRIKEOUTS
Cy Young BOS 158
Roy Patterson CHI...... 127
P. Dowling MIL, CLE... 124

SAVES
Bill Hoffer CLE 3
Ned Garvin MIL................ 2

COMPLETE GAMES
Joe McGinnity BAL 39
Cy Young BOS 38
three tied at................... 35

SHUTOUTS
Clark Griffith CHI............. 5
Cy Young BOS 5
three tied at..................... 4

GAMES PITCHED
Joe McGinnity BAL 48
P. Dowling MIL, CLE.... 43
Cy Young BOS 43

INNINGS PITCHED
Joe McGinnity BAL 382
Cy Young BOS 371
Roscoe Miller DET...... 332

1901 NL

	W	L	PCT	GB	R	OR	BA	FA	ERA
PITTSBURGH	90	49	.647	—	776	534	.286	.950	2.58
PHILADELPHIA	83	57	.593	7.5	668	543	.267	.954	2.87
BROOKLYN	79	57	.581	9.5	744	600	.288	.950	3.14
ST. LOUIS	76	64	.543	14.5	792	689	.285	.949	3.68
BOSTON	69	69	.500	20.5	531	556	.250	.952	2.90
CHICAGO	53	86	.381	37	578	699	.258	.943	3.33
NEW YORK	52	85	.380	37	544	755	.255	.941	3.87
CINCINNATI	52	87	.374	38	561	818	.251	.940	4.17
					5194	5194	.268	.947	3.32

BATTING AVERAGE
Jesse Burkett STL ..... .382
Ed Delahanty PHI ...... .357
W. Keeler BKN............ .355

HITS
Jesse Burkett STL 228
W. Keeler BKN............. 209
J. Sheckard BKN 197

DOUBLES
Jake Beckley CIN 39
Ed Delahanty PHI 39
Tom Daly BKN 38

TRIPLES
Jimmy Sheckard BKN... 19
three tied at.................... 17

HOME RUNS
Sam Crawford CIN........ 16
Jimmy Sheckard BKN... 11
Jesse Burkett STL 10

RUNS BATTED IN
Honus Wagner PIT 126
Ed Delahanty PHI 108
two tied at 104

SLUGGING AVERAGE
J. Sheckard BKN .... .536
Ed Delahanty PHI ...... .533
Sam Crawford CIN..... .528

STOLEN BASES
Honus Wagner PIT 49
Topsy Hartsel CHI 41
Sammy Strang NY 40

RUNS SCORED
Jesse Burkett STL 139
W. Keeler BKN............. 123
G. Beaumont PIT........ 120

WINS
B. Donovan BKN........... 25
Jack Harper STL........... 23
two tied at 22

WINNING PERCENTAGE
Jack Chesbro PIT ...... .677
D. Phillippe PIT .... .647
Jesse Tannehill........... .643

EARNED RUN AVERAGE
Jesse Tannehill PIT ... 2.18
D. Phillippe PIT 2.22
Al Orth PHI.................. 2.27

STRIKEOUTS
Noodles Hahn CIN...... 239
B. Donovan BKN.......... 226
T. Hughes CHI 225

SAVES
Jack Powell STL 3
three tied at..................... 2

COMPLETE GAMES
Noodles Hahn CIN........ 41
Dummy Taylor NY 37
two tied at 36

SHUTOUTS
Vic Willis BOS................. 6
Jack Chesbro PIT 6
Al Orth PHI..................... 6

GAMES PITCHED
B. Donovan BKN........... 45
Jack Powell STL 45
Dummy Taylor NY 45

INNINGS PITCHED
Noodles Hahn CIN...... 375
Dummy Taylor NY 353
B. Donovan BKN.......... 351

1902 AL

	W	L	PCT	GB	R	OR	BA	FA	ERA
PHILADELPHIA	83	53	.610	—	775	636	.287	.953	3.29
ST. LOUIS	78	58	.574	5	619	607	.265	.953	3.34
BOSTON	77	60	.562	6.5	664	600	.278	.955	3.02
CHICAGO	74	60	.552	8	675	602	.268	.955	3.41
CLEVELAND	69	67	.507	14	686	667	.289	.950	3.28
WASHINGTON	61	75	.449	22	707	790	.283	.945	4.36
DETROIT	52	83	.385	30.5	566	657	.251	.943	3.56
BALTIMORE	50	88	.362	34	715	848	.277	.938	4.33
					5407	5407	.275	.949	3.57

BATTING AVERAGE
Ed Delahanty WAS .... .376
N. Lajoie PHI, CLE..... .366
Hickman BOS, CLE ... .363

HITS
Hickman BOS, CLE 194
Lave Cross PHI........... 191
Bill Bradley CLE.......... 187

DOUBLES
Ed Delahanty WAS....... 43
Harry Davis PHI 43
two tied at 39

TRIPLES
Jimmy Williams BAL 21
Buck Freeman BOS...... 19
two tied at 14

HOME RUNS
Socks Seybold PHI 16
three tied at................... 11

RUNS BATTED IN
Buck Freeman BOS.... 121
Hickman BOS, CLE 110
Lave Cross PHI........... 108

SLUGGING AVERAGE
Ed Delahanty WAS .... .590
N. Lajoie PHI, CLE..... .551
Hickman BOS, CLE ... .541

STOLEN BASES
Topsy Hartsel PHI......... 47
Sam Mertes CHI 46
Dave Fultz PHI.............. 44

RUNS SCORED
Topsy Hartsel PHI....... 109
Dave Fultz PHI........... 109
Sammy Strang CHI..... 108

WINS
Cy Young BOS 32
Rube Waddell PHI 24
two tied at 22

WINNING PERCENTAGE
B. Bernhard PHI, CLE.. .783
Rube Waddell PHI ...... .774
Cy Young BOS .... .744

EARNED RUN AVERAGE
Ed Siever DET 1.91
Rube Waddell PHI 2.05
Bernhard PHI, CLE 2.15

STRIKEOUTS
Rube Waddell PHI 210
Cy Young BOS 160
Jack Powell STL 137

SAVES
Jack Powell STL 2

COMPLETE GAMES
Cy Young BOS 41
Bill Dinneen BOS.......... 39
two tied at 36

SHUTOUTS
Addie Joss CLE 5
three tied at...................... 4

GAMES PITCHED
Cy Young BOS 45
Jack Powell STL 42
Bill Dinneen BOS.......... 42

INNINGS PITCHED
Cy Young BOS 385
Bill Dinneen BOS........ 371
Jack Powell STL 328

1902 NL

	W	L	PCT	GB	R	OR	BA	FA	ERA
PITTSBURGH	103	36	.741	—	775	440	.287	.958	2.30
BROOKLYN	75	63	.543	27.5	564	519	.257	.952	2.69
BOSTON	73	64	.533	29	572	516	.250	.959	2.61
CINCINNATI	70	70	.500	33.5	633	566	.282	.945	2.67
CHICAGO	68	69	.496	34	530	501	.251	.946	2.21
ST. LOUIS	56	78	.418	44.5	517	695	.258	.944	3.47
PHILADELPHIA	56	81	.409	46	484	649	.247	.946	3.50
NEW YORK	48	88	.353	53.5	401	590	.238	.943	2.82
					4476	4476	.259	.949	2.78

BATTING AVERAGE
G. Beaumont PIT .... .357
W. Keeler BKN .... .338
Sam Crawford CIN ..... .333

HITS
G. Beaumont PIT 194
W. Keeler BKN 188
Sam Crawford CIN 185

DOUBLES
Honus Wagner PIT 33
Fred Clarke PIT 27
Duff Cooley BOS 26

TRIPLES
Sam Crawford CIN 23
Tommy Leach PIT 22
Honus Wagner PIT 16

HOME RUNS
Tommy Leach PIT 6
Jake Beckley CIN 5
two tied at 4

RUNS BATTED IN
Honus Wagner PIT 91
Tommy Leach PIT 85
Sam Crawford CIN 78

SLUGGING AVERAGE
Honus Wagner PIT .... .467
Sam Crawford CIN ..... .461
Fred Clarke PIT .... .453

STOLEN BASES
Honus Wagner PIT 42
Jimmy Slagle CHI 40
Patsy Donovan STL 34

RUNS SCORED
Honus Wagner PIT 105
Fred Clarke PIT 104
G. Beaumont PIT 100

WINS
Jack Chesbro PIT 28
Togie Pittinger BOS 27
Vic Willis BOS 27

WINNING PERCENTAGE
Jack Chesbro PIT ...... .824
Ed Doheny PIT .... .800
Jesse Tannehill PIT ... .769

EARNED RUN AVERAGE
Jack Taylor CHI 1.33
Noodles Hahn CIN 1.77
Jesse Tannehill PIT ... 1.95

STRIKEOUTS
Vic Willis BOS 225
Doc White PHI 185
Togie Pittinger BOS ... 174

SAVES
Vic Willis BOS 3
Sam Leever PIT 2
nine tied at 1

COMPLETE GAMES
Vic Willis BOS 45
Togie Pittinger BOS 36
Noodles Hahn CIN 35

SHUTOUTS
Christy Mathewson NY ... 8
Jack Chesbro PIT 8
Jack Taylor CHI 8

GAMES PITCHED
Vic Willis BOS 51
Togie Pittinger BOS 46
Stan Yerkes STL 39

INNINGS PITCHED
Vic Willis BOS 410
Togie Pittinger BOS 389
Jack Taylor CHI 325

1903 AL

	W	L	PCT	GB	R	OR	BA	FA	ERA
★BOSTON	91	47	.659	—	708	504	.272	.959	2.57
PHILADELPHIA	75	60	.556	14.5	597	519	.264	.960	2.97
CLEVELAND	77	63	.550	15	639	579	.270	.946	2.66
NEW YORK	72	62	.537	17	579	573	.250	.953	3.08
DETROIT	65	71	.478	25	567	539	.268	.950	2.75
ST. LOUIS	65	74	.468	26.5	500	525	.242	.953	2.77
CHICAGO	60	77	.438	30.5	516	613	.247	.949	3.02
WASHINGTON	43	94	.314	47.5	437	691	.231	.954	3.82
					4543	4543	.256	.953	2.95

BATTING AVERAGE
Nap Lajoie CLE.......... .355
Sam Crawford DET.... .335
P. Dougherty BOS ..... .331

HITS
P. Dougherty BOS 195
Sam Crawford DET.... 184
Nap Lajoie CLE........... 173

DOUBLES
Socks Seybold PHI 45
Nap Lajoie CLE............. 40
Buck Freeman BOS....... 39

TRIPLES
Sam Crawford DET....... 25
Bill Bradley CLE............ 22
Buck Freeman BOS...... 20

HOME RUNS
Buck Freeman BOS...... 13
C. Hickman CLE 12
Hobe Ferris BOS 9

RUNS BATTED IN
Buck Freeman BOS.... 104
C. Hickman CLE 97
Nap Lajoie CLE............. 93

SLUGGING AVERAGE
Nap Lajoie CLE.......... .533
C. Hickman CLE .... .502
Buck Freeman BOS.... .496

STOLEN BASES
Harry Bay CLE.............. 45
Ollie Pickering PHI........ 40
two tied at 35

RUNS SCORED
P. Dougherty BOS 108
Bill Bradley CLE.......... 103
two tied at 95

WINS
Cy Young BOS 28
Eddie Plank PHI............ 23
four tied at..................... 21

WINNING PERCENTAGE
Cy Young BOS .... .757
Tom Hughes BOS...... .741
Earl Moore CLE .... .679

EARNED RUN AVERAGE
Earl Moore CLE 1.77
Cy Young BOS 2.08
Bill Bernhard CLE 2.12

STRIKEOUTS
Rube Waddell PHI 302
Bill Donovan DET 187
two tied at 176

SAVES
five tied at 2

COMPLETE GAMES
Bill Donovan DET 34
Cy Young BOS 34
Rube Waddell PHI 34

SHUTOUTS
Cy Young BOS 7
Bill Dinneen BOS............ 6
George Mullin DET 6

GAMES PITCHED
Eddie Plank PHI............ 43
George Mullin DET 41
three tied at................... 40

INNINGS PITCHED
Cy Young BOS 342
Eddie Plank PHI........... 336
Jack Chesbro NY........ 325

1903 NL

	W	L	PCT	GB	R	OR	BA	FA	ERA
PITTSBURGH	91	49	.650	—	793	613	.287	.951	2.91
NEW YORK	84	55	.604	6.5	729	567	.272	.951	2.95
CHICAGO	82	56	.594	8	695	599	.275	.942	2.77
CINCINNATI	74	65	.532	16.5	765	656	.288	.946	3.07
BROOKLYN	70	66	.515	19	667	682	.265	.951	3.44
BOSTON	58	80	.420	32	578	699	.245	.937	3.34
PHILADELPHIA	49	86	.363	39.5	617	738	.268	.947	3.97
ST. LOUIS	43	94	.314	46.5	505	795	.251	.940	3.76
					5349	5349	.269	.946	3.27

BATTING AVERAGE
Honus Wagner PIT .... .355
Fred Clarke PIT .... .351
Mike Donlin CIN .... .351

HITS
G. Beaumont PIT 209
Cy Seymour CIN 191
George Browne NY 185

DOUBLES
Sam Mertes NY 32
Harry Steinfeldt CIN 32
Fred Clarke PIT 32

TRIPLES
Honus Wagner PIT 19
Mike Donlin CIN............ 18
Tommy Leach PIT 17

HOME RUNS
Jimmy Sheckard BKN..... 9
six tied at.......................... 7

RUNS BATTED IN
Sam Mertes NY 104
Honus Wagner PIT 101
Jack Doyle BKN............ 91

SLUGGING AVERAGE
Fred Clarke PIT .... .532
Honus Wagner PIT .... .518
Mike Donlin CIN.......... .516

STOLEN BASES
Jimmy Sheckard BKN... 67
Frank Chance CHI........ 67
two tied at 46

RUNS SCORED
G. Beaumont PIT........ 137
Mike Donlin CIN.......... 110
George Browne NY...... 105

WINS
Joe McGinnity NY 31
C. Mathewson NY 30
Sam Leever PIT............. 25

WINNING PERCENTAGE
Sam Leever PIT.......... .781
D. Phillippe PIT .... .774
Jake Weimer CHI........ .700

EARNED RUN AVERAGE
Sam Leever PIT......... 2.06
C. Mathewson NY 2.26
Jake Weimer CHI....... 2.30

STRIKEOUTS
C. Mathewson NY....... 267
Joe McGinnity NY 171
Ned Garvin BKN 154

SAVES
Carl Lundgren CHI.......... 3
Roscoe Miller NY 3
six tied at.......................... 2

COMPLETE GAMES
Joe McGinnity NY 44
C. Mathewson NY......... 37
Togie Pittinger BOS 35

SHUTOUTS
Sam Leever PIT............... 7
Henry Schmidt BKN........ 5
Noodles Hahn CIN.......... 5

GAMES PITCHED
Joe McGinnity NY 55
C. Mathewson NY......... 45
Togie Pittinger BOS 44

INNINGS PITCHED
Joe McGinnity NY 434
C. Mathewson NY 366
Togie Pittinger BOS 352

1904 AL

	W	L	PCT	GB	R	OR	BA	FA	ERA
BOSTON	95	59	.617	—	608	466	.247	.962	2.12
NEW YORK	92	59	.609	1.5	598	526	.259	.958	2.57
CHICAGO	89	65	.578	6	600	482	.242	.964	2.30
CLEVELAND	86	65	.570	7.5	647	482	.262	.959	2.22
PHILADELPHIA	81	70	.536	12.5	557	503	.249	.959	2.35
ST. LOUIS	65	87	.428	29	481	604	.239	.960	2.83
DETROIT	62	90	.408	32	505	627	.231	.959	2.77
WASHINGTON	38	113	.252	55.5	437	743	.227	.951	3.62
					4433	4433	.245	.959	2.60

BATTING AVERAGE
Nap Lajoie CLE.......... .381
W. Keeler NY .... .343
Harry Davis PHI .... .309

HITS
Nap Lajoie CLE............ 211
W. Keeler NY 186
Bill Bradley CLE........... 182

DOUBLES
Nap Lajoie CLE............. 50
Jimmy Collins BOS 33
four tied at...................... 31

TRIPLES
Joe Cassidy WAS 19
Buck Freeman BOS...... 19
Chick Stahl BOS 19

HOME RUNS
Harry Davis PHI 10
Buck Freeman BOS....... 7
Danny Murphy PHI 7

RUNS BATTED IN
Nap Lajoie CLE............ 102
Buck Freeman BOS...... 84
Bill Bradley CLE............ 83

SLUGGING AVERAGE
Nap Lajoie CLE.......... .554
Harry Davis PHI .... .490
Elmer Flick CLE .... .453

STOLEN BASES
Elmer Flick CLE............. 42
Harry Bay CLE 38
Emmet Heidrick STL..... 35

RUNS SCORED
Dougherty BOS, NY.....113
Elmer Flick CLE............. 97
Bill Bradley CLE............. 94

WINS
Jack Chesbro NY 41
Eddie Plank PHI............. 26
Cy Young BOS 26

WINNING PERCENTAGE
Jack Chesbro NY .... .774
J. Tannehill BOS......... .656
Frank Smith CHI .... .640

EARNED RUN AVERAGE
Addie Joss CLE 1.59
Rube Waddell PHI 1.62
Otto Hess CLE............ 1.67

STRIKEOUTS
Rube Waddell PHI 349
Jack Chesbro NY 239
Jack Powell NY 202

SAVES
Casey Patten WAS 3
eight tied at 1

COMPLETE GAMES
Jack Chesbro NY 48
George Mullin DET 42
Cy Young BOS 40

SHUTOUTS
Cy Young BOS 10
Rube Waddell PHI 8
three tied at...................... 7

GAMES PITCHED
Jack Chesbro NY 55
Jack Powell NY 47
Rube Waddell PHI 46

INNINGS PITCHED
Jack Chesbro NY........ 455
Jack Powell NY 390
Rube Waddell PHI 383

1904 NL

	W	L	PCT	GB	R	OR	BA	FA	ERA
NEW YORK	106	47	.693	—	744	476	.262	.956	2.17
CHICAGO	93	60	.608	13	599	517	.248	.954	2.30
CINCINNATI	88	65	.575	18	695	547	.255	.954	2.35
PITTSBURGH	87	66	.569	19	675	592	.258	.955	2.89
ST. LOUIS	75	79	.487	31.5	602	595	.253	.952	2.64
BROOKLYN	56	97	.366	50	497	614	.232	.945	2.70
BOSTON	55	98	.359	51	491	749	.237	.946	3.43
PHILADELPHIA	52	100	.342	53.5	571	784	.248	.937	3.39
					4874	4874	.249	.950	2.73

BATTING AVERAGE
Honus Wagner PIT .... .349
M. Donlin CIN, NY ..... .329
Jake Beckley STL .... .325

HITS
G. Beaumont PIT 185
Jake Beckley STL 179
Honus Wagner PIT 171

DOUBLES
Honus Wagner PIT 44
Sam Mertes NY 28
Joe Delahanty BOS 27

TRIPLES
Harry Lumley BKN 18
Honus Wagner PIT 14
three tied at 13

HOME RUNS
Harry Lumley BKN 9
Dave Brain STL 7
four tied at 6

RUNS BATTED IN
Bill Dahlen NY 80
Sam Mertes NY 78
Harry Lumley BKN 78

SLUGGING AVERAGE
Honus Wagner PIT .... .520
Mike Grady STL .... .474
M. Donlin CIN, NY ..... .457

STOLEN BASES
Honus Wagner PIT 53
Bill Dahlen NY 47
Sam Mertes NY 47

RUNS SCORED
George Browne NY 99
Honus Wagner PIT 97
Ginger Beaumont PIT ... 97

WINS
Joe McGinnity NY 35
C. Mathewson NY 33
Jack Harper CIN 23

WINNING PERCENTAGE
Joe McGinnity NY ...... .814
C. Mathewson NY ...... .733
Jack Harper CIN .... .719

EARNED RUN AVERAGE
Joe McGinnity NY 1.61
Ned Garvin BKN 1.68
T. Brown CHI 1.86

STRIKEOUTS
C. Mathewson NY 212
Vic Willis BOS 196
Jake Weimer CHI 177

SAVES
Joe McGinnity NY 5
Red Ames NY 3
Hooks Wiltse NY 3

COMPLETE GAMES
Jack Taylor STL 39
Vic Willis BOS 39
two tied at 38

SHUTOUTS
Joe McGinnity NY 9
Jack Harper CIN 6
two tied at 5

GAMES PITCHED
Joe McGinnity NY 51
C. Mathewson NY 48
Oscar Jones BKN 46

INNINGS PITCHED
Joe McGinnity NY 408
Oscar Jones BKN 377
C. Mathewson NY 368

1905 AL

	W	L	PCT	GB	R	OR	BA	FA	ERA
PHILADELPHIA	92	56	.622	—	623	492	.255	.958	2.19
CHICAGO	92	60	.605	2	612	451	.237	.968	1.99
DETROIT	79	74	.516	15.5	512	602	.243	.957	2.83
BOSTON	78	74	.513	16	579	564	.234	.953	2.84
CLEVELAND	76	78	.494	19	567	587	.255	.963	2.85
NEW YORK	71	78	.477	21.5	586	622	.248	.952	2.93
WASHINGTON	64	87	.424	29.5	559	623	.223	.951	2.87
ST. LOUIS	54	99	.353	40.5	511	608	.232	.955	2.74
					4549	4549	.241	.957	2.65

BATTING AVERAGE
Elmer Flick CLE .... .306
W. Keeler NY .... .302
Harry Bay CLE .... .298

HITS
George Stone STL 187
Sam Crawford DET 171
Harry Davis PHI 171

DOUBLES
Harry Davis PHI 47
Sam Crawford DET 40
two tied at 37

TRIPLES
Elmer Flick CLE 19
Hobe Ferris BOS 16
Terry Turner CLE 14

HOME RUNS
Harry Davis PHI 8
George Stone STL........... 7
four tied at 6

RUNS BATTED IN
Harry Davis PHI 83
Lave Cross PHI............. 77
Jiggs Donahue CHI....... 76

SLUGGING AVERAGE
Elmer Flick CLE .... .466
Frank Isbell CHI .... .440
Sam Crawford DET .... .433

STOLEN BASES
Danny Hoffman PHI...... 46
Dave Fultz NY 44
Jake Stahl WAS............ 41

RUNS SCORED
Harry Davis PHI 92
Fielder Jones CHI 91
Harry Bay CLE.............. 90

WINS
Rube Waddell PHI 26
Eddie Plank PHI............ 25
Ed Killian DET.............. 23

WINNING PERCENTAGE
Andy Coakley PHI........ .741
J. Tannehill BOS.......... .710
Rube Waddell PHI .... .703

EARNED RUN AVERAGE
Rube Waddell PHI 1.48
Doc White CHI 1.76
Cy Young BOS 1.82

STRIKEOUTS
Rube Waddell PHI 287
Eddie Plank PHI.......... 210
Cy Young BOS 210

SAVES
Jim Buchanan STL 2
Bill Wolfe WAS................ 2

COMPLETE GAMES
Eddie Plank PHI........... 36
Harry Howell STL.......... 35
George Mullin DET 35

SHUTOUTS
Ed Killian DET................. 8
Rube Waddell PHI 7
two tied at 6

GAMES PITCHED
Rube Waddell PHI 46
George Mullin DET 44
two tied at 42

INNINGS PITCHED
George Mullin DET 348
Eddie Plank PHI.......... 347
Frank Owen CHI 334

1905 NL

	W	L	PCT	GB	R	OR	BA	FA	ERA
★NEW YORK	105	48	.686	—	778	505	.273	.960	2.39
PITTSBURGH	96	57	.627	9	692	570	.266	.961	2.86
CHICAGO	92	61	.601	13	667	442	.245	.962	2.04
PHILADELPHIA	83	69	.546	21.5	708	602	.260	.957	2.81
CINCINNATI	79	74	.516	26	735	698	.269	.953	3.01
ST. LOUIS	58	96	.377	47.5	535	734	.248	.957	3.59
BOSTON	51	103	.331	54.5	468	731	.234	.951	3.52
BROOKLYN	48	104	.316	56.5	506	807	.246	.936	3.76
					5089	5089	.255	.954	2.99

BATTING AVERAGE
Cy Seymour CIN........ .377
Honus Wagner PIT .... .363
Mike Donlin NY .... .356

HITS
Cy Seymour CIN......... 219
Mike Donlin NY 216
Honus Wagner PIT 199

DOUBLES
Cy Seymour CIN............ 40
John Titus PHI 36
Honus Wagner PIT 32

TRIPLES
Cy Seymour CIN........... 21
Sam Mertes NY 17
Sherry Magee PHI 17

HOME RUNS
Fred Odwell CIN 9
Cy Seymour CIN............. 8
three tied at..................... 7

RUNS BATTED IN
Cy Seymour CIN......... 121
Sam Mertes NY 108
Honus Wagner PIT 101

SLUGGING AVERAGE
Cy Seymour CIN......... .559
Honus Wagner PIT .... .505
Mike Donlin NY .... .495

STOLEN BASES
Billy Maloney CHI 59
Art Devlin NY 59
Honus Wagner PIT 57

RUNS SCORED
Mike Donlin NY 124
Roy Thomas PHI 118
Miller Huggins CIN...... 117

WINS
C. Mathewson NY......... 31
Togie Pittinger PHI....... 23
two tied at 22

WINNING PERCENTAGE
C. Mathewson NY...... .795
Sam Leever PIT......... .760
Red Ames NY .... .733

EARNED RUN AVERAGE
C. Mathewson NY 1.27
Ed Reulbach CHI 1.42
Bob Wicker CHI 2.02

STRIKEOUTS
C. Mathewson NY....... 206
Red Ames NY 198
Orval Overall CIN........ 173

SAVES
Claude Elliott NY............. 6
Joe McGinnity NY 3
Hooks Wiltse NY............. 3

COMPLETE GAMES
Irv Young BOS............... 41
Vic Willis BOS 36
Chick Fraser BOS......... 35

SHUTOUTS
C. Mathewson NY 8
Irv Young BOS................. 7
three tied at..................... 5

GAMES PITCHED
Togie Pittinger PHI........ 46
Joe McGinnity NY 46
two tied at 43

INNINGS PITCHED
Irv Young BOS............. 378
Vic Willis BOS 342
C. Mathewson NY....... 339

1906 AL

	W	L	PCT	GB	R	OR	BA	FA	ERA
★CHICAGO	93	58	.616	—	570	460	.230	.963	2.13
NEW YORK	90	61	.596	3	644	543	.266	.957	2.78
CLEVELAND	89	64	.582	5	663	482	.279	.967	2.09
PHILADELPHIA	78	67	.538	12	561	542	.247	.956	2.60
ST. LOUIS	76	73	.510	16	558	498	.247	.954	2.23
DETROIT	71	78	.477	21	518	599	.242	.959	3.06
WASHINGTON	55	95	.367	37.5	518	664	.238	.955	3.25
BOSTON	49	105	.318	45.5	462	706	.239	.949	3.41
					4494	4494	.249	.958	2.69

BATTING AVERAGE
George Stone STL ...... .358
Nap Lajoie CLE .... .355
Hal Chase NY .... .323

HITS
Nap Lajoie CLE 214
George Stone STL 208
Elmer Flick CLE 194

DOUBLES
Nap Lajoie CLE 49
Harry Davis PHI 42
Elmer Flick CLE 34

TRIPLES
Elmer Flick CLE 22
George Stone STL 20
Sam Crawford DET 16

HOME RUNS
Harry Davis PHI 12
C. Hickman WAS 9
George Stone STL 6

RUNS BATTED IN
Harry Davis PHI 96
Nap Lajoie CLE 91
George Davis CHI 80

SLUGGING AVERAGE
George Stone STL ...... .501
Nap Lajoie CLE .... .460
Harry Davis PHI .... .459

STOLEN BASES
Elmer Flick CLE 39
John Anderson WAS 39
two tied at 37

RUNS SCORED
Elmer Flick CLE 98
Topsy Hartsel PHI 96
Wee Willie Keeler NY ... 96

WINS
Al Orth NY 27
Jack Chesbro NY 24
two tied at 22

WINNING PERCENTAGE
Eddie Plank PHI .... .760
Doc White CHI .... .750
Addie Joss CLE .... .700

EARNED RUN AVERAGE
Doc White CHI 1.52
Barney Pelty STL 1.59
Addie Joss CLE 1.72

STRIKEOUTS
Rube Waddell PHI 196
Cy Falkenberg WAS ... 178
Ed Walsh CHI 171

SAVES
Otto Hess CLE 3
Chief Bender PHI 3
seven tied at 2

COMPLETE GAMES
Al Orth NY 36
George Mullin DET 35
Otto Hess CLE 33

SHUTOUTS
Ed Walsh CHI 10
Addie Joss CLE 9
Rube Waddell PHI 8

GAMES PITCHED
Jack Chesbro NY 49
Al Orth NY 45
two tied at 43

INNINGS PITCHED
Al Orth NY 339
Otto Hess CLE 334
George Mullin DET 330

1906 NL

	W	L	PCT	GB	R	OR	BA	FA	ERA
CHICAGO	116	36	.763	—	705	381	.262	.969	1.76
NEW YORK	96	56	.632	20	625	510	.255	.963	2.49
PITTSBURGH	93	60	.608	23.5	623	470	.261	.964	2.21
PHILADELPHIA	71	82	.464	45.5	528	564	.241	.956	2.58
BROOKLYN	66	86	.434	50	496	625	.236	.955	3.13
CINCINNATI	64	87	.424	51.5	533	582	.238	.959	2.69
ST. LOUIS	52	98	.347	63	470	607	.235	.957	3.04
BOSTON	49	102	.325	66.5	408	649	.226	.947	3.17
					4388	4388	.244	.959	2.63

BATTING AVERAGE
Honus Wagner PIT .... .339
Harry Steinfeldt CHI... .327
Harry Lumley BKN ..... .324

HITS
Harry Steinfeldt CHI.... 176
Honus Wagner PIT 175
Seymour CIN, NY 165

DOUBLES
Honus Wagner PIT 38
Sherry Magee PHI 36
Kitty Bransfield PHI....... 28

TRIPLES
Wildfire Schulte CHI...... 13
Fred Clarke PIT 13
two tied at 12

HOME RUNS
Tim Jordan BKN 12
Harry Lumley BKN 9
Cy Seymour CIN, NY...... 8

RUNS BATTED IN
Jim Nealon PIT 83
Harry Steinfeldt CHI...... 83
Cy Seymour CIN, NY.... 80

SLUGGING AVERAGE
Harry Lumley BKN ...... .477
Honus Wagner PIT .... .459
Sammy Strang NY ..... .435

STOLEN BASES
Frank Chance CHI........ 57
Sherry Magee PHI 55
Art Devlin NY 54

RUNS SCORED
Frank Chance CHI 103
Honus Wagner PIT 103
Jimmy Sheckard CHI ... 90

WINS
Joe McGinnity NY 27
T. Brown CHI 26
three tied at................... 22

WINNING PERCENTAGE
Ed Reulbach CHI .... .826
T. Brown CHI .... .813
Sam Leever PIT .... .759

EARNED RUN AVERAGE
T. Brown CHI 1.04
Jack Pfiester CHI 1.56
Ed Reulbach CHI 1.65

STRIKEOUTS
F. Beebe CHI, STL 171
Big Jeff Pfeffer BOS... 158
Red Ames NY 156

SAVES
George Ferguson NY...... 6
Hooks Wiltse NY 5
Elmer Stricklett BKN 5

COMPLETE GAMES
Irv Young BOS.............. 37
Big Jeff Pfeffer BOS...... 33
four tied at...................... 32

SHUTOUTS
T. Brown CHI 10
Lefty Leifield PIT............. 8
Jake Weimer CIN............ 7

GAMES PITCHED
Joe McGinnity NY 45
Irv Young BOS.............. 43
two tied at 42

INNINGS PITCHED
Irv Young BOS............. 358
Joe McGinnity NY 340
Vic Willis PIT............... 322

1907 AL

	W	L	PCT	GB	R	OR	BA	FA	ERA
DETROIT	92	58	.613	—	694	532	.266	.959	2.33
PHILADELPHIA	88	57	.607	1.5	582	511	.255	.958	2.35
CHICAGO	87	64	.576	5.5	588	474	.237	.966	2.22
CLEVELAND	85	67	.559	8	530	525	.241	.960	2.26
NEW YORK	70	78	.473	21	605	665	.249	.947	3.03
ST. LOUIS	69	83	.454	24	542	555	.253	.959	2.61
BOSTON	59	90	.396	32.5	464	558	.234	.959	2.45
WASHINGTON	49	102	.325	43.5	506	691	.243	.952	3.11
					4511	4511	.247	.958	2.54

BATTING AVERAGE
Ty Cobb DET .... .350
Sam Crawford DET.... .323
George Stone STL .... .320

HITS
Ty Cobb DET 212
George Stone STL 191
Sam Crawford DET 188

DOUBLES
Harry Davis PHI 36
Sam Crawford DET 34
two tied at 30

TRIPLES
Elmer Flick CLE 18
Sam Crawford DET 17
Ty Cobb DET 15

HOME RUNS
Harry Davis PHI 8
Socks Seybold PHI 5
Ty Cobb DET 5

RUNS BATTED IN
Ty Cobb DET 116
Socks Seybold PHI 92
Harry Davis PHI 87

SLUGGING AVERAGE
Ty Cobb DET .... .473
Sam Crawford DET.... .460
Elmer Flick CLE .... .412

STOLEN BASES
Ty Cobb DET 49
Wid Conroy NY 41
Elmer Flick CLE 41

RUNS SCORED
Sam Crawford DET 102
Davy Jones DET 101
Ty Cobb DET 97

WINS
Addie Joss CLE 27
Doc White CHI 27
two tied at 25

WINNING PERCENTAGE
Bill Donovan DET ...... .862
Jimmy Dygert PHI ...... .724
Addie Joss CLE .... .711

EARNED RUN AVERAGE
Ed Walsh CHI 1.60
Ed Killian DET............. 1.78
Addie Joss CLE 1.83

STRIKEOUTS
Rube Waddell PHI 232
Ed Walsh CHI 206
Eddie Plank PHI.......... 183

SAVES
Ed Walsh CHI 4
Tom Hughes WAS........... 4
Bill Dinneen BOS, STL ... 4

COMPLETE GAMES
Ed Walsh CHI 37
George Mullin DET 35
Addie Joss CLE 34

SHUTOUTS
Eddie Plank PHI............. 8
Doc White CHI 7
Rube Waddell PHI 7

GAMES PITCHED
Ed Walsh CHI 56
Doc White CHI 46
George Mullin DET 46

INNINGS PITCHED
Ed Walsh CHI 422
George Mullin DET 357
Eddie Plank PHI.......... 344

1907 NL

	W	L	PCT	GB	R	OR	BA	FA	ERA
★CHICAGO	107	45	.704	—	572	390	.250	.967	1.73
PITTSBURGH	91	63	.591	17	634	510	.254	.959	2.30
PHILADELPHIA	83	64	.565	21.5	512	476	.236	.957	2.43
NEW YORK	82	71	.536	25.5	574	510	.251	.963	2.45
BROOKLYN	65	83	.439	40	446	522	.232	.959	2.38
CINCINNATI	66	87	.431	41.5	526	519	.247	.963	2.41
BOSTON	58	90	.392	47	502	652	.243	.961	3.33
ST. LOUIS	52	101	.340	55.5	419	606	.232	.947	2.70
					4185	4185	.243	.959	2.46

BATTING AVERAGE
Honus Wagner PIT ..... .350
Sherry Magee PHI ..... .328
G. Beaumont BOS ..... .322

HITS
G. Beaumont BOS 187
Honus Wagner PIT 180
Tommy Leach PIT 166

DOUBLES
Honus Wagner PIT 38
Sherry Magee PHI 25
two tied at 25

TRIPLES
W. Alperman BKN......... 16
John Ganzel CIN 16
two tied at 14

HOME RUNS
Dave Brain BOS 10
Harry Lumley BKN 9
Red Murray STL 7

RUNS BATTED IN
Sherry Magee PHI 85
Honus Wagner PIT 82
Ed Abbaticchio PIT 82

SLUGGING AVERAGE
Honus Wagner PIT .... .513
Sherry Magee PHI ..... .455
Harry Lumley BKN ..... .425

STOLEN BASES
Honus Wagner PIT....... 61
Johnny Evers CHI......... 46
Sherry Magee PHI 46

RUNS SCORED
Spike Shannon NY 104
Tommy Leach PIT 102
Honus Wagner PIT....... 98

WINS
C. Mathewson NY 24
Orval Overall CHI.......... 23
two tied at 22

WINNING PERCENTAGE
Ed Reulbach CHI .... .810
T. Brown CHI .... .769
Orval Overall CHI....... .742

EARNED RUN AVERAGE
Jack Pfiester CHI 1.15
Carl Lundgren CHI.... 1.17
T. Brown CHI 1.39

STRIKEOUTS
C. Mathewson NY 178
Buck Ewing CIN.......... 147
Red Ames NY 146

SAVES
Joe McGinnity NY 4
T. Brown CHI 3
Orval Overall CHI............ 3

COMPLETE GAMES
Stoney McGlynn STL.... 33
Buck Ewing CIN............ 32
C. Mathewson NY 31

SHUTOUTS
Christy Mathewson NY ... 8
Orval Overall CHI............ 8
Carl Lundgren CHI.......... 7

GAMES PITCHED
Joe McGinnity NY 47
Stoney McGlynn STL.... 45
two tied at 41

INNINGS PITCHED
S. McGlynn STL............ 352
Buck Ewing CIN.......... 333
C. Mathewson NY 316

1908 AL

	W	L	PCT	GB	R	OR	BA	FA	ERA
DETROIT	90	63	.588	—	647	547	.264	.953	2.40
CLEVELAND	90	64	.584	.5	568	457	.239	.962	2.02
CHICAGO	88	64	.579	1.5	537	470	.224	.966	2.22
ST. LOUIS	83	69	.546	6.5	544	483	.245	.964	2.15
BOSTON	75	79	.487	15.5	564	513	.246	.955	2.27
PHILADELPHIA	68	85	.444	22	486	562	.223	.957	2.57
WASHINGTON	67	85	.441	22.5	479	539	.235	.958	2.34
NEW YORK	51	103	.331	39.5	459	713	.236	.947	3.16
					4284	4284	.239	.958	2.39

BATTING AVERAGE
Ty Cobb DET .... .324
Sam Crawford DET.... .311
Doc Gessler BOS .... .308

HITS
Ty Cobb DET 188
Sam Crawford DET..... 184
two tied at 168

DOUBLES
Ty Cobb DET 36
Sam Crawford DET....... 33
C. Rossman DET 33

TRIPLES
Ty Cobb DET 20
Sam Crawford DET....... 16
Jake Stahl BOS, NY 16

HOME RUNS
Sam Crawford DET......... 7
Bill Hinchman CLE.......... 6
three tied at..................... 5

RUNS BATTED IN
Ty Cobb DET 108
Sam Crawford DET....... 80
two tied at 74

SLUGGING AVERAGE
Ty Cobb DET .... .475
Sam Crawford DET.... .457
Doc Gessler BOS .... .423

STOLEN BASES
Patsy Dougherty CHI 47
Charlie Hemphill NY 42
G. Schaefer DET 40

RUNS SCORED
Matty McIntyre DET.... 105
Sam Crawford DET..... 102
G. Schaefer DET 96

WINS
Ed Walsh CHI 40
Addie Joss CLE 24
Ed Summers DET......... 24

WINNING PERCENTAGE
Ed Walsh CHI .... .727
Bill Donovan DET ...... .720
Addie Joss CLE .... .686

EARNED RUN AVERAGE
Addie Joss CLE 1.16
Cy Young BOS 1.26
Ed Walsh CHI 1.42

STRIKEOUTS
Ed Walsh CHI 269
Rube Waddell STL...... 232
Tom Hughes WAS 165

SAVES
Ed Walsh CHI 6
Tom Hughes WAS 4
Rube Waddell STL.......... 3

COMPLETE GAMES
Ed Walsh CHI 42
Cy Young BOS 30
Addie Joss CLE 29

SHUTOUTS
Ed Walsh CHI 11
Addie Joss CLE 9
two tied at 6

GAMES PITCHED
Ed Walsh CHI 66
Rube Vickers PHI 53
Jack Chesbro NY.......... 45

INNINGS PITCHED
Ed Walsh CHI 464
Addie Joss CLE 325
Harry Howell STL........ 324

1908 NL

	W	L	PCT	GB	R	OR	BA	FA	ERA
★CHICAGO	99	55	.643	—	624	461	.249	.969	2.14
NEW YORK	98	56	.636	1	652	456	.267	.962	2.14
PITTSBURGH	98	56	.636	1	585	469	.247	.964	2.12
PHILADELPHIA	83	71	.539	16	504	445	.244	.963	2.10
CINCINNATI	73	81	.474	26	489	544	.227	.959	2.37
BOSTON	63	91	.409	36	537	622	.239	.962	2.79
BROOKLYN	53	101	.344	46	377	516	.213	.961	2.47
ST. LOUIS	49	105	.318	50	371	626	.223	.946	2.64
					4139	4139	.239	.961	2.35

BATTING AVERAGE
Honus Wagner PIT .... .354
Mike Donlin NY .... .334
Larry Doyle NY .... .308

HITS
Honus Wagner PIT 201
Mike Donlin NY 198
two tied at 167

DOUBLES
Honus Wagner PIT 39
Sherry Magee PHI 30
Frank Chance CHI 27

TRIPLES
Honus Wagner PIT 19
Hans Lobert CIN 18
two tied at 16

HOME RUNS
Tim Jordan BKN 12
Honus Wagner PIT 10
Red Murray STL 7

RUNS BATTED IN
Honus Wagner PIT 109
Mike Donlin NY 106
Cy Seymour NY 92

SLUGGING AVERAGE
Honus Wagner PIT .... .542
Mike Donlin NY .... .452
Sherry Magee PHI ..... .417

STOLEN BASES
Honus Wagner PIT 53
Red Murray STL 48
Hans Lobert CIN 47

RUNS SCORED
Fred Tenney NY 101
Honus Wagner PIT 100
Tommy Leach PIT 93

WINS
C. Mathewson NY 37
T. Brown CHI 29
Ed Reulbach CHI 24

WINNING PERCENTAGE
Ed Reulbach CHI .... .774
C. Mathewson NY .... .771
T. Brown CHI .... .763

EARNED RUN AVERAGE
C. Mathewson NY 1.43
T. Brown CHI 1.47
G. McQuillan PHI 1.53

STRIKEOUTS
C. Mathewson NY 259
Nap Rucker BKN 199
Orval Overall CHI 167

SAVES
T. Brown CHI 5
Christy Mathewson NY ... 5
Joe McGinnity NY 4

COMPLETE GAMES
C. Mathewson NY 34
Kaiser Wilhelm BKN 33
G. McQuillan PHI 32

SHUTOUTS
C. Mathewson NY 12
T. Brown CHI 9
four tied at....................... 7

GAMES PITCHED
C. Mathewson NY 56
G. McQuillan PHI 48
Bugs Raymond STL 48

INNINGS PITCHED
C. Mathewson NY 391
G. McQuillan PHI 360
Nap Rucker BKN 333

1909 AL

	W	L	PCT	GB	R	OR	BA	FA	ERA
DETROIT	98	54	.645	—	666	493	.267	.959	2.26
PHILADELPHIA	95	58	.621	3.5	605	408	.257	.961	1.92
BOSTON	88	63	.583	9.5	597	550	.263	.955	2.60
CHICAGO	78	74	.513	20	492	463	.221	.964	2.04
NEW YORK	74	77	.490	23.5	590	587	.248	.948	2.68
CLEVELAND	71	82	.464	27.5	493	532	.241	.957	2.39
ST. LOUIS	61	89	.407	36	441	575	.232	.958	2.88
WASHINGTON	42	110	.276	56	380	656	.223	.957	3.04
					4264	4264	.244	.957	2.47

BATTING AVERAGE
Ty Cobb DET .... .377
Eddie Collins PHI .... .346
Nap Lajoie CLE .... .324

HITS
Ty Cobb DET 216
Eddie Collins PHI 198
Sam Crawford DET 185

DOUBLES
Sam Crawford DET 35
Nap Lajoie CLE 33
Ty Cobb DET 33

TRIPLES
Frank Baker PHI 19
Danny Murphy PHI 14
Sam Crawford DET 14

HOME RUNS
Ty Cobb DET 9
Tris Speaker BOS 7
two tied at 6

RUNS BATTED IN
Ty Cobb DET 107
Sam Crawford DET 97
Frank Baker PHI 85

SLUGGING AVERAGE
Ty Cobb DET .... .517
Sam Crawford DET .... .452
Eddie Collins PHI .... .449

STOLEN BASES
Ty Cobb DET 76
Eddie Collins PHI 67
Donie Bush DET 53

RUNS SCORED
Ty Cobb DET 116
Donie Bush DET 114
Eddie Collins PHI 104

WINS
George Mullin DET 29
Frank Smith CHI 25
Ed Willett DET 21

WINNING PERCENTAGE
George Mullin DET .... .784
Harry Krause PHI .... .692
Chief Bender PHI .... .692

EARNED RUN AVERAGE
Harry Krause PHI 1.39
Ed Walsh CHI 1.41
Chief Bender PHI 1.66

STRIKEOUTS
Frank Smith CHI 177
W. Johnson WAS 164
Heinie Berger CLE 162

SAVES
Frank Arellanes BOS 8
Jack Powell STL 3

COMPLETE GAMES
Frank Smith CHI 37
Cy Young CLE 30
George Mullin DET 29

SHUTOUTS
Ed Walsh CHI 8
Harry Krause PHI 7
Frank Smith CHI 7

GAMES PITCHED
Frank Smith CHI 51
Frank Arellanes BOS 45
Bob Groom WAS 44

INNINGS PITCHED
Frank Smith CHI 365
George Mullin DET 304
W. Johnson WAS 297

1909 NL

	W	L	PCT	GB	R	OR	BA	FA	ERA
★PITTSBURGH	110	42	.724	—	699	447	.260	.964	2.07
CHICAGO	104	49	.680	6.5	635	390	.245	.961	1.75
NEW YORK	92	61	.601	18.5	623	546	.255	.954	2.27
CINCINNATI	77	76	.503	33.5	606	599	.250	.952	2.52
PHILADELPHIA	74	79	.484	36.5	516	518	.244	.961	2.44
BROOKLYN	55	98	.359	55.5	444	627	.229	.954	3.10
ST. LOUIS	54	98	.355	56	583	731	.243	.950	3.41
BOSTON	45	108	.294	65.5	435	683	.223	.947	3.20
					4541	4541	.244	.955	2.59

BATTING AVERAGE
Honus Wagner PIT .... .339
Mike Mitchell CIN .... .310
Dick Hoblitzell CIN ..... .308

HITS
Larry Doyle NY 172
Eddie Grant PHI.......... 170
Honus Wagner PIT 168

DOUBLES
Honus Wagner PIT 39
Sherry Magee PHI 33
Dots Miller PIT 31

TRIPLES
Mike Mitchell CIN.......... 17
Sherry Magee PHI 14
Ed Konetchy STL.......... 14

HOME RUNS
Red Murray NY 7
three tied at..................... 6

RUNS BATTED IN
Honus Wagner PIT 100
Red Murray NY 91
Dots Miller PIT 87

SLUGGING AVERAGE
Honus Wagner PIT .... .489
Mike Mitchell CIN .... .430
Larry Doyle NY .... .419

STOLEN BASES
Bob Bescher CIN 54
Red Murray NY 48
Dick Egan CIN 39

RUNS SCORED
Tommy Leach PIT 126
Fred Clarke PIT 97
two tied at 92

WINS
T. Brown CHI 27
Howie Camnitz PIT 25
C. Mathewson NY 25

WINNING PERCENTAGE
C. Mathewson NY ...... .806
Howie Camnitz PIT .... .806
T. Brown CHI .... .750

EARNED RUN AVERAGE
C. Mathewson NY 1.14
T. Brown CHI 1.31
Orval Overall CHI....... 1.42

STRIKEOUTS
Orval Overall CHI........ 205
Nap Rucker BKN 201
Earl Moore PHI 173

SAVES
T. Brown CHI 7
Doc Crandall NY 4
four tied at........................ 3

COMPLETE GAMES
T. Brown CHI 32
George Bell BKN 29
Nap Rucker BKN 28

SHUTOUTS
Orval Overall CHI............ 9
C. Mathewson NY........... 8
T. Brown CHI 8

GAMES PITCHED
T. Brown CHI 50
Al Mattern BOS............. 47
two tied at 44

INNINGS PITCHED
T. Brown CHI 343
Al Mattern BOS........... 316
Nap Rucker BKN 309

1910 AL

	W	L	PCT	GB	R	OR	BA	FA	ERA
★PHILADELPHIA	102	48	.680	—	673	441	.266	.965	1.79
NEW YORK	88	63	.583	14.5	626	557	.248	.956	2.59
DETROIT	86	68	.558	18	679	582	.261	.956	3.00
BOSTON	81	72	.529	22.5	638	564	.259	.954	2.46
CLEVELAND	71	81	.467	32	548	657	.244	.964	2.89
CHICAGO	68	85	.444	35.5	457	479	.211	.954	2.01
WASHINGTON	66	85	.437	36.5	501	550	.236	.959	2.46
ST. LOUIS	47	107	.305	57	451	743	.220	.944	3.09
					4573	4573	.243	.956	2.53

BATTING AVERAGE
Ty Cobb DET 385
Nap Lajoie CLE 384
Tris Speaker BOS 340

HITS
Nap Lajoie CLE 227
Ty Cobb DET 196
Eddie Collins PHI 188

DOUBLES
Nap Lajoie CLE............. 51
Ty Cobb DET................ 36
Duffy Lewis BOS........... 29

TRIPLES
Sam Crawford DET....... 19
Danny Murphy PHI 18
Bris Lord CLE, PHI 18

HOME RUNS
Jake Stahl BOS 10
Ty Cobb DET 8
Duffy Lewis BOS............. 8

RUNS BATTED IN
Sam Crawford DET..... 120
Ty Cobb DET 91
Eddie Collins PHI 81

SLUGGING AVERAGE
Ty Cobb DET .... .554
Nap Lajoie CLE........... .514
Tris Speaker BOS ...... .468

STOLEN BASES
Eddie Collins PHI.......... 81
Ty Cobb DET 65
two tied at 49

RUNS SCORED
Ty Cobb DET 106
Nap Lajoie CLE............. 92
Tris Speaker BOS......... 92

WINS
Jack Coombs PHI 31
Russ Ford NY 26
Walter Johnson WAS.... 25

WINNING PERCENTAGE
Chief Bender PHI........ .821
Russ Ford NY .... .813
Jack Coombs PHI .... .775

EARNED RUN AVERAGE
Ed Walsh CHI 1.27
Jack Coombs PHI 1.30
W. Johnson WAS........ 1.35

STRIKEOUTS
W. Johnson WAS........ 313
Ed Walsh CHI 258
Jack Coombs PHI 224

SAVES
Ed Walsh CHI 5
Frank Browning DET 3

COMPLETE GAMES
Walter Johnson WAS.... 38
Jack Coombs PHI 35
Ed Walsh CHI 33

SHUTOUTS
Jack Coombs PHI 13
Russ Ford NY 8
Walter Johnson WAS...... 8

GAMES PITCHED
Walter Johnson WAS.... 45
Ed Walsh CHI 45
Jack Coombs PHI 45

INNINGS PITCHED
W. Johnson WAS........ 373
Ed Walsh CHI 370
Jack Coombs PHI 353

1910 NL

	W	L	PCT	GB	R	OR	BA	FA	ERA
CHICAGO	104	50	.675	—	712	499	.268	.963	2.51
NEW YORK	91	63	.591	13	715	567	.275	.955	2.68
PITTSBURGH	86	67	.562	17.5	655	576	.266	.961	2.83
PHILADELPHIA	78	75	.510	25.5	674	639	.255	.960	3.05
CINCINNATI	75	79	.487	29	620	684	.259	.955	3.08
BROOKLYN	64	90	.416	40	497	623	.229	.964	3.07
ST. LOUIS	63	90	.412	40.5	639	718	.248	.959	3.78
BOSTON	53	100	.346	50.5	495	701	.246	.954	3.22
					5007	5007	.256	.959	3.02

BATTING AVERAGE
Sherry Magee PHI ..... .331
Vin Campbell PIT ..... .326
Solly Hofman CHI ...... .325

HITS
Bobby Byrne PIT......... 178
Honus Wagner PIT 178
two tied at 172

DOUBLES
Bobby Byrne PIT........... 43
Sherry Magee PHI 39
Zack Wheat BKN 36

TRIPLES
Mike Mitchell CIN.......... 18
Sherry Magee PHI 17
two tied at 16

HOME RUNS
Fred Beck BOS............. 10
Wildfire Schulte CHI...... 10
two tied at 8

RUNS BATTED IN
Sherry Magee PHI 123
Mike Mitchell CIN 88
Red Murray NY 87

SLUGGING AVERAGE
Sherry Magee PHI ..... .507
Solly Hofman CHI ...... .461
Wildfire Schulte CHI... .460

STOLEN BASES
Bob Bescher CIN........... 70
Red Murray NY 57
Dode Paskert CIN......... 51

RUNS SCORED
Sherry Magee PHI 110
Miller Huggins STL 101
Bobby Byrne PIT......... 101

WINS
C. Mathewson NY......... 27
T. Brown CHI 25
Earl Moore PHI 22

WINNING PERCENTAGE
King Cole CHI............. .833
Doc Crandall NY .... .810
C. Mathewson NY...... .750

EARNED RUN AVERAGE
G. McQuillan PHI 1.60
King Cole CHI 1.80
T. Brown CHI 1.86

STRIKEOUTS
Earl Moore PHI 185
C. Mathewson NY 184
S. Frock PIT, BOS 171

SAVES
T. Brown CHI 7
Harry Gaspar CIN 5
two tied at 4

COMPLETE GAMES
T. Brown CHI 27
C. Mathewson NY......... 27
Nap Rucker BKN 27

SHUTOUTS
T. Brown CHI 7
three tied at..................... 6

GAMES PITCHED
Al Mattern BOS............. 51
Harry Gaspar CIN 48
three tied at.................... 46

INNINGS PITCHED
Nap Rucker BKN 320
C. Mathewson NY........ 318
George Bell BKN 310

1911 AL

	W	L	PCT	GB	R	OR	BA	FA	ERA
★PHILADELPHIA	101	50	.669	—	861	601	.296	.965	3.01
DETROIT	89	65	.578	13.5	831	776	.292	.951	3.73
CLEVELAND	80	73	.523	22	691	712	.282	.954	3.37
CHICAGO	77	74	.510	24	719	624	.269	.961	3.01
BOSTON	78	75	.510	24	680	643	.275	.949	2.73
NEW YORK	76	76	.500	25.5	684	724	.272	.949	3.54
WASHINGTON	64	90	.416	38.5	625	766	.258	.953	3.52
ST. LOUIS	45	107	.296	56.5	567	812	.239	.945	3.83
					5658	5658	.273	.953	3.34

BATTING AVERAGE
Ty Cobb DET .... .420
Joe Jackson CLE .... .408
Sam Crawford DET.... .378

HITS
Ty Cobb DET 248
Joe Jackson CLE 233
Sam Crawford DET..... 217

DOUBLES
Ty Cobb DET 47
Joe Jackson CLE.......... 45
Frank Baker PHI 40

TRIPLES
Ty Cobb DET 24
Birdie Cree NY 22
Joe Jackson CLE.......... 19

HOME RUNS
Frank Baker PHI 11
Ty Cobb DET 8
Tris Speaker BOS........... 8

RUNS BATTED IN
Ty Cobb DET 144
Frank Baker PHI 115
Sam Crawford DET..... 115

SLUGGING AVERAGE
Ty Cobb DET .... .621
Joe Jackson CLE .... .590
Sam Crawford DET.... .526

STOLEN BASES
Ty Cobb DET 83
Clyde Milan WAS....... 58
Birdie Cree NY 48

RUNS SCORED
Ty Cobb DET 147
Joe Jackson CLE........ 126
Donie Bush DET 126

WINS
Jack Coombs PHI 28
Ed Walsh CHI 27
Walter Johnson WAS.... 25

WINNING PERCENTAGE
Chief Bender PHI........ .773
Vean Gregg CLE .... .767
Eddie Plank PHI......... .742

EARNED RUN AVERAGE
Vean Gregg CLE 1.81
W. Johnson WAS....... 1.89
Joe Wood BOS 2.02

STRIKEOUTS
Ed Walsh CHI 255
Joe Wood BOS 231
W. Johnson WAS........ 207

SAVES
Eddie Plank PHI.............. 4
Charley Hall BOS............ 4
Ed Walsh CHI 4

COMPLETE GAMES
Walter Johnson WAS.... 36
Ed Walsh CHI 33
two tied at 26

SHUTOUTS
Eddie Plank PHI.............. 6
Walter Johnson WAS...... 6
three tied at.................... 5

GAMES PITCHED
Ed Walsh CHI 56
Jack Coombs PHI 47
Joe Wood BOS 44

INNINGS PITCHED
Ed Walsh CHI 369
Jack Coombs PHI 337
W. Johnson WAS........ 323

1911 NL

	W	L	PCT	GB	R	OR	BA	FA	ERA
NEW YORK	99	54	.647	—	756	542	.279	.959	2.69
CHICAGO	92	62	.597	7.5	757	607	.260	.960	2.90
PITTSBURGH	85	69	.552	14.5	744	557	.262	.963	2.84
PHILADELPHIA	79	73	.520	19.5	658	669	.259	.963	3.30
ST. LOUIS	75	74	.503	22	671	745	.252	.960	3.68
CINCINNATI	70	83	.458	29	682	706	.261	.955	3.26
BROOKLYN	64	86	.427	33.5	539	659	.237	.962	3.39
BOSTON	44	107	.291	54	699	1021	.267	.947	5.08
					5506	5506	.260	.958	3.39

BATTING AVERAGE
Honus Wagner PIT .... .334
Dots Miller BOS .... .333
Chief Meyers NY .... .332

HITS
Dots Miller BOS 192
Dick Hoblitzell CIN 180
Jake Daubert BKN 176

DOUBLES
Ed Konetchy STL 38
Dots Miller BOS 36
Owen Wilson PIT 34

TRIPLES
Larry Doyle NY 25
Mike Mitchell CIN 22
Wildfire Schulte CHI...... 21

HOME RUNS
Wildfire Schulte CHI...... 21
Fred Luderus PHI 16
Sherry Magee PHI 15

RUNS BATTED IN
Wildfire Schulte CHI.... 121
Owen Wilson PIT 107
Fred Luderus PHI 99

SLUGGING AVERAGE
Wildfire Schulte CHI... .534
Larry Doyle NY .... .527
Honus Wagner PIT ... .507

STOLEN BASES
Bob Bescher CIN 81
Josh Devore NY............ 61
Fred Snodgrass NY 51

RUNS SCORED
J. Sheckard CHI.......... 121
Miller Huggins STL 106
Bob Bescher CIN 106

WINS
Grover Alexander PHI... 28
C. Mathewson NY......... 26
Rube Marquard NY....... 24

WINNING PERCENTAGE
Rube Marquard NY.... .774
Doc Crandall NY .... .750
King Cole CHI .... .720

EARNED RUN AVERAGE
C. Mathewson NY...... 1.99
Lew Richie CHI 2.31
Babe Adams PIT........ 2.33

STRIKEOUTS
Rube Marquard NY..... 237
G. Alexander PHI........ 227
Nap Rucker BKN 190

SAVES
T. Brown CHI 13
Doc Crandall NY 5
four tied at...................... 4

COMPLETE GAMES
Grover Alexander PHI... 31
C. Mathewson NY......... 29
Bob Harmon STL........... 28

SHUTOUTS
Grover Alexander PHI..... 7
Babe Adams PIT............. 7
four tied at...................... 5

GAMES PITCHED
T. Brown CHI 53
Bob Harmon STL 51
two tied at 48

INNINGS PITCHED
G. Alexander PHI......... 367
Bob Harmon STL........ 348
Lefty Leifield PIT 318

1912 AL

	W	L	PCT	GB	R	OR	BA	FA	ERA
★BOSTON	105	47	.691	—	799	544	.277	.957	2.76
WASHINGTON	91	61	.599	14	698	581	.256	.954	2.69
PHILADELPHIA	90	62	.592	15	779	658	.282	.959	3.32
CHICAGO	78	76	.506	28	638	646	.255	.956	3.06
CLEVELAND	75	78	.490	30.5	676	680	.273	.954	3.30
DETROIT	69	84	.451	36.5	720	777	.267	.950	3.78
ST. LOUIS	53	101	.344	53	552	764	.249	.947	3.71
NEW YORK	50	102	.329	55	630	842	.259	.940	4.13
					5492	5492	.265	.952	3.34

BATTING AVERAGE
Ty Cobb DET .... .410
Joe Jackson CLE .... .395
Tris Speaker BOS ...... .383

HITS
Ty Cobb DET 227
Joe Jackson CLE 226
Tris Speaker BOS 222

DOUBLES
Tris Speaker BOS 53
Joe Jackson CLE 44
Frank Baker PHI 40

TRIPLES
Joe Jackson CLE 26
Ty Cobb DET 23
two tied at 21

HOME RUNS
Frank Baker PHI 10
Tris Speaker BOS 10
Ty Cobb DET 7

RUNS BATTED IN
Frank Baker PHI 133
Duffy Lewis BOS 109
Sam Crawford DET 109

SLUGGING AVERAGE
Ty Cobb DET .... .586
Joe Jackson CLE .... .579
Tris Speaker BOS ...... .567

STOLEN BASES
Claude Milan WAS 88
Eddie Collins PHI 63
Ty Cobb DET 61

RUNS SCORED
Eddie Collins PHI 137
Tris Speaker BOS 136
Joe Jackson CLE 121

WINS
Joe Wood BOS 34
Walter Johnson WAS.... 32
Ed Walsh CHI 27

WINNING PERCENTAGE
Joe Wood BOS .... .872
Eddie Plank PHI......... .813
W. Johnson WAS........ .727

EARNED RUN AVERAGE
W. Johnson WAS....... 1.39
Joe Wood BOS 1.91
Ed Walsh CHI 2.15

STRIKEOUTS
W. Johnson WAS........ 303
Joe Wood BOS 258
Ed Walsh CHI 254

SAVES
Ed Walsh CHI 10
four tied at 3

COMPLETE GAMES
Joe Wood BOS 35
Walter Johnson WAS... 34
Ed Walsh CHI 32

SHUTOUTS
Joe Wood BOS 10
Walter Johnson WAS...... 7
Ed Walsh CHI 6

GAMES PITCHED
Ed Walsh CHI 62
Walter Johnson WAS... 50
two tied at 43

INNINGS PITCHED
Ed Walsh CHI 393
W. Johnson WAS......... 368
Joe Wood BOS 344

1912 NL

	W	L	PCT	GB	R	OR	BA	FA	ERA
NEW YORK	103	48	.682	—	823	571	.286	.956	2.58
PITTSBURGH	93	58	.616	10	751	565	.284	.972	2.85
CHICAGO	91	59	.607	11.5	756	668	.277	.960	3.42
CINCINNATI	75	78	.490	29	656	722	.256	.960	3.42
PHILADELPHIA	73	79	.480	30.5	670	688	.267	.963	3.25
ST. LOUIS	63	90	.412	41	659	830	.268	.957	3.85
BROOKLYN	58	95	.379	46	651	754	.268	.959	3.64
BOSTON	52	101	.340	52	693	861	.273	.954	4.17
					5659	5659	.272	.960	3.40

BATTING AVERAGE
H. Zimmerman CHI.... .372
Chief Meyers NY........ .358
Bill Sweeney BOS...... .344

HITS
H. Zimmerman CHI..... 207
Bill Sweeney BOS....... 204
Vin Campbell BOS...... 185

DOUBLES
H. Zimmerman CHI....... 41
Dode Paskert PHI......... 37
Honus Wagner PIT 35

TRIPLES
Owen Wilson PIT 36
Honus Wagner PIT 20
Red Murray NY 20

HOME RUNS
H. Zimmerman CHI....... 14
Wildfire Schulte CHI...... 13
three tied at................... 11

RUNS BATTED IN
H. Zimmerman CHI.... 103
Honus Wagner PIT 102
Bill Sweeney BOS....... 100

SLUGGING AVERAGE
H. Zimmerman CHI.... .571
Owen Wilson PIT .... .513
Honus Wagner PIT .... .496

STOLEN BASES
Bob Bescher CIN 67
Max Carey PIT 45
Fred Snodgrass NY 43

RUNS SCORED
Bob Bescher CIN 120
Max Carey PIT............ 114
two tied at 102

WINS
Larry Cheney CHI 26
Rube Marquard NY....... 26
Claude Hendrix PIT 24

WINNING PERCENTAGE
Claude Hendrix PIT .... .727
Larry Cheney CHI .... .722
Jeff Tesreau NY.......... .708

EARNED RUN AVERAGE
Jeff Tesreau NY.......... 1.96
C. Mathewson NY 2.12
Nap Rucker BKN 2.21

STRIKEOUTS
G. Alexander PHI........ 195
Claude Hendrix PIT 176
Rube Marquard NY..... 175

SAVES
Slim Sallee STL 6
Nap Rucker BKN 4
Christy Mathewson NY ... 4

COMPLETE GAMES
Larry Cheney CHI 28
C. Mathewson NY 27

SHUTOUTS
Nap Rucker BKN 6
Marty O'Toole PIT........... 6
George Suggs CIN 5

GAMES PITCHED
Rube Benton CIN.......... 50
Slim Sallee STL 48
Grover Alexander PHI.... 46

INNINGS PITCHED
G. Alexander PHI........ 310
C. Mathewson NY 310
two tied at 303

1913 AL

	W	L	PCT	GB	R	OR	BA	FA	ERA
★PHILADELPHIA	96	57	.627	—	794	592	.280	.966	3.19
WASHINGTON	90	64	.584	6.5	596	561	.252	.960	2.72
CLEVELAND	86	66	.566	9.5	633	536	.268	.962	2.52
BOSTON	79	71	.527	15.5	631	610	.269	.961	2.93
CHICAGO	78	74	.513	17.5	488	498	.236	.960	2.33
DETROIT	66	87	.431	30	624	716	.265	.954	3.41
NEW YORK	57	94	.377	38	529	668	.237	.954	3.27
ST. LOUIS	57	96	.373	39	528	642	.237	.954	3.06
					4823	4823	.256	.959	2.93

BATTING AVERAGE
Ty Cobb DET .... .390
Joe Jackson CLE .... .373
Tris Speaker BOS ...... .363

HITS
Joe Jackson CLE 197
Sam Crawford DET 193
Frank Baker PHI 190

DOUBLES
Joe Jackson CLE 39
Tris Speaker BOS 35
Frank Baker PHI 34

TRIPLES
Sam Crawford DET 23
Tris Speaker BOS 22
Joe Jackson CLE 17

HOME RUNS
Frank Baker PHI 12
Sam Crawford DET 9
Ping Bodie CHI 8

RUNS BATTED IN
Frank Baker PHI 126
Duffy Lewis BOS 90
Stuffy McInnis PHI 90

SLUGGING AVERAGE
Joe Jackson CLE .... .551
Ty Cobb DET .... .535
Tris Speaker BOS ...... .533

STOLEN BASES
Clyde Milan WAS 75
Danny Moeller WAS 62
Eddie Collins PHI 55

RUNS SCORED
Eddie Collins PHI 125
Frank Baker PHI 116
Joe Jackson CLE 109

WINS
Walter Johnson WAS ... 36
Cy Falkenberg CLE 23
Reb Russell CHI 22

WINNING PERCENTAGE
W. Johnson WAS .... .837
Joe Boehling WAS ..... .708
Ray Collins BOS .... .704

EARNED RUN AVERAGE
W. Johnson WAS 1.09
Eddie Cicotte CHI 1.58
Willie Mitchell CLE 1.74

STRIKEOUTS
W. Johnson WAS 243
Vean Gregg CLE 166
Cy Falkenberg CLE 166

SAVES
Chief Bender PHI 13
Tom Hughes WAS 6
Hugh Bedient BOS 5

COMPLETE GAMES
W. Johnson WAS 29
Reb Russell CHI 26
Jim Scott CHI 25

SHUTOUTS
Walter Johnson WAS 11
Reb Russell CHI 8
Eddie Plank PHI 7

GAMES PITCHED
Reb Russell CHI 51
Jim Scott CHI 48
Chief Bender PHI 48

INNINGS PITCHED
W. Johnson WAS 346
Reb Russell CHI 316
Jim Scott CHI 312

1913 NL

	W	L	PCT	GB	R	OR	BA	FA	ERA
NEW YORK	101	51	.664	—	684	515	.273	.961	2.43
PHILADELPHIA	88	63	.583	12.5	693	636	.265	.968	3.15
CHICAGO	88	65	.575	13.5	720	625	.257	.959	3.13
PITTSBURGH	78	71	.523	21.5	673	585	.263	.964	2.90
BOSTON	69	82	.457	31.5	641	690	.256	.957	3.19
BROOKLYN	65	84	.436	34.5	595	613	.270	.961	3.13
CINCINNATI	64	89	.418	37.5	607	717	.261	.961	3.46
ST. LOUIS	51	99	.340	49	523	755	.247	.965	4.24
					5136	5136	.262	.962	3.20

BATTING AVERAGE
Jake Daubert BKN ..... .350
Gavvy Cravath PHI .... .341
two tied at .... .317

HITS
Gavvy Cravath PHI 179
Jake Daubert BKN 178
George Burns NY 173

DOUBLES
Red Smith BKN............. 40
George Burns NY 37
Sherry Magee PHI 36

TRIPLES
Vic Saier CHI 21
Dots Miller PIT 20
Ed Konetchy STL.......... 17

HOME RUNS
Gavvy Cravath PHI 19
Fred Luderus PHI 18
Vic Saier CHI 14

RUNS BATTED IN
Gavvy Cravath PHI 128
H. Zimmerman CHI....... 95
Vic Saier CHI 92

SLUGGING AVERAGE
Gavvy Cravath PHI .... .568
B. Becker CIN, PHI .... .502
H. Zimmerman CHI .... .490

STOLEN BASES
Max Carey PIT.............. 61
Hy Myers BOS 57
Hans Lobert PHI 41

RUNS SCORED
Max Carey PIT.............. 99
Tommy Leach CHI........ 99
Hans Lobert PHI 98

WINS
Tom Seaton PHI 27
C. Mathewson NY 25
Rube Marquard NY 23

WINNING PERCENTAGE
Bert Humphries CHI... .800
G. Alexander PHI........ .733
Rube Marquard NY .... .697

EARNED RUN AVERAGE
C. Mathewson NY 2.06
Babe Adams PIT......... 2.15
Jeff Tesreau NY 2.17

STRIKEOUTS
Tom Seaton PHI 168
Jeff Tesreau NY.......... 167
G. Alexander PHI........ 159

SAVES
Larry Cheney CHI 11
T. Brown CIN 6
Doc Crandall NY 6

COMPLETE GAMES
Lefty Tyler BOS 28
C. Mathewson NY......... 25
Larry Cheney CHI 25

SHUTOUTS
Grover Alexander PHI..... 9
Tom Seaton PHI 6

GAMES PITCHED
Larry Cheney CHI 54
Tom Seaton PHI 52
Slim Sallee STL 49

INNINGS PITCHED
Tom Seaton PHI 322
Babe Adams PIT......... 314
two tied at 306

1914 AL

	W	L	PCT	GB	R	OR	BA	FA	ERA
PHILADELPHIA	99	53	.651	—	749	529	.272	.966	2.78
BOSTON	91	62	.595	8.5	589	511	.250	.963	2.35
WASHINGTON	81	73	.526	19	572	519	.244	.961	2.54
DETROIT	80	73	.523	19.5	615	618	.258	.958	2.86
ST. LOUIS	71	82	.464	28.5	523	615	.243	.952	2.85
CHICAGO	70	84	.455	30	487	560	.239	.955	2.48
NEW YORK	70	84	.455	30	538	550	.229	.963	2.81
CLEVELAND	51	102	.333	48.5	538	709	.245	.953	3.21
					4611	4611	.248	.959	2.73

BATTING AVERAGE
Ty Cobb DET .... .368
Eddie Collins PHI .... .344
two tied at .... .338

HITS
Tris Speaker BOS 193
Sam Crawford DET 183
Frank Baker PHI 182

DOUBLES
Tris Speaker BOS 46
Duffy Lewis BOS 37
two tied at 34

TRIPLES
Sam Crawford DET 26
Larry Gardner BOS 19
Tris Speaker BOS 18

HOME RUNS
Frank Baker PHI 9
Sam Crawford DET 8
two tied at 6

RUNS BATTED IN
Sam Crawford DET 104
Frank Baker PHI 97
Stuffy McInnis PHI 95

SLUGGING AVERAGE
Ty Cobb DET .... .513
Tris Speaker BOS ...... .503
Sam Crawford DET .... .483

STOLEN BASES
Fritz Maisel NY 74
Eddie Collins PHI 58
Tris Speaker BOS 42

RUNS SCORED
Eddie Collins PHI 122
Eddie Murphy PHI 101
Tris Speaker BOS 101

WINS
Walter Johnson WAS 28
Harry Coveleski DET 22
Ray Collins BOS 20

WINNING PERCENTAGE
Chief Bender PHI .... .850
Dutch Leonard BOS .... .792
Eddie Plank PHI .... .682

EARNED RUN AVERAGE
Dutch Leonard BOS... 1.01
Rube Foster BOS 1.65
W. Johnson WAS 1.72

STRIKEOUTS
W. Johnson WAS 225
Willie Mitchell CLE 179
Dutch Leonard BOS 174

SAVES
five tied at 4

COMPLETE GAMES
W. Johnson WAS 33
Harry Coveleski DET 23
two tied at 22

SHUTOUTS
Walter Johnson WAS 9
Chief Bender PHI 7
Dutch Leonard BOS 7

GAMES PITCHED
Walter Johnson WAS 51
Doc Ayers WAS 49
two tied at 48

INNINGS PITCHED
W. Johnson WAS 372
H. Coveleski DET 303
two tied at 302

1914 NL

	W	L	PCT	GB	R	OR	BA	FA	ERA
BOSTON	94	59	.614	—	657	548	.251	.963	2.74
NEW YORK	84	70	.545	10.5	672	576	.265	.961	2.94
ST. LOUIS	81	72	.529	13	558	540	.248	.964	2.38
CHICAGO	78	76	.506	16.5	605	638	.243	.951	2.71
BROOKLYN	75	79	.487	19.5	622	618	.269	.961	2.82
PHILADELPHIA	74	80	.481	20.5	651	687	.263	.950	3.06
PITTSBURGH	69	85	.448	25.5	503	540	.233	.966	2.70
CINCINNATI	60	94	.390	34.5	530	651	.236	.952	2.94
					4798	4798	.251	.958	2.78

BATTING AVERAGE
Jake Daubert BKN ..... .329
Beals Becker PHI .... .325
two tied at .... .319

HITS
Sherry Magee PHI 171
George Burns NY 170
Zack Wheat BKN 170

DOUBLES
Sherry Magee PHI 39
H. Zimmerman CHI 36
George Burns NY 35

TRIPLES
Max Carey PIT 17
three tied at 12

HOME RUNS
Gavvy Cravath PHI 19
Vic Saier CHI 18
Sherry Magee PHI 15

RUNS BATTED IN
Sherry Magee PHI 103
Gavvy Cravath PHI 100
Zack Wheat BKN 89

SLUGGING AVERAGE
Sherry Magee PHI ..... .509
Gavvy Cravath PHI .... .499
Joe Connolly BOS ..... .494

STOLEN BASES
George Burns NY 62
Buck Herzog CIN 46
Cozy Dolan STL............ 42

RUNS SCORED
George Burns NY 100
Sherry Magee PHI 96
Jake Daubert BKN 89

WINS
Dick Rudolph BOS........ 27
Grover Alexander PHI... 27
two tied at 26

WINNING PERCENTAGE
Bill James BOS........... .788
Bill Doak STL .... .769
Dick Rudolph BOS...... .730

EARNED RUN AVERAGE
Bill Doak STL 1.72
Bill James BOS........... 1.90
Jeff Pfeffer BKN 1.97

STRIKEOUTS
G. Alexander PHI........ 214
Jeff Tesreau NY 189
Hippo Vaughn CHI...... 165

SAVES
Red Ames CIN................ 6
Slim Sallee STL 6
Larry Cheney CHI 5

COMPLETE GAMES
Grover Alexander PHI... 32
Dick Rudolph BOS........ 31
Bill James BOS............. 30

SHUTOUTS
Jeff Tesreau NY.............. 8
Bill Doak STL 7
three tied at..................... 6

GAMES PITCHED
Larry Cheney CHI 50
Erskine Mayer PHI 48
Red Ames CIN............... 47

INNINGS PITCHED
G. Alexander PHI 355
Dick Rudolph BOS...... 336
Bill James BOS............ 332

1915 AL

	W	L	PCT	GB	R	OR	BA	FA	ERA
★BOSTON	101	50	.669	—	668	499	.260	.964	2.39
DETROIT	100	54	.649	2.5	778	597	.268	.961	2.86
CHICAGO	93	61	.604	9.5	717	509	.258	.965	2.43
WASHINGTON	85	68	.556	17	569	491	.244	.964	2.31
NEW YORK	69	83	.454	32.5	584	588	.233	.966	3.09
ST. LOUIS	63	91	.409	39.5	521	679	.246	.949	3.07
CLEVELAND	57	95	.375	44.5	539	670	.241	.957	3.13
PHILADELPHIA	43	109	.283	58.5	545	888	.237	.947	4.33
					4921	4921	.248	.959	2.94

BATTING AVERAGE
Ty Cobb DET .... .369
Eddie Collins CHI .... .332
two tied at .... .322

HITS
Ty Cobb DET 208
Sam Crawford DET..... 183
Bobby Veach DET 178

DOUBLES
Bobby Veach DET 40
four tied at..................... 31

TRIPLES
Sam Crawford DET....... 19
Jack Fournier CHI......... 18
three tied at................... 17

HOME RUNS
Braggo Roth CHI, CLE ... 7
Rube Oldring PHI............ 6

RUNS BATTED IN
Bobby Veach DET 112
Sam Crawford DET..... 112
Ty Cobb DET 99

SLUGGING AVERAGE
Jack Fournier CHI...... .491
Ty Cobb DET .... .487
M. Kavanagh DET ..... .452

STOLEN BASES
Ty Cobb DET 96
Fritz Maisel NY 51
Eddie Collins CHI.......... 46

RUNS SCORED
Ty Cobb DET 144
Eddie Collins CHI........ 118
Ossie Vitt DET 116

WINS
Walter Johnson WAS.... 28
three tied at................... 24

WINNING PERCENTAGE
Joe Wood BOS .... .750
Rube Foster BOS .... .704
Ernie Shore BOS .... .704

EARNED RUN AVERAGE
Joe Wood BOS 1.49
W. Johnson WAS....... 1.55
Ernie Shore BOS 1.64

STRIKEOUTS
W. Johnson WAS........ 203
Red Faber CHI.......... 182
John Wyckoff PHI 157

SAVES
Carl Mays BOS 7

COMPLETE GAMES
W. Johnson WAS.......... 35
Ray Caldwell NY........... 31
Hooks Dauss DET 27

SHUTOUTS
Walter Johnson WAS..... 7
Jim Scott CHI................. 7
Guy Morton CLE 6

GAMES PITCHED
Harry Coveleski DET ... 50
Red Faber CHI.............. 50
two tied at 48

INNINGS PITCHED
W. Johnson WAS........ 337
H. Coveleski DET 313
Hooks Dauss DET 310

1915 NL

	W	L	PCT	GB	R	OR	BA	FA	ERA
PHILADELPHIA	90	62	.592	—	589	463	.247	.966	2.17
BOSTON	83	69	.546	7	582	545	.240	.966	2.57
BROOKLYN	80	72	.526	10	536	560	.248	.963	2.66
CHICAGO	73	80	.477	17.5	570	620	.244	.958	3.11
PITTSBURGH	73	81	.474	18	557	520	.246	.966	2.60
ST. LOUIS	72	81	.471	18.5	590	601	.254	.964	2.89
CINCINNATI	71	83	.461	20	516	585	.253	.966	2.84
NEW YORK	69	83	.454	21	582	628	.251	.960	3.11
					4522	4522	.248	.964	2.75

BATTING AVERAGE
Larry Doyle NY .... .320
Fred Luderus PHI .... .315
two tied at .... .307

HITS
Larry Doyle NY 189
Tommy Griffith CIN 179
Bill Hinchman PIT 177

DOUBLES
Larry Doyle NY 40
Fred Luderus PHI 36
Vic Saier CHI 35

TRIPLES
Tommy Long STL 25
Honus Wagner PIT 17
Tommy Griffith CIN 16

HOME RUNS
Gavvy Cravath PHI 24
Cy Williams CHI 13
Wildfire Schulte CHI...... 12

RUNS BATTED IN
Gavvy Cravath PHI 115
Sherry Magee BOS....... 87
Tommy Griffith CIN 85

SLUGGING AVERAGE
Gavvy Cravath PHI .... .510
Fred Luderus PHI ...... .457
Tommy Long STL .... .446

STOLEN BASES
Max Carey PIT 36
Buck Herzog CIN 35
two tied at 29

RUNS SCORED
Gavvy Cravath PHI 89
Larry Doyle NY 86
Dave Bancroft PHI 85

WINS
G. Alexander PHI........... 31
Dick Rudolph BOS........ 22
two tied at 21

WINNING PERCENTAGE
G. Alexander PHI........ .756
Al Mamaux PIT .... .724
Fred Toney CIN .... .714

EARNED RUN AVERAGE
G. Alexander PHI....... 1.22
Fred Toney CIN 1.58
Al Mamaux PIT 2.04

STRIKEOUTS
G. Alexander PHI........ 241
Jeff Tesreau NY 176
Tom Hughes BOS....... 171

SAVES
Rube Benton CIN, NY..... 5
Tom Hughes BOS.......... 5
Wilbur Cooper PIT 4

COMPLETE GAMES
Grover Alexander PHI.... 36
Dick Rudolph BOS........ 30
Jeff Pfeffer BKN 26

SHUTOUTS
Grover Alexander PHI... 12
Al Mamaux PIT 8
Jeff Tesreau NY.............. 8

GAMES PITCHED
Tom Hughes BOS.......... 50
Grover Alexander PHI... 49
Gene Dale CIN 49

INNINGS PITCHED
G. Alexander PHI........ 376
Dick Rudolph BOS...... 341
Jeff Tesreau NY.......... 306

1916 AL

	W	L	PCT	GB	R	OR	BA	FA	ERA
★BOSTON	91	63	.591	—	550	480	.248	.972	2.48
CHICAGO	89	65	.578	2	601	497	.251	.968	2.36
DETROIT	87	67	.565	4	670	595	.264	.968	2.97
NEW YORK	80	74	.519	11	577	561	.246	.967	2.77
ST. LOUIS	79	75	.513	12	588	545	.245	.963	2.58
CLEVELAND	77	77	.500	14	630	602	.250	.965	2.89
WASHINGTON	76	77	.497	14.5	536	543	.242	.964	2.66
PHILADELPHIA	36	117	.235	54.5	447	776	.242	.951	3.84
					4599	4599	.248	.965	2.81

BATTING AVERAGE
Tris Speaker CLE ...... .386
Ty Cobb DET.............. .371
Joe Jackson CHI........ .341

HITS
Tris Speaker CLE 211
Joe Jackson CHI........ 202
Ty Cobb DET 201

DOUBLES
Jack Graney CLE........ 41
Tris Speaker CLE 41
Joe Jackson CHI.......... 40

TRIPLES
Joe Jackson CHI.......... 21
Eddie Collins CHI.......... 17
two tied at 15

HOME RUNS
Wally Pipp NY 12
Frank Baker NY 10
two tied at 7

RUNS BATTED IN
Del Pratt STL 103
Wally Pipp NY 93
Bobby Veach DET 91

SLUGGING AVERAGE
Tris Speaker CLE ...... .502
Joe Jackson CHI........ .495
Ty Cobb DET .... .493

STOLEN BASES
Ty Cobb DET 68
A. Marsans STL 46
Burt Shotton STL 41

RUNS SCORED
Ty Cobb DET 113
Jack Graney CLE........ 106
Tris Speaker CLE 102

WINS
Walter Johnson WAS.... 25
Bob Shawkey NY 24
Babe Ruth BOS 23

WINNING PERCENTAGE
Eddie Cicotte CHI ...... .682
Babe Ruth BOS .... .657
H. Coveleski DET ...... .656

EARNED RUN AVERAGE
Babe Ruth BOS 1.75
Eddie Cicotte CHI 1.78
W. Johnson WAS....... 1.89

STRIKEOUTS
W. Johnson WAS........ 228
Elmer Myers PHI......... 182
Babe Ruth BOS 170

SAVES
Bob Shawkey NY............ 8
Allan Russell NY 6
Dutch Leonard BOS....... 6

COMPLETE GAMES
W. Johnson WAS.......... 36
Elmer Myers PHI........... 31
Joe Bush PHI................ 25

SHUTOUTS
Babe Ruth BOS 9
Joe Bush PHI.................. 8
Dutch Leonard BOS....... 6

GAMES PITCHED
Dave Davenport STL 59
Reb Russell CHI 56
Bob Shawkey NY.......... 53

INNINGS PITCHED
W. Johnson WAS........ 371
H. Coveleski DET 324
Babe Ruth BOS 324

1916 NL

	W	L	PCT	GB	R	OR	BA	FA	ERA
BROOKLYN	94	60	.610	—	585	471	.261	.965	2.12
PHILADELPHIA	91	62	.595	2.5	581	489	.250	.963	2.36
BOSTON	89	63	.586	4	542	453	.233	.967	2.19
NEW YORK	86	66	.566	7	597	504	.253	.966	2.60
CHICAGO	67	86	.438	26.5	520	541	.239	.957	2.65
PITTSBURGH	65	89	.422	29	484	586	.240	.959	2.76
CINCINNATI	60	93	.392	33.5	505	617	.254	.965	3.10
ST. LOUIS	60	93	.392	33.5	476	629	.243	.957	3.14
					4290	4290	.247	.963	2.61

BATTING AVERAGE
Hal Chase CIN .... .339
Jake Daubert BKN ..... .316
Bill Hinchman PIT ...... .315

HITS
Hal Chase CIN 184
Dave Robertson NY 180
Zack Wheat BKN 177

DOUBLES
Bert Niehoff PHI 42
Zack Wheat BKN 32
Dode Paskert PHI 30

TRIPLES
Bill Hinchman PIT 16
three tied at 15

HOME RUNS
Dave Robertson NY 12
Cy Williams CHI 12
Gavvy Cravath PHI 11

RUNS BATTED IN
Zimmerman CHI, NY ... 83
Hal Chase CIN 82
Bill Hinchman PIT 76

SLUGGING AVERAGE
Zack Wheat BKN .... .461
Hal Chase CIN .... .459
Cy Williams CHI .... .459

STOLEN BASES
Max Carey PIT 63
Benny Kauff NY 40
Bob Bescher STL 39

RUNS SCORED
George Burns NY 105
Max Carey PIT 90
Dave Robertson NY 88

WINS
Grover Alexander PHI... 33
Jeff Pfeffer BKN 25
Eppa Rixey PHI 22

WINNING PERCENTAGE
Tom Hughes BOS ...... .842
G. Alexander PHI .... .733
Jeff Pfeffer BKN .... .694

EARNED RUN AVERAGE
G. Alexander PHI 1.55
R. Marquard BKN 1.58
Eppa Rixey PHI 1.85

STRIKEOUTS
G. Alexander PHI 167
Larry Cheney BKN 166
Al Mamaux PIT 163

SAVES
Red Ames STL 7
three tied at 5

COMPLETE GAMES
G. Alexander PHI 38
Jeff Pfeffer BKN 30
Dick Rudolph BOS 27

SHUTOUTS
Grover Alexander PHI... 16
Lefty Tyler BOS 6
Jeff Pfeffer BKN 6

GAMES PITCHED
Lee Meadows STL 51
G. Alexander PHI 48
two tied at 45

INNINGS PITCHED
G. Alexander PHI 389
Jeff Pfeffer BKN 329
Dick Rudolph BOS 312

1917 AL

	W	L	PCT	GB	R	OR	BA	FA	ERA
★CHICAGO	100	54	.649	—	656	464	.253	.967	2.16
BOSTON	90	62	.592	9	555	454	.246	.972	2.20
CLEVELAND	88	66	.571	12	584	543	.245	.964	2.52
DETROIT	78	75	.510	21.5	639	577	.259	.964	2.56
WASHINGTON	74	79	.484	25.5	543	566	.241	.961	2.77
NEW YORK	71	82	.464	28.5	524	558	.239	.965	2.66
ST. LOUIS	57	97	.370	43	510	687	.245	.957	3.20
PHILADELPHIA	55	98	.359	44.5	529	691	.254	.961	3.27
					4540	4540	.248	.964	2.66

BATTING AVERAGE
Ty Cobb DET .... .383
George Sisler STL ..... .353
Tris Speaker CLE .... .352

HITS
Ty Cobb DET 225
George Sisler STL 190
Tris Speaker CLE 184

DOUBLES
Ty Cobb DET 44
Tris Speaker CLE 42
Bobby Veach DET 31

TRIPLES
Ty Cobb DET 23
Joe Jackson CHI 17
Joe Judge WAS 15

HOME RUNS
Wally Pipp NY 9
Bobby Veach DET 8
two tied at 7

RUNS BATTED IN
Bobby Veach DET 103
Ty Cobb DET 102
Happy Felsch CHI 102

SLUGGING AVERAGE
Ty Cobb DET .... .571
Tris Speaker CLE .... .486
Bobby Veach DET ..... .457

STOLEN BASES
Ty Cobb DET 55
Eddie Collins CHI 53
Ray Chapman CLE 52

RUNS SCORED
Donie Bush DET 112
Ty Cobb DET 107
Ray Chapman CLE 98

WINS
Eddie Cicotte CHI 28
Babe Ruth BOS 24
two tied at 23

WINNING PERCENTAGE
Reb Russell CHI .... .750
Carl Mays BOS .... .710
Eddie Cicotte CHI ...... .700

EARNED RUN AVERAGE
Eddie Cicotte CHI 1.53
Carl Mays BOS 1.74
Stan Coveleski CLE ... 1.81

STRIKEOUTS
W. Johnson WAS 188
Eddie Cicotte CHI 150
Dutch Leonard BOS.... 144

SAVES
Dave Danforth CHI 9
Jim Bagby CLE 7
Bernie Boland DET 6

COMPLETE GAMES
Babe Ruth BOS 35
Walter Johnson WAS.... 30
Eddie Cicotte CHI 29

SHUTOUTS
Stan Coveleski CLE........ 9
Walter Johnson WAS...... 8
Jim Bagby CLE 8

GAMES PITCHED
Dave Danforth CHI 50
Jim Bagby CLE 49
Eddie Cicotte CHI 49

INNINGS PITCHED
Eddie Cicotte CHI 347
W. Johnson WAS........ 328
Babe Ruth BOS 326

1917 NL

	W	L	PCT	GB	R	OR	BA	FA	ERA
NEW YORK	98	56	.636	—	635	457	.261	.968	2.27
PHILADELPHIA	87	65	.572	10	578	500	.248	.967	2.46
ST. LOUIS	82	70	.539	15	531	567	.250	.967	3.03
CINCINNATI	78	76	.506	20	601	611	.264	.962	2.66
CHICAGO	74	80	.481	24	552	567	.239	.959	2.62
BOSTON	72	81	.471	25.5	536	552	.246	.966	2.77
BROOKLYN	70	81	.464	26.5	511	559	.247	.962	2.78
PITTSBURGH	51	103	.331	47	464	595	.238	.961	3.01
					4408	4408	.249	.964	2.70

BATTING AVERAGE
Edd Roush CIN .... .341
R. Hornsby STL .... .327
Zack Wheat BKN .... .312

HITS
Heinie Groh CIN 182
George Burns NY 180
Edd Roush CIN 178

DOUBLES
Heinie Groh CIN 39
F. Merkle BKN, CHI 31
Red Smith BOS 31

TRIPLES
Rogers Hornsby STL 17
Gavvy Cravath PHI 16
Hal Chase CIN.............. 15

HOME RUNS
Dave Robertson NY...... 12
Gavvy Cravath PHI 12
Rogers Hornsby STL 8

RUNS BATTED IN
H. Zimmerman NY 102
Hal Chase CIN.............. 86
Gavvy Cravath PHI 83

SLUGGING AVERAGE
R. Hornsby STL .... .484
Gavvy Cravath PHI .... .473
Edd Roush CIN .... .454

STOLEN BASES
Max Carey PIT 46
George Burns NY 40
Benny Kauff NY 30

RUNS SCORED
George Burns NY 103
Heinie Groh CIN 91
Benny Kauff NY 89

WINS
Grover Alexander PHI... 30
Fred Toney CIN 24
Hippo Vaughn CHI........ 23

WINNING PERCENTAGE
Ferdie Schupp NY ..... .750
Slim Sallee NY............ .720
Pol Perritt NY .... .708

EARNED RUN AVERAGE
F. Anderson NY 1.44
G. Alexander PHI........ 1.86
Pol Perritt NY 1.88

STRIKEOUTS
G. Alexander PHI........ 201
Hippo Vaughn CHI...... 195
Phil Douglas CHI 151

SAVES
Slim Sallee NY................ 4
five tied at 3

COMPLETE GAMES
Grover Alexander PHI... 35
Fred Toney CIN 31
two tied at 27

SHUTOUTS
Grover Alexander PHI..... 8
Wilbur Cooper PIT 7
Fred Toney CIN 7

GAMES PITCHED
Phil Douglas CHI 51
Jesse Barnes BOS 50
Pete Schneider CIN...... 46

INNINGS PITCHED
G. Alexander PHI......... 388
Pete Schneider CIN.... 342
Fred Toney CIN 340

1918 AL

	W	L	PCT	GB	R	OR	BA	FA	ERA
★BOSTON	75	51	.595	—	474	380	.249	.971	2.31
CLEVELAND	73	54	.575	2.5	504	447	.260	.962	2.63
WASHINGTON	72	56	.563	4	461	412	.256	.960	2.14
NEW YORK	60	63	.488	13.5	493	475	.257	.970	3.03
ST. LOUIS	58	64	.475	15	426	448	.259	.963	2.75
CHICAGO	57	67	.460	17	457	446	.256	.967	2.69
DETROIT	55	71	.437	20	476	557	.249	.960	3.40
PHILADELPHIA	52	76	.406	24	412	538	.243	.959	3.22
					3703	3703	.254	.964	2.77

BATTING AVERAGE
Ty Cobb DET .... .382
George Burns PHI ..... .352
George Sisler STL ...... .341

HITS
George Burns PHI 178
Ty Cobb DET 161
two tied at 154

DOUBLES
Tris Speaker CLE 33
Harry Hooper BOS........ 26
Babe Ruth BOS 26

TRIPLES
Ty Cobb DET 14
Harry Hooper BOS........ 13
Bobby Veach DET 13

HOME RUNS
Tilly Walker PHI 11
Babe Ruth BOS 11
two tied at 6

RUNS BATTED IN
Bobby Veach DET 78
George Burns PHI 70
Frank Baker NY 68

SLUGGING AVERAGE
Babe Ruth BOS .... .555
Ty Cobb DET .... .515
George Burns PHI ..... .467

STOLEN BASES
George Sisler STL 45
Braggo Roth CLE.......... 35
Ty Cobb DET 34

RUNS SCORED
Ray Chapman CLE....... 84
Ty Cobb DET 83
Harry Hooper BOS 81

WINS
Walter Johnson WAS.... 23
Stan Coveleski CLE...... 22
two tied at 21

WINNING PERCENTAGE
Sam Jones BOS .... .762
W. Johnson WAS........ .639
Stan Coveleski CLE... .629

EARNED RUN AVERAGE
W. Johnson WAS....... 1.27
Stan Coveleski CLE.... 1.82
Allen Sothoron STL.... 1.94

STRIKEOUTS
W. Johnson WAS........ 162
Jim Shaw WAS........... 129
Joe Bush BOS 125

SAVES
George Mogridge NY...... 7
Jim Bagby CLE............... 6
two tied at 4

COMPLETE GAMES
Carl Mays BOS 30
Scott Perry PHI 30
Walter Johnson WAS.... 29

SHUTOUTS
Carl Mays BOS 8
Walter Johnson WAS...... 8
Joe Bush BOS 7

GAMES PITCHED
Jim Bagby CLE.............. 45
George Mogridge NY.... 45
Scott Perry PHI............. 44

INNINGS PITCHED
Scott Perry PHI 332
W. Johnson WAS........ 325
Stan Coveleski CLE.... 311

1918 NL

	W	L	PCT	GB	R	OR	BA	FA	ERA
CHICAGO	84	45	.651	—	538	393	.265	.966	2.18
NEW YORK	71	53	.573	10.5	480	415	.260	.970	2.64
CINCINNATI	68	60	.531	15.5	530	496	.278	.964	3.00
PITTSBURGH	65	60	.520	17	466	412	.248	.966	2.48
BROOKLYN	57	69	.452	25.5	360	463	.250	.963	2.81
PHILADELPHIA	55	68	.447	26	430	507	.244	.961	3.15
BOSTON	53	71	.427	28.5	424	469	.244	.965	2.90
ST. LOUIS	51	78	.395	33	454	527	.244	.962	2.96
					3682	3682	.254	.965	2.76

BATTING AVERAGE
Zack Wheat BKN .... .335
Edd Roush CIN .... .333
Heinie Groh CIN .... .320

HITS
C. Hollocher CHI......... 161
Heinie Groh CIN 158
Edd Roush CIN........... 145

DOUBLES
Heinie Groh CIN 28
Les Mann CHI............... 27
Gavvy Cravath PHI 27

TRIPLES
Jake Daubert BKN 15
three tied at.................. 13

HOME RUNS
Gavvy Cravath PHI 8
Walt Cruise STL............ 6
Cy Williams PHI 6

RUNS BATTED IN
Sherry Magee CIN 76
George Cutshaw PIT 68
Fred Luderus PHI 67

SLUGGING AVERAGE
Edd Roush CIN.......... .455
Jake Daubert BKN...... .429
R. Hornsby STL .... .416

STOLEN BASES
Max Carey PIT.............. 58
George Burns NY 40
Charlie Hollocher CHI... 26

RUNS SCORED
Heinie Groh CIN 88
George Burns NY 80
Max Flack CHI 74

WINS
Hippo Vaughn CHI........ 22
four tied at.................... 19

WINNING PERCENTAGE
Claude Hendrix CHI... .731
E. Mayer PHI, PIT... .696
Hippo Vaughn CHI..... .688

EARNED RUN AVERAGE
Hippo Vaughn CHI..... 1.74
Lefty Tyler CHI............ 2.00
Wilbur Cooper PIT 2.11

STRIKEOUTS
Hippo Vaughn CHI...... 148
Wilbur Cooper PIT 117
B. Grimes BKN 113

SAVES
four tied at........................ 3

COMPLETE GAMES
Art Nehf BOS 28
Hippo Vaughn CHI........ 27
Wilbur Cooper PIT 26

SHUTOUTS
Hippo Vaughn CHI.......... 8
Lefty Tyler CHI............... 8
Burleigh Grimes BKN...... 7

GAMES PITCHED
Burleigh Grimes BKN.... 40
Wilbur Cooper PIT 38
Hod Eller CIN................ 37

INNINGS PITCHED
Hippo Vaughn CHI...... 290
Art Nehf BOS 284
Wilbur Cooper PIT 273

1919 AL

	W	L	PCT	GB	R	OR	BA	FA	ERA
CHICAGO	88	52	.629	—	667	534	.287	.969	3.04
CLEVELAND	84	55	.604	3.5	636	537	.278	.965	2.92
NEW YORK	80	59	.576	7.5	578	506	.267	.968	2.78
DETROIT	80	60	.571	8	618	578	.283	.964	3.30
ST. LOUIS	67	72	.482	20.5	533	567	.264	.963	3.13
BOSTON	66	71	.482	20.5	564	552	.261	.975	3.30
WASHINGTON	56	84	.400	32	533	570	.260	.960	3.01
PHILADELPHIA	36	104	.257	52	457	742	.244	.956	4.26
					4586	4586	.268	.965	3.21

BATTING AVERAGE
Ty Cobb DET .... .384
Bobby Veach DET ...... .355
George Sisler STL ...... .352

HITS
Bobby Veach DET 191
Ty Cobb DET 191
Joe Jackson CHI 181

DOUBLES
Bobby Veach DET 45
Tris Speaker CLE 38
Ty Cobb DET 36

TRIPLES
Bobby Veach DET 17
George Sisler STL 15
Harry Heilmann DET..... 15

HOME RUNS
Babe Ruth BOS 29
three tied at.................... 10

RUNS BATTED IN
Babe Ruth BOS 114
Bobby Veach DET 101
Joe Jackson CHI 96

SLUGGING AVERAGE
Babe Ruth BOS .... .657
George Sisler STL ...... .530
Bobby Veach DET ...... .519

STOLEN BASES
Eddie Collins CHI........... 33
George Sisler STL 28
Ty Cobb DET 28

RUNS SCORED
Babe Ruth BOS 103
George Sisler STL 96
Ty Cobb DET 92

WINS
Eddie Cicotte CHI 29
Stan Coveleski CLE...... 24
Lefty Williams CHI 23

WINNING PERCENTAGE
Eddie Cicotte CHI ...... .806
Hooks Dauss DET ..... .700
Lefty Williams CHI ..... .676

EARNED RUN AVERAGE
W. Johnson WAS........ 1.49
Eddie Cicotte CHI 1.82
Carl Weilman STL....... 2.07

STRIKEOUTS
W. Johnson WAS........ 147
Jim Shaw WAS............ 128
Lefty Williams CHI 125

SAVES
Allan Russell NY, BOS ... 5
three tied at..................... 4

COMPLETE GAMES
Eddie Cicotte CHI 30
Walter Johnson WAS.... 27
Lefty Williams CHI 27

SHUTOUTS
Walter Johnson WAS...... 7

GAMES PITCHED
Jim Shaw WAS.............. 45
A. Russell NY, BOS 44
two tied at 43

INNINGS PITCHED
Eddie Cicotte CHI 307
Jim Shaw WAS............. 307
Lefty Williams CHI 297

1919 NL

	W	L	PCT	GB	R	OR	BA	FA	ERA
★CINCINNATI	96	44	.686	—	577	401	.263	.974	2.23
NEW YORK	87	53	.621	9	605	470	.269	.964	2.70
CHICAGO	75	65	.536	21	454	407	.256	.969	2.21
PITTSBURGH	71	68	.511	24.5	472	466	.249	.970	2.88
BROOKLYN	69	71	.493	27	525	513	.263	.972	2.73
BOSTON	57	82	.410	38.5	465	563	.253	.966	3.17
ST. LOUIS	54	83	.394	40.5	463	552	.256	.963	3.23
PHILADELPHIA	47	90	.343	47.5	510	699	.251	.963	4.17
					4071	4071	.258	.968	2.91

BATTING AVERAGE
Edd Roush CIN........... .321
R. Hornsby STL .... .318
Ross Youngs NY .... .311

HITS
Ivy Olsen BKN 164
R. Hornsby STL 163
two tied at 162

DOUBLES
Ross Youngs NY 31
George Burns NY 30
Fred Luderus PHI 30

TRIPLES
Billy Southworth PIT 14
Hy Myers BKN 14

HOME RUNS
Gavvy Cravath PHI 12
Benny Kauff NY 10
Cy Williams PHI 9

RUNS BATTED IN
Hy Myers BKN 73
Edd Roush CIN 71
Rogers Hornsby STL 71

SLUGGING AVERAGE
Hy Myers BKN .... .436
Larry Doyle NY .... .433
two tied at .... .431

STOLEN BASES
George Burns NY 40
George Cutshaw PIT 36
Carson Bigbee PIT 31

RUNS SCORED
George Burns NY 86
Jake Daubert CIN 79
Heinie Groh CIN 79

WINS
Jesse Barnes NY 25
Slim Sallee CIN.............. 21
Hippo Vaughn CHI........ 21

WINNING PERCENTAGE
Dutch Ruether CIN .... .760
Slim Sallee CIN.......... .750
Jesse Barnes NY .... .735

EARNED RUN AVERAGE
G. Alexander CHI....... 1.72
Hippo Vaughn CHI..... 1.79
Dutch Ruether CIN 1.82

STRIKEOUTS
Hippo Vaughn CHI...... 141
Hod Eller CIN.............. 137
G. Alexander CHI........ 121

SAVES
Oscar Tuero STL 4
five tied at 3

COMPLETE GAMES
Wilbur Cooper PIT 27
Jeff Pfeffer BKN 26
Hippo Vaughn CHI........ 25

SHUTOUTS
Grover Alexander CHI 9
Babe Adams PIT............. 7
Hod Eller CIN.................. 7

GAMES PITCHED
Oscar Tuero STL 45
Meadows PHI, STL........ 40
three tied at................... 38

INNINGS PITCHED
Hippo Vaughn CHI...... 307
Jesse Barnes NY 296
Wilbur Cooper PIT 287

1920 AL

	W	L	PCT	GB	R	OR	BA	FA	ERA
★CLEVELAND	98	56	.636	—	857	642	.303	.971	3.41
CHICAGO	96	58	.623	2	794	665	.295	.968	3.59
NEW YORK	95	59	.617	3	838	629	.280	.970	3.31
ST. LOUIS	76	77	.497	21.5	797	766	.308	.963	4.03
BOSTON	72	81	.471	25.5	650	698	.269	.972	3.82
WASHINGTON	68	84	.447	29	723	802	.290	.963	4.17
DETROIT	61	93	.396	37	652	833	.270	.965	4.04
PHILADELPHIA	48	106	.312	50	558	834	.252	.959	3.93
					5869	5869	.283	.966	3.79

BATTING AVERAGE
George Sisler STL ..... .407
Tris Speaker CLE ...... .388
Joe Jackson CHI........ .382

HITS
George Sisler STL 257
Eddie Collins CHI....... 224
Joe Jackson CHI......... 218

DOUBLES
Tris Speaker CLE 50
George Sisler STL 49
Joe Jackson CHI........... 42

TRIPLES
Joe Jackson CHI........... 20
George Sisler STL 18
Harry Hooper BOS........ 17

HOME RUNS
Babe Ruth NY 54
George Sisler STL 19
Tilly Walker PHI 17

RUNS BATTED IN
Babe Ruth NY 137
B. Jacobson STL 122
George Sisler STL 122

SLUGGING AVERAGE
Babe Ruth NY............. .847
George Sisler STL ..... .632
Joe Jackson CHI........ .589

STOLEN BASES
Sam Rice WAS............. 63
George Sisler STL 42
Braggo Roth WAS 24

RUNS SCORED
Babe Ruth NY............. 158
George Sisler STL 137
Tris Speaker CLE 137

WINS
Jim Bagby CLE 31
Carl Mays NY................ 26
Stan Coveleski CLE..... 24

WINNING PERCENTAGE
Jim Bagby CLE .... .721
Carl Mays NY............. .703
Dickie Kerr CHI .... .700

EARNED RUN AVERAGE
Bob Shawkey NY........ 2.45
Stan Coveleski CLE.., 2.49
Urban Shocker STL ... 2.71

STRIKEOUTS
Stan Coveleski CLE... 133
Lefty Williams CHI 128
Bob Shawkey NY........ 126

SAVES
Dickie Kerr CHI 5
Urban Shocker STL 5
Bill Burwell STL............... 4

COMPLETE GAMES
Jim Bagby CLE 30
Red Faber CHI.............. 28
Eddie Cicotte CHI 28

SHUTOUTS
Carl Mays NY.................. 6
Urban Shocker STL 5
Bob Shawkey NY............. 5

GAMES PITCHED
Jim Bagby CLE 48
Doc Ayers DET 46
two tied at 45

INNINGS PITCHED
Jim Bagby CLE 340
Red Faber CHI........... 319
Stan Coveleski CLE.... 315

1920 NL

	W	L	PCT	GB	R	OR	BA	FA	ERA
BROOKLYN	93	61	.604	—	660	528	.277	.966	2.62
NEW YORK	86	68	.558	7	682	543	.269	.969	2.80
CINCINNATI	82	71	.536	10.5	639	569	.277	.968	2.84
PITTSBURGH	79	75	.513	14	530	552	.257	.971	2.89
CHICAGO	75	79	.487	18	619	635	.264	.965	3.27
ST. LOUIS	75	79	.487	18	675	682	.289	.961	3.43
BOSTON	62	90	.408	30	523	670	.260	.964	3.54
PHILADELPHIA	62	91	.405	30.5	565	714	.263	.964	3.63
					4893	4893	.270	.966	3.13

BATTING AVERAGE
R. Hornsby STL .... .370
Ross Youngs NY .... .351
Edd Roush CIN.......... .339

HITS
R. Hornsby STL 218
Milt Stock STL............. 204
Ross Youngs NY 204

DOUBLES
Rogers Hornsby STL 44
three tied at................... 36

TRIPLES
Hy Myers BKN 22
Rogers Hornsby STL 20
Edd Roush CIN............. 16

HOME RUNS
Cy Williams PHI 15
Irish Meusel PHI 14
George Kelly NY 11

RUNS BATTED IN
George Kelly NY 94
Rogers Hornsby STL 94
Edd Roush CIN............. 90

SLUGGING AVERAGE
R. Hornsby STL .... .559
Cy Williams PHI.......... .497
Ross Youngs NY .... .477

STOLEN BASES
Max Carey PIT.............. 52
Edd Roush CIN............. 36
Frankie Frisch NY 34

RUNS SCORED
George Burns NY 115
D. Bancroft PHI, NY 102
Jake Daubert CIN 97

WINS
G. Alexander CHI.......... 27
Wilbur Cooper PIT 24
Burleigh Grimes BKN.... 23

WINNING PERCENTAGE
B. Grimes BKN .... .676
G. Alexander CHI........ .659
Fred Toney NY .... .656

EARNED RUN AVERAGE
G. Alexander CHI........ 1.91
Babe Adams PIT.......... 2.16
B. Grimes BKN 2.22

STRIKEOUTS
G. Alexander CHI........ 173
Hippo Vaughn CHI...... 131
B. Grimes BKN 131

SAVES
Bill Sherdel STL.............. 6
Grover Alexander CHI 5
Hugh McQuillan BOS...... 5

COMPLETE GAMES
G. Alexander CHI.......... 33
Wilbur Cooper PIT 28
two tied at 25

SHUTOUTS
Babe Adams PIT............. 8
G. Alexander CHI............ 7

GAMES PITCHED
Jesse Haines STL.......... 47
G. Alexander CHI.......... 46
Phil Douglas NY............ 46

INNINGS PITCHED
G. Alexander CHI........ 363
Wilbur Cooper PIT 327
B. Grimes BKN 304

1921 AL

	W	L	PCT	GB	R	OR	BA	FA	ERA
NEW YORK	98	55	.641	—	948	708	.300	.965	3.79
CLEVELAND	94	60	.610	4.5	925	712	.308	.967	3.90
ST. LOUIS	81	73	.526	17.5	835	845	.304	.964	4.62
WASHINGTON	80	73	.523	18	704	738	.277	.963	3.97
BOSTON	75	79	.487	23.5	668	696	.277	.975	3.98
DETROIT	71	82	.464	27	883	852	.316	.963	4.40
CHICAGO	62	92	.403	36.5	683	858	.283	.969	4.94
PHILADELPHIA	53	100	.346	45	657	894	.274	.958	4.60
					6303	6303	.292	.965	4.28

BATTING AVERAGE
Harry Heilmann DET .. .394
Ty Cobb DET .... .389
Babe Ruth NY .... .378

HITS
Harry Heilmann DET ... 237
Jack Tobin STL 236
George Sisler STL 216

DOUBLES
Tris Speaker CLE 52
Babe Ruth NY 44
two tied at 43

TRIPLES
Howard Shanks WAS ... 19
Jack Tobin STL 18
George Sisler STL 18

HOME RUNS
Babe Ruth NY 59
Ken Williams STL 24
Bob Meusel NY 24

RUNS BATTED IN
Babe Ruth NY 171
Harry Heilmann DET ... 139
Bob Meusel NY 135

SLUGGING AVERAGE
Babe Ruth NY .... .846
Harry Heilmann DET .. .606
Ty Cobb DET .... .596

STOLEN BASES
George Sisler STL ... 35
Bucky Harris WAS 29
Sam Rice WAS 25

RUNS SCORED
Babe Ruth NY 177
Jack Tobin STL 132
R. Peckinpaugh NY 128

WINS
Carl Mays NY 27
Urban Shocker STL 27
Red Faber CHI 25

WINNING PERCENTAGE
Carl Mays NY .... .750
Urban Shocker STL ... .692
Joe Bush BOS .... .640

EARNED RUN AVERAGE
Red Faber CHI 2.48
G. Mogridge WAS 3.00
Carl Mays NY 3.05

STRIKEOUTS
W. Johnson WAS 143
Urban Shocker STL 132
Bob Shawkey NY 126

SAVES
Jim Middleton DET 7
Carl Mays NY 7
four tied at 4

COMPLETE GAMES
Red Faber CHI 32
Urban Shocker STL 31
Carl Mays NY 30

SHUTOUTS
Sad Sam Jones BOS 5
three tied at 4

GAMES PITCHED
Carl Mays NY 49
Urban Shocker STL 47
Bill Bayne STL 47

INNINGS PITCHED
Carl Mays NY 337
Red Faber CHI 331
Urban Shocker STL 327

1921 NL

	W	L	PCT	GB	R	OR	BA	FA	ERA
★NEW YORK	94	59	.614	—	840	637	.298	.971	3.55
PITTSBURGH	90	63	.588	4	692	595	.285	.973	3.17
ST. LOUIS	87	66	.569	7	809	681	.308	.965	3.62
BOSTON	79	74	.516	15	721	697	.290	.969	3.90
BROOKLYN	77	75	.507	16.5	667	681	.280	.964	3.70
CINCINNATI	70	83	.458	24	618	649	.278	.969	3.46
CHICAGO	64	89	.418	30	668	773	.292	.974	4.39
PHILADELPHIA	51	103	.331	43.5	617	919	.284	.955	4.48
					5632	5632	.289	.967	3.78

BATTING AVERAGE
R. Hornsby STL .... .397
Edd Roush CIN........... .352
Austin McHenry STL... .350

HITS
R. Hornsby STL 235
Frankie Frisch NY 211
Carson Bigbee PIT 204

DOUBLES
Rogers Hornsby STL 44
George Kelly NY 42
Jimmy Johnston BKN ... 41

TRIPLES
Rogers Hornsby STL 18
Ray Powell BOS 18
three tied at................... 17

HOME RUNS
George Kelly NY 23
Rogers Hornsby STL 21
Cy Williams PHI 18

RUNS BATTED IN
R. Hornsby STL 126
George Kelly NY 122
two tied at 102

SLUGGING AVERAGE
R. Hornsby STL .... .639
Austin McHenry STL... .531
George Kelly NY .... .528

STOLEN BASES
Frankie Frisch NY 49
Max Carey PIT.............. 37
Jimmy Johnston BKN ... 28

RUNS SCORED
R. Hornsby STL 131
Frankie Frisch NY 121
Dave Bancroft NY 121

WINS
Burleigh Grimes BKN.... 22
Wilbur Cooper PIT 22
two tied at 20

WINNING PERCENTAGE
Bill Doak STL .... .714
Art Nehf NY................. .667
B. Grimes BKN .... .629

EARNED RUN AVERAGE
Bill Doak STL.............. 2.59
Babe Adams PIT........ 2.64
Whitey Glazner PIT.... 2.77

STRIKEOUTS
B. Grimes BKN 136
Wilbur Cooper PIT 134
Dolf Luque CIN 102

SAVES
Lou North STL 7
Jesse Barnes NY 6
Hugh McQuillan BOS...... 5

COMPLETE GAMES
Burleigh Grimes BKN.... 30
Wilbur Cooper PIT 29
Dolf Luque CIN 25

SHUTOUTS
eight tied at 3

GAMES PITCHED
Jim Scott BOS 47
Joe Oeschger BOS....... 46
Hugh McQuillan BOS.... 45

INNINGS PITCHED
Wilbur Cooper PIT 327
Dolf Luque CIN 304
B. Grimes BKN 302

1922 AL

	W	L	PCT	GB	R	OR	BA	FA	ERA
NEW YORK	94	60	.610	—	758	618	.287	.975	3.39
ST. LOUIS	93	61	.604	1	867	643	.313	.968	3.38
DETROIT	79	75	.513	15	828	791	.305	.970	4.27
CLEVELAND	78	76	.506	16	768	817	.292	.968	4.60
CHICAGO	77	77	.500	17	691	691	.278	.975	3.93
WASHINGTON	69	85	.448	25	650	706	.268	.969	3.81
PHILADELPHIA	65	89	.422	29	705	830	.269	.966	4.59
BOSTON	61	93	.396	33	598	769	.260	.965	4.30
					5865	5865	.284	.969	4.03

BATTING AVERAGE
George Sisler STL ..... .420
Ty Cobb DET .... .401
Tris Speaker CLE .... .378

HITS
George Sisler STL 246
Ty Cobb DET 211
Jack Tobin STL 207

DOUBLES
Tris Speaker CLE 48
Del Pratt BOS 44
two tied at 42

TRIPLES
George Sisler STL 18
Ty Cobb DET 16
B. Jacobson STL 16

HOME RUNS
Ken Williams STL 39
Tilly Walker PHI 37
Babe Ruth NY 35

RUNS BATTED IN
Ken Williams STL 155
Bobby Veach DET 126
Marty McManus STL... 109

SLUGGING AVERAGE
Babe Ruth NY .... .672
Ken Williams STL ...... .627
Tris Speaker CLE ...... .606

STOLEN BASES
George Sisler STL 51
Ken Williams STL 37
Bucky Harris WAS 25

RUNS SCORED
George Sisler STL 134
Lu Blue DET 131
Ken Williams STL 128

WINS
Eddie Rommel PHI 27
Joe Bush NY 26
Urban Shocker STL 24

WINNING PERCENTAGE
Joe Bush NY .... .788
Eddie Rommel PHI .... .675
Bob Shawkey NY .... .625

EARNED RUN AVERAGE
Red Faber CHI............ 2.80
H. Pillette DET 2.85
Bob Shawkey NY 2.91

STRIKEOUTS
Urban Shocker STL 149
Red Faber CHI............ 148
Bob Shawkey NY 130

SAVES
Sad Sam Jones NY 8
Hub Pruett STL 7
Rasty Wright STL............ 5

COMPLETE GAMES
Red Faber CHI.............. 31
Urban Shocker STL 29
two tied at 23

SHUTOUTS
George Uhle CLE 5

GAMES PITCHED
Eddie Rommel PHI 51
George Uhle CLE 50
Urban Shocker STL 48

INNINGS PITCHED
Red Faber CHI............ 353
Urban Shocker STL 348
Bob Shawkey NY 300

1922 NL

	W	L	PCT	GB	R	OR	BA	FA	ERA
★NEW YORK	93	61	.604	—	852	658	.305	.970	3.45
CINCINNATI	86	68	.558	7	766	677	.296	.968	3.53
PITTSBURGH	85	69	.552	8	865	736	.308	.970	3.98
ST. LOUIS	85	69	.552	8	863	819	.301	.961	4.44
CHICAGO	80	74	.519	13	771	808	.293	.968	4.34
BROOKLYN	76	78	.494	17	743	754	.290	.967	4.05
PHILADELPHIA	57	96	.373	35.5	738	920	.282	.965	4.64
BOSTON	53	100	.346	39.5	596	822	.263	.965	4.37
					6194	6194	.292	.967	4.10

BATTING AVERAGE
R. Hornsby STL .... .401
Ray Grimes CHI.......... .354
Hack Miller CHI.......... .352

HITS
R. Hornsby STL 250
Carson Bigbee PIT 215
Dave Bancroft NY 209

DOUBLES
Rogers Hornsby STL 46
Ray Grimes CHI........... 45
Pat Duncan CIN........... 44

TRIPLES
Jake Daubert CIN 22
Irish Meusel NY 17
two tied at 15

HOME RUNS
R. Hornsby STL 42
Cy Williams PHI 26
two tied at 17

RUNS BATTED IN
R. Hornsby STL 152
Irish Meusel NY 132
Zack Wheat BKN 112

SLUGGING AVERAGE
R. Hornsby STL .... .722
Ray Grimes CHI.......... .572
Cliff Lee PHI............... .540

STOLEN BASES
Max Carey PIT............. 51
Frankie Frisch NY 31
George Burns CIN 30

RUNS SCORED
R. Hornsby STL 141
Max Carey PIT............ 140
two tied at 117

WINS
Eppa Rixey CIN 25
Wilbur Cooper PIT 23
Dutch Ruether BKN 21

WINNING PERCENTAGE
Pete Donohue CIN..... .667
Eppa Rixey CIN .... .658
Johnny Couch CIN..... .640

EARNED RUN AVERAGE
P. Douglas NY 2.63
Rosy Ryan NY 3.01
Pete Donohue CIN..... 3.12

STRIKEOUTS
Dazzy Vance BKN 134
Wilbur Cooper PIT 129
Jimmy Ring PHI 116

SAVES
Claude Jonnard NY 5
Lou North STL 4
four tied at....................... 3

COMPLETE GAMES
Wilbur Cooper PIT 27
Dutch Ruether BKN 26
Eppa Rixey CIN 26

SHUTOUTS
Dazzy Vance BKN 5
Johnny Morrison PIT....... 5
two tied at 4

GAMES PITCHED
Lou North STL 53
Bill Sherdel STL............ 47
two tied at 46

INNINGS PITCHED
Eppa Rixey CIN 313
Wilbur Cooper PIT 295
Johnny Morrison PIT... 286

1923 AL

	W	L	PCT	GB	R	OR	BA	FA	ERA
★NEW YORK	98	54	.645	—	823	622	.291	.977	3.66
DETROIT	83	71	.539	16	831	741	.300	.968	4.09
CLEVELAND	82	71	.536	16.5	888	746	.301	.964	3.91
WASHINGTON	75	78	.490	23.5	720	747	.274	.966	3.99
ST. LOUIS	74	78	.487	24	688	720	.281	.971	3.93
PHILADELPHIA	69	83	.454	29	661	761	.271	.965	4.08
CHICAGO	69	85	.448	30	692	741	.279	.971	4.03
BOSTON	61	91	.401	37	584	809	.261	.963	4.20
					5887	5887	.282	.968	3.99

BATTING AVERAGE
H. Heilmann DET .... .403
Babe Ruth NY .... .393
Tris Speaker CLE ...... .380

HITS
C. Jamieson CLE 222
Tris Speaker CLE 218
Harry Heilmann DET... 211

DOUBLES
Tris Speaker CLE 59
George Burns BOS....... 47
Babe Ruth NY 45

TRIPLES
Goose Goslin WAS....... 18
Sam Rice WAS 18
two tied at 15

HOME RUNS
Babe Ruth NY 41
Ken Williams STL 29
Harry Heilmann DET..... 18

RUNS BATTED IN
Babe Ruth NY 131
Tris Speaker CLE 130
Harry Heilmann DET... 115

SLUGGING AVERAGE
Babe Ruth NY .... .764
H. Heilmann DET .... .632
Ken Williams STL ...... .623

STOLEN BASES
Eddie Collins CHI.......... 47
Johnny Mostil CHI......... 41
Bucky Harris WAS 23

RUNS SCORED
Babe Ruth NY 151
Tris Speaker CLE 133
C. Jamieson CLE........ 130

WINS
George Uhle CLE 26
Sad Sam Jones NY 21
Hooks Dauss DET 21

WINNING PERCENTAGE
Herb Pennock NY .... .760
Sad Sam Jones NY ... .724
Waite Hoyt NY .... .654

EARNED RUN AVERAGE
Stan Coveleski CLE... 2.76
Waite Hoyt NY 3.02
Allan Russell WAS..... 3.03

STRIKEOUTS
W. Johnson WAS........ 130
Joe Bush NY............... 125
Bob Shawkey NY........ 125

SAVES
Allan Russell WAS.......... 9
Jack Quinn BOS 7
Slim Harriss PHI 6

COMPLETE GAMES
George Uhle CLE 29
Howard Ehmke BOS..... 28
Urban Shocker STL 24

SHUTOUTS
Stan Coveleski CLE...... 5
Elam Vangilder STL....... 4
Hooks Dauss DET 4

GAMES PITCHED
Eddie Rommel PHI 56
George Uhle CLE 54
two tied at 52

INNINGS PITCHED
George Uhle CLE 358
Howard Ehmke BOS... 317
Hooks Dauss DET 316

1923 NL

	W	L	PCT	GB	R	OR	BA	FA	ERA
NEW YORK	95	58	.621	—	854	679	.295	.972	3.90
CINCINNATI	91	63	.591	4.5	708	629	.285	.969	3.21
PITTSBURGH	87	67	.565	8.5	786	696	.295	.971	3.87
CHICAGO	83	71	.539	12.5	756	704	.288	.967	3.82
ST. LOUIS	79	74	.516	16	746	732	.286	.963	3.87
BROOKLYN	76	78	.494	19.5	753	741	.285	.955	3.73
BOSTON	54	100	.351	41.5	636	798	.273	.964	4.22
PHILADELPHIA	50	104	.325	45.5	748	1008	.278	.966	5.30
					5987	5987	.286	.966	3.99

BATTING AVERAGE
R. Hornsby STL .... .384
Jim Bottomley STL..... .371
two tied at .... .351

HITS
Frankie Frisch NY 223
Jigger Statz CHI........... 209
Pie Traynor PIT........... 208

DOUBLES
Edd Roush CIN............. 41
G. Grantham CHI.......... 36
C. Tierney PIT, PHI....... 36

TRIPLES
Pie Traynor PIT............. 19
Max Carey PIT.............. 19
Edd Roush CIN............. 18

HOME RUNS
Cy Williams PHI 41
Jack Fournier BKN........ 22
Hack Miller CHI............. 20

RUNS BATTED IN
Irish Meusel NY 125
Cy Williams PHI 114
Frankie Frisch NY 111

SLUGGING AVERAGE
R. Hornsby STL .... .627
Jack Fournier BKN..... .588
Cy Williams PHI .... .576

STOLEN BASES
Max Carey PIT.............. 51
G. Grantham CHI.......... 43
two tied at 32

RUNS SCORED
Ross Youngs NY 121
Max Carey PIT............. 120
Frankie Frisch NY 116

WINS
Dolf Luque CIN 27
Johnny Morrison PIT..... 25
G. Alexander CHI.......... 22

WINNING PERCENTAGE
Dolf Luque CIN .... .771
Rosy Ryan NY .... .762
Jack Scott NY .... .696

EARNED RUN AVERAGE
Dolf Luque CIN 1.93
Eppa Rixey CIN 2.80
Vic Keen CHI 3.00

STRIKEOUTS
Dazzy Vance BKN 197
Dolf Luque CIN 151
B. Grimes BKN 119

SAVES
Claude Jonnard NY 5
Rosy Ryan NY 4

COMPLETE GAMES
Burleigh Grimes BKN.... 33
Dolf Luque CIN 28
Johnny Morrison PIT..... 27

SHUTOUTS
Dolf Luque CIN 6
J. Barnes NY, BOS......... 5
Hugh McQuillan NY 5

GAMES PITCHED
Rosy Ryan NY 45
Claude Jonnard NY 45
Joe Oeschger BOS........ 44

INNINGS PITCHED
B. Grimes BKN 327
Dolf Luque CIN 322
Jimmy Ring PHI 313

1924 AL

	W	L	PCT	GB	R	OR	BA	FA	ERA
★WASHINGTON	92	62	.597	—	755	613	.294	.972	3.35
NEW YORK	89	63	.586	2	798	667	.289	.974	3.86
DETROIT	86	68	.558	6	849	796	.298	.971	4.19
ST. LOUIS	74	78	.487	17	764	797	.294	.969	4.55
PHILADELPHIA	71	81	.467	20	685	778	.281	.971	4.39
CLEVELAND	67	86	.438	24.5	755	814	.296	.967	4.40
BOSTON	67	87	.435	25	725	801	.277	.967	4.36
CHICAGO	66	87	.431	25.5	793	858	.288	.963	4.75
					6124	6124	.290	.969	4.23

BATTING AVERAGE
Babe Ruth NY............ .378
C. Jamieson CLE........ .359
Bibb Falk CHI.............. .352

HITS
Sam Rice WAS 216
C. Jamieson CLE........ 213
Ty Cobb DET 211

DOUBLES
Harry Heilmann DET.... 45
Joe Sewell CLE 45
two tied at 41

TRIPLES
Wally Pipp NY............... 19
Goose Goslin WAS....... 17
Harry Heilmann DET..... 16

HOME RUNS
Babe Ruth NY.............. 46
Joe Hauser PHI 27
B. Jacobson STL 19

RUNS BATTED IN
Goose Goslin WAS..... 129
Babe Ruth NY............. 121
Bob Meusel NY........... 120

SLUGGING AVERAGE
Babe Ruth NY............. .739
H. Heilmann DET........ .533
Ken Williams STL .... .533

STOLEN BASES
Eddie Collins CHI........ 42
Bob Meusel NY............ 26
Sam Rice WAS 24

RUNS SCORED
Babe Ruth NY............. 143
Ty Cobb DET 115
Eddie Collins CHI........ 108

WINS
Walter Johnson WAS... 23
Herb Pennock NY......... 21
two tied at 20

WINNING PERCENTAGE
W. Johnson WAS........ .767
Herb Pennock NY....... .700
Earl Whitehill DET...... .654

EARNED RUN AVERAGE
W. Johnson WAS........ 2.72
Tom Zachary WAS 2.75
Herb Pennock NY....... 2.83

STRIKEOUTS
W. Johnson WAS........ 158
Howard Ehmke BOS.... 119
Bob Shawkey NY........ 114

SAVES
Firpo Marberry WAS ... 15
Allan Russell WAS......... 8
Jack Quinn BOS 7

COMPLETE GAMES
Sloppy Thurston CHI 28
Howard Ehmke BOS..... 26
Herb Pennock NY 25

SHUTOUTS
Walter Johnson WAS.... 6
Dixie Davis STL 5
three tied at..................... 4

GAMES PITCHED
Firpo Marberry WAS 50
Ken Holloway DET........ 49
two tied at 46

INNINGS PITCHED
Howard Ehmke BOS... 315
S. Thurston CHI 291
Herb Pennock NY 286

1924 NL

	W	L	PCT	GB	R	OR	BA	FA	ERA
NEW YORK	93	60	.608	—	857	641	.300	.971	3.62
BROOKLYN	92	62	.597	1.5	717	675	.287	.968	3.64
PITTSBURGH	90	63	.588	3	724	588	.287	.971	3.27
CINCINNATI	83	70	.542	10	649	579	.290	.966	3.12
CHICAGO	81	72	.529	12	698	699	.276	.966	3.83
ST. LOUIS	65	89	.422	28.5	740	750	.290	.969	4.15
PHILADELPHIA	55	96	.364	37	676	849	.275	.972	4.87
BOSTON	53	100	.346	40	520	800	.256	.973	4.46
					5581	5581	.283	.970	3.87

BATTING AVERAGE
R. Hornsby STL .... .424
Zack Wheat BKN .... .375
Ross Youngs NY .... .356

HITS
R. Hornsby STL 227
Zack Wheat BKN 212
Frankie Frisch NY 198

DOUBLES
R. Hornsby STL 43
Zack Wheat BKN 41
George Kelly NY 37

TRIPLES
Edd Roush CIN............. 21
Rabbit Maranville PIT ... 20
Glenn Wright PIT 18

HOME RUNS
Jack Fournier BKN....... 27
Rogers Hornsby STL 25
Cy Williams PHI............ 24

RUNS BATTED IN
George Kelly NY 136
Jack Fournier BKN...... 116
two tied at 111

SLUGGING AVERAGE
R. Hornsby STL .... .696
Cy Williams PHI............ .552
Zack Wheat BKN .... .549

STOLEN BASES
Max Carey PIT.............. 49
Kiki Cuyler PIT 32
Cliff Heathcote CHI 26

RUNS SCORED
Frankie Frisch NY 121
R. Hornsby STL 121
Max Carey PIT............ 113

WINS
Dazzy Vance BKN 28
Burleigh Grimes BKN.... 22
two tied at 20

WINNING PERCENTAGE
Emil Yde PIT .... .842
Dazzy Vance BKN ..... .824
Jack Bentley NY .... .762

EARNED RUN AVERAGE
Dazzy Vance BKN 2.16
Hugh McQuillan NY ... 2.69
Eppa Rixey CIN 2.76

STRIKEOUTS
Dazzy Vance BKN 262
B. Grimes BKN 135
Dolf Luque CIN 86

SAVES
Jackie May CIN............... 6
Rosy Ryan NY 5
Claude Jonnard NY 5

COMPLETE GAMES
Dazzy Vance BKN 30
Burleigh Grimes BKN.... 30
Wilbur Cooper PIT 25

SHUTOUTS
six tied at.......................... 4

GAMES PITCHED
Ray Kremer PIT 41
Johnny Morrison PIT...... 41
Vic Keen CHI 40

INNINGS PITCHED
B. Grimes BKN 311
Dazzy Vance BKN 309
Wilbur Cooper PIT 269

1925 AL

	W	L	PCT	GB	R	OR	BA	FA	ERA
WASHINGTON	96	55	.636	—	829	669	.303	.972	3.67
PHILADELPHIA	88	64	.579	8.5	830	714	.307	.966	3.89
ST. LOUIS	82	71	.536	15	897	909	.298	.964	4.85
DETROIT	81	73	.526	16.5	903	829	.302	.972	4.61
CHICAGO	79	75	.513	18.5	811	771	.284	.968	4.34
CLEVELAND	70	84	.455	27.5	782	810	.297	.967	4.49
NEW YORK	69	85	.448	28.5	706	774	.275	.974	4.33
BOSTON	47	105	.309	49.5	639	921	.266	.957	4.97
					6397	6397	.292	.968	4.39

BATTING AVERAGE
H. Heilmann DET....... .393
Tris Speaker CLE ...... .389
Al Simmons PHI.......... .384

HITS
Al Simmons PHI.......... 253
Sam Rice WAS............ 227
Harry Heilmann DET... 225

DOUBLES
Marty McManus STL..... 44
Earl Sheely CHI 43
Al Simmons PHI 43

TRIPLES
Goose Goslin WAS....... 20
Johnny Mostil CHI......... 16
George Sisler STL 15

HOME RUNS
Bob Meusel NY.............. 33
Ken Williams STL 25
Babe Ruth NY................ 25

RUNS BATTED IN
Bob Meusel NY............ 138
Harry Heilmann DET... 133
Al Simmons PHI........... 129

SLUGGING AVERAGE
Ken Williams STL ...... .613
Ty Cobb DET .... .598
Al Simmons PHI.......... .596

STOLEN BASES
Johnny Mostil CHI.......... 43
Sam Rice WAS.............. 26
Goose Goslin WAS....... 26

RUNS SCORED
Johnny Mostil CHI....... 135
Al Simmons PHI.......... 122
Earle Combs NY 117

WINS
Eddie Rommel PHI 21
Ted Lyons CHI.............. 21
two tied at 20

WINNING PERCENTAGE
Stan Coveleski WAS... .800
W. Johnson WAS........ .741
D. Ruether WAS .... .720

EARNED RUN AVERAGE
S. Coveleski WAS...... 2.84
Herb Pennock NY 2.96
W. Johnson WAS....... 3.07

STRIKEOUTS
Lefty Grove PHI 116
W. Johnson WAS........ 108
two tied at 95

SAVES
Firpo Marberry WAS..... 15
Jess Doyle DET.............. 8
Sarge Connally CHI........ 8

COMPLETE GAMES
Sherry Smith CLE......... 22
Howard Ehmke BOS..... 22
Herb Pennock NY 21

SHUTOUTS
Ted Lyons CHI................. 5
Joe Giard STL................. 4
Sam Gray PHI................. 4

GAMES PITCHED
Firpo Marberry WAS..... 55
Rube Walberg PHI........ 53
two tied at 52

INNINGS PITCHED
Herb Pennock NY 277
Ted Lyons CHI............. 263
Eddie Rommel PHI 261

1925 NL

	W	L	PCT	GB	R	OR	BA	FA	ERA
★PITTSBURGH	95	58	.621	—	912	715	.307	.964	3.87
NEW YORK	86	66	.566	8.5	736	702	.283	.968	3.94
CINCINNATI	80	73	.523	15	690	643	.285	.968	3.38
ST. LOUIS	77	76	.503	18	828	764	.299	.966	4.36
BOSTON	70	83	.458	25	708	802	.292	.964	4.39
BROOKLYN	68	85	.444	27	786	866	.296	.966	4.77
PHILADELPHIA	68	85	.444	27	812	930	.295	.966	5.02
CHICAGO	68	86	.442	27.5	723	773	.275	.969	4.41
					6195	6195	.292	.966	4.27

BATTING AVERAGE
R. Hornsby STL .... .403
Jim Bottomley STL..... .367
Zack Wheat BKN .... .359

HITS
Jim Bottomley STL...... 227
Zack Wheat BKN 221
Kiki Cuyler PIT 220

DOUBLES
Jim Bottomley STL..... 44
Kiki Cuyler PIT 43
Zack Wheat BKN 42

TRIPLES
Kiki Cuyler PIT 26
three tied at................... 16

HOME RUNS
Rogers Hornsby STL 39
Gabby Hartnett CHI 24
Jack Fournier BKN........ 22

RUNS BATTED IN
R. Hornsby STL 143
Jack Fournier BKN...... 130
Jim Bottomley STL...... 128

SLUGGING AVERAGE
R. Hornsby STL .... .756
Kiki Cuyler PIT .... .593
Jim Bottomley STL..... .578

STOLEN BASES
Max Carey PIT.............. 46
Kiki Cuyler PIT 41
Sparky Adams CHI 26

RUNS SCORED
Kiki Cuyler PIT 144
R. Hornsby STL 133
Zack Wheat BKN 125

WINS
Dazzy Vance BKN 22
Eppa Rixey CIN 21
Pete Donohue CIN........ 21

WINNING PERCENTAGE
Bill Sherdel STL .... .714
Dazzy Vance BKN ..... .710
Vic Aldridge PIT .... .682

EARNED RUN AVERAGE
Dolf Luque CIN 2.63
Eppa Rixey CIN 2.88
Art Reinhart STL 3.05

STRIKEOUTS
Dazzy Vance BKN 221
Dolf Luque CIN 140
two tied at 93

SAVES
Johnny Morrison PIT....... 4
Guy Bush CHI 4
four tied at........................ 3

COMPLETE GAMES
Pete Donohue CIN......... 27
Dazzy Vance BKN 26
two tied at 22

SHUTOUTS
Dolf Luque CIN 4
Dazzy Vance BKN 4
Hal Carlson PHI 4

GAMES PITCHED
Johnny Morrison PIT..... 44
Pete Donohue CIN........ 42
Guy Bush CHI................ 42

INNINGS PITCHED
Pete Donohue CIN...... 301
Dolf Luque CIN 291
Eppa Rixey CIN 287

1926 AL

	W	L	PCT	GB	R	OR	BA	FA	ERA
NEW YORK	91	63	.591	—	847	713	.289	.966	3.86
CLEVELAND	88	66	.571	3	738	612	.289	.972	3.40
PHILADELPHIA	83	67	.553	6	677	570	.269	.972	3.00
WASHINGTON	81	69	.540	8	802	761	.292	.969	4.34
CHICAGO	81	72	.529	9.5	730	665	.289	.973	3.74
DETROIT	79	75	.513	12	793	830	.291	.969	4.41
ST. LOUIS	62	92	.403	29	682	845	.276	.963	4.66
BOSTON	46	107	.301	44.5	562	835	.256	.970	4.72
					5831	5831	.281	.969	4.02

BATTING AVERAGE
Heinie Manush DET... .378
Babe Ruth NY .... .372
two tied at .... .367

HITS
Sam Rice WAS 216
George Burns CLE 216
Goose Goslin WAS..... 201

DOUBLES
George Burns CLE 64
Al Simmons PHI............ 53
Tris Speaker CLE 52

TRIPLES
Lou Gehrig NY 20
C. Gehringer DET 17
two tied at 15

HOME RUNS
Babe Ruth NY 47
Al Simmons PHI............ 19
Tony Lazzeri NY 18

RUNS BATTED IN
Babe Ruth NY 145
George Burns CLE 114
Tony Lazzeri NY 114

SLUGGING AVERAGE
Babe Ruth NY .... .737
Al Simmons PHI.......... .566
Heinie Manush DET.... .564

STOLEN BASES
Johnny Mostil CHI........ 35
Sam Rice WAS.............. 25
Bill Hunnefield CHI....... 24

RUNS SCORED
Babe Ruth NY 139
Lou Gehrig NY 135
Johnny Mostil CHI....... 120

WINS
George Uhle CLE 27
Herb Pennock NY 23
Urban Shocker NY........ 19

WINNING PERCENTAGE
George Uhle CLE .... .711
Herb Pennock NY ...... .676
Urban Shocker NY ..... .633

EARNED RUN AVERAGE
Lefty Grove PHI 2.51
George Uhle CLE 2.83
Ted Lyons CHI........... 3.01

STRIKEOUTS
Lefty Grove PHI 194
George Uhle CLE 159
Tommy Thomas CHI... 127

SAVES
Firpo Marberry WAS 22
Hooks Dauss DET 9
two tied at 6

COMPLETE GAMES
George Uhle CLE 32
Ted Lyons CHI.............. 24
Walter Johnson WAS... 22

SHUTOUTS
Ed Wells DET 4

GAMES PITCHED
Firpo Marberry WAS..... 64
Joe Pate PHI.................. 47
Lefty Grove PHI 45

INNINGS PITCHED
George Uhle CLE 318
Ted Lyons CHI............. 284
Herb Pennock NY 266

1926 NL

	W	L	PCT	GB	R	OR	BA	FA	ERA
★ST. LOUIS	89	65	.578	—	817	678	.286	.969	3.67
CINCINNATI	87	67	.565	2	747	651	.290	.972	3.42
PITTSBURGH	84	69	.549	4.5	769	689	.285	.965	3.67
CHICAGO	82	72	.532	7	682	602	.278	.974	3.26
NEW YORK	74	77	.490	13.5	663	668	.278	.970	3.77
BROOKLYN	71	82	.464	17.5	623	705	.263	.963	3.82
BOSTON	66	86	.434	22	624	719	.277	.967	4.03
PHILADELPHIA	58	93	.384	29.5	687	900	.281	.964	5.19
					5612	5612	.280	.968	3.84

BATTING AVERAGE
B. Hargrave CIN .... .353
C. Christenson CIN .... .350
Earl Smith PIT .... .346

HITS
Eddie Brown BOS 201
Kiki Cuyler PIT 197
Sparky Adams CHI 193

DOUBLES
Jim Bottomley STL 40
Edd Roush CIN 37
Hack Wilson CHI 36

TRIPLES
Paul Waner PIT 22
Curt Walker CIN 20
Pie Traynor PIT 17

HOME RUNS
Hack Wilson CHI 21
Jim Bottomley STL 19
Cy Williams PHI 18

RUNS BATTED IN
Jim Bottomley STL 120
Hack Wilson CHI 109
Les Bell STL 100

SLUGGING AVERAGE
Cy Williams PHI .... .568
Hack Wilson CHI .... .539
Paul Waner PIT .... .528

STOLEN BASES
Kiki Cuyler PIT 35
Sparky Adams CHI 27
two tied at 23

RUNS SCORED
Kiki Cuyler PIT 113
Paul Waner PIT 101
two tied at 99

WINS
four tied at 20

WINNING PERCENTAGE
Ray Kremer PIT .... .769
Flint Rhem STL .... .741
Lee Meadows PIT ...... .690

EARNED RUN AVERAGE
Ray Kremer PIT 2.61
Charlie Root CHI 2.82
Jesse Petty BKN 2.84

STRIKEOUTS
Dazzy Vance BKN 140
Charlie Root CHI 127
two tied at 103

SAVES
Chick Davies NY 6
Ray Kremer PIT 5
Jack Scott NY 5

COMPLETE GAMES
Carl Mays CIN 24
Jesse Petty BKN 23
Charlie Root CHI 21

SHUTOUTS
Pete Donohue CIN 5
Sheriff Blake CHI 4
Bob Smith BOS 4

GAMES PITCHED
Jack Scott NY 50
C. Willoughby PHI 47
Pete Donohue CIN 47

INNINGS PITCHED
Pete Donohue CIN 286
Carl Mays CIN 281
Jesse Petty BKN 276

1927 AL

	W	L	PCT	GB	R	OR	BA	FA	ERA
★NEW YORK	110	44	.714	—	975	599	.307	.969	3.20
PHILADELPHIA	91	63	.591	19	841	726	.303	.970	3.95
WASHINGTON	85	69	.552	25	782	730	.287	.969	3.95
DETROIT	82	71	.536	27.5	845	805	.289	.968	4.12
CHICAGO	70	83	.458	39.5	662	708	.278	.971	3.91
CLEVELAND	66	87	.431	43.5	668	766	.283	.968	4.27
ST. LOUIS	59	94	.386	50.5	724	904	.276	.960	4.95
BOSTON	51	103	.331	59	597	856	.259	.964	4.68
					6094	6094	.285	.967	4.12

BATTING AVERAGE
H. Heilmann DET .... .398
Al Simmons PHI......... .392
Lou Gehrig NY .... .373

HITS
Earle Combs NY 231
Lou Gehrig NY 218
two tied at 201

DOUBLES
Lou Gehrig NY 52
George Burns CLE 51
Harry Heilmann DET..... 50

TRIPLES
Earle Combs NY 23
Heinie Manush DET...... 18
Lou Gehrig NY 18

HOME RUNS
Babe Ruth NY 60
Lou Gehrig NY 47
Tony Lazzeri NY 18

RUNS BATTED IN
Lou Gehrig NY 175
Babe Ruth NY 164
two tied at 120

SLUGGING AVERAGE
Babe Ruth NY .... .772
Lou Gehrig NY .... .765
Al Simmons PHI.......... .645

STOLEN BASES
George Sisler STL 27
Bob Meusel NY 24
three tied at................... 22

RUNS SCORED
Babe Ruth NY 158
Lou Gehrig NY 149
Earle Combs NY 137

WINS
Waite Hoyt NY 22
Ted Lyons CHI.............. 22
Lefty Grove PHI 20

WINNING PERCENTAGE
Waite Hoyt NY .... .759
Urban Shocker NY ..... .750
Wilcy Moore NY .... .731

EARNED RUN AVERAGE
Wilcy Moore NY 2.28
Waite Hoyt NY 2.63
Urban Shocker NY 2.84

STRIKEOUTS
Lefty Grove PHI 174
Rube Walberg PHI...... 136
Tommy Thomas CHI... 107

SAVES
G. Braxton WAS 13
Wilcy Moore NY 13
two tied at 9

COMPLETE GAMES
Ted Lyons CHI.............. 30
Tommy Thomas CHI..... 24
Waite Hoyt NY 23

SHUTOUTS
Hod Lisenbee WAS 4

GAMES PITCHED
G. Braxton WAS 58
Firpo Marberry WAS 56
Lefty Grove PHI 51

INNINGS PITCHED
Tommy Thomas CHI... 308
Ted Lyons CHI............. 308
Willis Hudlin CLE 265

1927 NL

	W	L	PCT	GB	R	OR	BA	FA	ERA
PITTSBURGH	94	60	.610	—	817	659	.305	.969	3.66
ST. LOUIS	92	61	.601	1.5	754	665	.278	.966	3.57
NEW YORK	92	62	.597	2	817	720	.297	.969	3.97
CHICAGO	85	68	.556	8.5	750	661	.284	.971	3.65
CINCINNATI	75	78	.490	18.5	643	653	.278	.973	3.54
BROOKLYN	65	88	.425	28.5	541	619	.253	.963	3.36
BOSTON	60	94	.390	34	651	771	.279	.963	4.22
PHILADELPHIA	51	103	.331	43	678	903	.280	.972	5.35
					5651	5651	.282	.969	3.91

BATTING AVERAGE
Paul Waner PIT .... .380
Rogers Hornsby NY .... .361
Lloyd Waner PIT .... .355

HITS
Paul Waner PIT 237
Lloyd Waner PIT 223
Frankie Frisch STL 208

DOUBLES
R. Stephenson CHI....... 46
Paul Waner PIT 40
two tied at 36

TRIPLES
Paul Waner PIT 17
Jim Bottomley STL........ 15
F. Thompson PHI........... 14

HOME RUNS
Hack Wilson CHI............ 30
Cy Williams PHI 30
Rogers Hornsby NY 26

RUNS BATTED IN
Paul Waner PIT 131
Hack Wilson CHI......... 129
Rogers Hornsby NY ... 125

SLUGGING AVERAGE
Chick Hafey STL........ .590
Rogers Hornsby NY ... .586
Hack Wilson CHI........ .579

STOLEN BASES
Frankie Frisch STL 48
Max Carey BKN 32
Harvey Hendrick BKN... 29

RUNS SCORED
Lloyd Waner PIT 133
Rogers Hornsby NY.... 133
Hack Wilson CHI......... 119

WINS
Charlie Root CHI........... 26
Jesse Haines STL......... 24
Carmen Hill PIT 22

WINNING PERCENTAGE
L. Benton BOS, NY.... .708
Jesse Haines STL...... .706
two tied at .... .704

EARNED RUN AVERAGE
Ray Kremer PIT 2.47
G. Alexander STL 2.52
Dazzy Vance BKN 2.70

STRIKEOUTS
Dazzy Vance BKN 184
Charlie Root CHI......... 145
Jackie May CIN........... 121

SAVES
Bill Sherdel STL.............. 6
George Mogridge BOS ... 5
Art Nehf CIN, CHI 5

COMPLETE GAMES
Dazzy Vance BKN 25
Jesse Haines STL......... 25
Lee Meadows PIT......... 25

SHUTOUTS
Jesse Haines STL........... 6
Red Lucas CIN 4
Charlie Root CHI............. 4

GAMES PITCHED
Charlie Root CHI........... 48
Jack Scott PHI 48
Rube Ehrhardt BKN...... 46

INNINGS PITCHED
Charlie Root CHI......... 309
Jesse Haines STL....... 301
Lee Meadows PIT....... 299

1928 AL

	W	L	PCT	GB	R	OR	BA	FA	ERA
★NEW YORK	101	53	.656	—	894	685	.296	.968	3.74
PHILADELPHIA	98	55	.641	2.5	829	615	.295	.970	3.36
ST. LOUIS	82	72	.532	19	772	742	.274	.969	4.17
WASHINGTON	75	79	.487	26	718	705	.284	.972	3.88
CHICAGO	72	82	.468	29	656	725	.270	.970	3.98
DETROIT	68	86	.442	33	744	804	.279	.965	4.32
CLEVELAND	62	92	.403	39	674	830	.285	.965	4.47
BOSTON	57	96	.373	43.5	589	770	.264	.971	4.39
					5876	5876	.281	.969	4.04

BATTING AVERAGE
Goose Goslin WAS.... .379
Heinie Manush STL ... .378
Lou Gehrig NY .... .374

HITS
Heinie Manush STL 241
Lou Gehrig NY 210
Sam Rice WAS 202

DOUBLES
Lou Gehrig NY 47
Heinie Manush STL 47
Bob Meusel NY 45

TRIPLES
Earle Combs NY 21
Heinie Manush STL 20
C. Gehringer DET 16

HOME RUNS
Babe Ruth NY 54
Lou Gehrig NY 27
Goose Goslin WAS 17

RUNS BATTED IN
Lou Gehrig NY 142
Babe Ruth NY 142
Bob Meusel NY 113

SLUGGING AVERAGE
Babe Ruth NY .... .709
Lou Gehrig NY .... .648
Goose Goslin WAS ..... .614

STOLEN BASES
Buddy Myer BOS 30
Johnny Mostil CHI......... 23
Harry Rice DET............. 20

RUNS SCORED
Babe Ruth NY 163
Lou Gehrig NY 139
Earle Combs NY 118

WINS
Lefty Grove PHI 24
George Pipgras NY....... 24
Waite Hoyt NY 23

WINNING PERCENTAGE
G. Crowder STL.......... .808
Waite Hoyt NY .... .767
Lefty Grove PHI .... .750

EARNED RUN AVERAGE
G. Braxton WAS 2.51
Herb Pennock NY 2.56
Lefty Grove PHI 2.58

STRIKEOUTS
Lefty Grove PHI 183
George Pipgras NY..... 139
Tommy Thomas CHI... 129

SAVES
Waite Hoyt NY 8
Willis Hudlin CLE 7
two tied at 6

COMPLETE GAMES
Red Ruffing BOS 25
Lefty Grove PHI 24
Tommy Thomas CHI.... 24

SHUTOUTS
Herb Pennock NY 5
four tied at........................ 4

GAMES PITCHED
Firpo Marberry WAS 48
Ed Morris BOS.............. 47
George Pipgras NY....... 46

INNINGS PITCHED
George Pipgras NY..... 301
Red Ruffing BOS 289
Tommy Thomas CHI...283

1928 NL

	W	L	PCT	GB	R	OR	BA	FA	ERA
ST. LOUIS	95	59	.617	—	807	636	.281	.974	3.38
NEW YORK	93	61	.604	2	807	653	.293	.972	3.67
CHICAGO	91	63	.591	4	714	615	.278	.975	3.40
PITTSBURGH	85	67	.559	9	837	704	.309	.967	3.95
CINCINNATI	78	74	.513	16	648	686	.280	.974	3.94
BROOKLYN	77	76	.503	17.5	665	640	.266	.965	3.25
BOSTON	50	103	.327	44.5	631	878	.275	.969	4.83
PHILADELPHIA	43	109	.283	51	660	957	.267	.971	5.52
					5769	5769	.281	.971	3.98

BATTING AVERAGE
R. Hornsby BOS .... .387
Paul Waner PIT .... .370
F. Lindstrom NY .... .358

HITS
F. Lindstrom NY 231
Paul Waner PIT 223
Lloyd Waner PIT 221

DOUBLES
Paul Waner PIT 50
Chick Hafey STL 46
two tied at 42

TRIPLES
Jim Bottomley STL....... 20
Paul Waner PIT 19
Lloyd Waner PIT 14

HOME RUNS
Hack Wilson CHI........... 31
Jim Bottomley STL........ 31
Chick Hafey STL............ 27

RUNS BATTED IN
Jim Bottomley STL...... 136
Pie Traynor PIT........... 124
Hack Wilson CHI......... 120

SLUGGING AVERAGE
R. Hornsby BOS .... .632
Jim Bottomley STL..... .628
Chick Hafey STL........ .604

STOLEN BASES
Kiki Cuyler CHI 37
Frankie Frisch STL 29
two tied at 19

RUNS SCORED
Paul Waner PIT 142
Jim Bottomley STL...... 123
Lloyd Waner PIT 121

WINS
Larry Benton NY 25
Burleigh Grimes PIT 25
Dazzy Vance BKN 22

WINNING PERCENTAGE
Larry Benton NY .... .735
Jesse Haines STL....... .714
Guy Bush CHI.............. .714

EARNED RUN AVERAGE
Dazzy Vance BKN 2.09
Sheriff Blake CHI 2.47
Art Nehf CHI 2.65

STRIKEOUTS
Dazzy Vance BKN 200
Pat Malone CHI 155
Charlie Root CHI......... 122

SAVES
Bill Sherdel STL.............. 5
Hal Haid STL 5
two tied at 4

COMPLETE GAMES
Burleigh Grimes PIT 28
Larry Benton NY 28
Dazzy Vance BKN 24

SHUTOUTS
five tied at 4

GAMES PITCHED
Burleigh Grimes PIT 48
Ray Kolp CIN 44
Eppa Rixey CIN 43

INNINGS PITCHED
Burleigh Grimes PIT ... 331
Larry Benton NY 310
Eppa Rixey CIN 291

1929 AL

	W	L	PCT	GB	R	OR	BA	FA	ERA
★PHILADELPHIA	104	46	.693	—	901	615	.296	.975	3.44
NEW YORK	88	66	.571	18	899	775	.295	.971	4.17
CLEVELAND	81	71	.533	24	717	736	.294	.968	4.05
ST. LOUIS	79	73	.520	26	733	713	.276	.975	4.08
WASHINGTON	71	81	.467	34	730	776	.276	.968	4.34
DETROIT	70	84	.455	36	926	928	.299	.961	4.96
CHICAGO	59	93	.388	46	627	792	.268	.970	4.41
BOSTON	58	96	.377	48	605	803	.267	.965	4.43
					6138	6138	.284	.969	4.24

BATTING AVERAGE
Lew Fonseca CLE ..... .369
Al Simmons PHI......... .365
Heinie Manush STL ... .355

HITS
Dale Alexander DET ... 215
C. Gehringer DET 215
Al Simmons PHI.......... 212

DOUBLES
Roy Johnson DET......... 45
C. Gehringer DET 45
Heinie Manush STL 45

TRIPLES
C. Gehringer DET 19
Russ Scarritt BOS......... 17
Bing Miller PHI.............. 16

HOME RUNS
Babe Ruth NY............... 46
Lou Gehrig NY 35
Al Simmons PHI............ 34

RUNS BATTED IN
Al Simmons PHI.......... 157
Babe Ruth NY.............. 154
Dale Alexander DET ... 137

SLUGGING AVERAGE
Babe Ruth NY............. .697
Al Simmons PHI........... .642
Jimmie Foxx PHI.......... .625

STOLEN BASES
C. Gehringer DET 28
Bill Cissell CHI 26
Bing Miller PHI.............. 24

RUNS SCORED
C. Gehringer DET 131
Roy Johnson DET....... 128
Lou Gehrig NY 127

WINS
G. Earnshaw PHI 24
Wes Ferrell CLE 21
Lefty Grove PHI 20

WINNING PERCENTAGE
Lefty Grove PHI .... .769
G. Earnshaw PHI .... .750
Wes Ferrell CLE .... .677

EARNED RUN AVERAGE
Lefty Grove PHI 2.81
F. Marberry WAS 3.06
T. Thomas CHI 3.19

STRIKEOUTS
Lefty Grove PHI 170
G. Earnshaw PHI 149
George Pipgras NY..... 125

SAVES
Firpo Marberry WAS 11
Wilcy Moore NY 8
Bill Shores PHI................ 7

COMPLETE GAMES
Tommy Thomas CHI..... 24
George Uhle DET 23
Sam Gray STL............... 23

SHUTOUTS
four tied at....................... 4

GAMES PITCHED
Firpo Marberry WAS 49
G. Earnshaw PHI 44
two tied at 43

INNINGS PITCHED
Sam Gray STL.............. 305
Willis Hudlin CLE 280
Lefty Grove PHI 275

1929 NL

	W	L	PCT	GB	R	OR	BA	FA	ERA
CHICAGO	98	54	.645	—	982	758	.303	.975	4.16
PITTSBURGH	88	65	.575	10.5	904	780	.303	.970	4.36
NEW YORK	84	67	.556	13.5	897	709	.296	.975	3.97
ST. LOUIS	78	74	.513	20	831	806	.293	.971	4.66
PHILADELPHIA	71	82	.464	27.5	897	1032	.309	.969	6.13
BROOKLYN	70	83	.458	28.5	755	888	.291	.968	4.92
CINCINNATI	66	88	.429	33	686	760	.281	.974	4.41
BOSTON	56	98	.364	43	657	876	.280	.967	5.12
					6609	6609	.294	.971	4.71

BATTING AVERAGE
Lefty O'Doul PHI .... .398
Babe Herman BKN .... .381
R. Hornsby CHI .... .380

HITS
Lefty O'Doul PHI 254
Lloyd Waner PIT 234
Rogers Hornsby CHI... 229

DOUBLES
J. Frederick BKN........... 52
Rogers Hornsby CHI..... 47
Chick Hafey STL 47

TRIPLES
Lloyd Waner PIT 20
Curt Walker CIN............ 15
Paul Waner PIT 15

HOME RUNS
Chuck Klein PHI............ 43
Mel Ott NY 42
two tied at 39

RUNS BATTED IN
Hack Wilson CHI......... 159
Mel Ott NY 151
Rogers Hornsby CHI... 149

SLUGGING AVERAGE
R. Hornsby CHI........... .679
Chuck Klein PHI.......... .657
Mel Ott NY .... .635

STOLEN BASES
Kiki Cuyler CHI 43
Evar Swanson CIN 33
Frankie Frisch STL 24

RUNS SCORED
Rogers Hornsby CHI.... 156
Lefty O'Doul PHI 152
Mel Ott NY 138

WINS
Pat Malone CHI 22
Red Lucas CIN 19
Charlie Root CHI........... 19

WINNING PERCENTAGE
Charlie Root CHI........ .760
Guy Bush CHI............. .720
B. Grimes PIT .... .708

EARNED RUN AVERAGE
Bill Walker NY............ 3.09
B. Grimes PIT 3.13
Charlie Root CHI........ 3.47

STRIKEOUTS
Pat Malone CHI 166
Watty Clark BKN......... 140
Dazzy Vance BKN 126

SAVES
Johnny Morrison BKN..... 8
Guy Bush CHI.................. 8
Lou Koupal BKN, PHI 6

COMPLETE GAMES
Red Lucas CIN 28

SHUTOUTS
Pat Malone CHI 5
F. Fitzsimmons NY 4
Charlie Root CHI............. 4

GAMES PITCHED
Guy Bush CHI............... 50
C. Willoughby PHI......... 49
three tied at................... 43

INNINGS PITCHED
Watty Clark BKN......... 279
Charlie Root CHI......... 272
Guy Bush CHI............. 271

1930 AL

	W	L	PCT	GB	R	OR	BA	FA	ERA
★PHILADELPHIA	102	52	.662	—	951	751	.294	.975	4.28
WASHINGTON	94	60	.610	8	892	689	.302	.974	3.96
NEW YORK	86	68	.558	16	1062	898	.309	.965	4.88
CLEVELAND	81	73	.526	21	890	915	.304	.962	4.88
DETROIT	75	79	.487	27	783	833	.284	.967	4.70
ST. LOUIS	64	90	.416	38	751	886	.268	.970	5.07
CHICAGO	62	92	.403	40	729	884	.276	.962	4.71
BOSTON	52	102	.338	50	612	814	.264	.968	4.70
					6670	6670	.288	.968	4.65

BATTING AVERAGE
Al Simmons PHI......... .381
Lou Gehrig NY .... .379
two tied at .... .359

HITS
Johnny Hodapp CLE... 225
Lou Gehrig NY 220
Al Simmons PHI.......... 211

DOUBLES
Johnny Hodapp CLE..... 51
Manush STL, WAS 49
two tied at 47

TRIPLES
Earle Combs NY 22
Carl Reynolds CHI 18
Lou Gehrig NY 17

HOME RUNS
Babe Ruth NY............... 49
Lou Gehrig NY 41
two tied at 37

RUNS BATTED IN
Lou Gehrig NY 174
Al Simmons PHI........... 165
Jimmie Foxx PHI......... 156

SLUGGING AVERAGE
Babe Ruth NY............ .732
Lou Gehrig NY .... .721
Al Simmons PHI.......... .708

STOLEN BASES
Marty McManus DET 23
C. Gehringer DET 19
three tied at................... 17

RUNS SCORED
Al Simmons PHI........... 152
Babe Ruth NY............. 150
C. Gehringer DET 144

WINS
Lefty Grove PHI 28
Wes Ferrell CLE 25
two tied at 22

WINNING PERCENTAGE
Lefty Grove PHI .... .848
F. Marberry WAS........ .750
Sam Jones WAS........ .682

EARNED RUN AVERAGE
Lefty Grove PHI 2.54
Wes Ferrell CLE 3.31
Lefty Stewart STL 3.45

STRIKEOUTS
Lefty Grove PHI 209
G. Earnshaw PHI........ 193
Bump Hadley WAS 162

SAVES
Lefty Grove PHI 9
G. Braxton WAS, CHI 6
Jack Quinn PHI................ 6

COMPLETE GAMES
Ted Lyons CHI............... 29
Crowder STL, WAS 25
Wes Ferrell CLE 25

SHUTOUTS
George Pipgras NY......... 3
George Earnshaw PHI.... 3

GAMES PITCHED
Lefty Grove PHI 50
G. Earnshaw PHI 49
two tied at 44

INNINGS PITCHED
Ted Lyons CHI 298
Wes Ferrell CLE 297
G. Earnshaw PHI 296

1930 NL

	W	L	PCT	GB	R	OR	BA	FA	ERA
ST. LOUIS	92	62	.597	—	1004	784	.314	.970	4.40
CHICAGO	90	64	.584	2	998	870	.309	.973	4.80
NEW YORK	87	67	.565	5	959	814	.319	.974	4.59
BROOKLYN	86	68	.558	6	871	738	.304	.972	4.03
PITTSBURGH	80	74	.519	12	891	928	.303	.965	5.24
BOSTON	70	84	.455	22	693	835	.281	.971	4.91
CINCINNATI	59	95	.383	33	665	857	.281	.973	5.08
PHILADELPHIA	52	102	.338	40	944	1199	.315	.962	6.71
					7025	7025	.303	.970	4.97

BATTING AVERAGE
Bill Terry NY .... .401
Babe Herman BKN .... .393
Chuck Klein PHI .... .386

SLUGGING AVERAGE
Hack Wilson CHI .... .723
Chuck Klein PHI .... .687
Babe Herman BKN .... .678

STRIKEOUTS
Bill Hallahan STL 177
Dazzy Vance BKN 173
Pat Malone CHI 142

HITS
Bill Terry NY 254
Chuck Klein PHI 250
Babe Herman BKN 241

STOLEN BASES
Kiki Cuyler CHI 37
Babe Herman BKN 18
Paul Waner PIT 18

SAVES
Hi Bell STL 8
Joe Heving NY 6
Watty Clark BKN 6

DOUBLES
Chuck Klein PHI 59
Kiki Cuyler CHI 50
Babe Herman BKN 48

RUNS SCORED
Chuck Klein PHI 158
Kiki Cuyler CHI 155
Woody English CHI 152

COMPLETE GAMES
Erv Brame PIT 22
Pat Malone CHI 22
Larry French PIT 21

TRIPLES
Adam Comorosky PIT ... 23
Paul Waner PIT 18
two tied at 17

WINS
Ray Kremer PIT 20
Pat Malone CHI 20
F. Fitzsimmons NY 19

SHUTOUTS
Charlie Root CHI 4
Dazzy Vance BKN 4
two tied at 3

HOME RUNS
Hack Wilson CHI 56
Chuck Klein PHI 40
Wally Berger BOS 38

WINNING PERCENTAGE
F. Fitzsimmons NY .... .731
Pat Malone CHI .... .690
Erv Brame PIT .... .680

GAMES PITCHED
Hal Elliot PHI 48
Phil Collins PHI 47
Guy Bush CHI 46

RUNS BATTED IN
Hack Wilson CHI 190
Chuck Klein PHI 170
Kiki Cuyler CHI 134

EARNED RUN AVERAGE
Dazzy Vance BKN 2.61
Carl Hubbell NY 3.76
Bill Walker NY 3.93

INNINGS PITCHED
Ray Kremer PIT 276
Larry French PIT 275
Pat Malone CHI 272

1931 AL

	W	L	PCT	GB	R	OR	BA	FA	ERA
PHILADELPHIA	107	45	.704	—	858	626	.287	.976	3.47
NEW YORK	94	59	.614	13.5	1067	760	.297	.972	4.20
WASHINGTON	92	62	.597	16	843	691	.285	.976	3.76
CLEVELAND	78	76	.506	30	885	833	.296	.963	4.63
ST. LOUIS	63	91	.409	45	772	870	.271	.963	4.76
BOSTON	62	90	.408	45	625	800	.262	.970	4.60
DETROIT	61	93	.396	47	651	836	.268	.964	4.56
CHICAGO	56	97	.366	51.5	704	939	.260	.961	5.05
					6355	6355	.278	.968	4.38

BATTING AVERAGE
Al Simmons PHI......... .390
Babe Ruth NY............ .373
Ed Morgan CLE .... .351

HITS
Lou Gehrig NY 211
Earl Averill CLE........... 209
Al Simmons PHI.......... 200

DOUBLES
Earl Webb BOS 67
Dale Alexander DET 47
Red Kress STL 46

TRIPLES
Roy Johnson DET......... 19
Lou Gehrig NY 15
Lu Blue CHI 15

HOME RUNS
Lou Gehrig NY 46
Babe Ruth NY............... 46
Earl Averill CLE............. 32

RUNS BATTED IN
Lou Gehrig NY 184
Babe Ruth NY............. 163
Earl Averill CLE........... 143

SLUGGING AVERAGE
Babe Ruth NY............ .700
Lou Gehrig NY .... .662
Al Simmons PHI.......... .641

STOLEN BASES
Ben Chapman NY......... 61
Roy Johnson DET......... 33
Jack Burns STL 19

RUNS SCORED
Lou Gehrig NY 163
Babe Ruth NY............. 149
Earl Averill CLE........... 140

WINS
Lefty Grove PHI 31
Wes Ferrell CLE 22
two tied at 21

WINNING PERCENTAGE
Lefty Grove PHI .... .886
F. Marberry WAS .... .800
Roy Mahaffey PHI...... .789

EARNED RUN AVERAGE
Lefty Grove PHI 2.06
Lefty Gomez NY 2.63
Bump Hadley WAS.... 3.06

STRIKEOUTS
Lefty Grove PHI 175
G. Earnshaw PHI........ 152
Lefty Gomez NY 150

SAVES
Wilcy Moore BOS 10
Bump Hadley WAS 8
two tied at 7

COMPLETE GAMES
Lefty Grove PHI 27
Wes Ferrell CLE 27
G. Earnshaw PHI.......... 23

SHUTOUTS
Lefty Grove PHI 4
G. Earnshaw PHI............. 3

GAMES PITCHED
Bump Hadley WAS....... 55
Wilcy Moore BOS 53
Pat Caraway CHI.......... 51

INNINGS PITCHED
Rube Walberg PHI...... 291
Lefty Grove PHI 289
G. Earnshaw PHI........ 282

1931 NL

	W	L	PCT	GB	R	OR	BA	FA	ERA
★ST. LOUIS	101	53	.656	—	815	614	.286	.974	3.45
NEW YORK	87	65	.572	13	768	599	.289	.974	3.30
CHICAGO	84	70	.545	17	828	710	.289	.973	3.97
BROOKLYN	79	73	.520	21	681	673	.276	.969	3.84
PITTSBURGH	75	79	.487	26	636	691	.266	.968	3.66
PHILADELPHIA	66	88	.429	35	684	828	.279	.966	4.58
BOSTON	64	90	.416	37	533	680	.258	.973	3.90
CINCINNATI	58	96	.377	43	592	742	.269	.973	4.22
					5537	5537	.277	.971	3.86

BATTING AVERAGE
Chick Hafey STL........ .349
Bill Terry NY............... .349
Jim Bottomley STL...... .348

HITS
Lloyd Waner PIT......... 214
Bill Terry NY................ 213
two tied at 202

DOUBLES
Sparky Adams STL....... 46
Wally Berger BOS......... 44
three tied at.................... 43

TRIPLES
Bill Terry NY.................. 20
Babe Herman BKN 16
Pie Traynor PIT............. 15

HOME RUNS
Chuck Klein PHI............ 31
Mel Ott NY 29
Wally Berger BOS.......... 19

RUNS BATTED IN
Chuck Klein PHI............ 121
Mel Ott NY 115
Bill Terry NY................. 112

SLUGGING AVERAGE
Chuck Klein PHI.......... .584
R. Hornsby CHI........... .574
Chick Hafey STL......... .569

STOLEN BASES
Frankie Frisch STL........ 28
Babe Herman BKN 17
two tied at 16

RUNS SCORED
Chuck Klein PHI.......... 121
Bill Terry NY................. 121
Woody English CHI.... 117

WINS
Bill Hallahan STL 19
Heinie Meine PIT 19
Jumbo Elliott PHI 19

WINNING PERCENTAGE
Paul Derringer STL..... .692
Bill Hallahan STL .... .679
Guy Bush CHI............. .667

EARNED RUN AVERAGE
Bill Walker NY............ 2.26
Carl Hubbell NY 2.66
Ed Brandt BOS 2.92

STRIKEOUTS
Bill Hallahan STL 159
Carl Hubbell NY 156
Dazzy Vance BKN 150

SAVES
Jack Quinn BKN 15
Jim Lindsey STL 7
Jumbo Elliott PHI 5

COMPLETE GAMES
Red Lucas CIN 24
Ed Brandt BOS 23
Heinie Meine PIT 22

SHUTOUTS
Bill Walker NY................. 6
three tied at..................... 4

GAMES PITCHED
Jumbo Elliott PHI 52
Syl Johnson CIN........... 42
Phil Collins PHI............. 42

INNINGS PITCHED
Heinie Meine PIT 284
Larry French PIT......... 276
Syl Johnson CIN......... 262

1932 AL

	W	L	PCT	GB	R	OR	BA	FA	ERA
★NEW YORK	107	47	.695	—	1002	724	.286	.969	3.98
PHILADELPHIA	94	60	.610	13	981	752	.290	.979	4.45
WASHINGTON	93	61	.604	14	840	716	.284	.979	4.16
CLEVELAND	87	65	.572	19	845	747	.285	.969	4.12
DETROIT	76	75	.503	29.5	799	787	.273	.969	4.30
ST. LOUIS	63	91	.409	44	736	898	.276	.969	5.01
CHICAGO	49	102	.325	56.5	667	897	.267	.958	4.82
BOSTON	43	111	.279	64	566	915	.251	.963	5.02
					6436	6436	.277	.969	4.48

BATTING AVERAGE
Alexander DET, BOS. .367
Jimmie Foxx PHI .364
Lou Gehrig NY .349

HITS
Al Simmons PHI 216
Heinie Manush WAS 214
Jimmie Foxx PHI 213

DOUBLES
Eric McNair PHI 47
C. Gehringer DET 44
Joe Cronin WAS 43

TRIPLES
Joe Cronin WAS 18
Tony Lazzeri NY 16
Buddy Myer WAS 16

HOME RUNS
Jimmie Foxx PHI 58
Babe Ruth NY 41
Al Simmons PHI 35

RUNS BATTED IN
Jimmie Foxx PHI 169
Lou Gehrig NY 151
Al Simmons PHI 151

SLUGGING AVERAGE
Jimmie Foxx PHI .749
Babe Ruth NY .661
Lou Gehrig NY .621

STOLEN BASES
Ben Chapman NY 38
Gee Walker DET 30
Johnson DET, BOS 20

RUNS SCORED
Jimmie Foxx PHI 151
Al Simmons PHI 144
Earle Combs NY 143

WINS
G. Crowder WAS 26
Lefty Grove PHI 25
Lefty Gomez NY 24

WINNING PERCENTAGE
Johnny Allen NY .810
Lefty Gomez NY .774
Red Ruffing NY .720

EARNED RUN AVERAGE
Lefty Grove PHI 2.84
Red Ruffing NY 3.09
Ted Lyons CHI 3.28

STRIKEOUTS
Red Ruffing NY 190
Lefty Grove PHI 188
Lefty Gomez NY 176

SAVES
Firpo Marberry WAS 13
Wilcy Moore BOS, NY 8
two tied at 7

COMPLETE GAMES
Lefty Grove PHI 27
Wes Ferrell CLE 26
Red Ruffing NY 22

SHUTOUTS
Tommy Bridges DET 4
Lefty Grove PHI 4

GAMES PITCHED
Firpo Marberry WAS 54
Sam Gray STL 52
G. Crowder WAS 50

INNINGS PITCHED
G. Crowder WAS 327
Lefty Grove PHI 292
Wes Ferrell CLE 288

1932 NL

	W	L	PCT	GB	R	OR	BA	FA	ERA
CHICAGO	90	64	.584	—	720	633	.278	.973	3.44
PITTSBURGH	86	68	.558	4	701	711	.285	.969	3.75
BROOKLYN	81	73	.526	9	752	747	.283	.971	4.28
PHILADELPHIA	78	76	.506	12	844	796	.292	.968	4.47
BOSTON	77	77	.500	13	649	655	.265	.976	3.53
NEW YORK	72	82	.468	18	755	706	.276	.969	3.83
ST. LOUIS	72	82	.468	18	684	717	.269	.971	3.97
CINCINNATI	60	94	.390	30	575	715	.263	.971	3.79
					5680	5680	.276	.971	3.88

BATTING AVERAGE
Lefty O'Doul BKN .... .368
Bill Terry NY .... .350
Chuck Klein PHI .... .348

HITS
Chuck Klein PHI 226
Bill Terry NY 225
Lefty O'Doul BKN 219

DOUBLES
Paul Waner PIT 62
Chuck Klein PHI 50
R. Stephenson CHI 49

TRIPLES
Babe Herman CIN 19
Gus Suhr PIT 16
Chuck Klein PHI 15

HOME RUNS
Chuck Klein PHI 38
Mel Ott NY 38
Bill Terry NY 28

RUNS BATTED IN
Don Hurst PHI 143
Chuck Klein PHI 137
Pinky Whitney PHI 124

SLUGGING AVERAGE
Chuck Klein PHI .... .646
Mel Ott NY .... .601
Bill Terry NY .... .580

STOLEN BASES
Chuck Klein PHI 20
Tony Piet PIT 19
two tied at 18

RUNS SCORED
Chuck Klein PHI 152
Bill Terry NY 124
Lefty O'Doul BKN 120

WINS
Lon Warneke CHI 22
Watty Clark BKN 20
Guy Bush CHI 19

WINNING PERCENTAGE
Lon Warneke CHI ...... .786
Guy Bush CHI .... .633
two tied at .... .625

EARNED RUN AVERAGE
Lon Warneke CHI 2.37
Carl Hubbell NY 2.50
Huck Betts BOS 2.80

STRIKEOUTS
Dizzy Dean STL 191
Carl Hubbell NY 137
Pat Malone CHI 120

SAVES
Jack Quinn BKN 8
Ray Benge PHI 6
two tied at 5

COMPLETE GAMES
Red Lucas CIN 28
Lon Warneke CHI 25
Carl Hubbell NY 22

SHUTOUTS
Dizzy Dean STL 4
Steve Swetonic PIT 4
Lon Warneke CHI 4

GAMES PITCHED
Larry French PIT 47
Dizzy Dean STL 46
Tex Carleton STL 44

INNINGS PITCHED
Dizzy Dean STL 286
Carl Hubbell NY 284
Lon Warneke CHI 277

1933 AL

	W	L	PCT	GB	R	OR	BA	FA	ERA
WASHINGTON	99	53	.651	—	850	665	.287	.979	3.82
NEW YORK	91	59	.607	7	927	768	.283	.972	4.36
PHILADELPHIA	79	72	.523	19.5	875	853	.285	.966	4.81
CLEVELAND	75	76	.497	23.5	654	669	.261	.974	3.71
DETROIT	75	79	.487	25	722	733	.269	.971	3.96
CHICAGO	67	83	.447	31	683	814	.272	.970	4.45
BOSTON	63	86	.423	34.5	700	758	.271	.966	4.35
ST. LOUIS	55	96	.364	43.5	669	820	.253	.976	4.82
					6080	6080	.273	.972	4.28

BATTING AVERAGE
Jimmie Foxx PHI......... .356
H. Manush WAS .... .336
Lou Gehrig NY .... .334

HITS
Heinie Manush WAS... 221
C. Gehringer DET 204
Jimmie Foxx PHI......... 204

DOUBLES
Joe Cronin WAS 45
Bob Johnson PHI.......... 44
Jack Burns STL 43

TRIPLES
Heinie Manush WAS..... 17
Earl Averill CLE 16
Earle Combs NY 16

HOME RUNS
Jimmie Foxx PHI......... 48
Babe Ruth NY 34
Lou Gehrig NY 32

RUNS BATTED IN
Jimmie Foxx PHI......... 163
Lou Gehrig NY 139
Al Simmons CHI 119

SLUGGING AVERAGE
Jimmie Foxx PHI......... .703
Lou Gehrig NY .... .605
Babe Ruth NY .... .582

STOLEN BASES
Ben Chapman NY 27
Gee Walker DET 26
Evar Swanson CHI 19

RUNS SCORED
Lou Gehrig NY 138
Jimmie Foxx PHI......... 125
Heinie Manush WAS... 115

WINS
Lefty Grove PHI 24
G. Crowder WAS 24
Earl Whitehill WAS........ 22

WINNING PERCENTAGE
Lefty Grove PHI .... .750
Earl Whitehill WAS..... .733
Lefty Stewart WAS..... .714

EARNED RUN AVERAGE
M. Pearson CLE 2.33
Mel Harder CLE 2.95
T. Bridges DET 3.09

STRIKEOUTS
Lefty Gomez NY 163
Bump Hadley STL...... 149
Red Ruffing NY........... 122

SAVES
Jack Russell WAS 13
Chief Hogsett DET.......... 9
Wilcy Moore NY 8

COMPLETE GAMES
Lefty Grove PHI 21
Bump Hadley STL........ 19
Earl Whitehill WAS........ 19

SHUTOUTS
Oral Hildebrand CLE....... 6
Lefty Gomez NY 4
G. Blaeholder STL 3

GAMES PITCHED
G. Crowder WAS 52
Jack Russell WAS 50
Johnny Welch BOS....... 47

INNINGS PITCHED
Bump Hadley STL........ 317
G. Crowder WAS 299
Lefty Grove PHI 275

1933 NL

	W	L	PCT	GB	R	OR	BA	FA	ERA
★NEW YORK	91	61	.599	—	636	515	.263	.973	2.71
PITTSBURGH	87	67	.565	5	667	619	.285	.972	3.27
CHICAGO	86	68	.558	6	646	536	.271	.973	2.93
BOSTON	83	71	.539	9	552	531	.252	.978	2.96
ST. LOUIS	82	71	.536	9.5	687	609	.276	.973	3.37
BROOKLYN	65	88	.425	26.5	617	695	.263	.971	3.73
PHILADELPHIA	60	92	.395	31	607	760	.274	.970	4.34
CINCINNATI	58	94	.382	33	496	643	.246	.971	3.42
					4908	4908	.266	.973	3.34

BATTING AVERAGE
Chuck Klein PHI......... .368
Spud Davis PHI .... .349
Tony Piet PIT .... .323

HITS
Chuck Klein PHI......... 223
Chick Fullis PHI 200
Paul Waner PIT 191

DOUBLES
Chuck Klein PHI......... 44
Joe Medwick STL 40
F. Lindstrom PIT 39

TRIPLES
Arky Vaughan PIT........ 19
Paul Waner PIT 16
two tied at 12

HOME RUNS
Chuck Klein PHI......... 28
Wally Berger BOS........ 27
Mel Ott NY 23

RUNS BATTED IN
Chuck Klein PHI......... 120
Wally Berger BOS....... 106
Mel Ott NY 103

SLUGGING AVERAGE
Chuck Klein PHI......... .602
Wally Berger BOS...... .566
Babe Herman CHI ..... .502

STOLEN BASES
Pepper Martin STL...... 26
Chick Fullis PHI 18
Frankie Frisch STL 18

RUNS SCORED
Pepper Martin STL...... 122
Chuck Klein PHI.......... 101
Paul Waner PIT 101

WINS
Carl Hubbell NY 23
three tied at................... 20

WINNING PERCENTAGE
Ben Cantwell BOS ..... .667
Carl Hubbell NY .... .657
Heinie Meine PIT .... .652

EARNED RUN AVERAGE
Carl Hubbell NY 1.66
Lon Warneke CHI 2.00
H. Schumacher NY 2.16

STRIKEOUTS
Dizzy Dean STL.......... 199
Carl Hubbell NY 156
Tex Carleton STL........ 147

SAVES
Phil Collins PHI 6
three tied at...................... 5

COMPLETE GAMES
Dizzy Dean STL............. 26
Lon Warneke CHI 26
Ed Brandt BOS 23

SHUTOUTS
Carl Hubbell NY 10
Hal Schumacher NY 7
Larry French PIT............. 5

GAMES PITCHED
Dizzy Dean STL............. 48
Larry French PIT........... 47
two tied at 45

INNINGS PITCHED
Carl Hubbell NY 309
Dizzy Dean STL.......... 293
Larry French PIT........ 291

1934 AL

	W	L	PCT	GB	R	OR	BA	FA	ERA
DETROIT	101	53	.656	—	958	708	.300	.974	4.06
NEW YORK	94	60	.610	7	842	669	.278	.973	3.76
CLEVELAND	85	69	.552	16	814	763	.287	.972	4.28
BOSTON	76	76	.500	24	820	775	.274	.969	4.32
PHILADELPHIA	68	82	.453	31	764	838	.280	.967	5.01
ST. LOUIS	67	85	.441	33	674	800	.268	.969	4.49
WASHINGTON	66	86	.434	34	729	806	.278	.974	4.68
CHICAGO	53	99	.349	47	704	946	.263	.966	5.41
					6305	6305	.279	.970	4.50

BATTING AVERAGE
Lou Gehrig NY .... .363
C. Gehringer DET ...... .356
H. Manush WAS .... .349

HITS
C. Gehringer DET 214
Lou Gehrig NY 210
Hal Trosky CLE............ 206

DOUBLES
Hank Greenberg DET ... 63
C. Gehringer DET 50
Earl Averill CLE.............. 48

TRIPLES
Ben Chapman NY 13
Heinie Manush WAS..... 11

HOME RUNS
Lou Gehrig NY 49
Jimmie Foxx PHI........... 44
Hal Trosky CLE.............. 35

RUNS BATTED IN
Lou Gehrig NY 165
Hal Trosky CLE............ 142
H. Greenberg DET 139

SLUGGING AVERAGE
Lou Gehrig NY .... .706
Jimmie Foxx PHI........ .653
H. Greenberg DET..... .600

STOLEN BASES
Bill Werber BOS............ 40
Jo-Jo White DET........... 28
Ben Chapman NY......... 26

RUNS SCORED
C. Gehringer DET 134
Bill Werber BOS.......... 129
two tied at 128

WINS
Lefty Gomez NY 26
S. Rowe DET 24
Tommy Bridges DET 22

WINNING PERCENTAGE
Lefty Gomez NY .... .839
S. Rowe DET .... .750
Firpo Marberry DET ... .750

EARNED RUN AVERAGE
Lefty Gomez NY 2.33
Mel Harder CLE 2.61
Johnny Murphy NY 3.12

STRIKEOUTS
Lefty Gomez NY 158
T. Bridges DET 151
two tied at 149

SAVES
Jack Russell WAS 7
Lloyd Brown CLE............ 6
Bobo Newsom STL........ 5

COMPLETE GAMES
Lefty Gomez NY 25
Tommy Bridges DET 23
Ted Lyons CHI.............. 21

SHUTOUTS
Mel Harder CLE.............. 6
Lefty Gomez NY 6
Red Ruffing NY.............. 5

GAMES PITCHED
Jack Russell WAS 54
Bobo Newsom STL....... 47
two tied at 45

INNINGS PITCHED
Lefty Gomez NY 282
T. Bridges DET 275
S. Rowe DET 266

1934 NL

	W	L	PCT	GB	R	OR	BA	FA	ERA
★ST. LOUIS	95	58	.621	—	799	656	.288	.972	3.69
NEW YORK	93	60	.608	2	760	583	.275	.972	3.19
CHICAGO	86	65	.570	8	705	639	.279	.977	3.76
BOSTON	78	73	.517	16	683	714	.272	.972	4.11
PITTSBURGH	74	76	.493	19.5	735	713	.287	.975	4.20
BROOKLYN	71	81	.467	23.5	748	795	.281	.970	4.48
PHILADELPHIA	56	93	.376	37	675	794	.284	.966	4.76
CINCINNATI	52	99	.344	42	590	801	.266	.970	4.37
					5695	5695	.279	.972	4.06

BATTING AVERAGE
Paul Waner PIT .... .362
Bill Terry NY .... .354
Kiki Cuyler CHI .... .338

HITS
Paul Waner PIT 217
Bill Terry NY 213
Ripper Collins STL 200

DOUBLES
Kiki Cuyler CHI 42
Ethan Allen PHI 42
Arky Vaughan PIT 41

TRIPLES
Joe Medwick STL 18
Paul Waner PIT 16
Gus Suhr PIT 13

HOME RUNS
Mel Ott NY 35
Ripper Collins STL 35
Wally Berger BOS 34

RUNS BATTED IN
Mel Ott NY 135
Ripper Collins STL 128
Wally Berger BOS 121

SLUGGING AVERAGE
Ripper Collins STL ..... .615
Mel Ott NY .... .591
Wally Berger BOS ...... .546

STOLEN BASES
Pepper Martin STL 23
Kiki Cuyler CHI 15
Dick Bartell PHI 13

RUNS SCORED
Paul Waner PIT 122
Mel Ott NY 119
Ripper Collins STL 116

WINS
Dizzy Dean STL 30
Hal Schumacher NY 23
Lon Warneke CHI 22

WINNING PERCENTAGE
Dizzy Dean STL .... .811
Waite Hoyt PIT .... .714
H. Schumacher NY .... .697

EARNED RUN AVERAGE
Carl Hubbell NY 2.30
Dizzy Dean STL 2.66
Waite Hoyte NY 2.93

STRIKEOUTS
Dizzy Dean STL 195
Van Mungo BKN 184
Paul Dean STL 150

SAVES
Carl Hubbell NY 8
Dizzy Dean STL 7
Dolf Luque NY 7

COMPLETE GAMES
Dizzy Dean STL 24
Carl Hubbell NY 23
Lon Warneke CHI 23

SHUTOUTS
Dizzy Dean STL 7
Carl Hubbell NY 5
Paul Dean STL 5

GAMES PITCHED
Curt Davis PHI 51
Dizzy Dean STL 50
Snipe Hansen PHI 50

INNINGS PITCHED
Van Mungo BKN 315
Carl Hubbell NY 313
Dizzy Dean STL 312

1935 AL

	W	L	PCT	GB	R	OR	BA	FA	ERA
★DETROIT	93	58	.616	—	919	665	.290	.978	3.82
NEW YORK	89	60	.597	3	818	632	.280	.974	3.60
CLEVELAND	82	71	.536	12	776	739	.284	.972	4.15
BOSTON	78	75	.510	16	718	732	.276	.969	4.05
CHICAGO	74	78	.487	19.5	738	750	.275	.976	4.38
WASHINGTON	67	86	.438	27	823	903	.285	.972	5.25
ST. LOUIS	65	87	.428	28.5	718	930	.270	.970	5.26
PHILADELPHIA	58	91	.389	34	710	869	.279	.968	5.12
					6220	6220	.280	.972	4.45

BATTING AVERAGE
Buddy Myer WAS .... .349
Joe Vosmik CLE .... .348
Jimmie Foxx PHI........ .346

HITS
Joe Vosmik CLE 216
Buddy Myer WAS 215
Doc Cramer PHI 214

DOUBLES
Joe Vosmik CLE 47
Hank Greenberg DET ... 46
M. Solters BOS, STL 45

TRIPLES
Joe Vosmik CLE 20
John Stone WAS 18
Hank Greenberg DET ... 16

HOME RUNS
Hank Greenberg DET ... 36
Jimmie Foxx PHI........... 36
Lou Gehrig NY 30

RUNS BATTED IN
H. Greenberg DET...... 170
Lou Gehrig NY 119
Jimmie Foxx PHI........ 115

SLUGGING AVERAGE
Jimmie Foxx PHI........ .636
H. Greenberg DET..... .628
Lou Gehrig NY .... .583

STOLEN BASES
Bill Werber BOS............ 29
Lyn Lary WAS, STL 28
Mel Almada BOS 20

RUNS SCORED
Lou Gehrig NY 125
C. Gehringer DET 123
H. Greenberg DET...... 121

WINS
Wes Ferrell BOS........... 25
Mel Harder CLE 22
T. Bridges DET 21

WINNING PERCENTAGE
Eldon Auker DET .... .720
Johnny Broaca NY..... .682
T. Bridges DET .... .677

EARNED RUN AVERAGE
Lefty Grove BOS......... 2.70
Ted Lyons CHI........... 3.02
Red Ruffing NY 3.12

STRIKEOUTS
T. Bridges DET 163
S. Rowe DET............... 140
Lefty Gomez NY 138

SAVES
Jack Knott STL 7
five tied at 5

COMPLETE GAMES
Wes Ferrell BOS........... 31
Lefty Grove BOS........... 23
Tommy Bridges DET 23

SHUTOUTS
Schoolboy Rowe DET..... 6
Tommy Bridges DET 4
Mel Harder CLE.............. 4

GAMES PITCHED
R. Van Atta NY, STL..... 58
Jim Walkup STL 55
Ivy Andrews STL........... 50

INNINGS PITCHED
Wes Ferrell BOS......... 322
Mel Harder CLE.......... 287
Earl Whitehill WAS..... 279

1935 NL

	W	L	PCT	GB	R	OR	BA	FA	ERA
CHICAGO	100	54	.649	—	847	597	.288	.970	3.26
ST. LOUIS	96	58	.623	4	829	625	.284	.972	3.54
NEW YORK	91	62	.595	8.5	770	675	.286	.972	3.78
PITTSBURGH	86	67	.562	13.5	743	647	.285	.968	3.42
BROOKLYN	70	83	.458	29.5	711	767	.277	.969	4.22
CINCINNATI	68	85	.444	31.5	646	772	.265	.966	4.30
PHILADELPHIA	64	89	.418	35.5	685	871	.269	.963	4.76
BOSTON	38	115	.248	61.5	575	852	.263	.967	4.93
					5806	5806	.277	.968	4.02

BATTING AVERAGE
Arky Vaughan PIT...... .385
Joe Medwick STL ...... .353
Gabby Hartnett CHI ... .344

HITS
Billy Herman CHI........ 227
Joe Medwick STL 224

DOUBLES
Billy Herman CHI.......... 57
Ethan Allen PHI 46
Joe Medwick STL 46

TRIPLES
Ival Goodman CIN 18
Lloyd Waner PIT........... 14
Joe Medwick STL 13

HOME RUNS
Wally Berger BOS......... 34
Mel Ott NY 31
Dolf Camilli PHI............ 25

RUNS BATTED IN
Wally Berger BOS....... 130
Joe Medwick STL 126
Ripper Collins STL...... 122

SLUGGING AVERAGE
Arky Vaughan PIT...... .607
Joe Medwick STL ...... .576
Mel Ott NY .... .555

STOLEN BASES
Augie Galan CHI........... 22
Pepper Martin STL........ 20
F. Bordagaray BKN....... 18

RUNS SCORED
Augie Galan CHI......... 133
Joe Medwick STL 132
Pepper Martin STL...... 121

WINS
Dizzy Dean STL............ 28
Carl Hubbell NY........... 23
Paul Derringer CIN 22

WINNING PERCENTAGE
Bill Lee CHI................. .769
Slick Castleman NY ... .714
Dizzy Dean STL......... .700

EARNED RUN AVERAGE
Cy Blanton PIT........... 2.58
Bill Swift PIT.............. 2.70
H. Schumacher NY 2.89

STRIKEOUTS
Dizzy Dean STL.......... 190
Carl Hubbell NY 150
two tied at 143

SAVES
Dutch Leonard BKN........ 8
Waite Hoyt PIT.............. 6
Syl Johnson PHI 6

COMPLETE GAMES
Dizzy Dean STL............. 29
Carl Hubbell NY 24
Cy Blanton PIT............. 23

SHUTOUTS
five tied at 4

GAMES PITCHED
Orville Jorgens PHI....... 53
Dizzy Dean STL............ 50
Jim Biven PHI 47

INNINGS PITCHED
Dizzy Dean STL.......... 325
Carl Hubbell NY 303
Paul Derringer CIN 277

1936 AL

	W	L	PCT	GB	R	OR	BA	FA	ERA
★NEW YORK	102	51	.667	—	1065	731	.300	.973	4.17
DETROIT	83	71	.539	19.5	921	871	.300	.975	5.00
CHICAGO	81	70	.536	20	920	873	.292	.973	5.06
WASHINGTON	82	71	.536	20	889	799	.295	.970	4.58
CLEVELAND	80	74	.519	22.5	921	862	.304	.971	4.83
BOSTON	74	80	.481	28.5	775	764	.276	.972	4.39
ST. LOUIS	57	95	.375	44.5	804	1064	.279	.969	6.24
PHILADELPHIA	53	100	.346	49	714	1045	.269	.965	6.08
					7009	7009	.289	.971	5.04

BATTING AVERAGE
Luke Appling CHI .... .388
Earl Averill CLE .... .378
Bill Dickey NY .... .362

HITS
Earl Averill CLE 232
C. Gehringer DET 227
Hal Trosky CLE 216

DOUBLES
C. Gehringer DET 60
Gee Walker DET 55
two tied at 50

TRIPLES
Earl Averill CLE 15
Red Rolfe NY 15
Joe DiMaggio NY 15

HOME RUNS
Lou Gehrig NY 49
Hal Trosky CLE 42
Jimmie Foxx BOS 41

RUNS BATTED IN
Hal Trosky CLE 162
Lou Gehrig NY 152
Jimmie Foxx BOS 143

SLUGGING AVERAGE
Lou Gehrig NY .... .696
Hal Trosky CLE .... .644
Jimmie Foxx BOS ...... .631

STOLEN BASES
Lyn Lary STL 37
J. Powell WAS, NY 26
Bill Werber BOS............ 23

RUNS SCORED
Lou Gehrig NY 167
Harlond Clift STL........ 145
C. Gehringer DET 144

WINS
Tommy Bridges DET 23
Vern Kennedy CHI 21
three tied at................... 20

WINNING PERCENTAGE
Monte Pearson NY .... .731
Vern Kennedy CHI..... .700
T. Bridges DET .... .676

EARNED RUN AVERAGE
Lefty Grove BOS........ 2.81
Johnny Allen CLE 3.44
Pete Appleton WAS ... 3.53

STRIKEOUTS
T. Bridges DET 175
Johnny Allen CLE 165
Bobo Newsom WAS ... 156

SAVES
Pat Malone NY................. 9
Jack Knott STL 6
two tied at 5

COMPLETE GAMES
Wes Ferrell BOS........... 28
Tommy Bridges DET 26
Red Ruffing NY............. 25

SHUTOUTS
Lefty Grove BOS............. 6
Tommy Bridges DET 5
three tied at..................... 4

GAMES PITCHED
Russ Van Atta STL 52
Jack Knott STL 47

INNINGS PITCHED
Wes Ferrell BOS........... 301
T. Bridges DET 295
Bobo Newsom WAS ... 286

1936 NL

	W	L	PCT	GB	R	OR	BA	FA	ERA
NEW YORK	92	62	.597	—	742	621	.281	.974	3.46
CHICAGO	87	67	.565	5	755	603	.286	.976	3.53
ST. LOUIS	87	67	.565	5	795	794	.281	.974	4.48
PITTSBURGH	84	70	.545	8	804	718	.286	.967	3.89
CINCINNATI	74	80	.481	18	722	760	.274	.969	4.22
BOSTON	71	83	.461	21	631	715	.265	.971	3.94
BROOKLYN	67	87	.435	25	662	752	.272	.966	3.98
PHILADELPHIA	54	100	.351	38	726	874	.281	.959	4.64
					5837	5837	.278	.969	4.02

BATTING AVERAGE
Paul Waner PIT .... .373
Babe Phelps BKN ..... .367
Joe Medwick STL ...... .351

HITS
Joe Medwick STL 223
Paul Waner PIT 218
Frank Demaree CHI 212

DOUBLES
Joe Medwick STL 64
Billy Herman CHI 57
Paul Waner PIT 53

TRIPLES
Ival Goodman CIN 14
Dolf Camilli PHI 13
Joe Medwick STL 13

HOME RUNS
Mel Ott NY 33
Dolf Camilli PHI............. 28
two tied at 25

RUNS BATTED IN
Joe Medwick STL 138
Mel Ott NY 135
Gus Suhr PIT 118

SLUGGING AVERAGE
Mel Ott NY .... .588
three tied at................ .577

STOLEN BASES
Pepper Martin STL........ 23
three tied at.................. 17

RUNS SCORED
Arky Vaughan PIT....... 122
Pepper Martin STL...... 121
Mel Ott NY 120

WINS
Carl Hubbell NY 26
Dizzy Dean STL............ 24
Paul Derringer CIN 19

WINNING PERCENTAGE
Carl Hubbell NY .... .813
Red Lucas PIT .... .789
Larry French CHI .... .667

EARNED RUN AVERAGE
Carl Hubbell NY 2.31
D. MacFayden BOS.... 2.87
Frank Gabler NY........ 3.12

STRIKEOUTS
Van Mungo BKN.......... 238
Dizzy Dean STL.......... 195
Cy Blanton PIT............ 127

SAVES
Dizzy Dean STL............. 11
Don Brennan CIN 9
Bob Smith BOS............... 8

COMPLETE GAMES
Dizzy Dean STL............. 28
Carl Hubbell NY 25
Van Mungo BKN........... 22

SHUTOUTS
seven tied at 4

GAMES PITCHED
Dizzy Dean STL............. 51
Paul Derringer CIN 51
Claude Passeau PHI 49

INNINGS PITCHED
Dizzy Dean STL.......... 315
Van Mungo BKN......... 312
Carl Hubbell NY 304

1937 AL

	W	L	PCT	GB	R	OR	BA	FA	ERA
★NEW YORK	102	52	.662	—	979	671	.283	.972	3.65
DETROIT	89	65	.578	13	935	841	.292	.976	4.87
CHICAGO	86	68	.558	16	780	730	.280	.971	4.17
CLEVELAND	83	71	.539	19	817	768	.280	.974	4.39
BOSTON	80	72	.526	21	821	775	.281	.970	4.48
WASHINGTON	73	80	.477	28.5	757	841	.279	.972	4.58
PHILADELPHIA	54	97	.358	46.5	699	854	.267	.967	4.85
ST. LOUIS	46	108	.299	56	715	1023	.285	.972	6.00
					6503	6503	.281	.972	4.62

BATTING AVERAGE
C. Gehringer DET .... .371
Lou Gehrig NY .... .351
Joe DiMaggio NY .... .346

HITS
Beau Bell STL 218
Joe DiMaggio NY 215
Gee Walker DET 213

DOUBLES
Beau Bell STL 51
Hank Greenberg DET ... 49
Wally Moses PHI 48

TRIPLES
Dixie Walker CHI 16
Mike Kreevich CHI 16
two tied at 15

HOME RUNS
Joe DiMaggio NY 46
Hank Greenberg DET ... 40
Lou Gehrig NY 37

RUNS BATTED IN
H. Greenberg DET 183
Joe DiMaggio NY 167
Lou Gehrig NY 159

SLUGGING AVERAGE
Joe DiMaggio NY .... .673
H. Greenberg DET ..... .668
Rudy York DET .... .651

STOLEN BASES
Chapman WAS, BOS ... 35
Bill Werber PHI 35
Gee Walker DET 23

RUNS SCORED
Joe DiMaggio NY 151
Red Rolfe NY 143
Lou Gehrig NY 138

WINS
Lefty Gomez NY 21
Red Ruffing NY 20
Roxie Lawson DET 18

WINNING PERCENTAGE
Johnny Allen CLE .... .938
Monty Stratton CHI .... .750
Red Ruffing NY .... .741

EARNED RUN AVERAGE
Lefty Gomez NY 2.33
Monty Stratton CHI 2.40
Johnny Allen CLE 2.55

STRIKEOUTS
Lefty Gomez NY 194
Newsom WAS, BOS ... 166
Lefty Grove BOS 153

SAVES
Clint Brown CHI 18
Johnny Murphy NY 10
Jack Wilson BOS 7

COMPLETE GAMES
W. Ferrell BOS, WAS ... 26
Lofty Gomez NY 25
Red Ruffing NY 22

SHUTOUTS
Lefty Gomez NY 6
Monty Stratton CHI 5

GAMES PITCHED
Clint Brown CHI 53
Jack Wilson BOS 51
two tied at 41

INNINGS PITCHED
Ferrell BOS, WAS 281
Lefty Gomez NY 278
Newsom WAS, BOS ... 275

1937 NL

	W	L	PCT	GB	R	OR	BA	FA	ERA
NEW YORK	95	57	.625	—	732	602	.278	.974	3.43
CHICAGO	93	61	.604	3	811	682	.287	.975	3.97
PITTSBURGH	86	68	.558	10	704	646	.285	.970	3.56
ST. LOUIS	81	73	.526	15	789	733	.282	.973	3.95
BOSTON	79	73	.520	16	579	556	.247	.975	3.22
BROOKLYN	62	91	.405	33.5	616	772	.265	.964	4.13
PHILADELPHIA	61	92	.399	34.5	724	869	.273	.970	5.06
CINCINNATI	56	98	.364	40	612	707	.254	.966	3.94
					5567	5567	.272	.971	3.91

BATTING AVERAGE
Joe Medwick STL .... .374
Johnny Mize STL........ .364
two tied at .... .354

HITS
Joe Medwick STL 237
Paul Waner PIT 219
Johnny Mize STL........ 204

DOUBLES
Joe Medwick STL 56
Johnny Mize STL.......... 40
Dick Bartell NY.............. 38

TRIPLES
Arky Vaughan PIT......... 17
Gus Suhr PIT 14
two tied at 12

HOME RUNS
Joe Medwick STL 31
Mel Ott NY 31
Dolf Camilli PHI............. 27

RUNS BATTED IN
Joe Medwick STL.... 154
Frank Demaree CHI.... 115
Johnny Mize STL........ 113

SLUGGING AVERAGE
Joe Medwick STL .... .641
Johnny Mize STL........ .595
Dolf Camilli PHI.......... .587

STOLEN BASES
Augie Galan CHI........... 23
Stan Hack CHI.............. 16
four tied at..................... 13

RUNS SCORED
Joe Medwick STL 111
Stan Hack CHI 106
Billy Herman CHI 106

WINS
Carl Hubbell NY 22
three tied at................... 20

WINNING PERCENTAGE
Carl Hubbell NY .... .733
Cliff Melton NY........... .690
two tied at .... .667

EARNED RUN AVERAGE
Jim Turner BOS......... 2.38
Cliff Melton NY.......... 2.61
Dizzy Dean STL......... 2.69

STRIKEOUTS
Carl Hubbell NY 159
Lee Grissom CIN 149
Cy Blanton PIT............ 143

SAVES
Mace Brown PIT 7
Cliff Melton NY................ 7
Lee Grissom CIN 6

COMPLETE GAMES
Jim Turner BOS............. 24
Lou Fette BOS 23
Bob Weiland STL.......... 21

SHUTOUTS
Jim Turner BOS................ 5
Lou Fette BOS 5
Lee Grissom CIN 5

GAMES PITCHED
Hugh Mulcahy PHI........ 56
Orville Jorgens PHI....... 52

INNINGS PITCHED
C. Passeau PHI 292
Bill Lee CHI................. 272
Bob Weiland STL........ 264

1938 AL

	W	L	PCT	GB	R	OR	BA	FA	ERA
★NEW YORK	99	53	.651	—	966	710	.274	.973	3.91
BOSTON	88	61	.591	9.5	902	751	.299	.968	4.46
CLEVELAND	86	66	.566	13	847	782	.281	.974	4.60
DETROIT	84	70	.545	16	862	795	.272	.976	4.79
WASHINGTON	75	76	.497	23.5	814	873	.293	.970	4.94
CHICAGO	65	83	.439	32	709	752	.277	.967	4.36
ST. LOUIS	55	97	.362	44	755	962	.281	.975	5.80
PHILADELPHIA	53	99	.349	46	726	956	.270	.965	5.48
					6581	6581	.281	.971	4.79

BATTING AVERAGE
Jimmie Foxx BOS .... .349
Jeff Heath CLE .... .343
Ben Chapman BOS ... .340

HITS
Joe Vosmik BOS......... 201
Doc Cramer BOS........ 198
two tied at 197

DOUBLES
Joe Cronin BOS............ 51
George McQuinn STL.... 42
two tied at 40

TRIPLES
Jeff Heath CLE 18
Earl Averill CLE 15
Joe DiMaggio NY......... 13

HOME RUNS
Hank Greenberg DET ... 58
Jimmie Foxx BOS 50
Harlond Clift STL 34

RUNS BATTED IN
Jimmie Foxx BOS....... 175
H. Greenberg DET...... 146
Joe DiMaggio NY........ 140

SLUGGING AVERAGE
Jimmie Foxx BOS ...... .704
H. Greenberg DET..... .683
Jeff Heath CLE .... .602

STOLEN BASES
Frank Crosetti NY 27
Lyn Lary CLE 23
Bill Werber PHI 19

RUNS SCORED
H. Greenberg DET...... 144
Jimmie Foxx BOS 139
C. Gehringer DET 133

WINS
Red Ruffing NY............. 21
Bobo Newsom STL....... 20
Lefty Gomez NY 18

WINNING PERCENTAGE
Red Ruffing NY........... .750
Monty Pearson NY..... .696
Mel Harder CLE.......... .630

EARNED RUN AVERAGE
Lefty Grove BOS........ 3.08
Red Ruffing NY 3.31
Lefty Gomez NY 3.35

STRIKEOUTS
Bob Feller CLE 240
Bobo Newsom STL..... 226
Lefty Mills STL 134

SAVES
Johnny Murphy NY 11
Archie McKain BOS 6
John Humphries CLE...... 6

COMPLETE GAMES
Bobo Newsom STL....... 31
Red Ruffing NY 22
three tied at................... 20

SHUTOUTS
Red Ruffing NY............... 4
Lefty Gomez NY 4
two tied at 3

GAMES PITCHED
John Humphries CLE.... 45
Bobo Newsom STL....... 44
three tied at................... 43

INNINGS PITCHED
Bobo Newsom STL..... 330
George Caster PHI 280
Bob Feller CLE 278

1938 NL

	W	L	PCT	GB	R	OR	BA	FA	ERA
CHICAGO	89	63	.586	—	713	598	.269	.978	3.37
PITTSBURGH	86	64	.573	2	707	630	.279	.974	3.46
NEW YORK	83	67	.553	5	705	637	.271	.973	3.62
CINCINNATI	82	68	.547	6	723	634	.277	.971	3.62
BOSTON	77	75	.507	12	561	618	.250	.972	3.40
ST. LOUIS	71	80	.470	17.5	725	721	.279	.967	3.84
BROOKLYN	69	80	.463	18.5	704	710	.257	.973	4.07
PHILADELPHIA	45	105	.300	43	550	840	.254	.966	4.93
					5388	5388	.267	.972	3.78

BATTING AVERAGE
Ernie Lombardi CIN ... .342
Johnny Mize STL .... .337
F. McCormick CIN ..... .327

HITS
F. McCormick CIN 209
Stan Hack CHI 195
Lloyd Waner PIT 194

DOUBLES
Joe Medwick STL 47
F. McCormick CIN 40
two tied at 36

TRIPLES
Johnny Mize STL 16
Don Gutteridge STL..... 15
Gus Suhr PIT 14

HOME RUNS
Mel Ott NY 36
Ival Goodman CIN 30
Johnny Mize STL 27

RUNS BATTED IN
Joe Medwick STL 122
Mel Ott NY 116
Johnny Rizzo PIT........ 111

SLUGGING AVERAGE
Johnny Mize STL .... .614
Mel Ott NY .... .583
Joe Medwick STL ...... .536

STOLEN BASES
Stan Hack CHI 16
Ernie Koy BKN.............. 15
C. Lavagetto BKN 15

RUNS SCORED
Mel Ott NY 116
Stan Hack CHI 109
Dolf Camilli BKN 106

WINS
Bill Lee CHI.................... 22
Paul Derringer CIN 21
Clay Bryant CHI 19

WINNING PERCENTAGE
Bill Lee CHI.................. .710
Clay Bryant CHI .... .633
Mace Brown PIT .... .625

EARNED RUN AVERAGE
Bill Lee CHI................. 2.66
Charlie Root CHI........ 2.86
Paul Derringer CIN 2.93

STRIKEOUTS
Clay Bryant CHI 135
Paul Derringer CIN ... 132
Vander Meer CIN........ 125

SAVES
Dick Coffman NY 12
Charlie Root CHI............. 8
two tied at 6

COMPLETE GAMES
Paul Derringer CIN 26
Jim Turner BOS 22
B. Walters PHI, CIN ... 20

SHUTOUTS
Bill Lee CHI..................... 9
D. MacFayden BOS........ 5
two tied at 4

GAMES PITCHED
Dick Coffman NY 51
Mace Brown PIT 51
Bill McGee STL............. 47

INNINGS PITCHED
Paul Derringer CIN 307
Bill Lee CHI.................. 291
Clay Bryant CHI 270

1939 AL

	W	L	PCT	GB	R	OR	BA	FA	ERA
★NEW YORK	106	45	.702	—	967	556	.287	.978	3.31
BOSTON	89	62	.589	17	890	795	.291	.970	4.56
CLEVELAND	87	67	.565	20.5	797	700	.280	.970	4.08
CHICAGO	85	69	.552	22.5	755	737	.275	.972	4.31
DETROIT	81	73	.526	26.5	849	762	.279	.967	4.29
WASHINGTON	65	87	.428	41.5	702	797	.278	.966	4.60
PHILADELPHIA	55	97	.362	51.5	711	1022	.271	.964	5.79
ST. LOUIS	43	111	.279	64.5	733	1035	.268	.968	6.01
					6404	6404	.279	.969	4.62

BATTING AVERAGE
Joe DiMaggio NY .... .381
Jimmie Foxx BOS ...... .360
Bob Johnson PHI .... .338

HITS
Red Rolfe NY 213
G. McQuinn STL 195
Ken Keltner CLE 191

DOUBLES
Red Rolfe NY 46
Ted Williams BOS......... 44
Hank Greenberg DET ... 42

TRIPLES
Buddy Lewis WAS 16
B. McCoskey DET 14
two tied at 13

HOME RUNS
Jimmie Foxx BOS 35
Hank Greenberg DET ... 33
Ted Williams BOS......... 31

RUNS BATTED IN
Ted Williams BOS....... 145
Joe DiMaggio NY 126
Bob Johnson PHI........ 114

SLUGGING AVERAGE
Jimmie Foxx BOS ...... .694
Joe DiMaggio NY........ .671
H. Greenberg DET...... .622

STOLEN BASES
George Case WAS 51
Mike Kreevich CHI 23
Pete Fox DET 23

RUNS SCORED
Red Rolfe NY 139
Ted Williams BOS....... 131
Jimmie Foxx BOS 130

WINS
Bob Feller CLE 24
Red Ruffing NY 21
two tied at 20

WINNING PERCENTAGE
Lefty Grove BOS......... .789
Red Ruffing NY .... .750
Bob Feller CLE .... .727

EARNED RUN AVERAGE
Lefty Grove BOS........ 2.54
Ted Lyons CHI 2.76
Bob Feller CLE 2.85

STRIKEOUTS
Bob Feller CLE 246
Newsom STL, DET 192
T. Bridges DET 129

SAVES
Johnny Murphy NY 19
Clint Brown CHI 18
two tied at 7

COMPLETE GAMES
Newsom STL, DET 24
Bob Feller CLE 24
Red Ruffing NY 22

SHUTOUTS
Red Ruffing NY 5
Bob Feller CLE 4
Newsom STL, DET 3

GAMES PITCHED
Clint Brown CHI 61
Chubby Dean PHI......... 54
E. Dickman BOS........... 48

INNINGS PITCHED
Bob Feller CLE 297
Newsom STL, DET 292
Dutch Leonard WAS ... 269

1939 NL

	W	L	PCT	GB	R	OR	BA	FA	ERA
CINCINNATI	97	57	.630	—	767	595	.278	.974	3.27
ST. LOUIS	92	61	.601	4.5	779	633	.294	.971	3.59
BROOKLYN	84	69	.549	12.5	708	645	.265	.972	3.64
CHICAGO	84	70	.545	13	724	678	.266	.970	3.80
NEW YORK	77	74	.510	18.5	703	685	.272	.975	4.07
PITTSBURGH	68	85	.444	28.5	666	721	.276	.972	4.15
BOSTON	63	88	.417	32.5	572	659	.264	.971	3.71
PHILADELPHIA	45	106	.298	50.5	553	856	.261	.970	5.17
					5472	5472	.272	.972	3.92

BATTING AVERAGE
Johnny Mize STL........ .349
F. McCormick CIN ..... .332
Joe Medwick STL ...... .332

HITS
F. McCormick CIN 209
Joe Medwick STL 201
Johnny Mize STL........ 197

DOUBLES
Enos Slaughter STL...... 52
Joe Medwick STL 48
Johnny Mize STL.......... 44

TRIPLES
Billy Herman CHI 18
Ival Goodman CIN 16
Johnny Mize STL.......... 14

HOME RUNS
Johnny Mize STL 28
Mel Ott NY 27
Dolf Camilli BKN 26

RUNS BATTED IN
F. McCormick CIN 128
Joe Medwick STL 117
Johnny Mize STL......... 108

SLUGGING AVERAGE
Johnny Mize STL .... .626
Mel Ott NY .... .581
Hank Leiber CHI .... .556

STOLEN BASES
Lee Handley PIT 17
Stan Hack CHI 17
Bill Werber CIN 15

RUNS SCORED
Bill Werber CIN 115
Stan Hack CHI 112
Billy Herman CHI 111

WINS
Bucky Walters CIN........ 27
Paul Derringer CIN 25
Curt Davis STL 22

WINNING PERCENTAGE
Paul Derringer CIN .... .781
Bucky Walters CIN...... .711
Larry French CHI .... .652

EARNED RUN AVERAGE
Bucky Walters CIN...... 2.29
Bob Bowman STL........ 2.60
Carl Hubbell NY 2.75

STRIKEOUTS
Passeau PHI, CHI....... 137
Bucky Walters CIN...... 137
Mort Cooper STL 130

SAVES
Bob Bowman STL............ 9
Clyde Shoun STL............ 9
three tied at..................... 7

COMPLETE GAMES
Bucky Walters CIN........ 31
Paul Derringer CIN 28
Bill Lee CHI 20

SHUTOUTS
Lou Fette BOS 6
Bill Posedal BOS 5
Paul Derringer CIN 5

GAMES PITCHED
Clyde Shoun STL 53
Rip Sewell PIT 52
Bob Bowman STL......... 51

INNINGS PITCHED
Bucky Walters CIN...... 319
Paul Derringer CIN 301
Bill Lee CHI 282

1940 AL

	W	L	PCT	GB	R	OR	BA	FA	ERA
DETROIT	90	64	.584	—	888	717	.286	.968	4.01
CLEVELAND	89	65	.578	1	710	637	.265	.975	3.63
NEW YORK	88	66	.571	2	817	671	.259	.975	3.89
BOSTON	82	72	.532	8	872	825	.286	.972	4.89
CHICAGO	82	72	.532	8	735	672	.278	.969	3.74
ST. LOUIS	67	87	.435	23	757	882	.263	.974	5.12
WASHINGTON	64	90	.416	26	665	811	.271	.968	4.59
PHILADELPHIA	54	100	.351	36	703	932	.262	.960	5.22
					6147	6147	.271	.970	4.38

BATTING AVERAGE
Joe DiMaggio NY .... .352
Luke Appling CHI .... .348
Ted Williams BOS ...... .344

HITS
Rip Radcliff STL 200
Doc Cramer BOS 200
B. McCoskey DET 200

DOUBLES
Hank Greenberg DET ... 50
Lou Boudreau CLE 46
Rudy York DET 46

TRIPLES
B. McCoskey DET 19
Lou Finney BOS 15
Charlie Keller NY 15

HOME RUNS
Hank Greenberg DET ... 41
Jimmie Foxx BOS 36
Rudy York DET 33

RUNS BATTED IN
H. Greenberg DET 150
Rudy York DET 134
Joe DiMaggio NY 133

SLUGGING AVERAGE
H. Greenberg DET ..... .670
Joe DiMaggio NY .... .626
Ted Williams BOS .... .594

STOLEN BASES
George Case WAS 35
Gee Walker WAS 21
Joe Gordon NY 18

RUNS SCORED
Ted Williams BOS 134
H. Greenberg DET 129
B. McCoskey DET 123

WINS
Bob Feller CLE 27
Bobo Newsom DET 21
Al Milnar CLE 18

WINNING PERCENTAGE
S. Rowe DET .... .842
Bobo Newsom DET ... .808
Bob Feller CLE .... .711

EARNED RUN AVERAGE
Bob Feller CLE 2.61
Bobo Newsom DET ... 2.83
Johnny Rigney CHI 3.11

STRIKEOUTS
Bob Feller CLE 261
Bobo Newsom DET 164
Johnny Rigney CHI 141

SAVES
Al Benton DET 17
Clint Brown CHI 10
Johnny Murphy NY 9

COMPLETE GAMES
Bob Feller CLE 31
Thorton Lee CHI 24
Dutch Leonard WAS 23

SHUTOUTS
Bob Feller CLE 4
Ted Lyons CHI 4
Al Milnar CLE 4

GAMES PITCHED
Bob Feller CLE 43
Al Benton DET 42
two tied at 41

INNINGS PITCHED
Bob Feller CLE 320
Dutch Leonard WAS ... 289
Johnny Rigney CHI 281

1940 NL

	W	L	PCT	GB	R	OR	BA	FA	ERA
★CINCINNATI	100	53	.654	—	707	528	.266	.981	3.05
BROOKLYN	88	65	.575	12	697	621	.260	.970	3.50
ST. LOUIS	84	69	.549	16	747	699	.275	.971	3.83
PITTSBURGH	78	76	.506	22.5	809	783	.276	.966	4.36
CHICAGO	75	79	.487	25.5	681	636	.267	.968	3.54
NEW YORK	72	80	.474	27.5	663	659	.267	.977	3.79
BOSTON	65	87	.428	34.5	623	745	.256	.970	4.36
PHILADELPHIA	50	103	.327	50	494	750	.238	.970	4.40
					5421	5421	.264	.972	3.85

BATTING AVERAGE
Debs Garms PIT .... .355
Ernie Lombardi CIN ... .319
J. Cooney BOS .... .318

HITS
F. McCormick CIN 191
Stan Hack CHI 191
Johnny Mize STL 182

DOUBLES
F. McCormick CIN 44
Arky Vaughan PIT........ 40
Jim Gleeson CHI........... 39

TRIPLES
Arky Vaughan PIT......... 15
Chet Ross BOS 14
three tied at.................. 13

HOME RUNS
Johnny Mize STL 43
Bill Nicholson CHI 25
Rizzo PIT, CIN, PHI 24

RUNS BATTED IN
Johnny Mize STL 137
F. McCormick CIN 127
M. Van Robays PIT..... 116

SLUGGING AVERAGE
Johnny Mize STL .... .636
Bill Nicholson CHI ...... .534
Dolf Camilli BKN .... .529

STOLEN BASES
Lonny Frey CIN............. 22
Stan Hack CHI 21
Terry Moore STL........... 18

RUNS SCORED
Arky Vaughan PIT....... 113
Johnny Mize STL 111
Bill Werber CIN 105

WINS
Bucky Walters CIN........ 22
Paul Derringer CIN 20
Claude Passeau CHI 20

WINNING PERCENTAGE
Fitzsimmons BKN .... .889
Rip Sewell PIT .... .762
Bucky Walters CIN...... .688

EARNED RUN AVERAGE
Bucky Walters CIN...... 2.48
C. Passeau CHI 2.50
Rip Sewell PIT 2.80

STRIKEOUTS
Kirby Higbe PHI 137
Whit Wyatt BKN 124
C. Passeau CHI........... 124

SAVES
Jumbo Brown NY............. 7
Joe Beggs CIN................. 7
Mace Brown PIT 7

COMPLETE GAMES
Bucky Walters CIN........ 29
Paul Derringer CIN 26
Hugh Mulcahy PHI 21

SHUTOUTS
Manny Salvo BOS 5
Bill Lohrman NY.............. 5
Whit Wyatt BKN.............. 5

GAMES PITCHED
Clyde Shoun STL 54
Mace Brown PIT 48
Claude Passeau CHI 46

INNINGS PITCHED
Bucky Walters CIN...... 305
Paul Derringer CIN 297
Kirby Higbe PHI 283

1941 AL

	W	L	PCT	GB	R	OR	BA	FA	ERA
★NEW YORK	101	53	.656	—	830	631	.269	.973	3.53
BOSTON	84	70	.545	17	865	750	.283	.972	4.19
CHICAGO	77	77	.500	24	638	649	.255	.971	3.52
CLEVELAND	75	79	.487	26	677	668	.256	.976	3.90
DETROIT	75	79	.487	26	686	743	.263	.969	4.18
ST. LOUIS	70	84	.455	31	765	823	.266	.975	4.72
WASHINGTON	70	84	.455	31	728	798	.272	.969	4.35
PHILADELPHIA	64	90	.416	37	713	840	.268	.967	4.83
					5902	5902	.266	.972	4.15

BATTING AVERAGE
Ted Williams BOS...... .406
Cecil Travis WAS....... .359
Joe DiMaggio NY....... .357

HITS
Cecil Travis WAS........ 218
Jeff Heath CLE 199
Joe DiMaggio NY........ 193

DOUBLES
Lou Boudreau CLE 45
Joe DiMaggio NY......... 43
Walt Judnich STL.......... 40

TRIPLES
Jeff Heath CLE 20
Cecil Travis WAS.......... 19
Ken Keltner CLE........... 13

HOME RUNS
Ted Williams BOS......... 37
Charlie Keller NY 33
Tommy Henrich NY 31

RUNS BATTED IN
Joe DiMaggio NY........ 125
Jeff Heath CLE 123
Charlie Keller NY 122

SLUGGING AVERAGE
Ted Williams BOS...... .735
Joe DiMaggio NY........ .643
Jeff Heath CLE .... .586

STOLEN BASES
George Case WAS 33
Joe Kuhel CHI.............. 20
Jeff Heath CLE 18

RUNS SCORED
Ted Williams BOS...... 135
Joe DiMaggio NY....... 122
Dom DiMaggio BOS ... 117

WINS
Bob Feller CLE 25
Thorton Lee CHI 22
Dick Newsome BOS ... 19

WINNING PERCENTAGE
Lefty Gomez NY .... .750
Al Benton DET .... .714
Red Ruffing NY........... .714

EARNED RUN AVERAGE
Thorton Lee CHI 2.37
Al Benton DET 2.97
C. Wagner BOS 3.07

STRIKEOUTS
Bob Feller CLE 260
Bobo Newsom DET 175
Thorton Lee CHI 130

SAVES
Johnny Murphy NY 15
Tom Ferrick PHI............. 7
Al Benton DET 7

COMPLETE GAMES
Thonton Lee CHI 30
Bob Feller CLE 28
Eddie Smith CHI 21

SHUTOUTS
Bob Feller CLE 6
three tied at..................... 4

GAMES PITCHED
Bob Feller CLE 44
Bobo Newsom DET 43
Clint Brown CLE 41

INNINGS PITCHED
Bob Feller CLE 343
Thorton Lee CHI 300
Eddie Smith CHI 263

1941 NL

	W	L	PCT	GB	R	OR	BA	FA	ERA
BROOKLYN	100	54	.649	—	800	581	.272	.974	3.14
ST. LOUIS	97	56	.634	2.5	734	589	.272	.973	3.19
CINCINNATI	88	66	.571	12	616	564	.247	.975	3.17
PITTSBURGH	81	73	.526	19	690	643	.268	.968	3.48
NEW YORK	74	79	.484	25.5	667	706	.260	.974	3.94
CHICAGO	70	84	.455	30	666	670	.253	.970	3.72
BOSTON	62	92	.403	38	592	720	.251	.969	3.95
PHILADELPHIA	43	111	.279	57	501	793	.244	.969	4.50
					5266	5266	.258	.972	3.63

BATTING AVERAGE
Pete Reiser BKN........ .343
J. Cooney BOS .... .319
Joe Medwick BKN...... .318

HITS
Stan Hack CHI 186
Pete Reiser BKN......... 184
Danny Litwhiler PHI 180

DOUBLES
Pete Reiser BKN........... 39
Johnny Mize STL........... 39
Johnny Rucker NY........ 38

TRIPLES
Pete Reiser BKN........... 17
Elbie Fletcher PIT 13
Johnny Hopp STL.......... 11

HOME RUNS
Dolf Camilli BKN 34
Mel Ott NY 27
Bill Nicholson CHI 26

RUNS BATTED IN
Dolf Camilli BKN 120
Bobby Young NY 104
two tied at 100

SLUGGING AVERAGE
Pete Reiser BKN........ .558
Dolf Camilli BKN .... .556
Johnny Mize STL........ .535

STOLEN BASES
Danny Murtaugh PHI 18
Stan Benjamin PHI 17
two tied at 16

RUNS SCORED
Pete Reiser BKN......... 117
Stan Hack CHI 111
Joe Medwick BKN....... 100

WINS
Kirby Higbe BKN........... 22
Whit Wyatt BKN............. 22
two tied at 19

WINNING PERCENTAGE
Elmer Riddle CIN .... .826
Kirby Higbe BKN......... .710
Ernie White STL.......... .708

EARNED RUN AVERAGE
Elmer Riddle CIN 2.24
Whit Wyatt BKN 2.34
Ernie White STL.......... 2.40

STRIKEOUTS
J. Vander Meer CIN 202
Whit Wyatt BKN 176
Bucky Walters CIN...... 129

SAVES
Jumbo Brown NY............. 8
Hugh Casey BKN............. 7
Bill Crouch PHI, STL....... 7

COMPLETE GAMES
Bucky Walters CIN....... 27
Whit Wyatt BKN 23
two tied at 20

SHUTOUTS
Whit Wyatt BKN 7
J. Vander Meer CIN 6
two tied at 5

GAMES PITCHED
Kirby Higbe BKN........... 48
Ike Pearson PHI............. 46
Hugh Casey BKN........... 45

INNINGS PITCHED
Bucky Walters CIN...... 302
Kirby Higbe BKN 298
Whit Wyatt BKN 288

1942 AL

	W	L	PCT	GB	R	OR	BA	FA	ERA
NEW YORK	103	51	.669	—	801	507	.269	.976	2.91
BOSTON	93	59	.612	9	761	594	.276	.974	3.44
ST. LOUIS	82	69	.543	19.5	730	637	.259	.972	3.59
CLEVELAND	75	79	.487	28	590	659	.253	.974	3.59
DETROIT	73	81	.474	30	589	587	.246	.969	3.13
CHICAGO	66	82	.446	34	538	609	.246	.970	3.58
WASHINGTON	62	89	.411	39.5	653	817	.258	.962	4.58
PHILADELPHIA	55	99	.357	48	549	801	.249	.969	4.48
					5211	5211	.257	.971	3.66

BATTING AVERAGE
Ted Williams BOS...... .356
Johnny Pesky BOS.... .331
Stan Spence WAS..... .323

HITS
Johnny Pesky BOS..... 205
Stan Spence WAS...... 203
two tied at 186

DOUBLES
Don Kolloway CHI......... 40
Harlond Clift STL 39
Jeff Heath CLE 37

TRIPLES
Stan Spence WAS........ 15
Jeff Heath CLE 13
Joe DiMaggio NY.......... 13

HOME RUNS
Ted Williams BOS.......... 36
Chet Laabs STL............. 27
Charlie Keller NY 26

RUNS BATTED IN
Ted Williams BOS....... 137
Joe DiMaggio NY........ 114
Charlie Keller NY 108

SLUGGING AVERAGE
Ted Williams BOS...... .648
Charlie Keller NY .... .513
Walt Judnich STL........ .499

STOLEN BASES
George Case WAS 44
Mickey Vernon WAS..... 25
two tied at 22

RUNS SCORED
Ted Williams BOS....... 141
Joe DiMaggio NY........ 123
Dom DiMaggio BOS ... 110

WINS
Tex Hughson BOS........ 22
Ernie Bonham NY......... 21
two tied at 17

WINNING PERCENTAGE
Ernie Bonham NY....... .808
Hank Borowy NY .... .789
Tex Hughson BOS..... .786

EARNED RUN AVERAGE
Ted Lyons CHI............ 2.10
Ernie Bonham NY...... 2.27
Spud Chandler NY..... 2.38

STRIKEOUTS
Bobo Newsom WAS ... 113
Tex Hughson BOS...... 113
two tied at 110

SAVES
Johnny Murphy NY 11
Mace Brown BOS 6
Joe Haynes CHI.............. 6

COMPLETE GAMES
Ernie Bonham NY 22
Tex Hughson BOS........ 22
Ted Lyons CHI............... 20

SHUTOUTS
Ernie Bonham NY 6

GAMES PITCHED
Joe Haynes CHI............ 40
George Castor STL....... 39

INNINGS PITCHED
Tex Hughson BOS...... 281
Jim Bagby CLE 271
Eldon Auker STL......... 249

1942 NL

	W	L	PCT	GB	R	OR	BA	FA	ERA
ST. LOUIS	106	48	.688	—	755	482	.268	.972	2.55
BROOKLYN	104	50	.675	2	742	510	.265	.977	2.84
NEW YORK	85	67	.559	20	675	600	.254	.977	3.31
CINCINNATI	76	76	.500	29	527	545	.231	.971	2.82
PITTSBURGH	66	81	.449	36.5	585	631	.245	.969	3.58
CHICAGO	68	86	.442	38	591	665	.254	.973	3.60
BOSTON	59	89	.399	44	515	645	.240	.976	3.76
PHILADELPHIA	42	109	.278	62.5	394	706	.232	.968	4.12
					4784	4784	.249	.973	3.31

BATTING AVERAGE
Ernie Lombardi BOS .. .330
Enos Slaughter STL ... .318
Stan Musial STL .... .315

HITS
Enos Slaughter STL...... 188
Bill Nicholson CHI 173
three tied at 166

DOUBLES
Marty Marion STL 38
Joe Medwick BKN 37
Stan Hack CHI 36

TRIPLES
Enos Slaughter STL 17
Bill Nicholson CHI 11
Stan Musial STL 10

HOME RUNS
Mel Ott NY 30
Johnny Mize NY............ 26
Dolf Camilli BKN 26

RUNS BATTED IN
Johnny Mize NY.......... 110
Dolf Camilli BKN 109
Enos Slaughter STL...... 98

SLUGGING AVERAGE
Johnny Mize NY .... .521
Mel Ott NY .... .497
Enos Slaughter STL.... .494

STOLEN BASES
Pete Reiser BKN........... 20
N. Fernandez BOS 15
Pee Wee Reese BKN .. 15

RUNS SCORED
Mel Ott NY 118
Enos Slaughter STL.... 100
Johnny Mize NY........... 97

WINS
Mort Cooper STL 22
Johnny Beazley STL..... 21
two tied at 19

WINNING PERCENTAGE
Larry French BKN ...... .789
J. Beazley STL............ .778
Mort Cooper STL .... .759

EARNED RUN AVERAGE
Mort Cooper STL 1.78
J. Beazley STL............ 2.13
Curt Davis BKN.......... 2.36

STRIKEOUTS
J. Vander Meer CIN 186
Mort Cooper STL 152
Kirby Higbe BKN......... 115

SAVES
Hugh Casey BKN.......... 13
Ace Adams NY 11
Joe Beggs CIN................ 8

COMPLETE GAMES
Jim Tobin BOS............. 28
Claude Passeau CHI 24
Mort Cooper STL 22

SHUTOUTS
Mort Cooper STL 10
three tied at...................... 5

GAMES PITCHED
Ace Adams NY 61
Hugh Casey BKN.......... 50
two tied at 43

INNINGS PITCHED
Jim Tobin BOS............. 288
Mort Cooper STL 279
C. Passeau CHI 278

1943 AL

	W	L	PCT	GB	R	OR	BA	FA	ERA
★NEW YORK	98	56	.636	—	669	542	.256	.974	2.93
WASHINGTON	84	69	.549	13.5	666	595	.254	.971	3.18
CLEVELAND	82	71	.536	15.5	600	577	.255	.975	3.15
CHICAGO	82	72	.532	16	573	594	.247	.973	3.20
DETROIT	78	76	.506	20	632	560	.261	.971	3.00
ST. LOUIS	72	80	.474	25	596	604	.245	.975	3.41
BOSTON	68	84	.447	29	563	607	.244	.976	3.45
PHILADELPHIA	49	105	.318	49	497	717	.232	.973	4.05
					4796	4796	.249	.973	3.30

BATTING AVERAGE
Luke Appling CHI........ .328
Dick Wakefield DET... .316
Ralph Hodgin CHI....... .314

HITS
Dick Wakefield DET.... 200
Luke Appling CHI........ 192
Doc Cramer DET 182

DOUBLES
Dick Wakefield DET...... 38
George Case WAS 36
two tied at 35

TRIPLES
Johnny Lindell NY......... 12
Wally Moses CHI 12
two tied at 11

HOME RUNS
Rudy York DET............. 34
Charlie Keller NY 31
Vern Stephens STL 22

RUNS BATTED IN
Rudy York DET........... 118
Nick Etten NY 107
Billy Johnson NY........... 94

SLUGGING AVERAGE
Rudy York DET.......... .527
Charlie Keller NY .... .525
Vern Stephens STL ... .482

STOLEN BASES
George Case WAS 61
Wally Moses CHI 56
Thurman Tucker CHI.... 29

RUNS SCORED
George Case WAS 102
Charlie Keller NY 97
Dick Wakefield DET...... 91

WINS
Spud Chandler NY 20
Dizzy Trout DET 20
Early Wynn WAS 18

WINNING PERCENTAGE
Spud Chandler NY ...... .833
Al Smith CLE .... .708
Ernie Bonham NY .... .652

EARNED RUN AVERAGE
Spud Chandler NY 1.64
Ernie Bonham NY 2.27
M. Haefner WAS........ 2.29

STRIKEOUTS
Allie Reynolds CLE 151
Hal Newhouser DET... 144
Spud Chandler NY...... 134

SAVES
G. Maltzberger CHI....... 14
Mace Brown BOS 9
Joe Heving CLE.............. 9

COMPLETE GAMES
Spud Chandler NY........ 20
Tex Hughson BOS........ 20
three tied at................... 18

SHUTOUTS
Spud Chandler NY.......... 5
Dizzy Trout DET 5
two tied at 4

GAMES PITCHED
Mace Brown BOS 49
Dizzy Trout DET 44
Roger Wolff PHI............ 41

INNINGS PITCHED
Jim Bagby CLE........... 273
Tex Hughson BOS...... 266
Early Wynn WAS 257

1943 NL

	W	L	PCT	GB	R	OR	BA	FA	ERA
ST. LOUIS	105	49	.682	—	679	475	.279	.976	2.57
CINCINNATI	87	67	.565	18	608	543	.256	.980	3.13
BROOKLYN	81	72	.529	23.5	716	674	.272	.972	3.88
PITTSBURGH	80	74	.519	25	669	605	.262	.973	3.06
CHICAGO	74	79	.484	30.5	632	600	.261	.973	3.24
BOSTON	68	85	.444	36.5	465	612	.233	.972	3.25
PHILADELPHIA	64	90	.416	41	571	676	.249	.969	3.79
NEW YORK	55	98	.359	49.5	558	713	.247	.973	4.08
					4898	4898	.258	.974	3.37

BATTING AVERAGE
Stan Musial STL .... .357
Billy Herman BKN ...... .330
Walker Cooper STL ... .318

HITS
Stan Musial STL 220
Mickey Witek NY......... 195
Billy Herman BKN 193

DOUBLES
Stan Musial STL 48
Vince DiMaggio PIT 41
Billy Herman BKN 41

TRIPLES
Stan Musial STL 20
Lou Klein STL 14
two tied at 12

HOME RUNS
Bill Nicholson CHI 29
Mel Ott NY 18
Ron Northey PHI........... 16

RUNS BATTED IN
Bill Nicholson CHI....... 128
Bob Elliott PIT 101
Billy Herman BKN 100

SLUGGING AVERAGE
Stan Musial STL .... .562
Bill Nicholson CHI...... .531
Walker Cooper STL ... .463

STOLEN BASES
Arky Vaughan BKN....... 20
Peanuts Lowrey CHI..... 13
three tied at.................... 12

RUNS SCORED
Arky Vaughan BKN..... 112
Stan Musial STL 108
Bill Nicholson CHI 95

WINS
Elmer Riddle CIN 21
Mort Cooper STL 21
Rip Sewell PIT 21

WINNING PERCENTAGE
Mort Cooper STL .... .724
Rip Sewell PIT .... .700
Max Lanier STL .... .682

EARNED RUN AVERAGE
Howie Pollet STL 1.75
Max Lanier STL 1.90
Mort Cooper STL 2.30

STRIKEOUTS
J. Vander Meer CIN 174
Mort Coope. STL 141
Al Javery BOS 134

SAVES
Les Webber BKN 10
Ace Adams NY 9
Clyde Shoun CIN 7

COMPLETE GAMES
Rip Sewell PIT 25
Jim Tobin BOS.............. 24
Mort Cooper STL 24

SHUTOUTS
Hi Bithorn CHI.................. 7
Mort Cooper STL 6

GAMES PITCHED
Ace Adams NY 70
Les Webber BKN 54
Ed Head BKN 47

INNINGS PITCHED
Al Javery BOS 303
J. Vander Meer CIN 289
Nate Andrews BOS..... 284

1944 AL

	W	L	PCT	GB	R	OR	BA	FA	ERA
ST. LOUIS	89	65	.578	—	684	587	.252	.972	3.17
DETROIT	88	66	.571	1	658	581	.263	.970	3.09
NEW YORK	83	71	.539	6	674	617	.264	.974	3.39
BOSTON	77	77	.500	12	739	676	.270	.972	3.82
CLEVELAND	72	82	.468	17	643	677	.266	.974	3.65
PHILADELPHIA	72	82	.468	17	525	594	.257	.971	3.26
CHICAGO	71	83	.461	18	543	662	.247	.970	3.58
WASHINGTON	64	90	.416	25	592	664	.261	.964	3.49
					5058	5058	.260	.971	3.43

BATTING AVERAGE
Lou Boudreau CLE .... .327
Bobby Doerr BOS ...... .325
Bob Johnson BOS ..... .324

HITS
S. Stirnweiss NY 205
Lou Boudreau CLE 191
Stan Spence WAS 187

DOUBLES
Lou Boudreau CLE 45
Ken Keltner CLE 41
Bob Johnson BOS 40

TRIPLES
Johnny Lindell NY 16
Snuffy Stirnweiss NY 16
Don Gutteridge STL 11

HOME RUNS
Nick Etten NY 22
Vern Stephens STL 20
three tied at 18

RUNS BATTED IN
Vern Stephens STL 109
Bob Johnson BOS 106
Johnny Lindell NY 103

SLUGGING AVERAGE
Bobby Doerr BOS ...... .528
Bob Johnson BOS ...... .528
Johnny Lindell NY ...... .500

STOLEN BASES
Snuffy Stirnweiss NY 55
George Case WAS 49
Glenn Myatt WAS 26

RUNS SCORED
S. Stirnweiss NY 125
Bob Johnson BOS 106
Roy Cullenbine CLE 98

WINS
Hal Newhouser DET 29
Dizzy Trout DET 27
Nels Potter STL 19

WINNING PERCENTAGE
Tex Hughson BOS ...... .783
H. Newhouser DET .... .763
Nels Potter STL .... .731

EARNED RUN AVERAGE
Dizzy Trout DET 2.12
H. Newhouser DET 2.22
Tex Hughson BOS 2.26

STRIKEOUTS
Hal Newhouser DET ... 187
Dizzy Trout DET 144
Bobo Newsom PHI 142

SAVES
Joe Berry PHI 12
G. Maltzberger CHI 12
George Caster STL 12

COMPLETE GAMES
Dizzy Trout DET 33
Hal Newhouser DET 25
four tied at 19

SHUTOUTS
Dizzy Trout DET 7
Hal Newhouser DET 6
two tied at 4

GAMES PITCHED
Joe Heving CLE............. 63
Joe Berry PHI 53
Dizzy Trout DET 49

INNINGS PITCHED
Dizzy Trout DET 352
Hal Newhouser DET ... 312
Bobo Newsom PHI 265

1944 NL

	W	L	PCT	GB	R	OR	BA	FA	ERA
ST. LOUIS	105	49	.682	—	772	490	.275	.982	2.67
PITTSBURGH	90	63	.588	14.5	744	662	.265	.970	3.44
CINCINNATI	89	65	.578	16	573	537	.254	.978	2.97
CHICAGO	75	79	.487	30	702	669	.261	.970	3.59
NEW YORK	67	87	.435	38	682	773	.263	.971	4.29
BOSTON	65	89	.422	40	593	674	.246	.971	3.67
BROOKLYN	63	91	.409	42	690	832	.269	.966	4.68
PHILADELPHIA	61	92	.399	43.5	539	658	.251	.972	3.64
					5295	5295	.261	.972	3.61

BATTING AVERAGE
Dixie Walker BKN ...... .357
Stan Musial STL .... .347
Joe Medwick NY .... .337

HITS
Phil Cavarretta CHI 197
Stan Musial STL 197
T. Holmes BOS 195

DOUBLES
Stan Musial STL 51
Augie Galan BKN 43
T. Holmes BOS 42

TRIPLES
Johnny Barrett PIT 19
Bob Elliott PIT 16
Phil Cavarretta CHI 15

HOME RUNS
Bill Nicholson CHI 33
Mel Ott NY 26
Ron Northey PHI 22

RUNS BATTED IN
Bill Nicholson CHI 122
Bob Elliott PIT 108
Ron Northey PHI 104

SLUGGING AVERAGE
Stan Musial STL .... .549
Bill Nicholson CHI ...... .545
Mel Ott NY .... .544

STOLEN BASES
Johnny Barrett PIT 28
Tony Lupien PHI 18
Roy Hughes CHI 16

RUNS SCORED
Bill Nicholson CHI 116
Stan Musial STL 112
Jim Russell PIT 109

WINS
Bucky Walters CIN 23
Mort Cooper STL 22
two tied at 21

WINNING PERCENTAGE
Ted Wilks STL .... .810
H. Brecheen STL .... .762
Mort Cooper STL .... .759

EARNED RUN AVERAGE
Ed Heusser CIN 2.38
Bucky Walters CIN 2.40
Mort Cooper STL 2.46

STRIKEOUTS
Bill Voiselle NY 161
Max Lanier STL 141
Al Javery BOS 137

SAVES
Ace Adams NY 13
Xavier Rescigno PIT 5
Freddie Schmidt STL 5

COMPLETE GAMES
Jim Tobin BOS 28
Bucky Walters CIN 27
Bill Voiselle NY 25

SHUTOUTS
Mort Cooper STL 7
Bucky Walters CIN 6
three tied at 5

GAMES PITCHED
Ace Adams NY 65
Les Webber BKN 48
Xavier Rescigno PIT 48

INNINGS PITCHED
Bill Voiselle NY 313
Jim Tobin BOS 299
Rip Sewell PIT 286

1945 AL

	W	L	PCT	GB	R	OR	BA	FA	ERA
★DETROIT	88	65	.575	—	633	565	.256	.975	2.99
WASHINGTON	87	67	.565	1.5	622	562	.258	.970	2.92
ST. LOUIS	81	70	.536	6	597	548	.249	.976	3.14
NEW YORK	81	71	.533	6.5	676	606	.259	.971	3.45
CLEVELAND	73	72	.503	11	557	548	.255	.977	3.31
CHICAGO	71	78	.477	15	596	633	.262	.970	3.69
BOSTON	71	83	.461	17.5	599	674	.260	.973	3.80
PHILADELPHIA	52	98	.347	34.5	494	638	.245	.973	3.62
					4774	4774	.255	.973	3.36

BATTING AVERAGE
S. Stirnweiss NY .... .309
T. Cuccinello CHI .... .308
J. Dickshot CHI .... .302

HITS
S. Stirnweiss NY 195
Wally Moses CHI 168
Vern Stephens STL 165

DOUBLES
Wally Moses CHI 35
Snuffy Stirnweiss NY 32
George Binks WAS 32

TRIPLES
Snuffy Stirnweiss NY ... 22
Wally Moses CHI 15
Joe Kuhel WAS 13

HOME RUNS
Vern Stephens STL 24
three tied at 18

RUNS BATTED IN
Nick Etten NY 111
Cullenbine CLE, DET.... 93
Vern Stephens STL 89

SLUGGING AVERAGE
S. Stirnweiss NY .... .476
Vern Stephens STL ... .473
Cullenbine CLE, DET. .444

STOLEN BASES
Snuffy Stirnweiss NY 33
George Case WAS 30
Glenn Myatt WAS 30

RUNS SCORED
S. Stirnweiss NY 107
Vern Stephens STL 90
Cullenbine CLE, DET.... 83

WINS
Hal Newhouser DET 25
Boo Ferriss BOS 21
Roger Wolff WAS 20

WINNING PERCENTAGE
H. Newhouser DET.... .735
D. Leonard WAS .... .708
Steve Gromek CLE.... .679

EARNED RUN AVERAGE
H. Newhouser DET.... 1.81
Al Benton DET 2.02
Roger Wolff WAS....... 2.12

STRIKEOUTS
Hal Newhouser DET ... 212
Nels Potter STL 129
Bobo Newsom PHI 127

SAVES
Jim Turner NY 10
Joe Berry PHI 8

COMPLETE GAMES
Hal Newhouser DET ... 29
Boo Ferriss BOS 26
three tied at 21

SHUTOUTS
Hal Newhouser DET 8
Boo Ferriss BOS 5
Al Benton DET 5

GAMES PITCHED
Joe Berry PHI 52
Allie Reynolds CLE 44
Marino Pieretti WAS..... 44

INNINGS PITCHED
Hal Newhouser DET ... 313
Boo Ferriss BOS 265
Bobo Newsom PHI 257

1945 NL

	W	L	PCT	GB	R	OR	BA	FA	ERA
CHICAGO	98	56	.636	—	735	532	.277	.980	2.98
ST. LOUIS	95	59	.617	3	756	583	.273	.977	3.24
BROOKLYN	87	67	.565	11	795	724	.271	.962	3.70
PITTSBURGH	82	72	.532	16	753	686	.267	.971	3.76
NEW YORK	78	74	.513	19	668	700	.269	.973	4.06
BOSTON	67	85	.441	30	721	728	.267	.969	4.04
CINCINNATI	61	93	.396	37	536	694	.249	.976	4.00
PHILADELPHIA	46	108	.299	52	548	865	.246	.962	4.64
					5512	5512	.265	.971	3.80

BATTING AVERAGE
Phil Cavarretta CHI.... .355
T. Holmes BOS.......... .352
Goody Rosen BKN .... .325

HITS
T. Holmes BOS........... 224
Goody Rosen BKN 197
Stan Hack CHI 193

DOUBLES
Tommy Holmes BOS 47
Dixie Walker BKN 42
two tied at 36

TRIPLES
Luis Olmo BKN 13
Andy Pafko CHI 12
two tied at 11

HOME RUNS
Tommy Holmes BOS 28
Chuck Workman BOS.... 25
B. Adams PHI, STL........ 22

RUNS BATTED IN
Dixie Walker BKN 124
T. Holmes BOS............ 117
two tied at 110

SLUGGING AVERAGE
T. Holmes BOS........... .577
W. Kurowski STL .... .511
Phil Cavarretta CHI.... .500

STOLEN BASES
R. Schoendienst STL.... 26
Johnny Barrett PIT........ 25
Dain Clay CIN............... 19

RUNS SCORED
Eddie Stanky BKN 128
Goody Rosen BKN 126
T. Holmes BOS............ 125

WINS
R. Barrett BOS, STL 23
Hank Wyse CHI 22
Ken Burkhart STL 19

WINNING PERCENTAGE
Ken Burkhart STL .... .704
Hank Wyse CHI .... .688
Barrett BOS, STL......... .657

EARNED RUN AVERAGE
Hank Borowy CHI 2.13
Ray Prim CHI.............. 2.40
C. Passeau CHI 2.46

STRIKEOUTS
Preacher Roe PIT 148
Hal Gregg BKN 139
Bill Voiselle NY 115

SAVES
Ace Adams NY 15
Andy Karl PHI 15
Xavier Rescigno PIT 9

COMPLETE GAMES
R. Barrett BOS, STL 24
Hank Wyse CHI 23
Claude Passeau CHI 19

SHUTOUTS
Claude Passeau CHI 5
four tied at........................ 4

GAMES PITCHED
Andy Karl PHI 67
Ace Adams NY 65
J. Hutchings BOS 57

INNINGS PITCHED
R. Barrett BOS, STL ... 285
Hank Wyse CHI 278
Hal Gregg BKN............ 254

1946 AL

	W	L	PCT	GB	R	OR	BA	FA	ERA
BOSTON	104	50	.675	—	792	594	.271	.977	3.38
DETROIT	92	62	.597	12	704	567	.258	.974	3.22
NEW YORK	87	67	.565	17	684	547	.248	.975	3.13
WASHINGTON	76	78	.494	28	608	706	.260	.966	3.74
CHICAGO	74	80	.481	30	562	595	.257	.972	3.10
CLEVELAND	68	86	.442	36	537	637	.245	.975	3.62
ST. LOUIS	66	88	.429	38	621	711	.251	.974	3.95
PHILADELPHIA	49	105	.318	55	529	680	.253	.971	3.90
					5037	5037	.256	.973	3.50

BATTING AVERAGE
M. Vernon WAS.......... .353
Ted Williams BOS....... .342
Johnny Pesky BOS...... .335

HITS
Johnny Pesky BOS..... 208
Mickey Vernon WAS... 207
Luke Appling CHI........ 180

DOUBLES
Mickey Vernon WAS..... 51
Stan Spence WAS......... 50
Johnny Pesky BOS....... 43

TRIPLES
Hank Edwards CLE 16
Buddy Lewis WAS 13
three tied at................... 10

HOME RUNS
Hank Greenberg DET ... 44
Ted Williams BOS.......... 38
Charlie Keller NY 30

RUNS BATTED IN
H. Greenberg DET....... 127
Ted Williams BOS........ 123
Rudy York BOS 119

SLUGGING AVERAGE
Ted Williams BOS....... .667
H. Greenberg DET..... .604
Charlie Keller NY .... .533

STOLEN BASES
George Case CLE 28
Snuffy Stirnweiss NY 18
Eddie Lake DET............ 15

RUNS SCORED
Ted Williams BOS....... 142
Johnny Pesky BOS..... 115
Eddie Lake DET.......... 105

WINS
Hal Newhouser DET 26
Bob Feller CLE 26
Boo Ferriss BOS........... 25

WINNING PERCENTAGE
Boo Ferriss BOS........ .806
H. Newhouser DET.... .743
Spud Chandler NY ..... .714

EARNED RUN AVERAGE
H. Newhouser DET.... 1.94
Spud Chandler NY 2.10
Bob Feller CLE 2.18

STRIKEOUTS
Bob Feller CLE 348
Hal Newhouser DET ... 275
Tex Hughson BOS...... 172

SAVES
Bob Klinger BOS.............. 9
Earl Caldwell CHI............ 8
Johnny Murphy NY 7

COMPLETE GAMES
Bob Feller CLE 36
Hal Newhouser DET 29
Boo Ferriss BOS........... 26

SHUTOUTS
Bob Feller CLE 10
four tied at...................... 6

GAMES PITCHED
Bob Feller CLE 48
Boo Ferriss BOS........... 40
Bob Savage PHI 40

INNINGS PITCHED
Bob Feller CLE 371
Hal Newhouser DET ... 292
Tex Hughson BOS...... 278

1946 NL

	W	L	PCT	GB	R	OR	BA	FA	ERA
ST. LOUIS*	98	58	.628	—	712	545	.265	.980	3.01
BROOKLYN	96	60	.615	2	701	570	.260	.972	3.05
CHICAGO	82	71	.536	14.5	626	581	.254	.976	3.24
BOSTON	81	72	.529	15.5	630	592	.264	.972	3.37
PHILADELPHIA	69	85	.448	28	560	705	.258	.975	3.99
CINCINNATI	67	87	.435	30	523	570	.239	.975	3.07
PITTSBURGH	63	91	.409	34	552	668	.250	.970	3.72
NEW YORK	61	93	.396	36	612	685	.255	.973	3.92
					4916	4916	.256	.974	3.42

*Defeated Brooklyn in a playoff 2 games to 0

BATTING AVERAGE
Stan Musial STL .... .365
Johnny Hopp BOS ..... .333
Dixie Walker BKN .... .319

HITS
Stan Musial STL 228
Dixie Walker BKN 184
Enos Slaughter STL.... 183

DOUBLES
Stan Musial STL 50
Tommy Holmes BOS 35
Whitey Kurowski STL.... 32

TRIPLES
Stan Musial STL 20
Phil Cavarretta CHI....... 10
Pee Wee Reese BKN ... 10

HOME RUNS
Ralph Kiner PIT 23
Johnny Mize NY............ 22
Enos Slaughter STL...... 18

RUNS BATTED IN
Enos Slaughter STL..... 130
Dixie Walker BKN 116
Stan Musial STL 103

SLUGGING AVERAGE
Stan Musial STL .... .587
Del Ennis PHI .... .485
Enos Slaughter STL.... .465

STOLEN BASES
Pete Reiser BKN........... 34
Bert Haas CIN............... 22
Johnny Hopp BOS 21

RUNS SCORED
Stan Musial STL 124
Enos Slaughter STL.... 100
Eddie Stanky BKN 98

WINS
Howie Pollet STL 21
Johnny Sain BOS 20
Kirby Higbe BKN........... 17

WINNING PERCENTAGE
Murry Dickson STL ..... .714
Kirby Higbe BKN.......... .680
Howie Pollet STL .... .677

EARNED RUN AVERAGE
Howie Pollet STL 2.10
Johnny Sain BOS 2.21
Joe Beggs CIN............ 2.32

STRIKEOUTS
Johnny Schmitz CHI ... 135
Kirby Higbe BKN......... 134
Johnny Sain BOS 129

SAVES
Ken Raffensberger PHI... 6
four tied at....................... 5

COMPLETE GAMES
Johnny Sain BOS 24
Howie Pollet STL 22
Dave Koslo NY 17

SHUTOUTS
Ewell Blackwell CIN......... 6
Harry Brecheen STL....... 5
J. Vander Meer CIN........ 5

GAMES PITCHED
Ken Trinkle NY.............. 48
Murry Dickson STL 47
Hank Behrman BKN 47

INNINGS PITCHED
Howie Pollet STL 266
Dave Koslo NY 265
Johnny Sain BOS 265

1947 AL

	W	L	PCT	GB	R	OR	BA	FA	ERA
★NEW YORK	97	57	.630	—	794	568	.271	.981	3.39
DETROIT	85	69	.552	12	714	642	.258	.975	3.57
BOSTON	83	71	.539	14	720	669	.265	.977	3.81
CLEVELAND	80	74	.519	17	687	588	.259	.983	3.44
PHILADELPHIA	78	76	.506	19	633	614	.252	.976	3.51
CHICAGO	70	84	.455	27	553	661	.256	.975	3.64
WASHINGTON	64	90	.416	33	496	675	.241	.976	3.97
ST. LOUIS	59	95	.383	38	564	744	.241	.977	4.33
					5161	5161	.256	.977	3.7

BATTING AVERAGE
Ted Williams BOS...... .343
B. McCoskey PHI........ .328
two tied at .... .324

HITS
Johnny Pesky BOS..... 207
George Kell DET......... 188
Ted Williams BOS....... 181

DOUBLES
Lou Boudreau CLE 45
Ted Williams BOS......... 40
Tommy Henrich NY 35

TRIPLES
Tommy Henrich NY 13
Mickey Vernon WAS..... 12
Dave Philley CHI........... 11

HOME RUNS
Ted Williams BOS......... 32
Joe Gordon CLE........... 29
Jeff Heath STL.............. 27

RUNS BATTED IN
Ted Williams BOS....... 114
Tommy Henrich NY 98
Joe DiMaggio NY.......... 97

SLUGGING AVERAGE
Ted Williams BOS...... .634
Joe DiMaggio NY .... .522
Joe Gordon CLE .... .496

STOLEN BASES
Bob Dillinger STL........... 34
Dave Philley CHI........... 21
two tied at 12

RUNS SCORED
Ted Williams BOS....... 125
Tommy Henrich NY 109
Johnny Pesky BOS..... 106

WINS
Bob Feller CLE 20
Allie Reynolds NY 19
Phil Marchildon PHI 19

WINNING PERCENTAGE
Allie Reynolds NY ...... .704
Joe Dobson BOS .... .692
Phil Marchildon PHI ... .679

EARNED RUN AVERAGE
Joe Haynes CHI.......... 2.42
Spud Chandler NY..... 2.46
Bob Feller CLE 2.68

STRIKEOUTS
Bob Feller CLE 196
Hal Newhouser DET ... 176
W. Masterson WAS 135

SAVES
Joe Page NY................. 17
Eddie Klieman CLE....... 17
Russ Christopher PHI ... 12

COMPLETE GAMES
Hal Newhouser DET 24
Early Wynn WAS 22
Eddie Lopat CHI 22

SHUTOUTS
Bob Feller CLE 5
three tied at................... 4

GAMES PITCHED
Eddie Klieman CLE....... 58
Joe Page NY................. 56
Earl Johnson BOS 45

INNINGS PITCHED
Bob Feller CLE 299
Hal Newhouser DET 285
Phil Marchildon PHI 277

1947 NL

	W	L	PCT	GB	R	OR	BA	FA	ERA
BROOKLYN	94	60	.610	—	774	668	.272	.978	3.82
ST. LOUIS	89	65	.578	5	780	634	.270	.979	3.53
BOSTON	86	68	.558	8	701	622	.275	.974	3.62
NEW YORK	81	73	.526	13	830	761	.271	.974	4.44
CINCINNATI	73	81	.474	21	681	755	.259	.977	4.41
CHICAGO	69	85	.448	25	567	722	.259	.975	4.10
PHILADELPHIA	62	92	.403	32	589	687	.258	.974	3.96
PITTSBURGH	62	92	.403	32	744	817	.261	.975	4.68
					5666	5666	.265	.976	4.07

BATTING AVERAGE
H. Walker STL, PHI ... .363
Bob Elliott BOS .... .317
Phil Cavarretta CHI ..... .314

HITS
T. Holmes BOS 191
H. Walker STL, PHI 186
two tied at 183

DOUBLES
Eddie Miller CIN 38
Bob Elliott BOS 35
two tied at 33

TRIPLES
H. Walker STL, PHI 16
Stan Musial STL 13
Enos Slaughter STL 13

HOME RUNS
Ralph Kiner PIT 51
Johnny Mize NY 51
Willard Marshall NY 36

RUNS BATTED IN
Johnny Mize NY 138
Ralph Kiner PIT 127
Walker Cooper NY 122

SLUGGING AVERAGE
Ralph Kiner PIT .... .639
Johnny Mize NY .... .614
Walker Cooper NY ..... .586

STOLEN BASES
Jackie Robinson BKN ... 29
Pete Reiser BKN 14
two tied at 13

RUNS SCORED
Johnny Mize NY 137
J. Robinson BKN 125
Ralph Kiner PIT 118

WINS
Ewell Blackwell CIN 22
four tied at 21

WINNING PERCENTAGE
Larry Jansen NY .... .808
G. Munger STL .... .762
Ewell Blackwell CIN .... .733

EARNED RUN AVERAGE
Warren Spahn BOS ... 2.33
Ewell Blackwell CIN ... 2.47
Ralph Branca BKN 2.67

STRIKEOUTS
Ewell Blackwell CIN 193
Ralph Branca BKN 148
Johnny Sain BOS 132

SAVES
Hugh Casey BKN 18
Harry Gumbert CIN 10
Ken Trinkle NY 10

COMPLETE GAMES
Ewell Blackwell CIN 23
Johnny Sain BOS 22
Warren Spahn BOS 22

SHUTOUTS
Warren Spahn BOS 7
George Munger STL 6
Ewell Blackwell CIN 6

GAMES PITCHED
Ken Trinkle NY 62
Kirby Higbe BKN, PIT ... 50
H. Behrman PIT, BKN... 50

INNINGS PITCHED
Warren Spahn BOS 290
Ralph Branca BKN 280
Ewell Blackwell CIN 273

1948 AL

	W	L	PCT	GB	R	OR	BA	FA	ERA
★CLEVELAND*	97	58	.626	—	840	568	.282	.982	3.22
BOSTON	96	59	.619	1	907	720	.274	.981	4.20
NEW YORK	94	60	.610	2.5	857	633	.278	.979	3.75
PHILADELPHIA	84	70	.545	12.5	729	735	.260	.981	4.43
DETROIT	78	76	.506	18.5	700	726	.267	.974	4.15
ST. LOUIS	59	94	.386	37	671	849	.271	.972	5.01
WASHINGTON	56	97	.366	40	578	796	.244	.974	4.65
CHICAGO	51	101	.336	44.5	559	814	.251	.974	4.89
					5841	5841	.266	.977	4.28

* Defeated Boston in a 1-game playoff

BATTING AVERAGE
Ted Williams BOS...... .369
Lou Boudreau CLE .... .355
Dale Mitchell CLE ...... .336

HITS
Bob Dillinger STL........ 207
Dale Mitchell CLE 204
Lou Boudreau CLE 199

DOUBLES
Ted Williams BOS........ 44
Tommy Henrich NY 42
Hank Majeski PHI 41

TRIPLES
Tommy Henrich NY 14
B. Stewart NY, WAS 13
three tied at................... 11

HOME RUNS
Joe DiMaggio NY.......... 39
Joe Gordon CLE............ 32
Ken Keltner CLE............ 31

RUNS BATTED IN
Joe DiMaggio NY........ 155
Vern Stephens BOS ... 137
Ted Williams BOS....... 127

SLUGGING AVERAGE
Ted Williams BOS...... .615
Joe DiMaggio NY........ .598
Tommy Henrich NY ... .554

STOLEN BASES
Bob Dillinger STL........... 28
Gill Coan WAS.............. 23
Mickey Vernon WAS..... 15

RUNS SCORED
Tommy Henrich NY 138
Dom DiMaggio BOS ... 127
two tied at 124

WINS
Hal Newhouser DET 21
Gene Bearden CLE 20
Bob Lemon CLE 20

WINNING PERCENTAGE
Jack Kramer BOS ...... .783
Gene Bearden CLE .... .741
Vic Raschi NY .... .704

EARNED RUN AVERAGE
Gene Bearden CLE ... 2.43
Scarborough WAS..... 2.82
Bob Lemon CLE 2.82

STRIKEOUTS
Bob Feller CLE 164
Bob Lemon CLE 147
Hal Newhouser DET ... 143

SAVES
R. Christopher CLE....... 17
Joe Page NY................. 16
two tied at 10

COMPLETE GAMES
Bob Lemon CLE 20
Hal Newhouser DET 19
two tied at 18

SHUTOUTS
Bob Lemon CLE 10
Gene Bearden CLE 6
Vic Raschi NY................. 6

GAMES PITCHED
Joe Page NY................. 55
Al Widmar STL.............. 49
Frank Biscan STL 47

INNINGS PITCHED
Bob Lemon CLE 294
Bob Feller CLE 280
Hal Newhouser DET ... 272

1948 NL

	W	L	PCT	GB	R	OR	BA	FA	ERA
BOSTON	91	62	.595	—	739	584	.275	.976	3.38
ST. LOUIS	85	69	.552	6.5	742	646	.263	.980	3.91
BROOKLYN	84	70	.545	7.5	744	667	.261	.973	3.75
PITTSBURGH	83	71	.539	8.5	706	699	.263	.977	4.15
NEW YORK	78	76	.506	13.5	780	704	.256	.974	3.93
PHILADELPHIA	66	88	.429	25.5	591	729	.259	.964	4.08
CINCINNATI	64	89	.418	27	588	752	.247	.973	4.47
CHICAGO	64	90	.416	27.5	597	706	.262	.972	4.00
					5487	5487	.261	.974	3.95

BATTING AVERAGE
Stan Musial STL .... .376
Richie Ashburn PHI ... .333
T. Holmes BOS.......... .325

HITS
Stan Musial STL 230
T. Holmes BOS............ 190
Stan Rojek PIT............ 186

DOUBLES
Stan Musial STL 46
Del Ennis PHI 40
Alvin Dark BOS............. 39

TRIPLES
Stan Musial STL 18
Johnny Hopp PIT 12
Enos Slaughter STL...... 11

HOME RUNS
Johnny Mize NY............ 40
Ralph Kiner PIT 40
Stan Musial STL 39

RUNS BATTED IN
Stan Musial STL 131
Johnny Mize NY.......... 125
Ralph Kiner PIT 123

SLUGGING AVERAGE
Stan Musial STL .... .702
Johnny Mize NY.......... .564
Sid Gordon NY............ .537

STOLEN BASES
Richie Ashburn PHI 32
Pee Wee Reese BKN ... 25
Stan Rojek PIT.............. 24

RUNS SCORED
Stan Musial STL 135
Whitey Lockman NY ... 117
Johnny Mize NY.......... 110

WINS
Johnny Sain BOS 24
Harry Brecheen STL..... 20
two tied at 18

WINNING PERCENTAGE
H. Brecheen STL .... .741
Sheldon Jones NY ..... .667
Johnny Sain BOS .... .615

EARNED RUN AVERAGE
H. Brecheen STL 2.24
Dutch Leonard PHI 2.51
Johnny Sain BOS 2.60

STRIKEOUTS
Harry Brecheen STL... 149
Rex Barney BKN......... 138
Johnny Sain BOS 137

SAVES
Harry Gumbert CIN....... 17
Ted Wilks STL 13
Kirby Higbe PIT............. 10

COMPLETE GAMES
Johnny Sain BOS 28
Harry Brecheen STL.... 21
Johnny Schmitz CHI 18

SHUTOUTS
Harry Brecheen STL..... 7
four tied at....................... 4

GAMES PITCHED
Harry Gumbert CIN....... 61
Ted Wilks STL 57
Kirby Higbe PIT............. 56

INNINGS PITCHED
Johnny Sain BOS 315
Larry Jansen NY 277
Warren Spahn BOS.... 257

1949 AL

	W	L	PCT	GB	R	OR	BA	FA	ERA
★NEW YORK	97	57	.630	—	829	637	.269	.977	3.69
BOSTON	96	58	.623	1	896	667	.282	.980	3.97
CLEVELAND	89	65	.578	8	675	574	.260	.983	3.36
DETROIT	87	67	.565	10	751	655	.267	.978	3.77
PHILADELPHIA	81	73	.526	16	726	725	.260	.976	4.23
CHICAGO	63	91	.409	34	648	737	.257	.977	4.30
ST. LOUIS	53	101	.344	44	667	913	.254	.971	5.21
WASHINGTON	50	104	.325	47	584	868	.254	.973	5.10
					5776	5776	.263	.977	4.20

BATTING AVERAGE
George Kell DET......... .343
Ted Williams BOS......... .343
Bob Dillinger STL........ .324

HITS
Dale Mitchell CLE 203
Ted Williams BOS....... 194
Dom DiMaggio BOS ... 186

DOUBLES
Ted Williams BOS......... 39
George Kell DET........... 38
Dom DiMaggio BOS 34

TRIPLES
Dale Mitchell CLE 23
Bob Dillinger STL........... 13
Elmer Valo PHI 12

HOME RUNS
Ted Williams BOS........ 43
Vern Stephens BOS 39
four tied at...................... 24

RUNS BATTED IN
Vern Stephens BOS ... 159
Ted Williams BOS....... 159
Vic Wertz DET 133

SLUGGING AVERAGE
Ted Williams BOS...... .650
V. Stephens BOS........ .539
Tommy Henrich NY ... .526

STOLEN BASES
Bob Dillinger STL........... 20
Phil Rizzuto NY............. 18
Elmer Valo PHI 14

RUNS SCORED
Ted Williams BOS....... 150
Eddie Joost PHI 128
Dom DiMaggio BOS ... 126

WINS
Mel Parnell BOS 25
Ellis Kinder BOS 23
Bob Lemon CLE 22

WINNING PERCENTAGE
Ellis Kinder BOS .... .793
Mel Parnell BOS .... .781
Allie Reynolds NY .... .739

EARNED RUN AVERAGE
Mike Garcia CLE......... 2.36
Mel Parnell BOS 2.77
Virgil Trucks DET........ 2.81

STRIKEOUTS
Virgil Trucks DET........ 153
Hal Newhouser DET ... 144
two tied at 138

SAVES
Joe Page NY................. 27
Al Benton CLE 10
Tom Ferrick STL............. 6

COMPLETE GAMES
Mel Parnell BOS 27
Bob Lemon CLE 22
Hal Newhouser DET 22

SHUTOUTS
Ellis Kinder BOS 6
Virgil Trucks DET............. 6
Mike Garcia CLE............. 5

GAMES PITCHED
Joe Page NY................. 60
Dick Welteroth WAS 52
Tom Ferrick STL............ 50

INNINGS PITCHED
Mel Parnell BOS 295
Hal Newhouser DET ... 292
Bob Lemon CLE 280

1949 NL

	W	L	PCT	GB	R	OR	BA	FA	ERA
BROOKLYN	97	57	.630	—	879	651	.274	.980	3.80
ST. LOUIS	96	58	.623	1	766	616	.277	.976	3.45
PHILADELPHIA	81	73	.526	16	662	668	.254	.974	3.89
BOSTON	75	79	.487	22	706	719	.258	.976	3.99
NEW YORK	73	81	.474	24	736	693	.261	.973	3.82
PITTSBURGH	71	83	.461	26	681	760	.259	.978	4.57
CINCINNATI	62	92	.403	35	627	770	.260	.977	4.33
CHICAGO	61	93	.396	36	593	773	.256	.970	4.50
					5650	5650	.262	.975	4.04

BATTING AVERAGE
J. Robinson BKN .... .342
Stan Musial STL .... .338
Enos Slaughter STL.... .336

HITS
Stan Musial STL 207
J. Robinson BKN 203
Bobby Thomson NY.... 198

DOUBLES
Stan Musial STL 41
Del Ennis PHI 39
two tied at 38

TRIPLES
Stan Musial STL 13
Enos Slaughter STL...... 13
Jackie Robinson BKN ... 12

HOME RUNS
Ralph Kiner PIT 54
Stan Musial STL 36
Hank Sauer CIN, CHI ... 31

RUNS BATTED IN
Ralph Kiner PIT 127
J. Robinson BKN 124
Stan Musial STL 123

SLUGGING AVERAGE
Ralph Kiner PIT .... .658
Stan Musial STL .... .624
J. Robinson BKN .... .528

STOLEN BASES
Jackie Robinson BKN ... 37
P. Reese BKN............... 26
four tied at..................... 12

RUNS SCORED
P. Reese BKN............. 132
Stan Musial STL 128
J. Robinson BKN 122

WINS
Warren Spahn BOS 21
Howie Pollet STL 20
K. Raffensberger CIN ... 18

WINNING PERCENTAGE
Preacher Roe BKN .... .714
Howie Pollet STL .... .690
two tied at .... .680

EARNED RUN AVERAGE
Dave Koslo NY 2.50
Gerry Staley STL 2.73
Howie Pollet STL 2.77

STRIKEOUTS
Warren Spahn BOS 151
D. Newcombe BKN..... 149
Larry Jansen NY 113

SAVES
Ted Wilks STL 9
Jim Konstanty PHI 7
Nels Potter BOS 7

COMPLETE GAMES
Warren Spahn BOS 25
K. Raffensberger CIN ... 20
Don Newcombe BKN.... 19

SHUTOUTS
four tied at....................... 5

GAMES PITCHED
Ted Wilks STL 59
Jim Konstanty PHI 53
Erv Palica BKN 49

INNINGS PITCHED
Warren Spahn BOS 302
Raffensberger CIN...... 284
Larry Jansen NY 260

1950 AL

	W	L	PCT	GB	R	OR	BA	FA	ERA
★NEW YORK	98	56	.636	—	914	691	.282	.980	4.15
DETROIT	95	59	.617	3	837	713	.282	.981	4.12
BOSTON	94	60	.610	4	1027	804	.302	.981	4.88
CLEVELAND	92	62	.597	6	806	654	.269	.978	3.74
WASHINGTON	67	87	.435	31	690	813	.260	.972	4.66
CHICAGO	60	94	.390	38	625	749	.260	.977	4.41
ST. LOUIS	58	96	.377	40	684	916	.246	.967	5.20
PHILADELPHIA	52	102	.338	46	670	913	.261	.974	5.49
					6253	6253	.271	.976	4.58

BATTING AVERAGE
Billy Goodman BOS... .354
George Kell DET........ .340
Dom DiMaggio BOS .. .328

HITS
George Kell DET......... 218
Phil Rizzuto NY 200
Dom DiMaggio BOS ... 193

DOUBLES
George Kell DET........... 56
Vic Wertz DET 37
Phil Rizzuto NY 36

TRIPLES
Dom DiMaggio BOS 11
Bobby Doerr BOS.......... 11
Hoot Evers DET............ 11

HOME RUNS
Al Rosen CLE 37
Walt Dropo BOS 34
Joe DiMaggio NY 32

RUNS BATTED IN
Vern Stephens BOS ... 144
Walt Dropo BOS 144
Yogi Berra NY 124

SLUGGING AVERAGE
Joe DiMaggio NY .... .585
Walt Dropo BOS .... .583
Hoot Evers DET......... .551

STOLEN BASES
Dom DiMaggio BOS 15
Elmer Valo PHI 12
Phil Rizzuto NY............. 12

RUNS SCORED
Dom DiMaggio BOS ... 131
Vern Stephens BOS ... 125
Phil Rizzuto NY 125

WINS
Bob Lemon CLE 23
Vic Raschi NY 21
Art Houtteman DET 19

WINNING PERCENTAGE
Vic Raschi NY .... .724
Eddie Lopat NY.......... .692
Early Wynn CLE .... .692

EARNED RUN AVERAGE
Early Wynn CLE 3.20
Ned Garver STL......... 3.39
Bob Feller CLE 3.43

STRIKEOUTS
Bob Lemon CLE 170
Allie Reynolds NY 160
Vic Raschi NY............. 155

SAVES
Mickey Harris WAS....... 15
Joe Page NY 13
Tom Ferrick STL, NY 11

COMPLETE GAMES
Ned Garver STL............ 22
Bob Lemon CLE 22
two tied at 21

SHUTOUTS
Art Houtteman DET 4

GAMES PITCHED
Mickey Harris WAS....... 53
Ellis Kinder BOS 48
three tied at................... 46

INNINGS PITCHED
Bob Lemon CLE 288
Art Houtteman DET 275
Ned Garver STL.......... 260

1950 NL

	W	L	PCT	GB	R	OR	BA	FA	ERA
PHILADELPHIA	91	63	.591	—	722	624	.265	.975	3.50
BROOKLYN	89	65	.578	2	847	724	.272	.979	4.28
NEW YORK	86	68	.558	5	735	643	.258	.977	3.71
BOSTON	83	71	.539	8	785	736	.263	.970	4.14
ST. LOUIS	78	75	.510	12.5	693	670	.259	.978	3.97
CINCINNATI	66	87	.431	24.5	654	734	.260	.976	4.32
CHICAGO	64	89	.418	26.5	643	772	.248	.968	4.28
PITTSBURGH	57	96	.373	33.5	681	857	.264	.977	4.96
					5760	5760	.261	.975	4.14

BATTING AVERAGE
Stan Musial STL .... .346
J. Robinson BKN .... .328
Duke Snider BKN....... .321

HITS
Duke Snider BKN....... 199
Stan Musial STL 192
Carl Furillo BKN 189

DOUBLES
R. Schoendienst STL.... 43
Stan Musial STL 41
Jackie Robinson BKN ... 39

TRIPLES
Richie Ashburn PHI 14
Gus Bell PIT................. 11
Duke Snider BKN.......... 10

HOME RUNS
Ralph Kiner PIT 47
Andy Pafko CHI 36
two tied at 32

RUNS BATTED IN
Del Ennis PHI 126
Ralph Kiner PIT 118
Gil Hodges BKN.......... 113

SLUGGING AVERAGE
Stan Musial STL .... .596
Andy Pafko CHI .... .591
Ralph Kiner PIT .... .590

STOLEN BASES
Sam Jethroe BOS......... 35
Pee Wee Reese BKN ... 17
Duke Snider BKN.......... 16

RUNS SCORED
Earl Torgeson BOS...... 120
Eddie Stanky NY......... 115
Ralph Kiner PIT 112

WINS
Warren Spahn BOS 21
Robin Roberts PHI........ 20
Johnny Sain BOS 20

WINNING PERCENTAGE
Sal Maglie NY .... .818
Jim Konstanty PHI ..... .696
Curt Simmons PHI ..... .680

EARNED RUN AVERAGE
Jim Hearn STL, NY.... 2.49
Sal Maglie NY 2.71
Ewell Blackwell CIN ... 2.97

STRIKEOUTS
Warren Spahn BOS 191
Ewell Blackwell CIN 188
Larry Jansen NY 161

SAVES
Jim Konstanty PHI 22
Bill Werle PIT 8
two tied at 7

COMPLETE GAMES
Vern Bickford BOS......... 27
Warren Spahn BOS 25
Johnny Sain BOS 25

SHUTOUTS
four tied at....................... 5

GAMES PITCHED
Jim Konstanty PHI 74
Murry Dickson PIT 51
Bill Werle PIT................. 48

INNINGS PITCHED
Vern Bickford BOS...... 312
Robin Roberts PHI....... 304
Warren Spahn BOS.... 293

1951 AL

	W	L	PCT	GB	R	OR	BA	FA	ERA
★NEW YORK	98	56	.636	—	798	621	.269	.975	3.56
CLEVELAND	93	61	.604	5	696	594	.256	.978	3.38
BOSTON	87	67	.565	11	804	725	.266	.977	4.14
CHICAGO	81	73	.526	17	714	644	.270	.975	3.50
DETROIT	73	81	.474	25	685	741	.265	.973	4.29
PHILADELPHIA	70	84	.455	28	736	745	.262	.978	4.47
WASHINGTON	62	92	.403	36	672	764	.263	.973	4.49
ST. LOUIS	52	102	.338	46	611	882	.247	.971	5.17
					5716	5716	.262	.975	4.12

BATTING AVERAGE
Ferris Fain PHI............ .344
Minoso CLE, CHI .326
George Kell DET........ .319

SLUGGING AVERAGE
Ted Williams BOS...... .556
Larry Doby CLE .... .512
two tied at .... .511

STRIKEOUTS
Vic Raschi NY............. 164
Early Wynn CLE 133
Bob Lemon CLE 132

HITS
George Kell DET......... 191
Dom DiMaggio BOS ... 189
Nellie Fox CHI............. 189

STOLEN BASES
M. Minoso CLE, CHI..... 31
Jim Busby CHI.............. 26
Phil Rizzuto NY............. 18

SAVES
Ellis Kinder BOS 14
Carl Scheib PHI 10
Lou Brissie PHI, CLE...... 9

DOUBLES
Sam Mele WAS 36
George Kell DET........... 36
Eddie Yost WAS 36

RUNS SCORED
Dom DiMaggio BOS ... 113
Minoso CLE, CHI 112
two tied at 109

COMPLETE GAMES
Ned Garver STL............ 24
Early Wynn CLE 21
Eddie Lopat NY............. 20

TRIPLES
M. Minoso CLE, CHI..... 14
Nellie Fox CHI............... 12
R. Coleman STL, CHI ... 12

WINS
Bob Feller CLE 22
Eddie Lopat NY............. 21
Vic Raschi NY............... 21

SHUTOUTS
Allie Reynolds NY........... 7
Eddie Lopat NY............... 5
two tied at 4

HOME RUNS
Gus Zernial CHI, PHI 33
Ted Williams BOS......... 30
Eddie Robinson CHI 29

WINNING PERCENTAGE
Bob Feller CLE .... .733
Eddie Lopat NY.......... .700
Allie Reynolds NY ...... .680

GAMES PITCHED
Ellis Kinder BOS 63
Lou Brissie PHI, CLE.... 56
Mike Garcia CLE........... 47

RUNS BATTED IN
G. Zernial CHI, PHI..... 129
Ted Williams BOS....... 126
Eddie Robinson CHI ... 117

EARNED RUN AVERAGE
Rogovin DET, CHI 2.78
Eddie Lopat NY.......... 2.91
Early Wynn CLE 3.02

INNINGS PITCHED
Early Wynn CLE 274
Bob Lemon CLE 263
Vic Raschi NY............. 258

1951 NL

	W	L	PCT	GB	R	OR	BA	FA	ERA
NEW YORK*	98	59	.624	—	781	641	.260	.972	3.48
BROOKLYN	97	60	.618	1	855	672	.275	.979	3.88
ST. LOUIS	81	73	.526	15.5	683	671	.264	.980	3.95
BOSTON	76	78	.494	20.5	723	662	.262	.976	3.75
PHILADELPHIA	73	81	.474	23.5	648	644	.260	.977	3.81
CINCINNATI	68	86	.442	28.5	559	667	.248	.977	3.70
PITTSBURGH	64	90	.416	32.5	689	845	.258	.972	4.78
CHICAGO	62	92	.403	34.5	614	750	.250	.971	4.34
					5552	5552	.260	.975	3.96

*Defeated Brooklyn in a playoff 2 games to 1

BATTING AVERAGE
Stan Musial STL .... .355
Richie Ashburn PHI ... .344
J. Robinson BKN .... .338

HITS
Richie Ashburn PHI 221
Stan Musial STL 205
Carl Furillo BKN 197

DOUBLES
Alvin Dark NY 41
Ted Kluszewski CIN...... 35
two tied at 33

TRIPLES
Stan Musial STL 12
Gus Bell PIT.................. 12
Monte Irvin NY 11

HOME RUNS
Ralph Kiner PIT 42
Gil Hodges BKN............ 40
Roy Campanella BKN... 33

RUNS BATTED IN
Monte Irvin NY 121
Sid Gordon BOS 109
Ralph Kiner PIT 109

SLUGGING AVERAGE
Ralph Kiner PIT .... .627
Stan Musial STL .... .614
R. Campanella BKN... .590

STOLEN BASES
Sam Jethroe BOS......... 35
Richie Ashburn PHI 29
Jackie Robinson BKN... 25

RUNS SCORED
Stan Musial STL 124
Ralph Kiner PIT 124
Gil Hodges BKN.......... 118

WINS
Sal Maglie NY 23
Larry Jansen NY 23
two tied at 22

WINNING PERCENTAGE
Preacher Roe BKN .... .880
Sal Maglie NY .... .793
D. Newcombe BKN.... .690

EARNED RUN AVERAGE
Chet Nichols BOS...... 2.88
Sal Maglie NY 2.93
Warren Spahn BOS... 2.98

STRIKEOUTS
Warren Spahn BOS 164
D. Newcombe BKN..... 164
Sal Maglie NY 146

SAVES
Ted Wilks STL, PIT....... 13
Frank Smith CIN 11
Jim Konstanty PHI 9

COMPLETE GAMES
Warren Spahn BOS...... 26
Robin Roberts PHI........ 22
Sal Maglie NY 22

SHUTOUTS
Warren Spahn BOS........ 7
Robin Roberts PHI......... 6
K. Raffensberger CIN 5

GAMES PITCHED
Ted Wilks STL, PIT....... 65
Bill Werle PIT................ 59
Jim Konstanty PHI 58

INNINGS PITCHED
Robin Roberts PHI...... 315
Warren Spahn BOS.... 311
Sal Maglie NY 298

1952 AL

	W	L	PCT	GB	R	OR	BA	FA	ERA
★NEW YORK	95	59	.617	—	727	557	.267	.979	3.14
CLEVELAND	93	61	.604	2	763	606	.262	.975	3.32
CHICAGO	81	73	.526	14	610	568	.252	.980	3.25
PHILADELPHIA	79	75	.513	16	664	723	.253	.977	4.15
WASHINGTON	78	76	.506	17	598	608	.239	.978	3.37
BOSTON	76	78	.494	19	668	658	.255	.976	3.80
ST. LOUIS	64	90	.416	31	604	733	.250	.974	4.12
DETROIT	50	104	.325	45	557	738	.243	.975	4.25
					5191	5191	.253	.977	3.67

BATTING AVERAGE
Ferris Fain PHI............ .327
Dale Mitchell CLE ...... .323
two tied at .... .311

HITS
Nellie Fox CHI............ 192
Bobby Avila CLE......... 179
two tied at 176

DOUBLES
Ferris Fain PHI.............. 43
Mickey Mantle NY 37
two tied at 33

TRIPLES
Bobby Avila CLE........... 11
three tied at.................. 10

HOME RUNS
Larry Doby CLE 32
Luke Easter CLE........... 31
Yogi Berra NY 30

RUNS BATTED IN
Al Rosen CLE 105
Eddie Robinson CHI ... 104
Larry Doby CLE 104

SLUGGING AVERAGE
Larry Doby CLE .... .541
Mickey Mantle NY...... .530
Al Rosen CLE .... .524

STOLEN BASES
Minnie Minoso CHI 22
Jim Rivera STL, CHI 21
J. Jensen NY, WAS 18

RUNS SCORED
Larry Doby CLE 104
Bobby Avila CLE.......... 102
Al Rosen CLE 101

WINS
Bobby Shantz PHI.........24
Early Wynn CLE 23
two tied at 22

WINNING PERCENTAGE
Bobby Shantz PHI ..... .774
Vic Raschi NY .... .727
Allie Reynolds NY ...... .714

EARNED RUN AVERAGE
Allie Reynolds NY 2.06
Mike Garcia CLE........ 2.37
Bobby Shantz PHI 2.48

STRIKEOUTS
Allie Reynolds NY 160
Early Wynn CLE 153
Bobby Shantz PHI 152

SAVES
Harry Dorish CHI 11
Satchel Paige STL 10
Johnny Sain NY 7

COMPLETE GAMES
Bob Lemon CLE 28
Bobby Shantz PHI 27
Allie Reynolds NY 24

SHUTOUTS
Allie Reynolds NY 6
Mike Garcia CLE............. 6
two tied at 5

GAMES PITCHED
Bill Kennedy CHI........... 47
Mike Garcia CLE........... 46
Satchel Paige STL........ 46

INNINGS PITCHED
Bob Lemon CLE 310
Mike Garcia CLE......... 292
Early Wynn CLE 286

1952 NL

	W	L	PCT	GB	R	OR	BA	FA	ERA
BROOKLYN	96	57	.627	—	775	603	.262	.982	3.53
NEW YORK	92	62	.597	4.5	722	639	.256	.974	3.59
ST. LOUIS	88	66	.571	8.5	677	630	.267	.977	3.66
PHILADELPHIA	87	67	.565	9.5	657	552	.260	.975	3.07
CHICAGO	77	77	.500	19.5	628	631	.264	.976	3.58
CINCINNATI	69	85	.448	27.5	615	659	.249	.982	4.01
BOSTON	64	89	.418	32	569	651	.233	.975	3.78
PITTSBURGH	42	112	.273	54.5	515	793	.231	.970	4.65
					5158	5158	.253	.976	3.73

BATTING AVERAGE
Stan Musial STL .... .336
F. Baumholtz CHI ...... .325
Ted Kluszewski CIN... .320

HITS
Stan Musial STL 194
Schoendienst STL 188
Bobby Adams CIN 180

DOUBLES
Stan Musial STL 42
Schoendienst STL 40
Roy McMillan CIN 32

TRIPLES
Bobby Thomson NY...... 14
Enos Slaughter STL...... 12
Ted Kluszewski CIN...... 11

HOME RUNS
Hank Sauer CHI............ 37
Ralph Kiner PIT 37
Gil Hodges BKN............ 32

RUNS BATTED IN
Hank Sauer CHI.......... 121
Bobby Thomson NY.... 108
Del Ennis PHI 107

SLUGGING AVERAGE
Stan Musial STL .... .538
Hank Sauer CHI.......... .531
Ted Kluszewski CIN.... .509

STOLEN BASES
Pee Wee Reese BKN ... 30
Sam Jethroe BOS......... 28
Jackie Robinson BKN... 24

RUNS SCORED
Stan Musial STL 105
Solly Hemus STL.......... 105
J. Robinson BKN 104

WINS
Robin Roberts PHI....... 28
Sal Maglie NY 18
three tied at.................. 17

WINNING PERCENTAGE
Hoyt Wilhelm NY......... .833
Robin Roberts PHI..... .800
Joe Black BKN............ .789

EARNED RUN AVERAGE
Hoyt Wilhelm NY........ 2.43
Warren Hacker CHI ... 2.58
Robin Roberts PHI..... 2.59

STRIKEOUTS
Warren Spahn BOS 183
Bob Rush CHI.............. 157
Robin Roberts PHI...... 148

SAVES
Al Brazle STL................ 16
Joe Black BKN............. 15
two tied at 11

COMPLETE GAMES
Robin Roberts PHI........ 30
Murry Dickson PIT 21
Warren Spahn BOS...... 19

SHUTOUTS
Curt Simmons PHI.......... 6
K. Raffensberger CIN 6

GAMES PITCHED
Hoyt Wilhelm NY........... 71
Joe Black BKN.............. 56
Eddie Yuhas STL........... 54

INNINGS PITCHED
Robin Roberts PHI...... 330
Warren Spahn BOS.... 290
Murry Dickson PIT 278

1953 AL

	W	L	PCT	GB	R	OR	BA	FA	ERA
★NEW YORK	99	52	.656	—	801	547	.273	.979	3.20
CLEVELAND	92	62	.597	8.5	770	627	.270	.979	3.64
CHICAGO	89	65	.578	11.5	716	592	.258	.980	3.41
BOSTON	84	69	.549	16	656	632	.264	.975	3.59
WASHINGTON	76	76	.500	23.5	687	614	.263	.979	3.66
DETROIT	60	94	.390	40.5	695	923	.266	.978	5.25
PHILADELPHIA	59	95	.383	41.5	632	799	.256	.977	4.67
ST. LOUIS	54	100	.351	46.5	555	778	.249	.974	4.48
					5512	5512	.262	.978	4.00

BATTING AVERAGE
M. Vernon WAS .... .337
Al Rosen CLE .... .336
two tied at .... .313

HITS
Harvey Kuenn DET 209
Mickey Vernon WAS ... 205
Al Rosen CLE 201

DOUBLES
Mickey Vernon WAS 43
George Kell BOS 41
Sammy White BOS 34

TRIPLES
Jim Rivera CHI 16
Mickey Vernon WAS 11
two tied at 9

HOME RUNS
Al Rosen CLE 43
Gus Zernial PHI 42
Larry Doby CLE 29

RUNS BATTED IN
Al Rosen CLE 145
Mickey Vernon WAS ... 115
Boone CLE, DET 114

SLUGGING AVERAGE
Al Rosen CLE .... .613
Gus Zernial PHI .... .559
Yogi Berra NY .... .523

STOLEN BASES
Minnie Minoso CHI 25
Jim Rivera CHI 22
Jackie Jensen WAS 18

RUNS SCORED
Al Rosen CLE 115
Eddie Yost WAS 107
Mickey Mantle NY 105

WINS
Bob Porterfield WAS 22
Bob Lemon CLE 21
Mel Parnell BOS 21

WINNING PERCENTAGE
Eddie Lopat NY .... .800
Whitey Ford NY .... .750
Mel Parnell BOS .... .724

EARNED RUN AVERAGE
Eddie Lopat NY 2.42
Billy Pierce CHI 2.72
Trucks STL, CHI 2.93

STRIKEOUTS
Billy Pierce CHI 186
V. Trucks STL, CHI 149
Early Wynn CLE 138

SAVES
Ellis Kinder BOS 27
Harry Dorish CHI 18
Allie Reynolds NY 13

COMPLETE GAMES
Bob Porterfield WAS 24
Bob Lemon CLE 23
Mike Garcia CLE 21

SHUTOUTS
Bob Porterfield WAS 9
Billy Pierce CHI 7
three tied at 5

GAMES PITCHED
Ellis Kinder BOS 69
Marlan Stuart STL 60
Morrie Martin PHI 58

INNINGS PITCHED
Bob Lemon CLE 287
Mike Garcia CLE 272
Billy Pierce CHI 271

1953 NL

	W	L	PCT	GB	R	OR	BA	FA	ERA
BROOKLYN	105	49	.682	—	955	689	.285	.980	4.10
MILWAUKEE	92	62	.597	13	738	589	.266	.976	3.30
PHILADELPHIA	83	71	.539	22	716	666	.265	.975	3.80
ST. LOUIS	83	71	.539	22	768	713	.273	.977	4.23
NEW YORK	70	84	.455	35	768	747	.271	.975	4.25
CINCINNATI	68	86	.442	37	714	788	.261	.978	4.64
CHICAGO	65	89	.422	40	633	835	.260	.967	4.79
PITTSBURGH	50	104	.325	55	622	887	.247	.973	5.22
					5914	5914	.266	.975	4.29

BATTING AVERAGE
Carl Furillo BKN .... .344
Schoendienst STL ...... .342
Stan Musial STL .... .337

HITS
Richie Ashburn PHI 205
Stan Musial STL 200
Duke Snider BKN........ 198

DOUBLES
Stan Musial STL 53
Alvin Dark NY 41
two tied at 38

TRIPLES
Jim Gilliam BKN............. 17
Bill Bruton MIL 14
two tied at 11

HOME RUNS
Eddie Mathews MIL 47
Duke Snider BKN.......... 42
Roy Campanella BKN... 41

RUNS BATTED IN
R. Campanella BKN.... 142
Eddie Mathews MIL 135
Duke Snider BKN........ 126

SLUGGING AVERAGE
Duke Snider BKN........ .627
Eddie Mathews MIL ... .627
R. Campanella BKN... .611

STOLEN BASES
Bill Bruton MIL.............. 26
Pee Wee Reese BKN ... 22
Jim Gilliam BKN............. 21

RUNS SCORED
Duke Snider BKN........ 132
Stan Musial STL 127
Alvin Dark NY 126

WINS
Warren Spahn MIL........ 23
Robin Roberts PHI........ 23
two tied at 20

WINNING PERCENTAGE
Carl Erskine BKN....... .769
Warren Spahn MIL...... .767
two tied at .... .750

EARNED RUN AVERAGE
Warren Spahn MIL....... 2.10
Robin Roberts PHI 2.75
Bob Buhl MIL 2.97

STRIKEOUTS
Robin Roberts PHI...... 198
Carl Erskine BKN........ 187
V. Mizell STL............... 173

SAVES
Al Brazle STL............... 18
Hoyt Wilhelm NY........... 15
Jim Hughes BKN 9

COMPLETE GAMES
Robin Roberts PHI........ 33
Warren Spahn MIL........ 24
two tied at 19

SHUTOUTS
Harvey Haddix STL.......... 6
Robin Roberts PHI.......... 5
Warren Spahn MIL.......... 5

GAMES PITCHED
Hoyt Wilhelm NY........... 68
Al Brazle STL................ 60
Johnny Hetki PIT 54

INNINGS PITCHED
Robin Roberts PHI...... 347
Warren Spahn MIL...... 266
Harvey Haddix STL..... 253

1954 AL

	W	L	PCT	GB	R	OR	BA	FA	ERA
CLEVELAND	111	43	.721	—	746	504	.262	.979	2.78
NEW YORK	103	51	.669	8	805	563	.268	.979	3.26
CHICAGO	94	60	.610	17	711	521	.267	.982	3.05
BOSTON	69	85	.448	42	700	728	.266	.972	4.01
DETROIT	68	86	.442	43	584	664	.258	.978	3.81
WASHINGTON	66	88	.429	45	632	680	.246	.977	3.84
BALTIMORE	54	100	.351	57	483	668	.251	.975	3.88
PHILADELPHIA	51	103	.331	60	542	875	.236	.972	5.18
					5203	5203	.257	.977	3.72

BATTING AVERAGE
Ted Williams BOS...... .345
Bobby Avila CLE......... .341
Minnie Minoso CHI .... .320

HITS
Nellie Fox CHI............. 201
Harvey Kuenn DET....... 201
Bobby Avila CLE......... 189

DOUBLES
Mickey Vernon WAS... 33
Minnie Minoso CHI 29
Al Smith CLE 29

TRIPLES
Minnie Minoso CHI 18
Pete Runnels WAS....... 15
Mickey Vernon WAS..... 14

HOME RUNS
Larry Doby CLE 32
Ted Williams BOS......... 29
Mickey Mantle NY......... 27

RUNS BATTED IN
Larry Doby CLE 126
Yogi Berra NY............. 125
Jackie Jensen BOS 117

SLUGGING AVERAGE
Ted Williams BOS...... .635
Minnie Minoso CHI .... .535
Mickey Mantle NY....... .525

STOLEN BASES
Jackie Jensen BOS 22
Jim Rivera CHI.............. 18
Minnie Minoso CHI 18

RUNS SCORED
Mickey Mantle NY....... 129
Minnie Minoso CHI 119
Bobby Avila CLE......... 112

WINS
Bob Lemon CLE 23
Early Wynn CLE 23
Bob Grim NY................. 20

WINNING PERCENTAGE
S. Consuegra CHI...... .842
Bob Grim NY.............. .769
Bob Lemon CLE .... .767

EARNED RUN AVERAGE
Mike Garcia CLE........ 2.64
S. Consuegra CHI...... 2.69
Bob Lemon CLE 2.72

STRIKEOUTS
Bob Turley BAL............ 185
Early Wynn CLE 155
Virgil Trucks CHI......... 152

SAVES
Johnny Sain NY 22
Ellis Kinder BOS 15
Ray Narleski CLE 13

COMPLETE GAMES
Bob Porterfield WAS..... 21
Bob Lemon CLE 21
Early Wynn CLE 20

SHUTOUTS
Virgil Trucks CHI.............. 5
Mike Garcia CLE.............. 5

GAMES PITCHED
S. Dixon WAS, PHI 54
three tied at.................... 48

INNINGS PITCHED
Early Wynn CLE 271
Virgil Trucks CHI......... 265
Mike Garcia CLE......... 259

1954 NL

	W	L	PCT	GB	R	OR	BA	FA	ERA
★NEW YORK	97	57	.630	—	732	550	.264	.975	3.09
BROOKLYN	92	62	.597	5	778	740	.270	.978	4.31
MILWAUKEE	89	65	.578	8	670	556	.265	.981	3.19
PHILADELPHIA	75	79	.487	22	659	614	.267	.975	3.59
CINCINNATI	74	80	.481	23	729	763	.262	.977	4.50
ST. LOUIS	72	82	.468	25	799	790	.281	.976	4.50
CHICAGO	64	90	.416	33	700	766	.263	.974	4.51
PITTSBURGH	53	101	.344	44	557	845	.248	.971	4.92
					5624	5624	.265	.976	4.07

BATTING AVERAGE
Willie Mays NY .... .345
Don Mueller NY .... .342
Duke Snider BKN .... .341

HITS
Don Mueller NY 212
Duke Snider BKN 199
two tied at 195

DOUBLES
Stan Musial STL 41
three tied at.................. 39

TRIPLES
Willie Mays NY.............. 13
Granny Hamner PHI 11
Duke Snider BKN.......... 10

HOME RUNS
Ted Kluszewski CIN...... 49
Gil Hodges BKN............ 42
two tied at 41

RUNS BATTED IN
Ted Kluszewski CIN.... 141
Gil Hodges BKN.......... 130
Duke Snider BKN........ 130

SLUGGING AVERAGE
Willie Mays NY .... .667
Duke Snider BKN........ .647
Ted Kluszewski CIN.... .642

STOLEN BASES
Bill Bruton MIL 34
Johnny Temple CIN 21
Dee Fondy CHI 20

RUNS SCORED
Duke Snider BKN........ 120
Stan Musial STL 120
Willie Mays NY............ 119

WINS
Robin Roberts PHI........ 23
Johnny Antonelli NY 21
Warren Spahn MIL........ 21

WINNING PERCENTAGE
Johnny Antonelli NY ... .750
B. Lawrence STL .... .714
Ruben Gomez NY...... .654

EARNED RUN AVERAGE
J. Antonelli NY 2.30
Lew Burdette MIL........ 2.76
Curt Simmons PHI 2.81

STRIKEOUTS
Robin Roberts PHI..... 185
Harvey Haddix STL..... 184
Carl Erskine BKN........ 166

SAVES
Jim Hughes BKN 24
Frank Smith CIN 20
Marv Grissom NY 19

COMPLETE GAMES
Robin Roberts PHI........ 29
Warren Spahn MIL 23
Curt Simmons PHI 21

SHUTOUTS
Johnny Antonelli NY 6

GAMES PITCHED
Jim Hughes BKN 60
Al Brazle STL................ 58
Johnny Hetki PIT 58

INNINGS PITCHED
Robin Roberts PHI...... 337
Warren Spahn MIL...... 283
two tied at 260

1955 AL

	W	L	PCT	GB	R	OR	BA	FA	ERA
NEW YORK	96	58	.623	—	762	569	.260	.978	3.23
CLEVELAND	93	61	.604	3	698	601	.257	.981	3.39
CHICAGO	91	63	.591	5	725	557	.268	.981	3.37
BOSTON	84	70	.545	12	755	652	.264	.977	3.72
DETROIT	79	75	.513	17	775	658	.266	.976	3.79
KANSAS CITY	63	91	.409	33	638	911	.261	.976	5.35
BALTIMORE	57	97	.370	39	540	754	.240	.972	4.21
WASHINGTON	53	101	.344	43	598	789	.248	.974	4.62
					5491	5491	.258	.977	3.96

BATTING AVERAGE
Al Kaline DET .... .340
Vic Power KC .... .319
George Kell CHI .... .312

HITS
Al Kaline DET 200
Nellie Fox CHI 198
two tied at 190

DOUBLES
Harvey Kuenn DET 38
Vic Power KC 34
Billy Goodman BOS 31

TRIPLES
Andy Carey NY 11
Mickey Mantle NY 11
Vic Power KC 10

HOME RUNS
Mickey Mantle NY 37
Gus Zernial KC 30
Ted Williams BOS 28

RUNS BATTED IN
Ray Boone DET 116
Jackie Jensen BOS 116
Yogi Berra NY 108

SLUGGING AVERAGE
Mickey Mantle NY .... .611
Al Kaline DET .... .546
Gus Zernial KC .... .508

STOLEN BASES
Jim Rivera CHI 25
Minnie Minoso CHI 19
Jackie Jensen BOS 16

RUNS SCORED
Al Smith CLE 123
Al Kaline DET 121
Mickey Mantle NY 121

WINS
Whitey Ford NY 18
Bob Lemon CLE 18
Frank Sullivan BOS 18

WINNING PERCENTAGE
Tommy Byrne NY .... .762
Whitey Ford NY .... .720
Billy Hoeft DET .... .696

EARNED RUN AVERAGE
Billy Pierce CHI 1.97
Whitey Ford NY 2.63
Early Wynn CLE 2.82

STRIKEOUTS
Herb Score CLE 245
Bob Turley NY 210
Billy Pierce CHI 157

SAVES
Ray Narleski CLE 19
Tom Gorman KC 18
Ellis Kinder BOS 18

COMPLETE GAMES
Whitey Ford NY 18
Billy Hoeft DET 17

SHUTOUTS
Billy Hoeft DET 7
three tied at 6

GAMES PITCHED
Ray Narleski CLE 60
Don Mossi CLE............. 57
Tom Gorman KC........... 57

INNINGS PITCHED
Frank Sullivan BOS 260
Whitey Ford NY 254
Bob Turley NY 247

1955 NL

	W	L	PCT	GB	R	OR	BA	FA	ERA
★BROOKLYN	98	55	.641	—	857	650	.271	.978	3.68
MILWAUKEE	85	69	.552	13.5	743	668	.261	.975	3.85
NEW YORK	80	74	.519	18.5	702	673	.260	.976	3.77
PHILADELPHIA	77	77	.500	21.5	675	666	.255	.981	3.93
CINCINNATI	75	79	.487	23.5	761	684	.270	.977	3.95
CHICAGO	72	81	.471	26	626	713	.247	.975	4.17
ST. LOUIS	68	86	.442	30.5	654	757	.261	.975	4.56
PITTSBURGH	60	94	.390	38.5	560	767	.244	.972	4.39
					5578	5578	.259	.976	4.04

BATTING AVERAGE
Richie Ashburn PHI ... .338
Willie Mays NY .... .319
Stan Musial STL .... .319

HITS
Ted Kluszewski CIN.... 192
Hank Aaron MIL 189
Gus Bell CIN 188

DOUBLES
Hank Aaron MIL............ 37
Johnny Logan MIL 37
Duke Snider BKN.......... 34

TRIPLES
Willie Mays NY 13
Dale Long PIT 13
Bill Bruton MIL 12

HOME RUNS
Willie Mays NY 51
Ted Kluszewski CIN...... 47
Ernie Banks CHI 44

RUNS BATTED IN
Duke Snider BKN........ 136
Willie Mays NY............ 127
Del Ennis PHI 120

SLUGGING AVERAGE
Willie Mays NY............ .659
Duke Snider BKN....... .628
Eddie Mathews MIL ... .601

STOLEN BASES
Bill Bruton MIL 25
Willie Mays NY 24
Ken Boyer STL 22

RUNS SCORED
Duke Snider BKN........ 126
Willie Mays NY 123
two tied at 116

WINS
Robin Roberts PHI........ 23
Don Newcombe BKN..... 20
two tied at 17

WINNING PERCENTAGE
D. Newcombe BKN.... .800
Robin Roberts PHI..... .622
Joe Nuxhall CIN......... .586

EARNED RUN AVERAGE
Bob Friend PIT............ 2.83
D. Newcombe BKN...... 3.20
Bob Buhl MIL 3.21

STRIKEOUTS
Sam Jones CHI............ 198
Robin Roberts PHI...... 160
Harvey Haddix STL..... 150

SAVES
Jack Meyer PHI 16
Ed Roebuck BKN.......... 12
two tied at 11

COMPLETE GAMES
Robin Roberts PHI....... 26
Don Newcombe BKN.... 17
Warren Spahn MIL 16

SHUTOUTS
Joe Nuxhall CIN.............. 5
Murry Dickson PHI 4
Sam Jones CHI............... 4

GAMES PITCHED
Clem Labine BKN 60
Hoyt Wilhelm NY........... 59
Paul LaPalme STL........ 56

INNINGS PITCHED
Robin Roberts PHI...... 305
Joe Nuxhall CIN........... 257
Warren Spahn MIL...... 246

1956 AL

	W	L	PCT	GB	R	OR	BA	FA	ERA
★NEW YORK	97	57	.630	—	857	631	.270	.977	3.63
CLEVELAND	88	66	.571	9	712	581	.244	.978	3.32
CHICAGO	85	69	.552	12	776	634	.267	.979	3.73
BOSTON	84	70	.545	13	780	751	.275	.972	4.17
DETROIT	82	72	.532	15	789	699	.279	.976	4.06
BALTIMORE	69	85	.448	28	571	705	.244	.977	4.20
WASHINGTON	59	95	.383	38	652	924	.250	.972	5.33
KANSAS CITY	52	102	.338	45	619	831	.252	.973	4.86
					5756	5756	.260	.975	4.16

BATTING AVERAGE
Mickey Mantle NY ...... .353
Ted Williams BOS ...... .345
Harvey Kuenn DET .... .332

HITS
Harvey Kuenn DET 196
Al Kaline DET 194
Nellie Fox CHI............. 192

DOUBLES
Jimmy Piersall BOS 40
Al Kaline DET 32
Harvey Kuenn DET 32

TRIPLES
four tied at 11

HOME RUNS
Mickey Mantle NY 52
Vic Wertz CLE 32
Yogi Berra NY 30

RUNS BATTED IN
Mickey Mantle NY 130
Al Kaline DET 128
Vic Wertz CLE 106

SLUGGING AVERAGE
Mickey Mantle NY ...... .705
Ted Williams BOS ...... .605
two tied at .... .534

STOLEN BASES
Luis Aparicio CHI 21
Jim Rivera CHI 20
Bobby Avila CLE............ 17

RUNS SCORED
Mickey Mantle NY 132
Nellie Fox CHI 109
Minnie Minoso CHI 106

WINS
Frank Lary DET 21
five tied at 20

WINNING PERCENTAGE
Whitey Ford NY .... .760
three tied at................ .690

EARNED RUN AVERAGE
Whitey Ford NY 2.47
Herb Score CLE 2.53
Early Wynn CLE 2.72

STRIKEOUTS
Herb Score CLE.......... 263
Billy Pierce CHI............ 192
Paul Foytack DET....... 184

SAVES
George Zuverink BAL ... 16
Tom Morgan NY 11
Don Mossi CLE............. 11

COMPLETE GAMES
Billy Pierce CHI 21
Bob Lemon CLE 21
Frank Lary DET 20

SHUTOUTS
Herb Score CLE 5

GAMES PITCHED
George Zuverink BAL ... 62
Jack Crimian KC 54
Tom Gorman KC........... 52

INNINGS PITCHED
Frank Lary DET 294
Early Wynn CLE 278
Billy Pierce CHI........... 276

1956 NL

	W	L	PCT	GB	R	OR	BA	FA	ERA
BROOKLYN	93	61	.604	—	720	601	.258	.981	3.57
MILWAUKEE	92	62	.597	1	709	569	.259	.979	3.11
CINCINNATI	91	63	.591	2	775	658	.266	.981	3.85
ST. LOUIS	76	78	.494	17	678	698	.268	.978	3.97
PHILADELPHIA	71	83	.461	22	668	738	.252	.975	4.20
NEW YORK	67	87	.435	26	540	650	.244	.976	3.78
PITTSBURGH	66	88	.429	27	588	653	.257	.973	3.74
CHICAGO	60	94	.390	33	597	708	.244	.976	3.96
					5275	5275	.256	.977	3.77

BATTING AVERAGE
Hank Aaron MIL.......... .328
Bill Virdon STL, PIT ... .319
R. Clemente PIT .... .311

HITS
Hank Aaron MIL.......... 200
Richie Ashburn PHI 190
Bill Virdon STL, PIT 185

DOUBLES
Hank Aaron MIL........... 34
three tied at.................. 33

TRIPLES
Bill Bruton MIL 15
Hank Aaron MIL............ 14
two tied at 11

HOME RUNS
Duke Snider BKN.......... 43
Frank Robinson CIN 38
Joe Adcock MIL 38

RUNS BATTED IN
Stan Musial STL 109
Joe Adcock MIL 103
Ted Kluszewski CIN.... 102

SLUGGING AVERAGE
Duke Snider BKN....... .598
Joe Adcock MIL .... .597
two tied at .... .558

STOLEN BASES
Willie Mays NY.............. 40
Jim Gilliam BKN............. 21
Bill White NY................. 15

RUNS SCORED
Frank Robinson CIN ... 122
Duke Snider BKN........ 112
Hank Aaron MIL........... 106

WINS
Don Newcombe BKN.... 27
Warren Spahn MIL 20
Johnny Antonelli NY 20

WINNING PERCENTAGE
D. Newcombe BKN....... .794
Bob Buhl MIL .... .692
two tied at .... .655

EARNED RUN AVERAGE
Lew Burdette MIL........ 2.70
Warren Spahn MIL 2.78
J. Antonelli NY 2.86

STRIKEOUTS
Sam Jones CHI........... 176
Haddix STL, PHI 170
Bob Friend PIT............ 166

SAVES
Clem Labine BKN 19
Hersh Freeman CIN...... 18
Turk Lown CHI.............. 13

COMPLETE GAMES
Robin Roberts PHI 22
Warren Spahn MIL....... 20
Bob Friend PIT.............. 19

SHUTOUTS
Johnny Antonelli NY 6
Lew Burdette MIL............. 6
Don Newcombe BKN...... 5

GAMES PITCHED
Roy Face PIT................. 68
Hersh Freeman CIN...... 64
Hoyt Wilhelm NY........... 64

INNINGS PITCHED
Bob Friend PIT............. 314
Robin Roberts PHI...... 297
Warren Spahn MIL...... 281

1957 AL

	W	L	PCT	GB	R	OR	BA	FA	ERA
NEW YORK	98	56	.636	—	723	534	.268	.980	3.00
CHICAGO	90	64	.584	8	707	566	.260	.982	3.35
BOSTON	82	72	.532	16	721	668	.262	.976	3.88
DETROIT	78	76	.506	20	614	614	.257	.980	3.56
BALTIMORE	76	76	.500	21	597	588	.252	.981	3.46
CLEVELAND	76	77	.497	21.5	682	722	.252	.974	4.05
KANSAS CITY	59	94	.386	38.5	563	710	.244	.979	4.19
WASHINGTON	55	99	.357	43	603	808	.244	.979	4.85
					5210	5210	.255	.979	3.79

BATTING AVERAGE
Ted Williams BOS...... .388
Mickey Mantle NY...... .365
G. Woodling CLE........ .321

HITS
Nellie Fox CHI............. 196
Frank Malzone BOS ... 185
Minnie Minoso CHI 176

DOUBLES
Billy Gardner BAL 36
Minnie Minoso CHI 36
Frank Malzone BOS 31

TRIPLES
Harry Simpson KC, NY ... 9
Gil McDougald NY 9
Hank Bauer NY 9

HOME RUNS
Roy Sievers WAS 42
Ted Williams BOS......... 38
Mickey Mantle NY......... 34

RUNS BATTED IN
Roy Sievers WAS 114
Vic Wertz CLE 105
three tied at................. 103

SLUGGING AVERAGE
Ted Williams BOS....... .731
Mickey Mantle NY...... .665
Roy Sievers WAS ...... .579

STOLEN BASES
Luis Aparicio CHI 28
Minnie Minoso CHI 18
Jim Rivera CHI.............. 18

RUNS SCORED
Mickey Mantle NY....... 121
Nellie Fox CHI............. 110
Jimmy Piersall BOS 103

WINS
Jim Bunning DET.......... 20
Billy Pierce CHI............. 20
three tied at................... 16

WINNING PERCENTAGE
Dick Donovan CHI ..... .727
Tom Sturdivant NY .... .727
Jim Bunning DET....... .714

EARNED RUN AVERAGE
Bobby Shantz NY 2.45
Tom Sturdivant NY 2.54
Jim Bunning DET....... 2.69

STRIKEOUTS
Early Wynn CLE 184
Jim Bunning DET........ 182
C. Johnson BAL.......... 177

SAVES
Bob Grim NY................ 19
Ray Narleski CLE 16
Ike Delock BOS 11

COMPLETE GAMES
Dick Donovan CHI 16
Billy Pierce CHI............. 16
Tom Brewer BOS.......... 15

SHUTOUTS
Jim Wilson CHI 5
Billy Pierce CHI................ 4
Bob Turley NY 4

GAMES PITCHED
George Zuverink BAL ... 56
Tex Clevenger WAS 52
Dick Hyde WAS 52

INNINGS PITCHED
Jim Bunning DET........ 267
Early Wynn CLE 263
Billy Pierce CHI........... 257

1957 NL

	W	L	PCT	GB	R	OR	BA	FA	ERA
★MILWAUKEE	95	59	.617	—	772	613	.269	.981	3.47
ST. LOUIS	87	67	.565	8	737	666	.274	.979	3.78
BROOKLYN	84	70	.545	11	690	591	.253	.979	3.35
CINCINNATI	80	74	.519	15	747	781	.269	.982	4.62
PHILADELPHIA	77	77	.500	18	623	656	.250	.976	3.80
NEW YORK	69	85	.448	26	643	701	.252	.974	4.01
CHICAGO	62	92	.403	33	628	722	.244	.975	4.13
PITTSBURGH	62	92	.403	33	586	696	.268	.972	3.88
					5426	5426	.260	.977	3.88

BATTING AVERAGE
Stan Musial STL .... .351
Willie Mays NY............ .333
two tied at .... .322

HITS
Schoendienst NY, MIL 200
Hank Aaron MIL.......... 198
Frank Robinson CIN ... 197

DOUBLES
Don Hoak CIN............... 39
Stan Musial STL 38
Ed Bouchee PHI 35

TRIPLES
Willie Mays NY............. 20
Bill Virdon PIT 11
two tied at 9

HOME RUNS
Hank Aaron MIL............ 44
Ernie Banks CHI 43
Duke Snider BKN.......... 40

RUNS BATTED IN
Hank Aaron MIL.......... 132
Del Ennis STL............. 105
two tied at 102

SLUGGING AVERAGE
Willie Mays NY............ .626
Stan Musial STL .... .612
Hank Aaron MIL.......... .600

STOLEN BASES
Willie Mays NY............. 38
Jim Gilliam BKN............ 26
Don Blasingame STL.... 21

RUNS SCORED
Hank Aaron MIL.......... 118
Ernie Banks CHI 113
Willie Mays NY............ 112

WINS
Warren Spahn MIL........ 21
Jack Sanford PHI.......... 19
Bob Buhl MIL 18

WINNING PERCENTAGE
Bob Buhl MIL .... .720
Jack Sanford PHI........ .704
Warren Spahn MIL...... .656

EARNED RUN AVERAGE
J. Podres BKN 2.66
Don Drysdale BKN....... 2.69
Warren Spahn MIL...... 2.69

STRIKEOUTS
Jack Sanford PHI........ 188
Dick Drott CHI............. 170
Moe Drabowsky CHI... 170

SAVES
Clem Labine BKN 17
Marv Grissom NY 14
Turk Lown CHI.............. 12

COMPLETE GAMES
Warren Spahn MIL........ 18
Bob Friend PIT.............. 17
Ruben Gomez NY......... 16

SHUTOUTS
Johnny Podres BKN 6
three tied at...................... 4

GAMES PITCHED
Turk Lown CHI.............. 67
Roy Face PIT................. 59
Clem Labine BKN 58

INNINGS PITCHED
Bob Friend PIT............. 277
Warren Spahn MIL...... 271
Lew Burdette MIL........ 257

1958 AL

	W	L	PCT	GB	R	OR	BA	FA	ERA
★**NEW YORK**	92	62	.597	—	759	577	.268	.978	3.22
CHICAGO	82	72	.532	10	634	615	.257	.981	3.61
BOSTON	79	75	.513	13	697	691	.256	.976	3.92
CLEVELAND	77	76	.503	14.5	694	635	.258	.974	3.73
DETROIT	77	77	.500	15	659	606	.266	.982	3.59
BALTIMORE	74	79	.484	17.5	521	575	.241	.980	3.40
KANSAS CITY	73	81	.474	19	642	713	.247	.979	4.15
WASHINGTON	61	93	.396	31	553	747	.240	.980	4.53
					5159	5159	.254	.979	3.77

BATTING AVERAGE
Ted Williams BOS...... .328
Pete Runnels BOS..... .322
Harvey Kuenn DET.... .319

HITS
Nellie Fox CHI............. 187
Frank Malzone BOS ... 185
Vic Power KC, CLE..... 184

DOUBLES
Harvey Kuenn DET....... 39
Vic Power KC, CLE...... 37
Al Kaline DET 34

TRIPLES
Vic Power KC, CLE.... 10
three tied at.................... 9

HOME RUNS
Mickey Mantle NY......... 42
Rocky Colavito CLE..... 41
Roy Sievers WAS 39

RUNS BATTED IN
Jackie Jensen BOS 122
Rocky Colavito CLE.... 113
Roy Sievers WAS 108

SLUGGING AVERAGE
Rocky Colavito CLE... .620
Bob Cerv KC............... .592
Mickey Mantle NY...... .592

STOLEN BASES
Luis Aparicio CHI......... 29
Jim Rivera CHI.............. 21
Jim Landis CHI 19

RUNS SCORED
Mickey Mantle NY....... 127
Pete Runnels BOS...... 103
Vic Power KC, CLE....... 98

WINS
Bob Turley NY 21
Billy Pierce CHI............. 17
two tied at 16

WINNING PERCENTAGE
Bob Turley NY .... .750
Cal McLish CLE......... .667
Billy Pierce CHI.......... .607

EARNED RUN AVERAGE
Whitey Ford NY 2.01
Billy Pierce CHI.......... 2.68
J. Harshman BAL....... 2.89

STRIKEOUTS
Early Wynn CHI 179
Jim Bunning DET........ 177
Bob Turley NY 168

SAVES
Ryne Duren NY............. 20
Dick Hyde WAS 18
Leo Kiely BOS 12

COMPLETE GAMES
Bob Turley NY 19
Billy Pierce CHI............. 19
Frank Lary DET 19

SHUTOUTS
Whitey Ford NY 7
Bob Turley NY 6
three tied at..................... 4

GAMES PITCHED
Tex Clevenger WAS 55
D. Tomanek CLE, KC ... 54
Dick Hyde WAS 53

INNINGS PITCHED
Frank Lary DET 260
Pedro Ramos WAS..... 259
Dick Donovan CHI 248

1958 NL

	W	L	PCT	GB	R	OR	BA	FA	ERA
MILWAUKEE	92	62	.597	—	675	541	.266	.980	3.21
PITTSBURGH	84	70	.545	8	662	607	.264	.978	3.56
SAN FRANCISCO	80	74	.519	12	727	698	.263	.975	3.98
CINCINNATI	76	78	.494	16	695	621	.258	.983	3.73
CHICAGO	72	82	.468	20	709	725	.265	.975	4.22
ST. LOUIS	72	82	.468	20	619	704	.261	.974	4.12
LOS ANGELES	71	83	.461	21	668	761	.251	.975	4.47
PHILADELPHIA	69	85	.448	23	664	762	.266	.978	4.32
					5419	5419	.262	.977	3.95

BATTING AVERAGE
Richie Ashburn PHI ... .350
Willie Mays SF .... .347
Stan Musial STL .... .337

HITS
Richie Ashburn PHI 215
Willie Mays SF 208
Hank Aaron MIL........... 196

DOUBLES
Orlando Cepeda SF...... 38
Dick Groat PIT 36
Stan Musial STL 35

TRIPLES
Richie Ashburn PHI 13
three tied at.................... 11

HOME RUNS
Ernie Banks CHI 47
Frank Thomas PIT 35
two tied at 31

RUNS BATTED IN
Ernie Banks CHI 129
Frank Thomas PIT 109
Harry Anderson PHI...... 97

SLUGGING AVERAGE
Ernie Banks CHI .... .614
Willie Mays SF .... .583
Hank Aaron MIL.......... .546

STOLEN BASES
Willie Mays SF 31
Richie Ashburn PHI 30
Tony Taylor CHI............. 21

RUNS SCORED
Willie Mays SF 121
Ernie Banks CHI 119
Hank Aaron MIL........... 109

WINS
Bob Friend PIT.............. 22
Warren Spahn MIL........ 22
Lew Burdette MIL.......... 20

WINNING PERCENTAGE
Warren Spahn MIL..... .667
Lew Burdette MIL....... .667
Bob Friend PIT............ .611

EARNED RUN AVERAGE
Stu Miller SF 2.47
Sam Jones STL 2.88
Lew Burdette MIL....... 2.91

STRIKEOUTS
Sam Jones STL 225
Warren Spahn MIL....... 150
two tied at 143

SAVES
Roy Face PIT................ 20
Clem Labine LA 14
Dick Farrell PHI............. 11

COMPLETE GAMES
Warren Spahn MIL........ 23
Robin Roberts PHI........ 21
Lew Burdette MIL.......... 19

SHUTOUTS
Carl Willey MIL................ 4
four tied at........................ 3

GAMES PITCHED
Don Elston CHI 69
Klippstein CIN, LA.......... 57
Roy Face PIT................. 57

INNINGS PITCHED
Warren Spahn MIL...... 290
Lew Burdette MIL........ 275
Bob Friend PIT............ 274

1959 AL

	W	L	PCT	GB	R	OR	BA	FA	ERA
CHICAGO	94	60	.610	—	669	588	.250	.979	3.29
CLEVELAND	89	65	.578	5	745	646	.263	.978	3.75
NEW YORK	79	75	.513	15	687	647	.260	.978	3.60
DETROIT	76	78	.494	18	713	732	.258	.978	4.20
BOSTON	75	79	.487	19	726	696	.256	.978	4.17
BALTIMORE	74	80	.481	20	551	621	.238	.976	3.56
KANSAS CITY	66	88	.429	28	681	760	.263	.973	4.35
WASHINGTON	63	91	.409	31	619	701	.237	.973	4.01
					5391	5391	.253	.977	3.86

BATTING AVERAGE
Harvey Kuenn DET .... .353
Al Kaline DET .... .327
Pete Runnels BOS..... .314

HITS
Harvey Kuenn DET 198
Nellie Fox CHI............. 191
Pete Runnels BOS....... 176

DOUBLES
Harvey Kuenn DET 42
Frank Malzone BOS 34
Nellie Fox CHI............... 34

TRIPLES
Bob Allison WAS............. 9
Gil McDougald NY 8

HOME RUNS
Rocky Colavito CLE...... 42
H. Killebrew WAS 42
Jim Lemon WAS 33

RUNS BATTED IN
Jackie Jensen BOS 112
Rocky Colavito CLE.... 111
H. Killebrew WAS 105

SLUGGING AVERAGE
Al Kaline DET .... .530
H. Killebrew WAS ...... .516
Mickey Mantle NY ...... .514

STOLEN BASES
Luis Aparicio CHI.......... 56
Mickey Mantle NY......... 21
two tied at 20

RUNS SCORED
Eddie Yost DET 115
Mickey Mantle NY....... 104
Vic Power CLE............ 102

WINS
Early Wynn CHI 22
Cal McLish CLE............ 19
Bob Shaw CHI 18

WINNING PERCENTAGE
Bob Shaw CHI .... .750
Cal McLish CLE.......... .704
Early Wynn CHI .... .688

EARNED RUN AVERAGE
Hoyt Wilhelm BAL 2.19
C. Pascual WAS 2.64
Bob Shaw CHI 2.69

STRIKEOUTS
Jim Bunning DET........ 201
C. Pascual WAS 185
Early Wynn CHI 179

SAVES
Turk Lown CHI.............. 15
three tied at.................... 14

COMPLETE GAMES
Camilo Pascual WAS.... 17
Don Mossi DET............. 15
Milt Pappas BAL 15

SHUTOUTS
Camilo Pascual WAS...... 6
Early Wynn CHI 5
Milt Pappas BAL 4

GAMES PITCHED
George Staley CHI........ 67
Turk Lown CHI.............. 60
Tex Clevenger WAS 50

INNINGS PITCHED
Early Wynn CHI 256
Jim Bunning DET........ 250
Paul Foytack DET....... 240

1959 NL

	W	L	PCT	GB	R	OR	BA	FA	ERA
LOS ANGELES*	88	68	.564	—	705	670	.257	.981	3.79
MILWAUKEE	86	70	.551	2	724	623	.265	.979	3.51
SAN FRANCISCO	83	71	.539	4	705	613	.261	.974	3.47
PITTSBURGH	78	76	.506	9	651	680	.263	.975	3.90
CHICAGO	74	80	.481	13	673	688	.249	.977	4.01
CINCINNATI	74	80	.481	13	764	738	.274	.978	4.31
ST. LOUIS	71	83	.461	16	641	725	.269	.975	4.34
PHILADELPHIA	64	90	.416	23	599	725	.242	.973	4.27
					5462	5462	.260	.977	3.95

* Defeated Milwaukee in a playoff 2 games to 0

BATTING AVERAGE
Hank Aaron MIL.......... .355
J. Cunningham STL.... .345
Orlando Cepeda SF.... .317

HITS
Hank Aaron MIL.......... 223
Vada Pinson CIN 205
Orlando Cepeda SF.... 192

DOUBLES
Vada Pinson CIN 47
Hank Aaron MIL............. 46
Willie Mays SF 43

TRIPLES
Charlie Neal LA............. 11
Wally Moon LA.............. 11
three tied at.................... 9

HOME RUNS
Eddie Mathews MIL....... 46
Ernie Banks CHI 45
Hank Aaron MIL............. 39

RUNS BATTED IN
Ernie Banks CHI 143
Frank Robinson CIN ... 125
Hank Aaron MIL.......... 123

SLUGGING AVERAGE
Hank Aaron MIL.......... .636
Ernie Banks CHI .... .596
Eddie Mathews MIL ... .593

STOLEN BASES
Willie Mays SF.............. 27
three tied at.................... 23

RUNS SCORED
Vada Pinson CIN 131
Willie Mays SF 125
Eddie Mathews MIL 118

WINS
Lew Burdette MIL.......... 21
Sam Jones SF 21
Warren Spahn MIL........ 21

WINNING PERCENTAGE
Roy Face PIT .... .947
Vern Law PIT .... .667
Johnny Antonelli SF... .655

EARNED RUN AVERAGE
Sam Jones SF 2.83
Stu Miller SF 2.84
Bill Buhl MIL................ 2.86

STRIKEOUTS
Don Drysdale LA......... 242
Sam Jones SF 209
Sandy Koufax LA........ 173

SAVES
Lindy McDaniel STL...... 15
Don McMahon MIL 15
Don Elston CHI 13

COMPLETE GAMES
Warren Spahn MIL....... 21
Vern Law PIT 20
Lew Burdette MIL.......... 20

SHUTOUTS
seven tied at 4

GAMES PITCHED
Bill Henry CHI 65
Don Elston CHI 65
Lindy McDaniel STL...... 62

INNINGS PITCHED
Warren Spahn MIL....... 292
Lew Burdette MIL......... 290
Johnny Antonelli SF.... 282

1960 AL

	W	L	PCT	GB	R	OR	BA	FA	ERA
NEW YORK	97	57	.630	—	746	627	.260	.979	3.52
BALTIMORE	89	65	.578	8	682	606	.253	.982	3.52
CHICAGO	87	67	.565	10	741	617	.270	.982	3.60
CLEVELAND	76	78	.494	21	667	693	.267	.978	3.95
WASHINGTON	73	81	.474	24	672	696	.244	.973	3.77
DETROIT	71	83	.461	26	633	644	.239	.977	3.64
BOSTON	65	89	.422	32	658	775	.261	.976	4.62
KANSAS CITY	58	96	.377	39	615	756	.249	.979	4.38
					5414	5414	.255	.978	3.87

BATTING AVERAGE
Pete Runnels BOS..... .320
Al Smith CHI .... .315
Minnie Minoso CHI .... .311

HITS
Minnie Minoso CHI 184
Nellie Fox CHI............. 175
B. Robinson BAL 175

DOUBLES
Tito Francona CLE........ 36
Bill Skowron NY 34
two tied at 32

TRIPLES
Nellie Fox CHI............... 10
Brooks Robinson BAL..... 9

HOME RUNS
Mickey Mantle NY 40
Roger Maris NY 39
Jim Lemon WAS 38

RUNS BATTED IN
Roger Maris NY 112
Minnie Minoso CHI 105
Vic Wertz BOS............. 103

SLUGGING AVERAGE
Roger Maris NY .... .581
Mickey Mantle NY ...... .558
two tied at .... .534

STOLEN BASES
Luis Aparicio CHI 51
Jim Landis CHI 23
Lenny Green WAS........ 21

RUNS SCORED
Mickey Mantle NY 119
Roger Maris NY 98
two tied at 89

WINS
Jim Perry CLE............... 18
Chuck Estrada BAL 18
Buddy Daley KC 16

WINNING PERCENTAGE
Jim Perry CLE............. .643
Art Ditmar NY............. .625
Chuck Estrada BAL ... .621

EARNED RUN AVERAGE
F. Baumann CHI........ 2.67
Jim Bunning DET....... 2.79
two tied at 3.06

STRIKEOUTS
Jim Bunning DET........ 201
Pedro Ramos WAS..... 160
Early Wynn CHI 158

SAVES
Mike Fornieles BOS...... 14
J. Klippstein CLE 14
Ray Moore CHI, WAS... 13

COMPLETE GAMES
Frank Lary DET 15
Pedro Ramos WAS....... 14
Ray Herbert KC 14

SHUTOUTS
Jim Perry CLE................. 4
Whitey Ford NY 4
Early Wynn CHI 4

GAMES PITCHED
Mike Fornieles BOS 70
Gerry Staley CHI........... 64
Tex Clevenger WAS 53

INNINGS PITCHED
Frank Lary DET 274
Pedro Ramos WAS..... 274
Jim Perry CLE............. 261

1960 NL

	W	L	PCT	GB	R	OR	BA	FA	ERA
PITTSBURGH	95	59	.617	—	734	593	.276	.979	3.49
MILWAUKEE	88	66	.571	7	724	658	.265	.976	3.76
ST. LOUIS	86	68	.558	9	639	616	.254	.976	3.64
LOS ANGELES	82	72	.532	13	662	593	.255	.979	3.40
SAN FRANCISCO	79	75	.513	16	671	631	.255	.972	3.44
CINCINNATI	67	87	.435	28	640	692	.250	.979	4.00
CHICAGO	60	94	.390	35	634	776	.243	.977	4.35
PHILADELPHIA	59	95	.383	36	546	691	.239	.974	4.01
					5250	5250	.255	.977	3.76

BATTING AVERAGE
Dick Groat PIT .... .325
Willie Mays SF .... .319
R. Clemente PIT .... .314

HITS
Willie Mays SF 190
Vada Pinson CIN 187
Dick Groat PIT 186

DOUBLES
Vada Pinson CIN 37
Orlando Cepeda SF 36
two tied at 33

TRIPLES
Bill Bruton MIL 13
Willie Mays SF 12
Vada Pinson CIN 12

HOME RUNS
Ernie Banks CHI 41
Hank Aaron MIL............. 40
Eddie Mathews MIL 39

RUNS BATTED IN
Hank Aaron MIL........... 126
Eddie Mathews MIL 124
Ernie Banks CHI 117

SLUGGING AVERAGE
F. Robinson CIN .... .595
Hank Aaron MIL.......... .566
Ken Boyer STL .... .562

STOLEN BASES
Maury Wills LA.............. 50
Vada Pinson CIN 32
Tony Taylor CHI, PHI.... 26

RUNS SCORED
Bill Bruton MIL 112
Eddie Mathews MIL 108
two tied at 107

WINS
Ernie Broglio STL.......... 21
Warren Spahn MIL........ 21
Vern Law PIT................ 20

WINNING PERCENTAGE
Ernie Broglio STL........ .700
Vern Law PIT .... .690
Warren Spahn MIL...... .677

EARNED RUN AVERAGE
Mike McCormick SF... 2.70
Ernie Broglio STL....... 2.74
Don Drysdale LA........ 2.84

STRIKEOUTS
Don Drysdale LA......... 246
Sandy Koufax LA........ 197
Sam Jones SF 190

SAVES
Lindy McDaniel STL...... 26
Roy Face PIT................ 24
Bill Henry CIN 17

COMPLETE GAMES
Warren Spahn MIL........ 18
Vern Law PIT 18
Lew Burdette MIL.......... 18

SHUTOUTS
Jack Sanford SF 6
Don Drysdale LA............. 5

GAMES PITCHED
Roy Face PIT................ 68
Lindy McDaniel STL...... 65
Don Elston CHI 60

INNINGS PITCHED
Larry Jackson STL....... 282
Lew Burdette MIL......... 276
Bob Friend PIT............. 276

1961 AL

	W	L	PCT	GB	R	OR	BA	FA	ERA
★NEW YORK	109	53	.673	—	827	612	.263	.980	3.46
DETROIT	101	61	.623	8	841	671	.266	.976	3.55
BALTIMORE	95	67	.586	14	691	588	.254	.980	3.22
CHICAGO	86	76	.531	23	765	726	.265	.980	4.06
CLEVELAND	78	83	.484	30.5	737	752	.266	.977	4.15
BOSTON	76	86	.469	33	729	792	.254	.977	4.29
MINNESOTA	70	90	.438	38	707	778	.250	.971	4.28
LOS ANGELES	70	91	.435	38.5	744	784	.245	.969	4.31
KANSAS CITY	61	100	.379	47.5	683	863	.247	.972	4.74
WASHINGTON	61	100	.379	47.5	618	776	.244	.975	4.23
					7342	7342	.256	.976	4.02

BATTING AVERAGE
Norm Cash DET .... .361
Al Kaline DET .... .324
Jimmy Piersall CLE.... .322

HITS
Norm Cash DET 193
B. Robinson BAL ... 192
Al Kaline DET 190

DOUBLES
Al Kaline DET 41
Tony Kubek NY.............. 38
Brooks Robinson BAL... 38

TRIPLES
Jake Wood DET............. 14
Marty Keough WAS 9
Jerry Lumpe KC.............. 9

HOME RUNS
Roger Maris NY 61
Mickey Mantle NY......... 54
two tied at 46

RUNS BATTED IN
Roger Maris NY 142
Jim Gentile BAL........... 141
Rocky Colavito DET.... 140

SLUGGING AVERAGE
Mickey Mantle NY...... .687
Norm Cash DET .... .662
Jim Gentile BAL.......... .646

STOLEN BASES
Luis Aparicio CHI........... 53
Dick Howser KC............. 37
Jake Wood DET............. 30

RUNS SCORED
Roger Maris NY 132
Mickey Mantle NY....... 132
Rocky Colavito DET.... 129

WINS
Whitey Ford NY 25
Frank Lary DET 23
Steve Barber BAL 18

WINNING PERCENTAGE
Whitey Ford NY .... .862
Ralph Terry NY .... .842
Luis Arroyo NY............ .750

EARNED RUN AVERAGE
Dick Donovan WAS ... 2.40
Bill Stafford NY 2.68
Don Mossi DET.......... 2.96

STRIKEOUTS
Camilo Pascual MIN ... 221
Whitey Ford NY 209
Jim Bunning DET........ 194

SAVES
Luis Arroyo NY.............. 29
Hoyt Wilhelm BAL.......... 18
Mike Fornieles BOS...... 15

COMPLETE GAMES
Frank Lary DET 22
Camilo Pascual MIN 15
Steve Barber BAL 14

SHUTOUTS
Camilo Pascual MIN 8
Steve Barber BAL 8
three tied at...................... 4

GAMES PITCHED
Luis Arroyo NY.............. 65
Tom Morgan LA............. 59
Turk Lown CHI............... 59

INNINGS PITCHED
Whitey Ford NY 283
Frank Lary DET 275
Jim Bunning DET........ 268

1961 NL

	W	L	PCT	GB	R	OR	BA	FA	ERA
CINCINNATI	93	61	.604	—	710	653	.270	.977	3.78
LOS ANGELES	89	65	.578	4	735	697	.262	.975	4.04
SAN FRANCISCO	85	69	.552	8	773	655	.264	.977	3.77
MILWAUKEE	83	71	.539	10	712	656	.258	.982	3.89
ST. LOUIS	80	74	.519	13	703	668	.271	.972	3.74
PITTSBURGH	75	79	.487	18	694	675	.273	.975	3.92
CHICAGO	64	90	.416	29	689	800	.255	.970	4.48
PHILADELPHIA	47	107	.305	46	584	796	.243	.976	4.61
					5600	5600	.262	.976	4.03

BATTING AVERAGE
R. Clemente PIT .... .351
Vada Pinson CIN .... .343
Ken Boyer STL .... .329

HITS
Vada Pinson CIN 208
R. Clemente PIT 201
Hank Aaron MIL.......... 197

DOUBLES
Hank Aaron MIL.......... 39
Vada Pinson CIN 34
three tied at.................. 32

TRIPLES
George Altman CHI 12
three tied at.................. 11

HOME RUNS
Orlando Cepeda SF...... 46
Willie Mays SF 40
Frank Robinson CIN 37

RUNS BATTED IN
Orlando Cepeda SF.... 142
Frank Robinson CIN ... 124
Willie Mays SF 123

SLUGGING AVERAGE
F. Robinson CIN .... .611
Orlando Cepeda SF... .609
Hank Aaron MIL......... .594

STOLEN BASES
Maury Wills LA.............. 35
Vada Pinson CIN 23
Frank Robinson CIN 22

RUNS SCORED
Willie Mays SF 129
Frank Robinson CIN ... 117
Hank Aaron MIL.......... 115

WINS
Joey Jay CIN 21
Warren Spahn MIL........ 21
Jim O'Toole CIN 19

WINNING PERCENTAGE
Johnny Podres LA ..... .783
Jim O'Toole CIN .... .679
Joey Jay CIN .... .677

EARNED RUN AVERAGE
Warren Spahn MIL.... 3.02
Jim O'Toole CIN 3.10
Curt Simmons STL 3.13

STRIKEOUTS
Sandy Koufax LA........ 269
Stan Williams LA......... 205
Don Drysdale LA......... 182

SAVES
Stu Miller SF 17
Roy Face PIT 17
two tied at 16

COMPLETE GAMES
Warren Spahn MIL........ 21
Sandy Koufax LA 15
two tied at 14

SHUTOUTS
Joey Jay CIN 4
Warren Spahn MIL......... 4

GAMES PITCHED
Jack Baldschun PHI...... 65
Stu Miller SF 63
Roy Face PIT................. 62

INNINGS PITCHED
Lew Burdette MIL......... 272
Warren Spahn MIL....... 263
Don Cardwell CHI 259

1962 AL

	W	L	PCT	GB	R	OR	BA	FA	ERA
★NEW YORK	96	66	.593	—	817	680	.267	.979	3.7
MINNESOTA	91	71	.562	5	798	713	.260	.979	3.8
LOS ANGELES	86	76	.531	10	718	706	.250	.972	3.7
DETROIT	85	76	.528	10.5	758	692	.248	.974	3.8
CHICAGO	85	77	.525	11	707	658	.257	.982	3.7
CLEVELAND	80	82	.494	16	682	745	.245	.977	4.1
BALTIMORE	77	85	.475	19	652	680	.248	.980	3.6
BOSTON	76	84	.475	19	707	756	.258	.979	4.2
KANSAS CITY	72	90	.444	24	745	837	.263	.979	4.7
WASHINGTON	60	101	.373	35.5	599	716	.250	.978	4.0
					7183	7183	.255	.978	3.9

BATTING AVERAGE
Pete Runnels BOS..... .326
Floyd Robinson CHI... .312
Chuck Hinton WAS .... .310

HITS
B. Richardson NY 209
Jerry Lumpe KC.......... 193
B. Robinson BAL 192

DOUBLES
Floyd Robinson CHI..... 45
C. Yastrzemski BOS..... 43
Ed Bressoud BOS......... 40

TRIPLES
Gino Cimoli KC 15
three tied at................... 10

HOME RUNS
H. Killebrew MIN........... 48
Norm Cash DET 39
two tied at 37

RUNS BATTED IN
H. Killebrew MIN 126
Norm Siebern KC........ 117
Rocky Colavito DET.... 112

SLUGGING AVERAGE
H. Killebrew MIN .... .545
Rocky Colavito DET... .514
Norm Cash DET .... .513

STOLEN BASES
Luis Aparicio CHI 31
Chuck Hinton WAS 28
Jake Wood DET............. 24

RUNS SCORED
Albie Pearson LA........ 115
Norm Siebern KC........ 114
Bob Allison MIN 102

WINS
Ralph Terry NY 23
three tied at................... 20

WINNING PERCENTAGE
Ray Herbert CHI .... .690
Whitey Ford NY .... .680
two tied at .... .667

EARNED RUN AVERAGE
Hank Aguirre DET...... 2.21
Robin Roberts BAL 2.78
Whitey Ford NY 2.90

STRIKEOUTS
Camilo Pascual MIN ... 20
Jim Bunning DET........ 18
Ralph Terry NY 17

SAVES
Dick Radatz BOS.......... 2
Marshall Bridges NY ... 1
Terry Fox DET 1

COMPLETE GAMES
Camilo Pascual MIN 1
Jim Kaat MIN 1
Dick Donovan CLE 1

SHUTOUTS
Camilo Pascual MIN ......
Dick Donovan CLE ....
Jim Kaat MIN ....

GAMES PITCHED
Dick Radatz BOS.......... 6
John Wyatt KC.............. 5

INNINGS PITCHED
Ralph Terry NY 29
Jim Kaat MIN 26
Jim Bunning DET........ 25

1962 NL

	W	L	PCT	GB	R	OR	BA	FA	ERA
SAN FRANCISCO*	103	62	.624	—	878	690	.278	.977	3.79
LOS ANGELES	102	63	.618	1	842	697	.268	.970	3.62
CINCINNATI	98	64	.605	3.5	802	685	.270	.977	3.75
PITTSBURGH	93	68	.578	8	706	626	.268	.976	3.37
MILWAUKEE	86	76	.531	15.5	730	665	.252	.980	3.68
ST. LOUIS	84	78	.519	17.5	774	664	.271	.979	3.55
PHILADELPHIA	81	80	.503	20	705	759	.260	.977	4.28
HOUSTON	64	96	.400	36.5	592	717	.246	.973	3.83
CHICAGO	59	103	.364	42.5	632	827	.253	.977	4.54
NEW YORK	40	120	.250	60.5	617	948	.240	.967	5.04
*Defeated Los Angeles in a playoff 2 games to 1					7278	7278	.261	.975	3.94

BATTING AVERAGE
Tommy Davis LA .... .346
F. Robinson CIN .... .342
Stan Musial STL .... .330

HITS
Tommy Davis LA 230
Frank Robinson CIN ... 208
Maury Wills LA............ 208

DOUBLES
Frank Robinson CIN 51
Willie Mays SF 36
Dick Groat PIT 34

TRIPLES
four tied at..................... 10

HOME RUNS
Willie Mays SF 49
Hank Aaron MIL............ 45
Frank Robinson CIN 39

RUNS BATTED IN
Tommy Davis LA 153
Willie Mays SF 141
Frank Robinson CIN ... 136

SLUGGING AVERAGE
F. Robinson CIN .... .624
Hank Aaron MIL........ .618
Willie Mays SF .... .615

STOLEN BASES
Maury Wills LA............ 104
Willie Davis LA............. 32
two tied at 26

RUNS SCORED
Frank Robinson CIN ... 134
Maury Wills LA........... 130
Willie Mays SF 130

WINS
Don Drysdale LA........... 25
Jack Sanford SF 24
Bob Purkey CIN 23

WINNING PERCENTAGE
Bob Purkey CIN .... .821
Jack Sanford SF .... .774
Don Drysdale LA........ .735

EARNED RUN AVERAGE
Sandy Koufax LA 2.54
Bob Shaw MIL 2.80
Bob Purkey CIN 2.81

STRIKEOUTS
Don Drysdale LA......... 232
Sandy Koufax LA........ 216
Bob Gibson STL 208

SAVES
Roy Face PIT 28
Ron Perranoski LA........ 20
Stu Miller SF 19

COMPLETE GAMES
Warren Spahn MIL........ 22
Art Mahaffey PHI 20
Billy O'Dell SF.............. 20

SHUTOUTS
Bob Gibson STL 5
Bob Friend PIT................ 5

GAMES PITCHED
Ron Perranoski LA....... 70
Jack Baldshun PHI 67
Ed Roebuck LA............. 64

INNINGS PITCHED
Don Drysdale LA.......... 314
Bob Purkey CIN 288
Billy O'Dell SF.............. 281

1963 AL

	W	L	PCT	GB	R	OR	BA	FA	ER
NEW YORK	104	57	.646	—	714	547	.252	.982	3.0
CHICAGO	94	68	.580	10.5	683	544	.250	.979	2.9
MINNESOTA	91	70	.565	13	767	602	.255	.976	3.2
BALTIMORE	86	76	.531	18.5	644	621	.249	.984	3.4
CLEVELAND	79	83	.488	25.5	635	702	.239	.977	3.7
DETROIT	79	83	.488	25.5	700	703	.252	.981	3.9
BOSTON	76	85	.472	28	666	704	.252	.978	3.9
KANSAS CITY	73	89	.451	31.5	615	704	.247	.980	3.9
LOS ANGELES	70	91	.435	34	597	660	.250	.974	3.5
WASHINGTON	56	106	.346	48.5	578	812	.227	.971	4.4
					6599	6599	.247	.978	3.6

BATTING AVERAGE
C. Yastrzemski BOS .. .321
Al Kaline DET .... .312
Rich Rollins MIN .... .307

HITS
C. Yastrzemski BOS ... 183
Pete Ward CHI............. 177
Albie Pearson LA 176

DOUBLES
C. Yastrzemski BOS 40
Pete Ward CHI.............. 34
three tied at.................. 32

TRIPLES
Zoilo Versalles MIN....... 13
Jim Fregosi LA.............. 12
Chuck Hinton WAS 12

HOME RUNS
H. Killebrew MIN........... 45
Dick Stuart BOS............ 42
Bob Allison MIN 35

RUNS BATTED IN
Dick Stuart BOS.......... 118
Al Kaline DET 101
H. Killebrew MIN 96

SLUGGING AVERAGE
H. Killebrew MIN .... .555
Bob Allison MIN .... .533
Elston Howard NY ..... .528

STOLEN BASES
Luis Aparicio BAL 40
Chuck Hinton WAS 25
two tied at 18

RUNS SCORED
Bob Allison MIN 99
Albie Pearson LA 92
three tied at.................. 91

WINS
Whitey Ford NY 24
Jim Bouton NY.............. 21
Camilo Pascual MIN 21

WINNING PERCENTAGE
Whitey Ford NY .... .774
Jim Bouton NY........... .750
Dick Radatz BOS....... .714

EARNED RUN AVERAGE
Gary Peters CHI 2.33
Juan Pizarro CHI 2.39
C. Pascual MIN.......... 2.46

STRIKEOUTS
Camilo Pascual MIN ... 20
Jim Bunning DET........ 19
Dick Stigman MIN 19

SAVES
Stu Miller BAL.............. 2
Dick Radatz BOS.......... 2
three tied at.................. 2

COMPLETE GAMES
Ralph Terry NY 1
Camilo Pascual MIN ... 1
Dick Stigman MIN 1

SHUTOUTS
Ray Herbert CHI ....
Jim Bouton NY.................

GAMES PITCHED
Stu Miller BAL.............. 7
Dick Radatz BOS.......... 6
Bill Dailey MIN 6

INNINGS PITCHED
Whitey Ford NY 26
Ralph Terry NY 26
Monbouquette BOS 26

1963 NL

	W	L	PCT	GB	R	OR	BA	FA	ERA
LOS ANGELES	99	63	.611	—	640	550	.251	.975	2.85
ST. LOUIS	93	69	.574	6	747	628	.271	.976	3.32
SAN FRANCISCO	88	74	.543	11	725	641	.258	.975	3.35
PHILADELPHIA	87	75	.537	12	642	578	.252	.978	3.09
CINCINNATI	86	76	.531	13	648	594	.246	.978	3.29
MILWAUKEE	84	78	.519	15	677	603	.244	.980	3.26
CHICAGO	82	80	.506	17	570	578	.238	.976	3.08
PITTSBURGH	74	88	.457	25	567	595	.250	.972	3.10
HOUSTON	66	96	.407	33	464	640	.220	.974	3.44
NEW YORK	51	111	.315	48	501	774	.219	.967	4.12
					6181	6181	.245	.975	3.29

BATTING AVERAGE
Tommy Davis LA .... .326
R. Clemente PIT .... .320
two tied at .... .319

HITS
Vada Pinson CIN 204
Hank Aaron MIL............ 201
Dick Groat STL 201

DOUBLES
Dick Groat STL 43
Vada Pinson CIN 37
three tied at.................. 36

TRIPLES
Vada Pinson CIN 14
Tony Gonzalez PHI....... 12
three tied at.................. 11

HOME RUNS
Willie McCovey SF........ 44
Hank Aaron MIL............ 44
Willie Mays SF 38

RUNS BATTED IN
Hank Aaron MIL.......... 130
Ken Boyer STL 111
Bill White STL 109

SLUGGING AVERAGE
Hank Aaron MIL.......... .586
Willie Mays SF............ .582
Willie McCovey SF..... .566

STOLEN BASES
Maury Wills LA.............. 40
Hank Aaron MIL............ 31
Vada Pinson CIN 27

RUNS SCORED
Hank Aaron MIL........... 121
Willie Mays SF 115
Curt Flood STL 112

WINS
Sandy Koufax LA........... 25
Juan Marichal SF.......... 25
two tied at 23

WINNING PERCENTAGE
Ron Perranoski LA..... .842
Sandy Koufax LA .... .833
two tied at .... .767

EARNED RUN AVERAGE
Sandy Koufax LA 1.88
Dick Ellsworth CHI 2.11
Bob Friend PIT........... 2.34

STRIKEOUTS
Sandy Koufax LA 306
Jim Maloney CIN 265
Don Drysdale LA.......... 251

SAVES
Lindy McDaniel CHI...... 22
Ron Perranoski LA........ 21
two tied at 16

COMPLETE GAMES
Warren Spahn MIL........ 22
Sandy Koufax LA 20
Dick Ellsworth CHI 19

SHUTOUTS
Sandy Koufax LA 11
Warren Spahn MIL.......... 7
two tied at 6

GAMES PITCHED
Ron Perranoski LA........ 69
Jack Baldschun PHI...... 65
Larry Bearnarth NY....... 58

INNINGS PITCHED
Juan Marichal SF........ 321
Don Drysdale LA......... 315
Sandy Koufax LA 311

1964 AL

	W	L	PCT	GB	R	OR	BA	FA	ERA
NEW YORK	99	63	.611	—	730	577	.253	.983	3.15
CHICAGO	98	64	.605	1	642	501	.247	.981	2.72
BALTIMORE	97	65	.599	2	679	567	.248	.985	3.16
DETROIT	85	77	.525	14	699	678	.253	.982	3.84
LOS ANGELES	82	80	.506	17	544	551	.242	.978	2.91
CLEVELAND	79	83	.488	20	689	693	.247	.981	3.75
MINNESOTA	79	83	.488	20	737	678	.252	.977	3.57
BOSTON	72	90	.444	27	688	793	.258	.977	4.50
WASHINGTON	62	100	.383	37	578	733	.231	.979	3.98
KANSAS CITY	57	105	.352	42	621	836	.239	.974	4.71
					6607	6607	.247	.980	3.63

BATTING AVERAGE
Tony Oliva MIN .... .323
B. Robinson BAL .... .317
Elston Howard NY ..... .313

HITS
Tony Oliva MIN 217
B. Robinson BAL 194
B. Richardson NY 181

DOUBLES
Tony Oliva MIN 43
Ed Bressoud BOS......... 41
Brooks Robinson BAL... 35

TRIPLES
Rich Rollins MIN 10
Zoilo Versalles MIN....... 10
three tied at..................... 9

HOME RUNS
H. Killebrew MIN 49
Boog Powell BAL 39
Mickey Mantle NY 35

RUNS BATTED IN
B. Robinson BAL 118
Dick Stuart BOS........... 114
two tied at 111

SLUGGING AVERAGE
Boog Powell BAL .... .606
Mickey Mantle NY ...... .591
Tony Oliva MIN .... .557

STOLEN BASES
Luis Aparicio BAL 57
Al Weis CHI 22
Vic Davalillo CLE 21

RUNS SCORED
Tony Oliva MIN 109
Dick Howser CLE........ 101
H. Killebrew MIN 95

WINS
Gary Peters CHI 20
Dean Chance LA 20
three tied at................... 19

WINNING PERCENTAGE
Wally Bunker BAL...... .792
Whitey Ford NY .... .739
Gary Peters CHI .... .714

EARNED RUN AVERAGE
Dean Chance LA 1.65
Joe Horlen CHI 1.88
Whitey Ford NY 2.13

STRIKEOUTS
Al Downing NY............ 217
Camilo Pascual MIN ... 213
Dean Chance LA 207

SAVES
Dick Radatz BOS.......... 29
Hoyt Wilhelm CHI 27
Stu Miller BAL 23

COMPLETE GAMES
Dean Chance LA 15
Camilo Pascual MIN 14
three tied at.................. 13

SHUTOUTS
Dean Chance LA 11
Whitey Ford NY 8
Milt Pappas BAL 7

GAMES PITCHED
John Wyatt KC 81
Dick Radatz BOS.......... 79
Hoyt Wilhelm CHI 73

INNINGS PITCHED
Dean Chance LA 278
Gary Peters CHI 274
Jim Bouton NY............ 271

1964 NL

	W	L	PCT	GB	R	OR	BA	FA	ERA
ST. LOUIS	93	69	.574	—	715	652	.272	.973	3.43
CINCINNATI	92	70	.568	1	660	566	.249	.979	3.07
PHILADELPHIA	92	70	.568	1	693	632	.258	.975	3.36
SAN FRANCISCO	90	72	.556	3	656	587	.246	.975	3.19
MILWAUKEE	88	74	.543	5	803	744	.272	.977	4.12
LOS ANGELES	80	82	.494	13	614	572	.250	.973	2.95
PITTSBURGH	80	82	.494	13	663	636	.264	.972	3.52
CHICAGO	76	86	.469	17	649	724	.251	.975	4.08
HOUSTON	66	96	.407	27	495	628	.229	.976	3.41
NEW YORK	53	109	.327	40	569	776	.246	.974	4.25
					6517	6517	.254	.975	3.54

BATTING AVERAGE
R. Clemente PIT .... .339
Hank Aaron MIL........ .328
Joe Torre MIL .... .321

HITS
Curt Flood STL 211
R. Clemente PIT 211
two tied at 201

DOUBLES
Lee Maye MIL............... 44
R. Clemente PIT 40
Billy Williams CHI......... 39

TRIPLES
Dick Allen PHI............... 13
Ron Santo CHI.............. 13
two tied at 11

HOME RUNS
Willie Mays SF............... 47
Billy Williams CHI......... 33
three tied at................... 31

RUNS BATTED IN
Ken Boyer STL 119
Ron Santo CHI............. 114
Willie Mays SF............. 111

SLUGGING AVERAGE
Willie Mays SF .... .607
Ron Santo CHI............. .564
Dick Allen PHI............. .557

STOLEN BASES
Maury Wills LA 53
Lou Brock CHI, STL...... 43
Willie Davis LA.............. 42

RUNS SCORED
Dick Allen PHI............. 125
Willie Mays SF............. 121
Lou Brock CHI, STL.... 111

WINS
Larry Jackson CHI 24
Juan Marichal SF.......... 21
Ray Sadecki STL.......... 20

WINNING PERCENTAGE
Sandy Koufax LA .... .792
Juan Marichal SF........ .724
Jim O'Toole CIN .... .708

EARNED RUN AVERAGE
Sandy Koufax LA 1.74
Don Drysdale LA........ 2.18
Chris Short PHI.......... 2.20

STRIKEOUTS
Bob Veale PIT............. 250
Bob Gibson STL 245
Don Drysdale LA......... 237

SAVES
Hal Woodeshick HOU... 23
Al McBean PIT.............. 22
Jack Baldschun PHI...... 21

COMPLETE GAMES
Juan Marichal SF.......... 22
Don Drysdale LA........... 21
Larry Jackson CHI 19

SHUTOUTS
Sandy Koufax LA 7
four tied at...................... 5

GAMES PITCHED
Bob Miller LA 74
Ron Perranoski LA........ 72
Jack Baldschun PHI...... 71

INNINGS PITCHED
Don Drysdale LA......... 321
Larry Jackson CHI 298
Bob Gibson STL 287

1965 AL

	W	L	PCT	GB	R	OR	BA	FA	ERA
MINNESOTA	102	60	.630	—	774	600	.254	.973	3.14
CHICAGO	95	67	.586	7	647	555	.246	.980	2.99
BALTIMORE	94	68	.580	8	641	578	.238	.980	2.98
DETROIT	89	73	.549	13	680	602	.238	.981	3.35
CLEVELAND	87	75	.537	15	663	613	.250	.981	3.30
NEW YORK	77	85	.475	25	611	604	.235	.978	3.28
CALIFORNIA	75	87	.463	27	527	569	.239	.981	3.17
WASHINGTON	70	92	.432	32	591	721	.228	.976	3.93
BOSTON	62	100	.383	40	669	791	.251	.974	4.24
KANSAS CITY	59	103	.364	43	585	755	.240	.977	4.24
					6388	6388	.242	.978	3.46

BATTING AVERAGE
Tony Oliva MIN .... .321
C. Yastrzemski BOS .. .312
Vic Davalillo CLE .... .301

HITS
Tony Oliva MIN 185
Zoilo Versalles MIN..... 182
Rocky Colavito CLE 170

DOUBLES
C. Yastrzemski BOS 45
Zoilo Versalles MIN....... 45
Tony Oliva MIN 40

TRIPLES
Bert Campaneris KC 12
Zoilo Versalles MIN....... 12
Luis Aparicio BAL 10

HOME RUNS
Tony Conigliaro BOS 32
Norm Cash DET 30
Willie Horton DET 29

RUNS BATTED IN
Rocky Colavito CLE.... 108
Willie Horton DET 104
Tony Oliva MIN 98

SLUGGING AVERAGE
C. Yastrzemski BOS .. .536
T. Conigliaro BOS ...... .512
Norm Cash DET .... .512

STOLEN BASES
Bert Campaneris KC 51
Jose Cardenal CAL....... 37
Zoilo Versalles MIN....... 27

RUNS SCORED
Zoilo Versalles MIN..... 126
Tony Oliva MIN 107
Tom Tresh NY 94

WINS
Mudcat Grant MIN 21
Mel Stottlemyre NY 20
Jim Kaat MIN 18

WINNING PERCENTAGE
Mudcat Grant MIN ..... .750
Denny McLain DET.... .727
Mel Stottlemyre NY.... .690

EARNED RUN AVERAGE
Sam McDowell CLE... 2.18
Eddie Fisher CHI 2.40
Sonny Siebert CLE 2.43

STRIKEOUTS
Sam McDowell CLE...... 325
Mickey Lolich DET 226
Denny McLain DET..... 192

SAVES
Ron Kline WAS 29
Eddie Fisher CHI 24
Stu Miller BAL 24

COMPLETE GAMES
Mel Stottlemyre NY....... 18
Mudcat Grant MIN 14
Sam McDowell CLE...... 14

SHUTOUTS
Mudcat Grant MIN 6
four tied at...................... 4

GAMES PITCHED
Eddie Fisher CHI 82
Ron Kline WAS 74
Bob Lee CAL 69

INNINGS PITCHED
Mel Stottlemyre NY 291
Sam McDowell CLE.... 273
Mudcat Grant MIN 270

1965 NL

	W	L	PCT	GB	R	OR	BA	FA	ERA
LOS ANGELES	97	65	.599	—	608	521	.245	.979	2.81
SAN FRANCISCO	95	67	.586	2	682	593	.252	.976	3.20
PITTSBURGH	90	72	.556	7	675	580	.265	.977	3.01
CINCINNATI	89	73	.549	8	825	704	.273	.981	3.88
MILWAUKEE	86	76	.531	11	708	633	.256	.978	3.52
PHILADELPHIA	85	76	.528	11.5	654	667	.250	.975	3.53
ST. LOUIS	80	81	.497	16.5	707	674	.254	.979	3.77
CHICAGO	72	90	.444	25	635	723	.238	.974	3.78
HOUSTON	65	97	.401	32	596	711	.237	.974	3.84
NEW YORK	50	112	.309	47	495	752	.221	.974	4.06
					6558	6558	.249	.977	3.54

BATTING AVERAGE
R. Clemente PIT .... .329
Hank Aaron MIL .... .318
Willie Mays SF .... .317

HITS
Pete Rose CIN 209
Vada Pinson CIN 204
Billy Williams CHI 203

DOUBLES
Hank Aaron MIL 40
Billy Williams CHI 39
two tied at 35

TRIPLES
Johnny Callison PHI 16
three tied at 14

HOME RUNS
Willie Mays SF 52
Willie McCovey SF 39
Billy Williams CHI 34

RUNS BATTED IN
Deron Johnson CIN 130
Frank Robinson CIN ... 113
Willie Mays SF 112

SLUGGING AVERAGE
Willie Mays SF .... .645
Hank Aaron MIL .... .560
Billy Williams CHI .... .552

STOLEN BASES
Maury Wills LA 94
Lou Brock STL 63
Jimmy Wynn HOU 43

RUNS SCORED
Tommy Harper CIN 126
Willie Mays SF 118
Pete Rose CIN 117

WINS
Sandy Koufax LA 26
Tony Cloninger MIL 24
Don Drysdale LA 23

WINNING PERCENTAGE
Sandy Koufax LA .... .765
Jim Maloney CIN .... .690
Sammy Ellis CIN .... .688

EARNED RUN AVERAGE
Sandy Koufax LA 2.04
Juan Marichal SF 2.13
Vern Law PIT 2.15

STRIKEOUTS
Sandy Koufax LA 382
Bob Veale PIT 276
Bob Gibson STL 270

SAVES
Ted Abernathy CHI 31
Billy McCool CIN 21
Frank Linzy SF 21

COMPLETE GAMES
Sandy Koufax LA 27
Juan Marichal SF 24
two tied at 20

SHUTOUTS
Juan Marichal SF 10
Sandy Koufax LA 8
three tied at 7

GAMES PITCHED
Ted Abernathy CHI 84
Woodeshick HOU, STL.. 78
Lindy McDaniel CHI 71

INNINGS PITCHED
Sandy Koufax LA 336
Don Drysdale LA 308
Bob Gibson STL 299

1966 AL

	W	L	PCT	GB	R	OR	BA	FA	ERA
★BALTIMORE	97	63	.606	—	755	601	.258	.981	3.32
MINNESOTA	89	73	.549	9	663	581	.249	.977	3.13
DETROIT	88	74	.543	10	719	698	.251	.980	3.85
CHICAGO	83	79	.512	15	574	517	.231	.976	2.68
CLEVELAND	81	81	.500	17	574	586	.237	.977	3.23
CALIFORNIA	80	82	.494	18	604	643	.232	.979	3.56
KANSAS CITY	74	86	.463	23	564	648	.236	.977	3.55
WASHINGTON	71	88	.447	25.5	557	659	.234	.977	3.70
BOSTON	72	90	.444	26	655	731	.240	.975	3.92
NEW YORK	70	89	.440	26.5	611	612	.235	.977	3.42
					6276	6276	.240	.978	3.44

BATTING AVERAGE
F. Robinson BAL......... .316
Tony Oliva MIN .... .307
Al Kaline DET .... .288

HITS
Tony Oliva MIN 191
Frank Robinson BAL..... 182
Luis Aparicio BAL 182

DOUBLES
C. Yastrzemski BOS 39
Brooks Robinson BAL... 35
Frank Robinson BAL..... 34

TRIPLES
Bobby Knoop CAL 11
Bert Campaneris KC 10
Ed Brinkman WAS 9

HOME RUNS
Frank Robinson BAL..... 49
H. Killebrew MIN 39
Boog Powell BAL 34

RUNS BATTED IN
Frank Robinson BAL... 122
H. Killebrew MIN 110
Boog Powell BAL 109

SLUGGING AVERAGE
F. Robinson BAL......... .637
H. Killebrew MIN .... .538
Al Kaline DET .... .534

STOLEN BASES
Bert Campaneris KC..... 52
Don Buford CHI 51
Tommy Agee CHI 44

RUNS SCORED
Frank Robinson BAL... 122
Tony Oliva MIN 99
two tied at 98

WINS
Jim Kaat MIN 25
Denny McLain DET....... 20
E. Wilson BOS, DET..... 18

WINNING PERCENTAGE
Sonny Siebert CLE .... .667
Jim Kaat MIN .... .658
E. Wilson BOS, DET... .621

EARNED RUN AVERAGE
Gary Peters CHI 1.98
Joe Horlen CHI 2.43
Steve Hargan CLE....... 2.48

STRIKEOUTS
Sam McDowell CLE.... 225
Jim Kaat MIN 205
E. Wilson BOS, DET ... 200

SAVES
Jack Aker KC 32
Ron Kline WAS............. 23
Larry Sherry DET.......... 20

COMPLETE GAMES
Jim Kaat MIN 19
Denny McLain DET....... 14
E. Wilson BOS, DET..... 13

SHUTOUTS
Luis Tiant CLE 5
Sam McDowell CLE........ 5
Tommy John CHI............ 5

GAMES PITCHED
E. Fisher CHI, BAL 67
Casey Cox WAS 66
Jack Aker KC 66

INNINGS PITCHED
Jim Kaat MIN 305
Denny McLain DET..... 264
E. Wilson BOS, DET... 264

1966 NL

	W	L	PCT	GB	R	OR	BA	FA	ERA
LOS ANGELES	95	67	.586	—	606	490	.256	.979	2.62
SAN FRANCISCO	93	68	.578	1.5	675	626	.248	.974	3.24
PITTSBURGH	92	70	.568	3	759	641	.279	.978	3.52
PHILADELPHIA	87	75	.537	8	696	640	.258	.982	3.57
ATLANTA	85	77	.525	10	782	683	.263	.976	3.68
ST. LOUIS	83	79	.512	12	571	577	.251	.977	3.11
CINCINNATI	76	84	.475	18	692	702	.260	.980	4.08
HOUSTON	72	90	.444	23	612	695	.255	.972	3.76
NEW YORK	66	95	.410	28.5	587	761	.239	.975	4.17
CHICAGO	59	103	.364	36	644	809	.254	.974	4.33
					6624	6624	.256	.977	3.61

BATTING AVERAGE
Matty Alou PIT .... .342
Felipe Alou ATL .... .327
Rico Carty ATL .... .326

HITS
Felipe Alou ATL 218
Pete Rose CIN 205
R. Clemente PIT 202

DOUBLES
Johnny Callison PHI 40
Pete Rose CIN 38
Vada Pinson CIN 35

TRIPLES
Tim McCarver STL........ 13
Lou Brock STL.............. 12
R. Clemente PIT 11

HOME RUNS
Hank Aaron ATL 44
Dick Allen PHI............... 40
Willie Mays SF 37

RUNS BATTED IN
Hank Aaron ATL 127
R. Clemente PIT 119
Dick Allen PHI.............. 110

SLUGGING AVERAGE
Dick Allen PHI............. .632
Willie McCovey SF..... .586
Willie Stargell PIT ...... .581

STOLEN BASES
Lou Brock STL.............. 74
Sonny Jackson HOU 49
Maury Wills LA.............. 38

RUNS SCORED
Felipe Alou ATL 122
Hank Aaron ATL 117
Dick Allen PHI............... 112

WINS
Sandy Koufax LA 27
Juan Marichal SF 25
two tied at 21

WINNING PERCENTAGE
Juan Marichal SF........ .806
Sandy Koufax LA......... .750
Gaylord Perry SF .... .724

EARNED RUN AVERAGE
Sandy Koufax LA 1.73
Mike Cuellar HOU 2.22
Juan Marichal SF....... 2.23

STRIKEOUTS
Sandy Koufax LA 317
Jim Bunning PHI 252
Bob Veale PIT.............. 229

SAVES
Phil Regan LA................ 21
Billy McCool CIN........... 18
Roy Face PIT................. 18

COMPLETE GAMES
Sandy Koufax LA.......... 27
Juan Marichal SF.......... 25
Bob Gibson STL 20

SHUTOUTS
six tied at......................... 5

GAMES PITCHED
Clay Carroll ATL 73
Pete Mikkelsen PIT....... 71
Darold Knowles PHI...... 69

INNINGS PITCHED
Sandy Koufax LA 323
Jim Bunning PHI 314
Juan Marichal SF........ 307

1967 AL

	W	L	PCT	GB	R	OR	BA	FA	ERA
BOSTON	92	70	.568	—	722	614	.255	.977	3.36
DETROIT	91	71	.562	1	683	587	.243	.979	3.32
MINNESOTA	91	71	.562	1	671	590	.240	.978	3.14
CHICAGO	89	73	.549	3	531	491	.225	.979	2.45
CALIFORNIA	84	77	.522	7.5	567	587	.238	.982	3.19
BALTIMORE	76	85	.472	15.5	654	592	.240	.980	3.32
WASHINGTON	76	85	.472	15.5	550	637	.223	.978	3.38
CLEVELAND	75	87	.463	17	559	613	.235	.981	3.25
NEW YORK	72	90	.444	20	522	621	.225	.976	3.24
KANSAS CITY	62	99	.385	29.5	533	660	.233	.978	3.68
					5992	5992	.236	.979	3.23

BATTING AVERAGE
C. Yastrzemski BOS .. .326
F. Robinson BAL........ .311
Al Kaline DET .... .308

HITS
C. Yastrzemski BOS ... 189
Cesar Tovar MIN 173
two tied at 171

DOUBLES
Tony Oliva MIN.............. 34
Cesar Tovar MIN 32
C. Yastrzemski BOS 31

TRIPLES
Paul Blair BAL............... 12
Don Buford CHI 9

HOME RUNS
H. Killebrew MIN 44
C. Yastrzemski BOS 44
Frank Howard WAS 36

RUNS BATTED IN
C. Yastrzemski BOS ... 121
H. Killebrew MIN 113
Frank Robinson BAL..... 94

SLUGGING AVERAGE
C. Yastrzemski BOS .. .622
F. Robinson BAL........ .576
H. Killebrew MIL.......... .558

STOLEN BASES
Bert Campaneris KC..... 55
Don Buford CHI 34
Tommy Agee CHI 28

RUNS SCORED
C. Yastrzemski BOS ... 112
H. Killebrew MIN 105
Cesar Tovar MIN 98

WINS
Jim Lonborg BOS 22
Earl Wilson DET 22
Dean Chance MIN 20

WINNING PERCENTAGE
Joe Horlen CHI .... .731
Jim Lonborg BOS .... .710
Earl Wilson DET .... .667

EARNED RUN AVERAGE
Joe Horlen CHI 2.06
Gary Peters CHI 2.28
Sonny Siebert CLE 2.38

STRIKEOUTS
Jim Lonborg BOS 246
Sam McDowell CLE.... 236
Dean Chance MIN 220

SAVES
Minnie Rojas CAL 27
John Wyatt BOS 20
Bob Locker CHI 20

COMPLETE GAMES
Dean Chance MIN 18
Jim Lonborg BOS 15
Steve Hargan CLE 15

SHUTOUTS
five tied at 6

GAMES PITCHED
Bob Locker CHI 77
Minnie Rojas CAL 72
Bill Kelso CAL................ 69

INNINGS PITCHED
Dean Chance MIN 284
Jim Lonborg BOS 273
Earl Wilson DET 264

1967 NL

	W	L	PCT	GB	R	OR	BA	FA	ERA
★ST. LOUIS	101	60	.627	—	695	557	.263	.978	3.05
SAN FRANCISCO	91	71	.562	10.5	652	551	.245	.979	2.92
CHICAGO	87	74	.540	14	702	624	.251	.981	3.48
CINCINNATI	87	75	.537	14.5	604	563	.248	.980	3.05
PHILADELPHIA	82	80	.506	19.5	612	581	.242	.978	3.10
PITTSBURGH	81	81	.500	20.5	679	693	.277	.978	3.74
ATLANTA	77	85	.475	24.5	631	640	.240	.978	3.47
LOS ANGELES	73	89	.451	28.5	519	595	.236	.975	3.21
HOUSTON	69	93	.426	32.5	626	742	.249	.974	4.03
NEW YORK	61	101	.377	40.5	498	672	.238	.975	3.73
					6218	6218	.249	.978	3.38

BATTING AVERAGE
R. Clemente PIT .... .357
Tony Gonzalez PHI.... .339
Matty Alou PIT .... .338

HITS
R. Clemente PIT 209
Lou Brock STL 206
Vada Pinson CIN 187

DOUBLES
Rusty Staub HOU 44
Orlando Cepeda STL.... 37
Hank Aaron ATL 37

TRIPLES
Vada Pinson CIN 13
Lou Brock STL 12
Billy Williams CHI......... 12

HOME RUNS
Hank Aaron ATL 39
Jimmy Wynn HOU 37
two tied at 31

RUNS BATTED IN
O. Cepeda STL............ 111
R. Clemente PIT 110
Hank Aaron ATL 109

SLUGGING AVERAGE
Hank Aaron ATL .... .573
Dick Allen PHI............. .566
R. Clemente PIT .... .554

STOLEN BASES
Lou Brock STL 52
Maury Wills PIT 29
Joe Morgan HOU 29

RUNS SCORED
Lou Brock STL............. 113
Hank Aaron ATL 113
Ron Santo CHI............ 107

WINS
Mike McCormick SF...... 22
F. Jenkins CHI 20
two tied at 17

WINNING PERCENTAGE
Dick Hughes STL........ .727
Mike McCormick SF... .688
Bob Veale PIT............. .667

EARNED RUN AVERAGE
Phil Niekro ATL 1.87
Jim Bunning PHI........ 2.29
Chris Short PHI.......... 2.39

STRIKEOUTS
Jim Bunning PHI......... 253
F. Jenkins CHI 236
Gaylord Perry SF........ 230

SAVES
Ted Abernathy CIN 28
Frank Linzy SF.............. 17
Roy Face PIT................ 17

COMPLETE GAMES
F. Jenkins CHI 20
three tied at................... 18

SHUTOUTS
Jim Bunning PHI.............. 6
three tied at..................... 5

GAMES PITCHED
Ron Perranoski LA........ 70
Ted Abernathy CIN 70
Ron Willis STL 65

INNINGS PITCHED
Jim Bunning PHI......... 302
Gaylord Perry SF 293
F. Jenkins CHI 289

1968 AL

	W	L	PCT	GB	R	OR	BA	FA	ERA
★DETROIT	103	59	.636	—	671	492	.235	.983	2.71
BALTIMORE	91	71	.562	12	579	497	.225	.981	2.66
CLEVELAND	86	75	.534	16.5	516	504	.234	.979	2.66
BOSTON	86	76	.531	17	614	611	.236	.979	3.33
NEW YORK	83	79	.512	20	536	531	.214	.979	2.79
OAKLAND	82	80	.506	21	569	544	.240	.976	2.94
MINNESOTA	79	83	.488	24	562	546	.237	.973	2.89
CALIFORNIA	67	95	.414	36	498	615	.227	.977	3.43
CHICAGO	67	95	.414	36	463	527	.228	.977	2.75
WASHINGTON	65	96	.404	37.5	524	665	.224	.976	3.64
					5532	5532	.230	.978	2.98

BATTING AVERAGE
C. Yastrzemski BOS .. .301
Danny Cater OAK ...... .290
Tony Oliva MIN .... .289

HITS
B. Campaneris OAK ... 177
Cesar Tovar MIN 167
two tied at 164

DOUBLES
Reggie Smith BOS........ 37
Brooks Robinson BAL... 36
C. Yastrzemski BOS..... 32

TRIPLES
Jim Fregosi CAL 13
Tom McCraw CHI 12
two tied at 10

HOME RUNS
Frank Howard WAS...... 44
Willie Horton DET 36
Ken Harrelson BOS 35

RUNS BATTED IN
Ken Harrelson BOS 109
Frank Howard WAS 106
Jim Northrup DET 90

SLUGGING AVERAGE
Frank Howard WAS ... .552
Willie Horton DET .... .543
Ken Harrelson BOS ... .518

STOLEN BASES
B. Campaneris OAK ... 62
Jose Cardenal CLE...... 40
Cesar Tovar MIN 35

RUNS SCORED
Dick McAuliffe DET....... 95
C. Yastrzemski BOS 90
two tied at 89

WINS
Denny McLain DET....... 31
Dave McNally BAL........ 22
two tied at 21

WINNING PERCENTAGE
Denny McLain DET.... .838
Ray Culp BOS .... .727
Luis Tiant CLE .... .700

EARNED RUN AVERAGE
Luis Tiant CLE 1.60
Sam McDowell CLE... 1.81
Dave McNally BAL..... 1.95

STRIKEOUTS
Sam McDowell CLE.... 283
Denny McLain DET..... 280
Luis Tiant CLE 264

SAVES
Al Worthington MIN....... 18
Wilbur Wood CHI 16
Dennis Higgins WAS 13

COMPLETE GAMES
Denny McLain DET....... 28
Luis Tiant CLE 19
Mel Stottlemyre NY....... 19

SHUTOUTS
Luis Tiant CLE 9

GAMES PITCHED
Wilbur Wood CHI 88
Hoyt Wilhelm CHI 72
Bob Locker CHI 70

INNINGS PITCHED
Denny McLain DET.... 336
Dean Chance MIN 292
Mel Stottlemyre NY 279

1968 NL

	W	L	PCT	GB	R	OR	BA	FA	ERA
ST. LOUIS	97	65	.599	—	583	472	.249	.978	2.49
SAN FRANCISCO	88	74	.543	9	599	529	.239	.975	2.71
CHICAGO	84	78	.519	13	612	611	.242	.981	3.41
CINCINNATI	83	79	.512	14	690	673	.273	.978	3.56
ATLANTA	81	81	.500	16	514	549	.252	.980	2.92
PITTSBURGH	80	82	.494	17	583	532	.252	.979	2.74
LOS ANGELES	76	86	.469	21	470	509	.230	.977	2.69
PHILADELPHIA	76	86	.469	21	543	615	.233	.980	3.36
NEW YORK	73	89	.451	24	473	499	.228	.979	2.72
HOUSTON	72	90	.444	25	510	588	.231	.975	3.26
					5577	5577	.243	.978	2.99

BATTING AVERAGE
Pete Rose CIN............ .335
Matty Alou PIT .... .332
Felipe Alou ATL .... .317

HITS
Pete Rose CIN............ 210
Felipe Alou ATL 210
Glenn Beckert CHI...... 189

DOUBLES
Lou Brock STL 46
Pete Rose CIN.............. 42
Johnny Bench CIN 40

TRIPLES
Lou Brock STL 14
R. Clemente PIT 12
Willie Davis LA.............. 10

HOME RUNS
Willie McCovey SF........ 36
Dick Allen PHI............... 33
Ernie Banks CHI 32

RUNS BATTED IN
Willie McCovey SF...... 105
Billy Williams CHI.......... 98
Ron Santo CHI.............. 98

SLUGGING AVERAGE
Willie McCovey SF..... .545
Dick Allen PHI............. .520
Billy Williams CHI....... .500

STOLEN BASES
Lou Brock STL 62
Maury Wills PIT............. 52
Willie Davis LA.............. 36

RUNS SCORED
Glenn Beckert CHI........ 98
Pete Rose CIN.............. 94
Tony Perez CIN 93

WINS
Juan Marichal SF.......... 26
Bob Gibson STL 22
F. Jenkins CHI 20

WINNING PERCENTAGE
Steve Blass PIT .... .750
Juan Marichal SF....... .743
Bob Gibson STL .... .710

EARNED RUN AVERAGE
Bob Gibson STL 1.12
Bobby Bolin SF 1.99
Bob Veale PIT............. 2.05

STRIKEOUTS
Bob Gibson STL 268
F. Jenkins CHI 260
Bill Singer LA 227

SAVES
Phil Regan LA, CHI....... 25
Joe Hoerner STL 17
Clay Carroll ATL, CIN ... 17

COMPLETE GAMES
Juan Marichal SF.......... 30
Bob Gibson STL 28
F. Jenkins CHI 20

SHUTOUTS
Bob Gibson STL 13
Don Drysdale LA............. 8
two tied at 7

GAMES PITCHED
Ted Abernathy CIN....... 78
Phil Regan LA, CHI....... 73
Clay Carroll ATL, CIN ... 68

INNINGS PITCHED
Juan Marichal SF........ 326
F. Jenkins CHI 308
Bob Gibson STL 305

1969 AL

EAST	W	L	PCT	GB	R	OR	BA	FA	ERA
●BALTIMORE	109	53	.673	—	779	517	.265	.984	2.83
DETROIT	90	72	.556	19	701	601	.242	.979	3.32
BOSTON	87	75	.537	22	743	736	.251	.975	3.93
WASHINGTON	86	76	.531	23	694	644	.251	.978	3.49
NEW YORK	80	81	.497	28.5	562	587	.235	.979	3.23
CLEVELAND	62	99	.385	46.5	573	717	.237	.976	3.94

WEST	W	L	PCT	GB	R	OR	BA	FA	ERA
MINNESOTA	97	65	.599	—	790	618	.268	.977	3.25
OAKLAND	88	74	.543	9	740	678	.249	.978	3.71
CALIFORNIA	71	91	.438	26	528	652	.230	.978	3.55
KANSAS CITY	69	93	.426	28	586	688	.240	.975	3.72
CHICAGO	68	94	.420	29	625	723	.247	.981	4.21
SEATTLE	64	98	.395	33	639	799	.234	.974	4.35
					7960	7960	.246	.978	3.63

BATTING AVERAGE
Rod Carew MIN................ .332
Reggie Smith BOS .... .309
Tony Oliva MIN................. .309

HITS
Tony Oliva MIN................. 197
Horace Clarke NY 183
Paul Blair BAL 178

DOUBLES
Tony Oliva MIN................... 39
Reggie Jackson OAK........... 36
Davey Johnson BAL........... 34

TRIPLES
Del Unser WAS 8
Horace Clarke NY 7
Reggie Smith BOS 7

HOME RUNS
Harmon Killebrew MIN 49
Frank Howard WAS............ 48
Reggie Jackson OAK 47

RUNS BATTED IN
Harmon Killebrew MIN 140
Boog Powell BAL 121
Reggie Jackson OAK 118

SLUGGING AVERAGE
Reggie Jackson OAK ...... .608
Rico Petrocelli BOS.......... .589
Harmon Killebrew MIN .... .584

STOLEN BASES
Tommy Harper SEA 73
Bert Campaneris OAK........ 62
Cesar Tovar MIN 45

RUNS SCORED
Reggie Jackson OAK........ 123
Frank Howard WAS 111
Frank Robinson BAL......... 111

WINS
Denny McLain DET 24
Mike Cuellar BAL 23
four tied at 20

WINNING PERCENTAGE
Jim Palmer BAL .... .800
Jim Perry MIN .... .769
Dave McNally BAL .... .741

EARNED RUN AVERAGE
Dick Bosman WAS.......... 2.19
Jim Palmer BAL 2.34
Mike Cuellar BAL 2.38

STRIKEOUTS
Sam McDowell CLE 279
Mickey Lolich DET 271
Andy Messersmith CAL 211

SAVES
Ron Perranoski MIN........ 31
Ken Tatum CAL 22
Sparky Lyle BOS 17

COMPLETE GAMES
Mel Stottlemyre NY 24
Denny McLain DET 23
two tied at........................... 18

SHUTOUTS
Denny McLain DET 9
Jim Palmer BAL 6
Mike Cuellar BAL 5

GAMES PITCHED
Wilbur Wood CHI 76
Ron Perranoski MIN.......... 75
Sparky Lyle BOS 71

INNINGS PITCHED
Denny McLain DET 325
Mel Stottlemyre NY 303
Mike Cuellar BAL 291

1969 NL

EAST	W	L	PCT	GB	R	OR	BA	FA	ERA
★NEW YORK	100	62	.617	—	632	541	.242	.980	2.99
CHICAGO	92	70	.568	8	720	611	.253	.979	3.34
PITTSBURGH	88	74	.543	12	725	652	.277	.975	3.61
ST. LOUIS	87	75	.537	13	595	540	.253	.978	2.94
PHILADELPHIA	63	99	.389	37	645	745	.241	.978	4.17
MONTREAL	52	110	.321	48	582	791	.240	.971	4.33

WEST	W	L	PCT	GB	R	OR	BA	FA	ERA
ATLANTA	93	69	.574	—	691	631	.258	.981	3.53
SAN FRANCISCO	90	72	.556	3	713	636	.242	.974	3.25
CINCINNATI	89	73	.549	4	798	768	.277	.973	4.13
LOS ANGELES	85	77	.525	8	645	561	.254	.980	3.09
HOUSTON	81	81	.500	12	676	668	.240	.975	3.60
SAN DIEGO	52	110	.321	41	468	746	.225	.975	4.24
					7890	7890	.250	.977	3.60

BATTING AVERAGE
Pete Rose CIN .... .348
Roberto Clemente PIT .... .345
Cleon Jones NY .... .340

HITS
Matty Alou PIT 231
Pete Rose CIN 218
Lou Brock STL 195

DOUBLES
Matty Alou PIT 41
Don Kessinger CHI 38
three tied at 33

TRIPLES
Roberto Clemente PIT 12
Pete Rose CIN 11
three tied at 10

HOME RUNS
Willie McCovey SF 45
Hank Aaron ATL 44
Lee May CIN 38

RUNS BATTED IN
Willie McCovey SF 126
Ron Santo CHI 123
Tony Perez CIN 122

SLUGGING AVERAGE
Willie McCovey SF .... .656
Hank Aaron ATL .... .607
Dick Allen PHI .... .573

STOLEN BASES
Lou Brock STL 53
Joe Morgan HOU 49
Bobby Bonds SF 45

RUNS SCORED
Pete Rose CIN 120
Bobby Bonds SF 120
Jimmy Wynn HOU 113

WINS
Tom Seaver NY 25
Phil Niekro ATL 23
two tied at 21

WINNING PERCENTAGE
Tom Seaver NY .... .781
Juan Marichal SF .... .656
two tied at .... .654

EARNED RUN AVERAGE
Juan Marichal SF 2.10
Steve Carlton STL 2.17
Bob Gibson STL 2.18

STRIKEOUTS
Ferguson Jenkins CHI 273
Bob Gibson STL 269
Bill Singer LA 247

SAVES
Fred Gladding HOU 29
Wayne Granger CIN 27
Cecil Upshaw ATL 27

COMPLETE GAMES
Bob Gibson STL 28
Juan Marichal SF 27
Gaylord Perry SF 26

SHUTOUTS
Juan Marichal SF 8
Ferguson Jenkins CHI 7
Claude Osteen LA 7

GAMES PITCHED
Wayne Granger CIN 90
Dan McGinn MON 74
two tied at 71

INNINGS PITCHED
Gaylord Perry SF 325
Claude Osteen LA 321
Bill Singer LA 316

1970 AL

EAST	W	L	PCT	GB	R	OR	BA	FA	ERA
★BALTIMORE	108	54	.667	—	792	574	.257	.981	3.15
NEW YORK	93	69	.574	15	680	612	.251	.980	3.25
BOSTON	87	75	.537	21	786	722	.262	.974	3.90
DETROIT	79	83	.488	29	666	731	.238	.978	4.09
CLEVELAND	76	86	.469	32	649	675	.249	.979	3.91
WASHINGTON	70	92	.432	38	626	689	.238	.982	3.80

WEST	W	L	PCT	GB	R	OR	BA	FA	ERA
MINNESOTA	98	64	.605	—	744	605	.262	.980	3.23
OAKLAND	89	73	.549	9	678	593	.249	.977	3.30
CALIFORNIA	86	76	.531	12	631	630	.251	.980	3.48
KANSAS CITY	65	97	.401	33	611	705	.244	.976	3.78
MILWAUKEE	65	97	.401	33	613	751	.242	.978	4.20
CHICAGO	56	106	.346	42	633	822	.253	.975	4.54
					8109	8109	.250	.978	3.72

BATTING AVERAGE
Alex Johnson CAL............ .329
Carl Yastrzemski BOS..... .329
Tony Oliva MIN................ .325

HITS
Tony Oliva MIN................. 204
Alex Johnson CAL............ 202
Cesar Tovar MIN 195

DOUBLES
Cesar Tovar MIN 36
Tony Oliva MIN................... 36
Amos Otis KC..................... 36

TRIPLES
Cesar Tovar MIN 13
Mickey Stanley DET 11
Amos Otis KC....................... 9

HOME RUNS
Frank Howard WAS............ 44
Harmon Killebrew MIN 41
Carl Yastrzemski BOS........ 40

RUNS BATTED IN
Frank Howard WAS.......... 126
Tony Conigliaro BOS 116
Boog Powell BAL.............. 114

SLUGGING AVERAGE
Carl Yastrzemski BOS..... .592
Boog Powell BAL .... .549
Harmon Killebrew MIN .... .546

STOLEN BASES
Bert Campaneris OAK........ 42
Tommy Harper MIL............. 38
Sandy Alomar CAL............. 35

RUNS SCORED
Carl Yastrzemski BOS...... 125
Cesar Tovar MIN 120
two tied at........................ 109

WINS
Dave McNally BAL 24
Jim Perry MIN 24
Mike Cuellar BAL 24

WINNING PERCENTAGE
Mike Cuellar BAL .... .750
Dave McNally BAL .... .727
two tied at........................ .667

EARNED RUN AVERAGE
Diego Segui OAK 2.56
Jim Palmer BAL 2.71
Clyde Wright CAL............ 2.83

STRIKEOUTS
Sam McDowell CLE 304
Mickey Lolich DET 230
Bob Johnson KC 206

SAVES
Ron Perranoski MIN.......... 34
Lindy McDaniel NY............ 29
two tied at......................... 27

COMPLETE GAMES
Mike Cuellar BAL 21
Sam McDowell CLE 19
Jim Palmer BAL 17

SHUTOUTS
Jim Palmer BAL 5
Chuck Dobson OAK............. 5
three tied at......................... 4

GAMES PITCHED
Wilbur Wood CHI 77
Mudcat Grant OAK............. 72
Darold Knowles WAS......... 71

INNINGS PITCHED
Sam McDowell CLE 305
Jim Palmer BAL 305
Mike Cuellar BAL 298

1970 NL

EAST	W	L	PCT	GB	R	OR	BA	FA	ERA
PITTSBURGH	89	73	.549	—	729	664	.270	.979	3.70
CHICAGO	84	78	.519	5	806	679	.259	.978	3.76
NEW YORK	83	79	.512	6	695	630	.249	.979	3.46
ST. LOUIS	76	86	.469	13	744	747	.263	.977	4.05
PHILADELPHIA	73	88	.453	15.5	594	730	.238	.981	4.17
MONTREAL	73	89	.451	16	687	807	.237	.977	4.50

WEST	W	L	PCT	GB	R	OR	BA	FA	ERA
●CINCINNATI	102	60	.630	—	775	681	.270	.976	3.71
LOS ANGELES	87	74	.540	14.5	749	684	.270	.978	3.82
SAN FRANCISCO	86	76	.531	16	831	826	.262	.973	4.50
HOUSTON	79	83	.488	23	744	763	.259	.978	4.23
ATLANTA	76	86	.469	26	736	772	.270	.977	4.35
SAN DIEGO	63	99	.389	39	681	788	.246	.975	4.38
					8771	8771	.258	.977	4.05

BATTING AVERAGE
Rico Carty ATL .... .366
Joe Torre STL.................. .325
Manny Sanguillen PIT ..... .325

HITS
Billy Williams CHI 205
Pete Rose CIN 205
Joe Torre STL................... 203

DOUBLES
Wes Parker LA 47
Willie McCovey SF 39
Pete Rose CIN 37

TRIPLES
Willie Davis LA 16
Don Kessinger CHI 14
two tied at............................ 10

HOME RUNS
Johnny Bench CIN 45
Billy Williams CHI 42
Tony Perez CIN 40

RUNS BATTED IN
Johnny Bench CIN 148
Billy Williams CHI 129
Tony Perez CIN 129

SLUGGING AVERAGE
Willie McCovey SF .... .612
Tony Perez CIN .... .589
Johnny Bench CIN .... .587

STOLEN BASES
Bobby Tolan CIN 57
Lou Brock STL 51
Bobby Bonds SF 48

RUNS SCORED
Billy Williams CHI 137
Bobby Bonds SF 134
Pete Rose CIN 120

WINS
Gaylord Perry SF 23
Bob Gibson STL................. 23
Ferguson Jenkins CHI........ 22

WINNING PERCENTAGE
Bob Gibson STL............... .767
Gary Nolan CIN................. .720
Luke Walker PIT............... .714

EARNED RUN AVERAGE
Tom Seaver NY 2.81
Wayne Simpson CIN 3.02
Luke Walker PIT.............. 3.04

STRIKEOUTS
Tom Seaver NY 283
Bob Gibson STL................ 274
Ferguson Jenkins CHI...... 274

SAVES
Wayne Granger CIN........... 35
Dave Giusti PIT 26
Jim Brewer LA................... 24

COMPLETE GAMES
Ferguson Jenkins CHI........ 24
Gaylord Perry SF 23
Bob Gibson STL................. 23

SHUTOUTS
Gaylord Perry SF 5
four tied at 4

GAMES PITCHED
Ron Herbel SD, NY 76
Dick Selma PHI 73
two tied at 67

INNINGS PITCHED
Gaylord Perry SF 329
Ferguson Jenkins CHI...... 313
Bob Gibson STL................ 294

1971 AL

EAST	W	L	PCT	GB	R	OR	BA	FA	ERA
● BALTIMORE	101	57	.639	—	742	530	.261	.981	3.00
DETROIT	91	71	.562	12	701	645	.254	.983	3.64
BOSTON	85	77	.525	18	691	667	.252	.981	3.83
NEW YORK	82	80	.506	21	648	641	.254	.981	3.45
WASHINGTON	63	96	.396	38.5	537	660	.230	.977	3.70
CLEVELAND	60	102	.370	43	543	747	.238	.981	4.28

WEST	W	L	PCT	GB	R	OR	BA	FA	ERA
OAKLAND	101	60	.627	—	691	564	.252	.981	3.06
KANSAS CITY	85	76	.528	16	603	566	.250	.978	3.25
CHICAGO	79	83	.488	22.5	617	597	.250	.975	3.13
CALIFORNIA	76	86	.469	25.5	511	576	.231	.980	3.10
MINNESOTA	74	86	.463	26.5	654	670	.260	.980	3.82
MILWAUKEE	69	92	.429	32	534	609	.229	.977	3.38
					7472	7472	.247	.980	3.47

BATTING AVERAGE
Tony Oliva MIN .... .337
Bobby Murcer NY .... .331
Merv Rettenmund BAL .... .318

HITS
Cesar Tovar MIN 204
Sandy Alomar CAL 179
Rod Carew MIN 177

DOUBLES
Reggie Smith BOS 33
Paul Schaal KC 31
two tied at 30

TRIPLES
Freddie Patek KC 11
Rod Carew MIN 10
Paul Blair BAL 8

HOME RUNS
Bill Melton CHI 33
Norm Cash DET 32
Reggie Jackson OAK 32

RUNS BATTED IN
Harmon Killebrew MIN 119
Frank Robinson BAL 99
Reggie Smith BOS 96

SLUGGING AVERAGE
Tony Oliva MIN .... .546
Bobby Murcer NY .... .543
Norm Cash DET .... .531

STOLEN BASES
Amos Otis KC 52
Freddie Patek KC 49
Sandy Alomar CAL 39

RUNS SCORED
Don Buford BAL 99
Bobby Murcer NY 94
Cesar Tovar MIN 94

WINS
Mickey Lolich DET 25
Vida Blue OAK 24
Wilbur Wood CHI 22

WINNING PERCENTAGE
Dave McNally BAL .... .808
Vida Blue OAK .... .750
Chuck Dobson OAK .... .750

EARNED RUN AVERAGE
Vida Blue OAK 1.82
Wilbur Wood CHI 1.91
Jim Palmer BAL 2.68

STRIKEOUTS
Mickey Lolich DET 308
Vida Blue OAK 301
Joe Coleman DET 236

SAVES
Ken Sanders MIL 31
Ted Abernathy KC 23
Fred Scherman DET 20

COMPLETE GAMES
Mickey Lolich DET 29
Vida Blue OAK 24
Wilbur Wood CHI 22

SHUTOUTS
Vida Blue OAK 8
Mel Stottlemyre NY 7
Wilbur Wood CHI 7

GAMES PITCHED
Ken Sanders MIL 83
Fred Scherman DET 69
Tom Burgmeier KC 67

INNINGS PITCHED
Mickey Lolich DET 376
Wilbur Wood CHI 334
Vida Blue OAK 312

1971 NL

EAST	W	L	PCT	GP	R	OR	BA	FA	ERA
★PITTSBURGH	97	65	.599	—	788	599	.274	.979	3.31
ST. LOUIS	90	72	.556	7	739	699	.275	.978	3.87
CHICAGO	83	79	.512	14	637	648	.258	.980	3.61
NEW YORK	83	79	.512	14	588	550	.249	.981	3.00
MONTREAL	71	90	.441	25.5	622	729	.246	.976	4.12
PHILADELPHIA	67	95	.414	30	558	688	.233	.981	3.71

WEST	W	L	PCT	GB	R	OR	BA	FA	ERA
SAN FRANCISCO	90	72	.556	—	706	644	.247	.972	3.33
LOS ANGELES	89	73	.549	1	663	587	.266	.979	3.23
ATLANTA	82	80	.506	8	643	699	.257	.977	3.75
CINCINNATI	79	83	.488	11	586	581	.241	.984	3.35
HOUSTON	79	83	.488	11	585	567	.240	.983	3.13
SAN DIEGO	61	100	.379	28.5	486	610	.233	.974	3.23
					7601	7601	.252	.979	3.47

BATTING AVERAGE
Joe Torre STL .... .363
Ralph Garr ATL .... .343
Glenn Beckert CHI .... .342

HITS
Joe Torre STL 230
Ralph Garr ATL 219
Lou Brock STL 200

DOUBLES
Cesar Cedeno HOU 40
Lou Brock STL 37
two tied at 34

TRIPLES
Joe Morgan HOU 11
Roger Metzger HOU 11
Willie Davis LA 10

HOME RUNS
Willie Stargell PIT 48
Hank Aaron ATL 47
Lee May CIN 39

RUNS BATTED IN
Joe Torre STL 137
Willie Stargell PIT 125
Hank Aaron ATL 118

SLUGGING AVERAGE
Hank Aaron ATL .... .669
Willie Stargell PIT .... .628
Joe Torre STL .... .555

STOLEN BASES
Lou Brock STL 64
Joe Morgan HOU 40
Ralph Garr ATL 30

RUNS SCORED
Lou Brock STL 126
Bobby Bonds SF 110
Willie Stargell PIT 104

WINS
Ferguson Jenkins CHI 24
three tied at 20

WINNING PERCENTAGE
Don Gullett CIN .... .727
Steve Carlton STL .... .690
Al Downing LA .... .690

EARNED RUN AVERAGE
Tom Seaver NY 1.76
Dave Roberts SD 2.10
Don Wilson HOU 2.45

STRIKEOUTS
Tom Seaver NY 289
Ferguson Jenkins CHI 263
Bill Stoneman MON 251

SAVES
Dave Giusti PIT 30
Mike Marshall MON 23
Jim Brewer LA 22

COMPLETE GAMES
Ferguson Jenkins CHI 30
Tom Seaver NY 21
two tied at 20

SHUTOUTS
four tied at 5

GAMES PITCHED
Wayne Granger CIN 70
Jerry Johnson SF 67
Mike Marshall MON 66

INNINGS PITCHED
Ferguson Jenkins CHI 325
Bill Stoneman MON 295
Tom Seaver NY 286

1972 AL

EAST	W	L	PCT	GB	R	OR	BA	FA	ERA
DETROIT	86	70	.551	—	558	514	.237	.984	2.96
BOSTON	85	70	.548	.5	640	620	.248	.978	3.47
BALTIMORE	80	74	.519	5	519	430	.229	.983	2.54
NEW YORK	79	76	.510	6.5	557	527	.249	.978	3.05
CLEVELAND	72	84	.462	14	472	519	.234	.981	2.97
MILWAUKEE	65	91	.417	21	493	595	.235	.977	3.45

WEST	W	L	PCT	GB	R	OR	BA	FA	ERA
★OAKLAND	93	62	.600	—	604	457	.240	.979	2.58
CHICAGO	87	67	.565	5.5	566	538	.238	.977	3.12
MINNESOTA	77	77	.500	15.5	537	535	.244	.974	2.86
KANSAS CITY	76	78	.494	16.5	580	545	.255	.980	3.24
CALIFORNIA	75	80	.484	18	454	533	.242	.981	3.06
TEXAS	54	100	.351	38.5	461	628	.217	.972	3.53
					6441	6441	.239	.979	3.07

BATTING AVERAGE
Rod Carew MIN .... .318
Lou Piniella KC .... .312
two tied at .... .308

HITS
Joe Rudi OAK 181
Lou Piniella KC 179
Bobby Murcer NY 171

DOUBLES
Lou Piniella KC 33
Joe Rudi OAK 32
Bobby Murcer NY 30

TRIPLES
Joe Rudi OAK 9
Carlton Fisk BOS 9
Paul Blair BAL 8

HOME RUNS
Dick Allen CHI 37
Bobby Murcer NY 33
two tied at 26

RUNS BATTED IN
Dick Allen CHI 113
John Mayberry KC 100
Bobby Murcer NY 96

SLUGGING AVERAGE
Dick Allen CHI .... .603
Carlton Fisk BOS .... .538
Bobby Murcer NY .... .537

STOLEN BASES
Bert Campaneris OAK 52
Dave Nelson TEX 51
Freddie Patek KC 33

RUNS SCORED
Bobby Murcer NY 102
Joe Rudi OAK 94
Tommy Harper BOS 92

WINS
Wilbur Wood CHI 24
Gaylord Perry CLE 24
Mickey Lolich DET 22

WINNING PERCENTAGE
Catfish Hunter OAK .... .750
Blue Moon Odom OAK .... .714
Luis Tiant BOS .... .714

EARNED RUN AVERAGE
Luis Tiant BOS 1.91
Gaylord Perry CLE 1.92
Catfish Hunter OAK 2.04

STRIKEOUTS
Nolan Ryan CAL 329
Mickey Lolich DET 250
Gaylord Perry CLE 234

SAVES
Sparky Lyle NY 35
Terry Forster CHI 29
Rollie Fingers OAK 21

COMPLETE GAMES
Gaylord Perry CLE 29
Mickey Lolich DET 23
two tied at 20

SHUTOUTS
Nolan Ryan CAL 9
Wilbur Wood CHI 8
Mel Stottlemyre NY 7

GAMES PITCHED
Paul Lindblad TEX 66
Rollie Fingers OAK 65
Wayne Granger MIN 63

INNINGS PITCHED
Wilbur Wood CHI 377
Gaylord Perry CLE 343
Mickey Lolich DET 327

1972 NL

EAST	W	L	PCT	GB	R	OR	BA	FA	ERA
PITTSBURGH	96	59	.619	—	691	512	.274	.978	2.81
CHICAGO	85	70	.548	11	685	567	.257	.979	3.22
NEW YORK	83	73	.532	13.5	528	578	.225	.980	3.27
ST. LOUIS	75	81	.481	21.5	568	600	.260	.977	3.42
MONTREAL	70	86	.449	26.5	513	609	.234	.978	3.60
PHILADELPHIA	59	97	.378	37.5	503	635	.236	.981	3.67

WEST	W	L	PCT	GB	R	OR	BA	FA	ERA
CINCINNATI	95	59	.617	—	707	557	.251	.982	3.21
HOUSTON	84	69	.549	10.5	708	636	.258	.980	3.77
LOS ANGELES	85	70	.548	10.5	584	527	.256	.974	2.78
ATLANTA	70	84	.455	25	628	730	.258	.974	4.27
SAN FRANCISCO	69	86	.445	26.5	662	649	.244	.974	3.70
SAN DIEGO	58	95	.379	36.5	488	665	.227	.976	3.78
					7265	7265	.248	.978	3.46

BATTING AVERAGE
Billy Williams CHI .... .333
Ralph Garr ATL .... .325
Cesar Cedeno HOU .... .320

HITS
Pete Rose CIN 198
Lou Brock STL 193
Billy Williams CHI 191

DOUBLES
Cesar Cedeno HOU 39
Willie Montanez PHI........... 39
Ted Simmons STL............... 36

TRIPLES
Larry Bowa PHI 13
Pete Rose CIN 11
three tied at 8

HOME RUNS
Johnny Bench CIN 40
Nate Colbert SD 38
Billy Williams CHI 37

RUNS BATTED IN
Johnny Bench CIN 125
Billy Williams CHI.............. 122
Willie Stargell PIT 112

SLUGGING AVERAGE
Billy Williams CHI .... .606
Willie Stargell PIT............ .558
Johnny Bench CIN .... .541

STOLEN BASES
Lou Brock STL 63
Joe Morgan CIN................. 58
Cesar Cedeno HOU 55

RUNS SCORED
Joe Morgan CIN 122
Bobby Bonds SF 118
Jimmy Wynn HOU 117

WINS
Steve Carlton PHI 27
Tom Seaver NY 21
two tied at 20

WINNING PERCENTAGE
Gary Nolan CIN................. .750
Steve Carlton PHI .... .730
Milt Pappas CHI .... .708

EARNED RUN AVERAGE
Steve Carlton PHI 1.97
Gary Nolan CIN................ 1.99
Don Sutton LA.................. 2.08

STRIKEOUTS
Steve Carlton PHI 310
Tom Seaver NY 249
Bob Gibson STL................ 208

SAVES
Clay Carroll CIN 37
Tug McGraw NY 27
Dave Giusti PIT 22

COMPLETE GAMES
Steve Carlton PHI 30
Ferguson Jenkins CHI........ 23
Bob Gibson STL................. 23

SHUTOUTS
Don Sutton LA...................... 9
Steve Carlton PHI 8
Fred Norman SD 6

GAMES PITCHED
Mike Marshall MON............ 65
Clay Carroll CIN 65
Pedro Borbon CIN.............. 62

INNINGS PITCHED
Steve Carlton PHI 346
Ferguson Jenkins CHI...... 289
Phil Niekro ATL 282

1973 AL

EAST	W	L	PCT	GB	R	OR	BA	FA	ERA
BALTIMORE	97	65	.599	—	754	561	.266	.981	3.07
BOSTON	89	73	.549	8	738	647	.267	.979	3.65
DETROIT	85	77	.525	12	642	674	.254	.982	3.90
NEW YORK	80	82	.494	17	641	610	.261	.976	3.34
MILWAUKEE	74	88	.457	23	708	731	.253	.977	3.98
CLEVELAND	71	91	.438	26	680	826	.256	.978	4.58

WEST	W	L	PCT	GB	R	OR	BA	FA	ERA
★OAKLAND	94	68	.580	—	758	615	.260	.978	3.29
KANSAS CITY	88	74	.543	6	755	752	.261	.974	4.21
MINNESOTA	81	81	.500	13	738	692	.270	.978	3.77
CALIFORNIA	79	83	.488	15	629	657	.253	.975	3.57
CHICAGO	77	85	.475	17	652	705	.256	.977	3.86
TEXAS	57	105	.352	37	619	844	.255	.974	4.64
					8314	8314	.259	.977	3.82

BATTING AVERAGE
Rod Carew MIN .350
George Scott MIL .306
Tommy Davis BAL .306

HITS
Rod Carew MIN 203
Dave May MIL 189
Bobby Murcer NY 187

DOUBLES
Sal Bando OAK 32
Pedro Garcia MIL 32
three tied at 30

TRIPLES
Rod Carew MIN 11
Al Bumbry BAL 11
Jorge Orta CHI 10

HOME RUNS
Reggie Jackson OAK 32
Frank Robinson CAL 30
Jeff Burroughs TEX 30

RUNS BATTED IN
Reggie Jackson OAK 117
George Scott MIL 107
John Mayberry KC 100

SLUGGING AVERAGE
Reggie Jackson OAK .531
Sal Bando OAK .498
Frank Robinson CAL .489

STOLEN BASES
Tommy Harper BOS 54
Billy North OAK 53
Dave Nelson TEX 43

RUNS SCORED
Reggie Jackson OAK 99
three tied at 98

WINS
Wilbur Wood CHI 24
Joe Coleman DET 23
Jim Palmer BAL 22

WINNING PERCENTAGE
Catfish Hunter OAK .808
Jim Palmer BAL .710
Vida Blue OAK .690

EARNED RUN AVERAGE
Jim Palmer BAL 2.40
Bert Blyleven MIN 2.52
Bill Lee BOS 2.74

STRIKEOUTS
Nolan Ryan CAL 383
Bert Blyleven MIN 258
Bill Singer CAL 241

SAVES
John Hiller DET 38
Sparky Lyle NY 27
Rollie Fingers OAK 22

COMPLETE GAMES
Gaylord Perry CLE 29
Nolan Ryan CAL 26
Bert Blyleven MIN 25

SHUTOUTS
Bert Blyleven MIN 9
Gaylord Perry CLE 7
Jim Palmer BAL 6

GAMES PITCHED
John Hiller DET 65
Rollie Fingers OAK 62
Doug Bird KC 54

INNINGS PITCHED
Wilbur Wood CHI 359
Gaylord Perry CLE 344
Nolan Ryan CAL 326

1973 NL

EAST	W	L	PCT	GB	R	OR	BA	FA	ERA
● NEW YORK	82	79	.509	—	608	588	.246	.980	3.27
ST. LOUIS	81	81	.500	1.5	643	603	.259	.975	3.25
PITTSBURGH	80	82	.494	2.5	704	693	.261	.976	3.74
MONTREAL	79	83	.488	3.5	668	702	.251	.974	3.73
CHICAGO	77	84	.478	5	614	655	.247	.975	3.66
PHILADELPHIA	71	91	.438	11.5	642	717	.249	.979	4.00

WEST	W	L	PCT	GB	R	OR	BA	FA	ERA
CINCINNATI	99	63	.611	—	741	621	.254	.982	3.43
LOS ANGELES	95	66	.590	3.5	675	565	.263	.981	3.00
SAN FRANCISCO	88	74	.543	11	739	702	.262	.974	3.79
HOUSTON	82	80	.506	17	681	672	.251	.981	3.78
ATLANTA	76	85	.472	22.5	799	774	.266	.974	4.25
SAN DIEGO	60	102	.370	39	548	770	.244	.973	4.16
					8062	8062	.254	.977	3.67

BATTING AVERAGE
Pete Rose CIN .... .338
Cesar Cedeno HOU .... .320
Garry Maddox SF .... .319

HITS
Pete Rose CIN 230
Ralph Garr ATL 200
Lou Brock STL 193

DOUBLES
Willie Stargell PIT 43
Al Oliver PIT 38
three tied at 36

TRIPLES
Roger Metzger HOU 14
Garry Maddox SF 10
Gary Matthews SF 10

HOME RUNS
Willie Stargell PIT 44
Davey Johnson ATL 43
Darrell Evans ATL 41

RUNS BATTED IN
Willie Stargell PIT 119
Lee May HOU 105
two tied at 104

SLUGGING AVERAGE
Willie Stargell PIT .... .646
Darrell Evans ATL .... .556
Davey Johnson ATL .... .546

STOLEN BASES
Lou Brock STL 70
Joe Morgan CIN 67
Cesar Cedeno HOU 56

RUNS SCORED
Bobby Bonds SF 131
Joe Morgan CIN 116
Pete Rose CIN 115

WINS
Ron Bryant SF 24
Tom Seaver NY 19
Jack Billingham CIN 19

WINNING PERCENTAGE
Tommy John LA .... .696
Don Gullett CIN .... .692
Ron Bryant SF .... .667

EARNED RUN AVERAGE
Tom Seaver NY 2.08
Don Sutton LA 2.42
Wayne Twitchell PHI 2.50

STRIKEOUTS
Tom Seaver NY 251
Steve Carlton PHI 223
Jon Matlack NY 205

SAVES
Mike Marshall MON 31
Tug McGraw NY 25
two tied at 20

COMPLETE GAMES
Tom Seaver NY 18
Steve Carlton PHI 18
Jack Billingham CIN 16

SHUTOUTS
Jack Billingham CIN 7
Dave Roberts HOU 6
two tied at 5

GAMES PITCHED
Mike Marshall MON 92
Pedro Borbon CIN 80
Elias Sosa SF 71

INNINGS PITCHED
Steve Carlton PHI 293
Jack Billingham CIN 293
Tom Seaver NY 290

1974 AL

EAST	W	L	PCT	GB	R	OR	BA	FA	ERA
BALTIMORE	91	71	.562	—	659	612	.256	.980	3.27
NEW YORK	89	73	.549	2	671	623	.263	.977	3.32
BOSTON	84	78	.519	7	696	661	.264	.977	3.72
CLEVELAND	77	85	.475	14	662	694	.255	.977	3.80
MILWAUKEE	76	86	.469	15	647	660	.244	.980	3.77
DETROIT	72	90	.444	19	620	768	.247	.975	4.17

WEST	W	L	PCT	GB	R	OR	BA	FA	ERA
★OAKLAND	90	72	.556	—	689	551	.247	.977	2.95
TEXAS	84	76	.525	5	690	698	.272	.974	3.82
MINNESOTA	82	80	.506	8	673	669	.272	.976	3.64
CHICAGO	80	80	.500	9	684	721	.268	.977	3.94
KANSAS CITY	77	85	.475	13	667	662	.259	.976	3.51
CALIFORNIA	68	94	.420	22	618	657	.254	.977	3.52
					7976	7976	.258	.977	3.62

BATTING AVERAGE
Rod Carew MIN.............. .364
Jorge Orta CHI .... .316
Hal McRae KC .... .310

HITS
Rod Carew MIN................ 218
Tommy Davis BAL............ 181
Don Money MIL................ 178

DOUBLES
Joe Rudi OAK 39
George Scott MIL 36
Hal McRae KC 36

TRIPLES
Mickey Rivers CAL 11
Amos Otis KC.................... 9

HOME RUNS
Dick Allen CHI 32
Reggie Jackson OAK 29
Gene Tenace OAK 26

RUNS BATTED IN
Jeff Burroughs TEX 118
Sal Bando OAK 103
Joe Rudi OAK 99

SLUGGING AVERAGE
Dick Allen CHI .... .563
Reggie Jackson OAK ...... .514
Jeff Burroughs TEX......... .504

STOLEN BASES
Billy North OAK 54
Rod Carew MIN................ 38
John Lowenstein CLE 36

RUNS SCORED
Carl Yastrzemski BOS........ 93
Bobby Grich BAL................ 92
Reggie Jackson OAK 90

WINS
Catfish Hunter OAK............ 25
Ferguson Jenkins TEX........ 25
four tied at 22

WINNING PERCENTAGE
Mike Cuellar BAL .... .688
Catfish Hunter OAK......... .676
Ferguson Jenkins TEX.... .676

EARNED RUN AVERAGE
Catfish Hunter OAK......... 2.49
Gaylord Perry CLE........... 2.52
Andy Hassler CAL............ 2.61

STRIKEOUTS
Nolan Ryan CAL 367
Bert Blyleven MIN 249
Ferguson Jenkins TEX..... 225

SAVES
Terry Forster CHI.............. 24
Tom Murphy MIL 20
Bill Campbell MIN.............. 19

COMPLETE GAMES
Ferguson Jenkins TEX........ 29
Gaylord Perry CLE 28
Mickey Lolich DET 27

SHUTOUTS
Luis Tiant BOS 7
Catfish Hunter OAK............. 6
Ferguson Jenkins TEX......... 6

GAMES PITCHED
Rollie Fingers OAK.............. 76
Tom Murphy MIL 70
Steve Foucault TEX 69

INNINGS PITCHED
Nolan Ryan CAL 333
Ferguson Jenkins TEX..... 328
Gaylord Perry CLE 322

1974 NL

EAST	W	L	PCT	GB	R	OR	BA	FA	ERA
PITTSBURGH	88	74	.543	—	751	657	.274	.975	3.49
ST. LOUIS	86	75	.534	1.5	677	643	.265	.977	3.48
PHILADELPHIA	80	82	.494	8	676	701	.261	.976	3.92
MONTREAL	79	82	.491	8.5	662	657	.254	.976	3.60
NEW YORK	71	91	.438	17	572	646	.235	.975	3.42
CHICAGO	66	96	.407	22	669	826	.251	.969	4.28

WEST	W	L	PCT	GB	R	OR	BA	FA	ERA
LOS ANGELES	102	60	.630	—	798	561	.272	.975	2.97
CINCINNATI	98	64	.605	4	776	631	.260	.979	3.42
ATLANTA	88	74	.543	14	661	563	.249	.979	3.05
HOUSTON	81	81	.500	21	653	632	.263	.982	3.48
SAN FRANCISCO	72	90	.444	30	634	723	.252	.972	3.80
SAN DIEGO	60	102	.370	42	541	830	.229	.973	4.61
					8070	8070	.255	.976	3.62

BATTING AVERAGE
Ralph Garr ATL .... .353
Al Oliver PIT .... .321
Two tied at .... .314

HITS
Ralph Garr ATL 214
Dave Cash PHI 206
Steve Garvey LA 200

DOUBLES
Pete Rose CIN 45
Al Oliver PIT 38
Johnny Bench CIN 38

TRIPLES
Ralph Garr ATL 17
Al Oliver PIT 12
Dave Cash PHI 11

HOME RUNS
Mike Schmidt PHI 36
Johnny Bench CIN 33
Jimmy Wynn LA 32

RUNS BATTED IN
Johnny Bench CIN 129
Mike Schmidt PHI 116
Steve Garvey LA 111

SLUGGING AVERAGE
Mike Schmidt PHI ...... .546
Willie Stargell PIT .... .537
Reggie Smith STL .... .528

STOLEN BASES
Lou Brock STL 118
Davey Lopes LA 59
Joe Morgan CIN 58

RUNS SCORED
Pete Rose CIN 110
Mike Schmidt PHI 108
Johnny Bench CIN 108

WINS
Phil Niekro ATL 20
Andy Messersmith LA 20
two tied at 19

WINNING PERCENTAGE
Andy Messersmith LA ..... .769
Don Sutton LA .... .679
Buzz Capra ATL .... .667

EARNED RUN AVERAGE
Buzz Capra ATL 2.28
Phil Niekro ATL 2.38
Jon Matlack NY 2.41

STRIKEOUTS
Steve Carlton PHI 240
Andy Messersmith LA 221
Tom Seaver NY 201

SAVES
Mike Marshall LA 21
Randy Moffitt SF 15
Pedro Borbon CIN 14

COMPLETE GAMES
Phil Niekro ATL 18
Steve Carlton PHI 17
Jim Lonborg PHI 16

SHUTOUTS
Jon Matlack NY 7
Phil Niekro ATL 6

GAMES PITCHED
Mike Marshall LA 106
Larry Hardy SD 76
Pedro Borbon CIN 73

INNINGS PITCHED
Phil Niekro ATL 302
Andy Messersmith LA 292
Steve Carlton PHI 291

1975 AL

EAST	W	L	PCT	GB	R	OR	BA	FA	ERA
● BOSTON	95	65	.594	—	796	709	.275	.977	3.99
BALTIMORE	90	69	.566	4.5	682	553	.252	.983	3.17
NEW YORK	83	77	.519	12	681	588	.264	.978	3.29
CLEVELAND	79	80	.497	15.5	688	703	.261	.978	3.84
MILWAUKEE	68	94	.420	28	675	793	.250	.971	4.34
DETROIT	57	102	.358	37.5	570	786	.249	.972	4.29

WEST	W	L	PCT	GB	R	OR	BA	FA	ERA
OAKLAND	98	64	.605	—	758	606	.254	.977	3.29
KANSAS CITY	91	71	.562	7	710	649	.261	.976	3.49
TEXAS	79	83	.488	19	714	733	.256	.971	3.90
MINNESOTA	76	83	.478	20.5	724	736	.271	.973	4.05
CHICAGO	75	86	.466	22.5	655	707	.255	.978	3.93
CALIFORNIA	72	89	.447	25.5	628	723	.246	.971	3.89
					8281	8281	.258	.975	3.79

BATTING AVERAGE
Rod Carew MIN	.359
Fred Lynn BOS	.331
Thurman Munson NY	.318

HITS
George Brett KC	195
Rod Carew MIN	192
Thurman Munson NY	190

DOUBLES
Fred Lynn BOS	47
Reggie Jackson OAK	39
three tied at	38

TRIPLES
Mickey Rivers CAL	13
George Brett KC	13
Jorge Orta CHI	10

HOME RUNS
George Scott MIL	36
Reggie Jackson OAK	36
John Mayberry KC	34

RUNS BATTED IN
George Scott MIL	109
John Mayberry KC	106
Fred Lynn BOS	105

SLUGGING AVERAGE
Fred Lynn BOS	.566
John Mayberry KC	.547
George Scott MIL	.515

STOLEN BASES
Mickey Rivers CAL	70
C. Washington OAK	40
Amos Otis KC	39

RUNS SCORED
Fred Lynn BOS	103
John Mayberry KC	95
Bobby Bonds NY	93

WINS
Jim Palmer BAL	23
Catfish Hunter NY	23
Vida Blue OAK	22

WINNING PERCENTAGE
Mike Torrez BAL	.690
Dennis Leonard KC	.682
Jim Palmer BAL	.676

EARNED RUN AVERAGE
Jim Palmer BAL	2.09
Catfish Hunter NY	2.58
Dennis Eckersley CLE	2.60

STRIKEOUTS
Frank Tanana CAL	269
Bert Blyleven MIN	233
G. Perry CLE, TEX	233

SAVES
Goose Gossage CHI	26
Rollie Fingers OAK	24
Tom Murphy MIL	20

COMPLETE GAMES
Catfish Hunter NY	30
Jim Palmer BAL	25
Gaylord Perry CLE, TEX	25

SHUTOUTS
Jim Palmer BAL	10
Catfish Hunter NY	7

GAMES PITCHED
Rollie Fingers OAK	75
Paul Lindblad OAK	68
Goose Gossage CHI	62

INNINGS PITCHED
Catfish Hunter NY	328
Jim Palmer BAL	323
G. Perry CLE, TEX	306

1975 NL

EAST	W	L	PCT	GB	R	OR	BA	FA	ERA
PITTSBURGH	92	69	.571	—	712	565	.263	.976	3.02
PHILADELPHIA	86	76	.531	6.5	735	694	.269	.976	3.82
NEW YORK	82	80	.506	10.5	646	625	.256	.976	3.39
ST. LOUIS	82	80	.506	10.5	662	689	.273	.973	3.58
CHICAGO	75	87	.463	17.5	712	827	.259	.972	4.57
MONTREAL	75	87	.463	17.5	601	690	.244	.973	3.73

WEST	W	L	PCT	GB	R	OR	BA	FA	ERA
★ CINCINNATI	108	54	.667	—	840	586	.271	.984	3.37
LOS ANGELES	88	74	.543	20	648	534	.248	.979	2.92
SAN FRANCISCO	80	81	.497	27.5	659	671	.259	.976	3.74
SAN DIEGO	71	91	.438	37	552	683	.244	.971	3.51
ATLANTA	67	94	.416	40.5	583	739	.244	.972	3.93
HOUSTON	64	97	.398	43.5	664	711	.254	.979	4.05
					8014	8014	.257	.976	3.63

BATTING AVERAGE
Bill Madlock CHI .... .354
Ted Simmons STL .... .332
Manny Sanguillen PIT ..... .328

HITS
Dave Cash PHI 213
Steve Garvey LA 210
Pete Rose CIN 210

DOUBLES
Pete Rose CIN 47
Dave Cash PHI 40
two tied at 39

TRIPLES
Ralph Garr ATL 11
four tied at 10

HOME RUNS
Mike Schmidt PHI 38
Dave Kingman NY 36
Greg Luzinski PHI 34

RUNS BATTED IN
Greg Luzinski PHI 120
Johnny Bench CIN 110
Tony Perez CIN 109

SLUGGING AVERAGE
Dave Parker PIT .... .541
Greg Luzinski PHI .... .540
Mike Schmidt PHI .... .523

STOLEN BASES
Davey Lopes LA 77
Joe Morgan CIN 67
Lou Brock STL 56

RUNS SCORED
Pete Rose CIN 112
Dave Cash PHI 111
Davey Lopes LA 108

WINS
Tom Seaver NY 22
Randy Jones SD 20
Andy Messersmith LA 19

WINNING PERCENTAGE
Don Gullet CIN .... .789
Tom Seaver NY .... .710
Burt Hooton CHI, LA .... .667

EARNED RUN AVERAGE
Randy Jones SD 2.24
Andy Messersmith LA 2.29
Tom Seaver NY 2.38

STRIKEOUTS
Tom Seaver NY 243
John Montefusco SF 215
Andy Messersmith LA 213

SAVES
Rawley Eastwick CIN 22
Al Hrabosky STL 22
Dave Giusti PIT 17

COMPLETE GAMES
Andy Messersmith LA 19
Randy Jones SD 18
two tied at 15

SHUTOUTS
Andy Messersmith LA 7
Randy Jones SD 6
Jerry Reuss PIT 6

GAMES PITCHED
Gene Garber PHI 71
Will McEnaney CIN 70
two tied at 67

INNINGS PITCHED
Andy Messersmith LA 322
Randy Jones SD 285
Tom Seaver NY 280

1976 AL

EAST	W	L	PCT	GB	R	OR	BA	FA	ERA
● NEW YORK	97	62	.610	—	730	575	.269	.980	3.19
BALTIMORE	88	74	.543	10.5	619	598	.243	.982	3.31
BOSTON	83	79	.512	15.5	716	660	.263	.978	3.52
CLEVELAND	81	78	.509	16	615	615	.263	.980	3.48
DETROIT	74	87	.460	24	609	709	.257	.974	3.87
MILWAUKEE	66	95	.410	32	570	655	.246	.975	3.64

WEST	W	L	PCT	GB	R	OR	BA	FA	ERA
KANSAS CITY	90	72	.556	—	713	611	.269	.978	3.21
OAKLAND	87	74	.540	2.5	686	598	.246	.977	3.26
MINNESOTA	85	77	.525	5	743	704	.274	.973	3.72
CALIFORNIA	76	86	.469	14	550	631	.235	.977	3.36
TEXAS	76	86	.469	14	616	652	.250	.976	3.47
CHICAGO	64	97	.398	25.5	586	745	.255	.979	4.25
					7753	7753	.256	.977	3.52

BATTING AVERAGE
George Brett KC.............333
Hal McRae KC 332
Rod Carew MIN...............331

HITS
George Brett KC.............215
Rod Carew MIN...............200
Chris Chambliss NY 188

DOUBLES
Amos Otis KC...................40
four tied at 34

TRIPLES
George Brett KC................14
Phil Garner OAK 12
Rod Carew MIN.................12

HOME RUNS
Graig Nettles NY 32
Sal Bando OAK 27
Reggie Jackson BAL 27

RUNS BATTED IN
Lee May BAL....................109
Thurman Munson NY 105
Carl Yastrzemski BOS...... 102

SLUGGING AVERAGE
Reggie Jackson BAL 502
Jim Rice BOS...................482
Graig Nettles NY 475

STOLEN BASES
Billy North OAK 75
Ron LeFlore DET 58
Bert Campaneris OAK...... 54

RUNS SCORED
Roy White NY...................104
Rod Carew MIN................. 97
Mickey Rivers NY.............. 95

WINS
Jim Palmer BAL 22
Luis Tiant BOS 21
Wayne Garland BAL............ 20

WINNING PERCENTAGE
Bill Campbell MIN............773
Wayne Garland BAL.........741
Doc Ellis NY 680

EARNED RUN AVERAGE
Mark Fidrych DET 2.34
Vida Blue OAK 2.36
Frank Tanana CAL 2.44

STRIKEOUTS
Nolan Ryan CAL 327
Frank Tanana CAL 261
B. Blyleven MIN, TEX....... 219

SAVES
Sparky Lyle NY................. 23
Dave LaRoche CLE 21
two tied at..................... 20

COMPLETE GAMES
Mark Fidrych DET 24
Frank Tanana CAL 23
Jim Palmer BAL 23

SHUTOUTS
Nolan Ryan CAL 7
three tied at 6

GAMES PITCHED
Bill Campbell MIN............. 78
Rollie Fingers OAK............ 70
Paul Lindblad OAK............ 65

INNINGS PITCHED
Jim Palmer BAL 315
Catfish Hunter NY 299
Vida Blue OAK 298

1976 NL

EAST	W	L	PCT	GB	R	OR	BA	FA	ERA
PHILADELPHIA	101	61	.623	—	770	557	.272	.981	3.10
PITTSBURGH	92	70	.568	9	708	630	.267	.975	3.37
NEW YORK	86	76	.531	15	615	538	.246	.979	2.94
CHICAGO	75	87	.463	26	611	728	.251	.978	3.93
ST. LOUIS	72	90	.444	29	629	671	.260	.973	3.61
MONTREAL	55	107	.340	46	531	734	.235	.976	3.99

WEST	W	L	PCT	GB	R	OR	BA	FA	ERA
CINCINNATI	102	60	.630	—	857	633	.280	.984	3.51
LOS ANGELES	92	70	.568	10	608	543	.251	.980	3.02
HOUSTON	80	82	.494	22	625	657	.256	.978	3.55
SAN FRANCISCO	74	88	.457	28	595	686	.246	.971	3.53
SAN DIEGO	73	89	.451	29	570	662	.247	.978	3.65
ATLANTA	70	92	.432	32	620	700	.245	.973	3.87
					7739	7739	.255	.977	3.50

BATTING AVERAGE
Bill Madlock CHI .... .339
Ken Griffey CIN .... .336
Garry Maddox PHI .... .330

HITS
Pete Rose CIN 215
W. Montanez SF, ATL 206
Steve Garvey LA 200

DOUBLES
Pete Rose CIN 42
Jay Johnstone PHI 38
two tied at 37

TRIPLES
Dave Cash PHI 12
Cesar Geronimo CIN 11
two tied at 10

HOME RUNS
Mike Schmidt PHI 38
Dave Kingman NY 37
Rick Monday CHI 32

RUNS BATTED IN
George Foster CIN 121
Joe Morgan CIN 111
Mike Schmidt PHI 107

SLUGGING AVERAGE
Joe Morgan CIN .... .576
George Foster CIN .... .530
Mike Schmidt PHI .... .524

STOLEN BASES
Davey Lopes LA 63
Joe Morgan CIN 60
two tied at 58

RUNS SCORED
Pete Rose CIN 130
Joe Morgan CIN 113
Mike Schmidt PHI 112

WINS
Randy Jones SD 22
Jerry Koosman NY 21
Don Sutton LA 21

WINNING PERCENTAGE
Steve Carlton PHI .... .741
John Candelaria PIT .... .696
two tied at .... .677

EARNED RUN AVERAGE
John Denny STL 2.52
Doug Rau LA 2.57
Tom Seaver NY 2.59

STRIKEOUTS
Tom Seaver NY 235
J.R. Richard HOU 214
Jerry Koosman NY 200

SAVES
Rawley Eastwick CIN 26
Skip Lockwood NY 19
Ken Forsch HOU 19

COMPLETE GAMES
Randy Jones SD 25
Jerry Koosman NY 17
Jon Matlack NY 16

SHUTOUTS
Jon Matlack NY 6
John Montefusco SF 6
two tied at 5

GAMES PITCHED
Dale Murray MON 81
Charlie Hough LA 77
Butch Metzger SD 77

INNINGS PITCHED
Randy Jones SD 315
J.R. Richard HOU 291
two tied at 271

1977 AL

EAST	W	L	PCT	GB	R	OR	BA	FA	ERA
★NEW YORK	100	62	.617	—	831	651	.281	.979	3.61
BALTIMORE	97	64	.602	2.5	719	653	.261	.983	3.74
BOSTON	97	64	.602	2.5	859	712	.281	.978	4.16
DETROIT	74	88	.457	26	714	751	.264	.978	4.13
CLEVELAND	71	90	.441	28.5	676	739	.269	.979	4.10
MILWAUKEE	67	95	.414	33	639	765	.258	.978	4.32
TORONTO	54	107	.335	45.5	605	882	.252	.974	4.57

WEST	W	L	PCT	GB	R	OR	BA	FA	ERA
KANSAS CITY	102	60	.630	—	822	651	.277	.978	3.52
TEXAS	94	68	.580	8	767	657	.270	.982	3.56
CHICAGO	90	72	.556	12	844	771	.278	.974	4.25
MINNESOTA	84	77	.522	17.5	867	776	.282	.978	4.36
CALIFORNIA	74	88	.457	28	675	695	.255	.976	3.76
SEATTLE	64	98	.395	38	624	855	.256	.976	4.83
OAKLAND	63	98	.391	38.5	605	749	.240	.970	4.05
					10247	10247	.266	.977	4.07

BATTING AVERAGE
Rod Carew MIN .388
Lyman Bostock MIN .336
Ken Singleton BAL .328

HITS
Rod Carew MIN 239
Ron LeFlore DET 212
Jim Rice BOS 206

DOUBLES
Hal McRae KC 54
Reggie Jackson NY 39
two tied at 38

TRIPLES
Rod Carew MIN 16
Jim Rice BOS 15
Al Cowens KC 14

HOME RUNS
Jim Rice BOS 39
Graig Nettles NY 37
Bobby Bonds CAL 37

RUNS BATTED IN
Larry Hisle MIN 119
Bobby Bonds CAL 115
Jim Rice BOS 114

SLUGGING AVERAGE
Jim Rice BOS .593
Rod Carew MIN .570
Reggie Jackson NY .550

STOLEN BASES
Freddie Patek KC 53
Mike Page OAK 42
two tied at 41

RUNS SCORED
Rod Carew MIN 128
Carlton Fisk BOS 106
George Brett KC 105

WINS
Jim Palmer BAL 20
Dave Goltz MIN 20
Dennis Leonard KC 20

WINNING PERCENTAGE
Paul Splittorff KC .727
Ron Guidry NY .696
Tom Johnson MIN .696

EARNED RUN AVERAGE
Frank Tanana CAL 2.54
Bert Blyleven TEX 2.72
Nolan Ryan CAL 2.77

STRIKEOUTS
Nolan Ryan CAL 341
Dennis Leonard KC 244
Frank Tanana CAL 205

SAVES
Bill Campbell BOS 31
Sparky Lyle NY 26
Lerrin LaGrow CHI 25

COMPLETE GAMES
Jim Palmer BAL 22
Nolan Ryan CAL 22
two tied at 21

SHUTOUTS
Frank Tanana CAL 7
three tied at 5

GAMES PITCHED
Sparky Lyle NY 72
Tom Johnson MIN 71
Bill Campbell BOS 69

INNINGS PITCHED
Jim Palmer BAL 319
Dave Goltz MIN 303
Nolan Ryan CAL 299

1977 NL

EAST	W	L	PCT	GB	R	OR	BA	FA	ERA
PHILADELPHIA	101	61	.623	—	847	668	.279	.981	3.71
PITTSBURGH	96	66	.593	5	734	665	.274	.977	3.61
ST. LOUIS	83	79	.512	18	737	688	.270	.978	3.81
CHICAGO	81	81	.500	20	692	739	.266	.977	4.01
MONTREAL	75	87	.463	26	665	736	.260	.980	4.01
NEW YORK	64	98	.395	37	587	663	.244	.978	3.77

WEST	W	L	PCT	GB	R	OR	BA	FA	ERA
LOS ANGELES	98	64	.605	—	769	582	.266	.981	3.22
CINCINNATI	88	74	.543	10	802	725	.274	.984	4.22
HOUSTON	81	81	.500	17	680	650	.254	.978	3.54
SAN FRANCISCO	75	87	.463	23	673	711	.253	.972	3.75
SAN DIEGO	69	93	.426	29	692	834	.249	.971	4.43
ATLANTA	61	101	.377	37	678	895	.254	.972	4.85
					8556	8556	.262	.977	3.91

BATTING AVERAGE
Dave Parker PIT .338
Garry Templeton STL .322
George Foster CIN .320

HITS
Dave Parker PIT 215
Pete Rose CIN 204
Garry Templeton STL 200

DOUBLES
Dave Parker PIT 44
Dave Cash MON 42
two tied at 41

TRIPLES
Garry Templeton STL 18
three tied at 11

HOME RUNS
George Foster CIN 52
Jeff Burroughs ATL 41
Greg Luzinski PHI 39

RUNS BATTED IN
George Foster CIN 149
Greg Luzinski PHI 130
Steve Garvey LA 115

SLUGGING AVERAGE
George Foster CIN .631
Greg Luzinski PHI .594
Reggie Smith LA .576

STOLEN BASES
Frank Taveras PIT 70
Cesar Cedeno HOU 61
Gene Richards SD 56

RUNS SCORED
George Foster CIN 124
Ken Griffey CIN 117
Mike Schmidt PHI 114

WINS
Steve Carlton PHI 23
Tom Seaver NY, CIN 21
four tied at 20

WINNING PERCENTAGE
John Candelaria PIT .800
Tom Seaver NY, CIN .778
Larry Christenson PHI .760

EARNED RUN AVERAGE
John Candelaria PIT 2.34
Tom Seaver NY, CIN 2.58
Burt Hooton LA 2.62

STRIKEOUTS
Phil Niekro ATL 262
J.R. Richard HOU 214
Steve Rogers MON 206

SAVES
Rollie Fingers SD 35
Bruce Sutter CHI 31
Goose Gossage PIT 26

COMPLETE GAMES
Phil Niekro ATL 20
Tom Seaver NY, CIN 19
two tied at 17

SHUTOUTS
Tom Seaver NY, CIN 7
Rick Reuschel CHI 4
Steve Rogers MON 4

GAMES PITCHED
Rollie Fingers SD 78
Dan Spillner SD 76
Dave Tomlin SD 76

INNINGS PITCHED
Phil Niekro ATL 330
Steve Rogers MON 302
Steve Carlton PHI 283

1978 AL

EAST	W	L	PCT	GB	R	OR	BA	FA	ERA
★NEW YORK*	100	63	.613	—	735	582	.267	.982	3.18
BOSTON	99	64	.607	1	796	657	.267	.977	3.54
MILWAUKEE	93	69	.574	6.5	804	650	.276	.977	3.65
BALTIMORE	90	71	.559	9	659	633	.258	.982	3.56
DETROIT	86	76	.531	13.5	714	653	.271	.981	3.64
CLEVELAND	69	90	.434	29	639	694	.261	.980	3.97
TORONTO	59	102	.366	40	590	775	.250	.979	4.55

WEST	W	L	PCT	GB	R	OR	BA	FA	ERA
KANSAS CITY	92	70	.568	—	743	634	.268	.976	3.44
CALIFORNIA	87	75	.537	5	691	666	.259	.978	3.65
TEXAS	87	75	.537	5	692	632	.253	.976	3.42
MINNESOTA	73	89	.451	19	666	678	.267	.977	3.69
CHICAGO	71	90	.441	20.5	634	731	.264	.977	4.22
OAKLAND	69	93	.426	23	532	690	.245	.971	3.62
SEATTLE	56	104	.350	35	614	834	.248	.978	4.72
* Defeated Boston in a 1-game playoff					9509	9509	.261	.978	3.77

BATTING AVERAGE
Rod Carew MIN.............. .333
Al Oliver TEX................. .324
Jim Rice BOS................. .315

HITS
Jim Rice BOS 213
Ron LeFlore DET 198
Rod Carew MIN.............. 188

DOUBLES
George Brett KC.............. 45
Carlton Fisk BOS 39
Hal McRae KC 39

TRIPLES
Jim Rice BOS.................. 15
Rod Carew MIN................ 10
Dan Ford MIN.................. 10

HOME RUNS
Jim Rice BOS.................. 46
Larry Hisle MIL 34
Don Baylor CAL 34

RUNS BATTED IN
Jim Rice BOS.................. 139
Rusty Staub DET 121
Larry Hisle MIL 115

SLUGGING AVERAGE
Jim Rice BOS................. .600
Larry Hisle MIL .... .533
Doug DeCinces BAL .... .526

STOLEN BASES
Ron LeFlore DET 68
Julio Cruz SEA 59
Bump Wills TEX 52

RUNS SCORED
Ron LeFlore DET 126
Jim Rice BOS................. 121
Don Baylor CAL 103

WINS
Ron Guidry NY 25
Mike Caldwell MIL............ 22
two tied at........................ 21

WINNING PERCENTAGE
Ron Guidry NY .... .893
Bob Stanley BOS .... .882
Larry Gura KC .... .800

EARNED RUN AVERAGE
Ron Guidry NY 1.74
Jon Matlack TEX 2.27
Mike Caldwell MIL 2.36

STRIKEOUTS
Nolan Ryan CAL 260
Ron Guidry NY 248
Dennis Leonard KC.......... 183

SAVES
Goose Gossage NY 27
Dave LaRoche CAL 25
Don Stanhouse BAL......... 24

COMPLETE GAMES
Mike Caldwell MIL............ 23
Dennis Leonard KC.......... 20
Jim Palmer BAL 19

SHUTOUTS
Ron Guidry NY 9
Mike Caldwell MIL............ 6
Jim Palmer BAL 6

GAMES PITCHED
Bob Lacey OAK................ 74
Dave Heaverlo OAK 69
Elias Sosa OAK................ 68

INNINGS PITCHED
Jim Palmer BAL 296
Dennis Leonard KC.......... 295
Mike Caldwell MIL............ 293

1978 NL

EAST	W	L	PCT	GB	R	OR	BA	FA	ERA
PHILADELPHIA	90	72	.556	—	708	586	.258	.983	3.33
PITTSBURGH	88	73	.547	1.5	684	637	.257	.973	3.41
CHICAGO	79	83	.488	11	664	724	.264	.978	4.05
MONTREAL	76	86	.469	14	633	611	.254	.979	3.42
ST. LOUIS	69	93	.426	21	600	657	.249	.978	3.58
NEW YORK	66	96	.407	24	607	690	.245	.979	3.87

WEST	W	L	PCT	GB	R	OR	BA	FA	ERA
LOS ANGELES	95	67	.586	—	727	573	.264	.978	3.12
CINCINNATI	92	69	.571	2.5	710	688	.256	.978	3.81
SAN FRANCISCO	89	73	.549	6	613	594	.248	.977	3.30
SAN DIEGO	84	78	.519	11	591	598	.252	.975	3.28
HOUSTON	74	88	.457	21	605	634	.258	.978	3.63
ATLANTA	69	93	.426	26	600	750	.244	.975	4.08
					7742	7742	.254	.978	3.58

BATTING AVERAGE
Dave Parker PIT .... .334
Steve Garvey LA .... .316
Jose Cruz HOU .... .315

HITS
Steve Garvey LA 202
Pete Rose CIN 198
Enos Cabell HOU 195

DOUBLES
Pete Rose CIN 51
Jack Clark SF 46
Ted Simmons STL 40

TRIPLES
Garry Templeton STL 13
Dave Parker PIT 12
Gene Richards SD 12

HOME RUNS
George Foster CIN 40
Greg Luzinski PHI 35
Dave Parker PIT 30

RUNS BATTED IN
George Foster CIN 120
Dave Parker PIT 117
Steve Garvey LA 113

SLUGGING AVERAGE
Dave Parker PIT .... .585
Reggie Smith LA .... .559
George Foster CIN .... .546

STOLEN BASES
Omar Moreno PIT 71
Frank Taveras PIT 46
Davey Lopes LA 45

RUNS SCORED
Ivan DeJesus CHI 104
Pete Rose CIN 103
Dave Parker PIT 102

WINS
Gaylord Perry SD 21
Ross Grimsley MON 20
two tied at 19

WINNING PERCENTAGE
Gaylord Perry SD .... .778
Burt Hooton LA .... .655
Ross Grimsley MON .... .645

EARNED RUN AVERAGE
Craig Swan NY 2.43
Steve Rogers MON 2.47
Pete Vuckovich STL 2.55

STRIKEOUTS
J.R. Richard HOU 303
Phil Niekro ATL 248
Tom Seaver CIN 226

SAVES
Rollie Fingers SD 37
Kent Tekulve PIT 31
Doug Bair CIN 28

COMPLETE GAMES
Phil Niekro ATL 22
Ross Grimsley MON 19
two tied at 16

SHUTOUTS
Bob Knepper SF 6
four tied at 4

GAMES PITCHED
Kent Tekulve PIT 91
Mark Littell STL 72
Donnie Moore CHI 71

INNINGS PITCHED
Phil Niekro ATL 334
J.R. Richard HOU 275
Ross Grimsley MON 263

1979 AL

EAST	W	L	PCT	GB	R	OR	BA	FA	ERA
● BALTIMORE	102	57	.642	—	757	582	.261	.980	3.26
MILWAUKEE	95	66	.590	8	807	722	.280	.980	4.03
BOSTON	91	69	.569	11.5	841	711	.283	.977	4.03
NEW YORK	89	71	.556	13.5	734	672	.266	.981	3.83
DETROIT	85	76	.528	18	770	738	.269	.981	4.26
CLEVELAND	81	80	.503	22	760	805	.258	.978	4.57
TORONTO	53	109	.327	50.5	613	862	.251	.975	4.82

WEST	W	L	PCT	GB	R	OR	BA	FA	ERA
CALIFORNIA	88	74	.543	—	866	768	.282	.978	4.34
KANSAS CITY	85	77	.525	3	851	816	.282	.977	4.44
TEXAS	83	79	.512	5	750	698	.278	.979	3.86
MINNESOTA	82	80	.506	6	764	725	.278	.979	4.1
CHICAGO	73	87	.456	14	730	748	.275	.972	4.1
SEATTLE	67	95	.414	21	711	820	.269	.978	4.5
OAKLAND	54	108	.333	34	573	860	.239	.972	4.75
					10527	10527	.270	.978	4.2

BATTING AVERAGE
Fred Lynn BOS .... .333
George Brett KC .... .329
Brian Downing CAL .... .326

HITS
George Brett KC 212
Jim Rice BOS 201
Buddy Bell TEX 200

DOUBLES
Cecil Cooper MIL 44
Chet Lemon CHI 44
three tied at 42

TRIPLES
George Brett KC 20
Paul Molitor MIL 16
two tied at 13

HOME RUNS
Gorman Thomas MIL 45
Fred Lynn BOS 39
Jim Rice BOS 39

RUNS BATTED IN
Don Baylor CAL 139
Jim Rice BOS 130
Gorman Thomas MIL 123

SLUGGING AVERAGE
Fred Lynn BOS .... .637
Jim Rice BOS .... .596
Sixto Lezcano MIL .... .573

STOLEN BASES
Willie Wilson KC 83
Ron LeFlore DET 78
Julio Cruz SEA 49

RUNS SCORED
Don Baylor CAL 120
George Brett KC 119
Jim Rice BOS 117

WINS
Mike Flanagan BAL 23
Tommy John NY 21
Jerry Koosman MIN 20

WINNING PERCENTAGE
Mike Caldwell MIL .... .727
Mike Flanagan BAL .... .719
Jack Morris DET .... .708

EARNED RUN AVERAGE
Ron Guidry NY 2.78
Tommy John NY 2.97
Dennis Eckersley BOS 2.99

STRIKEOUTS
Nolan Ryan CAL 223
Ron Guidry NY 20
Mike Flanagan BAL 19

SAVES
Mike Marshall MIN 32
Jim Kern TEX 29
two tied at 2

COMPLETE GAMES
Dennis Martinez BAL 18
three tied at 1

SHUTOUTS
Dennis Leonard KC ....
Mike Flanagan BAL ....
Nolan Ryan CAL ....

GAMES PITCHED
Mike Marshall MIN 90
Sid Monge CLE 7
Jim Kern TEX 7

INNINGS PITCHED
Dennis Martinez BAL 29
Tommy John NY 27
Mike Flanagan BAL 26

1979 NL

EAST	W	L	PCT	GB	R	OR	BA	FA	ERA
PITTSBURGH	98	64	.605	—	775	643	.272	.979	3.41
MONTREAL	95	65	.594	2	701	581	.264	.979	3.14
ST. LOUIS	86	76	.531	12	731	693	.278	.980	3.72
PHILADELPHIA	84	78	.519	14	683	718	.266	.983	4.16
CHICAGO	80	82	.494	18	706	707	.269	.975	3.88
NEW YORK	63	99	.389	35	593	706	.250	.978	3.84

WEST	W	L	PCT	GB	R	OR	BA	FA	ERA
CINCINNATI	90	71	.559	—	731	644	.264	.980	3.58
HOUSTON	89	73	.549	1.5	583	582	.256	.978	3.19
LOS ANGELES	79	83	.488	11.5	739	717	.263	.981	3.83
SAN FRANCISCO	71	91	.438	19.5	672	751	.246	.974	4.16
SAN DIEGO	68	93	.422	22	603	681	.242	.978	3.69
ATLANTA	66	94	.413	23.5	669	763	.256	.970	4.18
					8186	8186	.261	.978	3.73

BATTING AVERAGE
Keith Hernandez STL...... .344
Pete Rose PHI .331
Ray Knight CIN .... .318

HITS
Garry Templeton STL 211
Keith Hernandez STL....... 210
Pete Rose PHI 208

DOUBLES
Keith Hernandez STL......... 48
Warren Cromartie MON 46
Dave Parker PIT................. 45

TRIPLES
Garry Templeton STL 19
three tied at 12

HOME RUNS
Dave Kingman CHI 48
Mike Schmidt PHI.............. 45
Dave Winfield SD 34

RUNS BATTED IN
Dave Winfield SD 118
Dave Kingman CHI........... 115
Mike Schmidt PHI.............. 114

SLUGGING AVERAGE
Dave Kingman CHI .... .613
Mike Schmidt PHI............ .564
Dave Winfield SD .... .558

STOLEN BASES
Omar Moreno PIT 77
Billy North SF 58
two tied at.......................... 44

RUNS SCORED
Keith Hernandez STL 116
Omar Moreno PIT............. 110
three tied at 109

WINS
Phil Niekro ATL 21
Joe Niekro HOU 21
three tied at 18

WINNING PERCENTAGE
Tom Seaver CIN.............. .727
Joe Niekro HOU .... .656
Silvio Martinez STL .... .652

EARNED RUN AVERAGE
J.R. Richard HOU 2.71
Tom Hume CIN................. 2.76
Dan Schatzeder MON 2.83

STRIKEOUTS
J.R. Richard HOU 313
Steve Carlton PHI 213
Phil Niekro ATL 208

SAVES
Bruce Sutter CHI............... 37
Kent Tekulve PIT............... 31
Gene Garber ATL............... 25

COMPLETE GAMES
Phil Niekro ATL 23
J.R. Richard HOU 19
two tied at.......................... 13

SHUTOUTS
Tom Seaver CIN.................. 5
Steve Rogers MON 5
Joe Niekro HOU 5

GAMES PITCHED
Kent Tekulve PIT............... 94
Enrique Romo PIT............. 84
Grant Jackson PIT 72

INNINGS PITCHED
Phil Niekro ATL 342
J.R. Richard HOU 292
Joe Niekro HOU 264

1980 AL

EAST	W	L	PCT	GB	R	OR	BA	FA	ERA
NEW YORK	103	59	.636	—	820	662	.267	.978	3.58
BALTIMORE	100	62	.617	3	805	640	.273	.985	3.64
MILWAUKEE	86	76	.531	17	811	682	.275	.977	3.71
BOSTON	83	77	.519	19	757	767	.283	.977	4.38
DETROIT	84	78	.519	19	830	757	.273	.979	4.25
CLEVELAND	79	81	.494	23	738	807	.277	.983	4.68
TORONTO	67	95	.414	36	624	762	.251	.979	4.19

WEST	W	L	PCT	GB	R	OR	BA	FA	ERA
●KANSAS CITY	97	65	.599	—	809	694	.286	.978	3.83
OAKLAND	83	79	.512	14	686	642	.259	.979	3.46
MINNESOTA	77	84	.478	19.5	670	724	.265	.977	3.93
TEXAS	76	85	.472	20.5	756	752	.284	.977	4.02
CHICAGO	70	90	.438	26	587	722	.259	.973	3.92
CALIFORNIA	65	95	.406	31	698	797	.265	.978	4.52
SEATTLE	59	103	.364	38	610	793	.248	.977	4.38
					10201	10201	.269	.978	4.03

BATTING AVERAGE
George Brett KC.............. .390
Cecil Cooper MIL .... .352
Miguel Dilone CLE .... .341

HITS
Willie Wilson KC............... 230
Cecil Cooper MIL 219
Mickey Rivers TEX........... 210

DOUBLES
Robin Yount MIL................ 49
Al Oliver TEX..................... 43
Jim Morrison CHI 40

TRIPLES
Willie Wilson KC................ 15
Alfredo Griffin TOR............ 15
two tied at........................ 11

HOME RUNS
Reggie Jackson NY............ 41
Ben Oglivie MIL 41
Gorman Thomas MIL 38

RUNS BATTED IN
Cecil Cooper MIL 122
George Brett KC............... 118
Ben Oglivie MIL............... 118

SLUGGING AVERAGE
George Brett KC.............. .664
Reggie Jackson NY.......... .597
Ben Oglivie MIL............... .563

STOLEN BASES
R. Henderson OAK 100
Willie Wilson KC................ 79
Miguel Dilone CLE 61

RUNS SCORED
Willie Wilson KC.............. 133
Robin Yount MIL.............. 121
Al Bumbry BAL................ 118

WINS
Steve Stone BAL................ 25
Tommy John NY................. 22
Mike Norris OAK 22

WINNING PERCENTAGE
Steve Stone BAL.............. .781
Rudy May NY .... .750
Scott McGregor BAL .... .714

EARNED RUN AVERAGE
Rudy May NY 2.47
Mike Norris OAK 2.54
Britt Burns CHI 2.84

STRIKEOUTS
Len Barker CLE................ 187
Mike Norris OAK 180
Ron Guidry NY................. 166

SAVES
Dan Quisenberry KC 33
Goose Gossage NY 33
Ed Farmer CHI 30

COMPLETE GAMES
Rick Langford OAK 28
Mike Norris OAK 24
Matt Keough OAK 20

SHUTOUTS
Tommy John NY 6
Geoff Zahn MIN 5
three tied at 4

GAMES PITCHED
Dan Quisenberry KC 75
Doug Corbett MIN 73
two tied at......................... 67

INNINGS PITCHED
Rick Langford OAK 290
Mike Norris OAK 284
Larry Gura KC.................. 283

1980 NL

EAST	W	L	PCT	GB	R	OR	BA	FA	ERA
PHILADELPHIA	91	71	.562	—	728	639	.270	.979	3.43
MONTREAL	90	72	.556	1	694	629	.257	.977	3.48
PITTSBURGH	83	79	.512	8	666	646	.266	.978	3.58
ST. LOUIS	74	88	.457	17	738	710	.275	.981	3.93
NEW YORK	67	95	.414	24	611	702	.257	.975	3.85
CHICAGO	64	98	.395	27	614	728	.251	.974	3.89

WEST	W	L	PCT	GB	R	OR	BA	FA	ERA
HOUSTON*	93	70	.571	—	637	589	.261	.978	3.10
LOS ANGELES	92	71	.564	1	663	591	.263	.981	3.24
CINCINNATI	89	73	.549	3.5	707	670	.262	.983	3.85
ATLANTA	81	80	.503	11	630	660	.250	.975	3.77
SAN FRANCISCO	75	86	.466	17	573	634	.244	.975	3.46
SAN DIEGO	73	89	.451	19.5	591	654	.255	.980	3.65
					7852	7852	.259	.978	3.60

*Defeated Los Angeles in a 1-game playoff

BATTING AVERAGE
Bill Buckner CHI 324
Keith Hernandez STL 321
Garry Templeton STL 319

HITS
Steve Garvey LA 200
Gene Richards SD 193
Keith Hernandez STL 191

DOUBLES
Pete Rose PHI 42
Bill Buckner CHI 41
Andre Dawson MON 41

TRIPLES
Rodney Scott MON 13
Omar Moreno PIT 13
two tied at 11

HOME RUNS
Mike Schmidt PHI 48
Bob Homer ATL 35
Dale Murphy ATL 33

RUNS BATTED IN
Mike Schmidt PHI 121
George Hendrick STL 109
Steve Garvey LA 106

SLUGGING AVERAGE
Mike Schmidt PHI .... .624
Jack Clark SF .... .517
Dale Murphy ATL .... .510

STOLEN BASES
Ron LeFlore MON 97
Omar Moreno PIT 96
Dave Collins CIN 79

RUNS SCORED
Keith Hernandez STL 111
Mike Schmidt PHI 104
Dale Murphy ATL 98

WINS
Steve Carlton PHI 24
Joe Niekro HOU 20
Jim Bibby PIT 19

WINNING PERCENTAGE
Jim Bibby PIT .... .760
Jerry Reuss LA .... .750
Steve Carlton PHI .... .727

EARNED RUN AVERAGE
Don Sutton LA 2.21
Steve Carlton PHI 2.34
Jerry Reuss LA 2.52

STRIKEOUTS
Steve Carlton PHI 286
Nolan Ryan HOU 200
Mario Soto CIN 182

SAVES
Bruce Sutter CHI 28
Tom Hume CIN 25
Rollie Fingers SD 23

COMPLETE GAMES
Steve Rogers MON 14
Steve Carlton PHI 13
two tied at 11

SHUTOUTS
Jerry Reuss LA 6
J.R. Richard HOU 4
Steve Rogers MON 4

GAMES PITCHED
Dick Tidrow CHI 84
Tom Hume CIN 78
Kent Tekulve PIT 78

INNINGS PITCHED
Steve Carlton PHI 304
Steve Rogers MON 281
Phil Niekro ATL 275

1981 AL

EAST	W	L	PCT	GB	R	OR	BA	FA	ERA
MILWAUKEE**	62	47	.569	—	493	459	.257	.982	3.91
BALTIMORE	59	46	.562	1	429	437	.251	.983	3.70
●NEW YORK*†	59	48	.551	2	421	343	.252	.982	2.90
DETROIT	60	49	.550	2	427	404	.256	.984	3.53
BOSTON	59	49	.546	2.5	519	481	.275	.979	3.81
CLEVELAND	52	51	.505	7	431	442	.263	.978	3.88
TORONTO	37	69	.349	23.5	329	466	.226	.975	3.82

WEST	W	L	PCT	GB	R	OR	BA	FA	ERA
OAKLAND*†	64	45	.587	—	458	403	.247	.980	3.30
TEXAS	57	48	.543	5	452	389	.270	.984	3.40
CHICAGO	54	52	.509	8.5	476	423	.272	.979	3.47
KANSAS CITY**	50	53	.485	11	397	405	.267	.982	3.56
CALIFORNIA	51	59	.464	13.5	476	453	.256	.977	3.70
SEATTLE	44	65	.404	20	426	521	.251	.979	4.23
MINNESOTA	41	68	.376	23	378	486	.240	.978	3.98
					6112	6112	.256	.980	3.66

BATTING AVERAGE
Carney Lansford BOS ..... .336
Tom Paciorek SEA .... .326
Cecil Cooper MIL .... .320

HITS
R. Henderson OAK 135
Carney Lansford BOS 134
two tied at 133

DOUBLES
Cecil Cooper MIL 35
Al Oliver TEX 29
Tom Paciorek SEA 28

TRIPLES
John Castino MIN 9
four tied at 7

HOME RUNS
four tied at 22

RUNS BATTED IN
Eddie Murray BAL 78
Tony Armas OAK 76
Ben Oglivie MIL 72

SLUGGING AVERAGE
Bobby Grich CAL .... .543
Eddie Murray BAL .... .534
Dwight Evans BOS .... .522

STOLEN BASES
Rickey Henderson OAK 56
Julio Cruz SEA 43
Ron LeFlore CHI 36

RUNS SCORED
Rickey Henderson OAK 89
Dwight Evans BOS 84
Cecil Cooper MIL 70

WINS
four tied at 14

WINNING PERCENTAGE
Pete Vuckovich MIL .... .778
Mike Torrez BOS .... .769
Dennis Martinez BAL .... .737

EARNED RUN AVERAGE
Steve McCatty OAK 2.32
Sammy Stewart BAL 2.33
Dennis Lamp CHI 2.41

STRIKEOUTS
Len Barker CLE 127
Britt Burns CHI 108
two tied at 107

SAVES
Rollie Fingers MIL 28
Goose Gossage NY 20
Dan Quisenberry KC 18

COMPLETE GAMES
Rick Langford OAK 18
Steve McCatty OAK 16
Jack Morris DET 15

SHUTOUTS
four tied at 4

GAMES PITCHED
Doug Corbett MIN 54
Rollie Fingers MIL 47
Shane Rawley SEA 46

INNINGS PITCHED
Dennis Leonard KC 202
Jack Morris DET 198
Rick Langford OAK 195

1981 NL

EAST	W	L	PCT	GB	R	OR	BA	FA	ERA
ST. LOUIS	59	43	.578	—	464	417	.265	.981	3.63
MONTREAL**†	60	48	.556	2	443	394	.246	.980	3.30
PHILADELPHIA*	59	48	.551	2.5	491	472	.273	.980	4.05
PITTSBURGH	46	56	.451	13	407	425	.257	.979	3.56
NEW YORK	41	62	.398	18.5	348	432	.248	.968	3.55
CHICAGO	38	65	.369	21.5	370	483	.236	.974	4.01

WEST	W	L	PCT	GB	R	OR	BA	FA	ERA
CINCINNATI	66	42	.611	—	464	440	.267	.981	3.73
LOS ANGELES*†	63	47	.573	4	450	356	.262	.980	3.01
HOUSTON**	61	49	.555	6	394	331	.257	.980	2.66
SAN FRANCISCO	56	55	.505	11.5	427	414	.250	.977	3.28
ATLANTA	50	56	.472	15	395	416	.243	.976	3.45
SAN DIEGO	41	69	.373	26	382	455	.256	.977	3.72
					5035	5035	.255	.978	3.49

*Winner of first half **Winner of second half †Winner of playoff

---

BATTING AVERAGE
Bill Madlock PIT .... .341
Pete Rose PHI .... .325
Dusty Baker LA .... .320

HITS
Pete Rose PHI 140
Bill Buckner CHI 131
Dave Concepcion CIN 129

DOUBLES
Bill Buckner CHI 35
Ruppert Jones SD 34
Dave Concepcion CIN 28

TRIPLES
Craig Reynolds HOU 12
Gene Richards SD 12
Tommy Herr STL 9

HOME RUNS
Mike Schmidt PHI 31
Andre Dawson MON 24
two tied at 22

RUNS BATTED IN
Mike Schmidt PHI 91
George Foster CIN 90
Bill Buckner CHI 75

SLUGGING AVERAGE
Mike Schmidt PHI .... .664
Andre Dawson MON .... .553
George Foster CIN .... .519

STOLEN BASES
Tim Raines MON 71
Omar Moreno PIT 39
Rodney Scott MON 30

RUNS SCORED
Mike Schmidt PHI 78
Pete Rose PHI 73
Andre Dawson MON 71

WINS
Tom Seaver CIN 14
Steve Carlton PHI 13
F. Valenzuela LA 13

WINNING PERCENTAGE
Tom Seaver CIN .... .875
Steve Carlton PHI .... .765
Jerry Reuss LA .... .714

EARNED RUN AVERAGE
Nolan Ryan HOU 1.69
Bob Knepper HOU 2.18
Burt Hooton LA 2.28

STRIKEOUTS
F. Valenzuela LA 180
Steve Carlton PHI 179
Mario Soto CIN 151

SAVES
Bruce Sutter STL 25
Greg Minton SF 21
Neil Allen NY 18

COMPLETE GAMES
F. Valenzuela LA 11
Mario Soto CIN 10
Steve Carlton PHI 10

SHUTOUTS
Fernando Valenzuela LA 8
Bob Knepper HOU 5
Burt Hooton LA 4

GAMES PITCHED
Gary Lucas SD 57
Greg Minton SF 55
two tied at 51

INNINGS PITCHED
F. Valenzuela LA 192
Steve Carlton PHI 190
Mario Soto CIN 175

1982 AL

EAST	W	L	PCT	GB	R	OR	BA	FA	ERA
● MILWAUKEE	95	67	.586	—	891	717	.279	.980	3.98
BALTIMORE	94	68	.580	1	774	687	.266	.984	3.99
BOSTON	89	73	.549	6	753	713	.274	.981	4.03
DETROIT	83	79	.512	12	729	685	.266	.981	3.80
NEW YORK	79	83	.488	16	709	716	.256	.979	3.99
CLEVELAND	78	84	.481	17	683	748	.262	.980	4.11
TORONTO	78	84	.481	17	651	701	.262	.978	3.95

WEST	W	L	PCT	GB	R	OR	BA	FA	ERA
CALIFORNIA	93	69	.574	—	814	670	.274	.983	3.82
KANSAS CITY	90	72	.556	3	784	717	.285	.979	4.08
CHICAGO	87	75	.537	6	786	710	.273	.976	3.87
SEATTLE	76	86	.469	17	651	712	.254	.978	3.88
OAKLAND	68	94	.420	25	691	819	.236	.974	4.54
TEXAS	64	98	.395	29	590	749	.249	.981	4.28
MINNESOTA	60	102	.370	33	657	819	.257	.982	4.72
					10163	10163	.264	.980	4.07

BATTING AVERAGE
Willie Wilson KC .... .332
Robin Yount MIL .... .331
Rod Carew CAL .... .319

HITS
Robin Yount MIL 210
Cecil Cooper MIL 205
Paul Molitor MIL 201

DOUBLES
Robin Yount MIL 46
Hal McRae KC 46
Frank White KC 45

TRIPLES
Willie Wilson KC 15
Larry Herndon DET 13
Robin Yount MIL 12

HOME RUNS
Reggie Jackson CAL 39
Gorman Thomas MIL 39
Dave Winfield NY 37

RUNS BATTED IN
Hal McRae KC 133
Cecil Cooper MIL 121
Andre Thornton CLE 116

SLUGGING AVERAGE
Robin Yount MIL .... .578
Dave Winfield NY .... .560
Eddie Murray BAL .... .549

STOLEN BASES
R. Henderson OAK 130
Damaso Garcia TOR 54
Julio Cruz SEA 46

RUNS SCORED
Paul Molitor MIL 136
Robin Yount MIL 129
Dwight Evans BOS 122

WINS
LaMarr Hoyt CHI 19
three tied at 18

WINNING PERCENTAGE
Pete Vuckovich MIL .... .750
Jim Palmer BAL .... .750
Geoff Zahn CAL .... .692

EARNED RUN AVERAGE
Rick Sutcliffe CLE 2.96
Bob Stanley BOS 3.10
Jim Palmer BAL 3.13

STRIKEOUTS
Floyd Bannister SEA 209
Len Barker CLE 187
Dave Righetti NY 163

SAVES
Dan Quisenberry KC 35
Goose Gossage NY 30
Rollie Fingers MIL 29

COMPLETE GAMES
Dave Stieb TOR 19
Jack Morris DET 17
Rick Langford OAK 15

SHUTOUTS
Dave Stieb TOR 5
Geoff Zahn CAL 4
Ken Forsch CAL 4

GAMES PITCHED
Ed Vande Berg SEA 78
Tippy Martinez BAL 76
Dan Quisenberry KC 72

INNINGS PITCHED
Dave Stieb TOR 288
Jim Clancy TOR 267
Jack Morris DET 266

1982 NL

EAST	W	L	PCT	GB	R	OR	BA	FA	ERA
ST. LOUIS	92	70	.568	—	685	609	.264	.981	3.37
PHILADELPHIA	89	73	.549	3	664	654	.260	.981	3.61
MONTREAL	86	76	.531	6	697	616	.262	.980	3.31
PITTSBURGH	84	78	.519	8	724	696	.273	.977	3.81
CHICAGO	73	89	.451	19	676	709	.260	.979	3.92
NEW YORK	65	97	.401	27	609	723	.247	.972	3.88

WEST	W	L	PCT	GB	R	OR	BA	FA	ERA
ATLANTA	89	73	.549	—	739	702	.256	.979	3.82
LOS ANGELES	88	74	.543	1	691	612	.264	.979	3.26
SAN FRANCISCO	87	75	.537	2	673	687	.253	.973	3.64
SAN DIEGO	81	81	.500	8	675	658	.257	.976	3.52
HOUSTON	77	85	.475	12	569	620	.247	.978	3.41
CINCINNATI	61	101	.377	28	545	661	.251	.980	3.66
					7947	7947	.258	.978	3.60

BATTING AVERAGE
Al Oliver MON .... .331
Bill Madlock PIT .... .319
Leon Durham CHI .... .312

HITS
Al Oliver MON 204
Bill Buckner CHI 201
Andre Dawson MON 183

DOUBLES
Al Oliver MON 43
Terry Kennedy SD 42
Andre Dawson MON 37

TRIPLES
Dickie Thon HOU 10
three tied at 9

HOME RUNS
Dave Kingman NY 37
Dale Murphy ATL 36
Mike Schmidt PHI 35

RUNS BATTED IN
Dale Murphy ATL 109
Al Oliver MON 109
Bill Buckner CHI 105

SLUGGING AVERAGE
Mike Schmidt PHI............ .547
Pedro Guerrero LA.......... .536
Leon Durham CHI .... .521

STOLEN BASES
Tim Raines MON................ 78
Lonnie Smith STL.............. 68
Omar Moreno PIT 60

RUNS SCORED
Lonnie Smith STL............. 120
Dale Murphy ATL.............. 113
Mike Schmidt PHI............. 108

WINS
Steve Carlton PHI 23
Steve Rogers MON 19
F. Valenzuela LA 19

WINNING PERCENTAGE
Phil Niekro ATL .... .810
Steve Rogers MON .... .704
Steve Carlton PHI .... .676

EARNED RUN AVERAGE
Steve Rogers MON 2.40
Joe Niekro HOU 2.47
Joaquin Andujar STL....... 2.47

STRIKEOUTS
Steve Carlton PHI 286
Mario Soto CIN................. 274
Nolan Ryan HOU 245

SAVES
Bruce Sutter STL................ 36
Greg Minton SF................. 30
Gene Garber ATL............... 30

COMPLETE GAMES
Steve Carlton PHI 19
F. Valenzuela LA 18
Joe Niekro HOU 16

SHUTOUTS
Steve Carlton PHI 6
Joaquin Andujar STL............ 5
Joe Niekro HOU 5

GAMES PITCHED
Kent Tekulve PIT 85
Greg Minton SF................. 78
Rod Scurry PIT................... 76

INNINGS PITCHED
Steve Carlton PHI 296
F. Valenzuela LA 285
Steve Rogers MON 277

1983 AL

EAST	W	L	PCT	GB	R	OR	BA	FA	ERA
★BALTIMORE	98	64	.605	—	799	652	.269	.981	3.63
DETROIT	92	70	.568	6	789	679	.274	.980	3.80
NEW YORK	91	71	.562	7	770	703	.273	.978	3.85
TORONTO	89	73	.549	9	795	726	.277	.981	4.12
MILWAUKEE	87	75	.537	11	764	708	.277	.982	4.02
BOSTON	78	84	.481	20	724	775	.270	.979	4.34
CLEVELAND	70	92	.432	28	704	785	.265	.980	4.43

WEST	W	L	PCT	GB	R	OR	BA	FA	ERA
CHICAGO	99	63	.611	—	800	650	.262	.981	3.67
KANSAS CITY	79	83	.488	20	696	767	.271	.974	4.25
TEXAS	77	85	.475	22	639	609	.255	.982	3.31
OAKLAND	74	88	.457	25	708	782	.262	.974	4.35
CALIFORNIA	70	92	.432	29	722	779	.260	.977	4.31
MINNESOTA	70	92	.432	29	709	822	.261	.980	4.67
SEATTLE	60	102	.370	39	558	740	.240	.978	4.12
					10177	10177	.266	.979	4.06

BATTING AVERAGE
Wade Boggs BOS .... .361
Rod Carew CAL .... .339
Lou Whitaker DET .... .320

HITS
Cal Ripken BAL 211
Wade Boggs BOS 210
Lou Whitaker DET 206

DOUBLES
Cal Ripken BAL 47
Wade Boggs BOS 44
two tied at 42

TRIPLES
Robin Yount MIL 10
three tied at 9

HOME RUNS
Jim Rice BOS 39
Tony Armas BOS 36
Ron Kittle CHI 35

RUNS BATTED IN
Cecil Cooper MIL 126
Jim Rice BOS 126
Dave Winfield NY 116

SLUGGING AVERAGE
George Brett KC .... .563
Jim Rice BOS .... .550
Eddie Murray BAL .... .538

STOLEN BASES
R. Henderson OAK 108
Rudy Law CHI 77
Willie Wilson KC 59

RUNS SCORED
Cal Ripken BAL 121
Eddie Murray BAL 115
Cecil Cooper MIL 106

WINS
LaMarr Hoyt CHI 24
Rich Dotson CHI 22
Ron Guidry NY 21

WINNING PERCENTAGE
Rich Dotson CHI .... .759
Scott McGregor BAL .... .720
LaMarr Hoyt CHI .... .706

EARNED RUN AVERAGE
Rick Honeycutt TEX 2.42
Mike Boddicker BAL 2.77
Dave Stieb TOR 3.04

STRIKEOUTS
Jack Morris DET 232
Floyd Bannister CHI 193
Dave Stieb TOR 187

SAVES
Dan Quisenberry KC 45
Bob Stanley BOS 33
Ron Davis MIN 30

COMPLETE GAMES
Ron Guidry NY 21
Jack Morris DET................. 20
Dave Stieb TOR 14

SHUTOUTS
Mike Boddicker BAL 5
Britt Burns CHI 4
Dave Stieb TOR 4

GAMES PITCHED
Dan Quisenberry KC 69
Ed Vande Berg SEA........... 68
Ron Davis MIN 66

INNINGS PITCHED
Jack Morris DET 294
Dave Stieb TOR 278
Dan Petry DET 266

1983 NL

EAST	W	L	PCT	GB	R	OR	BA	FA	ERA
PHILADELPHIA	90	72	.556	—	696	635	.249	.976	3.34
PITTSBURGH	84	78	.519	6	659	648	.264	.982	3.55
MONTREAL	82	80	.506	8	677	646	.264	.981	3.58
ST. LOUIS	79	83	.488	11	679	710	.270	.976	3.79
CHICAGO	71	91	.438	19	701	719	.261	.982	4.07
NEW YORK	68	94	.420	22	575	680	.241	.976	3.68

WEST	W	L	PCT	GB	R	OR	BA	FA	ERA
LOS ANGELES	91	71	.562	—	654	609	.250	.974	3.10
ATLANTA	88	74	.543	3	746	640	.272	.978	3.67
HOUSTON	85	77	.525	6	643	646	.257	.977	3.45
SAN DIEGO	81	81	.500	10	653	653	.250	.979	3.62
SAN FRANCISCO	79	83	.488	12	687	697	.247	.973	3.70
CINCINNATI	74	88	.457	17	623	710	.239	.981	3.98
					7993	7993	.255	.978	3.63

BATTING AVERAGE
Bill Madlock PIT .... .323
Lonnie Smith STL .... .321
two tied at .... .318

HITS
Jose Cruz HOU 189
Andre Dawson MON 189
Rafael Ramirez ATL 185

DOUBLES
Al Oliver MON 38
Johnny Ray PIT................... 38
Bill Buckner CHI 38

TRIPLES
Brett Butler ATL 13
Omar Moreno HOU 11
two tied at........................... 10

HOME RUNS
Mike Schmidt PHI.............. 40
Dale Murphy ATL 36
two tied at.......................... 32

RUNS BATTED IN
Dale Murphy ATL 121
Andre Dawson MON 113
Mike Schmidt PHI............. 109

SLUGGING AVERAGE
Dale Murphy ATL .... .540
Andre Dawson MON .... .539
Pedro Guerrero LA .... .531

STOLEN BASES
Tim Raines MON................ 90
Alan Wiggins SD 66
Steve Sax LA 56

RUNS SCORED
Tim Raines MON.............. 133
Dale Murphy ATL 131
two tied at......................... 104

WINS
John Denny PHI 19
three tied at 17

WINNING PERCENTAGE
John Denny PHI .... .760
three tied at .... .652

EARNED RUN AVERAGE
Atlee Hammaker SF 2.25
John Denny PHI 2.37
Bob Welch LA 2.65

STRIKEOUTS
Steve Carlton PHI 275
Mario Soto CIN................. 242
Larry McWilliams PIT 199

SAVES
Lee Smith CHI 29
Al Holland PHI 25
Greg Minton SF................. 22

COMPLETE GAMES
Mario Soto CIN.................. 18
Steve Rogers MON 13
Bill Gullickson MON 10

SHUTOUTS
Steve Rogers MON 5
three tied at 4

GAMES PITCHED
Bill Campbell CHI 82
Kent Tekulve PIT 76
G. Hernandez CHI, PHI...... 74

INNINGS PITCHED
Steve Carlton PHI 284
Mario Soto CIN................. 274
Steve Rogers MON 273

1984 AL

EAST	W	L	PCT	GB	R	OR	BA	FA	ERA
★DETROIT	104	58	.642	—	829	643	.271	.979	3.49
TORONTO	89	73	.549	15	750	696	.273	.980	3.86
NEW YORK	87	75	.537	17	758	679	.276	.977	3.78
BOSTON	86	76	.531	18	810	764	.283	.977	4.18
BALTIMORE	85	77	.525	19	681	667	.252	.981	3.72
CLEVELAND	75	87	.463	29	761	766	.265	.977	4.25
MILWAUKEE	67	94	.416	36.5	641	734	.262	.978	4.06

WEST	W	L	PCT	GB	R	OR	BA	FA	ERA
KANSAS CITY	84	78	.519	—	673	686	.268	.979	3.91
CALIFORNIA	81	81	.500	3	696	697	.249	.980	3.96
MINNESOTA	81	81	.500	3	673	675	.265	.980	3.85
OAKLAND	77	85	.475	7	738	796	.259	.975	4.48
CHICAGO	74	88	.457	10	679	736	.247	.981	4.13
SEATTLE	74	88	.457	10	682	774	.258	.979	4.31
TEXAS	69	92	.429	14.5	656	714	.261	.977	3.91
					10027	10027	.264	.979	3.99

BATTING AVERAGE
Don Mattingly NY .... .343
Dave Winfield NY .... .340
Wade Boggs BOS .... .325

HITS
Don Mattingly NY 207
Wade Boggs BOS 203
Cal Ripken BAL 195

DOUBLES
Don Mattingly NY 44
Larry Parrish TEX 42
George Bell TOR 39

TRIPLES
Dave Collins TOR 15
Lloyd Moseby TOR 15
two tied at 10

HOME RUNS
Tony Armas BOS 43
Dave Kingman OAK 35
three tied at 33

RUNS BATTED IN
Tony Armas BOS 123
Jim Rice BOS 122
Dave Kingman OAK 118

SLUGGING AVERAGE
Harold Baines CHI .... .541
Don Mattingly NY .... .537
Dwight Evans BOS .... .532

STOLEN BASES
Rickey Henderson OAK 66
Dave Collins TOR 60
Brett Butler CLE 52

RUNS SCORED
Dwight Evans BOS 121
R. Henderson OAK 113
Wade Boggs BOS 109

WINS
Mike Boddicker BAL 20
Bert Blyleven CLE 19
Jack Morris DET 19

WINNING PERCENTAGE
Doyle Alexander TOR ..... .739
Bert Blyleven CLE .... .731
Dan Petry DET .... .692

EARNED RUN AVERAGE
Mike Boddicker BAL 2.79
Dave Stieb TOR 2.83
Bert Blyleven CLE 2.87

STRIKEOUTS
Mark Langston SEA 204
Dave Stieb TOR 198
Mike Witt CAL 196

SAVES
Dan Quisenberry KC 44
Bill Caudill OAK 36
G. Hernandez DET 32

COMPLETE GAMES
Charlie Hough TEX 17
Mike Boddicker BAL 16
Rich Dotson CHI 14

SHUTOUTS
Geoff Zahn CAL 5
Bob Ojeda BOS 5
two tied at 4

GAMES PITCHED
G. Hernandez DET 80
Dan Quisenberry KC 72
Aurelio Lopez DET 71

INNINGS PITCHED
Dave Stieb TOR 267
Charlie Hough TEX 266
Doyle Alexander TOR 262

1984 NL

EAST	W	L	PCT	GB	R	OR	BA	FA	ERA
CHICAGO	96	65	.596	—	762	658	.260	.981	3.75
NEW YORK	90	72	.556	6.5	652	676	.257	.979	3.60
ST. LOUIS	84	78	.519	12.5	652	645	.252	.982	3.58
PHILADELPHIA	81	81	.500	15.5	720	690	.266	.975	3.62
MONTREAL	78	83	.484	18	593	585	.251	.978	3.31
PITTSBURGH	75	87	.463	21.5	615	567	.255	.980	3.11

WEST	W	L	PCT	GB	R	OR	BA	FA	ERA
SAN DIEGO	92	70	.568	—	686	634	.259	.978	3.48
ATLANTA	80	82	.494	12	632	655	.247	.978	3.57
HOUSTON	80	82	.494	12	693	630	.264	.979	3.32
LOS ANGELES	79	83	.488	13	580	600	.244	.975	3.17
CINCINNATI	70	92	.432	22	627	747	.244	.977	4.16
SAN FRANCISCO	66	96	.407	26	682	807	.265	.973	4.39
					7894	7894	.255	.978	3.59

BATTING AVERAGE
Tony Gwynn SD .... .351
Lee Lacy PIT .... .321
Chili Davis SF .... .315

HITS
Tony Gwynn SD 213
Ryne Sandberg CHI 200
Tim Raines MON 192

DOUBLES
Johnny Ray PIT 38
Tim Raines MON 38
two tied at 36

TRIPLES
Juan Samuel PHI 19
Ryne Sandberg CHI 19
Jose Cruz HOU 13

HOME RUNS
Dale Murphy ATL 36
Mike Schmidt PHI 36
Gary Carter MON 27

RUNS BATTED IN
Gary Carter MON 106
Mike Schmidt PHI 106
Dale Murphy ATL 100

SLUGGING AVERAGE
Dale Murphy ATL .... .547
Mike Schmidt PHI .... .536
Ryne Sandberg CHI .... .520

STOLEN BASES
Tim Raines MON 75
Juan Samuel PHI 72
Alan Wiggins SD 70

RUNS SCORED
Ryne Sandberg CHI 114
Tim Raines MON 106
Alan Wiggins SD 106

WINS
Joaquin Andujar STL 20
Mario Soto CIN 18
Dwight Gooden NY 17

WINNING PERCENTAGE
Rick Sutcliffe CHI .... .941
Mario Soto CIN .... .720
Dwight Gooden NY .... .654

EARNED RUN AVERAGE
Alejandro Pena LA 2.48
Dwight Gooden NY 2.60
Orel Hershiser LA 2.66

STRIKEOUTS
Dwight Gooden NY 276
F. Valenzuela LA 240
Nolan Ryan HOU 197

SAVES
Bruce Sutter STL 45
Lee Smith CHI 33
Jesse Orosco NY 31

COMPLETE GAMES
Mario Soto CIN 13
F. Valenzuela LA 12
Joaquin Andujar STL 12

SHUTOUTS
Alejandro Pena LA 4
Joaquin Andujar STL 4
Orel Hershiser LA 4

GAMES PITCHED
Ted Power CIN 78
Gary Lavelle SF 77
Greg Minton SF 74

INNINGS PITCHED
Joaquin Andujar STL 261
F. Valenzuela LA 261
Joe Niekro HOU 248

1985 AL

EAST	W	L	PCT	GB	R	OR	BA	FA	ERA
TORONTO	99	62	.615	—	759	588	.269	.980	3.31
NEW YORK	97	64	.602	2	839	660	.267	.979	3.69
DETROIT	84	77	.522	15	729	688	.253	.977	3.78
BALTIMORE	83	78	.516	16	818	764	.263	.979	4.38
BOSTON	81	81	.500	18.5	800	720	.282	.977	4.06
MILWAUKEE	71	90	.441	28	690	802	.263	.977	4.39
CLEVELAND	60	102	.370	39.5	729	861	.265	.977	4.91

WEST	W	L	PCT	GB	R	OR	BA	FA	ERA
★KANSAS CITY	91	71	.562	—	687	639	.252	.980	3.49
CALIFORNIA	90	72	.556	1	732	703	.251	.982	3.91
CHICAGO	85	77	.525	6	736	720	.253	.982	4.07
MINNESOTA	77	85	.475	14	705	782	.264	.980	4.48
OAKLAND	77	85	.475	14	757	787	.264	.977	4.41
SEATTLE	74	88	.457	17	719	818	.255	.980	4.68
TEXAS	62	99	.385	28.5	617	785	.253	.980	4.56
					10317	10317	.261	.979	4.15

BATTING AVERAGE
Wade Boggs BOS .... .368
George Brett KC .... .335
Don Mattingly NY .... .324

HITS
Wade Boggs BOS 240
Don Mattingly NY 211
Bill Buckner BOS 201

DOUBLES
Don Mattingly NY 48
Bill Buckner BOS 46
Wade Boggs BOS 42

TRIPLES
Willie Wilson KC 21
Brett Butler CLE 14
Kirby Puckett MIN 13

HOME RUNS
Darrell Evans DET 40
Carlton Fisk CHI................. 37
Steve Balboni KC 36

RUNS BATTED IN
Don Mattingly NY 145
Eddie Murray BAL 124
Dave Winfield NY 114

SLUGGING AVERAGE
George Brett KC.............. .585
Don Mattingly NY .... .567
Jesse Barfield TOR .... .536

STOLEN BASES
Rickey Henderson NY 80
Gary Pettis CAL 56
Brett Butler CLE 47

RUNS SCORED
Rickey Henderson NY 146
Cal Ripken BAL 116
Eddie Murray BAL............. 111

WINS
Ron Guidry NY 22
Bret Saberhagen KC 20
two tied at.......................... 18

WINNING PERCENTAGE
Ron Guidry NY .... .786
Bret Saberhagen KC .... .769
Charlie Leibrandt KC........ .654

EARNED RUN AVERAGE
Dave Stieb TOR 2.48
Charlie Leibrandt KC......... 2.69
Bret Saberhagen KC......... 2.87

STRIKEOUTS
B. Blyleven CLE, MIN....... 206
Floyd Bannister CHI 198
Jack Morris DET............... 191

SAVES
Dan Quisenberry KC 37
Bob James CHI.................. 32
two tied at.......................... 31

COMPLETE GAMES
Bert Blyleven CLE, MIN 24
Charlie Hough TEX 14
Mike Moore SEA 14

SHUTOUTS
Bert Blyleven CLE, MIN 5
Jack Morris DET................... 4
Britt Burns CHI 4

GAMES PITCHED
Dan Quisenberry KC........... 84
Ed Vande Berg SEA........... 76
two tied at.......................... 74

INNINGS PITCHED
B. Blyleven CLE, MIN....... 294
Oil Can Boyd BOS 272
Dave Stieb TOR 265

1985 NL

EAST	W	L	PCT	GB	R	OR	BA	FA	ERA
ST. LOUIS	101	61	.623	—	747	572	.264	.983	3.10
NEW YORK	98	64	.605	3	695	568	.257	.982	3.11
MONTREAL	84	77	.522	16.5	633	636	.247	.981	3.55
CHICAGO	77	84	.478	23.5	686	729	.254	.979	4.16
PHILADELPHIA	75	87	.463	26	667	673	.245	.978	3.68
PITTSBURGH	57	104	.354	43.5	568	708	.247	.979	3.97

WEST	W	L	PCT	GB	R	OR	BA	FA	ERA
LOS ANGELES	95	67	.586	—	682	579	.261	.974	2.96
CINCINNATI	89	72	.553	5.5	677	666	.255	.980	3.71
HOUSTON	83	79	.512	12	706	691	.261	.976	3.66
SAN DIEGO	83	79	.512	12	650	622	.255	.980	3.41
ATLANTA	66	96	.407	29	632	781	.246	.976	4.19
SAN FRANCISCO	62	100	.383	33	556	674	.233	.976	3.61
					7899	7899	.252	.979	3.59

BATTING AVERAGE
Willie McGee STL .... .353
Pedro Guerrero LA.......... .320
Tim Raines MON .... .320

HITS
Willie McGee STL 216
Dave Parker CIN 198
Tony Gwynn SD 197

DOUBLES
Dave Parker CIN 42
Glenn Wilson PHI.............. 39
Tommy Herr STL 38

TRIPLES
Willie McGee STL 18
Juan Samuel PHI 13
Tim Raines MON 13

HOME RUNS
Dale Murphy ATL 37
Dave Parker CIN 34
two tied at......................... 33

RUNS BATTED IN
Dave Parker CIN 125
Dale Murphy ATL 111
Tommy Herr STL 110

SLUGGING AVERAGE
Pedro Guerrero LA.......... .577
Dave Parker CIN .... .551
Dale Murphy ATL .... .539

STOLEN BASES
Vince Coleman STL 110
Tim Raines MON................ 70
Willie McGee STL 56

RUNS SCORED
Dale Murphy ATL.............. 118
Tim Raines MON............... 115
Willie McGee STL.............. 114

WINS
Dwight Gooden NY 24
John Tudor STL 21
Joaquin Andujar STL.......... 21

WINNING PERCENTAGE
Orel Hershiser LA............. .864
Dwight Gooden NY .... .857
Bryn Smith MON .... .783

EARNED RUN AVERAGE
Dwight Gooden NY 1.53
John Tudor STL 1.93
Orel Heshiser LA............. 2.03

STRIKEOUTS
Dwight Gooden NY 268
Mario Soto CIN................. 214
Nolan Ryan HOU 209

SAVES
Jeff Reardon MON 41
Lee Smith CHI................... 33
two tied at......................... 27

COMPLETE GAMES
Dwight Gooden NY 16
F. Valenzuela LA 14
John Tudor STL 14

SHUTOUTS
John Tudor STL 10
Dwight Gooden NY 8
two tied at........................... 5

GAMES PITCHED
Tim Burke MON.................. 78
Mark Davis SF................... 77
Scott Garrelts SF............... 74

INNINGS PITCHED
Dwight Gooden NY 277
John Tudor STL 275
F. Valenzuela LA 272

1986 AL

EAST	W	L	PCT	GB	R	OR	BA	FA	ERA
● BOSTON	95	66	.590	—	794	696	.271	.979	3.93
NEW YORK	90	72	.556	5.5	797	738	.271	.979	4.11
DETROIT	87	75	.537	8.5	798	714	.263	.982	4.02
TORONTO	86	76	.531	9.5	809	733	.269	.984	4.08
CLEVELAND	84	78	.519	11.5	831	841	.284	.975	4.57
MILWAUKEE	77	84	.478	18	667	734	.255	.976	4.01
BALTIMORE	73	89	.451	22.5	708	760	.258	.978	4.30

WEST	W	L	PCT	GB	R	OR	BA	FA	ERA
CALIFORNIA	92	70	.568	—	786	684	.255	.983	3.84
TEXAS	87	75	.537	5	771	743	.267	.980	4.11
KANSAS CITY	76	86	.469	16	654	673	.252	.980	3.82
OAKLAND	76	86	.469	16	731	760	.252	.978	4.31
CHICAGO	72	90	.444	20	644	699	.247	.981	3.93
MINNESOTA	71	91	.438	21	741	839	.261	.980	4.77
SEATTLE	67	95	.414	25	718	835	.253	.975	4.65
					10449	10449	.262	.979	4.18

BATTING AVERAGE
Wade Boggs BOS .... .357
Don Mattingly NY .... .352
Kirby Puckett MIN .... .328

HITS
Don Mattingly NY 238
Kirby Pucket MIN 223
Tony Fernandez TOR 213

DOUBLES
Don Mattingly NY 53
Wade Boggs BOS 47
three tied at 39

TRIPLES
Brett Butler CLE 14
Ruben Sierra TEX 10
two tied at............................ 9

HOME RUNS
Jesse Barfield TOR 40
Dave Kingman OAK 35
Gary Gaetti MIN 34

RUNS BATTED IN
Joe Carter CLE 121
Jose Canseco OAK 117
Don Mattingly NY 113

SLUGGING AVERAGE
Don Mattingly NY .... .573
Jesse Barfield TOR .... .559
Kirby Puckett MIN .... .537

STOLEN BASES
Rickey Henderson NY 87
Gary Pettis CAL 50
John Cangelosi CHI 50

RUNS SCORED
Rickey Henderson NY 130
Kirby Puckett MIN............ 119
Don Mattingly NY 117

WINS
Roger Clemens BOS.......... 24
Jack Morris DET................ 21
Ted Higuera MIL................ 20

WINNING PERCENTAGE
Roger Clemens BOS....... .857
Dennis Rasmussen NY ... .750
Jack Morris DET.............. .724

EARNED RUN AVERAGE
Roger Clemens BOS....... 2.48
Ted Higuera MIL................ 2.79
Mike Witt CAL 2.84

STRIKEOUTS
Mark Langston SEA 245
Roger Clemens BOS........ 238
Jack Morris DET............... 223

SAVES
Dave Righetti NY 46
Don Aase BAL.................... 34
Tom Henke TOR 27

COMPLETE GAMES
Tom Candiotti CLE 17
Bert Blyleven MIN 16
two tied at.......................... 15

SHUTOUTS
Jack Morris DET.................. 6
Bruce Hurst BOS................ 4
Ted Higuera MIL.................. 4

GAMES PITCHED
Mitch Williams TEX 80
Dave Righetti NY 74
Greg Harris TEX................ 73

INNINGS PITCHED
Bert Blyleven MIN 272
Mike Witt CAL 269
Jack Morris DET............... 267

1986 NL

EAST	W	L	PCT	GB	R	OR	BA	FA	ERA
★NEW YORK	108	54	.667	—	783	578	.263	.978	3.11
PHILADELPHIA	86	75	.534	21.5	739	713	.253	.978	3.85
ST. LOUIS	79	82	.491	28.5	601	611	.236	.981	3.37
MONTREAL	78	83	.484	29.5	637	688	.254	.979	3.78
CHICAGO	70	90	.438	37	680	781	.256	.980	4.49
PITTSBURGH	64	98	.395	44	663	700	.250	.978	3.90

WEST	W	L	PCT	GB	R	OR	BA	FA	ERA
HOUSTON	96	66	.593	—	654	569	.255	.979	3.15
CINCINNATI	86	76	.531	10	732	717	.254	.978	3.91
SAN FRANCISCO	83	79	.512	13	698	618	.253	.977	3.33
SAN DIEGO	74	88	.457	22	656	723	.261	.978	3.99
LOS ANGELES	73	89	.451	23	638	679	.251	.971	3.76
ATLANTA	72	89	.447	23.5	615	719	.250	.978	3.97
					8096	8096	.253	.978	3.72

BATTING AVERAGE
Tim Raines MON............. .334
Steve Sax LA .... .332
Tony Gwynn SD .... .329

HITS
Tony Gwynn SD................ 211
Steve Sax LA 210
Tim Raines MON.............. 194

DOUBLES
Von Hayes PHI.................. 46
Steve Sax LA 43
Sid Bream PIT 37

TRIPLES
Mitch Webster MON........... 13
Juan Samuel PHI 12
Tim Raines MON............... 10

HOME RUNS
Mike Schmidt PHI............... 37
Glenn Davis HOU............... 31
Dave Parker CIN 31

RUNS BATTED IN
Mike Schmidt PHI............. 119
Dave Parker CIN 116
Gary Carter NY 105

SLUGGING AVERAGE
Mike Schmidt PHI............. .547
Darryl Strawberry NY ...... .507
Kevin McReynolds SD .... .504

STOLEN BASES
Vince Coleman STL 107
Eric Davis CIN.................... 80
Tim Raines MON................ 70

RUNS SCORED
Tony Gwynn SD 107
Von Hayes PHI 107
two tied at.......................... 97

WINS
F. Valenzuela LA 21
Mike Krukow SF 20
two tied at.......................... 18

WINNING PERCENTAGE
Bob Ojeda NY .... .783
Dwight Gooden NY .... .739
Sid Fernandez NY........... .727

EARNED RUN AVERAGE
Mike Scott HOU 2.22
Bob Ojeda NY 2.57
Ron Darling NY 2.81

STRIKEOUTS
Mike Scott HOU 306
F. Valenzuela LA 242
Floyd Youmans MON 202

SAVES
Todd Worrell STL 36
Jeff Reardon MON 35
Dave Smith HOU................ 33

COMPLETE GAMES
F. Valenzuela LA 20
Rick Rhoden PIT 12
Dwight Gooden NY 12

SHUTOUTS
Mike Scott HOU 5
Bob Knepper HOU 5
two tied at............................ 3

GAMES PITCHED
Craig Lefferts SD................ 83
Roger McDowell NY........... 75
two tied at.......................... 74

INNINGS PITCHED
Mike Scott HOU 275
F. Valenzuela LA 269
Bob Knepper HOU 258

1987 AL

EAST	W	L	PCT	GB	R	OR	BA	FA	ERA
DETROIT	98	64	.605	—	896	735	.272	.980	4.02
TORONTO	96	66	.593	2	845	655	.269	.982	3.74
MILWAUKEE	91	71	.562	7	862	817	.276	.976	4.62
NEW YORK	89	73	.549	9	788	758	.262	.983	4.36
BOSTON	78	84	.481	20	842	825	.278	.982	4.77
BALTIMORE	67	95	.414	31	729	880	.258	.982	5.01
CLEVELAND	61	101	.377	37	742	957	.263	.975	5.28

WEST	W	L	PCT	GB	R	OR	BA	FA	ERA
★ MINNESOTA	85	77	.525	—	786	806	.261	.984	4.63
KANSAS CITY	83	79	.512	2	715	691	.262	.979	3.86
OAKLAND	81	81	.500	4	806	789	.260	.977	4.32
SEATTLE	78	84	.481	7	760	801	.272	.980	4.48
CHICAGO	77	85	.475	8	748	746	.258	.981	4.29
CALIFORNIA	75	87	.463	10	770	803	.252	.981	4.38
TEXAS	75	87	.463	10	823	849	.266	.976	4.63
					11112	11112	.265	.980	4.46

BATTING AVERAGE
Wade Boggs BOS .... .363
Paul Molitor MIL .... .353
Alan Trammell DET .... .343

HITS
Kevin Seitzer KC 207
Kirby Puckett MIN 207
Alan Trammell DET 205

DOUBLES
Paul Molitor MIL 41
Wade Boggs BOS 40

TRIPLES
Willie Wilson KC 15
Luis Polonia OAK 10
Phil Bradley SEA 10

HOME RUNS
Mark McGwire OAK 49
George Bell TOR................ 47
four tied at 34

RUNS BATTED IN
George Bell TOR............... 134
Dwight Evans BOS........... 123
Mark McGwire OAK........... 118

SLUGGING AVERAGE
Mark McGwire OAK .... .618
George Bell TOR.............. .605
Wade Boggs BOS .... .588

STOLEN BASES
Harold Reynolds SEA 60
Willie Wilson KC................. 59
Gary Redus CHI................. 52

RUNS SCORED
Paul Molitor MIL 114
George Bell TOR 111
two tied at 110

WINS
Roger Clemens BOS.......... 20
Dave Stewart OAK 20
Mark Langston SEA 19

WINNING PERCENTAGE
Roger Clemens BOS....... .690
Jimmy Key TOR .... .680
two tied at........................ .643

EARNED RUN AVERAGE
Jimmy Key TOR 2.76
Frank Viola MIN 2.90
Roger Clemens BOS....... 2.97

STRIKEOUTS
Mark Langston SEA 262
Roger Clemens BOS........ 256
Ted Higuera MIL............... 240

SAVES
Tom Henke TOR 34
Jeff Reardon MIN 31
Dave Righetti NY............... 31

COMPLETE GAMES
Roger Clemens BOS.......... 18
Bruce Hurst BOS............... 15
Bret Saberhagen KC 15

SHUTOUTS
Roger Clemens BOS............ 7
Bret Saberhagen KC 4

GAMES PITCHED
Mark Eichhorn TOR 89
Mitch Williams TEX 85
Dale Mohorcic TEX 74

INNINGS PITCHED
Charlie Hough TEX 285
Roger Clemens BOS........ 282
Mark Langston SEA 272

1987 NL

EAST	W	L	PCT	GB	R	OR	BA	FA	ERA
● ST. LOUIS	95	67	.586	—	798	693	.263	.982	3.91
NEW YORK	92	70	.568	3	823	698	.268	.978	3.84
MONTREAL	91	71	.562	4	741	720	.265	.976	3.92
PHILADELPHIA	80	82	.494	15	702	749	.254	.980	4.18
PITTSBURGH	80	82	.494	15	723	744	.264	.980	4.20
CHICAGO	76	85	.472	18.5	720	801	.264	.979	4.55

WEST	W	L	PCT	GB	R	OR	BA	FA	ERA
SAN FRANCISCO	90	72	.556	—	783	669	.260	.980	3.68
CINCINNATI	84	78	.519	6	783	752	.266	.979	4.25
HOUSTON	76	86	.469	14	648	678	.253	.981	3.84
LOS ANGELES	73	89	.451	17	635	675	.252	.975	3.72
ATLANTA	69	92	.429	20.5	747	829	.258	.982	4.63
SAN DIEGO	65	97	.401	25	668	763	.260	.976	4.27
					8771	8771	.261	.979	4.08

BATTING AVERAGE
Tony Gwynn SD .... .370
Pedro Guerrero LA .... .338
Tim Raines MON .... .330

HITS
Tony Gwynn SD 218
Pedro Guerrero LA 184
Ozzie Smith STL 182

DOUBLES
Tim Wallach MON 42
Ozzie Smith STL 40
Andres Galarraga MON 40

TRIPLES
Juan Samuel PHI 15
Tony Gwynn SD 13
two tied at 11

HOME RUNS
Andre Dawson CHI 49
Dale Murphy ATL 44
Darryl Strawberry NY 39

RUNS BATTED IN
Andre Dawson CHI 137
Tim Wallach MON 123
Mike Schmidt PHI 113

SLUGGING AVERAGE
Jack Clark STL .... .597
Eric Davis CIN .... .593
Darryl Strawberry NY ...... .583

STOLEN BASES
Vince Coleman STL 109
Tony Gwynn SD 56
Billy Hatcher HOU 53

RUNS SCORED
Tim Raines MON 123
Vince Coleman STL 121
Eric Davis CIN 120

WINS
Rick Sutcliffe CHI 18
Shane Rawley PHI 17
two tied at 16

WINNING PERCENTAGE
Dwight Gooden NY .... .682
Rick Sutcliffe CHI .... .643
Bob Welch LA .... .625

EARNED RUN AVERAGE
Nolan Ryan HOU 2.76
Mike Dunne PIT 3.03
Orel Hershiser LA 3.06

STRIKEOUTS
Nolan Ryan HOU 270
Mike Scott HOU 233
Bob Welch LA 196

SAVES
Steve Bedrosian PHI 40
Lee Smith CHI 36
Todd Worrell STL 33

COMPLETE GAMES
Rick Reuschel PIT, SF 12
F. Valenzuela LA 12
Orel Hershiser LA 10

SHUTOUTS
Rick Reuschel PIT, SF 4
Bob Welch LA 4

GAMES PITCHED
Kent Tekulve PHI 90
Rob Murphy CIN 87
Frank Williams CIN 85

INNINGS PITCHED
Orel Hershiser LA 265
Bob Welch LA 252
F. Valenzuela LA 251

1988 AL

EAST	W	L	PCT	GB	R	OR	BA	FA	ERA
BOSTON	89	73	.549	—	813	689	.283	.984	3.97
DETROIT	88	74	.543	1	703	658	.250	.982	3.71
MILWAUKEE	87	75	.537	2	682	616	.257	.981	3.45
TORONTO	87	75	.537	2	763	680	.268	.982	3.80
NEW YORK	85	76	.528	3.5	772	748	.263	.978	4.26
CLEVELAND	78	84	.481	11	666	731	.261	.980	4.16
BALTIMORE	54	107	.335	34.5	550	789	.238	.980	4.54

WEST	W	L	PCT	GB	R	OR	BA	FA	ERA
●OAKLAND	104	58	.642	—	800	620	.263	.983	3.44
MINNESOTA	91	71	.562	13	759	672	.274	.986	3.93
KANSAS CITY	84	77	.522	19.5	704	648	.259	.980	3.66
CALIFORNIA	75	87	.463	29	714	771	.261	.979	4.31
CHICAGO	71	90	.441	32.5	631	757	.244	.976	4.12
TEXAS	70	91	.435	33.5	637	735	.252	.979	4.05
SEATTLE	68	93	.422	35.5	664	744	.257	.980	4.15
					9858	9858	.259	.981	3.97

BATTING AVERAGE
Wade Boggs BOS .... .366
Kirby Puckett MIN .... .356
Mike Greenwell BOS .... .325

HITS
Kirby Puckett MIN 234
Wade Boggs BOS 214
Mike Greenwell BOS 192

DOUBLES
Wade Boggs BOS 45
three tied at 42

TRIPLES
Willie Wilson KC 11
Harold Reynolds SEA 11
Robin Yount MIL 11

HOME RUNS
Jose Canseco OAK 42
Fred McGriff TOR 34
Mark McGwire OAK 32

RUNS BATTED IN
Jose Canseco OAK 124
Kirby Puckett MIN 121
Mike Greenwell BOS 119

SLUGGING AVERAGE
Jose Canseco OAK .... .569
Fred McGriff TOR .... .552
Gary Gaetti MIN .... .551

STOLEN BASES
Rickey Henderson NY 93
Gary Pettis DET 44
Paul Molitor MIL 41

RUNS SCORED
Wade Boggs BOS 128
Jose Canseco OAK 120
Rickey Henderson NY 118

WINS
Frank Viola MIN 24
Dave Stewart OAK 21
Mark Gubicza KC 20

WINNING PERCENTAGE
Frank Viola MIN .... .774
Bruce Hurst BOS .... .750
Mark Gubicza KC .... .714

EARNED RUN AVERAGE
Allan Anderson MIN 2.45
Ted Higuera MIL 2.45
Frank Viola MIN 2.64

STRIKEOUTS
Roger Clemens BOS 291
Mark Langston SEA 235
Frank Viola MIN 193

SAVES
Dennis Eckersley OAK 45
Jeff Reardon MIN 42
Doug Jones CLE 37

COMPLETE GAMES
Roger Clemens BOS 14
Dave Stewart OAK 14
Bobby Witt TEX 13

SHUTOUTS
Roger Clemens BOS 8
three tied at 4

GAMES PITCHED
Chuck Crim MIL 70
Bobby Thigpen CHI 68
Mitch Williams TEX 67

INNINGS PITCHED
Dave Stewart OAK 276
Mark Gubicza KC 270
Roger Clemens BOS 264

1988 NL

EAST	W	L	PCT	GB	R	OR	BA	FA	ERA
NEW YORK	100	60	.625	—	703	532	.256	.981	2.91
PITTSBURGH	85	75	.531	15	651	616	.247	.980	3.47
MONTREAL	81	81	.500	20	628	592	.251	.978	3.08
CHICAGO	77	85	.475	24	660	694	.261	.980	3.84
ST. LOUIS	76	86	.469	25	578	633	.249	.981	3.47
PHILADELPHIA	65	96	.404	35.5	597	734	.239	.976	4.14

WEST	W	L	PCT	GB	R	OR	BA	FA	ERA
★LOS ANGELES	94	67	.584	—	628	544	.248	.977	2.97
CINCINNATI	87	74	.540	7	641	596	.246	.980	3.35
SAN DIEGO	83	78	.516	11	594	583	.247	.981	3.28
SAN FRANCISCO	83	79	.512	11.5	670	626	.248	.980	3.39
HOUSTON	82	80	.506	12.5	617	631	.244	.978	3.40
ATLANTA	54	106	.338	39.5	555	741	.242	.976	4.09
					7522	7522	.248	.979	3.45

BATTING AVERAGE
Tony Gwynn SD 313
Rafael Palmeiro CHI 307
Andre Dawson CHI 303

HITS
A. Galarraga MON 184
Andre Dawson CHI 179
Rafael Palmeiro CHI 178

DOUBLES
Andres Galarraga MON 42
Rafael Palmeiro CHI 41
Chris Sabo CIN 40

TRIPLES
Andy Van Slyke PIT 15
Vince Coleman STL 10
three tied at 9

HOME RUNS
Darryl Strawberry NY 39
Glenn Davis HOU...............30
two tied at............................29

RUNS BATTED IN
Will Clark SF 109
Darryl Strawberry NY 101
two tied at..........................100

SLUGGING AVERAGE
Darryl Strawberry NY ...... .545
A. Galarraga MON .... .540
Will Clark SF .... .508

STOLEN BASES
Vince Coleman STL 81
Gerald Young HOU 65
Ozzie Smith STL 57

RUNS SCORED
Brett Butler SF...................109
Kirk Gibson LA 106
Will Clark SF 102

WINS
Orel Hershiser LA................23
Danny Jackson CIN 23
David Cone NY 20

WINNING PERCENTAGE
David Cone NY .... .870
Tom Browning CIN .... .783
two tied at........................ .742

EARNED RUN AVERAGE
Joe Magrane STL............ 2.18
David Cone NY 2.22
Orel Hershiser LA............ 2.26

STRIKEOUTS
Nolan Ryan HOU 228
David Cone NY 213
Jose DeLeon STL 208

SAVES
John Franco CIN 39
Jim Gott PIT 34
Todd Worrell STL 32

COMPLETE GAMES
Orel Hershiser LA...............15
Danny Jackson CIN 15
Eric Show SD 13

SHUTOUTS
Orel Hershiser LA.................8
Tim Leary LA 6
Danny Jackson CIN 6

GAMES PITCHED
Rob Murphy CIN 76
Jeff Robinson PIT 75
Juan Agosto HOU 75

INNINGS PITCHED
Orel Hershiser LA...............267
Danny Jackson CIN 261
Tom Browning CIN 251

1989 AL

EAST	W	L	PCT	GB	R	OR	BA	FA	ERA
TORONTO	89	73	.549	—	731	651	.260	.980	3.58
BALTIMORE	87	75	.537	2	708	686	.252	.986	4.00
BOSTON	83	79	.512	6	774	735	.277	.980	4.01
MILWAUKEE	81	81	.500	8	707	679	.259	.975	3.80
NEW YORK	74	87	.460	14.5	698	792	.269	.980	4.50
CLEVELAND	73	89	.451	16	604	654	.245	.981	3.65
DETROIT	59	103	.364	30	617	816	.242	.979	4.53

WEST	W	L	PCT	GB	R	OR	BA	FA	ERA
★ OAKLAND	99	63	.611	—	712	576	.261	.979	3.09
KANSAS CITY	92	70	.568	7	690	635	.261	.982	3.55
CALIFORNIA	91	71	.562	8	669	578	.256	.985	3.28
TEXAS	83	79	.512	16	695	714	.263	.978	3.91
MINNESOTA	80	82	.494	19	740	738	.276	.982	4.28
SEATTLE	73	89	.451	26	694	728	.257	.977	4.00
CHICAGO	69	92	.429	29.5	693	750	.271	.975	4.23
					9732	9732	.261	.980	3.88

BATTING AVERAGE
Kirby Puckett MIN .... .339
Carney Lansford OAK ..... .336
Wade Boggs BOS .... .330

HITS
Kirby Puckett MIN 215
Wade Boggs BOS 205
Steve Sax NY 205

DOUBLES
Wade Boggs BOS 51
Kirby Puckett MIN 45
Jody Reed BOS 42

TRIPLES
Ruben Sierra TEX 14
Devon White CAL 13
Phil Bradley BAL 10

HOME RUNS
Fred McGriff TOR 36
Joe Carter CLE 35
Mark McGwire OAK 33

RUNS BATTED IN
Ruben Sierra TEX 119
Don Mattingly NY 113
Nick Esasky BOS 108

SLUGGING AVERAGE
Ruben Sierra TEX .... .543
Fred McGriff TOR .... .525
Robin Yount MIL .... .511

STOLEN BASES
R. Henderson NY, OAK 77
Cecil Espy TEX 45
Devon White CAL 44

RUNS SCORED
R. Henderson NY, OAK 113
Wade Boggs BOS 113
two tied at 101

WINS
Bret Saberhagen KC 23
Dave Stewart OAK 21
two tied at 19

WINNING PERCENTAGE
Bret Saberhagen KC .... .793
Bert Blyleven CAL .... .773
Storm Davis OAK .... .731

EARNED RUN AVERAGE
Bret Saberhagen KC 2.16
Chuck Finley CAL 2.57
Mike Moore OAK 2.61

STRIKEOUTS
Nolan Ryan TEX 301
Roger Clemens BOS 230
Bret Saberhagen KC 193

SAVES
Jeff Russell TEX 38
Bobby Thigpen CHI 34
three tied at 33

COMPLETE GAMES
Bret Saberhagen KC 12
Jack Morris DET 10
Chuck Finley CAL 9

SHUTOUTS
Bert Blyleven CAL 5
Kirk McCaskill CAL 4
Bret Saberhagen KC 4

GAMES PITCHED
Chuck Crim MIL 76
Rob Murphy BOS 74
Kenny Rogers TEX 73

INNINGS PITCHED
Bret Saberhagen KC 262
Dave Stewart OAK 258
Mark Gubicza KC 255

1989 NL

EAST	W	L	PCT	GB	R	OR	BA	FA	ERA
CHICAGO	93	69	.574	—	702	623	.261	.980	3.43
NEW YORK	87	75	.537	6	683	595	.246	.976	3.29
ST. LOUIS	86	76	.531	7	632	608	.258	.982	3.36
MONTREAL	81	81	.500	12	632	630	.247	.979	3.48
PITTSBURGH	74	88	.457	19	637	680	.241	.975	3.64
PHILADELPHIA	67	95	.414	26	629	735	.243	.979	4.04

WEST	W	L	PCT	GB	R	OR	BA	FA	ERA
SAN FRANCISCO	92	70	.568	—	699	600	.250	.982	3.30
SAN DIEGO	89	73	.549	3	642	626	.251	.976	3.38
HOUSTON	86	76	.531	6	647	669	.239	.977	3.65
LOS ANGELES	77	83	.481	14	554	536	.240	.981	2.95
CINCINNATI	75	87	.463	17	632	691	.247	.980	3.73
ATLANTA	63	97	.394	28	584	680	.234	.976	3.70
					7673	7673	.246	.978	3.50

BATTING AVERAGE
Tony Gwynn SD .... .336
Will Clark SF .... .333
Lonnie Smith ATL............ .315

HITS
Tony Gwynn SD 203
Will Clark SF 196
Roberto Alomar SD 184

DOUBLES
Pedro Guerrero STL............ 42
Tim Wallach MON 42
Howard Johnson NY 41

TRIPLES
Robby Thompson SF 11
Bobby Bonilla PIT 10
three tied at 9

HOME RUNS
Kevin Mitchell SF 47
Howard Johnson NY 36
two tied at 34

RUNS BATTED IN
Kevin Mitchell SF 125
Pedro Guerrero STL.......... 117
Will Clark SF 111

SLUGGING AVERAGE
Kevin Mitchell SF .... .635
Howard Johnson NY .... .559
Will Clark SF .... .546

STOLEN BASES
Vince Coleman STL 65
Juan Samuel PHI, NY 42
Roberto Alomar SD 42

RUNS SCORED
Howard Johnson NY 104
Will Clark SF 104
Ryne Sandberg CHI 104

WINS
Mike Scott HOU 20
Greg Maddux CHI 19
two tied at........................ 18

WINNING PERCENTAGE
Mike Bielecki CHI .... .720
D. Martinez MON .... .696
Rick Reuschel SF............. .680

EARNED RUN AVERAGE
Scott Garrelts SF............. 2.28
Orel Hershiser LA............ 2.31
Mark Langston MON 2.39

STRIKEOUTS
Jose DeLeon STL 201
Tim Belcher LA.................. 200
Sid Fernandez NY............ 198

SAVES
Mark Davis SD 44
Mitch Williams CHI 36
John Franco CIN 32

COMPLETE GAMES
Tim Belcher LA................... 10
Bruce Hurst SD 10
three tied at 9

SHUTOUTS
Tim Belcher LA..................... 8
Doug Drabek PIT 5
three tied at 4

GAMES PITCHED
Mitch Williams CHI.............. 76
Rob Dibble CIN 74
Jeff Parrett PHI.................. 72

INNINGS PITCHED
Orel Hershiser LA............. 257
Tom Browning CIN 250
two tied at......................... 245

1990 AL

EAST	W	L	PCT	GB	R	OR	BA	FA	ERA
BOSTON	88	74	.543	—	699	664	.272	.980	3.72
TORONTO	86	76	.531	2	767	661	.265	.986	3.84
DETROIT	79	83	.488	9	750	754	.259	.979	4.39
CLEVELAND	77	85	.475	11	732	737	.267	.981	4.26
BALTIMORE	76	85	.472	11.5	669	698	.245	.985	4.04
MILWAUKEE	74	88	.457	14	732	760	.256	.976	4.08
NEW YORK	67	95	.414	21	603	749	.241	.980	4.21

WEST	W	L	PCT	GB	R	OR	BA	FA	ERA
●OAKLAND	103	59	.636	—	733	570	.254	.986	3.18
CHICAGO	94	68	.580	9	682	633	.258	.980	3.61
TEXAS	83	79	.512	20	676	696	.259	.979	3.83
CALIFORNIA	80	82	.494	23	690	706	.260	.978	3.79
SEATTLE	77	85	.475	26	640	680	.259	.979	3.69
KANSAS CITY	75	86	.466	27.5	707	709	.267	.980	3.93
MINNESOTA	74	88	.457	29	666	729	.265	.983	4.12
					9746	9746	.259	.981	3.91

BATTING AVERAGE
George Brett KC .... .329
R. Henderson OAK .... .325
Rafael Palmeiro TEX .... .319

HITS
Rafael Palmeiro TEX 191
Wade Boggs BOS 187
Roberto Kelly NY 183

DOUBLES
George Brett KC 45
Jody Reed BOS 45
two tied at 44

TRIPLES
Tony Fernandez TOR 17
Sammy Sosa CHI 10
three tied at 9

HOME RUNS
Cecil Fielder DET 51
Mark McGwire OAK 39
Jose Canseco OAK 37

RUNS BATTED IN
Cecil Fielder DET 132
Kelly Gruber TOR 118
Mark McGwire OAK 108

SLUGGING AVERAGE
Cecil Fielder DET .... .592
R. Henderson OAK .... .577
Jose Canseco OAK .... .543

STOLEN BASES
R. Henderson OAK 65
Steve Sax NY 43
Roberto Kelly NY 42

RUNS SCORED
Rickey Henderson OAK ... 119
Cecil Fielder DET 104
Harold Reynolds SEA 100

WINS
Bob Welch OAK 27
Dave Stewart OAK 22
Roger Clemens BOS 21

WINNING PERCENTAGE
Bob Welch OAK .... .818
Roger Clemens BOS .... .778
Dave Stieb TOR .... .750

EARNED RUN AVERAGE
Roger Clemens BOS 1.93
Chuck Finley CAL 2.40
Dave Stewart OAK 2.56

STRIKEOUTS
Nolan Ryan TEX 232
Bobby Witt TEX 221
Erik Hanson SEA 211

SAVES
Bobby Thigpen CHI 57
Dennis Eckersley OAK 48
Doug Jones CLE 43

COMPLETE GAMES
Jack Morris DET 11
Dave Stewart OAK 11
five tied at 7

SHUTOUTS
Roger Clemens BOS 4
Dave Stewart OAK 4
three tied at 3

GAMES PITCHED
Bobby Thigpen CHI 77
Jeff Montgomery KC 73
Duane Ward TOR 73

INNINGS PITCHED
Dave Stewart OAK 267
Jack Morris DET 250
Bob Welch OAK 238

1990 NL

EAST	W	L	PCT	GB	R	OR	BA	FA	ERA
PITTSBURGH	95	67	.586	—	733	619	.259	.979	3.40
NEW YORK	91	71	.562	4	775	613	.256	.978	3.42
MONTREAL	85	77	.525	10	662	598	.250	.982	3.37
CHICAGO	77	85	.475	18	690	774	.263	.980	4.34
PHILADELPHIA	77	85	.475	18	646	729	.255	.981	4.07
ST. LOUIS	70	92	.432	25	599	698	.256	.979	3.87

WEST	W	L	PCT	GB	R	OR	BA	FA	ERA
★ CINCINNATI	91	71	.562	—	693	597	.265	.983	3.39
LOS ANGELES	86	76	.531	5	728	685	.262	.979	3.72
SAN FRANCISCO	85	77	.525	6	719	710	.262	.983	4.08
HOUSTON	75	87	.463	16	573	656	.242	.978	3.61
SAN DIEGO	75	87	.463	16	673	673	.257	.977	3.68
ATLANTA	65	97	.401	26	682	821	.250	.974	4.58
					8173	8173	.256	.980	3.79

BATTING AVERAGE
Willie McGee STL .... .335
Eddie Murray LA .... .330
Dave Magadan NY .... .328

HITS
Brett Butler SF 192
Lenny Dykstra PHI 192
Ryne Sandberg CHI 188

DOUBLES
Gregg Jefferies NY 40
Bobby Bonilla PIT 39
Chris Sabo CIN 38

TRIPLES
Mariano Duncan CIN 11
Tony Gwynn SD 10
three tied at 9

HOME RUNS
Ryne Sandberg CHI 40
Darryl Strawberry NY 37
Kevin Mitchell SF 35

RUNS BATTED IN
Matt Williams SF 122
Bobby Bonilla PIT............. 120
Joe Carter SD................... 115

SLUGGING AVERAGE
Barry Bonds PIT............... .565
Ryne Sandberg CHI .... .559
Kevin Mitchell SF .... .544

STOLEN BASES
Vince Coleman STL 77
Eric Yelding HOU 64
Barry Bonds PIT................. 52

RUNS SCORED
Ryne Sandberg CHI 116
Bobby Bonilla PIT............. 112
Brett Butler SF.................. 108

WINS
Doug Drabek PIT 22
Ramon Martinez LA 20
Frank Viola NY 20

WINNING PERCENTAGE
Doug Drabek PIT .... .786
Ramon Martinez LA .... .769
Dwight Gooden NY .... .731

EARNED RUN AVERAGE
Danny Darwin HOU......... 2.21
Zane Smith MON, PIT...... 2.55
Ed Whitson SD................ 2.60

STRIKEOUTS
David Cone NY 233
Dwight Gooden NY 223
Ramon Martinez LA 223

SAVES
John Franco NY 33
Randy Myers CIN............... 31
Lee Smith STL 27

COMPLETE GAMES
Ramon Martinez LA 12
Doug Drabek PIT 9
Bruce Hurst SD 9

SHUTOUTS
Mike Morgan LA 4
Bruce Hurst SD 4

GAMES PITCHED
Juan Agosto HOU 82
Paul Assenmacher CHI...... 74
Greg Harris SD.................. 73

INNINGS PITCHED
Frank Viola NY 250
Greg Maddux CHI 237
Ramon Martinez LA 234

1991 AL

EAST	W	L	PCT	GB	R	OR	BA	FA	ERA
TORONTO	91	71	.562	—	684	622	.257	.980	3.50
BOSTON	84	78	.519	7	731	712	.269	.981	4.01
DETROIT	84	78	.519	7	817	794	.247	.983	4.51
MILWAUKEE	83	79	.512	8	799	744	.271	.981	4.14
NEW YORK	71	91	.438	20	674	777	.256	.979	4.42
BALTIMORE	67	95	.414	24	686	796	.254	.985	4.59
CLEVELAND	57	105	.352	34	576	759	.254	.976	4.23

WEST	W	L	PCT	GB	R	OR	BA	FA	ERA
★MINNESOTA	95	67	.586	—	776	652	.280	.985	3.69
CHICAGO	87	75	.534	8	758	681	.262	.982	3.79
TEXAS	85	77	.525	10	829	814	.270	.979	4.47
OAKLAND	84	78	.519	11	760	776	.248	.982	4.57
SEATTLE	83	79	.512	12	702	674	.255	.983	3.79
KANSAS CITY	82	80	.506	13	727	722	.264	.980	3.92
CALIFORNIA	81	81	.500	14	653	649	.255	.984	3.69
					10172	10172	.260	.981	4.09

BATTING AVERAGE
Julio Franco TEX............. .341
Wade Boggs BOS .... .332
two tied at......................... .327

HITS
Paul Molitor MIL 216
Cal Ripken BAL................. 210
two tied at......................... 203

DOUBLES
Rafael Palmeiro TEX........... 49
Cal Ripken BAL.................. 46
Ruben Sierra TEX............... 44

TRIPLES
Lance Johnson CHI............ 13
Paul Molitor MIL................. 13
Roberto Alomar TOR.......... 11

HOME RUNS
Cecil Fielder DET 44
Jose Canseco OAK 44
Cal Ripken BAL................... 34

RUNS BATTED IN
Cecil Fielder DET 133
Jose Canseco OAK 122
Ruben Sierra TEX 116

SLUGGING AVERAGE
Danny Tartabull KC .... .593
Cal Ripken BAL................ .566
Jose Canseco OAK.......... .556

STOLEN BASES
Rickey Henderson OAK 58
Roberto Alomar TOR 53
Tim Raines CHI 51

RUNS SCORED
Paul Molitor MIL 133
Jose Canseco OAK 115
Rafael Palmeiro TEX........ 115

WINS
Scott Erickson MIN............. 20
Bill Gullickson DET............. 20
Mark Langston CAL 19

WINNING PERCENTAGE
Scott Erickson MIN............ .714
Mark Langston CAL .... .704
Bill Gullickson DET........... .690

EARNED RUN AVERAGE
Roger Clemens BOS....... 2.62
T. Candiotti CLE,TOR....... 2.65
Bill Wegman MIL.............. 2.84

STRIKEOUTS
Roger Clemens BOS........ 241
Randy Johnson SEA 228
Nolan Ryan TEX 203

SAVES
Bryan Harvey CAL 46
Dennis Eckersley OAK....... 43
Rick Aguilera MIN 42

COMPLETE GAMES
Jack McDowell CHI............. 15
Roger Clemens BOS........... 13
two tied at............................ 10

SHUTOUTS
Roger Clemens BOS............. 4
four tied at 3

GAMES PITCHED
Duane Ward TOR................. 81
Mike Jackson SEA 72
Gregg Olson BAL................ 72

INNINGS PITCHED
Roger Clemens BOS........ 271
Jack McDowell CHI 254
Jack Morris MIN 247

1991 NL

EAST	W	L	PCT	GB	R	OR	BA	FA	ERA
PITTSBURGH	98	64	.605	—	768	632	.263	.981	3.44
ST. LOUIS	84	78	.519	14	651	648	.255	.982	3.69
PHILADELPHIA	78	84	.481	20	629	680	.241	.981	3.86
CHICAGO	77	83	.481	20	695	734	.253	.982	4.03
NEW YORK	77	84	.478	20.5	640	646	.244	.977	3.56
MONTREAL	71	90	.441	26.5	579	655	.246	.979	3.64

WEST	W	L	PCT	GB	R	OR	BA	FA	ERA
ATLANTA	94	68	.580	—	749	644	.258	.978	3.49
LOS ANGELES	93	69	.574	1	665	565	.253	.980	3.06
SAN DIEGO	84	78	.519	10	636	646	.244	.982	3.57
SAN FRANCISCO	75	87	.463	19	649	697	.246	.982	4.03
CINCINNATI	74	88	.457	20	689	691	.258	.979	3.83
HOUSTON	65	97	.401	29	605	717	.244	.974	4.00
					7955	7955	.250	.980	3.68

BATTING AVERAGE
Terry Pendleton ATL........ .319
Hal Morris CIN................. .318
Tony Gwynn SD .... .317

HITS
Terry Pendleton ATL........ 187
Brett Butler LA................ 182
Chris Sabo CIN 175

DOUBLES
Bobby Bonilla PIT............. 44
Felix Jose STL 40
two tied at....................... 36

TRIPLES
Ray Lankford STL 15
Tony Gwynn SD 11
Steve Finley HOU 10

HOME RUNS
Howard Johnson NY 38
Matt Williams SF 34
Ron Gant ATL 32

RUNS BATTED IN
Howard Johnson NY 117
Barry Bonds PIT 116
Will Clark SF................... 116

SLUGGING AVERAGE
Will Clark SF .... .536
Howard Johnson NY .... .535
Terry Pendleton ATL........ .517

STOLEN BASES
Marquis Grissom MON....... 76
Otis Nixon ATL 72
Delino DeShields MON 56

RUNS SCORED
Brett Butler LA 112
Howard Johnson NY 108
Ryne Sandberg CHI 104

WINS
John Smiley PIT 20
Tom Glavine ATL 20
Steve Avery ATL............... 18

WINNING PERCENTAGE
Jose Rijo CIN .... .714
John Smiley PIT .... .714
Steve Avery ATL............... .692

EARNED RUN AVERAGE
Dennis Martinez MON..... 2.39
Jose Rijo CIN 2.51
Tom Glavine ATL 2.55

STRIKEOUTS
David Cone NY 241
Greg Maddux CHI 198
Tom Glavine ATL............. 192

SAVES
Lee Smith STL 47
Rob Dibble CIN 31
two tied at....................... 30

COMPLETE GAMES
Tom Glavine ATL................. 9
Dennis Martinez MON......... 9
Terry Mulholland PHI........... 8

SHUTOUTS
Dennis Martinez MON......... 5
Ramon Martinez LA 4
three tied at 3

GAMES PITCHED
Barry Jones MON.............. 77
Paul Assenmacher CHI...... 75
Mike Stanton ATL.............. 74

INNINGS PITCHED
Greg Maddux CHI 263
Tom Glavine ATL............. 247
Mike Morgan LA 236

1992 AL

EAST	W	L	PCT	GB	R	OR	BA	FA	ERA
★TORONTO	96	66	.593	—	780	682	.263	.985	3.91
MILWAUKEE	92	70	.568	4	740	604	.268	.986	3.43
BALTIMORE	89	73	.549	7	705	656	.259	.985	3.79
CLEVELAND	76	86	.469	20	674	746	.266	.978	4.11
NEW YORK	76	86	.469	20	733	746	.261	.982	4.21
DETROIT	75	87	.463	21	791	794	.256	.981	4.60
BOSTON	73	89	.451	23	599	669	.246	.978	3.58

WEST	W	L	PCT	GB	R	OR	BA	FA	ERA
OAKLAND	96	66	.593	—	745	672	.258	.979	3.73
MINNESOTA	90	72	.556	6	747	653	.277	.985	3.70
CHICAGO	86	76	.531	10	738	690	.261	.979	3.82
TEXAS	77	85	.475	19	682	753	.250	.975	4.09
CALIFORNIA	72	90	.444	24	579	671	.243	.979	3.84
KANSAS CITY	72	90	.444	24	610	667	.256	.980	3.81
SEATTLE	64	98	.395	32	679	799	.263	.982	4.55
					9802	9802	.259	.981	3.94

BATTING AVERAGE
Edgar Martinez SEA .... .343
Kirby Puckett MIN .... .329
Frank Thomas CHI .... .323

HITS
Kirby Puckett MIN 210
Carlos Baerga CLE 205
Paul Molitor MIL 195

DOUBLES
Edgar Martinez SEA........... 46
Frank Thomas CHI 46
two tied at 40

TRIPLES
Lance Johnson CHI............. 12
Mike Devereaux BAL.......... 11
Brady Anderson BAL.......... 10

HOME RUNS
Juan Gonzalez TEX 43
Mark McGwire OAK 42
Cecil Fielder DET 35

RUNS BATTED IN
Cecil Fielder DET 124
Joe Carter TOR 119
Frank Thomas CHI 115

SLUGGING AVERAGE
Mark McGwire OAK .... .585
Edgar Martinez SEA........ .544
Frank Thomas CHI .... .536

STOLEN BASES
Kenny Lofton CLE 66
Pat Listach MIL 54
Brady Anderson BAL.......... 53

RUNS SCORED
Tony Phillips DET 114
Frank Thomas CHI 108
Roberto Alomar TOR 105

WINS
Kevin Brown TEX 21
Jack Morris TOR 21
Jack McDowell CHI 20

WINNING PERCENTAGE
Mike Mussina BAL .... .783
Jack Morris TOR .... .778
Juan Guzman TOR .... .762

EARNED RUN AVERAGE
Roger Clemens BOS 2.41
Kevin Appier KC 2.46
Mike Mussina BAL 2.54

STRIKEOUTS
Randy Johnson SEA 241
Melido Perez NY 218
Roger Clemens BOS........ 208

SAVES
Dennis Eckersley OAK...... 51
Rick Aguilera MIN 41
Jeff Montgomery KC 39

COMPLETE GAMES
Jack McDowell CHI 13
Roger Clemens BOS.......... 11
Kevin Brown TEX 11

SHUTOUTS
Roger Clemens BOS............. 5
Mike Mussina BAL ....
Dave Fleming SEA...............

GAMES PITCHED
Kevin Rogers TEX............... 81
Duane Ward TOR 79
Steve Olin CLE 72

INNINGS PITCHED
Kevin Brown TEX 266
Bill Wegman MIL 262
Jack McDowell CHI 260

1992 NL

EAST	W	L	PCT	GB	R	OR	BA	FA	ERA
PITTSBURGH	96	66	.593	—	693	595	.255	.984	3.35
MONTREAL	87	75	.537	9	648	581	.252	.980	3.25
ST. LOUIS	83	79	.512	13	631	604	.262	.985	3.38
CHICAGO	78	84	.481	18	593	624	.254	.982	3.39
NEW YORK	72	90	.444	24	599	653	.235	.981	3.66
PHILADELPHIA	70	92	.432	26	686	717	.253	.978	4.11

WEST	W	L	PCT	GB	R	OR	BA	FA	ERA
ATLANTA	98	64	.605	—	682	569	.254	.982	3.14
CINCINNATI	90	72	.556	8	660	609	.260	.984	3.46
SAN DIEGO	82	80	.506	16	617	636	.255	.982	3.56
HOUSTON	81	81	.500	17	608	668	.246	.981	3.72
SAN FRANCISCO	72	90	.444	26	574	647	.244	.982	3.61
LOS ANGELES	63	99	.389	35	548	636	.248	.972	3.41
					7539	7539	.252	.981	3.50

BATTING AVERAGE
Gary Sheffield SD .... .330
Andy Van Slyke PIT .... .324
John Kruk PHI .... .323

HITS
Terry Pendleton ATL......... 199
Andy Van Slyke PIT 199
Ryne Sandberg CHI 186

DOUBLES
Andy Van Slyke PIT 45
three tied at 40

TRIPLES
Deion Sanders ATL 14
Steve Finley HOU 13
Andy Van Slyke PIT 12

HOME RUNS
Fred McGriff SD 35
Barry Bonds PIT 34
Gary Sheffield SD 33

RUNS BATTED IN
Darren Daulton PHI 109
Terry Pendleton ATL 105
Fred McGriff SD 104

SLUGGING AVERAGE
Barry Bonds PIT .... .624
Gary Sheffield SD .... .580
Fred McGriff SD .... .556

STOLEN BASES
Marquis Grissom MON....... 78
Delino DeShields MON 46
two tied at............................ 44

RUNS SCORED
Barry Bonds PIT............... 109
Dave Hollins PHI 104
Andy Van Slyke PIT 103

WINS
Greg Maddux CHI 20
Tom Glavine ATL 20
four tied at 16

WINNING PERCENTAGE
Bob Tewksbury STL .... .762
Tom Glavine ATL.............. .714
Charlie Liebrandt ATL ..... .682

EARNED RUN AVERAGE
Bill Swift SF 2.08
Bob Tewksbury STL 2.16
Greg Maddux CHI 2.18

STRIKEOUTS
John Smoltz ATL 215
David Cone NY 214
Greg Maddux CHI 199

SAVES
Lee Smith STL 43
Randy Myers SD 38
John Wetteland MON......... 37

COMPLETE GAMES
Terry Mulholland PHI.......... 12
Doug Drabek PIT 10
Curt Schilling PHI.............. 10

SHUTOUTS
David Cone NY 5
Tom Glavine ATL.................. 5

GAMES PITCHED
Joe Boever HOU 81
Doug Jones HOU 80
two tied at............................ 77

INNINGS PITCHED
Greg Maddux CHI 268
Doug Drabek PIT 257
John Smoltz ATL 247

1993 AL

EAST	W	L	PCT	GB	R	OR	BA	FA	ERA
★TORONTO	95	67	.586	—	847	742	.279	.980	4.21
NEW YORK	88	74	.543	7	821	761	.279	.981	4.35
BALTIMORE	85	77	.525	10	786	745	.267	.983	4.31
DETROIT	85	77	.525	10	899	837	.275	.981	4.65
BOSTON	80	82	.494	15	686	698	.264	.979	3.77
CLEVELAND	76	86	.469	19	790	813	.275	.985	4.58
MILWAUKEE	69	93	.426	26	733	792	.258	.976	4.45

WEST	W	L	PCT	GB	R	OR	BA	FA	ERA
CHICAGO	94	68	.580	—	776	664	.265	.985	3.70
TEXAS	86	76	.531	8	835	751	.267	.982	4.28
KANSAS CITY	84	78	.519	10	675	694	.263	.985	4.0
SEATTLE	82	80	.506	12	734	731	.260	.986	4.20
CALIFORNIA	71	91	.438	23	684	770	.260	.983	4.3
MINNESOTA	71	91	.438	23	693	830	.264	.980	4.7
OAKLAND	68	94	.420	26	715	846	.254	.984	4.9
					10674	10674	.266	.981	4.3

BATTING AVERAGE
John Olerud TOR .... .363
Paul Molitor TOR .... .332
Roberto Alomar TOR .... .326

HITS
Paul Molitor TOR 211
Carlos Baerga CLE 200
John Olerud TOR 200

DOUBLES
John Olerud TOR 54
Devon White TOR 42
two tied at 40

TRIPLES
Lance Johnson CHI 14
Joey Cora CHI 13
David Hulse TEX 10

HOME RUNS
Juan Gonzalez TEX 46
Ken Griffey SEA 45
Frank Thomas CHI 41

RUNS BATTED IN
Albert Belle CLE 129
Frank Thomas CHI 128
Joe Carter TOR 121

SLUGGING AVERAGE
Juan Gonzalez TEX .... .632
Ken Griffey SEA .... .617
Frank Thomas CHI .... .607

STOLEN BASES
Kenny Lofton CLE 70
Roberto Alomar TOR 55
Luis Polonia CAL 55

RUNS SCORED
Rafael Palmeiro TEX 124
Paul Molitor TOR 121
two tied at 116

WINS
Jack McDowell CHI 22
Randy Johnson SEA 19
Pat Hentgen TOR 19

WINNING PERCENTAGE
Jimmy Key NY .... .750
Randy Johnson SEA .... .704
Kevin Appier KC .... .692

EARNED RUN AVERAGE
Kevin Appier KC 2.56
Wilson Alvarez CHI 2.95
Jimmy Key NY 3.00

STRIKEOUTS
Randy Johnson SEA 30
Mark Langston CAL 19
Juan Guzman TOR 19

SAVES
Jeff Montgomery KC 4
Duane Ward TOR 4
Tom Henke TEX 4

COMPLETE GAMES
Chuck Finley CAL 1
Kevin Brown TEX 1
two tied at 1

SHUTOUTS
Jack McDowell CHI ....
three tied at ....

GAMES PITCHED
Greg Harris BOS 8
Scott Radinsky CHI 7
three tied at 7

INNINGS PITCHED
Cal Eldred MIL 25
Jack McDowell CHI 25
Mark Langston CAL 25

1993 NL

EAST	W	L	PCT	GB	R	OR	BA	FA	ERA
PHILADELPHIA	97	65	.599	—	877	740	.274	.980	3.95
MONTREAL	94	68	.580	3	732	682	.257	.977	3.55
ST. LOUIS	87	75	.537	10	758	744	.272	.982	4.09
CHICAGO	84	78	.519	13	738	739	.270	.982	4.18
PITTSBURGH	75	87	.463	22	707	806	.267	.982	4.77
FLORIDA	64	98	.395	33	581	724	.248	.978	4.13
NEW YORK	59	103	.364	38	672	744	.248	.977	4.05

WEST	W	L	PCT	GB	R	OR	BA	FA	ERA
ATLANTA	104	58	.642	—	767	599	.262	.981	3.14
SAN FRANCISCO	103	59	.636	1	808	636	.276	.982	3.61
HOUSTON	85	77	.525	19	716	630	.267	.980	3.49
LOS ANGELES	81	81	.500	23	675	662	.261	.979	3.50
CINCINNATI	73	89	.451	31	722	785	.264	.981	4.51
COLORADO	67	95	.414	37	758	927	.273	.974	5.41
SAN DIEGO	61	101	.377	43	679	772	.252	.977	4.23
					10190	10190	.264	.980	4.04

BATTING AVERAGE
Andres Galarraga COL ... .370
Tony Gwynn SD .... .358
Gregg Jefferies STL .... .342

HITS
Lenny Dykstra PHI 194
Mark Grace CHI 193
Marquis Grissom MON 188

DOUBLES
Charlie Hayes COL 45
Lenny Dykstra PHI 44
Dante Bichette COL 43

TRIPLES
Steve Finley HOU 13
Brett Butler LA 10
tied at 9

HOME RUNS
Barry Bonds SF 46
David Justice ATL 40
Matt Williams SF 38

RUNS BATTED IN
Barry Bonds SF 123
David Justice ATL 120
Ron Gant ATL................... 117

SLUGGING AVERAGE
Barry Bonds SF .... .677
Andres Galarraga COL ... .602
Matt Williams SF .... .561

STOLEN BASES
Chuck Carr FLA 58
Marquis Grissom MON 53
Otis Nixon ATL 47

RUNS SCORED
Lenny Dykstra PHI 143
Barry Bonds SF................ 129
Ron Gant ATL 113

WINS
Tom Glavine ATL............... 22
John Burkett SF 22
Billy Swift SF 21

WINNING PERCENTAGE
Mark Portugal HOU......... .818
Tommy Greene PHI......... .800
Tom Glavine ATL............. .786

EARNED RUN AVERAGE
Greg Maddux ATL 2.36
Jose Rijo CIN 2.48
Mark Portugal HOU 2.77

STRIKEOUTS
Jose Rijo CIN 227
John Smoltz ATL............... 208
Greg Maddux ATL 197

SAVES
Randy Myers CHI 53
Rod Beck SF 48
Bryan Harvey FLA............. 45

COMPLETE GAMES
Greg Maddux ATL 8
five tied at........................... 7

SHUTOUTS
Pete Harnisch HOU.............. 4
Ramon Martinez LA 3

GAMES PITCHED
Mike Jackson SF................. 81
Rod Beck SF 76
David West PHI.................. 76

INNINGS PITCHED
Greg Maddux ATL 267
Jose Rijo CIN 257
John Smoltz ATL 244

1994 AL

EAST	W	L	PCT	GB	R	OR	BA	FA	ER
NEW YORK	70	43	.619	—	670	534	.290	.982	4.3
BALTIMORE	63	49	.563	6.5	589	497	.272	.986	4.3
TORONTO	55	60	.478	16	566	579	.269	.981	4.7
BOSTON	54	61	.470	17	552	621	.263	.981	4.9
DETROIT	53	62	.465	18	652	671	.265	.981	5.3
CENTRAL	**W**	**L**	**PCT**	**GB**	**R**	**OR**	**BA**	**FA**	**ER**
CHICAGO	67	46	.593	—	633	498	.287	.981	3.9
CLEVELAND	66	47	.584	1	679	562	.290	.980	4.3
KANSAS CITY	64	51	.557	4	574	532	.269	.982	4.2
MINNESOTA	53	60	.469	14	594	688	.276	.982	5.6
MILWAUKEE	53	62	.461	15	547	586	.263	.981	4.6
WEST	**W**	**L**	**PCT**	**GB**	**R**	**OR**	**BA**	**FA**	**ER**
TEXAS	52	62	.456	—	613	697	.280	.976	5.4
OAKLAND	51	63	.447	1	549	589	.260	.979	4.8
SEATTLE	49	63	.438	2	569	616	.269	.977	4.9
CALIFORNIA	47	68	.409	5.5	543	660	.264	.983	5.4
					8330	8330	.273	.981	4.8

BATTING AVERAGE
Paul O'Neill NY .... .359
Albert Belle CLE .... .357
Frank Thomas CHI .... .353

HITS
Kenny Lofton CLE 160
Paul Molitor TOR 155
Albert Belle CLE 147

DOUBLES
Chuck Knoblauch MIN 45
Albert Belle CLE 35
two tied at 34

TRIPLES
Lance Johnson CHI 14
Vince Coleman KC 12
Kenny Lofton CLE 9

HOME RUNS
Ken Griffey Jr. SEA 40
Frank Thomas CHI 38
Albert Belle CLE 36

RUNS BATTED IN
Kirby Puckett MIN 112
Joe Carter TOR 103
two tied at 101

SLUGGING AVERAGE
Frank Thomas CHI .... .729
Albert Belle CLE .... .714
Ken Griffey Jr. SEA .... .674

STOLEN BASES
Kenny Lofton CLE 60
Vince Coleman KC 50
Otis Nixon BOS 42

RUNS SCORED
Frank Thomas CHI 106
Kenny Lofton CLE 105
Ken Griffey Jr. SEA 94

WINS
Jimmy Key NY 17
David Cone KC 16
Mike Mussina BAL 16

WINNING PERCENTAGE
Jason Bere CHI .... .857
Jimmy Key NY .... .810
Mark Clark CLE .... .786

EARNED RUN AVERAGE
Steve Ontiveros OAK 2.65
Roger Clemens BOS 2.85
David Cone KC 2.94

STRIKEOUTS
Randy Johnson SEA 20
Roger Clemens BOS 16
Chuck Finley CAL 14

SAVES
Lee Smith BAL ....
Jeff Montgomery KC ....
Rick Aguilera MIN ....

COMPLETE GAMES
Randy Johnson SEA ....
Chuck Finley CAL ....
Dennis Martinez CLE ....

SHUTOUTS
Randy Johnson SEA ....
five tied at ....

GAMES PITCHED
Bob Wickman NY ....
Jose Mesa CLE ....
two tied at ....

INNINGS PITCHED
Chuck Finley CAL 1
Jack McDowell CHI 1
Cal Eldred MIL 1

1994 NL

EAST	W	L	PCT	GB	R	OR	BA	FA	ERA
MONTREAL	74	40	.649	—	585	454	.278	.979	3.56
ATLANTA	68	46	.596	6	542	448	.267	.982	3.57
NEW YORK	55	58	.487	18.5	506	526	.250	.980	4.13
PHILADELPHIA	54	61	.470	20.5	521	497	.262	.978	3.85
FLORIDA	51	64	.443	23.5	468	576	.266	.978	4.50
CENTRAL	**W**	**L**	**PCT**	**GB**	**R**	**OR**	**BA**	**FA**	**ERA**
CINCINNATI	66	48	.579	—	609	448	.286	.983	3.78
HOUSTON	66	49	.574	.5	602	503	.278	.983	3.97
PITTSBURGH	53	61	.465	13	466	580	.263	.980	4.64
ST. LOUIS	53	61	.465	13	535	621	.263	.982	5.14
CHICAGO	49	64	.434	16.5	500	549	.259	.982	4.47
WEST	**W**	**L**	**PCT**	**GB**	**R**	**OR**	**BA**	**FA**	**ERA**
LOS ANGELES	58	56	.509	—	532	509	.270	.980	4.17
SAN FRANCISCO	55	60	.478	3.5	504	500	.249	.985	3.99
COLORADO	53	64	.453	6.5	573	638	.274	.981	5.15
SAN DIEGO	47	70	.402	12.5	479	531	.275	.975	4.08
					7422	7422	.267	.980	4.21

BATTING AVERAGE
Tony Gwynn SD 394
Jeff Bagwell HOU 367
Moises Alou MON 339

HITS
Tony Gwynn SD 165
Jeff Bagwell HOU 147
Dante Bichette COL 147

DOUBLES
Craig Biggio HOU 44
Larry Walker MON 44
two tied at 35

TRIPLES
Darren Lewis SF 9
Brett Butler LA.....................9
Raul Mondesi LA..................8

HOME RUNS
Matt Williams SF 43
Jeff Bagwell HOU 39
Barry Bonds SF 37

RUNS BATTED IN
Jeff Bagwell HOU 116
Matt Williams SF 96
Dante Bichette COL 95

SLUGGING AVERAGE
Jeff Bagwell HOU 750
Kevin Mitchell CIN............681
Barry Bonds SF 647

STOLEN BASES
Craig Biggio HOU................39
Deion Sanders ATL, CIN....38
Marquis Grissom MON.......36

RUNS SCORED
Jeff Bagwell HOU 104
Marquis Grissom MON.....96
two tied at.........................89

WINS
Ken Hill MON 16
Greg Maddux ATL 16
two tied at.........................14

WINNING PERCENTAGE
Marvin Freeman COL........ .833
Bret Saberhagen NY .... .778
Ken Hill MON .... .762

EARNED RUN AVERAGE
Greg Maddux ATL 1.56
Bret Saberhagen NY 2.74
Doug Drabek HOU 2.84

STRIKEOUTS
Andy Benes SD.................189
Jose Rijo CIN 172
Greg Maddux ATL.............156

SAVES
John Franco NY 30
Rod Beck SF......................28
Doug Jones PHI 27

COMPLETE GAMES
Greg Maddux ATL...............10
Doug Drabek HOU 6
Tom Candiotti LA...................5

SHUTOUTS
Ramon Martinez LA 3
Greg Maddux ATL 3
two tied at.............................2

GAMES PITCHED
Steve Reed COL 61
Mel Rojas MON...................58
Jose Bautista CHI 58

INNINGS PITCHED
Greg Maddux ATL...............202
Danny Jackson PHI...........179
Bret Saberhagen NY 177

AL MOST VALUABLE PLAYER VOTING

PLAYER	1st	2nd	3rd	Tot
Frank Thomas CHI	24	4	-	372
Ken Griffey Jr. SEA	3	8	7	233
Albert Belle CLE	-	13	8	225
Kenny Lofton CLE	1	3	4	181
Paul O'Neill NY	-	-	5	150
Jimmy Key NY	-	-	4	102
Kirby Puckett MIN	-	-	-	100
Julio Franco CHI	-	-	-	49
David Cone KC	-	-	-	40
Joe Carter TOR	-	-	-	35
Jose Canseco TEX	-	-	-	27
Cal Ripken BAL	-	-	-	24
Wade Boggs NY	-	-	-	19
Lee Smith BAL	-	-	-	18
Will Clark TEX	-	-	-	17
Rafael Palmeiro BAL	-	-	-	11
Mo Vaughn BOS	-	-	-	10
Don Mattingly NY	-	-	-	9
Paul Molitor TOR	-	-	-	9
Chuck Knoblauch MIN	-	-	-	8
Mike Mussina BAL	-	-	-	8
Chili Davis CAL	-	-	-	3
Jason Bere CHI	-	-	-	1
Ruben Sierra OAK	-	-	-	1

NL MOST VALUABLE PLAYER VOTING

PLAYER	1st	2nd	3rd	Tot
Jeff Bagwell HOU	28	-	-	392
Matt Williams SF	-	11	5	28
Moises Alou MON	-	9	4	18
Barry Bonds SF	-	1	6	144
Greg Maddux ATL	-	5	2	133
Mike Piazza LA	-	1	2	12
Tony Gwynn SD	-	1	2	11
Fred McGriff ATL	-	-	3	9
Kevin Mitchell CIN	-	-	2	8
Andres Galarraga COL	-	-	-	4
Larry Walker MON	-	-	-	2
Ken Hill MON	-	-	-	2
Marquis Grissom MON	-	-	-	2
Dante Bichette COL	-	-	-	1
Hal Morris CIN	-	-	-	1
Craig Biggio HOU	-	-	1	1
Gregg Jefferies STL	-	-	-	
Jeff Conine FLA	-	-	-	
Tim Wallach LA	-	-	-	
John Franco NY	-	-	-	
Bret Boone CIN	-	-	-	
Andy Benes SD	-	-	-	
Brett Butler LA	-	-	-	
Bret Saberhagen NY	-	-	-	

AL CY YOUNG AWARD VOTING

PLAYER	1st	2nd	3rd	Tot
David Cone KC	15	10	3	108
Jimmy Key NY	10	14	4	96
Randy Johnson SEA	2	2	8	24
Mike Mussina BAL	1	2	12	23
Lee Smith BAL	-	-	1	1

NL CY YOUNG AWARD VOTING

PLAYER	1st	2nd	3rd	Tot
Greg Maddux ATL	28	-	-	14
Ken Hill MON	-	16	8	5
Bret Saberhagen NY	-	11	9	4
Marvin Freeman COL	-	1	1	
Doug Drabek HOU	-	-	4	
Danny Jackson PHI	-	-	3	
John Franco NY	-	-	2	
Rod Beck SF	-	-	1	

AL ROOKIE OF THE YEAR VOTING

PLAYER	1st	2nd	3rd	Tot
Bob Hamelin KC	25	3	-	134
Manny Ramirez CLE	-	12	8	44
Rusty Greer TEX	3	7	8	42
Darren Hall TOR	-	3	-	9
Chris Gomez DET	-	1	3	6
Bill Risley SEA	-	-	6	6
Brian Anderson CAL	-	1	1	4
Jim Edmonds CAL	-	-	2	2
Jose Valentin MIL	-	-	1	1

NL ROOKIE OF THE YEAR VOTING

PLAYER	1st	2nd	3rd	Tot
Raul Mondesi LA	28	-	-	14
John Hudek HOU	-	8	3	
Ryan Klesko ATL	-	6	7	
Steve Traschel CHI	-	6	4	
Cliff Floyd MON	-	2	4	
Joey Hamilton SD	-	2	4	
Bill VanLandingham SF	-	2	3	
Hector Carrasco CIN	-	1	-	
Bobby Jones NY	-	1	-	
Javier Lopez ATL	-	-	2	
Shane Reynolds HOU	-	-	1	